HANDBOOK
of
SOCIAL THEORY

HANDBOOK
of
SOCIAL THEORY

Edited by
GEORGE RITZER AND BARRY SMART

SAGE Publications
London • Thousand Oaks • New Delhi

Contents

List of contributors

Mark Abrahamson, Department of Sociology, University of Connecticut, US

Robert J. Antonio, Department of Sociology, University of Kansas, Lawrence, US

Barry Barnes, Department of Sociology, Exeter University, UK

Peter Beilharz, Sociology Department, Harvard University, US; School of Sociology and Anthropology, La Trobe University, Bundoora, Australia

Richard Harvey Brown, Department of Sociology, University of Maryland – College Park, US

Craig Calhoun, Department of Sociology, New York University, US

Stephen Crook, School of Anthropology, Archaeology and Sociology, James Cook University, Australia

Mitchell Dean, Department of Sociology, Macquarie University, Sydney, Australia

Gerard Delanty, Department of Sociology, University of Liverpool, UK

Anthony Elliott, Centre for Critical Theory, University of the West of England, UK

Harvie Ferguson, Department of Sociology, University of Glasgow, UK

Gary Alan Fine, Department of Sociology, Northwestern University, Evanston, US

Mike Gane, Department of Social Sciences, Loughborough University, UK

Douglas Goodman, Department of Sociology, University of Maryland – College Park, US

Peter Halfpenny, Department of Sociology, University of Manchester, UK

Douglas D. Heckathorn, Department of Sociology, Cornell University, US

Robert Holton, School of Social Science, Flinders University, Bedford Park, Australia

Hans Joas, John F. Kennedy Institut, Freve University of Berlin, Germany and University of Chicago, US

Joseph Karaganis, Department of Sociology, New York University, US

Douglas Kellner, Graduate School of Education, UCLA, US

David Kettler, Scholar in Residence, Bard Center, New York, US

Karin Knorr Cetina, Department of Sociology, University of Bielefeld, Germany

Charles Lemert, Department of Sociology, Wesleyan University, Middletown, US

Patricia Madoo Lengermann, Department of Sociology, George Washington University, Washington, US

Daniel D. Martin, Department of Sociology, Gerontology and Anthropology, Miami University, Oxford, US

Gregor McLennan, Department of Sociology, University of Bristol, UK

Volker Meja, Department of Sociology, Memorial University of Newfoundland, Canada

Linda D. Molm, Department of Sociology, University of Arizona, US

Birgitta Nedelmann, Institute of Sociology, Johannes Gutenberg University Mainz, Germany

John O'Neill, Department of Sociology, York University, Canada

Jill Niebrugge-Brantley, Department of Sociology, George Washington University, Washington, US

George Ritzer, Department of Sociology, University of Maryland – College Park, US

Roland Robertson, Department of Sociology, University of Aberdeen, Scotland, UK

Mary F. Rogers, Department of Sociology, University of West Florida, Pensacola, US

John Rundell, The T.R. Ashworth Centre for Social Theory, University of Melbourne, Australia

Kent L. Sandstrom, Department of Sociology, Anthropology and Criminology, University of Northern Iowa, Cedar Falls, US

Wes Sharrock, Department of Sociology, University of Manchester

Chris Shilling, School of Social and Historical Studies, University of Portsmouth, UK

Barry Smart, School of Social and Historical Studies, University of Portsmouth, UK

Nico Stehr, Sociologiska Institutionen, Göteborg, Sweden

Jonathan H. Turner, Department of Sociology, University of California – Riverside, US

Robert van Krieken, Department of Sociology, University of Sydney, Australia

Sam Whimster, Department of Sociology, London Guildhall University, UK

Wendy Wiedenhoft, Department of Sociology, University of Maryland, US

Shanyang Zhao, Department of Sociology, Temple University, Philadelphia, US

1

Introduction: Theorists, Theories and Theorizing

GEORGE RITZER AND BARRY SMART

THE PROBLEM OF THE CANON AND THE
INTERPRETATION OF TRADITIONS OF SOCIAL
THOUGHT

Handbooks, by their very nature, serve to define a field of study, to map out, at least for a time and for at least some scholars, the analytic parameters, key figures, perspectives and concerns associated with the field. The present *Handbook of Social Theory* is no different, and even if the editors did not intend it, it will play a role in helping to define social theory at the dawn of a new millennium. However, such an exercise is not without controversy, for developments within social thought, in particular the construction of postmodern, feminist and multicultural perspectives, have rendered the very activity of defining the key figures and perspectives to be found in the field as problematic, as representing something like the constitution of a canon, itself a potentially reprehensible act. We are all now acutely aware of the fact that defining a field is regarded by some commentators as a potentially dangerous political act, not only for what is defined as important through inclusion, but, perhaps more significantly, for what is implicitly defined as unimportant through exclusion. Fraught with difficulty as the exercise might be there is a sense in which the constitution of something like a canon – in the form of recognized thinkers, perspectives and concerns – is a corollary of discipline-differentiated intellectual enquiry. Specification of the field of social theory, its constitution as a discursive formation with particular concepts, objects and types of enunciation, is bound up with the identification of particular key figures, texts, analytic perspectives and concerns. The process of specification is difficult for the field of social theory is constituted from contributions emanating from a number of disciplines, including sociology, political economy, philosophy, psychoanalysis and linguistics, as well as from theoretical developments in feminism and cultural studies. Notwithstanding the controversy surrounding such an exercise, there is a surprising degree of agreement within the community of social theorists about the range of perspectives encountered in the field, although there continues to be a healthy debate, and not infrequently strong disagreements are expressed, about the relative merit or value of many of them. While at one level social theory may be described as lacking an agreed paradigm and as fragmented insofar as there are a range of different, at times competing if not conflicting, conceptions of, perspectives on and approaches to the study of social phenomena, nevertheless there is a significant body of work that is recognized as central to, if not foundational for the practice of social theory, a body of work to which analysts have returned and referred over and over again. This body of work is not completely fixed and it is not sacred, and to that extent the notion of a canon with its ecclesiastical connotations may not be entirely appropriate. For our purposes the notion of the canon serves, at best, as a metaphor, as indicating the significance of particular works, which are nevertheless open to reinterpretation and addition with the identification of formerly neglected or new texts and studies, and specific analysts and authors, again open to change with the recognition of relevant others. The discursive formation of social theory is not a fixed unity, it is dynamic, subject to reconstitution in the light of new interpretative moves, retrievals of forgotten or marginalized thinkers and works, innovations and novel syntheses, changing relationships to cognate formations such as philosophy, linguistics and political economy and in response to transformed social conditions.

Notwithstanding the various criticisms of alleged 'Eurocentrism', 'logocentrism', 'sexism' and so on, social theory continues to have its 'great' texts and authors, its key works and significant analysts. Generally, it is a body of analyses described as 'classics' that have provided the foundations of social theory, that is the works of key nineteenth-century figures who were attempting to make sense of the 'great transformation' (Polanyi, 1980), specifically the emergence of modern forms of social life, through the development of novel forms of social analysis. However, the sense of the canon to be found in the *Handbook* extends beyond the works of the classical thinkers to encompass not only contemporary theoretical perspectives that have been developed in response to the perceived limits and limitations of the classical tradition, but also the contributions of analysts and perspectives critical of the very idea of a canon.

The *Handbook* has been constructed in full awareness of the problems associated with the idea of a canon. This is manifest, among other places, in the effort to be as inclusive as possible within the limits to which the exercise is subject, in particular ensuring the inclusion of those perspectives that have been most critical of the idea of canonical works. However, inclusion of contributions on postmodernism, feminism and multiculturalism is not simply a matter of editorial choice; any contemporary attempt to map out the field of social theory, to specify the range of perspectives utilized by social theorists, would need to acknowledge the capacity of the canon to accommodate critical approaches. Especially important in this regard are the chapters by Stephen Crook on postmodern social theory, Charles Lemert's address of multiculturalism as both a theory and a social reality, Douglas Kellner's overview of cultural studies and its relevance to social theory, and the chapters by Patricia Lengermann and Jill Niebrugge-Brantley on classical feminist theory and Mary Rogers on contemporary feminist theory. These chapters deal with approaches that frequently have been marginalized or excluded. The *Handbook* also includes chapters on theoretical contributions to substantive topics that have been similarly neglected. Barry Smart, Chris Shilling and Anthony Elliott in their respective discussions of ethics and morality, the body and sexuality are acutely aware of the historic tendency to marginalize or deny the relevance of the topics of concern to them. Smart draws attention to the way in which questions of ethics and morality have tended to be regarded as virtually inadmissible within a sociological discourse bent on promoting its modern scientific credentials and argues for a critical sociological address of the social production of immorality to help promote a regeneration of ethical life. Shilling argues that the embodied basis of social life has been devalued and marginalized within the sociological tradition and that a theoretical understanding of embodiment is central to a more effective understanding of the constitution of society. In a comparable manner, Elliott comments on the relative neglect of sex and sexuality in modern social thought and then proceeds to outline the turn to sexuality in social theory in the wake of social protests and movements in the 1960s and 1970s. This theme of neglect is also central to the chapter by George Ritzer, Douglas Goodman and Wendy Wiedenhoft who argue that the productivist bias of most classical and contemporary social theory has led to theories of consumption being inappropriately relegated to a position of relative unimportance. Their chapter seeks to identify the theoretical roots of a consumption problematic in the work of the classics and to argue that we are currently witnessing a flowering of theoretical and empirical work on consumption.

While careful consideration has been given to the need to be as inclusive as possible of significant approaches and themes that have tended to be neglected or marginalized, of necessity the *Handbook* tends to be dominated by chapters dealing with very familiar theorists – for example, Marx (McLennan), Weber (Whimster), Durkheim (Gane), Simmel (Nedelmann), Freud (O'Neill) and Mead (Joas) – and well-established theoretical approaches – for example, structural functionalism (Abrahamson), critical theory (Calhoun and Karaganis), symbolic interactionism (Sandstrom, Martin and Fine) and exchange theory (Molm).

This is not surprising, it simply reflects the fact that there are key theoretical figures and approaches about which social theorists need to be knowledgeable whatever particular theoretical preferences they may have. In short, as far as the question of a definition of the field is concerned our contention is that there is a greater degree of common ground (or collective understanding) between social theorists than is generally recognized to be the case. Argument and debate in social theory generally takes place on the basis of a set of shared assumptions about the texts and thinkers that have had the most significant impact on the analysis and understanding of modernity, although judgement of the analytic value and explanatory relevance of the works of particular thinkers and texts varies considerably and an over-riding commitment to a particular perspective can often lead to other approaches receiving, at best, highly selective attention. As Robert Merton has noted, as social theory has developed there has been a tendency for perspectives to become associated with camps of followers who close themselves off from 'ideas and information at odds with their own conceptions', the upshot of which is that they become 'less and less motivated to examine' (1972: 40) other perspectives.

Theoretical reflection on social life has changed significantly as late nineteenth-century attempts to constitute a new discipline of sociology were followed in the course of the twentieth century by an institutionalization of sociological teaching and research, most prominently within the distinctive intellectual and cultural traditions of universities in the United States and Europe, and by a subsequent proliferation of forms of social inquiry and research. Differences between American and European traditions were noted by Weber in his Munich University speech on 'Science as a Vocation' (1970 [1918]), but while he identified signs of an 'Americanization' of intellectual life and anticipated that a process of cultural colonization would become a more prominent feature, important differences have remained between European and American traditions of social thought. For example, while it is possible to argue that functionalism constituted the dominant paradigm for a period (approximately 1945–68) in American sociology (Gouldner, 1971), it is clear that functionalism never held the same compelling influence over social enquiry in Europe. Likewise, the traditions of Marxist thought and critical theory never exercised quite the same influence in the United States that they had in Europe over the same period (Poster, 1975).

Cross-cultural differences are also evident in the ways in which new perspectives or paradigms emerge and the works of particular thinkers are read. For example, postmodernism first achieved prominence in the United States in the 1960s, specifically in relation to the perceived neutralization of the critical potential of modernism. In his mapping of the postmodern Huyssen (1984) outlines the complex trajectory of the term from literary criticism in the United States in the late 1950s to architecture, dance, theatre, painting, music and film by the mid-1970s and then its subsequent migration to European social thought 'via Paris and Frankfurt' in the late 1970s. Significant differences have also been identified in

the reception Foucault's work has received in the United States and France. It has been argued that whereas in the US Foucault's Nietzscheanism (see Antonio's chapter in this volume) is reduced to a residual element and his work is set up in opposition to that of Habermas, in France Foucault is regarded as radically Nietzschean and his work tends to be set in opposition to phenomenology (Descombes, 1987). It is a striking fact that the key influential figures in contemporary social thought have tended to be French, the respective works of Foucault (see Dean's chapter in this volume), Lyotard, Baudrillard, Bourdieu and Derrida featuring prominently, and German, with the respective contributions of Habermas (see Brown and Goodman in this volume), Beck and Luhmann being particularly significant. The general issue of different interpretations and understandings of the works of particular thinkers is explored in a number of contributions to this volume.

The editing of a volume like this one carries with it an enormous responsibility. Identifying the theorists, theoretical approaches and examples of thematic forms of theorizing for inclusion is a daunting process, a process of selection and judgement which, while it does not court controversy, is likely to encounter it. Controversy comes with the territory and a degree of ambivalence and unease about an exercise such as this is to be expected. Undoubtedly some readers/colleagues will be less than totally happy with our selection and will argue against the inclusion of particular theorists, theories or forms of theorizing and/or will advocate the inclusion of others that we have appeared to neglect. Such differences of opinion are the lifeblood of social thought and are not only to be expected but are to be welcomed, uncomfortable as that might be for those on the receiving end. Criticism is not an optional extra; it is an intrinsic part of the practice of social science. Indeed it would be very helpful to have the responses of colleagues critical of our attempt to re-define the field and re-codify something like a canon, particularly as social theory is likely to continue to change in the coming years as theoretical perspectives and the topics of concern to all of us ebb and flow and we as editors prepare revisions for subsequent editions of the *Handbook*. To that end we have provided our e-mail addresses at the end of this introductory chapter.

(DE)/(RE)CONSTRUCTING THE CANON

From the outset, the practice of social theory has been characterized by change and fluctuation. The initial analytic focus of social theory, the accelerating erosion of traditional forms of life and emergence of the modern world, was from the beginning a moving target, and the features initially ascribed to that modern world – '[c]onstant revolutionizing of production, uninterrupted disturbance of all social conditions, everlasting uncertainty and agitation' (Marx and Engels, 1968: 83) – have become more pronounced and more prominent with the passage of time. Unavoidably, then, the object of social theory is a changing world, a modern world in perpetual motion, a (post)modern world in which it seems the only certainty is that things will be different tomorrow. And insofar as social theory cannot be 'kept insulated from its "subject matter"' (Giddens, 1987: 31), it is really no surprise to find that the field of social theory is characterized by transformation and uncertainty. One significant consequence of the change and fluctuation to which social theory has been exposed has been the identification of a proliferation of perspectives or recognition of the existence of a 'diversity of theoretical standpoints'. Whether diversity constitutes an intrinsic feature of the field has been a matter of some disagreement, with conflicting views being expressed about future prospects. Is there going to be a continuing 'proliferation of theoretical traditions' or is there a realistic prospect of a convincing new synthesis (Giddens, 1987)? What is abundantly clear from this volume is that the field of social theory is almost constantly in flux. Below is an enumeration of some of the major types of changes that have precipitated a reconsideration of the canon of social theory.

1 *Innovation* – new theories and syntheses are continually coming to the fore. For example, Barry Barnes in his chapter on macro/micro theory discusses the importance of a new theoretical perspective, actor–network theory; and Stephen Crook documents the way in which a series of analytic and aesthetic developments have been identified as exemplifying a distinctive postmodern approach.

2 *Retrieval* – older theories (or aspects of them) are being rediscovered and retrieved on a regular basis. This is nowhere clearer than in Patricia Lengermann and Jill Niebrugge-Brantley's discussion of a number of classical feminist theories that are just now being rediscovered and given the status and attention they deserve. In a parallel fashion, Robert van Krieken argues that Norbert Elias' work was ignored for decades before it was rediscovered and accorded appropriate recognition. Elias' work has subsequently had a significant impact on social theory. Similarly, Robert Antonio details the current resurgence of interest in Nietzsche's work.

3 *Translation* – new works of classical theorists, or translations of works that have never been translated before, give new life to classical theories and lead to new interpretations of those theories. For example, the translation into English of Simmel's *Philosophy of Money* in 1978 led to a rapid acceleration of interest in his work and to a dramatic alteration of the sense and understanding of Simmel's theory in the English-speaking world. Birgitta Nedelmann makes the point that the complete corpus of Simmel's work is soon to be published in German for the first time. Such an event will undoubtedly generate further interest in Simmel's work among German speakers and stimulate a reappraisal of his work as a whole and our understanding of its significance. Reappraisal will undoubtedly continue when Simmel's corpus is translated into other languages.

4 *Reinterpretation* – dominant interpretations of classical theories are subject to change over time as they are re-read in new social contexts and in the light of new intellectual concerns and understandings of specific classical texts. As interpretations change new types of theory may be generated, as Mike Gane demonstrates through his discussion of Durkheim's work in which an argument is presented for a shift of emphasis in its designation from structural functionalism to cultural sociology.

5 *Changing intellectual priorities* – the prominence and profile of perspectives fluctuate over time; even out-of-vogue perspectives are sustained by their community of practitioners. Unlike Kuhn's notion of the scientific community practising 'normal' science, generally working in a focused manner within an agreed paradigm, and only disturbed by exceptional periods of 'revolutionary' science that eventually lead to an alternative agreed paradigm, social theory is multiparadigmatic (Ritzer, 1975/1980). Older paradigms do not die or wither away, they merely add to the level of intellectual diversity.

In his chapter Shanyang Zhao observes that metatheorizing periodically seems to enjoy a burst of interest, only to retreat for a time into the theoretical shadows. However, whether or not it is explicitly addressed by social theorists, metatheorizing, Zhao argues, constitutes a significant part of the practice of social theory. It might be argued that metatheorizing is inherent in all social theory, and that what Bourdieu calls reflexive exploration of the 'unthought categories' of our thinking that serve to limit and predetermine what is thought should be regarded as a central feature of social theory. In short, it is through reflecting constantly on their own work that theorists can achieve an appropriate degree of epistemological vigilance and thereby become aware of, come to terms with, and begin to neutralize to some extent the particular determinisms to which their work is subject. However, again as Bourdieu makes clear, thinking about limits does not enable us to think without limits and to that extent the practice of epistemic reflexivity, and what Zhao terms metatheorizing, is a vital ongoing part of the practice of social theory. All of the chapters in this handbook are of necessity metatheoretical in character to some degree.

6 *Changing social conditions* – the experience and conceptualization of social changes frequently leads to significant transformations in social thought. As the sociology of knowledge demonstrates, the relationship between changes in social conditions and developments in social thought is a complex matter and the precise connection between particular events and specific theoretical narratives constitutes an important focus for empirical research. A number of chapters in our collection allude to the impact of events on social thought. For example, evidence of transformations to which the modern nation-state has been exposed under conditions of globalization leads Gerard Delanty to argue that we are witnessing a decoupling of nation from state and to theorize the idea of post-nationalism. Accumulating signs of a relative decline in the significance of production and evidence of a concomitant increase in the social, economic and cultural importance of consumption lead Ritzer, Goodman and Wiedenhoft to argue that greater attention needs to be directed to theories of consumption. Relatedly, the increased importance accorded to knowledge in the contemporary world has led Nico Stehr to theorize the notion of a knowledge society. In a comparable manner it can be argued that the feminist social movement has played a key role in the dramatic growth in feminist social theory. Likewise Charles Lemert carefully explores the close articulation between multiculturalism as a social movement and as a theory. The increasing importance of the process of globalization is reflected in Roland Robertson's chapter on globalization theory. Finally, the growing importance of technologically mediated relationships (for example, those conducted over the Internet) is reflected in Karin Knorr Cetina's chapter on postsocial theory.

Reappraisal of historic events is also closely articulated with changes in social thought. For example, the late twentieth-century generation of theoretical interest in the abuses of Nazism and in particular the Holocaust not only drew attention to the relative marginalization and neglect of these concerns but also called into question prevailing understandings of both modern social thought and the social formation of modernity itself. These issues are raised in Smart's discussion of the increasing prominence accorded to questions of morality and ethics in the work of social theorists concerned to counter the silence surrounding moral and ethical matters in sociological enquiry. In a comparable manner, recognition of the excesses of Soviet-style communism, in particular its 'terrors', with the Gulag serving as an appropriate emblem, and in turn that these matters have not received the analytic attention their gravity warrants, has served to undermine both the political notion of socialism and Marxism as a political discourse. In response to the discrediting of socialism as a politics, a form of political life that seems to be a part of the past, Peter Beilharz proceeds in his chapter to suggest that the idea of socialism may nevertheless be retrieved, that it can continue to operate in a critical register, as the counter-culture of modernity. Likewise, Gregor McLennan responds to the notion that Marxism as a vital intellectual project might have had its day by providing a strong argument for the continuing contemporary relevance of Marx's analysis of the capitalist mode of production. With the globalization of capitalism there is fresh scope for a reappraisal of the value of Marx's work and McLennan maintains that while orthodox Marxism has justifiably been discredited and consigned to the dustbin of history the relevance of Marx's work has never been greater than it is now. The complex historical events associated with the Holocaust and the collapse of the Communist bloc, and associated claimed manifestations of a socialist alternative, have been retrieved, reinterpreted and subsequently considered to signify the limitations of the modern project, a diagnosis that is closely articulated with the development of postmodern forms of social theory discussed by Crook.

As modernity has continued to develop and change and the consequences of living in a runaway modern world have emerged, social analysts have been required to respond by introducing new concepts with which to theorize the transformed social conditions encountered. With the diffusion of the institutional features of modernity throughout the world conventional sociological understandings of 'society' have been problematized. As a number of analysts have noted, the globalization of economic and cultural life in particular raises questions about the appropriateness of the received idea of 'society' (Robertson, 1992; Touraine, 1989). The globalization of modernity not only introduces a world-wide extension of social relations across space and time, it also exerts an influence on local events and processes (see Robertson's chapter in this volume).

As modern life has continued to be subject to complex processes of transformation, the very terms employed to conceptualize existing formations and conditions have been called into

question. Reflecting on the historical development of modernity analysts have argued that
'industrial society' is merely a semi-modern
society and that currently we are living through a
process of reflexive modernization that is
introducing not simply more modernity, but is
leading to a radicalized modernity. It is argued
that the process of reflexive modernization has
given rise to a new type of post-traditional
society, one which has been designated a 'risk
society' (Beck, 1992; Beck et al., 1994). Yet
another fine example of the responsiveness of
social theory to the rapidly changing social
environment that constitutes its subject matter is
provided by the notion of the 'network society',
a term introduced to enhance understanding of
the new social structure emerging from the
introduction of information technology and the
effects of its articulation with a global capitalist
economy, a 'culture of real virtuality' and a
nation-state system that is held to be in crisis
(Castells, 1996; Smart, 2000).

7 *Developments in cognate fields of enquiry* –
can also have an important impact on social
theory. A good example is to be found in
Kellner's chapter on cultural studies and its
increasing importance in social theory. A similar
conclusion can be drawn from Harvie Ferguson's chapter on phenomenological philosophy
and John O'Neill's discussion of psychoanalytic
theory. More broadly, it is clear that developments in philosophy, in particular the works of
philosophers of science (for example, Popper,
Kuhn and Feyerabend) and the writings of continental philosophers (for example, Foucault,
Lyotard and Derrida), have precipitated what
has been described as 'a return to ontological/
epistemological issues' (Mouzelis, 1991: 2). The
philosophical works of Foucault, Lyotard and
Derrida have also contributed powerfully to the
debate over the modern situation and what has
been termed the postmodern predicament
(Bernstein, 1991; Huyssen, 1984).

The activity of theoretically reflecting on and
attempting to reason about human existence and
the complex ways in which the lives of individuals
and communities have been organized has a long
history. A sustained and developing series of
theoretical narratives on social life, on the socius,
emerged with the Enlightenment, with the
philosophers of the Enlightenment era, as John
Rundell demonstrates in his chapter. A preoccupation with an agenda of issues that derive
from Enlightenment thought informs the work of
the classical founders of social theory and
continues through the proliferating narratives
of contemporary social thought. The shadow of
Enlightenment thought can be detected in the
contrasting writings of key contemporary social
theorists such as Habermas and Foucault and it

provides the background against which the
debate over contending modern and postmodern
orientations to social thought tends to be played
out.

The emergence of formal theories about social
life, theories offering different perspectives on
'the social', conceptualizing the study of social
phenomena in a variety of different ways – social
facts (Durkheim), social action (Weber), sociation (Simmel), forces and social relations of
production (Marx) – accelerated with the constitution of the modern epistemological configuration and the formation of the social sciences
in general and sociology in particular. It is here,
in the second half of the nineteenth century with
the increasing institutionalization of modern
forms of life, with the increasing diffusion of that
form of life we now identify as modernity, that
the discipline of sociology established itself and
took root, and a distinctive practice of social
theorizing first began to emerge. It is through a
reconsideration of the epistemological context in
which sociology emerged and theorizing about
the social became a possibility within the field of
knowledge that an understanding of the indeterminate and fragmentary character of contemporary social theory may be achieved.

The parameters of the epistemological context
within which sociological reflection on social
conditions and processes developed have been
identified as mathematical formalization, the
adoption of models and concepts derived from
biology, economics and the sciences of language,
and philosophical reflection (Foucault, 1973). It
is within this complex epistemological space and
in relation to the different planes of thought that
are a corollary that different styles of sociological reflection have emerged and developed.
For example, consider the pursuit of mathematical formalization evident in more positivisti-
cally orientated forms of social enquiry, the
adoption of concepts and models from biology
evident in forms of functionalist analysis, the
impact of political economy on social analysis
and the significance linguistics has assumed in
the development of structuralist and post-
structuralist approaches. The complexity of the
epistemological context has led to the constitution of a range of different sociologies, exemplified most clearly by the contrasting formative
attempts of such key figures as Emile Durkheim
and Max Weber, and to a lesser extent Georg
Simmel, to make the case for the distinctiveness
of sociology as a form of enquiry with its own
subject matter and methodology, literally to
situate the discipline in relation to other social
sciences. The precariousness that has been a
feature of this process of determining the distinctiveness of sociology is effectively exemplified by the omission of a key figure from the

previous statement. Karl Marx is justifiably regarded as a 'founding father' of the discipline, one of 'the trinity', yet at no point does he attempt to make the case for a distinctive socio-logical approach and when he does make explicit reference to the discipline it is in the context of a brief criticism of Auguste Comte's 'trashy positivism'. It is worth adding that Weber was opposed to the establishment of chairs of socio-logy and late in life he was inclined to refer to himself as a 'political economist'. In a compar-able manner, Simmel described himself as a philosopher and spoke of philosophy as his 'life's task', the practice of sociology constituting a mere 'sideline' (Lepenies, 1988: 243). It is perhaps possible to recognize here an early trace of a tension that has become more pro-nounced as the volume of analytic reflection on social life has increased; a tension exemplified by a far from clearly drawn distinction between sociological and social theory.

Theorizing about social life is not confined to the discipline of sociology, indeed it might be argued that increasingly it has been analysts who, much like Marx, are not operating within a sociological paradigm who have had the most powerful impact on the development of con-temporary social thought and the generation of more persuasive understandings of social condi-tions. For example, the respective works of philosophers like Foucault, Derrida and Lyo-tard, and to a lesser extent Deleuze and Guattari, and Virilio, the controversial writings of Baud-rillard, the narratives of literary and cultural analysts such as Jameson and Bhaba, the psy-choanalytic reflections of Lacan and Kristeva, and the contributions of feminist analysts and those working in interdisciplinary areas like cultural studies are now regularly invoked in analyses of contemporary social life.

As we have noted, social theory is a very varied discourse, internally diverse, character-ized by a variety of schools and traditions of enquiry. A number of the schools and traditions of enquiry derive from the distinctive qualities of perspectives introduced by key founding figures (notably Marx, Weber, Durkheim, Simmel and Freud), individuals whose works continue to be reinterpreted in the light of present conditions (see the chapters by McLennan, Gane, Whim-ster, Nedelmann and O'Neill), theorists whose works remain a significant foundation resource of ideas for making sense of late modern social life. Other schools and traditions of enquiry have developed in response to the perceived limits and limitations of what is frequently described as classical social theory, but the works of the classics endure and continue to be reinterpreted and regarded as relevant to an understanding of late modern social life.

One of the ways in which the history of modern social theory can be read is as a continuing search for the definitive theory or synthesis, for the approach that effectively orders and appropri-ately explains the social. The continuing pro-liferation of perspectives demonstrates the resistance of social phenomena to such a theor-etical ordering. There always seems to be a remainder, always another perspective that defies inclusion and that cannot be silenced, and although this resembles the line to be found in positions frequently identified as postmodern, the emergence of such a 'perspective' in response to the perceived limits and limitations of modern social theory has not concluded the debate or brought to an end the process of development of 'new' forms and styles of theorizing. To the contrary, postmodern social theory now seems to have become a part of the very canon it itself sought to discredit.

Without doubt the field of social theory has been subject to change but it is difficult to sustain the idea of cumulative progress in social thought. The notion of a progressive accumulation of knowledge about the social world represented by the displacement of a prevailing theoretical paradigm by an alternative one better equipped to explain and account for anomalies does not represent an adequate description of the field of social theory. The relationship between social thought and modern social life is more complex than the 'instrumental' conception acknowl-edges. The idea that social thought constitutes an instrument for exercising control over social institutions and processes and that improvements and advances can be gained and recognized through the achievement of greater control and predictability constitutes an inappropriate, if not an impoverished view of the relationship between social analysis and social processes. As Giddens explains, a social science like sociology does not 'develop cumulative knowledge in the same way as the natural sciences' (1990: 16), rather the relationship it has to its subject matter is that of a 'double hermeneutic'. Social knowledge stands in a complex relationship to its subject matter, it is not independent or detached from the social world. To the contrary, ideas, conceptions and explanations infiltrate the very social contexts that they seek to describe or account for and in the process social knowledge and the social world that is its object are both transformed. Such an understanding of the practice of social enquiry leads David Kettler and Volker Meja to suggest in their analysis of the theories of Karl Mannheim that we are not beneficiaries of any 'progress' in social thought. The inappropriateness of the idea that the history of social thought might be read in terms of a narrative of progress, with theorizing advancing from a more primitive state to one which is increasingly more refined is further undermined by Rundell's identification of the clear presence of modern sociological issues in the respective works of such pre-sociologists as Ferguson and Schiller.

The history of social theory reveals the presence of many different schools and approaches and a significant range of them appear in this volume. For some social theorists the existence of contrasting schools and approaches constitutes a challenge to which the appropriate response is the pursuit of a synthesis, theoretical overview or totalization promising a renewed coherence. The respective works of Parsons (see Holton's chapter in this volume), Giddens (1984, 1987) and Habermas (see Brown and Goodman) provide significant examples of attempts to overcome the problems associated with a continually proliferating range of theoretical traditions. However, not all analysts share this view of the field: for example, Van Krieken makes the point that Elias rejected the idea of a grand synthesis and notwithstanding the efforts of contemporary analysts such as Giddens, Habermas, Mouzelis and Runciman, social theory continues to be characterized by a wide variety of more specific theoretical perspectives. In short, alongside attempts to develop syntheses, there continues to be a proliferation of specific narratives on topics like consumption, the body and sexuality, a tendency exemplified by some of the contributors to the final section of this volume.

Just as a narrative of progress can no longer be regarded as appropriate or adequate for telling the story of social theory, so positivism no longer constitutes a guiding principle for the practice of social thought. While there are those who still adhere to a positivistic approach (for example see Peter Halfpenny's chapter on positivism; Jonathan Turner's chapter on Comte and Spencer; Douglas Heckathorn's on rational choice theory; and Linda Molm's discussion of exchange theory), the majority of social theorists have eschewed such an approach. Very few of the chapters in this volume adopt a positivistic perspective, but each of them, to use the notion introduced by Kettler and Meja, offer a 'thoughtful encounter' with the work of a particular theorist, a specific theoretical perspective or approach, or an idea or issue worth theorizing. Such thoughtful encounters generate insights, sometimes some striking and new insights, into the topics being examined. However, it would be a mistake for readers to restrict their 'thoughtful encounters' purely to such secondary sources, for there is even more to be gained by engaging directly with the primary source material to which our contributors have directed their attentions. We hope that reading the chapters in this volume will prove to be a 'thoughtful encounter', one that

will stimulate the reader's interest in the key figures, perspectives and themes that currently constitute the field of contemporary social theory. But it is more than a thoughtful encounter that we intend, as satisfying as that might appear to be.

In so far as the *Handbook* returns to, reviews and reinterprets the works associated with a representative range of classical and contemporary theorists, critically explores prominent theoretical perspectives, and in addition offers examples of significant forms of theorizing on selected themes and issues, the reader can begin to appreciate the rich diversity of contemporary social thought, and begin to take a necessary first step towards an address of the problem of 'selective inattention' that so concerned Merton (1972). Increasing specialization is probably destined to remain a feature of social scientific enquiry and insofar as that is the case it is likely that fragmentation and the absence of a core problematic will remain prominent and potentially problematic features of the field of social theory.

However, while it is the case that the field is characterized by contrasting and at times conflicting theoretical perspectives and concerns, there is evidence of, if not a new synthesis, certainly a radically regenerated preoccupation with the transformation of modernity, what Bernstein has termed a 'new constellation' of analytic concern that is not reducible to 'a common denominator, essential core, or generative first principle' (1991: 8), a preoccupation that is effectively exemplified by Bauman's powerful series (1987, 1989, 1991) of analytic engagements with the complex reality and uneven consequences of modern social life.

Social theory, as the chapters in the *Handbook* demonstrate, continues to accommodate to and to account for the new forms of social life emerging with the transformation of modernity. Mirroring the preoccupations of the classical founders of social thought, contemporary social theory continues to engage with fundamental questions concerning the respects in which the social world is changing and the forms or styles of analysis that are required to generate effective explanations of the transformed social conditions in which we now find ourselves living. This constitutes the central task of social theory, its mission, and it represents the common underlying focus to which the different chapters in this volume are directed.

REFERENCES

Bauman, Z. (1987) *Legislators and Interpreters – On Modernity, Postmodernity and Intellectuals*. Cambridge: Polity Press.

Bauman, Z. (1989) *Modernity and the Holocaust*. Cambridge: Polity Press.

Bauman, Z. (1991) *Modernity and Ambivalence*. Cambridge: Polity Press.

Beck, U. (1992) *Risk Society – Towards a New Modernity*. London: Sage.

Beck, U., Giddens, A. and Lash, S. (1994) *Reflexive Modernization – Politics, Tradition and Aesthetics in the Modern Social Order*. Cambridge: Polity Press.

Bernstein, R.J. (1991) *The New Constellation – The Ethical-Political Horizons of Modernity/Postmodernity*. Cambridge: Polity Press.

Castells, M. (1996) *The Information Age: Economy, Society and Culture*, Vol. 1: *The Rise of the Network Society*. Oxford: Blackwell.

Descombes, V. (1987) 'Je m'en Foucault', *London Review of Books*, 5 (9): 20–1.

Foucault, M. (1973) *The Order of Things – An Archaeology of the Human Sciences*. New York: Vintage Books.

Giddens, A. (1984) *The Constitution of Society*. Cambridge: Polity Press.

Giddens, A. (1987) *Social Theory and Modern Sociology*. Cambridge: Polity Press.

Giddens, A. (1990) *The Consequences of Modernity*. Cambridge: Polity Press.

Gouldner, A. (1971) *The Coming Crisis of Western Sociology*. London: Heinemann.

Habermas, J. (1984) *The Theory of Communicative Action*, Vol. 1: *Reason and the Rationalisation of Society*. London: Heinemann.

Habermas, J. (1987) *The Theory of Communicative Action*, Vol. 2: *Lifeworld and System: A Critique of Functionalist Reason*. Cambridge: Polity Press.

Huyssen, A. (1984) 'Mapping the Postmodern', *New German Critique*, No. 33 (Fall): 5–52.

Lepenies, W. (1988) *Between Literature and Science: The Rise of Sociology*. Cambridge: Cambridge University Press.

Marx, K. and Engels, F. (1968) *The Communist Manifesto*. Harmondsworth: Penguin.

Merton, R. (1972) 'Insiders and Outsiders: A Chapter in the Sociology of Knowledge', *American Journal of Sociology*, 78 (1): 9–47.

Mouzelis, N.P. (1991) *Back to Sociological Theory – The Construction of Social Orders*. London: Macmillan.

Polanyi, K. (1980) *The Great Transformation*. New York: Octagon Books.

Poster, M. (1975) *Existential Marxism in Post-war France: From Sartre to Althusser*. Princeton, NJ: Princeton University Press.

Ritzer, G. (1975/1980) *Sociology: A Multiple Paradigm Science*. Boston, MA: Allyn and Bacon.

Robertson, R. (1992) *Globalization: Social Theory and Global Culture*. London: Sage.

Runciman, W.G.A. (1983) *Treatise on Social Theory: The Methodology of Social Theory* (Vol. 1). Cambridge: Cambridge University Press.

Runciman, W.G.A. (1989) *Treatise on Social Theory: Substantive Social Theory* (Vol. 2). Cambridge: Cambridge University Press.

Runciman, W.G.A. (1997) *Treatise on Social Theory: Applied Social Theory* (Vol. 3). Cambridge: Cambridge University Press.

Smart, B. (2000) 'A Political Economy of New Times? Critical Reflections on the Network Society and the Ethos of Informational Capitalism', *European Journal of Social Theory*, 3 (1): 51–65.

Touraine, A. (1989) 'Is Sociology Still the Study of Society?', *Thesis Eleven*, 23.

Weber, M. (1970 [1918]) 'Science as a Vocation' in *From Max Weber: Essays in Sociology*, edited with an introduction by H.H. Gerth and C. Wright Mills. Routledge and Kegan Paul, London.

E-MAIL ADDRESSES FOR CORRESPONDENCE

ritzer@socy.umd.edu

barry.smart@port.ac.uk

Part One
CLASSICAL SOCIAL THEORY

2

Modernity, Enlightenment, Revolution and Romanticism: Creating Social Theory

JOHN RUNDELL

Social theory is often thought of as the intellectual child of the major changes in society that occurred in the nineteenth century due to industrialization, the formation of the nation-state, realignments between the state and civil society, and the capitalist transformation of social relations. Up until the formation of the discipline of sociology late in the nineteenth century, analyses and critiques of these changes took place from the vantage point of political philosophy, philosophy, history and political economy, at least in the universities. Once the paradigm of society took shape, especially in the writings of Emile Durkheim in France and Max Weber in Germany, these disciplines gave way to social theory as the register through which social critique was voiced (Lévi-Strauss, 1945; Salomon, 1945).

While this general outline is correct for the development of social theory, once it is professionalized under the umbrella of sociology, many of these dimensions of social life mentioned above were already present during the seventeenth and eighteenth centuries. The aim of this chapter is to explore some of the critiques of these changes, critiques that were often voiced in political and philosophical registers. These critiques helped to create, draw on and reinterpret three major intellectual currents of the eighteenth century. These currents were, following Seidman, the sociocentric current of the Enlightenment, the revolutionary tradition, and Romanticism (Seidman, 1983: 21–77; see also Saiedi, 1993; Zeitlin, 1997).

The Enlightenment can be divided into two broad currents – an objectivistic one, which combines rationalism and empiricism, and a sociocentric current, which begins with the assumption that humans are only formed in society. Seidman points out that the sociocentric current vehemently criticized the individualism inherent in social contract theories, as well as the presocial images of the individual inherent in many of them, especially Hobbes' *Leviathan* and Rousseau's *The Social Contract* (Seidman, 1983: 21–41; Taylor, 1975: 3–29).

The revolutionary tradition can be divided into four broad currents: one that radicalizes the value category of freedom, which encompasses Marxism and anarchism; the radical egalitarianism of Jacobinism, which is articulated in the works of Babeuf and Blanqui (see below); radicalized ideals of authentic community, which also draws from Romanticism (see below) and includes Nazism; and socialism, which ranges from the work of Saint-Simon and the social democracy of Bernstein. Each current thematized the idea that the world could be built anew – the central motif of the revolutionary tradition. Prior to the French Revolution, the meaning of revolution referred to astronomical cycles. Only with the French Revolution did the word begin to refer to sudden and fundamental changes to a society's social and political conditions (Arendt, 1973; Scocpol and Kestnbaum, 1990: 13). Apart from the modern image of rapid and fundamental change, the revolutionary tradition also contributed to the social theoretical critiques of natural law and utilitarianism, and to sociology as a reformist discipline in its concern with social injustice, inequality and the analysis of forms of domination, whether they be articulated in class or gender terms. By the end of the eighteenth century class and gender domination were already being critiqued, and they found their critics in, for example, the French utopian socialists, Fourrier, Proudhon and the English Jacobin-feminist Mary Wollstonecraft. Both Marxism and feminism inherited and critically worked with and against these various revolutionary currents (Hearnshaw, 1928; Seidman, 1983: 64–73; Vogel, 1986).

Romanticism emerged in Germany at the end of the eighteenth century and became the primary voice through which the excesses of rationalism and instrumentalism were voiced. Whilst it originated in Germany, it also took root in France, England and Russia during the nineteenth century, and is still a major cultural force today. Romanticism encompassed a wider cultural movement of not only literature, especially poetry, art and music, but also blurred the boundaries between these forms of expression and philosophy itself.[1] In this context, Saiedi's reading of the Romantic legacy to social theory, which emphasizes its subjectivism and relativism, can be extended to encompass three other concerns (Saiedi, 1993). These concerns are historiography and aesthetics, both of which are underpinned by a philosophical anthropology or a human self-image of 'the creative–imaginative self' (see Abrams, 1953; Kearney, 1988; Taylor, 1975).

In the midst of this complex and diverse intellectual and political ferment people hotly debated the shape of the societies in which they found themselves, and the nature of their lives. This intellectual ferment helped to shape modernity, and developed a conceptual vocabulary specific to this eighteenth-century context. During the eighteenth century three terms gained currency in order to make sense of, and have conceptual purchase on, the features of modernity, and became common points of reference across the Enlightenment, and the revolutionary and romantic traditions. These terms were civil society, civilization and culture.

Civil society came to refer to a part of society separate from the state in which people engaged in commercial and/or political life as citizens. Civilization and culture, in particular, emerge as two competing notions that stand apart, and because of national differences, give different weight, value and emphasis to different aspects of *modern* social life. During the eighteenth century, civilization was deployed as a term that was used, in part, in the same way that people use the term society today. In conventional sociological language it encompassed, in the Western tradition at least, civil society (given its etymology) as well as state forms from absolutism to the nation-state. However, it referred not only to social

processes and institutions, but also to the conduct of manners, as well as the images (such as the savage) through which an elite portrayed its own society, or projected it onto another (Elias, 1996; Febvre, 1998; Rundell and Mennell, 1998: 6–11). Culture or *Kultur*, alternatively, referred to the activity and products of *reflexive* thought, irrespective of whether or not they took the form of religion, art or science (in the broader German meaning of the word). Increasingly, it came to refer to the activities of artists, and to the worthiness of high art. In this context, especially, culture was viewed as separate and distanced from the institutional worlds of commerce, state power and bureaucratic rule, worlds viewed by those of culture as mundane, tedious and perverse (Berlin, 1999; Goethe, 1989; Rundell and Mennell, 1998: 12–14).

Eighteenth-century thinkers invoked the conceptual currencies of civil society, civilization and culture in order to present and carry forward ideas about modernity. Within the current of the Enlightenment, civilization and civil society were interpreted as idioms through which the progress of humankind could be posited. Within the revolutionary current civilization and civil society were critically reconstructed in order to bring forward and accomplish the political utopias of freedom and equality that were the hallmarks of the American and French Revolutions. In the current of Romanticism, civilization and civil society were often viewed as the alienated, counter-worlds to the authentic one of culture. It is here that Romanticism came into its own, with its emphasis on the creative, imaginative and poetic powers that would unite subjects alienated from one another and themselves.

The Enlightenment, the revolutionary tradition and Romanticism, and each of the thinkers who are discussed below, leave a legacy that becomes a point of reference, in either positive or negative terms, which finds its way into the social-theoretical imagination. In other words, each current and each of the thinkers discussed reaches forward with questions and issues that are addressed, often with a sense of urgency, by social theorists and sociologists alike.

THE ENLIGHTENMENT AND ADAM FERGUSON'S POLITICAL SOCIOLOGY: THE TEMPERS OF CIVIL SOCIETY AND CIVILIZATION

The famous question, 'What is Enlightenment?', debated so heatedly in the German press in the 1780s, and to which Kant's equally famous essay by the same name was a contribution, had already preoccupied European thinkers for almost one hundred and fifty years. The intellectual curiosity and critique of the philosophers who participated in this intellectual movement cannot be tied to one specific European location. France, Italy, Germany and England, more specifically Scotland, developed specific Enlightenments, drawing on their own traditions, and their arguments against others, all in the light of the particular modernity which they confronted and in which they participated (Bierstedt, 1978; Fletcher, 1971).

Nor can the Enlightenment philosophers' curiosity and critique be tied to one particular preoccupation. Rather, Bierstedt, for example, reconstructs their intellectual range in terms of four propositions around which they argued, and which captured the spirit of the times. In the first proposition, it was argued that reason, and science in particular, was superior to religion, in explaining the nature of reality, whether it be natural or social. Given this confidence in reason as a mode of explanation, it was also argued that all natural and social problems that confronted humankind could be solved through the application of scientific principles. Moreover, the Enlightenment philosophers' confidence in reason's ability to solve all problems sat neatly with a third proposition – that humankind was, in principle, perfectible, and that it (humankind) was progressively moving on a path towards perfection. Imperfection was identified not only with those forms of knowledge and societies that were viewed as backward, but also those that were viewed as corrupt. Corruption, itself, also entailed a fourth set of issues – those that addressed the problem of government and related to this, issues of negative freedoms and rights (Bierstedt, 1978: 5).

However, as Taylor and Seidman have suggested, these four propositions or sets of arguments, tend to boil down to two major intellectual lines of development. Taylor terms these the objectivistic and the subjectivistic currents of the Enlightenment (Taylor, 1975: 11–30).

In the objectivistic Enlightenment version, modernity became identified with the development of objectified knowledge, that is, with the development of modern rationalist, scientific thinking. Epistemologically, knowledge of the social and natural worlds is gleaned and explained through a methodology of empirical rationalism. Under its aegis the view of the natural world shifted from one in which human beings projected a cosmological, holistic meaning onto it, to one in which it was viewed as neutral and contingent. Nature, including internal nature or the soul, became viewed as simply constituted by properties and things, which themselves were viewed atomistically. Relations

between these atomistically construed properties and things were viewed in mechanistic terms. Causal effects between things and properties were, thus, no longer viewed as necessary, but rather only related to their contingent aspects that became evident in the release or demonstration of either efficient or inefficient energies when one thing or property came in contact with another. The representatives of this tradition are Descartes, Bacon and Locke (Taylor, 1975: 7–10).

Through the philosophies of rationalism and empiricism, society is conceived as a conglomerate of separate, private individuals who construct private bonds prior to the advent of society itself. The search for a rational analysis of society begins with single, observable phenomena found in history and social life. General systems of conduct and governance are then formed inductively from these observations. In other words, the mechanistic and atomistic view affected the way in which political and social relations were perceived. Human beings were not only part of nature, and in this sense could be manipulated by a range of social techniques, but were also in a state of nature, that is, faced one another as atomistic, disconnected individuals. The background assumption, articulated, for example, by Hobbes' *Leviathan* about the origins of civil society, is that individuals exist in a presocial state of nature, and that their association creates the problem. Here, self-identity and its formation refer to an image of contractualism between the state, which guarantees safety, and isolated individuals as they 'enter' society. Civil society was viewed as the social space in which private and egoistic individuals pursued their own private interests. Here, private property became both the symbol of, and medium through which these individualistic assumptions of social relations were pursued under the protective umbrella of the state, to forge the image of the 'contractual self' (Hobbes, 1968; Taylor, 1989: 159–76).

Seidman convincingly argues that the other subjectivist current is more important and relevant to the genealogy and development of social theory (Seidman, 1983: 28–34). The subjectivist current can be termed a critical or philosophical anthropology with a practical intent to both understand how human beings live together, and to change the conditions under which they do so. According to Taylor, who gives his account a philosophical and political focus, this current emphasized humankind's ability to free itself from all types of external constraints, especially nature, the state and the church (Taylor, 1975: 9). However, what is significant about this current is that it combines this notion of self-activating freedom with views that were both sociocentric and historical. The breakthrough to the social sciences of humankind in the subjectivist current, of which Montesquieu, Voltaire, D'Alembert, Hume and Ferguson are representative figures, occurs once rationalism and historiography are interpreted from the subjectivist standpoint and united (Seidman, 1983: 25–8).

As we have seen, objectivistic rationalism makes the world accessible only through the principles of method, principles identified with reason itself. In the historiographical tradition prior to its subjectivistic reorientation, historiography 'singled out the unique historical "event" as a rudimentary unit of analysis and employed narration as the means to achieve conceptual order' (Seidman, 1983: 26). However, under the umbrella of subjectivism, both sides were transformed. Rational principles became subject to the recognition of the diversity of historical and social conditions. Montesquieu, Condorcet and Voltaire, in their own ways, declared that the object of study was humankind in its diversity. Historiography came under the sway of subjectivistic principles. Writing universal history became possible as all epochs and regions of the world could be reconstructed in terms of developmental paths that gave a narrative unity to otherwise disconnected events. The result of this was the formation of philosophies of history that often deployed the language of civilization as its unifying idea (Seidman, 1983: 25–30).

Accompanying this historiographical reorientation was another that actually underpinned it. In contrast to the image of 'the contractual self', a philosophical anthropology emerged that could be termed the 'societal self', and was based on human association. Whilst Montesquieu, Voltaire and Hume all point to this crucial aspect of social life in their critiques of the philosophical fiction of the atomistic individual in the presocial state of nature (Hobbes and Rousseau), it is Ferguson who presents a proto-social theory that begins and builds systematically on the image of 'the societal self'. He posits that '[humankind is] to be taken in groups, as they have always subsisted' (Ferguson, 1991: 4). Ferguson's *An Essay on the History of Civil Society* sits at this particularly important point in the genealogy of social theory. Writing in 1767, Ferguson systematically develops a sociocentric and associative perspective, which also provides him with a vantage point to critically assess modern society. For him modern society was already being torn by the creation of wealth and moral disintegration, which resulted from increased commercial activity and specialization within the division of labour. His work prefigures that of Marx, Spencer and Durkheim, and because of this he is often referred to as 'the father of sociology' in a

way that the above thinkers cannot be (MacRae, 1969: 17–26; Swingewood, 1991).[2]

The correct study of humankind, for Ferguson is both the study of social individuals in groups and societies, and the types of associations and actions by these social individuals. Ferguson goes on to say that 'the history of the individual is but a detail of the sentiments and thoughts he has entertained in the view of his species: and every experiment relative to this subject should be made with entire societies, not with single men' (Ferguson, 1991: 4). Elsewhere he states, simply, that 'Man is by nature, a member of a community', which entails that it is society that is the human being's 'state of nature' (Ferguson, 1991: 59; Kettler, 1965: 188).

In this context, the methodologically and a priori notion of reason shifts to one that is essentially pragmatic – it is the result of interaction in the world of both natural and human affairs. Ferguson terms this type of reasoning 'reflection' and 'insight', both of which are only articulated and formulated through specific patterns of human interaction (Ferguson, 1991: 11). Reflection and insight denote a capacity to achieve a critical distance from a particular situation. According to Ferguson, though, it is the patterns of human association that enable a critical distance to be achieved. In other words, social interaction provides the conditions for reasoned action, and not the other way round. He singles out and gives primacy to two patterns of social interaction – those that foster affection, and those that are based on aversion and hostility. Both patterns of interaction foster social solidarity (Ferguson, 1991: 18, 20, 24).[3]

The interpenetration of society and the individual, association and reasoning means that Ferguson also develops a model of socialization that presages many of the versions that emerge in the social-theoretical tradition. Like the later sociologists, Emile Durkheim, especially in *Suicide*, and Norbert Elias in *The Civilizing Process*, Ferguson posits a model of socialization in which there is a close homology between the structure of society and the structure of the personality. Self-identity has a strong parallel with social identity. Ferguson, like Elias, deploys his version of socialization through his notion of civilization. All human beings, because they are social, must undergo a civilizing process that encompasses learning and practising virtues, reflection and insight. In a manner that also presages Elias' work in his much later study *The Civilizing Process*, the more unmediated and undifferentiated the society, the more unmediated and undifferentiated the personality. In Ferguson's view more intense patterns of mutual affection and aversion occur in societies where patterns of social conduct (which he terms virtues) are not greatly differentiated. The differentiation of society generates both a differentiation and specialization of virtues, and, thus, less intense patterns of interaction (Ferguson, 1991: 81–107).

Ferguson's philosophical anthropology also grounds his historical survey and critique of the formation of civil society. In Ferguson's view, civil society is a particularly complex form of civilization, which he terms *polished society*, as distinct from *rude* ones, which are those societies that are not yet differentiated in terms of their functions or manners and styles of life. In contrast, polished societies are those that have undergone a historical shift that amounts to a civilizational breakthrough in the history of humankind. This breakthrough, to put it in terms of social-theoretical language after Ferguson, occurs as a process of societal differentiation that takes place along three axes – the development of specialized realms of economy (what Ferguson terms 'commerce'), culture (what Ferguson terms 'arts'), and statecraft (which is analysed under the term 'subordination'). Importantly, in an eighteenth-century context of both teleological and proto-biological philosophies of history, and later theories of social evolution, Ferguson argues that the history of humankind cannot be grounded in ontogenetic metaphors of childhood, maturity and old age. Civilizations are both contingent and reversible. They are a product of a combination of factors (which includes reflection and insight), and in ever-present danger of political and social corruption and disintegration (Ferguson, 1991: 232–72).

In Ferguson's view, the corruption or reversibility of the civilization of modern societies is an indication of the tensions within the division of labour and factional conflicts in republicanism, tensions that may result in a form of corruption that combines both cultural and social decadence and political despotism. The greatest danger that the modern division of labour poses is a loss of public spirit. In an analysis to which Marx was drawn and which also presages much of Durkheim's work, the divisions between public administration and private citizens, soldiers and citizens, entrepreneurs and workers erodes the bonds of civil society, and the sociability through which civil society is constituted. Civil society dissolves and is 'made to consist of parts of which none is animated with the spirit of society itself' (Ferguson, 1991: 218). Peaceful and temperate conduct simply become masks of politeness as men (and women) of commerce lapse into self-interest. Later, Marx in his *1844 Manuscripts*, would portray this world as an alienated one, whilst Durkheim, in his 1897 *The Division of Labour in Society*, would portray it as one of pathological differentiation. Ferguson constructs a telling portrait of a new commercial class who, without the normative and cultural resources of traditional aristocratic classes with their codes of honour, conspicuously consumes and turns productive time into idle time, expressing itself through an emotional economy of jealousy, meanness and envy (Ferguson, 1991: 248–61). In this analysis, 'the personality [is] impoverished even as it [is] enriched', and as Pocock further points out, 'we are at the point [within the history of this argument] where the classical concept of corruption merges into the modern concept of alienation, and the humanist roots of early Marxism become visible' (Pocock, 1975: 502).

In the political sphere corruption arises when monarchies or democracies become despotic. Ferguson sees despotism, 'as a form of oligarchic state which pacifies its subjects and divests them of their traditional civil rights, if necessary by bureaucratic regulation, fraud and military force' (Keane, 1988: 42). In an aside once again directed to Hobbes, Ferguson remarks that the state of nature is to be found only in a despotic state (Ferguson, 1991: 64, 73). In a context of a *political* proto-social theory, Ferguson's remark foreshadows the difficulties that modern civilization and its civic cultures run into. His analysis of the corruption of civic virtues can be seen as a prelude to de Tocqueville's analysis of American political culture in *Democracy in America*, where, in part, political virtues and public life are neglected and eroded once capitalism takes hold (Ferguson, 1991: 263; de Tocqueville, 1990: 316–30).

'CRUDE COMMUNISM': THE JACOBIN CURRENT OF THE REVOLUTIONARY TRADITION

Notwithstanding Ferguson's political sensitivity to the problems of corruption and despotic government, he could not have foreseen the invention of a new political imagination, organization and ideal that grew out of the political crisis and turmoil of the French revolutionary period. There have been a variety of interpretations that see the French Revolution as a specific 'event', or as part of a longer-term set of historical processes, interpretations that cannot be discussed here (Furet, 1981, 1990; Wallerstein, 1990). Moreover, the French Revolution is also hailed as a watershed of modernity, and as such has achieved the status of a modern myth in the minds of democrats, nationalists and revolutionaries alike. From a democratic perspective, it is viewed as a breakthrough to *modern* constitutional republican government, which from a nationalist perspective ties popular sovereignty to the soil of the people (Baker, 1989: 844–59).

However, from a revolutionary perspective, of both the left and the right, it is not the ability to institute principles of formal democracy through constitutions, or to invoke the image of the nation that is important. Rather, the myth of the French Revolution invoked the ability of a society to transform itself *ideologically* (Feher, 1987; Furet, 1981). The notion of ideology grew out of the French Revolutionary context and was introduced into the lexicon of politics by Destutt de Tracy. He viewed it as a 'science of ideas' that could be used for human improvement, and could be taught through a system of national education. In this context, ideology linked a system of ideas with a specific programme of social reform that was instituted by the state.[4]

Feher argues in his *The Frozen Revolution: An Essay on Jacobinism* that the egalitarian or Jacobin revolutionary current had a lasting impact at this particular moment in the history of European modernity on both the revolutionary tradition as a whole, and social theory. In this context, the other three versions of the revolutionary tradition mentioned above, although they have antecedents in the eighteenth century, are more fully expressed in the nineteenth, especially the libertarian currents that are found in Marx's own version of communism, anarchism and the complex history of social democracy. The exception is radical communitarianism, which as we will see below could be seen to belong equally to Romanticism.

There were four aspects that combined to make the Jacobin version have a lasting impact on modernity and the ways it was organized and thought about. First, according to Feher, and in agreement with Durkheim in *Saint-Simon and Socialism*, the modernity of this version of the revolutionary tradition was not only its anticapitalism, but also that it introduced the 'social question' or the redistribution of social wealth (property) into political discourse (Feher, 1987: 134). Secondly, and related to this, is the development of the ideal of ideology as a driving force for social transformation. Thirdly, and as importantly, it invented a technology of power in the form of the dictatorship of the Committee of Public Safety and the Terror that inverted the relation between civil society and the state, making the state predominant — under the modern umbrella of 'directed democracy'. Later Marx would term this version 'crude communism' – a communism grounded in the politics of envy, in 'Private Property and Communism' (Marx, 1981: 301–14). Moreover, his notion of 'crude communism' can also be extended to include his critique, in *The Holy Family*, of

Robespierre's 'guillotine politics', where freedoms were annihilated with the ease of signing a death warrant (Marx and Engels, 1980: 148–54).

Fourthly, the invention of the vocational and professional revolutionary is related to the ideal of ideologically driven social transformation. This aspect was to find its fullest expression in the Russian revolutionary tradition. Chernashevsky, for example, portrays the vocational revolutionary in his original *What is to be Done?*, which is subsequently critiqued by Dostoevsky in *The Possessed*. Russian Jacobinism, though, combines ideological motivation with the monopolization and transformation of the state as a vehicle for social transformation, which becomes the forerunner of Leninism (Bescançon, 1981; Rundell, 1990; Venturi, 1960; Walicki, 1979). The combination of these dimensions established the groundwork for, and development of totalitarianism, which has remained an undertheorized aspect of modernity despite its historical significance (Feher, 1987: 68–96).[5]

Equality, rather than freedom, was singled out as the principal value in the Jacobin vocabulary, becoming the basis for a generalized social critique. The development of a world increasingly ruled by money disrupted the homogeneity of what was viewed as the natural, taken-forgranted order. Based on a negative anthropology, Jacobinism had a vehement anti-capitalism and distrust of private property, which was based on the conviction that bourgeois man, as economic man, once granted freedom of economic action, would inevitably act from motives of gain. Capitalism invoked a crisis of the basis of 'the good' and a crisis of the community. French society was seen, by such critics as Rousseau, and in the civilizational terms described above, as *artificial* (Driver, 1930; Martin, 1956; Rousseau, 1974).

Jacobinism also gave birth to a politicalideological attitude to rulership based on the conflation of representation and truth, the result of which was the idea of *directed* democracy. It stemmed from Rousseau's doubt concerning the feasibility of direct democracy, which he viewed as fragmentary and insufficient (Feher, 1987: 80). The Jacobin ideology established the exclusive rule of true opinion, an exclusive rule that was based on a prefabricated consensus. The prefabricated consensus resulted from not only invoking the formal rules by which decisions were made, but also, on this basis, claiming that the decision arrived at represented society as a whole. In other words, revolutionary democracy came to mean the extension of the prefabricated consensus from a politicized group to society as a whole, which includes the state, and the control of the state by a militant minority group who ascribe for themselves a new legitimacy based on the conflation between truth and democracy (Feher, 1987: 68–96).[6]

Moreover, Jacobin revolutionary democracy also nurtured and sustained an anthropological dualism: the faith in the perfectibility of Man in the tradition of the French Enlighteners, and a moral pessimism. These come together in a secular version of the 'second coming'. Jacobin Enlightened revolutionaries would lead the economically fallen and dispossessed out of the corrupted, atomistic and artificial civilization of capitalism, and create a new collective morality. This new collective morality would be achieved by inventing a new public sphere, not of public political argument and opinion and decision-making, but of political festival. This new public sphere would destroy not only the atomism of the 'artificial' civilization of capitalism, but also create a politicized morality in which new collective ties would be forged. However, in the wake of the capitalization of social life, and in the absence of traditional communal ties, the transposition of the democratically oriented public sphere to one of festivals entails that the political function of the public disappears. This function is given over to the state – it now provides the moral foundation for collective action as well as leadership and decision-making for the community.

Both Martin (1956), in his *The Rise of French Liberal Thought*, and Driver in 'Morelly and Mably' point to the anti-capitalist and anti-civilizational views of eighteenth-century French revolutionary thinkers, and especially the now forgotten figures of Mably, Morelly and Linguet, who articulated communisms that were egalitarian in nature (Driver, 1930: 217–53; Martin, 1956: 220–58). As Durkheim points out in his *Socialism and Saint-Simon*, these figures, especially, sit at a watershed that separates pre-modern revolutionary utopias from their modern variants in that 'they assert categorically that things must be as they expound them' (Durkheim, 1958: 51). In other words, social change was possible and based on an ideology that would transform society. In this context, one can disagree with Martin when he says that 'socialism in the eighteenth century was primarily moral, and only incidentally economic [and] found its inspiration in the conception of a natural state of communism' (Martin, 1956: 237). Durkheim points out that this moral critique shifted from one grounded in the description of inequalities to a critique of property itself (Durkheim, 1958: 50). Whilst Morelly and Mably articulate this modern position, Robespierre, Babeuf, Buonarotti and Blanqui stand in their wake as the political actors who bequeathed this legacy of Jacobin egalitarianism to the revolutionary tradition.

Grachus Babeuf – whom Marx refers to directly as 'the crude communist' in his *1844 Manuscripts* – left a legacy as the first conspiratorial and egalitarian revolutionary. By positing an image of revolution based on the idea of the 'empirical' inequality of the people, and linking this internally to the universally driven *ideal and criteria* of equality, Babeuf obliterated the distinction between concrete, empirical actions and demands, and abstract universalizable principles. Revolutionary and dictatorial political action was viewed as being above reproach in that the abstract claim of humanity was tied and reduced to an empirical defence, in this instance, of equality. Moreover, the distinction between the political claim and the social group to whom the claim is addressed was also obliterated – revolutionary political action was always on behalf of a beleaguered society that could not, unguided, perceive or pursue its ultimate interests – equality (Marcuse, 1972: 98; Scott, 1972: 40, 46, 52–3).[7]

Babeuf invoked the new, modern idea of a self-appointed enlightened vanguard and married this to the principle of popular sovereignty. The people, although sovereign citizens of their nation, were seen only as a passive and resigned mass. According to Babeuf, only an enlightened leadership could mediate sovereignty and equality, and take over all decision-making functions and imperatives in which authority, wisdom and sovereignty are united and consummated. The ideological justification for the dissolution of formal democracy was that it protected the French Revolution and the welfare of the people in the form of a dictatorship that exercised power on behalf of a deluded and dispossessed majority (Buonarotti, 1965: 388). In this way, and within the logic of Babeuf's position, the dictatorial politics of the general will did not constitute an offence against the state – democratic or otherwise – but a defensive response on behalf of a concrete validation of the radicalized Enlightenment claim for equality (Babeuf, 1972: 34; Marcuse, 1972: 102–3).

The Jacobin current within the revolutionary tradition can be viewed as a counter-current or movement that preoccupied classical social theory with the issues and problems it bequeathed – the value of absolute equality, revolutionary dictatorship and the re-institution of collective bonds. In this sense, and unlike Ferguson's (and the subjectivistic Enlightenment's) sociocentric contribution to the heritage of social theory, the Jacobin legacy is indirect. It does not concern a particular writer (or writers) whose work gives expression to a body of ideas that are explicitly *socio-theoretical*. Rather, Jacobinism bequeaths a *particular image of modernity as radically transformative*. Through this image Jacobinsm, as well as the myths associated with the French Revolution generally, opened the modern landscape to a series of long-lasting debates concerning the nature of social transformation and the relative importance given to particular aspects of the modern constellation. The Jacobin image of revolution simultaneously collapsed together issues regarding the structure of modern state power, the relation between popular sovereignty and the form of state rule, and the social question of distributive justice. As such, it introduced the phenomenon of viewing society as a totality – and hence of viewing social change in a totalizing manner. It also introduced the negative anthropology that underlaid the idea of dictatorship – the theorist imputes to his/her addressee (class, group, gender etc.) either passivity or a blindness – a false consciousness. He/she must, then, lead and re-educate them in their own best interests.

It is at this precise point that this aspect of the French Revolution becomes theoretically significant for classical social theory. Marx, Durkheim, Mauss and Weber all understood that under the sway of the Jacobin dictatorship, *formal democracy*, which can be viewed as an institutional form that mediates the diversity and complexity of social powers that are internal to modernity, dissolved. As already mentioned, for Marx, Jacobinism represented the annihilation of democracy and the victory of the state over society. As his own principle value is that of freedom, and not equality, his critique of 'crude communism' is one that belonged to the modernity of the subjectivist current of the Enlightenment. He is at the same time one of modernity's greatest champions, as well as one of its great critics: a champion, because of modernity's freedoms that destroy all institutions and ways of life that were once solid, and a critic, because under capitalism, these freedoms remain only partially realized (Marx and Engels, 1967).

Durkheim's constant political point of reference throughout his work was the unfinished, problematic nature of the French Revolution, especially represented by its Jacobin dimension. For him, in 'Individualism and the Intellectuals', a negative individualism simply mirrors the atomistic individualism of utilitarianism, the result of which is a political anomie (Durkheim, 1969; see also Mauss, 1992). According to Durkheim in *Professional Ethics and Civic Morals*, political anomie can only be overcome by a democratic, although corporatist mediation within civil society, and between it and the state (Durkheim, 1992). The French Revolution, for him, also points to the necessity of creating and sustaining festive and sacred dimensions of modern political life, a theme which is central to

The Elementary Forms of Religious Life (Durkheim, 1976).

Weber, also, implicitly recognized the political consequences of Jacobinism and its denial of the mundane work of politics, including the work that is entailed once democratic opposition is accepted. As importantly, though, for Weber, Lenin's own version, in which he replaced the value of equality with the value of industrialization, represented an attempt to artificially re-unify, under the auspices of the party/state, the spheres of life that had become differentiated from one another. This differentiation had become a hallmark of the modern condition. Leninism, so Weber also argued, introduced the personalization of political force, once again, into modern political life. Rule of law became arbitrary rather than existed as an abstract formal–legal principle. As he suggested in 'Socialism' and especially in 'Politics as a Vocation', this form of politics, whether expressed from the left or the right, represented the denial of the complexity of modern life. It was also an expression of the danger to modern society when one value, as an absolute one, was invoked in the face of modernity's value pluralization (Weber, 1970: 77–128; 1975: 251–62).

ROMANTICISM'S CRITIQUE OF MODERNITY: 'STRANGERS TO THE WORLD OF SENSE'

Romanticism, in part, emerged as a critical response to the crises of the French Revolution and its programme of political reform. This was especially the case as European intellectuals, who had initially heralded it, became increasingly alarmed in the wake of its political disasters. For example, Schiller's *On the Aesthetic Education of Man* was written in 1794 and published in 1795 as a direct response to this crisis, as well as the despair and loss of confidence brought about by it. He argued that two contrasting, yet ultimately complementary, self-inflicted wounds occurred – one from above and one from below – that indicated that modernity was still an unfulfilled promise. The wound to the Revolution from above was inflicted by the self-appointed revolutionary elite who, in their commitment to the principle of the Revolution, turned these principles into absolute goals. The French Revolution had also failed because *le peuple* or *les misérables* had expressed their economic and cultural poverty as resentment when they had entered the political arena. *Le peuple* were driven by unconstrained resentful passions and emotions, which, for Schiller, indicated a state of barbarism rather than freedom.

Barbarism, in Schiller's deployment of the term, indicated a modern condition in which egalitarian maxims took root and were expressed through the unconstrained, resentful voice of the crowd (Schiller, 1967: 25–9).[8]

However, it is not Romanticism's response to the French Revolution that is our central concern here, but two further concerns it placed on the intellectual map, which were to have lasting significance. The first concern was its critique of reason. The second concern was the development of its counter-position based in a naturalistic holism, which moved towards a pantheistic oneness with Nature. This naturalistic holism moved in two directions. One was inward and emphasized the creative imagination, affects and emotions. This inner movement also entailed the disjunction between the individual and society. Unlike Ferguson's sociocentric idea of the individual, which some versions of social theory have also taken as paradigmatic, the Romantic one did not view him/her as infinitely malleable, but rather subject to irrational forces. Moreover, this self-conception of the Romantic individual was related to the other direction – an outward one that emphasized an intense oneness achieved through the sensual and embodied union of like-minded souls. This idea of like-minded union moved in two directions. One direction privileged the emotional economy of love as the paradigm of like-minded union. The other direction took as its point of reference historical, ethnic or regional myths and narratives for not only their critiques of modernity, but also as the basis to posit their own versions of modernity that referred to national identity and forms of community.

The Romantic background has not been addressed in much of the literature on social theory and as such remains a suppressed tradition, although it may misleadingly be discussed under the heading of 'Conservatism', which emphasizes its communitarian and anti-modern agrarian dimension (Nisbet, 1976: 80–117). Gouldner, Seidman and Saiedi all argue that Romanticism's fuller heritage to social theory be acknowledged as much as the Enlightenment and revolutionary ones (Gouldner, 1973; Saiedi, 1991; Seidman, 1983).[9] The following remarks on Romanticism, which emphasize the significance of the first generation German Romantics, will concentrate on the legacies that are bequeathed to social theory, but are often drawn on as unstated assumptions and points of reference. These legacies are, first, the image of the 'creative imaginary self', and in relation to this, the disjunction between the individual and society through its specific ideal of the genius, which provides the backdrop to the development of psychoanalysis. The second legacy, which will be

highlighted here, is Romanticism's historicization of cultures and societies, which places an emphasis on community and national identity. This historicization, and especially the communitarianism that accompanies it, finds its way into social theory's anxiety about the fate of collective ties in the modern world. All of this stands in the midst of Romanticism's redefinition of Nature as an organic source of vital energy and identity, rather than as a passive object.

Unlike Kant, the first generation of German Romantic thinkers, among them Schiller, Friedrich and August Schlegel, Schelling, did not share his confidence that the powers of reason would both ground and guarantee that humans would progress. In Schiller's view, for example, the Kantian construction of transcendental reason wrenched apart feeling and good judgement, reason and imagination and left humankind a cold, technical animal. Under the regime of reason, the human being had become a dissecting animal, left only with the cold heart of objectivity, which sees reality as a passive object about to be portioned into pieces under the knife of methodical principles. As such, the modern subject becomes soulless and fragmented; not only a stranger and at war with nature, but also a stranger and at war with him or herself (Schiller, 1967: 21, 39; Taylor, 1975: 35).

The beautiful and the sublime became the motifs through which the Romantics addressed the fractured and crisis-ridden nature of social and political life, as well as the vivisectionist attitude of the objectivistic Enlighteners towards Nature. The Romantics searched for an internal source apart from Reason that answered the call of human freedom, but was not grounded in principles of rational method. Berlin, in The Roots of Romanticism, argues that Kant's idea of radical freedom or autonomy, which was central to his moral philosophy, became, in turn, the beacon for Romanticism. For Kant, radical freedom fell under the principles of Reason and was opposed to nature, which must be moulded by it (Berlin, 1999: 76).

Yet, it is not Kant's notion of reason that the Romantics became interested in, but the idea of nature as internal force. In Kant's work, especially in his Critique of Judgement, this internal force was identified as the creative imagination, which for him was a human faculty and not part of nature per se. In the hands of the Romantics, though, the notion of the creative imagination tied together an idea of natural force with radical freedom, because such a force was viewed as unbounded, pure creativity, as well as natural because it was viewed as an inner force, which was part of nature. Nature was no longer viewed as a passive object, but rather viewed as an activated energy and force. The artist, in the form of the genius, was viewed as both the repository of this force and power, and its activator. The artist combined in him or herself the elements of both nature and art. He or she relied on blind spontaneity outside his or her control, and produced art by both relying on this spontaneity and freely choosing means that would produce it. The creative imagination became identified as this internal force. It 'became the way to unify [humankind's] psyche and by extension [humankind] with Nature, to return by the paths of self-consciousness, to a state of higher nature, a state of the sublime where senses, mind and spirit elevate the world around them even as they elevate themselves' (Engell, 1981: 8; see also Abrams, 1953; Kearney, 1988).

Schelling, for example, answered the need for beauty, harmony and integration with the idea of marrying the notion of creative subjectivity with a poetic vision of Nature. In his *System of Transcendental Idealism*, written in 1800, Schelling argued that Nature was the unconscious product of subjectivity. In his view, subjectivity gave birth to two worlds – one of Nature, and one of moral action and history. Since they have the same foundation they strive to join one another, but from different starting points. The subject in Nature is *life*, which becomes more complex as it realizes itself. However, it cannot do this in a conscious manner. This is done from the other side, on the side of human beings. Conscious subjectivity reaches out to incorporate nature and this is obtained in art where nature and freedom meet. The ideal of the beautiful is the apex because it is evidence of the unfolding subjectivity. For Schelling, beauty is the completion of an organic circle in which the creative life of thought and the creative life of nature are united. As such, he articulates the Romantic sensibility to Nature. Nature is known not by dissecting it, but by communing with it, and once having achieved this, human beings come in contact with their own spiritual force, which is *internal* Nature, or Nature as an internal source (Schelling, 1978).

Whilst Schiller's *On the Aesthetic Education of Man* is multifaceted, his psychological theory, or in his terms, anthropological revolution, attempted to reconcile both the external and internal dimensions of the human being. Schiller points to the pathological conditions that occur when there is an imbalance between social and inner life. When the imbalance occurs on the side of the social, the self becomes dominated by society (or civilization), resulting in a loss of creativity and the reduction of the self to merely a social role. When the imbalance occurs on the side of inner life, the result is an equally powerful, yet different pathology, one of a self-

enclosure in one's own psychic life at the expense of sociability with others. Schiller's importance, then, is that he investigates the way in which the drama of modernity is played out in the relation between the social and internal lives of the self. As he says:

> man can be at odds with himself in two ways: either as a savage, when feeling predominates over principle; or as a barbarian, when principle destroys feeling. The savage despises civilization, and acknowledges Nature as his sovereign mistress. The barbarian derides and dishonours nature, but, more contemptible than the savage, as often as not continues to be the slave of his slave. (Schiller, 1967: 21)

In Schiller's view, the harmonization of Nature and Freedom occurs through play. Play takes us beyond the strain and tyranny of our oppositions and corresponds to an ideal of integrated, undivided and non-conflictual self-expression. Chytry notes that in formulating a basic play drive in human beings, Schiller makes the most important advance in the theory of play since Plato (Chytry, 1989: 82). In fact, Schiller's theory of play represents an equally important attempt to posit a theory of the self-formation of human beings which accounts for the inner life, and links this account to its expression in the best possible social conditions – creative associations with others. In this sense, Schiller's aim is to posit 'a harmonious blending of the sensuous and the rational' – the result of which is beauty. Accordingly, for him, it is only through beauty that our experiences and our need to order these are brought into harmony. His idea of an anthropological revolution is the basis for his culturally oriented response in which 'the man of Culture makes a friend of Nature, and honours her freedom whilst curbing her caprice' (Schiller, 1967: 21). The conceptual currency of culture is the medium through which Schiller's critique of modernity and his social psychology are articulated. For him, the Romantic creative-imaginative self finds his or her home in high culture where inner and social life should meet in harmony.

Schelling's theory of unconscious nature and Schiller's notion of play provide one of the foundation stones for later psychoanalytic theories of the unconscious, which explicitly critiques the image of socialization that posits a homology between individual and society. Schiller's work is of interest here also because it already points to the dangers of what later social theory has termed 'the over-socialized conception of man' (Wrong, 1976: 21–30; 55–70). This conception, formulated predominantly in functionalist social theory refers to the social actor's learned ability to participate in his or her social environment by taking on roles. As mentioned above, Schiller had already pointed to the one-dimensionality of the role-playing self – for him, the self of barbarous civilization. In positing his notion of the three drives – the form drive, the sense drive and the play drive – human beings exist multidimensionally in a tense relation between the drives, and each other, a relation that can only be resolved aesthetically.

Both Schiller and Schelling, though, naturalize the idea of imaginative creative force. Schiller interprets imaginative freedom or play as a drive, and Schelling interprets creativity as a natural inwardly derived *force*. In this way, both lay the ground for those psychoanalytic interpretations of the self that posit freedom of unconscious drives in a naturalistic manner. Ellenberger, in *The Discovery of the Unconscious*, points to the way in which the philosophy of Nature takes root, through Schelling's work in particular, in the early psychoanalytic theories of the nineteenth century, especially von Schubert, Schopenhauer and von Hartman. According to von Schubert, humankind lived in a primordial state of harmony with Nature before separating itself from it through a self-love. Yet a longing remains to return to this primordial state. Schopenhauer's philosophy of the will privileged the force of Nature as the constitutive internal, yet unknown territory of the human animal. For him, the irrational forces consist of two drives or instincts, one for preservation, the other for sex. It is, though, von Hartman who, in his 1869 *Philosophy of the Unconscious*, gives this swelling, primordial naturalized state a respectable home – the unconscious (Ellenberger, 1970: 202–10). Whilst Nietzsche's notion of the eternal return finds its way into Freud's psychoanalytic theory, this naturalization of internal life is a central aspect of his metapsychology. His notion of the id harks back to these earlier formulations. Even in his later *Outline of Psychoanalysis*, it represents the pre-linguistic and irrational energetic force of nature by which, according to him, we are all driven, and which remains in permanent conflict with our social self (Freud, 1969).

The distinction that Irving Singer makes between benign and pessimistic romanticism in his *The Nature of Love* can be usefully introduced in order to more fully outline Romanticism's second set of legacies to social theory. This second set of legacies are more outwardly directed than the first set, and emphasize particular styles of life and forms of identity, again, as responses to the Enlightenment's version of modernity.

Benign Romanticism, which could also be called remedial Romanticism, emphasized the possibility of eliminating what was destructive in society or oneself, and achieving, either through beauty or love, reconciliation with oneself and with others, as we have seen with Schiller's work (Singer, 1984: 376–431). Moreover, Romanticism became the basis for a proto-feminist critique of the objectivistic current of the Enlightenment and the structures of the patriarchal way of life through the development of the specifically new Romantic ideal of love. Notwithstanding feminism's critique of Romantic love as a bastion of patriarchal ways of life, Vogel, in her 'Rationalism and Romanticism: two strategies for women's liberation' points to Romanticism's notion of affective autonomy as a forming background notion for feminist social theory (Johnson, 1995; Vogel, 1986).

In Friedrich Schlegel's *Lucinde*, women's oppression is not a violation of moral or cognitive principles in the first instance but an assault on the aesthetic ideal of femininity in which reason and feeling, desire for knowledge, and the free expression of sensuality are all brought into harmony. Schlegel's ideal of independent femininity lies in the quest for individuality, diversity and organic wholeness. In *Lucinde* he posited a counter-model to the prevailing stereotype of 'pure femininity' in which a woman's individuality is reduced to domesticity, false modesty and dependence on men. 'Pure femininity' would not allow for the extensive and unconstrained development of the individual potential of each woman. In reconstructing a history of independent womanhood in Sparta, Schlegel's account of Spartan femininity challenged the belief in an immutable sexual nature, and posited an alternative model based in a woman's capacity to harmonize experience and knowledge from an inner centre of intuitive understanding and reflective feeling (Schlegel, 1971). This was the specificity of female reason – as against 'the Man of Reason' (Lloyd, 1984).

Female identity could be associated with emotive qualities because the Romantic ideal of self-realization demanded the cultivation and exercise of all human faculties – feeling, desire and passion, no less than understanding. The paradigm of Romantic love became important because it was

> credited with the power to encourage the discovery of the self. To love is to inspire another person's development; each releases in the other energies that will bring them closer towards what they might achieve as human beings. Since freedom is understood as a process of self-creation in which all individual faculties and endeavors are activated, and since the polarity of female and male nature can act as stimulus upon such development, love constitutes the proper sphere of emancipation. (Vogel, 1986: 41)

Romantic love articulated the free expression and development of what can be termed the autonomous, impassioned self – a self that was impassioned both sensually and culturally.

In other words, those Romantic thinkers who viewed Romanticism as a remedy to the fragmented emptiness and barbarism of modern civilization invoked ideals of either beauty or love through which sentiment and reason, desire and freedom could be re-united. As Kain has pointed out, this remedial image also found its way into Marx's utopianism of a world beyond work and necessity through Schiller's notion of beauty based on aesthetic play in *On the Aesthetic Education of Man* (Kain, 1982). Notwithstanding this particular Romantic utopianism, the languages of alienation and fragmentation long held sway as idioms through which the ills of modernity could be presented, from Simmel to the neo-Marxism of Lukács, in his *History and Class Consciousness* (1968), and the Frankfurt School, especially Horkheimer and Adorno's *Dialectic of Enlightenment* (1972).

Pessimistic romanticism, as with pessimistic romantic love, defines the quest for human wholeness as also ennobling, but as leading ultimately to death – to nothingness. Love redeems the evils of the world (fragmented selves, functional relations, alienation), but only in the act of death, and after a descent into madness (Singer, 1984: 432–81). Whilst this is the fate, for example, of Goethe's Werther in his *The Sorrows of Young Werther* (1989), this image of an individual's fate at the hands of Romantic love is also transposed from a pessimistic individualistic motif to an equally pessimistic communal one. It is not love that is the culprit here – but modernity itself, for in its wake communal bonds are eroded. Pessimistic Romanticism points towards not only the historicization and relativization of cultures and societies, but also, and unlike the sociocentric Enlightenment's versions, to a historicization and relativization that contained a commitment to the ideal of the collective identity of the group or nation as a principal value.

Against the unilinear and evolutionary views of progress, historical periods and other societies were viewed as unique. The past was brought into the present as a benchmark against which the modern world was judged. Ancient Greece, especially the period of classical Athens, was a favourite point of comparison for Schiller, Friedrich and August Schlegel and Hölderlin (Shalin, 1986: 73–123; Webb, 1982: 1–32). For Schiller, the Athenian Greeks represented the image of unity whose life threw the vicissitudes of the modern period into relief. They represented natural humanity, 'for they were wedded to all the delights of art and all the dignity of wisdom, without . . . falling prey to their seduction . . . In fullness of form no less than of content, at once philosophic and creative, sensitive and energetic, the Greeks combined the first youth of imagination with the manhood of reason in a glorious manifestation of humanity' (Schiller, 1967: 31). Antiquity, though, was not the only point of reference; the Christian Middle Ages as well as pre-Christian mythology and folklore became ones also. There was a glorification of peasant mentality, the nameless builders of the Gothic cathedrals, the nameless authors of plays and epics. These nameless people were viewed as truer and deeper creators than the writers and artists of modern civilization, in touch with their communities, neither disconnected from them nor reliant on the market for their livelihood and recognition. According to Friedrich Schlegel, for example, there were two types of languages and cultures. One was dynamic and identified with cultures that were viewed as original and self-constructing such as Sanskrit, German and Celtic, whilst the others were non-dynamic, and identified with languages that were viewed as linguistic hybrids, and thus were either dead or mechanical (Latin and English) (Blom Hansen, 1997: 26).

The Romantic interest in the authenticity of other cultures and epochs was also motivated by the particularly German experience of its own modernity. Politically, Romanticism emerged 'as a movement of national renovation in line with the principles of nationalities' (Ellenberger, 1970: 198). Early German Romanticism gave vent to a frustration of a 'Germany' without a state – a culture threatened by (especially French) foreign influence, and divided into a multiplicity of small sovereign states. The articulation of this frustration was voiced through a defensive image of community or *Gemeinschaft* that was based, philosophically, on the outward image of a naturalistic human holism. This defensive conceptual strategy makes this particular Romanticism pessimistic because without the bulwark of nationalism to sustain it, there was a sense that 'Germany' would perish at the hands of the French invaders. In this way, the ideal of community became the basis for a critique of not only what the Romantics saw as modernity's capitalism, and its image of the solitary and egoistic 'contractual self', but also of a civilization built on artiface. By contrast, the ideal of community was constructed as 'a fusion of feeling and thought, of tradition and commitment, of membership and volition. It may be found in a given symbolic expression, by loyalty, religion, nation, race, occupation or crusade. Its archetype both historically and symbolically, is the family' (Nisbet, 1966: 48).

Freidrich Schlegel, and Fichte, are the principal German contributors to this current, which finds its way into social theory. Each contributes to an image of a mythologized dividing line that separates premodernity from modernity. This dividing line is articulated as one between *community*, which is transposed by each into the idea of the nation, and *society*, or in the older language, civilization. In this way, nationalist aspirations are tied to a critique of modernity, the outcome of which, in the German case at least, is a preoccupation with images of organic, holistic primordiality (Berlin, 1999: 93–117; Minogue, 1967: 53–80; Saiedi, 1991: 126–30; Schmitt, 1986: 109–44). This is particularly the case with Fichte, who in his *Addresses to the German Nation*, written in the wake of Napoleon's defeat of the Prussian army at Jena in 1806 and delivered in Berlin in 1807–08, argued that the ideal of the nation was based on a cultural-linguistic *originality* and integrity. The ideas of freedom and creativity were transposed and tied to an ideal of a primary *ethnie*, which is defined as the culturally authentic group. This image of cultural authenticity, as he sees it, becomes the basis of identity and, hence, the dividing line between inclusion and exclusion and of a self-enclosed state that both structures and guarantees it (Fichte, 1889).[10]

The other side of Friedrich Schlegel's affective Romanticism, which as we have seen in his benignly Romantic *Lucinde*, is found in his idealization of the Christian Middle Ages. For him there was no paradox here; love, faith and feeling are the basis for a loyalty to authority. As he says, '[the] Christian state must rest on the basis of the religious feelings . . . the government founded on religion, is one in which sentiment, personal spirit and personal character are the primary and ruling elements, and not the dead letter, and the written formula of a mere artificial constitution [read civilization]' (F. Schlegel, quoted in Saiedi, 1993: 130). In his view, the Christian state is the truly natural one in which the different parts of society are organically integrated, and each has a necessary and vital function. In this context, for him, the political structure of modernity should replicate the organic forms of the medieval corporations and estates that linked individual members together, and enabled the state to reproduce itself and live as a nation, and not as a dismembered polity.[11] The result of Friedrich Schlegel's perspective is an *affective* political Romanticism that rejected the principles of popular sovereignty and formal abstract law.

This dividing line is given a fuller voice in a social-theoretical register by Tönnies in *Gemeinschaft und Gesellschaft* (Community and Society). Tönnies is emphatic that with the development of capitalism, industrialization and city cultures with their cosmopolitanism, the community-based forms of association would collapse. Once, established, once the historical watershed to 'society' is crossed, human associations would no longer be based on a prior existing and continuous unity. Actions performed by individuals would no longer capture the will and spirit of collective life, nor could these actions be viewed as taking place on its behalf (Tönnies, 1963). What for Marx in his *1844 Manuscripts* is an alienation that can only be overcome by a move to a world beyond capitalism – the realm of freedom, what for Durkheim, in his *The Social Division of Labour in Society*, is a condition of anomie that can only be overcome by reinventing collective ties and organizations, is for Tönnies a fixed historical condition that can only be responded to *nostalgically*.

CONCLUDING REMARKS

This in-built nostalgia informs the very basis of the construction of the typologies of, and attitudes towards modernity developed by classical social theory, in particular, the current that ends with Parsons' own idiosyncratic synthesis of Durkheim, Weber and Pareto, first in *The Structure of Social Action*, and later in *The Social System*. The legacy of community and national identity, as idealizations, and irrespective of their empirical content, are symptoms of a myth that has been so deeply absorbed into modern consciousness that it appears as a truism. The myth contains two aspects – that there is a stark dividing line between the premodern and the modern, which is drawn sometime in the eighteenth century. The other myth is that premodern societies are harmonious and integrated, and without cultural change and conflict. It is only modern societies that are ridden with power, are diverse and transformative. As Nisbet states in his *The Sociological Tradition*, which can be taken as a representative text that articulated many of the social-theoretical prejudices that were absorbed by classical social theory and synthesized in the Parsonian tradition, the eighteenth century *alone* was the dividing line between premodern and the modern. According to him, 'old Europe', that is the European world based on kinship, land, religion, local communities and monarchical power, and which stretches from the Middle Ages to the eighteenth century, gave way under the weight of the blows struck by democratization and industrialization (Nisbet, 1976: 21).

As this chapter has tried to show, though, the creation of social theory was part of a broader reflection than one that concerned the processes of only industrialization and democratization. This creation also included reflections and debates concerning the capitalization of social life which had been part of European modernity since the Middle Ages, nation-state formation, which had also been present since at least the absolutist states of the seventeenth century, and aesthetic modernization. These reflections both originated and were produced by, an intellectual ferment of diverse creative inventions and challenges, which included hidden evaluations, perspectives and interpretations. This chapter has highlighted three such perspectives and interpretations with their own hidden evaluations that became the basis for social theory – the Enlightenment, the revolutionary tradition and Romanticism. Each spoke not only about the past and the present, but also reached into the future – to us.

NOTES

1 The Romantic era is conventionally seen as that period in European culture approximately between 1780 and 1850. Following Barzun's *Classic, Romantic, Modern* (1975), there are three subsequent periods, 1850–1885 – the realist movement; 1875–1905 – impressionism, symbolism and naturalism; 1960s to the present – mass Romantic counter-movements, including postmodernity.

2 Adam Ferguson, *An Essay on the History of Civil Society*, with a new Introduction by Louis Schneider (1991). See also Robert Bierstedt, 'Sociological Thought in the Eighteenth Century' (1978), pp. 3–38; Donald G. MacRae, 'Adam Ferguson', in Timothy Raison (ed.), *The Founding Fathers of Sociology* (1969), pp. 17–26; W.C. Lehmann's major and indispensable study, *Adam Ferguson and the Beginnings of Modern Sociology* (1930). David Kettler's fine analysis, *The Social and Political Thought of Adam Ferguson* (1965); Alan Swingewood, *A Short History of Sociological Thought* (1991).

3 Mutual affection fosters temperance, fortitude, generosity and candor, whilst mutual aversion fosters courage, competition and group identity.

4 We can leave to one side the ways that the notion of ideology was transformed by Marx and the Marxian tradition and then again by Mannheim. In the context of the revolutionary tradition as a whole, the term can be delimited to Destutt de Tracy's original conception to refer to a way of thinking that encompasses a comprehensive explanatory theory of the human condition and the social world, an explanatory theory that is underlain by a principal value that is viewed as absolute, for example, freedom, equality, nation, race. Furthermore, ideologies are programmatic in that they set out a manifesto or plan of social and political

organization, and it considers that this manifesto or plan can only be realized on the basis of a political struggle that occurs outside political institutions. Whilst they address a wider public, ideologies seek to recruit loyal adherents, and in so doing generate an expectation of commitment, often in terms of a leadership over society that is imputed to the group as a whole. This gives ideologies a closed form of thinking, which is often replicated in their organizational structures (Cranston, 1976: 194; Feher, 1987).

5 It is the technology of power, in particular, which is inherited, and given institutional form by Lenin, especially in his 'What is to be Done?'. Lenin, though, replaces equality with industrialization as the primary value. On the undertheorized dimension of the totalitarian current of modernity see J.P. Arnason, 'Totalitarianism and Modernity' (1998).

6 The unification of truth and the directed democracy of the revolutionary elite enables the distinction to be drawn between citizens and non-citizens, that is between friends and enemies. Rather than identifying oppositional factions, or a multiplicity of social forces and social powers, opposition is identified with enemy. Society is internally relegated to a permanent or semi-permanent state of war.

7 Babeuf was a member of the Society of Equals, which defended the principles of the French constitution of 1793 and conspired to overthrow the Revolutionary executive because he thought the French Revolution had not fulfilled its egalitarian promise. Babeuf states that 'nature has endowed very man with an equal right to the use of nature's gifts, the function of society is to defend this equality of right from the unending attacks of those who, in the state of nature, are wicked and strong, and to enhance by collective action, collective happiness' (Scott, 1972: 46). See also Buonarroti, *Babeuf's Conspiracy for Equality* (1965: 29) for a clear statement of this 'naturalized' anthropology.

In his defence before the High Court at Vendôme in April 1797 he reiterates the basic tenets of The Rights of Man:

1 The natural right and destiny of man are life, liberty and the pursuit of happiness.
2 Society is created in order to guarantee the enjoyment of this natural right.
3 In the event that this right is not guaranteed at all, the social compact is at an end.
4 To prevent the dissolution of this compact, a fundamental right is reserved to the individual.
5 This is none other than the right of every citizen to be vigilant against violations of the compact, to alert others when they occur, to be the first to resist tyranny and to urge others to follow the same course.

The Defense of Grachus Babeuf (ed. and trans. J.A. Scott) (1972: 52–3).

8 Schiller's portrayal of the French Revolution is also an astute analysis of the role of intellectuals in

social change, and one of the first. It was only much later that social theory became interested in the role of intellectuals as a group or a class. See, for example, Mannheim's *Ideology and Utopia* (1985); Bauman's *Legislators and Interpreters* (1987); and Konrad and Szelenyi's *The Intellectuals on the Road to Class Power* (1979).

Moreover, his critique of the mob is also as prescient as his critique of intellectuals. As Schiller's analysis shows, while not confined to modernity, the crowd's political dimension throws into relief the nature of its actions. From this perspective, crowd behaviour became an important topic for sociology, not only in terms of collective behaviour and violence, but also collective psychology. Freud in *Group Psychology and the Analysis of the Ego*, New York: W.W.Norton (1959); Canetti, *Crowds and Power* (tr. Carol Stewart), London: Penguin (1973); Arendt, *The Origins of Totalitarianism*, 3rd edn, London: G. Allen & Unwin (1967); Elias, *Involvement and Detachment* (tr. Edmund Jephcott), Oxford: Blackwell (1987) all studied this phenomenon of civil society in which an agglomeration that transcends the private individuals who constitute it, generates its own form of identity and emotional economy.

9 Norbert Elias is one sociologist who has interpreted Romanticism *sociologically* as a result of the construction of the particular group identity of the Germans. See his *The Germans* (1996). However, if the Romantic heritage is only implicitly acknowledged in social theory it has, by way of intellectual and institutional migration, become a central feature of psychoanalysis, feminism and postmodernism. In one way or another, they all draw on Romantic motifs with their emphasis on the irrational and pre-symbolic or pre-linguistic domains of human experience, relativism and difference, and forms of embodiment. See J.-F. Lyotard, *The Postmodern Condition*, Minneapolis: University of Minnesota Press (1979); Philippe Lacoue-Labarthe and Jean Luc Nancy, *The Literary Absolute*, New York: New York University Press (1988); E. Marks and I. de Courtivron (eds), *New French Feminisms*, London: Harvester (1981).

10 Fichte's model of a state-centred Romanticism is seen in his *The Closed Commercial State*, which, as both Feher and Schmitt point out, combines a Romantic attitude with a Jacobin politics. The state organizes social life, including the distribution of property and social functions (Feher, 1987: 133; Schmitt, 1986: 111).

11 F. Schlegel goes on to say that 'when thus resolved into its constituent atoms and numbered off in succession, a nation is reduced to an elementary mass . . . It is only when a state or nation historically lives on, further develops and vitally maintains itself in its organic members, i.e., in its several estates and essential corporations, that it can be said to form a living whole, and to be as it were one great individual' (quoted in Saiedi, 1991: 128).

REFERENCES

Abrams, M.H. (1953) *The Mirror and the Lamp*. New York: Oxford University Press.

Alexander, J.C. (1995) *Sociology after the Crisis*. Boulder, CO: Westview Press.

Arendt, H. (1973) *On Revolution*. Harmondsworth: Penguin.

Arnason, J.P. (1998) 'Totalitarianism and Modernity', *Poznán Studies in Philosophy of the Social Sciences and the Humanities*, 65: 151–79.

Baker, K.M. (1989) 'Sovereignty', in F. Furet and M. Ozouf (eds), *A Critical Dictionary of the French Revolution*. Cambridge, MA: The Belknap Press at Harvard University Press. pp. 844–59.

Barzun, J. (1975) *Classic, Romantic and Modern*, 2nd edn. Chicago: University of Chicago Press.

Bauman, Z. (1987) *Legislators and Interpreters: On Modernity, Postmodernity and Intellectuals*. Cambridge: Polity Press.

Berlin, I. (1999) *The Roots of Romanticism* (ed. H. Hardy). Princeton, NJ: Princeton University Press.

Bescançon, A. (1981) *The Intellectual Origins of Leninism* (trans. Sarah Matthews). Oxford: Basil Blackwell.

Bierstedt, R. (1978) 'Sociological Thought in the Eighteenth Century', in T. Bottomore and R. Nisbet (eds), *A History of Sociological Analysis*. London: Heinemann Educational Books.

Blom Hansen, T. (1997) 'Inside the Romantic Episteme', *Thesis Eleven*, 48: 21–42.

Bowie, A. (1995) '"Non-Identity": The German Romantics, Schelling and Adorno', in T. Rajan and D.L. Clark (eds), *Intersections: Nineteenth Century Philosophy and Contemporary Theory*. Albany. NY: State University of New York Press.

Buonarotti, N. (ed.) (1965) *Babeuf's Conspiracy for Equality*. New York: Kelly.

Cassirer, E. (1971) *The Myth of the State*. New Haven, CT: Yale University Press.

Chytry, J. (1989) *The Aesthetic State: A Quest in Modern German Thought*. Berkeley, CA: University of California Press.

Cranston, M. (1976) 'Ideology', in *The Encyclopaedia Britannica*, vol. 9. Chicago: Encyclopaedia Britannica Inc.

de Tocqueville, A. (1990) *Democracy in America*, vol. 2. New York: Vintage Books.

Driver, C.H. (1930) 'Morelly and Mably', in F.J.C. Hearnshaw (ed.), *The Social and Political Ideas of Some Great French Thinkers in the Age of Reason*. London: George G. Harrap and Company Ltd.

Durkheim, E. (1958) *Socialism and Saint-Simon*. Yellow Springs, OH: The Antioch Press.

Durkheim, E. (1969) 'Individualism and the Intellectuals', *Political Studies*, XVII: 14–30.

Durkheim, E. (1976) *The Elementary Forms of Religious Life* (trans. J.W. Swain). London: George Allen and Unwin.

Durkheim, E. (1992) *Professional Ethics and Civic Morals*. London: Routledge.

Elias, N. (1996) *The Germans: Power Struggles and the Development of Habitus in the Nineteenth and Twentieth Centuries* (trans. E. Dunning and S.J. Mennell). Cambridge: Polity Press.

Ellenberger, H.F. (1970) *The Discovery of the Unconscious*. London: Allen Lane, The Penguin Press.

Engell, J. (1981) *The Creative Imagination*. Cambridge, MA: Harvard University Press.

Febvre, L. (1998) 'Civilization: Evolution of a Word and a Group of Ideas', in J. Rundell and S.J. Mennell (eds), *Classical Readings in Culture and Civilization*. London: Routledge. pp. 160–90.

Feher, F. (1987) *The Frozen Revolution: An Essay on Jacobinism*. Cambridge: Cambridge University Press.

Feher, F. (1990) *The French Revolution and the Birth of Modernity*. Berkeley, CA: University of California Press.

Ferguson, A. (1991) *An Essay on the History of Civil Society*. New Brunswick, NJ: Transaction Publishers.

Fichte, J.G. (1889) *The Popular Works of Johann Gottlieb Fichte* (trans. W. Smith). London: Trübner and Co.

Fletcher, R. (1971) *The Making of Sociology*. London: Michael Joseph.

Freud, S. (1969) *Outline of Psychoanalysis* (trans. J. Strachey). London: Hogarth Press.

Furet, F. (1981) *Interpreting the French Revolution* (trans. E. Forste). Cambridge/New York: Cambridge University Press.

Furet, F. (1990) 'Transformations in the Historiography of the Revolution', in F. Feher (ed.), *The French Revolution and the Birth of Modernity*. Berkeley, CA: University of California Press.

Furst, L.R. (1979) *The Contours of European Romanticism*. London: Macmillan.

Gane, M. (1992) *The Radical Sociology of Durkheim and Mauss*. London: Michael Joseph.

Goethe, J.W. von (1989) *The Sorrows of Young Werther*. London: Penguin.

Gouldner, A.W. (1973) *For Sociology: Renewal and Critique in Sociology Today*. Harmondsworth: Penguin.

Hawthorn, G. (1976) *Enlightenment and Despair*. Cambridge: Cambridge University Press.

Hearnshaw, F.J.C. (1928) *A Survey of Socialism*. London: Macmillian and Co.

Hearnshaw, F.J.C. (1930) *The Social and Political Ideas of Some Great French Thinkers of the Age of Reason*. London: George C. Harrap and Co.

Heilbron, J. (1995) *The Rise of Social Theory* (trans. S. Gogol). Cambridge: Polity Press.

Hobbes, T. (1968) *Leviathan*. Harmondsworth: Penguin.

Horkheimer, M. and Adorno, T. (1972) *Dialectic of Enlightenment*. New York: Searbury Press.

Johnson, P. (1995) 'The Quest for the Self: Feminism's Appropriation of Romanticism', *Thesis Eleven*, 41: 76–93.

Kain, P.J. (1982) *Schiller, Hegel and Marx*. Montreal: McGill–Queens University Press.

Keane, J. (1988) *Civil Society and the State*. London: Verso.

Kearney, R. (1988) *The Wake of the Imagination*. London: Hutchinson.

Kettler, D. (1965) *The Social and Political Thought of Adam Ferguson*. Columbus, OH: Ohio State University Press.

Konrad, G. and Szelenyi, I. (1979) *The Intellectuals on the Road to Class Power* (trans. A. Arato and R.E. Allen). Brighton: Harvester Press.

Lehmann, W.C. (1930) *Adam Ferguson and the Beginnings of Modern Sociology*. New York: Columbia University Press.

Lemert, C. (1995) *Sociology After the Crisis*. Boulder, CO: Westview Press.

Lévi-Strauss, C. (1945) 'French Sociology', in G. Gurvitch and W.E. Moore (eds), *Twentieth Century Sociology*. New York: The Philosophical Library.

Lloyd, G. (1984) *The Man of Reason*. London: Methuen.

Lockridge, L. (1989) *The Ethics of Romanticism*. Cambridge: Cambridge University Press.

Lukács, G. (1968) *History and Class Consciousness*. London: Merlin Press.

MacRea, D.G. (1969) 'Adam Ferguson', in T. Raison (ed.), *The Founding Fathers of Sociology*. Harmondsworth: Penguin.

Mannheim, K. (1985) *Ideology and Utopia: An Introduction to the Sociology of Knowledge*. San Diego: Harcourt Brace Jovanovitch.

Marcuse, H. (1972) 'Thoughts on the Defense of Grachus Babeuf', in J.A. Scott (ed.), *The Defense of Grachus Babeuf*. New York: Schocken Books.

Markus, G. (1994) 'A Sociology of Culture: the Constitution of Modernity', in G. Robinson and G. Rundell (eds), *Rethinking Imagination*. London: Routledge. pp. 15–29.

Martin, K. (1956) *The Rise of French Liberal Thought*. New York: New York University Press.

Marx, K. (1979) *Capital*, vol. 1. Harmondsworth: Penguin.

Marx, K. (1981) *Early Writings*. London: Penguin.

Marx, K. and Engels, F. (1967) *The Communist Manifesto*. Harmondsworth: Penguin.

Marx, K. and Engels, F. (1980) *The Holy Family or Critique of Critical Criticism*. Moscow: Progress Publishers.

Mauss, M. (1992) 'A Sociological Assessment of Bolshevism', in Mike Gane (ed.), *The Radical Sociology of Durkheim and Mauss*. London: Routledge.

Minogue, K.R. (1967) *Nationalism*. London: B.T. Batsford.

Nisbet, R. (1996) *The Sociological Tradition*. London: Heinemann.

Nisbet, R. (1976) 'Conservatism', in T. Bottomore and R. Nisbet (eds), *A History of Sociological Analysis*. London: Heinemann Educational Books.

Pocock, J.G.A. (1975) *The Machiavellian Moment: Florentine Political Thought and the Atlantic Republican Tradition*. Princeton, NJ: Princeton University Press.

Robinson, G. and Rundell, J. (eds) (1994) *Rethinking Imagination*. London: Routledge.

Rousseau, J.J. (1974) *The Social Contract*. London: Penguin.

Rundell, J.F. (1987) *Origins of Modernity: The Origins of Modern Social Theory from Kant to Hegel to Marx*. Cambridge: Polity Press.

Rundell, J.F. (1990) 'The Jacobin Critique of Modernity: The Case of Petr Tkachev', *Thesis Eleven*, 7: 125–51.

Rundell, J. and Mennell, S.J. (eds) (1998) 'Introduction: Civilization, Culture and the Human Self-image', *Classical Readings in Culture and Civilization*. London: Routledge.

Saiedi, N. (1993) *The Birth of Social Theory: Social Thought in Enlightenment and Romanticism*. Lanham, MD: University Press of America.

Salomon, A. (1945) 'German Sociology', in G. Gurvitch and W.E. Moore (eds), *Twentieth Century Sociology*. New York: The Philosophical Inquiry.

Schelling, F.W.J. (1978) *System of Transcendental Idealism (1800)*. Charlottesville, VA: University Press of Virginia.

Schiller, F. (1967) *On the Aesthetic Education of Man* (trans. E.M. Wilkinson and L.A. Willoughby). Oxford: Oxford University Press.

Schlegel, F. (1971) *Lucinde and the Fragments* (trans. P. Firchow). Minneapolis: University of Minnesota Press.

Schmitt, C. (1986) *Political Romanticism* (trans. G. Oakes). Cambridge, MA: The MIT Press.

Scocpol, T. and Kestnbaum, M. (1990) 'Mars Unshackled: The French Revolution in World Historical Perspective', in F. Feher (ed.), *The French Revolution and the Birth of Modernity*. Berkeley, CA: University of California Press.

Scott, J.A. (ed.) (1972) *The Defense of Grachus Babeuf*. New York: Schocken Books.

Seidman, S. (1983) *Liberalism and the Origins of European Social Theory*. Berkeley, CA: University of California Press.

Shalin, D. (1986) 'Romanticism and the Rise of Sociological Hermeneutics', *Social Research*, 53: 77–123.

Singer, I. (1984) *The Nature of Love*, vol. 2. Chicago: Chicago University Press.

Swingewood, A. (1991) *A Short History of Sociological Thought*, 2nd edn. New York: St Martin's Press.

Taylor, C. (1975) *Hegel*. Cambridge: Cambridge University Press.

Taylor, C. (1989) *Sources of the Self*. Cambridge, MA: The MIT Press.

Tönnies, F. (1963) *Community and Society* (trans. C. Loomis). New York: Harper and Row.

Venturi, F. (1960) *Roots of Revolution*. Chicago: University of Chicago Press.

Vogel, U. (1986) 'Rationalism and Romanticism: Two Strategies for Women's Liberation', in J. Evans (ed.), *Feminism and Political Theory*. London: Sage.

Walicki, A. (1979) *A History of Russian Thought from the Enlightenment to Marxism*. Stanford, CA: Stanford University Press.

Wallerstein, I. (1990) 'The French Revolution as a World-historical Event', in F. Feher (ed.), *The French Revolution and the Birth of Modernity*. Berkeley, CA: University of California Press.

Webb, T. (1982) *English Romantic Hellenism, 1700–1824*. Manchester: Manchester University Press.

Weber, M. (1970) *From Max Weber*. London: Routledge and Kegan Paul.

Weber, M. (1975) *Weber: Essays in Translation* (ed. W.G. Runciman). Cambridge: Cambridge University Press.

Wrong, D.H. (1976) *Skeptical Sociology*. New York: Columbia University Press.

Zeitlin, I.M. (1997) *Ideology and the Development of Social Theory*. Englewood Cliffs, NJ: Prentice Hall.

3

The Origins of Positivism: The Contributions of Auguste Comte and Herbert Spencer

By the beginning of the nineteenth century, the social world was increasingly viewed by Enlightenment thinkers as part of the natural universe; and indeed, many were coming to the conclusion that the natural *and* social sciences could be used to promote human progress. This perspective was not accepted by all; and in fact, it took well over a century for the various social sciences to become institutionalized inside and outside of academia. Still, for well over a century, beginning in the early 1700s, the idea that human beings and their social world could be studied scientifically had been gaining momentum; and by the time that Auguste Comte began to publish his *Course of Positive Philosophy* (1830–42) and to proclaim that the day of sociology had arrived, this was no longer such a radical idea.

THE ORIGINS OF COMTE'S POSITIVISM

The young Comte was, like most scholars of his time on the European continent, a child of the Enlightenment, especially the Scientific Revolution which had begun to offer the hope that science could be used in the name of human progress. By the time that Comte had begun to write, the moral fervor of the French Philosophers had been combined and tempered with the view that science could be the tool for reconstructing society along more humane and just lines. While Sir Francis Bacon (1561–1626) had

been the first figure in the Enlightenment to give articulate expression to the modern scientific method, legitimating the great achievements in astronomy during the sixteenth and seventeenth centuries, it was Isaac Newton's law of gravity that provided a vision of what scientific inquiry could be: formal laws stating the fundamental relationships among basic properties of the universe. It would take over a century to see clearly that the discovery of such laws could better the conditions of humankind, but Newton provided the model of how elegant science could be. Comte would take the slowly accumulating recognition of science as the means for human progress and forge this recognition into sociological positivism.

The first clear evidence of the transition to seeing science as the key to reconstructing society can be found in the works of Charles Montesquieu (1689–1755), who engaged in analysis that suggested the possibilities for a science of society resembling Newton's great law. In his *The Spirit of the Laws* (1748), Montesquieu advocated that society must be considered a 'thing'; and as such, its fundamental properties and dynamics could be discovered through systematic observation and analysis. Many of the ideas in Comte's synthesis in the next century – the search for laws, the hierarchy of the sciences, the movement of societies through stages, for example – are to be found in rudimentary form in Montesquieu. Later thinkers, particularly Jacques Turgot (1727–81) and Jean Condorcet (1743–94), further instilled in Comte the idea of human progress through stages, especially the movement of systems of ideas. These thinkers also codified the French Philosophers' notions of social justice and societal betterment into a more scientific form of expression.[1] Thus, a science of society was becoming not only possible, but in true Enlightenment fashion, it was to be used to construct a better society and, thereby, further human progress.

After leaving the Ecole Polytechnique,[2] Comte began his collaboration with Claude-Henri de Saint-Simon (1760–1825). It was during this somewhat tumultuous collaboration, first as Saint-Simon's secretary later as a junior peer, that most of the ideas that were to appear in *The Course of Positive Philosophy* took definite form. Comte felt that Saint-Simon and his ardent followers, known as the 'Saint-Simonians', were too prone to ameliorative efforts without proper scientific understanding of the dynamics of human social organization. Still, Saint-Simon's works provided the foundation for Comte's *Positive Philosophy*. For, it was Saint-Simon who used the term 'positive' science to describe a study of humankind and society based upon empirical observations; it was Saint-Simon who had revitalized the organismic analogy, seeing society as a kind of organism whose laws of development and organization could be discovered and whose pathologies could be treated like those of a biological organism; it was Saint-Simon who postulated a law of history moving from a religious to positivistic basis; it was Saint-Simon who understood that positivism penetrated the sciences at different rates, first into physics and chemistry and later into physiology (including both biological and sociocultural organisms); and it was Saint-Simon who advocated a 'terrestrial morality' based upon a positivistic view of using observations to develop, test and implement the laws of human organization. Just where Saint-Simon's work leaves off and Comte's begins is not clear, but there can be no doubt that Comte took much from his mentor before their irrevocable break in 1824 — a break that left Comte an intellectual isolate at the very time he was beginning to write *The Course of Positive Philosophy*. Indeed, Comte was reduced to menial teaching and tutoring jobs that were considerably beneath his intellect; and so, he was to pay a very high price for his abrasive personality.

In desperation, Comte proposed a series of public lectures to recapture his fading esteem; and even though several dozen eminent scientists subscribed to the lectures, he gave only three before the pressure of the enterprise proved too much and made him ill. Even when the lectures were revived later, some of the early subscribers once again appeared but were soon driven away by Comte's personality. Thus, as Comte was writing the first serialized instalments of *Positive Philosophy*, he was becoming an intellectual outcast; and even when the first volume of this work appeared to critical acclaim, his ideas did not attract wide attention and his acclaim was short-lived. He had alienated almost everyone and had become the enemy of the Saint-Simonians. His marriage and friends began to fail him, and by the time that the last volume of *Positive Philosophy* was published, not a single review of it appeared in the French press. The founder of positivism and sociology was, therefore, to be a failure in his host country, although British social philosophers like John Stuart Mill and, most importantly, Herbert Spencer had read Comte with great interest. Thus, positivism was created and given its most articulate expression by a failing scholar, one whose star had fallen and one who would later become a pathetic figure proclaiming himself the Great Priest of Humanity and preaching to rag-tag groups of followers.[3]

THE POSITIVE PHILOSOPHY OF AUGUSTE COMTE

In 1822, Auguste Comte published the first clear statement of his positive philosophy in an article titled 'Plan of the Scientific Operations Necessary for Reorganizing Society'. For Comte, it was essential to create a 'positive science' like other sciences, and this science would be based upon empirical observations that would be used to generate and test abstract laws of human organization. This new science was to be called 'social physics'[4] and once the laws of human organization have been discovered and formulated, they should be used to direct the operation of society. Scientists of society were, therefore, to guide the course and direction of human organization. One of the most fundamental laws of human organization was the 'law of the three stages' – an idea which he clearly borrowed from Turgot, Condorcet and Saint-Simon – with each stage being typified by a particular kind of 'spirit' – a notion that first appeared in Montesquieu's *The Spirit* and was reinforced by Condorcet and Saint-Simon. These well-known stages were the 'theological-military', 'metaphysical-judicial', and 'scientific-industrial' or positivistic. Society had now entered the last stage, and hence, it was possible to have a true science of social organization. For Comte, the age of sociology had arrived; and it was to be very much like Newtonian physics in the formulation of abstract laws on the forces of the social universe that could then be used to reconstruct society. This first important essay, written independently of Saint-Simon, presented in broad strokes the outline of Comte's more ambitious *Course of Positive Philosophy*.

The Course of Positive Philosophy is a long work; and its goal was to unify all of the sciences, while advocating a place for sociology among the sciences. In many ways, *Positive Philosophy* is a history of science through the prism of the law of three stages and an effort to establish a program for the new science of society with respect to (1) theory, (2) methods, (3) substance and (4) advocacy. Each of these points of emphasis will guide the review of how Comte formulated his positivism.

The nature of sociological theory

The opening pages of *Positive Philosophy* are filled with statements about the nature of theory in the new science. Comte was, like all thinkers of the Enlightenment, impressed with Newton's law of gravity, and he felt that sociology could develop similar laws. As he emphasized (Comte, 1854: 5–6).[5]

> The first characteristic of Positive Philosophy is that it regards all phenomena as subject to invariable natural laws. Our business is – seeing how vain is any research into what are called *Causes* whether first or final – to pursue an accurate discovery of these Laws, with a view to reducing them to the smallest possible number. By speculating upon causes, we could solve no difficulty about origins and purpose. Our real business is to analyse accurately the circumstances of phenomena, and to connect them by the natural relations of succession and resemblance. The best illustration of this is in the case of the doctrine of Gravitation.

This short quotation introduces a number of important issues which are critical to the positivist project as it was to unfold over the next one hundred and fifty years. First, there is the obvious reference to the goal of all theory: to articulate abstract laws about the operation of the social universe.

Second, is the nature of these laws, but here matters become a bit vague. In the context of Comte's time, the reference to 'first causes' had several meanings: (a) *first* in the sense of God, (b) *first* in the sense of what initiated a phenomenon in the distant past and (c) *first* in the sense of the more proximate forces that set a phenomenon in motion. Search for such causes creates problems of placing trust in non-worldly entities (that is, God), of seeking the 'Big Bang' of a social phenomenon in the ultimate past, and

of engaging in an infinite causal regress (that is, if A is caused by B, what caused B? Perhaps C, which was caused by D, and so on in a constant regress). In place of a concern with causality, Comte offered the notion of 'natural relations of succession and resemblance'. But, what does this mean? If the Law of Gravitation is the ideal, then it must mean that a law states relations among basic forces, as is the case where the magnitude of gravitation is postulated to be a function (multiplied by a constant) of the relative size of the respective bodies and their distance from each other. There is no causal connection postulated, at least not in the sense typically used by sociologists. There is simply a statement of equivalence: one force is related to other properties of the universe. To this day, the issue of what sociological laws should look like haunts theory. We often speak in the language of causality, but at the more abstract level where empirical context is removed from a principle, causality gives way to basic relations among forces in the universe. It is not evident that Comte had a very sophisticated view of causality and its pitfalls in mind, but his words pull us into a debate that has never been resolved, either at a philosophical level or at the level of the actual practice of science.

Third, the reference to final causes is vague. He states that he means 'purpose', but does he mean some ultimate goal or a function? It simply is not clear; and if he means function, he did not follow his own advice, since Comte reintroduced functional analysis into social theory.

Fourth is a clearly stated view that sociological theory will have relatively few laws, because abstract statements should be reduced to 'the smallest number possible'. Comte thus had an image of sociological theory as resembling the astrophysics of his time; indeed, as was also the case with Spencer, positivism emerges as an effort to emulate astrophysics in generating very abstract laws that state the basic nature of relations among generic forces in the social universe.

Yet, Comte also recognized that these abstract laws need to be applied to specific empirical contexts; and he proposed a kind of division of labor in the natural sciences and, hence, in sociology:

> we must distinguish between the two classes of Natural science – the abstract or general, which have for their object the discovery of laws which regulate phenomena in all conceivable *cases*, and the concrete, particular, or descriptive, which are sometimes called Natural sciences in a restricted sense, whose function is to apply these laws to the actual history of existing beings. The first are fundamental, and our business is with them alone; as the second

are derived, and however important, they do not rise to the rank of our subjects of contemplation. (Comte, 1854: 23)

In this passage, emphasis on the abstract, general and generic is maintained, but Comte implies something else: deductions from these abstract laws to particular cases. From its beginnings, then, positivism held to a view of theory as highly abstract but, at the same time, as amenable to translations to particular contexts.

Curiously, positivism is often equated in the contemporary commentaries with 'raw empiricism', especially with the use of 'hard' methods and quantitative data analyses. Such a portrayal is then used to condemn positivism, but as is obvious, this portrayal is a gross distortion of what Comte intended. For he recognized that 'if it is true that every theory must be based upon observed *facts*, it is equally true that facts cannot be observed without the guidance of some theory' (Comte, 1854: 4) Thus, empiricism is impossible since there is always some theory, implicit or explicit, guiding what one sees, but more fundamentally, empirical inquiry alone stifles the development of a true positive science:

> The next great hindrance to the use of observation is the empiricism which is introduced into it by those who, in the name of impartiality, would interdict the use of any theory whatever. No other dogma could be more thoroughly irreconcilable with the spirit of positive philosophy – No real observation of any kind of phenomena is possible, except in as far as it is directed, and finally interpreted, by some theory. (Comte, 1854: v.2:242)

Thus, the portrayal of positivism as empiricism, *per se*, is patently false, and Comte (1854: v.2:243) went on to make sure that there was no misunderstanding about the matter:

> Hence it is clear that, scientifically speaking, all isolated, empirical observation is idle, and even radically uncertain; that science can use only those observations which are connected, at least hypothetically, with some law.

In sum, then, positivism was at its very beginning a view of sociology *as* a theory-driven science, devoted to (1) discovering the fundamental properties that are always present when humans organize and (2) formulating abstract laws on the forces governing the operation of these properties. It was never data collection for its own sake, despite contemporary pejorative portrayals, but a view of sociology as a natural science whose goal was to develop general and abstract laws. Still, these laws need to be tested against data; and at times, the collection of data can help in the formulation of a law. Thus,

Comte's positivism was also concerned with general methodological strategies for data collection.

The basic methodological strategies

While the goal of positivism is to develop the laws of human organization, Comte took seriously the methodological question of how to collect data in order to test theories and, at times, in order to induct theoretical principles from systematically collected and analysed data. Yet, his discussion of methods is rather superficial, presenting a case for four basic methodological strategies.

One strategy is observation; and here he draws upon Montesquieu's idea of considering social phenomena as 'things' or, as he phrased the matter, as 'social facts'.[6] When viewing the social as a thing or fact, observations stay away from biased moral judgement and, instead, focus on the statical and dynamical properties of social forces. Sociology was, therefore, to be the science of social *facts*.

Another strategy is experimentation. Comte did not have in mind laboratory experiments but, rather, naturally occurring situations where a pathological force interrupts the normal flow of events. Under these conditions, where the normal state of the social organism is interrupted by a pathological condition, it becomes possible to see how the more normal social processes reassert themselves in an effort to manage the pathology. Comte analogized to the physician, arguing that sociologists could do much the same thing for the 'body social'; for just as the physician can learn about normal body functioning by observing disease, so the sociologist could understand the normal functioning of society by observing social pathologies. Of course, just what would constitute 'normal' and 'pathological' for the social organism would open up the door to moral judgement about the social world. Comte would, of course, have rejected this conclusion, but it unfortunately follows from this rather limited view of experimentation.

A third strategy is comparison, and here Comte also had a biological view of comparative anatomy (or structure and dynamics) between societies. But he also had a view of comparison between different types of social forms evident among 'lower' animals, as well as comparisons with past and present social forms of human organization. By such comparisons, it becomes possible to see what is similar and dissimilar and what is present and absent across various forms; and from these types of comparisons, knowledge about the fundamental properties of the social world of humans would be revealed.

The final methodological strategy proposed by Comte is historical analysis, which is a variant of the comparative method. His law of the three *stages* is such a historical method, examining the movement of ideas and corresponding structural arrangements across history. In looking at societies over time, Comte argued, their dynamical qualities are revealed; and it is these that will be formulated into laws of human organization.

Comte's strategies seem rather simplistic today, but for their time, these were important insights. There is little attention to how data are to be collected within each of these four strategies, but Comte was nonetheless making a strong case for a science built upon the formulation and testing of general theoretical principles through the unbiased assessment of data.

The substance of sociology: statics, dynamics and the organismic analogy

Like Saint-Simon, Comte saw sociology as an extension of biology in its study of organisms. Sociology was to be the study of social *organization*, with an emphasis on social wholes. For 'there can be no scientific study of society, either in its conditions or its movements, if it is separated into portions, and its divisions are studied apart' (Comte, 1854: 225). Thus, while the basic goal of sociology was to produce laws like those in the astrophysics of his time, the subject matter was an extension of biology. Hints of this emphasis come from his interest in studying social pathologies or in comparing the anatomy of diverse social forms. In seeing the social organism as the subject matter of sociology, Comte reintroduces functional analysis into sociology: social facts are to be studied with reference to their consequences for maintaining the normal states of the social whole. Thus, positivism in sociology was originally very much married to functional analysis; subsequent positivists like Herbert Spencer and Emile Durkheim would continue this alliance of searching for laws like those in physics on a subject matter defined in biological terms.

Comte divided sociological analysis of social organisms into 'statics' and 'dynamics'. He wanted to study structure (statics), but true to his Enlightenment ideals, he also wanted to view society as progressing (dynamics). Statics is, in essence, the analysis of functions of social parts to the whole. The parts to be analysed by sociology were not individuals (these were to be the subject matter of biology[7]), but the units organizing individuals. The 'family' composed minimally of husband and wife is, in Comte's functional view, the most elementary unit of social organization, with this elementary unit becoming the basic

building block for larger social units. Late in his career, long after he abandoned science, Comte [1851–54] 1875: 221–76) elaborated on this analysis, engaging in analogies between biological organisms and social organism. But in *Positive Philosophy*, emphasis is on examining structures in terms of (1) how various social units become collated into larger units and (2) how these larger units operate to sustain the 'body social'. His analysis is highly flawed, but he introduces ideas that dominate functional analysis to the present day. Social organisms are highly differentiated, and as such, it is important to know how they are held together or integrated; the key mechanisms of such integration are common morality or spirit, mutual interdependence and exchange, and centralization of power to coordinate functions. These points of emphasis were to constitute the agenda of functional sociology for over a hundred and fifty years.

Social dynamics is, unfortunately, confined to the law of the three stages in which the nature of ideas, structural forms and their modes of integration are examined for the theological, metaphysical and positivistic *stages*. The details of this law are not as interesting as the basic approach to social change: examine the units of the social whole; assess their modes of integration; explore the nature of the idea systems and leaders who articulate these ideas over time; examine change in the nature of units, patterns of integration, and use of symbol systems. The historical trend is for ever more differentiation of structural units and new forms of integration (i.e. power, mutual dependence, and more generalized cultural symbols). Comte even hints at the key forces driving such differentiation: increases in the size of a population and the material density of individuals (ideas that he took from Montesquieu and that were later adopted by Durkheim (1893) in *The Division of Labor in Society*).

ADVOCACY AND THE RECONSTRUCTION OF SOCIETY

Comte's positivism always contained a basic line of advocacy: science is superior to any other system of thought for examining the structure and dynamics of society; laws of these dynamic properties can provide the tools for reconstructing society. Sociology is the 'queen science' because it has been the last to go positivistic, but with its emergence, all domains of the universe can now be examined scientifically. As a result, the laws of the universe – physical, biological and social – can be used to make a better society. Such is, of course, the essence of the Enlightenment project, but it begs an important issue: who is to decide, and in terms of what moral premises, how the laws of science are to be used to construct what type of universe? Comte simply assumed, it appears, that the laws themselves would inform policy-makers of the proper direction of the social order. Obviously, this is a very naive position, but the critical point is that early positivism always contained a vision of laws being used to reconstruct the social world.

From its beginnings, then, positivism had an engineering component, or if one prefers, an emphasis on social practice.[8] The laws of human organization were not just to be discovered for their own sake; they are to be used and applied to problematic conditions. Ironically, sociological practice as it has evolved in sociology over the past one hundred years often mounts critiques of positivism, whereas in fact, the thrust of positivism was always to use general laws for engineering applications.[9]

Comte in retrospect

In many ways we hold Comte in more respect today than his colleagues did at his death. Yet, we still view Comte in a kind of bemused fashion, as one who postulated the law of the three stages, the hierarchy of sciences with sociology as the queen science, and the now often rejected view that sociology could be a true natural science. We can ask if this is any way to treat a founder, but there can be little doubt that the founder of sociology is not highly regarded today. There is, of course, some basis for this low regard, but his advocacy for positivism remains sound. Sociology can be a natural science; the subject matter of this science is social structures (statics) and social processes (dynamics); the goal of sociology is to develop abstract general laws on the forces that explain the operative dynamics of this subject matter; these laws should be constantly assessed against the empirical facts; and the verified laws of sociology should be used in engineering applications. Comte's positivism is simply an advocacy for what all scientific disciplines do; our retrospective view of Comte as a flawed figure comes not only from the fact that Comte was indeed an odd man, but also from contemporary sociology's ambivalence over its scientific prospects.[10]

THE ORIGINS OF HERBERT SPENCER'S POSITIVISM

In 1864, almost a decade before Herbert Spencer entered sociology, he published an article titled 'Reasons for Dissenting from the Philosophy of M. Comte'. In this essay, Spencer (1864) stressed that he disagreed with Comte on the following issues: that societies pass through three stages of development; that causality is less important than relations of affinity in stating laws; that government can use the laws of sociology to reconstruct society; and that psychology is merely a subdiscipline of biology. He did, however, agree that knowledge comes from observations of facts and that laws about the invariant properties of the universe could be formulated. Spencer also accepted Comte's label for the discipline, sociology, and he gave Comte credit for re-introducing the organismic analogy back into social thought, although he was quick to point out that Plato and Hobbes had made similar analogies and that von Baer had greatly influenced Comte's views. This article almost reads as if Spencer is 'protesting too much', but it is hard to know for sure since at the time Spencer had not yet written any of his major sociological works. But like Comte, his sociology was to emphasize the search of laws of the universe and to employ a mode of functional analysis inspired by an organismic analogy. And so, to the extent that Spencer can be seen as the carrier of positivism from the 1870s to the turn of the century, sociological laws in Spencerian sociology were (1) to be deduced from the laws of nineteenth century physics and (2) to address a subject matter conceptualized as 'superorganic' systems.

Spencer saw himself as a philosopher, and his goal was to develop what he termed a *Synthetic Philosophy* that encompassed all domains of the universe, social and natural, and including morals. There was, then, always a moral component in Spencer's work, and indeed, our retrospective appreciation of Spencer is diminished by his ideological biases that are considered highly conservative today but, in fact, were very liberal in Spencer's time. If we ignore the moral works, which mark the beginning and very end of Spencer's career,[11] we can see that he converted Comte's crude organismic analogy and simple view of scientific laws into a highly sophisticated sociology. Like Comte, this sociology was very much influenced by the Newtonian revolution, but equally significantly, Spencer was influenced by the emerging biological sciences – indeed, he wrote one of the major treatises on the topic. He had read Thomas Malthus (1766–1834), who was not, of course, a biologist but a political philosopher whose influence on biology was none the less profound; and more directly in biology, he read William Harvey, Ernst von Baer and Charles Darwin. Moreover, Spencer associated in London clubs with the most eminent scientists of his time, a good portion of whom were biologists. Thus, by the time Comte's career had come to an end, Spencer had spent decades absorbing real science; and this greater familiarity[12] with the advances in science during the decades of the nineteenth century enabled Spencer to develop positivism on both substantive and methodological grounds.

The rather strange vocabulary of Spencer's model of human evolution[13] is partly the result of his effort to subsume all the sciences, and ethics as well, under what he termed 'first principles'. These were published in 1862 in a book by this name, and the goal was to delineate the *cardinal* or *first principles* that govern the operation of the universe. These are borrowed from the physics of his time and concerned such issues as (a) the indestructibility of matter, (b) the continuity of motion in a given direction, (c) the persistence of force behind movement of matter, (d) the transferability of force from one type of matter to another, (e) the tendency of motion to pass along the line of least resistance, and (f) the rhythmic nature of motion. All other principles relevant to a particular domain of the universe – physical, chemical, biological, psychological, sociological, or ethical – could be deduced from these first principles. The details of translating these ideas to specific areas of inquiry are less interesting today than the intent: to create a unified general systems theory for all domains of the universe. This unity came from highly abstract – and obviously rather vague – ideas about matter, motion and force. Spencer's positivism was thus even more grandiose than Comte's because he believed that the same laws could be used to understand every realm of the universe; all that was necessary was to translate these first principles and, then, add necessary refinements as inquiry into a particular realm of the universe is undertaken. By the time Spencer was actively engaged in sociology during the 1870s, he had written not only *First Principles* (1862) but also *The Principles of Psychology* (1855–1872) and *The Principles of Biology* (1864–1867).[14]

THE POSITIVISM OF HERBERT SPENCER

Spencer's methodological work

Spencer's sociology can be broken down into two major components, one methodological and the other substantive. Spencer began his foray into sociology with two important methodological efforts. One was the publication of *The Study of Sociology*[15] in 1873, and the other was the compilation and collation of comparative historical and ethnographic works into *Descrip-*tive *Sociology*. By the time that *The Study of Sociology* was published, work on *Descriptive Sociology* was well under way, with the first volume published in the same year as *The Study of Sociology*. The multiple volumes of *Descriptive Sociology* that were to appear over the next sixty years[16] represented an effort to pursue the comparative method advocated by Comte by assembling data on what was then known about populations all over the world, both literate and pre-literate. For literate populations with a written history, Spencer hired professional scholars to compile a history of a society; for pre-literature, he employed scholars to compile the data from anthropologists and travelogs on diverse populations. The goal, as Spencer noted in the preface of Volume I on *The English* (1873: vi), was to provide data for *The Principles of Sociology*:

> In preparation for *The Principles of Sociology*, requiring as bases of induction large accumulations of data, fitly arranged for comparison, I commenced by proxy the collection and organization of facts presented by societies of different types, past and present . . . the facts collected and arranged for easy reference and convenient study of their relations, being so presented, apart from hypotheses, as to aid all students of social science in testing such conclusions as they have drawn and in drawing others.

Thus, Spencer's positivism was to rest, like Comte's advocacy, on 'social facts' induced from the data available on diverse populations; and the analysis of super-organic bodies was to be comparative, examining different types of societies and, it should be added, different species of animals that are organized in terms of a division of labor (that is, the social insects). Unlike Comte, who merely advocated a comparative methodology, Spencer executed it. In all of the volumes of *Descriptive Sociology*, a common category system is used to list facts.[17] These categories allow for comparison of one society across its history or for the comparison of different societies in the past or present. And as Spencer emphasizes in the quote above, these comparative data formed the basis for induction of theoretical principles. Thus, for Spencer, as one moves from highly general 'first principles' to specific realms of the universe, it becomes necessary to array the data in systematic ways. With the array of data, generalizations can be inducted that can help develop the more abstract laws connecting the 'first principles' to the social world. In Spencer's sociology, then, deduction *and* induction are critical; they both can facilitate the formulation of general theoretical laws that, on the one side, apply the first principles and, on the other, make them sufficiently concrete so as to explain the operative dynamics of a particular subject matter.

The Principles of Sociology is such a long work because it is filled with data. The actual theoretical statements take only a few hundred pages; the rest is example after example from *Descriptive Sociology* as well as findings from the other sciences, particularly the data assembled for *The Principles of Biology*. Thus, Spencerian positivism is highly theoretical, but it seeks to formulate theories that have been disciplined and assessed by social facts from a wide variety of sources. For if laws are to be truly general and universal, Spencer appears to have argued, they must explain the data from a wide range of specific empirical cases.[18]

The other major methodological work in Spencer's positivism is *The Study of Sociology*, which represented both a call to scientific sociology and an effort to quiet critics of social science in general. In this work, Spencer was to address not only the sources of bias inherent in humans studying human society, but perhaps more fundamentally, he anticipated many of the criticisms against efforts to develop general scientific laws in sociology. For those who would argue against the existence of fundamental forces directing human organization, Spencer argued that policy-makers and lay persons alike constantly make this assumption when they presume that their remedies for social ills will indeed solve problems; otherwise, if they did not feel that the social world had basic forces that could be shaped to their will, they would not be so adamant in their advocacy for particular policies and programs.

What lay persons implicitly assume, sociologists must explicitly pursue. Human organization is guided by generic forces that operate in a lawful manner, and 'it behooves us to use all diligence in ascertaining what the forces are, what are their laws, and what are the ways in which they cooperate' (Spencer, 1873: 47). For those who argue that sociology cannot be an 'exact science', like the natural sciences, Spencer countered that many of the insights of the 'hard' sciences are stated verbally and that the methods used by researchers in these sciences are often qualitative. For when scientists must work in natural systems and are, therefore, unable to measure precisely variables nor to control for their interaction effects, it becomes impossible to engage in purely quantitative analysis. But, these constraints do not make research or theory any less scientific, nor do they make laws less powerful. For it is evident that in many situations, 'factors so numerous and so hard to measure, that to develop our knowledge of their relations into quantitative form will be extremely difficult, if not impossible' (Spencer, 1873: 45).

In these opening passages of *The Study of Sociology*, Spencer thus removes the burden of quantification from positivism. The goal is to isolate the forces of the social universe, state their operation in laws, and seek to understand their relations to each other. Such activity need not be stated as a mathematical equation, as in Newton's law of gravity, nor do the data collected to assess the plausibility of a law need to be quantitatively measured. Additionally, sociologists should not use prediction of events as the criterion of a science, since in complex natural systems, such efforts become difficult; instead, the criterion of all science should be: Do the laws on the basic forces of the universe lead to an understanding of why an event occurred? When an affirmative answer can be made to this question, it then becomes possible to have a scientific explanation for a specific empirical event, even if these events could not be predicted with any precision.

The rest of *The Study of Sociology* addresses sources of bias that need not be reviewed in detail here, except when Spencer's detailed discussion bears on the nature of positivism. Spencer argued that the data collected in science should be directly relevant to formulating or testing the laws on the timeless forces that govern the social universe. Research problems selected for other purposes – for example, the desires of benefactors and funding agents, the dictates of public opinion, the commitment to a research technique or research paradigm, the dominance of particular agents and programs, and the social positions of researchers themselves – should not distort the collection of data away from the fundamental, basic, generic and universal forces governing the operation of the social world. Futhermore, the collection and analysis of data should not be biased by a cherished hypothesis and ideological commitments which keep researchers from assessing objectively and critically the plausibility of their theories. Finally, it is important to collect data over time in order to see processes unfold rather than to take only a cross-section of data that does not give a sense for process. If all these sources of bias can be overcome, then it is possible to have a true science of society.

Spencer's substantive analysis of super-organic bodies

Spencer is most famous for his organismic analogy and functionalism, and as a result, early positivism is somewhat tainted by this association with what some see today as a discredited approach. But, if we take literally, as Spencer did, the title of his work 'The *Principles* of

Sociology', functional analysis on super-organic bodies was designed to produce abstract laws of human organization. Added to this functional analysis was an evolutionary approach in which Spencer traced the long-term development of human societies from hunting and gathering to industrial forms of organization.[19] This too, for a time, stigmatized positivism as it became associated with models of evolution which, by the early twentieth century, were in fast decline. Yet, if we look more closely, Spencer's heuristics for analysing society – that is, functionalism and evolutionism – were designed to generate abstract laws of human organization that followed from his 'first principles'. Detailed analyses of the sociological principles derived from the first or cardinal principles and induced from the data arrayed in *Descriptive Sociology* can be found in a number of places (for example, Turner, 1984; 1985; 1998: 74–7; 2000), and so they need not be enumerated here. Instead, we can simply summarize the basic intent and substantive thrust of the principles.

For Spencer, long-term evolution involved increasing differentiation of a population and the structures organizing the activities of this population. The basic cause of this differentiation was population growth which placed escalated logistical loads on basic social functions: production, reproduction, distribution, and regulation. That is, as populations grow, they generate selection pressures[20] for new ways to expand production, to assure adequate reproduction of human capital, to distribute goods, resources, services and information, and to coordinate and regulate the increased number and expanded volume of societal activity. Those populations that cannot meet these new challenges will face dissolution and will, therefore, de-evolve,[21] whereas those that do, will become more differentiated with respect to the economic division of labor, the diversification of reproductive structures, the extensiveness of transportation and communication infrastructures as well as market exchanges, and the consolidation of political power. These are, in Spencer's eye, fundamental forces of human organization; and their interrelated dynamics explain much of what occurs in super-organic systems. These forces also set off certain dialectical dynamics. One of these is growing inequality associated with expanded production and concentrated power; and as inequality increases, internal threats increase and place new logistical loads on regulatory structures. As threats mount, ever more power is concentrated which only ratchets up the level of inequality and escalates the threats to new levels, eventually placing enormous disintegrative pressure on the society. Another dialectical dynamic is the external threat from the geopolitical arena, which increases the concentration of power which in turn only serves to escalate the level of inequality and, hence, the potential for internal threats. Moreover, as more territory is conquered, the level of inequality increases as does the diversity of the conquered populations, thereby increasing internal threats. All these ideas are developed as an abstract series of first principles, and they constitute some of sociology's most important laws of human organization, although most contemporary sociologists often do not recognize that Spencer was the first to articulate these basic laws. Spencer also engaged in a more detailed analysis of institutional systems, applying these general laws and, at the same time, producing lower-level generalizations about institutional dynamics during the course of human evolution.[22]

Thus, in contrast to Comte who had only advocated a search for general laws and their application to the dynamics of social organisms, Spencer actually executed the strategy, generating some of sociology's basic laws about the relations among the fundamental forces of human organization: population, power, production, reproduction, distribution, geopolitics, inequality and conflict. These laws were illustrated with many examples drawn from *Descriptive Sociology*, and so, Spencer's positivism was both a highly abstract theoretical exercise at discovering fundamental laws and a comprehensive effort to illustrate the plausibility of these laws with empirical examples drawn from a wide range of sources.

THE TRANSFIGURATION OF POSITIVISM IN THE TWENTIETH CENTURY

To the extent that we consider Comte and Spencer the founders of sociological positivism, it is clear what they advocated: search for the general laws of human organization and assess these against empirical facts. Positivism, in their eyes, is simply the equivalent of producing general theory, through derivations from other theoretical principles and through inductions from empirical generalizations, or both. This was positivism, plain and simple.

One of the more interesting historical questions is how positivism became associated with either raw empiricism and data analysis employing quantitative methods or, in the eyes of critical theorists, with anti-humanism legitimating the systems of power in a society and the status quo. Comte and Spencer clearly did not advocate the view of positivism as mere data collection, and Comte obviously saw positivism as supporting humanistic ends and goals, and if necessary, as challenging the status quo. Even Spencer was highly critical of concentrated power, and he argued strongly against the use of power to extend a society's geopolitical boundaries.[23] In closing this review of early positivism, then, it might be useful to examine this transfiguration of positivism to connote in the minds of many an approach so different from what Comte and Spencer championed.

The Vienna Circle is the key to the change in positivism; and although Ernst Mach (1893) was not part of this circle, he is still a key figure in the circle's deliberations. Mach had argued that science should not speculate on unobservables, rejecting the kinds of 'natural laws' postulated by positivists. Instead, theory should be mathematical descriptions of immediate sense data. This line of argument framed much of the debate within the Vienna Circle which, for the most part, was concerned with logic and systems of formal thought. But soon, in light of Mach's advocacy, a split developed over the relative merits of data or logic in generating understanding of the universe. The radical faction argued that truth can be 'measured by logical coherence of statements', whereas the more moderate group stressed the need for a 'material truth of observation', supplementing any 'formal truths' generated by logic (Johnson, 1983: 189). Karl Popper (1959, 1969), who was a somewhat marginal figure in the Vienna Circle in the 1930s, was the most famous mediator of this split, suggesting that a formal theory can never be proven and, therefore, must be constantly subject to empirical tests to sustain its plausibility.

How did this debate within the Vienna Circle transfigure the meaning of positivism? The answer resides in America, where there was a compulsive concern with sociology's status as a science in the early decades of the twentieth century (Turner and Turner, 1990). Both Mach's and Popper's arguments were appealing, because they legitimated the kind of variable analysis (for example, cross tabulations and the beginnings of Pearsonian correlations) that was emerging in American sociology in the late 1920s and 1930s. By the 1930s, sampling, scaling and statistical analysis were increasingly becoming mainstays of the discipline. The Vienna Circle had, in the meantime, invented a redundant term – logical positivism – to describe the process of deducing hypotheses from abstract theoretical formulations which, for Comte and Spencer, was simply positivism. But this division between logical deduction on one side, and empirical generalization on the other, gave legitimation to quantitative data analysis that was to test hypotheses deduced from abstract laws; and since no theory is ever proven (à la Popper), it must constantly

be assessed with quantitatively analysed data. Thus, the collection of data and their quantitative analysis were essential to carrying out the mandate of 'logical positivism'. This position was not very different from that argued by Comte and Spencer, but the emphasis on quantification went against Spencer's advocacy and, more significantly, began to convert positivism toward the collection and analysis of data *per se*, without too much regard for theory or for the 'logic' of deduction.

Ironically, in the 1970s, a theory construction movement swept over American sociology with the production of texts on how to 'build' and 'construct' theory.[24] Here was logical positivism converted into 'cook books' about procedures for building theory, but these books were too mechanical. They sought to do for the 'logical' part of positivism what statistics textbooks had done for data collection and analysis; and they soon fell into deserved obscurity. With their demise, the last remnants of the theoretical part of positivism gave way to quantitative sociology in the United States and as a result, positivism increasingly became associated with sampling, use of scaling techniques, statistical analyses of various sorts. The emergence of the computer, especially the desk-top computer, only accelerated a trend that was well under way in the late 1950s. Today, we are left with this legacy in the United States, although in Europe positivism is better appreciated for what its founders – Comte and Spencer – advocated. Still, in Europe, there tends to be considerable skepticism about the prospects for a true science of society, and so in a somewhat different way, positivism is often perceived in negative terms.

Thus, the promise of positivism trumpeted by Comte and Spencer has given way to considerable skepticism. Faith in the Enlightenment project is constantly assaulted by various waves of anti-science rhetoric, most recently by postmodernism. In this postmodern context, positivism is viewed as a failed epistemology, or as a misguided effort to create a Grand Narrative. And, of course, in the more American context, the association of positivism with compulsive quantitative data analysis offers another line of criticism. And for critical theorists in Europe and the United States, positivism is seen not only as inhumane but as an instrument of domination in which science is used to legitimate the status quo and current systems of power. Comte and Spencer would probably turn over in their graves if they could see how their vision has been so transfigured.

Still, despite these alterations to the original meaning of positivism, there remains in the discipline of sociology as a whole a belief that theory should guide research; and while this idea is rarely executed in practice, there is a sense that data should have more general theoretical implications. This connection between data and more general theoretical laws is the essence of positivism, and even if it is only an ideal that is only occasionally implemented, most sociologists today would at least confirm their faith in this ideal. Thus, even with the transfiguration of Comte's and Spencer's meaning, the essence of positivism lives on. Perhaps it is no longer called positivism, given the unsavory connotations of this term in the modern eye, but it is the spirit of what Comte and Spencer saw as the essence of sociology.

NOTES

1 All of the Philosophers – Volaire, Rousseau, Diderot and others – postulated that humans had certain 'natural rights' that stood in contradiction to existing institutional arrangements. Old institutional systems would, therefore, have to be abandoned and new ones constructed; and it is this vision of societal reconstruction that was to be incorporated into Comte's work and, indeed, most works of French thinkers in the nineteenth century.

2 Comte had established himself as a brilliant student, but also as a difficult one. Like most students, Comte had lost his faith in religion; and in its place, the university environment created a new faith in science and in the belief that scientific laws could be used in engineering applications to reconstruct the world, both the physical and social. The Ecole Polytechnique closed for a period in a dispute between students and faculty, on the one side, and the government, on the other; and when it reopened, Comte did not return, and in fact, he did not seek readmission, perhaps because he realized that he had made too many enemies. Comte's abrasive personality was to haunt his entire career, and in the end, it destroyed him.

3 Comte proclaimed that he was the Founder of Universal Religion, and he went about establishing churches advocating love as the unifying force of humanity. He tried to counsel political leaders in the way of past theologians; and he offered ritual ceremonies for the members of his religion. Comte was, in a word, insane; and his last work, *System of Positive Polity* (1851–1854) is full of the ramblings of a man gone crazy (although this work also contains important sociological insights).

4 In Comte's time, the term *physics* had not been wholly usurped by the contemporary discipline using this label. The notion of 'physics' was understood to mean 'to study the nature of'; and so, a social physics was to study the nature of social organization. But the Belgian statistician Adolphe Quetelet had already used this label for his kind of statistical work, which outraged Comte but which none the less forced him to adopt the label 'sociology' to describe the science of society.

5 Harriet Marineau, a very fine sociologist in her own right, translated and condensed Comte's original version of *The Course of Positive Philosophy* (which was published in serial form in five volumes between 1830 and 1842) into a three volume set, titled *The Positive Philosophy of Auguste Comte*, released in 1854. All page references are to this 1854 English edition.

6 Obviously, this phrase 'social facts' is taken by Durkheim as the cornerstone of his methodological approach in *The Rules of the Sociological Method* (1895).

7 Comte relegated psychology to biology and did not see psychology as a distinct science.

8 It is unlikely that Comte in his early writing would have approved of sociological 'practice' as it is currently performed. True, he had a kind of medical view of the social organism, but laws were to be the equivalent of those in physics. Hence, the use of sociology to reconstruct society was to be more like an engineering discipline than a medical one. Laws would be translated into rules of thumb that could be employed to rebuild society.

9 Not all of those engaged in social practice reject positivism, but many hold a more clinical view of such practice, emphasizing intuition and sensitivity to problems. Positivism posits a more hard-nosed view of practice as social engineering, a view that offends many sociologists. For a review of the issue, see Turner (1998).

10 If there is a criticism of Comte, it is not his view of scientific sociology, but his lack of substantive analysis of human societies beyond the rather crude law of the three stages. Comte provides leads about what to look for in analysing social process – for example, population size, density, differentiation, integration through mutual interdependence, power and common symbols – but he never develops these ideas to any great extent. Rather, it was the next generation who would take Comte's leads and forge them into a more profound sociology.

11 *Social Statics: or, the Conditions Essential to Human Happiness Specified, and the First of Them Developed* ([1851] 1888) and *The Principles of Ethics* ([1892–1898] 1978) are like bookends on Spencer's major works. In between these two highly charged moral statements, Spencer wrote important treatises on physics, biology, psychology and, last of all, sociology.

12 Comte had, fairly early on in his career, decided to pursue 'cerebral hygiene' and ignore others' works. Thus, with each passing decade, Comte became less familiar with science. Obviously, only a deranged man would pronounce that the age of positivism was here and then proceed to isolate himself from the advances in the sciences. Spencer did not read much either, but he learned a great deal through his associations with prominent scientists and through the work of his research assistants.

13 For Spencer, evolution in general is defined in *First Principles* (Spencer, [1862] 1880: 243) as 'a change from a less coherent form to a more coherent form, consequent on the dissipation of motion and integration of matter . . . leading to a change from a homogeneous to a heterogeneous state'. For social evolution, these ideas translated into a view of societies as differentiating along productive, reproductive, regulatory and distributive functions.

14 Almost all of Spencer's work first appeared in serial form as essays in prominent periodicals of his time. They were then published as books. These books and their serialized contents were among the most widely read volumes of the last century, a fact which is hard to grasp in light of how few contemporary sociologists or social thinkers ever read Spencer today.

15 Spencer had not intended to write *The Study of Sociology*, but the editor of *Popular Science Monthly*, who had been instrumental in serializing Spencer's work in his magazine and who had also been crucial in getting his work published as books under the Appleton–Century–Crofts nameplate, prevailed upon Spencer to write this initial work. Spencer reluctantly agreed, but when he was finished, he recognized the importance of this preliminary statement to overcome the view that sociology could not be a science.

16 Spencer had inherited a considerable fortune from his uncle who had educated him. This money was used to finance independent scholars to conduct the research for each of the volumes of *Descriptive Sociology*. Spencer left money in his will to continue the project after his death, with the last volume appearing in 1934, thirty-one years after his death in 1903.

17 In essence, Spencer created a Human Relations Area Files, some sixty years before George P. Murdock's efforts (Turner and Maryanski, 1988). There is a direct lineage between Spencer and Murdock, via Albert G. Keller, who used Spencer's ideas in his *Societal Evolution* (1915) as well as in his and William Graham Sumner's *The Science of Society* (1927) and who was Murdock's mentor at Yale.

18 Many reviews of Spencer's *The Principles of Sociology* complained that there was simply too much data. Thus, any view of Spencer's positivism as armchair theorizing ignores the actual contents of his works which, if anything, summarize too much data.

19 Spencer's *Descriptive Sociology* provided the data base for this analysis which was, by far, the most detailed and sophisticated of all the evolutionary schemes produced in the nineteenth century.

20 Spencer implied a selectionist argument, as Turner (1995) has made explicit. This argument is both Darwinian (i.e., competition for resources increases under population growth and ecological density) and functional (i.e., functional needs generate selection pressures for a population to discover solutions, by luck, chance, planning, borrowing, and other means, to basic and fundamental problems of survival). Both kinds of selection – Darwinian and functional – always operate on human populations.

21 *Dissolution* was seen by Spencer to be a fundamental property of the universe, and he gave it great emphasis in *First Principles* ([1862] 1888). For societal evolution, Spencer argued that if selection does not produce structures for dealing with basic problems created by population growth, then the population will disintegrate or dissolve.

22 Indeed, the vast majority of pages in *The Principles of Sociology* are devoted to this institutional analysis. For generalization from this analysis, see Turner (1985) and (2000).

23 Spencer emphasized in *The Principles of Sociology* that war had been a great force in human evolution, since the more productive and organized society usually wins a geopolitical conflict, and through this process, the level of human organization is constantly ratcheted up. But, he felt that once an industrial stage of development is reached, war works against expanded productivity and market dynamics, since it biases technological development and production to war-making which, in turn, concentrates power, aggravates inequality and promotes internal threats associated with inequality. Moreover, control of territories increases logistical loads and consumes capital for social control that might otherwise be used to increase domestic production. These do not sound like the ideas of a conservative supporting the status quo during the peak period of British Colonialism.

24 Jerald Hage (1994) has collected essays dealing with the theory construction movement in the context of its time.

REFERENCES

Comte, Auguste ([1822] 1975) 'Plan of the Scientific Operations Necessary for Reorganizing Society', in G. Lenzer (ed.), *Auguste Comte and Positivism: The Essential Writings*. New York: Harper Torchbooks. pp. 9–69.

Comte, Auguste ([1830–1842] 1854) *The Positive Philosophy of Auguste Comte* (trans. and condensed by Harriet Martineau), 3 vols. London: George Bell and Sons.

Comte, August [1851–1854] 1875) *System of Positive Polity*. New York: Burt Franklin.

Durkheim, Emile ([1893] 1947) *The Division of Labor in Society*. New York: Free Press.

Durkheim, Emile ([1895] 1938) *The Rules of the Sociological Method*. New York: Free Press.

Hage, Jerald R. (1994) *Formal Theory: Opportunity or Pitfall?* Albany, NY: State University of New York Press.

Johnson, William M. (1983) *The Austrian Mind: An Intellectual and Social History, 1848–1938*. Berkeley, CA: University of California Press.

Keller, Albert G. (1915) *Societal Evolution: A Study of the Evolutionary Basis of the Science of Society*. New York: Macmillan.

Mach, Ernst (1893) *The Science of Mechanics* (trans. T.J. McCormack). La Salle, IL: Open Court.

Montesquieu, Charles ([1748] 1900) *The Spirit of the Laws*. London: Colonial.

Popper, Karl (1959) *The Logic of Scientific Discovery*. London: Hutchinson.

Popper, Karl (1969) *Conjectures and Refutations*. London: Kegan and Paul.

Spencer, Herbert ([1851] 1888) *Social Statics: or the Conditions Essential to Human Happiness Specified, and the First of Them Developed*. New York: Appleton–Century–Crofts.

Spencer, Herbert ([1855–72] 1898) *The Principles of Psychology*. New York: Appleton–Century–Crofts.

Spencer, Herbert ([1862] 1880) *First Principles*. New York: A.L. Burt.

Spencer, Herbert ([1864–1867] 1898) *The Principles of Biology*. New York: Appleton–Century–Crofts.

Spencer, Herbert ([1864] 1968) *Reasons for Dissenting from the Philosophy of M. Comte and Other Essays*. Berkeley, CA: Glendessary.

Spencer, Herbert (1873) *The Study of Sociology*. London: Routledge, Kegan and Paul.

Spencer, Herbert ([1874–1896] 1898) *The Principles of Sociology*. New York: Appleton–Century–Crofts.

Spencer, Herbert ([1892–1898] 1978) *The Principles of Ethics*. Indianapolis, IN: Liberty Press.

Spencer, Herbert (1893–1934) *Descriptive Sociology*. 16 volumes with various authors and publishers.

Sumner, William Graham and Albert G. Keller (1927) *The Science of Society*. New Haven, CT: Yale University Press.

Turner, Jonathan H. (1984) 'Durkheim's and Spencer's Principles of Social Organization', *Sociological Perspectives*, 9: 283–91.

Turner, Jonathan H. (1985) *Herbert Spencer: A Renewed Appreciation*. Newbury Park, CA: Sage.

Turner, Jonathan H. (1995) *Macrodynamics: Toward a General Theory on the Organization of Human Populations*. New Brunswick, NJ: Rutgers University Press.

Turner, Jonathan H. (1998) 'Must Sociological Theory and Practice Be So Far Apart?', *Sociological Perspectives*, 41: 243–58.

Turner, Jonathan H. (2000) 'Herbert Spencer', in G. Ritzer (ed.), *Blackwell Companion to Major Social Theorists: Classical and Contemporary*. Oxford: Blackwell, in press.

Turner, Jonathan H. and Maryanski, Alexandra (1988) 'Sociology's Lost Human Relations Area Files', *Sociological Perspectives*, 31: 1934.

Turner, Stephen Park and Turner, Jonathan H. (1990) *The Impossible Science*. Newbury Park, CA: Sage.

4

Maintaining Marx

GREGOR McLENNAN

In this chapter I discuss Karl Marx's major concepts and some of the continuing debates around them. These are grouped into three overlapping sections, dealing with Marx's theories of history, his account of capitalism and class, and his philosophical or metatheoretical standpoint. Although several of Marx's key arguments are now widely regarded as either defective or indeterminate, he remains a thinker of signal importance and fertility for contemporary social understanding. This is indicated by the strong 'comeback' that Marx has made, following the collapse of the Soviet bloc countries during 1989–91, when many people thought, rather superficially, that the last nail in his intellectual coffin had finally been hammered in. Instead, on a substantive level, Marx's account of the basic logic and volatility of capitalist society looks as powerful as ever. As regards metatheory, the positivity and aspiration to integration that characterize Marx's approach to social scientific understanding went entirely out of fashion during the 1980s, as a wave of 'reflexivity' and 'deconstruction' washed over critical social theory. However, once again, there is a fresh appreciation of Marx's strengths at this level, partly as an antidote to widespread 'negativity' and excessive self-scrutiny on the part of intellectuals.

HISTORICAL MATERIALISM

As with other aspects of his ideas, controversy surrounds Marx's theories of human historical development, or 'materialist conception of history'. Did his reflections on history aspire to be anything as developed as a 'theory' or (even

grander) a 'philosophy' of history? Commentators can be found on all sides, from the interpretation of Marx as a 'teleological' inevitabilist propounding a God's-eye view of history's inner meaning, to his imaging as someone who believed, to the contrary, that history has *no* logic in itself, but is rather constructed and reconstructed according to present political needs and struggles. Two expressions or phases of Marx's thinking about history, nevertheless, are largely agreed upon.

Marx's reflections on human 'alienation' (1843–4), constitute one of these phases. Hegel's conception of the 'dialectical' *movement* of history was that of a contradictory but dynamic process in which the initial separation and antagonism of the different component 'moments' of Mind or Spirit are progressively overcome. Out of some apparently intractable tensions between the empirical and the conceptual, the finite and the infinite, the rational and the ineffable, Man and God, a spiral of encompassing developments in consciousness is posited, eventuating, in principle, in a complete higher fusion (= the 'Absolute Idea'). Drawing on, but going beyond, Ludwig Feuerbach's humanistic critique of Hegel, Marx inverted this schema in a materialist way whilst retaining something of its logical pattern. He objected to its religiosity, and derided Hegel's politically reactionary attempt to overcome its impossible abstractness by identifying as its 'expression' the progress of the actual Prussian state. Accordingly, in works such as the *Contribution to the Critique of Hegel's Philosophy of Right* Marx sought to demolish the anti-democratic implications of Hegel's theologically motivated political assertions, whilst in *On the Jewish Question* and journalistic work, he pursued the notion of emancipation beyond the attainment of liberal rights within civil society.

More generally, Marx interpreted available religious and political discourses as desperate expressions of the lack of human self-realization in the present state of society, a view spelled out in the *Economic and Philosophic Manuscripts* of 1844. From limited beginnings as a collective and conscious labouring species, humanity undergoes a progressively 'reified' and 'alienated' existence. Modern civil society is represented here as an experience of profound *estrangement*, principally due to the generalization of commodity production, including labour itself, under industrial conditions. Men as workers are necessarily forced to be, and to feel, separated from the product of their own work activity, from each other and from their higher 'species-being'. Moreover, the laws, rights and citizen activities achieved under conditions of alienation, whilst offering an important bulwark against tyranny, are severely limited, and indeed partially obstruct further societal and personal growth. Communism, on the other hand, is presented as nothing less than 'the riddle of history solved, and it knows itself to be this solution'. Communism marks 'the positive transcendence of human self-estrangement' and 'the *genuine* resolution of the conflict between man and nature', 'between man and man' and 'between freedom and necessity'.

Whilst 'alienation' is a powerful motivating idea, the 'history' that it conveys is possibly an over-moralized one, featuring something like the fall and redemption of Man's creative labouring essence. Notwithstanding its moral and political force, the 'alienation' and 'species self-realization' scenario is, ironically, somewhat 'idealist' in character and simplistic in its implied application across the board. *The German Ideology* of 1845–6 provided methodological protocols at once more solidly materialist, and yet also more responsive to historical specificity. Marx and Engels declare that the proper 'premises' of historical analysis are not grounded in a concern for consciousness or self-realization, but rather in the empirical grasp of 'real individuals', involved in 'definite social and political relations', these relations being in turn based upon 'the production of material life itself'. From that viewpoint, not only are speculative accounts of Man's essence and fate wrong, they constitute 'mystification', *illusory* expressions of the very material life processes in which they are embedded.

Perhaps, then, Marx is best regarded as an open-minded, empirical historian and sociologist rather than a philosopher of history as such? In that case, his 'materialist conception of history' would simply be a heuristic tool, not a sub-stantive doctrine. Marx sometimes presents himself that way, and his materialism at times is very generously conceived: it is the material 'life-process' as a whole that is being highlighted, a process in which men [*sic*] are *actively*, not passively, engaged. This strand in the discussion squares nicely with the activist and practical emphasis emerging from Marx's reflections in the *Theses on Feuerbach* at around the same time. Overall, though, Marx's perspective has to be judged as a prospective *theory* of society and history as a whole. The priority given to the production of the 'means of life' in understanding social organization and consciousness amounts to more than simply 'correcting' the excesses of idealism, as some cautious supporters have maintained. More plausibly, Marx is engaged on the ambitious business of 'expounding the real process of production' in order to *explain* 'the basis of all history', 'its action as State' (forms of consciousness, religion, philosophy, morality etc. etc.), so that 'the whole thing . . . can be depicted in its totality'. The way in which the material basis of a society is produced is associated with definite 'social forms of intercourse', and together these account for the character of the political and ideological 'superstructure', including the role that dominant ideas play in the rationalization of ruling class advantage.

Marx's 1859 'Preface to *A Contribution to the Critique of Political Economy*' summarizes the 'guiding principle' of his studies at the time of *The German Ideology*, and in this text, notoriously, historical materialism is expressed in sharper terms still, resulting in what is often designated 'productive forces determinism'. In this, the productive forces of a society (materials, technological capacity, level of knowledge, organizational 'energy') seem to provide the driving force for change in the social relations of production (property forms, appropriation of surplus product, class divisions, labour regimes). In combination, the forces and relations of production (= 'mode of production') account for the character and direction of the 'whole immense superstructure'. Across history, a relatively small number of modes of production have appeared, each having its own logic of social relations: in the Preface, Marx mentions the Asiatic, Ancient (slave), feudal and capitalist modes, but we must add from other writings a tribal communist mode, and of course a future advanced communist society. Marx envisages these generically distinctive modes of production and forms of social life as forming a definite sequence in time, and they develop into one another (during 'eras of social revolution') because of the inability of the prevailing social relations to cope with the developmental potential of the productive forces. This scenario is also present in the *Communist Manifesto* of 1848, and it underwrites Marx's greatest work, *Capital*, too, though in a more muted way. On the one hand, capitalism shows a relentless tendency to generate greater productive capacity; on the other hand, it is constitutively unable to use its technological breakthroughs for the good of society as a whole – by ending economic exploitation, ensuring less toil and enabling more creative work for all. Sooner or later, this fundamental contradiction is impossible to contain within the prevailing relations of production.

There are several important questions about the status of 'productive forces determinism'.The two main issues are: did Marx actually hold any strong version of this theory; and, how valid or credible is it, with or without Marx's endorsement? Neither question can be tackled properly without a great deal of specialist discussion, but a reasonable summary would be that productive forces determinism is invalid, and that although in many passages, Marx does appear to articulate the strong thesis, in other passages, and in his more substantive political writings, he undermines it again. The formula for 'mode of production' is often slippery, perhaps deliberately so. Thus, productive forces are sometimes rendered not as *technological* potential *per se*, but as 'social forces of production' and 'productive powers', and indeed in one or two places the forces seem to include not only the relationship of 'man to nature' but also of 'men to each other'. Another vital ambiguity lies in whether Marx placed work relations in the labour process, or the division of labour generally, within the productive *forces*, or as part of the *relations* of production, or somewhere in between the two. The relations of production, for their part, are also incompletely defined by Marx, sometimes coming out as forms of property ownership, sometimes as control over the production process, and sometimes more vaguely as 'forms of social intercourse'.

Apart from the definition of the component elements of the mode of production concept, there is the issue of the relationship between them. Marx is often accused of technological determinism, but it is doubtful that he saw the primacy of the forces of production in straight causal terms, as 'determinism' implies. Even his 'tough' formulations on this speak of the 'correspondence' between forces and relations, or the 'connections' and 'coupling' between them, rather than the forces being depicted as a separable and prior effective agency. Accordingly, the relationship has been reframed as a *functional* one, with a number of conceptual and empirical conundrums emerging around this in the literature. These concern the problem of distinguishing between valid and spurious functional explanations, and between causal mechanisms and the functions they are purported to fulfil. Under the rubric of functional explanation, the relations of production come into being *because* they promote the development of the productive forces. But if these elements are co-present and mutually functional, could the thesis not be reversed, so that certain productive forces come and go according to whether they promote or 'fetter' the maintenance or intensification of the relations of production themselves? And anyway, what exactly is being 'promoted' above all else in productive forces functionalism: is it the current *level* of the forces, or their potential *use* as they presently stand, or their *rate* of growth, or their optimum *possible* development, or something else? There is no decisive answer to this, either in Marx or in his sophisticated interpreters.

A further issue is that when Marx comes to explaining and describing major *historical* episodes, his accounts sometimes seem to favour the primacy of the forces, sometimes the primacy of the relations. For example, the fundamental technical change associated with the industrial revolution is portrayed as occuring *within* an already established capitalist social structure: no leadership role for the productive forces there. On the other hand, the transition from feudalism to capitalism, like the projected transition from capitalism to socialism, is to be understood as the result of impossible social contradictions stemming from the productive forces bursting through outdated property relations. Even in this latter case, though, it might be appropriate to see Marx as trying to establish the *necessary* but not *sufficient* conditions for modal transformation, because in all his accounts, class capacities and class action (which are co-terminous with the social relations of production) play a crucial role in historical outcomes. The famous rousing line in the *Communist Manifesto* – 'the history of all hitherto existing society is the history of class struggles' – would make little sense otherwise.

Marx's inconsistencies aside, productive forces determinism is generally held to be either false or undemonstrable in any strong formulation. This is the consensus, at least, amongst even Marxist historians, since there are too many notable counter-examples. Moreover, the idea that technological and scientific powers have an *independent* momentum throughout history, to which social relations must adapt, relies upon a dangerously narrow view of how human rationality expresses itself in circumstances of scarcity and conflict. Indeed, if Marx really held to this perspective, he would have to be deemed in thrall to the kind of 'transhistorical' philosophy of history that he spent much energy attacking. At the same time, though, it is incontestable that his 'mode of production' conception requires some kind of directionality if it is to be seen as a theory of history in any substantial sense at all. It is vital to see here that the assertion of inevitable *tendencies* persisting through time does *not* commit us to a foregone conclusion about what must inevitably happen, all things considered. That is why contemporary Marxists who do not advocate 'strong' historical materialism continue to put effort and skill into defending 'broader' or 'weaker' versions.

CAPITALISM AND CLASS ANALYSIS

Marx placed capitalism in historical perspective as one of a series of (transient) socioeconomic formations, but it was not *just* one of a series. The analysis of capital and the prospects for class struggle within and beyond it were his primary concerns. Marx read capitalism as an economic system characterized by the production and exchange of *commodities*. Crucially, human labour power itself is a commodity under capitalism, freely bought and sold on the market. Labour is 'free', but there is a dark irony about this. On the one hand, workers are able to offer their labour to, or withdraw it from, any particular employer, and so any labour market exchange is one struck between autonomous people, legally recognized as such. On the other hand, workers have been *forced* to be free, first, because the very availability of masses of labourers to work in capitalist enterprises was largely the result of the expulsion of rural labourers from their former lands and livelihoods. Marx graphically summarizes his account of this process in *Capital*, Volume I: The history of the peasants: 'expropriation is written in the annals of mankind in letters of blood and fire'. Secondly, moreover, the working class or proletariat under mature capitalism has no choice but to sell its labour power simply in order to live, whereas capitalists do not.

According to Marx in *Capital*, Volume III, it is 'the specific economic form in which unpaid surplus labour is pumped out of direct producers' that determines the relations of production in a given mode, 'the relationship of rulers and ruled'. How does this mechanism work under capitalism? The value of a commodity is determined, as Marx sees it, by the amount of socially necessary labour time that goes into its production. But assuming that commodities exchange at their values, it is something of a mystery as to how profit actually arises, and difficult to say

that anything particularly unfair or disadvantageous is going on when the buyers of commodities, including capitalists, come away from the exchange process with whatever gains they have transacted. This appearance of coherence and apparent fairness in exchange Marx dubbed 'the fetishism of commodities': people are mesmerized by the seeming objectivity and authority of The Market, and are inclined to be stumped by the question of how capital is generated and accumulated. Marx's answer was that profit arises not in commodity exchange at all, but in the production process itself, and in pursuing this he makes a decisive distinction between labour power and actual labour performed. The capitalist buys the labour *power* of the worker, whose value is determined by the labour time necessary to reproduce it, as measured by the average bundle of subsistence goods required, but sells the labour *product*. The product is of a higher value because the working day is typically longer than the time needed to reproduce the labourer's capacity to work, and so the extra labour contribution in the typical day's work represents *surplus value*. Surplus value is realized in market sale, producing profit. Marx has many bitingly witty passages in which he caricatures the individual capitalist as 'Mr. Moneybags', but this is what he terms a 'personification' only, because actually he sees capitalism as a *system*, driven by an impersonal logic of accumulation and 'expanded reproduction' rather than by personal greed or conspicuous consumption.

Capitalist firms do not operate in isolation: there are other firms seeking to make profits and they operate in particular industrial sectors, across which average rates of exploitation and average rates of profit are formed. In conditions of capitalist competition, there will be an initial tendency to seek market advantage through the extension of the working day, but this cannot continue indefinitely. Instead, gains are made through introducing greater intensity within the labour process, improving the productivity of labour. Marx sees this process in terms of the 'rising organic composition of capital', which names the steady increase of constant capital (plant, machinery = 'dead labour') in relation to variable capital (actual 'living labour'). But since it is only labour/variable capital that imparts value to other commodities, and in so doing creates surplus value – the source of profits – it follows that the *rate of profit* tends to fall, because variable capital is persistently diminishing as a proportion of total capital. Here is one of Marx's central 'contradictions' of capitalism. It is not true that Marx sees it as heralding, in itself, the complete breakdown of capitalism, because the *total amount* of surplus value (and therefore profit) might increase even if its *proportion* relative to fixed capital diminishes. Several other 'counter-tendencies' are also identified by Marx.

But the tendency of the rate of profit to fall does cause endemic volatility and crisis. In order to stay ahead or catch up, capitalists are driven to enhance productivity and reduce labour, with the result that more and more is produced, and periodically large numbers of workers are 'shed'. Eventually, too much productive capital is in play, and too many goods go unsold; firms go out of business altogether, and fixed capital may even have to be destroyed, all in likely social conditions of widespread hardship, class conflict and social unrest. On the other hand, with capitalists having cut back on orders for capital stock, and producing fewer commodities, the organic composition of capital within the sector will reduce, and there will be fewer firms around to take advantage of the associated rising rate of profit. A recovery ensues. In this way, Marx sees capitalism lurching from upswing to downturn, and from crisis to crisis. But these will progressively worsen: capital is, over time, concentrated in fewer and fewer big firms; higher levels of the productive forces progressively characterize the production process, so that each crisis is playing dice with more sophisticated and expensive resources; and each crisis increases the chances that workers will come to see that the irrationalities and exploitativeness of capitalism are intrinsic to it as a socioeconomic order. They will then unite to create a better one, one that is thoroughly cooperative and non-exploitative.

Both the dynamics of capitalism, and the emergence of any alternative to it, are couched by Marx in terms of tendencies, not necessities. This renders his theories more flexible than they often appear. For some readers, this is very annoying: Marx is making rather God-like pronouncements on the structure and future of capitalism, and banking on the raised consciousness of those who will replace it, yet it is not clear just what kind of evidence will ever justify this expectation. For supporters, there is no real problem here, and signal advantages. Social scientific explanation, they would say, is always partial, incomplete and 'diagnostic' in character – it provides the basis for investigation and action rather than proof. And there is no doubt that out of just a few central theses, Marx generates a massive research programme, full of political and ideological consequences of the greatest interest and significance. Warfare and welfare states, colonialism and imperialism, the relentless commodification of everything, the shift from production-based workforces to service-based labour, the psychology of uncertainty and agitation, the proletarianization of the middle class and the increased knowledge base of key productive workers – and much more – can all be tackled using Marx's conceptual and normative apparatus; and they can hardly be explained satisfactorily without it.

Still, there are major interpretative problems surrounding Marx's analysis, not the least of which concerns 'class' itself. Surprisingly, Marx wrote very little of a definitional nature about class. Famously, Engels, as editor of *Capital*, Volume III, noted simply that 'here the manuscript breaks off' after just a few paragraphs in which Marx, finally, began to address this elemental question. One conundrum concerns the nature of the working class itself. If the major classes of a society are the exploiters and exploited within a given mode of production, then the strict ruling on the proletariat is that it comprises only those workers who produce surplus value, the entire basis of exploitation in capitalism. But on this account, especially under the conditions of increasing labour productivity that Marx says are also definitive of capitalism, the proportion of a population that directly produces surplus value is bound to diminish steadily. This process is borne out of course by empirical trends, leading many sociologists to see Marxism as utterly outmoded. Under a 'labour market' definition, however, Marx's vision of progressive class polarization, with an ever-larger number of proletarians, can still be sustained. The key thing is that workers have to sell their labour power, whilst capitalists do not. But the cost of this broader approach is that Marx's special stress on the production of surplus value needs to be played down, and we need to be comfortable about including in the broad working class anyone who is not able to live reasonably on proceeds wholly derived from other people's efforts. This will be the vast majority of the population, including high-level professionals and managers as well as the more routinized 'middle class'.

The broad definition of the proletariat is defensible, but just like an excessively narrow definition, it does seem somewhat perverse in its *sociological* consequences. In Marx's account, bourgeoisie and proletariat are intrinsically opposed to one another, yet also symbiotically tied together, such that any other groups and classes within capitalism (*petit bourgeoisie*, landlords, speculators) can be understood only as subsidiary to that primary relationship. This 'relational' conception has, periodically, been deemed superior to 'descriptive' and 'hierarchical' conceptions which home in on the almost infinite number of sociologically significant distinctions of income, occupation and status that exist amongst empirical individuals. However, if we can include almost everyone in the working class, and if this is the most important thing about them, then a great deal of sociological interest is sidelined by Marxian class theory, and meanwhile there may be little empirical indication of 'situational' or 'activist' commonality across the ranks of the total 'collective worker'.

There are various ways of striking a middle way between the narrow and broad definitions of class. Especially, *effective control* over the means of production can be added to criteria of surplus value creation and property ownership. Indeed, some would interpret effective control as the essential content of capitalist 'possession'. This might be particularly important given the trend in capitalism (which Marx noted) away from individual total capital ownership and towards joint stock companies, pension fund investment and the 'managerial revolution'. A more recent contribution says that productive assets include not only large-scale ownership of means of production, but also lower-level 'property' such as *credentials* and *skills*. These forms of endowment can be used by some workers to take material advantage of less well endowed workers, whilst both remain to varying degrees jointly exploited by large-scale capitalists. Such amendments retain the concepts of exploitation, class and profit, but in a diluted or compounded form, thus claiming some kind of endorsement in Marx's own work, but looking more adequate to the perceived divisions of interest and identity within contemporary stratification processes. Overall, most Marxists, including Marx, use some mixture of property, labour market situation and reward, and power/control over and within the production process to try to defend or reconstruct the basic proposition that socioeconomic class is the primary form of social division.

Neo-Marxist ingenuity and breadth is required in another pivotal area of Marxian class analysis, namely the theory of value and surplus value. True, there are still Marxist economists, skilled in advanced mathematics, who are trying to 'crack' one persistent problem, namely, the difficulty of showing just how labour *values* translate into market *prices*. But apart from this 'transformation problem', Marx makes other assumptions which have been thoroughly challenged, especially since they are presented in such an a priori fashion. For example, he assumes that all the complex, combined and variably skilled labour tasks that characterize work under capitalism can be calculated in terms of their 'common denominator', simple average labour time. The counter-argument is that this equation just cannot be computed, and that there is no independent reason for its plausibility. Similarly, Marx takes it for granted that there is a strict equivalence of exchange values in the buying and selling of commodities, but again it is far from obvious that this takes place, even hypothetically. Finally, critics have had enough of Marx's theses that only human labour creates value, and that labour value alone must stand as the measure of commodity exchange. In principle, they say, any other commodity could play this measuring role: it is a romantic anthropological vision, not a 'scientific' discovery as such, that compels Marx to foreground labour's unique socioeconomic status.

Marx's class theory, and his 'anatomy' of capitalism, thus face serious objections. However, whenever social theorists discuss anything in terms of capitalism and class, and whenever they look up from their texts to try to appraise the state of the world as a whole, their debt to Marx is usually very evident. Accordingly, the effort that has gone into trying to reformulate Marx's theories – perhaps in a far 'broader' way than he would like – is not simply a gestural or religious quest to save the Master's reputation at all costs. Particularly important in this regard, since it generates the greatest number of accusations of conceptual breakdown, is the explanatory relation of socioeconomic class to political, cultural and ideological phenomena.

I have already intimated that Marx was neither a determinist, nor an 'inevitabilist' when it comes to connecting 'superstructural' features to 'basic' ones. Had he been, then questions of politics and ideology would have been much easier to deal with, one way or another. The problem for interpretation today is rather that of the 'relative autonomy' of politics and culture in terms of its degree of influence by the state of the relations of production. Many social scientists accept that there is some kind of broadly functional connection or elective affinity between economic imperatives and other aspects of social existence. The issue is: can we generalize consistently about the causal direction and empirical appearance of these 'connections'? Marx's own political and cultural writings are not decisive in this matter. At first, he seemed to imagine capitalism as relentlessly impoverishing the working class, to the point where some kind of revolutionary change would have to occur 'spontaneously'. The role of the state in this scenario is simply one of maintaining capitalist interests: 'the executive of the modern state is but a committee for managing the common affairs of the whole bourgeoisie', as the *Manifesto* puts it. As for ideology, the *German Ideology* insists that 'the ideas of the ruling class are in every epoch the ruling ideas'. Here, no doubt, the connections between base and superstructure, capitalism and social life, are too tightly drawn, though when regarded as summative hypotheses rather than an intended representation of the detailed facts, there is surely little to feel aggrieved about. At any rate, Marx was always optimistic about humanity's ability to 'solve' the problems it posed for itself, and about the way in which an apparently stable social equilibrium breaks down. Capitalism especially – the *Manifesto* again – produces 'uninterrupted disturbance of all social conditions, everlasting uncertainty and agitation', and so creates a culture in which 'all that is solid melts into air'. It is very unlikely, then, that Marx would have regarded people's class locations as configuring their forms of life and thought in every respect, or that the political and ideological realms would straightforwardly fulfil the functions that capitalism sets for them in principle. Thus, after about 1850, Marx explored without qualm the possibility that major concessions could be wrung out of the state, thereby improving the situation and consciousness of the working class, and taking the ultimate 'battle of democracy' forward.

Marx conducted a series of sustained analyses of French politics after 1848, in which we can see both a degree of 'reductionist' intent, and yet also the detailed undermining of any simple reductionism. In these studies, the actions of prominent individuals, the French state and a whole range of political groupings are framed as variously expressing essential class interests, themselves figured as part of the long, inexorable social revolution of the nineteenth century as a whole. Political and ideological strategies on the surface, Marx implies in the *Eighteenth Brumaire*, do little more than track the subterranean workings of the 'old mole' of history itself. Yet at the same time, these metaphors are conceits, and even if taken theoretically, they operate at an extremely general level. Ultimately, it is the complex and 'conjunctural' way in which Marx handles the interconnections amongst a large range of groupings, class fractions and forms of consciousness that stands out. The question then imposes itself: if there is no *necessary* connection between basic and superstructural elements, and no *direct* manifestation of the primacy of economic relationships within the cultural and political spheres, then how can Marxian class theory be maintained? It is important to point out that this issue can be pressed from a radical as well as a conservative standpoint. Indeed, from political leaders such as Lenin and Gramsci through to postmodern cultural thinkers, the idea of base determining superstructure has itself been regarded, precisely, as a *conservative*, not an *emancipatory* image. At a time when some commentators are perceiving a dramatic 'cultural turn' in society and theory alike, an outright 'superstructuralism' has developed today, with ideas and identities seeming to be primary in relation to socioeconomic materialities.

That attitude, whatever its merits, represents the abandonment rather than the modification of Marxism's theoretical core. In response, Marxists could rail against the absurdly 'radical' sense of contingency and plurality that such culturalism leads to, and specifically bemoan the loss of a materialist sense of the logic of capitalist society at a time when the latter finally pervades the entire globe. This latter point is polemically effective, because few critical theorists who challenge the primacy of class deny the power of global capital, or even dispute that there are deep and increasing inequalities in society today which are evidently class-related, even if they are not always class inequalities as such. The problem then becomes one of relating together people's various identities and situations rather than posing 'class' identities monolithically *against* other 'cultural' identities, as both 'vulgar Marxists' and 'post-Marxists' tend to do. One suggestion here, which I think could be Marx's own, is that whilst, of course, people must be recognized as having and pursuing various cultural identities, their lives and aspirations remain profoundly shaped and constrained by the fact that they have to earn their living *as workers, under capitalism*. This simple fact generates considerable commonality of situation and interest amongst otherwise different groups, a commonality that is consistently played down – mostly unconsciously, sometimes deliberately – by the workings and ideologies of capitalist institutions. Completing his train of thought, Marx offered a proposition that continues to be intellectually intriguing as well as normatively inspiring: that only in a classless society can the positive differences amongst otherwise equal and free persons be fully recognized and celebrated.

'SCIENCE' AND METHOD IN MARX

As well as developing scenarios of social order and historical change, social theorists invoke or presume conceptions about what sorts of things *exist* (ontology), and about the legitimacy of the *type of knowledge* they are producing (epistemology). Projects which are avowedly *critical* of reigning intellectual and political orthodoxies, as Marx's was, tend to be particularly self-conscious of these epistemological and ontological dimensions, seeking radically to revise our very understandings of social knowledge and being as part of changing our views about the way society is structured. But there is a difficulty in coming to terms with Marx's philosophical position, because he was an anti-philosophical philosopher: he distrusted the systematic presentation of abstract general concepts, when separated out from substantive and political argumentation. Not only was stand-alone philosophy *idealist* in that sense, it quintessentially embodied the condition of *alienation*, in that creative ideas take on an apparently transcendent life of their own, an eternal thing-like status, separated off from the concrete human needs and activities in which they are rooted. Consistent with this attitude, Marx's more particular philosophical preferences tend to be found embedded within his substantive investigations and critiques, or expressed in pithy occasional 'theses'.

It makes sense to approach Marx's metatheories 'negatively', in terms of their nonconformity with alternative philosophical traditions. One of the most obvious contrasts in this respect is with the *empiricist* strand in the social sciences. Crudely, empiricism refers to the idea that all knowledge stems from sensory *perceptions* of reality, and that when our observations are marshalled in a disciplined and cumulative way, then 'the facts' of the world present themselves to us as both palpable and indubitable. Theories in science certainly provide interpretative hypotheses that help make sense of the facts, but it is the facts that are 'sovereign', since theories are to be judged successful or not by reference to the data of observation. Now Marx's works exhibit a healthy respect for 'the facts', and he enthusiastically absorbed a wide range of dry empirical 'data' in the course of his studies. More programmatically, *The German Ideology* tells us that it is only 'empirical observation' that can bring out 'the connection of the social and political structure with production'. Yet this is misleading, since Marx's strategy in that text and elsewhere was clearly to chart a path *between* the fallacies of idealism on the one hand – 'the imagined activity of imagined subjects' – and those of empiricism on the other – the 'collection of dead facts'. Indeed, Marx deeply objected to the passive and individualized conception of human intellectual activity that is presumed in the empiricist notion that external sensory information directly impresses itself upon the *tabula rasa* of the mind. If the form of appearance of things, he announced in *Capital*, Volume III, coincided with their essence, there would be no need for science.

Positivism is sometimes regarded as an extreme version of empiricism, and so it is perhaps even less likely that Marx could be associated with that philosophical outlook. However, this is not right. It is true that positivism is more rigorous than empiricism in general, but whereas empiricism is often portrayed as healthy commonsense philosophy, positivism involves a principled commitment to 'science'. This commitment expresses itself in the greater role that

theory plays in positivist conceptions of knowledge-formation. Also, positivism develops as something of a cultural campaign: to articulate and praise the image of 'objective' science in modern Western society, so that the dangers of irrationality, superstition and ignorance can be progressively eliminated. These two central tenets of positivism are closely linked, because all science, including social science, is thought to reveal a *unified method*, one which pursues general causal laws as expressed through observed empirical regularities.

Aspects of Marx's thinking are congruent with positivism. In *The German Ideology* Marx and Engels express the Comtean sentiment that 'where speculation ends begins real, positive science'. Philosophy then 'loses its medium of existence' and becomes, at most, the 'summing up of the most general results' of substantive knowledge. In addition to this marked hostility to metaphysical understanding, Marx also presents a view of humanity which pictures it as continuous with the natural world. Hence his emphasis on the process of production as the way in which societies survive and thrive in their struggle with nature. This naturalism is reinforced by Marx's striking suggestion that only with the onset of advanced classless society will we be able to talk of humanity's emergence from its 'prehistory'. And a central feature of that transition is the harnessing of science and technology in the reduction of human toil. In terms of methodological protocol, Marx delivers several ringing pronouncements about the way in which the historical laws and inner dynamics of capitalist society work themselves out 'with iron necessity', and clearly he saw the achievement of his own work as having uncovered a large part of these deep workings. It is thus hard to get around Marx's tough 'objectivism' in relation to how the social world operates, and his resounding critiques of bourgeois pseudo-social science as *ideology* make little sense without this claim to science on his part.

However, it is doubtful whether these positivistic *sentiments* can be taken as a subscription to any sort of systematic positivistic philosophy, though some later 'orthodox' Marxists – beginning with Engels – moved further in that direction. For Marx, whilst human beings were, as material creatures, subject to various natural laws, it was also part of their very nature to be *more* than merely natural-material beings. Human existence involves the kind of consciousness and social labour which enable people, collectively, to manipulate and even counteract the regimes of purely natural necessity. For that reason, without denying the applicability of natural scientific methods and results across many domains, Marx is primarily interested in accounting for, and surpassing, *historical and social* 'necessities', and these operate in ways which do not match any strict positivist understanding. For one thing, historical laws in Marx are not 'universal' laws: they pertain to particular domains or aspects of social life that are limited and transitory. Secondly, they operate as 'tendencies' – Marx makes no assumption that social laws express themselves as causal regularities. His sort of laws, then, can be neither analysed nor 'confirmed' through the observational or experimental categories of the natural sciences. Rather, social theory has to rely upon 'the force of abstraction' alone, as the Preface to *Capital*, Volume I puts it. Thirdly, social laws operating as tendencies encounter, and sometimes intrinsically generate, *counter-tendencies*, with no a priori assumption that the designated principal tendencies are bound to prevail. The tendency of productive forces to develop and the tendency of the rate of profit to fall are examples of this relative open-endedness.

Today, the philosophical label which typically combines a general naturalism across the sciences with acknowledgement of the particularity of the objects and methods of social sciences is known as 'critical realism', and not surprisingly Marx has been claimed as belonging to that camp. Marx's assertion in *Capital*, Volume III that 'all science would be superfluous if the outward appearance and essence of things directly coincided' has often been taken as a prime expression of his commitment to realism. Realists see both the natural and social worlds as comprising a multiplicity of domains governed by essential tendencies and mechanisms operating through strings of complex interactive processes. Unlike positivists, realists have no expectation that – in the kind of 'open systems' characteristic of the complex sciences – these inner workings can be easily or regularly observed, nor do they regard causation, as positivists do, as clear-cut dependencies between separable entities and events. Rather, there exists a wide range of relationships, concatenations and syndromes amongst particular things and processes. Realism, in this sense, can be construed as an update of 'dialectical materialism', an older term used to describe Marx's ontology and epistemology. From his early writings in the 1840s, Marx rejected idealist notions that 'reality' is constituted by human consciousness: the world was independent of mind, he believed, and had an intractable material character. However, Marx also regularly inveighed against vulgar materialists, who conceived reality as thing-like, static and overwhelming. Instead, Marx clearly had a view of reality – whether social or natural – as essentially *processual*, requiring ongoing human deciphering through active engagement with it.

Realism has persistently come under fire from a 'pragmatist' direction. Realism talks floridly about the essential processes and mechanisms in the world, but its anti-positivism renders these unobservable and unrealized, and its sense of complex causation rules out any definitive depiction of them. But if this is so, how do we ever *know* what is *really* 'essential', and how do we even know *that* the world is indeed 'deeply' structured by these nominal generative mechanisms? The history of science and humanity, after all, tells us precisely that what one epoch might regard as indubitably real and essential, the next one overturns in its thinking and practice. The very presumption that is built into realism – that we can know and show at a given point how 'reality in itself' is 'essentially' constituted – therefore comes into serious question. And intriguingly, Marx himself provides some supportive ammunition for scepticism here. Famously, in his *Theses on Feuerbach*, Marx rejected 'contemplative' theoretical solutions of problems featuring the abstract 'reality' status of thought and its objects. 'The dispute over the reality or non-reality of thinking which is isolated from practice is a purely scholastic question.' Rather, the issue of the truth, which is one of 'reality and power', is 'a *practical* question'.

Marx's pragmatism, like the philosophical pragmatism that has sprung into life again in recent years, can be taken in different directions. One of these remains firmly realist, because whilst Marx is saying that truth and reality are operational only in terms of our practical agenda, the latter, when successfully fulfilled, can reasonably be taken as yielding reliable indications of the nature of all kinds of independent structures. Alternatively, Marx has been understood as saying that we must *forget* questions of ultimate truth and reality, since their natures always present themselves in a humanly mediated form. All we have, and all we need, are 'local' and practical forms of knowledge. This is a *non-realist* view, but it is not necessarily *anti-realist*. But there is also an anti-realist line of pragmatist argument, and at a pinch Marx can sometimes be aligned with this. The point is that our understandings of nature, the past, society, etc. are not only *framed within*, but are actively *constituted by*, discourses that are constructed so as to satisfactorily resolve certain theoretical and practical problems that we face.

Influential 'Western Marxists' such as Gramsci and Lukács held views akin to this radical discursive pragmatism, and the question is: Can Marx himself, with all his scathing dismissals of 'absolute idealism', be signed up for this kind of constructionist outlook? To some extent he can. In the 1857 Introduction to the *Grundrisse*, Marx tells us that he is looking back on the past sequence of modes of production from the point of view of the categories we need to understand present capitalist society. Analogously, we are interested in the anatomy of the ape from the point of view of the clues we might retrospectively pick up concerning the functioning of Man. Marx thus suggests that we look back at the charms of Greek art, for instance, in the way that grown-ups reflect upon their childhood expressions. These can never be authentically retrieved as such, and we know this, being interested in this reflective process only if it can teach us some 'lessons' about the way we are now.

In further support of the 'non-realist' Marx, we can recall Marx's presentation of his theoretical work as the critique of prevalent *categories*, especially those of the political economists. Marx, perhaps, was not so much providing an account of social reality, so that it could be compared favourably with mistaken bourgeois categories. Rather, he was engaging in a kind of immanent and therapeutic deconstruction of bourgeois categories, which, actually, he believed were never 'illusory' as such, but part of a certain type of practical engagement within capitalist social relations themselves. This construal of Marx's method has been labelled in different ways, as a kind of 'immanent' critique, as a kind of revolutionary 'idealism', and as the 'philosophy of praxis'. As with rival readings of Marx's metatheoretical outlook, these versions can neither be demonstrated conclusively nor ruled out of court.

CONCLUSION: MARX, 'MARX' AND THE MULTIPLE MARXES

Marx is back, and for good reason. But Marx is not 'back' in any straightforward way. For one thing, it is *Marx* rather than *Marxism* whose strengths are being appreciated anew: his diagnosis of ceaseless capitalist dynamism and instability; his prescient sketches of globalization and colonialism; his marvellous rhetorical variety and skill, his synthetic, interdisciplinary range; his formidable sense of rigour and his diamond-like political insistency. Here it is the individual Marx that is being (re)canonized – quite properly in a sense, but with the effect that the systematic and generalized aspects of a world-view are being reduced to the admired personality traits of their author, or to a few classic 'texts' for revered consumption only. Secondly, there is no longer one single, definitive canon, but a proliferation of them – there is even a venerable post-structuralist canon of canon-deconstructors. In our case, it is interesting to reflect how a gradual separating-out of sociology

from sociological theory or general social theory produces rather different canonical lists, with Marx himself probably figuring as a stronger fixture within the latter than the former. Inevitably, these discursive formations change their character and emphasis as time passes, and their canonical figures will vary accordingly.

Thirdly, although we might think that it is high time that Marx's intellectual personality was allowed to speak for itself now that Official Marxism is gone, ultimately this is a naive view. From the earliest days of the tradition, Marx has been known and debated as 'Marx', whether as constructed by Engels, Bolshevism and Stalinism, or as heroically depicted through embittered and dogged opposition to that dominant historical filtering. Accordingly, no anti-orthodox or revisionist reconstruction of Marx today – for example, that he was really a radical democrat or libertarian rather than a state centralist, or that he intimated a 'capitalist road to communism' rather than a transitional revolutionary regime, or that he was a methodological constructionist rather than a realist – none of these interpretations can fail to be a retrospective appraisal of the legend, governed by the discursive and political fortunes of Marxism over time and in the present.

The conclusion suggests itself that we are dealing with an ineradicably textualized 'Marx', whose identity and significance are heavily governed by our own intellectual problems and political priorities, which are different from those of Marx. This line leads us not only from Marx to 'Marx' but on further to the idea of Multiple Marxes, for there is arguably no way of deciding, or necessarily *wanting* to decide, how all these inputs can be calibrated. The strength of this approach to Marx as unstable and 'produced' is that it confronts the question of *pluralism*. In our globalized and multicultural times, the suggestion that there is no singular, essential condition of existence, identity or method in terms of which we can forge a univocal social metaphysics or politics, has really taken root, and for good sociological reasons. Academically, this means that, across the board, we need to be ultra-sensitive to the dangers of false closure, dogmatic 'essentialism' and ethnocentric bias. Marx, by contrast, given the more 'monistic' *Zeitgeist* of his time, might have seen things very differently. So quite plausibly, these gaps in mood and appraisal can only be closed up on the basis of personal, contingent readings, none of which can claim any greater general adequacy than any other.

Yet, whilst salutary in many ways, such an argument borders on gratuitous defeatism. It underestimates, for one thing, Marx's own significant grappling with problems of pluralism;

problems of reconciling difference and unity in both theory and practice. Relatedly, the post-modern line exaggerates how comfortable current consciousness – intellectual or lay – is with any consistent or 'rampant' pluralism: most people, on most issues, still want to draw some kind of line when it comes to the *acceptable range* of programmes or interpretations. Even to argue that Marx is Multiple involves a singular effort to de-legitimate readings which argue for a different, more unified Marx. Finally, it is important to remember that a properly historical perspective – and we have learned this as much from Marx as anyone – can have the effect of tempering as well as stimulating our sense of what is genuinely novel and plural about our current situation. That we happen sometimes to *feel* that our kind of pluralism and situation is entirely new does not necessarily mean that the world today, duly considered, is any more intrinsically complex or undecipherable than in other epochs, that there are no substantial overlaps with previous epochs, or that previous theoretical categories have suddenly become entirely inapplicable.

In Marx's day as in ours, then, the challenge is how best to achieve integrative theoretical solutions out of manifest empirical diversity. Indeed, this would appear to be the very *raison d'être* of sociological theory itself. Emblematically, this is what fuels the ever-interesting question of the relationship between Marx's project and that of Weber. Marx, conscious of pluralist pressures rather than ignorant or dismissive of them, remains the theorist most undauntedly – and in many ways still most persuasively – in pursuit of a singular (if complex) account of *the logic of the social* in modern times. Without something like the latter as its goal, sociological theory would seem to have no rationale, other than as a form of contemporary moralism or anchorless description. Weber, on the other hand, well aware of the seduction and even necessity of powerful conceptions of societal logic, insistently reminds us that there are in principle always a number of such 'logics', and that they all face a number of contrary empirical and evaluative considerations. We have not moved altogether beyond that matrix of debate, whether in general sociological theory or in the understanding of particular perspectives, such as Marx's own.

SELECTED FURTHER READING

Ball, T. and Farr, J. (1984) *After Marx*. Cambridge: Cambridge University Press.

Barrett, M. (1991) *The Politics of Truth: From Marx to Foucault*. Cambridge: Polity Press.

Berlin, I. (1978) *Karl Marx: His Life and Environment*, 4th edn. Oxford: Oxford University Press.

Callinicos, A. (1996) *The Revolutionary Ideas of Karl Marx*, 2nd edn. London: Bookmarks.

Carter, A. (1988) *Marx: A Radical Critique*. Brighton: Harvester Wheatsheaf.

Carver, T. (ed.) (1993) *The Cambridge Companion to Marx*. Cambridge: Cambridge University Press.

Carver, T. (1998) *The Postmodern Marx*. Manchester: Manchester University Press.

Cohen, G.A. (1979) *Karl Marx's Theory of History: A Defence*. Oxford: Oxford University Press.

Conway, D. (1987) *A Farewell to Marx*. Harmondsworth: Pelican.

Craib, I. (1997) *Classical Sociological Theory*. Oxford: Oxford University Press.

Dahrendorf, R. (1959) *Class and Conflict in Industrial Societies*. London: Routledge and Kegan Paul.

Elster, J. (1985) *Making Sense of Marx*. Cambridge: Cambridge University Press.

Fine, B. and Harris, L. (1979) *Rereading Capital*. Basingstoke: Macmillan.

Gamble, A., Marsh, D. and Tant, T. (1999) *Marxism and Social Science*. Basingstoke: Macmillan.

Geras, N. (1984) *Marx and Human Nature: Refutation of a Legend*. London: Verso.

Gilbert, A. (1981) *Marx's Politics*. Oxford: Martin Robertson.

Graham, K. (1992) *Karl Marx: Our Contemporary*. Hemel Hempstead: Harvester/Wheatsheaf.

Grossberg, L. and Nelson, C. (eds) (1989) *Marxism and the Interpretation of Culture*. London: Macmillan.

Marx, K. and Engels, F. (1975 on) *Collected Works*. New York and London: Lawrence & Wishart.

McLennan, G. (1989) *Marxism, Pluralism and Beyond*. Cambridge: Polity Press.

Meikle, S. (1985) *Essentialism in the Thought of Karl Marx*. London: Duckworth.

Miller, R. (1984) *Analysing Marx*. Princeton, NJ: Princeton University Press.

Norman, R. and Sayers, S. (1980) *Marx, Hegel and Dialectic*. Brighton: Harvester Press.

Ollman, B. (1976) *Alienation: Marx's Conception of Man in Capitalist Society*. Cambridge: Cambridge University Press.

Parkin, F. (1981) *Marxism and Class Theory: A Bourgeois Critique*. London: Tavistock.

Pierson, C. (ed.) (1997) *The Marx Reader*. Cambridge: Polity Press.

Rigby, S.H. (1987) *Marx and History: A Critical Introduction*. Manchester: Manchester University Press.

Sayer, D. (1979) *Marx's Method*. Brighton: Harvester Press.

Wood, A. (1981) *Karl Marx*. London: Routledge and Kegan Paul.

Wright, E.O. et al. (1989) *The Debate on Classes*. London: Verso.

Wright, E.O., Levine, A. and Sober, E. (1992) *Reconstructing Marxism*. London: Verso.

5

Max Weber: Work and Interpretation

SAM WHIMSTER

It is now increasingly recognized just how extensive, complex and multidisciplinary Weber's
writings are. This has come about through the
work of Weber scholarship and interpretation
over the past fifteen years, in particular due to
the ongoing publication of all his writings by the
Max Weber Gesamtausgabe. One result is that
the understanding and use of Weber is becoming
less legislative and more interpretive. The
days are gone when a lone authority such as
Aron (1950), Bendix (1960), Parsons (1937), or
Winckelmann (1957) would inform generations
of students what were the core ideas and
approach of Max Weber. Instead, we are faced
with a more polysemic legacy where complexities
are not simplified and antinomies of his thought
are respected. This is part of the coming of age of
social theory itself, in which it has learned not to
foreclose the hermeneutic door on its own long
history. I therefore divide this present work into
the exposition and the reception of Weber's
thought.

WEBER'S WORK

I will set out in brief Weber's works in order of
their appearance. (For a full bibliography, see
Käsler, 1988: 242–75.) Weber's postgraduate
dissertations and first publications showed his
precocious ability to work with the methods of
one discipline and produce results relevant to
another. Weber studied law, which was heavily
biased to the historical development of its
respective Roman, German and communal
origins. His first publication (1889) on medieval
trading companies analysed the social and legal
forms through which the modern business

concepts of risk and return on capital and
investment were to develop. Medieval shipping
ventures could be immensely profitable but due
to piracy and shipwreck were highly risky. Risk
could be spread through partnerships and the
limiting of liability to types of investors. Weber's
research identified the legal and social factors
that enabled these early 'companies' to trade.

His next publication (1891) was on Roman
agrarian history. Again Weber used legal and
historical sources to advance what was in effect
an understanding of agrarian developments
through the interests and needs of different
social groups and classes. Weber adopted the
position, from the German agrarian historian Dr
Meitzen, that public land was distributed and
held communally. The plebian class excluded
from the first distribution turned Roman policy
to territorial conquest in order to satisfy their
hunger for land. With this emerged the concept
of private property and the legal titles to enable
the exchange of property. It was a development
that favoured the large property holder over the
smaller and led to the establishment of Rome's
first real estate exchange. The further history of
private property in the Roman Empire saw the
establishment of large estates with slaves, their
ignoring of the fiscal demands of the towns, and
the gradual move toward a manorial economy.
Although in no way a systematic presentation,
Weber's exposition pointed to world historical
moments: the transition from communal to
private property, and the turn to manorialism
and the anticipation of feudalism. He gave a
narrative form to this analysis in a later lecture
on the decline of antiquity (1896a/1976).

Over the 1890s Weber developed a public
reputation as an agricultural expert and policy

adviser in the field of contemporary society. Germany was experiencing deep structural changes as the agricultural sector lost its predominance to industry and the younger generation left farming occupations for jobs in the cities. Germany's main academic policy association, the *Verein für Sozialpolitik*, commissioned a nation-wide survey on conditions in the farming sector. Weber was chosen to analyse and write up the results of the data, mainly from questionnaires to landowners, for the region East of the Elbe. His study (1892) went deeper than relaying information on crops, wage levels, output, productivity and labour shortages. He analysed the types of labour contracts. The East lacked a population of independent small farmers; instead very large estates employed farm labourers on servant contracts. The contract between *Instmann* and landowner had been the main pattern in the nineteenth century. The *Instmann* had his own small-holding on the lord's estate and was obligated to work in summer on cereal production and in winter on threshing. He was paid in kind and the amount was directly linked to the profitability of the harvest. By the 1890s the *Instmann* had all but disappeared, replaced instead by the immigrant contract labourer who was paid in wages, accommodated in dormitories and who returned across the border to Poland and Galicia at the end of the season.

Weber was surprisingly sympathetic to the *Instmann*–landowner relationship. It had the disadvantage that it was patriarchal, with the landowner having legal powers of master over servant. But, said Weber, it offered an identity of interests, community and patriarchal responsibility. The seasonal contract by contrast reduced the personalized labour relationship to a short-term wage contract, where landowners felt no obligation for the living conditions of labourers. Weber extended his empirical knowledge of the subject with a survey of country parsons, who were seen as a more valid source of information than the landowner.

Armed with the knowledge of the rural economy and society, Weber advanced himself into major political and policy debates. This culminated in his deliberatively provocative inaugural lecture at Freiburg University (1896b/ 1989). He accused the Prussian landowners of abusing their leading position in government to subsidize through tariffs and loans their economically failing estates. He accused them of acting against the national interest by using Poles and Ruthenes instead of German farmworkers, so undermining the basis of army recruitment and de-Germanizing the Eastern frontier. In a reference to Darwinist principles of selection, he pointed out that foreign workers were more adaptable to lower wages, so undermining the higher cultural level of Germans. Weber saw it as his place to champion the cultural values of the German nation. Turning to his new discipline of economics (*Nationalökonomie*), he said that its value standards could not be derived from science and that the highest value standards were those of the national state. Weber later offered a retraction of some of these statements and the period reflects not only his work in social research but also an ambition to be directly involved in politics (see Wolfgang J. Mommsen, 1993: 59–60, 540).

As an economist, he was one of the few German economists to include Austrian marginalism (the basis of neoclassical economics) into his lecture courses; likewise he supported the stock exchanges' right to trade in agricultural futures – a measure that was rejected by the agrarian politicians. He tempered his views on free trade, however, with the acceptance of low tariffs. He believed that Germany should have a greater imperial place in the world and for this it had to be a power state with a strong army and navy. This should be accompanied internally by liberal reforms in key areas as trade unions, political parties, welfare and women's rights. But he did not think welfare should be a matter of ethics or charity but instead part of the modernization of society in which social classes had the freedom legally and politically to pursue their own interests. This phase of Weber's life ended in 1899 with an illness and long convalescence that ended his involvement in policy questions as well as his role as a full-time university professor. (For a detailed account of Weber's life, see Marianne Weber, 1988.)

The next phase was signalled by Weber's involvement in the *Archiv für Sozialwissenschaft und Sozialpolitik*, which he co-edited with the economic historian Werner Sombart and the banking expert Edgar Jaffé. In his previous period Weber had tended to use social research as a vehicle for his own political views, whereas now he recognized a greater differentiation between science and politics. In his convalescence Weber had achieved a deeper understanding of these issues through his association with the Baden philosophers Windelband, Rickert and Lask, who were known as neo-Kantians (Oakes, 1987: 434–46).

In its day neo-Kantianism struggled to assert itself against the predominance of the physical and life sciences which had extended their ascendancy into the historical and cultural sciences. Material determinism and the laws of science were seen as the goals of science. Through successes such as Helmholtz's discovery of entropy, Mach in physics, Haeckel in the life sciences, materialism and monism was taken up by Wundt in psychology, and by Lamprecht and Breysig in history and culture. Monism denied the split between a material and an ideal world; rather the latter could be scientifically explained through the laws of matter. The purpose of science was to discover the laws of matter. This methodology became highly influential in economics, sociology, psychology, anthropology, history and art studies and assumed explanation resided in the discovery of laws. Equally, however, the pretensions of a naturalistic understanding of the world were greatly resented and resisted by a defensive population of philosophers, historians, sociologists and others in the humanities who argued in favour of the cardinality of the mind, subjective experience, creativity and free will. Academic knowledge, therefore, was divided between the partisanship of a strong form of positivism and the primacy of idealism.

In a series of essays that culminated in '"Objectivity" in Social Science and Social Policy' (1904) and 'Critical Studies in the Logic of the Cultural Sciences' (1905) (in Weber, 1949), Weber vigorously combated the claims of monism, arguing instead that a gulf separated the mind's representation of the world and brute reality itself. It had to be accepted that mind and physical reality were two separate realities and what needed to be done was to develop methodologies that would produce reliable knowledge. Weber's solution drew on modern epistemology 'which ultimately derives from Kant' (1949: 106). Scientists cannot capture the full complexity of the world but they can select aspects of reality using criteria of cultural significance, so providing a point of purchase for scientific investigation. Weber combated positivism and the claim that explanation lay in the discovery of laws by arguing that the infinite complexity of concrete reality could never be fully explained through laws, as though social reality could be deduced from scientific axioms of human behaviour.

Weber characterized the social and historical sciences as cultural sciences and he presented his own methodological instrument, the ideal type, as a way of making sense of the infinite diversity of empirical reality. In selecting an aspect of reality for study according to the investigator's cultural interest, it was open to the scientist to shape and model cultural phenomena into an artificial form that would present an account of the world in a logically pure way. Competitive market behaviour as an economic theory was in Weber's terms an ideal type. Actual behaviour only approximated to the theory's rational axioms of behaviour. Weber combined this conceptual constructivism with an insistence on a cause and effect understanding of individual acts. Events had causes that had to be ascertained 'through the study of precise empirical data' (1949: 69).

In 'Critical Studies in the Logic of the Cultural Sciences' (Weber, 1949), Weber turned his fire away from the positivists to the idealists. His main target, which he treated very respectfully, was historians who believed in the primacy of the fact (over theory) and the freedom of the will (over determination). Weber argued these historians suppressed and failed to recognize their own theoretical presuppositions when they established the particular causes and antecedents of events. It was the role of theory, and sociology in particular, to make these presuppositions apparent and logical. This activity in no way detracted from the value of the historians' own work. On free will Weber argued that historians subscribed to a form of romanticism and irrationalism. His own position, which is traceable back to Spinoza, held that to act rationally was to act in accordance with knowledge of the forces influencing one's behaviour. An absolute freedom denies any determination upon the individual, which is absurd. To act in wilful ignorance of determination is irrational.

So-called value-neutrality or value-freedom (*Wertfreiheit*) is a plurality of positions. Cultural scientists require their own values in order to create a value relation to the world. But the truth of individual events has a universal validity independent of particular value viewpoints. Science, while it can establish individual truth, cannot justify a person's view of the world. One can show, for example, the causes of poverty but it does not scientifically follow that welfare measures are justified. Welfare measures are justified in terms of the citizen's own values: whether they are considered good depends on the morality and value standards of citizens themselves. Scientific social policy studies cannot prescribe policy solutions. In short, an analysis of 'what is' cannot by itself be converted into a normative statement of what 'should be'. Weber summarized the purpose of his own journal (of social science and social policy) as 'the education of judgement about practical social problems' (1949: 50).

The Protestant Ethic and the Spirit of Capitalism (hereafter *PE*) appeared at the same time as the 'Objectivity' essay. Started during his illness and departure from academic life, the study is the basis of Weber's enormous reputation. At the start of his illness he reflected to his wife on how he had been a driven man in his energetic commitment to so many academic and political issues in the 1890s. The *PE* is a study of what drove the early Puritan to create the economic, social and psychological conditions on which modern capitalism was built. It also revealed the major advances Weber made in combining history with social theory, for he successfully demonstrated that large cultural themes could be addressed without abandoning the causal adequacy of the thesis put forward. Weber defined his field by asking a new question – what is the influence of religion on everyday economic life? This was his value relation to history and to judge by the work's success it was a cultural question that found a large audience. Weber acknowledged that his viewpoint was by no means the only one and that materialist conceptions of history (for example, Marx's theory of class conflict) were equally pertinent (Sayer, 1991: 92–133). In pursuing his study Weber had to draw a picture of the way in which religious ideas dominated the everyday life of Puritans and here he presented ideal typical accounts of Calvinist religious ideas in the behaviour of different groups of Puritans. The causal adequacy of the thesis has attracted much subsequent attention. How would it be possible to isolate this set of ideal factors as responsible for the accelerating impact of capitalism in early modernity from other contingent and objective factors? The *PE* failed to treat this issue at length, and in his later work Weber came to realize just what an immense task it would be to isolate early modern capitalism as a phenomenon and establish its major causal antecedents. The *PE* concludes with the deepest cultural forebodings about how Protestant conscience still haunts modern man (1930: 178–83).

Weber's next major piece of writing reported and analysed the revolution of 1904 in Russia and the political events of 1905 when the czarist autocracy eventually conceded limited constitutional reforms (Weber, 1995). Weber provided a comprehensive account of Russia's social and economic development, its social classes, the various political movements and their aim, an analysis of autocracy and the backward role of the Church, and what he called Russia's lack of history. Weber describes the new world historical forces as capitalism, science and human rights, and he held that it was inevitable that Russian autocracy would be weakened by each confrontation with these forces. Weber, however, noted the absence of Western values of law, constitutionalism and human rights and in this light he remained pessimistic about the chances of a bourgeois democracy establishing itself in the face of a bureaucratic autocracy in conflict with the more radical political forces such as the socialists.

In 1907 Weber returned to social research with a large-scale study of the social psychology of industrial workers. The research was conducted with members of the *Verein für Sozialpolitik* and Weber wrote up the research in 1908–9 in the *Archiv für Sozialwissenschaft und Sozialpolitik*.

Like much of industrial sociology, its relevance was contemporary. Weber was closely involved in the research design and its methodology. One part of the study examined the influence of large factory production on the character of the workers, their occupational chances and life style. Another part researched the output of the worker as a dependent variable and its interaction with the various factors of factory conditions and the social, cultural and ethical background of workers. The study clarified Weber's thinking on the place of objective social research, in particular in relation to psychology, which was concerned with human perceptions and motivation as well as physiological effects upon behaviour. He distanced his interpretive method from both the empathetic method of understanding motives, which was derived from Dilthey, and the natural scientific orientation of physiological psychology. The study also forced Weber to think about whether patterns of work followed a worker's rational calculation or belonged to unthinking habituation. (See Wolfgang Schluchter's editorial introduction to Weber, 1995: 1–58.)

In 1909 Weber published a book-length encyclopedia article entitled 'The Agrarian Sociology of Ancient Civilizations' (1896a/ 1976: 37–366). At one sight a descriptive round tour of the societies of the Mediterranean basin, it in fact offers an analysis of capitalism in the perspective of comparative civilizations. Weber established that extensive markets for wealth, land and commodities existed in the ancient world and he also revised his previous emphasis on slave production, so stressing the importance of free labour. His agrarian sociology allowed him to pose the question why modern capitalism appeared in Western Europe at the end of the Middle Ages, while ancient capitalism, though richer in resources, failed to move to a self-expanding capitalist dynamic. His answer turned on the respective roles of the townspeople. In antiquity they were subservient to the bureaucratic force of the state, whereas the medieval towns created the conditions of economic and legal freedom. Unlike his later comparative work, Weber restricts his use of ideal types, which he used as a device for denying evolutionary patterns, and instead permits a comparative and developmental logic to appear.

His 'Agrarian Sociology' provided the platform for the last decade of his life, when he attained an astonishing intellectual power in his comparison of civilizations. Chronological exposition of his writings, however, starts to break down at this point. He pursued two major projects. One was the comparative study of the economic ethics of world religions whose publication can be traced and dated in the *Archiv für*

Sozialwissenschaft und Sozialpolitik. The other project was his editorship of the hugely ambitious *Grundriß der Sozialökonomik* that was only partially realized as a multi-volume conspectus of German language social science knowledge. Partly because of the First World War many contributors failed to deliver and Weber himself took over the writing of parts of the series. Unfortunately, he died in 1920 when he had proofread only three chapters. These form the start of the work that in English is known as *Economy and Society* (1968). Otherwise all that is reliably known, so far, is that he started work on the *Grundriß der Sozialökonomik* in January of 1909 (Weber, 1994: 2). The so-called 'Economy and Society' contains a range of special sociologies (the state, rulership, music, law, the city, religion, the economy), but these have not yet been dated, and many were left in draft form. This circumstance has left considerable uncertainty about how the various parts of his writings were intended to relate to each other.

The editors of the *Max Weber Gesamtausgabe* have decided not to follow the decision of previous editors (Marianne Weber followed by Johannes Winckelmann) to publish together both the manuscripts Weber had prepared for publication in 1919 and 1920 (the so-called Part 1) and the earlier manuscripts written before 1914 (the so-called Part 2). As Marianne Weber wrote in the foreword to her editing of *Wirtschaft und Gesellschaft*, 'No plan existed for the construction of the whole.' Instead the *Gesamtausgabe* intend to published the 'Part 1' under the title 'Wirtschaft und Gesellschaft. Soziologie. Unvollendet 1919–1920'. And it will publish what they deem to be the rest of 'Economy and Society' as five separate titles: 'Gemeinschaften', 'Religiöse Gemeinschaften', 'Recht', 'Herrschaft' and 'Die Stadt'. (On these editorial plans see Weber, 1999: VII–XVII).

The 'Economic Ethics of World Religions' grew out of the work he was contributing for the *Grundriß der Sozialökonomik*. In his Introduction, written in 1913, to the former, Weber indicates how the two projects fitted together. His research problem was to show how religions produced ethics in the sphere of practical everyday activity. Equally, Weber recognized the reverse causal sequence: how religions are influenced by material factors. By this he did not mean that religion is the ideology of social class, as argued by Marxists. Instead, he used Nietzsche's observation that Christianity is the 'slave revolt in morals' to argue that Christianity, which developed religious prophecy from a background of magical practices, flourished within the plebeian sectors of urban populations. Religious doctrines are adjusted to religious needs. Weber developed the idea of a social

theodicy. Religions explain the irrational outcomes of good and bad fortune in life. The urban masses who through no choice of their own suffer from sickness, poverty, or distress can be offered the religious illusion of salvation. In rural-based magic, misfortune is a sign of cultic impurity. By these means the inequalities and injustices of the world are explained and justified (Weber, 1948: 267–301).

Hence religion has a social function, but it is not automatically functional. Priests and magicians belong to certain sectors within a society's social stratification. A Confucian ethic is practised by an elite educated class in China. In India a high caste of Brahmins act as cultic and spiritual advisers to the communities. The development of the Western Church, as opposed to the early communal stage of primitive Christianity, was determined by the role of priests within the higher ranks of society. Religion, therefore, interlinks with political sociology where secular and religious power is competed for. Bourdieu has analysed this process as a struggle over legitimation (1987). 'Economy and Society' seeks to provide an analysis of these complex interactions. Economic behaviour is influenced by religious ethics; likewise religions are influenced by the factors of social stratification and of political rulership. The chain of interactions has the potential to extend endlessly. 'Economy and Society' distances itself to an extent from the sheer historical complexity through the imposition of ideal types placed together as schemas. This produces in the field of rulership the typology of traditional, charismatic and legal rational authority. In the field of economics he outlines the main categories of economic action. In the field of stratification Weber provides a typology of social class and estates. In the field of religion Weber provides a typology of magic and religion, and of different types of salvation and ascetic practices. In the field of law he outlines a typology of rational and irrational types of law and their formal and substantive rationalization. In the field of music Weber offers a typology of rational and non-rational harmony.

The typologies are cross-cultural and operate across civilizations. As ideal types they are used to orientate the researcher's interest in the face of the infinite complexity of empirical reality. Weber's advice on causal understanding still stands, as already mentioned. If a researcher wishes to establish the exact sequence of interactions in a particular society, then she or he has to move from ideal typical orientation to concrete empirical research of the selected question that has cultural relevance.

Through the monumental labour of his typologies in conjunction with his accounts of the economic ethics of the world religions (Confucianism, Hinduism, Buddhism, Christianity, Islam and Judaism), Weber returned to his starting point of the Protestant Ethic. In a prefatory essay to his *Gesammelte Aufsätze zur Religionssoziologie* (1920) he posed a dual question: one of origins and one of cultural significance. What was the combination of circumstances, which had occurred in Western civilization alone, that had led to cultural phenomena to produce a line of development that had '*universal* significance and value'? (1930, 13).

In 'Basic Sociological Terms', which forms Chapter One of *Economy and Society*, Weber formulated his final version of his theory of social action. He reduced and distilled his ideal types to four types of action: instrumental rationality, value rationality, affectual action and traditional action. 'Basic' here does mean basic. The four types are the fundamental orientating types for investigating all societies and civilizations. Instrumental rationality evaluates rationally the means and ends of actions as well as the values of the different possible ends of actions. It represents the completion of man's ability to reflect upon the ways and purposes of his behaviour. It is present in all societies but emerges to predominance in advanced capitalist societies. Value rationality is characteristic of early modern societies and civilizations that have not made the transition to high modernity. Social action achieves high levels of rationality but is unable to reflect upon the value or worth of the ends of actions themselves. This ultimate stage of reflexivity is denied by adherence to strong belief systems. Affectual action recognizes the place of emotion in human action. Traditional action represents unthinking habitual behaviour.

In 'Basic Sociological Terms' Weber restated the need for the researcher to arrive at a dual explanation. Social action had to be comprehended in terms of the meanings governing people's actions, and it had to be explained in terms of causal antecedents and their effects. The latter task has to be established through exact empirical research (Weber, 1968: 3–26).

RECEPTION AND MAIN DIRECTIONS OF INTERPRETATION

The current bibliography of Max Weber contains over 300 items (books, articles, speeches and newspaper articles). Despite the extent and complexity of his output, Weber never established a corpus of work in his lifetime or a Weberian school of sociology. His work was gathered together for posterity by his widow, Marianne Weber, in the six years after his death. Its publication drew little response in Germany and was virtually ignored until he was rediscovered and taken up in the 1950s and 1960s. In a sense this was a form of ostracism both nationally and internationally. Weber was a leading member of the educated middle-class elite, one of whose major functions was to provide cultural legitimation and leadership to the new German nation-state. Although Weber was personally very critical of the authoritarian nature of Prussian leadership and the role of Kaiser Wilhelm II in government, the whole of the academic caste was severely discredited in the eyes of the German public after the unexplained defeat of November 1918 and the humiliation of the Treaty of Versailles of 1919 (Ay, 1999). After the war intellectuals and academics had to find new ways and Weber's work was largely ignored. Symptomatic of the time was Heidegger and Gadamer's critique of neo-Kantianism, which severely disparaged the whole tradition on which Weber's work rested (Gadamer, 1989: xxix; Safranski, 1998: 98). In the 1930s sociology's tasks and substance were in thrall to National Socialist ideology and Weber's work was considered unacceptable (Mommsen, 1989: 178–9).

The recovery of Weber's legacy has, therefore, been a piecemeal operation and owes much to English-speaking as well as German scholars. Foremost in the rehabilitation of Weber's reputation was Talcott Parsons' translation of *The Protestant Ethic and the Spirit of Capitalism* (1930) and the incorporation of Weber's theory of social action in Parsons' own modern sociological classic, *The Structure of Social Action* (1937). This placed Weber in a prized position at the centre of American social science with an incalculable benefit to his reputation (Mommsen, 1989: 181). This also had a number of interesting side effects. Publication of the *PE* in English triggered the huge 'religion and the rise of capitalism' debate. (See Green, 1959, for an overview.) Weber was treated in a severely Anglo-historical manner, with little understanding of what was meant by ideal types. Either the book contained a thesis to be confirmed or one to be rejected. Weber's later writing on just how difficult a historical problem this was and the development of a comparative method remained to be explored. Equally the theme of the cultural significance of modern capitalism simply did not fit the frame of values of Anglo critics. In the post 1945 world democracy and capitalism were emblematic of progress. Hence, how could knowledge and science disenchant, and how could modernization possess a tragic side? Protestantism as the source of progress was argued in Robert Merton's very influential study of the congruence of Puritan religious orientation and the development of science in the seventeenth century (Merton, 1957).

The other interesting side effect of Parsons' championing of Weber occurred during the expansion of sociology as an academic discipline in the 1960s and 1970s. Parsons' own intellectual success, which placed his version of social and system theory at the heart of American social science, triggered two critical responses. One attack stressed conflict instead of cohesion and Marx was used as a big stick to belabour Parsons and Weber. The other attack, or rather more of a divergence, was to radicalize the theory of social action and to strip it of any presumption of what Parsons referred to as central values. These two tendencies had a self-image of Marxism and phenomenology respectively. Weber in his Parsonian guise became part of a three-cornered debate. Undoubtedly these debates were constitutive of the formation of sociology. But in retrospect we can see that each corner of the debate – Marx and conflict theories, Parsons and consensual values, phenomenological theories – was interpreted through the curious yet distinctive filter of the 1960s and 1970s. (On the Marx–Weber relationship, see Sayer, 1991, and Antonio and Glassman, 1985.)

Looking to the current state of Weberian interpretation the following, somewhat discrepant, directions can be noted. It should be added that these interpretations are, as always, subject to change. It is difficult to second-guess the direction of change but two factors are relevant. First, as indicated in the exposition above, a considerable amount of scholarship on Weber and his context is being undertaken which has the potential to recast received views of Weber. Second, one could judge the current field of social theory as being held between the two opposed poles of hermeneutics and naturalism in an evolutionist guise. This is very much akin to the situation that Weber found himself in: on the one side hermeneutics, values and the idiographic, and on the other, science, the nomological and objectivity. And Weber's response, as will be recalled, was to create a series of methodological solutions.

1   The modernity debate and historical sociology

This is an expansion of the original 'religion and the rise of capitalism' debate in which the terms have been widened to include the constitution of modernity and why in the West there arose the distinctively rational institutions of the firm, markets, finance, the state, the nation, bureaucracy and law. Again it was Talcott Parsons who provided the impetus for the debate by casting his explanation for what he took to be the progressiveness of Western civilization in terms of social system theory. This theory placed a premium not only on unified accounts of societies and the dynamics of their change but also placed priority on cultural values, elaborated by Parsons as pattern variables. System theory was used by historical sociologists (Smelser, 1959) and developmental theorists (Eisenstadt, 1973). This reading of Western civilization provoked a number of attacks that introduced an array of structural historical actors: the peasantry, the people, ruling classes, elites, the intelligentsia, the religious powers. Conflict was emphasized over consensus, and the origins of modern institutions and their values were traced back to historical actors who were characterized more by ruthlessness and goal attainment than liberal tolerance. Barrington Moore's *Social Origins of Democracy and Dictatorship* (1967) was both symptomatic and influential. Although it was un-Weberian in its concern for social justice, it showed the way to a realist approach to historical sociology in which conflict, class struggles, power, legitimacy and legitimations, and rationalization were made prominent. Weber's definition of the state as the legitimate monopoly of the means of violence received great currency, for example from Giddens' *The Nation-state and Violence* (1985). From Ernest Gellner's 'Patterns of History' seminar at the London School of Economics issued John Hall's *Powers and Liberties* (1985) that analysed the historical conditions of liberty and Michael Mann's *The Sources of Social Power* (1993) that described the course of Western modernization as the outcome between populist forces from below in conflict with other social forces within the frame of state and inter-state systems. In 1988 Gellner's own neo-Weberian account of comparative history appeared. *Plough, Sword and Book: The Structure of Human History* offers a trans-historical structuring of societies in terms of the social division of labour vectored on production, coercion and cognition. Gellner concedes that it might well have been the Puritan Reformation that occasioned the epochal move from agrarian to industrial society, but he goes on to note that the number of potential factors involved make the Weberian thesis impossible to verify. Gellner's contribution to the very large question of transition is to consider how the varieties of production, coercion and cognition have a built-in tendency to lock societies into the agrarian phase. Warriors and priests have no interest in handing autonomy and economic freedom to the producers. Hence to achieve the breakthrough to modernity must have involved a strange and fortuitous configuration in the social division of labour.

Randall Collins' *Weberian Sociological Theory* (1986), aside from the notable intellectual feat of predicting the demise of the Soviet system, argued that Weber's last lecture course (posthumously published as the *General Economic History*, 1961) contained a fully developed account of modern capitalism, which was more than the equal of Immanuel Wallerstein's world system theory. In the same vein, John Rex had re-directed sociology toward an acceptance of a theory of social action that took account of conflict, interests, power and resources (1961). Likewise, in Germany Lepsius advocated a sociology that elucidated the interplay of power, ideas and interests (1990). And Stephen Kalberg has shown how Weber's theory of social action can be integrated with historical sociology (1994).

2   Another modernity

This label has to be treated with care for it signals a non-unitary tendency. While in section (1) above modernity is seen to have unequivocally arrived as a determining *force majeure* in all our lives, another modernity signals incompleteness, reluctance and the aporetic quality of modernity. Its central Weberian idea is disenchantment, most clearly seen in Weber's account of science. The rise of the modern world owes much to scientific knowledge and man's ability to know and dominate nature and the social world. But ultimate aspects of reality simply remain beyond science and belong instead to the illusions of culture, art and magic. Knowledge always brings with it a sense of dissatisfaction and disenchantment. In this way Weber drew on Nietzsche's denunciation of knowledge as reducible to science and the call for the Superman to re-seed cardinal values independent of the forces of modernity.

Weber himself explored the aporetic in his comments on art and culture. While the 'iron cage' has become famous as a metaphor for the wholesale rationalization of the world, it is also the case that Weber remained curiously attached to ideas of re-enchanting the world, or as Scaff has put it, 'fleeing the iron cage' (1989). However, while he explores possibilities of escape – most notably in his 'Zwischenbetrachtung' essay – he relentlessly hauls himself and his readers back from the beguilements of religion, art and the erotic (Weber, 1949: 323–59). Modernity may be incomplete, but it is ultimately a form of escapism to believe that the demands of the modern economy and politics can be ignored. This distinguishes Weber from his friend Georg Simmel, who saw culture and art as the only remaining source of ultimate values. Simmel regarded the individual as a cultural being who constantly creates the forms of social life as a type of artistic creation (Scaff, 1989: 186–201).

The Nietzschean cultural dimension has been eloquently represented in Germany, first by Karl Löwith and recently by Wilhelm Hennis. For them the modern individual still remains a 'Kulturmensch', a cultural being who confers values upon the world in his or her choices and decisions. The theory of social action, while reflecting the world of beliefs, norms, interests and powers, never absolves the individual from becoming the passive entity of *homo sociologicus*. Löwith asserts an existentialist faith that the human being generates his or her own values and beliefs (Löwith, 1982). Hennis has a more political grasp of the same question (1988). He re-poses Weber's question, what sort of person do we want to see emerge from the current social order and political powers? Hennis frames his question in the tradition of Weber's lecture 'Politics as a Vocation' (1948: 77–128). It is the duty of the politician to consider the overall framework of society and to ask, critically, what sort of person is thereby produced. The politician must have his own values and convictions and seek to ground them within the orders of society. In contemporary Germany Hennis has pointedly asked of the German political class what is their thinking about the reunification of the German nation, its governing institutions and what sort of person is desired (1999).

The figure of Michel Foucault has also been widely seen in the tradition of Nietzsche and Weber, as has been argued by Owen (1994). In comparison, though, to Hennis Foucault belongs more to anarchism and certainly not to the political class. In addition, he has taken the aporetic to an extreme in declaring the human subject an illusory product of a subject–object epistemology. Foucault has effaced the human subject as part of his strategy of oblique avoidance of the institutions of power and their discourses. Weber respected anarchists, because they withdrew so completely from the mechanisms of power and conforming social order. They were 'Kulturmenschen' because they invoked their own convictions with no prospect of success and tried to shape their own lives against the grain of modern rationalizing society, which as a process remained blind to cultural values (Whimster, 1999: 1–40). The ubiquity of power and its forms are themes common to both Foucault and Weber, but ultimately this similarity breaks down. This is not so much because Weber was a German nationalist and committed to the power of the state, and that Foucault was subversive of all power. Rather different times produce different choices and a strong commonality overrides the two historical contexts. Both men were committed to forms of freedom for the person in the face of rationalizing forces (Weber) and/or discursive practices (Foucault). Instead the comparison fails on their respective understanding of knowledge. Foucault argued the modern era was inaugurated by a contrived epistemology of subject and object, whereas for Weber the rationalization of knowledge is no recent event but was built into very long-run accounts of religion and knowledge. Against the odds, Weber still holds onto ideas of autonomy, and the values of the individual human being. For Foucault the individual is constituted by a subjectivizing discourse (his birth of modernity) and the humanist language of *Menschlichkeit* is compromised from the start. Foucault's ludic strategems seek to confound the subjection to knowledge and power. Weber remained pessimistic. His view of disenchantment is based on its ineluctability and is bound up with concepts of fate and tragedy.

The pervasive influence of rationalization into all spheres of life over the course of the twentieth century has been investigated by Ritzer (1993), although recently there has been a move away from assuming this leads to disenchantment. Re-enchantment may turn out to be the dominant cultural process (Ritzer, 1999).

3   Back to Kant

As stated above, neo-Kantianism was a methodological solution as to how knowledge is constituted. The infinity of reality is divided up according to disciplinary interests and each discipline generates its own rules of investigation and standards of validity. This was more a reflection of the organization of knowledge in the contemporary university than a return to Kant's original attempt to give foundations to how we can be correct about out knowledge of the world and how this is compatible with our freedom of action and beliefs. Kant was trying to provide assurance in the face of Hume's scepticism which held that what we understand about the world and what actually occurs in the world are two entirely separate matters that can never be ultimately reconciled. In Enlightenment Germany, where reason had been allotted the place of underpinning man's planning and control of the world, reason had to secure the copper-bottomed guarantees that previously religion had supplied. Kant was almost immediately seen to have failed to provide those guarantees (Beiser, 1987). Over the nineteenth century various other underpinnings were sought: in hermeneutics starting with Schleiermacher, historical dialectics with Hegel, and with Helmholtz and Wundt's psychological naturalism. Neo-Kantianism can hardly be called

a solution for it was more a pragmatic resolution, and Weber himself was aware of two major problems. Science needed to secure truth, and values had to be defended against the charge of relativism. If both of these could be secured, then the Kantian problem was re-stabilized, even though Weber sharply dichotomized each world. Scientific truth cannot underpin our value and beliefs about the world. The lecture 'Science as a Vocation' is the strongest version of this standpoint (1948: 129–56). Weber argued that science could establish scientific truth, universally. Science could inform us about the world but it could not tell us what we ought to do. Hence the value judgements we make about the world have no necessary scientific ordering, either in truth or in prioritization. This then admits a plurality of value judgements and, seemingly, value relativism. Weber meets the objection of relativism by arguing that each individual is responsible for deciding according to his or her values and meeting their demands absolutely.

Habermas, in line with the Frankfurt School, mounted a critique of Weber for reducing reason to individual instrumental action. He took Weber's position of value judgements to be decisionist, where no value consensus of universal claims can be secured. Consensus is replaced by the play of interests and power. Habermas, in addition, was critical of Weber's adherence to science as upholding truth as a value in itself. Habermas combined hermeneutics with left radicalism to point out that in the twentieth century science has become embedded within powerful corporate and governmental institutions. This was a possibility that Weber had never seriously envisioned with respect to capitalism, although he did see the danger of the state suborning the freedom of academics to express their views. In an unequal world, the appearance of academic neutrality, argued Habermas, creates a bias towards vested interests.

Weber's neo-Kantianism rested on the counterbalancing of science, as an independent realm of truth, and values as subjective but informed by science and reason. Given the embeddedness of both subjective values and science by power and interests, Habermas looked for a new Kantian solution. The claims of science to truth, of values to validity, and reason to emancipation can only be realized through an acceptance of their respective embeddedness and the referral of the different spheres to a high level procedure through which rationality is secured through communication (Habermas, 1984: 273–399). This position contrasts markedly with Weber's own fundamental position, which regarded any new transcendental unification of science, politics and beauty as illusory. Each of these spheres would proceed separately, and the condition of modernity was the fracturing of what Kant had tried to make coherent (Weber, 1948: 143–8).

The work of Schluchter is notable for trying to rescue Weber for the Kantian tradition and to negate some of Habermas' criticisms. Schluchter's pivotal discussion concerns ethics and scientific knowledge. These two realms are dichotomous for Weber. Science concerns truth, ethics is a matter of judgement and belief. Schluchter, however, effects a reconciliation. In the contemporary world individuals are educated and have access to reliable knowledge of the world. Instrumental rational action is in itself a very high level of rationality. It is not crudely expedient and opportunist, as charged by the Frankfurt School. Rather, it can assess the value of goals and anticipate the results of actions. Weber allowed that one distinctive ethical outlook was an ethic of responsibility. This was a rational ethic. Had Weber left ethics in this category alone, then some reconcilability of ethics with science would be possible. However, Weber also stipulated an ethic of conviction. This is a lesser form of rationality unable to assess goals or take into account the consequences of action. Its inspiration is Lutheran: 'here I stand, I can do no other'. One can adapt to the world to an extent, but the conviction ethic demands no adjustment of core beliefs. Weber was adamant that if certain, superior, people did not possess these core beliefs, then the world of autonomous values and beliefs would be completely rationalized and negated.

Schluchter's response to the imperfections of the conviction ethic is to argue that under conditions of modern society, unreflexive conviction is no longer an option. Convictions involve assessment, and with more than a nod towards Habermas' process of communicative rationality, Schluchter feels able to reground the conviction ethic as reconcilable with rational knowledge and judgement (1996: 48–101).

4 Sense and reference

In section (3) above the underlying problem is hermeneutics. The sovereign individual establishing the truth of the world around him is undermined by the fact that no individual has sovereign command of language, beliefs, values, or autonomy. All social worlds are intersubjective, therefore knowledge is forced to be a reflection of that intersubjectivity. There is no universal truth, only truth relative to the social surround of a person's world. This is a powerful current of thought in social theory and includes such major figures as Heidegger, Gadamer, Habermas and, it is said, the later Wittgenstein.

Hermeneutics is built into the fabric of Weber's methodology. *Verstehen*, or interpretative understanding, is based on intuition and empathy. One does not have to be Caesar to understand his thinking, said Weber. It is a transcendental presupposition that we can put ourselves in the place of anyone in the world and re-live their values and choices. Weber resisted the imputation of relativism nevertheless by insisting at the same time on the possibility of scientific truth. But, as seen in section (3), these protestations have been regarded as untenable by leading members of the hermeneutic tradition.

Contemporary analytic philosophy, however, would not regard Weber's position as anomalous. We need to go back to an argument that was first secured by Frege in 1891, which was almost certainly unbeknown to Weber. Frege used the example of the 'morning star' and the 'evening star' that appear at first light and twilight as bright 'stars' dominating the sky. In fact, as astronomers eventually discovered, these two 'stars' are one and the same planet, Venus. Frege pointed out that different expressions are used for the same object, and the sense of these expressions could be very different. The object to which these different names and senses refer is the planet Venus, and Venus is therefore the reference. There is only one Venus therefore a reference can be unambiguously true – what Frege called truth-value, whereas the senses of the object held by people can be multiple. Runciman has brought this argument to the defence of Weber's methodology (1972). Ideal types are concerned with meaning and the clarification of meaning and in this regard they contribute to our interpretative understanding of a situation. This allows us to make intelligible the actions of people. The truth of how people act in the world, however, proceeds for Weber through correct attribution of cause and effect. Following Frege, sense is the meaning people attribute to their actions; reference is the action itself which is a unique event open to verification. Hermeneutics, as Gellner has pointed out, wish to privilege meaning as the exclusive source of validity, while ignoring the task of relating expressions to the objects and actions to which they refer (1973: 50–77).

Contemporary analytic philosophy also shares Weber's distrust of general or covering laws of causality. Weber was unable to see how the regularity of causal occurrences amounted to an explanatory statement. For him what counted was the specific occurrence, or what analytical philosophy now calls the singular rather than the generic cause, and he criticized the belief in causal laws as positivism (Cartwright, 1983). Weber is now frequently referred to as a 'positivist' but it would be more accurate to designate him as allowing the truth of singular events to be established.

The above four directions leave the interpretation and evaluation of Weber's work as controversial as ever. It pays to keep in mind that his work cannot be reduced to unifying catchphrases such as 'rationalization', 'value freedom' or '*Verstehen*' and that each of these concepts are only part of more complex bundles of ideas. Are the four directions outlined above divergent? And what challenges do they present to social theory? The four directions certainly appear to cover very different ground and debates. In a very broad sense, however, they are aspects of the large question of modernity: how it originated, how it impacts upon our mode of life, how it coheres as an idea, and what its dominant cognitive mode is. These questions present one of the liveliest challenges to contemporary social theory, and Weber as an empirical social scientist would have been the first to admit that his work was only a start that would soon be superseded. As a social theorist, though, he does give us answers of a peculiar sort. He does not tell us precisely how he obtained his answers, they are presented with great confidence, and they are answers which are given in the form of antinomies. They are not answers in the sense of a harmonious resolution of a problem. Instead we are presented with the antinomies of freedom and ethics, fundamentalism and reason, happiness and vocation, ethical pacifism and violence, form and substance, concept and reality, and so on. Weber's challenge to the social theorist is that these antinomies are not resolvable through recourse to some higher unity or clever harmonization. They are the closest expression that we can get of the nature of things and social existence. The social theorist, like the citizen, is forced to make choices and to commit something of his- or herself in understanding the social world.

REFERENCES

Antonio, Robert and Glassman, Ronald M. (1985) *A Weber–Marx Dialogue*. Lawrence, KS: University Press of Kansas.

Aron, Raymond (1950) *La sociologie allemande contemporaine*. Paris: Alcan.

Ay, Karl-Ludwig (1999) 'Max Weber: a German Intellectual and the Question of War Guilt after the Great War', in S. Whimster (ed.), *Max Weber and the Culture of Anarchy*. Basingstoke: Macmillan.

Beiser, Frederick C. (1987) *The Fate of Reason. German Philosophy from Kant to Fichte*. Cambridge, MA: Harvard University Press.

Bendix, Reinhard (1960) *Max Weber. An Intellectual Portrait*. New York: Doubleday.

Bourdieu, Pierre (1987) 'Legitimation and Structured Interests in Weber's Sociology of Religion', in S. Whimster and S. Lash (eds), *Max Weber, Rationality and Modernity*. London: Allen and Unwin.

Cartwright, Nancy (1983) *How the Laws of Physics Lie*. Oxford: Clarendon Press.

Collins, Randall (1986) *Weberian Sociological Theory*. Cambridge: Cambridge University Press.

Eisenstadt, S.N. (1973) *Tradition, Change and Modernity*. New York: Free Press.

Gadamer, Hans-Georg (1989) *Truth and Method*. London: Sheed and Ward.

Gellner, Ernest (1973) 'The New Idealism – Cause and Meaning in the Social Sciences', in *Cause and Meaning in the Social Sciences*. London: Routledge and Kegan Paul.

Gellner, Ernest (1988) *Plough, Sword and Book: The Structure of Human History*. London: Collins Harvill.

Giddens, Anthony (1985) *The Nation-state and Violence*. Cambridge: Polity Press.

Green, Robert W. (1959) *Protestantism and Capitalism. The Weber Thesis and its Critics*. Lexington, MA: Heath.

Habermas, Jürgen (1984) *The Theory of Communicative Action. Reason and the Rationalization of Society* (trans. Thomas McCarthy). London: Heinemann.

Hall, J. (1985) *Powers and Liberties*. Oxford: Blackwell.

Hennis, Wilhelm (1988) *Max Weber. Essays in Reconstruction* (trans. K. Tribe). London: Allen and Unwin. (Revised edition, *Max Weber's Central Question*. Newbury: Threshold Press, 2000.)

Hennis, Wilhelm (1999) 'Max Weber's "Politik als Beruf" in der Berliner Republik', *Frankfurter Allgemeine Zeitung*, 2 October 1999.

Kalberg, Stephen (1994) *Max Weber's Comparative-Historical Sociology*. Cambridge: Polity Press.

Käsler, Dirk (1988) *Max Weber. An Introduction to his Life and Work*. Cambridge: Polity Press.

Lepsius, Rainer M. (1990) *Interessen, Ideen und Institutionen*. Opladen: Westdeutscher Verlag.

Löwith, Karl (1982) *Max Weber and Karl Marx*. London: George Allen and Unwin.

Mann, Michael (1993) *The Sources of Social Power*, Volume II: *The Rise of Classes and Nation-states, 1760–1914*. Cambridge: Cambridge University Press.

Merton, Robert (1957) *Social Theory and Social Structure*. New York: Free Press.

Mommsen, Wolfgang J. (1989) *The Political and Social Theory of Max Weber*. Cambridge: Polity Press.

Mommsen, Wolfgang, J. (1993) 'Einleitung', *Max Weber Gesamtausgabe*, I (4). Tübingen: Mohr/Siebeck.

Moore, Barrington (1967) *Social Origins of Democracy and Dictatorship. Lord and Peasant in the Making of the Modern World*. London: Allen Lane.

Oakes, Guy (1987) 'Weber and the Southwest German

School: the Genesis of the Concept of the Historical Individual', in W.J. Mommsen and J. Osterhammel (eds), *Max Weber and his Contemporaries*. London: Allen and Unwin.

Owen, David (1994) *Maturity and Modernity. Nietzsche, Weber and Foucault and the Ambivalence of Reason*. London: Routledge.

Parsons, Talcott (1937) *The Structure of Social Action*. New York: The Free Press.

Rex, John (1961) *Key Problems of Sociological Theory*. London: Routledge and Kegan Paul.

Ritzer, George (1993) *The McDonaldization of Society. The Changing Character of Contemporary Life*. Newbury Park, CA: Pine Forge Press.

Ritzer, George (1999) *Enchanting a Disenchanted World. Revolutionizing the Means of Consumption*. Thousand Oaks, CA: Pine Forge Press.

Runciman, W.G. (1972) *A Critique of Max Weber's Methodology of the Social Sciences*. Cambridge: Cambridge University Press.

Safranski, Rüdiger (1998) *Martin Heidegger. Between Good and Evil*. Cambridge, MA and London: Harvard University Press.

Sayer, Derek (1991) *Capitalism and Modernity*. London and New York: Routledge.

Scaff, Lawrence (1989) *Fleeing the Iron Cage. Culture, Politics, and Modernity in the Thought of Max Weber*. Berkeley, CA: University of California Press.

Schluchter, Wolfgang (1996) *Paradoxes of Modernity. Culture and Conduct in the Theory of Max Weber* (trans. Neil Solomon). Stanford, CA: Stanford University Press.

Smelser, N.J. (1959) *Social Change in the Industrial Revolution. An Application of Theory to the Lancashire Cotton Industry, 1770–1840*. London: Routledge and Kegan Paul.

Weber, Marianne (1988) *Max Weber. A Biography*. New Brunswick, NJ and Oxford: Transaction Books.

Weber, Max (1889) *Zur Geschichte der Handelsgesellschaften im Mittelalter*. Stuttgart: F. Enke.

Weber, Max (1891/1986) *Die römische Agrargeschichte in ihrer Bedeutung für das Staats- und Privatrecht*, in *Max Weber Gesamtausgabe* I (2). Tübingen: Mohr/Siebeck.

Weber, Max (1892/1984) *Die Lage der Landarbeiter im ostelbischen Deutschland, in Max Weber Gesamtausgabe* I (3). Tübingen: Mohr/Siebeck.

Weber, Max (1896a/1976) 'The Social Causes of the Decline of Ancient Civilization', in *The Agrarian Sociology of Ancient Civilizations*. London: NLB. pp. 387–411.

Weber, Max (1896b/1989) 'The National State and Economic Policy' in K. Tribe (ed.), *Reading Weber*. London: Routledge. pp. 188–209.

Weber, Max (1920) *Gesammelte Aufsätze zur Religionssoziologie*. Tübingen: Mohr/Siebeck.

Weber, Max (1930) *The Protestant Ethic and the Spirit of Capitalism* (trans. Talcott Parsons). London: Allen and Unwin.

Weber, Max (1948) *From Max Weber* (ed. Hans Gerth and C.W. Mills). London: Routledge and Kegan Paul.

Weber, Max (1949) *The Methodology of the Social Sciences* (trans. and ed. E. Shils and H. Finch). New York: Free Press.

Weber, Max (1961) *General Economic History* (trans. F. Knight). New York: Collier-Macmillan.

Weber, Max (1968) *Economy and Society. An Outline of Interpretive Sociology* (ed. Guenther Roth and Claus Wittich). New York: Bedminster Press.

Weber, Max (1994) *Max Weber Gesamtausgabe, Briefe*, II (6) (ed. R. Lepsius and W.J. Mommsen). Tübingen: Mohr/Siebeck.

Weber, Max (1995) *The Russian Revolutions* (trans. and ed. G.C. Wells and P. Baehr). Cambridge: Polity Press.

Weber, Max (1995) *Zur Psychophysik der industriellen Arbeit*, in *Max Weber Gesamtausgabe* I (11). Tübingen: Mohr/Siebeck.

Weber, Max (1999) *Max Weber Gesamtausgabe. Wirtschaft und Gesellschaft. Die Stadt*. 1/22–5 (ed. W. Nippel). Tübingen: Mohr/Siebeck.

Whimster, Sam (1999) 'Introduction to Weber, Ascona and Anarchism', in S. Whimster (ed.), *Max Weber and the Culture of Anarchy*. London: Macmillan.

Winckelmann, J. (1957) *Legitimität und Legalität in Max Webers Herrschaftssoziologie*. Tübingen: Mohr/Siebeck.

6

The Continuing Relevance of Georg Simmel: Staking Out Anew the Field of Sociology[1]

BIRGITTA NEDELMANN

The century has run its course,
but the single individual has to start
all over again.

(Goethe: epigraph of Simmel's
dissertation)[2]

WHY SHOULD ONE STAKE OUT ANEW THE FIELD OF SOCIOLOGY?

At the beginning of the twenty-first century, we sociologists are well advised to go back to the foundations of sociology laid by our classics at the turn of the last century. Among them, Georg Simmel's efforts at staking out the field of sociology and of establishing it, together with Max Weber, Ferdinand Tönnies and others, as an autonomous academic discipline are especially suited to help correct some of the main flaws of contemporary sociology. But just how can the acute problems we are confronted with today be cured by reminding ourselves of the sociological foundations laid by Simmel a hundred years ago? How can the present be cured with the past?

The solution of this riddle cannot consist in attempting to prove the 'actuality' of Simmel's sociological *oeuvre*. The empirical problems Simmel dealt with differed considerably from those challenging us sociologists today. Claiming the 'actuality' of Simmel's *oeuvre* would, therefore, be a contradiction in itself. Re-reading it under the assumption that it will offer us the

solutions to our problems is a futile exercise. It is tantamount to placing Simmel, or other classics, in an exegetic Procrustean bed from which they are only released if we find in them the answers we already knew before, but which we then can advance more authoritatively in their names.

There must be other reasons for claiming that present problems can be solved by past solutions. These reasons are intimately linked to the highly problematic way in which sociology presents itself today as an academic discipline. The foundations of contemporary sociology are shaking and its boundaries with other disciplines are becoming blurred. What can Simmel's efforts at staking out the field of sociology a hundred years ago contribute to restaking our field today? When consulting Simmel, we do this out of our deep concern about the future of our discipline in the new millennium. We believe that re-reading Simmel will give us insights that will help to repair at least some of the deficiencies of our discipline. Which deficiencies do we have in mind more specifically and which remedy can Simmel offer?

First, many critiques of sociology agree that ever-increasing specialization endangers our discipline's internal cohesion and integration. The claim advanced here is that restaking the sociological field with the help of Simmel's conceptual frame of reference can contribute to reintegrating sociology and preventing its premature dissolution. Secondly, what eminent scholars have observed before deserves being stressed again, namely, that one-dimensional thinking still dominates contemporary socio-logical thought. The specific attention Simmel has given to dualism can help, in my belief, to correct the one-dimensional bias in contem-porary sociological thought. Thirdly, theories of individualization and globalization are experi-encing a boom in social theory. One of the consequences of the fatal attraction to these theories is a double flight from the core prob-lematic of sociology, that is, the mediation between individuals and supraindividual forms (or institutions). Reminding researchers of the leitmotiv in Simmel's sociology may contribute to stopping this flight. Last but not least, it is claimed that ongoing efforts at either moralizing or trivializing the task of our discipline can be cured by learning at least three lessons from Simmel.

The first and the fourth issues I have men-tioned are related to sociology as an academic discipline; the second and third deal with more substantive issues. In what follows, the first problem will be given special attention, since it constitutes the basis for the discussion of the other three problems.

SIMMEL'S CONCEPTUAL FRAME OF REFERENCE

Leading scholars of our discipline, such as Donald N. Levine (1997a), have criticized social theory in the United States as 'marked internally by pluralistic confusion and externally by dimin-ishing support'. His observation holds true of sociology as an academic discipline world-wide. The accelerated process of specialization has supported a flight from the foundations of socio-logy. As a consequence, sociology is in danger of losing its identity and autonomy. It has always been difficult to find consensus among sociolo-gists as to where the boundaries of our discipline are in relation to our neighboring disciplines. Today, there seems to be a general tendency towards voluntarily running over ever-so feeble disciplinary fences and to mix with other aca-demic fields. As a consequence, sociology is more and more becoming an indistinguishable ingre-dient in the large melting pot of the 'social sciences'. Some social scientists welcome this development in the name of 'inter-disciplinarity', thus overlooking the fact that there can only be 'inter- and multi-*disciplinarity*', if there are autonomous academic disciplines able to interact with each other. If sociology is to survive as an autonomous scientific discipline in the next century, we have to re-engage in a task which is not much different from the one the founding

fathers of sociology successfully dealt with at the turn of the last century: we have to (re-)define *the field of sociology*.

It was exactly this effort in defining the field of sociology which gave rise to Simmel's landmark first chapter *Das Gebiet der Soziologie* in his *Grundfragen der Soziologie* (his so-called 'Little Sociology' written in 1917; GSG 16).[3] Re-reading this important work today helps remind ourselves of the specificity of socio-logical enquiry, of its main working instruments and of the *Problemstellung*, the problematic, typical of sociology and sociology only. I will reconstruct what could be called Simmel's conceptual frame of reference, drawing not only on his *Field of Sociology* but also on other of his works.

Before undertaking this task a word of clari-fication is needed. How can a classic theorist like Simmel, it may be asked, notorious for his 'incoherence' and 'unsystematic' way of thought, offer a conceptual frame of reference and contribute to reintegrating the fragmented field of contemporary sociology? Both among Sim-mel's contemporaries and Simmel scholars today, his work is known because of its alleged lack of coherence and systematic approach. This dubious reputation has given rise to two contradictory types of reactions: severe criticism and even rejection of his work on the one hand, and enthusiastic praise because of Simmel's 'post-modern(ized) style' (Weinstein and Wein-stein, 1993)[4] on the other. Attempts have been made, both in Simmel's time and today, at demonstrating that the judgement of the incoherence of Simmel's work is wrong and, accordingly, both types of reactions are inap-propriate. Among contemporary Simmel scho-lars, Levine (1997b: 196) has shown convincingly 'that Simmel's sociology evinced a greater degree of coherence than those of his illustrious con-temporaries'.[5] Among Simmel's contemporaries, Heinrich Rickert has coined an appropriate label when calling Simmel *'der Systematiker der Unsystematik'*, the 'systematizer of the unsyste-matic' (quoted after Marcuse, 1958: 190). This gives us a clue to understanding his sociological methodology.

Wechselwirkung as a guiding principle

The label of Simmel as the systematizer of the unsystematic mirrors Simmel's conviction that it is the modern world which is lacking internal coherence and order. Therefore, the sociologist, like any other scientist, has to use an artificial trick, a *Kunstgriff*, in order to systematize the chaos he or she is exposed to. This artificial trick consists of selecting one main concept and assigning it the function of a *guiding concept*. Under the guidance of this concept, sociology has to fulfill a two-step task of, first, taking the individual existences apart (*zerlegen*) and, then, recomposing (*neu zusammenfassen*) them in the light of its (i.e. sociology's) own conception (GSG 16: 71; Simmel, 1976: 64). For Simmel, the concept of *Wechselwirkung*, interaction, functions as such a guiding concept for both sociological analysis *and* recomposition. His choice is based on the undeniable and fundamental empirical fact that individuals interact. Equipped with this guiding concept, the sociologist can now risk exposing himself or herself to the chaotic world. The breadth of Simmel's empirical work shows that he did not shy away from treating a surprisingly great variety of topics and themes. It is exactly by strictly applying the concept of interaction that he masters the empirical chaos he, or anybody else studying society, exposes himself to.

For Simmel, *Wechselwirkung* not only functioned as a guiding concept, but also as a guiding *principle* of sociology. There are at least three imperatives for sociological research implied in this concept. First, it is a commitment to studying the relations *between* individuals or collective actors. Emphasizing the *relational* aspect, Simmel elegantly overcomes the controversy between individualism and collectivism, between micro- and macro-sociology, which was going on at his time and is still absorbing academic energies today. Simmel's answer to the eternal question of whether the individual or the society is more 'real' and therefore more privileged than the other to be the 'object of sociology' is that neither of them can claim to be more 'real' than the other. Neither of them constitutes the 'object of sociology'. Moreover, Simmel rejects defining academic disciplines by an 'object of experience' (*Erfahrungsobjekt*) of their own. Like any other science, sociology has to specify the analytical perspective with which it analyses an 'object of experience' and recomposes it into an 'object of cognition' (*Erkenntnisobjekt*). The concept of interaction functions as the analytical principle under the guidance of which objects of experience are transformed into objects of cognition.

Secondly, the concept of *Wechselwirkung* expresses Simmel's special attention to one type of sociological explanation which – at least at his time – was unconventional, that is, explanation in terms of *zirkuläre Verursachung*, circular causation, or self-referentiality. An example of this type of explanation can be taken from his 'On the Self-maintenance of Social Groups' (GSG 16: 335): If the stressed city dweller finds recreation in the countryside, it cannot be explained by the countryside being the cause of the recreational effect. This explanation is, following Simmel, incorrect, or at least incomplete, because we have, first, 'laid our feelings, depths, meanings into the landscape, and, only then, we receive comfort, consolation and inspiration from it' (GSG 16: 335; my translation). Whenever studying self-referential processes of *Wechselwirkung*, Simmel examines the possibility of different sequences of circular causation giving rise to either vicious or virtuous circles.

Thirdly, for Simmel, the concept of *Wechselwirkung* stands for his rejection of reification and mystification of supraindividual social units (GSG 5: 225) and his commitment to *process analysis*. In his unfinished autobiographical note he declares that scientific activity consists in dissolving what seems to be fixed and stable into the fluidity of its dynamic relations (Simmel, 1958: 9; my translation). Consequently, there is yet another reason for rejecting both the individual and the society as the given 'objects' of sociology. What we experience as if it were a social unity, is in reality composed of permanently ongoing processes. With reference to the concept of 'society' it is, therefore, inappropriate to define it as a fixed unity; rather, it refers to dynamic and gradual processes of 'sociation', *Vergesellschaftung*, resulting in 'more or less society' (GSG 16: 70).

In sum, *relationality, self-reflexivity* and *process analysis* are the main imperatives for sociological research implied in the concept of interaction understood as a guiding principle of sociology. A set of sub-concepts are intimately linked to this guiding concept of *Wechselwirkung*, making up what can be called Simmel's *conceptual frame of reference* (see Figure 6.1).[6]

The sub-concepts of interaction

Although Simmel did not use formal definitions or conceptual schemes for staking out *The Field of Sociology*, he repeatedly used the concepts included in the scheme presented in Figure 6.1 throughout his empirical research. In contrast to his contemporary, Max Weber, Simmel did not devote his intellectual energies to scholarly exercises in conceptual definitions. Perhaps, Simmel may not even have been enthusiastic about an attempt at restructuring his *Field of Sociology* a posteriori in the form of a schematic overview. Be that as it may, I believe that it helps us both clarify his sociological approach and stake out anew the field of sociology today.

The exegetic work of eminent Simmel scholars has already contributed to a deeper understanding of the different concepts underlying Simmel's empirical sociological work (Dahme, 1981;

VARIABLES

1 **Number**
1.1 Dyad
1.2 Triad
1.3 Three and more

2 **Space**
2.1 Close – Distant
2.2 Sedentary – Mobile
2.3 Narrow Borders – Broad Borders

3 **Time**
3.1 Synchronic – Diachronic
3.2 Speed – Rhythm

4 **Dualism**
4.1 Contradiction
4.2 Ambivalence
4.3 Contrast

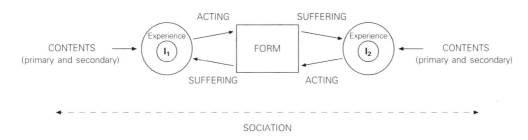

Figure 6.1 *Simmel's conceptual frame of reference*

Frisby and Featherstone, 1997; Köhnke, 1996; Levine, 1971, 1979, 1981, 1997b; Rammstedt 1992, 1999). As far as I can see, less effort has been made so far at showing how the different Simmelian concepts are linked together.[7] I shall try to show that these concepts actually can be combined into a *frame* of reference for socio-logical analysis.

The concept of *Wechselwirkung* guides two conceptual pairs, 'form' and 'contents', and 'acting' (*Tun*) and 'suffering' (*Leiden*), the latter concept referring to *receiving* the effects emanat-ing from previous interaction sequences. The constituent parts of each pair mutually condition each other. Forms can only come into social being if individuals strive to realize their wishes, needs, interests, or desires (primary contents); and, vice versa, contents can only be realized through and within social forms. Concerning the second conceptual pair, 'acting' is the necessary pre-condition for 'receiving' interactional effects; and, vice versa, 'receiving' stimulates further new ways of 'acting'. However, there is an important transformatory mechanism linking the two conceptual pairs together, that is, experience (*Erleben*) (Nedelmann, 1990). Actors evaluate the effects they receive with the interior side of their individuality. As a result, different kinds of experience are shaped which, in their turn, transform 'primary contents' into 'secondary contents', that is, into *socially formed* interests, needs, wishes or desires. Secondary contents again can give rise to actions that modify old social forms or create new ones.

The four sub-processes of sociation

Filtered through different ways of experiencing, acting and receiving, (primary and secondary) contents and form stimulate each other recipro-cally *and* crosswise, thus setting into motion four different sub-processes. In their combination, they constitute the overall process of *sociation*. Going beyond Simmel's terminology, we call the first process 'externalization'; it is related to the concept of 'acting'. The second process is called 'internalization'; it is related to the concept of 'receiving'. The third process, 'institutionaliza-tion', refers to the concept of 'form' and means the process of constructing, shaping and reshap-ing social institutions. The fourth process, finally, 'interest-formation', is related to the con-cept of 'contents' and means the dynamics of shaping and reshaping social interests, needs, wishes or emotions. I have to limit myself to making a few remarks about what these four sub-processes of sociation mean more precisely and how they are linked to each other.

Externalization and internalization

The processes of 'externalization' and 'internal-ization' are the dynamic aspects of interaction, of mutually reciprocating effects. In stressing these two processes, Simmel looks at the individual (or collective) actor from two different points of view. He, first, sees him or her as the 'creator' of processes of sociation, and, secondly, as the receiver or addressee of the social effects emerging from previous interaction sequences. Externalization refers to processes of social productivity, internalization to the elaboration of emergent social effects through experience. 'What happens to men', Simmel (1976: 64) asks in *The Field of Sociology*, '. . . in so far as they form groups and are determined by their group existence because of interaction?' To look at the agent from these two aspects must not be confounded with emphasizing an active and a passive aspect. Both processes demand active individuals, but there are different kinds of activity demanded from them. Simmel's example from the *Metropolis* (GSG 7: 116–31) may help explain what is meant by experience as an activity. The attitude of aloofness (*blasé*) results from the very fact that the inhabitant of the metropolis is exposed to a permanent over-stimulation of his (or her) senses. To display the attitude of aloofness *vis-à-vis* the co-citizens results from consciously filtering the effects received from the urban environment and stylizing them into a distinct social attitude. Different ways of experiencing the world do not simply emanate from passively absorbing the environmental effects. They have to be selected and culturally stylized under the guidance of *both* individual and supraindividual categories. In shaping externally visible ways of experience, the interiority of the individuality functions, as it were, as a battleground between the ever-conflicting principles of individuality and generality. Aesthetic, erotic, ethical and other ways of experience are characterized by Simmel by the proportions in which these two conflicting principles are represented in them.

At this point, it may be advisable to take into consideration a warning made by Margaret S. Archer (1995) against conflationary theorizing. Although both processes, externalization and internalization, are linked together empirically, they have to be treated as *analytically* independent, producing different effects in different interaction sequences and for different actors. It is exactly this type of non-conflationary theorizing Simmel demonstrates in his empirical work. Just take as an example his sociology of culture: 'Objective culture' is the emergent product of previous interaction sequences in which individuals have externalized their cultural interests by creating cultural forms. The longer these forms exist, the more they produce emergent properties conditioning in their turn the individuals' cultural interests. Following Archer's advice, it is important to make clear which actors are exposed to these emergent effects at which point in time. Different groups or generations of actors may and, as a rule, do react differently to being conditioned in their interest realization. As Simmel described, some may protest against the overwhelming powers of objective culture (for example, against the institution of marriage) and revolt against 'forms' as such, in the futile attempt at trying to realize their sexual desires outside any social institutions. Other types and actors may at other points in time adapt more easily to being culturally conditioned, limiting themselves to reforming the given cultural institutions. Bringing back this Simmelian sociological approach to the ongoing theoretical debate may help overcome the controversy between individualism and collectivism and strengthen the arguments presented in Archer's morphogenetic theory against 'conflationism' and 'elisionism'.

Institutionalization

The third and fourth processes, institutionalization and interest-formation, are related to Simmel's famous (but often misunderstood) distinction between form and contents. The investigation of the forms of sociation is the core task Simmel assigns to sociology. His 'Great Sociology' is an attempt at demonstrating the scientific fertility of this type of formal or institutional analysis.[8] Departing from Levine's (1971: xxiv–xxvii) distinction between four different forms in Simmel's work – (1) the forms of elementary social interaction; (2) institutionalized structures; (3) the generic forms of society itself, and (4) autonomous 'play' forms[9] – the 'Great Sociology' can also be re-read as a contribution to the sociology of institutions and institutionalization. The decisive criterion of progressive institutionalization is the degree in which forms are 'condensed' (*verdichtet*) or crystallized. Increasing condensation means that social forms become increasingly autonomous in relation to their original creators. Accordingly, three different levels of institutionalization can be distinguished. The *first* level of institutionalization is made up of patterned everyday mundane interactions. On this level, the actors autonomously negotiate and control the ways in which they realize their interests. Individual deviations from the negotiated patterns of interaction can be made at a relatively low social cost. The more these elementary forms crystallize and start defining their own laws of behavior, the more the individuals feel restricted in their ability to realize their interests spontaneously. The higher the degree of institutionalization, the higher the social costs for individual freedom.

The *second* level of institutionalization is characterized by interactions within institutionalized structures. The very quality of a higher degree of crystallization is felt by the actors as an increasing constraint on their individual choice. On this level of institutionalization, we find the essential characteristic of social institutions proper, defined by Jepperson (1991: 146) in a Simmelian manner as 'freedom within constraint': individual action is free within the constraints of institutionalized structures. Throughout his 'Great Sociology', Simmel pays special attention to the question of how the tension emanating from this duality between freedom and constraint expresses itself socially. He emphasizes that the very *social* quality of forms results only from the struggle between opposite poles, such as freedom and constraint. This is one reason why institutionalized structures are *socially* productive. Another reason for the social productivity of social institutions consists in the very fact that institutions offer action alternatives which individuals could not have chosen without institutions. This fundamental insight into the social productivity of institutions helps us correct the widespread prejudice held among many contemporary social theorists against institutional analysis as being biased against individual freedom. Among the themes to be researched further in institutional theory today is the social productivity of institutionalized structures.

The *third* level of institutionalization is made up by the 'generic forms of society itself'. Rephrased in Weberian terms as 'social spheres', they can be characterized by the dominance of one criterion of rationality (for example, maximization of profit in the sphere of economics), thus putting a relatively high price on those individually chosen action alternatives which deviate from this criterion of rationality. Deviations from the institutionalized criterion of rationality are followed up by sanctions and control mechanisms, making it increasingly difficult, although not impossible, to act against the logics implicit in institutionalized social spheres.

Applying Simmel's dynamic perspective, the three types of institutions can be understood as a continuum of increasing institutionalization (or de-institutionalization), in which the costs of individual freedom (in the sense of deviations from the institutionalized criterion of social action) are gradually increasing (or decreasing). Contemporary institutional analysis could largely profit from this kind of dynamic reinterpretation of Simmel's contribution to the sociology of social forms. The increasing costs for individual choice can be seen as an emergent property of increasing institutionalization, institutional change thus becoming a more and more 'expensive' enterprise. Contemporary critiques of institutional analysis have stressed the bias towards stability and constraint and the neglect of the individual actor in conventional sociological approaches to institutional analysis. Reinterpreting institutions in the Simmelian dynamic

way helps correct this bias. It contributes to enriching contemporary institutional analysis in yet another sense. We have said that condensation also refers to a gradual process in which social forms become increasingly abstract. As Neil J. Smelser puts it, patterns of interaction become increasingly 'imagined', meaning 'that they are not "seen" in any immediate sense, in the way that neighbors, policemen on the beat, the corner grocery store, and the local school are seen' (Smelser, 1997: 46). In this process of increasing 'imaginedness', individuals do not disappear from the stage of institutional interaction, but they take over more and more the role of representatives of the institution in question. As institutional representatives, 'institutionalized individuals' become the very carriers of institutions. We can only agree with Smelser (1997: 47) that this aspect of institutional representation deserves more systematic investigation in future.

The *fourth* type of form, autonomous 'play forms', is perhaps Simmel's most original contribution to the analysis of social institutions. Simmel scholars have either overlooked this type or treated it as a rare, or even exotic, social form. The importance of Simmel's analysis of sociability (GSG 16: 103–121) goes beyond its being a brilliant example of 'pure' sociology, as Simmel calls it. I rather classify sociability as a *vertical* type of institution, a type which deserves being integrated systematically into contemporary sociological theories of institutions. Whereas the three types of institutions mentioned so far refer to *horizontal* processes of institutionalization, this fourth type is related to a vertical dimension of patterned interaction. What do we mean by patterned vertical processes of interaction? In play forms, the forms represented in 'real' life (such as super- and subordination, conflict and secrecy) are transformed into objects of playful discourse. To play, as it were, with the forms of social life presupposes the individual's ability to take a distance from the seriousness of 'real' life and to reflect about it lightly on a meta-societal level. In sociable encounters, the real 'heavy' society and the playful 'light' society are related to each other vertically. In picking out society and its forms of interaction as a central theme of sociable discourse, sociable people playfully turn the social forms characteristic of society upside down: in sociable encounters, powerholders play as if they were equals among equals, subordinates jokingly imitate their superiors, or men and women flirt with love. As Simmel stresses, sociable encounters are not limited to the sphere of sociability proper. Just as the form of, for example, super- and subordination permeates many (if not all) social phenomena (GSG 8: 180), so play forms also permeate almost all social spheres. Taken together, they constitute what could be called the light social superstructure of social life. It contributes to smoothing the functioning of the heavy social substructure. So, for example, political decision-making is eased by sociable meetings among politicians; decisions over life and death in hospitals are transformed into routine with the help of joking rituals (as Erving Goffman has described so brilliantly); and the 'iron cage' (Weber) of bureaucracy is felt as a lighter burden if clients teasingly allude to its built-in problems when dealing with functionaries. Vertical processes of institutionalization function as supporting mechanisms of horizontal processes of institutionalization in yet another sense: they are a socializing mechanism in so far as they playfully teach their participants how social forms function in 'real' life. Taking the supportive and socializing functions of sociability together, it could be said that vertical playforms contribute to increasing the 'flexibility management' (Nedelmann, 1995a: 21) of social institutions. An institution that is suffused by playforms increases the range of interpretation within which it has to control deviations from its rules and norms. A more systematic integration of this vertical type of institution into the analysis of the other three types of horizontal institutionalization would certainly enrich present theories in this field of research. It would also help include a range of empirical phenomena which, so far, have lived in isolation from 'real' institutional analysis, that is, joking rituals and social games.

Interest-formation

Let us now turn to the fourth process that is related to the concept of secondary contents, interest-formation. Simmel gives a prominent example of this type of process in his *excursus* on *Treue und Dankbarkeit* (GSG 11: 652–70). The emotions of fidelity and gratitude emerge from interactions within social institutions. They constitute the emotional bond between individuals and institutions, thus making up the 'cement of society' (Elster, 1989). Why is it of relevance for contemporary sociological theory to pay attention to such processes of emerging secondary contents, or, interest-formation? The great success rational choice theory enjoys at present among sociologists has as its consequence the narrowing of our awareness for processes of interest-formation and transformation. Looking through Simmel's sociological glasses, interests are permanently formed and transformed within and through social institutions. In the example mentioned, Simmel analyses the dialectics between love and fidelity in marriage: love (primary content), first, giving rise to

fidelity (secondary content), which, then, reactivates feelings of love, which appear now as institutionally generated emotions. Institutionally mediated contents can, accordingly, follow a dialectical process of succession of primary and secondary contents, the institution itself functioning both as generator and terminator of contents (Nedelmann, 1984: 99–101).

The problem of how institutions can generate interests and feelings is a highly important one in many areas of institutional analysis today. Just take the example of institutional design in politics. How can, for example, the institutional setting of the European Union generate feelings of belongingness among us Europeans, just as the old institution of the nation-state once gave rise to feelings of belonging to the same 'community of fate' (Weber)? Having introduced the European Monetary Union, how can we trust the new currency, the Euro? Or how can people trust the newly designed democratic institutions in Eastern Europe (Sztompka, 1998)? The Simmelian approach certainly does not give us a ready-made answer to these questions. But his explicit awareness of institutionally generated interests and feelings helps us formulate a sociological problematic which is highly important for contemporary institutional analysis: how are processes of institutionalization linked to processes of interest-formation? And how do they feed back upon each other?[10]

THE IMPORTANCE OF AMBIVALENCE

Let us now turn to the set of variables Simmel repeatedly used in his empirical research (formally speaking, to the upper part in Figure 6.1).[11] The broad spectrum of empirical subjects Simmel researched is held together not only by a leitmotiv to which he returns over and over again (and to which we will turn later), but also by his interest in studying them with reference to recurrently reappearing variables. In their combination, they make up a coherent research program which Simmel followed himself. For us contemporary Simmel scholars this set of variables can function as a scheme for systematically reinterpreting his sociological *oeuvre*. Although impressive work has already been undertaken with relation to some of these variables, each of them deserves more systematic exploration. In this context, I wish to highlight especially variable (4), dualism.

The meaning of dualism goes beyond being an empirical variable. It characterizes Simmel's way of thinking throughout his sociological work. After having followed one way of interpretation, Simmel typically starts all over again by unfolding the opposite direction of interpretation. Witnesses of his university lectures report that these shifts from one line of thought to the opposite were marked by a 'silent second of self-oblivion in which he inwardly annihilated' what he had just said before (Marcuse, 1958: 191; my translation). This 'silent second' is translated in his written texts into phrasings with which he typically opens the next paragraph, such as 'on the other hand . . .', 'the opposite direction . . .', or 'a totally different picture presents itself . . .'. They only insufficiently prepare the reader to meet an author whose body of thought is based on unfolding contradictions, dualisms and opposites which he stubbornly refuses to merge into one predominant statement. As frustrating as this reading experience may be for the student who yearns for salvation by discovering *one* truth and *one* theory, it is stimulating for the enlightened scholar who looks for progress by accumulating refutations.

Dualism has yet another, more substantive meaning. As has been hinted at above, it is Simmel's conviction that forms of interaction acquire a *social* quality only if dualistic or opposite social forces are at work. 'It was Simmel's repeatedly expressed view that the condition for the existence of any aspect of life is the coexistence of a diametrically opposed element' (Levine, 1971: xxxv). The coexistence of dualistic social forces gives rise to social tension, which, in its turn, causes the dynamics of social forms. So, for example, processes of change in forms of super- and subordination are based on the permanent conflict between obedience and opposition; intimate relations get their momentum from the very fact that feelings of both attraction and repulsion, love and indifference are at work. These examples already illustrate what Simmel means: without the co-presence of dualistic forces, there is neither *social* life, nor social *life*.

Simmel distinguishes different social phenomena according to the way in which these dualistic forces are related more precisely to each other. Here, we wish to emphasize only one type, *ambivalence*. Levine (1985), Robert K. Merton (1976), and Ann-Mari Sellerberg (1994) belong to those scholars who, departing from Simmel, already have done systematic research in this area. But in spite of their efforts, contemporary sociologists are still reluctant to integrate sociological ambivalence systematically into social theory.[12] The importance of ambivalence has, therefore, to be highlighted again.

Generally speaking, ambivalence can be defined in the following way: in contrast to social phenomena which are structured by a contradiction between 'A' and 'non-A' (such as, freedom and constraint in super- and subordination), ambivalent social forces are at work if 'A'

and 'non-A' are present simultaneously. Simmel's highly complicated study on *Flirtation* (1984) can be read as a model for ambivalence as a *form* of interaction. Mutually reciprocating ambivalent messages ('yes' *and* 'no') in one and the same action unit are not only characteristic of gender relations, but also of interactions between other types of actors and in other social areas, such as politics, law or business. In my own research, I have distinguished between ambivalence (a) as a *form* and (b) as a *norm* of interaction, the latter one referring to Merton's (1976: 6) core type of sociological ambivalence. The difference between these two types consists in the very fact that ambivalence does not necessarily have to be integrated into the role structure and thus be normatively prescribed. Ambivalence can also be a form of interaction which is chosen deliberately as an action alternative without being normatively expected. The preference for ambivalence as a form of interaction increases both present and future alternatives of action. This is especially so in decision-making on highly sensitive political issues. The German law on abortion is an excellent case in point. After unification, it became necessary to rewrite legislation on abortion. Whereas abortion was defined as an illegal act in the old Federal Republic, it was not in the former DDR. In the new legislation, abortion is, on the one hand, defined as a criminal act to be prosecuted legally; *but*, it is, on the other hand and in the very same paragraph, not considered criminal and not prosecutable, if certain conditions are fulfilled. Ambivalent decision-making is a widely used strategy of conflict management without which peace agreements, resolutions on the labor market, or family conflicts could not be handled. In these areas, ambivalence is not normatively prescribed, but deliberately chosen as a way out of the restrictions implied in any unambiguous decision-making. Combining this Simmelian type of ambivalence as a *form* of interaction with the Mertonian type of ambivalence as a *norm* of interaction, we arrive at a third type of ambivalence, that is, *normative forms* of ambivalence. Professional politics, especially diplomacy, is an excellent area in which this third type could be studied further (Nedelmann, 1997). By making more systematic investigations in these social areas, we could not only hope for gaining new empirical insights, but also for correcting the bias of one-dimensionality still dominating contemporary theories of social action. The argument I am stressing here differs from the one often held against the onesidedness of present theories of social action, namely, that they have to take into consideration both rational and emotional motives. Instead, I am arguing for a theory of social action that is built on the actors' *simultaneous* orientation towards two, equally valent criteria of action (be they rational, affective, traditional or whatever). The Weberian types of social action and the Parsonian pattern alternatives are excellent starting points for elaborating further such a theory of ambivalent social action. They can be reinterpreted as possible 'mixes' of ambivalent action orientations in which the extreme poles of action orientation are fused into equally valent action alternatives. Social interaction based on ambivalence can be understood as an exchange process in which the actors reciprocate ambivalences.

STOPPING THE FLIGHT FROM SOCIOLOGY BY REINTRODUCING SIMMEL'S LEITMOTIV

At the turn of this millennium, there are two different theories enjoying particular attraction among sociologists – individualization and globalization. The followers of each theory are 'fleeing the iron cage' (Scaff, 1989) of 'society' in two opposite directions: individualization theorists into the direction of the individual, globalization theorists into the opposite direction of imagined global networks.[13] In a truly Simmelian manner, this flight from society could be described as a double process of centripetally fleeing theorists of individualization, on the one hand, and centrifugally fleeing theorists of globalization, on the other. There could hardly be a stronger manifestation of one-dimensional thought in present social theory-building than the fashionable upswing of these two diametrically opposed theoretical streams. Together they leave behind a vacuum in contemporary sociology. Both evade, although in different ways, the encounter with the 'vexacious fact of society' (Archer, 1995: 2), that is, in Simmelian terms, with the fact that supraindividual social forms (or social institutions in the four meanings discussed above) emerge from interactions *between* individuals. Whereas globalization theorists evade the encounter with social institutions by escaping into the meta-societal atmosphere of imagined global networks, individualization theorists crawl back under the institutional level finding comfort from the 'vexacious fact of society' in the closeness of face-to-face interactions. One of the main puzzles our discipline has tried to solve since its beginning, the emergence of individually caused supraindividual institutions, is precipitously abandoned even before it has been solved satisfactorily. As a consequence, both theoretical directions contribute in their way to deconstructing sociology. Globalization theorists have started a frenetic

clearing-out activity of some of the basic sociological concepts replacing those 'which reflected an older order, such as society, class, state' (Albrow et al., 1994: 371) with new ones, such as 'community, socioscapes and milieux' (Albrow, 1996: 155–9). Individualization theorists have declared the beginning of the so-called 'second modernity' (Beck, 1997a), before having fully profited from the contributions our classics made to the analysis of the 'first modernity'. Johannes Weiß (1998: 418–19) rightly observes that the way in which Ulrich Beck talks about 'individuality' or 'individualization' is surprisingly undifferentiated, reflecting even a stubborn unwillingness to differentiate it further. At best, Simmel's highly differentiated theories of individualization are alluded to, but no systematic efforts are made at integrating them into their theorizing. Thus, Simmel's own prophecy has come true that he will not leave behind any heirs – but it has come true not because he did not leave behind any heritage, but, on the contrary, because we contemporary sociologists have not fully discovered his heritage, which offers us 'one of the most sophisticated perspectives on social interaction that we possess' (Levine 1997b: 202).

I believe that the double flight from the core problem of sociology could be slowed down, if not stopped altogether, by remembering the leitmotiv of Simmel's sociology. Given the broad range of empirical subjects he dealt with, Simmel scholars have asked themselves if it is at all possible to identify a general problem in Simmel's sociological opus. I claim that this is indeed possible. As has already been mentioned above, Simmel's sociological program was to investigate the forms of sociation. Over and over again he asked himself how autonomous social forms emerging from interactions between individuals could be mediated with their creators' interests and desires. Dealing with such highly different topics as the *Metropolis* (GSG 7: 116–31) or *The Picture-Frame* (GSG 7: 101–8), Simmel was intrigued by the question of how to find a balanced relationship between the single individual and cultural institutions. Let me just take the example of *The Picture Frame*.[14] For Simmel, the relations between the painting, the frame and the cultural environment function as a metaphor for discussing the fundamental sociological problematic of how to mediate between the individual and culture. It is the frame, says Simmel, which has to take over the function of mediating between the piece of art and the individual in his or her role as art consumer, by both separating *and* uniting, 'the task on which, in analogy to history, *the individual and the society crush each other*' (GSG 7: 108; my emphasis and translation). The leitmotiv reappears here as the problematic of 'social framing'

(Nedelmann, 2000), that is, of finding inter-mediary institutions between the 'individual' and objectified social institutions. Also the study of the metropolis is marked by Simmel's deep concern about how the city dweller can avoid being crushed in his or her individuality by the overwhelming objective power of modern urban life. One mediating instance is here the develop-ment of stylized attitudes towards fellow citizens, such as aloofness. Without being able to go into further detail, Simmel's leitmotiv could be summarized in the following question: how is it possible to mediate between the single individual and social institutions without either of the two sides having to sacrifice its underlying principles of existence? His diagnosis of the modern era was that such mediating instances were missing. As a consequence, the relationship between the individual and the cultural world was distorted, 'individualization', 'exaggeration' and 'paralyza-tion' representing only three of the problems of modern culture (Nedelmann, 1991). It is exactly because this leitmotiv forces us to look at both sides of sociation, to individual interaction and emerging social institutions, that it lends itself self-evidently as a sociological problematic bridging, and perhaps even integrating, indivi-dualization and globalization theories.

OVERCOMING MORALIZING AND TRIVIALIZING SOCIOLOGY BY LEARNING SIMMEL'S LESSONS

The present internal fragmentation of our discipline has not only increased the uncertainty of how to legitimize sociology internally, but also externally. There are two extreme ways in which contemporary sociologists typically react to the weakening of external support. They either trivialize or moralize the role of sociology in contemporary society. Whereas the first type of reaction underestimates the task of our discipline, the second one overestimates it by deliberately taking over political and moral competences we sociologists are not trained for. Both trivialization and moralization are unpro-fessional scientific strategies for filling the legitimacy gap.

It is not only by his merits, but also by his obvious weaknesses that Simmel can teach we contemporary sociologists how to react profes-sionally in such a situation of legitimacy crisis. As founders not only of sociology but also of the German Association of Sociology, Simmel and his contemporaries took special care in defining sociology as an autonomous academic field obeying its own set of rules. Not moral rules, but only the ethics of science itself were considered by them as the basis of sociology. When Weber, Simmel, Sombart and others jointly left the German Association of Sociology in 1912, they did it in protest against attempts at moralizing sociology and thereby deconstructing our field as an independent self-regulating academic disci-pline. Their declaration of *Werturteilsfreiheit* was a commitment towards sociology as a discipline that refrains from making value-judgements, simply because it is beyond the competence of professional sociologists to decide moral values.

As is well known, Simmel broke with this professional rule when he, in 1914, started lecturing about the war and propagated militar-ism as a solution to the cultural problems of modernity. His *Kriegsschriften* (GSG 16: 7–58), published in 1917, are a warning of how even the most brilliant and sharp sociological thought can be deconstructed by one-sided political judge-ments. Therefore, and only therefore, his writings on the war deserve re-reading whenever voices are raised today for moralizing or politicizing our discipline. The fact that Simmel wrote *The Field of Sociology* in the same year (1917) shows that his commitment to the professional role dominated his temporary aberrations in the field of political judgements. Let us, therefore, by way of conclusion, return to Simmel the professional sociologist, in order to see what positive lessons we can learn from him.

The *first* lesson to be learned could be summarized as consisting in the principle of *theoretical homelessness*. The greater the frag-mentation of our discipline, the greater the felt need among sociologists to find, as it were, a theoretical home. The belongingness to one theoretical home helps identify ourselves and others in a situation in which it is more and more difficult (if not impossible) to get an overview of our field. The security of belonging to a theor-etical home has a high price. We limit our perspective of how to look at the empirical world by wanting the latter to fit our theory and to stabilize our theoretical fortress. Not seeking shelter under any theoretical roof, Simmel can teach us to take higher risks as theoretically homeless sociologists. Instead of only looking for empirical facts confirming his findings, he also searched for those contradicting them. He systematically practiced (in the 'silent second' mentioned above) a procedure which, following Popper, could be called the procedure of 'conjecture and self-refutation'. By refusing to integrate his contradictory findings into a closed theoretical system, he expressed his resistance against any kind of dogmatic thinking. He consciously exposed himself to the risk that goes hand in hand with self-refutation and theoretical homelessness, that is, of not being easily identified in the midst of a sociological landscape made up of closed theory buildings. The present tendencies towards dogmatic self-closure and fragmentation could be overcome by taking higher professional risks and following Simmel's principle of theoretical homelessness and the procedure of self-refutation.

There is a *second* lesson to be learned from Simmel. As a *problem-finder*, he presents the counter-type to present theory builders who consider their main role as consisting in solving problems. Simmel's sociology does not teach us how to solve problems, but rather how to *find* problems (Krähnke, 1999: 100). As we have argued here, Simmel's problem-finding activities are systematically guided by his conceptual frame of reference and by a set of recurrently used variables. In his 'Notes on Problem-Finding in Sociology', Merton (1959: ix) quotes the experience of scientists according to which 'it is often more difficult to find and formulate a problem than to solve it'. To this it could be added that it is also more difficult for the student to follow problem-finding than problem-solving scientific activities. Ready-made theory constructions are easier to pass on to next generations of scholars than ever-so systematic procedures of problem-finding. Problem-finding activities are generally less gratifying than problem-solving activities. The way in which empirical research is institutionalized today has as a natural consequence to put a premium on solving problems others have defined for us. This is why skills in problem-finding are less cultivated in contemporary sociology. Re-reading Simmel could correct this shortcoming and bring back the figure of the sociologist as a problem-finder. In autonomously finding and defining our problems, we could raise the autonomy of our discipline and, as a consequence, also its internal and external legitimacy.

The *third* lesson to be learned by Simmel is his sociological glance. In his concluding paragraph of *The Self-Maintenance of Social Groups* (GSG 5: 371/2; my translation), Simmel stresses: 'What is most important is to sharpen the glance for that which is sociological in a particular phenomenon and that which belongs into the realm of other sciences – in order for sociology to finally stop digging in an already occupied territory.' To sharpen the sociological glance today is more important than ever, unless sociology wants to run the risk of being dissolved in the great melting pot of the social sciences. If our sociological glance is obscured by moral concepts, we dig in fields already occupied by professional politics; if we trivialize our professional role, our eyes can only grasp a small fraction of sociologically relevant phenomena. To sharpen the sociological glance means,

following Simmel, to look at the empirical world through the perspective of *interaction* (including the research implications of relationality, self-referentiality and process-analysis). This may seem a modest, perhaps too modest, sociological perspective. But, as Simmel writes in concluding his study on the *Metropolis* (GSG 7: 131), it is neither our task to accuse, nor to forgive, but only to understand. Simmel's Goethe epigraph quoted at the outset can also function as a motto for Simmel scholars in the next century: 'The century has run its course, but the single individual has to start all over again.' German-reading students are encouraged to start their Simmel research all over again by the fact that the edition of Simmel's *oeuvre* will soon be completed. However, they are well advised to integrate into their work, more than they have done before, the foundations laid especially by Levine in the past three decades for a better understanding of Simmel's sociology. Concerning students who are dependent upon English translations of Simmel's texts, Alan Sica (1997: 294) may be right when saying: 'The chance that a hermeneutically competent rendering of Simmel will glide into the canon . . . is small, . . . until Levine or a similarly knowledgeable expert displaces the earlier definitive texts with new ones more reflective of the "complete" Simmel that begins to emerge from Levine's characterization.'

NOTES

1 I wish to thank Sabetai Unguru for style editing and valuable comments, and Ursula Külheim for drawing the graphic.

2 Quoted after Köhnke, 1996: 43; my translation.

3 GSG (*Georg Simmel Gesamtausgabe*) refers to Georg Simmel's *oeuvre* edited by Otthein Rammstedt. At time of writing (May 2000), 13 out of 21 planned volumes of the GSG are available.

4 For a critique of Weinstein and Weinstein (1993), see Nedelmann (1995b) and Jaworsky (1997: 109–23).

5 See also Krähnke's (1999) attempt at demonstrating what he considers Simmel's research program.

6 The following comments are a further elaboration of the conceptual scheme I have presented earlier (Nedelmann, 1999: 133).

7 Levine's (1997b: 198) 'Neo-Simmelian Schema of Social Forms' aims at 'construing the great variety of forms that he [Simmel] treats in terms of relations, processes, roles, collectivities, dynamic patterns, or structural variables'. My attempt at constructing a Simmelian conceptual scheme of reference is more modest: I wish to show how the different concepts Simmel used in his sociological work are linked

together and which main dimensions or variables he used in his empirical research.

8 Simmel makes very explicit that he does not attempt to give a complete description of all the social forms constituting the society (GSG 11: 62).

9 For the present purpose, I have reordered Levine's distinctions between form (3) and (4).

10 See also Smelser (1997: 20–7), who highlights Simmel's contribution to a sociology of emotions, especially trust.

11 I am drawing here both on Levine's numerous works (1971, 1979, 1981, 1997b) and on my own previous attempts (Nedelmann, 1980, 1999).

12 An indication of this fact is the neglect of Merton's concept of sociological ambivalence both by Sztompka (1986) and Clark et al. (1990).

13 I have in mind especially Ulrich Beck and his many followers who, first, propagated theories of individualization and, then, under the label of 'second modernity', theories of globalization (Beck, 1997a, b).

14 For a more detailed analysis of 'The Picture Frame', see Nedelmann (2000).

REFERENCES

Albrow, Martin (1996) *The Global Age. State and Society Beyond Modernity.* Cambridge: Polity Press.

Albrow, Martin, Eade, J., Washbourne, N. and Durrschmidt, J. (1994) 'The Impact of Globalization on Sociological Concepts: Community, Culture and Milieu', *Innovation,* 7 (4): 371–89.

Archer, Margaret S. (1995) *Realist Social Theory: The Morphogenetic Approach.* Cambridge: Cambridge University Press.

Beck, Ulrich (1997a) *Kinder der Freiheit.* Frankfurt a.M.: Suhrkamp.

Beck, Ulrich (1997b) *Was ist Globalisierung? Irrtümer des Globalismus – Antworten auf Globalisierung.* Frankfurt a.M.: Suhrkamp.

Clark, Jon, Modgil, C. and Modgil, S. (eds) (1990) *Robert K. Merton. Consensus and Controversy.* London: The Falmer Press.

Dahme, H.-J. (1981) *Soziologie als exakte Wissenschaft. Georg Simmels Ansatz und seine Bedeutung in der gegenwärtigen Soziologie. Teil I: Simmel im Urteil der Soziologie. Teil II: Simmels Soziologie im Grundriß.* Stuttgart: Enke.

Elster, Jon (1989) *The Cement of Society. A Study of Social Order.* Cambridge: Cambridge University Press.

Frisby, David and Featherstone, M. (1997) 'Introduction to the Texts', in D. Frisby and M. Featherstone (eds), *Simmel on Culture.* London: Sage. pp. 1–31.

GSG 5 (1992) *Georg Simmel: Aufsätze und Abhandlungen 1894 bis 1900* (ed. H.J. Dahme and D. Frisby).

Georg Simmel Gesamtausgabe (ed. O. Rammstedt). Frankfurt a.M.: Suhrkamp.

GSG 7 (1995) *Georg Simmel: Aufsätze und Abhandlungen 1901 bis 1908. Band 1* (ed. R. Kramme, A. Rammstedt and O. Rammstedt). *Georg Simmel Gesamtausgabe* (ed. O. Rammstedt). Frankfurt a.M.: Suhrkamp.

GSG 8 (1993) *Georg Simmel: Aufsätze und Abhandlungen 1901 bis 1908. Band 2* (ed. A. Cavalli and V. Krech). *Georg Simmel Gesamtausgabe* (ed. O. Rammstedt). Frankfurt a.M.: Suhrkamp.

GSG 11 (1992) *Soziologie* (ed. O. Rammstedt). *Georg Simmel Gesamtausgabe* (ed. O. Rammstedt). Frankfurt a.M.: Suhrkamp.

GSG 16 (1999) *Der Krieg und die geistigen Entscheidungen. Grundfragen der Soziologie. Vom Wesen des historischen Verstehens. Der Konflikt der modernen Kultur. Lebensanschauung* (ed. G. Fitzi and O. Rammstedt). *Georg Simmel Gesamtausgabe* (ed. O. Rammstedt). Frankfurt a.M.: Suhrkamp.

Jaworsky, Gary (1997) *Georg Simmel and the American Prospect.* New York: State University of New York Press.

Jepperson, Ronald L. (1991) 'Institutions, Institutional Effects, and Institutionalism', in W.W. Powell and P.J. DiMaggio (eds), *The New Institutionalism in Organizational Analysis.* Chicago: University of Chicago Press. pp. 143–63.

Köhnke, Klaus Ch. (1996) *Der junge Simmel in Theoriebeziehungen und sozialen Bewegungen.* Frankfurt a.M.: Suhrkamp.

Krähnke, Uwe (1999) 'Dynamisierte Theoriebildung. Das Forschungsprogramm von Georg Simmel', *Berliner Journal für Soziologie,* 9 (1): 85–104.

Levine, Donald N. (1971) 'Introduction', in D.N. Levine (ed.), *Georg Simmel on Individuality and Social Forms.* Chicago: University of Chicago Press. pp. ix–lxv.

Levine, Donald N. (1979) 'Simmel at a Distance: On the History and Systematics of the Sociology of the Stranger', in W.A. Shack and E.P. Skinner (eds), *Strangers in African Societies.* Berkeley, CA: University of California Press. pp. 21–36.

Levine, Donald N. (1981) 'Sociology's Quest for the Classics: The Case of Georg Simmel', in B. Rhea (ed.), *The Future of the Sociological Classics.* London: Allen and Unwin. pp. 60–80.

Levine, Donald N. (1985) *The Flight from Ambiguity: Essays in Social and Cultural Theory.* Chicago: University of Chicago Press.

Levine, Donald N. (1997a) 'Social Theory as Vocation', *Perspectives. The ASA Theory Section Newsletter,* 19 (2) (no pagination).

Levine, Donald N. (1997b) 'Simmel Reappraised: Old Images, New Scholarship', in Ch. Camic (ed.), *Reclaiming the Sociological Classics.* Oxford: Blackwell. pp. 173–207.

Marcuse, Ludwig (1958) 'Erinnerungen an Simmel', in K. Gassen and M. Landmann (eds), *Buch des Dankes an Georg Simmel. Briefe, Erinnerungen, Bibliographie.* Berlin: Duncker and Humblot. pp. 188–92.

Merton, Robert K. (1959) 'A Note on Problem-Finding in Sociology', in R.K. Merton, L. Broom and L.S. Cottrell Jr (eds), *Sociology today. Problems and Prospects.* New York: Basic Books. pp. ix–xxxiv.

Merton, Robert K. (1976) *Sociological Ambivalence and Other Essays.* New York: The Free Press.

Nedelmann, Birgitta (1980) 'Strukturprinzipien der soziologischen Denkweise Georg Simmels', *Kölner Zeitschrift für Soziologie und Sozialpsychologie,* 32 (3): 559–73.

Nedelmann, Birgitta (1984) 'Georg Simmel als Klassiker soziologischer Prozeßanalyse', in O. Rammstedt and H.-J. Dahme (eds), *Georg Simmel und die Moderne.* Frankfurt a.M.: Suhrkamp. pp. 91–115.

Nedelmann, Birgitta (1990) 'On the Concept of "Erleben" in Georg Simmel's Sociology', in M. Kaern, B.S. Phillips and R.S. Cohen (eds), *Georg Simmel and Contemporary Sociology.* Dordrecht: Kluwer Academic Publishers. pp. 225–41.

Nedelmann, Birgitta (1991) 'Individualization, Exaggeration and Paralysation: Simmel's Three Problems of Culture', *Theory, Culture and Society,* 8 (3): 169–93.

Nedelmann, Birgitta (1995a) 'Gegensätze und Dynamik politischer Institutionen', in B. Nedelmann (ed.), *Politische Institutionen im Wandel.* Opladen: Westdeutscher Verlag. pp. 15–40.

Nedelmann, Birgitta (1995b) Review essay: 'Sellerberg, Ann-Mari: *A Blend of Contradictions. Georg Simmel in Theory and Practice*' in Deena Weinstein and Michael A. Weinstein: *Postmodern(ized) Simmel'.* New York: Routledge 1993, *Contemporary Sociology,* 23 (6): 403–5.

Nedelmann, Birgitta (1997) 'Ambivalenz als Interaktionsform und Interaktionsnorm', in H.O. Luthe, and R.E. Wiedenmann (eds), *Ambivalenz.* Opladen: Leske and Budrich. pp. 149–63.

Nedelmann, Birgitta (1999) 'Georg Simmel (1858–1918)', in D. Kaesler (ed.), *Klassiker der Soziologie.* Munich: C.H. Beck. pp. 127–49.

Nedelmann, Birgitta (2000) 'At the Turn of the Centuries: Georg Simmel Then and Now', in M. Kohli and A. Woodward (eds), *European Societies: Inclusion/Exclusion.* London: Routledge, forthcoming.

Rammstedt, Otthein (1992) 'Editorischer Bericht', in GSG 11: 877–905.

Rammstedt, Otthein (1999) 'Editorischer Bericht', in GSG 16: 426–42.

Scaff, Lawrence A. (1989) *Fleeing the Iron Cage. Culture, Politics, and Modernity in the Thought of Max Weber.* Berkeley, CA: University of California Press.

Sellerberg, Ann-Mari (1994) *A Blend of Contradictions. Georg Simmel in Theory and Practice.* New Brunswick, NJ: Transaction Books.

Sica, Alan (1997) 'Acclaiming the Reclaimers: the Trials of Writing Sociology's History', in Ch. Camic (ed.), *Reclaiming the Sociological Classics.* London: Blackwell. pp. 282–98.

Simmel, Georg (1958) 'Anfang einer unvollendeten Selbstdarstellung', in K. Gassen and M. Landmann (eds), *Buch des Dankes an Georg Simmel. Briefe, Erinnerungen, Bibliographie.* Berlin: Duncker and Humblot. pp. 9–10.

Simmel, Georg (1976) 'The Field of Sociology', in *Georg Simmel: Sociologist and European* (ed. P.A. Lawrence). Sunbury-on-Thames: Nelson.

Simmel, Georg (1984) 'Flirtation', in G. Simmel, *On Women, Sexuality and Love* (trans. and ed. G. Oakes). New Haven, CT: Yale University Press. pp. 133–52.

Smelser, Neil J. (1997) *Problematics of Sociology. The Georg Simmel Lectures, 1995.* Berkeley, CA: University of California Press.

Sztompka, Piotr (1986) *Robert K. Merton: An Intellectual Profile.* Basingstoke: Macmillan.

Sztompka, Piotr (1998) 'Trust, Distrust and Two Paradoxes of Democracy', *European Journal of Social Theory,* 1 (1): 19–32.

Weinstein, Deena and Weinstein, M.A. (1993) *Postmodern(ized) Simmel.* New York: Routledge.

Weiß, Johannes (1998) 'Die Zweite Moderne – eine neue Suhrkamp-Edition', *Soziologische Revue,* 21 (4): 415–26.

7

Durkheim's Project for a Sociological Science

MIKE GANE

Durkheim did not claim to be the founder of sociology, but he did claim to have made a decisive modification to the intellectual tradition that originates from Saint-Simon and Comte. There is today considerable interest in the precise balance of influences on Durkheim's thought and the complexity of his cultural and religious origins (see Strenski, 1997, which fills a gap in the standard biography by Steven Lukes, 1973). Discoveries of more texts from all periods of his career have opened up more lines of enquiry (e.g. Durkheim, 1996, 1997). These new materials are likely to be influential in making interpretation of Durkheim's intellectual career more sensitive to the way Durkheim's sociology intervened in the currents of French thought and politics in the period of the Third Republic, as they show the emergence of a sophisticated confrontation with the positivist tradition on the one hand, and idealist, neo-Kantian schools on the other (Gross, 1996). These reassessments are part of a considerable shift in the evaluation of Durkheimian sociology from one dominated by identifying Durkheim as a crude functionalist, either of the extreme left, centre or right, to one that recognizes the radical theoretical and political complexity of the Durkheimian project. It is this continuing interest in Durkheim which attests to the importance of the intellectual challenges and puzzles created in his sociological and philosophical writings.

Durkheim's sociology belongs to a tradition which was evolutionist and holistic, and because of this refused to acknowledge a break between anthropology and sociology. It believed the role of social science was to provide guidance for specific kinds of social intervention. Crucial for the success of this project was for sociology to align itself with the other more established sciences within the institutional orbit of the higher educational system, the universities, a relatively autonomous haven for research which could remain free from direct political partisanship, particularly where scientific knowledge and practice arises within a democratic society basing itself on popular sovereignty. As part of this endeavour, the concept of social pathology was given considerable importance, revealing the extent to which Durkheim's sociology was consciously modelled on the medical ideal of therapeutic intervention. There was no fundamental philosophical reason why sociology could not define and legitimate in its own special way social and moral norms. An essential part of Durkheim's project was to work out specific rules for determining the distinction between normal and pathological social phenomena. In this respect Durkheim went much further in a direction outlined in principle by Comte and Spencer.

Although Durkheim secured a position teaching social sciences at the University of Bordeaux from 1887, his initial formation was in philosophy and he had taught philosophy at Lycées (Sens, Saint-Quentin and Troyes). His position at Bordeaux and later in Paris (from 1902) also required that he teach courses in education as well as sociology. The corpus of Durkheim's work consists of major books (*The Division of Labour in Society*, *The Rules of Sociological Method*, *Suicide* and *The Elementary Forms of the Religious Life*), a small number of minor books (on *Montesquieu*, *Primitive Classification* (with Mauss), *Moral Education*), but also important lecture courses that were published posthumously (*Socialism, Professional Ethics, The Evolution of Educational Thought in France*) and courses which are based on notes taken by students (*Pragmatism*). There are also a large number of journal articles, some of which were gathered into collections, there are verbatim reports of debates, book reviews and letters (his letters to Marcel Mauss, for example, were published for the first time in 1998). But Durkheim did not work alone or in isolation, he founded a school of sociology organized around the journal called *L'Année Sociologique*. The aim of the project thus organized was to ensure the implantation of sociology within the universities as a reputable discipline with a vital role to play in the identification of the normal forms of the emerging institutional structures of modern societies.

A notable feature of Durkheim's sociological writing is its highly rationalist idioms. This is particularly clear in his methodological requirements, with their demand for clear and precise conceptual definition, rigorous formulation of problems, careful consideration for quality of evidence, canons of proof. The demand is that sociology should break with the prevailing ideological methods and establish a scientific rigour that can facilitate the discovery of the basic social laws governing social development and the formation of different modes of social solidarity. It is clear in this respect that Durkheim follows in general the aims outlined by Comte in his *Cours de philosophie positive* (1830–42), yet Durkheim criticized in detail the specific forms of Comte's analyses and their results. It is very striking, for example, that Durkheim first of all focused on what he called 'moral facts' as against the emphasis on cognition in Comte's law of the three states. Indeed, Durkheim's studies reveal something missing in Comte: a serious absence of any sociological consideration of morals, laws, norms, sanctions, in the treatment of religion, culture and social development.

Durkheim's emphasis seems to reflect a new awareness of the importance of Kant's work and the problem of the relation between the individual and society, and can be seen as an attempt to unify within the sociological project the perspectives, transformed in a certain way, of both Kant and Comte (and Spencer). In Durkheim's work on social categories, the sociology of knowledge and sociology of religion there is also a broader concern to deal with the philosophical problems raised by these two earlier writers and to place their ideas, suitably reconstructed, into a single analytical frame.

Durkheim repeated several times that he was 'following the path opened up' by Comte ([1907]

1980: 77), but was doing so in a specific way. He remained highly critical of Comtean epistemology and the way Comte's law of the three states was formulated: 'if, as Comte thought, historical development is unilinear, if it is constituted by a single and unique series which begins with humanity itself and continues without end, it is evident that, since all terms of comparison are lacking, it cannot be reduced to laws' ([1906] 1980: 73). The law of the three social states, theological, metaphysical and positive, was not for Durkheim an adequate conceptualization of social species: it was essentially arbitrary – for why should evolution stop at the third state? Yet if Durkheim was hostile to the general form of Comte's sociology he affirmed very specifically Comte's analysis of European history since the middle ages: 'Comte's law correctly describes the way modern societies have developed from the tenth to the nineteenth century – but it does not apply to the entire course of human evolution' ([1928] 1962: 268). And rather than adopt Comte's terminology of the three states, he opted for a modified version of the morphological classification developed by Herbert Spencer, a classification by mode and degree of complexity of social composition, from segmental to organized societal forms. Durkheim was at pains to insist the form was not unilinear, but involved genuine non-teleological diversity: 'the genealogical tree of organized beings, instead of having the form of a geometric line, resembles more nearly a very bushy tree whose branches, issuing haphazardly all along the trunk, shoot out capriciously in all directions' ([1888] 1978: 53). Thus Durkheim made a fine distinction between the genealogical analysis within a single real continuous society (historical sequence), a comparative analysis within a single society and societies of the same type, and a much more abstract comparative cross-cultural analysis leading to the construction of theoretical evolutionary typologies.

It is important to specify what is involved in these distinctions. Wallwork (1984) has attempted to specify a six-stage model of Durkheim's evolutionary conception at the beginning of his career: the elementary horde, simple clan-based tribe, tribal confederation, ancient city-state, medieval society, modern industrial nation. In this perspective Durkheim divides these societies into two basic types, and in this respect he departs from Spencer: the societies that are 'mechanical' accretions of elements (kinship groups) as 'compound' or 'doubly compound' in Spencer's terms, as against those societies that are organized on the basis of an 'organic' division of labour and interdependent specialization of function (comprising medieval society and the modern nation). The idea of basing a classification on what is called social morphology, or what has become since Spencer known as social structure, is quite different from one based on cultural configuration such as can be found in Comte's sociology. For Comte, rather as for Marx, it was essentially one decisive element in society, its determining element, the method of knowing, which should form the basis of classification. Comte's classification, in effect, followed a parallel five-stage model: fetishist, polytheist, monotheist, metaphysical and positive societal types, in a single logical sequence explained by the struggle of positive reason against theological reason. Marx, of course, also had a five-stage model: primitive communism, slave, feudal, capitalist and higher communist societies, a sequence determined by the economic mode of production and class struggle.

There are notable differences between the models of Marx and Comte on the one hand, and Spencer and Durkheim on the other. In the first place, for Marx and Comte the final stage is a messianic logical construction of a future utopian state. For Spencer and Durkheim the sequence contains no reference to the future, which remains in principle open and unknowable. The Spencer–Durkheim scheme is descriptively and empirically holistic: it does not depend on a presumed part–whole form of causal theory. Thirdly, when theory is introduced, both Spencer and Durkheim reject the idea that there is a simple development of forms of social inequality through the sequence. Such stratification is affected not only by degree of social complexity, but by the distribution of power in society and this is decisively determined by the condition and form of social mobilization: for war, external or civil, or peace and industry. In other words, Spencer and Durkheim reorganized the Comtean evolutionary thesis that society moves from warlike to industrial occupations, to one in which these can be found as modal states at any stage of development.

PROBLEMS OF METHOD

Following in Comte's footsteps, Durkheim attempted to specify the unique domain of sociological phenomena within the branches of the scientific division of labour. It is tempting to suggest that this is an attempt to align sociology within the rationalist tradition stemming from Bacon and Descartes. But Durkheim insists that rules of method are strictly parallel with other ethical and moral rules: 'methodological rules are for science what rules of law and custom are for conduct', and whereas the natural sciences appear to form common ground, the

'moral and social sciences' are in a state of anomie: 'the jurist, the psychologist, the anthropologist, the economist, the statistician, the linguist, the historian, proceed with their investigations as if the different orders of fact they study constituted so many different worlds' ([1893] 1964: 368). Rules of method are far more than rules for gathering information. They organize and regulate the field and identify the ground for scientific strategies and legitimate the way these strategies should be assessed. Durkheim's writings on methodology, not surprisingly, have given rise to important controversies. These are of two kinds. The first concern the orientation and content of some of the rules. The second the apparent conflict between certain rules.

The methodological orientation is from the start one which strives for maximal objectivity of investigation. As if traumatized by a surfeit of individual and subjective introspection, even the primary definition of the terrain of sociology itself, the very object of social analysis, Durkheim formulated as 'any way of acting, whether fixed or not, capable of exerting over the individual an external constraint' ([1895] 1982: 59). In this argument, *The Rules of Sociological Method* seems intent on correcting an apparent weakness in previous sociological practice, for the emphasis is insistent: all preconceptions must be discarded, never assume the voluntary character of a social institution, always study social phenomena which are detached from individual forms. The fundamental rule for observing social phenomena is 'to consider social facts as things' ([1895] 1982: 60). It is evident that Durkheim considered the common ideological formation of the sociologist as modern citizen in a sense, and paradoxically, both a support and a fundamental obstacle to social research. His critical judgement is that 'instead of observing, describing and comparing things, we . . . reflect on our ideas . . . Instead of a science which deals with realities, we carry out no more than an ideological analysis' (p. 60). It is no wonder that this particular text has been read as a revolutionary manifesto in sociology, for it essentially demands that each sociologist reverse habitual and everyday forms of thought. In this sense it is a fundamental text in a tradition that includes Comte and Marx as central figures: social science comes into being in a revolutionary, epistemological break with ideological methods.

The very specific character of Durkheim's method is that it carries the idea of objectivity into the very conceptualization of its object, the social itself. The terms social exteriority, constraint, collective, are transcendent as against individual manifestation, and are clearly conceived as decisive for the investigator and for social research in general: the most objective of objects are the fixed social forms and these are to be given priority because they offer a privileged route for investigative analysis. Durkheim is, however, very clear and explicit: these terms are provisional. They are to be adopted in the first instance because they offer the best chance of avoiding significant obstacles to social science. It is clear that as a manifesto, this system of rules does call for a revolutionary transformation in the mode of practice of sociologists, and calls for a commitment to sociology as a vocation. This vision is not concerned with the isolated and lonely genius, but with a collective practice, organized and disciplined within the modern educational system. Sociological research is a collective procedure, its ideas are subjected to rational rules of evidence and verification, unique to sociology. These rules mark out and define a territory for study against competing claims: the domain of social facts.

It is clear, however, that these rules are also closely bound up with Durkheim's own ideas about the content of social analysis, and indeed his own changing and developing research priorities: what seems at first to be an attempt to produce a definitive text on methodology, *The Rules of Sociological Method*, is more complex than its appears. Many of its major formulations had already appeared as the first Introduction to *The Division of Labour in Society* (edition of 1893). This Introduction was replaced in the second edition of 1902, but can be found, as an appendix, in the English translation of 1964 (but not in the second translation of 1984). The first formulation of the field of study is developed in terms not of social but moral facts: 'moral facts consist in a rule of sanctioned conduct' (1964: 425). Durkheim adopts this definition since the study of moral evolution no longer depends on the study of norms but also of sanctions which he conceives as 'an external fact reflecting [an] internal state' (p. 425). His aim remains consistent: the development of the 'positive science of morality is a branch of sociology, for every sanction is principally a social thing' (p. 428). In this first Introduction there is a very clearly demarcated separation between those forms of action which are moral obligations and other 'gratuitous acts' which are at the free choice of the individual and which Durkheim assigns to the domain of aesthetics and art (pp. 430–1).

What happens between this first Introduction to *The Division of Labour* and the appearance of the essays called *The Rules of Sociological Method* which were published separately as articles in 1894 (before appearing in modified book form in 1895), is that all the characteristics of the moral fact are displaced and incorporated into the category of the social fact. It is

significant to note for instance that Durkheim in 1893 referred to a group of acts as 'gratuitous' and outside morals: 'the refinements of worldly urbanity, the ingenuities of politeness . . . the gifts, affectionate words or caresses between friends or relatives, up to the heroic sacrifices that no duty demands . . . The father of a family risks his life for a stranger; who would dare to say that was useful' ([1893] 1964: 430–1). In *The Rules*, however, Durkheim specifies a whole new range of ways in which external constraint occurs from informal sanctions of ridicule and social ostracism to technical and organizational necessities. Moral obligation and sanction form the first object of Durkheim's methodological reflection, but constraint and circumstantial necessity broaden this into the essential characteristics of social facts in general. In these 1894 formulations it is made clear none the less that the sociologist must choose to give primacy to the study of facts from 'a viewpoint where they present a sufficient degree of consolidation' (Durkheim, 1988: 138). By the time the book version of *The Rules* was published in 1895 with a large number of revisions, this particular injunction was changed to the rule that the sociologist 'must strive to consider [social facts] from a viewpoint where they present themselves in isolation from their individual manifestations' (1982: 82–3). It seems clear that Durkheim had altered his research priorities and was edging towards the full scale study of suicide statistics, published in 1897 not long after *The Rules*. Towards the end of *The Rules*, Durkheim gives suicide as an example of a problematic social fact: 'if suicide depends on more than one cause it is because in reality there are several kinds of suicide' (p. 150). The existence of suicide statistics makes it possible for sociologists to study social currents as phenomena that are 'independent of their individual manifestations'. Because the study concerns social rates of suicide there is something more to the phenomena than random 'gratuitous acts'. It is apparent then that far from being a fixed and unique definition of the object of sociology, Durkheim in fact has a number of options which are refocused and specified according to the task at hand. He does not seem to be worried if he does not follow to the letter his own hastily conceived prescriptive rules, as long as he remains consistent at a higher level of epistemological theory.

There was a strong injunction throughout the methodological writings to this point (1895), that the sociologist must start from things not ideas, indeed the sociologist must start from 'a group of phenomena defined beforehand by certain common external characteristics' ([1895] 1982: 75). This strategy demands analysis works from these external features towards an understanding of their internal causal relationships. When investigating suicide statistics Durkheim seems to have started in this way as prescribed by his rules. The procedure required that he group together those suicides with the same external features (for example, how suicides were committed) and 'would admit as many suicide currents as there were distinct types, then seek to determine their causes' ([1897] 1970: 146). In the analysis published as *Suicide* ([1897] 1970), Durkheim says this procedure could not be used, rather he was 'able to determine the social types of suicide by classifying them not directly by their preliminarily described characteristics, but by the causes which produce them' (p. 147). Durkheim uses what he calls 'this reverse method'. Instead of proceeding from the characteristics in the facts themselves, he says 'once the nature of the causes is known we shall try to deduce that nature of the effects . . . Thus we shall descend from causes to effects and our aetiological classification will be completed by a morphological one' (p. 147). It comes as something of a surprise to learn that the social causes of suicides (anomic, egoistic, altruistic) are already known, since the concept of altruism (of Comtean origin of course) has hardly figured in Durkheim's sociology up to this point. It is also surprising that Durkheim could reverse the order of analysis, prescribed so insistently in his recent writings, with such ease and assurance. In the study of suicide rates Durkheim does not group suicides according to an external characteristic of the act of suicide as his previous rules required: he classifies them according to his theory of the major social causes of suicide.

Apart from the problems of orientation and inconsistency of usage, there is also a profound problem concerning the relation of theory to method: are the two independent or dependent? Clearly Durkheim did not think method completely separate from theory but developed alongside the progress of substantive sociology itself. At least in one crucial instance a conflict between a substantive thesis and methodological principle can be identified. This conflict arises in the central chapter (Chapter 3) of *The Rules*, in a discussion which deals with the problem of determining the difference between normal and pathological social facts. It is clear from the social analysis presented in *The Division*, and especially its famous second Introduction to the edition of 1902, that Durkheim considered French society to be in a grave condition of malaise, due to a social structural abnormality: with the abolition of the guild system in the eighteenth century a severe structural imbalance had been introduced into French society. The severe political oscillations which had occurred in French society since then were ultimately a result of this social structural imbalance: only by re-introducing some modern equivalent of the guilds, towards a pattern he called an 'institutional socialism', could the normal system of counter-weights be restored.

The methodological problem posed at the heart of the Durkheimian project was to define unambiguously the way such a question could be resolved. His primary rule is clear: if the social fact is general in the average form of the social species under consideration the fact is to be judged normal. But he introduced another much more theoretical consideration, requiring a demonstration for a normal fact 'that the general character of the phenomenon is related to the general conditions of collective life in the social type under consideration' and this 'verification is necessary when this fact relates to a social species which has not yet gone through its complete evolution' ([1895] 1982: 97). These two rules tend to contradict each other in the case under discussion. If the anomic forms of the division of labour are a continuation of a feature of segmental society, and 'now increasingly dying out, we shall be forced to conclude that this now constitutes a morbid state, however universal it may be' (p. 95). In other words the theoretical analysis of the forms and functions of regulation suggest that economic anomie is pathological even if it is general; the principal rule would suggest its generality indicates normality. This problem goes to the heart of modern Durkheimian scholarship. On the one hand, those Durkheimians who follow the primary empirical rule would be forced to conclude that the modern democratic state with its absence of guild forms has proven to be a normal social type. On the other, those Durkheimians who follow more strictly his theoretical analysis of modern societies with their lack of solidarity see a proliferation of many kinds of social pathological phenomena.

THEORY

Durkheim's basic theory developed and changed over the course of his career, as did his methodological reflections. In the earlier writings he held that primitive societies were characterized by similitudes and passions, while the advanced societies by individualism and calm restraint. He later revised this view completely. One example of this can be seen in his writing on education. In his early lectures on moral education (1973) he argued that there was a plague of violent punishment in the schools of the middle ages, and the lash remained in constant use up until the eighteenth century. After researching his lectures on educational thought in France ([1938] 1977), he describes the idea of the violent medieval colleges as simply 'a legend'. The reason for this, he argues, was that the educational communities remained essentially democratic and these forms 'never have very harsh disciplinary regimes' because 'he who is today judged may tomorrow become the judge' ([1938] 1977: 155–7). The new analysis suggests that the turn towards a more oppressive disciplinary regime began at the end of the sixteenth century, just at the moment when the schools and colleges in France became centralized and cut off from the outside community. In these circumstances, he says, the whip became a regular feature of college life.

In his lectures to teachers Durkheim discussed the problem of how to arrive at a rational approach to discipline and punishment in school. Between the offence and the punishment he observed there is a hidden continuity, for they are not 'two heterogeneous things coupled artificially' ([1925] 1973: 179). Because the mediating term is obscure, a series of misleading theories of punishment arises. One such misleading theory sees punishment as expiation or atonement, another sees it primarily as a way of intimidating or inhibiting further offences. From a pedagogical point of view the problem concerns the capacity to neutralize the demoralizing effects of an infringement of group norms. The true objective of punishment, he argues, is a moral one. Its effectiveness should be judged by how far it contributes to the solidarity of the group as a whole. The problem is that certain kinds of punishment can contribute to the creation of further immoral acts (p. 199), and once applied, punishment seems to lose something of its power. A reign of terror is, in the end, a very weak system of sanctions, even driven to extremes by its own ineffectiveness. The recourse to corporal punishment seems to involve a counter-productive attack on the dignity of the individual, a dignity valued and fostered in modern societies.

The central theoretical issue here was addressed once again in his attempt to reconstruct the theses of *The Division of Labour in Society*, in an article of 1900 called 'Two Laws of Penal Evolution' (1978: 153–80). Durkheim criticizes Spencer for thinking that the degree of absoluteness of governmental power is related to the number of functions it undertakes, but he works towards a very Spencerian formulation: 'the more or less absolute character of the government is not an inherent characteristic of any given social type' (p. 157). Indeed, it is here that Durkheim presents an account of French society that can be seen to be diametrically opposed to that of Marx: 'seventeenth-century France and nineteenth-century France belong to the same type' (p. 157). To think there has been a

change of type is to mistake a conjunctural feature of the society with its fundamental structure, for governmental absolutism arises, not from the constituent features of a social form, but from 'individual, transitory and contingent conditions' in social evolution (p. 157). It is this very complication which makes analysis of social type and analysis of the logic of this type taken with the specific form of governmental power extremely complex, since transitory forms of power can neutralize long run social organization.

Durkheim's argument suggests social theory is often mistaken in thinking the state as either a purely repressive machine, or that the purely political division of powers can deliver political and social liberty in the fullest sense. For Durkheim, the thesis that freedom is freedom from the state ignores the fact that it is the state 'that has rescued the child from family tyranny [and] the citizen from feudal groups and later from communal groups'. Indeed, Durkheim argues the state must not limit itself to the administration of 'prohibitive justice . . . [it] must deploy energies equal to those for which it has to provide a counter-balance' ([1950] 1992: 64). Against the political illusion of power, for example as found in Montesquieu, Durkheim in effect tries to show that liberty is based on a particular form of the total social division of power: the state 'must even permeate all those secondary groups of family, trade and professional association, Church, regional areas, and so on . . .' ([1950] 1992: 64) if the full potentialities of human development are to be realized.

But the state can become too strong and develop its own pathological dimensions and capacities. In his pamphlet *'Germany Above All': German Mentality and War* (1915) he presented a critique of the ideas of the German political philosopher Heinrich Treitschke, which he took to be representative of the mentality that brought war not just to France and Europe in 1914. He was careful in fact to say that he was not analysing the causes of war, only one of the manifestations of a condition of social pathology (1915: 46). Durkheim contrasts the democratic idea in which there is a continuity between government and people with Treitschke's thesis that there is a radical antagonism between state and civil society. This latter idea requires a state power capable of enforcing a mechanical obedience from its citizens – their first duty is to obey its dictates – and leaders who are possessed of enormous ambition, unwavering determination, with personalities characterized by aspects that have 'something harsh, caustic, and more or less detestable' about them (pp. 30–4). In practice these states flout international law and conventions, and their idea of war pushes the development of military technologies which are almost 'exempt from the laws of gravity . . . [t]hey seem to transport us into an unreal world, where nothing can any longer resist the will of man' (p. 46).

This analysis of the German war mentality draws on Durkheim's crucial concept of anomic states, developed most clearly with respect to anomic forms of the division of labour ([1893] 1964: 353–73) and anomic suicides ([1897] 1970: 241–76). It is evident from Durkheim's first formulations of this idea that it is derived from Comte, who developed it in relation to an analysis of the unregulated division of the modern sciences. Durkheim also follows Comte's conception (itself derived from Broussais) of pathological facts as exceptional phenomena, that is exhibiting exceptionally high or low intensities. Thus crime, for example, is not in itself an abnormal feature of human societies: the sociologist has to determine normal and abnormal rates of crime. Changing intensities of social facts in Durkheimian theory are determined in relation to modifications in the power dynamics of social systems. Where there is a shift towards the concentration of power in the state, as occurs in wartime, the structures protecting individual values are weakened. In wartime there is to be expected not only an increase in altruistic suicide, most commonly associated with military organization (1970: 228ff.), but also an increase in civil homicides since the individual as such is less protected in moral value (1992: 110–20).

It seems clear that there is a long-term continuity in Durkheim's interest in moral statistics from the early essay on variations in birth rates through a range of studies of family, divorce, to political statistics (Turner, 1993). This aspect of his sociology has attracted attention as installing an experimental rationalism as a founding moment in the modern discipline (see Berthelot, 1995: 75–105). But this is to overlook the dependence of this methodology on the theoretical frame derived in large measure from Comte, and acknowledged by Durkheim. Whereas Comte focused on a single line of evolution unifying the historical experience of humanity as a whole, Durkheim investigated the dispersive branchings of social evolution and this strategy may have legitimized a more experimental and comparative methodological inventiveness. There is also a marked difference in the conception of the role of theory in sociology between Durkheim and Comte. For the latter, the aim of analysis is to be able to construct a hierarchical system of laws of co-variation: no reference to causal explanation is required; for Durkheim the role of theory is paramount in the search for causes, and is essential for a complete sociological explanation

of social laws. Durkheim, it must be stressed, still embraced the aim of discovering basic social laws, and many of these are formulated in his early works. These are always related to a causal or aetiological analysis, which even becomes the explicit organizing principle, as is the case in *Suicide*.

Durkheim's theoretical frame did not remain static, as has already be indicated. The most evident development of theory in Durkheim's work can be found by comparing the depiction of early societies in the two studies at each end of his career: *The Division of Labour in Society* ([1893]) and *The Elementary Forms of the Religious Life* ([1912] 1995). In the first study the fundamental fact of the early societies is that they are held together by 'bonds of similitude' and characterized by intense and violent reactions to infringements of the highly uniform 'collective consciousness'. There is little in the way of social differentiation, even the gender division of labour is so slight there is no contractual regulation between the sexes. The era of 'mechanical solidarity' was one of sexual promiscuity ([1893] 1964: 57–8). Durkheim's investigations into Australian tribal society led him to change this view fundamentally. He came to see kinship organization as complex, and based on deeply embedded forms of sexual and age divisions. He came to see social structure as the complex outcome of symbolic practices, particularly those crystallized in ritual traditions. He established the thesis that ritual beliefs were structured on knowledge categories which were socially produced and reproduced. Fundamental to such systems of religious categories were the concepts of the sacred and profane, good and evil, which were involved both in organizing such rituals and being at the same time produced by them. Instead of elaborating or criticizing Comte's theory of early societies as being characterized by forms of fetishism (worship organized in relation to charged objects), Durkheim suggested that the earliest form of religion was totemistic (group kinship and religious practices were organized in relation to a hierarchy of objects: the totemic emblem, the totemic group, the totemic species). The practices of the group produced widely different forms of experience, for example, religious effervescent, high-energy ceremonials contrasted with low-energy utilitarian food gathering. These socially produced distinctions formed the material basis for category differentiation. In this way Durkheim thought he could arrive at a definitive sociological critique of Kantian a priorism on the one hand, and Spencerian individualism on the other. Durkheim tried to identify those groups which could draw moral strength from the solidarities produced by sacred rituals, and those with weaker solidarity who would then be vulnerable to the process of scapegoating, for example misfortunes befalling the group were blamed on women ([1912] 1995: 404).

Durkheim developed a theory of the fundamental importance of gender as he encountered the materials on Australian totemism. These also led to a theory of sacred categories, of good and evil, on top of the distinction between the sacred and profane social spheres, a distinction which Durkheim showed to be drawn in ritual practice. This investigation also tried to show that the idea of the individual soul was intimately linked to the structure of social groups and their internal differentiation (in some groups for example, women did not have souls). Because Durkheim's attention had shifted to these symbolic processes and practices of intervention in and reproduction of such symbolic materials, it has been assumed in some interpretations that his whole sociology had itself become a subjective exercise in symbolic interactionism (Stone and Farberman, 1967). It seems clear from the text of *The Elementary Forms*, in fact, that there was no break in continuity of methodological reflection and prescription. However, the focus of analysis was no longer on the transcendent external modes of sanctioned conduct (moral facts), but had moved to social epistemology, or what he called 'the sociology of knowledge and religion' which examined the way immanent infrastructures imposed their exigencies on action. In other words, Durkheim had moved to a large scale and empirically based study of the cognitive structures of the earliest societies: Comtean terrain, but Durkheim locates his discussion almost entirely with respect to post-Comtean theory, and in a very different theoretical strategy.

THE CURRENT SITUATION

If we review the reception of Durkheim's work among anthropologists and sociologists it is very apparent that there has been a good deal of theoretical confusion as to the precise nature and meaning of Durkheim's methodology. The adoption of structural functionalism in America showed that the methodology could be adapted for social analysis in an advanced democracy. But there was a reaction which can be seen in Lukes' extreme introduction to the second English translation (1982). More recent discussion, particularly the balanced accounts in the conference proceedings of the centennial meeting in Bordeaux (Cuin, 1997), point to the epistemological sophistication of Durkheim's interventions.

Method is increasingly seen as the key to understanding the strategic connections in Durkheim's sequence of studies. Against this continuity, the studies themselves have come under considerable substantive criticism. *The Division of Labour in Society*, for example, came under considerable critical attack in the writings of Sheleff (1975), and Lukes and Scull (in Durkheim, 1983). *Suicide* came under severe criticism by subjectivist trends in sociology, particularly social constructionists, from Douglas (1967), Pope (1976) to Atkinson (1978). *The Elementary Forms of Religious Life* has had an equally problematic career. After the text appeared, its central theses were frontally attacked by a range of writers. Adam Kuper has reviewed these criticisms and concludes that the 'model of a segmentary structure based on unilineal descent groups is a sociological fantasy' (Kuper, 1985: 235). Other critics have argued that the whole problematic of totemic society is as false as that of Comte's theory of fetishism. The paradox is, therefore, why does Durkheim's work remain significant? Kuper suggests the 'apparently paradoxical fruitfulness of Durkheim's work, despite its substantive failure, is . . . due to the power of certain elements of his methodology; to the importance of some of the questions which he set on the agenda of the next generation; and, above all, to the sense which he communicated of the richness, complexity and sociological interest of ethnographic materials' (1985: 235).

From the 1960s different styles of Durkheimian scholarship were pursued against the trend of Durkheim criticism. These included most notably the work of Jeffrey Alexander in cultural theory (1988), Frank Pearce in politics and law (1989), Steve Taylor on suicide (1982), Mike Gane on method (1988) and institutional socialism (1992), Jennifer Lehmann in gender theory (1994), W.S.F. Pickering in the sociology of religion (1984), Mark Cladis on ethics and liberalism (1992), W. Watts Miller on ethics and politics (1996), S. Mestrovic on postmodern culture (1988, 1991, 1992) and Warren Schmaus on methodology (1994). There were a number of thematic collections which attempted to address certain themes; collections edited by Stephen Turner on religion and morality (1993), Allen, Pickering and Watts Miller's collection on *The Elementary Forms* (1998). Further collections on *Suicide*, and on *Collective Representations*, are in press. Pickering and Martins' *Debating Durkheim* (1994) addressed a wide range of issues in dispute. Many of these debates and publications have been organized by the British Centre for Durkheimian Studies, directed by W.S.F. Pickering, at Oxford. During this period there have been a number of introductions to Durkheim's works which have been far more positive than that of Anthony Giddens, particularly those by Ken Thompson (1982), Robert Alun Jones (1986) and Frank Parkin (1992). A move towards a *rapprochement* between the Weberian and Durkheimian traditions is now well under way (see Boudon, 1995).

It seems clear in retrospect, however, that Durkheim's work entered in the 1960s a period of intense critical scrutiny after being, in the United States particularly, the dominant sociological paradigm (see Parsons, 1937 and Merton, 1949). The point at which the rejection of Durkheim's method and theory reached its height was perhaps at around 1980 with three essays: a 'Critical Commentary' on Durkheim's work by Anthony Giddens (Giddens, 1978: 101–20), an assessment of the adequacy of Durkheim's theory as an 'integrated sociological paradigm' (Ritzer and Bell, 1981), and the vitriolic introduction by Steven Lukes to the second (1982) translation of *The Rules of Sociological Method*. In the 1990s a series of conferences and theme-based publications produced a complex *fin de siècle* balance sheet. At first sight the question might seem to be whether these publications mark the end of a period, or announce a rebirth of Durkheimian perspectives. But the issue is probably more complex and less heroic. On the one hand, after a period in which the core sociological problems were related to Marx, Durkheim and Weber (see Morrison, 1995), there is likely to be a recovery of the wider band of influences on social theory, back into the eighteenth century as a way of contextualizing the irruption of sociology at the beginning of the nineteenth century (Comte, Mill, Littre, Spencer), and a wider appreciation of the theorists at the beginning of the twentieth century (including Pareto, Tönnies, Simmel and others). Twentieth-century sociology is marked by a division arising out of the legacy of the Durkheim school: the direction taken by structural modernist sociology, and another direction, influenced by Georges Bataille, leading towards postmodernism.

What is the significance of the Durkheimian legacy in this picture? Although Durkheim himself stressed the role of decisive discoveries in the progression of a science, it seems there is another important critical function in the growth of sociological knowledge. As against making discoveries this might be called learning from errors. It might thus be the case, and paradoxically, that Durkheim's empirical analyses have been shown to be at best only partially successful. The great strength of these studies was that they were experimental, and in important respects Durkheim often tried to improve his analyses where they became evidently untenable. He did this with great theoretical skill and

inventiveness, always aware of the importance of reconstructing his conceptual schemes and methodological controls. His analytic scheme is not confused with empirical evidence and this makes it possible to check and correct, or reject his analyses. This process has become an essential element of modern sociology. It was not inaugurated by Durkheim, whose treatment of Comte for example was not exemplary. It was inaugurated by scholars working on the Durkheim corpus, and became an essential moment in the formation of all modern sociologists.

BIBLIOGRAPHICAL NOTE

The standard reference source for Durkheim's publications is Steven Lukes' *Emile Durkheim* (1973) and updated in the second edition (1992).

There have been a number of special issues on Durkheim. Three notable and useful ones are:
Social Forces, 1981, vol. 59, no. 4
Studies in the History and Philosophy of Science, 1982, vol. 13, no. 4
Journal of the History of the Behavioural Sciences, 1996, vol. 32, no. 4

There have also been two sets (each of four volumes) of *Emile Durkheim: Critical Assessments*, edited by Peter Hamilton (1990 and 1995, published by Routledge).

Bibliographical listings of Durkheim-related material can be found in:
Revue Française de Sociologie, 1976, vol. 17, pp. 343–53
Revue Française de Sociologie, 1979, vol. 20, pp. 293–9
Etudes Durkheimiennes (ed. P. Besnard), Paris, 1977–87 (12 issues; ISSN: 0154 9413)
Etudes Durkheimiennes/Durkheim Studies (ed. R.A. Jones), 1991–4
Durkheimian Studies (ed. Watts Miller), 1995 (ISSN 1362-024X)

REFERENCES

Alexander, Jeffrey (1988) *Durkheimian Sociology: Cultural Studies*. Cambridge: Cambridge University Press.
Allen, N., Pickering, W.S.F. and Watts Miller, W. (eds) (1998) *On Durkheim's 'Elementary Forms of Religious Life'*. London: Routledge.
Atkinson, J.M. (1978) *Discovering Suicide: Studies in the Organisation of Sudden Death*. London: Macmillan.
Berthelot, Jean-Michel (1995) *1895: Durkheim: l'avènement de la sociologie scientifique*. Toulouse: Presses Universitaires du Mirail.

Boudon, Raymond, (1995) 'Weber and Durkheim: Beyond the Differences. A Common Important Paradigm?', *Revue Internationale de Philosophie*, 192: 221–39.

Cladis, Mark (1992) *A Communitarian Defense of Liberalism. Emile Durkheim and Contemporary Social Theory*. Stanford, CA: Stanford University Press.

Cuin, Charles-Henri (ed.) (1997) *Durkheim d'un Siècle à l'autre*. Paris: Presses Universitaires de France.

Douglas, Jack (1967) *The Social Meanings of Suicide*. Princeton, NJ: Princeton University Press.

Durkheim, Emile ([1893] 1964) *The Division of Labour in Society*. London: Collier.

Durkheim, Emile ([1895] 1982) *The Rules of Sociological Method*. London: Macmillan.

Durkheim, Emile ([1895] 1988) *Les Règles de la methode sociologique* (ed. J.-M. Berthelot). Paris: Flammarion.

Durkheim, Emile ([1897] 1970) *Suicide*. London: Routledge.

Durkheim, Emile ([1912] 1995) *The Elementary Forms of the Religious Life*. New York: The Free Press.

Durkheim, Emile (1915) *'Germany Above All': German Mentality and War*. Paris: Armand Colin.

Durkheim, Emile ([1925] 1973) *Moral Education*. New York: The Free Press.

Durkheim, Emile ([1928] 1962) *Socialism*. New York: Collier.

Durkheim, Emile ([1938] 1977) *The Evolution of Educational Thought in France*. London: Routledge and Kegan Paul.

Durkheim, Emile ([1950] 1992) *Professional Ethics and Civic Morals*. London: Routledge.

Durkheim, Emile (1978) *Durkheim on Institutional Analysis* (ed. M. Traugott). Chicago: University of Chicago Press.

Durkheim, Emile (1980) *Emile Durkheim: Contributions to 'L'Année Sociologique'*. New York: The Free Press.

Durkheim, Emile (1983) *Durkheim and the Law* (edited and introduced by S. Lukes and A. Scull). Oxford: Martin Robertson.

Durkheim, Emile (1996) 'Cours de Philosophie fait au Lycée de Sens en 1883–4'. In *Durkheimian Studies*, 2 (n.s.): 5–30.

Durkheim, Emile (1997) 'French Rebut Germany's Bad Faith', *Durkheimian Studies*, 3 (n.s.): 3–10.

Gane, Mike (1988) *On Durkheim's Rules of Sociological Method*. London: Routledge.

Gane, Mike (ed.) (1992) *The Radical Sociology of Durkheim and Mauss*. London: Routledge.

Giddens, Anthony (1978) *Durkheim*. London: Fontana.

Gross, Neil (1996) 'A Note on the Sociological Eye and the Discovery of a New Durkheim Text', *Journal of the History of the Behavioural Sciences*, 32 (2): 408–23.

Jones, Robert Alun (1986) *Emile Durkheim*. London: Sage.

Kuper, Adam (1985) 'Durkheim's Theory of Kinship', *British Journal of Sociology*, 36 (2): 224–37.

Lehmann, Jennifer (1994) *Durkheim and Women*. Lincoln, NB: University of Nebraska Press.

Lukes, Steven (1973) *Emile Durkheim*. London: Allen Lane.

Merton, Robert (1949) *Social Theory and Social Structure*. New York: The Free Press.

Mestrovic, Stjepan (1988) *Emile Durkheim and the Reformation of Sociology*. NJ: Rowman and Littlefield.

Mestrovic, Stjepan (1991) *The Coming Fin de Siècle: An Application of Durkheim's Sociology to Modernity and Postmodernism*. London: Routledge.

Mestrovic, Stjepan (1992) *Durkheim and Postmodern Culture*. New York: Aldine de Gruyter.

Morrison, K. (1995) *Marx, Durkheim, Weber: Formations of Modern Thought*. London: Sage.

Parkin, Frank (1992) *Durkheim*. Oxford: Oxford University Press.

Parsons, Talcott (1937) *The Structure of Social Action*. New York: The Free Press.

Pearce, Frank (1989) *The Radical Durkheim*. London: Unwin Hyman.

Pickering, W.S.F. (1984) *Durkheim's Sociology of Religion: Themes and Theories*. London: Routledge and Kegan Paul.

Pickering, W.S.F. and Martins, Herminio (1994) *Debating Durkheim*. London: Routledge.

Pope, W. (1976) *Durkheim's 'Suicide': A Classic Analysed*. Chicago: University of Chicago Press.

Ritzer, George and Bell, Richard (1981) 'Emile Durkheim: Exemplar for an Integrated Sociological Paradigm?', *Social Forces*, 59 (4): 966–95.

Schmaus, Warren (1994) *Durkheim's Philosophy of Science and the Sociology of Knowledge*. Chicago: University of Chicago Press.

Sheleff, L.S. (1975) 'From Restitutive Law to Repressive Law: Durkheim's *The Division of Labour in Society* Revisited', *Archives, Européenes de Sociologie*, 16: 16–45.

Stone, Gregory and Farberman, H. (1967) 'On the Edge of Rapprochement: Was Durkheim Moving towards the Perspective of Symbolic Interaction?', *Sociological Quarterly*, 8: 149–64.

Strenski, Ivan (1997) *Durkheim and the Jews of France*. Chicago: University of Chicago Press.

Taylor, Steve (1982) *Durkheim and the Study of Suicide*. London: Macmilllan.

Thompson, Ken (1982) *Emile Durkheim*. London: Tavistock.

Turner, Stephen (ed.) (1993) *Emile Durkheim: Sociologist and Moralist*. London: Routledge.

Wallwork, Ernest (1984) 'Religion and Social Structure in *The Division of Labor*', *American Anthropologist*, 86 (1): 43–64.

Watts Miller, Willie (1996) *Durkheim, Morals and Modernity*. London: UCL Press.

8

The Emergence of the New: Mead's Theory and Its Contemporary Potential

HANS JOAS

In his contribution to a volume representing and celebrating 'the revival of pragmatism' in American social thought, law and culture, Alan Wolfe – one of the leading contemporary American sociologists – has pointed out that this revival has so far only slightly influenced the practice of the social sciences.[1] Although he is quite willing to welcome a potential revival 'for its insistence on the importance of human beings, its emphasis on indeterminacy, language, and skepticism', he is also worried that it could prove counter-productive; for him, pragmatism has never been realistic in the sense of getting reality right, and thus its revival could become yet another version of that type of social science that is tempted 'to substitute longings for a better world for the need to understand this one first'. Alan Wolfe plays with the double meaning of the term 'pragmatic' when he concludes: 'Our most pragmatic response ought to be to welcome the revival of pragmatism, and then go back to our business, appreciating its qualities, but refusing to turn it into a panacea for the dilemmas that are at the heart of social science enquiry.'

Every contemporary re-examination of major pragmatist thinkers probably has to deal with this suspicion. Does going back to the pragmatists mean to be attracted by an idealistic vision of a better world – which might be a positive trait of a person, but not a necessary precondition for good social science? Or does the old equivocation of meanings in the term 'pragmatic' foster misunderstandings of the philosophy of pragmatism and thus cover up the true importance of this approach? The following interpretation of

George Herbert Mead's work is, of course, highly selective with respect to these questions. Mead is only one of the pragmatists, but at least for historical reasons one can call his work the bridge between pragmatism and sociology. So a re-examination of his life and work and an evaluation of his influence in social theory may lead us to an at least partial answer concerning the question of what sociologists and social theorists today can learn from pragmatist thinking.

LIFE AND CONTEXT

George Herbert Mead was born into a Congregationalist pastor's home in South Hadley, Massachusetts, on 27 February 1863. His childhood and youth were spent in the surroundings of Oberlin College, Ohio, where his father went in 1869 to take up a professorship in homiletics and which the son himself later entered as a student. Mead's development occurred at a time when the sciences were gaining more space on American college syllabuses, and thus coming into conflict with dogmatically religious claims to explain the world. Typically, the key experience of Mead's generation was the encounter with Darwin's theory of evolution and its compelling proof of the mythological character of the Christian doctrine of creation. Unlike many of his contemporaries, however, the young Mead did not draw social-Darwinist or determinist consequences from this. The question he asked himself was how the moral values of socially committed American Protestantism could be preserved without outdated theological dogma and beyond the narrowness of Puritan life. After he finished college in 1883, Mead spent four years moving between jobs and then, in 1887, braved all the economic risks to study philosophy at Harvard. His most important influence there was the Christian neo-Hegelian Josiah Royce, one of the best authorities in the United States on classical German idealism. Royce passed on to him the outlines of a philosophy of history which interpreted the Kingdom of Heaven as the historical realization of a community of all human beings in which there is universal communication among them. But although Mead never lost his admiration for this teacher from his university days, he soon came to regard as inadequate a philosophy that kept aloof from the sciences and the social problems of the age. It seemed to him a graft from European culture, rather than an authentic interpretation of American life or a guide to action in contemporary American conditions.

In 1888 Mead switched to the study of (physiological) psychology, because it promised an empirical clarification of philosophical problems and offered greater intellectual independence. From 1888 to 1891 he studied in Germany, first for a semester in Leipzig (with Wilhelm Wundt et al.), then in Berlin (under Friedrich Paulsen, Wilhelm Dilthey et al.). One of his special interests was the psychology of the child's early moral development and – as part of a dissertation project – research into the perception and constitution of space that went beyond the theories of Kant. Outside academia, he was impressed by Social Democracy and by the efficiency of local administration in Germany.

In 1891 Mead took up an offer to teach psychology at the University of Michigan in Ann Arbor, and departed from Germany full of plans concerning philosophy and psychology on one hand and social reform on the other. In 1894 he moved at John Dewey's request to the newly founded University of Chicago, where he remained until his death in 1931.

The new university had two ambitious goals: to combine research and teaching more closely (as in the German model), but also to ensure that both were strongly geared to practical tasks, preferably in the local community. At that time Chicago was one of the fastest-growing industrial cities, its population largely made up of unskilled or semi-skilled first-generation immigrants. Mead became part of an interdisciplinary network of major Chicago academics who, especially in the 'Progressive Era' before the First World War, involved themselves in numerous social reform projects (for example, at Hull House, run as part of the social settlement movement by Jane Addams, the future winner of

the Nobel Peace Prize). Mead responded to the world war with political and journalistic activity, in favour of President Wilson and American entry into the conflict. In the period before the war, his academic work had as its core the development of an anthropological theory of communication and a related social psychology, which together assure Mead of a place among the major thinkers in the history of sociology and social psychology.

After the war, Mead turned more to various questions in the philosophy of science and of nature, and his work for political and social reform largely receded into the background in the 1920s. He died on 26 April 1931, embittered by a dispute over university policy that had even led him to decide to abandon the university and the city where he had been so active.

George Herbert Mead occupies a special position among those who are today recognized beyond dispute as the classical sociological theorists. By the time of his death he had not published a single book, and was scarcely known outside the circle of his students and immediate colleagues. Moreover, he had never actually taught in the sociology faculty: his life's work was in the fields of philosophy and psychology, and his sociological influence was at first almost entirely limited to the course on social psychology that he gave for decades in Chicago. This course, which presented his specific approach to the subject, became part of sociological instruction at what was for a long time the most influential American department in the field. The posthumous publication of Mead's writings, together with the compilation of students' lecture notes in book form, has subsequently established his reputation to an extent that is still growing today.

THE WORK

In his foundations of social psychology, Mead starts not from the behaviour of the individual organism but from a cooperating group of distinctively human organisms; not from an isolated, Crusoe-like actor who must first enter into social relationships and constitute collectively binding values, but from the complex activities of a group, from what he called the 'social act'.

Groups of human organisms are subject to conditions that differ fundamentally from those of pre-human stages. In contrast to insect colonies, for example, a strict division of labour is no longer assured through physiological differentiation. Even the regulation of group life by instinct-bound forms of behaviour which are only modified in processes of status acquisition within a unilinear hierarchy of dominance – a principle which applies to societies of vertebrates – is ruled out by the organic preconditions of the human species. For human societies, the problem is how individual behaviour not fixed by nature can be differentiated yet also, via mutual expectations, be integrated into group activity. Mead's anthropological theory of the origins of specifically human communication seeks to uncover the mechanism that makes such differentiation and reintegration possible. Communication thus moves to the centre of the analysis, but it would be a mistake to accuse Mead of limiting his concept of society to processes of communication. 'The mechanism of human society,' he states quite clearly, 'is that of bodily selves who assist or hinder each other in their cooperative acts by the manipulation of physical things.'[2]

Darwin's analysis of expressive animal behaviour and Wundt's concept of gestures were crucial stimuli for Mead's own thinking on this matter. He shares with them the idea that a 'gesture' is a 'syncopated act', the incipient phase of an action that may be employed for the regulation of social relationships. Such regulation is possible when an animal reacts to another animal's action during this incipient phase as it would react to the action as a whole – for example, when the baring of a dog's teeth in preparation for attack is 'answered' by another dog's flight or by the baring of its own teeth. If such a connection is working properly, the early phase of the action can become the 'sign' for the whole action and serve to replace it. Mead does not agree with Darwin's assumption, however, that expressive goals lie behind such gestures: the animal is not trying to express anything; its action is simply an uncontrollable discharge of instinctual energy. Nor does he share Wundt's assumption that the emotion expressed in one animal's gestures is triggered in the other animal through imitation of those gestures. The weakness of Wundt's hypothesis is that it sees imitation as a simple instinctive mechanism which can be unproblematically employed for the purposes of explanation. For Mead, the opposite is true: imitation itself is an achievement that requires explanation. How does it happen, then, that gestures have the same semantic content for both sides involved in communication?

For a gesture to have this same meaning, its originator must be able to trigger in himself the reaction that he will excite in the partner to communication, so that the other's reaction is already represented inside himself. In other words, it must be possible for the gesture to be perceived by its actual originator. Among human beings, this is the case particularly with a type of gesture that can also be most widely varied according to the precise situation: namely, vocal gestures. Contrary to a widespread view, Mead did not attach excessive weight to vocal gestures; for him, they were not the most frequent gestures, but the ones most suited for such a self-perception. They are a necessary condition for the emergence of self-consciousness in the history of the species, but not a sufficient condition (otherwise the path of self-consciousness would, for example, have been open to birds as well).

Mead also regarded as crucial the typically human uncertainty of response, and the hesitancy facilitated by the structure of the nervous system. These entail that the originator's virtual reaction to his own gesture does not just take place simultaneously with the reaction of his partner, but actually *precedes* that reaction. His own virtual reaction is also registered in its incipient phase and can be checked by other reactions, even before it finds expression in behaviour. Thus, *anticipatory* representation of the other's behaviour is possible. Perception of one's own gestures leads not to the emergence of signs as substitute stimuli, but to the bursting of the whole stimulus–response schema of behaviour and to the constitution of '*significant symbols*'. It thus becomes possible to gear one's own behaviour to the potential reactions of others, and intentionally to associate different actions with one another. Action is here oriented to expectations of behaviour. And since, in principle, one's communicative partners have the same capacity, a binding pattern of reciprocal behavioural expectations becomes the premise of collective action.

This anthropological analysis, which Mead extends into a comparison between human and animal sociality, provides the key concepts of his social psychology. The concept of 'role' designates precisely a pattern of behavioural expectation; 'taking the role of the other' means to anticipate the other's behaviour, and not to assume the other's place in an organized social context. This inner representation of the other's behaviour entails that different instances take shape within the individual. The individual makes his own behaviour (like his partner's behaviour) the object of his perception; he sees himself from the other's point of view. Alongside the dimension of instinctive impulses, there appears an evaluative authority made up of expectations about how the other will react to an expression of those impulses.

Mead speaks of an '*I*' and a '*me*'. The '*I*' refers in the traditional philosophical sense to the principle of creativity and spontaneity, but in Mead it also refers biologically to man's instinctual make-up. This duality in Mead's usage of the term is often experienced as contradictory, since 'instinct', 'impulse', or 'drive' are associated with a dull natural compulsion. Mead, however, considers that human beings are endowed with a 'constitutional surplus of impulses' (Arnold Gehlen), which – beyond any question of satisfaction – creates space for itself in fantasy and can be only channelled by normativization. The '*me*' refers to my idea of how the other sees me or, at a more primal level, to my internalization of what the other expects me to do or be. The '*me*', qua precipitation within myself of a reference person, is an evaluative authority for my structuring of spontaneous impulses and a basic element of my developing self-image. If I encounter several persons who are significant references for me, I thus acquire several different '*me*'s', which must be synthesized into a unitary self-image for consistent behaviour to be possible. If this synthesization is successful, the '*self*' comes into being: that is, a unitary self-evaluation and action-orientation which allows interaction with more and more communicative partners; and at the same time, a stable personality structure develops which is certain of its needs. Mead's model, unlike Freud's, is oriented to dialogue between instinctual impulses and social expectations. Culturally necessary repression and anarchic satisfaction of needs do not form an alternative from which there is no escape. Rather, Mead sees a possibility of open-ended argument, in which social norms are susceptible of communicative modification and the instinctual impulses can be reoriented in a voluntary (because satisfying) direction.

Mead's theory of personality passes into a developmental logic of the formation of the self that is applicable to both species and individual. Central here are the two forms of children's conduct designated by the terms '*play*' and '*game*'. '*Play*' is ludic interaction with an imagined partner in which the child uses behavioural anticipation to act out both sides; the other's conduct is directly represented and complemented by the child's own conduct. The child reaches this stage when it becomes capable of interacting with different individual reference-persons and adopting the other's perspective – that is, when the reference-person at whom the child's instinctual impulses are mainly directed is no longer the only one who counts. The child then also develops a capacity for group '*game*', where anticipation of an individual partner's behaviour is no longer enough and action must be guided by the conduct of all other participants. These others are by no means disjointed parts, but occupy functions within groups organized in accordance with a purposive division of labour. The individual actor must orient himself by a goal that is valid for all the other actors – a

goal which Mead, with its psychical foundations in mind – calls the '*generalized other*'. The behavioural expectations of this generalized other are, for instance, the rules of the game, or, more generally, the norms and values of a group. Orientation to a particular 'generalized other' reproduces at a new stage the orientation to a particular concrete other. The problem of orienting to ever-broader generalized others thus becomes the guiding thought in Mead's *ethical* theory.

If Mead's introductory lectures on social psychology published as *Mind, Self, and Society* (1934), and the great series of essays that developed his basic ideas for the first time between 1908 and 1912, are taken as his answer to how cooperation and individuation are possible, then the much less well-known collection of Mead's remaining papers – *The Philosophy of the Act* (1938) – represents an even more fundamental starting point. The problem that Mead addresses here is how instrumental action itself is possible.[3] In particular, he considers the essential prerequisite for any purposive handling of things: that is, the constitution of permanent objects. His analysis of the ability for role-taking as an important precondition for the constitution of the 'physical thing' is a major attempt to combine the development of communicative and instrumental capabilities within a theory of socialization.

In Mead's model, action is made up of four stages: impulse, perception, manipulation and (need-satisfying) consummation. The most distinctively human of these is the third, the stage of manipulation, whose interposition and independence express the reduced importance of the instincts in man and provide the link for the emergence of thought. In animals, contact experience with objects is totally integrated into activities aimed at the satisfaction of needs. Even in apes, the locomotive function of the hand is stronger than its role in feeling things; only in man does it develop into an organ of manipulation no longer directly tied to needs. Hand *and* speech are for Mead the two roots of the development from ape to man. Along with the differentiation and accumulation of contact experiences made possible by the autonomy of the hand, man disposes of several distance receptors (such as eyes and ears) and the brain as their internal apparatus. If impressions of distance initially trigger a response only in movements of the body, the retardation of response due to distance and the autonomy of the sphere of contact experience then make possible a reciprocal relationship between eye and hand: the two cooperate and control each other. Intelligent perception and the constitution of objects take place, in Mead's view, when distance experience is consciously related to contact experience. But this becomes possible, he further argues, only when the role-taking capability develops to the point where it can be transferred to non-social objects. How are we to understand this?

A thing is perceived as a thing only when we attribute to it an 'inside' that exerts pressure on us as soon as we touch it. This 'inside' capable of exerting pressure can never be conveyed to us through dissection (which only ever leads to new surfaces); it must always be attributed. I attribute it in accordance with the schema of pressure and counter-pressure, which I learn through self-perception of the pressure that I exert upon myself – for example, in playing with both hands. I can then transfer this experience to things, by representing as coming from the object a pressure that is as great as my own pressure but is moving in the opposite direction. Mead calls this 'taking the role of the thing'. If I also succeed in doing this by anticipation, I will be able to deal with things in a controlled manner and accumulate experiences of manipulative action. Combined with the cooperation of eye and hand, this means that the body's distance senses can and actually do trigger the experience of resistance proper to manipulation. The distant object is then perceived as an anticipated 'contact value'; the thing *looks* heavy, hard or hot.

For Mead, of course, what is primary is not conscious self-perception of the pressure I exert upon myself, but a self-perception analogous to the perception of sound produced by myself. In order that this can be transferred to objects and a counter-pressure be anticipated, the basic role-taking capability, so Mead argues, must have already been acquired. Only interactive experience allows what stands before me to appear as active (as 'pressing'). If this is correct, social experience is the premise upon which the diversity of sense perception can be synthesized into 'things'. Mead thereby also explains why at first – that is, in the consciousness of the infant or of primitive cultures – all things are perceived as living partners in a schema of interaction, and why it is only later that social objects are differentiated from physical objects. The constitution of permanent objects is, in turn, the precondition for the separation of the organism from other objects and its self-reflective development as a unitary body. Self-identity is thus formed in the same process whereby 'things' take shape for actors.

Mead is trying to grasp the social constitution of things without falling prey to a linguistically restricted concept of meaning. His attempt to join together the development of communicative and instrumental capabilities outlines a solution

to the problem that remains unsolved in other major conceptions of instrumental action (those of Arnold Gehlen or Jean Piaget, for example).

To some extent, Mead develops a slightly different formulation of the same ideas in those of his works that connect up with philosophical discussions of relativity theory and which make central use of the concept of 'perspective'. For him, the theory of relativity finally lays to rest the idea that perspectives are merely subjective, for it is precisely as subjective that they are objectively present. 'The conception of the perspective as there in nature is in a sense an unexpected donation by the most abstruse physical science to philosophy. They are not distorted perspectives of some perfect patterns, nor do they lie in consciousness as selections among things whose reality is to be found in a noumenal world.'[4] Mead then asks how it is possible that man does not remain a prisoner to the perspective centred on his own body, but is able to have two or more perspectives *simultaneously*. The main problem – and here Mead avoids drawing relativist consequences from pragmatism – is how man is capable of universality in grasping the object. Mead bases the capacity for perspectival change upon role-taking, upon the capacity to place oneself in the perspective of others. In role-taking, two perspectives are simultaneously present within me, and I must integrate them into a many-sided picture of the object, much as I have to synthesize a number of different 'me's. By transposition to others and eventually to a generalized other, I arrive at a comprehensive picture of the object, and finally at a reconstruction of the structural context that contains both myself and my perspective. Not only the constitution of things but also the growing adequacy of their perception are thus bound up with the development of personal identity. Damage to that identity also puts at risk my free contact with things.

Mead's ethics and moral psychology are as much grounded upon his theory of action and his social psychology as they set an axiological framework for these scientific parts of his work. Mead's approach to ethics develops from a critique of both the utilitarian and Kantian positions: he does not regard as satisfactory an orientation simply to the results of action or simply to the intentions of the actor; he wants to overcome both the utilitarian lack of interest in motives and the Kantian failure to deal adequately with the goals and objective results of action. He criticizes the psychological basis common to both ethical theories. Mead argues that the separation between motive and object of the will is a consequence of the empiricist concept of experience, and that beneath the surface this also characterizes Kant's concept of inclination.

> We are now free from the restrictions of the Utilitarian and Kantian if we recognize that desire is directed toward the object instead of toward pleasure. Both Kant and the Utilitarian are fundamentally hedonists, assuming that our inclinations are toward our own subjective states – the pleasure that comes from satisfaction. If that is the end, then of course our motives are all subjective affairs. From Kant's standpoint they are bad, and from the Utilitarian standpoint they are the same for all actions and so neutral. But on the present view, if the object itself is better, then the motive is better. (1934: 384–5)

Mead, then, imports his theory of the social constitution of objects into the realm of ethics; his aim is to move beyond Kant's grounding of universality upon the *form* of the will.

Mead's position is not easily accessible from within present-day ethical debate. First, through its original linkage of the concept of value with the concept of action, it frees itself from all the aporias concerning the deducibility of an ought from an is. For Mead, the value of an object is associated with the consummatory stage of the action, so that value is experienced as obligation or desire. What he wants to show is that the relation expressed in the concept of value cannot be limited either to subjective evaluation or to an objective quality of value; that it results from a relationship between subject and object which should not, however, be understood as a relationship of knowledge. The value relation is thus an objectively existing relation between subject and object, which differs structurally from the perception of primary or secondary qualities not through a higher degree of subjective arbitrariness, but simply by virtue of its reference to the phase of need satisfaction rather than the phase of manipulation or perception. The claim to objectivity on the part of scientific knowledge bound up with perception or manipulation is, therefore, a matter of course also as far as moral action is concerned. This does not mean that Mead reduces ethics to one more science among others. For science, in his analysis, investigates the relations of ends and means, whereas ethics investigates the relationship among ends themselves.

Mead's starting point is the idea that there are neither secure biological roots for moral conduct nor a fixed value system by which action can always be oriented. Biologically determined behaviour (including quasi-moral caring) and norm-bound behaviour are each prior to the genuinely moral situation, which arises when different motives and values come into conflict with one another and have to be assessed in the light of their anticipated results. Analysis of the moral situation lies at the heart of Mead's ethics.

Epigrammatically, one might say that for Mead the moral situation is a personality crisis. It confronts the personality with a conflict between various of its own values, or between its own values and those of direct partners or the generalized other, or between its own values and impulses. This conflict brings action to a standstill; the unexpected problem tends toward the disintegration of identity. This crisis can be overcome only by one's own creative, and hence ever-risky, actions. Mead's ethics, then, seek not to prescribe rules of conduct but to elucidate the situation in which 'moral discoveries' are necessary. Expectations and impulses must be restructured, so that it becomes possible to rebuild an integral identity and to outline a moral strategy appropriate to the situation. If this is done successfully, the self is raised to a higher stage, since regard for further interests has now been incorporated into conduct.

Mead attempts to describe stages of self-formation as stages of moral development and, at the same time, as stages in the development of society toward freedom from domination. Orientation to a concrete other is followed by orientation to organized others within a group. Beyond this stage and beyond conflicts between different generalized others, there is an orientation to ever-more comprehensive social units, and finally to a universalist perspective with an ideal of full development of the human species. We attain this universalist perspective by attempting to understand all values that appear before us – not relativistically in a non-judgemental juxtaposition, but by assessing them in the light of a universalist community based upon communication and cooperation. Comprehensive communication with partners in the moral situation, and rational conduct oriented to achievement of the ideal community, are thus two rules to be applied in solving the crisis. This perspective lifts us outside any concrete community or society and leads to ruthless questioning of the legitimacy of all prevailing standards. In each, moral decision is a reference to a better society.[5]

The moral value of a given society is shown in the degree to which it involves rational procedures for the reaching of agreement and an openness of all institutions to communicative change. Mead uses the term 'democracy' for such a society; democracy is for him institutionalized revolution. Individuals do not acquire their identity within it through identification with the group or society as such in its struggle against internal or external enemies. In a number of analyses, Mead investigated the power-stabilizing and socially integrative functions of punitive justice, and looked at patriotism as an ethical and psychological problem. He recognized that both are functionally necessary in a society which, because not everyone can publicly express their needs, requires an artificial unity. Nor did he overlook the fact that national patriotism may have progressive effects in the overcoming of particularist group orientations. For Mead, the generation of a universalist perspective is by no means just a moral demand; he is aware of its material foundations and sees that it is achievable only when all human beings share a real context in which to act – something that can come about by means of the world market.

Mead's philosophy of history is based not on a pious trust in the reasonable character of evolution, but on a belief in the definite mutability of all institutions, on creative individuality and open-ended historical progress. He rejects with verve not only all deterministic conceptions that eliminate the potential for human action, but also teleological assumptions of a fixed goal of history as a utopia to be made real. For him, the philosophies of history in both Hegel and Marx fall under that category.

In his philosophy of history, Mead returns again and again to the dynamic of scientific progress and contributes a number of major new insights into it.[6] Scientific progress takes on this central role for him because it offers the possibility of proving the non-predictability of the future. Mead tries to show that a new scientific paradigm cannot, in principle, be predicted on the basis of an old one; its emergence is necessary in the sense of a solution to a problem, but not in that of a causal chain. For it to come about, individual thinkers have to perform their creative tasks. The starting point here is not solipsistic sense data but a conflict between the thinker's own experience and the interpretation of the world current in his society and deposited in his own prejudices. If he does not wish to renounce his own experiential evidence, his explanation of it must advance a hypothesis with claims not just to individual but to universal validity. It too must become intersubjective; it must gain collective acceptance and prove its success in collective action.

Mead's concern is to uncover the constitution of scientific experience within everyday experience, and thus to avoid either irrationalist disablement of science as such or scientistic burying of any aesthetic or axiological reference to reality and the distinctive character of social science. This problem acquires greater topicality for Mead because of certain philosophical attempts to deal with relativity theory as the most important development in the natural sciences. He remarks how, on one hand, relativity theory is itself interpreted relativistically, but he also notes how, on the other hand, in the multidimensional space–time framework of the 'Minkowski world', relativity theory again produces the idea of a world-in-itself statically transparent for an infinite consciousness and thereby undermines his anti-determinist orientation to changes in the world and to collective constitution of our world picture. This seems to him all the more intolerable in that relativity theory precisely offers the chance for a scientifically produced confirmation of the pragmatic concept of science, and for a 'dialectical' conception of the non-eliminability of the subject from the research process. Alfred North Whitehead's interpretations become for Mead the most important issue in the whole controversy; he grants the productive aspects of Whitehead's approach, but wants to avoid its idealist consequences. It is not possible to give an adequate account of this dispute here, which was not over when Mead died. It should be noted, however, that Mead regarded Whitehead's concept of perspective as the great opportunity to develop a new concept of objectivity that involved objectification of the observing subject; that Mead's lifelong interest in Aristotle and other non-mechanistic theories of nature leads towards a rehabilitation of qualitative, non-quantifying experience of nature; and that his discussion of time begins in relation to the philosophy of science, but goes on to develop a reconstructive concept of history and biography. Mead's later work resembles Edmund Husserl's in many of its themes, without sharing his transcendental philosophical orientation; and it resembles Whitehead's work, without taking over his cosmology or his theory of ideas.

MEAD'S INFLUENCE IN SOCIAL THEORY

During Mead's lifetime, his influence was almost entirely limited to his students and a few colleagues in Chicago, and to his friend, the leading pragmatist philosopher John Dewey, who taught at Columbia University in New York after 1904. It is almost impossible to reconstruct the details, because the paths of influence joining pragmatist philosophy, functionalist psychology, institutionalist economics, empirical sociology and progressive social reformism cannot really be disentangled from one another.[7] Since Chicago played the decisive role in the early professionalization of American sociology, the importance of Mead's views for American sociologists all over the country became considerable. In the history of philosophy, Mead's main service is to have developed a pragmatist analysis of social interaction and individual self-reflection. This same achievement enabled him, in the age of classical sociological theory, to clear a way for it to escape fruitless oppositions such as that between individualism and collectivism. Mead's grasp of the unity of individuation and socialization defines his place in the history of sociology.

After Mead's death, the school of 'symbolic interactionism' played a decisive role in assuring his influence in sociology. Herbert Blumer, a former student of Mead, became the founder and key organizer in the USA of a rich sociological research tradition which turned against the dominance of behaviourist psychology, quantitative methods of empirical social research and social theories that abstracted from the action of members of society. This school, by contrast, emphasized the openness of social structures, the creativity of social actors and the need for interpretation of the data of social science. Mead thus came to be seen as the school's progenitor and classical reference, although his work was consulted only fragmentarily. Certainly, some of the leading symbolic interactionists like Anselm Strauss and David Maines published important interpretations of Mead's work and elaborated his ideas in creative ways; but in general it can be said that those parts of his work which do not fall into the field of social psychology remained almost completely ignored. In the dominant postwar theory of Talcott Parsons, Mead's ideas remained rather marginal; they were mentioned, alongside the works of Durkheim, Freud and Cooley, as important for the understanding of the internalization of norms.

There are other currents of social thought and social science which paid attention to Mead's work and tried to incorporate it into their own approaches. Mead's self-characterization as a 'behaviourist' has continually led to claims from this school of psychology that the symbolic interactionist interpretation distorts Mead's intentions, but it cannot be overlooked that Mead used the term 'behaviourism' in a way that is rather different from what has become its established meaning. Phenomenological (and pragmatist) philosophers have contributed to the discussion about similarities and dissimilarities between their theoretical orientation and Mead's work or pragmatism in general; it is particularly the work of the French social phenomenologist Maurice Merleau-Ponty which allows fruitful comparison with Mead. Feminist scholars have started to reinterpret Mead's life and work in the light of his interest for feminist questions and his social activism in this regard. Representatives of different and rival approaches in sociological theory – from Randall Collins' 'conflict sociology' to Jeffrey

Alexander's 'neofunctionalism' – attach fundamental importance to a discussion of his work now – a clear sign that Mead has become considered not just the originator of one sociological approach among many, that is, symbolic interactionism, but a classical theorist of the whole discipline. The renaissance of pragmatism, however, that is working itself out in philosophy and public life, has focused attention on John Dewey and has not reached Mead yet. The same is true for the debate about communitarianism in which some authors articulate views that are astonishingly close to Mead's, but with few exceptions (like Philip Selznick) do not refer to Mead at all. The popularity of post-structuralism and the topic of postmodernism have sparked a controversy within symbolic interactionism about the relationship between the two 'discourses'; though there are attempts to interpret Mead's thinking as a kind of post-structuralism *avant la lettre*, the predominant contributions make a clear distinction and defend the superiority of the Meadian tradition of a social constructionism regarding the self.

Outside of the USA – particularly, but not only, in Eastern Europe – the way to Mead is often prepared by two figures, the important Russian psychologist Lev Vygotsky or the outstanding Russian literary theorist Mikhail Bakhtin. A particularly important receptive strand can be found in Germany, where Arnold Gehlen, one of the leading thinkers of so-called philosophical anthropology, was the first to attach major importance to Mead's work. This has to be seen in the context of a specific interest in American pragmatism among German National Socialist thinkers; the focus here was not on Mead's intersubjectivist approach. Jürgen Habermas, who is deeply influenced by the school of philosophical anthropology, has, from an early phase of his development, referred to the semiotic superiority of Mead's theory of communication and its importance for socialization research. In his magnum opus of 1981 (*The Theory of Communicative Action*) he dedicated a long chapter to Mead and identified him as the main inspirer of the paradigm shift 'from purposive to communicative action' which Habermas himself proposed. In later writings he kept returning to Mead, and offered another interpretation of his work in his book on *Post-metaphysical Thinking* (1992). German sociology and theology have produced a series of books on Mead, comparing his work to Martin Buber, Alfred Schütz, Niklas Luhmann, Talcott Parsons, structuralists and others.

I myself have tried to sound the potential of Mead's work and American pragmatism in general for a revision of sociological action theory, the theory of norms and values, and macro-sociological theory. The innovative potential of Mead's theory is, in my view, evident – far beyond the field of qualitative micro-sociological research, for which large parts of symbolic interactionism has primarily laid claim.

But this innovative potential has to be located on the right logical level. It is not to be found, as Alan Wolfe seems to assume, either on the level of the discovery of new empirical facts nor on a purely normative level; it is to be found in Mead's fundamental theoretical and metatheoretical approach. Since Habermas' theory of communicative action, because of its undeniable affinity with some aspects of Mead's work, might also overshadow the other approach, it makes sense briefly to spell out some differences between these two important contributions to social theory.

The affinity between the two clearly consists in the common emphasis on human communication and interaction and particularly on the symbolically mediated character of this interaction. But (1) whereas Habermas almost exclusively focuses on linguistic communication, Mead is much more interested in the *corporeal* dimension. His analysis of language in terms of vocal gestures makes it clear that, for him, language is based in corporeal expressivity. This is probably a mere difference in emphasis (and not in principle), since both theorists would accept continuity and discontinuity in the relationship between corporeal expressivity and fully developed linguistic communication.

(2) A much deeper difference can be detected when we compare the place of communication within the whole of an action-theoretical approach. Whereas Habermas is exclusively interested in contrasting communicative action with other types of human action, particularly with merely strategic action toward other actors and with instrumental action toward material objects, Mead's interest is in the character of human action as such and in what distinguishes it from animal behaviour. That is the reason why Mead's theory of the 'taking the role of the thing' is of crucial theoretical importance; it shows not only how cognitive and communicative abilities and their developments are intertwined, but also that the notion of instrumental action must not become a mere residual category characterized mostly by its difference from communicative action. Mead's theory of action, as the understanding of action in pragmatist thinking in general, is focused on the *creativity* of action. His understanding of the specificities of human communication is the elaboration of one aspect of this creativity.

(3) This emphasis on creativity leads to an interest in the dynamics of human *experience* in

its openness and rich variety. One can contrast this quasi-phenomenological side of pragmatism with the concentration on problems of rationality in Habermas. Again it would be wrong to overstate the difference, particularly to assume that rationality plays no role in Mead's pragmatist approach. But the relationship between a theory of action and a theory of rationality is much more indirect in Mead than in Habermas. Whereas Habermas develops his theory of action out of his interest in the elaboration of the concept of communicative rationality, Mead's point of departure is an understanding of the creativity of action, and thus he comes to the problem of rationality, as his ethical theory demonstrates, in a second step, namely, at the point when creative solutions to action problems are made the subject matter of discourses about justification.

(4) Mead's moral theory is an 'ethics from the perspective of actors', not a theory about the objectivity of justifications; it is also not reduced to the dimension of norms and the possibilities of their universalization – as Habermas' discourse ethics is – but it contains additionally the dimension of *values* and their universalization. The universalization of values is not identical with the universalization of norms since values are more closely tied to the contingencies of human experiences than norms.

(5) On the macro-sociological level, we have to draw on Mead's political writings because there is no elaborate macro-sociological theory in his work. If we are allowed to extrapolate the fundamentals of such a theory from these writings we can say that there are no traces of a Habermasian dualism between 'system' and 'life-world', between functionalism and hermeneutics, in Mead's approach. He remains consistently *action-theoretical* in his orientation, but he is able to construct a tension between different dimensions of on-going processes of universalization. For him there is the universalization of economic and social processes on the one hand epitomized in the world market, but also in international relationships and transnational institutions – and there is the universalization of norms and values on the other hand as expressed in universalist morality and universalist value systems in the world religions. Mead sees his epoch characterized by a tension between rapid progress in economic universalization and slow progress in the adaptation of universalist value systems to these changing conditions of social life. And

(6) social change is hence not analysed by Mead following the thread of 'rationalization', be it 'monologic' rationalization in Weber's style or 'communicative' rationalization in Habermas' sense. The anti-teleological and anti-evolutionist

thrust of Mead's philosophy of history leads to an emphasis on the *contingency* of historical processes, both as an increase of individual options for action and as an increase in the awareness of historical contingency itself. Such an orientation does not ignore processes of rationalization, but it makes us see these processes as contingent. Mead's historical perspective is not centred on a process of on-going rationalization, but on the constant and unpredictable emergence of the new.

These brief remarks can neither exhaust the problems of a systematic comparison between Meadian pragmatism and Habermasian 'theory of communicative action' nor the substantive questions involved in each single area of debate. They can only point to broader attempts to elaborate Mead's approach in all these directions (Joas, 1996, 2000).

But they may be able to answer the question about the contemporary relevance of pragmatism for sociology and social theory. I do indeed claim that Meadian pragmatist ideas about the creativity of human action and the contingency of human experience and social change can provide a serious and innovative competitor to other synthetic approaches in social theory today.

NOTES

1 For this and the following quotations in this paragraph, see Alan Wolfe, 1998; here see p. 205.

2 'The Objective Reality of Perspectives' (1927), in Mead, 1964: 313.

3 See also George Herbert Mead, 'The Physical Thing', in Mead, 1932: 119–39; Joas, 1985.

4 George Herbert Mead, 'The Objective Reality of Perspectives', in Mead, 1964: 308.

5 See George Herbert Mead, 'Philanthrophy from the Point of View of Ethics', in Mead, 1964: 392–407. On the further development of this theory of moral value, see Joas, 2000.

6 See, for example, George Herbert Mead, 'Scientific Method and Individual Thinker' (1917), in Mead, 1964: 171–211.

7 See Hans Joas, *Pragmatism in American Sociology*, in Joas, 1993: 14–54.

REFERENCES AND FURTHER READING

Aboulafia, Mitchell (1986) *The Mediating Self: Mead, Sartre, and Self-Determination*. New Haven, CT: Yale University Press.

Aboulafia, Mitchell (1995) 'Habermas and Mead: On Universality and Individuality', *Constellations*, 2: 93–113.

Alexander, Jeffrey (1987) 'Pragmatism and the Legacy of G.H. Mead', in Jeffrey Alexander, *Twenty Lectures: Sociological Theory since 1945*. New York: Columbia University Press. pp. 195–214.

Baldwin, John D. (1986) *George Herbert Mead. A Unifying Theory for Sociology*. London: Sage.

Blumer, Herbert (1966) 'Sociological Implications of the Thought of G.H. Mead', *American Journal of Sociology*, 71: 535–44.

Blumer, Herbert (1981) 'G.H. Mead', in Buford Rhea (ed.), *The Future of the Sociological Classics*. London: Sage. pp. 136–69.

Campbell, James (1992) *The Community Reconstructs: The Meaning of Pragmatic Social Thought*. Urbana, IL: University of Illinois Press.

Collins, Randall (1989) 'Toward a Neo-Meadian Sociology of Mind', *Symbolic Interaction*, 12: 1–32.

Cook, Gary Allan (1993) *G.H. Mead: The Making of a Social Pragmatist*. Urbana, IL: University of Illinois Press.

Corti, Walter Robert (ed.) (1973) *The Philosophy of G.H. Mead*. Winterthur: Amriswiler Bücherei.

Coser, Lewis (1971) 'G.H. Mead', in Lewis Coser, *Masters of Sociological Thought*. New York: Harcourt Brace Jovanich. pp. 333–55.

Dodds, Agnes E., Lawrence, Jeannette A. and Valsiner, Jan (1997) 'The Personal and the Social. Mead's Theory of the "Generalized Other"', *Theory and Psychology*, 7: 483–503.

Dunn, Robert G. (1997) 'Self, Identity, and Difference: Mead and the Poststructuralists', *Sociological Quarterly*, 38: 687–705.

Fisher, Berenice M. and Strauss, Anselm L. (1979) 'G.H. Mead and the Chicago Tradition of Sociology', *Symbolic Interaction*, 2: 9–25.

Glock, Hans-Joachim (1986) 'Vygotsky and Mead on the Self, Meaning, and Internalisation', *Studies in Soviet Thought*, 31: 131–48.

Habermas, Jürgen (1987) *The Theory of Communicative Action*, vol. 2. Boston, MA: Beacon Press.

Habermas, Jürgen (1992) *Postmetaphysical Thinking*. Cambridge, MA: MIT Press.

Hamilton, Peter (ed.) (1992) *G.H. Mead. Critical Assessments*, 4 vols. London/New York: Routledge.

Hanson, Karen (1986) *The Self Imagined: Philosophical Reflections on the Social Character of Psyche*. New York: Routledge and Kegan Paul.

Joas, Hans (1985a) *G.H. Mead. A Contemporary Re-examination of His Thought* (2nd edn 1997). Cambridge, MA: MIT Press.

Joas, Hans (ed.) (1985b) *Das Problem der Intersubjektivität. Neuere Beiträge zum Werk George Herbert Meads*. Frankfurt a.M: Suhrkamp.

Joas, Hans (1993) *Pragmatism and Social Theory*. Chicago: University of Chicago Press.

Joas, Hans (1996) *The Creativity of Action*. Chicago: University of Chicago Press.

Joas, Hans (1998) 'The Autonomy of the Self. The Meadian Heritage and Its Postmodern Challenge', *European Journal of Social Theory*, 1: 7–18.

Joas, Hans (2000, forthcoming) *The Genesis of Values.* Cambridge: Polity Press.

Joas, Hans and Honneth, Axel (1988) *Social Action and Human Nature.* Cambridge: Cambridge University Press.

Jung, Matthias (1995) 'From Dilthey to Mead and Heidegger: Systematic and Historical Relations', *Journal of the History of Philosophy*, 33: 661–77.

Koczanowicz, Leszek (1994) 'G.H. Mead and L.S. Vygotsky on Meaning and the Self', *Journal of Speculative Philosophy*, 8: 262–75.

Lewis, G. David and Smith, Richard L. (1980) *American Sociology and Pragmatism. Mead, Chicago Sociology, and Symbolic Interaction.* Chicago: University of Chicago Press. (Cf. the excellent review symposium on this book with contributions by H. Blumer, E. Rochberg-Halton, J. Campbell and the rejoinder by Lewis and Smith in: *Symbolic Interaction*, 6 (1983): 123–74.)

Leys, Ruth (1994) 'Mead's Voices: Imitation as Foundation, or the Struggle against Mimesis', in Dorothy Ross (ed.), *Modernist Impulses in the Human Sciences 1870–1930.* Baltimore, MD: Johns Hopkins University Press. pp. 210–35.

Maines, David, Surgrue, Noreen and Katovich, Michael (1983) 'The Sociological Import of G.H. Mead's Theory of the Past', *American Sociological Review*, 48: 161–73.

McCarthy, E. Doyle (1984) 'Toward a Sociology of the Physical World: Mead on Physical Objects', *Studies in Symbolic Interaction*, 5: 105–21.

Mead, G.H. (1932) *The Philosophy of the Present* (ed. by Arthur Murphy). La Salle, IL: The Open Court.

Mead, G.H. (1934) *Mind, Self, and Society* (ed. by Charles Morris). Chicago: University of Chicago Press.

Mead, G.H. (1936) *Movements of Thought in the Nineteenth Century* (ed. by Merritt Moore). Chicago: University of Chicago Press.

Mead, G.H. (1938) *The Philosophy of the Act* (ed. by Charles Morris et al.). Chicago: University of Chicago Press.

Mead, G.H. (1964) *Selected Writings* (ed. by Andrew Reck). Indianapolis: Bobbs-Merrill.

Miller, David L. (1973) *G.H. Mead: Self, Language, and the World.* Austin, TX: University of Texas Press.

Moran, Jon S. (1973) 'Mead on the Self and Moral Situations', *Tulane Studies in Philosophy*, 22: 63–78.

Moran, Jon S. (1996) 'Bergsonian Sources of Mead's Philosophy', *Transactions of the Charles S. Peirce Society*, 32: 41–63.

Natanson, Maurice (1956) *The Social Dynamics of G.H. Mead.* Washington: Public Affairs Press.

Pfuetze, Paul E. (1961) *Self, Society, Existence. Human Nature and Dialogue in the Thought of G.H. Mead and Martin Buber.* New York: Harper and Brothers.

Rosenthal, Sandra and Bourgeois, Patrick L. (1991) *Mead and Merleau-Ponty: Toward a Common Vision.* Albany. NY: State University of New York Press.

Shalin, Dmitri (1984) 'The Romantic Antecedents of Meadian Social Psychology', *Symbolic Interaction*, 7: 43–65.

Shalin, Dmitri N. (1986) 'Pragmatism and Social Interactionism', *American Sociological Review*, 51: 9–29.

Shalin, Dmitri N. (1987/88) 'G.H. Mead, Socialism, and the Progressive Agenda', *American Journal of Sociology*, 93: 913–51.

Shalin, Dmitri (2000) 'G.H. Mead', in George Ritzer (ed.), *A Companion to Major Social Theorists.* Cambridge, MA: Blackwell.

Tugendhat, Ernst (1986) *Self-Consciousness and Self-Determination.* Cambridge, MA: MIT Press.

Wolfe, Alan (1998) 'The Missing Pragmatic Revival in American Social Science', in Morris Dickstein (ed.), *The Revival of Pragmatism.* Durham, NC: Duke University Press. pp. 199–206.

9

Karl Mannheim and the Sociology of Knowledge

DAVID KETTLER AND VOLKER MEJA

Max Scheler coined the expression 'sociology of knowledge' [*Wissenssoziologie*] in 1924, and Karl Mannheim appropriated it almost immediately, in 1925, applying the term to his own proposed alternative to Scheler's approach (Mannheim, [1925] 1993; Scheler 1924). The critical differences between them carry forward to present-day disputes about the point of uncovering 'the relations between knowledge and other existential factors in the society and culture' (Merton, [1945] 1957).[1] For Scheler, the sociology of knowledge bears on the 'knowledge' it studies only insofar as it explains the time and circumstances of its emergence, acceptance, or obscuration. Its sad lesson is the 'impotence of the human spirit'. Mannheim's sociology of knowledge, in contrast, has a dual program. On the one hand, it may limit itself to Scheler's questions, although, in contrast to Scheler, it draws on Marxist ideas about ideology formation rather than Scheler's micro-sociological analyses of knowledge institutions, and, most important, Mannheim's empirical sociology of knowledge specifies its subject matter in a Weberian rather than Platonic manner. Knowledge, for the purpose of sociological study, is what is considered to be knowledge. Alongside of this 'value-free' conception of relations between organized claims about the truth of things and the social activity environing such cultural productions, Mannheim contends that sociological understanding of knowledge stands as a 'massive fact' that any philosophical theory of knowledge must recognize, and that the sociology of knowledge consequently comes upon central epistemological and metaphysical problems of knowledge, even if it begins with the more modest ambitions in the manner of academic sociology. Writing in the last year of his life, long after his work seems to many commentators to have abandoned unduly 'speculative' philosophical extrapolations from empirical sociology, Mannheim told Kurt H. Wolff:

> [What] happens is that in our empirical investigation we become aware of the fact that we are observing the world from a moving staircase, from a dynamic platform, and, therefore, the image of the world changes with the changing frames of reference which various cultures create. On the other hand, epistemology still only knows of a static platform where one doesn't become aware of the possibility of various perspectives and, from this angle, it tries to deny the existence and the right of such dynamic thinking. There is a culture lag between our empirical insight into the nature of knowing and the premises upon which the traditional idealists' epistemology is built. Instead of perspectivism, the out-of-date epistemology wants to set up a veto against the emerging new insights, according to which man can only see the world in perspective, and there is no view which is absolute in the sense that it represents the thing in itself beyond perspective. (Wolff, [1959] 1974: 557–8; Mannheim, [1925] 1993; [1931] 1936)

The present chapter will not retry the philosophical case frequently made against Mannheim's undertaking. We are content to note that the case has in fact been dramatically reopened, most recently in the name of post-structuralist and postmodernist movements of thought. We proceed to a reconstruction of Mannheim's sociology of knowledge secure in the belief that he is exemplary in his honesty about difficulties encountered in the attempt to distinguish his unfinished philosophical project from an uncritical surrender to mere relativism or rhetoric. In this respect, if no other, Mannheim offers a sobering partner for the negotiations that a commentator has recently placed on the agenda of the sociological profession, the confrontation with the 'radical Weimar posture regarding the reflexivity and situatedness of all knowledge', which is, in his view, currently given vital expression, 'by feminist standpoint epistemology, constructivist science studies, and Bourdieu's reflexive praxeology of culture' (Pels, 1996a: 1776; cf. Pels, 1996b). Going beyond this, we suggest that proponents of these and similar current movements would also do well to open themselves to conversations with Mannheim's own attentively reflexive writings, so lacking in arrogance towards Marx, Weber and their successors.

Mannheim's project can indeed be likened to postmodern questioning of the premises of his own knowledge – including the concept of a project – but we argue here that this does not make him a prophet of the end of modernism. Few writers, after all, fit most models of modernism more closely, certainly in the last decade of his life. When Martin Albrow writes, '[T]he modern is the abstract quality of a historical period, in which the rational and the new form a dynamic alliance,' he could be summarizing Mannheim's claims on behalf of 'thinking at the level of planning'. Yet Albrow might also be recapitulating Mannheim's design for a sociology of knowledge when he writes, in the same context, that his own 'post-modern' proposal for a kind of thinking appropriate to the global age 'tends to identify the way new experience recasts our understanding of old concepts and encourages us to develop new ones', characterizing it as a 'pragmatic universalism which remains skeptical about the possibilities of ever discovering timeless truth in human or natural affairs, while recognizing the necessity to affirm truths on the best understanding available to our own time.'[2] Mannheim, in fact, attempts to incorporate an even thicker – less 'modernist' – slice of skeptical complexity. We treat Mannheim as one of the important figures whose work calls into question the stereotyped – and frequently ideologized – present-day confrontation between modern and postmodern.

SOCIOLOGY AS CULTIVATION

Born in 1893, the son of prosperous Jewish parents, Karl Mannheim spent his first twenty-six years in Budapest, where he graduated in philosophy and precociously participated in the intellectual life of the remarkable Hungarian 'second reform generation' born a decade earlier (Gluck, 1985; Horvath, 1966; Kadarkay, 1991; Káradi and Vezér, 1985; Kettler, 1971). The advanced thinkers of the time were divided between proponents of modernization oriented to French and English social thought and prophets of radical cultural rebirth inspired mainly by Russian and German models. Like many others, Mannheim did not think that his dedication to the latter group, led by the philosopher Georg Lukács, entailed a blanket rejection of the former, under the sociologist Oscar Jászi. Lukács' wartime 'Sunday Circle' in Budapest may have devoted its meetings to Dostoevsky and Meister Eckhardt, with Mannheim in eager attendance, but Lukács was also proud of his acceptance in the Max Weber Circle when he was in Heidelberg. Analogously, Mannheim, during a visiting semester in Berlin in 1914, selected as his master the sociologist Georg Simmel, a subtle mediator between cultural philosophy and sociology. Mannheim's intellectual location at the time is well captured by an essay on Goethe's *Wilhelm Meister* by Lukács.[3] The task that confronted – and confounded – the great German classicist, Lukács maintained, was to transcend the opposition between the modern Idealism epitomized by Kant and the new counter-current of Romanticism. Lukács decided in 1918 that the Communist revolution represented the fulfillment of this classical mission. Mannheim never accepted Lukács' solution, but he was eventually inspired to a selective appropriation of Lukács' Marx, and he was politically compromised in the aftermath by Lukács' patronage during the brief months of the Hungarian Soviet regime. His early apprenticeship to Lukács was fateful.

Mannheim lived in Germany from 1919, when he fled the counter-revolutionary regime in Hungary, until 1933, when National Socialist decrees forced him out of the university. Within a few years of his transfer from the Budapest intellectual scene to German university life, and notwithstanding the rapid publication of several philosophical writings derived from his Hungarian doctoral dissertation on the structure of epistemology, Mannheim began work in Heidelberg on a habilitation thesis in cultural sociology under Alfred Weber.[4] In that year, he also married a fellow-exile, Juliska Láng, a graduate in psychology, whose interests and ideas influenced Mannheim, although the extent of her collaboration cannot be reconstructed. Mannheim's sociological interpretation of the rise and self-differentiation of conservatism, accepted by the faculty in 1925, was subtitled 'A Contribution to the Sociology of Knowledge', and its submission coincided with Mannheim's publication of an article devoted to his critical encounter with Max Scheler, whose *Problems of a Sociology of Knowledge* (1924) had, as noted, brought the concept into discussion during the preceding year. Mannheim's inaugural address as habilitated university instructor set out the parameters of 'the contemporary state of sociology in Germany' as he saw them: he dealt with Max Weber, Ernst Troeltsch and Max Scheler. His opinion of the weight of these sociological thinkers in German intellectual life can be judged from the fact that he planned to publish his three essays on their work in a volume he wanted to call 'On the State of Contemporary Thought'. Sociology, he believed, provided the frame of reference for twentieth-century thinking as a whole.

His aloofness, however, from the specialized 'state of sociology' question as it was debated by the German Sociological Association, as well as his equation of the main currents of all contemporary thought with the leading sociological theories, indicate that his move from philosophy to sociology cannot be understood as a simple change of academic specialization. Sociology, in his view, was a more comprehensive undertaking than the academic discipline taking form under leading professors like Leopold von Wiese at Cologne. Goaded in 1929 by a charge of 'sociologism' against *Ideologie und Utopie* ([1929] 1952) made by the noted literary scholar Ernst Robert Curtius ([1929] 1990), Mannheim invoked the heritage of Max Weber, Ernst Troeltsch and Max Scheler against the literary scholar's accusation of treason to humanism.[5] Mannheim speaks of the sociologists' writings as modern German classics, characterizing them as 'a great heritage, a tradition that must be built upon' (Mannheim, [1929a] 1993). Mannheim's hope of persuading proponents of humanistic education that his broad conception of sociology represents a timely adaptation of the older ideal of *Bildung* is also documented in his occasional correspondence with Eduard Spranger, a popular philosopher active in the controversy about the reform of secondary education in Weimar (Spranger Papers; Loader, 1985: 19, 234–5). In January 1929, Mannheim had visited Spranger to solicit a book for Mannheim's new series of books on topics lying in boundary regions between philosophy and sociology, a series initiated by Scheler. Mannheim wrote to Spranger a few months later to thank him for his promise of cooperation and to urge Spranger to read the forthcoming *Ideologie und Utopie*. Contrary to the denigration of the spirit found in naturalistic sociology, he assures Spranger, his own work is designed to complement the under-

standing of spiritual development that is provided by the cultural studies Spranger is promoting. The social is a mode of the spiritual, Mannheim argues, and a sociological view is not identical with Marxism: 'It is not Marxism but a thoroughgoing sociological approach that alone is capable of bringing to full consciousness the situation which breeds the crisis – I would say, with you, the generative crisis – which you have so brilliantly characterized at the level of world views (Spranger Papers).' Mannheim closes by invoking their close, even fraternal, affinities, and he throws himself on Spranger's judgement, however stern. Unpersuaded, Spranger harshly denounces the 'sociologism' of Mannheim's thought when he reviews *Ideologie und Utopie* a year later (Meja and Stehr, 1990: 239–40), using the same pejorative as Curtius.

When Mannheim projects a sociology that will partly displace philosophy and literature as a foundation of the cultivation (*Bildung*) that German cultural writers carefully distinguished from science (*Wissenschaft*), he clearly does not mean to transfer sociology to academic secondary schools, the traditional site of cultivation. Nor does he mean to deny all legitimacy to the more narrowly defined university discipline. He published a number of professional papers, after all, that accepted the conventional academic constraints.[6] At its highest level, however, he thought, sociology must address the puzzles about the historical diversity and variability of knowledge – specifically social and political knowledge – that philosophy alone can no longer hope to unriddle. He states his case for the multiple levels of sociology most extensively in the introductory course he offered during his first semester after assuming the professorship at Frankfurt in the spring of 1930 (Mannheim, [1930] 2000).[7] Mannheim focuses on the modern experience of distantiation from direct participation in collective moral or cognitive norms, and he contends that all sociology expresses and exacerbates the condition of living an 'experimental' life. Only cultivated sociology, to paraphrase Hegel, can heal the wounds that popular sociology inflicts. Rather than disqualifying human groups from action, as distantiation threatens to do, sociology – and specifically sociology of knowledge – constitutes a mode of encountering life in terms of a new, reflective practice. He rejects the forms of 'reprimitivization' that attempt to deny distance – instancing fascism and orthodox Marxism (in both socialist or communist variants), but he acknowledges the need, from time to time, to reach a conditional accommodation with one or the other of these socio-cognitive eruptions. The common current of distantiation interconnects sociology as comprehensive attitude, sociology as method for historical and similar studies, and sociology as specialized academic discipline. Enabling reflective persons to participate in sociology as comprehensive practice is the new cultivation (*Bildung*).

GERMAN IDEOLOGIES

The novelty in Mannheim's approach to the sociology of knowledge is neither the social interpretation of political ideas nor its extension to a wide range of cultural productions not usually considered political. These he accepts as the achievements of a line of thinkers, culminating in Marx and Weber. Mannheim makes three distinctive claims, epitomized in his later *Ideologie und Utopie* in the concept of total ideology. First, and perhaps most controversial, is the contention that boundaries between manifestly ideological and ostensibly scientific modes of explaining the cultural as well as the social world are porous, with sociology of knowledge emerging in the border region, as a reflexive therapy for both domains. Second, is the concomitant conception of ideologies as cognitive structures. They are variously flawed, limited, perspectivistically one-sided, subject to drastic correction from other perspectives, and nevertheless productive of knowledge. The third original claim, then, is that the sociology of knowledge bears on the answers to substantive questions addressed by ideologies and that it consequently contributes directly to political orientation. It does so, in Mannheim's view, not because knowledge of social genesis can in itself determine judgements of validity, but because the systematic pursuit of such knowledge will foster a synthesis of the valid elements in the ideologies, relocating them in a developmental context that will not so much falsify particularistic ideologies as cognitive structures as render them obsolete – displacing them with a new comprehensive vision. Mannheim's sociology of knowledge, at its most ambitious, is a method for attaining social and political knowledge (that is, a way to such knowing). By requiring sociological thinkers to explicate the diverse intellectual formations competing in the ideological field, correlating them with one another and with the social situation within which the ideological field is located, the study carries inquirers through the topics they must consider before they can realistically diagnose their own time. And inquirers who pursue this course gain a new readiness for comprehensive knowledge. They are freed from illusions about ideologies – and liberated from the disorientation bred of

distantiation. They experience a new form of mastery that is, in turn, incapable of domination.

Mannheim's sociology of knowledge strategy involves two steps. First, the variety of ideas in the modern world is classified according to a scheme of historical ideological types, few in number, in keeping with Mannheim's thesis that the ideological field has moved from a period of atomistic diversity and competition to a period of concentration. Liberalism, conservatism and socialism are the principal types. Second, each of these ideologies is interpreted as a function of some specific way of being in the social world, as defined by location within the historically changing patterns of class and generational stratification. Liberalism is thus referred to the capitalist bourgeoisie in general, and various stages in its development are referred to generational changes. Similar analyses connect conservatism to social classes harmed by the rise to power of the bourgeoisie, and socialism to the new industrial working class. Approaches in the human sciences (*Geisteswissenschaften*) – and notably the social sciences among them (*Sozialwissenschaften*) – have their own ideological lineages, albeit in more sublimated form.[8]

Each of the ideologies is said to manifest a characteristic 'style' of thinking, a distinctive complex of responses to the basic issues that systematic philosophy has identified as constitutive of human consciousness, such as conceptions of time and space, the structure of reality, human agency and knowledge itself. The political judgements and recommendations on the surface of purely ideological texts must be taken in that larger structural context. Not every ideology elaborates such a philosophy, and the elaborated philosophies associated with an ideology may not provide an adequate account of the underlying ideological structures. Such philosophical statements are ideological texts like others, and require structural analysis and sociological interpretation to be fully comprehended. The style of thinking is most apparent in the way concepts are formed, according to Mannheim, and in the logic by which they are interlinked. These are the features that must be uncovered to identify the distinctive style.

Each of the styles, in turn, expresses some distinctive design upon the world vitally bound up with the situation of one of the social strata present in the historical setting. Mannheim is emphatic in his original German texts, but not in his later English revisions, that this design cannot be simply equated to a group 'interest', not least because he disavows the theory of motivation and the indifference to social psychological group processes associated with the stress on interest.[9] The sociologist of knowledge has no direct authoritative information about the formative will he or she postulates as the principle of integration and immanent development in ideological wholes. The self-explanations offered by groups in their ideologies and utopias are the starting points for knowledge about underlying styles and principles, along with such social theories as may be available to expound the logic of their social location, not excluding theories of interests. It is the view of the 'totality' that is the objective. Sociology of knowledge seeks to give an account of the whole ideological field, in its historical interaction and change, together with an account of the historically changing class and generational situations that the ideologies interpret to the groups involved. To have a method for seeing all this, according to Mannheim, means to be able to see in a unified and integrated way what each of the ideologically oriented viewers can only see in part. It is to have the capacity for viewing the situation at a distance and as a whole, without its losing the quality of being a situation in which actions matter. Choice gains in importance as a central feature of the experimental life, which is the epitome of the sociological attitude.

Mannheim draws on Marxism for a conception of politics as a process of dialectical interplay among factors more 'real' than the competing opinions of liberal theory. But neither the proletariat nor any other socio-political force is bearer of a transcendent rationality, historically destined to reintegrate all the struggling irrationalities in a higher, pacified order. The contesting social forces and their projects in the world are complementary and in need of a synthesis that will incorporate elements of their diverse social wills and visions. Syntheses in political vision and *Sozialwissenschaften* are interdependent. Sociology of knowledge presages and fosters both.

Despite the distance Mannheim put between his position and Marxist politics, as such, two of his three promoters, Alfred Weber and Carl Brinckmann, assailed him as a 'historical materialist' at major professional meetings shortly after his habilitation; but the patronage of the third, Emil Lederer, helped Mannheim to a successful start as habilitated instructor in Heidelberg and then, in 1930, to a professorship at Frankfurt. Mannheim's call to Frankfurt would not have been possible, of course, without the remarkable recognition earned by his further work in sociology of knowledge. A presentation on 'Competition' at the Sixth Conference of German Sociologists in 1928 overshadowed the conceptual explication of competition as social mechanism by the most influential proponent of sociology as a specialized discipline, Leopold von Wiese (Mannheim, [1929b] 1993; von Wiese, 1929). Mannheim audaciously used the value-

judgement controversy in recent sociology to illustrate his theses about the connectedness to existence (*Seinsverbundenheit*) of social thought and the operations of socially grounded competition to generate syntheses that transcend intellectual conflict. Mannheim emerged as the 'star' of the meetings, even if many senior sociologists remained distrustful. When a publisher chose Mannheim as Scheler's successor in the editorship of a series on Philosophy and Sociology, Mannheim seized the opportunity. The first book he brought out in the series was his own *Ideologie und Utopie* ([1929] 1952), consisting of an essay on 'politics as a science,' possibly intended for the now abandoned collection on Weber, Troeltsch and Scheler, an essay on Utopian consciousness, written for Alfred Weber's sixtieth birthday in 1928, and a new essay to explicate the concepts of 'ideology' and to tie it, however loosely, to the concept of 'utopia.' Only the first reviews had appeared when Mannheim received the Frankfurt appointment, but the excitement generated by the book launched Mannheim in his new setting, recognized in the wider intellectual community as a significant and controversial personality.[10]

The debate about *Ideologie und Utopie* ([1929] 1952) was mainly philosophical and political, with the focus, first, on Mannheim's hope of overcoming both ideology and political distrust through sociology of knowledge; second, on his conception of the intelligentsia as the social stratum uniquely equipped and even destined for this task; and third, on his activist conception of sociological knowledge, its inherent mediation, as a mode of public consciousness-raising, between theory and practice. Almost all commentators recognized the special importance of Mannheim's essay on Max Weber, 'Is Politics as Science Possible? (The Problem of Theory and Practice) [*Ist Politik als Wissenschaft Möglich? (Das Problem der Theorie und Praxis)*]' (Mannheim, [1929] 1952). In it, Mannheim argues that the comprehensive social knowledge capable of diagnosing the historical situation and grounding a scientific politics is generated by social interpretation of the clashing ideologies rending the political terrain.

In his lecture on 'Science as a Vocation' (1922), Max Weber distinguishes between words in politics and in science, likening the former to weapons for overpowering opponents and the latter to ploughshares for cultivating knowledge. Mannheim offers the sociology of knowledge as a way of bringing about the biblical transformation of swords into pruning hooks prophesied by Isaiah. He claims that the sociology of knowledge constitutes the 'organon for politics as a science'. It provides an instrument for operating on the ideological views active in politics so as to give them a new character, constituting a field of knowledge with a structure appropriate to this dimension of reality and to the work that knowing performs in it. Although Mannheim nominally defers to Weber's conception of politics as a sphere governed by choices no knowledge can dictate, his conception of the political involvement implicit in gaining insight into political situations shifts the meaning of the Weberian formulas he invokes. Political knowledge takes on elements of Hegelian consciousness. Mannheim credits Weber with uncovering that the Marxist method for exposing the social provenance and function of political ideas applies no less to the proletarian view of the world. But rendered non-partisan, the method can now reveal its constructive powers. While the disillusioning discoveries of the earlier generation have to be preserved, they gain new positive functions. When Weber quotes Isaiah's admonition to watchmen in the night, he intends to reproach those who wait in vain for prophets of salvation instead of soberly meeting the demands of the day. Mannheim uses the same passage to call intellectuals to a mission of guardianship (Mannheim, [1929] 1952: 140; Weber, 1922: 613). Mannheim's proposals were widely canvassed in the leading periodical reviews and subjected to intense criticism, but his reading of the intellectual situation was almost universally applauded. In the cultivated Weimar public for political-literary topics, as among the participants in what has been labeled the 'Weimar conversation' about the situation of social thought after Nietzsche and Marx, *Ideologie und Utopie* ([1929] 1952) figured as the representative book of its time, whether as symptom of cultural crisis or as promise of a way out.

During his five semesters as professor in Frankfurt, Mannheim in effect declined the role of public intellectual. He separated the professional aspects of his activities from his public reputation. Only one of his critics received an answer, and then only a rejoinder to the charge of trespassing beyond the bounds of sociology. While he drew close to Paul Tillich and his circle of religious socialists in private discussions, his publications and organizational efforts concentrated on strengthening his legitimacy in the sociology chair. His classes attracted a large and comparatively diverse audience, including many women students and male students of diverse but active political commitments. Mannheim's strategy in his courses was to build on the generalized popular 'sociological' attitude he expected them to bring with them, but to argue the need for a move towards rigor in method and specificity in research work. Celebrated and embattled as an 'intellectual,' he defined himself ever more as a professional sociologist. His 1931

article on 'Sociology of Knowledge' in a professional handbook was philosophically more cautious than *Ideologie und Utopie* ([1929] 1952), hiving off speculations about political or philosophical implications from problems of empirical enquiry. In 1932, he found himself providing a comprehensive guide to the 'present tasks of sociology' for teachers. While expanding the boundaries of the field to include contemporary political studies and cultural approaches that might have been left out by others, he took great care to respect the territorial rights of the major figures in the discipline and avoided anything like his earlier polemics against Positivism. In conjunction with his friend, the economist Adolf Löwe, he organized an interdisciplinary research seminar on Liberalism, and together, as is evident from coordinated presentations they made in the Netherlands in 1933, they began an enquiry into planning as a counter to the evident crisis of liberalism. Mannheim clearly did not want to become a man of one book.

Mannheim was caught unawares by the Nazi measure that deprived him of his professorship on grounds of his foreign birth and Jewish ethnicity. He had not exposed himself politically. *Ideologie und Utopie* ([1929] 1952) had been generously treated in the Socialist periodical *Die Gesellschaft*, but the four articles published there were all more critical than the reception that his work received in *Die Tat*, a periodical of the activist right. The hard left treated him as a betrayer of Marxism. In advising a young Communist about the conditions of matriculating for study with him, he wrote, two weeks before Hitler became Chancellor, that the student would find 'a rather intensive study group, close contact with the lecturers, but little dogmatic commitment, we do not think of ourselves as a political party but must act as if we had a lot of time and could calmly discuss the pros and cons of every matter' (OJP: Letter to G. Jászi, 16 January, 1933).[11] Three months later, Mannheim was a refugee in Amsterdam. Neither his sociology nor his politics had anything to do with his exile from Germany.

SOCIOLOGY IN AN AGE OF
REPRIMITIVIZATION

In the summer of 1933, Mannheim was appointed to a special lectureship at the London School of Economics, the beneficiary of a fund for exiled scholars. He was selected by the political theorist Harold Laski, and the sociologist Morris Ginsberg, above all for his well-known work on sociology of knowledge, which Ginsberg saw as a continental version of the evolutionary sociology of rationality associated with his own mentor, Leonard Hobhouse. Mannheim soon concluded, however, that neither the times nor his situation were conducive to pursuing sociology of knowledge studies. It was necessary to compact with a less than fully reflective public knowledge. He saw it as his mission to diagnose the general crisis he held responsible for the German disaster and to promote prophylactic and therapeutic measures in Britain. His sense of urgency and his grand theoretical ambitions enthused many students, but they rapidly estranged the beleaguered small core of professional sociologists led by Morris Ginsberg, who were engaged in a difficult fight to found the academic respectability of a discipline widely dismissed by the English university establishment as a dilettante pursuit. Although Mannheim was marginalized at the London School of Economics, the only British institution with a chair in Sociology, he was able to make a place for himself as a public intellectual, especially after his acceptance by a circle of Christian thinkers whose periodic discussions and publications centered on a theme of cultural crisis hospitable to Mannheim's sociological interpretations (Kettler and Meja, 1995; Loader, 1985).

Mannheim continued to focus on the relationship between knowledge and society, his lifelong topic. The core problem, however, is no longer presented as a conflict among hypostatized partial views vainly competing to monopolize the definition of a social situation that can only be adequately grasped as socially diverse and intellectually multifaceted. Writing in *Man and Society in an Age of Reconstruction* (1940), a work that was no less influential in the postwar years than *Ideology and Utopia* (1936), he claims that the sociology of knowledge has lost its strategic centrality with the demise of ideological competition (Mannheim, 1940). Mannheim asks for 'a new experimental attitude in social affairs,' in view of the 'practical deterioration of the ideals of Liberalism, Communism, and Fascism'. He continues:

> But one can only learn if one has belief in the power of reason. For a time it was healthy to see the limitations of *ratio*, especially in social affairs. It was healthy to realize that thinking is not powerful if it is severed from the social context and ideas are only strong if they have their social backing, that it is useless to spread ideas which have no real function and are not woven into the social fabric. But this sociological interpretation of ideas may also lead to complete despair, discouraging the individual from thinking about issues which will definitely become the concern of the day. This discouragement of the

intelligentsia may lead them to too quick a resignation of their proper function as the thinkers and forerunners of the new society, may become even more disastrous in a social setting where more depends on what the leading elites have in mind than in other periods of history. (Mannheim, 1940: 365)

The theory of the social determination of ideas properly applied to the age of war and dictatorship, Mannheim continues, shows that everything depends on 'whether or not sound thinking goes on today and whether it reaches the ruling elites'.[12] When these passages are read in the light of his continued eagerness to see the sociology of knowledge project carried forward, as expressed in his 1946 letter to Kurt H. Wolff (Wolff, [1959] 1974: 557–8), it is difficult to escape the conclusion that his wartime statements represent the sort of conditional bargain with the least harmful forms of reprimitivized thought that he acknowledged in 1930 (Mannheim, [1930] 2000) as necessary whenever unconditional action was imperative.

The National Socialist dictatorship, he now argues, exploits a socially unconscious mass response to a worldwide crisis in the institutions of liberal civilization, involving the obsolescence of its regulative social technologies – from markets to parliaments to elitist humanistic education. Mannheim pleads for a preemptive move to a planned social order that strategically utilizes, instead of vainly resisting, the new social technologies that undermine the spontaneous self-ordering of the previous epoch. A discriminating, consensual reconstruction could save many human qualities and diversities earlier privileged by liberalism, unlike the violent homogenization imposed by Communist or National Socialist control through command. Without anachronistic confidence in obsolete forms of liberalism, planning for freedom would rely as far as possible on manipulated field controls (more recently known as steering by induced self-regulation) and other unbureaucratic techniques for coordinating activities that proceed best when experienced as spontaneous. Timely action guided by awareness of the impending crisis taken by leading strata whose positions are still sheltered from the full force of the devastating changes under way, notably the English elite of gentlemanly professionals, can tame the processes that would otherwise destroy the old liberal civilization and condition mass populations for dictatorial domination. Planning for freedom presupposes a reorientation among traditional elites, their acceptance of a sociological diagnosis of the times and their willingness to learn prophylactic and therapeutic techniques. Mannheim now claims for sociology the ability to ground and coordinate interdisciplinary approaches to the problems encountered in planning. If British sociologists were skeptical about this proposed redirection of their discipline, Mannheim's lectures and writings on 'planning' won him an interested audience, especially during the war and immediate postwar years, and his conception of a post-ideological age was never altogether submerged by the Cold War. As his wartime slogan of 'militant democracy' justified German measures against leftists during the middle decades of the century, his slogan of the 'Third Way' is heard at the turn of the millennium in support of political designs he would have found quite familiar.

SOCIOLOGY AS SCIENCE: LOSING THE WAR

Among sociologists, however, Mannheim's standing was defined by the reception of *Ideology and Utopia* ([1931] 1936), a redacted translation of *Ideologie und Utopie* ([1929] 1952) published in collaboration with the American sociologist Louis Wirth (and his assistant, Edward Shils), framed by a new beginning and a new end: a new justification of the enterprise by Mannheim and a republication of his 1931 sociological handbook article. In his preface, Wirth casts the work primarily as a contribution to objectivity in social science. By systematizing the work of discounting for the effects of interests in social judgements, the sociology of knowledge can rebuild a working agreement on the facts among social scientists divided by conflicting social values. Mannheim's program for understanding action through socially grounded motivations, moreover, provides a framework for objective study of phenomena that cannot be understood without empathy with the human actors under examination. This does not entail an abandonment of the determinism that is integral to a usable science, Wirth maintains, but merely the elaboration of disciplinary techniques, sketchy as Mannheim's psychology might be, appropriate to the comprehension of a determination through motives. Wirth's emphasis on the methodological bearing of Mannheim's work inadvertently contributed to the result that he and Mannheim were especially eager to avoid. *Ideology and Utopia* was debated among American sociologists first of all as a challenge to value-free and empirical sociology.[13]

The original terms of American discussion were set by reviews in the principal sociological journals by German sociologists in America. Most influential – and most disappointing for Mannheim – was an essay by Alexander von Schelting, who had already assailed the

philosophical ambitions of the original German publication on the basis of neo-Kantian epistemological teachings, and who once again charges Mannheim with lapsing into a relativist vicious circle by virtue of an elementary confusion between the meaning and the validity of the ideas he subjected to sociological interpretation. Although Mannheim thought that he could counter such objections with the help of John Dewey's pragmatism, Louis Wirth chose instead, when confronted with this argument at a session on Mannheim's book at the 1937 meeting of the Sociological Research Association, to deprecate the attention paid to Mannheim's peripheral philosophical speculations in assessing the work. Wirth insists, quoting *Ideology and Utopia*, that for Mannheim the 'principal problem' of the sociology of knowledge is 'the purely empirical investigation through description and structural analysis of the ways in which social relationships, in fact, influence thought' (Mannheim, [1931] 1936: 239).[14] By this time, Wirth had already abandoned 'sociology of knowledge' as the name of his course at the University of Chicago, in favor of 'sociology of intellectual life'.[15] Wirth's shift in emphasis anticipated the terms on which Mannheim was ultimately recognized as a contributor to American sociological discussion.

The professional consensus is formalized in Robert K. Merton's authoritative essay on 'The Sociology of Knowledge' (Merton, ([1945] 1957).[16] Merton includes Mannheim in a group of social theorists from Karl Marx to Pitirim Sorokin, whose diverse approaches to 'the relations between knowledge and other existential factors in the society and culture' he relates to a syllabus of questions and alternative answers, which lays down, in turn, an agenda for the theoretical clarification and empirical research required to build a proper subdiscipline of sociology. Merton's 'Paradigm' for the Sociology of Knowledge sets out five key issues: the existential basis of mental productions, the varieties and aspects of mental productions subject to sociological analysis, the specific relationship(s) between mental productions and existential basis, the functions of existentially conditioned mental productions, and the conditions under which the imputed relations obtain. Crediting Mannheim with having 'sketched the broad contours of the sociology of knowledge with remarkable skill and insight', Merton nevertheless found his theory very loose, needlessly burdened with dubious philosophical claims, and strikingly unclear in identifying the range of mental productions considered *seinsverbunden* – notably with regard to the exact sciences – as well as imprecise and inconsistent in specifying the exact character of this relationship. Merton was unpersuaded by Mannheim's speculations about the bearing of sociology of knowledge on epistemological issues, and, more importantly, he was convinced that the question only arose for Mannheim because of confusion about the principal philosophical import of his own theses. In substance, Merton contends, Mannheim's arguments about the social sciences, logically imply nothing more, despite his denials, than Max Weber's neo-Kantian awareness of the value-relevance (*Wertbezogenheit*) of problem choice. 'Mannheim's procedures and substantial findings clarify relations between knowledge and social structure which have hitherto remained obscure,' Merton concludes in 1941, but only after they are 'shorn of their epistemological impedimenta, with their concepts modified by the lessons of further empirical inquiry and with occasional logical inconsistencies eliminated' (Merton, [1941] 1957: 508; cf. Swidler and Arditi, 1994).

Despite some uncertainty in the matter, the condition for Mannheim's acceptance as a deserving pioneer of sociology was the discarding of the concept of total ideology, his way of calling into question both social science and social knowledge, the epitome of the problem constellation which had energized Mannheim's engagement with sociology of knowledge and the prime stimulus for the excitement following the original publication of *Ideologie und Utopie* ([1929] 1952). Mannheim had reserved the empirical option that was taken up and he had given it added prominence in the changes introduced in *Ideology and Utopia* ([1931] 1936), but he always considered it a mere temporizing with an inevitable problem; and he was seemingly content to let matters rest while he pursued, until his premature death in 1947, his more urgent advocacy of planning, which presupposed confidence in an unproblematic sociological science.[17] In editing and introducing three posthumous collections of Mannheim's essays, his intimate friends, the noted social scientists Paul Kecskemeti and Adolph Loewe, reinforced the consensus view. As Mannheim became better acquainted with Anglo-American social science, they argued, empirical social psychology had steadily displaced the stimulating but misleading continental philosophies as the theoretical framework for his thinking about knowledge and society, and his early writings merit consideration primarily as brilliant anticipations of these promising developments, cut off too soon. In Robert Merton's sociological theory classes during the 1950s, *Ideology and Utopia* often followed Machiavelli's *Prince* in the syllabus, as source material for an exercise in transmuting suggestive ideas into testable propositions.

TAKING COUNSEL WITH MANNHEIM

Shall we master the globe's inner stresses, or
are we shipwrecked upon our own history?

Karl Mannheim, 1930

Stretching Thomas Kuhn's concept of a scientific paradigm, as was commonly done by optimistic social scientists in the years after the publication of his *Structure of Scientific Revolutions* (1970), it could be said that Mannheim's work had joined the list of historical authorities celebrated in stereotyped simplicity as legitimating precursors of a settled way of defining and doing sociology. Yet Kuhn also called attention to the critical reassessment of historical texts when a dominant paradigm is unsettled by inassimilable findings or unorthodox novelties. If we accept Kuhn's language of scientific paradigm as metaphor for a broader range of related cultural configurations, we can trace the renewal of attention to the historical social thinker Karl Mannheim to the renewed conflicts about the subject matter, method and attitude of sociology that erupted in the 1960s. The connection is not simple, since the attack on the disciplinary consensus, where historical models were involved, was more likely to call on Marxist writers or on figures like Theodor W. Adorno, Max Horkheimer and Herbert Marcuse, who had been among Mannheim's harshest contemporary critics. The effect, nevertheless, was to relegitimate questions about the historicity of social knowledge, the problem of relativism, and the paths of reflexivity open to social thinkers – the issues filtered out of Mannheim's thought in his American reception – and to provide a new point of connection for Kurt H. Wolff and some other sociologists, who had quietly continued puzzling over the issues debated when *Ideologie und Utopie* ([1929] 1952) first appeared. In this newly fluid state of questions appropriate for sociological theory, Mannheim's famous book no longer stands alone among Mannheim's writings and his insistence on its essayistic experimentalism is no longer ignored. And Mannheim is considered more as a bargaining partner than as a model, with recent theoretical interlocutors finding value in bringing him into conversations with Rorty, Foucault, Bakhtin or Bourdieu. There are no propositions to be distilled out of Mannheim's work; there is just the thoughtful encounter with it. Mannheim's prediction about the consequences of uncovering the 'massive fact' of knowledge in society and society in knowledge has been borne out. Yet we are not beneficiaries of any 'progress' in thought, as postmodernists paradoxically often suppose: we may well have to think deeply about old texts, however we class them.

NOTES

1 Kurt H. Wolff circumscribes the 'peculiar viewpoint of the sociology of knowledge' as one of seeing 'mental events in their relative social setting', in the first of the series of self-questioning reflections initiated early in his career (Wolff, [1943] 1974: 476).

2 Albrow, 1997: 81. Among writings on sociology and the supposed end of modernism that inform this chapter, we single out Alexander and Sztompka, 1990 and Albrow, 1997. We have also benefited from conference papers, as yet unpublished, by Claudia Honegger and Anna Wessely (see contributions by the editors in Endreß and Srubar, 1999).

3 The essay on Goethe is found in Lukács' *The Theory of the Novel*, the subject of Mannheim's first German publication, an admiring review (Mannheim, [1920] 1993).

4 Mannheim scholarship, including Kettler and Meja, 1995, has overlooked evidence that Mannheim almost certainly followed up his semester with Heidegger in Freiburg with several semesters under Jaspers and Rickert at Heidelberg. In his tribute to Alfred Weber, written in 1937, Mannheim recalls that he had made several efforts to habilitate with 'a bearded professor' – probably Rickert – before he abandoned this dictatorial sponsor in favor of Weber. For Mannheim's immersion in the philosophical debates of the time, see the essay by Reinhard Laube in Endreß and Srubar 1999.

5 Mannheim's original version of his best-known book will be cited throughout as *Ideologie und Utopie*. The translation (1936) was revised in several important respects and will be cited by its English title. See Kettler and Meja, 1995: 213–16.

6 For example, Mannheim published an abridgement of his habilitation thesis in a version consistent with Alfred Weber's conception of cultural sociology (Mannheim, 1927), and a conceptual analysis of the sociological problem of generations that comes very close in its starting point to Leopold von Wiese, whose closely held journal also provided the outlet (Mannheim, [1928] 1993). Cf. Loader and Kettler, 2001.

7 The text was recently found in the papers of the noted sociologist Hans Gerth. English translation by Colin Loader and David Kettler (Mannheim, 2000).

8 A major conclusion of Mannheim's habilitation thesis is the filiation of philosophy of life (*Lebensphilosophie*) and historicism, movements he considers quite radical in their intellectual consequences, to conservative ideology.

9 Mannheim analyses the limitations of interpretations grounded on 'interest' and argues the case for 'engagement' in Mannheim, [1925] 1993: 377. The synoptic overview of Mannheim's philosophical hopes for sociology of knowledge offered here draws not only on writings he published in his lifetime, but also the posthumous treatises (Mannheim, [1922–24] 1982). The anthologized essays (Mannheim, [1924] 1952 and Mannheim, [1926] 1993), draw on these more systematically argued texts.

10 Mannheim won the attention of a remarkable sample of the younger thinkers who came to prominence during the ensuing years, if only in emigration. *Die Gesellschaft*, the theoretical journal of the SPD, provides the most striking example. In the last issue of 1929 and the first issue of 1930, it brought long, critical articles on *Ideologie und Utopie* ([1929] 1952) by Paul Tillich, Hannah Arendt, Herbert Marcuse and Hans Speier (see Meja and Stehr, 1990). The best German reception survey is Wolff, 1978.

11 In this correspondence, Mannheim was counseling the son of his own mentor, Oscar Jászi, at the father's request. Mannheim's conception of a political education for choice is developed in *Ideologie und Utopie* ([1929] 1952). See also Mannheim, [1932] 1993 and his 1930 lecture notes (Mannheim, [1930] 1999). On 'political education' see Mannheim (2000) and Loader and Kettler (2001). As Louis Wirth suggests in a memo (LWP, 65: 4), there is reason to believe that Mannheim's conceptions influenced the development of the Berlin *Hochschule für Politik*, founded in the mid-1920s, whose program embraced 'synthesis' through multi-partisanship. A survey of the press published in 1931 and 1932 by the Research Division of the *Hochschule* expressly sought to factor out the ideological element in the diverse news coverages it analyzed (RF: 1: 717).

12 As a measure of Mannheim's influence at the time, we suggest that three seminal books of the 1950s are best understood as critical responses to Mannheim's writings on planning: Friedrich Hayek's *Counter-Revolution of Science*, Karl Popper's *The Poverty of Historicism*, and Robert Dahl and Charles Lindblom's *Politics, Economics and Welfare*.

13 For Mannheim's reception in America, see Wolff, [1943] 1974; Nelson, 1990; Rüschemeyer, 1981. Cf. Kettler and Meja, 1995.

14 The passage quoted by Wirth illustrates the adjustments Mannheim made in revising the English translation. In the German version, the empirical aspect of the sociology of knowledge is characterized as a matter of **phenomenological** description and the transition to epistemological enquiry is treated as a logical step that can be delayed or avoided but not called into question (Mannheim, [1931] 1952: 229).

15 'During the coming year,' Wirth wrote in mid-1937, 'I shall again give a course on the Sociology of Intellectual Life, which I am coming to think is a better translation of *Wissenssoziologie* than the Sociology of Knowledge' (LWP, 7/11: 17.8.37). Wirth's interest in *Wissenssoziologie* was strongly supported by his brilliant assistant, Edward Shils, whose detailed

studies of German social theory equipped him to probe more deeply than Wirth into Mannheim's work. Archival evidence confirms Shils' recollection that he was in fact the translator of *Ideology and Utopia*. Wirth's 'Preface' (Mannheim, 1936), his contributions to the Sociological Research Association discussion of Mannheim, and his University of Chicago lecture course have detailed memoranda from Shils as their bases. Shils did not agree with Wirth's narrowing of the issues (LWP).

16 Merton's views on Mannheim, codified in 1945 in his magisterial survey of the sub-field, were first set forth in a 1941 essay that dealt with Mannheim's work alone. Both of these essays, grouped with a paper summarizing Merton and Lazarsfeld's wartime 'Studies on Radio and Film Propaganda' and introduced by an introduction justifying the bracketing as a way of posing the problem of mediating between 'European' and 'American' ways of studying relations between social structures and communications, are included in Merton's *Social Theory and Social Structure* ([1945] 1957), the basic statement of Columbia sociology during the decades of its greatest influence.

17 It should be noted that the only dissertation completed under Mannheim's direction in England, Viola Klein's *The Feminine Character: History of an Ideology* (1946), was in fact an express application of *Wissenssoziologie* to nominally scientific theories, aspiring to extract an adequate understanding of the substantive issue through the sociological encounter with approaches exposed as ideological. Remarkably enough, Mannheim's preface to the published work, brought out in the series he was editing, slighted the sociology of knowledge aspect in favor of a concept of problem-centered interdisciplinarity, which Klein herself considered incidental.

REFERENCES

Albrow, Martin (1997) *The Global Age*. Stanford, CA: Stanford University Press.
Alexander, Jeffrey C. and Sztompka, Piotr (eds) (1990) *Rethinking Progress*. Boston, MA: Unwin Hyman.
Curtius, Ernst Robert ([1929] 1990) 'Sociology – and its Limits', in Volker Meja and Nico Stehr (eds), *Knowledge and Politics*. London and New York: Routledge. pp. 113–20.
Endreß, Martin and Srubar, Ilja (eds) (1999) *Karl Mannheims Beitrag zur Analyse moderner Gesellschaften*. Opladen: Leske and Biedrich.
Gluck, Mary (1985) *Georg Lukács and his Generation, 1900–1918*. Cambridge, MA: Harvard University Press.
Horváth, Zoltán (1966) *Die Jahrhundertwende in Ungarn*. Budapest: Corvina.
Káradi, Eva and Vezér, Erzsébet (eds) (1985) *Georg Lukács, Karl Mannheim und der Sonntagskreis*. Frankfurt: Sendler.
Kadarkay, Arpad (1991) *Georg Lukács: Life, Thought, and Politics*. Cambridge, MA: Blackwell.
Kettler, David (1971) 'Culture and Revolution: Lukács in the Hungarian Revolutions of 1918/1919', *Telos*, 10: 35–92.
Kettler, David and Meja, Volker (1995) *Karl Mannheim and the Crisis of Liberalism: The Secret of These New Times*. New Brunswick, NJ: Transaction Books.
Klein, Viola (1946) *The Femine Character. History of an Ideology*. London: Routledge and Kegan Paul.
Loader, Colin (1985) *The Intellectual Development of Karl Mannheim: Culture, Politics, and Planning*. Cambridge: Cambridge University Press.
Loader, Colin and Kettler, David (2001) *Karl Mannheim's Sociology as Political Education*. New Brunswick, NJ: Transaction Books.
Louis Wirth Papers (LWP). Regenstein Library. University of Chicago.
Mannheim, Karl ([1920] 1993) 'A Review of Georg Lukács' *Theory of the Novel*', in Kurt H. Wolff (ed.) *From Karl Mannheim*. New Brunswick, NJ: Transaction Books. pp. 131–5.
Mannheim, Karl ([1922–24] 1982) *Structures of Thinking* (ed. David Kettler, Volker Meja and Nico Stehr). London: Routledge and Kegan Paul.
Mannheim, Karl ([1924] 1952) 'Historicism', *Essays in the Sociology of Knowledge*. London: Routledge and Kegan Paul. pp. 84–133.
Mannheim, Karl ([1925] 1993) 'The Problem of a Sociology of Knowledge', *From Karl Mannheim* (2nd expanded edition) (ed. Kurt H. Wolff). New Brunswick, NJ: Transaction Books. pp. 220–43.
Mannheim, Karl ([1926] 1993) 'The Ideological and the Sociological Interpretation of Intellectual Phenomena', *From Karl Mannheim* (2nd expanded edition) (ed. Kurt H. Wolff). New Brunswick, NJ: Transaction Books. pp. 244–59.
Mannheim, Karl (1927) 'Das konservative Denken', *Archiv für sozialwissenschaft und Sozialpolitik*, 57 (1): 68–142; (2): 470–95.
Mannheim, Karl ([1928] 1993) 'The Problem of Generations', *From Karl Mannheim* (2nd expanded edition) (ed. Kurt H. Wolff). New Brunswick, NJ: Transaction Books. pp. 355–95.
Mannheim, Karl ([1929] 1952) *Ideologie und Utopie*, 3rd edn. Frankfurt a.M.: Schulte–Bulmke.
Mannheim, Karl ([1929a] 1993) 'Problems of Sociology in Germany', *From Karl Mannheim* (2nd expanded edition) (ed. Kurt H. Wolff). New Brunswick, NJ: Transaction Books. pp. 438–56.
Mannheim, Karl ([1929b] 1993) 'Competition as a Cultural Phenomenon', *From Karl Mannheim* (2nd expanded edition) (ed. Kurt H. Wolff). New Brunswick, NJ: Transaction Books. pp. 399–437.
Mannheim, Karl ([1930] 2000) 'An Introduction to Sociology', Karl Mannheim, *Sociology as Political Education: Texts* (ed. Colin Loader and David Kettler). New Brunswick, NJ: Transaction Books.

Mannheim, Karl ([1931] 1936) 'The Sociology of Knowledge', *Ideology and Utopia*. London: Routledge and Kegan Paul. pp. 237–80.

Mannheim, Karl ([1931] 1952) 'Wissensoziologie', *Ideologie und Utopie*, 3rd edn. Frankfurt a.M.: Schulte–Bulmke.

Mannheim, Karl ([1932] 1993) 'The Sociology of Intellectuals', *Theory, Culture and Society*, 10 (3): 69–80.

Mannheim, Karl (1940) *Man and Society in an Age of Reconstruction*. London: Routledge and Kegan Paul.

Meja, Volker and Stehr, Nico (eds) (1990) *Knowledge and Politics*. London and New York: Routledge.

Merton, Robert K. ([1941] 1957) 'Karl Mannheim and the Sociology of Knowledge', *Social Theory and Social Structure* (revised and enlarged edition). Glencoe: The Free Press. pp. 489–508.

Merton, Robert K. ([1945] 1957) 'The Sociology of Knowledge', *Social Theory and Social Structure* (revised and enlarged edition). Glencoe: The Free Press. pp. 456–88.

Nelson, Rodney D. (1990) 'The Reception and Development of the Sociology of Knowledge in American Sociology, 1936–1960'. PhD dissertation, University of Toronto.

Oscar Jászi Papers (OJP). Rare Books and Manuscript Library, Columbia University.

Pels, Dick (1996a) '[Review of] *Karl Mannheim and the Crisis of Liberalism: The Secret of these New Times*, by David Kettler and Volker Meja', *American Journal of Sociology*, 101 (6): 1774–6.

Pels, Dick (1996b) 'Karl Mannheim and the Sociology of Scientific Knowledge: Towards a New Agenda', *Sociological Theory*, 14 (1): 30–48.

Rockefeller Foundation Archives (Paris Office) (RF), North Tarrytown, New York.

Rüschemeyer, Dietrich (1981) 'Die Nichtrezeption von Karl Mannheims Wissensoziologie in der amerikanischen Soziologie', in M. Rainer Lepsius (ed.), *Soziologie in Deutschland und Österreich 1918–1945*. Opladen: Westdeutscher Verlag. pp. 414–26.

Scheler, Max (ed.) (1924) *Versuche zu einer Soziologie des Wissens*. Munich: Duncker and Humblot.

Spranger Papers. Bundesarchiv, Koblenz, Germany.

Swidler, Ann and Arditi, Jorge (1994) 'The New Sociology of Knowledge', *Annual Review of Sociology*, 20: 305–29.

von Schelting, Alexander (1936) '[Review of Mannheim's] *Ideologie und Utopie*', *American Sociological Review*, 11 (4): 664–74.

von Wiese, Leopold (1929) 'Die Konkurrenz, vorwiegend in soziologisch-systematischer Betrachtung', *Verhandlungen des Sechstem deutschen Sozialogentages*. Tübingen: J.C.B. Mohr (Paul Siebeck). pp. 15–35.

Weber, Max (1922) 'Wissenschaft als Beruf', in *Wissenschaftslehre*. Tübingen: J.C.B. Mohr (Paul Siebeck).

Wolff, Kurt H. ([1943] 1974) 'The Sociology of Knowledge: Emphasis on an Empirical Attitude', in *Trying Sociology*. New York: John Wiley & Sons. pp. 461–86.

Wolff, Kurt H. ([1959] 1974) 'The Sociology of Knowledge and Sociological Theory', in *Trying Sociology*. New York: John Wiley & Sons. pp. 554–90.

Wolff, Kurt H. ([1967] 1974) 'The Sociology of Knowledge in the United States of America', in *Trying Sociology*. New York: John Wiley & Sons. pp. 609–46.

Wolff, Kurt H. (1978) 'Karl Mannheim', in Dirk Käsler (ed.), *Klassiker des Soziologischen Denkens*. Munich: Beck. pp. 289–362.

10

Psychoanalysis and Sociology: From Freudo-Marxism to Freudo-Feminism

JOHN O'NEILL

RECEPTION CONTEXTS

Universities continue to organize themselves around the division of faculties. This dictates the division of departments that in turn dictate the division of subjects which constitute their curricula. At the same time, universities are encouraged to espouse multidisciplinary research to which they respond precisely because their faculties and postgraduate students have long recognized the practice of mixed knowledge or blurred genres. The arts and sciences now borrow so freely from each other both on the level of theory and of method that the wall that once separated the two cultures is now more like an overstretched borderline crossed daily by sociologists, philosophers, literary and psycho-analytic theorists. Yet somehow these border-lines still serve to inspire cultural theorists to the celebration of transgression, law-breaking and dis-affiliation (O'Neill, 1995). Here, of course, cultural workers enjoy rights of renunciation, violation and transit not shared by other workers whose transfiguration is blocked or stalled in messianic time.

Our present enlightenment severely tests our previous enlightenment. It therefore strains sociology, which is a child of the Enlightenment. It thereby invites sociologists to turn to psycho-analysis like that elder child in their family whose wounded self-knowledge and painful submission to society may deepen their under-standing. The psychoanalysis turn may well appear to involve a retreat from sociology's determination to release us from pre-history, to let us out of the family, to unbind myth and emotion with knowledge and its freedoms. Hence, the wall between sociology and psycho-analysis. But it turns out that in its escape to freedom sociology may well have hurriedly packed its baggage with hasty notions of sub-jectivity, agency and law, of reason and imagi-nation, of sexuality and of language. The result has been that in the past forty years or so sociologists have been obliged to return to the hermeneutical sciences, in particular to psycho-analysis. There are many shifts within the linguistic turn. In sociology's case, the shifts are through ordinary language philosophy (Wittgenstein, 1958) to hermeneutics (Gadamer, 1975) to critical theory (Habermas, 1971) and to the linguistic return to Freud (Lacan, 1968), shifts that have restored the (un)conscious in reason's project (Ricouer, 1974).

What had to be challenged for Freud's socio-logical adaptation was his insistence upon universal knowledge of the human species and the primacy of internal over external factors in the determination of eventual behaviour. In 'Totem and Taboo', the struggle between the integrating force of Eros and the destructive force of primary masochism is tipped by the severity of the super-ego against individual desire in favour of the authority of institutions. Human prematurity and helplessness mean that aggression towards objects and others is the latent source of the aggression we form against ourselves in the name of external authorities. Clearly, Freud's position on the structure of the political unconscious is as hard on any utopian movement as it is upon totalitarian regimes even though it may appear to offer no remedy on either score. The Freudian position is that political ideologies are projections divorced from their unconscious drives and defence mechanisms which prevents their recognition of their internal source of failure. As the creations of a 'purified ego', political ideologies project conflict-free futures guaranteed by the expulsion of the evils located in the father or in the property system. From this perspective, illusion will always have a future but the future will never emerge from illusions.

Psychoanalytic theory entered the social sciences earlier in the United States than the United Kingdom (Bocock, 1976, 1983). It did so prematurely – the effect being realized only in the 1960s and as a carrier of student body-politics, whose failure repeated the earlier failure of prewar Marxism to realize love's body. The second wave of psychoanalytic reception in both the US and the UK had to wait out the rise of 'French Marx' in the 1980s, which was itself a disciplinary response to failed revolution. Meantime, critical attention turned to the analysis of the constitutional bond between knowledge and power, to the madness and oppression in the heart of rationality. In the UK, the works of Laing (1969) and Cooper (1971) developed an existential anti-psychiatry (Sedgwick, 1982), compared to the work of Goffman (1961) and Szasz (1961) in the US and to the work of Foucault (1973) and Deleuze/Guattari (1977) in France. But it is from France that we inherit the 'return to Freud', that is, a return to the classic texts of psychoanalysis, an effect that was then multiplied in literary, philosophical and socio-logical readings of Freudian psychoanalysis. These studies have inspired the politics of sexual and racial identity, driving the new industry of cultural studies that transgress conventional disciplinary boundaries. They have also con-tributed to the redefinition of the academic labour force and the larger culture of the university. Thus the 'marriage' between sociol-ogy and psychoanalysis which was produced by rethinking the failure of 'the revolution' has contributed to the implosion of 'minoritarian' movements in the past two decades.

Against this rather sweeping characterization of events that far exceeds the contextualization that I have imposed upon them, I shall now follow through 'analytically', as Parsons would say, where sociology took on board what is needed from psychoanalysis to accomplish its own agenda. The Parsonian assumption of Freud is given here in some detail because it provides a benchmark for many of the assertions and denials in the later, post-oedipal readings developed in particular by feminist theorists. The rubrics I shall have to employ are beholden to

the contexts generated by the interaction of sociology and psychoanalysis:

1 Socialization theory
2 Civilization theory
3 Post-oedipal theory

So it must be understood that these organiza-tional rubrics merely gesture towards 'encyclo-paedism'. This is because we now live in an age of broken knowledge and fragmented justice whose drive towards integrity and solidarity can take no giant step.

SOCIALIZATION THEORY

Parsons' basically Durkheimian theory of cul-ture necessarily sets aside Freud's instinctualism or biologism in order to bring psychoanalysis into the liberal voluntarist paradigm of social interaction. For this reason, he vehemently rejected Wrong's (1961) resurrection of the anti-social instincts and his 'undialectical' con-struct of the 'oversocialized man'. Parsons' integrative bias overrides Freud's view that ambivalence is the bottom character of our social relations and as such always leaves us open to the possibility of regression. The costs of sublimation and sacrifice on behalf of society are so high that Freud was pessimistic about our ability to sustain them. As we shall see, later theorists (Fromm, Marcuse, Brown) adopt various revisionist strategies on this issue. On the level of psycho-history, Freud's concept of religion as an obsessional neurosis entirely separates him from Parsons' liberal progressive conception of the reinforcements of religion and capitalism in the development of modern individualism. Here, too, Parsons' conception of the liberal professions in the production of health, education and social management places them on a broader stage than Freud's clinic (O'Neill, 1995) – not to mention Goffman (1961) and Foucault's studies of the asylum (1973).

Yet Parsons read Freud very closely for his own analytic purpose. Parsons was especially attracted to Lecture XXXI of the *New Intro-ductory Lecture on Psychoanalysis* (1933), where Freud takes up 'The Dissection of the Psychical Personality'. Here Freud re-enters the 'physical underworld' to revisit the forces that result in ego-splitting (the overlapping of self-observa-tion, judgement and punishment) that we attribute to the rule of conscience. Freud's phenomenon, however, is not Durkheim's social concept of conscience but that roller-coaster ride of moral depression and elation experienced by the melancholic. Nor is the super-ego Kant's heavenly lamp. It is a parental image through

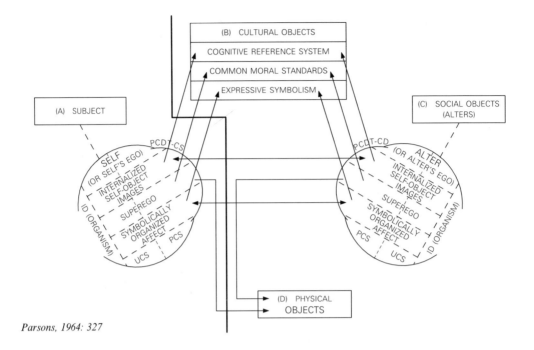

Parsons, 1964: 327

which the child becomes the severest judge of its fulfilment of the laws of perfection. Moreover, the super-ego cannot be located entirely on the level of ego-consciousness or of unconscious repression. Rather, both the ego and the super-ego are closer than not to the unconscious, or to the id. What is involved is a permeable psychic system whose subsystems 'translate' each other in the endless task of making more room for ego where there was once almost nothing but id (Freud, 1923). Human conduct is structured hierarchically so that inputs are symbolically re-presented on the levels of the id, ego and super-ego.

Parsons appropriates the Freudian psychic apparatus by opening it towards the socio-psychic and psychocultural systems:

> How can the fundamental phenomenon of the internalization of moral norms be analyzed in such a way as to maximize the generality of implications of the formulation, both for the theory of personality and for the theory of the social system? (Parsons, 1964: 19–20)

In this device Parsons makes several analytical moves:

1   the relocation of the super-ego midway between the ego and the cultural system (with the id located on the level of the organism);
2   the inclusion of the super-ego in the ego which internalizes three components (cogni-tive, moral and expressive) of common

culture which may be largely unconscious and subject to repression;
3   the self oriented cognitively and cathectically to a double environment of social and non-social objects within which
    (a)   only culture can be internal;
    (b)   emotions are symbolically generalized systems;
    (c)   only ego–alter relations can be mutual.

Parsons was extremely critical of Freud's alleged separation between the personality system and its cultural environment. Because he neglected their mutual cultural conditioning, Freud was obliged to restrict the ego to a purely cognitive reading of its external environment and to assign all the work of collective identification to the super-ego. The result was to make the super-ego a more remote moral sensor of ego's attachments than need be if their common culture were recognized. Freud's limitation in this respect, Parsons argues, was due to his restricted concept of affective symbolism which he located between the ego and the id. In turn, Freud's parental identification mechanism is too reductive to account for the cultural acquisition of the symbolically generalized system of emotions that integrate the personality system and the social system on the level of the family (Parsons and Bales, 1955).

The socialization process must be seen as a two-way process of the personality system by the social system (here the sociological concept of *role* is the key) and of the social system by the personality system (here the psychoanalytic theory of *identification*, object cathexis, internalization is the other key). Parsons argues that the Freudian key opens the levels of id, ego and super-ego to each other provided what drives the personality system is not the instincts but a social interaction that is already operative at the breast. Here infant and mother learn to interpret one another's reactions and to generalize their pattern. Thus there already occurs an exchange between the endo-psychic and socio-psychic organization of the dyad that prefigures, so to speak, all later socialization on the levels of ego and super-ego. Social reproduction is already at work on the level of metabolism inasmuch as its bare material, physical and instinctual elements of feeding are the site and source of a hermeneutics through which mother and infant inaugurate a level of expectable, sanctionable conduct of care and feeding (O'Neill, 1992).

Parsons' baby is a social actor from the first day it steps onto the family stage. Henceforth, it will live for a love whose conditions it will be taught to win or lose:

> I think it a legitimate interpretation of Freud to say that only when the *need for love* has been established as the paramount goal of the personality can a genuine ego be present. (Parsons, 1964: 90, emphasis in original)

Parsons nevertheless claims that Freud lost the generalizability in his discovery of infant eroticism by interpreting the identification process in terms of the infant's desire to *be* the mother – with all its oedipal complications. Rather, what a child learns is to interact with the mother in terms of collectively defined roles through which family membership is reproduced. The infant is at first a dependent subject in relation to the mother whose point of view it will come to adopt as its own. Thus the child's investment in the maternal object-choice is the vehicle of its internalization of the collective norms represented to it through the mother's sanctioning of its progressive maturation. Upon this first level of maternal identification, the child can then build identifications with the family as a collective category as well, with its categories of sexual and generational identity. In this process, the mother becomes a lost-object in exchange for membership in the wider family. Once this is achieved, the super-ego is in place:

> The super-ego, then, is primarily the normative pattern governing the behaviour of the different members in their different roles in the family as a system. (Parsons, 1964: 96)

Parsons also questioned the restricted symbolic significance of the father in Freud's theory of socialization. The infant has to learn sex-role differentiation as a cultural categorization akin to age and status categorization. At the same time, the child must learn to differentiate instrumental-adaptive and expressive-integrative functions in relation to age and sex categorization. Here, Parsons argues, the incest taboo may be regarded as a cultural mechanism that shifts infant erotic dependency upon intrafamilial models to extrafamilial attachments to peers among whom the child is one of a kind, neither more nor less. By the same token, the parent figures are relativized as competitors among other extrafamilial authority figures just as the family culture yields primacy to school and workplace culture. In this developmental sequence the primacy of the oedipal father yields to authority orientation in the wider society where, of course, it may play a role in attitudes of conformity and rebellion (as we shall see in the following sections).

CIVILIZATION THEORY

It was not until after the Second World War that America again read Freud. This time it was not so much to promote sociology's narrow professional identity, but America itself. The question of America's destiny seriously divided cultural theorists into optimists and pessimists. America had helped to save democracy from fascism as well as to put capitalism in first place and to leave communist/socialism a poor runner-up. In return for Marshall Aid to rebuild Europe, however, the United States imported many European scholars, from rocket scientists to critical Marxists and Freudians. For our story, the irony is that it was the Frankfurt School of critical theory that reintroduced Freud to America. It also imported a sophisticated form of Marxist philosophy of the social sciences and cultural analysis that underwrote the establishment of left academic in Anglo-America (Jay, 1973; Slater, 1977). The Frankfurt School had turned to psychoanalysis to examine the eclipse of the proletarian revolution by fascist and totalitarian state regimes in Europe. With some change, they made the same move to examine why American capitalism subordinated liberal democracy to a corporate agenda masked by an ideology of narcissistic individualism and aggression (Slater, 1970).

Marx and Freud are not, of course, an easy marriage. While it owes as much to the rethinking of psychoanalysis as of Marxism, the birth of 'Freudo-Marxism' introduced an unruly child into the house of theory. The heart of the matter is the temptation to reduce political revolution to sexual revolution (Chasseguet-Smirgel and

Grunberger, 1986). This demand requires two other moves, that is, to treat the *economy* as the source of an historically produced *scarcity* and to treat the *family* as the corresponding source of sexual *repression*. One can then reverse Marxist-analysis with psychoanalysis: emancipate sexually from the (bourgeois) family and the result will be happiness underwritten by an economy of abundance. Only Marx and Freud are left with a frown on their faces! This does not bring them any closer. We are back to the civilization question (Tester, 1992) or the question of the nature of human nature – is it rooted in biology or is its biology revisable? Is human nature anti-social and unhappy in civilization or is socialized humanity and its sublimations proof that human nature is only second nature? We should now consider how these arguments took their course in the works of Marcuse (1955), Brown (1959) and Rieff (1959, 1966).

What was needed was the elaboration of an historical materialist psychology to move beyond weak notions of false consciousness among the masses and conspiratorial theories of elite ideology which worked together to 'save' Marxist revolutionary theory from its historical failures. In current terms, it was necessary to spell out the intervening mechanisms through which the economic substructure determines the cultural superstructure in capitalist society. The turn to Freud was a turn from both 'vulgar Hegelian' and 'vulgar Marxist' accounts of the civilization relations between economy, society and personality. This turn was taken in the publication by the Frankfurt Institute of Social Research of *Studies in Authority and Family* (Forschungsberichte . . ., 1936). It was Erich Fromm who made the initial moves, drawing upon Freud's later cultural works (1920 onwards). These drew upon anthropology and social psychology to deal with the central issues of political authority, mass psychology and the role of the super-ego in the allegiance to cultural ideologies. In Freud's essays on 'Totem and Taboo' (1912–13), 'The Future of an Illusion' (1927), 'Civilization and its Discontents' (1930), for example, it is clear that the psyche is socially and historically conditioned, even though Freud seriously overweighs the present and future with the burden of the past. This, of course, is why the very notion of any alliance between Marxism and psychoanalysis has always appeared a retrograde step bound to mire critical theory in Freud's undialectical dualism of Eros and Thanatos (as Reich, 1945, and Marcuse, 1955, were to argue).

Fromm argued that the drives (instincts) are not what determine human history. Indeed, there would be no 'history', that is, no development of humanity without the mediation of institutions which socialize individuals to cathect

behaviour that is normative and thereby regular for given constellations of economy, polity and society. The periodization of these institutional contexts is the work of Marxist materialist history. This is not our concern in any detail except to note that historical 'laws' require what J.S. Mill calls 'middle principles' (*Logic*, BK VI) to connect with individual conduct. It is tempting to assign this work to the agency of religion, law and the police. But the analytic issue is how these forces of law and order achieve their purpose through behaviour that is more orderly than not. Why don't individuals withdraw their labour, play truant, abandon themselves to pleasure and perversion? How do they tolerate inequality, racism and genderism? Fromm's answer is that order is not achieved through 'vulgar Freudian' notions of repression and sublimation imposed on the drives by the collusion of the super-ego with the death instinct. Order is achieved through a libidinal adaptation to economic necessity translated through the family's class position, occupation and income. Fromm, following Reich (1945), shifted Freud's emphasis from the intrafamilial dynamics that shape individual fates to the broader structure of economic relations to which families must respond, thereby instituting a largely unconscious environment of possible and impossible conducts (character structure).

The analytic innovation here is the search for a concept of the sociological unconscious which is formed under the pressure of class position and expressed in attitudes towards authority, rebellion and ritualistic conformity in a wider range of cultural and personal behaviour (Richards, 1984). Fromm (1942, 1956, 1984) was concerned with the social contradiction between the ideological sovereignty of the individual and the psycho-social fact of individual impotence and its wide political consequences. The compensatory 'busyness' in everyone from the entrepreneur to the housewife and data-driven researcher – and even the psychoanalyst – is the mark of their alienation from productive humanity. Fromm may even have argued that this impotence underlies critical theory's own inability to connect theory and praxis. Its resolution to live with the 'non-identity thesis', that is, the divorce between empirical and transcendental history, remains the mark of intellectual impotence and its own surrender to repressive tolerance. In this regard, Fromm's early work (1937, 1970) on the administrative techniques of the German state, and school system and penal systems as a disciplinary regime that reinforces petty-bourgeois hegemony and mass submission (O'Brien, 1976), is well ahead of later work by Gramsci and Foucault. Fromm also anticipated the criticism that the

Freudian analyst–patient relationship abstains from reflection on the bourgeois character structure of repression and tolerance.

Prior to entering the Marcuse/Brown readings of Freud, it may be useful to insert Rieff's reading of the question to what extent successful psychoanalysis requires adjustment to or rejection of the civilizing process. Unlike Habermas (1971), Rieff separates psychotherapy from any overall emancipatory drive since this only reintroduces an illusion of salvation and community. 'Psychological man' operates on the basis of self-knowledge and world-knowledge, combining the strengths of a scientist and an entrepreneur in acting upon himself. Because he understands his internal dissatisfactions, he can steer through the obstacles set by civilization. For Rieff, Freud is a cultural hero. But not for long; a few years later he found that the psychologization of psychoanalysis had the upper hand:

> Where the family and nation once stood, or Church and Party, there will be hospital and theatre too, the normative institutions of the next culture. Trained to be incapable of sustaining sectarian satisfaction, psychological man cannot be susceptible to sectarian control. Religious man was born to be saved; psychological man is born to be pleased. The difference was established long ago when 'I believe', the cry of the ascetic, lost precedence to 'one feels', the caveat of the therapeutic. And if the therapeutic is to win out, then surely the psychotherapist will be his secular spiritual guide. (Rieff, 1966: 24–5)

The full sense of this observation would involve an extended analysis of arguments regarding the symbiosis between the politics of intimacy, the sexualization of economic life, and the mystification of the bases of social control and power in advanced capitalist society.

In fact this becomes the focus of Christopher Lasch's *The Culture of Narcissism* (1979), whose thesis is his concern with the displacement of the socialization functions of the bourgeois family onto professional, bureaucratic and state agencies. These agencies foster the narcissistic culture generated in the reduced families whose main function is consumption (aided by TV viewing) rather than production. The narcissistic personality is the perfect expression of the weakened family *vis-à-vis* the state and economy which recruit only privatized consumers. Thus Lasch argued that the schools, juvenile courts, health and welfare services, advertising and the media all function to erode the authority of the family. The result is that the family is increasingly a place where narcissistic individuals learn to compete with one another in the consumption of services and goods – emotional, political and economic – but with a diminished capacity for the competence required in their production.

Yet, when Lasch himself looked for a counterculture to narcissism, the best he himself could do was to locate it in the hard school of the very rich, realistic about privilege and victimization, busy in the pursuit of studies, music lessons, ballet, tennis and parties 'through which the propertied rich acquire discipline, courage, persistence, and self-possession' (Lasch, 1979: 371).

Whatever Freud's views on utopianism, his reflections on the high cost of 'civilization' permitted a second wave of Marxo-Freudianism in Marcuse's *Eros and Civilization* (1955) and Norman O. Brown's great renunciation of the spirit of Protestantism and capitalism in *Life Against Death* (1959) and *Love's Body* (1966). Both books, despite Marcuse's rejection of Brown's utopianism and Brown's dismissal of Marcuse's inability to get libidinal, became cult texts of the 1960s. The core issue between them – as between Freud and Reich – is over the concept of sublimation or the connection between culture and (infant) sexuality in the sacrifice of pleasure and the realization of society. The 'post-Freudian' solution is to drop the infantile psychic apparatus by historicizing the patriarchal family character to release full genitality, the body without organs (Deleuze and Guattari, 1977), the libidinal economy of jouissance (Lyotard, 1993) and (be)coming woman (Jardine, 1985). The danger in these moves is that they fall into the denunciation of institutions and authority in the name of fictionality and desire. Moreover, the relative autonomy of the cultural sphere guarantees that cultural politics will make headway in academia and the media. Thus particular cultural strategies like (de)constructionism and minoritarianism serve to redistribute symbolic capitals yet not necessarily alter the inequality that governs cultural capitalism (an issue to which we return in the final section of this chapter).

In *Life Against Death* Norman O. Brown attacked capitalism at its very foundations, that is, its excremental vision, its noxious composition of denunciation and denial of the body's gifts unless congealed in the fetishes of property, money and jewellery. Capitalism is therefore a neurosis built out of self-hatred. Its hold upon us deepens once it combines with the anal virtues of orderliness, parsimony and obstinacy prized in the Protestant ethic. Brown pursues the dead body of Protestant capitalism as the proper equivalent of Freud's death instinct which otherwise confounds social progress. He also traces the same life-denying impulses in the domination of science and technology, raising the question of what a life-affirmative or 'non-morbid' science would look like. Brown also looked at archaic economies that were not governed either by overproduction or scarcity. He questioned the Freudian principle of sublimation as a misreading of historical economies of non-enjoyment which conquered the archaic economies of the gift and social solidarity.

The economy of repressive sublimation and anality rests upon the death instinct, Brown argues, because we are *unable to die*. This is rooted in the infant's refusal to be separated from the mother-body and in the prolonged fetalization of human beings. It is the source of our combined morbidity and possessiveness. It is also the origin of our search for self-creation, of our quest for parthenogenesis, hermaphroditism and androgyny and of the current mythology of possessive sexual identities which in effect espouse death-in-life by fleeing from death:

> Science and civilization combine to articulate the core of the human neurosis, man's incapacity to live in the body, which is also his incapacity to die. (Brown, 1959: 303)

Curiously enough, there is a more profound historical analysis of capitalism in Brown than in Marcuse, to whose historicization of psychoanalysis we now turn. This is because Marcuse was preoccupied with a critique of the conservative consequences of liberalism (rather than fascism) in late capitalism. Mention must also be made of Marcuse's rehabilitation of the *revolutionary* philosophy of Hegel (Marcuse, 1960), if we are to understand his strategy of saving Freud for a revolutionary reading. Marcuse – like Horkheimer and Adorno – was therefore not entirely critical of the bourgeois family inasmuch as it was the site of the struggle between patriarchalism and radical invidualism. However, by the time of *One-Dimensional Man* (1964), Marcuse had abandoned the argument that the family was a critical site of emancipation. The corporate agenda now bypasses the family through direct media manipulation of individuals and the individualization of male, female and child labour driven by compulsive desires.

Marcuse adopted two analytical strategies in order to make his argument that psychological concepts are political concepts. The first was to historicize the psychic costs of civilization by placing them wholly on the side of the reality principle, that is, the social organization of an economy of scarcity, rather than on the side of the pleasure principle regarded as an innately anti-social and unsatisfiable drive. This move generated the second argument that repression is always surplus-regression created by the political failure to open up the liberal freedoms that would flow from an economy of abundance. Marcuse rescued the revolutionary principle of the pleasure principle, not only by arguing for a utopian future but by grounding it in a cognitive function of preserving the past critical memory of happiness as a standard for political change:

> If memory moves into the centre of psychoanalysis as a decisive mode of *cognition*, this is far more than a therapeutic device; the therapeutic role of memory derives from the *truth value* of memory. Its truth value lies in the specific function of memory to preserve promises and potentialities which are betrayed and even outlawed by the mature, civilized individual, but which had once been fulfilled in his dim past and which are never entirely forgotten. The reality principle restrains the cognitive function of memory – its commitment to the past experience of happiness which spurns the desire for its conscious recreation. The psychoanalytic liberation of memory explodes the rationality of the repressed individual. As cognitive gives way to re-cognition, the forbidden images and impulses of childhood begin to tell the truth that reason denies. Regression assumes a progressive function. The rediscovered past yields critical standards which are tabooed by the present. Moreover, the restoration of memory is accompanied by the restoration of the cognitive content of phantasy. Psychoanalytic theory removes these mental faculties from the noncommittal sphere of daydreaming and fiction and recaptures their strict truths. The weight of these discoveries must eventually shatter the framework in which they were made and confined. The liberation of the past does not end in its reconciliation with the present. Against the self-imposed restraint of the discoverer, the orientation on the past tends toward an orientation on the future. The *recherche du temps perdu* becomes the vehicle of future liberation. (Marcuse, 1955: 18, emphasis in original)

In this way Marcus released Freud's deadlock between Eros and Thanatos. He denied there is any social organization of the death instinct, although he conceded that aggression is a necessary byproduct of repression. In late capitalism social domination bypasses the patrarichal family. Domination becomes the work of the anonymous corporate administration of individualized desires that supply the content of happiness without creativity of the pleasure principle.

To resist what he calls 'the corporealization of the super-ego', Marcuse argued that phantasy serves a positive historical task of preserving the collective aspiration for happiness and security, preserved in the cultural myths of Orpheus and Narcissus rather than the productivist myth of Prometheus, which prolongs the conflict between man and nature. Against Freud, Marcuse reads Narcissus as a figure of subjective and world harmonization and non-repressive sublimation exercised in art, play and contemplation as truly human aspirations, and the basis for an alternative reality principle (see Alford, 1988 for critical discussion). So far from encouraging narcissism in any vulgar sense, Marcuse in fact drew upon the mythological and aesthetic tradition of Narcissus and Orpheus pitted against the tradition of Prometheus:

> The Orphic and Narcissistic experience of the world negates that which sustains the world of the performance principle. The opposition between man and nature, subject and object, is overcome. Being is experienced as gratification, which unites man and nature so that the fulfillment of man is at the same time the fulfillment, without voilence, of nature . . . This liberation is the work of Eros. The song of Orpheus breaks the petrification, moves the forests and the rocks – but moves them to partake in joy. (Marcuse, 1955: 150–1)

It is in terms of this aesthetic myth that Marcuse then adapted Freud's theory of *primary narcissism*, which he interpreted not as a neurotic symptom but as a constitutive element in the construction of reality and of a mature, creative ego with the potential for transforming the world in accordance with a *new science of nature*:

> The striking paradox that narcissism, usually understood as egotistic withdrawal from reality, here is connected with oneness with the universe, reveals the new depth of the conception: beyond all immature autoeroticism, narcissism denotes a fundamental relatedness to reality which may generate a comprehensive existential order. (Marcuse, 1955: 27)

In France the Marxist turn to Freud had to get past the official line of the Communist Party on psychoanalysis as a bourgeois subjectifying ideology. It has also to skirt Sartre's (1957) existentialist critique of the positivist bias of psychoanalytic explanation. Yet Sartre, especially through Laing and Cooper in the UK, was also the source of an anti-psychiatric movement, which picked up with Foucault (1973). In the course of events, psychoanalysis provided arguments for the anti-psychiatry movement but then fell foul of it as an establishment ideology of familized order and capitalist repression (Turkle, 1981). The principle work here is *Anti-Oedipus: Capitalism and Schizophrenia* (1977), in which Deleuze and Guattari excoriate oedipalism in the name of the schizoanalytic meltdown of Freudo-capitalism.

Desire must be released from the 'Daddy–Mommy–Me' nucleus of capitalist society where desire is constitutionally castrated, where it is always less than itself, always ready to be sacrificed to smaller and more sensible pleasures. Whereas Freud struggled to re-oedipalize the 'bodies-without-organs' he had discovered in his case histories, especially of Little Hans (1909), Wolf Man (1918) and Schreber (1911), Deleuze

and Guattari unleash them as the schizoid exemplars of post-capitalist desire;

> There is no such thing as the social production of reality on the one hand, and a desiring-production that is mere fantasy on the other. The only connections that could be established between these two productions would be secondary ones of introjection and projection, as though all social practices had their precise counterpart in introjected or internal mental practices, or as though mental practices were projected upon social systems, without either of the two sets of practices ever having any real or concrete effect upon the other. As long as we are content to establish a perfect parallel between money, gold, capital, and the capitalist triangle on the one hand, and the libido, the anus, the phallus, and the family triangle on the other, we are engaging in an enjoyable pastime, but the mechanisms of money remain totally unaffected by the anal projections of those who manipulate money. The Marx–Freud parallelism between the two remains utterly sterile and insignificant as long as it is expressed in terms that make them introjections or projections of each other without ceasing to be utterly alien to each other, as in the famous equation money = shit. The truth of the matter is that *social production is purely and simply desiring-production itself under determinate conditions*. We maintain that the social field is immediately invested by desire, that it is the historically determined product of desire, and that libido has no need of any mediation or sublimation, any psychic operation, any transformation, in order to invade and invest the productive forces and the relations of production. *There is only desire and the social, and nothing else.* (Deleuze and Guattari, 1977: 28–9, emphasis in original)

Schizoanalysis merely re-iterates the after-effect of capitalism's desperate attempt to simultaneously dam and to unbind unlimited desire, its invention of non-hierarchical bodies in endless states of agitation, flow, copulation and consumption.

The theoretical *rapprochement* between French Freud and French Marx was the work of Louis Althusser, who developed scientific, that is, structuralist and anti-humanist, accounts of Marx, Freud and Lacan. The common ground was found in the concept of ideology, which Althusser identified with the a-historical unconscious Žižek, 1989). Thus history has no subject-centre except through 'inter-pellation', or being called up by an ideological apparatus in which any subject (mis)recognizes itself as the subject of social practices and rituals:

> We observe that the structure of all ideology, interpellating individuals as subjects in the name of a Unique and Absolute Subject, is *speculary*, i.e., a mirror-structure, and *doubly* speculary: this mirror

duplication is constitutive of ideology and ensures its functioning. Which means that all ideology is *centred*, that the Absolute Subject occupies the unique place of the Centre, and interpellates around it the infinity of individuals into subjects in a double mirror-connexion such that it *subjects* the subjects to the Subject, while giving them in the Subject in which each subject can contemplate its own image (present and future) the *guarantee* that this really concerns them and Him, and that since everything takes place in the Family (the Holy Family: the Family is in essence Holy), 'God will *recognize* his own in it', i.e., those who have recognized God, and have recognized themselves in Him, will be saved.

Let me summarize what we have discovered about ideology in general.

The duplicate mirror-structure of ideology ensures simultaneously:

1. the interpellation of 'individuals' as subjects;
2. their subjection to the Subject;
3. the mutual recognition of subjects and Subject, the subjects' recognition of each other, and finally the Subject's recognition of himself;
4. The absolute guarantee that everything really is so, and that on condition that the subjects recognize what they are and behave accordingly, everything will be all right: Amen – '*So be it*'.

Result: caught in this quadruple system of inter-pellation as subjects, of subjection to the Subject, of universal recognition and of absolute guarantee, the subjects 'work', they 'work by themselves' in the vast majority of cases, with the exception of the 'bad subjects' who on occasion provoke the intervention of one of the detachments of the (repressive) State apparatus. (Althusser, 1971: 168–9)

Althusser's hybridization of Marxism and psychoanalysis brings us full circle. This time the individual is over-socialized through an ideo-logical mirror of subjectivity in which the indi-vidual sees subjection as how things are. We have lost the rebelliousness of the unconscious and surrendered transgressive desire to normalcy in the name of the state cultural apparatus. The insight of psychoanalysis is the blindness of sociology.

POST-OEDIPALISM

Here we will treat the main arguments in the reception/rejection of Freudian psychoanalysis that have played a role in the articulation of feminism as a particular strategy within the larger history of women's movements (Lovell, 1996; Mitchell, 1974). It need hardly be said that women experience inferiority, aggression and exploitation. Their sexual lives prior to and within marriage are largely controlled by patriarchal ideologies which in turn have domi-nated their economic and political lives (Ortner, 1974; Rubin, 1975). The specific exploitation of women has been a blind spot even in Marxist thought and has again necessitated a turn to Freud in order to rethink woman's sexuality, the sociopsychic costs of reproduction and the need to redefine heterosexual relations. It was neces-sary to historicize the second-sex ideology of woman's otherness (de Beauvoir, 1961; Rich, 1978; Wittig, 1973), the feminine mystique (Friedman, 1963) that confined women to Victorian hysteria, to patriarchalism (Eisten-stein, 1981; Figes, 1970) and, above all, to psychic and social castration (Greer, 1971). Feminist scholarship (Greene and Kahn, 1985) is now so vast and so well-received that it is impossible to summarize without losing the nuances of early Anglo-American feminism and of Franco-feminism fuelled by Lacanian psycho-analysis, deconstruction and semiotics (Marks and de Courtivron, 1980). The result has been to reconstruct patriarchal ideas of the feminine (Pateman, 1988), of mothering, household and child care in ways that encourage women to assume social and political agency in their own right/write.

The feminist fascination with Lacan has to be one of the most difficult relationships to under-stand – it is perhaps *the* enigma of the woman's movement (Benjamin, 1988; Cixous and Clem-ent, 1986; Flax, 1990; Gallop, 1982; Irigaray, 1985; Kofman, 1985; Ragland-Sullivan, 1987). Since all the versions cannot be satisfactorily explored, we must try to set out an analytic core in Lacan. Taken with the earlier accounts of Parsons and Althusser, this excursus may help the reader to estimate the balance of the feminist 'return to Freud'. Lacan re-read Freud and was in turn read into philosophy, psychoanalysis, anti-psychiatry, women's studies and so on, only to be rejected by critics of his own residual Freudianism! Lacan's departure was to revise Freudian psychologism just as Althusser rejected Marx's humanism and once again reconnected Marxism and psychoanalysis. Analytically, then, Lacan's contribution to sociology was to reject the search for influences or determinisms between individual behaviour and social institu-tions. Society is never beyond the individual because it dwells in the language each of us speaks and thereby appropriates subjectivity/objectivity, masculine/feminine etc. Society does not erase a state of nature with its imposition of Law. The categories of kinship and partriarchy are invoked in the oedipal family to shift the pre-oedipal infant from the imaginary order of maternal fusion to the symbolic order of social difference. For Lacan individualism is an illusion that originates in the (maternal) mirror and thereafter constitutes the subject as an endless question for its own return. This is the modus operandi of the subject of slavery and seduction, of the patient and student subject, of the consumer and political subject, in short of innumerable capital bodies that are the objects of psychoanalytically based culture criticism.

While the tension between psychoanalysis and feminism has been enormously creative, its source should not be overlooked. The feminist appropriation of psychoanalysis involved a political *volte face*. Jacqueline Rose puts the nub of the issue:

> The difficulty is to pull psychoanalysis . . . towards a recognition of the fully social constitute of identity and norms, and then back again to that point of tension between ego and unconscious where they are endlessly re-modeled and endlessly break. (Rose, 1986: 7)

To the extent that post-oedipal feminism abandons the pre-oedipal matrix, its anti-patriarchal politics of women's sexuality overlooks the pre-oedipal limits set by the unconscious to identity and plurality claims around sexual difference, patriarchal ideology and aggression as purely social constructs. Thus feminist legal theorists (Bower, 1991) have taken conflicting positions on the question of motherhood and the maternal in public life. In turn, the challenges of combining working and mothering, reproductive control, especially abortion practice, and affirmative action directed by women's identity politics has also led to considerable theoretical work by legal feminists (Cornell, 1991; Mackinnon, 1983), and even to a maternal jurisprudence (West, 1988).

It may be useful here to insert Kristeva's attempt to move beyond the alternatives represented by *liberal* feminism (equal access to symbolic capital) and *radical* feminism (deconstruction of symbolic capital) in the name of difference. Kristeva opens up a *metaphysical* deconstruction of the masculine/feminine dichotomy (Kristeva, 1981). In positive terms, Kristeva embraces marginality, subversion and dissidence grounded in the pre-oedipal mother-body and its semiotic transcendence of gender division. However, other feminists have not aligned with this position since, like Chodorow (1978), they start from the position that motherhood merely reproduces patriarchalism and commits daughters to an ideology of care and rearing from which they must be emancipated to become women. They have been even more reluctant to take on Kristeva's re-appropriation of religion and the trinitarian semiotics of maternal divinity (Crownfield, 1992).

Any remarks on the range of women's theorizing have to be qualified by conceding the problem of generalizing upon specific grounds and strategies of advancement that women have adopted in government, social policy, health, childcare, education and the workplace. Obviously, women have made major gains in redefining the institutions that affect their lives. Here the task is to estimate what has been the role of women's appropriation of psychoanalysis in their expanded socioeconomic and political lives. In the first place, women have broadened the distinction between 'pure knowledge' and 'political knowledge' (Haraway, 1991; Jardine, 1985) inasmuch as the realities they challenge prove to have been gendered constructions that privilege male interest. They have also broadened the male narrative that governed modernity, either to soften it with its own female side (Silverman, 1992) or to set out an open-ended female socio-narrative of becoming-woman (gynesis). More recently, Judith Butler (1993) has suggested that gay/lesbians adopt the strategy of appropriating the designation of 'queer', to extricate it from its normative stigma as pathological practice and to reassign its performative power through self-naming. A similar strategy has appealed to gays, lesbians, blacks and those with disabilities seeking to deconstruct and re-assign their place in a democratic society. Yet it cannot be presumed that there is no remainder of self-assigned difference within these groups. It remains a difficult matter to gauge the effectiveness of political theatre based upon 'acting up' underprivileged identities. The political tolerance (which includes funding) of its margins is at least as much a sign of the power of a social system as of its potential transformation.

In fairness, it must be noted that the work of deconstructing male/female dichotomies has engaged male theorists as much as female theorists. In the US the work of Stoller (1968) and of Money and Ehrhardt (1972) on the biological and cultural factors in sexual differentiation was path breaking. Once the door to social constructionism (Berger and Luckmann, 1967; Goffman, 1961) opened, a great deal of the programme was set for later gender and race studies. Women have demystified their self-concept, empowered themselves in the field of symbolic capital and implemented organizational forms of practical action whose development will be in their own hands. What is at stake are new formulations of politics, ethics and aesthetics, at one level, and new relations of authority, care and democracy in the lifeworld that will shift the intergenerational burdens of women.

The shift from early capitalist gendered economies (contemporaneous with traditional economies) to late capitalist economic sexism

(Illich, 1982) has not altered the contradiction between increased exploitation of women and their new freedom in the market place (O'Neill, 1991). Here the current reconfiguration of the welfare state is of enormous consequence for women and children in single parent households, for working women and elder women (O'Neill, 1994). It is important to remember that it is easier for academic women to make inroads on the canon, figurability and the erotic imagination, in short, to re-write and re-read 'woman', than it is for women outside of academia to achieve such voice.

CONCLUSION

Sociology cannot ignore its basic assumptions about human nature. All the same, sociologists do not wish to trade upon religious, philosophical and psychological conceptions of human nature. This is because sociologists suspect that any theory of human nature is a covert theory of social and political order. It turns out that all social thinkers have to make some fundamental decision on what we may call the *Hobbesian problem of order* (Carveth, 1984; O'Neill, 1972), that is, how far is human nature sociable, or other-regarding? We are divided between egoists and altruists; we are split between the parties of order and dis(order), between Eros and Thanatos. No theory is adequate that ignores the complexity of the relations between reason and the passions, or the costs of socialization and sublimation. No social theory can entirely separate history and structure without inviting deconstruction and revision. Thus sociology and psychoanalysis remain uneasy yet necessary partners.

REFERENCES

Alford, C. Fred (1988) *Narcissism: Socrates, the Frankfurt School, and Psychoanalytic Theory*. New Haven, CT: Yale University Press.
Althusser, Louis (1971) *Lenin and Philosophy and Other Essays*. London: New Left Books.
de Beauvoir, Simone (1961) *The Second Sex*. New York: Bantam.
Benjamin, Jessica (1988) *The Bonds of Love*. New York: Pantheon Books.
Berger, Peter and Luckmann, Thomas (1967) *The Social Construction of Reality*. New York: Doubleday.
Bocock, Robert (1976) *Freud and Modern Society: An Outline and Analysis of Freud's Sociology*. New York: Holmes and Meier.
Bocock, Robert (1983) *Sigmund Freud*. Chichester: Ellis Horwood Ltd.
Bower, Lisa C. (1991) 'Mother in Law: Conceptions of Mother and the Maternal in Feminisms and Feminist Legal Theory', *Differences: A Journal of Feminist Cultural Studies*, 3 (1): 20–38.
Brown, Norman O. (1959) *Life Against Death: The Psychoanalytical Meaning of History*. New York: Vintage Books.
Brown, Norman O. (1966) *Love's Body*. New York: Random House.
Butler, Judith (1993) *Bodies That Matter: On the Discursive Limits of 'Sex'*. New York: Routledge.
Carveth, Donald L. (1984) 'Psychoanalysis and Social Theory: The Hobbesian Problem Revisisted', *Psychoanalysis and Contemporary Thought*, 7 (1): 43–98.
Chasseguet-Smirgel, Janine and Grunberger, Béla (1986) *Freud or Reich? Psychoanalysis and Illusion* (trans. Claire Pajaczkowska). London: Free Association Books.
Chodorow, Nancy (1978) *The Reproduction of Mothering: Psychoanalysis and the Sociology of Gender*. Berkeley, CA: University of California Press.
Cixous, Hélène and Clement, Catherine (1986) *The Newly Born Woman*. Minneapolis: University of Minnesota Press.
Cooper, David (1971) *Psychiatry and Anti-Psychiatry*. New York: Ballantine Books.
Cornell, Drucilla P. (1991) *Beyond Accommodation: Ethical Feminism, Deconstruction, and the Law*. New York: Routledge.
Crownfield, David R. (ed.) (1992) *Body/Text in Julia Kristeva: Religion, Women, and Psychoanalysis*. Albany, NY: State University of New York Press.
Deleuze, Gilles and Guattari, Félix (1977) *Anti-Oedipus: Capitalism and Schizophrenia*. New York: The Viking Press.
Eisenstein, Zillah R. (1981) *The Radical Future of Liberal Feminism*. Boston, MA: Northeastern University Press.
Figes, Eva (1970) *Patriarchal Attitudes*. London: Faber and Faber.
Flax, Jane (1990) *Thinking Fragments: Psychoanalysis, Feminism, and Postmodernism in the Contemporary West*. Berkeley, CA: University of California Press.
Forschungsberichte aus dem Institut fur sozialforschung (1936) *Studien über Autorität und Familie*. Paris: Alcan.
Foucault, Michel (1973) *Madness and Civilization: A History of Insanity in the Age of Reason*. New York: Vintage Books.
Freud, Sigmund (1909) 'Analysis of a Phobia in a Five-Year-Old Boy', *SE*, vol. X.
Freud, Sigmund (1911) 'Psycho-Analytical Notes on an Autobiographical Account of a Case of Paranoia (Dementia Paranoides), *SE*, vol. XII.
Freud, Sigmund (1912–13) 'Totem and Taboo', in *Standard Edition (SE) of the Complete Psychological Works*. London: Hogarth Press. vol. XIII.

Freud, Sigmund (1918) 'From the History of an Infantile Neurosis', *SE*, vol. XVII.

Freud, Sigmund (1920) 'Beyond the Pleasure Principle', *SE*, vol. XVIII.

Freud, Sigmund (1923) 'The Ego and the Id', *SE*, vol. XIX.

Freud, Sigmund (1927) 'The Future of an Illusion', *SE*, vol. XXI.

Freud, Sigmund (1930) 'Civilization and its Discontents', *SE*, vol. XXI.

Freud, Sigmund (1933) 'New Introduction Lectures on Psychoanalysis', *SE*, vol. XXII.

Friedman, Betty (1963) *The Feminine Mystique*. New York: Dell Publishing.

Fromm, Erich (1937) 'Zum Gefuhl der Ohnmacht', *Zeitschift für sozialfurschung*, 6: 95–119.

Fromm, Erich (1942) *Escape from Freedom*. London: Routledge.

Fromm, Erich (1956) *The Sane Society*. London: Routledge.

Fromm, Erich (1970) *The Crisis of Psychoanalysis: Essays on Freud, Marx and Social Psychology*. New York: Henry Holt and Company.

Fromm, Erich (1984) *The Working Class in Weimar Germany: A Psychological and Sociological Study* (trans. Barbara Weinberger). Leamington Spa: Berg.

Gadamer, Hans-Georg (1975) *Truth and Method*. New York: The Seabury Press.

Gallop, Jane (1982) *The Daughter's Seduction: Feminism and Psychoanalysis*. Ithaca, NY: Cornell University Press.

Greene, Gayle and Kahn, Coppelia (1985) *Making a Difference: Feminist Literary Criticism*. London: Methuen.

Greer, Germaine (1971) *The Female Eunuch*. New York: McGraw-Hill.

Goffman, Irving (1961) *Asylums: Essays on the Social Situation of Mental Patients and Other Inmates*. New York: Doubleday, Anchor Books.

Habermas, Jürgen (1971) *Knowledge and Human Interests*. Boston, MA: Beacon Press.

Haraway, Donna J. (1991) *Simians, Cyborgs, and Women: The Reinvention of Nature*. New York: Routledge.

Illich, Ivan (1982) *Gender*. New York: Pantheon Books.

Irigaray, Luce (1985) *This Sex Which Is Not One*. Ithaca, NY: Cornell University Press.

Jardine, Alice A. (1985) *Gynesis: Configurations of Woman and Modernity*. Ithaca, NY: Cornell University Press.

Jay, Martin (1973) *The Dialectical Imagination: A History of the Frankfurt School and the Institute of Social Research, 1923–1950*. Boston, MA: Little, Brown and Company.

Kofman, Sarah (1985) *The Enigma of Woman: Woman in Freud's Writings*. Ithaca, NY: Cornell University Press.

Kristeva, Julia (1981) 'Women's Time', *Signs*, 7 (1): 13–35.

Lacan, Jacques (1968) *The Language of the Self: The Function of Language in Psychoanalysis*. New York: Dell Publishing.

Laing, R.D. (1969) *Politics of Experience*. Harmondsworth: Penguin.

Lasch, Christopher (1979) *The Culture of Narcissism: American Life in an Age of Diminishing Expectations*. New York: W.W. Norton.

Lovell, Terry (1996) 'Feminist Social Theory', in Bryan S. Turner (ed.), *The Blackwell Companion to Social Theory*. Oxford: Blackwell. pp. 307–39.

Lyotard, Jean-François (1993) *Libidinal Economy*. London: The Athlone Press.

Mackinnon, Catherine (1983) 'Feminism, Marxism, Method and the State: Toward Feminist Jurisprudence', *Signs*, 8: 635–58.

Marcuse, Herbert (1955) *Eros and Civilization: A Philosophical Inquiry into Freud*. Boston, MA: Beacon Press.

Marcuse, Herbert (1960) *Reason and Revolution: Hegel and the Rise of Social Theory*. Boston, MA: Beacon Press.

Marcuse, Herbert (1964) *One-Dimensional Man*. Boston, MA: Beacon Press.

Marks, Elaine and de Courtivron, Isabelle (1980) *New French Feminisms*. Amherst, MA: University of Massachusetts Press.

Mitchell, Juliet (1974) *Psychoanalysis and Feminism*. London: Penguin Books.

Money, John and Ehrhardt, Anke M. (1972) *Man and Woman Boy and Girl: The Differentiation and Dimorphism of Gender Identity from Conception to Maturity*. Baltimore, MD: The Johns Hopkins University Press.

O'Brien, Ken (1976) 'Death and Revolution: An Appraisal of Identity Theory', in John O'Neill (ed.), *On Critical Theory*. New York: The Seabury Press. pp. 104–28.

O'Neill, John (1972) *Sociology as a Skin Trade: Essays Towards a Reflexive Sociology*. London: Heinemann.

O'Neill, John (1991) 'Women as a Medium of Exchange: Defamilization and the Feminization of Law in Early and Late Capitalism', in *Plato's Cave: Desire, Power and the Specular Functions of the Media*. Norwood, NJ: Ablex Publishing Corporation. pp. 79–80.

O'Neill, John (1992) 'The Mother Tongue: Semiosis and Infant Transcription', in *Critical Convention: Interpretation in the Literary Arts and Sciences*. Norman, OK: University of Oklahoma Press. pp. 249–63.

O'Neill, John (1994) *The Missing Child in Liberal Theory: Towards a Covenant Theory of Family, Community, Welfare, and the Civic State*. Toronto: University of Toronto Press.

O'Neill, John (1995) *The Poverty of Postmodernism*. London: Routledge.

Ortner, Sherry B. (1974) 'Is Female to Male as Nature is to Culture?', in Michelle Rosaldo and Louise Lamphere (eds), *Women, Culture and Society*. Stanford, CA: Stanford University Press.

Parsons, Talcott (1964) *Social Structure and Person-ality*. New York: The Free Press.

Parsons, Talcott and Bales, Robert (1955) *Family, Socialization and Interaction Process*. New York: The Free Press.

Pateman, Carol (1988) *The Sexual Contract*. Oxford: Basil Blackwell.

Ragland-Sullivan, Ellie (1987) *Jacques Lacan and the Philosophy of Psychoanalysis*. Urbana, IL: University of Illinois Press.

Reich, Wilhelm (1945) *Character Analysis*. New York: Farrar, Straus and Giroux.

Rich, Adrienne (1978) *The Dream of a Common Language*. New York: Norton.

Richards, Barry (ed.) (1984) *Capitalism and Infancy: Essays on Psychoanalysis and Politics*. London: Free Association Books.

Ricouer, Paul (1974) *The Conflict of Interpretations*. Evanston, IL: Northwestern University Press.

Rieff, Philip (1959) *Freud: The Mind of the Moralist*. New York: Viking Press.

Rieff, Philip (1966) *The Triumph of the Therapeutic: Uses of Faith After Freud*. London: Chatto and Windus.

Rose, Jacqueline (1986) *Sexuality in the Field of Vision*. London: Verso.

Rubin, Gayle (1975) 'The Traffic in Women: Notes on the Political Economy of Sex', in Rayna Rapp Reiter (ed.), *Toward an Anthropology of Women*. New York: Monthly Review Press. pp. 157–210.

Sedgwick, Peter (1982) *Psychopolitics: Laing, Foucault,*

Goffman, Szasz and the Future of Mass Psychiatry. New York: Harper and Row.

Silverman, Kaja (1992) *Male Subjectivity at the Margins*. New York: Routledge.

Slater, Philip (1970) *The Pursuit of Loneliness: American Culture at the Breaking Point*. Boston, MA: Beacon Press.

Slater, Philip (1977) *Origin and Significance of the Frankfurt School: A Marxist Perspective*. London: Routledge, Kegan Paul.

Stoller, Richard J. (1968) *Sex and Gender: On the Development of Masculinity and Femininity*. New York: Science House.

Szasz, Thomas (1961) *The Myth of Mental Illness: Foundations of a Theory of Personal Conduct*. New York: Hoeber–Harper.

Tester, Keith (1992) *Civil Society*. London: Routledge.

Turkle, Sherry (1981) *Psychoanalytic Politics: Freud's French Revolution*. Cambridge, MA: The MIT Press.

West, Robin (1988) 'Jurisprudence and Gender', *University of Chicago Law Review*, 55: 1–72.

Wittgenstein, Ludwig (1958) *Philosophical Investigations*. Oxford: Clarendon Press.

Wittig, Monique (1973) *The Lesbian Body*. New York: Avon.

Wrong, Dennis (1961) 'The Oversocialized Conception of Man in Modern Sociology', *The American Sociological Review*, 26: 183–93.

Žižek, Slavoj (1989) *The Sublime Object of Ideology*. London: Verso.

11

Classical Feminist Social Theory

PATRICIA MADOO LENGERMANN AND JILL NIEBRUGGE-BRANTLEY

Classical feminist social theory has its intellectual origins in the development of Western political theory in the eighteenth century, the emergence in the nineteenth century of a faith that social amelioration was possible through a science of society, but above all in the age-old record of women's protest against their subordination, particularly as that protest coalesced in the nineteenth and early twentieth centuries, in both Europe and America, into a social movement centering on women's struggle for political rights – the so-called 'first wave' of feminist mobilization.

DEFINITIONAL ISSUES

In the context of this chapter, we will focus on classical feminist sociological theory, by which we shall mean works created between 1830 and 1930, by women who were reflectively exploring the ameliorative possibilities of social science while developing a systematic theory of society and social relations, a theory infused with a woman-centered consciousness and committed to a critique of domination. As primary exemplars of this tradition, we discuss the social theory of Harriet Martineau (British, 1802–76), Flora Tristan (French, 1803–44), Anna Julia Cooper (African American, 1858–1964), Beatrice Webb (British, 1858–1943), Jane Addams (European American, 1860–1935), Charlotte Perkins Gilman (European American, 1860–1935) and Marianne Weber (German, 1870–1954). Our definition allows us to distinguish the works of these women from the works of thinkers who shared some but not all of their concerns: from

feminist writers who wrote before the idea of social science became a part of Western thought – for example, Mary Astell (1668–1721), Mary Wortley Montagu (1689–1762), Catherine Macaulay (1731–91), Abigail Adams (1744–1818), Judith Sargent Murray (1751–1820), Mary Wollstonecraft (1759–97), Germaine De Staël (1766–1817); from contemporaries whose primary expression of feminist ideas was philosophical, political or literary rather than sociological – for example, Margaret Fuller, Harriet Taylor Mill and John Stuart Mill, Frances Wright, Sarah and Angelina Grimké, Maria Stewart, Frances Ellen Watkins Harper, Elizabeth Cady Stanton, Susan B. Anthony, Sojourner Truth, Mary Church Terrell, Ida B. Wells, Olive Schreiner, Virginia Woolf; from contemporary women social scientists who analysed a particular aspect of social life rather than constructing a general theory – for example, Elizabeth Blackwell, medical sociology; Florence Nightingale, health; Mary Van Kleeck, social organizations; Katherine Bement Davis, criminology; Sophonisba Breckinridge and Edith Abbott, urban social problems, and from theorists who wrote about domination and women's subordination but not from a woman-centered perspective, for example, Karl Marx, Friedrich Engels, Emma Goldman, Rosa Luxemburg.

BIOGRAPHY AND HISTORIOGRAPHY

Because the women theorists discussed in this review are relatively unknown to a social science readership, we introduce them in this section. Our introduction addresses a current debate in the historiography of sociology about the place of classical feminist theory in the sociological canon. We advance the claim made by one side in that debate – that a rich and lively production of feminist sociological theory occurred between 1830 and 1930, in the same period in which male-created sociology developed. Despite the pioneering work of scholars like Costin (1983), Deegan (1988), Fish (1981, 1985), Kandal (1988), Rosenberg (1982) and Terry (1983), this claim remains a contested one in mainstream discourses on sociology's history and theoretical traditions (see, for example, Crothers, 1998). Although some established texts on the history of sociological theory are beginning the incorporation of the women (for example, Lemert, 1995, 1999; Ritzer, [1996] 2000), others continue the decades-long practice of ignoring and marginalizing the feminist presence in sociology's classical period (see, for example, Ashley and Orenstein, 1998; Collins and Makowsky, 1998; Farganis, 1996; Levine, 1995).

Our introductory biographical sketches substantiate the claim of a feminist sociological heritage with five arguments: first, that the classical women theorists worked and wrote in an active relation to sociology as an organized area of scholarship and as a framework for social analysis; second, that the classical women theorists were important public figures and were known as social analysts to the men who created mainstream sociology in the period 1830–1930; third, that that male discourse group was at best ambivalent and more typically resistant to the women's presence and sociological production, largely because sexist attitudes made it difficult to accept women's intellectual work as authoritative; fourth, that these same dynamics, coupled with a growing contrast between the aspirations for an objective and generalizing science in male sociology and the critical, activist, grounded formulations of classical feminist social thought led, over time, to a complete erasure of this tradition's presence from the histories of sociology created out of various male historiographical frameworks; and fifth that this feminist presence is currently being recovered by a growing body of scholarship grounded in a new feminist historiography, a scholarship which is rediscovering these women as social theorists relevant to a range of contemporary academic fields, and which is now in sociology sufficiently dense to produce multiple interpretations of some of these women's work.

Current scholarship easily substantiates both the connections to sociology and the public visibility of the five women who were privileged by class and race – Martineau (e.g. Hoecker-Drysdale, 1992, 2000), Addams (e.g., Deegan, 1988), Gilman (e.g., Ceplair, 1991), Webb (e.g.,

Romano, 1998) and Weber (e.g., Roth, 1990). Martineau, who from the late 1820s was Britain's leading woman of letters primarily on the basis of her social analysis, has survived in sociology's records only for her 1853 translation and abridgement, *The Positive Philosophy of Auguste Comte*. But she was working on the construction of sociology from the 1830s, bringing out three extensive and interrelated works – *Society in America* ([1836, 1837] 1962) *How to Observe Morals and Manners* (1838b) and 'Domestic Service' (1838a). Hoecker-Drysdale (1992: 70–1) reports that in 1837 Martineau wrote of being asked to edit a new journal intending 'to treat of philosophical principles, abstract and applied, of sociology'.

Addams self-identified as a sociologist, taught sociology, was a member of the American Sociological Society, published in the *American Journal of Sociology*, wrote eight major books of social theory (including *Democracy and Social Ethics* ([1902] 1907), *Newer Ideals of Peace* (1907), *The Spirit of Youth and the City Streets* (1909), which were reviewed in the *AJS*) and had significant relationships with Mead, Park, W.I. Thomas, Small and Burgess (Deegan, 1988). From her base at Hull House, the social settlement she founded, with Ellen Gates Starr, in Chicago in 1889, she became a major spokesperson for progressive causes and was repeatedly voted one of the two or three most admired Americans in public opinion polls. Gilman was widely regarded as the leading feminist intellectual of her day but preferred to be known as a 'sociologist' (Degler, 1966: vi–vii). She wrote six book-length works of formal social theory – including *Women and Economics* (1898), *Human Work* (1904) and *The Man-Made World* (1911); published articles in the *American Journal of Sociology*, *Annals of the American Academy of Political and Social Science* and *Publications of the American Sociological Society*; held membership in the American Sociological Society from its foundation in 1895 (Keith, 1991), and maintained intellectual relationships with Lester Ward and E.A. Ross.

Webb's widely regarded autobiography *My Apprenticeship* (1926) describes her evolution into a 'social investigator'. She was tutored by Spencer, whose ideas she later rejected, taught sociology, worked as a social investigator on Charles Booth's *Life and Labour of the People of London*, and wrote her own independent investigations, climaxing in the socialist reform classic, *The Co-operative Movement in Great Britain* (1891). As part of a powerful scholarly and political partnership with her husband Sidney, Webb researched and co-authored eleven volumes of empirical sociology which helped lay the foundation for the British welfare state.

Marianne Weber lived at the center of German sociological circles and debated both Simmel and her husband Max in her own writings. She was a leader of the German feminist movement, the first woman to be elected to a German parliament, the author of eight books of social analysis and sociology, including the monumental work on the legal position of women, *Ehefrau und Mutter in der Rechtsentwicklung* [Marriage, Motherhood and the Law] (1907) – which was reviewed by Durkheim in *L'Année sociologique*, and the collected essays, *Frauenfragen und Frauengedanken* [Reflections on Women and Women's Issues] (1919). She secured Max's position within sociology after his death by editing and publishing ten volumes of his work and writing her important interpretive biography of him.

The two less privileged women – Tristan disadvantaged by class, and Cooper, by race – had real but more tangential relations to sociology (see, for example, Grogan, 1998, for Tristan; Lemert and Bahn, 1998, for Cooper).

Tristan wrote three book-length sociological studies – *Peregrinations of a Pariah* (1838), *Promenades in London* (1840) and *The Workers' Union* (1844), which were informed by the ideas of the utopian socialists Saint-Simon, Fourier, Considerant and Robert Owen – the last three of whom she knew personally. Marx and Engels defend her work in *The Holy Family* ([1845] 1956), and Marx was urged to meet her (and Georges Sands) when he took refuge in France in 1844. Tristan wrote with a knowledge of herself as a marginal person, a 'pariah', who spoke from the lived experience of the oppressed working-class woman. The daughter of a French woman of unknown origins and a Peruvian aristocrat, Tristan was left in poverty at the age of four when her father died. As a teenager she went to work in the printing trades for a French lithographer, with whom she had a brief, unhappy and abusive marriage. In her lifetime, Tristan's reputation was largely within socialist and working-class circles.

Cooper's major work *A Voice from the South by a Black Woman from the South* (1892) formulates principles of 'sociology' to explain race, gender and class relations in the United States; she refers to Comte and Spencer and incorporates the social theories of the French historians Taine and Guizot. Cooper was an associate of W.E.B. DuBois, the African American sociologist, whose sociology has also been neglected in histories of the discipline (Lemert, 2000). In 1925, she defended her dissertation, *Slavery and the French Revolutionists, 1789–1805*, at the Sorbonne before a committee that included Célestin Bouglé, one of the leading figures in French sociology of that time, whose ideas about race

and democracy Cooper attacked. *A Voice from the South* received superlative reviews from black and white publications alike and established her as a prominent intellectual and spokesperson among African Americans.

Despite their work as social theorists and their public visibility, the classical women sociologists were perceived only as a marginal presence in the male discourse groups constructing sociology in the period 1830–1930. The crucial barrier appears to have been patriarchal culture, which both in interaction and through social structures, denied women the authority necessary for recognition as serious participants in the discourse. For example, Cooper was well known to W.E.B. DuBois – and yet was cited by him only as 'a woman of the race' (Washington, 1988). Weber saw herself on a journey of intellectual development during her engagement and marriage to Max, but was advised by him to create a sure base for herself in domesticity when she turned to him for help in selecting theoretical and philosophical readings (Weber, [1926] 1975). Webb, who resisted acknowledging her gender as a social impediment, nevertheless reported how Alfred Marshall (whom Parsons (1937) treats as a major contributor to the sociological tradition) discouraged her from writing *The Co-operative Movement in Great Britain* (1891), telling her: '*A book by you on the Co-operative Movement I may get my wife to read to me in the evening to while away the time, but I shan't pay any attention to it*' (Webb, 1926: 352, original emphasis). The women theorists themselves explore the obstacles that their gender presented to their intellectual and social science aspirations. In the introduction to *Society in America*, Martineau answers the charge that being a woman made it difficult to do social research; she argues instead that as a woman, she has easier access to the sites of domestic life which are 'excellent schools in which to learn the morals and manners of a people' – and that anyone may learn about 'public and professional affairs . . . who really feel[s] an interest in them' (Martineau, [1836] 1962: I: xiii). Addams, in one of her earliest published works, focuses on the denial of authority to the female voice, likening the woman scholar's experience to that of Cassandra – 'to be in the right and always to be disbelieved and rejected' (1881: 37). Gilman constructs a major work, *The Man-Made World, or Our Androcentric Culture* (1911) around the thesis that women's meanings are denied and rendered inconsequential by patriarchal culture.

The women's erasure from subsequent histories of sociology and its theories resulted from the working out of this problem of authority in two interrelated politics – a politics of gender and a politics of knowledge. The politics of gender proceeded as described above; the politics of knowledge involved a struggle over the purpose of sociology and the social role of the sociologist. This recurring struggle – variously described as 'objectivity versus advocacy' (Furner, 1975), 'scientistic' timelessness versus historical specificity (Ross, 1991) or 'the objective service intellectual' versus 'the purposivist' reformer (Smith, 1994) – was first fought between 1890 and 1947. In this period, sociology's male academic elites moved to a consensus that the appropriate role for the sociologist is that of the objective service intellectual committed to scientific rigor, value-neutrality and formal abstraction. This consensus de-legitimated the work of the classical women theorists, and many men, who practiced a critical, activist sociology of advocacy. The primary explanation for the growing emphasis on scientistic expertise was sociology's move into the university as its 'legitimate' work site, a move that was part of its quest for professional authority, social status, and job and salary security – and a move which further marginalized the women who were accepted as students but not as faculty. Location in the academy produced a distinctive theoretical voice and a way of building theory which assumed theory to be an activity done in a particular part of one's life, where one purposively set out to find something to theorize, proceeding in linear fashion towards increasing abstraction and predictions subject to scientific verification. The classical women theorists offered an alternative way of doing theory, as an activity done as part of a larger project of social critique and amelioration, in which the theorist responds to situations in the everyday lifeworld, constructing 'weblike' accounts whose verification lies in the utility of the theory for the people who are its subjects. This difference in theoretical voice is a key factor in delegitimating the achievements of the classical women theorists and justifying their erasure from the canon.

Until the late 1980s no major sociological study recognized the feminist tradition in classical sociology. The scholarship of the classical women theorists was noted only when pertinent to the accomplishments of important male founders of the discipline – Martineau as Comte's translator, Weber as Max's biographer, Webb as Sidney's partner helping construct the British empirical tradition (Kent, 1981). The impetus for the recovery of the women discussed in this chapter, and of the tradition they represent, has come not from sociology itself but from a new feminist historiography born of the burgeoning scholarship of second wave feminism. Path-breaking work on the earlier tradition of feminist social science has been done by feminist historians (Caine, 1982; Fitzpatrick, 1990; Giddings, 1984; Hill, 1980, 1985, 1995;

Muncy, 1991; Rosenberg, 1982; Sklar, 1995). This new historiography now permeates most academic disciplines, so that the significance of various of the classical women theorists is being discussed by philosophers (e.g., Baker-Fletcher, 1994, on Cooper; Seigfried, 1996, on Addams), economists (e.g., Dimand, 1996, and Sheth and Prasch, 1996, on Gilman), political scientists (e.g., Silverberg, 1998), and literary scholars who have produced a vast literature on these women.

In sociology the first major products of this new historiography appeared in 1988, with Deegan's detailed argument for Addams' importance, and Kandal's carefully documented exploration of the uneasy relation between feminism and sociology in the nineteenth and early twentieth centuries. In the 1990s four key works have substantiated the claim for a feminist contribution to the construction of sociology: Deegan (1991), Lengermann and Niebrugge-Brantley (1998), McDonald (1994) and Reinharz (1992). Taken collectively, these texts provide the basic information about the women who are the subjects of this chapter. In addition to these key works, a growing literature on these women is proceeding unevenly, with some of the women still only sketchily explored, while others are now the subject of a lively literature that is producing multiple interpretations of their work. Weber, surprisingly – given her productivity and her relationship to Max – has to date had only preliminary attention. Little of her writing has been translated into English, except for her biography of Max ([1926] 1975) and three essays from her 1919 collection *Frauenfragen und Frauengedanken* (see Kirchen's translations in Lengermann and Niebrugge-Brantley, 1998). Available, too, in English are studies of her experiences with Max (Scaff, 1998), her position *vis à vis* Max's on gender (Thomas, 1985) and her theoretical debates with Simmel (Scaff, 1988; Tijssen, 1991). Wobbe's 1998 review of her general social theory is available only in German. Tristan, too, is still only partially visible to a sociological audience, although all her key works have been translated into English. Her social theory has been described by writers approaching her as a utopian socialist and feminist (Beik and Beik, 1993; Cross and Gray, 1992; Desanti, 1976); Grogan (1998) and McDonald (1998) have included brief assessments of her social science contributions. As with Tristan, Webb's sociological work can be in part discovered through current discussion of her feminism (Beilharz and Nyland, 1998). She has had direct attention as a sociologist from Broschart (1991), McDonald (1998) and Romano (1998).

The movement to incorporate Cooper and Gilman into the sociological canon is much further advanced, with Cooper being presented as almost paradigmatic of black feminist social theory (Collins, 1990; Lemert, 1999, 1995; Lemert and Bahn, 1998) and Gilman of white feminist social theory (Deegan and Hill, 1998; Lemert, 1995, 1999). There is some trend towards multiple interpretations of Gilman – as an analyst of women and health (Oakley, 1997), a materialist feminist (Walby, 1990) and as a feminist Darwinist (Doskow, 1997).

The two deepest areas of scholarship are those on Martineau and Addams. Martineau is being recovered both as a feminist (Yates, 1985) and as a sociologist (Hill and Hoecker-Drysdale, 2000; Hoecker-Drysdale, 2000) with major accomplishments as a methodologist (Hill, 1989; Lengermann and Niebrugge-Brantley, 2000), as a sociologist of work (Hoecker-Drysdale, 2000), and as a political sociologist (McDonald, 1998). A growing body of feminist work is exploring the complexities of Addams' social thought, seeing her as a critical pragmatist (Deegan, 1988), a feminist pragmatist (Seigfried, 1996), an empiricist (McDonald, 1994), a feminist sociologist (Lengermann and Niebrugge-Brantley, 1998, 2000), an interpretive theorist (Ross, 1998), and a theorist of war, peace and the state (McDonald, 1998).

THEMES

Despite the fact that the women theorists we discuss here represent two different generations and various national traditions in their relation to feminism and to sociology, and that each woman creates a distinctive social theory, those theories taken collectively reveal a coherent tradition of classical feminist sociological thought. The hallmarks of that tradition are apparent in the theorists' central problematic, methodological orientation, model of society, emphasis on social change and the explanatory significance assigned to the individual and to ideas.

The central problematic

The central problematic of the classical feminist sociological tradition is the description, analysis and critique of socially produced pain, and, as befits a critical theory, the exploration of the social conditions that produce happiness or joy. Probably no other sociological theory has been as explicit in its dedication to both these projects. Martineau argues in sociology's first treatise on methods, *How to Observe Morals and Manners* (1838b), that the project of sociology is to see how various peoples develop culturally diverse systems of 'morals and manners' around the great end of all social life, '[t]hat man should be

happy' (1838b: 25). Webb and Addams both sought to combine empirical observation with ethical mobilization – in Webb's case to study the 'poverty amidst riches' (1926: 216) generated by capitalism; in Addams', first, to understand and alleviate 'the stress and need of those who bear the brunt of the social injury' (1895: 183–4) and as a second purpose to urge that the modern world act to 'organize play' as it has organized work (1909). Tristan introduces her major work of social observation, her study of London, as a depiction of 'the suffering of the English people' intended 'to put a stop to abuses . . . trac[ing] them back to their causes' ([1840] 1980: xix). Sixty-four years later, Gilman would make much the same argument: 'our study of sociology is prefaced by social pathology [because] society feels first and most what hurts it; . . . [s]o unbearable is the amount of human pain that we alone among all animals manifest the remarkable phenomenon of suicide – a deliberate effort of a form of life to stop living because living hurts so much . . .' (Gilman, 1904: 10, 16).

In this tradition socially produced pain has many dimensions – the material experience of physical want, suffering and exhaustion caused by an unjust distribution of material resources and an unjust arrangement of the work of social production; the cognitive experience of lack of agency, stemming not from one's lack of will but from social arrangements that deny that will the opportunities for meaningful action; and emotional experiences of frustration, alienation and loneliness, whose causes also lie in social inequities. Joy is seen as realized in experiences of free creative agency and spontaneous sociability, for which some of the social prerequisites are material security, absence of stress, adequate leisure, education and a cultural endorsement of playfulness.

Methodology

The methodological stance of this sociological tradition is framed by a feminist awareness and anchored in the concerns of the central problematic with socially produced human pain. The early women theorists develop four key methodological strategies:

1   to affirm women's standpoint as a valid epistemological base for theoretical knowledge;
2   to construct theory in an ongoing movement between the standpoint of situated actors (the personal) and the formulation of generalized understandings (the theoretical);
3   to verify theory not only, nor most importantly, in this move to abstraction, but in the preservation within the theoretical account of the particulars of daily existence;

4   to be explicitly and rigorously reflexive about the theorist's relation to the theory, the authenticity of subjects' accounts, and the movement from those accounts to a theoretical construction.

The standpoint of women

The classical women sociologists affirmed that they approached the task of analysing society from their distinctive knowledge and experiences as women, and that this standpoint gave them particular advantages as theorists. Martineau's 'Introduction' to *Society in America* explicitly confronts the significance of her gender for her research. Discounting the frequently made charge 'that my being a woman was [a] disadvantage' ([1836] 1962: I: xiii), she asserts that women have an advantage over men as social researchers, for they know about and have easy access to domestic life, a key location from which to discover a people's morals and manners. Cooper begins *A Voice from the South* (1892) with a now famous claim for the necessity for the black woman's voice in any social analysis which wishes 'a clearer vision and truer pulse-beat in studying' the American dilemma of democratic aspiration and racial injustice (1892: ii). Moving from their own standpoint as women to the more general issue of the sociological value of women's understanding of the social world, the classical women theorists affirm women's standpoint as an essential lens for discovering the organization of society. Gilman repeatedly turns to women's experience in the home as a basis from which to critique not only the subordination of women but the corruption of society. Gilman (1898, 1903) makes the production of food – one of women's key experiences – the distinguishing feature of human social life. She uses food preparation to illustrate everything that is wrong with a society founded on the 'sexuo-economic relation', Gilman's term for gender stratification. First, food preparation is paradigmatic of the sexuo-economic relation in which the woman gives unpaid service of all sorts in exchange for a livelihood. Second, food preparation reveals the social isolation of the uninstructed and untrained woman in the patriarchal household. Third, food preparation illustrates the public sector vulnerability of women that results from this isolation, for as single purchasers of food, they can exercise little power in the market place. Fourth, this power imbalance between women as consumers and male-dominated capitalist production leads to the variety of social and cultural problems resulting from unfettered greed.

Situated vantage points

The women who created sociology's classic tradition of feminist theory moved from this general understanding that one's sex (they did not have the term 'gender') affected what one knew and experienced about the social world, to a more reflective exploration of the significance of differently situated standpoints for the social analyst's quest for knowledge. Since they worked from the feminist position that what women knew and experienced mattered, they focused particularly on the issue of differently situated women; since their theory was a critical one, built around a central concern with socially produced pain, the differences they most frequently explored were those produced by the inequalities of class, ethnicity, age and race. They sought to create a general theoretical understanding of social life which could capture this complexity of experience and viewpoint. In an early example of this theoretical method, Martineau explores the relation between employer and domestic servant as collisions in the vantage points of variously class-situated actors: '[W]ho that does not live by manual labor understands the feelings of those who do? How many of the hundreds of thousands of employers reflect on the early life of the servants they hire and make allowance for them accordingly? . . .' (1838a: 424). The maid servant in turn is uncomprehending of her employers' activities – reading and writing, for example, seem to her leisured frivolity (1838a: 424). Cooper's (1892) analysis of American race relations focuses significant attention on the ways those relations create and are reproduced by the different attitudes of white and black women, white and black feminists, and women, both white and black, of various class backgrounds. Weber consistently recognizes categorical differences among women produced by their various locations in social structure, of which location in the class structure seems to her the most important. She understands the profound differences between rural and urban women in the Germany of her day, and the distinctions between rural women themselves, which contain 'such diverse existences as those of the peasant landholder . . . the resident farm worker, the seasonal worker and the day laborer' ([1912b/1919] 1998: 46). In urban society, she argues, differences in class location produce material differences, and these turn into differences in life style, needs and perceptions. Weber is particularly concerned about the argument by privileged-class feminists – including Gilman – that all women can be emancipated and fulfilled through wage sector employment. She argues that within the realities of capitalist employment, most women's wage work, indeed, most people's wage work, is done out of necessity and is hard, 'fragmenting' and unfulfilling. Bearing the double burden of wage work and housework, women of most class positions lead lives in which the solution 'employment for all' will not produce utopia.

Dailiness

The strategy of building a social theory which incorporated the experiences and knowledge of different and unequal social actors allowed the early feminist sociologists to remain firmly oriented to their theoretical problematic – the social causes and the lived actualities of human pain. This orientation also produced a distinctive theoretical account, one which grounded itself in lived actualities by preserving within the theoretical account the details of people's daily lives. They did this by using what literary scholars call 'texture' – those details that remain in any text after the paraphrasable argument has been removed. The paraphrasable argument is of course the abstract proposition. The classical women theorists affirm a theoretical strategy directly at odds with that of Durkheim's foundational principle for male sociology: '*When, then, the sociologist undertakes the investigation of some order of social facts, he [sic] must endeavor to consider them from an aspect that is independent of their individual manifestations*' ([1895] 1938: 44–5; emphasis in original). Sometimes this inclusion of texture is done by a brief list of the concrete particularities of a subject's life – such as in Marianne Weber's summary of the work done by the housewife in her essays, 'Women and Objective Culture' ([1913] 1919) and 'Women's Special Cultural Tasks' ([1918/ 1919] 1998). Sometimes it is done by more extended descriptions of routine activities, such as Gilman's treatment of housework's many faces in *The Home* (1903) or in Webb's study of the dock workers of East London (1887). Sometimes we are presented with a brief but vivid snapshot, as with Cooper's notes on her traumatic train ride through the South. Sometimes these portraits are more detailed, as in Tristan's accounts of her tour of the London prisons and her visit to Ascot. But above all, the presentation of texture is done through storytelling or narrative. The purest example of this use can be found in Addams, who uses narrative to show a world in which differently situated standpoints collide (for example, housewife and servant, charity workers and their clients, settlement workers and their working class immigrant neighbors) and to offer a rich, often poignant, imagery of the body to evoke the intersection of class, gender, ethnicity and age in individual biography.

Reflexivity

The classic women theorists reject the theoretical stance in which the theorist locates her- or himself outside and apart from what he or she analyses, speaking as a disinterested and omniscient observer. Instead, they use three strategies for locating themselves in their social theory: they let the reader see the particular socioeconomic background from which they speak; they share with the reader their valuational and emotional responses to the situations they analyse, and they work where possible to have the subjects in those situations respond to their analyses. Additionally, they all write major autobiographical accounts – a reflexive practice that contrasts with the male counterparts of their generation. Weber discusses the particular privilege of women like herself – financially secure, educated, in marriages like her own with liberal minded husbands – or unmarried. She argues that this privilege brings responsibility: to represent women's experience in all its diversity in the growing male discourse of social science and to advocate policies for women that are not necessarily the 'most feminist' but that lend themselves most flexibly to the diverse circumstances under which women live. Cooper's major work of sociology, *A Voice from the South*, signals the autobiographical nexus of gender/ race/class from her opening pages: the volume's extended title, *A Voice from the South by a Black Woman of the South*, runs opposite a photo of Cooper, showing a well-dressed, clearly African American woman, seated at a table covered with a lace cloth on which several books await her attention. Webb (1926) argues that sociological knowledge can transcend class perspective; presenting herself as a person of extreme class privilege, she describes how her study of poverty leads her, against her class socialization and interests, from an individualistic to an increasingly collectivist interpretation. Tristan, who also identifies herself to us, cryptically in the title of her first major publication, *Peregrinations of a Pariah*, illustrates the recourse to emotional and valuational response which is a distinctive feature of classical feminist method: 'It was a pitiful sight, the courtyard of that hospital . . . dedication to suffering, which only a true religion inspires, is nowhere evident . . . [The sick] dying of thirst, uttered feeble, mournful cries . . . the sufferings . . . overwhelmed my whole being; I . . . deplored my own inability to help' ([1838] 1993: 19–20). Addams actively sought strategies for monitoring her accounts, making it a point never to speak to 'a Chicago audience on the subject of the Settlement and its vicinity without having a neighbor to go with me, that I might curb any hasty generalization by the consciousness that I had an auditor who knew conditions more intimately than I could hope to do' (1910: 96), and never allowing herself to forget 'the harrowing consciousness of the difference in economic condition between ourselves and our neighbors' (1910: 133–4).

The organization of society

The classical women theorists present a model of society as having a threefold organization: interactional, institutional and stratificational. In this model, the interactional order is the fundamental order; here, people relate out of interests, emotions, sociability, moving in and out of multiple relational sites and carrying with them, in transition, between sites and within sites, certain ideas about ethics and manners that they adjust situationally. For example, Gilman defines the subject of sociology as 'human social relation', a phrase she uses to describe the process of reciprocal action and inter-psychic orientation among individuals within the context of a shared collective membership (1900: 278). While much of social life is to be found purely at this ephemeral yet persistent level of association, human interactions also pattern into denser nodes around activities or functions essential to social life. Some of the functional or institutional areas named are the familiar 'key institutions' – economy, government, law, education, religion, family, media. But others are distinctive to this woman-centered approach – charity, recreation, friendship, domesticity and community. Martineau and Addams, for instance, both take as one of the key indicators of the efficacy of social organization the practice of charity in a society. Superimposed on or permeating interactions and institutions is the stratificational order – class inequality, race inequality, ethnic inequality, age inequality and, central to their analyses, gender inequality. One distinction among the theorists is the form of inequality on which they focus: Tristan focuses on class and gender; Martineau, on class, gender and race; Cooper, on race and gender; Addams, on class, ethnicity, age and gender; Gilman, and Weber on gender; and Webb, on class.

The feature of stratification which particularly concerns them is domination. Like any group of critical theorists, the classical women sociologists offer two visions of society – a vision of society as it ought to be organized and a vision of society as it is organized. The good society fosters human happiness through social arrangements that promote individual agency, moral autonomy and spontaneous sociability. Domination is a power relation whose most active feature is the denial of the subordinate's

subjectivity – that is, the subordinate's capacity for and right to agency, moral autonomy and spontaneous sociability.

Domination is presented as working both as a structure and a process, an underlying grammar of social relations. All the early women theorists offer definitions of domination. For Martineau the crucial issue in conceptualizing domination is always that of the enforced 'submission of one's will to another' (1838a: 411). For Cooper, it is the refusal to allow difference an equal place, the need to make difference – whether of gender, class, color or shade – the basis for hierarchy; in America, domination distorts difference to mean both departure from and subordinate to the norm of Anglo Saxon whiteness. For Weber, as for Addams, domination is the violation of a fundamental ethical principle – the duty to acknowledge the subjectivity of the other, a principle Weber summarizes: 'that each one must heed the command in every other human to become an end in oneself, that no person may regard a fellow human being *as simply the means to his/her own personal ends*. In practice there is hardly any conceivable human relationship that can disregard this principle if it wishes to be ethically sufficient . . .' (Weber, [1912a/1919] 1998: 217; emphasis in original). Domination, then, is a critical concept, that is, it is the social condition that must be ameliorated.

Significance of the individual

The human individual is given a dynamic and essential role in classical feminist social theory. Realization of the human potential is seen as a universal mandate for social organization; a key measure of societal efficacy is the degree to which human happiness is facilitated or subverted by social structure. The individual social actor is thus neither determined by nor independent of social organization; rather, social actor and social process relate in varying degrees of mutually satisfactory or unsatisfactory interdependence. Above all, for classical feminist social theory, the willful individual is not a problem to be solved by social structure but a living fact to be nourished and empowered.

The women theorists assign the individual a complex of qualities and capacities. Perhaps distinctive to feminist theoretical tradition is the understanding of the social actor as an embodied subjectivity; personhood exists in a physical body, bearing the signifiers of gender, class, race, age and health, and responding to enactments of domination with pain, exhaustion, debilitation. Here then is a major cause of socially produced human pain – social arrangements which are unkind to the human body. Descriptions of embodied human pain are to be found through-out the women's writings – the beating and mutilation of black slaves in America (Marti-neau), the physical collapse of convicts from intricately contrived hard labor (Tristan), aged working-class immigrants whose hands are gnarled by arthritis and overwork (Addams), housewives providing house-service on weary feet all day and deep into the night (Gilman and Weber), black washerwomen 'pinched and stooped' over their huge loads of laundry (Cooper), and dock workers bearing lumber on their 'hummies', neck callouses developed by and essential to their work (Webb).

These embodied people are characterized by a rich inner life marked by agentic subjectivity – by capacities to think and to will, by ethical orientation and by irrepressible desire. The actor is understood as having purposes of his or her own which the reformer and the social analyst must take into account: 'We are not content to include all men in our hopes, *but have become conscious that all men are hoping* and are part of the same movement of which we are a part' (Addams, [1902] 1907: 179; emphasis added). Addams' theory of human development revolves around the way this will is nourished, shaped and thwarted. In this theory, the human sense of ethics is seen as rooted in human propensities for sociability, kindness and aspiration towards the good. People wish to find themselves in right relation with others and with universal principles of good action: 'If there be any human power and business and privilege which is absolutely universal, it is the discovery and adoption of the principle and laws of duty' (Martineau, [1837] 1962: II: 229–30). The capacity of the human individual to hold on to will, desire and aspira-tion even in the most repressive and degrading of circumstances is a central faith in this theoretical tradition, an object of awe, and the underlying imperative behind their theoretical project of critique and change: 'It is that "Something" – that *Singing* Something, which distinguished the first Man from the last ape, which in a subtle way tagged him with the picturesque Greek title *anthropos*, the *upward face*, and which justifies the claim to equality by birthright . . .' (Cooper, [1925] 1998: 292–3).

Significance of ideas

In the tradition of classical feminist sociology, collective ideas serve as the key social mechan-ism linking the potentially willful, desirous, ethical human individual to a societal order which teeters between domination, on the one hand, and the facilitation of human happiness, on the other. Human beings, motivated by ideas which pattern interests and ethics, act in ways that reproduce or change social structures. Although individuals are understood to have the capacity to generate new ideas, in most routine social situations they acquire their ideas, and thus their motives for action, from the collectivities in which they live. But collective ideas are not necessarily reflective of the human potential for agency, sociability and ethical 'right relation'. Instead, much more frequently and pervasively, collective ideas arise out of prevail-ing forms of societal organization as those forms have evolved over history. Thus human beings may be motivated to act in ways that reproduce social structures inimical to their happiness.

The classical women theorists identify two major societal sources of wrong ideas: structures of domination and uneven social change. For Weber a major source of ethical distortion comes from patriarchy, the system of male domination. She shows how the doctrine of freedom of conscience became the basic moral claim in both the political revolutions of the eighteenth century and the philosophic achievement of German Idealism. Yet in looking at the marriage relation, the philosophers let the male desire for domination override the philosophical argument for moral autonomy, arguing that the woman in entering into marriage willingly agrees as part of that contract to relinquish her autonomy to the husband. For Gilman, human ideas have been distorted by the interaction of capitalist domina-tion with patriarchy. Together these have produced an 'androcentric culture', which has valued being male rather than being human (1911) and created a system of false economic concepts which have corrupted work – poten-tially the greatest source of joy – into an experience of deep alienation. Cooper locates the motivational pressure towards domination in American racism. She analyses the situation of the African American as the direct result of the Anglo American's confusion of belief: '[T]he problematical position at present occupied by descendants of Africans in the American social polity . . . grow[s] . . . out of the continued indecision in the mind of the more powerful descendants of the Saxons as to whether it is expedient to apply the maxims of their religion to their civil and political relationships' (1892: 185). Ideas also become misaligned with human needs and aspiration because of historic social change. For Martineau, an 'anomaly' may arise between the morals a society formally upholds and the manners or routinized practices it creates over time. She finds such anomalies in the United States between the founding moral principle of the society, the principle of equality of claim to inalienable rights, and the institutio-nalized practices of slavery, the subjugation of women, the tyranny of public opinion, and the fetishism of wealth. For Addams, the chief problem in United States society in her day is what she terms the 'belatedness' of the relation between industrial production and ethics; while material production has become increasingly 'socialized', ethics have remained rooted in the restrictive values of individual morality, militarism and loyalty to the family. The thesis that distorted thinking sustains domination, while right ideas can initiate ameliorative social change towards the good society, undergirds the classical women theorists' understanding of their social role as theorists: they will create ideas that can help produce the good society.

Social change

Classical feminist social theory was in large measure created because the early women sociologists wished to bring about positive social change to alleviate human pain and actively promote human joy. The women theorists saw their theoretical work as having three roles in the production of ameliorative social change: as a catalyst for changes already in motion, as a pressure on the state for social reform, and as a project of radical transformation through an appeal to the disempowered. Martineau, Gilman and Cooper all argue that their social critiques would help clarify and accelerate changes already under way. They see the potential for ameliorative change in the lines of tension existing in American society, in the anomalous situation between formally proclaimed morals of equality and routinized practices of domination (Martineau), in the clash between a patriarchal-capitalist system of widespread alienation and the irrepressible human impulses for self-actualization through work and sociability (Gilman), and in the racial and gender power struggles triggered by the newly enfranchised African Americans' drive for self-improvement and the increasingly mass-based women's movement for political rights (Cooper). They all saw their own theoretical analyses as intended to add clarity and energy to these emergent critiques. Cooper, for example, argues that 'from her peculiar coigne of vantage as a quiet observer . . . [t]he colored woman . . . is watching the movements of the contestants . . . and is all the better qualified, perhaps, to weight and judge and advise because not herself in the excitement of the race' (1892: 138).

Of theorists who sought to bring pressure on the state, Weber believed that the legal system was potentially a neutral but powerful mechanism for ameliorative social change and that with the pressure of feminist mobilization it could be turned away from patriarchal practices and towards policies making for greater gender equality. Webb argued that social experiments in alternative social organization were taking place all the time as collectivities, businesses and governments try different actions to see if they will produce desired effects on various groups of people. She sought through social science research to analyse those social experiments that bring political democracy to economic life, as for example, the consumer cooperative movement and municipal government efforts to procure a collective rather than an individual good – such as roads and parks (the latter done with her husband Sidney). Her sociological strategy was to systematize and promulgate these 'natural' strategies for communitarian group life.

Still other theorists called for the radical repatterning of social relationships. Gilman, for example, argued for a fundamental restructuring of the heterosexual household in order to give everyone a genuine home from which they could develop their fullest potential. Tristan and Addams both sought the transformation of capitalism into a socialized democracy. Tristan's approach was militant: 'Workers, . . . the day has come where you must *act* . . . in the interest of your own cause. At stake are your very lives – or death, that horrible, ever-menacing death: misery and starvation. . . . You have but one legal and legitimate recourse permissible before God and man: THE UNIVERSAL UNION OF WORKING MEN AND WOMEN' ([1844] 1983: 27–8). Addams' approach was reformist and moderately stated yet hers may have been the most pervasively radical theory of ameliorative social change. In the context of contemporary American society, Addams states that what is called for is a 'social ethic' – a truly democratic and collectivist culture – to both mirror the new socialized forms of production and to curb its excesses. This ethical transformation requires, first, a change in consciousness and habits of interaction so that people learn to identify their individual interests with the common good. Second, to acquire these new habits of thought and relationship people must invent new forms and sites of association: settlement houses, trades unions, educational clubs, consumer leagues, study groups, investigative task forces and cooperatives. Third, people under the impetus of the social ethic and of these new associations must pressure the state to formulate socially responsible policies. Addams, thus, called for an entirely new arrangement of culture, group life, government and production – one in which the individual, social organizations and government act out of concern for the well-being of the full, and fully differentiated, community.

SIGNIFICANCE OF CLASSICAL FEMINIST SOCIAL THEORY

The rediscovery of classical feminist sociological theory, as outlined above, has several important implications for sociological theory and the history of sociology. It shows us that the contemporary burgeoning of feminist sociology and feminist sociological theory can claim a heritage in sociology's history. It expands our understanding of the nature of theory construction, the ways theory is written, and the places where it is created. It leads us to recover some of these forgotten sites for sociological work, such as the settlement movement and the social science movement. It expands the tradition of sociology as a critical science. And, it shows the writing of the history of sociology as a complex construction involving multiple politics, including a politics of gender.

REFERENCES

Addams, Jane (1881) 'Cassandra', in *Essays of Class of 1881, Rockford Seminary*. DeKalb, IL: 'News' Steam Press. pp. 36–9.

Addams, Jane (1895) 'The Settlement as a Factor in the Labor Movement', *Hull-House Maps and Papers by the Residents of Hull-House, A Social Settlement*. New York: Crowell. pp. 183–204.

Addams, Jane (1896) 'A Belated Industry', *American Journal of Sociology*, 1: 536–50.

Addams, Jane ([1902] 1907) *Democracy and Social Ethics*. New York: Macmillan.

Addams, Jane (1907) *Newer Ideals of Peace*. New York: Macmillan.

Addams, Jane (1909) *The Spirit of Youth and the City Streets*. New York: Macmillan.

Addams, Jane (1910) *Twenty Years at Hull-House*. New York: Macmillan.

Ashley, David and Orenstein, David Michael (1998) *Sociological Theory: Classical Statements*. Boston, MA: Allyn and Bacon.

Baker-Fletcher, Karen (1994) *A Singing Something: Womanist Reflections on Anna Julia Cooper*. New York: Crossroad.

Beik, Doris and Beik, Paul (1993) 'Introduction to Her Life', in D. Beik and P. Beik (trans. and eds), *Flora Tristan: Utopian Feminist*. Bloomington, IN: Indiana University Press. pp. v–xxi.

Beilharz, Peter and Nyland, Chris (eds) (1998) *The Webbs, Fabianism and Feminism*. Aldershot: Ashgate Publishing.

Caine, Barbara (1982) 'Beatrice Webb and the Woman Question', *History Workshop Journal*, 14: 23–43.

Ceplair, Larry (ed.) (1991) *Charlotte Perkins Gilman: A Non-Fiction Reader*. New York: Columbia University Press.

Collins, Randall and Makowsky, Michael (1998) *The Discovery of Society*, 6th edn. New York: McGraw-Hill.

Cooper, Anna Julia (1892) *A Voice from the South by a Black Woman from the South*. Xenia, OH: Aldine.

Cooper, Anna Julia ([1925] 1988) *Slavery and the French Revolutionists (1788–1805)* (trans. Frances Richardson Keller). Queenston, Ontario: Edwin-Mellen Press.

Cooper, Anna Julia ([1925] 1988) 'Equality of Races and the Democratic Movement', in Charles Lemert and Esme Bahn (eds), *The Voice of Anna Julia Cooper*. Lanham, MD: Rowman and Littlefield. pp. 291–8.

Costin, Lela (1983) *Two Sisters for Social Justice: A Biography of Edith and Grace Abbott*. Urbana, IL: University of Illinois.

Cross, Maire and Gray, Tim (1992) *The Feminism of Flora Tristan*. Oxford: Berg.

Crothers, Charles (1998) 'Engaging with Exemplars', *Perspectives*, 20 (2): 1, 8.

Deegan, Mary Jo (1988) *Jane Addams and the Men of the Chicago School, 1892–1913*. New Brunswick, NJ: Transaction Books.

Deegan, Mary Jo (1991) *Women in Sociology: A Bio-Bibliographical Sourcebook*. Westport, CT: Greenwood Press.

Deegan, Mary Jo and Hill, Michael (eds) (1998) *Charlotte Perkins Gilman: With Her in Ourland*. Westport, CT: Praeger.

Degler, Carl (1966) 'Introduction' to 1966 edition of Charlotte Perkins Gilman, *Women and Economics*. New York: Harper and Row.

Diamand, Mary-Ann (1996) 'Women and Economics: The Economic Factor between Men and Women as a Factor in Social Evolution', *Feminist Economics*, 2 (3): 167–74.

Doskow, Minna (1997) 'Charlotte Perkins Gilman: The Female Face of Social Darwinism', *Weber-Studies*, 14 (3): 9–22.

Durkheim, Emile ([1895] 1938) *The Rules of Sociological Method* (ed. George E.G. Catlin, trans. Sarah A. Solovay and John H. Mueller). New York: The Free Press.

Farganis, James (1996) *Readings in Social Theory: The Classic Tradition*. New York: McGraw-Hill.

Fish, Virginia Kemp (1981) 'Annie Marion MacLean: A Neglected Part of the Chicago School', *Journal of the History of Sociology*, 3: 43–62.

Fish, Virginia Kemp (1985) 'Hull House: Pioneer in Urban Research During its Creative Years', *History of Sociology*, 6 (1): 33–54.

Fitzpatrick, Ellen (1990) *Endless Crusade: Women Social Scientists and Progressive Reform*. New York: Oxford University Press.

Furner, Mary (1975) *Advocacy and Objectivity: A Crisis in the Professionalization of American Social Science, 1865–1905*. Lexington, KY: University of Kentucky Press.

Giddings, Paula (1984) *Where and When I Enter: The*

Impact of Black Women on Race and Sex in America. New York: William Murrow.

Gilman, Charlotte Perkins (1898) *Women and Economics.* Boston, MA: Small and Maynard.

Gilman, Charlotte Perkins (1900) *Concerning Children.* Boston, MA: Small and Maynard.

Gilman, Charlotte Perkins (1903) *The Home: Its Work and Influence.* New York: Macmillan.

Gilman, Charlotte Perkins (1904) *Human Work.* New York: McClure and Phillips.

Gilman, Charlotte Perkins (1911) *The Man-Made World, or Our Androcentric Culture.* London: Fisher Unwin.

Grogan, Susan (1998) *Flora Tristan: Life Stories.* New York: Routledge.

Hill, Mary A. (1980) *Charlotte Perkins Gilman: The Making of a Radical Feminist, 1860–1896.* Philadelphia: Temple University Press.

Hill, Mary A. (ed.) (1985) *Endure: The Diaries of Charles Walter Stetson* (ed. Mary A. Hill). Philadelphia: Temple University Press.

Hill, Mary A. (1995) *A Journey From Within: The Love Letters of Charlotte Perkins Gilman, 1897–1900* (ed. Mary A. Hill). Lewisburg, PA: Bucknell University Press.

Hill, Michael R. (1989) 'Empiricism and Reason in Harriet Martineau's Sociology', Introduction by Michael Hill, editor, to *How to Observe Morals and Manners* by Harriet Martineau. New Brunswick, NJ: Transaction Books.

Hill, Michael and Hoecker-Drysdale, Susan (2000) *Harriet Martineau: Theoretical and Methodological Perspectives.* New York: Garland.

Hoecker-Drysdale, Susan (1992) *Harriet Martineau: First Woman Sociologist.* New York: Berg Press.

Hoecker-Drysdale, Susan (2000) 'Harriet Martineau', in George Ritzer (ed.), *The Blackwell Companion to Major Social Theorists.* Oxford and Cambridge, MA: Blackwell.

Kandal, Terry R. (1988) *The Woman Question in Classical Sociological Theory.* Miami: International Universities Press.

Keith, Bruce (1991) 'Charlotte Perkins Gilman', in Mary Jo Deegan (ed.), *Women in Sociology: A Bio-bibliography Sourcebook.* Westport, CT: Greenwood Press. pp. 148–56.

Kent, Raymond A. (1981) *A History of British Empirical Sociology.* Aldershot: Gower Press.

Kirchen, Elizabeth (1998) 'Translations from Marianne Weber's *Frauenfragen und Frauengedanke*', in P. Lengermann and J. Niebrugge-Brantley (eds), *The Women Founders: Sociology and Social Theory, 1830–1898.* New York: McGraw-Hill. pp. 215–28.

Lemert, Charles (1995) *Sociology After the Crisis.* Boulder, CO: Westview Press.

Lemert, Charles (1999) *Sociology: The Multicultural and Classic Readings.* Boulder, CO: Westview Press.

Lemert, Charles (2000) 'W.E.B. DuBois', in George Ritzer (ed.), *The Blackwell Companion to Major Social Theorists.* Oxford and Cambridge, MA: Blackwell.

Lemert, Charles and Bahn, Esme (eds) (1998) *The Voice of Anna Julia Cooper.* Lanham, MD: Rowman and Littlefield.

Lengermann, Patricia and Niebrugge-Brantley, Jill (1998) *The Women Founders: Sociology and Social Theory, 1830–1930.* New York: McGraw-Hill.

Lengermann, Patricia and Niebrugge-Brantley, Jill (2000) 'The Meaning of "Things". Harriet Martineau and Emile Durkheim on Sociological Method', in Michael R. Hill and Susan Hoecker-Drysdale (eds), *Harriet Martineau: Theoretical and Methodological Perspectives.* New York: Garland.

Levine, Donald (1995) *Visions of the Sociological Tradition.* Chicago, IL: University of Chicago Press.

Livingston, Beverly (1983) 'Translator's Introduction', in Flora Tristan, *The Workers' Union.* Urbana, IL: University of Illinois Press. pp. vii–xxvi.

Martineau, Harriet ([1836/1837] 1962) *Society in America* (2 vols). New York: Saunders and Otley.

Martineau, Harriet (1838a) 'Domestic Service', *London and Westminster Review*, 29: 405–32.

Martineau, Harriet (1838b) *How to Observe Morals and Manners.* London: Charles Fox.

Martineau, Harriet (1853) *The Positive Philosophy of Auguste Comte, freely translated and condensed by Harriet Martineau.* London: John Chapman.

Marx, Karl and Engels, Friedrich ([1845] 1956) *The Holy Family.* Moscow: Foreign Language Press.

McDonald, Lynn (1994) *The Women Founders of the Social Sciences.* Ottawa, Canada: Carleton University Press.

McDonald, Lynn (ed.) (1998) *Women Theorists on Society and Politics.* Waterloo, Ontario: Wilfred Laurier University Press.

Muncy, Robyn (1991) *Creating a Female Dominion of Reform.* New York: Oxford University Press.

Oakley, Anne (1997) 'Beyond *The Yellow Wallpaper*', *Reproductive Health Matters*, 10: 29–39.

Parsons, Talcott (1937) *The Structure of Social Action.* New York: The Free Press.

Reinharz, Shulamit (ed.) (1992) *Feminist Methods in Social Research.* New York: Oxford University Press.

Ritzer, George ([1996] 2000) *Classical Sociological Theory.* New York: McGraw-Hill.

Romano, Mary Ann (1998) *Beatrice Webb (1858–1943): The Socialist with a Sociological Imagination.* Lampeter, Wales: Edwin Mellen.

Rosenberg, Rosalind (1982) *Beyond Separate Spheres: Intellectual Roots of Modern Feminism.* New Haven, CT: Yale University Press.

Ross, Dorothy (1991) *The Origins of American Social Science.* Cambridge: Cambridge University Press.

Ross, Dorothy (1998) 'Gendered Social Knowledge: Domestic Discourse, Jane Addams, and the Possibilities of Social Science', in Helene Silverberg (ed.), *Gender and American Social Science: The*

Formative Years. Princeton, NJ: Princeton University Press. pp. 235–64.

Roth, Gunther (1990) 'Marianne Weber and Her Circle', *Society*, 127: 63–70.

Scaff, Lawrence A. (1988) 'Weber, Simmel, and the Sociology of Culture', *Sociological Review*, 36 (1): 1–30.

Scaff, Lawrence A. (1998) 'The "Cool Objectivity of Sociation": Max Weber and Marianne Weber in America', *History of the Human Sciences*, 11 (2): 61–82.

Seigfried, Charlene Haddock (1996) *Pragmatism and Feminism: Reweaving the Social Fabric*. Chicago: University of Chicago Press.

Sheth, Falgani and Prasch, Robert (1996) 'Charlotte Perkins Gilman: Reassessing Her Significance for Feminism and Social Economics', *Review of Social Economy*, 64 (3): 323–35.

Silverberg, Helene (ed.) (1998) *Gender and American Social Science*. Princeton, NJ: Princeton University Press.

Sklar, Kathryn Kish (1995) *Florence Kelley and the Nation's Work 1830–1900*. New Haven, CT: Yale University Press.

Smith, Mark C. (1994) *Social Science in the Crucible*. Durham, NC: Duke University Press.

Terry, James L. (1983) 'Bringing Women . . . In: A Modest Proposal', *Teaching Sociology*, 10 (2): 251–61.

Thomas, J.J.R. (1985) 'Rationalization and the Status of Gender Divisions', *Sociology*, 19 (1): 409–20.

Tijssen, Lietake van Vucht (1991) 'Women and Objective Culture: George Simmel and Marianne Weber', *Theory, Culture and Society*, 8: 203–18.

Tristan, Flora ([1838] 1993) 'From *Peregrinations of a Pariah*', in D. Beik and P. Beik (trans. and eds), *Flora Tristan: Utopian Feminist*. Bloomington, IN: Indiana University Press. pp. 9–33.

Tristan, Flora ([1840] 1980) *London Journal* [or *Promenade London*] (trans. Dennis Palmer and Giselle Picentl). Charleston, MA: Charles River Books.

Tristan, Flora ([1844] 1983) *The Workers Union* (trans. Beverly Livingston). Urbana, IL: University of Illinois Press.

Walby, Sylvia (1990) 'Historical Roots of Contemporary Materialist Feminism', Paper presented at the International Sociological Association, Amsterdam.

Washington, Mary Helen (1988) 'Introduction to *A Voice from the South by Anna Julia Cooper*'. Schomburg Library of Nineteenth-Century Black Women Writers. New York: Oxford University Press.

Webb, Beatrice Potter (1887) 'The Dock Life of East London', *Nineteenth Century*, 22: 483–99.

Webb, Beatrice Potter (1891) *The Co-operative Movement in Great Britain*. London: Swan, Sonnenschein, and Company.

Webb, Beatrice Potter (1926) *My Apprenticeship*. London: Longmans, Green.

Weber, Marianne ([1905] 1919) 'Jobs and Marriage', in *Frauenfragen und Frauengedanken*. Tübingen: J.C.B. Mohr. pp. 20–37.

Weber, Marianne (1907) *Ehefrau und Mutter in der Rechtsentwicklung*. Tübingen: J.C.B. Mohr.

Weber, Marianne ([1912a/1919] 1998) 'Authority and Autonomy in Marriage', in Elizabeth Kirchen (trans.), 'Selections from *Marianne Weber's Reflections on Women and Women's Issues*', unpublished manuscript, pp. 27–41. (Originally published in *Frauenfragen und Frauengedanken*. Tübingen: J.C.B. Mohr. pp. 67–79.)

Weber, Marianne ([1912b/1919] 1998) 'On the Valuation of Housework', in Elizabeth Kirchen (trans.), 'Selections from *Marianne Weber's Reflections on Women and Women's Issues*', unpublished manuscript, pp. 42–58. (Originally published in *Frauenfragen und Frauengedanken*. Tübingen: J.C.B. Mohr. pp. 80–94.)

Weber, Marianne ([1913] 1919) 'Women and Objective Culture', in *Frauenfragen und Frauengedanken*. Tübingen: J.C.B. Mohr. pp. 95–134.

Weber, Marianne ([1918/1919] 1998) 'Women's Special Cultural Tasks', in Elizabeth Kirchen (trans.), 'Selections from *Marianne Weber's Reflections on Women and Women's Issues*', unpublished manuscript, pp. 1–26. (Originally published in *Frauenfragen und Frauengedanken*. Tübingen: J.C.B. Mohr. pp. 238–61.)

Weber, Marianne (1919) *Frauenfragen und Frauengedanken* [Reflections on Women and Women's Issues]. Tübingen: J.C.B. Mohr.

Weber, Marianne ([1926] 1975) *Max Weber: A Biography* (trans. Harry Zohn). New York: Wiley.

Wobbe, Theresa (1998) 'Ideen, Interessen und Geschlect: Marianne Weber's Kultursoziologische Fragestellung' [Ideas, Interests and Gender: Marianne Weber's Cultural-Sociological Inquiry], *Berliner-Journal-fur-Soziologie*, 8 (1): 105–23.

Yates, Gayle Graham (ed.) (1985) *Harriet Martineau on Women*. New Brunswick, NJ: Rutgers University Press.

Part Two
CONTEMPORARY
SOCIAL THEORY

12

Functional, Conflict and Neofunctional Theories

MARK ABRAHAMSON

Between roughly the mid 1940s and the late 1960s, structural functionalism was the dominant theoretical perspective in sociology. Talcott Parsons was its major figure, and so great was his influence that even the sharpest critics among his contemporaries conceded that they had to define their own intellectual positions in relation to his (Alexander, 1983). The abstractness of Parsons' theorizing and his grandiloquent writing style were, during his time of prominence, widely discussed and debated; but sociologists were generally less reflective about many of the distinctive suppositions of Parsons' structural functionalism. Perhaps the distinguishing features of the perspective remained in the background due to the relative absence of competing paradigms (cf. Ritzer, 1980). In any case, Kingsley Davis' presidential address to the American Sociological Association probably reflected the views of most of his contemporaries when he insisted that functional and sociological analyses were, in fact, virtually identical (Davis, 1959). Anyone who thought functionalism involved any special assumptions, Davis concluded, believed in a myth.

Current, multiple paradigm sociology has obviously changed very much in the latter decades of the twentieth century. The place of functionalism and neofunctionalism in the contemporary theoretical mix is one of the major topics to be assessed in this chapter. We will also examine the important historical interplays between structural functional and (non-Marxian) conflict theories. Before turning to the changes that occurred over the last one-third of the twentieth century, however, it will be instructive first to look back at how diverse conceptual contributions converged to become the structural functional paradigm in the middle of the twentieth century.

To state where any school of thought began necessarily requires arbitrary decisions, because no matter where one chooses to begin it would almost always be possible to find some still earlier, relevant statement. Therefore, let us simply say that one logical place to begin is with the writings of a group of eighteenth-century Scottish scholars – including Adam Smith and David Hume, in particular – who later came to be collectively referred to as the Scottish Moralists.

SCOTTISH MORALISTS

Several theoretical notions shared by most of the Scots had particular impact upon the development of functional theory in sociology (and anthropology). To begin, they all tended to emphasize a conceptual distinction between levels of analysis in which collective units, such as the economy or society, were seen as possessing qualities that were separate from the individuals that comprised them. Further, the Scots claimed, a collectivity could not be entirely fashioned by the conscious volition of individual participants because they only partly understood it, at best. In Adam Smith's view, genuine comprehension and explanation required that the analyst be distanced from the routine workings of a society or economy (cf. Copley, 1995).

However, neither Smith nor the other Scots regarded social organization as adversely affected by its separation from human agency. Smith's discussion of how an 'invisible hand' anomolously promotes social ends, despite people's selfish and hedonistic intents, may be the exemplar of this position. To illustrate, he explained how the vanity of large land and factory owners combined with the eager entrepreneurship of merchants to produce an industrial and commercial revolution that benefited everyone:

> A revolution of the greatest importance to the public happiness was . . . brought about by two different orders of people, who had not the least intention to serve the public . . . To gratify the most childish vanity was the sole motive of the great proprietors. The merchants . . . acted merely from a . . . principle of turning a penny whenever a penny was to be got. Neither of them had either knowledge or foresight of that great revolution which the folly of the one, and the industry of the other, was gradually bringing about. (Smith, [1863] 1967: 199)

The Scots' separation of intent and consequence proved to have enormous analytical and methodological implications. It meant that social practices could not necessarily be judged according to any intrinsic or introspective standard that involved people's motives. Instead, a social analyst had (metaphorically at least) to stand aside, and observe the actual collective consequences of individuals' behavior. An interesting illustration is provided by David Hume's analysis of courtship and marriage patterns. After observing differences among societies, he wondered what accounted for the variation in civil laws and moral sentiments.

Hume was able to answer this question, at least partially, by examining the consequences of particular matings. For example, among royalty, what harm would come from a widow marrying her deceased husband's brother? In the circle of great princes, he reasoned, marriage is more ceremonial and commercial than sexual, so rules which prohibit such marriages among non-royalty need not apply to them. Furthermore, if the widow and her brother-in-law come from different nations, then their marriage may help to cement an alliance, even if it violates a conventional marital taboo. Therefore, Hume concluded, 'there is less reason for extending toward them the full rigour of the rule . . .' (Hume, 1879: 95).[1]

In sum, the Scottish Moralists presented several inter-related points that were especially important with respect to the development of structural functional theory in sociology: an emphasis upon an outsider's examination of the consequences of people's behavior; a conceptual distinction between individuals and collectivities as units which act and are acted upon; and the assumption that the parts of societies or economies will generally be well integrated, despite their tendency to be removed from individual volition. All of the above notions were elaborated by the French theorist, Emile Durkheim, and they became the early cornerstones of his new science of sociology.

EMILE DURKHEIM

The primary topic in Durkheim's first classic provided him with a great opportunity to polemicize against earlier theories which viewed the *collective* division of labor as a product of *individuals'* calculations (cf. Luhmann 1982). Correspondingly, Durkheim began *The Division of Labor in Society* ([1893] 196; hereafter cited as *DoL*) with an acknowledgement of Adam Smith's influence, especially Smith's insights into the advantages of the division of labor. By contrast, elsewhere in *DoL* Durkheim went to some lengths to stress the uniqueness of his own contributions, especially in relation to Comte and Spencer.

In a brief introductory passage, Durkheim states that the first problem is, 'To determine the function of the division of labor, that is to say, what social need it satisfies' (*DoL*: 45). Then in Chapter One he turns to a clarification of what the term 'function' implies, beginning with why some seemingly identical words can not be used as synonyms. An 'aim', for example, would presuppose intent, and (like the Scots) he does not want to go in that direction. 'Effect' is not an acceptable substitute either because it does not necessarily indicate a correspondence between any particular result and the needs of the society; but function has this implication for Durkheim. At the end of the first chapter he offers the book's major hypothesis: divisions of labor normally function to provide the 'order, harmony, and social solidarity' that society needs (*DoL*: 63).

The rest of *DoL* provides insightful analyses of change across diverse institutions. Many, if not most, of Durkheim's arguments and interpretations are functional, and he seems to take special pleasure in pointing out what Merton ([1949a] 1968a) later termed latent functions; that is, how a social practice or activity contributed to social integration in ways which people neither intended nor recognized. For example, Durkheim argued that crime has the (latent) consequence of enhancing solidarity among the non-deviant, and that the punishment of a criminal paradoxically reinvigorates the norm that the offender violated. He completed this classical functional interpretation by arguing that crime and punishment meet such fundamental social needs that it is difficult to image a society in which they are absent.

Durkheim's ([1895] 1964) most formal and elaborate presentation of functional methodology came later, in *The Rules of Sociological Method* (hereafter cited as *The Rules*). In this book he explicitly places individual needs and motives outside the proper realm of sociological enquiry and identifies the social order and the 'things' which comprise it – social facts – as the appropriate subject matters. Then he poses as the central question, How are these social facts to be explained? No personal characteristic could logically explain a religious belief, a rate of marriage, or the like because these social facts transcend individual lifetimes. Each generation encounters an institutional arrangement it did not make. Therefore, he concludes, the explanation of social facts must lie in previously established social facts.

In the first four chapters of *The Rules*, Durkheim presents canons for observing and classifying social facts, building toward Chapter Five in which he outlines the protocol by which they are to be explained. Unfortunately, this key chapter includes a number of statements that are, in my opinion, either confusing or untenable, and the similarities or differences that Durkheim envisioned between functional and causal analyses of social facts are at the heart of the problem.

Durkehim begins his description of the rules of explanation by offering the observation that some law or pattern of behavior might retain essentially the same form or content over hundreds of years, but serve different functions at different times. So, 'the causes of its existence are, then, independent of the ends it serves' (*The Rules*: 91). On the one hand this statement may mean just what it appears to mean, namely, that function and cause are two different things. On the other hand, he goes on to define 'ends' in this context as referring to *individual* utilities. Function, by contrast, is again defined as entailing practices that satisfy the general needs of the *social* organism. Thus, rather than being intended to separate function and cause, the quotation in question may really be nothing more than a restatement of his non-reducibility dictum.

In later pages of *The Rules* Durkheim appears to oscillate, sometimes clearly separating function and cause, sometimes fusing them. For example, to explain a social phenomenon, he states, 'we must seek separately the efficient cause which produces it and the function it fulfills'. That seems clear, but then he adds, 'the bond which united the cause to the effect is reciprocal . . . the . . . cause needs its effect' (*The Rules*: 95.) To illustrate, Durkheim proposes that the punishment of a crime 'is due to' (that is, caused by) the collective sentiments that are offended by the crime. The punishment, he continues, is also functional for maintaining those sentiments because unless they are periodically activated and expressed through punishments, the sentiments, themselves, will diminish in intensity.

Durkheim's writings on causality and function leave more questions unanswered than we could hope to address here. However, a few of the issues need to be at least noted. To begin, did Durkheim mean to say that *whenever* a causal relationship is shown, one should expect to find that the dependent variable 'needs' the independent variable? To answer this question one would first have to clarify what Durkheim meant by cause, and sometimes he confused causal inference with simple correlation. Other times he may be using causal to mean that some behavior seems patterned, hence amenable to law-like descriptions in which the causal connections among terms might remain implicit (Turner, 1990; see also Faia, 1986).

Perhaps the most consistent interpretation is that Durkheim conceptualized a highly integrated social system in which simple correlations among social facts reflected both functional and causal interconnections. Function and cause were to be kept conceptually separate, even if one could not readily tell them apart in the analysis. Certainly he did regard society, in its normal state, as an organic whole in which the parts were harmoniously integrated. He most clearly presented this view in his analysis of 'survivals': practices which once served a function, do not seem to do so now, but persist anyway. (Inferring survivals creates a quandary for functionalists because an alternative interpretation is always possible, namely, that a latent function will later surface.) In reflecting upon the prevalence of survivals, Durkheim states that to maintain non-functioning social facts still cost effort. Because they do not benefit the society, though, such survivals are 'parasitic' to the budget of the social organism. No society could afford to carry very many of them. Thus, Durkheim concludes, it will typically be possible to show that social facts, 'combine in such a way as to put society in harmony with itself and with the environment external to it' (*The Rules*: 97).

Durkheim had previously argued that it was normal for the parts of a society to fit together and to function to maintain solidarity. For example, he identified the first abnormal, or pathological, type of division of labor as 'anomic'. He defined it as overly fragmented, entailing differentiation in which specialization does not lead to solidarity because, 'social functions are not adjusted to one another' (*DoL*: 354). To illustrate, Durkheim described the serious labor conflicts that can occur in large-scale industry when workers and employers become too separate from each other. However, such instances were exceptional and temporary, in his view, and tended to be self-correcting by a 'spontaneous consensus of parts'. Further, if the parts of a society did not fit, there was typically little anyone could do about the resultant problems until, in effect, the social system re-equilibrated itself. 'We cannot adjust these functions to one another and make them concur harmoniously if they do not concur of themselves' (*DoL*: 360).[2]

In sum, note that all the major parts of Durkheim's theory and method were in close accord with the main assumptions of the Scottish Moralists. Specifically, they shared:

1   A preference for outsiders' inferences to insiders' understandings, or introspection. (They viewed participants as likely to be overwhelmed by a multitude of detail.)
2   A strong conceptual distinction between the attributes of individuals and of collectivities. They also insisted that variables related to individuals cannot be causal with regard to larger social units, but characteristics of collectivities were often assigned causal status with regard to individual behavior.
3   An assumption of social integration, in which the parts of a society (that is, the social facts) fit with each other and fulfill the needs of the collectivity, without the tinkering of would-be social engineers.

TALCOTT PARSONS[3]

Parsons consistently acknowledged that he was strongly indebted to four theorists: Durkheim, Pareto, Weber and Freud. He not only fused their insights, but his early book (Parsons, 1937) also brought their work to the attention of many American sociologists. We have discussed Durkheim at length because of his continued importance as a social theorist, quite apart from Parsons. Following that logic, our treatment of Pareto will be brief because, although he greatly influenced Parsons, he is no longer among the more widely read theorists in sociology. Weber and Freud will not be examined at all due to their limited contributions to structural functionalism. Although Freud's incipient system perspective influenced Parsons, his primary interest in Freud and Weber was probably more substantive, for their insights into the role of the non-rational. Sciulli (1991: 281) claims that all of Parsons' work can be summarized by saying, 'he was a theorist preoccupied with non-rational social action'.

Pareto's influence upon Parsons' structural functionalism was great primarily because of the former's efforts to view society in system terms. (And a system conception, or its equivalent, is probably essential for any analysis that focuses upon the patterned consequences of action in an integrated structure.) Like Durkheim, Pareto ([1916] 1963) emphasized the distinction between function and cause, but he had less interest in causal inference than Durkheim because he felt that, for sociologists, it required erroneous assumptions. Many social variables tend to be so strongly interrelated, in Pareto's view, that it is not fruitful to try to isolate specific relationships and explain them in causal terms. He proposed instead that sociologists examine the interrelated parts of government, religion and the like in order to deduce their common functions.

In the Preface to *The Social System*, Parsons (1951: vii) wrote that his book's title was the most indebted to 'Pareto's great work'.[4] As sociologists, Parsons stated, we are primarily interested in the social system, but cultural and personality systems were seen as impinging so directly on the social system that their influences could be partitioned out only in arbitrary conceptualizations. Furthermore, the way these three systems (or subsystems) interpenetrated was the key to Parsons' theory of social integration – and he saw integration as the foremost function of the social system. Specifically, he conceptualized an ideal type society in which cultural values were institutionalized in the social system and norms were, in turn, internalized in the personality system. Individuals will then comply with social expectations, in this view, because they regard the rules as legitimate (given their source) and because the rules are consistent with their own internalized values. In addition, because norms are derived from common value orientations, they possess a 'harmonious character', so competing expectations will not often lead people to face internal conflicts.

While Parsons did not expect the ideal type condition of perfect congruence among the three systems to be attained by any actual society, a substantial degree of accord was considered both necessary and inevitable – or the society could not persist. Correspondingly, Parsons and several of his contemporaries (cf. Aberle et al., [1950 1967; Parsons and Smelser, 1956) deduced functional prerequisites, or necessary conditions, of society. Included at the top of everyone's list were social control mechanisms designed to safeguard the socialization process in order to ensure that each cohort of youngsters internalized the norms and was motivated to play conventional roles.

The 'danger' to the stable equilibrium among the three subsystems in the ideal type society that Parsons conceptualized early in his career was social change. In the final chapter of *The Social System*, Parsons (1951) claims to have deliberately exaggerated system stability in order to devise a base line from which to examine transformations. However, he assumed that each subsystem normally had the means to resist alterations, and most of his core theoretical writings regarded change as worrisome because it could compromise system imperatives. Further, Parsons (like Durkheim and the Scottish Moralists) was concerned that the consequences of even a seemingly minor change might be more far reaching (and worse) than anyone reckoned.

When, later in his career, Parsons (1966) explicitly analysed change, it was from an orderly, evolutionary perspective. Societal complexity, in this view, entailed the greater differentiation of sub-systems, and transformations occurred as a result of system tensions which increased because of malintegration among the components. Thus, societies were described as moving through stages of temporary equilibrium, but change followed an orderly sequence and continued to be patterned in accordance with self-regulating system needs.

Viewing change apprehensively, especially if it was deliberately enacted, was one quality that gave structural functionalism a conservative tilt. A second involved a tendency not to consider the possibility that traditional practices differentially benefit some parts of a society. For Durkheim, it will be recalled, the 'beneficiary' of functional practices was the society, which he conceptualized as a thing apart (and which therefore could not be equated with any specific segment or group). In Parsons' view, internalization of a common value system led to a situation in which virtually everyone in a society shared a strong affectual commitment to seeing institutionalized practices continue. Robert K. Merton, a student and colleague of Parsons, suggested that sociologists explicitly consider the possibility that what is functional for some segments of a society might not be functional for others. However, Merton's own case studies usually wound up showing how diverse groups, in fact, benefited from the same practice (Abrahamson, 1978; Merton, [1949a] 1968a).

The third pillar on which the conservativeness of Parsons' structural functionalism rested was a disinclination to accord an important place to conflict, opposition or power. The closest Durkheim came to dealing with these phenomena was in his description of how society behaved coercively, prodding people to a moral way of life. However, when he saw a clash between the wishes of individuals and the needs of the collectivity, he did not consider the differential interests of divergent groups, so power remained a neglected variable (cf. Giddens, 1993). Even this limited type of power and opposition was largely absent from Parsons' conceptions, though. Despite his abiding interest in Freud, Parsons regarded internalization as likely to correct any potential individual 'versus' society antagonism.

In addition, because of the interpenetration of the sub-systems, people in Parsons' theory did not have to force each other to comply with legitimate expectations. They wanted to obey. Even the tendency of most of the functionalists not to allow much room for survivals was part of their blindness to conflict, in Gouldner's (1970) view. Had they really examined survivals, he wrote, they would have had to confront the existence of unequal exchanges, and then they could not have avoided the role of force and opposition in maintaining exploitative relationships.

In order to show the ways and degrees to which Parsons' writing continued in a functionalist tradition, let us examine his positions on the three main assumptions previously used to summarize the continuity between Durkheim and the Scottish Moralists.

1 The preference for outsider's inferences. Because Parsons contended that individuals internalized the same core values, their reflections might provide valid social indicators. Hence, participants' views might be taken more seriously by Parsons than Durkheim or Adam Smith; but the terms in Parsons' scheme were so abstract that the potential relevance of insiders' observations was extremely limited.

2 A distinction between individuals and collectivities. Parsons certainly emphasized their separation, and the irreducibility of the social system, and he also saw the social system impinging upon, or penetrating, the personality system.

3 Social integration, without 'tinkering', was a very central supposition in Parsons' scheme. The parts fit, in his view, and once equilibrium was attained, its continuation did not require the stipulation of any special mechanisms.

The previously described criticisms – from Merton and others working within structural functionalism – did not lead to any substantial changes in structural functionalism. The perspective retained Parsons' imprint well into the 1960s, and then it was slowly 'overwhelmed' by the criticisms of theorists working within other paradigms that were then evolving. Functionalism left center stage, and nearly left the stage entirely. Nearly two decades later, however, neofunctionalism appeared, and Parsons was again viewed as its major spokesperson. Before examining these more recent changes, however, it is important to note most of the paradigms whose insights were utilized to criticize structural functionalism were developed in large part as polemics against Parsonian structural functionalism. Among the most important of these paradigms were:

- Exchange: George Homans (1958), who had been part of the Pareto Circle with Parsons, made seminal contributions to this perspective, largely because he thought the macro-Durkheimian emphasis in Parsons paid insufficient attention to the psychological underpinnings of social structures.
- Ethnomethodology: Harold Garfinkel (1964), a former student of Parsons', made significant contributions to this paradigm in part to rectify what he regarded as Parsons' view of people as oversocialized dopes.
- Feminist-gender: The functionalists' very traditional views of women and women's roles was an important impetus to new theories about gender differences and the sexual division of labor (cf. Johnson, 1989).

Still other sociologists polemicized against the tendency – shared by most functionalists from Durkheim to Parsons – to downplay the role of conflict in society. They developed a conflict school that probably depended more upon a polemic against structural functionalism for its inception than any of the other theoretical paradigms. Before Parsons' emphasis upon order and stability, Alexander (1998: 95) comments, 'there was no such beast as "conflict theory"'.

CONFLICT THEORY

To keep the record straight, we should note that some conflict theories pre-dated Parsons. Marx, discussed elsewhere in this volume, is the obvious example. Simmel may also be a good example, depending upon how his writings are interpreted. His essays (1908; in Levine, 1971) examined such issues as superordination and subordination, conflicts and contradictions. However, Simmel was interested in the form of solidarity, friendship and other forms of relationship in addition to conflict; hence, Simmel can be interpreted as having offered a theory *of* conflict rather than a conflict theory (Collins, 1990).

It is also important to note that the major structural functionalists did not entirely ignore power and conflict (cf. Lockwood, 1992). For example, Durkheim ([1893] 1964) described class conflicts in modern society, with a reference to Marx no less! And Parsons' (1951) analysis of need dispositions included a discussion of dominance and submission. However, their attention to such matters was generally brief and they de-emphasized conflict and differential power by placing them into 'special' (i.e. out-of-the-ordinary) categories. Thus, Durkheim discussed class conflict under the heading, 'abnormal forms' of the division of labor, and Parsons discussed domination under the rubric, 'deviant orientation'. In reaction, some mid-twentieth-century theorists urged a more prominent treatment of conflict, and one that regarded it as a more normal part of any society.

The advocates of conflict theory quickly found themselves caught between theoretical behemoths. On one side was structural functionalism, with Parsons' emphasis upon normative and value consensus, and a harmonious relationship among the parts. There was, of course, a readily available rendition of conflict theory: Marxian. However, it entailed a number of suppositions these proponents found little better than the structural functionalism they were criticizing. Specifically, all the versions of Marxian theory tended to emphasize intense struggles that had a material basis and could not be resolved without fundamentally changing the society that engendered them. The conflict theorists were not comfortable embracing Marxism because they contended that: the roots of social conflicts were as often normative as material, the intensity and tractability of these conflicts were explicitly variable, and the competing interests of different groups might be reconciled without necessarily altering fundamental properties of the society.

Two of the most influential early advocates of conflict theory were Ralf Dahrendorf and Lewis Coser. The degree of convergence between their views declined over time, however, and their positions essentially came largely to define the two poles within which conflict theories developed. Dahrendorf initially tried to present an outline of a theory of social conflict that examined the intensity of conflict as variable, influenced by such considerations as: the number of dimensions on which people were deprived, how organized they were, the relations between a group's leaders and followers, and so on (Dahrendorf, 1959). Although he was very critical of Parsons' emphasis upon consensus, he was primarily interested in trying to strike a balance that would equalize the treatment of consensus and conflict. Coser (1956) professed a similar objective, namely, balancing consensus and stability, on the one hand, with conflict and change, on the other. Correspondingly, he argued that some of Marx's ideas should be incorporated into structural functionalism in order to compensate for that paradigm's neglect of power and conflict.

Claiming to steer a middle ground, Coser criticized both Marx and Durkheim; but the latter fared a lot better than the former in Coser's hands. For example, he claimed that Marx was 'historically obsolete', but Coser thought it appropriate to forgive him because it was not Marx's fault he was born in the wrong century (Coser, 1967: 150). He also wrote that while Marx's analysis was analytically powerful, it was too narrow in its focus upon the economic realm, and that it could and should be recast in functionalist terms. Coser's criticisms of Durkheim were much milder; for example, he claimed that Durkheim's theories were too conservative. However, even these gentle rebukes were usually offset by what followed, in which Coser either stated that he really meant only to praise Durkheim or that Durkheim's influence upon his thinking remained unsurpassed.

In the end, Coser tried to add just a little conflict to a functionalist perspective more than he tried to add a little consensus to a conflict theory. Thus, his analyses focused upon functions of social conflict and tried to show its positive consequences; for example, reducing tension which thereby permitted systems to continue. Perhaps in response, Dahrendorf's (1968) later writing became more critical of functionalism, Parsons in particular, and described society as more characterized by conflict than consensus.

There continues to be some sociological writing that one can identify as falling within a non-Marxian conflict perspective. One of the distinguishing features of much of this work is that, at least implicitly, Parsons' ghost seems to hover in its background. For example, James Hunter's (1991, 1996) influential writing on America's cultural wars sees conflict as endemic, and based upon competing values and beliefs that are explicitly not class-based, in a Marxian sense. The only resolution Hunter sees will require the development of a new normative consensus. To illustrate further, Beteille's analysis of contemporary India makes explicit use of Parsons' paradigm, and shows how the tension between consensus and conflict has continued to characterize conflict theory. After reviewing the ways in which institutionalized values in India seem incompatible with each other, he concluded that a society's normative structure 'is designed to regulate conflicts of interest between . . . its constituent parts. But what is to regulate the conflicts that inhere in the normative structure itself?' (Beteille, 1998: 286).

In recent years, conflict theory has been nibbled at from two sides by the convergence of neo-Marxian and neofunctional theories. Its always tenuous boundaries, between Marx and Parsons, have become still more vague and its attempt to provide a balanced picture of conflict and order – the distinctive thrust of mid-century conflict theory – has lost much of its distinctiveness. Within the larger discipline it may continue to inform efforts at micro-macro synthesis, and provide a framework for empirical research (cf. Collins, 1990). However, the more neofunctional and neo-Marxian paradigms converge, the more difficult it is for me to envision the conflict perspective occupying an important place in sociological theory.

Collins (1990) presents a very different prognosis, however. He contends that after conflict theory's mid-century theoretical debates with functionalism, conflict theory developed in relation to empirical, macro-historical research, and such major substantive areas as social movements, organizations and stratification. The theory's emphasis upon domination, power and change has, in Collins' view, permeated enquiry, though not in a theoretically self-conscious manner. Thus, as research in these diverse areas continues to accumulate, the development of conflict theory may quietly and simultaneously proceed.

NEOFUNCTIONALISM

During the 1970s, the criticism and defense of Parsons and of structural functionalism declined. The burial of the man (in 1979) could easily have been viewed as symbolizing the end of his influence as well. It turned out to be only a brief hiatus, however, because during the 1980s there was a revival of interest in Parsons' writing. Some of the renewed attention had little to do with structural functionalism. Rather, it was the result of sociologists again recognizing his importance in synthesizing the work of classical theorists and using it to advance such disparate areas as family sociology (cf. Smith, 1993) and economy and society (cf. Holton and Turner, 1986). Of more direct relevance to the concerns of this chapter, there was also a resurgence of interest in Parsonian structural functionalism, first in Germany and then in the United States (Alexander, 1983). Almost all of the efforts, on both sides of the Atlantic, sought to merge aspects of structural functionalism with other paradigms that had better developed critical and behavioral perspectives. The objective was to create a 'hybrid' that built upon the conceptual strengths of each of the merged perspectives in order to provide more balanced treatments of such (potentially) disparate tendencies as:

equilibrium and change, cohesion and conflict, social structure and agency (Alexander and Colomy, 1990).

Two of the leading figures in the German revival were Niklas Luhmann and Jürgen Habermas. The two collaborated in 1971 on a theory of social engineering in modern society, then subsequently worked separately, though along some parallel tracks, and with frequent reference to each other's work. Luhmann had been formally trained in law, but read sociology and spent a year studying with Parsons at Harvard (in 1960). At the time of his collaboration with Habermas, much of Luhmann's work followed a framework that was sympathetic to Parsonian structural functionalism. In marked contrast, Habermas was a major figure in the Frankfurt School, dominated by critical theorists for whom Marx's writings were central and for whom Parsons was an anathema.

Luhmannn moved *from* Parsons: the title of one of his major theoretical books – *Social Systems* – clearly reflects Parsons' influence; so did Luhmann's self-conscious use of ego and alter as referents. However, Luhmann's book incorporated perspectives on systems from such diverse sources as linguistics and cognitive sciences. He contended that relationships between systems and their environments were more complex than Parsons' description implied, and he conceived of sub-systems more as differentiated problem-solving units (Luhmann, [1984] 1995). Perhaps his most explicit disagreement with Parsons concerned the options normally available to ego and alter as concrete human beings. Parsons' emphases upon value consensus and the social system's penetration of the personality system, according to Luhmann, limited the kinds of social relationships and human behavior that a theorist could analyse outside of a deviant category. To open more alternatives, he conceptually moved people out of the social system and into a 'societal environment' that he described both as more complex and less restrictive than the social system. It accords people more freedom, Luhmann ([1984] 1995: 213) wrote, 'especially freedom for irrational and immoral behavior'.

Habermas, on the other hand, moved *toward* Parsons. His early writings, like those of most critical theorists, treated Parsons disparagingly. He was especially sharp in his criticisms of Parsons' proclivity for objectifying and elevating system imperatives. In juxtaposition, he emphasized action and the 'lifeworld'. However, without attributing dominance to system properties or adopting Durkheimian notions about system integration, Habermas did initially accord a place in his critical theory to cultural, social and personality systems; and his conceptualization of their interrelationships was consistent with Parsons' view (Habermas, 1975). Corresponding with these three systems, Habermas described the lifeworld as a parallel, intersubjective realm for experiencing and communicating about culture, society and personality.

As societies become more complex, he later wrote, lifeworld and structural systems become increasingly separated from each other because people find it more difficult to predict the consequences of their actions. Therefore, Habermas (1987) concluded, to explain most contemporary societies may require the Parsonian inference of self-regulating systems, though requirements of the lifeworld continue to set parameters within which systems evolve. It is this assumption of (at least partly) self-regulating systems that is probably the most unambiguously neofunctional feature in Habermas' intentionally eclectic theory. However, some critics have been reluctant to let him hedge on this issue, and contend that any assumption of self-regulation is fundamentally incompatible with Habermas' view that systems are dependent upon the conceptions and actions of individual participants (cf. Schwinn, 1998).

Within the United States, most of the major contributions to neofunctionalism came from theorists who were sympathetic to Parsonian structural functionalism. Especially notable was the writing of Jeffrey Alexander whose volume on Parsons helped again to focus the attention of sociologists upon Parsons' framework (Alexander, 1983; see also Camic, 1987). In that volume Alexander praised Parsons as a synthesizer of grand theory without equal, and claimed that his influence continued to be enormous. At the same time, Alexander was critical of Parsons' theory on several grounds, agreeing that it posed an overly deterministic stance and lacked sufficient attention to conflict and strain. In his subsequent essays on neofunctionalism, however, Alexander (1985; Alexander and Colomy, 1990) contended that the theory's deficiencies were not irreversible. In other words, conflict and subjective meaning could be introduced; and system integration and the interpenetration of sub-systems could be regarded as tendencies, open to enquiry rather than assumed, as givens.

The response to the efforts of Alexander and others to revive functionalist notions in the guise of neofunctionalism has been markedly varied. Echoing the disapproval of Habermas' consolidations, some critics felt there were limits to how far any theoretical perspective could go in accommodating incompatible notions, and still retain its name and lineage. Noefunctionalism, to these critics, was eviscerated from its heritage (Turner and Maryanski, 1988); but others saw clear continuity (Colomy, 1990). Coming from an opposite direction, still other antagonists felt the recent changes were more cosmetic than real because neofunctionalism remained imbued with the features that distinguished functionalism, from the Scottish Moralists to Durkheim. Specifically, the 'objective' view of outsiders continued to predominate, people were still regarded as reactors to systems more than actors, and conflict remained secondary. Blasi (1987: 187) claimed the supporters of neofunctionalism failed to realize that they had not made substantive alterations to functionalism because, 'orthodoxies rest on presuppositions which are invisible to the orthodox adherents themselves'.

AN EMPIRICAL REFERENT?

If Alexander's predictions about the future of social theory are correct, the criticisms of neofunctionalism (or functionalism) are merely final gasps from the past. In his most recent book (Alexander, 1998), he tried to describe what the sociological landscape might look like 'after neofunctionalism'. He concluded that the polemics have run their course. There will be grand theory in the future, he foresees, it will be important and it will be truly multidimensional with respect to macro–micro, conflict–order and the other polarities which divided theorists in the past. Neofunctionalism, after further 'hybridization', will necessarily be a still less distinctive paradigm if Alexander is correct.

If neofunctionalism, or some other descendent of functionalism, persists, will it be developed in relation to empirical research? In other words, will theory and research be expected to bear upon each other in the future? These questions introduce another potentially important polarity, namely, how much the referent for any theory ought to be other theory rather than empirical research. These particular poles may have been moved further apart even as other polarities were presumably diminishing.

The current emphasis upon synthesis accentuates the importance of conceptual analyses of how paradigms and suppositions previously thought to be at variance with each other can now be combined. There may also be some empirical referent in these efforts to construct or deconstruct theories, but it is of trivial importance except insofar as one wants to include the theoretical writings of others *as though* they represented empirical observations (cf. Parsons, 1949). When the culture of social theorists stresses synthesis it is likely to be better for the advancement of metatheory than for extending the links between theory and research. As Ritzer

(1991) notes, there are diverse types of metatheory, different from each other in their ambitions. None of them takes enhancement of the interplay between theory and research as a major objective, though.

Another major reason for the neofunctionalists' relative neglect of empirical linkages lies in the predilections of its most influential figure, Jeffrey Alexander, and those who have worked most closely with him.[5] While not anti-empirical, Alexander (1998) is explicitly suspicious of empirically based inferences, arguing that social science is fundamentally different from natural science because theoretical traditions always permeate everything social scientists see and do. He further states, and this is the nub of the matter, that given the differences in the nature of the two types of science, sociological theory can be scientifically significant independently of its capacity to explain empirical observations (Alexander, 1998, esp. ch. 8).

Minimizing the importance of the interplay between theory and empirical research sounds, to me, more like the past than the future. It will put the discipline at risk of experiencing what worried Merton ([1949b] 1968b) half of a century ago, namely, that one group of theorists will absurdly contemplate each other's abstractions while a totally separate group of researchers carry out mindless modeling and abstracted empiricism. Would it not be ironic to characterize the division of labor in sociology as anomic?

NOTES

1 His conclusions regarding marriage among royalty was one of several analyses in which Hume was influenced by Mandeville's earlier contention that private vices can lead to public virtues (Baier, 1991).

2 In addition to describing a condition in which the parts did not fit, Durkheim also affixed anomie to situations in which the norms did not regulate people's aspirations or desires. For further clarification of types of anomie, see Abrahamson, 1980, and Merton, 1995. What ties these two types of anomie together is Durkheim's contention that it is precisely when there is an imbalance among the parts that the social norms fail to regulate.

3 Sequeing from Durkheim to Parsons helps to illuminate their continuity, but it leaves out the way Durkheim influenced social anthropologists, and how they, in turn, influenced subsequent sociologists. Especially notable, to round out this picture, are Radcliffe-Brown, 1955, and Malinowski, 1927.

4 Along with Robert K. Merton, George C. Homans and others, Parsons belonged to a 'Pareto Circle' that regularly met at Harvard during the 1930s (cf. Heyl, 1968).

5 There are exceptions, of course, and especially notable is the comparative analysis of educational institutions by Parsons' former student and collaborator, Neil Smelser (1985).

REFERENCES

Aberle, David, F., Cohen, Albert K., Davis, Allison K. and Levy, Marion J. ([1950] 1967) 'The Functional Prerequisites of a Society', in Nicholas Demerath and Richard Peterson (eds), *System, Change and Conflict*. New York: The Free Press. pp. 317–31.

Abrahamson, Mark (1978) *Functionalism*. Englewood Cliffs, NJ: Prentice-Hall.

Abrahamson, Mark (1980) 'Sudden Wealth, Gratification and Attainment: Durkheim's Anomie of Affluence Reconsidered', *American Sociological Review*, 45 (1): 49–58.

Alexander, Jeffrey C. (1983) *The Modern Reconstruction of Classical Thought: Talcott Parsons*. Berkeley, CA: University of California Press.

Alexander, Jeffrey C. (1985) *Neofunctionalism*. Beverly Hills, CA: Sage.

Alexander, Jeffrey C. (1998) *Neofunctionalism and After*. Malden, MA: Blackwell.

Alexander, Jeffrey C. and Colomy, Paul (1990) 'Neofunctionalism Today', in George Ritzer (ed.), *Frontiers of Social Theory*. New York: Columbia University Press. pp. 33–67.

Baier, Annette C. (1991) *A Progress of Sentiments*. Cambridge, MA: Harvard University Press.

Beteille, Andre (1998) 'The Conflict of Norms and Values in Contemporary Indian Society', in Peter L. Berger (ed.), *The Limits of Social Cohesion*. Boulder, CO: Westview Press. pp. 265–92.

Blasi, Anthony J. (1987) 'Review of Neofunctionalism', *Sociological Analysis*, 48 (2): 186–7.

Camic, Charles (1987) 'The Making of a Method', *American Sociological Review*, 52 (2): 421–39.

Collins, Randall (1990) 'Conflict Theory and the Advance of Macro-Historical Sociology', in George Ritzer (ed.), *Frontiers of Social Theory*. New York: Columbia University Press. pp. 68–87.

Colomy, Paul (1990) 'Introduction', in Paul Colomy (ed.), *Neofunctionalist Sociology*. Brookfield, VT: Elgar Publishing. pp. xi–lxii.

Copley, Stephen (1995) 'Introduction', in Stephen Copley and Kathryn Sutherland (eds), *Adam Smith's Wealth of Nations*. Manchester: Manchester University Press. pp. 1–22.

Coser, Lewis (1956) *The Functions of Social Conflict*. New York: The Free Press.

Coser, Lewis (1967) *Continuities in the Study of Social Conflict*. New York: The Free Press.

Dahrendorf, Ralf (1959) *Class and Class Conflict in Industrial Society*. Stanford, CA: Stanford University Press.

Dahrendrof, Ralf (1968) *Essays in the Theory of Society*. Stanford, CA: Stanford University Press.

Davis, Kingsley (1959) 'The Myth of Functional Analysis as a Special Method in Sociology and Anthropology', *American Sociological Review*, 24 (3): 757–72.

Durkheim, Emile ([1893] 1964) *The Division of Labor in Society*. New York: The Free Press.

Durkheim, Emile ([1895] 1964) *The Rules of Sociological Method*. New York: The Free Press.

Faia, Michael A. (1986) *Dynamic Functionalism*. Cambridge: Cambridge University Press.

Garfinkel, Harold (1964) 'The Studies of the Routine Grounds of Everyday Activity', *Social Problems*, 11 (2): 225–50.

Giddens, Anthony (1993) *New Rules of Sociological Method*. Stanford, CA: Stanford University Press.

Gouldner, Alvin W. (1970) *The Coming Crises in Western Sociology*. New York: Basic Books.

Habermas, Jürgen (1975) *Legitimation Crisis*. Boston, MA: Beacon Press.

Habermas, Jürgen (1987) *The Theory of Communicative Action*. Boston, MA: Beacon Press.

Heyl, Barbara S. (1968) 'The Harvard Pareto Circle', *Journal of the History of the Behavioral Sciences*, 4: 316–34.

Holton, Robert J. and Turner, Bryan S. (1986) *Talcott Parsons on Economy and Society*. London: Routledge and Kegan Paul.

Homans, George C. (1958) 'Social Behavior as Exchange', *American Journal of Sociology*, 63 (3): 597–606.

Hume, David (1879) *The History of England*. New York: Harper.

Hunter, James D. (1991) *Culture Wars*. New York: Basic Books.

Hunter, James D. (1996) 'Response to Davis and Robinson: Remembering Durkheim', *Journal for the Scientific Study of Religion*, 35 (3): 246–8.

Johnson, Miriam (1989) 'Feminism and the Theories of Talcott Parsons', in Ruth A. Wallace (ed.), *Feminism and Sociological Theory*. Newbury Park, CA: Sage. pp. 101–18.

Levine, Donald (ed.) (1971) *Georg Simmel*. Chicago: University of Chicago Press.

Lockwood, David (1992) *Solidarity and Schism*. Oxford: Oxford University Press.

Luhmannn, Niklas (1982) *The Differentiation of Society*. New York: Columbia University Press.

Luhmannn, Niklas ([1984] 1995) *Social Systems*. Stanford, CA: Stanford University Press.

Malinowski, Bronislaw (1927) *Sex and Repression in Savage Society*. New York: Harcourt, Brace.

Merton, Robert K. ([1949a] 1968a) 'Manifest and Latent Functions', in Robert K. Merton, *Social Theory and Social Structure*. New York: The Free Press. pp. 73–138.

Merton, Robert K. ([1949b] 1968b) 'The Bearing of Sociological Theory on Empirical Research' and 'The Bearing of Empirical Research on Sociological

Theory', in Robert K. Merton, *Social Theory and Social Structure*. New York: The Free Press. pp. 83–111.

Merton, Robert K. (1995) 'Opportunity Structure', in Freda Adler and William S. Laufer (eds), *The Legacy of Anomie Theory*. New Brunswick, NJ: Transaction Books. pp. 3–78.

Pareto, Vilfredo ([1916] 1963) *The Mind and Society*. New York: Dover Publications.

Parsons, Talcott (1937) *The Structure of Social Action*. New York: McGraw-Hill.

Parsons, Talcott (1949) *The Structure of Social Action*, 2nd edn. New York: McGraw-Hill.

Parsons, Talcott (1951) *The Social System*. New York: The Free Press.

Parsons, Talcott (1966) *Societies*. Englewood Cliffs, NJ: Prentice-Hall.

Parsons, Talcott and Smelser, Neil J. (1956) *Economy and Society*. New York: The Free Press.

Radcliffe-Brown, A.R. (1955) *Structure and Function in Primitive Society*. New York: The Free Press.

Ritzer, George (1980) *Sociology: A Multiple Paradigm Science*, rev. edn. Boston, MA: Allyn and Bacon.

Ritzer, George (1991) *Metatheorizing in Sociology*. Lexington, MA: Lexington Books.

Schwinn, Thomas (1998) 'False Connections: Systems and Action Theories in Neofunctionalism and in Jürgen Habermas', *Sociological Theory*, 16 (1): 75–95.

Sciulli, David (1991) *Theory of Societal Constitutionalism*. Cambridge: Cambridge University Press.

Smelser, Neil J. (1985) 'Evaluating the Model of Structural Differentiation in Relation to Educational Change in the Nineteenth Century', in Jeffrey C. Alexander (ed.), *Neofunctionalism*. Beverly Hills, CA: Sage Publications. pp. 113–29.

Smith, Adam ([1863] 1967) *The Wealth of Nations*. Edinburgh: Adam and Charles Black.

Smith, Dorothy E. (1993) 'The Standard North American Family', *Journal of Family Issues*, 14 (1): 50–65.

Turner, Jonathan H. (1990) 'Emile Durkheim's Theory of Social Organization', *Social Forces*, 68 (4): 1089–103.

Turner, Jonathan H. and Maryanski, Alexandra Z. (1988) 'Is "Neofunctionalism" Really Functional?', *Sociological Theory*, 6 (1): 110–21.

13

Talcott Parsons: Conservative Apologist or Irreplaceable Icon?

ROBERT J. HOLTON

Talcott Parsons is one of the most important, yet also most controversial social theorists of the twentieth century. His career spanned the five decades from the late 1920s to the late 1970s. He is possibly best known for his postwar theories of normative order, for the construction of a grand theoretical edifice labelled structural functionalism, and for a tendency to write impenetrable prose. Many of the critical commentaries on these aspects of Parsons' work, however, lack a broader appreciation of the insights and subtleties of his work. These emerge, to take only three examples, from his early work on social action and economic life in the 1930s, his synthesis of social theory and psychoanalysis in the 1950s, as well as later work on the human condition published just before his death in 1979.

Parsons' project for social theory contrasts with many of the prevailing modes of theoretical endeavour as we enter the twenty-first century. Social theory today is typically fragmented in scope, anti-foundational in temper, riven with epistemological conflict and unsure of its relationship with social and political action. Parsons, by contrast, sought nothing less than the construction of a unified map of the social. His irrepressible usage of the vocabulary of structured systems, determinate input–output relations and boundary interchanges, in these endeavours, contrasts markedly with the anti-canonical iconoclasm of the present day. Parsons, by contrast, is an iconic figure, offering an iconic style of social theory. This aspired to coherence not merely in its internal logic and architecture, but also in its account of the relationship between the social, the metaphysical and the natural worlds.

These wider concerns reflect both his liberal Protestant origins, and early career ambitions to become a biological scientist. These influences underlie Parsons' concern to provide an account of social action, capable of acknowledging both the place of human autonomy driven by ultimate values, and the importance of socialization and forms of structural dependency on the biological organism. His map of the social is therefore positioned between two external environments, the 'inner' environment of ultimate meaning and purpose, and the 'outer' environment of the natural (physicochemical and organic) worlds.

This perspective on the social means, amongst other things, that Parsons' social theory gives a prominent place to the sociology of values (including religious values), to the sociology of material life (including economic institutions), and to the sociology of health and sickness (including connections between materiality and values). These broad interests were pursued in the Departments of Sociology and Social Relations at Harvard University, where Parsons taught from the early 1930s. There are few social theorists writing today with Parsons' synthetic boldness of interdisciplinary vision. This may partly explain the exaggerated contemporary success of sociobiology in colonizing the territory where biology meets sociology. Parsons, by contrast with most contemporary social theorists, was not content merely to claim that biology is mediated through sociality, a position that leaves the territory vulnerable to occupation by others.

The political implications of Parsons' social theory are also worth clarifying, in view of the criticisms made of him as merely an apologist for

American conservatism. It is certainly the case that Parsons grounded a good deal of his social theory on institutional and interpersonal patterns of life evident in American society. These include the multiple and cross-cutting sets of civil associations, and the relative freedom from traditional ties of status that he believed had impeded upward social mobility, undermined social consensus and created class conflicts in Europe. As postwar reconstruction and social stabilization proceeded in the 1950s, many social theorists like Parsons developed evolutionary theories of social change around concepts of modernization, and the emergence of industrial society. These centred on the politics of liberal democratic reform, and the further extension of citizenship rights through inclusion of groups hitherto excluded from imperfectly democratic institutions.

Within these overoptimistic assumptions, Parsons' political agenda centred domestically on a fuller social citizenship in areas such as the inclusion of African Americans. In the same spirit he opposed elements of anti-semitic exclusion within the institutions of academia. Very little attention, by contrast was given to issues of gender exclusion. In foreign affairs, meanwhile, his basic approach was that of assimilation of the underdeveloped world within what he saw as the superior Western institutions of democracy, the market and the rule of law. Support for American policy in the Vietnam War followed from this. His interest in achieving social order through normative consensus rather than violence and coercion none the less made him critical of the superpower conflicts of the Cold War. While fearful of nuclear war, Parsons' theoretical expectations encouraged him to look for the possible emergence of international forms of normative order within the United Nations, and intermediary groups between the great powers, such as the Non-Aligned Movement (Parsons, 1961). These thoughts remained undeveloped, however, and in most respects Parsons like most other sociologists of his generation, remained wedded to the national-focused comparative sociology of individual societies, rather than to the global perspectives that have since become more prominent.

PARSONS' SOCIAL THEORY

There is always a tendency to overestimate the internal consistency of a social theorist's work, and this is no less true of Parsons than anyone else. His sociological endeavour shifted around in many of its interests and emphases as he encountered new issues, or was confronted with intellectual challenges and social changes that appeared to challenge aspects of his previous thinking. For all of this, we may say that Parsons' work was concerned with two core theoretical issues above all else. These may be labelled the problem of social action, and the problem of social order (Alexander, 1983). The problem of social action asks why human actors act in the way that they do, how far their actions are structured by influences outside their control, and what consequences, intentional or unintended, follow. The problem of social order asks how it is possible for a multiplicity of social actions to produce some kind of coordinated social patterning, and how far such patterning depends on force or compulsion, as against consensus.

These two problems come together, under modern conditions and within Western liberal traditions, around the issues of self-interest and rationality in social life. If the rational pursuit of self-interest is advanced as an answer to the problem of social action, there remains the difficulty of explaining how it is that self-interest can generate social order. If social action is explained, on the other hand, in terms of the determining influence of structures beyond individual control, then what place is left for human autonomy and rationality, perception and judgement in social life? These issues had, of course, been around for a long time. Parsons' virtuoso strategy for dealing with their seeming intractability was to try to reconcile structure and agency, the 'macro' institutions and rules underlying social order, with the 'micro' personality or self, within some kind of new theoretical synthesis.

In the early part of his career Parsons account of social action was developed through a critique of the utilitarian assumptions which lay at the heart of neoclassical economics. Social action involves both 'ends' and 'means', but how were they connected? Economic theory typically took the ends of action as given and probably unknowable. It was concerned rather with the logic whereby actors select and implement those means that will achieve given ends in the most efficient or rational ways. This approach was defective, according to Parsons, for two main reasons. First, it excluded enquiry into the social origins of ends, including questions such as the part played by social values and meaning in determining ends. Secondly, it failed to account for social order, relying on the dubious assumption that the pursuit of self-interest by a mass of individuals would somehow create order in a spontaneous fashion, as in Adam Smith's celebrated metaphor of the invisible hand guiding market transactions.

There had been many critics of economic theory before Parsons who had identified the same set of problems. His response differed, however, from many of his predecessors. Whereas the so-called institutional school of economists adopted a somewhat ad hoc approach, showing how economists' assumptions failed to operate in a range of individual cases, Parsons sought a theoretical response. This should somehow incorporate explanation of both the values and norms that went into the determination of ends, and an account of the material processes whereby economic resources were appropriated and made available as means to satisfy ends.

Against this background, there is a consistency running through all his work. This applies to major theoretical statements in *The Structure of Social Action* (1937) and *The Social System* (1951), through collaborations such as *Towards a General Theory of Action* (Parsons and Shils, 1951), to compilations of essays such as *Social Structure and Personality* (1964a), *Sociological Theory and Modern Society* (1967) and *Action Theory and the Human Condition* (1978), a number of which deal with empirical issues such as 'Christianity and Modern Industrial Society', or 'Full Citizenship for the Negro American'. This unifying thread concerns the construction of an action theory of both the social system and the wider human condition. The ambition here was to explain how social action was at one and the same time structured in systemic ways, and yet expressive of, and functional to the autonomy of particular individuals and households. This in turn required that attention be given to the meaning of action in terms of human purpose, as well as recognition of the organic exigencies of life.

If this is the underlying logic of Parsons' position, then it is equally the case that different moments in his career find him exploring one line of argument, such as structural or systemic determination of action, as far as it may be taken. In this particular example, his most deterministic writing, as found in much of *The Social System*, was taken by his critics to be definitive and final. Parsons, it was said, saw individuals as bearers of social rules that were typically internalized within the personality and processes of social reproduction. Social consensus was thus the normal modus operandi, and deviance episodic and pathological. Parsons labelled this 'structural functional analysis', rather than structural functionalism, as such. Structural functional analysis was conceived as a highly generalized mode of theory-building, founded on the analytical significance of variations in the structural bases of social systems, and their relations with the performance of functions essential to social life (Parsons, 1951: 19–22).

The charge that Parsons held to an oversocialized (Wrong, 1961), or overintegrated (Lockwood, 1956), conception of social life, was to stay with him for the remainder of his life. And as his theory had come to be articulated in the mid-1950s, there was much merit in the criticism. From a longer-term perspective, none the less, the charge is not consistent either with his intentions, or with much that he wrote at earlier or later points in his life. It is certainly true that Parsons, in company with most of the classical nineteenth century sociologists thought that social relationships and institutions performed social functions. The problem lies rather with the attachment of functionalism to the idea of structuralism. This association tends to play down the voluntaristic, meaning-oriented aspect of Parsons' attempted theoretical synthesis. The centrality of social action, in his thinking helps explain why Parsons moved away from the idea of structural functional analysis in his later work (Parsons, 1977: 100–17), even while his critics gleefully perpetuated it as a false totem to be excised from the sociological pantheon. By the end of his career, Parsons had come to regard the social system, the notion at the heart of structural functionalism, as a component part of the action system rather than the other way around. Meanwhile the action system is itself only one component of the human condition. The idea of structural functionalism is then unhelpful to a balanced understanding of the general thrust of Parsons' work.

MAPPING THE SOCIAL: BEYOND STRUCTURAL FUNCTIONALISM

Key moves in the elaboration of Parsons' social theory involved identification of the multiple exigencies that faced social actors, and which set the challenges that social systems faced if they were to secure social stability. Parsons argued such exigencies were complex and differentiated rather than singular or unitary. The route by which he arrived at this conclusion, built first on the idea of 'pattern variables' that characterized both 'traditional' and 'modern' societies (Parsons et al., 1953). Five sets of pattern variables were located, namely particularism and universalism, ascription and achievement, specificity and diffuseness, affectivity and neutrality, and collectivity-orientation as contrasted with self-orientation. While designed primarily for analytical purposes, Parsons' conception of modernity was associated with the second term in each of these pairs.

The substance of the pattern variables drew in part on the conventional dichotomies of classical sociology, such as Tönnies' contrast between 'traditional' *Gemeinschaft* (involving community or collectivity-orientation), and 'modern' Gesellschaft (involving the association of self-interested individuals). But it also introduced new elements deriving from interdisciplinary collaboration at

Harvard, and from empirical research that Parsons had conducted into both the sociology of the professions, and the sociology of health and illness. The dichotomies between 'traditional' affectivity and particularism and 'modern' neutrality and universalism, for example, were influenced by his analysis of the role of professional–client relations in medicine. Here the clinician's professionalism was seen as depending on a dispassionate and detached neutrality, differentiated from any emotional or affective attachment to the patient, and integrated within the universalistic norms of service.

Taken overall, then, the transition from tradition to modernity meant a differentiation and specialization of social roles and institutions. The individual was increasingly separated from the strong bonds of community, and emotion was to be detached from rationality. At the household level, this resulted in a very conservative and controversial reading of the gender division of labour, where modern women were seen as specializing in affective roles, leaving men to specialize in the detached and rational realms of professional life and public rationality. Over the past forty years, the entire edifice of the pattern variables has come under the most scathing criticism, both for its ahistorical and uncritical approach toward differentiation, and for its use of exaggerated and misleading conceptual dichotomies between the traditional and the modern.

The multiple forms of social differentiation represented in Parsons' pattern variables were developed in both a theoretical and historical direction. Theoretically they were a bridge into the four-function or AGIL paradigm which remained at the heart of his theoretical endeavours until his death (Parsons and Smelser, 1956). This highly abstract system defined social life in terms of four major exigencies. These may be listed as follows, but in no particular order of priority. The adaptive (A) challenge, comprises interaction between society and outer nature, generating resources available for social distribution. The goal-attainment (G) challenge involves the setting of resources to meet human goals. The integration (I) challenge is concerned with the harmonization of the entire social system, including A, I and L elements, through effective norms. The final component of this account is the latent pattern-maintenance (L) challenge, which involves interaction with society and the inner metaphysical environment, and is concerned with the stabilization of the ultimate values held by individuals into patterns of social values. These are projected as latent insofar as they become taken for granted rather than explicit.

The functioning of social systems involves complex patterns of interchange or input–output

relations between the four functional components. A highly simplified version of how this is supposed to work is as follows. The A sub-system, for example, delivers resource outputs to the G sub-system, which are reciprocated through inputs of capital from the G sub-system back to the A sub-system. Meanwhile, outputs of social goods from the G sub-system require legitimation according to value outputs from the L system, with the whole network of exchanges regulated through institutionalized norms emanating from the I system. A vast edifice of further elaboration was designed to clarify the nature of system interchange through generalized media such as money, power and influence.

This AGIL system, it should be emphasized is an analytical construct rather than an empirical description of social life. Its analytical significance is that it offers a theoretical map of the social that is located between outer nature and the metaphysical realm, and internally differentiated in terms of four exigencies or challenges faced by any social system. While we might loosely identify A with the economy, G with the polity, I with law and L with cultural values, these associations would be somewhat misleading. The analytical reason for this is that Parsons sub-divided each of the four individual AGIL categories, into four sub-categories. In the case of the A sub-system, for example, this was further divided into an adaptive sub-system (Aa), a goal-setting sub-system (Ag), an integration sub-system (Ai) and a latent-pattern maintenance sub-system (Al). The process of production (Aa), could thus be differentiated from strategic goal-setting (Ag), the entrepreneurial integration of factors of production (Ai) and economic values (Al). In this way Parsons, sought, amongst other things, to emphasize the interpenetration of the four functional exigencies or challenges throughout the social system. Put more simply, values were not exclusive to culture, nor was integration exclusive to law (for further elaboration see Holton and Turner, 1986: ch. 2).

A final issue in the elaboration of Parsons' grand theory, is the status of the term social system. This was defined in far broader terms than the conventional association of social systems with national societies. For Parsons, any entity that was relatively self-subsistent with respect to an environment qualified as a social system. The AGIL framework was thereby potentially applicable to social organizations both within (for example, universities and government departments) as well as beyond nations (for example, the UN).

This whole exercise none the less raises the question as to the utility of such a proliferation of theoretical boxes. What is to be gained by the construction of such a complex theoretical apparatus, beyond the translation of familiar theoretical problems into a new terminology? Does Parsons' account of the multidimensional interpenetration of social functions, for example, improve on Weber's anti-reductionist comment that 'a banking history of a nation which adduces only economic motives for explanatory purposes is ... just as unacceptable as an explanation of the Sistine Madonna as a consequence of the socio-economic basis of the culture of the epoch in which it was created' (Weber, 1949: 71)?

One particular defence of Parsons, with relevance to economic life, is that his theoretical approach had within it the elements of an integrated research programme, capable of promoting many neglected issues in economic sociology. In a situation where conventional forms of economics neglected the social determination of ends, and radical political economy produced accounts that emphasized power and coercion at the expense of norms, Parsons' framework offers ways of bringing norms and values back in (Holton, 1992). This legacy (along with the earlier work of Durkheim upon which Parsons drew), has exerted a diffuse influence on later discussions of economic values, the social meaning of money and trust.

A more general issue raised by Parsons' four-function paradigm is its utility in understanding social change, and its capacity to illuminate the historical evolution of societies. Reacting against criticisms of excessively ahistorical abstraction, Parsons responded with two key books: *Societies: Evolutionary and Comparative Perspectives* (1966) and *The System of Modern Societies* (1971), preceded by a seminal article, 'Evolutionary Universals' (1964b). These more historically focused works were not grounded in empirical research. But they did at least offer a kind of conjectural history designed to explain the rise of Western institutions. A strength of this neglected body of work is Parsons' alertness to contrasts in the developmental significance of differing national and regional institutions and traditions. The major weakness is a triumphalist Occidental organizing framework, within which evidence of historical complexity is exquisitely tortured to fit Parsons' grand theoretical apparatus.

Parsons, like other postwar theorists of modernization, adopted an evolutionist stance towards processes of social change. This drew on biological accounts of the evolution of species in general and the notion of evolutionary advantage in particular. Just as the human species had gained advantages in meeting the exigencies of life, through the development of specialized organs such as the hand, so particular human societies gained adaptive advantages in developing institutions better able to meet the four AGIL challenges, outlined above. Specialization meant both the differentiation of social institutions from each other, as well as the development of specific institutional complexes within each specialized sub-system.

In the case of the A (adaptive) sub-system, this meant the market rather than the command economy, for the G (goal-attachment) system, democracy rather than authoritarianism, for the I (integration) sub-system, the rule of law rather than arbitrary procedures, and for the L (latent pattern maintenance) system, patterns of values that emphasized moral individualism rather than traditional community. The modern complex of institutions such as the market, democracy and so forth, represented a set of specialized institutions better able to meet the challenges of social life than the alternatives. In this sense they represent 'evolutionary universals'. From this perspective, liberal democratic market economies was seen as better adapted to meet such exigencies than less differentiated communist societies in which economic, legal and cultural organizations were integrated into a suffocating political authoritarianism. For Parsons it followed that the communist model would either collapse (as it has) or successfully converge with the liberal democratic capitalist model (which it has not).

One criticism of this kind of evolutionism is that it leads inexorably to what may be called an 'end of history' position. As articulated by Fukuyama (1989), this claims that liberal capitalism has won the evolutionary struggle with alternative social systems and ideologies. There is, in this sense, no alternative future beyond liberal democratic market society. Parsons' own position was not, however, quite as complacent as this. His earlier evolutionary optimism was soon to be profoundly shaken by the social radicalism of Western student movements in the late 1960s. This prompted a greater attention to what he regarded as strains and disturbances within broadly liberal democratic arrangements, as well as to the emergence of movements aiming at de-differentiation (Parsons, 1978: 148–53). Further elaboration of the idea of 'societal community' remained a preoccupation for the rest of his life, anticipating in many respects the recent revival of interest in civil society.

A key feature of the student challenge was opposition to the 'value neutrality' of academia, which Parsons had seen as a typically modern pattern variable. This suggested the immanence of a de-differentiating cultural revolution which would re-integrate communitarian values within institutions of higher education hitherto characterized by cognitive rationality. In the face of this prospect Parsons argued that further differentiation rather than de-differentiation was the more likely future. Students, after all, occupied a temporary social position, and could not be likened to more enduring social groupings, such as the social classes of Marxist theory. What the higher educational revolution had revealed was a certain failure of social integration. Parsons located this failure in the detachment of the specialized personality types generated in intellectual communities from 'a community-type societal nexus' (1978: 151). This was part of the more general problem of integrating the emergent importance of knowledge-holders and knowledge-based institutions (in Parsonian language 'the cognitive complex') with the broader social system.

This episode is instructive in demonstrating that Parsons' social theory posited continuing forms of disturbance and social strain within the process of social change. While he used the language of systems quite extensively, this was not meant to imply that nothing ever went wrong, or that social arrangements never broke down. Achievement of the evolutionary universals he identified in the early 1960s did not mean an end to history, for two reasons. First, social evolution continued, raising new integrative challenges. Secondly, there was no guarantee that individual societies would necessarily converge with the liberal democratic capitalist model. And in a wider sense, continuing crises of integration were likely to be manifest at the level of the individual personality, as well as at the level of the social system. While emphasizing a strong tendency for individuals to be socialized into coherent and stable normative patterns, Parsons equally perceived continuing problems of inadequate socialization, inasmuch as individuals are not socialized within the social system as such, but only within particular parts of that system, such as the family or the school.

While it is possible to defend Parsons' approach from 'end of history' complacency, there remains the almost inescapable conclusion that his theoretical apparatus set sharp limits to his capacity to explain social change, and thus to map the social. Take his response to the challenge of de-differentiation, for example (Parsons, 1978: 138–43). This was thoroughly unadventurous in that Parsons assumed virtually no limits to the capacity of differentiation processes to meet adaptive challenges. Other contemporaries, were not so sure. In the case of the relations between knowledge and society, for example, Parsons' assumptions of a unifying normative order and cultural system ruled out more adventurous possibilities, such as Daniel Bell's theory of the cultural contradictions of capitalism (Bell, 1976). For Bell, the emergence of a knowledge-based postindustrial society created sharp tensions between an older work ethic born of industrial society and a more recent culture of self-actualization and self-realization. Capitalism it seemed contained two divergent cultural patterns rather than one.

A more fundamental objection to Parsons' evolutionary universals may be linked with the rise of de-differentiating movements both within and beyond the West. Within the West, a good deal of the recent momentum behind discussions of de-differentiation, stems from reactions against the politics of the Reagan and Thatcher years, labelled as new right, monetarist, or economic rationalist. While attempts to press a market-based utilitarian model as far as it may be taken continue, their partial implementation has created counter-movements, represented theoretically within a resurgence of communitarianism. Much of this is similar to Parsons in temper, inasmuch as it is recognized that the market (or A sub-system), cannot operate independently of the remainder of society. Parsons would of course agree that markets need extra-economic normative (I sub-system) supports, as well as cultural (L sub-system) legitimacy. Significant differences emerge, however, around questions of power and inequality, and how they affect theories of relations between economy and society.

PARSONS ON POWER

Parsons' discussion of power is often seen as one of the weakest parts of his social theory. Giddens (1968), Parkin (1979: 51–4) and Alexander (1984: 198), for example, point to the way that Parsons' theoretical edifice neglects structural features of modern society, including the predominant power of private capital over both labour, and government. Other critics have claimed that Parsons neglected power relation in favour of normative explanations of social order. This has been linked to a downplaying of Marxist theory, in favour of a Durkheimian approach. Many issues are at stake here, pertaining both to empirical and theoretical questions.

In an empirical sense Parsons believed, with most modernization theorists, that the increasing separation of ownership from management rendered Marxian analyses of the power of private capital redundant. Management had become differentiated from ownership, and thus amenable, at least in principle, to normative regulation according to norms of professional service. There is little concern here, either for the issues to do with the profit-optimization logic of managerial activity, and the vulnerability of underperforming corporations to takeover, or for the de-differentiation of management and ownership through stock-option packages and management buyouts.

Parsons also gave great weight to extensions of political citizenship, around conceptions of social rights implemented within welfare state policies. These were regarded, following writers such as the English sociologist T.H. Marshall, as means of limiting or balancing economic activities with wider democratic political processes and objectives. While it might be said that neo-Marxists have underestimated the importance of citizenship, it is equally the case that Parsons failed to consider the possibility that welfare states might function more as agents of capitalist social control than as a limit on the power of holders of capital. Such debates are, however, difficult to resolve at a general conjectural level, and demand a far greater attention to historical and national variations between state and society than Parsons or his critics have often provided.

In a more theoretical sense, Parsons' treatment of power raises important issues about the relative importance of coercion, money, influence and value consensus in securing social order. The idea of social order is of course a very slippery term in its own right, part of a diffuse array of terms like integration, coherence, stability and equilibrium, whose meaning is by no means commonly agreed or clearly and consistently distinguished. Is order the same as social equilibrium and social stasis, or is order conceivable as a series of constantly shifting social arrangements, constituted by dynamic uncertainty? Does the integration of social institutions into a coherent pattern, necessarily entail the social integration of actors through strong ties of solidarity and consent? And beyond this lie questions arising from the highly normative status of social order as a concept. If there is more than one normative yardstick upon which perceptions of order rely, then it is possible that what is order from one social vantage point looks like disorder from another. Is a large street demonstration necessarily a manifestation of disorder, threatening violence and challenging the status quo, or is it rather to be seen as an orderly expression of hard-won civil rights, and solidarity for those involved? Those with an interest in the status quo may perceive order differently to those who feel excluded. Parsons' contribution to the theory of social order engaged with a number of these issues, but was conducted mostly within a highly abstract framework, difficult to operationalize in empirical analysis. He took as his reference points inadequacies in two major accounts of social order. In answer to the question 'How is social order constituted?', these stressed either coercion (the tradition of Hobbes and Marx), or harmony of interests (the tradition of utilitarianism). In the former case, insufficient attention was given to issues such as the role of consent, or the significance of beliefs in the legitimacy of a social order. In the case of utilitarianism, no account was provided of the processes whereby harmony of interests emerged within social institutions, and personality types.

Parsons' alternative involved a multidimensional version of social exchange theory. As we have already noted, the AGIL four-function paradigm entailed a multidimensional account of social life, based on the interpenetration of A, G, I and L elements. His account of the mechanisms of interaction within this system centred on what were called generalized media of exchange. It was here that Parsons' discussion of power was located, as one of several such media (Parsons, 1963). Others included money and influence.

Parsons offered a multiform definition of power as a 'generalized capacity to secure the performance of binding obligations by units in a system of collective organization when the obligations are legitimized with reference to their bearing on collective goals, and where there is a presumption of enforcement of negative situational sanctions' (Parsons, 1967: 308). In this way he combined issues of force or coercion with issues of legitimation and consent, rather than neglecting the former in favour of the latter. This enabled him to secure the idea of power as a circulating medium able to move across and between the four functional sub-systems of any social system. Power, in this sense, was connected both with economic property rights (the institutional structure of the market) and with symbolic patterns of normative commitment.

Interestingly, this multidimensional approach enabled Parsons to detach power from an exclusive relationship with the sovereign power of government, thereby leaving conceptual space for the operation of power through stable normative rules that required no explicit use of force. This insight was not, however, developed in a Foucauldian direction via a discursive construction of knowledge/power, operating within the play of language and performance, and as a micro-physics of power. This is partly because in thinking of the concrete forms in which power was institutionalized, Parsons assumed the necessity of highly integrated political systems. The underlying model here was that of the nation-state requiring 'some relatively paramount apex of power', thereby privileging sovereign power (1967: 344). It also connects with his relatively undeveloped discussion of epistemological issues to do with how truth is socially constructed. Parsons' social theory, for example, does not problematize language in any fundamental way.

As a neo-Kantian, Parsons accepted that knowledge is socially constructed, and built up from organizing or orienting categories and social facts. In analysing the relations between the two, he none the less wished to move beyond Kant's dichotomy between sense data 'emanating from the external world and the categories of the understanding, which are of transcendental grounding' (1967: 400). He felt this tended to diminish the status of sense data as random, putting the emphasis rather on categorical ordering in the construction of knowledge. This encouraged a kind of subjectivism, for if scientific knowledge of the empirical world is categorically driven and thus fictional, then reality becomes simply a matter of subjective experience. Parsons' alternative is to think of a differentiated set of relations between knowledge and the world, ranging from causal explanation designed to achieve empirical ordering of social facts, to world views providing transcendental ordering in matters to do with the ultimate metaphysical purposes of human action.

What is lacking here is further concrete elaboration of the relations between power and knowledge, within social practices and institutions. For all his interest in the self and in personality development, for example, Parsons' discussion of power lacks what might be called a micro-sociological dimension. At best, this amounts to what Alexander calls a 'macro-sociological theory of the micro foundations of behaviour' (Alexander, 1998: 212). Foucault's discourses of professional knowledge/power, that constrain as much as they enable, are re-allocated in Parsonian theory, as enabling features of the modern normative order, and associated with processes such as the work of universalistically competent professional actors.

The most critical theoretical issue in any assessment of Parsons on power remains his assumption of broadly symmetrical relationships between different sub-systems of the social order, implying a symmetry in the power of different social interests or collectivities. The architecture here is that of input–output relations between the different sub-systems of society, transmitted as it were through generalized media of exchange. Parsons typically thinks in terms of a tendency towards a symmetrical balancing of the four functional exigencies faced by any society, if it is to evolve and be sustainable.

When challenged with the problem of concentrated power in the hands of any particular interest, the Parsonian response is to identify the inputs required from other parts of the social system for any one element in the system to operate effectively. In the case of private holders of capital, to take one example, these rely on inputs of political legitimacy, legal security and personalities socialized into the work ethic. Such inputs can only be sustained if capital holders can deliver goods available for political redistribution, and income to sustain those who offer their labour. Parsons' critics rightly see this type of argument as assuming rather than proving a level playing field between social actors within liberal democracies. If the initial conditions of the system are unequal, and if the operation of the system reproduces that inequality, then the mere functioning of the system does not entail symmetry in the power available to different collectivities within that system.

Parsons' more general treatment of power is, however, far more subtle, than the simplistic, exclusively normative caricature presented by some critics. The agenda of generic issues he elaborated, such as the connection between force and norms, or the degree to which power is a zero-sum game, remain at the centre of debate, both within sociology (Holmwood, 1996: 62–70) and more generally within rational choice theory. This applies even though the substance of much of his more concrete commentaries on power in modern society is widely regarded as implausible.

PARSONS, HIS CRITICS AND THE PARSONIAN LEGACY

Bryan Turner (Holton and Turner, 1986: 187) has made an important distinction between two contrasting modes of criticism of Parsons' work. The first, rather piecemeal approach, is to select particular features of his work (for example, professionalization, social change, power), for detailed critique. The second, more holistic, line of attack focuses on the overall structure and logic of his theory. One interesting feature of continuing debates around Parsons' work, foreshadowed in the discussion of power, is that key elements in his general theoretical project have proven more robust than many of the more specific component parts of his enterprise. The general features of his project that remain important influences are, first, his attempt to map the social, including boundary interchanges with the internal and external environments, and secondly, his attempt to develop a non-reductionist and hence multi-dimensional social theory inclusive of normative as well as coercive or instrumental elements.

Contemporary social theory contains more centrifugal than centripetal tendencies. Splitters implicated in fragmentation predominate over lumpers committed to synthesis. General theory is itself under fire from a number of directions. These range from those who see general theory as the pursuit of a philosophical chimera (Holmwood, 1996; Mouzelis, 1991), to those who reject it as a form of totalizing power/knowledge resting on the dubious epistemological hubris of Western reason. Yet among those still interested in a general mapping of the social,

Parsons remains a powerful reference point and theoretical resource.

One important example of this occurs around issues to do with relations between society and the biological organism, as they both affect the creation of the social self and construct the human condition. Parsons' early work on the sick role as a social construct, for example, made considerable inroads into purely biological accounts of human sickness. For all the detailed and substantive limitations of Parsons' argument, this helped open up a general line of argument in favour of medical sociology, that has never looked back. He also made a parallel contribution to the sociology of the personality, by re-casting Freudian psychoanalysis in more sociological directions. Themes discussed include the Oedipus problem (Parsons, 1953) and the incest taboo (Parsons, 1954).

This body of work has exerted a diffuse influence on subsequent feminist work such as Chodorow's analysis of the socialization processes involved in the gendering of personality (1978, 1989). Parsons' theoretical impact is evident here, even though he himself took a rather conservative position on the conventional gender division of labour. This centred on what he took as the functional significance of differentiation between public and private roles, which allocated men primarily to the 'public' industrial system, and women, operating as specialists in child socialization, to the isolated nuclear family. While Chodorow problematized this account of differentiated gender roles, she none the less, accepted that effective socialization processes around gender required analysis of the personality types and motivational elements involved. This led her to formulate and pursue the question, 'Why do most women want to be mothers?' in a manner typical of Parsons' psychoanalytically inflected sociology.

Having said this, it remains the case that feminism, in its varied theoretical manifestations, remains highly critical of the functionalist premises within which Parsons grounded his accounts of social differentiation. The public/private divide, and institutions such as the nuclear family, are typically interpreted, not as functionally adapted to personality formation and social order, but in more pathological terms. Their function is not to secure some kind of upgraded universalistic evolutionary advantage in the successful socialization of individuals into a stable set of roles, but to secure the reproduction of patriarchal domination. Under modern conditions this has become a de-stabilizing rather than an integrating force. Empirical evidence of de-differentiation in the gender division of labour, expressed in part through resistance to traditional gender roles, appears as a radical

challenge to Parsons' substantive analyses of the family and gender within modern society.

Another more fundamental area where Parsons' general social theory has proven extremely robust, even in the face of criticism of the more substantive levels of analysis, involves his use of system theory. In Germany, for example, both Luhmann and Habermas, have developed different versions of systems theory, sharing common generic features and the presuppositions if not the detailed substance of Parsons' work. For Luhmann (1990: 255), in particular, Parsons' systems theory is seen both as the only recent attempt to formulate a general social theory of sufficient complexity to be plausible, and as a project that remains largely unrefuted in its general parameters. Luhmann identifies a number of enduring characteristics of this project, including the often neglected point that systems theory is not the theory of a particular kind of empirical object (that is, systems). It is focused rather on the theorizing of entities that can be analytically distinguished from the environments in which they operate. Amongst other things, this clarification disposes of the objection that societies are too disorderly or exhibit too few stable and enduring patterns to warrant use of the idea of system in social theory.

Luhmann's appreciation of Parsons extends both to his account of the internal components of social systems, and to his treatment of the distinctions and connections between systems of various kinds and the environments in which they operate. In the former domain, Parsons' four-function paradigm is seen as rendering redundant the perpetuation of social theories claiming general priority for any single functional subsystem. In the latter, Luhmann welcomes Parsons' interdisciplinary attention to relations between systems and their environment, while arguing that this attention does not probe far enough. In his alternative approach, Luhmann asks whether and in what senses systems are open or closed with respect to an environment. In contrast with Parsons' account of openness to both the physical and metaphysical environments, Luhmann's perspective is more complex. In essence he sees social systems as causally open to wider environments, but cognitively or operationally closed in the sense of being self-referential. The medium of exchange which Parsons failed to discuss in this respect was communication.

Habermas, while writing in the iconoclastic traditions of critical theory, has none the less appropriated much of Parsons' general systems idiom. But like Luhmann he argues that communication, or in Habermas' terms, communicative rationality, is a crucial missing element in Parsons' social theory. While agreeing with much of the logic and conceptual architecture of Parsons' multidimensional systems theory, Habermas' substantive elaboration of its dynamics leads in somewhat divergent directions. In terms of common ground, Habermas, like Parsons, accepts that there are multiple aspects to social evolution, embracing both instrumental/economic and normative exigencies. Society, in this sense, evolves in both its capacity to generate material resources and in the learning of social rules and the construction of institutions embodying some kind of consensual order. Habermas diverges from Parsons in his account of the dynamics of evolution, his greater emphasis on conflict and crisis rather than order and integration, and his emancipatory search for a reconstructed public realm. This search is grounded on communicative interpersonal exchange within the lifeworld, that is, on forms of exchange beyond power and money. Both Habermas and Parsons draw on liberal democratic models of the public sphere (Calhoun, 1996: 455–7). Habermas, however, places explicit emphasis on the transcendental potential of language and speech as bases for the construction of public norms of validity, applying to truth, rightness and authenticity. Communicative rationality in this way is seen as anti-pathetical to the 'civic and familial privatism' that animates much of Parsons' work.

While some of his objections to Parsons are familiar, Habermas' critique is striking in the way that it remains within system theory, and tries to build a radical alternative from within. At the heart of this re-casting of system theory is a more communitarian, less individualistic and differentiated approach to normative order than that offered by Parsons. Yet in privileging of emergent norms arising within the speech-communities of the life-world, Habermas neglects the institutional frameworks of public life and normative order that occupy centre stage in Parsons' accounts of societal community. The result is a dualism between 'system' and 'life-world', rather than an integrated analysis of the macro and micro elements of public life.

In the case of system theory, as with theories of power, and of personality formation, Parsons' generic agenda remains a major though controversial reference point. While Luhmann may be right in stressing that Parsons' generic theoretical edifice has not been supplanted by any more powerful alternative, it remains unclear just how far grand theory of this kind has a future in contemporary social thought.

CONCLUDING THOUGHTS: PARSONS, NEO OR POST?

Social theories, and rhetorical styles of talking about theory seem to come and go. Parsons'

work was proclaimed to be flawed and inadequate in the late 1960s and 1970s, only to stage a comeback in the 1980s, even spawning a significant but ultimately transitory school of neofunctionalism around Jeff Alexander and his associates (Alexander, 1985, 1998). If Marx and Weber deserve schools of followers, so the argument went, then why not Parsons as well? The past few decades have, however, been an epoch of 'posts' (post-industrial, post-modern, post-structuralist, post-Marxist etc.), rather more than 'neos' (neo-realist, neo-Marxist and so forth). If this rhetoric is anything to go by, then theoretical renewal is less in vogue than a will to transcend past failures together with uncertainty about where the present is leading.

It is a measure of Parsons' stature as a social theorist that his work is relevant both for those of a 'neo' and those of a 'post' disposition. Parsons' 'neo-work' involved an immense synthesis not only of the classical sociological tradition, but also of a broader multidisciplinary body of work, embracing biology and cybernetics. His ambition to position social theory within a more overarching account of the human condition, including both organic and psychic elements, remains unmatched within the narrower more introverted discussions that currently occupy the terrain of social theory.

The syntheses developed in his general work on action-systems, and the social system, meanwhile, have defined most of the generic terrain upon which subsequent debates in system theory, social exchange theory and theories of power, order and conflict, personality formation and socialization have taken place. And within more substantive areas, Parsons, together with associates such as Neil Smelser, left areas such as economic sociology, the sociology of institutions, medical sociology and the sociology of personality very different from when he first encountered them. In this respect, his work may be seen as a creative renewal of the classical sociological tradition; if you like, a neo-classicism.

For 'postists' on the other hand, Parsons' legacy may be less evident. One of the strengths of 'postism' may be its impatience with excessive piety toward older inadequate bodies of theory, especially those that maintain the holy grail of a rationally constituted social theory of general validity. Contemporary social theory has been variously seen as post-modern, post-materialist, post-classical, or even post-neo-functional, implying a greater diversity and fragmentation. Against this, Parsons' strategy of building a single general theory out of new syntheses of past traditions appears rhetorically incorrect.

The wish to move beyond outmoded versions of social theory, characteristic of postism, has however proven less effectively iconoclastic than it would sometimes have us believe. Whatever the inadequacies of Parsons' sociology, of which there are many, analysts seem continually to return either to his statement of grand theory or at least the issues contained within it. This stems both from the continuing search for clarification (or 'cognitive ordering' as Parsons puts it), and from awareness of the inescapable presence of grand theoretical assumptions within any form of sociological reasoning. In this sense, albeit reluctantly, we are all Parsonians now. When liberated from negative stereotypes and read afresh, Parsons' theoretical reach, implacable curiosity and synthetic ingenuity remain a rich and underexplored legacy. His work is, however, a bounded resource. For more concrete, empirically grounded theory, capable, as Alexander (1998: 212) puts it, of tracking 'concrete, living, breathing actors making their way through space and time', it is necessary to look elsewhere.

REFERENCES

Alexander, Jeffrey C. (1983) *Theoretical Logic in Sociology. Positivism, Pre-Suppositions and Current Controversies*, vol 1. London: Routledge and Kegan Paul.

Alexander, Jeffrey C. (1984) *Theoretical Logic in Sociology. The Modern Reconstruction of Classical Thought: Talcott Parsons*, vol 4. London: Routledge and Kegan Paul.

Alexander, Jeffrey C. (ed.) (1985) *Neofunctionalism*. Beverly Hills, CA: Sage.

Alexander, Jeffrey C. (1998) *Neo functionalism and After*. Oxford: Blackwell.

Bell, Daniel (1976) *The Cultural Contradictions of Capitalism*. New York: Basic Books.

Calhoun, Craig (1996) 'Social Theory and the Public Sphere', in Bryan S. Turner (ed.) *The Blackwell Companion to Social Theory*, Oxford: Blackwell. pp. 429–470.

Chodorow, Nancy (1978) *The Reproduction of Mothering*. Berkeley, CA: University of California Press.

Chodorow, Nancy (1989) *Feminism and Psycho-Analytic Theory*, Newhaven, CT: Yale University Press.

Fukuyama, F. (1989) 'The End of History', *The National Interest*, 16: pp. 3–18.

Giddens, Anthony (1968) 'Power in the recent writings of Talcott Parsons', *Sociology*, 2(2): pp. 268–70.

Holmwood, John (1996) *Founding Sociology? Talcott Parsons and the idea of General Theory*. London: Longman.

Holton, Robert J. (1992) *Economy and Society*. London: Routledge.

Holton, Robert J. and Turner, Bryan S. (1986) *Talcott Parsons on Economy and Society*. London: Routledge.

Lockwood, David (1956) 'Some remarks on The Social System', *British Journal of Sociology*, 7(1): pp. 134–46.

Luhmann, Niklas (1990) 'General Theory and American Sociology', in Herbert J. Gans (ed.), *Sociology in America*. Newbury Park, CA: Sage. pp. 253–64.

Mouzelis, Nicos P. (1991) *Back to Sociological Theory*. London: MacMillan.

Parkin, Frank (1979) *Marxism and Class Theory: A Bourgeois Critique*. London: Tavistock.

Parsons, Talcott (1937) *The Structure of Social Action*. New York: McGraw Hill.

Parsons, Talcott (1951) *The Social System*. New York: Free Press.

Parsons, Talcott (1953) 'Psychoanalysis and Social Science with Special reference to the Oedipus problem', in Franz Alexander and Helen Ross (eds.) *Twenty years of Psychoanalysis*. New York: Norton. pp. 186–212.

Parsons, Talcott (1954) 'The Incest taboo in relation to Social Structure and the Socialization of the Child', *British Journal of Sociology*, 5(2): pp. 101-17.

Parsons, Talcott (1961) 'Polarisation of the World and International Order', *Berkeley Journal of Sociology*, VI(1): pp. 115–34.

Parsons, Talcott (1963) 'On the concept of Political Power', *Proceedings of the American Philosophical Society*, 107(3): pp. 232–62.

Parsons, Talcott (1964a) *Social Structure and Personality*. New York: Free Press.

Parsons, Talcott (1964b) 'Evolutionary Universals in Society', *American Sociological Review*, 29(3): pp. 339-57.

Parsons, Talcott (1966) *Societies: Evolutionary and Comparative Perspectives*. Englewood Cliffs, NJ: Prentice Hall.

Parsons, Talcott (1967) *Sociological Theory and Modern Society*. New York: Free Press.

Parsons, Talcott (1971) *The System of Modern Societies*. Englewood Cliffs, NJ: Prentice Hall.

Parsons, Talcott (1977) *Social Systems and the Evolution of Action Theory*. New York: Free Press.

Parsons, Talcott (1978) *Action Theory and the Human Condition*. New York: Free Press.

Parsons, Talcott, and Shils, Edward (1951) *Towards a General Theory of Action*. Cambridge, MA: Harvard University Press.

Parsons, Talcott, Bales, Robert, and Shils, Edward (1953) *Working papers in the Theory of Action*. New York: Free Press.

Parsons, Talcott and Smelser, Neil (1956) *Economy and Society*. New York: Free Press.

Weber, Max (1949) 'Objectivity in Social Science and Social Policy', in Max Weber, *The Methodology of the Social Sciences*. New York: Free Press. pp. 50–112.

Wrong, Dennis (1961) 'The over-socialised conception of man in modern sociology', *American Sociological Review*, 26: pp. 183–93

14

Nietzsche: Social Theory in the Twilight of the Millennium

ROBERT J. ANTONIO

Nietzsche revealed this primordial fact: once God had been killed by the bourgeoisie, the immediate result would be catastrophic confusion, emptiness, and even a sinister impoverishment.

(Georges Bataille, [1927–30] 1985: 38)

Prior to Nietzsche, all those who taught that man is a historical being presented . . . history as in one way or another progressive. After Nietzsche, a characteristic formula for describing our history is 'the decline of the West'.

(Allan Bloom 1987: 196)

I beg pardon for seeing Nietzsche everywhere, and only him.

(Thomas Mann, [1918] 1983: 366)[1]

THEORIZING WITH A HAMMER

I know my own fate. One day my name will be associated with the memory of something tremendous – a crisis without equal on earth, the most profound collision of conscience, a decision that was conjured up *against* everything that had

been believed, demanded, hallowed so far. I am no man, I am dynamite.

(Nietzsche, [1888] 1969: 326)

In this well-known, prescient passage, Nietzsche stated vividly the way his thought has come to be remembered. The exploitation of Nietzsche as a Nazi totem and claims that his ideas constituted a *Zeitgeist* of fascism seem to uphold his prophetic self-description. In this light, the famous pictures of Nietzsche's sister greeting Hitler at the doorway of the deceased philosopher's archives and Hitler posing and staring intently at his bust appear to be prima facie evidence of the tie between Nietzscheanism and fascism. Mussolini's Nietzscheanism manifested the same affinity (Aschheim, 1992: 133, 200–1, 315–30; Sluga, 1995: 29–52, 123–53, 179–86). But Nietzsche also had an 'antipolitical' side, treating mass politics as the bane of all 'culture' and rejecting fanaticism, especially the nationalistic sort. From the start, his 'open' texts have been read in many ways, inspiring liberal as well as radical critiques and flights from politics as well as intense political responses. However, diverse thinkers have seen him as 'the' harbinger of the twentieth century's deepest crises and as cultural dynamite. This often repeated theme is evident again, today, at the turn of the new millennium. I will address the connections between 'Nietzschean theories', modernization theory, Marxism and postmodernism, focusing especially on the convergence of radical 'left' and 'right' Nietzscheanisms in a 'totalizing critique of modernity' and contrasting this theme to a divergent, largely ignored 'anti-political Nietzscheanism'.[2]

NIETZSCHEAN THEORY AND EPOCHAL EXHAUSTION: AN END TO HISTORY?

Everything of today – it is falling, it is decaying: who would support it? But I want to push too!

(Nietzsche, [1883–1885] 1969: 226)

Nietzsche thinks nihilism as the 'inner logic' of Western history.

(Martin Heidegger, [1943] 1977: 67)

Although Nietzsche was largely ignored during his lifetime, very shortly after his death many people embraced his ideas. At the turn of the twentieth century, early Nietzscheans, like the current wave, stressed *fin de siècle* sensibilities about cultural decline. Also similar to today, many first-wave Nietzscheans were young people with strong romantic or aesthetic inclinations, who felt that bourgeois culture was too workaday, uninspiring and mediocre. After the loss of the First World War and the consequent erosion of national self-esteem and multiple crises, Max Weber addressed surging Nietzschean sensibilities among younger Germans. He warned that alienated refugees from the Youth Movement and idealistic revolutionaries lacked the 'ethic of responsibility', which he viewed, perhaps, as modernity's most precious cultural resource and ethical basis of the 'vocations' of politics and science (he hoped that they would moderate the fragmentation accompanying disenchanted mass democracy). However, Weber feared that the new Nietzschean generation, with its musical impatience for routine, was not up to facing the 'demands of the day', and would become fodder for authoritarian leaderships, already emergent and poised to forge 'a polar night of icy darkness and hardness' ([1918] 1958a: 127–8; [1918] 1958b: 134–5, 140–1 155–6; Marianne Weber, [1926] 1975: 318–20, 455–64).

Weber was probably right that a major part of his day's romantic antimodernism could be traced 'back to Nietzsche' (i.e., his vision of epochal cultural exhaustion, scathing critique of rational culture, and aestheticism) ([1921] 1958c: 393). But Nietzsche anticipated this appropriation, seeing self-proclaimed Nietzschean 'free spirits' as 'incorrigible blockheads and buffoons of "modern ideas"' and counting them among his worst enemies. In his view, they were pathetic 'last men', rather than the vaunted 'solitary', 'hard', 'aristocratic', 'sovereign individuals' that he believed would resist the 'herd's' all-pervasive

'decadence' and '*resentiment*' and its 'great men of the masses' and forge postmodern values and beings. Nietzsche opposed bitterly the manipulative moralizing, demagoguery of airy New Age sects and nationalist political fanatics, which his ideas ironically helped grow ([1886] 1966: 53–6; [1888] 1969: 280).

Karl Löwith asserted that: 'Nietzsche was a precursor to the German present, and at the same time its sharpest negation – "National Socialist" and "Cultural Bolshevik" – either, depending on how he was used' ([1939] 1994: 83). Regardless of Nietzsche's warnings about political fanaticism, his ideas gave rise to radical Nietzscheanisms of 'right' and 'left', which are often so dismissive of bourgeois culture and call for such a complete rupture from it that the new order is not prefigured in the present and must forged *de novo*. Their aesthetic anti-rationalism and ambiguous idea of the future, especially with regard to new social and political institutions, blur the line between right and left. Clear right and left theories, policy-regimes and parties are connected inextricably to the distinctly modern culture and societies that radical Nietzscheans hope to overcome. Operating in fluid cultural and political space, they escape definitive categorization or shift suddenly from one pole to the other (Aschheim, 1992; Kolnai, 1938: 113, 235–6).

A most famous, historically important example of radical Nietzscheanism, Oswald Spengler's *Decline of the West* ([1918–1922] 1991) captured the imagination of many Weimar-era Germans. Its aesthetic tone, prophetic qualities and ambiguous politics defied the conventional left and right. A rabid critic, Spengler lambasted Western modernity's drab economism, workaday emphasis on the machine and technique, imperialist tendencies, arid culture, confused people and 'barrack cities'. In his view, the West was in the 'autumnal' phase of a descending spiral from 'Culture' to 'Civilization'; a degenerate slide that signaled the imminent collapse of earlier sociocultural orders. Lacking any creative impulses and merely reproducing endless, superficially modified, decadent cultural forms, he argued, the West is a 'souless', 'rootless', 'nihilistic' shell of a culture. Spengler ([1918–1922] 1991: xxxi), acknowledged his great debt to Nietzsche and the Nietzschean facets of his work are easy to detect. Like almost all other 'Nietzscheans', however, he mixed themes from Nietzsche's texts with diverse and often opposed ideas of his own and ones borrowed from other theorists. Thus, 'Nietzschean' is a proximate label. For example, putting aside Nietzsche's scathing attacks on nationalism and the state, Spengler called for a corporatist-nationalist socialism to overcome class splits and unify the German people. His protofascism foreshadowed the German future, but, like other aristocratic, radical-right Nietzscheans, he rejected Nazism's plebeian philistinism, opposed the regime and was marginalized by it (Hughes, [1952] 1962: 59–64, 98–36).

Although Spengler does not rank among the most creative 'Nietzscheans', such as Heidegger, later Adorno, or Foucault, the thrust of his work manifests sharply a core theme in Nietzsche's thought and major point of convergence among radical Nietzscheans – the idea that Western culture is totally spent or moribund. The title of Spengler's magnum opus became, perhaps, the most famous signifier of this sensibility. Anticipating recent, post-Marxist 'end of modernity' discourses, Heidegger ([1961] 1991b: 6–9) held that Nietzsche heralded the 'conclusion of Western history or the counterpoint to another beginning'. His Nietzschean critique of 'technological civilization' exerted a major influence on key segments of the Weimar-era left, as well as his fellow 'radical conservatives' and, more recently, on post-structuralists as well as today's 'New Right'. Adorno and Horkheimer's 'dialectic of Enlightenment', Marcuse's 'one-dimensionality', and Foucault's 'carceral' stress a similar type of sweeping cultural exhaustion. The radical Nietzschean right and left contend that cultural homogenization and regimentation, rooted deeply in the West's distinctive rational features, are manifested, in the extreme, in 'advanced industrial society' or 'postindustrial society'. They decry consequent hegemonic economism and instrumentalism and destruction of the creative and aesthetic impulses that nurture animate types of culture, community, identity and politics.

DIALECTICS OF MODERNITY: NIETZSCHE VERSUS MARX

'The honesty of a contemporary scholar . . . can be measured by the position he takes *vis-à-vis* Nietzsche and Marx. . . . The intellectual world in which we live is a world which to a large extent bears the imprint of Marx and Nietzsche.'

Max Weber purportedly made this statement after a public debate with Spengler over *Decline of the West*.[3] Holding that theorists 'deceive' themselves and others when they fail to recognize their debt to the two masters, Weber implied that Marx and Nietzsche framed the core questions and problems that set limits for modern 'social theory'.[4] Although disagreeing about the worth and impacts of Marx's and Nietzsche's ideas, diverse thinkers have argued that the two made a basic and, perhaps, 'the' most fundamental

contribution to framing the project of modern social theory. For example, Heidegger held that Nietzsche heralded the 'consummation' of 'the modern age', while Marx represented its decline into technological civilization (1991b: 9); Karl Löwith stated that they 'made the decline of the bourgeois-Christian world the theme of . . . a fundamental analysis' ([1939] 1991: 175–6); Paul Ricoeur held that the two were framers of the hermeneutics of 'suspicion' (1970: 32–6); Leo Strauss saw them as the core theorists of the 'third wave of modernity' ([1975] 1989: 94–8); Michel Foucault said that 'It was Nietzsche who specified the power relation as the general focus . . . whereas for Marx it was the production relation' (1980: 53); and Wolfgang Baier called them 'polestars' of social theory (1981–2).

As Nancy Love has argued (1986), Marx and Nietzsche are leading 'theorists of modernity', making deeply problematic the shape, direction and value of the social formations and cultural complexes accompanying the emergence of modern capitalism and mass democracy. They addressed modernity's 'differentiating' and 'homogenizing' facets and their tensions and entwinement with the ideals of 'justice' and 'freedom'. Marx emphasized universalistic social struggles against inequality, rooted in developmental tendencies of sociocultural modernity, while Nietzsche stressed the mobilization of aesthetic sensibilities, rooted in the body and senses, to resist cultural homogenization and nurture human particularity. Transcending the particular historical moments in which the two theorists lived, their big questions reappear in times of sea-change, or when, as Weber held, 'the great cultural problems' shift and 'the road is lost in the twilight'. When the 'value' of specialized practices and concepts and middle-range or sociological theories is no longer taken-for-granted, Weber said, they are viewed from the 'heights of thought' ([1904] 1949: 112).

A century ago, Georg Simmel ([1900] 1978: 484) spoke of a 'secret restlessness' or 'helpless urgency' that pushes thinkers 'from socialism to Nietzsche'. Around mid-century, the Frankfurt School's 'dialectic of Enlightenment' phase suggested a similar shift, following the dashed revolutionary hopes after Stalinism, Nazism, the Holocaust and triumphant capitalism. Their view that the prevailing society lacked historical resources for liberation led them from a critique of capitalism to a cultural critique of Western rationality and a move from Marx to Nietzsche. Their ideas about all-embracing 'one-dimensionality' and 'negative dialectics' helped inspire the New Left's aesthetic radicalism, and foreshadowed postmodernism. Today's radical Nietzscheanisms amplify a similarly strong sense of cultural exhaustion.

Richard Wolin's (1990: 166) point about the relationship of Heideggerian Nietzscheanism to the Marxian tradition illuminates a core facet of the split between the two 'polestar' theorists:

> Ironically, for all his criticisms of Nietzsche, Heidegger's own position remains eminently 'Nietzschean' in at least one critical respect; he accepts without question the standpoint of 'total critique' that Nietzsche himself adopts *vis-à-vis* the failings of the modern age. Thus, for both thinkers, the essence of modernity is . . . a wholesale dissolution of the structures of value and belief that have traditionally made life meaningful. The method of 'immanent critique' is rejected insofar as there is essentially nothing about modernity as a social formation that is worth redeeming.

Heidegger rejected Marxian presuppositions about the fecundity of 'history'; the idea that modern sociocultural orders contain determinate resources for mapping, securing and creating more progressive, democratic, or emancipated institutions and culture. He held that hegemonic, technocratic-economistic instrumentalism and consequent 'darkening of the world' and 'always-the-sameness' characterize socialism as well as capitalism and that 'Europe lies in a pincers between Russia and America [polar capitals of economism], which are metaphysically the same . . .' ([1953] 1961: 36–9).

Young Marx asserted in a letter to his father, explaining his conversion to Hegelianism: 'I arrived at the point of seeking the idea in reality itself. If previously the gods had dwelt above the earth, now they became its center' ([1837] 1975: 18). Marx's famous 'inversion' of Hegel was supposed to radically historicize Hegelian 'immanent critique', making it concrete and social. Marx's 'materialist' version of the method, 'ideology critique', sought more determinate bases for emancipatory change and for justification of his normative standpoint 'within' actual or emergent sociocultural conditions. His move, however, like Hegel's, fashioned a *historicist* alternative to absolutist or transcendental normative arguments and rested, ultimately, on faith in history. Marx believed that modernity offers historical resources, which are refined by progressive rationalization, for a free, just, abundant society and culture. In his view, ideology critique follows history's tracks, locating its progressive facets, honing them theoretically, turning them against repressive conditions, and guiding emancipatory movements. Seeing the future to be prefigured in the present, he detected taints of socialism in late-capitalist science, firms and labor movements. Although often indirectly, other modern social theories express similar optimism about immanent or historicist bases for social progress and normative critique.

Nietzsche's contrary views about exhausted modernity and postmodern rupture offer an entirely different type of – or *aesthetic* – alternative to absolutism and transcendentalism (Antonio, 1981, 1989, 1990, 1995, 2000a; Antonio and Kellner, 1992; Benhabib, 1986; Wallerstein, 1998).

In recent years, intense theoretical debates and cultural wars over 'modernity' versus 'postmodernity' and Marx versus Nietzsche indicate that we may again be experiencing the type of rupture that Weber referred to a century ago. Mounting inequality in the wake of neoliberal globalization and rapid normalization after the 'Revolutions of 1989' dimmed soaring illusions about a 'second modernity' or postmodern 'progress' (an implicit idea, since the word is now taboo). A severe economic downturn would likely raise Marx from the dead once again; some theorists already see his 'specter'. However, in this millennial twilight time, with its over-ripe *fin de siècle* sensibilities, 'realism' about 'wasteful' social programs, restless ambivalence about the seamy underside and self-indulgent neglect of the stockholders' republic, and rampant ethnic-racial chauvinism and nationalism, I paraphrase Thomas Mann: 'I see Nietzsche, only Nietzsche'.

IN THE RUINS OF POSTWAR MODERNIZATION: NIETZSCHE RISING

> Just as in Nietzsche's day educated philistines believed in progress, the unfaltering elevation of the masses and the greatest possible happiness for the greatest possible number, so today they believe . . . in the opposite, the revocation of 1789, the incorrigibility of human nature, the anthropological impossibility of happiness – in other words, that the workers are too well off. The profound insights of the day before yesterday have been reduced to the ultimate in banality.

(Theodor Adorno, [1951] 1978: 188)

Although of enduring importance for 'social theory', Marx and Nietzsche were largely ignored by 'sociological theorists', during the rise and initial expansion of professional sociology (starting in the United States in the 1920s and elsewhere mostly after the Second World War). During much of the postwar era, Marxian ideas had wide impact outside the US, through successful labor and socialist parties, leftist youth movements and revolutionary politics. Although they sometimes were ideological dress for political power, they often provided sharp critiques of hegemonic forms of welfare liberalism, social democracy and post-war modernization projects, pushing for more 'socialization' or 'participation'. By the 1960s, Marxian questions, concepts and analyses were central to international sociological circles. Even in North America, where labor was weaker and socialist ideas had little currency, 'conflict theorists' (for example, C. Wright Mills, Lewis Coser, Alvin Gouldner) challenged dominant functionalist theories, especially the Parsonsian variety stressing 'normative consensus' and 'Americanization'. 'Conflict theory' was a loose collection of general approaches and normative sensibilities 'critical' of social 'scientific' arguments that Keynesian liberalism and the Pax Americana constituted a conflictless 'post-industrialism' and 'end of ideology'. They attacked the ideas that welfare capitalism overcame the divisions of industrial capitalism, which it supposedly superseded, and that it attained unparalleled, sweeping substantive legitimacy. 'Conflict theory' was identified with diverse theorists (for example, Simmel, Weber, Mead and others), but Marx was eventually portrayed as the main classical figure of this supposed 'alternative' to mainstream sociology.

By the later 1960s and early 1970s, many 'critical' social theorists and sociologists, often younger people active in the student and anti-war movements and New Left politics, forged new theory circles and journals (for example, *Telos, New German Critique, New Left Review*), stressing 'Western Marxist' theorists (for example, Lukács, Gramsci, Adorno, Althusser) and cultural issues. Breaking with orthodox Marxism, they argued that the Western working classes were conservative and integrated into the 'system', that Eurocommunism was bureaucratic and conformist, and that Soviet-style communism was repressive. Older Marxists embraced left versions of modernization theory, but the New Left, especially segments that fused radical politics with hippy culture or embraced 'revolutionary' Marxisms (for example, European Maoist and Red Guard factions), manifested romantic themes that suggested deep disenchantment with postwar modernity and prepared the way for 'post-Marxist' and 'postmodernist' approaches. Although weaned on Heidegger and Nietzsche, even Foucault allied, for a time, with the Maoist student-left (Miller, 1993: 165–207). By the early 1970s, Marxian ideas started to be engaged seriously in certain sub-areas of North American sociology (for example, stratification, sociology of development, sociology of work, sociological theory). Marx later joined Durkheim and Weber in the discipline's classical

theory canon or 'Holy Trinity'. Marx was the 'liminal' figure of the three and signifier for radical critique.

The 'revolutions of 1968' in Prague, Paris and Chicago and the Chinese cultural revolution lifted radical hopes, but were deflated almost immediately by a crushing normalization (that is, the Brezhnev Doctrine, Nixon election, American-Chinese accord, and Gaullist restoration) followed by more decisive defeats and neoliberal hegemony, during the later 1970s and 1980s (Anderson, 1998: 93–4). Anderson has held that, by the late 1970s, regardless of the success of empirically based Marxist sociology, Western Marxist theory had 'come to an end', being replaced, on the 'left' by postmodernist theory (1983: 20–7; Laclau and Mouffe, 1985; Wood, 1986). While Marxism was still gaining a foothold in North American sociology, the New Left was collapsing, neoconservatism was ascending, and new Nietzschean approaches, forged by Foucault and other 'new cultural theorists', were gaining in left-leaning theory circles. The much heralded 'cultural' or 'discursive' turn was most decisive in the humanities, where postmodernist theories were widely embraced by younger faculty and graduate students, dominant in many sub-areas and programs, and nearly everywhere the focus of intense generational splits and 'culture wars' over the canon, political correctness and cultural decline, which went beyond academe. In the 1980s, Marx's place in sociology's classical canon was well established. He was memorialized as the exemplar of one of the three main theoretical paradigms, but, as his sociological respectability grew and his ideas were applied in research programs, he faded as the main liminal figure of social and cultural theory. By the mid-1980s, Nietzsche replaced Marx.

The 'new social movements' (that is, ethnic, racial, feminist, gay and lesbian, and other forms of identity politics) rose to prominence and replaced the New Left. They emerged in the context of an international shift in emphasis from postwar-era national parties, labor-oriented leaderships, state-centered reforms, and social planning to 'local struggles', 'pluralistic alliances', 'cultural politics' and 'risk avoidance', and from emphasis on material needs, structure and class to 'cultural identity', 'agency' and 'discourse' (for example, Beck 1992; Beck et al., 1994; Giddens, 1994; Mellucci 1989, 1996a, 1996b; Sassoon, 1996: 647–90). The new social movements had diverse followings and standpoints, but movement theorists usually stressed an epiphanic break with Marxism as 'the' essential move in attaining a fresh awareness and 'ascending' to a 'politics of difference' (for example, Aronson, 1995; Nicholson and

Seidman, 1995). Their new cultural theories, often postmodernist positions, were fashioned to address the new sociopolitical and cultural context and they often converged, albeit often implicitly, with Nietzschean views about cultural homogenization and cultural pluralism (Antonio, 1998). They were highly critical of the theory and politics of postwar liberals and radicals, which they contend ignored and obscured cultural domination. They held that Marx was the master theorist or forerunner of the postwar era's overly ambitious planning and statism, insouciant disregard for minorities and women, and, overall, failed modernization, masking paternalistic domination as assistance, progress or emancipation. Similar themes appeared in sociology, especially among its left-leaning cultural theorists and movement activists. The sociological critics charged that the postwar left ignored non-class issues and cultural domination, upheld patriarchal, heterosexist and Eurocentrist tendencies of the mainstream, and, overall, propped-up the cultural, political, and disciplinary status quo. They saw the deficiencies of postwar theory and politics to be rooted in the classical canon's alleged retrograde blindspots; emblazoned on teeshirts at American Sociological Association meetings in the 1990s, the Holy Trinity became 'Dead White Males'.

Postmodernist Nietzscheanism appeared early in France, long before parallel changes occurred in the United States. Arguably one of the most creative predecessors of postmodernism, after Nietzsche, Henri Lefebvre, argued, in the early 1960s, that 'Marx's thought terminated' in 'dead ends' and that 'a new analysis and a new account' is needed to address the 'technicity' and 'scientism' that animate domination in socialist as well as capitalist regimes ([1962] 1995: 206–15). Following in Lefebvre's tracks, in the later 1960s and 1970s, Michel Foucault subverted incisively the normative and epistemological bases of postwar social theory and politics, albeit in a somewhat roundabout and historically indirect way. He described the eighteenth- and nineteenth-century rise of a 'panoptical' order, based on all-pervasive 'minute', 'meticulous' discipline and 'surveillance' or self-regulated and nearly total cultural control, clothed in the mantle of the 'human sciences' and exerted by various testing, measuring, and helping techniques ([1975] 1979). He implied that panopticism reached full maturity in the postwar era. Also, Jean-François Lyotard held that modern Western 'metanarratives' about freedom and science serve technocracy uncritically. Seeing Marx as the master theorist of this dead modern theory, Lyotard decried his 'totalizing model and . . . totalitarian effect'. In Lyotard's view, Marxian theory justifies 'totalizing' practices of

capitalist as well as socialist 'system managers' ([1979] 1984: 12–3, 46, 60–7). Foucault and Lyotard made basic contributions to an ascendent postmodernist vision of the repressive 'therapeutic state', which treated Keynsian liberalism, social democracy, and democratic socialism as manifestations of the same sweeping 'normalization'. Following Nietzsche, they argued that control mechanisms are now far more numerous, varied and deceptive, and, although less overtly and brutally coercive, much more economical and effective in exercising domination. In the 1980s and 1990s, postmodernists from North America and other parts of the world espoused similar lines, seeing postwar modernity as the high-tide of Western rationalization and as a cultural noose (earlier inscribed in Marx's abortive dream) that foreclosed all possibilities for liberation (for example, Bauman, 1992; Jencks, 1985: 180–1, 371–3).

After the ascendance of new cultural theory and its Holy Trinity or postmodernist canon of Foucault, Lyotard and Derrida, the neoconservative philosopher, Allan Bloom, held emphatically that 'Marx has become boring for' and 'does not speak to' young American intellectuals (1987: 217, 222). The chorus on the post-Marxist left sang the same tune that 'Marxism is over' (for example, Aronson, 1995: 40–67). But Bloom argued that 'so-called Marxist teachers' now employ a Nietzschean language and that a wholesale turn to Nietzsche began in the New Left era and is continued by postmodernism. He declared that: 'The New Left in America was a Nietzscheanized-Heideggerianized Left. The unthinking hatred of "bourgeois society" was exactly the same in both places.' He held that this 'mutant breed of Marxists . . . derationalize Marx and turn Nietzsche into a leftist' (1987: 222, 314). He saw this 'Nietzscheanized left' as a leading force in the 'decomposition' of American universities and culture. Although his estimation of the left's dubious achievements and claim that 'today virtually every Nietzschean as well as Heideggerian is a leftist' are grossly overblown, his point that Nietzsche has emerged again as a major figure for left-leaning social and cultural theorists has much credence. Postmodernists often identify Nietzsche as a most important precursor, but, more importantly, they take up, at least tacitly, his core positions on cultural exhaustion and difference. As suggested above, his very name is entwined with today's 'endings discourses' (that is, the 'end of history', 'end of the social', 'end of the political' 'end of left and right', and 'end of alternatives') and with views that equate postwar modernization with sterile and repressive technocracy, differing only by degree from the Holocaust and Gulag. Anderson may be right that the 'deeper sense' of these

Nietzschean claims about endings 'lies in cancellation of political alternatives', or a fundamental constriction of such possibilities (1998: 92).

WHEN HISTORY FAILS: THE 'BODY AGAINST THE MACHINE'

> That thirst for more of the intellectual 'war and laughter' that we find Nietzsche calling us to may bring us satisfactions that optimism-haunted philosophies could never bring. Malcontentedness may be the beginning of promise.
>
> (Randolph Bourne, [1917] 1964b: 64)

> The sky of modernity has seen several stars . . . ascendant, the sable sun of melancholy and ennui, disaster's pale moon, the red sun of joy. We are faced with an unforeseen astrological conjuncture, from which we are unable to calculate a horoscope.
>
> (Henri Lefebvre, [1962] 1995: 224)

Spiritual forerunner to the New Left and today's literary radicals, Randolph Bourne employed Nietzschean ideas of 'herd-instinct' and cultural regimentation in sharp critiques of US progressives, who justified US entry into the First World War with high-handed slogans about 'saving the world from subjugation' ([1917] 1964a: 7, 11, 13). In his Nietzschean-titled 'Twilight of the Idols', Bourne skewered his former teacher and hero, John Dewey, for giving into nationalist impulses and supporting participation in the war (1964b; Westbrook, 1991: 195–227). Bourne attacked incisively the optimistic posture that the war would increase social solidarity and lead to global democracy. He implied that Dewey's historicism was blind to the grim realities of the day. While praising democracy abstractly, Bourne held, such supporters of the war contribute to forces that silence the democratic opposition. With the help of a Nietzschean optic, he detected early signs of a wartime hysterical, propagandistic, reactionary erosion of democracy, which progressives missed. He held that their all-too-cheery liberalism and scientism confused the ideal and the real and ignored the underside of American life. But Bourne, qualifying his critique, asserted that he and others on the Nietzschean left were not 'cultural vandals' and that their 'skeptical, malicious, desperate,

ironical' mood was a 'sign of hope' and of 'more vivid and more stirring life fermenting in America today' (1964b: 63–4). Bourne did not break entirely with progressivism, but tried to make it much more critical.

Expressing Nietzschean opposition to Cold War-era Marxism, Lefebvre held that historicism had become a metalegitimation for a drab, uncritical, conformist, materialist, workerist lockstep, which capitulated to Soviet domination, French Communist Party bureaucrats and technocracy. Prefacing the work with a passage from Nietzsche, he lambasted Marxism's limp 'unconditional optimism, faith in the future' ([1962] 1995: 26–32). In his view, Marxism had degenerated into a philistine state 'religion' incapable of addressing critically or even seeing the new pattern of technocratic domination and history's contrary and divergent directions and tendencies. For Lefebvre, Marxist historicism had lost its analytical power as social theory and inspirational force as a political vision. He declared ([1962] 1995: 249):

> History, the historical? We . . . of the second half of the twentieth century are fed up . . . with it. We have lived through many historic hours, far too many, too often have we felt the passing winds of destiny . . . There are certain blinkered pedagogues who use Marxism as justification for treating us like naughty schoolchildren forced to keep our eyes on the blackboard. But there is something sickening about history as a spectacle, and the notion of history as action requires a great deal of patience – too much – and a lot of mutilations. The philosophy of history ends up making the very thought of history unbearable.

In the affluent United States, during the same period, the capital–labor compromise, standard consumer package and social security neutralized the classical Marxian scenario. Hanging on to 'Marxism' by a thread, Marcuse described a condition of euphoric alienation where workers embrace the system, legitimacy derives from the delivery of goods (not from grand 'ideologies'), and opposition to capitalism disappears. In his view, the 'distinguishing feature of advanced industrial society is its effective suffocation of those needs which demand liberation'. The 'absorption of ideology into reality', he held, evaporates the dialectical tension in modern history between the ideal and the real; two-dimensional culture is collapsed into one conformist horizon (1964: 11). He argued that 'domination is transfigured into administration' and that 'products indoctrinate and manipulate', promoting 'a false consciousness . . . immune against falsehood'; thus, Marx's revolutionary 'working class . . . no longer appears to be the living contradiction to the established society'

(1964: 11–12, 31–2). Regardless of political divergence, Marcuse's portrayal of stultifying homogeneity had taints of his former teacher Heidegger's vision of technological civilization.

Lefebvre amplified facets implicit in Marcuse's scenario, which foreclosed critique even more sharply. Lefebvre argued that new forms of media and information production reduce 'social reality' to a 'system of signs and significations'. Anticipating Baudrillardian 'simulation' or 'hyperreality', he held that 'social reality . . . loses all its solidity, its substantiality and its frames of reference; it begins to crumble – or rather, to evaporate'. Hence, arises a 'world of boredom' and 'nostalgia', dominated by the 'aleatory' or chance ([1962] 1995: 204, 222–3). In his view, modern theory's basic epistemological and normative distinctions (for example, ideal–real, truth–falsity, good–bad, base–superstructure, culture–society) are blurred so hopelessly that 'progressive' facets of history cannot be distinguished from their opposites. Lefebvre implies a near complete dissipation of historical sensibilities and the cultural bases for social theory. History and society dissolve into pure contingency, historicism fails and immanent critique comes up empty. Adorno described this moment, when 'culture' loses its 'salt of truth', as an 'open air prison' ([1967] 1981: 19–34).

In such 'pessimistic' times social theory often becomes a 'message in a bottle', cast out to sea with the hope that it might have some impact when history rights itself, if it ever rights itself. Thus, strategies for criticism often shift; some theorists move back to absolutism (for example, Leo Strauss), while others pose deontological or quasitranscendental positions (for example, John Rawls and Jürgen Habermas). But retreat from history is frequently the case. Such a climate is ripe also for Nietzschean alternatives; aesthetic critiques or 'negativity' anchored in 'bodily' or 'instinctive' capacities. Although not breaking entirely with historicism and immanent critique, Marcuse framed a Freudo-Marxist position, partially rooted in Nietzsche, stressing organically based needs and envisioning the 'aesthetic dimension' as an underground reservoir of resistance to domination that flows in the darkest of times. In his view, 'Eros' cannot be eradicated entirely by brutal repression or euphoric alienation; mounting unmet needs can spur the utopian imagination. Referring to Nietzsche, he urged turning 'the body against the machine'. He called for a Nietzschean 'gay science' to redirect 'advanced industrial society's vast productive forces from their linkage to repression and destruction to the service of life and joy. He wanted 'to activate arrested *organic*, biological needs: to make the human body an instrument of pleasure rather than labor'. He urged going beyond the depleted, regimented humanity that he criticized in his *One-Dimensional Man* and that he now depicted as 'the determinate negation of Nietzsche's superman' ([1955] 1966: xi, xiv–xv; also see 118–24). Marcuse's aesthetic radicalism was aimed to preserve the utopian impulse when the prospects for political change appeared to be blocked. Although lean with regard to concrete proposals for change, he helped expose the inauthenticity of a Marxist historicism perpetuated mainly as a catechism to discipline the faithful in the face of drastically changed historical conditions, which seemed contrary to the theory. The Nietzschean moves of Bourne, Lefebvre and Marcuse let light and air into the dank basement of the conformist left. Posing innovative critiques that illuminated conditions that others ignored, they paved the way for the New Left. Similarly, intellectually serious versions of today's new cultural theories, such as Foucauldian theory, helped stimulate new forms of resistance in the wake of moribund types of Marxism and the collapsed New Left. At least in part, intense battles over the new approaches derive from their critical force.

IN THE LAND OF 'ZERO OPTIONS': TWILIGHT-TIME NIETZSCHEANISM

All hopes have seemingly been betrayed. The Owl of Minerva which once flew at dusk has folded its wings, . . . the direction of History has been lost, and it knows not what to tell us.

(Daniel Bell, 1990: 43)

Nietzsche continues to be the epitome of German unreason, or what is called the German spirit. A gulf separates him from those who unscrupulously preach his message, yet he prepared the way for them that he himself did not follow.

(Karl Löwith, [1940] 1994: 5)

As Luc Ferry holds, Horkheimer's and Adorno's Nietzschean-influenced dialectic of Enlightenment 'was wary of any romantic escape from the modern era' (1990: 2). In my view, even the bolder Nietzschean moves of Lefebvre did not depart entirely from Enlightenment culture. Although Ferry would probably disagree (1994; Ferry and Renaut, 1990: 68–121; 1997), a similar claim could be made about the Holy Trinity of

Foucault, Lyotard and Derrida. Their deconstructive broadside of the liberal–left order is overblown, but their critiques of a moribund Althusserian left helped open the way for the new 'micropolitics'. Foucault's Nietzschean views about the entwinement of 'power and knowledge' supplemented structural theories of power, which did not illuminate the types of exclusion and disrespect stressed by the new politics of 'recognition' or 'difference'. He supplied an epistemological and normative alternative to postwar Marxism and a fresh lexicon (for example, 'totalitarian theories', 'normalization', 'local criticism' and 'subjugated knowledges') employed widely among 'new social movements' theorists (1980: 80–1, 107). As Julie Stephens argues, Foucault is 'an obvious reference point' for an 'antidisciplinary politics' that links postmodernism and the new social movements to their roots with the New Left (1998: 23).

However, leading postmodernist and Deweyean Richard Rorty recently posed a scalding critique of the US 'Foucauldian left', implying that their critical powers fizzle in today's historical context. Rorty concedes that they illuminate types of domination that were ignored by his generation and that their critiques of 'socially accepted sadism' and of 'humiliation' of disparaged minorities have made American society 'more civilized'. But his main emphasis is on the 'cultural left's' alleged 'dark side'. He claims that their Nietzschean ideas of cultural exhaustion and textualism produce 'spectatorial' ways and 'hopelessness'. Most importantly, Rorty argues that they ignore mounting 'economic inequality' and 'economic insecurity', beneath the prospering, stock-holding, professional middle classes and that they have no vision about how to rekindle battles for economic justice or to resist the protofascist tendencies emergent on the radical right (1998: 75–107). He still says that he concurs with the cultural left critique of 'Enlightenment rationalism' by 'Nietzsche, Heidegger, Foucault, and Derrida' and with the pluralist goals of the related politics of difference (1998: 96). And he remains a staunch anti-Marxist. However, he argues emphatically that the consequences of over twenty years of neoliberal restructuring and retreating welfare liberalism have immiserated very substantial segments of the populace and cry out for a revived 'reformist left' to engage material misery and revive social democracy.

Marxian theorists have posed sharper critiques, charging that postmodernists' celebratory claims about cultural autonomy or 'autoreferentiality' distort gravely the neoliberal context of eroded regulation, hypermobile global capital, recommodified public goods, and hypernitchified mass culture (for example, Eagleton, 1996; Jameson, 1991; Offe, 1996; Wood, 1995; Žižek, 1997). They charge that the sharp cultural turn and attacks on labor-centered politics make economic power and injustice invisible, which disappear in jargon-laden portrayals of a relativistic flatland of floating signifiers (where identity and consumption rule and needs are incommensurable). The critics argue that postmodernist approaches reflect the logic of neoliberal capitalism. Overall, they imply that the Nietzschean left addressed a postwar context that is now over. Marxist critics often agree that the cultural left's critiques of postwar politics pointed to genuine gaps and that their politics of difference have laudable goals, which still need to be realized. However, they criticize the failure to illuminate adequately increased economic inequality, eroded work conditions and reduced welfare rights. If they are right, the peak of Foucaldian theory is past and the climate is ripe for another return of Marx. Faint signs are already visible (for example, Cassidy, 1997; Derrida, 1994), but a Marx revival probably will take another (periodic) moderate to severe economic crisis.

By contrast to the post-structuralist Holy Trinity and the broader cultural left, a more extreme and politically ambiguous postmodernism breaks much more sharply with modern social theory (Antonio, 1998). Jean Baudrillard radicalized Lefebvre's early views about the 'aleatory' nature of media culture (e.g., 1983a, 1983b, 1987). His vision of 'hyperreality' and all-encompassing 'simulation' portrays a 'regime of signification' that evaporates the ability to stand back from, evaluate and judge events. He holds that the Foucauldian 'panopticon', or 'real' surveillance and normalization, is replaced by 'simulation' or purely semiotic control. Under these conditions, he contends, efforts to reform or revolutionize sociocultural life are blunted and reversed by the swirl of signifiers, cacophony of divergent voices and 'black hole' of the 'silent majorities'. In his view, Foucauldian 'micropolitics' merely create the appearance of responsiveness and uphold the all-controlling sign system. Implying a nightmare version of Nietzsche's 'eternal recurrence' or of Spengler's moribund last stage of decayed civilization, Baudrillard holds that simulation replays things '*ad infinitum*', imploding all meaning and defrocking historicism as 'our own mythology' (1987: 69). In the ruins of Enlightenment culture, he endorses the rule of hyperaestheticized, Nietzschean 'fascination' and 'seduction' (that is, living on the flat surface of culture and embracing its flow of aleatory images). This scenario implies total evaporation of the cultural resources for (including the epistemological and normative bases of) modern social theory and liberal democratic culture.

Baudrillard's playful rambling should not be accorded too much veracity or blame, but it does amplify a 'pathological' side of cultural postmodernization, manifested intensely in key areas of mass culture and consumption; common sensibilities about media events, politics and advertising being so staged and so tied to instantly changing, fragmented images that the lines between truth and falsity and illusion and reality are blurred totally. Because signs lack clear referents, we cannot distinguish between true and false information and simulated and 'real' events. For example, the endless series of tabloid stories stretching from Watergate to the death of Diana, Princess of Wales and Monicagate momentarily raise people's moral hackles, but fade rapidly, cause little change, and seem hard to distinguish from other cheap forms of 'entertainment'. Thus, critical theories and genuine politics may be, indeed, fading away, as Baudrillard claims, into a netherland of simulation, ennui and boredom, opening the way for a return of another type of Nietzscheanism, which Nietzsche himself feared, stressing myth, will and collective redemption.

The Weimar-era 'New Right' or 'radical conservatives' blended Nietzschean ideas of cultural exhaustion with a one-sided reading of Weber. Universalizing his 'iron cage' thesis, they ignored his many qualifications about the historical openness, ambiguities and different directions of rationalization and failed to entertain the implications of his crucial distinction between limited state power and total states and of his point that rationalized bureaucratic jurisdictions and centralized decision-making (that is, 'rule of small number'), within democratic regimes, block revolutionary change, but clarify responsibility and make reform possible. They also neglected his argument that distinctly modern cultural rationalization multiplies vastly specialized value and life spheres, rationalizing them according to their distinct internal logics, increasing differences and heightening capacities to detect them. Weber warned sternly that demagogic promises about eliminating the contradictions of rationalization could forge the very type of iron cage that they denounced in the abstract. Appearing on the left and the right in the 1920s writings of Marxist Georg Lukács and protofascist Carl Schmitt, this reading of Weber equated modern rationalization with descent into total administration, total meaninglessness and total cultural homogenization or evaporation of human particularity. This position was a sociological bridge linking Heidegger's technological civilization to the Frankfurt School's total administration, New Left's technocracy and postmodernists' therapeutic state. However, New Right Nietzscheans deployed this grim vision in a new position

claiming to go 'beyond left and right'. They criticized economic insecurity and class divisions, and exhorted a revival of social solidarity against bourgeois individualism and capitalist instrumentalism. Yet they attacked, just as strongly, decadent liberal democracy for its egalitarian mediocrity, cultural fragmentation and political paralysis from too much tolerance of difference and interest group conflict.

The Weimar-era New Right held that human particularity could be redeemed by reviving, cultivating, preserving and empowering national particularity. They called for a restoration of 'organic community' based on legitimate hierarchical-authority, natural inequality and mass military *ésprit* and discipline. They wedded the totalized Weber, stressing relentless capitalist liquidation of particularity, to a stripped-down Nietzsche, *sans* his affirmations of sovereign individuality and cultural hybridity and fulminations about the evils of the state, nationalism and cultural regimentation. For example, Heidegger described totally homogenized technocracy and saw its tonic to be a Nietzschean 'higher man' transmuted into a 'type' concept (precursors of which he saw as 'Prussian Soldiery and the Jesuit order'!) and 'collective artwork' that celebrates 'national community' and serves as '*the* religion' ([1961] 1991a: 85–6; 1991c: 99–100, emphasis in original).

The New Right saw advocacy of anti-Nietzschean nationalism and regimented collective-being as an essential Nietzschean move to escape all-pervasive nihilism.[5] Believing that revolutionary politics, rooted in mythologized national community, could resist capitalism and 'overcome' bourgeois humanity, they claimed to be heeding Nietzsche's musical call for a 'moment of decision', or 'great noontide', when 'preparatory human beings', choosing to 'live dangerously', exert their will, clear away the cultural debris of moribund civilization, and make way for a 'higher' humanity (*Übermenschen*) that live beyond bourgeois morality, its 'last men', and modernity ([1883–1885] 1969: 226–32, 279, 289–306; [1882] 1974: 228–9). Nietzsche's powerful aesthetic thread has had diverse impacts; Bourne expressed it in his vision of a new generation of young American radicals overcoming corrupt, spent establishment progressivism; writers such as Hesse, Rilke, Mann and Kazantakis implied it in literary departures from bourgeois life, and, albeit somewhat tepidly, Foucauldian posthumanism manifests it. Nietzsche's call to 'live dangerously' and seek 'heights' inspired Löwith's generation to try to forge authentic and meaningful lives. However, it also led, as Löwith asserted, 'in a roundabout and yet direct way . . . to Goebbels' heroic clichés about self-sacrifice' ([1940] 1994: 5).

First-generation radical conservatives (such as Heidegger, Carl Schmitt, Ernst Jünger) have been rehabilitated and are widely read and considered legitimate beyond radical-right circles (Dahl, 1996). Resurgent New Right Nietzscheans play the old tunes in a postmodern *fin de siècle* rhythm, offering an 'alternative' to gridlocked mass politics and modern social theory.[6] Exploiting the yearning for collective identity in a context where economic and cultural globalization erode the autonomy of nation-states, they amplify 'retribalization' or rampant ethnic-racial populism, separatism, nationalism and even 'ethnic cleansing' (for example, Barber, 1996; Betz, 1994; Betz and Immerfall, 1998). Their theories and politics have a seductive power deriving from their romantic references to the restoration of community, emphatic assertion of tabooed views of nationalism, race and immigration, and self-righteous indignation against 'political correctness'. They resurrect Schmittean 'friend–enemy' politics, criticizing liberal democratic citizenship and calling for majority-group nationalism. Schmitt saw political resistance to cultural homogenization to depend on nurturance of cultural particularity and collective identity, which, he believed, could be strong only when opposed to divergent cultural complexes and peoples. He argued that the heights of politics are reached only when a people grasp actively what they are *not* and share clear, specific, bitter, collective enemies. In his view, genuine cultures are incommensurable, and real communication is limited by 'ethnos' or to the circle of friends. His 'cultural theory' had a fateful affinity for the prevailing anti-semitism of his day ([1932] 1996). Today's New Right mix these Schmittean views deceptively with Gramscian references to 'cultural hegemony' and 'cultural struggle'. They offer bold and often intellectually sophisticated departures from postwar political frameworks, addressing the political-economic issues ignored by Foucauldian Nietzscheanism and the postmodern fragmentation, paralysis and ennui expressed by Baudrillardian Nietzscheanism. The New Right's enchanted and mythic allusions to 'ethnos', solidarity, morality and collective will strike at the prosaic heart of liberalism.

New Right theorists revive Heideggerian Nietzscheanism's equation of Western rationalization with all-encompassing homogenization. They acknowledge their debt to Nietzsche, but, like first-generation radical conservatives, they put aside the antiauthoritarian aspects of his thought. They argue that the primary 'cultural' and 'political' task is revival, nurturance and protection of cultural particularity or community, based on common 'ethnos', natural inequality (that is, genuine individual particu-

larity), shared mythology and general will. They speak with special urgency about the 'New World Order', or hegemonic neoliberalism, contending that this global, managerial-capitalist juggernaut is imposing universal markets hand-in-hand with universal human rights and leveling everything in its path. They see abstract universality, anchored now in a Janus-faced mix of economism and multiculturalism, to be creating a 'global midnight' or end-game of culture and individuality. They claim to be the genuine 'Third Way', gleaning the best facets of left and right and offering the only alternative to a morally bankrupt neoconservativism, toady for international bankers and managerial capitalism, and to the ersatz 'third way' politics of Clinton, Blair and Schröder, the leading-edge of the New World Order's neoliberal grim reaper and universal state.

Overall, New Right Nietzscheans subvert the foundations of modern social theory, liberal-left politics, and the democratic nation-state. Blurring left and right, they deploy skillfully postmodern sensibilities. They claim to represent 'the right to difference' or 'ethnopluralism' against cultureless, deracinated, identityless, disempowered victims of liberal democracy. In their view, 'real' diversity and identity require unified, politically empowered ethnic, racial and religious communities, resistant to the simulated difference and individuality based on manipulated and culturally impoverished mass consumption and egalitarianism. Their Nietzschean language of exerting political will, escaping ennui and overcoming liberal paralysis implies an exclusionary, hierarchical, postliberal or protofascist order. Although past history is not likely to be repeated, the New Right justifies existing trends toward parochial standpoint philosophy, cultural philistinism, ethnic and racial separatism and violence, and other authoritarian departures from liberal democracy.

ANTIPOLITICAL NIETZSCHE: AGAINST 'PSYCHIC PROLETARIANIZATION'

All great cultural epochs are epochs of political decline: that which is great in the cultural sense has been unpolitical, even *antipolitical* . . .

(Nietzsche, [1888] 1968, Vol 1: 63, emphasis in original)

'Truth' as every prophet, every sectarian, every latitudinarian, every socialist, every Churchman understands the word is conclusive proof that not so much as a start has been made on that disciplining of the intellect and self-overcoming necessary for the discovery of any truth, even the smallest.

(Nietzsche, [1888] 1968, Vol 2: 171).

Nietzsche referred to himself as 'the last *antipolitical* German' ([1888] 1969: 225, emphasis in original). This antipolitical theme runs counter to his impulsive aestheticism and vision of cultural exhaustion. By contrast to the Nietzschean right and left, he saw 'culture' and 'politics' to be contradictory domains. He criticized socialist, feminist and other mass democratic politics for putting a brake on cultural creativity, but he argued much more emphatically that the new politics of 'nationalism and race hatred' exert extreme narcotic, philistine, anti-cultural effects (e.g., [1873–1876] 1983: 3–8; [1887] 1969: 159; [1888] 1968: 60–3). He charged that 'national scabies of the heart' caused 'the nations of Europe to barricade themselves against each other' ([1882] 1974: 339). His vision of politics is informed by his broader views about the role of morality and '*ressentiment*' in sociocultural reproduction. He argued that Western modernity originated from a 'slave revolt'; 'ascetic priests' created a very harsh 'slave morality' (that is, Socratic philosophy and Christianity) to cope with disintegration following the collapse of pre-Socratic culture. Nietzsche contended that a much more sweeping type of cultural control was imposed by granting the 'soul' or 'mind' imperious lordship over the body and redirecting repressed instincts and feelings of inferiority, powerlessness and unjustified suffering into guilt; redemption required acquiescing to self-lacerating conscience, accepting spiritual regimentation and turning residual anger against divergent values and outsiders ([1887] 1969: 120–36; [1888] 1968: 29–34, 130–2).

Nietzsche anticipated Schmitt's vision of 'friend–enemy' politics, but he saw it as a perversion that controls people by making them 'sick'. He argued that mass politics preys on the weak, inward Western personality, made even more vulnerable by later modernity's homelessness, falsity and cheap mass culture. He held that extreme insecurity and overconcern with the 'self' and others' perceptions of it makes people easy targets for the predations of authoritarian demagogues. He stated that: 'the less one knows how to command [i.e., exert self-control], the more one covets someone who commands severely – a god, prince, class, physician, father confessor, dogma, or party conscience' (Nietzsche, [1882] 1974: 287, also see 175, 287–90, 338–40). The herd seeks 'leaders', who promise to end their suffering, vanquish their enemies, and redeem their souls. In this light, Nietzsche

considered appeals to collective subjectivity and national reawakening as leading to a nightmarish slave revolt and an even baser, more degraded herd, rather than to genuine community, identity and 'higher' people.

Nietzsche believed that moralism breeds fanaticism. He argued that the idea of morality operating 'above' and 'guiding' instrumental affairs (central to Western religion and philosophy) promotes ignorance about its effects and produces disastrous blindness and imprudence in political affairs. By contrast, he held that morality is entwined with power and knowledge, having an extremely pervasive, yet usually unexamined impact on nearly all action, blocking critical reflection and favoring instant responses ([1888] 1968: 65, 173). His declaration that 'we are unknown to ourselves' refers to morality's blinders ([1887] 1969: 15). Traveling a slippery slope later traversed by Weber, he warned about treating morality as a separate domain, but still called for restraining moralizing impulses to make obdurate cultural and corporeal 'realities' visible as well as to enhance life.

Especially in his later work, Nietzsche spoke passionately about living 'without illusions', 'saying Yes to reality', and the 'self-overcoming of morality' ([1886] 1966: 50; [1888] 1969: 218, 272, 328, 331). He praised highly a type of 'immoralism' or 'modesty' that allows us to 'see' and approach inconvenient, unexpected, strange, unpleasant 'realities', engage plural 'truths' and expose the 'limits of reason' ([1888] 1968: 62–6, 123–5, 162–75). He saw this realism as prefiguring postmodern beings, able to stand 'above morality' without 'anxious stiffness' or fear of 'falling' and, thus, to accept uncertainty, embrace diversity and exert responsibility ([1886] 1966: 145–98; [1882] 1974: 98, 164, 331–2). This immoralism, directed against the fanatic and true believer, manifests a facet of Nietzsche's thought that Marcuse embraced, stressing a more joyful, creative, rich, uninhibited life, in touch with the body and less constrained by political power.

Even if one finds Nietzsche's overall speculations about Western culture to be dubious, his antipolitical side encourages enquiry that goes beyond the manifest forms of material and ideological power, emphasizing the role of morality in creating psychic dependence and mass obedience *within* social movements and political organizations. He had a strong 'suspicion' of the moral vocabularies that claim to counter or overcome power, especially highhanded declarations about liberating people or defending community. Weber's Nietzschean points about 'pseudo-ethical self-righteousness' and 'psychic proletarianization' suggest a type of demagogic manipulation that regiments people by stirring up fanatical emotionalism, dulling sensitivity to consequences and cultivating hatred of enemies ([1918] 1958: 125). Nietzsche argued that political morality commands obedience by shame, censure and guilt, causing already resentful followers to act in obsequious ways, become more resentful and direct their self-degradation and anger outward toward conventional targets. In his view, such morality is a prime source of cheap and cowardly forms of aggression, passed off as good reputation or trustworthiness among friends. Like other complex aspects of culture, political morality, has multiple directions and felicitous as well as harmful sides. However, Nietzsche offered valuable insight into its usually ignored, yet very important relation to power.

From this Nietzschean standpoint, morality has operated centrally in Stalinism, the Holocaust, the slaughter in Kampuchea, Jonestown, Serbian ethnic cleansing, US racism and Christian anti-semitism. Nietzschean suspicion challenges claims that authoritarian politics originate from an absence of morality and is best resisted by moral crusades. It questions moralizing silences (for example, how righteous indignation about terror in the Middle East might dull us to the plight of Palestinians). It also exposes the 'kinder–gentler' types of demagoguery closer to home. For example, it detects a dynamic of resentment, guilt and hostility in the left-liberal politics of difference, voice and discursive democracy as well as among the hard right and mainstream liberals. The later twentieth-century cultural left deployed their deconstructive insights about power and morality *externally* as a political weapon to expose enemy depredations. These latter-day 'Nietzscheans' seldom 'problematized' their own moralizing discourse and its relations to power. Nietzschean suspicion should be strong in the circle of friends (a center of struggles for self-recognition and identity and of moralistic self-deception) as well as in enemy domains. Properly aimed, it generates complex types of criticism, yields surprises and exposes much more non-linear, ambiguous, contradictory moral terrain than is revealed in conventional deconstruction.

The Nietzschean antipolitical lens offers means for attuning ourselves to psychic proletarianization in our own thought and acts. For example, we 'critical theorists' might detect self-censoring forms of power and regimentation in our writing or speech as we couch words or accede to expected silences about ethically objectionable facets of our own groups and of favored thinkers in order to avoid being branded as 'reactionary', 'racist', or 'liberal' or to position ourselves in a politically or academically

propitious fashion. This lens may help us diminish the normalizing acts in our reading, writing, teaching and politics. Nietzschean immoralism is, ironically, a heightened form of ethical imagination, which might enhance our politics by making them more self-reflexive and critical. In the early twentieth century, Bourne and Dewey both argued that a powerful Puritan thread was still very much alive in North America, being manifested in progressive as well as establishment politics. The same is still true today. Nietzsche offers a valuable tool for decoding the high-handed ways of our micropolitics as well as our national politics. Yet it also sheds light on the protofascist 'politics of ethnos', which trots out Gramsci along with Nietzsche to seduce by moral means. The likely return of Marx need not push antipolitical Nietzscheanism into the grave. This side of Nietzsche might even be an ally of Marxism and critical social theory, combating repetition of the moral and political excesses of totalizing forms of theory and politics.

NOTES

Many detailed endnotes have had to be dropped, because of space limitations. The original essay is available from the author. Many thanks to George Ritzer for his critical comments. This chapter is dedicated to Pasquale and Maria Caracciolo, Nietzsche *aficionados* and no 'last men'.

1 Bracketed dates designate either the original date of publication or the approximate time when the work was written or formulated. These dates provide historical reference points for major works by important authors.

2 On Nietzsche and politics, see, e.g., Bataille, 1985: 182–96; Habermas, 1987; Hughes, [1958] 1977; Kaufmann, [1950] 1974; Lukács, [1962] 1980; Schutte, 1986; Strong, 1988; Thomas, 1986; Warren, 1988.

3 The passage as quoted here is from Schluchter, 1989: 316, and appeared in the original German in Baumgarten, 1964: 554.

4 This essay is about 'social theory'. By contrast to 'sociological theory's' primarily empirical, hermeneutic, or analytical intent and usual 'middle-range' disciplinary focus, 'social theory' has a strong, yet not exclusive, 'normative thrust', addressing issues of societal or trans-societal scope and posing questions about the 'value' of different directions or programs of sociocultural development, knowledge, and policy.

5 'Nietzscheans' often argue that even their departures from Nietzsche somehow remain Nietzschean. See, e.g., Heidegger, quoted in Krell, 1987: 293 and Foucault, 1989: 327.

6 The New Right emphasizes: the 'primacy of culture', 'cultural identity', 'cultural politics' and

'cultural hegemony'; a virulent 'anti-universalism' and bitter opposition to Enlightenment grand narratives and difference-blind social rights; all-pervasive power-knowledge; 'standpoint theories' that stress the incommensurability of culture and impossibility of communication, consensus and uncoerced cooperation across 'ethnos' or cultural groups; and the 'politics of ethnos' over the 'politics of demos' (Antonio, 2000b).

REFERENCES

Adorno, Theodor ([1951] 1978) *Minima Moralia: Reflections From a Damaged Life* (trans. E.F.N. Jephcott). London and New York: Verso.

Adorno, Theodor ([1967] 1981) *Prisms* (trans. Samuel and Shierry Weber). Cambridge, MA: MIT Press.

Anderson, Perry (1983) *In the Tracks of Historical Materialism*. London: Verso.

Anderson, Perry (1998) *The Origins of Postmodernity*. London and New York: Verso.

Antonio, Robert J. (1981) 'Immanent Critique as the Core of Critical Theory: Its Origins and Developments in Hegel, Marx and Contemporary Thought', *British Journal of Sociology*, 32: 330–45.

Antonio, Robert J. (1989) 'The Normative Foundations of Emancipatory Theory: Evolutionary Versus Pragmatic Perspectives', *American Journal of Sociology*, 94: 721–48.

Antonio, Robert J. (1990) 'The Decline of the Grand Narrative of Emancipatory Modernity: Crisis or Renewal in Neo-Marxian Theory?', in George Ritzer (ed.), *Frontiers of Social Theory: The New Syntheses*. New York: Columbia University Press. pp. 88–116.

Antonio, Robert J. (1995) 'Nietzsche's Antisociology: Subjectified Culture and the End of History', *American Journal of Sociology*, 101: 1–43.

Antonio, Robert J. (1998) 'Mapping Postmodern Social Theory', in Alan Sica (ed.), *What is Social Theory? The Philosophical Debates*. Malden, MA and Oxford: Blackwell. pp. 22–75.

Antonio, Robert J. (2000a) 'Karl Marx', in George Ritzer (ed.), *The Blackwell Companion to the Major Social Theorists*. Malden, MA and Oxford: Blackwell. pp. 105–43.

Antonio, Robert J. (2000b) 'After Postmodernism: Reactionary Tribalism', *American Journal of Sociology*.

Antonio, Robert J. and Kellner, Douglas (1992) 'Metatheorizing Historical Rupture: Classical Theory and Modernity', in George Ritzer (ed.), *Metatheorizing*. Newbury Park, CA and London: Sage. pp. 88–106.

Aronson, Ronald (1995) *After Marxism*. New York and London: Guilford Press.

Aschheim, Steven E. (1992) *The Nietzsche Legacy in Germany, 1890–1990*. Berkeley, CA: University of California Press.

Baier, Horst (1981–2) 'Die Gessellschaft – ein langer

Schatten des toten Gottes: Friedrich Nietzsche und die Entstehung der Soziologie aus dem Geist der "Décadence" und "Diskussion"', *Nietzsche Studien*, 10/11: 6–33.

Barber, Benjamin R. (1996) *Jihad vs. McWorld: How Globalism and Tribalism are Reshaping the World*. New York: Ballantine Books.

Bataille, Georges (1985) *Visions of Excess: Selected Writings, 1927–1939* (ed. Allan Stoekl, and trans. Allan Stoekl with Carl R. Lovitt and Donald M. Leslie Jr). Minneapolis: University of Minnesota Press.

Baudrillard, Jean (1983a) *Simulations* (trans. Paul Foss, Paul Patton and Phillip Beitchman). New York: Semiotext(e).

Baudrillard, Jean (1983b) *In the Shadow of the Silent Majorities or, The End of the Social and Other Essays* (trans. Paul Foss, John Johnston and Paul Patton). New York: Semiotext(e).

Baudrillard, Jean (1987) *Forget Foucault and Forget Baudrillard (An Interview with Sylvère Lotringer)*. New York: Semiotext(e).

Bauman, Zygmunt (1992) *Intimations of Postmodernity*. London and New York: Routledge.

Baumgarten, Eduard (1964) *Max Weber: Work and Person*. Tübingen: J.C.B. Mohr.

Beck, Ulrich (1992) *Risk Society: Towards a New Modernity* (trans. Mark Ritter). London: Sage.

Beck, Ulrich, Giddens, Anthony and Lash, Scott (1994) *Reflexive Modernization: Politics, Tradition and Aesthetics in the Modern Social Order*. Stanford, CA: Stanford University Press.

Bell, Daniel (1990) 'Resolving the Contradictions of Modernity and Modernism', *Society*, 27 (March/April): 43–50.

Benhabib, Seyla (1986) *Critique, Norm, and Utopia: A Study in the Foundations of Critical Theory*. New York: Columbia University Press.

Betz, Hans-George (1994) *Radical Right-Wing Populism in Western Europe*. New York: St Martin's Press.

Betz, Hans-George and Immerfall, Stefan (eds) (1998) *The New Politics of the Right: Neo-Populist Parties and Movements in Established Democracies*. New York: St Martin's Press.

Bloom, Allan (1987) *The Closing of the American Mind*. Touchstone Books: New York.

Bourne, Randolph S. ([1917] 1964a) 'The War and the Intellectuals', in Carl Resek (ed.), *War and the Intellectuals: Essays by Randolph S. Bourne, 1915–1919*. New York: Harper and Row. pp. 3–14.

Bourne, Randolph S. ([1917] 1946b) 'Twilight of the Idols', in Carl Resek (ed.), *War and the Intellectuals: Essays by Randolph S. Bourne, 1915–1919*. New York: Harper and Row. pp. 53–64.

Cassidy, John (1997) 'The Return of Karl Marx', *The New Yorker*, 20/27 October: 248–59.

Dahl, Göran (1996) 'Will "the Other God" Fail Again? On the Possible Return of the Conservative

Revolution', *Theory, Culture, and Society*, 13 (1): 25–50.

Derrida, Jacques (1994) *Specters of Marx: The State of the Debt, the Work of Mourning and the New International* (trans. Peggy Kamuf). New York and London: Routledge.

Eagleton, Terry (1996) *The Illusions of Postmodernism.* Oxford and Cambridge, MA: Blackwell.

Ferry, Luc (1994) 'The Three Phases of Modern Philosophy: Tasks for a Secularized Thought', *Thesis Eleven*, 37: 1–9.

Ferry, Luc and Renaut, Alain (1990) *French Philosophy of the Sixties: An Essay on Antihumanism* (trans. Mary H.S. Cattani). Amherst, MA: University of Massachusetts Press.

Ferry, Luc and Renaut, Alain (1997) 'What Must First be Proved is Worth Little', in L. Ferry and A. Renaut (eds), *Why We Are Not Nietzscheans* (trans. Robert de Loaiza). Chicago and London: University of Chicago Press. pp. 92–109.

Foucault, Michel (1980) *Power/Knowledge: Selected Interviews and Other Writings 1972–1977* (ed. Colin Gordon and trans. Colin Gordon, Leo Marshall, John Mepham, and Kate Soper). New York: Pantheon Books.

Foucault, Michel (1989) *Foucault Live: (Interviews 1966–84)* (ed. Sylvère Lotringer and trans. John Johnson). New York: Semiotext(e).

Giddens, Anthony (1994) *Beyond Left and Right: The Future of Radical Politics.* Stanford, CA: Stanford University Press.

Habermas, Jürgen (1987) *The Philosophical Discourse of Modernity* (trans. Frederick Lawrence). Cambridge, MA: MIT Press.

Heidegger, Martin ([1943] 1977) 'The Word of Nietzsche: "God is Dead"', in Martin Heidegger, *The Question Concerning Technology and Other Essays* (ed. and trans. William Lovitt). New York: Harper Torchbooks. pp. 53–112.

Heidegger, Martin ([1953] 1961) *An Introduction to Metaphysics* (trans. Ralph Manheim). Garden City, NY: Anchor Books.

Heidegger, Martin ([1961] 1991a) *The Will to Power as Art*, Vol. 1: *Nietzsche* (trans. David Farrell Krell). New York: HarperCollins.

Heidegger, Martin ([1961] 1991b) *The Will to Power as Knowledge and as Metaphysics*, Vol. 3: *Nietzsche* (ed. David Farrell Krell and trans. Joan Stambaugh, David Farrell Krell and Frank A. Capuzzi). New York: HarperCollins.

Heidegger, Martin ([1961] 1991c) *Nihilism*, Vol. 4: *Nietzsche* (ed. David Farrell Krell and trans. Frank A. Capuzzi). New York: HarperCollins.

Hughes, H. Stuart ([1952] 1962) *Oswald Spengler: A Critical Estimate.* New York: Charles Scribner's Sons.

Hughes, H. Stuart ([1958] 1977) *Consciousness and Society: The Reorientation of European Social Theory, 1890–1930.* New York: Vintage Books.

Jameson, Fredric (1991) *Postmodernism, or, The Cultural Logic of Late Capitalism.* Durham, NC: Duke University Press.

Jencks, Charles (1985) *Modern Movements in Architecture.* Harmondsworth: Penguin Books.

Kaufmann, Walter ([1950] 1974) *Nietzsche: Philosopher, Psychologist, Antichrist.* Princeton, NJ: Princeton University Press.

Kolnai, Aurel (1938) *The War Against the West.* New York: The Viking Press.

Krell, David Farrell (1987) 'Analysis', in Martin Heidegger ([1961] 1991) *Nihilism*, Vol. 4: *Nietzsche* (ed. David Farrell Krell and trans. Frank J. Capuzzi). New York: HarperCollins. pp. 253–94.

Laclau, Ernesto and Mouffe, Chantal (1985) *Hegemony and Socialist Strategy: Towards a Radical Democratic Politics.* London and New York: Verso.

Lefebvre, Henri ([1962] 1995) *Introduction to Modernity: Twelve Preludes, September 1959–May 1961* (trans. John Moore). London and New York: Verso.

Love, S. Nancy (1986) *Marx, Nietzsche, and Modernity.* New York: Columbia University Press.

Löwith, Karl ([1939] 1991) *From Hegel to Nietzsche: The Revolution in Nineteenth Century Thought* (trans. David E. Green). New York: Columbia University Press.

Löwith, Karl ([1940] 1994) *My Life in Germany Before and After 1933* (trans. Elizabeth King). Urbana, IL: University of Illinois Press.

Lukács, Georg ([1962] 1980) *The Destruction of Reason* (trans. Peter Palmer). London: The Merlin Press.

Lyotard, Jean-François ([1979] 1984) *The Postmodern Condition: A Report on Knowledge* (trans. Geoff Bennington and Brian Massumi). Minneapolis: University of Minnesota Press.

Mann, Thomas ([1918] 1983) *Reflections of a Non-political Man* (trans. Walter D. Morris). New York: Frederick Unger.

Marcuse, Herbert ([1955] 1966) *Eros and Civilization: A Philosophical Inquiry into Freud.* Boston, MA: Beacon Press.

Marcuse, Herbert (1964) *One-Dimensional Man: Studies in the Ideology of Advanced Industrial Society.* Boston, MA: Beacon Press.

Marx, Karl ([1837] 1975) 'Letter from Marx to his Father: in Trier', *Karl Marx Frederick Engels: Collected Works.* Vol. 1: *Karl Marx, 1835–1843.* New York: International Publishers. pp. 10–21.

Mellucci, Alberto (1989) *Nomads of the Present: Social Movements and Individual Needs in Contemporary Society.* Philadelphia: Temple University Press.

Mellucci, Alberto (1996a) *Challenging Codes: Collective Action in the Information Age.* Cambridge and New York: Cambridge University Press.

Mellucci, Alberto (1996b) *The Playing Self: Person and Meaning in the Planetary Society.* Cambridge and New York: Cambridge University Press.

Miller, James (1993) *The Passion of Michel Foucault.* New York and London: Anchor Books.

Nicholson, Linda and Seidman, Steven (1995) 'Introduction', in Linda Nicholson and Steven Seidman (eds), *Social Postmodernism: Beyond Identity Politics*. Cambridge and New York: Cambridge University Press. pp. 1–35.

Nietzsche, Friedrich ([1873–1876] 1983) *Untimely Meditations* (trans. R.J. Hollingdale). Cambridge: Cambridge University Press.

Nietzsche, Friedrich ([1882] 1974) *The Gay Science: With a Prelude in Rhymes and an Appendix of Songs* (trans. Walter Kaufmann). New York: Vintage Books.

Nietzsche, Friedrich ([1883–1885] 1969) *Thus Spoke Zarathustra* (trans. R.J. Hollingdale). London: Penguin Books.

Nietzsche, Friedrich ([1886] 1966) *Beyond Good and Evil: Prelude to a Philosophy of the Future* (trans. Walter Kauffmann). New York: Vintage Books.

Nietzsche, Friedrich ([1887] 1969) *On the Genealogy of Morals* (trans. Walter Kaufmann and R.J. Hollingdale). New York: Vintage Books.

Nietzsche, Friedrich ([1888] 1968) *Twilight of the Idols* (Vol 1) and *The Anti-Christ* (vol. 2), (trans. R.J. Hollingdale). London: Penguin Books.

Nietzsche, Friedrich ([1888] 1969) *Ecce Homo*, in Nietzsche, *On the Genealogy of Morals* (trans. Walter Kaufmann). New York: Vintage Books. pp. 199–335.

Offe, Claus (1996) *Modernity and the State: East, West*. Cambridge, MA: MIT Press.

Ricoeur, Paul (1970) *Freud and Philosophy: An Essay on Interpretation* (trans. Denis Savage). New Haven, CT: Yale University Press.

Rorty, Richard (1998) *Achieving Our Country: Leftist Thought in Twentieth-Century America*. Cambridge, MA and London: Harvard University Press.

Sassoon, Donald (1996) *One Hundred Years of Socialism: The West European Left in the Twentieth Century*. New York: The New Press.

Schluchter, Wolfgang (1989) *Rationalism, Religion, and Domination: A Weberian Perspective* (trans. Neil Solomon). Berkeley, CA: University of California Press.

Schmitt, Carl ([1932] 1996) *The Concept of the Political* (trans. George Schwab). Chicago and London: University of Chicago Press.

Schutte, Ofelia (1986) *Beyond Nihilism: Nietzsche Without Masks*. Chicago and London: University of Chicago Press.

Simmel, Georg ([1900] 1978) *The Philosophy of Money* (trans. Tom Bottomore and David Frisby). London: Routledge and Kegan Paul.

Sluga, Hans (1995) *Heidegger's Crisis: Philosophy and Politics in Nazi Germany*. Cambridge, MA and London: Harvard University Press.

Spengler, Oswald ([1918–1922] 1991) *The Decline of the West* (abridged edition by Helmut Werner and trans. Charles Francis Atkinson; ed. abridged English edition by Arthur Helps). New York and Oxford: Oxford University Press.

Stephens, Julie (1998) *Anti-Disciplinary Protest: Sixties Radicalism and Postmodernism*. Cambridge and New York: Cambridge University Press.

Strauss, Leo ([1975] 1989) *An Introduction to Political Philosophy: Ten Essays by Leo Strauss* (ed. Hilail Gildin). Detroit: Wayne State University Press.

Strong, Tracy B. (1988) *Friedrich Nietzsche and the Politics of Transformation: Expanded Edition*. Berkeley, CA: University of California Press.

Thomas, R. Hinton (1986) *Nietzsche in German Politics and Society, 1890–1918*. La Salle, IL: Open Court.

Wallerstein, Immanuel (1998) *Utopistics: Or, Historical Choices of the Twenty-First Century*. New York: The New Press.

Warren, Mark (1988) *Nietzsche and Political Thought*. Cambridge, MA: MIT Press.

Weber, Marianne ([1926] 1975) *Max Weber: A Biography* (trans. and ed. Harry Zohn). New York and London: John Wiley and Sons.

Weber, Max ([1904] 1949) '"Objectivity" in Social Science and Social Policy', in Edward A. Shils and Henry A. Finch (ed. and trans.), *The Methodology of the Social Sciences*. Glencoe, IL: The Free Press. pp. 49–112.

Weber, Max ([1918] 1958a) 'Politics as a Vocation', in H.H. Gerth and C. Wright Mills (ed. and trans.), *From Max Weber*. New York: Oxford University Press. pp. 77–128.

Weber, Max ([1918] 1958b) 'Science as a vocation', in H.H. Gerth and C. Wright Mills (ed. and trans.), *From Max Weber*. New York: Oxford University Press. pp. 129–56.

Weber, Max ([1921] 1958) 'National character and the Junkers', in H.H. Gerth and C. Wright Mills (ed. and trans.), *From Max Weber*. New York: Oxford University Press. pp. 386–95.

Westbrook, Robert B. (1991) *John Dewey and American Democracy*. Ithaca, NY and London: Cornell University Press.

Wolin, Richard (1990) *The Politics of Being: The Political Thought of Martin Heidegger*. New York: Columbia University Press.

Wood, Ellen Meiksins (1986) *The Retreat From Class: A New 'True' Socialism*. London: Verso.

Wood, Ellen Meiksins (1995) *Democracy Against Capitalism: Renewing Historical Materialism*. Cambridge and New York: Cambridge University Press.

Žižek, Slavoj (1997) 'Multiculturalism, or, the Cultural Logic of Multinational Capitalism', *New Left Review*, 225: 28–51.

15

Critical Theory

CRAIG CALHOUN AND JOSEPH KARAGANIS

The term 'critical theory' is generally associated with the group of German social theorists affiliated with the Institute for Social Research. Founded in Frankfurt in 1923, the Institute sought to conduct social research that would examine the contradictions of modernity, interrogate the limits of the present order, and overcome the limitations of modern social and philosophical thought. In pursuing these objectives, the 'Frankfurt School' (as the founders and early staff of the Institute came to be known) built on the combined foundations of Marxism, idealist philosophy and psychoanalysis as well as empirically oriented sociology.

The core members of the early Frankfurt School included Max Horkheimer, long-time director of the Institute, Theodore Adorno, and Herbert Marcuse. While the label 'critical theory' is sometimes used synonymously with their work (and they sometimes claimed to be the only truly critical theorists of their generation), it is misleading to use the label for the Frankfurt School exclusively. This makes critical theory appear to be much more rigid and fixed than it ever was or can be. Not only are there innovations by new generations of theorists – as with any vital theoretical tradition – the Frankfurt School founders insisted on a conception of critical theory as always embedded in processes of historical change, providing both an analytical perspective on the present and a lever on the future. In this, Horkheimer, Adorno and Marcuse were all influenced by Marx's dictum that 'the philosophers have only *interpreted* the world . . . the point, however, is to change it' (Marx, 1978: 145). Changing the world, as Marx had argued, did not imply rejecting theoretical enquiry in favor of action, but rather over-

coming that opposition. The idea of theory, Frankfurt theorists argued, needed to be recovered from a cerebral and abstract philosophical tradition that failed to challenge the social status quo; it needed to be made useful in movements that would bring about radical and liberatory social change.

From the Enlightenment on, philosophers and social theorists drew an opposition between tradition and modernity. This tended, however, to present modernity too simply and universally, as though it were internally homogenous and moved in only one direction. In the dialectical tradition of Hegel and Marx, the Frankfurt School argued that modernity was internally complex and even contradictory. It was necessary to grasp it as an unfolding of contradictory potentials in history which included Nazism and Stalinism as well as the rise of democracy and science. Speaking of history here means both being specific about differences within modernity and seeing theory itself as part of history, shaped by the conditions under which it is developed.

This is one reason why critical theory should not be identified exclusively with the original Frankfurt theorists. It is a more general project of reflection on the possibilities and realities of modernity in which a wider range of theorists participate. In the first place, the original Frankfurt theorists were often divided on important questions – especially the potential for revolutionary change. They also engaged closely with contemporaries such as Walter Benjamin, who were never strictly part of the Institute for Social Research. A second generation of the Frankfurt School – including most famously Jürgen Habermas, but also Albrecht

Wellmer and others – has directly and provocatively engaged earlier Frankfurt School work. A third generation has risen to prominence with theorists like Axel Honneth in Germany and Seyla Benhabib in the United States. But the project of critical theory – and aspects of the direct legacy of the original Frankfurt School – shapes a much wider range of work. In its broader sense, critical theory shares important ground with analyses of totalizing social processes and epochal change by Michel Foucault and François Lyotard, with Pierre Bourdieu's efforts to theorize the relationship between human action and the reproduction of social order, and with Jacques Derrida's critical approach to philosophical history.

This chapter focuses most intensively on the original Frankfurt School, partly because other chapters in the present book take up many of the relevant later theorists. We emphasize on the first generation of Frankfurt School critical theorists and their core ideas and contributions. We stress the interdisciplinary nature of the Institute's work, which tried – not always successfully – to create a framework for integrating philosophy, psychology, cultural criticism and empirical sociology.[1] The second section considers direct extensions of the Frankfurt School legacy, especially in the work of Habermas. The third considers the relationship of critical theory to Foucault, Bourdieu and other figures of postmodernism and post-structuralism.

FRANKFURT SCHOOL FOUNDATIONS

Though the Frankfurt theorists saw philosophy as limited by both its distance from social action and its distance from empirical enquiry, they drew heavily on conceptions of critique embedded in German philosophical traditions. Kant, Hegel and Nietzsche were all important alongside Marx, Weber, and Freud. In this tradition, 'critique' means not simply criticism, but rather a deep examination of the conditions under which any particular form of thinking could operate. Four dimensions of this project are crucial.

First, the conditions of knowledge itself are not self-evident but must be examined critically. While we certainly gain knowledge of the world from our senses, critical theory insists that this is hardly the whole story. Our visual sense organs respond differently to stimuli from different wavelengths of light. This is the basis for our perception of color. But in itself, it doesn't tell us how to divide the colors from each other – where, for example, blue shades into turquoise or teal. These distinctions depend on language

and on social learning that guides the use of language. Similarly, we can gain knowledge of mathematics with a kind of purity and certainty that is different from knowledge of the empirical world (though even mathematics does not allow perfect certainty and freedom from arbitrariness or contradiction). We also mean something different by 'knowing' an empirical fact like the number of pages in a book and 'knowing' whether a painting is beautiful or an action ethically right. The latter are examples of judgement and 'practical reason' that can be better or worse without necessarily being true or false. All this is important to various kinds of empirical and theoretical enquiry. Its specific importance for critical theory lies in the fact that human beings see the same empirical world, but use different languages, concepts, ideologies, and theories to understand it. Critical theory includes as part of its task the effort to analyse the effects of these different ways of knowing and judging the world.

Secondly, critical analysis reveals that reality itself is not simply a matter of surface appearances but of underlying causes and conditions, which are not adequately understood by empirical generalization. Theoretical analysis is required in order to understand why things are one way and not another – why for example capitalism predominates in the contemporary world, or why people rely on courts to resolve disputes. A critical understanding of the world as it exists is necessarily historical. It considers the conditions necessary for any particular patterns – biological or physical as well as social – to have arisen and persisted. In the case of society, this critical perspective is especially important, for it reveals the omnipresence of change, and thus the potential for the social world to be reshaped by social action. Capitalism, thus, is not simply a fact of nature but the result of historical processes. A key aspect of the Frankfurt School approach involved using critical theory to uncover 'reification', or the tendency for products of human action to appear as though they were 'things', products of nature rather than human choices.[2]

Thirdly, based in part on the first two senses of critique, critical theory seeks to analyse social theory itself in terms of the basic categories of understanding different theories employ. Theory develops historically not simply by rejecting earlier efforts, but by analysing them and uncovering their limits. It is in this sense that Marx subtitled his major work, Capital, 'a critique of political economy'. Marx did not mean simply a criticism, but rather an examination of classical political economy (the economics of his day) that sought to reveal the basic categories used and their limits. Through such an analysis, a critical theorist seeks not only to develop a better theory, one which can incorporate the advances of previous theory as well as innovations, but also to explain why other theories reached limits they could not transcend. Critical theory thus sees scientific theory in historical terms, not as uncovering timeless truths, but as analysing an ever-changing world by means of intellectual categories that may prove more or less adequate to grasping what is going on. Where such categories reflect an affirmation of the status quo, or of certain powerful interests, they may be criticized as ideologically biased. More generally, though, there are potential limits to the adequacy of all categories, and things they will obscure even while they reveal others.[3] For this reason, the critical theorist seeks always to apply this same sort of critical analysis to his or her own theoretical inheritance and work.

Fourthly, critical theory is shaped by a critical engagement with society. This means not simply that critical theorists have preferences and offer opinions about society. Rather, it means that critical theory seeks to achieve a unity of theory and practice (which the early Frankfurt Theorists followed Marx in calling *praxis*). Critical theory is thus developed with the knowledge that it is an action in society, not some kind of external view on society. Indeed, a central point of critical theory is that all scientific work is located inside society, not outside. Some social scientists pretend that their standpoints, histories, bases in social institutions and political engagements don't matter, but critical theory suggests that this is never altogether true. The task for social science is not to cut itself off from society, but to make explicit and criticizable the social bases on which it stands.[4] Critical theorists try to study topics that are of direct social importance, not of 'purely academic' interest, and to do so in ways that enable critical awareness to become more widespread. They try to offer less distorting, clearer and more adequate categories for understanding social phenomena.

The first generation of Frankfurt School critical theorists always insisted on the historical embeddedness of theory. They recurrently criticized those who presented theory as though it could adopt a position outside of history, and those who imagined that theory would somehow explain social change without itself being transformed by it. This was especially important for a theory that sought direct involvement in processes of social change. Looking at the world around them in the 1930s, Horkheimer and Adorno concluded, for example, that Nazism and Stalinism closed off certain historical possibilities – including the older Marxist idea of class struggle and proletarian revolution. Indeed, the experience of totalitarianism, the war against it and exile in America left Horkheimer and Adorno extremely pessimistic about the immediate prospects for radical social change. They took solace in considering their work a heritage (a 'message in a bottle') on which other theorists could build when changing historical conditions opened new possibilities. Like history itself, theoretical enquiry would remain open-ended.

All the Frankfurt theorists recognized the crisis that the rise of totalitarianism represented for Marxist theory. With the victories of Stalinism and Nazism, Marxist social theorists were confronted with seemingly incontestable evidence that the working class, long held to be the vehicle of social emancipation, had contributed to these disasters of Western civilization. Moreover, totalitarianism signaled the apparent demise not only of Marxism's liberatory promises, but also, in their view, those of liberalism and more generally the Enlightenment. Much of Horkheimer, Adorno and Marcuse's work of the late 1930s is an attempt to reconcile Marxism with this outcome, reconceiving the history of capitalism without the radically oppositional social position previously attributed to the working class.

Important, too, was the experience of exile in America, where the Frankfurt School relocated in 1934 after Hitler's rise to power. There, the relative integration and accommodation of working-class radicalism suggested the efficacy of other, less direct ways of suppressing social contradictions. Over time, the analysis of totalitarianism and American capitalism led the Frankfurt School away from the Marxist preoccupation with modes of production, class struggle, and the primacy of the economy toward a much more global and ultimately pessimistic cultural analysis. This centered on a critical analysis of the ways in which reason, a source of liberation in Enlightenment thought, had been harnessed to a project of rationalization that was potentially imprisoning. Indebted to Max Weber's image of an 'iron cage' of instrumental rationality, they analysed the ways in which both bureaucratic states and large-scale capitalism limited human potential. This led them to develop theories of the administered society. Tensions between government and capitalist corporations could be reduced and the two sides could collaborate in using techniques of mass persuasion (political campaigns, advertising) to create a population that sought material gains within the existing system rather than a more fundamental liberation from it. This new system allowed people to participate and feel that they had choices as consumers (of political candidates as well as industrial products), but the choices were limited by the emergence of mass culture and the deployment of its instruments by states and corporations. The limited choices offered only discouraged the development of real opposition to the existing order.

The key point of reference for these critiques was the reduction of the broad human capacity for reason to an instrument of domination – over nature, and increasingly over human beings. Enlightenment thinkers had seen reason as full of promise, because they thought people would use their reason to critically analyse all existing social institutions and create better ones. Subsequent history, however, showed capitalism and the state successfully harnessing reason to merely technical tasks in production and government. Instead of using reason to emancipate people from power relations and the constraints of material necessity, the dominant forces in society had created new institutions and processes – states, markets, that seemed beyond the control of human actors and increasingly beyond their power to critique or challenge them. People felt helpless before giant global corporations and capitalist markets as before totalitarian states – and indeed, this very feeling of helplessness and alienation was one of the reasons why people willingly acquiesced to totalitarian governments. The Frankfurt School sought to demonstrate how the liberation that might have attended the growth of human power had turned against itself, producing the horrors of the twentieth century.

This was the essence of Horkheimer and Adorno's critique of the Enlightenment and the culture industry in *Dialectic of Enlightenment* (1987). The problem was a simple one: 'the Enlightenment has always aimed at liberating men from fear and establishing their sovereignty. Yet the fully enlightened earth radiates disaster triumphant' (1987: 3). This contradiction underwrote much of the Frankfurt School work, from Freudian-inspired connections between paternal authority and fascism to Marcuse's later vision of one-dimensional society. And yet their writing constantly, if not always consistently, struggles against this totalization, seeking to identify resources for critique and social transformation. Here, despite obvious differences in scale, belong Adorno's interest in negative dialectics and the critical, utopian energy of modern art, Marcuse's hopes for a culture-wide 'desublimation' of libido, and Walter Benjamin's attention to the possibility of historical ruptures. The work of Jürgen Habermas is perhaps the dominant contemporary articulation of this search for liberatory resources, extending the analysis of the systemic integration of modern society, while re-establishing the consideration of emancipatory human agency and ethics.

In analysing these issues, the Frankfurt School developed a strongly interdisciplinary approach that drew from a range of sources, including Marxism, psychoanalysis, German idealism, romanticism, art history and aesthetics. The major early figures were somewhat less attentive to political economy, although Frankfurt School members such as Friedrich Pollack and Franz Neumann made important contributions in these areas.

Two broad issues will open up much of this complexity in the next pages: first, the constant concern among the Frankfurt critical theorists for the negative moment of social critique – the negation of the status quo that Marx had assigned to the proletariat, but which the Frankfurt theorists had enormous difficulty in attributing to any historical actors of the day. This inability had consequences not only for the prospects of social change but for the status of critical theory itself, which often self-reflexively examined the isolated character of modern intellectual activity. Negation would become a major subject of contention, too, in theories of post-structuralism and postmodernism, as we shall see.

The second issue is a recurring historical dynamic in the work of the Frankfurt theorists: the progressive loss of the structures that mediated between the individual and systems of economic, cultural and political power, to the point that individuality becomes a simple extension of integrated social forces. The early Frankfurt theorists explained the rise and efficacy of totalitarianism in terms of the emergence of increasingly direct forms of domination – forms that ruthlessly eliminated other sites of authority and resources for autonomy such as class, the family and law. Only the state, and its condensed expression in cults-of-personality remained. In their postwar work, the Frankfurt theorists extended this general principle toward the analysis of liberal society and the culture industry, crediting the latter with a dismaying power to channel diverse individual desires and needs into fundamentally equivalent consumer choices. Such analysis illuminates another of the Frankfurt School imperatives: the need to treat the present constellation of social power and human possibility as the product of historical and fundamentally human forces, in the hope that recognizing the roots of the present situation will allow people to identify and overcome its limits. Drawing on a long tradition of demystification from Marx to Nietzsche and Freud, critical theory has consistently opposed the reification of the present into an inevitable, natural order. At its best, it is a challenge to take the future seriously.

KANT AND REASON

In essays published in the Institute's journal *Zeitschrift* in the mid and late 1930s, Frankfurt School theorists, especially Horkheimer and Marcuse, began to reflect on the specificity and mission of critical theory – Horkheimer's term for their work. These program statements investigated the possibilities and limitations of contemporary social critique, and turned on the differences between critical theory and what Horkheimer called 'traditional philosophy'. Kant figures prominently in these investigations as the philosopher *par excellence*: both the thinker who culminates the philosophical agenda of Enlightenment, bringing reason fully to bear on the question of human consciousness, and the first representative of philosophical enquiry into the conditions of the age. For theorists as diverse as Michel Foucault and Jürgen Habermas this reflective turn is still seen as effectively inaugurating philosophical modernity.

For the Frankfurt theorists, Kant culminates Enlightenment thought on a number of fronts. He reduces the notion of selfhood to a minimum number of a priori logical categories which order the experience of the senses; he refounds ethics on the purely formal procedure of determining an act's compatibility with universal reason (the categorical imperative); and he justifies the break-up of reason into a series of autonomous domains – pure reason, practical reason and judgement. In so doing, Kant made reason synonymous with the proper categorizing of experience, both as a description of the self and as an ethical posture toward others – in Kantian terms, *duty*.

For Horkheimer, such a conception of ethics suffered from excessive formalism: the demand for universality had no positive content or claim on particular social arrangements; moreover it could justify diametrically opposed forms of behavior. Horkheimer and Adorno made this point in a shocking manner by juxtaposing Kant and the Marquis de Sade (the eighteenth-century contemporary who gave his name to sadism) as the two poles of the Enlightenment: 'What Kant grounded transcendentally . . . Sade realized empirically' (1987: 88). What Kant imagined as a system for achieving universal mutual respect for individuals, Sade imagined as a universal instrumentalization of the human body – of sexual domination and the free use of the other as a categorical and, as Sade demonstrated at length, infinitely categorizable imperative. Much in the same way that Hegel identified the French Revolution's exterminatory search for unanimity as the counterpoint of Kant's ethical formalism, Horkheimer and Adorno criticized Kant for

undermining reason's public function – for advocating a purely subjective form of reason which abandoned the critique of irrational forms of authority and the formulation of positive goals. As Horkheimer argued, 'When the idea of reason was conceived, it was intended to achieve more than the mere regulation of the relation between means and ends: it was regarded as the instrument for understanding the ends, for determining them' (1992a: 38).

Instead, Kant proposed that persons possessed shared capacities, but exercised them in isolation. For Horkheimer, this view exemplified the detached role of the philosopher in bourgeois society: 'The traditional ideal of theory is based on scientific activity as carried on within the division of labor at a particular stage in the latter's development. It corresponds to the activity of the scholar which takes place alongside all the other activities of a society but in no immediately clear connection to them' (1992b: 241–2). As Marcuse argued, this isolation was confirmed by the philosophical preoccupation with consciousness at the expense of explaining, and potentially challenging, concrete, external forms of domination:

> In the bourgeois period, economic conditions determine philosophical thought insofar as it is the emancipated, self-reliant individual who thinks . . . Correspondingly, he appears in philosophy only as an abstract subject, abstracted from his full humanity . . . (I)n every act of cognition the individual must once again re-enact the 'production of the world' and the categorical organization of experience. However, the process never gets any further because the restriction of 'productive' cognition to the transcendental sphere makes any new form of the world impossible. The constitution of the world occurs behind the backs of the individuals; yet it is their work. (Marcuse, 1992: 15)

In other words, Kant's transcendental philosophy 'aroused the belief that the realization of reason through factual transformation was unnecessary, since individuals could become rational and free within the established order' (Marcuse, 1992: 7). This is an area where critical theory strongly marked its difference from philosophies of consciousness, including latter-day versions such as existentialism and phenomenology. For the critical theorists, there could be no internal freedom without external freedom.

DIALECTICS AND NEGATIVITY

Hegelian dialectics, Horkheimer and Adorno noted, marked a major philosophical break with the linear narrative of Enlightenment progress –

the 'dissolution of myths and the substitution of knowledge for fancy' that would accompany the growth of human reason. Instead, Hegel emphasized the way in which Enlightenment reason had undermined itself and produced its opposite – quintessentially in the French revolutionary terror. He contended that this outcome reflected a dialectical process of history that generated opposition and synthesis. Dialectics furnished the law of historical movement and provided a way of contextualizing the disasters of reason (as well as such apparently universal theories of selfhood as Kant's) within a larger framework of human progress. His ascription of agency in this process to a depersonalized notion of 'Spirit', however, and his claims in late work such as *The Philosophy of Right* that objective reason had finally been achieved in the form of the Prussian state, opened the door to a range of critiques in the 1830s and 1840s by a group of scholars known as the Young Hegelians. Most prominent among these were Marx's radical appropriation of dialectics to reveal the contradictions of capitalism and his famous materialist critique of Spirit.

Major elements of this critique remained central to the work of the Frankfurt School (and indeed, to much of the French post-structural movement) a century later. Among these was Marx's revision of the concept of *praxis*. Aristotle, in *Metaphysics*, had distinguished between three basic forms of human activity: praxis, or action which is an end in itself, including the domains of ethics and politics; poiesis, or goal-oriented action, including forms of material production; and theoria, or the production of truth. This framework structured most scientific and philosophical enquiry from the classical era through to Hegel, who continued to endorse a distinction between practical and theoretical knowledge. Post-Hegelian thinkers, however, and especially Marx, substantially revised this model, rejecting the Hegelian effort to displace the unity of practical and theoretical knowledge to a higher level of speculative reality – that of Spirit. Marx described praxis as the creative activity through which human beings created and shaped their world, over and above the labor necessary for their simple survival. Praxis, in this view, was grounded within existing social activity. Theory, insofar as it aimed at transforming society and not at speculative truth about ultimate realities, became a form of praxis.

A fundamental implication of this attack on speculative philosophy was that critique had to proceed from within society, on an *immanent* basis. Contra Hegel, Marcuse observed that 'in [Marx's] work, the negativity of reality becomes a historical condition which cannot be

hypostatized as a metaphysical state of affairs' (1960: 314–15). Negativity – the critique of the present order – is consequently for Marx not an abstract opposition that emerges at the level of ideas, but a concrete opposition between groups – or more specifically, between classes distinguished by their relationship to the means of production. Insofar as the social order reflected the prerogatives of the owners of the means of production – the capitalists – negativity became the property of the working class, the consequence of their structural subordination.

Although the Frankfurt School had been founded with an explicit mandate to study the revolutionary potential of the German working class, Horkheimer's rise to the directorship signaled a shift toward skepticism about this structurally assigned role. The failure of the German left in the early 1930s contributed greatly to this mistrust, although related hopes for the Soviet experiment were not completely dashed – at least for Horkheimer – until the purge trials of the late 1930s. Dissatisfaction with the increasingly rigid and positivist doctrine of the Communist Party was another contributing factor. Following Engels' lead, Marxism in the early part of the century had hardened into a science of history that treated dialectics as an immutable natural logic. By returning to Marxism's foundational enquiry into the meaning and conditions of social negation, the Frankfurt School played a key role in the recovery of the philosophical dimension of Marxism – a recovery that passed through renewed interest in Hegel by Dilthey and even more significantly through Lukác's reconstruction of the theory of alienation and reification in *History and Class Consciousness.*[5]

From this perspective, the formative critical theory of the 1930s was characterized by a widening break with the Marxist account of negativity. This break presented the Frankfurt School writers with their principal theoretical dilemma: the question of whether negativity had any structural place in modern society – any inherent actor. If this was not the working class, or no longer the working class, then where was critical potential to be found? If structural negation was no longer a possibility, then what were the prospects of radical social action? This issue is one of the most significant points of differentiation among the major critical theorists. Horkheimer's early mission statement, 'Traditional and Critical Theory', for instance, tries to salvage working-class negativity from the increasingly stark evidence of its failure by positing an antagonistic relationship between intellectuals (such as himself) and the working class they represented: 'even the situation of the proletariat is, in this society, no guarantee of correct knowledge . . . This truth becomes clearly evident in the person of the theoretician; he exercises an aggressive critique not only against the conscious defenders of the status quo but also against distracting, conformist, or utopian tendencies within his own household . . .' (1992b: 248).

Although Horkheimer tried to reincorporate this antagonism into the Marxist concept of an intellectual vanguard of class struggle, something more fundamental than the proper role of the intellectual was at stake. The broad shift within critical theory toward instrumental reason as the motor of historical development departed from the assumptions of class struggle. No longer could liberation be conceived simply as a matter of reorganizing the relationship between workers and the means of production. The Soviet experience – which Pollack described as 'state capitalism' – was bringing into relief the larger contours of domination that survived such reorganization: the logic of technological mastery over nature and humanity alike, and the reduction of politics to a question of administration and planning. Always vague on the subject of the transition to communism, Marx's labor theory of value not only failed to account for these other dimensions, but embraced instrumentality as long as it remained in the right hands.

Here the Frankfurt theorists can be seen as integrating Marxist analysis with Max Weber's more developed sociological understanding of the state. Equally importantly, much of the Frankfurt theorists' work elaborated an account of rationalization close to Weber's own account of the loss of reason's liberatory potential and the emergence of the 'iron cage' of modernity where rationality meant only the rule-governed character of bureaucracy and the instrumental pursuit of economic gain. Like Weber, Horkheimer, Adorno and many of their colleagues saw this as a collapse of civilization, as the spiritual and aesthetic sides of human existence were sacrificed to the peculiar rationalities of state and market.

TOTALITARIANISM AND THE ANALYSIS OF THE STATE

It is no great exaggeration to see the Frankfurt School's work on mass culture and totalitarianism as an investigation of the forces that undermined negativity in modern society.[6] Marx had envisioned the development of capitalism as a process of intensifying contradiction. Capital would concentrate into fewer and fewer hands, impoverishing an ever-larger percentage of the population; increases in productivity in the form of new technologies would become ever-more costly, and productive capacities would vastly outstrip the power of internal and ultimately external markets to consume goods, leading to worsening cyclical crises of overproduction. On this basis, Marx identified the working class as the world-historical class – an increasingly powerful social force whose radical dispossession would eventually break the ideology of private property and the social order it supported. As capital concentrated in the hands of a few industrialists, the concept of private property, like Kant's notion of reason, achieved a purely formal status. As the Frankfurt theorists argued, it no longer functioned in any broad sense as the material basis for individual autonomy, as it had been in the progressive era of bourgeois society. Rather, the idea of private property mystified the difference between personal possessions and the holdings of impersonal corporations.

Totalitarianism brought this process to a culmination and delivered a decisive blow to the idea that Marx's labor theory underpinned a necessary solidarity of workers in the struggle against capitalism. The Frankfurt School theorists overwhelmingly understood this development as a further outcome of capitalism, although they differed in many particulars. They argued that as capitalism eroded the content of liberal individualism – not only property, but also the family and legal institutions – it undermined the conditions of bourgeois reason, including the basic bourgeois distinction between state and society. Classical liberalism treated society as the product of interaction and agreement among autonomous individuals, but in the mass society of the twentieth century, that kind of autonomous individual was rare. Instead, economic interdependence – with an accent on 'dependence', the opposite of autonomy – was the order of the day. The rise of the culture industry subjected what had once been realms of critical individuality to regimes of mass production. State management reached, moreover, into what had previously been considered private realms.

For the most part, the core Frankfurt School theorists focused on cultural, social psychological and philosophical concerns, which were indeed one dimension of this new pattern in modern society. Horkheimer, Adorno, Marcuse and Walter Benjamin did little empirical research into the finer grain of institutional history and other concrete developments within the capitalist era. They tended to treat state power as a special case of instrumental reason and authority as an objectification of psychological structures. The tasks of linking critical theory to political economy fell more to their colleagues in the Institute for Social Research, especially Friedrich Pollack and Franz Neumann. Other Institute writers – especially Horkheimer – used this work in support of their own, and many of its conclusions would later find a prominent place in the work of Jürgen Habermas among others.

Pollack was a pioneer in studies of the role of the state in modern economies. Throughout the 1930s, he studied the fundamental role of state planning, not only in the Soviet communist case where five-year plans were the rule, but also in the explicitly capitalist economies, including those with democratic regimes. In Western Europe and the United States an unprecedented expansion of the state's mandate in economic affairs was under way, largely in response to capitalism's latest crisis of overproduction, the Great Depression. Increasingly, this role went beyond mere regulation – the hallmark of progressivism in the United States and still an expression of faith in the market mechanism. Instead, the state became an active and even dominant actor in determining production. For Pollack, this new role represented a dramatic politicization of the economy. The state assumed functions previously reserved for the market: the determination of prices and wages, levels of employment and unemployment, and the balancing of supply and demand. This intervention opened the door to totalitarianism, Pollack argued, insofar as it tended toward a 'command economy' in which the mediating institution of the market was abolished. In this context, social relations were determined less by one's relationship to the means of production than by one's access to the power of the state – whence the emergence of state protection rackets and other forms of economic intimidation. Such politicization was manifestly not, in Pollack's view, a stage on the road to socialism, but rather what he called 'state capitalism' – a new social form in which the monopoly power of late capitalism was appropriated by the state in order to suppress the contradictions of the system.[7] Economic planning, forced employment, technological innovation and a large, surplus-absorbing military sector, Pollack argued, provided a durable set of techniques which could prolong the new social order, perhaps indefinitely. The only clear internal weakness of such regimes, he suggested – here echoing a number of Frankfurt School analyses of Nazism – was the irrational nature of the internal struggle for power, which obeyed no efficiency principle and tended toward gangsterism.

Franz Neumann's classic study of Nazism, *Behemoth*, developed a similar line of analysis, but characterized totalitarianism as an advanced form of monopoly capitalism rather than as a new, stable social order. Although he followed Pollack in crediting totalitarianism with the erosion of the distinction between state and economy, he argued that the Nazi regime had not entirely absorbed the economy – a claim evidenced by surviving market control over the 'economic circulation' of many goods and services and by the fact that industry remained, for the most part, in private hands. Moreover, Neumann saw totalitarian measures as primarily a response to the more intense contradictions and greater instability produced by a high degree of monopolization: 'The system has become so fully monopolized that it must by nature be hypersensitive to cyclical changes, and such disturbances must be avoided . . . In short, democracy would endanger the fully monopolized system. It is the essence of totalitarianism to stabilize it and fortify it' (1944: 354).

Although Pollack's and Neumann's analyses shared many elements, they offered rather different evaluations of the possibility of a transformational crisis of the system – a subject of considerable importance to the Frankfurt theorists. Pollack's more pessimistic account resonated strongly with Horkheimer and Adorno, who, by the 1940s, had concluded that there was little margin for meaningful opposition in modern society. Neumann's theory of intensified contradiction, on the other hand, found an ally in Marcuse, who continued to struggle well into the 1960s with the issues of libratory social action and privileged historical actors. Indeed, the protest movements of the 1960s were the first great wave of popular activism to challenge the social status quo since the 1930s. To some – including Marcuse – they suggested the possibility of renewing radical, emancipatory struggle for social change.

A distinctive contribution of the Frankfurt School approach to state capitalism was its effort to work out a unified explanation of modern capitalism that grasped the similarities between Soviet and Nazi totalitarianism. This was important not only for historical analyses of the mid twentieth century – showing how despite their ideological differences each totalitarian system pursued capital accumulation and exploitative productivity levels for labor – but also for understanding the importance of the state to modern capitalism generally.

THE AUTHORITARIAN PERSONALITY

While others worked on political and economic dimensions of totalitarianism, the core Frankfurt School theorists were increasingly drawn to psychological and cultural analyses. The emergence of an 'authoritarian personality' was one of the Institute's dominant themes of the 1930s and 1940s, involving numerous scholars in two major empirical studies: *Studien über Autorität und Familie* (*Studies in Authority and the Family*), and the better-known collection of works, including *The Authoritarian Personality* (Adorno et al., 1950), that formed the *Studies in Prejudice*. Again, in this work the decline of the economic framework of bourgeois autonomy played a crucial explanatory role – not this time at the macro level of the politicization of the economy, but at a micro level which corresponded to a perceived decline in paternal authority. Here Institute scholars placed less emphasis on the repressive characteristics of the bourgeois family than on the breakdown of the forms of individuation and socialization that characterized bourgeois family life. Although their specific accounts of the role of the family varied, the Frankfurt School theorists were consistent in arguing that insofar as the family constituted a viable private domain of relationships outside the reach of the state, it performed a 'negative' function with respect to society. On the one hand it prepared individuals (men, by default) for the liberal duties of self-restraint and democratic participation, and on the other provided a haven from the purely instrumental values of the marketplace. For Horkheimer, Adorno and Marcuse, the oedipal complex was the definitive account of this process.[8] They agreed, too, that monopoly capitalism posed a basic challenge to oedipalization insofar as bourgeois paternal authority rested on the father's status as an independent economic agent – the fully empowered individual of liberal civil society. As monopoly capitalism reduced the father to an increasingly impotent economic position, that authority crumbled, subjecting the family to increasing contradictions and greater determination by 'public power' (Marcuse, 1970: 15). These difficulties, in turn, had dire consequences for the socializing and individuating function of the family. In oedipal terms, the paternal function of interdiction – the key 'threat of castration' that crystallizes the development of the autonomous ego – loses its force. As a consequence, the internalization of authority – the oedipal outcome that reproduces the paternal role – fails to fully occur. In a society that lacks strong fathers, individual egos remain weak and in search of both a positive ideal and a sense of appropriate limits.

The Frankfurt theorists had no doubts about where the ego would find such an ideal: 'It is precisely the idealization of himself which the fascist leader tries to promote in his followers . . .' By playing the '"great little man", a person who

suggests both omnipotence and the idea that he is just one of the folks . . . [the] leader image gratifies the follower's twofold wish to submit to authority and to be the authority himself' (Adorno, 1992: 91). Fromm was the first to specify this basic masochistic structure of the authoritarian personality. The empirical studies of the Institute, initially directed by Fromm in Germany and subsequently expanded in the United States, were expected to support this conclusion by gathering data on prejudices and attitudes toward authority among the working and middle classes. Among the latter group of studies, however, only *The Authoritarian Personality*, co-authored by Adorno, Else Frenkel Brunswik, Daniel J. Levinson, and R. Nevitt Sanford, drew strong correlations between authoritarianism and ostensibly relevant forms of submissiveness, aggressiveness, anti-semitism, and 'Exaggerated concern with sexual "goings-on"' (Adorno et al., 1950: 228). Indeed, *The Authoritarian Personality* went so far as to offer a statistical model of authoritarian tendencies.[9]

The other dimension of psychoanalysis that proved central to the Frankfurt critical theorists was Freud's association of civilization with the repression of pleasure. The origins of this critique lay in Nietzsche's *Genealogy of Morals*, which transformed the theological notion of a paradise lost – still visible in Rousseau's secularized version of the fall into civilization – into a psychological model of originary repression. It was Nietzsche, moreover, who identified the greater stakes of this fall, to which Freud would return in late works such as *Civilization and Its Discontents*. These were not only the repression of spontaneous, unsanctioned desires – the super-ego internalization of the particular social order – but the role of societal force, once of the most brutal kind, in the creation of the internalized, divided and developed psyche. As Nietzsche argued:

> it needs only a glance at our ancient penal codes to impress on us what labor it takes to create a nation of thinkers . . . By such methods the individual was finally taught to remember five or six 'I won'ts' which entitled him to participate in the benefits of society; and indeed, with the aid of this sort of memory, people eventually 'came to their senses'. What an enormous price man had to pay for reason, seriousness, control over his emotions – those grand human prerogatives and cultural showpieces! How much blood and horror lies behind all 'good things'! (1956: 193–4)

If, for the Frankfurt theorists, Nietzsche was guilty of defending 'irrationalism' in his attack on the psychological foundations of civilization, Freud's account of this fundamental repression proved, to the contrary, enormously suggestive.

If civilization for Freud offered much the same bargain, demanding the deferral, narrowing, or prohibition of pleasure, this process none the less called into play a more complex adjustment of primal forces than Nietzsche allowed – an accommodation of life and death instincts, Eros and Thanatos.

Among the core Frankfurt theorists, Marcuse was perhaps the least interested in psycho-analytic considerations during the 1930s, pre-ferring to explore the terrain of Hegelian and Marxist dialectics. His postwar work, however, evidences a dramatic re-evaluation of Freud's significance – particularly for revolutionary theory. It explores at length and on diverse occasions the social dynamics of pleasure and repression, and goes furthest in expanding on Freud's relatively limited historicization of this process. In so doing, Marcuse takes up the Freudian account of primordial, presocial instinctual life. Where eros had originally been a generalized and undifferentiated principle of sexual pleasure – a 'polymorphously-perverse' extension of libidinal energy – the constitution of society around 'unpleasant' labor increasingly limited eros to the narrow construction of genital, and ultimately familial sexuality. Where the death instinct had been simply sub-ordinated to the life instinct in living creatures, the demands of civilization pressed it into other sublimations 'toward the outside world in the form of socially useful aggression – toward nature and sanctioned enemies – or, in the form of conscience, or morality, . . . by the superego for the socially useful mastery of one's own drives' (1970: 8). Here lies the crucial transition between the theory of repression and the critique of reason that marks Marcuse's work of the period. The death instinct, for Marcuse, becomes identified not only with the internalization of authority, but with instrumental reason directed at the world. Horkheimer, addressing the other side of this equation, made the homology explicit: 'objective reason . . . is accessible to him who takes upon himself the effort of dia-lectical thinking, or identically, who is capable of eros' (1992a: 38).[10]

Within this framework, the Frankfurt theor-ists ultimately diverged over whether the conflict between eros and the death instinct was resolvable. Once again, this disagreement found Horkheimer and Adorno in a position of growing pessimism – increasingly aligned with Freud's late conclusion that humanity tended toward self-destruction. Marcuse, on the other hand, continued to envision the liberation of human energies, hoping to 'emancipate' eros from the excessive and intensifying sublimation of the labor process. This was the task he set himself in *Eros and Civilization* and other writing

of the post-war period. When the 'libidinal revolution' arrived after a fashion in the 1960s, Marcuse was one of its heroes.

THE CULTURE INDUSTRY

The culture industry, Horheimer and Adorno claimed in the *Dialectic of Enlightenment*, provides a 'palliative' for this repression, offer-ing entertainment as a substitute for genuine pleasure. Culture becomes an industry not merely because it is organized along lines of mass production and distribution – of films and consumer goods, for example – but also because those products extend the logic of the labor process, controlling the forms of available diver-sion and integrating them into the cycle of pro-duction and consumption. Where leisure time once represented the limit of economically struc-tured activity, it now becomes another mechan-ism of control and source of profit. In the process, a new unity is achieved:

> by occupying men's senses from the time they leave the factory in the evening to the time they clock in again the next morning with matter that bears the impress of the labor process they themselves have to sustain throughout the day, this subsumption mockingly satisfies the concept of a unified culture which the philosophers of personality contrasted with mass culture. (Horkheimer and Adorno, 1987: 131)

The turn from active forms of cultural participa-tion to passive forms of cultural consumption is another dimension of this process. Older con-ceptions of culture 'still expected a contribution from the individual', positing the autonomous self's engagement with an externalized object or experience. The logic of technological innova-tion reduces this space of action. To an ever-growing extent, culture-producers are separated from culture-consumers. For Horkheimer and Adorno, 'The step from the telephone to the radio has clearly distinguished the roles. The former still allowed the subscriber to play the role of subject, and was liberal. The latter is democratic; it turns all participants into listeners and authoritatively subjects them to broadcast programs which are all exactly the same. No machinery of rejoinder has been devised . . .' (1987: 124, 122).[11]

Though Horkheimer and Adorno had devel-oped core elements of their critique of the culture industry while still in Europe, the *Dialectic of Enlightenment* also reflects the extremis of a second exile – this time to Southern California, where Horkheimer spent several years in the early 1940s in order to improve his health.

Hollywood, home to a large community of German exiles during the war, was the catalyst for this highly provocative, influential, problematic and ultimately deeply pessimistic account of the development of instrumental reason since the classical age. What began with Odysseus' cunning culminated in the emergence of the benign totalitarianism of American culture, which integrated all of the control of the totalitarian regimes without anything approaching the brutality. The joining of economic and cultural production, Horkheimer and Adorno asserted, had achieved a purely 'affirmative' culture in which real negation was a fiction and in which bourgeois autonomy was effectively abolished. The combination of technological and administrative power successfully overwhelms the weakened modern personality, which in the end comes to prefer its submission. In this context culture no longer provides an occasion for autonomous individual response but pre-emptively constructs the available choices, including those defined as oppositional. Such a world of prefabricated choice no longer requires coercion. Indeed as Marcuse noted it perversely realizes the bourgeois ambition of Kantian freedom – the final rationalization that establishes harmony between individual will and the social order. As Marcuse glossed this issue, 'All freedoms are predetermined and preformed by [society] and subordinated not so much to political force as to the rational demands of the apparatus' (1970: 16).

As the bourgeois subject weakens, the culture industry becomes the main purveyor of the *content* of personality: 'It is as though the free space which the individual has at his disposal for his psychic processes has been greatly narrowed down; it is no longer possible for something like an individual psyche with its own demands and decisions to develop; the space is occupied by public, social forces' (1970: 14). Hollywood, rather than the father, or for that matter the Führer, now provides the principal ego ideals – the heroes and heroines of popular narratives – as well as the appropriate cues for social behavior. Together with the disciplinary forces of the workplace, school and other institutions, Horkheimer and Adorno suggest, 'the individual is reduced to the nodal point of the conventional responses and modes of operation expected of him . . .' (1987: 28).

The patina of individuality survives, however, in the extreme segmentation of the mass public – indeed this reformulation of individuality is necessary to the system's efficiency and promise of freedom. No longer the province of family life and economic autonomy, individuality becomes a product, a matter of positioning among minutely differentiated consumer choices. As

Horkheimer and Adorno describe the process, 'Something is provided for all so that none may escape; the distinctions are emphasized and extended . . . Everybody must behave (as if spontaneously) in accordance with his previously determined and indexed level, and choose the category of mass product turned out for his type' (1987: 123). Such choices, as popular critiques of communist societies once made explicit, bear an increasingly large share of the meaning of freedom.

The totalization of this system lies not in the fact that it remains hidden, but in the fact that it no longer needs to hide: 'The triumph of advertising in the culture industry is that consumers feel compelled to buy and use products even though they see through them' (1987: 167). By the same token, ideology critique becomes an empty exercise, since the system is no longer perpetuated by mystification or false-consciousness. Worst of all, Horkheimer and Adorno see little evidence that the hollowing-out of individuality constitutes in any way a fatal or even intensifying contradiction:

> the popularity of the hero models comes partly from a secret satisfaction that the effort to achieve individuation has at last been replaced by the effort to imitate, which is admittedly more breathless. It is idle to hope that this self-contradictory disintegrating 'person' will not last for generations, that the system must collapse because of such a psychological split, or that the deceitful substitution of the stereotype for the individual will of itself become unbearable for mankind. Since Shakespeare's Hamlet, the unity of the personality has been seen through as a pretense . . . For centuries society has been preparing for Victor Mature and Mickey Rooney. By destroying, they come to fulfill. (1987: 156)

Still, even in this bleakest work, Horkheimer and Adorno resist granting the culture industry complete victory – if only because to do so would evacuate the rationale for their own critical reflections. Thus, even as witnesses to the reduction of social negativity to zero and of the resulting creation of a 'one-dimensional society' (as Marcuse would later describe it), they find hints of negativity in the most apparently trivial or compromised acts – the lack of attention commonly paid to movies, for instance, or the energy expended in the jitterbug. The nature of this instability became one of Adorno's chief preoccupations in the 1950s and 1960s, leading to his rejection of the totalizing capacity of thought in *Negative Dialectics*. It would be left, however, to the cultural studies movement of the 1960s and 1970s to explore and politically exploit this space of less than perfect transmission between cultural producers and consumers.[12] For Adorno, such practical possibilities remained insignificant. The dynamism of thought merely pointed to the 'theoretical' openness of the future.

The main refuge of negativity for Adorno was art. This reflected the importance that he and the other major figures accorded the imagination and 'fantasy' in negating the status quo – in imagining the truly different. If 'the universal criterion of merit' for objects of mass culture was 'the amount of "conspicuous production", of blatant cash investment', great art, by contrast, contained 'a negative truth' – 'a force of protest of the humane against the pressure of domineering institutions, religious and otherwise . . .' More generally, great art transcended banal period styles, pointing beyond the limits of the present (Horkheimer and Adorno, 1987: 124, 130). Modern art, Adorno argued, condenses these tendencies further, resulting in works whose formal difficulty sharply contrasts with the frictionless entertainments of the culture industry. Like many of the modernists themselves, Adorno equated difficulty with resistance to commodification. As a symbol of the negation of the present, art maintained the '*promesse de bonheur*' – the utopian promise of happiness – which stood against the rationalized present (Adorno, 1970: 430).[13] Adorno's celebration of the atonal musical compositions of Arthur Schönberg and his repeated, categorical attacks on jazz as a commodified musical form are the purest expressions of this position. They are also perhaps the clearest indicators of its limitations, making visible Adorno's retreat from the effort to find or imagine negativity among existing social actors, and demonstrating the tenuousness of the distinction between subjective taste and objective reason.[14]

HABERMAS

Without question, the most significant inheritor and interpreter of this tradition is Jürgen Habermas, a sometime protégé of Adorno and the leading figure of the second generation of Frankfurt School scholars. Much of this inheritance is reflected in Habermas' rebellion against the pessimism of *Dialectic of Enlightenment* which, to an unfortunate degree, set the terms and the tone for most of Horkheimer's and Adorno's work in the postwar period. For both, critical theory became an increasingly rearguard action dedicated to preserving critique for an all-too-vaguely identified future – a 'message in a bottle' thrown to future readers. We have seen, too, the ways in which Marcuse continued to seek an exit from many of the same structural conclusions about modern society. His project of

libidinal revolution and diagnoses of the false satisfactions of consumer society in *Eros and Civilization* and *One-Dimensional Man* made Marcuse a key figure for many 1960s radicals – though Marcuse himself was never convinced of the viability of student-led revolution. In many ways, Habermas was temperamentally closer to Marcuse. One of Habermas' major contributions was to recover something of the forward-looking, constructive dimension to critical theory that had been characteristic of the early Frankfurt School.

Habermas' contributions to critical theory are many. He has endeavored to place critical theory on solid epistemological ground, maintaining a dialectical relationship between 'objectivist' analysis of social systems and subjectivist or hermeneutic analysis of action.[15] Among his key arguments is the notion that technical and practical interests are not simply sources of distortion to knowledge that must be eliminated for a perfect, objective orientation to the truth to appear. On the contrary, knowledge is formed only on the basis of interests; these shape the ways in which it appears and it would be inaccessible without some such orientation. What is crucial is not the elimination of interest, but analysis of the knowledge-forming interests at work in any specific context (Habermas, 1971). Most basically, Habermas has refocused the critical analysis of modernity and its contradictions on an enquiry into the unfinished project and liberatory potential of modernity. This is the basis for some of Habermas' barbed exchanges with post-structuralist thinkers who have retained something of the older Frankfurt theorists' pessimism about emancipatory projects, often rejecting the very historical narratives that give them meaning as reflecting the effects of power over knowledge.

Habermas has focused on re-establishing emancipatory human reason as the principal stake of critical and political reflection. This is clearly an attempt to escape the blind alley in which Horkheimer and Adorno found themselves after the war. Equally, though, it involves a rejection of Marcuse's utopianism, which relegated hope for a rational society to an improbable radical transformation of human subjectivity. Instead, Habermas has attempted to isolate the necessary conditions of critical reason by means of an immanent critique of the actual historical institutions in which critical reason achieved political significance. In so doing, he has explored the possibility of reproducing or at least leveraging those values against the mechanisms of fabricated consent in modern democratic societies.

Habermas' early theory proceeded largely by a historically concrete analysis of the institutions and theoretical principles of the public sphere. These suggested that there was in fact an unrealized liberatory potential in the bourgeois project of democracy – and Habermas has argued resolutely against leftists who see democracy as only a sham covering up for the interests of capitalist elites. For Habermas, one of the historic but tragically ephemeral achievements of bourgeois society was the emergence of a public sphere organized around the principle of rational-critical discourse – a public sphere which could 'compel public authority to legitimate itself before public opinion' (Habermas, 1989: 25). New semi-public spaces and forms of sociability in the eighteenth century contributed to this development, from the coffeehouse to the newspaper and literary salon. So did the growth of civil society – the realm of social self-regulation which included but was not limited to the market, and within which the public sphere was located. The roughly simultaneous construction of family life as an intimate, private sphere both helped to define the borders of the public sphere and to support the ostensibly autonomous individuals who entered into it. Here Habermas noted the vast importance of the eighteenth-century sentimental novel in disseminating the models of intimacy and the vocabulary of interiority that came to define the private. Together, these developments provided a context for the exchange and evaluation of opinions in a space that lay between the private realm and the state, beginning in some cases with discussion of novels or local business, but increasingly inclusive of public matters. In this process, public opinion gradually acquired legitimacy as a reasoned form of access to truth.

The legitimacy of the public sphere in liberal thought depended on two factors. First, individuals must be autonomous; this was guaranteed initially but problematically by private property, which allowed the emergence of a class of men whose livelihoods did not depend on political power or patronage. Secondly, the discourse of the public sphere gained legitimacy from its 'rational-critical' character in which the best argument and not the highest ranking person was authoritative. This depended on a 'bracketing' or putting aside of differences of rank and background for the purposes of argument within the public sphere.

As Habermas recognized, access to the early public sphere was sharply restricted – typically to propertied men, although there was considerable diversity within this group. None the less, he argues that the rational-critical public sphere represented bourgeois universalism at its most progressive, if not democratic. Like earlier critical theorists, Habermas suggests that rational-critical discourse in the Enlightenment was oriented toward the concept of objective reason – the revealing of the rational laws which governed society – and to a form of social negativity which brought reason to bear against the traditional and still dominant authority of church and state. Also like earlier critical theorists, Habermas is highly critical of subsequent developments. In his account, the eighteenth-century era of rational-critical discourse slowly succumbs to the processes of rationalization which it itself had set into motion. These included the pressures of democratization, which achieved mass inclusion at the expense of the structures of economic and psychological autonomy that had, in principle, underwritten rational-critical discourse. They included, too, the expedient replacement of the goal of objective reason by the utilitarian process of balancing private interests characteristic of modern constitutionalism. Finally, they involved the breakdown of the constitutive distinction between state and society as the state became responsible for administering and correcting for increasingly large-scale organizations of capital. As far as public discourse is concerned, this situation results, Habermas argues, in a culture industry-like subsumption of the process of opinion formation, whereby 'rational-critical debate had a tendency to be replaced by consumption, and the web of public communication unraveled into acts of individuated reception, however uniform in mode' (1989: 161).

Whatever the potential of democracy, therefore, Habermas still confronted the challenge posed by Horkheimer and Adorno in the *Dialectic of Enlightenment*. The culture industry and the massification of society seemed to stand in the way of democratic progress through the public sphere. To meet this challenge, Habermas sought bases for utopian hope that lay deeper than historically specific social institutions. He drew sustenance for a time from Lawrence Kohlberg's psychological theories which suggested a natural development of capacities for ever more universalistic reasoning about justice.[16] His more enduring resolution to the theoretical dilemma, however, drew on theories of language. In the very ways in which human beings use language, Habermas saw commitments to intersubjective validity that provided a universal basis for progressive development of reason. Because such resources were implicit in the very capacity for speech, they would always be available as a basis for attempting to ground social life on something other than money and power – no matter what temporary setbacks the causes of liberation and solidarity might suffer in the meantime.

The universal grounding for critical theory and democratic hopes that Habermas found in language use is a counterweight to his insistence that theorists recognize that the systemic integration of modern society cannot simply be undone. The lives of billions of people depend on the market and state structures that have been created, and these are not simply one-sided instruments of elite power. They reflect also compromises that ordinary people have won over the years – from minimum wage laws to public health services. Following Weber, Habermas argues that it is necessary and inevitable that large and complex modern societies be differentiated into different value spheres organized according to different criteria. At a broad level of generality, we need to recognize that 'non-linguistic steering media' such as money and power organize much of our lives. We respond to them with instrumental and strategic action. But as critical theorists we need also to see the limits of such systems. In the first place, we need to see the human action that stands behind them and offers us the possibility of criticizing them.[17] More crucially, for Habermas, we need also to see that much of our lives remains organized in other ways. We have the capacity to resist the colonization of the everyday 'lifeworlds' we construct through communication with each other by the systemic imperatives and strategic action of markets and states.

Habermas first approached the double questions of how to secure a 'good' (or at least stable) social system, and how to preserve communicatively organized social life from reduction to systemic imperatives in *Legitimation Crisis* and other writings of the 1970s. In these he carried forward the classical Frankfurt School concern for the rapprochement of society and state. Habermas emphasized two major characteristics of the late-capitalist system: 'an increase in state intervention in order to secure the system's stability, and a growing interdependence of research and technology, which has turned the sciences into the leading productive force' (Habermas, 1992: 130). The former creates a compact between workers and the state, which increasingly assumes responsibility for their welfare. This process, Habermas argues, 'depoliticizes' the population, reducing politics to matters of technical administration such as the maintenance of economic growth and the buying-off of the economy's structural victims. The latter feature – the systematic pursuit of technological progress and efficiency – becomes the official ideology of this state of affairs. Scientific innovation, rather than intensified exploitation (that is, harder work) is increasingly recognized as the only guarantor of continued growth; meanwhile, the social displacements that technological revolution inevitably provokes are

themselves moderated by the state in a further exercise of rational administration.

In his magnum opus, *Theory of Communicative Action*, Habermas integrates his analysis of the power of systemic integration through the non-linguistic media of power and money with his analysis of the potentials for both resistance and transcendence inherent in communication. Specifically, he distinguishes two basic registers of language use and human action: the instrumental, oriented to accomplishing objectives, relating means to ends, and the communicative, oriented to reaching understanding. (Strategic action is an ambiguous case, close to instrumental action, but involving the attempt to accomplish ends through interaction with other people, as in games.) On this basis, Habermas introduces a distinction between *system world* and *lifeworld*.[18]

Although the larger field of instrumental action grows increasingly dominant and alienating, all speech is predicated on certain standards of validity that derive from the interpersonal realm of the lifeworld. Procedures for evaluating the truth of a statement, for instance, rely not only on the existence of a conceptual framework, but presuppose that speakers speak without manipulative intent. These aspects of communicative reason, Habermas argues, are marginalized by deeper and more extensive 'colonization of the lifeworld' by the system world – for example, the growing role of the state in family life. This intrusion, he argues further, produces many of the individual symptoms of alienation and disorientation in the face of modernity, as well as forms of social protest in defense of the lifeworld. Potentially, the latter provide the materials for a rational discussion of limits to the system world, though such coordination is rarely achieved. The key point, with regard to systemic incursions, is that the communicative basis of the lifeworld can not thereby be lost.

Habermas supports both an active rehabilitation of this underlying consensual structure of human communication and a loosely evolutionary schema that implies that communicative reason develops alongside its instrumental counterpart. The goal of both accounts is the recovery of genuine political discourse, understood as a process of unimpeded consensus formation, of 'communicatively achieved understanding'. Such consensus would be able to grapple with the social questions of large-scale organization without the distorting influences of abstract 'steering mechanisms' such as science and money. Directed by communicative rationality, social and cultural change could (and perhaps in evolutionary fashion would) multiply the occasions for actively informed consensus and in the process expand the field of the socially possible beyond existing ideological constraints.

Where earlier critical theory had effectively displaced the possibility of a privileged social actor (such as a class) beyond the historical horizon, Habermas reinscribes that opposition into a split between existing areas of social activity. Communicative action – action oriented to reflective understanding and the creation of social relations – provides a resource against instrumental action, which is embodied in the integrated economic, state and cultural networks of the system world.

Communicative action has been the central subject of Habermas' work of the past twenty years, informing his wide-ranging discussions of ethics, law, capitalism and the philosophical tradition. Indeed, in his analysis of modern legal systems, he has sought to integrate his early analysis of the public sphere with his later theory of communicative action (Habermas, 1996). Central to this is the attempt to reformulate both ethics and politics in terms of a thorough-going proceduralism – an attempt to keep distinct the concrete questions of what constitutes a good life and the more general (possibly universal) procedural questions of how agreements should be reached. This effort extended, indeed in a sense radicalized, the early Frankfurt School emphasis on theory that was at once historically embedded and necessarily open-ended. He harkens back to Kant, suggesting that the continual critique of the categories of knowledge is a necessary response to modernity, with its imperfectly predictable patterns of change: 'Modernity, now aware of its contingencies, depends all the more on a procedural reason, that is, on a reason that puts itself on trial' (1996: xli).

Habermas' linguistic turn has been greeted with skepticism by many critical theorists and fellow travelers, as much for the strict separation it seems to imply between lifeworld and system world as for its explicit idealization of speech and consensus. On the one hand, Habermas assumes that the lifeworld and its central institution, the family, are not also constituted by a specific organization of capitalism, and by extension not also subject to forms of power and oppression – in this case directed primarily against women. Any attempt to defend the family as the source of consensual and interpersonal reason must make some account of these traditional forms of domination – all the more so since they frequently involve the denial of equal terms in decision-making. In such a context, as Nancy Fraser (1992) has noted, it is not surprising that the system world can come to seem a liberating means of depersonalizing relations.

A more general problem with this division is that it reproduces the classical assumption that identities are somehow 'settled' prior to entry into the process of consensus formation. This allows Habermas to further assume that the entrants into public discussion will share the same 'generalizable interests' – that there is, in short, a single authoritative discourse about public affairs which can be separated out from the distortions of power and distinctions among groups. But such a claim is problematic for any number of reasons. For one, it assumes as settled in advance the question of what constitutes a political versus a private issue – a subject of contention in virtually every social movement since the eighteenth century, and which is inextricably part of the democratic process itself. It tends to assume also that identity is a static, unified object, neither internally divided nor shaped by participation in arenas outside the private realm, such as system world organizations or public processes of deliberation themselves. Here Habermas reverses earlier critical theory regarding the constitution of the subject by power relations – the notion of the individual as a 'nodal point' within a field of overlapping systems – and retreats from psychoanalytic insights into the complex, divided nature of identity and the experience of self.

Not least of all, questions arise about the extent to which Habermas' theory draws on liberal assumptions about the relationship of state to individuals. Habermas himself has argued that these assumptions are outmoded: 'The practical philosophy of modernity continued to assume that individuals belong to a society like members to a collectivity or parts to a whole – even if the whole is only supposed to constitute itself through the connection of its parts. However, modern societies have since become so complex that these two conceptual motifs – that of a society concentrated in the state and that of a society made up of individuals – can no longer be applied unproblematically' (1996: 1–2). Habermas suggests that the problematic assumptions about individuals and their autonomy derived from the philosophies of consciousness dominant throughout most of modernity and that his communicative theory avoids them by grasping persons as intersubjectively constituted. Likewise, he has argued that discourse theory provides an effective way to address concerns about what constitutes the relevant totality. This is important precisely because the state cannot be assumed in the traditional manner (for example, as Europe integrates). The growth of transnational politics (and transnational moral concerns like human rights) is precisely the kind of historical change that challenges the adequacy of existing theories.

Many such theories can be shown to depend, for example, on the category of the nation-state and liberal assumptions about how it relates to citizens. Habermas' critical theory is an innovation designed in part to address these concerns.

Not everyone is satisfied, of course. Of particular importance are two linked sets of questions. First, does Habermas' theory do justice to cultural, gender and other differences among human beings?[19] Secondly, does it presume a unified progressive notion of society that derives from the modern history of nationalism and state-making and is not sufficiently critical of it. The issues are linked, for example, by questions about how differences among citizens are given or denied legitimacy in the public sphere or by the constitutional arrangements of states. Habermas has addressed both issues, and indeed their interrelationship.[20] As we noted above, his reconstruction of liberalism (and of Kantian philosophy) emphasizes the separation of questions about the concrete content of the good life from questions about the potentially universalizable procedures by which justice is achieved. States should be ordered by the latter, he suggests, as the best way of guaranteeing respect or at least tolerance for people who differ from each other. Ethnicity may, for example, be salient in giving people different conceptions of the good life, but it ought not to be salient in how the law resolves disputes between people. Likewise, membership in a modern polity should be based on adherence to its constitution and not on ethnicity. Far from presuming the existing history of nation-states, Habermas argues, this would be the best way to move beyond it towards a European constitutional democracy.

POST-STRUCTURALISM AND POSTMODERNISM

Among those least persuaded by Habermas are a diverse range of theorists often lumped together under the labels 'post-structuralism' and 'post-modernism'. This is not the place to examine the relation between these terms or the different positions of these theorists. It is important to note, however, that post-structuralism and post-modernism both constitute alternative versions of critical theory in important respects, not only in terms of the broad approach to critique outlined above but also in the influence of early Frankfurt School theorists – especially Adorno – on their dominant articulations.

Like Habermas, post-structuralist and post-modernist theorists investigate the nature and margin of human freedom in an increasingly systematized world. Major post-structuralist and postmodernist figures such as Michel Foucault, François Lyotard and Jean Baudrillard have tended to reproduce the Frankfurt School's darkest assessments of modernity, seeing human subjectivity, whether by history or nature, as fundamentally constituted and defined by increasingly coherent structures of power – even, and in some cases, especially, where the dominant ideology emphasizes autonomy and freedom. As modernity extends and refines the power of systems to 'discipline' and routinize human behavior, the margin of human unpredictability – the only remaining measure of freedom on these terms – narrows to insignificance. At the logical endpoint of such speculations are postmodernists such as Baudrillard, who, in announcing the completion of the Enlightenment's undermining of its own categories of truth and value, find 'ironic detachment' to be the only available posture.[21]

The more common conclusion, however, is that criticism and theory are best used to enhance this margin, breaking the grip – if in only occasional ways – of predictable action and habit. 'It is important,' Lyotard suggests in his account of modernity as a set of language games, 'to increase displacement in the games, and even to disorient it, in such a way as to make an unexpected "move"' (1984: 16). Concern with programmed circuits of behavior is, as we have suggested, highly visible in the critical theory of Horkheimer, Adorno, Marcuse and, especially, Habermas, but it also has a long and relatively independent history in French social thought and philosophy from Bergson on. Indeed, breaking such circuits constitutes a virtual leitmotiv of the postwar generation of French structuralist and post-structuralist theorists, from Roland Barthes (1973) (in his attack on *myth*) to Foucault (in the notion of *resistance*) (1980)[22] and Gilles Deleuze (1990) (in the exploration of *sense*). Though their sources differ widely, this broad front against systematized thought suggests a common need to situate critique at a level below large-scale organization, which inevitably creates its own clichés and demands for conformity.

At the limit, this level is found in cognitive or bodily practices – in forms of micropolitics which take thought and the self as the first and, in some cases, only available battleground. It is here that many contemporary social theorists run the risk of reducing opposition to a ubiquitous, undifferentiated phenomenon, which provides no help in evaluating political and social alternatives. This charge has been leveled in different ways against Michel Foucault and Jacques Derrida, who, however great their differences, expressly part with a notion of reason which might ground liberatory projects.

Indeed, if Foucault's concept of resistance and Derrida's *différance* have an analog in the work of the Frankfurt School, it is in Adorno's notion of negative dialectics, which similarly asserts the inevitable dynamism of thought, and the consequent incompleteness of identity claims, concepts and categories, and mechanisms of social control.

Pierre Bourdieu also rejects the idea of a static social system but does focus on the ways in which social reproduction takes place and how it is accomplished through social action. His sociology has been perhaps uniquely successful in integrating theoretical development and empirical analysis. Indeed, Bourdieu has condemned the 'theoretical theory' of the Frankfurt School. Eschewing conceptual abstractions, his work is a minute exploration of forms of embodied behavior, the margins of improvisation in which individuals act, and the subtle shadings of structured and autonomous response. *Habitus* is his term for the regulated form of improvisation that characterizes daily life – the set of 'durable dispositions' which condenses tradition, knowledge and practices, and which guides choices without ever being strictly reducible to formal rules.[23] Bourdieu has organized his analyses of diverse fields of knowledge and social activity around the question of practices in order to reconstruct theory from the ground up, reaching conclusions about regularities and social structures on the basis of empirical research. For Bourdieu, this is the advantage of sociology over philosophy, but it is not a sufficient advantage. Echoing a by now familiar theme in this chapter, empirical work must be complemented by careful consideration of the role of the sociologist and the place of sociological knowledge in society, which like all forms of knowledge, Bourdieu argues, is produced by interested parties.[24] Only by making objectivity itself an object of analysis is it possible to avoid the 'theoretical distortion' associated with objectivity claims – the birds-eye view which reduces 'all social relations . . . to decoding operations' (1977: 1). Such an immanent critique of the role of the sociologist, Bourdieu argues, is not a threat to the truth of social science. On the contrary it makes social science more scientific, capable of accounting, finally, for its constitutive blind spot. The self-referentiality of this gesture completes the 'autonomization' of the social scientific field, much as the doctrine of 'art for art's sake' completes the autonomization of the artistic field.[25] Though in most respects they are hardly fellow-travelers, Bourdieu's analysis of the way in which interest may be mobilized to pursue truth through science is strikingly reminiscent of Habermas' analysis of knowledge-forming interests.

In *The Weight of the World* (1999b) and other recent work Bourdieu has relied on the legitimacy conferred by a reflexive analysis of knowledge production and a critical theory of struggles over categories of thought and action to draw attention to rhetorics that legitimate forms of injustice and inequality. None the less, it is difficult to see how his account of the *habitus* permits individual behavior to escape the essentially conservative limits of improvisation, or more generally how social transformation change occurs at all – except, as in his example of Kabyle society, through intervention from the outside. His analyses of social reproduction run the risk of treating society as an efficiently closed system. Struggle for money, prestige, legitimation and other forms of capital occurs, Bourdieu argues, at all levels of society and across a wide range of differently organized fields. But such contention appears as a universal social feature only nominally tied to developing historical or economic contradictions. Thus, if the utility of Bourdieu's sociology lies in its capacity to demystify social relations – claims often made for Foucault's and Derrida's methods as well – it begs the question, close to the heart of critical theory, of for whom? For what social actor and to what purpose? Bourdieu's leftist political sympathies, like Foucault's, provide an implicit answer: some groups are more dominated than others. While Bourdieu gives a compelling account of what empowers him as an actor in such political struggles, however, his theory does not in itself provide a rationale for or orientation to such activity. It is the basis for an extraordinarily productive empirical sociology, and it is clearly in many respects a critical theory, but if it is a theory with practical intent, the link between theory and practice remains underdeveloped.[26]

Michel Foucault's work furnishes one of the pre-eminent engagements with these issues in recent years. A enormously influential historian and analyst of modernity, Foucault's early work is very much a historicization of reason. His study, *The Order of Things* (1970), describes an epochal shift in the definition of the human (and a diremption in the idea of a unified nature) that occurred in the course of the eighteenth century. As Foucault demonstrated, classical thought was based on the idea of representation as an objective feature of the universe. Resemblances and recurrences among things provided the basis for knowledge, and could link an infinite range of similar phenomena (as the coincidence of dates informs connections in astrology). The modern *episteme* broke with this order of representation by introducing the idea of the finite human subject as basis for all knowledge, thereby also discovering 'man' as a separate object of enquiry. In the context of this shift, language became newly problematic. The relationship between word and thing was no longer transparent. So too the relationship between the human being as subject – maker of history – and object, alienated man, subject to powers greater than himself. Foucault refused the temptation to naturalize the modern perspective, to treat it as a superior reality which surpassed earlier forms of knowledge. Rather, he tried to study the historical change itself, especially as it issued in different kinds of projects of knowledge (sciences) which themselves had limits. Echoing the Frankfurt School, he stressed the historicity of the categories of knowledge. Foucault also echoed the Frankfurt theorists (and both followed Nietzsche) in seeing a central feature of the modern *episteme* as an orientation toward truths which enabled technical mastery over nature. But this logic eventually encounters its own limits. As for Horkheimer and Adorno, artistic modernism (for Foucault that of Antonin Artaud and Raymond Roussel) marks the symbolic end of this paradigm. Treating the sign as a material object rather than a marker of objectified and instrumentalized reality – as a range of modernist writers did – breaks the sign–object structure of truth and identity. These artistic tendencies, Foucault argued, tracked closely with a larger socioeconomic, political, scientific and metaphysical retreat from the claims of truth. Foucault then envisioned, somewhat loosely, another paradigm transition – 'Since man was constituted at a time when language was doomed to dispersion, will he not be dispersed when language recovers its unity?' Will he not disappear 'like a face drawn in sand at the edge of the sea?' (1970: 386, 387). We are left to ponder our own status as subjects transformed – or crucially, awaiting transformation – by a new relationship to knowledge.

Foucault's later work loses this potentially emancipatory teleology, moving toward the much starker account of power, technology and the cooption of opposition visible in *Discipline and Punish* ([1975] 1979). Here the gentle totalitarianism of liberal society is every bit as efficient as in the postwar work of Horkheimer and Adorno – indeed Foucault acknowledged regret at having encountered the Frankfurt School only late in the course of his own thinking on these issues (Wiggershaus, 1994: 4). His final investigations of sexuality, however, tread a discernible middle path on this point, envisioning society as characterized at all times by a constantly changing dynamic of power and resistance. In this respect, Foucault implied, ancient Greece differed little from eighteenth-century France or twenty-first-century America.

One general implication of this emphasis on the constitutive effects of power is that there can

be no strict distinction between instrumental and communicative reason – though Foucault did, at times, recognize the possibility of making *relative* distinctions on these grounds (1992: 311).[27] For a critical theorist such as Habermas, this presents a fundamental dilemma: without a critical ground on which to base emancipatory human action there are no criteria for distinguishing between legitimate and illegitimate power. The question of a qualitatively better future is either rejected or expelled beyond the historical horizon. Foucault shared this problem, in Habermas' view, with Horkheimer and Adorno.[28] Part of the difficulty, for Habermas, lies in approaches to modernity that imagine truth and value as a unified realm in which theories about the self, political economy, science and metaphysics depend upon the same forms of legitimation, and consequently suffer a collective disintegration in the passage to something like postmodernity.

This is in essence the crisis of truth and value postulated by Nietzsche, whose account of modernity has exercised a tremendous influence on French twentieth-century thought. Habermas' distinction between instrumental and communicative reason, however idealized, challenges this account by recognizing different modes of legitimation in different areas of human experience. The project of an absolutely unified knowledge is no longer tenable. There are instead different ways of establishing functional truths. If, for instance, uncertainty in particle physics proves relatively inconsequential to how persons construct reliable fabrics of human relations at a given time, then we may well have more resources and fewer epochal contradictions to rely on in imagining social change – and achieving social solidarity. As Habermas argued with respect to Derrida and Rorty, 'They are still battling against the "strong" concepts of theory, truth, and system that have actually belonged to the past for over a century and a half . . .' (Habermas, 1987b: 408). Critical theory is not the pursuit of a grand system of knowledge, perfected and closed to new influences. It is, rather, an approach to improving on existing understanding – theoretical and practical. It offers 'epistemic gain', not absolute truth. It offers it in an open-ended fashion, in the recognition that all existing theories will need to be revised – perhaps radically or perhaps rejected – in the light of new historical experience.

NOTES

1 There are a number of good general accounts of the Frankfurt School, including Martin Jay's *The Dialectical Imagination* (1973), David Held's *Introduction*

to *Critical Theory: Horkheimer to Habermas* (1980) and Rolf Wiggershaus' *The Frankfurt School: Its History, Theories, and Political Significance* (1994).

2 The Frankfurt theorists were influenced in this regard by Georg Lukács' analysis of reification in *History and Class Consciousness* (1922). A generation older than the Frankfurt theorists, Lukács similarly combined influences from idealist philosophy, Marx and Weber into a critical theory of society, and also focused largely on cultural analysis. The idea of reification has older roots as well, and is similar to Marx's analysis of the 'fetishism of commodities' (in *Capital*, vol. 1, ch. 1). Marx's term was an analogy to the way in which some religions treat physical objects as sacred in themselves, obscuring the extent to which they have gained this standing from social action and their capacity to serve as signs. The critique of reification is especially important in regard to capitalism, with its creation of labor markets and use of quantification to make labor itself appear as a 'thing' being exchanged rather than human action. See the analysis by the 'third generation' Frankfurt School theorist Moishe Postone in *Time, Labor and Social Domination* (1993).

3 It is common in social science to focus on explanation primarily as a matter of establishing relations of cause and effect (or at least more or less robust implication, cf. Boudon, 1974). Equally important, however, is the question of how adequate theoretical categories are to the phenomena they purport to describe. Much of the most important theoretical work necessarily involves figuring out the implications of the analytic categories or concepts employed – about which there are always choices.

4 This may involve claiming the standpoint of a social group, as Marx and Lukács claimed the standpoint of the proletariat and modern feminists have sometimes claimed the standpoint of women (or, less helpfully and pluralistically, of woman). But the idea of analysing the standpoint from which one works need not be a matter simply of identification with a group. It may involve analysing the way in which academic institutions affect the production of knowledge by professors, or the nature of one's own commitment to science or to society and how that shapes one's work. Most social theory is written implicitly from the standpoint of highly educated citizens in the world's richest societies. This no doubt shapes both theorists' choice of issues and the ways in which they approach those issues. The point is not to escape from this – which is quite impossible – but to achieve critical self-awareness and seek throughout one's work to examine the effects of one's perspective. See Calhoun, 1995: ch. 6.

5 These dimensions of Marx's thought were developed primarily in unpublished early works such as *The German Ideology* and *The Economic and Philosophical Manuscripts* of 1844. These works were only rediscovered in the 1920s and only widely disseminated in the 1930s. Lukács did not have access to them when he wrote *History and Class Consciousness* in 1922.

6 Or to see the ongoing search for a privileged historical actor as an attempt to refound it. In this vein Frankfurt School analyses explored the negative potential of the Jews, the 'wretched' of the Third World, and the student radicals of the 1960s.

7 Much of this argument is synthesized in Pollack's classic essay 'State Capitalism: Its Possibilities and Limitations' (1941).

8 Horkheimer, Adorno and Marcuse were all relatively orthodox in matters of Freudian psychoanalytical theory. The Institute did include other voices during the 1930s, though, especially Erich Fromm (whose 'revisionist', more social-constructionist approach to psychoanalysis Horkheimer and Adorno rejected). There was a wave of interest in sociocultural applications of psychoanalysis in the years before and after the Second World War. The Frankfurt theorists were influential, but always tended toward the defense of Freud against revisionists.

9 The other major works in the *Studies of Prejudice* dealt with a range of topics, but strongly confirmed the Institute's preoccupation with the link between antisemitism and authoritarianism. These were *Dynamics of Prejudice: A Psychological and Sociological Study of Veterans*, by Bruno Bettleheim and Morris Janowitz; *Anti-Semitism and Emotional Disorder: A Psychoanalytic Interpretation*, by Nathan W. Ackerman and Marie Jahoda; *Prophets of Deceit*, by Leo Lowenthal and Norbert Guterman; and *Rehearsal for Destruction*, by Paul Massing.

10 It is worth noting that the passage from Nietzsche cited above similarly illuminates this crucial intersection between the theory of repression and the critique of reason – although Nietzsche's blanket dismissal of reason earned him the charge of 'irrationalism'. For Nietzsche, the repression of pleasure is not merely the road to the internalization of authority; it also plays a fundamental role in the creation of human capacities – above all the duration of memory which makes man a social creature capable of making promises, and the development of reason, which displaces force as the arbiter of right.

11 It should be noted that the older forms of culture in which Horkheimer and Adorno see more participatory engagement were very limited in access, reaching mainly an educated and prosperous elite. The rise of the culture industry reflects the mass market that new recording and transmission technologies can reach. An unsolved puzzle (which resurfaces in Habermas' account of the structural transformations of the public sphere) is whether it is possible to have wider democratic access to cultural processes without losing interactivity, educated judgement, or other valued qualitative features.

12 Resulting in much closer attention to the dynamics of interpretation than the Frankfurt School thought necessary. Stuart Hall's model of encoding and decoding is one such model; reader–response

theory in the United States and reception theory in Germany provide numerous others. Horkheimer and Adorno remained somewhat divided on this issue. If they sometimes implied that such space existed, they unequivocally denied that it mattered.

13 Marcuse, too, endorsed the utopian potential of art when he returned to the subject in his final work, *The Aesthetic Dimension: Toward a Critique of Marxist Aesthetics* (1978).

14 Much of Adorno's work on art, negative dialectics, and the question of style (which plays a prominent part in his writing) shows the influence of Walter Benjamin, a peripheral member of the Frankfurt School who died while fleeing France in 1940. Benjamin stressed a more archaic, communal dimension to the artistic gesture – an 'aura' of authenticity that surrounded the singular artwork or performance. 'Mechanical reproduction', Benjamin argued, destroys this connection between culture and authenticity. With the loss of this ancient function, art, like the economy and the family, 'begins to be based on another practice – politics' (1969: 224). It's worth noting that, unlike the other Frankfurt School figures, Benjamin saw the potential, at least, for new forms of radicalism in this politicization.

15 Among other things, Habermas thus relates critical theory to two of the most prominent alternatives in contemporary intellectual life (especially in Germany): Luhmann's systems theory and Gadamer's hermeneutics. Though he incorporates features of both, he has been more resolute in keeping his distance from hermeneutics. More importantly, perhaps, he insists on the inevitability in the social sciences of a 'both/and' relationship between the two extremes of objectivist and interpretative analysis: 'Whereas the natural and the cultural or hermeneutic sciences are capable of living in a mutually indifferent, albeit more hostile than peaceful, coexistence, the social sciences must bear the tension of divergent approaches under one roof, for in them the very practice of research compels reflection on the relationship between analytic and hermeneutic research methodologies' (Habermas, 1967: 3).

16 See, e.g., *Communication and the Evolution of Society* (Habermas, 1979).

17 This can include offering a critique of the reification or fetishization involved in systems such as markets or states, revealing the human action that creates them. Habermas seems less interested in such a critique than earlier critical theorists, however, and in fact worried that those who undertake it will be led to imagine that the systems involved are less necessary than he thinks them to be. Others have argued that his theory would be improved by stressing this dimension more. See McCarthy, 1991 and Calhoun, 1988.

18 See *Communication and the Evolution of Society* (1979) and especially *Theory of Communicative Action*, vols. 1 and 2 (1984, 1987b).

19 Questions of identity loom very large for many of the 'third generation' Frankfurt School critical theorists. See for example Seyla Benhabib, *Situating the Self* (1992) and Axel Honneth, *The Struggle for Recognition* (1996). See also the debate occasioned by Charles Taylor's 'The Politics of Recognition,' including Habermas' response, collected in Gutman, 1992.

20 See especially the essays collected in *The Inclusion of the Other* (1998); also Habermas, 1996: esp. ch. 7 and the two appendices.

21 See especially *The Mirror of Production* (Baudrillard, 1975) and *For a Critique of the Political Economy of the Sign* (Baudrillard, 1981).

22 Foucault develops the idea of resistance to power in much of his later work, including *Power/ Knowledge: Selected Interviews and Other Writings, 1972–1977* (1980).

23 Bourdieu's corpus encompasses studies of numerous fields of intellectual and artistic production as well as social institutions such as class and education. His principal theoretical statements, however, are *Outline of a Theory of Practice* (1977) and *The Logic of Practice* (1990).

24 In this he is quite close to Habermas and, before him, Horkheimer, who always associated knowledge with a 'knowledge-creating interest' (*erkentnissenteresse*).

25 A case Bourdieu took up in *The Rules of Art: Genesis and Structure of the Literary Field* (1996).

26 One aspect of Bourdieu's critique of market-centered neoliberalism is that it courts reduction of the autonomy of different fields to a genuinely low common denominator, thereby sacrificing many historical gains; see *Acts of Resistance* (1999a). This is at least superficially similar to Habermas' defense of the differentiation of value spheres, and it suggests a link between critical analysis and normative judgement, but it is not clear how far Bourdieu wishes to make this argument.

27 This essay tries to bridge the gap between his theory of power as a constituting 'matrix' of subjectivity and a much more conventional set of distinctions between applied power, 'objective capacities', and communication; the latter, he suggests, 'support one another reciprocally, and use each other mutually as means to an end'.

28 See Habermas, 1987b. Foucault, in essays and interviews, tends more toward a more normative description of political action and allows a greater role for such buffering mechanisms as rights than he does in his major writings.

REFERENCES

Adorno, Theodor (1970) *Aesthetic Theory* (trans. C. Lenhardt). New York: Routledge and Kegan Paul.

Adorno, Theodor (1992) 'Freudian Theory and the Pattern of Fascist Propaganda', in David Ingram and Julia-Simon Ingram (eds), *Critical Theory: The*

Essential Readings. St Paul, MN: Paragon. pp. 84–102.

Adorno, Theodor, Frenkel Brunswick, Else, Levinson, Daniel J. and Sanford, R. Nevitt (1950) *The Authoritarian Personality*. New York: Harper.

Barthes, Roland (1973) *Mythologies*. New York: Noonday.

Baudrillard, J. (1975) *The Mirror of Production*. St Louis, MO: Telos Press.

Baudrillard, J. (1981) *For a Critique of the Political Economy of the Sign*. St Louis, MO: Telos Press.

Benhabib, Seyla (1992) *Situating the Self*. New York: Routledge.

Benjamin, Walter (1969) 'Art in the Age of Mechanical Reproduction', in *Illuminations: Walter Benjamin, Essays and Reflections* (trans. Harry Zohn). New York: Schocken Books.

Boudon, Raymond (1974) *The Logic of Sociological Explanation*. Harmondsworth: Penguin.

Bourdieu, Pierre (1977) *Outline of a Theory of Practice* (trans. R. Nice). Cambridge: Cambridge University Press.

Bourdieu, Pierre (1990) *The Logic of Practice*. Stanford, CA: Stanford University Press.

Bourdieu, Pierre (1996) *The Rules of Art: Genesis and Structure of the Literary Field*. Stanford, CA: Stanford University Press.

Bourdieu, Pierre (1999a) *Acts of Resistance*. New York: The New Press.

Bourdieu, Pierre (1999b) *The Weight of the World* (trans. P. Ferguson). Stanford, CA: Stanford University Press.

Calhoun, Craig (1988) 'Populist Politics, Communications Media, and Large Scale Social Integration', *Sociological Theory*, 6 (2): 219–41.

Calhoun, Craig (1995) *Critical Social Theory*. Oxford: Blackwell.

Deleuze, Gilles (1990) *The Logic of Sense* (trans. Mark Lester). New York: Columbia University Press.

Foucault, Michel (1970) *The Order of Things*. New York: Random House.

Foucault, Michel ([1975] 1979) *Discipline and Punish: The Birth of the Prison* (trans. Alan Sheridan). New York: Vintage Books.

Foucault, Michel (1980) *Power/Knowledge: Selected Interviews and Other Writings, 1972–1977*. New York: Pantheon.

Foucault, Michel (1992) 'The Subject and Power', in David Ingram and Julia-Simon Ingram (eds), *Critical Theory: The Essential Readings*. St Paul, MN: Paragon. pp. 303–19.

Fraser, Nancy (1992) 'What's Critical About Critical Theory?', in David Ingram and Julia-Simon Ingram (eds), *Critical Theory: The Essential Readings*. St Paul, MN: Paragon. pp. 357–87.

Gutman, A. (ed.) (1992) *Multiculturalism and the Politics of Recognition*. Princeton, NJ: Princeton University Press.

Habermas, Jürgen (1967) *On the Logic of the Social Sciences*. Cambridge, MA: MIT Press.

Habermas, Jürgen (1971) *Knowledge and Human Interests*. Boston, MA: Beacon Press.

Habermas, Jürgen (1974) 'Some Difficulties in the Attempt to Link Theory and Praxis', in *Theory and Practice*. London: Heinemann. pp. 1–40.

Habermas, Jürgen (1979) *Communication and the Evolution of Society*. Boston, MA: Beacon Press.

Habermas, Jürgen (1984) *The Theory of Communicative Action*, vol. 1: *Reason and the Rationalization of Society*. Boston, MA: Beacon Press.

Habermas, Jürgen (1987a) *The Theory of Communicative Action*, vol. 2: *Lifeworld and System: A Critique of Functionalist Reason*. Boston, MA: Beacon Press.

Habermas, Jürgen (1987b) *The Philosophical Discourse of Modernity* (trans. Frederick Lawrence). Cambridge, MA: MIT Press.

Habermas, Jürgen (1989) *The Structural Transformation of the Public Sphere*. Cambridge, MA: MIT Press.

Habermas, Jürgen (1992) 'Technology and Science as "Ideology"', in David Ingram and Julia-Simon Ingram (eds), *Critical Theory: The Essential Readings*. St Paul, MN: Paragon. pp. 117–50.

Habermas, Jürgen (1996) *Between Facts and Norms*. Cambridge, MA: MIT Press.

Habermas, Jürgen (1998) *The Inclusion of the Other*. Cambridge, MA: MIT Press.

Held, David (1980) *Introduction to Critical Theory: Horkheimer to Habermas*. Berkeley, CA: University of California Press.

Honneth, Axel (1996) *The Struggle for Recognition*. Cambridge, MA: MIT Press.

Horkheimer, Max (1941) 'Art and Mass Culture', *Studies in Philosophy and Social Science*, 9 (2): 290–304.

Horkheimer, Max (1992a) 'Means and Ends', in David Ingram and Julia-Simon Ingram (eds), *Critical Theory: The Essential Readings*. St Paul, MN: Paragon. pp. 36–48.

Horkheimer, Max (1992b) 'Traditional and Critical Theory', in David Ingram and Julia-Simon Ingram (eds), *Critical Theory: The Essential Readings*. St Paul, MN: Paragon. pp. 239–54.

Horkheimer, Max and Adorno, Theodor (1987) *Dialectic of Enlightenment* (trans. John Cumming). New York: Continuum.

Jay, Martin (1973) *The Dialectical Imagination*. Berkeley, CA: University of California Press.

Lukács, Georg (1922) *History and Class Consciousness*. Cambridge, MA: MIT Press.

Lyotard, François (1984) *The Postmodern Condition: A Report on Knowledge* (trans. Geoff Bennington and Brian Massumi). Minneapolis, MN: University of Minnesota Press.

Marcuse, Herbert (1960) *Reason and Revolution: Hegel and the Rise of Social Theory*. Boston, MA: Beacon Press.

Marcuse, Herbert (1970) 'Freedom and Freud's Theory of Instincts', in *Five Essays: Psychoanalysis, Politics, and Utopia* (trans. Jeremy Shapiro and Shierry Weber). Boston, MA: Beacon Press. pp. 1–27.

Marcuse, Herbert (1978) *The Aesthetic Dimension: Toward a Critique of Marxist Aesthetics.* Boston, MA: Beacon Press.

Marcuse, Herbert (1992) 'Philosophy and Critical Theory', in David Ingram and Julia-Simon Ingram (eds), *Critical Theory: The Essential Readings.* St Paul, MN: Paragon. pp. 5–19.

Marx, Karl (1978) 'Theses on Feuerbach', in *The Marx-Engels Reader* (ed. Robert C. Tucker). New York: W.W. Norton. pp. 143–5.

McCarthy, Thomas (1991) *Ideals and Illusions: On Reconstruction and Deconstruction in Contemporary Critical Theory.* Cambridge, MA: MIT Press.

Neumann, Franz (1944) *Behemoth: The Structure and Practice of National Socialism, 1933–1944.* New York: Harper Torchbooks.

Nietzsche, Friedrich (1956)'The Genealogy of Morals', in *The Birth of Tragedy and the Genealogy of Morals* (trans. Francis Golffing). Garden City, NY: Doubleday.

Pollack, Friedrich (1941) 'State Capitalism: Its Possibilities and Limitations', *Studies in Philosophy and Social Sciences*, IX (2): 200–25.

Postone, Moishe (1993) *Time, Labor and Social Domination.* New York: Cambridge University Press.

Wiggershaus, Rolf (1994) *The Frankfurt School: Its History, Theories, and Political Significance.* Cambridge, MA: MIT Press.

16

Jürgen Habermas' Theory of Communicative Action: An Incomplete Project

RICHARD HARVEY BROWN AND
DOUGLAS GOODMAN

As capitalism slouches into a new millennium, many of the most extreme predictions about it, both optimistic and pessimistic, appear to be coming true. For those within the advanced capitalist countries, it has provided material comfort that is as broad and enduring as any that humans have experienced. And, as a system, it continues to grow more efficient and pervasive. Capitalism's global reach is now unchecked by any rival order. It has conquered the world and, by many, been welcomed with open arms. If democracy and peace spread around the globe, it will likely be because they provide a good environment for capitalism more than for any intrinsic value.

However, it is also true that many of the most dire predictions of the critics of capitalism have been realized – Marx's prediction of alienation and fetishism of commodities, de Tocqueville's fear of a capitalist aristocracy, Weber's prediction of disenchantment and the iron cage of bureaucracy, Durkheim's anomie and loss of collective morality. As the technicians diligently fine-tune the machinery of economic prosperity, its supposed beneficiaries increasingly see capitalism as an uncontrollable juggernaut headed towards an uncertain destination.

Even as capitalism's progress seems inevitable, the concept of progress itself is looking more dubious. On both intellectual and political levels, the assumption of democratic progress through enlightenment rationality is increasingly difficult to believe. Rationality itself has been largely reduced in practice to technical calculation of efficient means without regard to the substantive rationality of ends, purposes, or values. This turns political and moral questions into technical or instrumental ones. Such a reduction of reason to calculations of efficiency tends to empower technical experts, to *de*power citizens, and to limit the public space available for civic discourse.

The triumph of capitalism and the technicization of reason has engendered a critique. Rationality itself is attacked from many directions. Post-structuralists insist that it is a form of power; feminists suggest that rationality disguises male domination; postmodernists argue that rationality is itself historical, a language game that constructs its own domains of application. But much of this criticism seems to be compromised by the rational arguments upon which they rely.

This is the situation that Jürgen Habermas attempts to address: the triumph of a seemingly indispensable capitalist system, the postmodern skepticism toward reason, and the failure of public discourse. Habermas aims to restore an ethical rationality to civic discourse by recovering rationality from its reduction to calculations of efficiency, on the one hand, and fending off postmodern skepticism on the other. He hopes that this would provide for a critique of capitalism and a revival of democracy.

Habermas' theory is first and foremost a critical theory. Critical theory is meant here in both the generic sense and in the specific sense of a theory that is derived from the Frankfurt School – that collection of neo-Marxists which includes among its more famous members Max Horkheimer, Theodor Adorno, Herbert Marcuse, Walter Benjamin and Erich Fromm. Habermas is generally considered to be the leader of the Frankfurt School's 'second generation'. He was deeply influenced not only by the Frankfurt School's concept of a critical theory, but also by the first generation's failure in achieving one.

Habermas sees his work as an attempt to appropriate Weber in the spirit of Western Marxism. The primary intent of Habermas' project is to provide an alternative to the formal, instrumental reason that Weber had shown to lead to both disenchantment and an iron cage of bureaucracy. According to Weber, Western culture has been characterized by the inescapable growth of a peculiar type of reasoning. While most forms of reason are tied to the accomplishment of a particular moral value, Western rationality is tied only to efficiency, calculability and control. This formal, instrumental rationality inevitably results in the loss of meaning and the growth of bureaucracy so evident in capitalist modernity.

Horkheimer and Adorno (1972) made Weber's pessimism even more radical. They argued that this formal, instrumental reason is the corrupt heart of the Enlightenment project. According to Horkheimer and Adorno, the inescapable conundrum of the Enlightenment is this: the reason which is needed to create the objective conditions of freedom ends up destroying freedom's subjective and intersubjective conditions. Because human beings have inescapable material needs, our freedom depends upon controlling nature. To better control nature, we control other people and, in the end, efficiency demands that we even control our own inner nature. The tragedy of 'dialectic of Enlightenment' is that we end up repressing and controlling the very human nature that is the motivation for our freedom. The opportunities opened up by our control of nature are confronted by a repressed and diminished subject.

Habermas believes that both Weber and the early Frankfurt School made the mistake of assuming that the only type of reason is one bent on control in order to satisfy material needs. Instead, for Habermas, the Enlightenment project encompasses the increasing rationalization of both an instrumental reason as well as a reason inherent to what Habermas calls communicative action. Habermas argues that communicative action can function as an alternative

way of relating to others that does not just use them as means to self-interested goals tied to the necessity of producing our material needs. Instead, the goal of communicative action is understanding and, as a form of reason, it does not lead to either the subjective crisis of repression or the objective crisis of the excrescence of bureaucracy.

In 1970, Habermas (1980: 189–90) laid out the path that he was to follow by identifying two ways in which a theory of communication could be critical. One way would be 'a rational reconstruction of a regulative system that adequately defines general linguistic competence'. This approach would start from an 'ideal' speech situation and use that as a standpoint to critique our current situation. The other way would be to start from the experienced crises of everyday communication and develop a model of how society needs to change in order to correct these pathologies. The first approach can be called a *theory of normalcy* since it specifies what the non-pathological condition would be. The second can be called a *theory of pathologies*.

The theory of normalcy and the theory of pathologies are closely related, but they are not reducible to each other. Indeed, the theory of pathologies requires that a theory of normalcy be established separately in order for experiences of crises to be defined as pathologies instead of, for example, necessary growing pains. We can all agree that war is a crisis, but that, in and of itself, is not an argument against war. We need a further explanation showing that war is not a necessary stage that must be passed through on our way to a just and peaceful society.

Conversely, the theory of normalcy requires a theory of pathologies. It is needed to make the reconstruction of the historical development of necessary competences for communicative action into a critical theory rather than a conservative one. For example, a theory that reconstructs the way in which children are socialized into competent gender performances based upon biological sexual characteristics is only a critical theory if it is agreed that these gender performances are pathological. Otherwise the theory could be taken as a model of how one should socialize children into traditional gender roles. This means that Habermas' diagnosis of modernity is critical only if he can show that the colonization of communicative action by an administrative system results in crises that are avoidable.

In the next section of this chapter, we present Habermas' theory of 'normalcy'. In using the term normalcy, we mean non-pathological rather than normative or regularly occurring. Clearly Habermas does not claim that what he calls communicative action occurs regularly in modern capitalism. Instead, the very rarity of its occurrence is central to its critical force. Neither do we use the term normalcy to mean related to a norm, although Habermas' theory of normalcy does have implications for norms and values. Instead, his argument is that what is 'normal' (1987b: 196) can be reconstructed from the necessary presuppositions for communication which is oriented toward understanding. Such a reconstruction demonstrates that communication has an inherent telos; and it also shows that other forms of communication presuppose such a telos even as they negate it in practice. This theory of normalcy allows Habermas to argue, in his theory of pathologies, that the experienced dilemmas of modernity are caused by the repression of communicative rationality. The theory of normalcy shows that the crises described in the theory of pathologies are not necessary stages.

HABERMAS' THEORY OF NORMAL COMMUNICATION

Habermas defines what is normal by reconstructing a communicative rationality that he argues is necessary to social reproduction and personal identity. The concept of a necessary communicative rationality has been a part of Habermas' thought from his first book. A main theme of *The Structural Transformation of the Public Sphere* (1991a) was that society has suffered from the dismantling of the arena for public communication to make way for a manufactured publicity that merely appears to be communication.

Habermas' first major theoretical work, *Knowledge and Human Interests* (1971), was an attempt to provide an epistemological justification for an alternative type of rationality that is distinct from instrumental reason. He developed the concept of cognitive interests in order to distinguish different types of rationalities. Communication with the aim of mutual understanding (the primary focus of Habermas' later work) is one of three primary interests that are the conditions for knowledge. The other two are an instrumental and an emancipatory interest. Part of Habermas' argument was for the autonomy of the communicative realm from the instrumental; however, his main focus in this early attempt was not the communicative, but the emancipatory interest which constituted the realm in which an ideology critique could function.

Ideology critique based on reflection was central to the critical theory of the early Habermas. However, the reliance on reflection was heavily criticized because Habermas could not explain how this seemingly interest-free, critical reflection was possible given his own theory of knowledge constitutive interests (Dallmayr, 1972; McCarthy, 1978; Ottmann, 1982). Consequently, the focus on ideology critique through reflection was abandoned in favor of a reconstruction of the necessary presuppositions for the reproduction of society through communication.

The reconstruction of the necessary presuppositions of such communication has two aims: first, to recover and validate the rationality that is embodied in everyday communication and necessary for social reproduction; and second, to establish the possibility of a context-transcending perspective within the current intellectual milieu that is skeptical of all such attempts to transcend contexts (Habermas, 1984: 137). In this way, Habermas proposes a theory of normalcy that is tied to everyday communication and yet transcends its local contexts.

Habermas proposes that the competences in the use of language that are presupposed in any communication can be reconstructed in what he calls a pragmatics of human communication. Such a pragmatics focuses on the formal (as opposed to substantive) properties of language use. He bases his reconstruction on the concrete use of language which is, of course, always bound to a particular context. By focusing on the abstract form of the necessary general competences, he hopes that he can define a concept of validity that does not simply reproduce the conventions of a particular society. It is upon the foundation of this context-transcendent validity that Habermas proposes to build his theory of normalcy.

The theory of communication that Habermas develops draws on the idea of George Herbert Mead and others that personal identity – our experience of our self as a self – is intersubjectively constructed through symbolic interaction, that is, communication. Because such communication constitutes our very selves, its necessary presuppositions are not to be viewed as norms, although they have a normative force (Habermas, 1979: 88). They do not represent 'a particular value, for or against which we can take sides' (Habermas, 1982: 226). Instead, the necessary presuppositions of communication are the source for our identity, as well as any position we might take and any norm to which we would accede. The intersubjective medium of language not only is the source of personal identity; it also is the medium through which we understand ourselves as a part of a social group and through which activity of individuals within such groups is coordinated.

For Habermas, language is intrinsically critical. Of course, any criticism of the status quo must be articulated through language. In this sense, language always has the potential to be critical. But Habermas means much more than that. For him, the necessary structure of communication contains an emancipatory goal latent within the concept of mutual understanding. This emancipatory goal inheres in normal communication, even though much use of language does not itself share this emancipatory perspective. Habermas' own theory therefore provides for a critique of current conditions to the extent that actual communication does not live up to its emancipatory potential.

Strategic and communicative action

According to Habermas, communication can be divided into two types, one which he labels 'strategic' and the second, a true 'communicative action' aimed at understanding. Only communicative action fits Habermas' concept of normal communication.

In strategic communication the goal of social action is pre-established and often hidden. The intent is not to reach agreement about the goals of the action but simply effectively to carry out the plans of the speaker, especially where the hearers may not agree with the speaker's intentions. Although strategic action uses language and involves other people, its goals are not inherent to language use and other people are treated as if they were objects. Social norms and even the speaker's own subjective expressions become tools to be used to further the speaker's predefined goals. The rationality of communication is judged in terms of its efficiency in getting others to do what the speaker wants them to do (Habermas, 1982: 264). Strategic communication is under the spell of instrumental reason and leads to all of the problems that Weber and the Frankfurt School predicted.

In contrast, communicative action aims at achieving understanding – which Habermas takes to be the 'inherent telos of human speech' (1984: 287). The key to what Habermas means by communicative action is his special use of the term 'understanding'. The German term *Verständigung* can mean both understanding and the process of coming to an understanding. Habermas connects these two senses: 'Reaching understanding [*Verständigung*] is considered to be a process of reaching agreement [*Einigung*] among speaking and acting subjects' (1984: 286–7).

In communicative action, human beings are not objects to be used to further predefined goals; instead, goals are mutually agreed upon through a process of communication that recognizes the autonomous humanity of all persons involved. Social action is coordinated through the process of understanding itself. That is, the very process through which understanding is achieved also generates cooperative goals and agreements. Communicative action thereby offers a form of rationality that escapes the spell of instrumental reason and provides a definition of non-pathological communication upon the basis of which social crises can be diagnosed as pathologies.

The difference between strategic and communicative action is not that one is goal-oriented and the other is not. Both forms involve coordinating action to achieve goals. The difference lies in the distinct relation between the goal pursued and the language used. In strategic action, the relation between language and goal is one of means to end, with language reduced to a mere instrument for achieving any posited goal. In communicative action, however, the goal is understanding and the precise nature of that goal is inseparable from the processes of language use through which it is achieved (Habermas, 1991b: 241). For example, in trying to get a child to rake the yard, one could either tell her that there is money under the leaves or one could try to discuss with her why raking the yard may or may not be an important thing to do. In the former case, language is just one means among others (paying her to do it, threatening her with punishment if she doesn't, etc.) to accomplish the goal of raking the yard. In the latter, understanding and coming to a consensus about the importance of raking is the goal, and this can only be done through language.

For Habermas, this distinction is not simply a matter of subjective attitude. He claims that communicative action requires a structure of presuppositions that is qualitatively different from linguistic interactions that simply manipulate others to achieve a predetermined goal. This is related to the different mechanisms for social coordination of strategic and communicative action. The distinction can be summed up as the difference between mutual understanding and mutual influencing. With communicative action, individuals are coordinated through building consensus that derives its coordinating force from 'the binding and bonding energies of language itself' (Habermas, 1998: 221). Strategic action, in comparison, is coordinated by complementing interest situations. Non-linguistic means are used to manipulate the situation so that it is in people's 'interest' to cooperate. The egocentric goals of strategic action could be pursued without communication. When language is used, it merely transmits information or expresses power. In communicative action, by contrast, language itself integrates action.

Certainly, all language transmits information and all language that integrates action also involves interests. However, Habermas (1998: 224) argues that, in communicative action, the transmission of information about interests that lie outside of language is interrupted, and there is a shift of 'perspective from the objectivating attitude of an actor oriented toward success who wants to realize some purpose in the world, to the performative attitude of a speaker who wants to reach understanding with a second person with regard to something in the world'. Consequently, Habermas (1998: 220) claims, 'both these types of action are "entwined" although they occur in "different constellations"'.

Since the mechanism for coordinating action is intrinsic to speech in communicative action, Habermas (1987b: 196) argues that we should look at communicative action as the normal use of language. In contrast, strategic action uses language simply as one among other means for social coordination, and is therefore parasitic upon normal language insofar as it presumes normalcy of communication for the very effectiveness of its manipulations.

Of course, such terms as 'parasitic' and 'normal' carry a normative charge. Yet we believe that Habermas' thought can be better understood if we take it primarily as a theory of normal and pathological communication, rather than as a normative argument against strategic and for communicative action. His is first a theory of normalcy and only secondarily a normative theory. Indeed, Habermas sees very well the attraction of strategic action. If our goals are clear and our cause is just, it is perhaps immoral to try to achieve them through such a risky and inefficient method as communicative action. In the causes of equality, justice and freedom – not to mention simply feeding hungry people – shouldn't we engage in strategic action wherever necessary? Habermas' question is why, given that, does communicative action still exist? Why hasn't the world, in pursuit of mostly laudable goals, been reduced, willy-nilly, to the instrumental action that Weber, Horkheimer and Adorno foresaw?

Notice that this is a more subtle argument than Habermas is usually interpreted as making. He is not just saying that Weber's, Horkheimer's and Adorno's pessimistic theoretical cul-de-sac must be countered with a theory of communicative action. Instead he is saying that their pessimism is historically inaccurate. Our culture has not been completely and irrevocably dominated by a formal instrumental reason. Communicative action is offered as a theory to explain why formal instrumental reason has not and ultimately cannot completely dominate a culture.

Understanding and validity claims

Habermas argues that communicative action continues to occur because even strategic action depends upon the kind of understanding that is tied to the idea of reaching an agreement. This is because, for Habermas, understanding cannot be adequately described as transferring meaning from the speaker to the hearer since meaning goes beyond the intention of the speaker. Nor can meaning be seen as awareness of the correspondence between the utterance and the world since this idea is based on a dubious copy theory of truth. Instead, understanding is an intersubjective process that occurs within the realm of language. It is language that provides both the medium and the telos of understanding.

To understand the meaning of a linguistic utterance is to take a stand in terms of its claims to being a valid statement, and such *validity claims* can only be justified linguistically. This linguistic justification takes the form of a rationally motivated agreement about something in the world. Even though understanding in strategic action may refer to reified norms or objects that appear to be external to language, these too ultimately depend upon rationally motivated agreement to the extent that they can be understood. The process of reaching an understanding means being able to rationally accept or reject the validity claims made by the speech act. This is the normal function of language and communicative action of this kind allows social action to be coordinated in a non-pathological way.

A validity claim coordinates social action because it is inherently intersubjective. It creates an intersubjective expectation for both speaker and hearer. There is a binding expectation upon the speaker to assume responsibility for reasonably justifying validity claims if challenged. There is also a binding expectation upon the hearer to agree or disagree with the validity claim and to be able to provide reasons for doing so. Seeing a statement as a validity claim implies that the participants are capable of bracketing the 'truth' of their statement and conceiving the statement as being open to challenge. This reciprocal openness to possible challenge and critique requires a reflective attitude on the part of both speaker and hearers.

Habermas' is primarily a theory of normalcy rather than a normative theory. Hence, this binding expectation imposed by validity claims characterizes the normal state of communication. Yet Habermas' formulation also has a normative force, because the binding expectation of communicative action makes an ethical demand upon speakers to assume responsibility for redeeming their validity claims through further communication and without resorting to external factors. This is the normative force intrinsic to understanding. Communicative action is distinguished by its attempt to comply with that norm whereas strategic action simply uses that expectation without intending to fulfill it.

The purpose of normal communication is the achievement of an agreement regarding the validity claim which does not necessarily conform to the expectations of either party. Habermas is not saying that the *ability* to reach agreement is built into everyday processes of communication, only that this ability is implicit or presupposed as part of the goal of understanding. All true communication takes the form of validity claims that call for a reflective attitude and bind social action through their demand for recognition. In practice, however, many communications fail to achieve this agreement. Understanding is part of the form of communicative action and does not require that actual agreements be reached.

Validity claims are not a specialized and uncommon form of communication. According to Habermas, all communication that is oriented to understanding implicitly raises validity claims which are part of the general structure of possible communication. A theory of communicative action can locate in these validity claims 'a gentle but obstinate, a never silent although seldom redeemed claim to reason, a claim that must be recognized de facto whenever and wherever there is to be consensual action' (Habermas, 1979: 97). Claims to validity are often not explicit, and it is even rarer for them to be explicitly redeemed. None the less, that possibility of redemption is built into the structure of understanding and represents the paradigm case.

Validity claims always occur in and are tied to specific contexts. Nevertheless, Habermas thinks that they transcend the contingencies of their local genesis to make universal claims. To make a claim to validity is, for Habermas, always to presuppose universality, that is, to suppose that any rational person would be motivated to agree. It is the presupposition of universality in any validity claim that gives them a certain transcendence over their particular context. In this sense, Habermas' theory of normalcy applies to any cultural context. Communicative action involving contestable validity claims is the normal form of speech and is able to provide a critical perspective on any society.

Necessary presuppositions of normal communication

The necessary presuppositions for communication function like strong idealizations. This is why Habermas has often referred to them as an 'ideal speech situation'. The presuppositions are not always realized, but they must be supposed by the participants if the interaction is to be one characterized as communication. Habermas is quite aware of the burden of proof if he is to escape the accusation that his necessary presuppositions simply reflect the prejudices of Western academic culture. He 'must show that these rules of discourse are not mere conventions; rather they are inescapable presuppositions' (Habermas, 1990: 89).

In response, Habermas proposes what he calls reconstructions. The idea of a reconstruction went through several formulations for Habermas, but it essentially means to make the implicit knowledge of competent subjects theoretically explicit. In this way, a reconstruction is only descriptive of normal communication. Therefore the relation that everyday knowledge has to a reconstructive science is different than to an objectivating science, such as a natural science. An objectivating science can and often does debunk everyday knowledge, but 'a proposal for reconstruction . . . can represent pretheoretical knowledge more or less explicitly or adequately, but it can never falsify it' (Habermas, 1979: 16).

The presuppositions are reconstructed from what competent actors must be assumed to be able to do given Habermas' theory of understanding and validity claims. Remember that Habermas believes that the purpose of communication is to achieve understanding and that understanding means the ability to take a stand in relation to a validity claim based only on the rationality of the argument. The reconstruction makes explicit what competent actors are able to do intuitively in order for communication to achieve its goal of understanding.

According to Habermas, all communication must presuppose an 'ideal speech situation' of unforced consensus. Thus, taking a stand regarding validity claims means presupposing a situation where the validity claims are challenged and defended by rational argumentation alone and not by recourse to status, money or power. This ideal speech situation is the core of communicative action and stands as a metaphor for the normal state of communication. Strategic action also requires imagining this ideal speech situation, at least as a counter-factual. Even in the worst forms of manipulation, speakers must imagine how people would come to agree without manipulation, if only in order to more effectively manipulate them.

From this conception of the ideal speech situation, we can formulate two distinct presuppositions of normal communication (and several associated characteristics). First, participants must be able to take a stand based only on the rationality of the argument; and second, there must be reciprocity predicated on the mutual recognition of all competent subjects.

The first presupposition is necessary if the goal of the communication is understanding. Understanding that is based on any force outside of communication is not, according to Habermas, true understanding. Let us say, for example, that a teacher tells a student that he will receive a 'C' for a class. There is no understanding of the meaning of the 'C' unless they can both bracket the external forces so that the student can take a stand only in terms of the rationality of the teacher's reasons for giving that 'C'. To the student, the 'C' might mean a lost scholarship. To the teacher, it might mean an average effort that fulfilled only the basic requirements. They understand one another only if the teacher sets aside her institutional authority and explains to the student her reasons for the 'C' and if the student sets aside the external pressures and takes a stand only in terms of the rationality of the teacher's reasons. When the goal is understanding, the social action of assigning a grade becomes a matter of reaching consensus based on rational argumentation.

The second presupposition requires that we recognize all competent subjects as equally legitimate sources of validity claims and challenges. Taking a stand on validity claims based only on the rationality of the argument requires the recognition that other viewpoints may be more rationally convincing than our own. In order for the most rational argument to dominate, no relevant argument can be suppressed or excluded. Every subject who is capable of speech and action is allowed to participate in discourse. Each is allowed to call into question any proposal. Each is allowed to introduce any proposal into the discourse. Each is allowed to express her attitudes, wishes and needs.

In his more recent works, Habermas suggests that these presuppositions are somewhat flexible. For example, he wants to drop the term 'ideal speech situation', because it 'tempts one to improperly hypostatize the system of validity claims on which speech is based' (1996: 323). What is essential here are not the specific presuppositions, but that there are some counterfactual presuppositions that 'open up a perspective allowing them to go beyond local practices of justification and to transcend the provinciality of their spatiotemporal contexts that are inescapable in action and experience' (1996: 323).

Habermas insists that to argue against the existence of these communicative presuppositions is to engage in a 'performative contradiction'. By this he means that actual engagement in the argument contradicts the proposition being asserted. For example, the presupposition of reciprocal recognition of all competent subjects implies that all arguments necessarily presuppose that any rational person would agree if only they understood. It is always possible to maintain that arguments do not necessarily make such an assumption, but by engaging in the argument even skeptics are assuming, through their performance, that any rational person would agree with their proposition. The skeptic's performance contradicts her position.

Of course, it could be imagined that these necessary presuppositions could be avoided by simply not engaging in real argumentation. However, Habermas believes that the type of socialization required to produce a human being necessarily includes communicative action, and this in itself makes it impossible to deny the universality of norms implied by such communication. As Habermas (1990: 100) put it, 'The skeptic may reject morality, but he cannot reject the ethical substance of the life circumstances in which he spends his waking hours, not unless he is willing to take refuge in suicide or serious mental illness.'

This is not to say that actual discourses do conform to these presuppositions, but they are intelligible only in terms of them. In this way, the presuppositions necessary for normal speech carry a normative force (Habermas, 1975: 120). For example, the presupposition of reciprocal recognition of every competent subject calls for democratic decision-making and stands as a criticism of all discussions that exclude some category of persons.

This is really the basis of Habermas' famous discourse ethics. He does not intend to provide any first principle or ultimate justification from outside the realm of argumentation, nor does he offer concrete precepts about what should, or should not, be done. He wants only to provide a methodological prescription about how moral decisions are to be made. 'To that extent, morality as grounded by discourse ethics is based on a pattern inherent in mutual understanding in language from the beginning' (Habermas, 1990: 163).

These necessary presuppositions of normal communication are a central part of Habermas' analytic and descriptive sociology. They provide an internal logic against which the contingent circumstances and the development of concrete communicative situations can be assessed. More importantly, these necessary presuppositions are the heart of his critical sociology. With them, Habermas is able to recover a standpoint from which the present situation can be critiqued. Habermas believes that this critical standpoint is missing in non-transcendental approaches because of their cultural relativism.

System and Lifeworld: the Theory of Pathologies

Habermas' critical theory springs from two intermingled but separate sources. The first, discussed above, is a theory of normalcy which defines a non-pathological situation in terms of the necessary presuppositions of communication. The second, which we now examine, begins from experiences of crises that Habermas theoretically diagnoses as pathologies of modernity. A theory of normalcy is necessary in order to show that current crises are pathologies and not merely unpleasant but necessary stages. Nevertheless, because the theory of necessary communicative presuppositions is a descriptive reconstruction from the status quo, it cannot possibly provide a critical approach to the status quo. For this reason, a critical theory of pathologies cannot simply be derived from the theory of normalcy. Instead, Habermas' critical theory depends upon the argument that crises which are actually experienced and apparently unrelated are best diagnosed as the result of a conflict between a 'lifeworld' that requires communicative action and a 'system' that both depends on the lifeworld and yet destructively encroaches upon it. We are motivated to realize the ideal speech situation of communicative action because essential lifeworld processes would fail if given entirely over to a system that bypasses understanding.

Much of Habermas' description of the crises of modernity is derived from Weber and the early Frankfurt School – loss of meaning, the growth of bureaucracy, alienation and reification to name a few. These manifest themselves as individual experiences of crises. But Habermas wants to theorize the crises as *avoidable* pathologies rather than as necessary stages or byproducts of modernity. Indeed, the criticality of his theory depends on this. Thus Habermas sees these crises as due to a particular relation between the system and the lifeworld that could be otherwise.

To grasp Habermas' theory of pathologies we need to understand precisely what he means by lifeworld and system and the pathological relation between them under advanced capitalism. The distinction between system and lifeworld is introduced in *Legitimation Crisis* (1975) but not fully developed until the second volume of *The Theory of Communicative Action* (1987a). It would be a mistake to simply assimilate it to such sociological divisions as that between macro and micro or structure and agency. Instead, it demarcates different spheres of social reproduction, different functions of integration and different contexts of action. Put briefly, the system is a specialized sphere of material reproduction which is integrated by interconnecting the consequences of actions that are embedded in a strategic context. In contrast, the lifeworld is primarily the sphere of symbolic reproduction integrated through mutual understanding embedded in a communicative context. System and lifeworld are always together in practice, but a full understanding of modernity requires that they be analytically separated. These two models provide a two-level concept of society with each level developing increasingly autonomous modes of operation. Starting from the premise that they are increasingly autonomous, much of Habermas' effort has been in trying to understand how the two are related.

Lifeworld

The lifeworld refers to those interpretive patterns that are culturally transmitted and linguistically organized, which for Habermas includes the formation of group identities and the development of individual personalities. According to Habermas, these all share the characteristics of being symbolically structured and dependent on linguistically mediated social reproduction.

Habermas (1984: 70) speaks of the lifeworld both as a set of 'more or less diffuse, always unproblematic, background convictions', and also as a form of integration. This corresponds to the two different perspectives from which the lifeworld can be examined: that of the participating subject, and that of sociological analysis. From the viewpoint of the participating subject, the lifeworld is a resource of implicit assumptions, pre-interpreted knowledge and traditional practices. As such, the lifeworld provides the necessarily assumed context for individual actions that are often in conflict with the actions of others. From the sociological perspective, the lifeworld coordinates social action not just in spite of, but also through, conflictual action. The lifeworld provides the necessarily assumed intersubjective grounds upon which all conflict is acted out (Habermas, 1991b: 247).

Strictly speaking, the lifeworld is precisely that part of society which cannot be thematized as an object of sociological study, although elements of it can be. In this sense, the lifeworld is the necessarily implicit background against which any given social object can appear. Habermas argues that the concept of the lifeworld only becomes sociologically fruitful when we focus on the functions that it performs in the reproduction of social life. He posits three forms of social reproduction. First, cultural reproduction in which participants reproduce and modify the stock of pre-interpreted knowledge upon which they draw in order to come to mutual understandings. Second, social integration through which participants manage interpersonal interactions and regulate membership in social groups to create societal solidarity. Third, socialization which reproduces the competences that make a subject capable of reciprocal participation in communicative processes. Habermas (1987a: 137–8) calls this set of competences a personality.

According to Habermas, the lifeworld requires normal communication in order to carry out these three functions of reproducing of social life. If the lifeworld cannot carry out these functions, social pathologies develop and manifest themselves as individual experiences of crises. Habermas argues that this is precisely what is happening in advanced capitalism as the system inappropriately takes over the functions of the lifeworld.

System

The system represents those parts of society where interpersonal actions are coordinated through their functional consequences in accordance with the adaptive goals of instrumental action. A system achieves social order through the functional integration of the consequences of actions of anonymous individuals based on abstract media.

The primary example of a system is a free market economy. If we try to discover, for example, who sets the price of a particular commodity in an ideal free market, we soon discover that no one really does. The price of the commodity is set by functionally relating the consequences of the actions of producers and suppliers with the actions of consumers, that is, by the coordination of supply and demand. The abstract medium for relating those actions is money. If the producer makes more of the commodity and the consumers' demand does not increase, then the price of the commodity goes down. In a sense, we could say that the producer caused the price to go down, but that was hardly the producer's intent. It makes more sense here to say that the functional relations that constitute the market set the price. Prices go up and down, companies prosper or fail, people are hired or fired, consumers are disappointed or satisfied all because of market actions that are impossible to trace to the intent of any particular person or even group.

Both conceptually and actually, systems are tied to processes in the lifeworld. In actuality, systems and the lifeworld are always intertwined and even when fully objectivated by sociological analysis, systems still must be seen as firmly anchored in the lifeworld. For example, the formal model of the market as a fully autonomous system is only an abstraction from the myriad informal relations that constitute the market. Prices are set not only by the functional relation of abstract media, but also by such lifeworld processes as mob psychology, con games, trust, personal competition, and the like.

A system is also tied to the lifeworld conceptually. A system represents those aspects of interpersonal processes that cannot be grasped as a product of communicative action in the lifeworld. The full extent of the system can only be discovered by starting hermeneutically with members' knowledge in the lifeworld and then, through an objectivating analysis, uncovering the conditions and constraints that go beyond the knowledge of participants themselves.

Nevertheless, Habermas (1987a: 233) argues that 'the systems model is no mere artifact'. Admittedly, most aspects of society can be viewed either as a lifeworld from the participants' viewpoints or as a functional system from an objectivating viewpoint. There are, however, some aspects of social reality that are not fully compatible with a lifeworld perspective. Habermas calls these 'steering media' and gives the examples of money and power. These media are the heart of a system and steer interpersonal relations without recourse to traditional norms or communicatively achieved consensus. In this sense, the system includes the operative mechanisms of society that function below or above the level of awareness of its members.

Systems such as the economy and political administration are primarily steered by money and power instead of by people. As the complexity of the system increases, its rationality no longer coincides with the rationality of any individual. People are able to pursue egoistic, even anti-social goals, that nevertheless result in the social order of the system. Indeed, people's agreement on the goals of the system through rational ethical argument becomes unnecessary for social order. Actors no longer need to agree with or even understand the goals of the system in order for their actions to assume a pattern in pursuit of those goals. This is what Habermas means by the uncoupling of the system from the lifeworld. The functionalist interrelations achieved through media such as money mean that the coordination of actions can be increasingly uncoupled from the lifeworld of communication and are able to work, in effect, behind people's backs.

Habermas argues that the current relationship between the lifeworld and the system is dangerously unbalanced, and that this imbalance leads to social pathologies. However, it would be wrong to interpret him as saying that any uncoupling of the system and lifeworld is necessarily bad. In fact, it may be inevitable given the complexities of the modern world. We simply cannot rely on our traditions to, for example, set the prices of commodities and we certainly do not wish to spend all of our time reaching a consensual agreement on the diverse prices.

Modern, complex societies are less and less able to coordinate action by a reservoir of traditional interpretations immune from criticism. Instead, any consensual agreement must be reached through rational discussions that often bring into question the very grounds for deciding any dispute. Consequently, agreements based on understanding are much more difficult to reach and much less stable if reached. Systems, such as economic markets, are able to coordinate actions in increasingly complex ways without the need for understanding or consensus. In our pluralistic society, it has become difficult to even imagine any other way to set the prices of commodities, to decide what will or will not be produced, what companies will or will not survive, who will or will not work. This is why Habermas sees the emergence of systems as an evolutionary advance.

Even though systems can be seen as increasingly uncoupled from the lifeworld, they must still be connected to processes in the lifeworld in the sense that the steering media of the system, such as money and power, need to be institutionally and motivationally anchored in the lifeworld. A capitalist system, for example, requires a lifeworld that esteems wealth and will define success in terms of its acquisition. Changes in the system also need to be grounded in the lifeworld for adherence and legitimation. Indeed, 'every new leading mechanism of system differentiation must be institutionalized [in the lifeworld] via family status, the authority of office, or bourgeois private law' (Habermas, 1987a: 173). For all these reasons, Habermas (1987a: 151) can say that 'the inner logic of the symbolic reproduction of the lifeworld . . . results in internal limitations on the reproduction of the societies we view from the outside as boundary-maintaining systems'.

In sum, despite the usefulness of the system model, society cannot be conceived simply as a boundary-maintaining system. None the less, parts of society, especially those dominated by steering media, can be modeled as systems so long as we remember that they emerge from the lifeworld and are never totally separate from its processes. Habermas maintains that it is only by using the model of a system that we are able to perceive the threat to the lifeworld posed by current conditions. The distinction between lifeworld and system is central to Habermas' theory of pathologies since it allows him to analyse the instrumental functions of the system, the communicative actions of the lifeworld and, most importantly, the pathological relation between the two.

Rationalization and differentiation

The primary difference between the system and the lifeworld lies in the distinct ways in which they coordinate interactions between people. Habermas refers to one as system integration and the other as social integration. The lifeworld's social integration coordinates interaction primarily through mutual understanding – whether traditionally secured or communicatively achieved – and depends on the conscious action orientation of individuals. System integration coordinates interaction by functional interrelation of consequences of actions, which is able to bypass the conscious intentions of individuals (Habermas, 1987a: 117). Habermas' theory of pathologies depends upon the idea that pathological effects may occur when the mode of integration characteristic of systems replaces or bypasses the mode of integration achieved through communicative action.

Habermas' theory contends that these two mechanisms of integration are not simply different perspectives for observing the same phenomena. Instead, he argues that they are two different forms that develop through distinct evolutionary processes. Thus Habermas presents the increasing complexity of the system and the increasing rationalization of the lifeworld as two separate but related processes. Habermas' theory of pathologies requires that we recognize the internal, evolutionary logic of their separate development. If we cannot grasp the *logic* of their separate development, we are unable to criticize the *actual* development as pathological.

The difference between the development of the system and the development of the lifeworld increases over time. Moreover, differentiation *within* the lifeworld also increases as different 'value spheres' of the lifeworld – such as the aesthetic, the scientific and the normative – develop their particular ways of evaluating validity claims. This is, for Habermas, the very definition of rationalization, the development of the internal logic of a particular mode of integrating interactions through discursively redeemable validity claims. Differentiation and rationalization are therefore connected by definition – especially since the internal logic of any given differentiated sphere becomes explicit and capable of being expressed as discursively defensible validity claims only because there are external standpoints in other differentiated and rationalized spheres from which the internal logic of the pertinent sphere can be observed. For example, the taken-for-granted assumptions of a religious domain become in need of discursive defense and therefore rationalized because they can be challenged from a separate scientific domain.

In the differentiated, rationalized lifeworld of modernity, traditions cannot guarantee mutual understanding. Instead, traditions can only remain viable if they are no longer simply assumed, but rather become the explicit subject of communicative action – in other words, to the extent that they cease to be real traditions. In our rationalized, pluralistic lifeworld, traditions tend to lose their unifying power and shrink down to individual subjective reason (Habermas, 1987a: 302). Rationalization in the lifeworld means that procedures of justification become increasingly independent from traditional normative criteria of validity and increasingly dependent on communicative action. Habermas (1984: 340) contends that 'a lifeworld can be regarded as rationalized to the extent that it permits inter-actions that are not guided by normatively ascribed agreement but – directly or indirectly – by communicatively *achieved* understanding'.

As interactions in the lifeworld become increasingly independent of traditional norma-tive contexts, they rely more on the risky and unstable integration of consensual agreement. Thus it is precisely the reliance on inherently unstable consensual agreement that leads to the need for integration at the systems level. Consequently, rationalization in the lifeworld leads to the emergence of systems.

Not only do value-spheres within the lifeworld differentiate and rationalize, but so do the three processes through which the lifeworld is reproduced. In cultural reproduction, expert knowledge replaces sacred traditions; in social integration, a legal system is differentiated from moral norms; in socialization, a post-conven-tional stage of moral autonomy allows indivi-duals to separate themselves from traditional norms and discursively defend their own moral choices.

The more the lifeworld and the processes for its reproduction are differentiated and rationa-lized, the more they come to depend on communicative action. However, it is also true that each of these areas of reproduction become separated from the everyday world of commu-nication. Expert knowledge is separated from popular knowledge; legal interpretations are separated from everyday concepts of justice; and ethical and religious systems become separate from everyday moral intuitions.

Reintegrating this expert knowledge back into the everyday world becomes a major problem in modern society. Expert knowledge in scientific, legal and religious institutions tends to become

reified into systems when separated from every-day communication. Questions of what to study, what laws are just, and what actions are moral are removed from the communicative contexts of everyday life and instead increasingly decided by functional relations based on money and power.

Furthermore, as the lifeworld becomes differentiated into distinct spheres of rationality, individual subjects become decentered. The functional and strategic rationality of the world of work, for instance, is so distinct from the communicative rationality of the family that individuals never feel at home in either one. This makes the subject vulnerable to what Habermas calls fragmentation – the feeling of being different people at work and at home.

The rationalization of the lifeworld provides the link between Habermas' theory of necessary presuppositions for communication and his theory of social pathologies. In former times, communicative understanding could be used merely as the means for passing on traditions in the lifeworld. Now, however, with the collapse of traditions in modernity, the lifeworld increas-ingly is *constituted* by communicative under-standing. The regulation of interpersonal interactions does not rely on understanding traditions so much as on understanding itself, that is on the interpretive accomplishments of the participating actors. The rationalized life-world requires communicative action for its reproduction.

As we have seen, however, communicative action is a risky and unstable method of social integration. It is vulnerable to many failures, but especially to having its essential functions taken over by the more efficient system. This is at the heart of Habermas' theory of pathologies. Under current conditions, the lifeworld and commu-nicative action are threatened by the expansion of systems.

Social pathologies

In contrast to the rationalization of the life-world, the system develops through increasing complexity, differentiation and expanded capa-cities of steering mechanisms. Although a considerably rationalized lifeworld is one of the initial conditions for the emergence of a system, the system's decoupling means the increasing complexity of the system is autonomous from the lifeworld's rationalization. The system constitutes a distinct internal logic that becomes pathological when it takes over or 'colonizes' the essential functions of the lifeworld.

The type of understanding that Habermas describes may not be necessary for all commu-nication, but he argues that it is at least necessary for communicative action which maintains the rationalized lifeworld and avoids pathologies. Habermas (1990: 102) claims that cultural reproduction, social integration, and socialization 'operate only in the medium of action oriented toward reaching an understanding. There is no other equivalent medium in which these functions can be fulfilled. Individuals acquire and sustain their identity through communicative interactions. They do not have the option of a long-term absence from contexts of action oriented toward reaching an understanding.' To withdraw from the communicative actions that constitute the lifeworld is to risk personal crises, such as schizophrenia or suicide, that are signs of social pathology.

Of course, it is not always clear whether individual crises are signs of social pathology. There is no obvious, universal definition of health in terms of which societies can be seen as pathological. The crux of Habermas' critical theory depends upon showing these developments to be pathological in some context-transcendent way. His argument is that these crises are generated by the failure of symbolic reproduction in the lifeworld, a failure caused by the subordination of communicative action and its necessary presuppositions.

From the viewpoint of communicative action, Western modernization has been a one-sided development of instrumental rationality and strategic communication. As system complexity increases at the expense of the lifeworld, the system takes over functions that it cannot possibly perform, such as cultural reproduction, social integration and socialization. 'These three functions can be fulfilled only via the medium of communicative action and not via the steering media of money and power: meaning can neither be bought nor coerced' (Habermas, 1991b: 259).

The systemic mechanisms based on power and money penetrate into areas, such as the socialization of children, that require a communicative coordination of action. For example, children increasingly are being socialized by television shows and advertising. However, the values, models and images that appear on TV are not a product of consensual discussion; instead they are decided by a market system using the medium of money. Habermas argues that while such a system may be very good at setting the price of commodities sold on TV, it cannot possibly be expected to properly socialize children, since it views them only strategically without any goal of reaching collaborative understanding.

This does not make the system inherently evil. It is not the uncoupling of the system from the lifeworld as such that Habermas sees as pathological, but the penetration of system processes into areas that are necessary to the symbolic reproduction of the lifeworld. These areas are forced to rely on economic and bureaucratic mechanisms that are inimical to mutual understanding. This is not, however, an inevitable process. The system and the lifeworld could uncouple in a way that would still allow the lifeworld to place restrictions on the functioning of the system. Instead, in advanced capitalist societies, it is the system that has restricted the lifeworld with pathological results.

Colonization of the lifeworld occurs when crises in the management of economic and political systems are avoided by disturbing the symbolic reproduction of the lifeworld. For example, the capitalist economic system inevitably develops problems that would lead to the failure of businesses and losses for investors. These dangers are now routinely minimized by government policies which often are not in the general public interest. In order to generate public support for such corporate welfare programs, public opinion comes to be viewed as something to be manufactured. In other words, the system is legitimized by top-down manipulations, rather than the bottom-up activity of citizens rationally and ethically debating the appropriateness of various public policies. Since consensus no longer emerges from communicative action in the lifeworld, democratic judgements are instead reduced to the aggregate opinions of isolated, atomized and easily manipulated individuals. Steering crises in the economic or bureaucratic sub-systems are avoided by colonizing the lifeworld which increases personal alienation, fragmentation of identity and the unsettling of democratic solidarities (Habermas, 1987a: 386).

The primary example of colonization discussed by Habermas is juridification. This is the redefinition of everyday situations so that they are subject to legal regulations. Like many of the effects of the system, juridification is both good and bad. On the one hand, juridification expands social rights; on the other, it creates a new type of dependency. The dependence of people on each other mediated by the lifeworld in families, communities, churches and schools, is replaced by dependence on legal or administrative bureaucracies with their own imperatives as systems. The orientation toward understanding and consensus that characterized the lifeworld is replaced by strategic relations to bureaucracies.

One recent example is the United States' Supreme Court decision in *Davis* v. *Monroe* that made school administrators liable for sexual harassment between children. This expands the rights of children, but also introduces a new type of dependency, so that potential problems are avoided by the institution of explicit regulations under the threat of legal sanctions rather than by more flexible lifeworld discussions involving parents, teachers and administrators.

Habermas recognizes that the lifeworld, based on dominating traditions, has its own problems, and that juridification is an attempt to solve these problems. For Habermas (1987a: 362), the irony is that juridification itself endangers the basis of freedom in civic discourse at the same time that it is being used to guarantee personal liberties and rights. For example, the welfare state helps to address the traditional gaps regarding the care of the poor, but in so doing it erodes earlier traditions of care, and the consensual mechanisms that coordinate it, by imposing a new welfare bureaucracy onto what formerly was a function of the lifeworld.

The cure for these pathologies is a more vigorous lifeworld which allows the free inter-play of the different systematized value spheres within everyday communication. The scientific, economic, legal and political spheres must be open to the uninhibited discursive challenges and reinterpretations of communicative action. This utopic vision stands as a criticism of present society because this free interplay is incompatible with advanced capitalism and a welfare state which must manage the lifeworld in order to manipulate public opinion. Nevertheless, Habermas claims that this vision is anticipated in everyday communication. Everyday communication necessarily refers to the presuppositions that Habermas believes characterize communicative action. The pathologies of modernity can only be avoided if communicative action is allowed to interpenetrate and curtail the workings of systems.

CRITICISMS

Habermas' theory of normalcy has been subjected to various attacks. Underlying many of these has been a skepticism toward any notion of normalcy. It is not likely that any concept of what is normal – even one that is tied to process rather than substance, and even one that deals with such a universal phenomenon as communication – can ever escape the charge of ethnocentrism. This is especially so since Habermas attempts to discern normalcy from a particular historical instance. His analysis of the ideal speech situation admittedly begins from 'idealised cases of the communicative action that is typical of everyday life *in modern societies*' (Habermas, 1982: 236; emphasis added). This is hardly a promising beginning for a theory that seeks to transcend any local context.

In particular, Habermas' contention that communicative action involving validity claims is the paradigm case of communication is not entirely convincing. Certainly, other forms of communication employ resources that are intrinsic to language. For example, rhetoric – which Habermas (1984: 331) clearly distinguishes from communicative action – may be the use of language *par excellence*. Rather than resorting to validity claims and a transcendental ethics of speech, rhetoric attains reasoned decisions through the persuasive powers of language itself. Habermas presents no reason why the expressive play of rhetoric is any less the inherent telos of communication than his conception of understanding. Clearly, there are cases where we may prefer communicative action's focus on validity claims, but it cannot be said that communicative action rather than rhetoric is the normal or even ideal use of language.

Whether or not communicative action is the normal state of communication, it is difficult to argue with the proposition that communication and understanding are necessary both to the individual and for social reproduction. However, Habermas' critical theory is not based on the necessity of an ordinary idea of understanding in everyday communication. He is only able to derive his necessary presuppositions from his special definitions of communication and understanding. Understanding a communication means, for Habermas, being able to take a stand on its validity claims that are motivated only by the rationality of the argument.

Even his friendliest critics have had a difficult time with Habermas' definition of understanding. As Thomas McCarthy (1985) points out, you do not have actually to take a position to understand. Similarly, Jeffrey Alexander (1991: 64) calls the identification of understanding with rational consensual agreement in regards to validity claims, 'a wishful equation'. Communication and understanding, as those words are normally used, do not necessitate consensual agreement free of all non-rational force. Therefore, complains Alexander, Habermas is just incorporating his utopian aspirations into his preliminary definitions.

Neither is communicative action essential to social integration. In fact, unquestioned traditional norms and non-rational sentiments integrate society much more effectively than validity claims, even in advanced capitalist societies. This appears to be as much a fact as any historical knowledge can be. Since Habermas can hardly deny that past societies have been successfully integrated with very little communicative action, his argument for the current necessity of communicative action rests on an unsupported evolutionary theory. He contends that, in the present situation, communicative presuppositions are necessary because now society can only be integrated on the basis of contestable validity claims.

This means that the core of Habermas' argument is not that the presuppositions are necessary to social reproduction – the historical record clearly shows they are not – but that their evolutionary development is inevitable. He therefore must contend that although contestable validity claims have not been necessary in the past and although in comparison they are less effective integrators, nevertheless evolutionary developments now make them necessary. The necessity of the communicative presuppositions can only be derived from the *inevitability* of the evolutionary development. Unfortunately, Habermas' theory of evolution is incomplete and, on the points he has clarified, dubious. (See, for example, Schmid, 1982; and for an immanent critique of the developmental logic of Habermas's evolutionary theory, see Strydom, 1992.)

In any case, inevitability cannot be logically derived from historical trends, especially if one wants to develop a theory that is able to critique such trends. Moreover, it is both contradictory and unsupported to say that the move from unquestioned traditional norms to communicative action is inevitable, but that the move from communicative action to system integration is not. The most that can be said is that, in our present historical situation, we prefer communicative action over both traditional norms and system integration, and that, therefore, presuppositions such as reciprocity are preferred by communicatively competent individuals in postconventional societies.

Furthermore, even in those modern situations where communication is most likely to take the form of validity claims, Habermas' presuppositions do not appear to be necessary. In scientific discussions, for example, not everyone who is capable of speech and action is allowed to participate in discourse, to put any proposal into discussion, or to express their attitudes, wishes and needs. There are some special qualifications for participating in scientific discussions and these appear to be very helpful in reaching consensus.

From a postmodernist viewpoint, it has been argued that Habermas' commitment to communicative rationality and evolutionary ethics is simply an attempt to portray controversial political judgements as a mythical metanarrative of emancipation (Redding, 1986; Rorty, 1985). Jean-Francois Lyotard (1984) holds that such metanarratives delegitimate other language games by defining truth in terms of a timeless universal pragmatics. This notion of an ideal truth based on consensus devalues the practical truths expressed by particular persons and groups – truths that emerge from their own creative activity. In addition, by requiring consensus for a statement to count as truth, universal pragmatics stifles new expressions, particularly by those who have traditionally been silent. For Lyotard, the only type of truth which is possible resides in the particular language games that create the heteromorphous, local narratives of everyday life, subject to heterogeneous sets of pragmatic rules. 'For this reason,' says Lyotard (1984: 65), 'it seems neither possible, nor even prudent, to follow Habermas in orienting our treatment of the problem of legitimation in the direction of a search for universal consensus.'

Habermas' response to this critique is that Lyotard is confusing different registers of rationality. The substantive rules that form the content of our reasoning are different from the formal rules *with which* we reason. The former are heterogeneous and may or may not encourage consensus. The latter – the rules *with which* we reason – are the necessary presuppositions that provide the framework of intelligibility and the possibility of any consensus or dissensus. However, it is doubtful that Habermas can make any such clear distinction between the content of the discourse and the rules that frame it. In fact, Habermas' own critical theory depends upon there being a strong connection between the formal rules and the substantive goals that society should pursue. He argues that the formal rules of communicative action are linked to the substantive goal of equal recognition for all participants to the discussion. Clearly, this *Diskursethik* is simply a philosophical version of the liberal values of fair play and procedural justice. It is a mystification to take these controversial political values and move them into the transcendental realm of necessary formal presuppositions.

Because the local and pragmatic character of communication is obscured by universalist pretensions, Habermas' critical theory comes across as convoluted and vague. His primary ideas, such as the ideal speech situation and reciprocity, are defined so abstractly as to have little of the normative force that Habermas ascribes to them. Even if, as Habermas claims, the ideal speech situation is universal and transcends local contexts, the actualization of such characteristics as reciprocity will vary widely depending on particular contexts of speech. Reciprocity in a tribal society must mean something very different than reciprocity in the functionally differentiated society of advanced capitalism.

Mendelson (1979: 73) argues that Habermas' concepts are so abstract as to be politically irrelevant. Rather than appealing to a theory of communication, 'one must . . . criticize these traditions immanently and not get sidetracked in an esoteric theoretical direction'. Since it is the concrete form of reciprocity that matters, discussion of abstract communicative universals is sociologically unrealistic and politically empty. Thus Habermas' core concepts are too vague to be practically meaningful or, if made practically meaningful, are no longer universal.

None of this is to be taken as an argument against the desirability of communicative action and its implied ideal speech situation of reciprocity. On the contrary, most democratically inclined persons share Habermas' preferences. This, however, does not make communicative action necessary or universal; it only shows that communicative action is a central property of certain cultures and situations. But if this is true, what is required is not an argument invoking normalcy and universality, but a discussion that spells out the full implications for the reflexive emergence and practical viability of communicative action.

However, once communicative action is not seen as normal or necessary, some of its disadvantages come into view. Specifically, many of the crises that Habermas refers to in his theory of pathologies can be seen as due more to the trend toward communicative action than to the growth of the system. Anomie, alienation and disenchantment are related to the weakening of traditional norms, which are questioned and thereby undermined by communicative action. These crises are caused by the failure of communicative action to adequately perform the functions of traditional norms rather than the failure of a system to perform the functions of communicative action. We can certainly still prefer communicative action to unquestioned traditional norms, but we cannot pretend that communicative action is the panacea for all the pathologies of modernity, even though it may be central to any democratic search for solutions.

Furthermore, we should realize that the adequacy of communicative action is situational, not universal or essential. Whether communicative action is preferred cannot be derived from a notion of communicative action's necessary functions. For example, the education of children can be done by a semi-bureaucratic system such as a school. The informal relations that actually make up such a system may be able to override the imperatives of money and power that guide the system. Certainly, as discussed above, juridifying the relation between school children carries considerable risks, but sometimes the persistence of regressive practices inclines us to take those risks. The dangers of sexual harassment between children may outweigh the dangers of juridification. In such cases, the formal ethics of a supposedly normal communication provide little guidance.

Habermas' critical theory would be somewhat weakened if communicative action were changed from a necessary presupposition to a method of prudent judgement in specific settings. At the very least, it becomes impossible for an objective analyst to prescribe what is to be done. But Habermas' analysis is still indispensable for understanding the full implications of our commitment to a democratic discourse. For example, his theory spells out the antagonistic relationship between interpersonal communication and such systemic structures as the economy. This means that the preservation of democratic communication requires a defense of the lifeworld from encroachments of such systems as the economy. Most importantly, Habermas' theory provides us with some of the cognitive tools and analytic categories for pursuing our democratic project under the complex and difficult situations of a systematized modernity.

Nevertheless, Habermas' theory of communicative action is not sufficient either to its intended task of critique nor to the practical requirements of democratic discourse. Indeed, Habermas' emphasis on rationality and consensus as an ideal seems to ignore the essentially political character of democratic life and of language use itself. Language's power to constitute an identity and to integrate social action does not lie in its formal presuppositions, but in the speech community that authorizes a language and invests certain users and usages with authority. Even less can these formal presuppositions provide our vision of what is to be done.

'Language is real, practical consciousness,' said Marx and Engels in *The German Ideology* (1970), and part of its being real and practical is that it masks as much as it reveals, suppresses as much as it expresses, takes as tacit more than it makes explicit. A critical theory cannot expect to find its telos in the formal presuppositions of language, because no theory of language can generate a practical program. Thus to accept Habermas' theories of normalcy and pathologies is not to accept, or even to know, the Habermasian solution. His sociological insights are not the same thing as a civic discourse, much less a political agenda. They do not tell us how to move from the analyst's 'is' toward the political 'ought'. In these important senses, for all its brilliance, Habermas' theory of communication is an incomplete project.

REFERENCES

Alexander, Jeffrey (1991) 'Habermas and Critical Theory: Beyond the Marxian Dilemma?', in A. Honneth and H. Joas (eds), *Communicative Action: Essays on Jürgen Habermas's The Theory of*

Communicative Action. Cambridge: Cambridge University Press. pp. 49–73.

Dallmayr, Fred R. (1972) 'Critical Theory Criticized: Habermas's Knowledge and Human Interest and its Aftermath', *Philosophy of the Social Sciences*, 2: 211–29.

Habermas, Jürgen (1971) *Knowledge and Human Interests*. Boston, MA: Beacon Press.

Habermas, Jürgen (1975) *Legitimation Crisis*. Boston, MA: Beacon Press.

Habermas, Jürgen (1979) *Communication and the Evolution of Society*. Boston, MA: Beacon Press.

Habermas, Jürgen (1980) 'The Hermeneutic Claim to Universality', in J. Bleicher (ed.), *Contemporary Hermeneutics: Hermeneutics as Method, Philosophy and Critique*. London: Routledge and Kegan Paul. pp. 181–211.

Habermas, Jürgen (1982) 'A Reply to My Critics', in J. Thompson and D. Held (eds), *Habermas: Critical Debates*. Cambridge, MA: MIT Press. pp. 219–83.

Habermas, Jürgen (1983) 'Modernity – An Incomplete Project', in Hal Foster (ed.), *The Anti-Aesthetic: Essays on Postmodern Culture*. Post Townsend, WA: Bay. pp. 3–15.

Habermas, Jürgen (1984) *The Theory of Communicative Action*. Vol. 1: *Reason and the Rationalization of Society*. Boston, MA: Beacon Press.

Habermas, Jürgen (1987a) *The Theory of Communicative Action*. Vol. 2: *Lifeworld and System: A Critique of Functionalist Reason*. Boston, MA: Beacon Press.

Habermas, Jürgen (1987b) *The Philosophical Discourse of Modernity: Twelve Lectures*. Cambridge, MA: MIT Press.

Habermas, Jürgen (1990) *Moral Consciousness and Communicative Action*. Cambridge, MA: MIT Press.

Habermas, Jürgen (1991a) *The Structural Transformation of the Public Sphere: An Inquiry into a Category of Bourgeois Society*. Cambridge, MA: MIT Press.

Habermas, Jürgen (1991b) 'A Reply', in A. Honneth and H. Joas (eds), *Communicative Action: Essays on Jürgen Habermas's The Theory of Communicative Action*. Cambridge, MA: MIT Press. pp. 215–64.

Habermas, Jürgen (1996) *Between Facts and Norms: Contributions to a Discourse Theory of Law and Democracy*. Cambridge, MA: MIT Press.

Habermas, Jürgen (1998) 'Actions, Speech Acts, Linguistically Mediated Interactions, and the Lifeworld', in M. Cooke (ed.), *On the Pragmatics of Communication*. Cambridge, MA: MIT Press. pp. 215–55.

Horkheimer, Max and Adorno, Theodor (1972) *Dialectic of Enlightenment*. New York: Continuum.

Lyotard, Jean-François (1984) *The Postmodern Condition: A Report on Knowledge* (trans. G. Bennington and B. Massumi). Minneapolis: University of Minnesota Press.

Marx, Karl and Engels, Freidrich (1970) *The German Ideology*. Part 1 (ed. C.J. Arthur). New York: International Publishers.

McCarthy, Thomas (1978) *The Critical Theory of Jürgen Habermas*. Cambridge, MA: MIT Press.

McCarthy, Thomas (1985) 'Reflections on Rationalization in the Theory of Communicative Action', in R.J. Bernstein (ed.), *Habermas and Modernity*. Cambridge, MA: MIT Press. pp. 176–91.

Mendelson, Jack (1979) 'The Habermas–Gadamer Debate', *New German Critique*, 18: 44–73.

Ottmann, Henning (1982) 'Cognitive Interests and Self-Reflection', in J. Thompson and D. Held (eds), *Habermas: Critical Debates*. Cambridge, MA: MIT Press. pp. 79–97.

Redding, P. (1986) 'Habermas, Lyotard, Wittgenstein: Philosophy at the Limits of Modernity', *Thesis Eleven*, 14: 9–25.

Rorty, Richard (1985) 'Habermas and Lyotard on Postmodernism', in R.J. Bernstein (ed.), *Habermas and Modernity*. Cambridge, MA: MIT Press. pp. 161–76.

Schmid, Michael (1982) 'Habermas's Theory of Social Evolution', in J. Thompson and D. Held (eds), *Habermas: Critical Debates*. Cambridge, MA: MIT Press. pp. 162–80.

Strydom, Piet (1992) 'The Ontogentic Fallacy: The Immanent Critique of Habermas's Developmental Logical Theory of Evolution', *Theory, Culture and Society*, 9: 65–93.

17

Symbolic Interactionism at the End of the Century

KENT L. SANDSTROM, DANIEL D. MARTIN AND GARY ALAN FINE

The turn of a new century has traditionally been a time of stock-taking. In terms of sociological theory there can be little doubt that the start of the twentieth century was dominated by important European thinkers, while at its conclusion American thinkers more than hold their own. The first and most distinctively American sociological theory was symbolic interactionism, a perspective on social life that is now more than sixty years old (Blumer, 1937). Symbolic interactionism is clearly linked to American intellectual traditions and, many would argue, to the American belief in the power of individual agency in the face of social structure.

Historically, symbolic interactionism emerged out of the American philosophical tradition of pragmatism, an approach elaborated in the late nineteenth century by Charles Peirce, William James and John Dewey. These thinkers challenged the mechanistic world-view and dualistic assumptions of classical rationalism, the dominant philosophy of their time (Shalin, 1991). Unlike the rationalists, they saw reality as dynamic, individuals as active knowers, meanings as linked to social action and perspectives, and knowledge as an instrumental force that enables people to solve problems and rearrange the world (Denzin, 1996a; Joas, 1996; Shalin, 1986; Thayer, 1981).

Pragmatist philosophy entered into sociology most directly through the writings and teachings of George Herbert Mead (1863–1931), who sought to translate pragmatism into a theory and method for the social sciences. In doing so, Mead drew not only on the ideas of the pragmatist founders, Charles Peirce and William James, but also on the psychological insights of Wilhelm Wundt, the sociological observations of Charles Horton Cooley and James Mark Baldwin, and the evolutionary theory of Charles Darwin. Mead derived his greatest inspiration, however, from the philosophical works of John Dewey (1922, 1925), his colleague at the University of Chicago. Building upon Dewey's seminal ideas, Mead developed a profoundly sociological account of human consciousness, selfhood and behavior – an account he conveyed in a series of social psychology lectures that became the basis for his best-known book, *Mind, Self, and Society* (1934).

The most important disseminator of Mead's ideas was his student Herbert Blumer, a former professional football player who later became a sociologist at Chicago and the University of California at Berkeley. Blumer championed the merits and applicability of Mead's theories for sociological analysis. Eventually Blumer compiled some of his own writings into a book entitled *Symbolic Interactionism* (1969b), which became recognized as the major explication of the symbolic interactionist perspective.

Along with one of his colleagues, Everett Hughes, Blumer had a major influence on a cohort of graduate students he taught at the University of Chicago in the 1940s and early 1950s. This cohort, which included such notable scholars as Howard Becker, Erving Goffman, Joseph Gusfield, Helena Lopata, Gregory Stone, Anselm Strauss and Ralph Turner, further developed the symbolic interactionist perspective and became known as the Second Chicago School (Fine, 1995).

THE GUIDING PREMISES OF SYMBOLIC INTERACTIONISM

Like the advocates of other sociological theories, symbolic interactionists regularly debate with one another about core beliefs, theoretical interpretations and methodological techniques. Yet, while having these areas of disagreement, they share several common assumptions. Central to their perspective are the following three premises articulated by Blumer:

> The first premise is that human beings act toward things on the basis of the meanings those things have for them ... The second premise is that the meaning of such things is derived from, or arises out of, the social interaction that one has with one's fellows. The third premise is that these meanings are handled in, and modified through, an interpretive process used by the person in dealing with the things he [or she] encounters. (1969b: 2)

Although Blumer's three premises serve as the cornerstones of the interactionist perspective, other implicit assumptions inform and guide this perspective, providing it with its philosophical foundations:

1 *People are unique creatures because of their ability to use symbols.* Drawing on the insights of Mead and the early pragmatists, symbolic interactionists stress the significance of people's symbolic capacities. Because people use and rely upon symbols, they do not usually respond to stimuli in a direct or automatic way; instead, they give meanings to the stimuli they experience and then act in terms of these meanings. Their behavior is thus distinctively different from that of other animals or organisms, who act in a more instinctive or reflex-based manner. Humans learn what things mean as they interact with one another. In doing so they rely heavily on language and the communicative processes it facilitates. In essence, they learn to see and respond to symbolically mediated 'realities' – realities that are socially constructed.

2 *People become distinctively human through their interaction.* Symbolic interactionists assume that people acquire distinctively human qualities, and become capable of distinctively human behavior, only through associating with others. According to interactionists, these uniquely human qualities and behaviors include the ability to use

symbols, to think and make plans, to take the role of others, to develop a sense of self, and to participate in complex forms of communication and social organization (Hall, 1972; Strauss, 1993). Interactionists do not believe that people are born human. Rather, they presume that people develop into distinctively human beings as they take part in social interaction. While acknowledging that people are born with certain kinds of biological 'hardware' (for example, a highly developed nervous system) that give them the potential to become fully human, interactionists stress that involvement in society is essential for realizing this potential.

3 *People are conscious and self-reflexive beings who actively shape their own behavior.* The most important capacities that people develop through their involvement in society, or social interaction, are the 'mind' and the 'self'. As Mead (1934) observed, we form minds and selves through communication and role-taking. That is, we develop the capacity to see and respond to ourselves as objects and, thus, to interact with ourselves, or think. Because we can think, we have a significant degree of autonomy in formulating our behavior. As Blumer (1969b: 63–4) asserted, our capacity for thought, or self-interaction, places us 'over against the world instead of merely in it, requires [us] to meet and handle the world through a defining process instead of merely responding to it, and forces [us] to construct [our] action instead of merely releasing it'. We stand over against the objects that make up our environment 'in both a logical and psychological sense', and this frees us from a coercive or predetermined response to those objects (Blumer, 1969b: 69). Our behavior, then, is not determined by the stimuli or objects we confront in our environment. Rather, it is built up and constructed, based on which stimuli and objects we take into account and how we define them. In making this assertion, interactionists embrace a voluntaristic image of human behavior. They suggest that people exercise an important element of freedom in their actions. This does not mean that interactionists think people's actions are unaffected by forces beyond their control. Interactionists clearly believe that a variety of social factors, such as language, race, class and gender, constrain people's interpretations and behaviors. In light of this, interactionists are best characterized as 'soft determinists'; they presume that people's actions are influenced but not determined by prior events or social and biological forces (Brissett and Edgley, 1990).

4 *People are purposive creatures who act in and toward situations.* According to interactionists, human beings don't 'release' their behavior, like tension in a spring, in response to biological drives, psychological needs, or social expectations. Rather, people act toward situations (Hall, 1972). We build up and construct our behavior based on the meaning we attribute to the situation in which we find ourselves. This meaning, or 'definition of the situation', emerges out of interactions with others. That is, we determine what meaning to give to a situation and how to act through taking account of the unfolding intentions, actions and expressions of others. As we negotiate and establish a definition of a situation, we also determine what goals we should pursue. We are purposive in our thoughts and actions; we select lines of behavior based on the presumption that these will lead to anticipated outcomes and desired goals. This is not to say that we are always accurate in appraising the consequences of our chosen actions. In acting purposefully, we do not necessarily act wisely or correctly. In addition, as we interact with others and create lines of action, we don't always pursue goals in a clearcut or single-minded way. Once we begin acting, we encounter obstacles and contingencies that may block or distract us from our original goals and direct us toward new ones.

5 *Human society consists of people engaging in symbolic interaction.* Interactionists differ from other sociologists in their view of the relationship between society and the individual. Following Blumer, interactionists conceive of society as a *fluid but structured process.* This process is grounded in individuals' abilities to assume each other's perspectives, adjust and coordinate their unfolding acts, and symbolically communicate and interpret these acts. In emphasizing that society consists of people acting and interacting symbolically, interactionists disagree with psychologistic theories that see society as existing primarily 'in our heads', either in the form of reward histories or socially shaped cognitions. Interactionists also depart from those structuralist perspectives that reify society, suggesting that it exists independently of us as individuals and that it dictates our actions through the rules, roles, statuses, or structures it imposes upon us. While acknowledging that we are born into a society that sets the framework for our actions through the patterns of meaning and rewards it provides, interactionists stress that we actively shape our identities and behaviors as we make plans, seek goals and

interact with others in specific situations. Society and its structures are human products; they are rooted in the joint acts we engage in with other people.

6 *To understand people's social acts, we need to use methods that enable us to discern the meanings they attribute to these acts.* Interactionists emphasize the significance of the fact that people act on the basis of the meanings they give to things in their world. In turn, interactionists believe it is essential to understand those worlds of meaning and to see them as the individuals or groups under investigation see them. To develop this insider's view, researchers must empathize with – or 'take the role of' – the individuals or groups they are studying (Blumer, 1969b). They also must observe and interact with these individuals or groups in an unobtrusive way. Through adopting such an approach, researchers can gain a deeper appreciation of how these social actors define, construct and act toward the 'realities' that constitute their everyday worlds (Glaser and Strauss, 1967).

MAJOR AREAS OF CONTRIBUTION

Theories gain renown through what their practitioners accomplish. The continuing growth and success of the interactionist approach depends upon the power of its lines of research. In the following survey, we consider some of the more significant lines of research engaged in by interactionists, highlighting the contributions they have made to six major areas of sociological concern: self and identity theory; emotions and emotion work; social coordination; social constructionism; culture and art; and macroanalysis.

Self and identity theory

Analysis of the self has always been central to interactionist sociology. The writings of Blumer (1962), Cooley ([1902] 1964), Mead (1934) and other founders of interactionism highlight the social nature of the self. As noted by these theorists, the self emerges, develops and is sustained through processes of social interaction. It is not present at birth nor is it an inevitable consequence of a person's biological development. Rather, an individual must learn who he or she is through interacting with others. Through these interactions a person comes to believe that he or she has a distinct and meaningful self. Put another way, an individual's 'self' develops out of his or her social relationships. Most importantly, this recognition that the self is fundamentally social represents a core insight of interactionism.

In analysing the self and its implications, interactionists focus on three themes: the genesis and development of the self, the self-concept and the presentation of self.

The genesis and development of the self

As noted earlier, George Herbert Mead developed a ground-breaking theoretical account of how the self arises from communication, interaction and role-taking. Yet, while paying homage to Mead, interactionists have identified gaps in his theory and offered refinements into the processes through which individuals develop selves. For instance, Norbert Wiley (1979) has formulated a theory of infant selfhood that offers a more detailed picture of the emergence of the self in a child's first year – a period that roughly equates to what Mead called the preparatory stage of self-development. Other interactionists such as Gregory Stone (1981) and William Corsaro (1985) have revised and extended Mead's ideas regarding the play stage of self-development, illustrating how playing at fantasy roles and dramas is as important to a child's self-development as playing at the visible roles that Mead highlighted. This type of play enables children not only to enhance their role-taking abilities, but also to learn communication strategies which help them to coordinate their actions with others, enlarge their behavioral repertoires and realize desired selves.

Interactionists have also clarified Mead's ideas about how individuals pass through the stages of self-development. Norman Denzin (1977) notes that Mead did not think people automatically pass from the play to game stages and, thus, did not specify the age sequence of these stages. Instead, Mead implied that 'some persons may never progress to the generalized other phase of taking the other's attitude' (Denzin, 1977: 81). Based on ethnographic research, Denzin proposes that children's movement from one stage of self-development to the next is shaped by their social context, with the most important factor being the patterns of interaction to which they are exposed. Children's self-development, then, is not tied directly to their chronological age but rather is linked to their *interactional* age.

The self-concept

While generally agreeing on how the self emerges and develops, interactionists part company on the relative weight of the 'self' versus the 'situation' in shaping action. Interactionists who place greater emphasis on the self focus on the salience of the self-concept. They ask: how do we conceive of ourselves and how does this change

over time? In addressing these questions, they rely on diverse methodologies, including in-depth interviews, open-ended questionnaires and survey research. Methodologically they are less 'interpretive' and 'qualitative' than their counterparts who emphasize situations. Indeed, self theorists such as Sheldon Stryker (1980) and Morris Rosenberg (1981) are scorned by some interactionists who contend that they reify the social reality of the self in their efforts to quantify that reality. Stryker and Rosenberg, who are sometimes referred to as 'structural symbolic interactionists', recognize the fluid and mutable nature of the self-concept, but they assume that the process through which it changes can be measured and predicted.

In contrast, Viktor Gecas (1982), Ralph Turner (1976) and Louis Zurcher (1977) highlight the fluidity and malleability of self-concepts, even while admitting that these concepts have spatial, institutional and temporal stability. These researchers do not propose predictive hypotheses of the social forces that lead people to conceive of themselves in different ways. Rather, they focus on the symbolic meaning of selves and their shifting social moorings. According to Turner and Zurcher, broad changes in American culture have produced significant alterations in where people anchor their most fundamental images of self. In the 1950s and 1960s, Americans tended to have fairly stable and consistent conceptions of self that were anchored in the social institutions to which they belonged, such as family, workplace, church or school. More recently Americans have developed a 'mutable' sense of self, anchored more in impulses than institutions and flexibly adaptive to the demands of a rapidly changing society.

The presentation of self

Another branch of interactionism downplays the self in favor of the situation. The sociology of Erving Goffman, which implies there is no deeply held 'real' self, only a set of masks and situated performances, serves as the prototype of this approach. In his dramaturgical theory of social life, Goffman claimed that everyday interactions could be better understood if we thought of people as actors on a stage. As actors they play at roles and manipulate props, settings, clothing and symbols to achieve advantageous outcomes, notably smooth interactions which lead to valued selves. As Goffman noted in his most famous work, *The Presentation of Self in Everyday Life* (1959), people have ideas about who they are, ideas they present to others. They are concerned about the images that others form of them. Only by influencing others' images can individuals predict or control how these others will respond to them. This process of tailoring their performances to different audiences is fundamental to social interaction. Goffman described it as *impression management* – the process by which individuals manipulate how others see and define a situation, generating expressive cues which lead others to behave in accordance with their plans.

Goffman's insights into self-presentation have had considerable impact on symbolic interactionists. Inspired by Goffman, theorists have examined everyday interaction and found masks (Strauss, 1959), performances (Messinger et al., 1962), appearances (Stone, 1970) and rhetorical strategies (Hewitt and Stokes, 1975; Scott and Lyman, 1968). In recent years, interactionists have applied and extended Goffman's ideas in elaborating the dynamics of *identity work* (Sandstrom, 1990, 1998; Snow and Anderson, 1987), or the techniques actors use to create and sustain identities. These researchers illustrate how strategies such as distancing, embracement, insulation and fictive story telling are used to offset stigma and preserve cherished selves.

Problems and potential directions in self theory

Self theory continues to be a central focus of interactionists, but it is the subject of vitriolic methodological and theoretical debates. While there are many sources of these debates, they are exacerbated by interactionism's failure to develop a standardized terminology about what the constructs of 'self', 'self-concept' and 'identity' mean. Despite the efforts of interactionists to define and distinguish the meanings of these constructs (Gecas, 1982; Rosenberg, 1979; Stone, 1970), the terms are used in confusing and contradictory ways.

Self theory should draw on insights from studies of the emotions, which demonstrate that the self is not simply a cognitive phenomenon. In addition, the theory could better address the growing interest of interactionists in organizational sociology. As Fine (1993) emphasizes, selves are lodged in and shaped by the organizations and institutions in which they are embedded – including the family, school and workplace. Goffman (1961b) recognized this point in his analysis of 'total institutions', but it has not been adequately incorporated into self theory. Like the rest of symbolic interaction, self theory will move away from being a purely social psychological perspective as it addresses the domains of macro-sociology.

Emotions and emotion work

Until about twenty-five years ago the study of emotions had been left to psychologists and was unconnected to social forces or organization. It was through the analyses of symbolic interactionists that emotions entered sociological discourse (Gordon, 1981; Shott, 1979). Interactionists understand emotions as embodied phenomena, connected to how human beings experience their physical and social reality. Emotions inform and mediate experience; as a form of cognitive evaluation, an aspect of affect control, and a resource individuals draw upon to coordinate their actions with others (Hochschild, 1983). Interactionists treat emotions as 'lived experience', as 'cognitive constructions' linked to meaning and identity, and as a form of labor integral to self-presentation and joint action. While these approaches are distinct, attempts have been made to synthesize them (Cahill and Eggleston, 1994; Johnson, 1992; Scheff, 1983, Thoits, 1989).

Emotional experience

Some interactionists stress how emotions are felt by human beings as bodily experiences – experiences that are not only filtered through social demands, but also affect one's existence and self-understandings. As Denzin (1983) proposes, emotion is *self-feeling* – affecting a lived body and given meaning by a reflexive actor. Emotion represents a window into the self, grounded in felt experience, simultaneously connecting it to community. Others highlight how the experiences of time (Flaherty, 1987) and nature (Fine, 1998a; Weigert, 1991) are shaped by self-feelings, such as anxiety, fear, boredom, and exhilaration. In a related vein, interactionists who examine the lived experience of illness accentuate how *feelings* of 'dis-ease', and not merely the social definitions given to the sick, evoke new self-understandings and, in many cases, transformations of identity (Charmaz, 1991; Karp, 1996; Sandstrom, 1996, 1998).

To appreciate the social psychological implications of emotion, a group of interactionists rely on 'systematic sociological introspection', a method to explore and describe their own emotions and lived experiences (Ellis, 1991). For example, Ellis (1995) crafted a poignant 'autoethnography' which described her partner's illness and death and its impact on her selffeelings. Similarly, Frank (1991) wrote an evocative account of the challenging emotions and self-changes he experienced as he faced cancer. Both Ellis' and Frank's analyses are designed to elicit a felt understanding in their readers, moving them to deeper awareness of the nature and ramifications of lived, emotional experience.

Affect control

A second interactionist approach to emotion is affect control theory (Heise, 1979; Smith-Lovin and Heise, 1988). This theory combines cognitive social psychology with identity theory, emphasizing the shared nature of meaning for identity. Affect control theorists propose that meanings can be measured through three dimensions: *evaluation* (good/bad), *potency* (powerful/powerless) and *activity* (active/inactive). Measurements of meaning (EPA profiles) are gleaned from asking subjects to rate identities and objects on a semantic differential scale.

Affect control theorists examine people's attitudes or 'fundamental sentiments' toward specific identities and behaviors and how people feel about changes in their identity or the identities of others (Smith-Lovin, 1990). These scholars argue that people construct interpretations of events to confirm the meanings they give to self and others, minimizing their need to readjust their feelings or behaviors. They also propose that emotions signal the degree to which events confirm or disconfirm meanings and identities. Emotional responses arise out of situational definitions and the recognized social identities of the definers. People feel distress, discomfort, or other negative sentiments when their interaction partners do not allow them to confirm their own identities through interaction (Smith-Lovin, 1990).

Ultimately, the affect control model construes the dynamics of emotion as primarily cognitive, emerging out of social definitions, rather than produced directly from experience. To measure these definitions, affect control theorists utilize quantitative methodology. Through adopting this approach, these theorists seek to link interactionist ideas about identity and emotion to experimental social psychology.

Emotion work

A third interactionist approach to emotions emphasizes how people manage and display their feelings in ongoing identity work. This approach draws heavily on Goffman's dramaturgical theory. From a dramaturgical viewpoint, emotions are strategic methods for managing identities and negotiating relationships. Through socialization people learn what emotions are appropriate to feel in a given situation and how to express them. As Hochschild (1983) notes, individuals develop skills in 'surface acting' (management of emotional displays) and 'deep acting' (management of feelings from which expressive displays follow). They also discover that emotion work is an integral aspect of identity negotiation. To announce and realize desired identities, social actors must manage sentiments in accord with appropriate feeling rules.

The emotion work that people do is shaped by the social definitions provided by the groups to which they belong (Kleinman, 1996; Thoits, 1996). Through interaction individuals learn unwritten guidelines that apply to feeling display. More crucially, they learn to manage their emotions in light of these guidelines. In doing so they proactively control their bodily sensations and emotional experiences. They respond to their emotions as *social objects* – objects they can shape and manipulate not only to meet others' expectations but also to influence and direct others' responses. Emotions, then, become a vital channel of communication through which individuals convey and negotiate definitions of self, others and situations.

Social coordination

One of the more ambitious research programs within interactionism, the search for universal principles of coordinated action, has been developed by Carl Couch and his students (Couch, 1989, 1992; Couch et al., 1986; Katovich and Couch, 1992). Since the early 1970s these researchers have addressed the processes and conditions through which people coordinate their conduct and create social order. Based on laboratory and field studies, Couch and his associates have found several features crucial for establishing relationships and developing social order. First, interactants must recognize that others are present and serve as an audience. Second, interactants must attend and respond to each other's actions. Third, interactants must create congruent identities that demonstrate they participate in the same social situation. Finally, interactants must create a shared focus and objective. In establishing a social relationship, parties create a shared past and a projected future (Katovich and Couch, 1992; Maines et al., 1983). A social relationship develops traditions and an 'idioculture' (Fine, 1979). The existence of shared pasts allows people to adjust their responses to each other quickly and without self-consciousness. Research finds that this coordination of responses is remarkably subtle, producing temporal symmetry in micro-interaction, as individuals respond instantaneously to each other's words and deeds (Gregory, 1983).

Aligning actions

While Couch and his followers have searched for generic principles of social coordination, others have focused on the strategies people use to align their actions in everyday interaction. When speaking of 'aligning actions' (Stokes and Hewitt, 1976), interactionists refer to verbal communications that produce shared reality. These include such linguistic strategies as accounts (Scott and Lyman, 1968) and disclaimers (Hewitt and Stokes, 1975). Interactionists are guided by Mills' (1940) notion of 'vocabularies of motive', Goffman's (1961a) concept of 'remedial work', and Burke's (1969) rhetorical dramaturgy. Vocabularies of motive, reflected in accounts and disclaimers, are techniques through which people manage the impressions of others and thereby facilitate ongoing interaction. In their daily rounds, individuals become enmeshed in various mistakes or wayward acts and need ready-made exits to sustain their reputations (Gross and Stone, 1964). By proposing an account after the fact or a prior disclaimer, people deflect or neutralize the negative implications for their identities. They demonstrate that they appreciate the perspectives of others and the moral legitimacy of those perspectives.

Constructions of deviance and social problems

Since its origins, symbolic interactionism has been linked to the study of deviance and social problems. In fact, interactionism emerged out of sociologists' desires to effect social and political reforms in Chicago during the early twentieth century (Fisher and Strauss, 1978). Much interactionist research addresses troubling social and political issues, informed by labeling theory and the 'construction of social problems' perspective.

Labeling theory

Unlike other sociological approaches, symbolic interactionism does not seek to explain why certain social actors engage in deviance. Instead, it focuses on questions such as: How is deviance produced by the creation and application of rules? Who makes these rules? How, when and why do they apply or enforce them? Why are some people more likely than others to be recognized and labeled as rule-breakers? How do their actions, interactions and self-concepts change after becoming labeled deviant?

Guided by these questions, interactionists concentrate on the processes through which deviant identities are created and sustained. In doing so they are informed by the tenets of 'labeling theory' (Becker, 1963; Lemert, 1951). Labeling theory suggests that rule-makers and

enforcers are at least as involved in the creation of deviance as the purported deviant. By passing powerful legislation (such as drug laws) and then applying this legislation to targeted groups, rule-makers actively participate in the production of deviance. They also 'dramatize the evils' associated with specific acts or attributes, increasing the likelihood of particular actors to become labeled as deviant.

A key premise of labeling theory is that the processes set in motion by the act of labeling confirm and strengthen a deviant identity. If others define a person as deviant, other identities fade into the background. Deviance becomes a master status, overriding others and defining the person. This commonly leads to 'secondary deviance', or deviance that results from the labeling process. For example, if individuals become defined as criminal they are apt to be stigmatized and rejected by friends, relatives and employers. In turn, they must look to other criminals for moral support and financial assistance. Once involved with these criminals, they are even more likely to form a self-image as deviant and to engage in additional rule-breaking behavior, fulfilling others' negative expectations. Ironically, then, the consequence of labeling an individual as deviant is to create a deviant behavior pattern and career.

The construction of social problems

While labeling theory describes the creation of deviance, an important extension of this theory – social constructionism – considers the creation of social problems (Schneider, 1985; Spector and Kitsuse, 1977). Drawing on this theory, interactionists examine the institutional formulation of social problems. They ask: Why are some patterns of behavior defined as 'problematic' while others, equally threatening, are 'normalized'? Why do particular issues become regarded as social problems, while others are ignored? Who has the power to make their definitions stick? Why, for example, is it legal to consume alcohol but illegal to use drugs? Why does social concern about the use of certain drugs ebb and flow across time?

The constructionist approach is the dominant contemporary interactionist orientation within social problems theory. This approach permits interactionists to analyse dynamic historical processes affecting society, such as the 'medicalization of deviance' (Conrad and Schneider, 1980). It also allows them to consider how people draw upon various metaphorical images and rhetorical strategies to define certain phenomena as social problems and to build consensus that action needs to be taken to constrain the behaviors of others (Best, 1990; Fine, 1998b).

Yet, while constructionism offers advantages, it is characterized by internal divisions and disputes. Some constructionist theorists emphasize that all meaning (and, therefore, the existence of any 'objective' social problem) is questionable (Woolgar and Pawluch, 1985). Such a claim implies that sociological knowledge is as constructed as the rhetoric or ideology of any social group. This view, referred to as *strong constructionism*, is disputed by those who accept the existence of objective conditions, while focusing on the social processes through which these conditions enter public debate (Best, 1993). This alternative approach is referred to as *contextual constructionism* or *cautious naturalism*. Those who embrace it presume that sociologists can, to some extent, be 'honest brokers'. These theorists consider how cultural conditions (Fine and Christoforides, 1991), structural realities (Hilgartner and Bosk, 1988), and the role of moral entrepreneurs (Pfohl, 1977) combine to determine which problems enter public debate and which are defined as requiring a societal response.

Culture and art

Because it emphasizes the importance of meaning, symbolic interactionism has always been conducive to the study of symbolic productions such as culture and art. In fact, Blumer's first empirical investigation was a study of the movies, produced under the auspices of the Payne Fund (Blumer, 1933). Film represents a reality that is quintessentially a form of symbolic interaction. Blumer's later work on fashion (1969a) reflects the same recognition of the social organization of the symbolic world.

While Blumer's studies blazed the path for interactionist investigations of culture and art, the most renowned analyses are those of Howard Becker, culminating in his book *Art Worlds* (1982). Becker proposed that segments of the 'art world' could be viewed as social worlds. He focused on both structural and interactional characteristics of the art world that led to the production of art, concluding that in order to organize their behavior, artists (like others) rely upon 'conventions', or standardized modes of doing things. These conventions are not immutable or unbreakable, but artists who violate them face significant consequences. 'Deviant' artists need support networks to make their convention-breaking decisions artistically significant.

Within the sociology of art, the predominant approach is the 'production of culture' perspective, which contends that the art world should be analysed like any industry that produces a product. This perspective involves two related

views, each of which examines the production of culture. The first is structural in orientation, focusing on organizational constraints in the production of culture (Hirsch, 1972; Peterson, 1979). The second view is more traditionally interactionist, analysing how culture is produced on the interactional, relational and interpersonal level (Faulkner, 1983). The most significant weakness of the 'production of culture' approach has been its reluctance to examine aesthetics. This weakness is rooted in the relativist assumption that one cannot distinguish cultural productions in terms of aesthetic value. But aesthetics do matter to producers and clients. The issue is not efficiency, but the sensory qualities of the outcomes. In conducting research on restaurants and trade school cooking programs, Fine (1985, 1996) discovered that students and workers are socialized into aesthetic appreciation, and that their desire to create aesthetically satisfying objects is shaped by the structural conditions of their work.

In contributing to the sociology of culture, symbolic interactionists must further explore and refine the connection between the two components of their name, addressing issues such as how symbols are a function of interaction and how interaction is a consequence of symbolic display. At the same time, scholars must make the meaning and aesthetics of cultural objects central to the analysis of culture.

Macro analysis: organizations and collective action

The most common criticism leveled against symbolic interactionism is that it is a micro-sociological perspective, lacking interest in structure without recognition of organizational and institutional power (Hall, 1987; Maines, 1988). This criticism has always been misleading. Even Blumer, chided for his 'astructural bias', wrote extensively about industrialization, power conflicts, race relations and collective action (Blumer, 1954, 1955).

In examining social organization, interactionists have focused on the level of mesostructure. This emphasis resulted from an influential survey article, 'Social Organization and Social Structure in Symbolic Interactionist Thought', by David Maines (1977) in the *Annual Review of Sociology*. Maines highlighted the interactionist concern with structure, institutions and organizations, emphasizing that interactionists *do* have concepts, such as negotiated order, constraint, collective action and commitment to organizations that allow them to analyse large-scale social units. Following Maines, other interactionists emphasized how constructs such as network (Faulkner, 1983; Fine and Kleinman, 1983), power (Hall, 1997), organizational culture (Fine, 1984), symbolic meaning (Manning, 1992) and frame alignment (Snow et al., 1986) provide symbolic interactionism with tools to engage in macro-level analysis.

In addition to directing greater research attention to organizations, interactionists have become increasingly interested in studying collective action and social movement organizations. For instance, David Snow (1979) and his colleagues (Snow et al., 1981, 1986) have demonstrated how social movements are organized as a consequence of the 'frames' and frame alignment processes that shape the outlooks and behavioral choices of participants. Snow contends that members of social movements are continually searching for frameworks of meaning that enable them to answer the question, 'What is going on here?' Some frames legitimate violent protest (the frame of oppression), whereas other frames (the frame of moral justice) diminish the probability of violence. Leaders within social movements commonly set a guiding tone for group definitions and actions. In some cases leaders have an official role but often they 'emerge' as movements face new challenges and problematic situations.

In an effort to extend Snow's frame alignment model, Robert Benford and Scott Hunt (1992) examine how movement actors utilize interrelated dramaturgical techniques – scripting, staging, performing and interpreting – to construct and communicate their conceptions of power. Through identifying and elaborating these techniques, Benford and Hunt offer illuminating insights into how power and power relations are defined, redefined and articulated by social movement participants. Benford and Hunt also demonstrate how an interactionist approach inspires a different genre of research questions regarding social movements, such as: How are the dramaturgical techniques used by a movement related to its effectiveness? How and when do various techniques mobilize support, neutralize antagonists and reshape power relations?

Despite the notable contributions that interactionists have made in the study of social organization, they must extend their perspective to make it more applicable to the analysis of political and economic structures. While having this limit, interactionism can illuminate how organizational fields and socioeconomic systems are structured through symbolic negotiation and, thus, are similar to smaller-scale negotiations. Even large-scale systems are ultimately anchored in the symbols that people utilize and the interactions they engage in as they cope with local realities.

Feminism

Like other sociological paradigms, symbolic interactionism has only hesitantly taken a 'feminist turn'. Recently, however, interactionists have become aware of concerns they share with feminist theorists. For instance, both interactionists and feminists conceive of gender as a set of social meanings, identities, relationships and practices through which sex differences are made salient (Laslett and Brenner, 1989; Thorne, 1993). Moreover, both feminists and interactionists explore how gender is constructed, enacted and reproduced through cultural beliefs, social arrangements and interpersonal relationships.

In addressing these concerns, some feminist researchers rely heavily upon interactionist ideas. For instance, Candace West and Don Zimmerman (1987) utilize interactionist (as well as ethnomethodological) insights to explicate how people 'do gender' through their routine practices and interactions. This approach illustrates how gender is performed and reproduced, individually and institutionally, through micro-level relations. It also suggests that the process of doing gender is characterized by indeterminacy that allows people to engage in agentive action.

Yet, while extending sociological analysis of gender, West and Zimmerman's approach has been criticized for its 'overly discursive bias' and its lack of attention to power. Chafetz (1999: 147) contends that this approach has failed to result in adequate theorizing of 'the contents of the two genders' (that is why some behaviors are defined as 'appropriate' to a given sex in a given context). Similarly other variants of feminist interactionism, although more sensitive to gender inequality, have assumed male power and neglected analysis of its sources. To their credit, these variants have highlighted processes through which male power connects to interaction and to the negotiation of gender identities and ideologies (Thorne, 1993).

In general, feminist interactionists have directed less attention to issues of power than other feminist scholars, particularly those guided by critical/radical theoretical perspectives. Nevertheless, feminist interactionists do not lack interest in the analysis of power. When studying cross-gender conversations, for example, they concentrate on issues of power, observing how men exercise and maintain conversational advantage through interruptions (West, 1984), topic changes (West and Garcia,

1988), and language style (Arlis, 1991). More-over, feminist interactionists have studied the 'sexual politics' that characterize family relation-ships (DeVault, 1991; Hochschild and Machung, 1989), organizational life (Hochschild, 1983) and a wide range of face-to-face communications (Henley, 1977). In addition to this, they have drawn upon and extended Goffman's (1979) incisive analyses of how people conceptualize gender, 'mark' gender differences publicly, and read gender displays as embodiments of the 'essential nature' of men and women (West, 1996).

While these contributions have influenced feminist theory, they have had less influence on interactionism itself. Still, one area where feminist interactionism has had a significant voice is in studies of the management of emo-tion. Based on research conducted in a variety of sites, including airlines (Hochschild, 1983), alternative health care clinics (Kleinman, 1996) and appearance associations (Martin, 2000), feminist-oriented interactionists offer revealing insights into how organizations manufacture sentiments and regulate emotional display. At the same time, these scholars illustrate how organizations require women to engage in unrecognized or devalued forms of emotional labor, perpetuating their subordination and reproducing gender inequality.

While sharing some areas of *rapprochement*, feminist and interactionists also disagree. A key source of tension is feminism's commitment to emancipatory research and social practice. Feminists often feel disenchanted with the less 'radical' epistemological and political stances characterizing interactionism as a whole. Unlike many of their colleagues, feminist interactionists do not merely regard research and theory as avenues for understanding social reality. Instead, they see research and theory as liberating social practices that ought to contribute to the elimination of gender inequality and oppression.

Critical interactionism

It is problematic for interactionists to stake any claim to a domain called 'critical interactionism'. As much as interactionists might claim 'critical ethnography', the radical scholars who write it do not identify with symbolic interactionism (Burawoy et al., 1991). Instead, they align them-selves with Marxist approaches that assume 'the central reason for bothering to do social theory and research is to contribute in some way to the realization of . . . emancipatory projects' (Wright, 1993: 40).

Yet, in spite of the critiques Marxist scholars have directed toward them, interactionists have certainly contributed to analyses of concerns such as inequality (Schwalbe et al., 1999), ideo-logy (Fine and Sandstrom, 1993), and agency and consciousness – topics connected to political economy. Perhaps the analyses that best fit under the rubric of 'critical' interactionism are those offered by Michael Schwalbe, particularly in *The Psychosocial Consequences of Natural and Alienated Labor* (1986). Schwalbe explores and synthesizes Marx's and Mead's theories of materialism in examining the dynamics of the labor process, consciousness and aesthetic experience. Guided by interest in the social pro-cesses through which inequality is reproduced, Schwalbe formulates an analytic approach that is firmly grounded in both interactionist studies of micro-politics and the emancipatory agenda of Marxism.

Surprisingly, given the interest in inequality that is shared among critical ethnographers, few symbolic interactionists have taken up Schwalbe's lead in theorizing dimensions of political economy. Topics that critical scholars consider central to the study of political econ-omy, such as ideology or 'the State', have been neglected by interactionists. By contrast, pro-ponents of the 'critical studies' paradigm have not overlooked key components of ideology such as moral commitment, practical action and emotion, also attended to by interactionists (Selinger, 1976).

A potential contribution of symbolic inter-actionism to 'critical studies' lies in the develop-ment of 'critical' or 'emancipatory' dramaturgy. In formulating the concept of 'frame', Goffman (1974: 10) turned his attention from the inter-action strategies that individuals use in everyday life to a concern with 'how definitions of situ-ations are built up in accordance with principles of organization which govern events – at least social ones – and our involvement in them'. As noted, interactionists investigating social move-ments have used this framework in under-standing how movement issues are politically constructed and given meanings that lead to the mobilization of movements.

The strength of frame analysis in the assess-ment of social movements lies in its view of humans as active agents who redefine and transform the obdurate structures and condi-tions in which they live. Still, despite the insights offered by such analysis, one might ask if dramaturgy or other variants of symbolic inter-actionism will ever be truly emancipatory. Can – or should – there be an 'emancipatory inter-actionism' whose analysis leads toward the transformation of capitalist political economies? If so, what would such an analysis look like? T.R. Young's work *The Drama of Social Life* (1990) provides a glimpse of the possibilities of an emancipatory dramaturgy, locating the performance strategies of people within the broader context of political economy. According to Young, 'capitalism has improved the means of production to the extent that the central problem is how to realize profit from those with discretionary income' (1990: 197). In part, this has been accomplished by a growing emphasis on appearances and the accoutrements needed in maintaining them. In evaluating this 'culture of appearances', critical-emancipatory dramaturgy has three key goals. First, it strives to offer theoretical insights into the sources of oppression and the mechanisms that maintain them, penetrating impressions 'given' and locating the interests of those producing them. Second, it seeks to stimulate praxis by offering theoretical insights oriented towards collective interests and collective action. Third, it attempts to identify fraudulent forms of politics and the actors behind these politics.

Ultimately, because of its radical goals, critical dramaturgy seems likely to have a minor impact on interactionism. Nevertheless, critical dramaturgy has successfully encouraged some interactionists to examine topics they had largely neglected. While this may not enhance 'human emancipation', it could benefit sociological theory.

Postmodernism

Over the past decade, the most significant challenges to mainstream interactionism have been posed by postmodern theorists. These analysts have emphasized that postmodernism is not a way of thinking (Lemert, 1997). Instead, it is a multidimensional term that describes the condition in which people find themselves in advanced capitalist countries. This condition is characterized by the rise of a consumption and media-oriented society, the growth of information technologies and culture industries, the commodification of images, the pluralization of social worlds, the decentering of selves and the crumbling of previously dominant modernist values. Above all, the postmodern condition is characterized by rapid social transformations that evoke a sense that the world has fundamentally changed.

'Postmodern interactionists' seek to make sense of this unique historical and social situation (Denzin, 1996b). In doing so they utilize an 'interpretive interactionist' approach informed by post-structuralist, feminist, neo-Marxist and cultural studies. They thereby distance themselves from traditional interactionism and its modernist theories and research projects. According to postmodern interactionists, the theories and projects of modernist interactionism should be rejected because they 'play directly into the hands of those who would politically manage the postmodern' (Denzin, 1996b: 349).

While challenging the intellectual agenda of mainstream interactionism, postmodern interactionists do share some of its central assumptions and emphases. For instance, they share interactionism's (and pragmatism's) suspicion of positivism and scientism, emphasizing that all social science is value-laden because it is shaped by the cultural and structural locations of the individuals who produce it (Gergen, 1991). In addition to this, postmodernists embrace interactionism's emphasis on interpretative scholarship and accentuate the contributions this form of scholarship has made to social theory. They also make language and information technology central to the social actors and dynamics they study (Maines, 1996).

Postmodern interactionists extend the interactionist perspective in several interesting ways. First, they introduce intriguing concepts for rethinking interpretive work, such as multivocality, hyper-reality, systems of discourse, the dying of the social, epiphanies and the saturated self. Secondly, postmodern interactionists highlight how writing is intrinsic to method (Maines, 1996). Writing is not something analysts do after collecting data, but rather it is constitutive of data and textual representations. In making this point, postmodern interactionists remind their mainstream colleagues to be keenly aware of the importance of metaphors, tropes and audiences. Through heeding this advice, they will not only become better writers, but also better knowers (Ellis and Bochner, 1996). Thirdly, postmodern interactionists have offered trenchant analyses of the changing nature of the self in 'late capitalist' societies. Gergen (1991) observes that the pace of life and communications is overwhelming people, leaving them with selves 'under siege'. He proposes that people are reaching a point of 'social saturation' with far-reaching implications for how they experience the self. Gergen's core argument is that identities have become fragmented and incoherent in postmodern societies. Under postmodern conditions, the concept of the self becomes uncertain and 'the fully saturated self becomes no self at all' (Gergen, 1991: 7). People face a daunting challenge in 'constructing and maintaining an integrated self because the social structures necessary to anchor the self have themselves become unstable and ephemeral' (Karp, 1996: 186).

While postmodern theory offers promising insights to interactionism, it is regarded as an irredeemably flawed enterprise by critics who embrace more traditional interactionist concepts and approaches (Maines, 1996; Snow and Morrill, 1995). According to these critics, the failings of postmodern interactionism include an unscientific orientation, a faulty epistemology, a flawed historiography, an inadequate theory of aesthetics and an overly political and moralistic agenda. Some critics also assert that postmodern interactionism is irrelevant for interactionist sociology because it essentially reiterates the longstanding views of traditional interactionism (Maines, 1996).

In responding to these critiques, postmodern interactionists, led by Norman Denzin (1996b,c), have urged their mainstream colleagues to return to the spirit of the early pragmatists, embracing their anti-realist and anti-reductionist understandings, their openness to innovation and their concern with fostering progressive social reforms. By taking this step interactionists could forge a *rapprochement* between the ideas of pragmatism and postmodernism, resulting in a 'prophetic post-pragmatism' that would merge interactionist theory with radical democratic practice (Denzin, 1996b).

THE (FRACTIOUS) FUTURE OF SYMBOLIC INTERACTIONISM

Perhaps postmodernists are correct: there is no center. Certainly this chapter has suggested that interactionism is a diverse enterprise. At the least, it appears that the contributions that symbolic interactionist theory have made to the discipline of sociology are consequential. Sociology would not be what it is today without the challenges and insights offered by generations of interactionist scholars. In the study of the self, interaction, culture, gender, emotion, organization, social movements and public problems, interactionist research has had significant reverberations. Of course, interactionism is not the only interpretivist sociology; instead, it is one perspective in dialogue with others. Is it the most valuable perspective? Clearly no single answer exists for this question. Even within the body of interactionism answers would vary widely. This is how it should be.

Will interactionism abide? Surely the issues that the perspective has raised will continue to feature prominently in sociological thought during this next century. Perhaps in a hundred years the label of interactionism will also remain notable in sociology – but perhaps not. Regardless, during its first sixty years, symbolic interactionism has clearly extended the discipline of sociology and addressed many of the most important social scientific questions of the twentieth century.

ACKNOWLEDGEMENT

The research for this chapter was supported in part by a grant from the Graduate School at the University of Northern Iowa. The authors wish to thank Vicki Kessler, Sherryl Kleinman, Ron Roberts and Jerry Stockdale for their helpful comments.

REFERENCES

Arlis, Laurie (1991) *Gender Communication.* Englewood Cliffs, NJ: Prentice-Hall.

Becker, Howard S. (1963) *Outsiders.* New York: The Free Press.

Becker, Howard S. (1982) *Art Worlds.* Berkeley, CA: University of California Press.

Benford, Robert and Hunt, Scott M. (1992) 'Dramaturgy and Social Movements: The Social Construction and Communication of Power', *Sociological Inquiry*, 62: 36–55.

Best, Joel (1990) *Threatened Children.* Chicago: Chicago University Press.

Blumer, Herbert (1933) *Movies and Conduct.* New York: Macmillan.

Blumer, Herbert (1937) 'Social Psychology', in Emerson Schmidt (ed.), *Man and Society.* New York: Prentice-Hall.

Blumer, Herbert (1954) 'Social Structure and Power Conflict', in A. Kornhauser, R. Dubin and A. Ross (eds), *Industrial Conflict.* New York: McGraw Hill. pp. 232–9.

Blumer, Herbert (1955) 'Reflections on Theory in Race Relations', in A. Lind (ed.), *Race Relations in World Perspective.* Honolulu: University of Hawaii Press. pp. 3–21.

Blumer, Herbert (1962) 'Society as Symbolic Interaction', in A.M. Rose (ed.), *Human Behavior and Social Processes.* Boston, MA: Houghton Mifflin.

Blumer, Herbert (1969a) 'Fashion: From Class Differentiation to Collective Selection', *The Sociological Quarterly*, 10: 275–91.

Blumer, Herbert (1969b) *Symbolic Interactionism.* Englewood Cliffs, NJ: Prentice-Hall.

Brissett, Dennis and Edgley, Charles (1990) *Life as Theater: A Dramaturgical Source Book*, 2nd edn. Chicago: Aldine.

Burawoy, Michael, Burton, Alice, Ferguson, Ann, Fox, Kathryn J., Gamson, Joshua, Gartell, Nadine, Hurst, Leslie, Hurzman, Charles, Salzinger, Leslie, Schiffman, Joseph and Vi, Shiori (1991) *Ethnography Unbound.* Berkeley, CA: University of California Press.

Burke, Kenneth (1969) *A Grammar of Motives.* Berkeley, CA: University of California Press.

Cahill, Spencer and Eggleston, Robin (1994) 'Managing Emotion in Public: The Case of Wheelchair Users', *Social Psychology Quarterly*, 57: 300–12.

Chafetz, Janet (1999) 'Structure, Consciousness, Agency and Social Change in Feminist Sociological Theories: A Conundrum', in Jennifer M. Lehmann (ed.), *Current Perspectives in Social Theory*. Stamford, CT: JAI Press. pp. 145–64.

Charmaz, Kathy (1991) *Good Days, Bad Days*. New Brunswick, NJ: Rutgers University Press.

Conrad, Peter and Schenider, Joseph W. (1980) *Deviance and Medicalization: From Badness to Sickness*. St Louis: Mosby.

Cooley, Charles Horton ([1902] 1964) *Human Nature and the Social Order*. New York: Scribner's.

Corsaro, William (1985) *Friendship and Peer Culture in the Early Years*. Norwood, NJ: Ablex.

Couch, Carl (1989) *Social Processes and Relationships: A Formal Approach*. Dix Hills, NY: General Hall.

Couch, Carl (1992) 'Toward a Formal Theory of Social Processes', *Symbolic Interaction*, 15: 117–34.

Couch, Carl J., Saxton, Stanley L. and Katovich, Michael A. (eds) (1986) *Studies in Symbolic Interaction: The Iowa School*, 2 vols. Greenwich, CT: JAI Press.

Denzin, Norman (1977) *Childhood Socialization*. San Francisco, CA: Jossey-Bass.

Denzin, Norman (1983) 'A Note on Emotionality, Self, and Interaction', *American Journal of Sociology*, 89: 402–9.

Denzin, Norman (1996a) 'Post-Pragmatism: A Review of Pragmatism and Social Theory', *Symbolic Interaction*, 19: 61–76.

Denzin, Norman (1996b) 'Prophetic Pragmatism and the Postmodern: A Comment on Maines', *Symbolic Interaction*, 19: 341–56.

Denzin, Norman (1996c) 'Sociology at the End of the Century', *The Sociological Quarterly*, 37: 743–52.

DeVault, Marjorie L. (1991) *Feeding the Family*. Chicago: University of Chicago Press.

Dewey, John (1922) *Human Nature and Conduct*. New York: Holt, Rinehart and Winston.

Dewey, John (1925) *Experience and Nature*. Chicago: Open Court.

Ellis, Carolyn (1991) 'Symbolic Introspection and Emotional Experience', *Symbolic Interaction*, 14: 23–50.

Ellis, Carolyn (1995) *Final Negotiations*. Philadelphia: Temple University Press.

Ellis, Carolyn and Bochner, Arthur (1996) *Composing Ethnography*. Thousands Oaks, CA: Alta Mira Press.

Faulkner, Robert R. (1983) *Music on Demand*. New Brunswick, NJ: Transaction Books.

Fine, Gary Alan (1979) 'Small Groups and Culture: Idioculture of Little League Baseball Teams', *American Sociological Review*, 44: 733–45.

Fine, Gary Alan (1984) 'Negotiated Orders and Organizational Cultures', *Annual Review of Sociology*, 10: 239–62.

Fine, Gary Alan (1985) 'Occupational Aesthetics: How Trade School Students Learn to Cook', *Urban Life*, 14: 3–32.

Fine, Gary Alan (1987) 'Working Cooks: The Dynamics of Professional Kitchens', in Helena Z. Lopata (ed.), *Current Research on Occupations and Professions*. Greenwich, CT: JAI Press.

Fine, Gary Alan (1993) 'The Sad Demise, Mysterious Disappearance, and Glorious Triumph of Symbolic Interactionism', *Annual Review of Sociology*, 19: 61–87.

Fine, Gary Alan (ed.) (1995) *A Second Chicago School? The Development of a Postwar American Sociology*. Chicago: University of Chicago Press.

Fine, Gary Alan (1996) *Kitchens: The Culture of Restaurant Work*. Berkeley, CA: University of California Press.

Fine, Gary Alan (1998a) *Morel Tales: The Culture of Mushrooming*. Cambridge, MA: Harvard.

Fine, Gary Alan (1998b) 'Scandal, Social Conditions, and the Creation of Public Attention: Fatty Arbuckle and the "Problem of Hollywood"', *Social Problems*, 44: 297–323.

Fine, Gary Alan and Kleinman, Sherryl (1983) 'Network and Meaning: An Interactionist Approach to Structure', *Symbolic Interaction*, 6: 97–110.

Fine, Gary Alan and Christoforides, Lazaros (1991) 'Dirty Birds, Filthy Immigrants, and the English Sparrow War: Metaphorical Linkage in Constructing Social Problems', *Symbolic Interaction*, 14: 375–93.

Fine, Gary Alan and Sandstrom, Kent (1993) 'Ideology in Action: A Pragmatic Approach to a Contested Concept', *Sociological Theory*, 11: 21–38.

Fisher, Berenice and Strauss, Anselm (1978) 'The Chicago Tradition and Social Change: Thomas, Park and Their Successors', *Symbolic Interaction*, 1: 5–23.

Flaherty, Michael (1987) 'Multiple Realities and the Experience of Duration', *Sociological Quarterly*, 28: 313–26.

Frank, Arthur (1991) *At the Will of the Body*. New York: Houghton-Mifflin.

Gecas, Viktor (1982) 'The Self-Concept', *Annual Review of Sociology*, 8: 1–33.

Gergen, Kenneth (1991) *The Saturated Self*. New York: Basic Books.

Glaser, Barney and Strauss, Anselm (1967) *The Discovery of Grounded Theory*. Chicago: Aldine.

Goffman, Erving (1959) *The Presentation of Self in Everyday Life*. Garden City, NY: Anchor.

Goffman, Erving (1961a) *Asylums*. New York: Anchor.

Goffman, Erving (1961b) *Encounters*. Indianapolis: Bobbs-Merrill.

Goffman, Erving (1974) *Frame Analysis*. New York: Harper and Row.

Goffman, Erving (1979) *Gender Advertisements*. New York: Harper and Row.

Gordon, Steven (1981) 'The Sociology of Sentiments and Emotion', in Morris Rosenberg and Ralph H. Turner (eds), *Social Psychology: Sociological Perspectives*. New York: Basic Books.

Gregory, S.W. Jr (1983) 'A Quantitative Analysis of

Temporal Symmetry in Microsocial Relations', *American Sociological Review*, 48: 129–35.

Gross, Edward and Stone, Gregory (1964) 'Embarrassment and the Analysis of Role Requirements', *American Journal of Sociology*, 70: 1–15.

Hall, Peter M. (1972) 'A Symbolic Interactionist Analysis of Politics', *Sociological Inquiry*, 42: 35–75.

Hall, Peter M. (1987) 'Interactionism and the Study of Social Organization', *The Sociological Quarterly*, 28: 1–22.

Hall, Peter M. (1997) 'Meta-Power, Social Organization, and the Shaping of Social Action', *Symbolic Interaction*, 20: 397–418.

Heise, David (1979) *Understanding Events: Affect and the Construction of Social Action*. New York: Cambridge University Press.

Henley, Nancy (1977) *Body Politics*. Englewood Cliffs, NJ: Prentice-Hall.

Hewitt, John and Stokes, Randall (1975) 'Disclaimers', *American Sociological Review*, 40: 1–11.

Hilgartner, S. and Bosk, C.L. (1988) 'The Rise and Fall of Social Problems: A Public Arenas Model', *American Journal of Sociology*, 94: 53–78.

Hirsch, Paul M. (1972) 'Processing Fads and Fashions: An Organization-Set Analysis of Cultural Industry Systems', *American Journal of Sociology*, 77: 639–59.

Hochschild, Arlie (1983) *The Managed Heart*. Berkeley, CA: University of California Press.

Hochschild, Arlie with Machung, Anne (1989) *The Second Shift*. New York: Avon Books.

Joas, Hans (1996) *The Creativity of Action*. Chicago: University of Chicago Press.

Johnson, Cathyrn (1992) 'The Emergence of the Emotional Self: A Developmental Theory', *Symbolic Interaction*, 15: 183–202.

Karp, David (1996) *Speaking of Sadness*. New York: Oxford University Press.

Katovich, Michael and Couch, Carl (1992) 'The Nature of Social Pasts and Their Use as Foundations for Situated Action', *Symbolic Interaction*, 15: 25–47.

Kleinman, Sherryl (1996) *Opposing Ambitions: Gender and Identity in an Alternative Organization*. Chicago: University of Chicago Press.

Laslett, Barbara and Brenner, Johanna (1989) 'Gender and Social Reproduction: Historical Perspectives', *Annual Review of Sociology*, 15: 381–404.

Lemert, Charles (1997) *Postmodernism Is Not What You Think*. Malden, MA: Blackwell.

Lemert, Edwin M. (1951) *Social Pathology*. New York: McGraw Hill.

Maines, David R. (1977) 'Social Organization and Social Structure in Symbolic Interactionist Thought', *Annual Review of Sociology*, 3: 235–59.

Maines, David (1988) 'Myth, Text and Interactionist Complicity in the Neglect of Blumer's Macrosociology', *Symbolic Interaction*, 11: 43–57.

Maines, David (1996) 'On Postmodernism, Pragmatism, and Plasterers: Some Interactionist Thoughts and Queries', *Symbolic Interaction*, 19: 323–40.

Maines, David, Sugrue, N. and Katovich, Michael

(1983) 'G.H. Mead's Theory of the Past', *American Sociological Review*, 48: 161–73.

Manning, Peter (1992) *Organizational Communications*. New York: Aldine.

Martin, Daniel D. (2000) 'Organizational Approaches to Shame: Management, Announcement, and Contestation', *The Sociological Quarterly*, 41 (1): 125–50.

Mead, George H. (1934) *Mind, Self, and Society*. Chicago: University of Chicago Press.

Messinger, Sheldon E., Sampson, Harold and Towne, Robert D. (1962) 'Life as Theater: Some Notes on the Dramaturgic Approach to Social Reality', *Sociometry*, 25: 98–110.

Mills, C. Wright (1940) 'Situated Actions and Vocabularies of Motive', *American Sociological Review*, 5: 904–13.

Peterson, Richard A. (1979) 'Revitalizing the Culture Concept', *Annual Review of Sociology*, 5: 137–66.

Pfohl, Steven (1977) 'The Discovery of Child Abuse', *Social Problems*, 24: 310–23.

Rosenberg, Morris (1979) *Conceiving the Self*. New York: Basic Books.

Rosenberg, Morris (1981) 'The Self-Concept: Social Product and Social Force', in Morris Rosenberg and Ralph H. Turner (eds), *Social Psychology: Sociological Perspectives*. New York: Basic Books.

Sandstrom, Kent (1990) 'Confronting Deadly Disease: The Drama of Identity Construction among Gay Men with AIDS', *Journal of Contemporary Ethnography*, 19: 271–94.

Sandstrom, Kent (1996) 'Redefining Sex and Intimacy: The Sexual Self-Images, Outlooks, and Relationships of Gay Men Living with HIV Disease', *Symbolic Interaction*, 19 (3): 241–62.

Sandstrom, Kent (1998) 'Preserving a Vital and Valued Self in the Face of AIDS', *Sociological Inquiry*, 68 (3): 354–71.

Schneider, Joseph (1985) 'Social Problems: The Constructionist View', *American Review of Sociology*, 11: 209–29.

Schwalbe, Michael L. (1986) *The Psychosocial Consequences of Natural and Alienated Labor*. Albany, NY: State University of New York.

Schwalbe, Michael, Godwin, Sandra, Holden, Daphne, Schrock, Douglas, Thompson, Shealy and Wolkomir, Michele (1999) 'Generic Processes in the Reproduction of Inequality: an Interactionist Theory', unpublished manuscript.

Scott, Marvin and Lyman, Stanford (1968) 'Accounts', *American Sociological Review*, 33: 46–62.

Selinger, Martin (1976) *Ideology and Politics*. London: George Allen and Unwin.

Shalin, Dmitri (1986) 'Pragmatism and Social Interactionism', *American Sociological Review*, 51: 9–29.

Shalin, Dmitri (1991) 'The Pragmatic Origins of Symbolic Interactionism and the Crisis of Classical Science', *Studies in Symbolic Interaction*, 12: 223–51.

Scheff, Thomas (1983) 'Toward Integration in the

Social Psychology of Emotions', *Annual Review of Sociology*, 9: 333–54.

Shott, Susan (1979) 'Emotion and Social Life: A Symbolic Interactionist Analysis', *American Journal of Sociology*, 84: 1317–34.

Smith-Lovin, Lynn (1990) 'Emotion as the Confirmation and Disconfirmation of Identity: An Affect Control Model', in T.D. Kemper (ed.), *Research Agendas in the Sociology of Emotion*. Albany, NY: State University of New York Press.

Smith-Lovin, Lynn and Heise, David (1988) *Analyzing Social Interaction: Advances in Affect Control Theory*. New York: Gordon Breach Science.

Snow, David A. (1979) 'A Dramaturgical Analysis of Movement Accommodation: Building Idiosyncrasy Credit as a Movement Mobilization Strategy', *Symbolic Interaction*, 2: 23–44.

Snow, David and Anderson, Leon (1987) 'Identity Work among the Homeless: the Verbal Construction and Avowal of Personal Identities', *American Journal of Sociology*, 92: 1336–71.

Snow, David and Morrill, Calvin (1995) 'Ironies, Puzzles, and Contradictions in Denzin and Lincoln's Vision of Qualitative Research', *Journal of Contemporary Ethnography*, 22: 358–62.

Snow, David A., Zurcher, Louis and Peters, Robert (1981) 'Victory Celebrations as Theater: A Dramaturgical Approach to Crowd Behavior', *Symbolic Interaction*, 4: 21–41.

Snow, David A., Burke Rochford Jr, E., Worden, Steven K. and Benford, Robert D. (1986) 'Frame Alignment Processes, Micromobilization and Movement Participation', *American Sociological Review*, 51: 464–81.

Spector, Malcolm and Kitsuse, John I. (1977) *Constructing Social Problems*. New York: Aldine.

Stokes, Randall and Hewitt, John (1976) 'Aligning Actions', *The American Sociological Review*, 46: 838–49.

Stone, Gregory P. (1970) 'Appearance and the Self', in Gregory P. Stone and Harvey Farberman (eds), *Social Psychology Through Symbolic Interaction*. New York: Wiley and Sons.

Stone, Gregory P. (1981) 'The Play of Little Children', in Gregory P. Stone and Harvey Farberman (eds), *Social Psychology Through Symbolic Interaction*, 2nd edn. New York: Wiley and Sons.

Strauss, Anselm (1959) *Mirrors and Masks*. Glencoe, IL: The Free Press.

Strauss, Anselm (1993) *Continual Permutations of Action*. Chicago: Aldine.

Stryker, Sheldon (1980) *Symbolic Interactionism: A Social Structural Version*. Reading, MA: Cummings.

Thayer, H.S. (1981) *Meaning and Action*. Cambridge: Hackett Publishing Company.

Thoits, Peggy (1989) 'The Sociology of Emotions', *Annual Review of Sociology*, 15: 317–42.

Thoits, Peggy (1996) 'Managing the Emotions of Others', *Symbolic Interaction*, 19: 85–109.

Thorne, Barrie (1993) *Gender Play*. New Brunswick, NJ: Rutgers University Press.

Turner, Ralph (1976) 'The Real Self: From Institution to Impulse', *American Journal of Sociology*, 81: 989–1016.

Weigert, Andrew (1991) 'Transverse Interaction: A Pragmatic Perspective on the Environment as Other', *Symbolic Interaction*, 14: 139–63.

West, Candace (1984) *Routine Complications*. Bloomington, IN: Indiana University Press.

West, Candace (1996) 'Goffman in Feminist Perspective', *Sociological Perspectives*, 39: 353–69.

West, Candace and Garcia, Angela (1988) 'Conversational Shift Work: A Study of Topical Transitions between Women and Men', *Social Problems*, 35: 551–75.

West, Candace and Zimmerman, Don H. (1983) 'Small Insults: A Study of Interruptions in Cross-Sex Conversations between Unacquainted Persons', in B. Thorne, N. Henley and C. Kramarae (eds), *Language, Gender, and Society*. Rowley, MA: Newbury House. pp. 102–17.

West, Candace and Zimmerman, Don H. (1987) 'Doing Gender', *Gender and Society*, 1: 125–51.

Wiley, Norbert (1979) 'Notes on Self-Genesis: From Me to We to I', in Norman Denzin (ed.), *Studies in Symbolic Interaction* (vol. 2). Greenwich, CT: JAI Press.

Woolgar, S. and Pawluch, D. (1985) 'Ontological Gerrymandering: The Anatomy of Social Problems', *Social Problems*, 32: 214–27.

Wright, Erik Ohlin (1993) 'Explanation and Emancipation in Marxism and Feminism', *Sociological Theory*, 11: 39–54.

Young, T.R (1990) *The Drama of Social Life*. New Brunswick, NJ: Transaction Publishers.

Zurcher, Louis (1977) *The Mutable Self*. Beverly Hills, CA: Sage.

18

Phenomenology and Social Theory

HARVIE FERGUSON

Spirit has not only lost its essential life; it is also conscious of this loss, and of the finitude that is its own content . . . and now demands from philosophy not so much *knowledge* of what it *is* as the recovery through its agency of that lost sense of solid and substantial being.

(G.W.F. Hegel, *Phenomenology of Spirit*, 1807)

The title of this chapter is deliberately disjunctive. The troubled relationship between phenomenology and social theory throughout the twentieth century renders dangerously misleading the seamless 'phenomenological social theory' or 'phenomenological sociology'. Indeed, if it were not for their short-lived union in the early writing of Hegel, it might well be judged advisable to treat phenomenology and social theory as two quite distinct and independent developments. For the most part shared indifference, interspersed with bouts of hostility, has characterized the relationship.

So, why raise the issue of their relationship at all? Because, first, in spite of mutual disdain, an important conceptual relation does exist here and, secondly, a tradition of genuine but implicit phenomenological social theory, though it has rarely made reference either to modern phenomenological philosophy or to the multiplying perspectives of a self-consciously theoretical sociology, has in fact emerged.

THE SOVEREIGNTY OF EXPERIENCE

In common language the 'phenomenal' is exceptional, incredible, extraordinary; a distant recollection of the early modern preoccupation with those many 'wonders', 'curiosities' and 'monstrosities' which stood on the margins of, and in stark contradiction to, the immanent order of Nature (Daston and Park, 1998). Without reason or purpose the 'phenomenal' just happened to exist. Throughout the modern period the region of fascinating monstrosities gradually shrank into nothingness while the sphere of an internally orderly and predictable domain of observable events expanded, in principle, to become coterminous with the infinity of empirical reality. There were no exceptions to Nature's universality and necessity. But empirical reality was immeasurably complex so that Nature's indubitable orderliness was expressed, as it were, in hidden and implicit ways. The phenomenal became the generally incomprehensible and ungraspable immediacy of actual existence in contrast to the intelligible order – the 'noumenal' – to which the chaos of particular and individual events was ultimately reducible. Reality was identical to existence; but existence remained stubbornly incomprehensible. The phenomenal, that is to say, no sooner acceded to the dignity of autonomous and exclusive being than it lost itself in its own overwhelming abundance; and became 'appearance' in contrast to 'reality'.

Not the least difficulty in understanding the philosophical movement known as phenomenology is the special sense in which this central term is used. In fact, and as distinct from any previous usage, phenomenology is that perspective within which no distinction between the phenomenal and the noumenal can arise. The aim is neither to explain nor revalue the 'phenomenal' but, rather, to return being to the undifferentiated unity of actual experience. Friedrich Nietzsche, thus, expresses the founding insight of phenomenology with characteristic pithiness: 'The antithesis "thing-in-itself" and "appearance" is untenable; with that, however, the concept "appearance" also disappears' (Nietzsche, 1967: 298).

Phenomenology is an essentially modern perspective on the human world and it is the philosophical movement most closely associated with the twentieth century. Its origins – like all Western philosophical movements – can be traced in exemplary ancient texts and, more significantly, has roots in medieval Scholasticism. However, phenomenological writers themselves, are generally content to take their point of departure in the writings of Edmund Husserl; and Husserl himself repeatedly draws attention to René Descartes' radical break with earlier philosophizing as the beginning of a decisively phenomenological perspective.

Husserl claims Descartes' rejection of all previous philosophical authority as the foundational act of modern phenomenology. Descartes' determination to doubt everything and accept as certain only that to which he was led by the exercise of his own reason, freely reflecting on its own experience, is not simply the methodological principle but (*in nuce*) the substantive content of the modern philosophical view of reality. Husserl recognizes the implication of Descartes' method of systematic doubt to be the elevation of experience as the real subject matter, as well as the ultimate arbiter, of philosophical truth. In terms of philosophy, indeed, modernity simply means the *sovereignty of experience*. In this sense all modern philosophical movements are phenomenological, though prior to Husserl's decisive thematizing of experience, they were so obscurely, being viewed as an important but external starting point for modern thought. The overthrowing of premodern authorities had been seen exclusively as an important social and political prelude to modern thought; its precondition rather than its genesis.

In general terms, then, for the modern view experience is the only source of knowledge and, because experience is not immediately lucid, it is simultaneously the very condition which makes knowledge necessary. Experience, that is to say, does not immediately offer itself as an indubitable guide to the world (including ourselves).

In its most general form, then, phenomenology is simply the 'subjective turn' which characterizes all modern thinking and brings clearly into awareness the insight that human consciousness is trapped in an endlessly self-referential system of representations; that consciousness is a system of *signs*. In a paradoxical fashion, however, modernity – as the sovereignty of *experience* – immediately divides itself into the mutually exclusive realms of subject and object; distinct forms of being which seem to deny, or to offer an

escape from, the solipsism to which the 'subjective turn' otherwise seems condemned. Significantly, Descartes himself draws attention to the curiously disjunctive character of subjectivity. He points out, for example, that, in dreaming, the waking world is banished but reappears, so to speak, within the dream itself when we dream the difference between waking and dreaming; indeed, it becomes difficult to specify precisely the experiential difference between being awake and only dreaming that we are awake. This dualism between subject and object – albeit a dualism that falls wholly within a broader conceptualization of subjectivity – is foundational to modernity and is the framework within which phenomenology is formed, and with which it seeks to deal (Judovitz, 1988).

Two major traditions of modern thought, therefore, seek to grasp the entire world of experience, alternatively, from the point of view of objectivity or of subjectivity. The objective empiricist tradition seeks to *explain* consciousness as a (somewhat imperfect) mirroring device in which is reflected the real structure of the world of objects which exist independently and outside of our awareness of it. Consciousness is here viewed as an *image* of a world apart from and alien to our immediate self-presence as sentient beings. In contrast, the subjective idealist tradition seeks to *interpret* the world in terms of the inherent *expressiveness* of consciousness. The former is preoccupied with problems of validating knowledge, the latter with issues of the authenticity of feeling, but both strive to bridge the abysmal gulf between reality and appearance; the rupture in being which is at the heart of modern experience.

Importantly both empiricist and idealist traditions (unlike premodern conceptualizations of being) view reality as crystallized at specific points; being concentrates itself in the actuality of exterior bodies, or in the interiority of the personal soul or psyche. The modern 'point-mass' conception of reality – paradigmatically formulated in Newton's mechanics and Rousseau's literary psychology – grasps being as essentially individual and particular and treats all 'higher order' realities as the outcome of complex interactions of analytically and actually discrete, naturally occurring, individuals. These modern traditions are also at one in the essential dynamism of their characterization of reality. The empiricist tradition regards the 'natural' condition of a body to be uniform rectilinear motion; while, for the idealist tradition, the natural condition of the soul is held to be teleological self-development or growth.

It is important to note that Husserl (or for that matter Nietzsche) does not claim for his phenomenology (as Hegel had done for his) a final resolution or solution to this problem; he does not claim to reveal a transcendental meeting ground in which object and subject are ultimately reconciled in a 'higher' unity; rather he seeks to direct our reflection towards a consciousness *prior* to that differentiation. Equally, it is important to realize that this is not an appeal to any premodern philosophical position. Rather, it is only by taking seriously Descartes' modern political demands (for the autonomy and authority of self-experience), as well as his novel philosophical ambition (the search for certainty), that Husserl is driven to reject the initial separation upon which modern thought had rested.

Husserl appeals to experience, and to the ultimate founding of certainty in self-experience, for philosophical clarity. Self-experience is independent of all external authority; 'each of us bears in himself the warrant of his absolute existence' (Husserl, 1931: 143). And in doing so rejects all hypothetical and theoretical constructions in favour of a return to 'pure' consciousness. In his view, *both* explanatory *and* interpretative schemas of consciousness are infected with doubt and gratuitous abstractions. Certainty rests neither on (constructed) appearance nor on (hypothetical) reality, but is given as *phenomena*.

Though now intimately associated with the work of one author, phenomenology, in its most general sense as the sovereignty of experience, permeates modern culture. In this sense, indeed, it might well be argued that the most distinctively phenomenological perspective, and one which directly challenged both scientific naturalism and romantic idealism, first found expression in the writings of Friedrich Nietzsche. What was so original and ultimately compelling in his fervent iconoclasm was the rigorous manner in which he made reflexive arguments against any conception of the experience of nature as terminating in simple pre-given 'objects', to which a variety of attributes might be attached. For Nietzsche, the self-certain 'subject', equally as the thingness of the 'object', is a fiction. All is phenomenal multiplicity and flux:

> I maintain the phenomenality of the inner world, too: everything of which we become conscious is arranged, simplified, schematized, interpreted through and through – the actual processes of inner 'perception', the causal connection between thoughts, feelings, desires, between subject and object, are absolutely hidden from us – and are perhaps purely imaginary. (Nietzsche, 1967: 264)

'Inner experience', therefore, is no more immediately graspable than is the remoteness of 'external reality'; indeed, it 'enters our consciousness only after it has found a language' (Nietzsche, 1967: 266).

In a properly phenomenological perspective all such crystallized forms dissolve:

> At last the 'thing-in-itself' also disappears, because this is fundamentally the conception of a 'subject-in-itself'. But we have grasped that the subject is a fiction. The antithesis 'thing-in-itself' and 'appearance' is untenable; with that, however, the concept 'appearance' also disappears. (Nietzsche, 1967: 298)

Nietzsche's unorthodox and often bewildering style as well as his marginal position in relation to academic institutions allowed his astonishing insights to pass into the general culture without academic comment. His influence, for many years unacknowledged, was none the less enormous and there is a sense in which the whole development of contemporary phenomenology takes place in dialogue with his submerged presence. In relation, however, to the emergence of Husserl's (stylistically austere) foundational works anticipatory hints of the direction of phenomenology can be traced in the less spectacular writings of his immediate teachers and academic predecessors.

Hermann Lotze, for example, in his *Microcosmus* (1885), anticipates in a less radical fashion some aspects of a new phenomenological attitude. He talks of experience as 'boundless in the wealth of its forms and events, unknown in its origins' (Lotze, 1885: 417). Still restricted to a subject/object conceptualization of experience, Lotze nevertheless suggests something of the distinctive character of phenomena; 'the lustre emitted by objects only seems to be emitted by *them*, and that it can even *seem* to come from them, only because our eyes are there, the receptive organs of a cognitive soul, to which appearances are possible' (Lotze, 1885: 157). He insists, indeed, that 'In all perception nothing is directly in our consciousness but that which it has itself created' (1885: 347). And, at the same time, these constructive acts are felt in terms of incipient emotions: 'Feelings of the most various kinds pervade all the manifold events of ideational life' (1885: 240). For him, the 'transfiguring radiance' of the senses is a reflected image of ourselves.

In a more significant and systematic way, however, phenomenological ideas emerged in the work of Franz Brentano, whom Husserl himself recognized as the real starting point for his own thought, and whose ideas, therefore, belong to the internal development of the movement itself.

CONSCIOUSNESS AS A 'FIELD'

Husserl's philosophy is best understood as a rigorous description of experience considered as an extended field, or fields, of consciousness in preference to its analysis in terms of point-mass concepts which had developed as one of the central assumptions of modernity. His philosophy is directly linked, therefore, not only to specific philosophical discussions within but, more generally, to the major cultural transformations of the late nineteenth century.

Within the empiricist and 'objectivist' account of reality – in the physical sciences themselves – new ideas had emerged during the second half of the nineteenth century which seriously challenged classical mechanism. The general features of wave phenomena had previously been studied in relation to some aspects of light and electricity, but in the bold and original work of James Clerk Maxwell a systematic foundation for a new view of the physical universe was successfully established. Maxwell's wave equations proved to be the starting point for new mechanical and dynamical concepts which came to dominate the development of twentieth-century physics. Rather than being viewed as localized in naturally individuated physical bodies – the bearers of 'primary qualities' – matter was viewed as extending through space, with which ultimately it became coterminous. 'Physical' reality was best understood as specific characteristics of space (Hendry, 1986).

At the same time, within the newly developing 'sciences' of the human soul, the psyche appeared in new ways. Its crystallization as a self-conscious and individuated ego, gave way to more diffuse characterizations of psychic life; at once 'material' as well as 'psychic', dispersed throughout, rather than localized within, space. Experience was redefined as a 'stream' or 'flux'. Anton Gurwitsch, thus, begins his appropriately titled presentation of phenomenology *The Field of Consciousness* with a discussion of William James (Gurwitsch, 1964). For James the psychic 'offers itself as something changing incessantly and necessarily, as if it were a stream with waves which fleetingly rise up and flow away again' (James, 1950: 79). It is 'Interest alone [which] gives accent and emphasis, light and shade, background and foreground'; a structure only emerges in experience secondarily as a result of the mind working on the 'primordial chaos of sensation' (1950: 288).

The unity and concreteness of reality might be regarded as reflecting, or even consequential upon, the experience of ourselves as coherent egos localized in singular bodies. But it was just this unity and coherence which seemed to be breaking down. More directly and dramatically than in Nietzsche's spectacular essays, the bourgeois ego fragmented and dissolved, giving rise to puzzling new phenomena; hysteria, hypnosis, fugue, multiple personality (Ellenberger, 1970; Hacking, 1995). The emergence of new field characterizations of reality, therefore, became a matter of practical urgency as well as an intellectual necessity.

ESSENTIAL IDEAS OF PHENOMENOLOGY

The phenomenological movement which emerges in the work of Husserl proclaims a radical commitment to the founding spirit of modernity. Not only must thought be genuinely grounded in experience (a much more stringent condition than is usually thought) it must not stray beyond the boundaries of experience. Phenomenology refuses to accept as 'real' the referents of many of the seemingly innocuous 'descriptive' terms common both in scientific discourse and in everyday language. The objection to all such terms is simply that they are not transparently grounded in experience and that, far from expressing self-evident truths, they introduce 'explanatory' or 'interpretative' schemas in an ultimately arbitrary manner.

The initial aim of phenomenology, therefore, is very simple; it is to describe what is given, what appears to consciousness, without attempting to 'explain' it in any way and without attributing 'significance' and 'meaning' where none exists. It is a specific application of the Cartesian method of doubt; to seek only that which presents itself indubitably. Stated thus it appears to be a trivial task. Why should it be at all difficult to reveal what is already given? Our normal way of thinking cannot help but look upon such a statement with suspicion. If something is given it must be known, if it is already known surely it is given? Phenomenology takes root in this apparent contradiction and, by clarifying its essential consistency, establishes a distinctive and original orientation towards reality.

Intentionality

Husserl's starting point and most general insight into the character of experience is expressed in his fundamental dictum of the 'intentionality' of consciousness. This means simply that consciousness is never without content: 'Conscious processes are also called *intentional*; but then the word intentionality signifies nothing else than this universal fundamental property of consciousness: to be conscious *of* something as a *cogito*; to bear within itself its *cogitatum*' (Husserl, 1950: 33).

We cannot experience consciousness in the empty form of, for example, 'seeing', 'hearing', 'feeling', 'willing' and so on; we can only be aware of seeing something, hearing something, feeling a particular way or willing something in particular. The occasionally voiced objection that characteristically contemporary feelings are not only vague in themselves but, as anxiety or guilt, are frequently 'objectless' is hardly an objection here (Strasser, 1977); we remain conscious of a feeling of fear or anger or guilt, though we may be unsure of its 'source'. This, indeed, is just Husserl's point. From the phenomenological perspective, no judgement is made as to the 'objective reality' or 'externality' of *any* contents of consciousness. Experience is analysed in its own terms 'as if' it were an autonomous realm: '*There is no conceivable place where the life of consciousness could break through or be broken through* so that we would encounter a transcendency that could have a sense other than that of an intentional unity appearing in the subjectivity of consciousness itself' (Husserl, 1970a: 236).

Husserl himself attributes the modern version of this notion to Brentano. Certainly, Brentano insisted that any adequate psychology must resist the temptation of reductionism and grasp consciousness in its own terms:

> Every psychical phenomenon is characterized by what the Scholastics of the middle ages called the intentional (also mental) inexistence of an object and what we would call – although not an entirely unambiguous term – relation to a content, direction toward an object (which is not to be understood here as something real), or an immanent objectivity. (Brentano, 1973: 124)

The 'objectivity' of consciousness has no implications beyond consciousness itself. The intentionality of consciousness means only that consciousness is so structured that we are always aware of its content as an 'object' of some sort. The distinction between subject and object, that is to say, is a general feature of consciousness itself; its content always appears as something 'outside' and 'independent' of ourselves as conscious subjects.

Brentano's conception, however, is restricted to the perceptual 'immanence' of consciousness. Along with the major empirical philosophies, Brentano is preoccupied with sensory experience; indeed, he 'regards sensory experience as the only form of experience' (de Boer, 1978: 79; Kockelmans, 1994: 93). Husserl enormously extends the range of intentional objects to be considered as aspects of experience. The intentional object is defined over and over again in terms of continually shifting perspectives and in relation to distinct modalities of its appearing. Our view of experience is thereby enormously enriched and complicated. Through a (potentially interminable) series of increasingly fine differentiations, gradations and interrelations of emotion, will, judgement, memory, sense etc.,

consciousness reveals itself in an inexhaustible variety of contents with their phases and transitions. And in this process the phenomenal character of experience becomes ever more firmly established.

For Husserl intentionality is the most penetrating insight into the modern sovereignty of experience. Empiricist and idealist traditions, in his view, are at fault not only in seeking to account for experience in terms other than consciousness, in doing so they have accepted an impoverished view of experience.

Lived experience

Consciousness, however, is to be understood as lived experience (acts) rather than as the detachable 'contents' of the mind. Husserl is eloquent in his pursuit of this fundamental insight:

> Dazed by the confusion between object and mental content, one forgets that the objects of which we are 'conscious', are not simply *in* consciousness as in a box, so that they can merely be found in it and snatched at in it; but that they are first *constituted* as being what they are for us, and as what they count as for us, in varying forms of objective intuition. (Husserl, 1970a: 385)

The peculiar intentionality of consciousness is not to be mistaken for an alien presence: 'Experience is not an opening through which a world, existing prior to all experience, shines into a room of consciousness; it is not a mere taking of something alien to consciousness into consciousness' (Husserl, 1970a: 232). The objects of consciousness are constituted as an aspect of consciousness itself: 'the object as having identity "within itself" during the flowing subjective process, does not come into the process from outside; on the contrary, it is included as a sense in the subjective process itself' (Husserl, 1950: 42). Normally we remain unaware of the constituting acts of consciousness and surrender to its immanent flow: 'The appearing of things does not itself appear to us, we live through it' (Husserl, 1970a: 538). Merleau-Ponty vividly expresses Husserl's insight: 'I am no more aware of being the true subject of my sensations than of my birth or my death' (Merleau-Ponty, 1962: 215).

Taken together, the notions of intentionality and lived experience, as elaborated by Husserl, are sufficient to indicate a further and highly important characteristic of consciousness; its contents are not formed into objects simply but into objects of sense:

> If we imagine a consciousness prior to all experience, it may very well have the same *sensations* as we have.

But it will intuit no things, and no events pertaining to things, it will perceive no trees and no houses, no flight of birds nor any barking dogs. One is at once tempted to express the situation by saying that its sensations *mean* nothing to such a consciousness, that they do not *count as signs* of the properties of an object, that their combination does not count as a sign of the object itself. They are merely lived through, without objectifying *interpretation* derived from experience. (Husserl, 1970a: 309)

Essences

Phenomenology is committed to experience, but rejects empiricism. Husserl's philosophy emerges primarily through a sustained criticism of what he called 'psychologism'; the view, exemplified, for example, by James Mill's *Logic*, that *all* knowledge is reducible to particular mental contents. This made logical and scientific 'truth' dependent on the contingency of the senses and distinct from direct perception only through the application of an ultimately mysterious process of 'empirical generalization'. Husserl's insight into, and commitment to, modernity found its clearest expression in his determination to clarify our capacity for 'apodictic' truth; that is, truths grasped with absolute transparency and self-certainty. Husserl began his professional career as a philosopher of mathematics, and mathematics presented the most compelling and accessible domain of such truth. Our knowledge, for example, that the sum of the internal angles of a triangle is two right angles does not depend on empirical investigation. It is inconceivable that early mathematicians directly measured thousands of different triangles and, invariably finding this to be the case, elevated their observations to a general principle. Equally, however, it made no sense whatever to suppose that some ideal or perfect triangle exists somehow 'in the mind' so that, reflecting upon this formal object, we can investigate its supposedly universal properties. The road to mathematical truth, Husserl points out, consists in the *arbitrary* construction of an exemplar which, being absolutely *freely* produced, represents *any* triangle.

The 'experience' which is the subject matter of a pure phenomenology 'has as its exclusive concern, experiences intuitively seizable and analysable in the pure generality of their essences' (Husserl, 1970a: 249). 'Essences' are not to be regarded as empirical generalizations or as actually existing Platonic forms but, rather, as 'intuitions'; and 'The intuition of essences includes no more difficulties or "mystical" secrets than perception' (quoted in de Boer, 1978: 243). Husserl aims, thus, at a general 'geometry of experience' (Husserl, 1973: 202).

Modalization

Essential insight is gained through *free variation* of intentional objects. It is the unconstrained character of mathematician's exemplary constructions which inspires confidence in the universality of the results they achieve. Husserl, it should be noted, rejects the modern romantic tradition in which apodictic truth is located in the realm of absolute freedom itself. An imaginative liberation from the constraints of empirical actualities is a necessary prelude to a rigorous investigation of eidetic objectivities, and does not itself guarantee (as is supposed in the uncontrolled self-production of *archetypes*) an immediate grasp of Truth (Gusdorf, 1985; Spariosu, 1989; Yack, 1992). Husserl insists that the search for apodictic truth should not be mistaken for 'a field of architectonic play' (Husserl, 1970a: 62).

For Husserl, '*every fact can be thought of merely as exemplifying a pure possibility*' (Husserl, 1950: 71). Not only the mathematician's freely chosen diagram, but all immediate unreflective experience, can be thought of as an arbitrary actualization drawn from an indeterminate variety of possibilities. Importantly, in addition to providing a route towards insight into essential aspects of experience (pure phenomenology), this idea is the starting point for new and enriched understanding of immediate experience. Empirical actuality continually points beyond itself or back from itself to the realm of possibilities from which it has appeared: 'All actual experience refers beyond itself to possible experiences, and so on *ad infinitum*' (Husserl, 1989: 147). And as '*every actuality involves its potentialities* which are not empty possibilities' (Husserl, 1977: 54) but possibilities lived through appropriate modalities given with experience itself, empirical reality is actualized, so to speak, under the sign of possibility. It is its vast penumbra of conditionality which lends to experience much of its characteristic colour and richness. Every actual experience involves 'the systematic shaping of pure fantasy' (Husserl, 1977: 54), and every perception 'thus acquired, floats in the air, so to speak – in the atmosphere of pure phantasiableness' (Husserl, 1950: 70).

Typically, Husserl points out, 'the active apprehension of the object immediately turns into contemplation; the ego, oriented toward the acquisition of knowledge, tends to penetrate the object, considering it not only from all sides but also in all of its particular aspects, thus, to *complicate* it' (Husserl, 1973: 103). Additionally, the ego freely modalizes its relation to the world oriented towards feeling, will, recollection and so forth, revealing in successive waves ever new objects and aspects of objects; ever new

phenomenological strata swim into view'
(Husserl, 1970a: 46).

The world of experience is made up not of
perceptions only, but of this continually expanding field of *co-present* objectivities, each with its
own mode of appearing and its own rich hinter-
land of possibilities. Any phenomenological analysis, therefore, seeks not only to grasp essential
objects but also 'by making present in phantasy
the potential perceptions that would make the
invisible visible' (Husserl, 1950: 48) both digni-
fies and relativizes the contingent present. The
world might indeed have been different but, in
being just what it is, essential realities are clothed
and take shape as actual experience. All actual
experience is an endless process of becoming;
'predelineated potentialities', appear with the
object itself and, through ever renewed modalization, reveal 'an *open infinity of thematic determination*' and continually changing 'schematic
horizons' (Husserl, 1973: 213).

Epoché

Husserl refers to his philosophical method,
which (however paradoxically) is nothing other
than a consistent application of the distinctively modern demand for the sovereignty of
experience, as the 'transcendental reduction' or
epoché. It is the requirement that the reflecting
subject temporarily withhold the conviction of
reality which normally and effortlessly arises
with perceptual images and other intentional
acts of consciousness. Specifically he seeks to
turn subjectivity away from the seeming
solidity and individually objectified forms of
'external' reality and return it to its own 'pre-
given' forms.

Overcoming the 'natural attitude' in which the
world appears to us as a well founded and
organized collection of objects requires not only
the suppression of all scientific and theoretical
abstractions through which these things are
interrelated, explained and interpreted but also,
and even more significantly, the dissolution of all
those objectifying assumptions, rooted in everyday life and thought, through which they are
originally constituted as experiential *things*:

> we must go from the scientific fundamental concepts
> back to the contents of 'pure experience', we must
> radically set aside all presumptions of exact science,
> all its peculiar conceptual superstructures – in other
> words, we must consider the world as if these
> sciences did not yet exist, the world precisely as life-
> world, just as it maintains its coherent existence in
> life throughout all its relativity, as it is constantly
> outlined in life in terms of validity. (Husserl, 1950:
> 216)

The 'inhibiting' of all existential position-taking
does not imply the complete emptying of
experience: 'On the contrary we gain possession
of something by it . . . my own living, with all the
pure subjective processes making this up . . . the
universe of "phenomena" in the (particular also
the wider) phenomenological sense. The *epoché*
can also be said to be the radical and universal
method by which I apprehend myself purely'
(Husserl, 1950: 20/1).

Consciousness is decisively shifted from an
orientation in which 'nothing of the psychic acts
and other subjective lived experiences which
comprise the varying consciousness of the object
occurs in the content of their sense itself'
(Husserl, 1977: 15), to one in which is established
'an inner viewing which discloses the lived
experiences of thinking (normally) hidden from
the thinker' (Husserl, 1977: 19).

In Husserl's view, the modern methodological
principle of 'detachment' as a precondition of
valid knowledge, when taken seriously, transforms things into phenomena. In the process
self-knowledge and self-understanding is placed
on a new foundation:

> The epoché creates a unique sort of philosophical
> solitude which is the fundamental methodical
> requirement for a truly radical philosophy. In this
> solitude I am not a single individual who has
> somehow wilfully cut himself off from the society of
> mankind . . . I am not *an* ego, who still has his *you*,
> his *we*, his total community of cosubjects in natural
> validity . . . All of mankind, and the whole
> distinction and ordering of the personal pronouns,
> has become a phenomen within my epoché . . . I can
> say nothing other than: it is I who practice the
> epoché . . . it is I who stand above all natural
> existence that has meaning for me. (Husserl, 1950:
> 184)

The *epoché* is a 'transcendental reduction'; it is
consciousness returned to its essential living form
which 'lays open . . . an infinite realm of being of
a new kind' (Husserl, 1950: 27).

TRANSCENDENTAL EXPERIENCE

What is essential to this 'infinite realm'? Can it
be assigned a positive content or must every
effort to furnish it with a structure be regarded
as an unwarranted compromise with the 'natural
attitude' which should more properly be
dissolved into the pure flux of appearing and
disappearing. One might well expect the *epoché*
to fall into incoherence and a bewildering flux
of conscious states. Husserl himself points out
that 'The universe of free-possibilities in general
is a *realm of disconnectedness*; it lacks unity of

content', and the Transcendental Reduction is founded upon just such 'free-possibilities' (Husserl, 1973: 356). Certainly, we cannot expect the empirical ego to be protected in some way from the general process of dissolution of the natural attitude. The 'transcendental residuum' contains no trace of the mundane ego as an 'external' observing subject which is, so to speak, assimilated to the self-identity of experience itself.

Significantly, however, Husserl also emphasizes that, in addition to our awareness of fluid and streaming life, 'we also experience equally well subjects with abiding psychic characteristics, as characteristics, that is, which manifest themselves as remaining during the multiple change of psychic doing and living' (Husserl, 1977: 79). And, more decisively, he insists the *eidos* is intuited through 'exemplary arbitrariness' the 'whim of passive imagination' (Husserl, 1973: 343); an essence which is directly linked to the *manifold* of experiences. The 'bracketing' of the natural attitude, that is to say, both in terms of contents and modalities, reveals a previously hidden structure rather than a phenomenal chaos. Husserl, in fact, confidently assures us that 'the bare identity of the "I am" is not the only thing given as indubitable in transcendental self-experience' (Husserl, 1950: 28).

Embodiment

The 'primal' givenness of experience consists, first of all, in its embodiment. The *epoché* does not detach 'pure' experience from the body – the critical error in the Platonic tradition is just the claim that it does – rather, it reveals the constitutive role of the body for the whole field of consciousness. Even for the natural attitude, in fact, the intimacy of body and soul never wholly decomposes into the estrangement of object and subject. A psychological analysis carried on wholly within the natural attitude already reveals that 'The qualities of material things are aestheta, such as they present themselves to me intuitively, prove to be dependent on my qualities, the make-up of the *experiencing subject*, and to be related to *my Body* and my "normal sensibility"'. In a completely general sense 'The Body is, in the first place, the *medium of all perception* . . . all that is thingly-real in the surrounding world of the Ego has its relation to the Body' (Husserl, 1989: 61; Strauss, 1963, 1966).

But, more properly understood, the mutual implication of body and soul is itself a phenomenological insight which shakes consciousness out of the natural attitude; Body and soul 'are bound and interwoven together, they flow into one another in layers and are possible only in

this unity of a stream. Nothing can be torn away from this stream; nothing can be separated off as, so to say, a thing for itself' (Husserl, 1989: 98). Equally, the natural attitude towards the ego or psyche as an empirical unity (itself a reflex of the natural attitude towards the body), is dissolved in the phenomena of embodiment:

> no attempt to separate off and objectify the soul – just as is the case with the thing itself, so the soul itself is nothing more than the unity of its properties; in its states it 'behaves' in such and such a way, in its properties it 'is' and each of its properties is a sheer ray of its being. (Husserl, 1989: 131)

Consciousness, that is to say, is a synthesis of a peculiar sort: 'The flux of psychic life has its unity in itself' (Husserl, 1989: 140). The directionality and orientation of consciousness – the fundamental intentionality of consciousness – finds its 'zero-point' in the phenomenon of embodiment; in the pre-givenness of the body as the centre of experience: 'I have all things over and against me; they are all "there" – with the exception of one and only one, namely the Body, which is always "here"' (Husserl, 1989: 166).

The embodied soul and the ensouled body are one and the same living being, a being distinct from either the body or the soul of the natural attitude:

> In a quite unique way the living body is constantly in the perceptual field quite immediately, with a completely unique ontic meaning . . . Thus, purely in terms of perception, physical body and living body [*Körper und Leib*] are essentially different. (Husserl, 1989: 107)

The body is more than the point of spatial orientation, it is the centre of the phenomenal world in all its modalities and is, therefore, uniquely related to the ego; it is *my* body:

> the Body has its special virtues compared with other things, and as a result it is 'subjective' in a pre-eminent sense, i.e., as bearer of fields of sense, as organ of free movements, and so as organ of the will, as bearer of the center and as seat of the fundamental directions of spatial orientation . . . this Body is *my* Body, and indeed mine in the palpable special sense, because I already am and in a certain sense bestow on it its special virtues. (Husserl, 1980: 224)

The fundamental directionality of consciousness, its *horizon* of expectation and appearing, in all its modes, is embodied and is orientated to the world primarily in terms of corporeality. It is also clear that the special intimacy of embodiment means that the 'free-variation' of experience, which is the key to grasping essential phenomena, here mutually reinforces the peculiarly 'given' quality of both Body and Soul. We cannot, even in imagination, divest ourselves of bodily form or enter a world other than that given to us as human experience; we can empathize with another person but not with a member of another species.

The phenomenological foundation in embodiment also provides a key point of differentiation from both idealist and empirical psychologies of self-identity. For the empiricist tradition personal identity remains fundamentally unexplicated and accidental; a mysterious accretion consequential on the various 'contacts' the body makes with its environment. The idealist tradition, alternatively, lodges identity with the soul and places it inside the body. Both traditions support a 'developmental' view in which authentic selfhood is progressively attained; either, because the body is brought under ever greater control by the rational intelligence adventitiously adhering to it, or because the interior soul succeeds finally in 'expressing itself' as spontaneous action. In both views development depends on a progressive concentration and, as it were, narrowing of the focus of personal characteristics. Authenticity is a process of gaining clarity and self-definition, of becoming more and more just the person we are and abandoning all the people we might have been.

Husserl decisively rejects these approaches which fatally confuse the transcendental and empirical ego. For him, self-identity, like all other aspects of consciousness, is phenomenal in character. Authenticity, the *essential* ego, as distinct from the continuous transitions of immediate experience, is a product of free-variation and modalization. The 'self' emerges as a result of continuously departing from and returning to itself; a process of continuous imaginative enrichment. It is in the endless multiplicity of open possibilities, rather than the enforced selection of the singular and decisive choice, that the self establishes its own validity. This, largely unexplored, implication of Husserl's work provides a potentially fertile approach to a realistic psychology of modern experience.

Temporality

Spatialization is an achievement of the body/ego; a construction and a psychical act. All experience must be orientated to 'here' or 'there', 'near/far', 'right/left', 'up/down', 'inside/outside' and so on. Spatialization, however, is not the most fundamental aspect of intentionality. Husserl shifts the perspective of post-Renaissance modern thought away from space and vision in which the 'natural attitude' of spectatorship emerged (Edgerton, 1991; Leppert, 1996; White,

1957) towards time and the original kinaesthesia of sensing. Temporality is given with every act of consciousness and is present 'first of all as an all-ruling, *passively* flowing synthesis, in the form of the *continuous consciousness of internal time*. Every subjective process has its internal temporality' (Husserl, 1993: 41). Husserl claims that 'Time-consciousness is the original seat of the unity of identity in general' (1993: 73) and that, consequently, 'For us temporality is a sufficient mark of reality'.

This is among the most challenging of Husserl's positions. Abandoning the natural attitude leaves the transcendental ego in a potentially timeless void. The fact that a continuous *flow* of phenomena make their appearance cannot be predicated on the empirical flux of actual events. 'Events' do not themselves disclose such a flow, nor, indeed, do they reveal with absolute clarity an 'arrow of time' as a condition of experience itself. Within the *epoché* there are no 'events' in the normal sense of the word. This might be thought of as closely related to Henri Bergson's notion of the experience of time as 'duration' (Bergson, 1991). Rather than begin with spatial categories (objects, events, changes of location) from which the necessity of time is deduced, the primordially given experience of temporality is itself the medium receptive to the construction of spatial categories.

Temporality is a pre-given and absolutely general condition of the transcendental ego. The transcendental reduction loses contact with empirically measured or 'objective' time, but is not empty of temporality. 'Now', 'before', 'earlier', are given phenomenological data from which Husserl develops a rich network of insights.

> temporal determinations of every sort are attached in a certain way and as a necessary consequence to every coming into being and passing away that occurs in the present. (Husserl, 1993: 15)

Retention in consciousness, furthermore, effects continuous and essential changes in its contents; every 'now point' has attached to it 'consciousness *of what has just been*' (Husserl, 1993: 34), then 'sinks' into the past with progressive loss of its determinations. We cannot avoid the flow of 'now points' and their continuous modification. Paul Ricoeur nicely emphasizes the point; 'we cannot stress too much the extent to which consciousness is disarmed and powerless before its own drift into the future' (Ricoeur, 1966: 52). The continuous process of modification means that an '*impressional* consciousness, constantly flowing, passes over into ever new *retentional* consciousness' (Husserl, 1993: 31):

> Ever new primal impressions continuously flash forth with ever new matter, now the same, now

changing. What distinguishes primal impression from primal impression is the individualizing moment of the impression of the original temporal position, which is something fundamentally different from the quality and other material moments of the content of sensation. (Husserl, 1993: 70)

We never experience 'empty' duration, but all experience requires a co-present and independently constituted temporal flow. Consciousness, indeed, is a 'double intentionality' bodying forth objectivities bearing essential temporal relations.

Husserl is at pains to reveal the complexity of actual time-consciousness in its varied forms and the subtle enrichment of consciousness effected by the work of retention, secondary memory and free phantasy, each introducing, and as it were, interleaving varied forms of temporality and constituting objectivities in their own distinctive ways.

Intersubjectivity

The existence of Other body/ego unities is also given originally in experience. Husserl himself discusses at considerable length, particularly in the fifth *Cartesian Meditation*, how this is to be understood. Making minimal assumptions, he argues that other bodies are perceived and enter our own experience as conscious contents. There is, however, a difficulty of grasping the sense in which the Other, which is alien from me, is none the less given as the centre of its own world and not just as another version of myself. The Other is always outside me, always 'there', as distinct from my 'here'. The Other as human subject, Husserl suggests, is inferred analogically on the basis of our own 'free-variation' – we can imaginatively take the position of the other body and see that it behaves 'as if' another (impenetrable) ego were located there. Making somewhat less minimal assumptions, we might prefer (with, for example, Max Scheler, 1973, or Ortega y Gassett, 1957), to say that the Other is given directly as Other (clearly we cannot directly enter into another's experience); that is, as another *person* without need of inference or deduction. In any event the world is experienced as intersubjective, as shared and available to Others. Indeed, the fact that my own essence can stand over against the Other 'presupposes that *not all my modes of consciousness are modes of self-consciousness*' (Husserl, 1950: 105).

There are two distinct senses in which intersubjectivity becomes important here. First, as what might be termed the interactive ego. The givenness of Others means that *my* world is constituted through communicative interaction and practical activity in relation to Others and not simply on the basis of experience considered from the point of view of some (illusory) individual consciousness. Secondly, transcendental experience (the modalities of sense, judgement, feeling and so on, as well as the general features of *epoché*) is intersubjective in the sense of being absolutely general and universal; in terms of essential phenomena my experience *must* be identical to every other person's. Husserl would probably have included in this universality the sense of self-identity as an individuated *monad*.

It is perhaps not surprising (though alternative approaches may well prove more promising) that it is in terms of some notion of interactive subjectivity that a fruitful point of contact between Husserl's work and sociological thought has most frequently been sought.

HISTORICAL SUBJECTIVITY

Husserl's last major work, *The Crisis in European Science* – like others published in his own lifetime subtitled 'An Introduction to Phenomenology' – is distinctive in presenting his ideas in a broad historical framework. This may be seen not simply as another 'way in' to phenomenological insights and methods but, rather, as an essential development of phenomenology itself (Carr, 1987). Once the intersubjective character of consciousness is recognized then the historical character of experience comes to light.

This, in fact, is no new departure for Husserl whose chosen method – a rigorous working through of the implications of Cartesian doubt – has tended to obscure the essentially historical character of his project as a whole. His philosophy had always been an explication of *modernity*; and, though the 'teleological-historical' account of phenomenology in the *Crisis* is not a genuinely new development, it is, certainly, an important and comprehensive reworking of basic insights. Here the historical context is supplied with a definite and impassioned statement of the origins of modernity in Galilean science's claim to Truth, and in the demand for human self-autonomy implicit in that claim. But the early promise of the modern sciences – the founding of a new radical and free philosophy as a coherent development of an all-embracing human reason – underwent curtailment, fragmentation and disillusionment. The primal establishment of the new 'philosophy' (of humanism) was the living demand of European humanity, 'which seeks to renew itself radically' (Husserl, 1970b: 12). Thus the crisis of philosophy implies the crisis of all modern sciences as members of the philosophical universe. This universe, however, was and remains grounded in actual experience; a point on which he had already insisted 'every particular scientific province must lead us back to a province in the original experiential world' (Husserl, 1977: 40). Consequently, the general crisis in philosophy – the fragmentation and emptying of Reason – represents 'at first a latent, then a more and more prominent crisis of European humanity itself in respect to the total meaningfulness of its cultural life'. The philosophical faith in reason – which had once been the most decisive statement of the modern commitment to the sovereignty of experience – has been shattered:

> It is reason which ultimately gives meaning to everything that is thought to be, all things, values, and ends – their meaning understood as the normative relatedness to what, since the beginning of philosophy, is meant by the word 'truth' – truth in itself . . . Along with this falls the faith in 'absolute' reason, through which the world has its meaning, the faith in the meaning of history, of humanity, the faith in man's freedom, that is, his capacity to secure rational meaning for his individual and common human existence. (Husserl, 1970b: 9)

Husserl wants to revive these great tasks of philosophy and reimbue it with the spirit of its first modern foundation, for, 'If man loses his faith, it means nothing less than the loss of faith "in himself" in his own true being.' True being remains a task and not an immediately given aspect of consciousness.

SPIRIT IN MODERNITY

It is not difficult to see that a concept of 'interactive' subjectivity supports an essentially historical understanding of experience; what is much more challenging, however, is the idea that the 'collective' or 'universal' subject, defined through the absolutely general results of the transcendental reduction, is also historical in character. The most rigorous reflection on our own apparently individuated and personal experience of the world reveals a pre-given structure of consciousness which reconnects us, so to speak, to the general world of humanity and, therefore, to its history. Such a view is already anticipated by Husserl in an important essay on psychology in which he associates his own views more closely to the historical hermeneutics of Wilhelm Dilthey (one feels he might well have mentioned Hegel in this regard).

The separation of the world of reason – as scientific idealization and rationality – from the world of primordial experience leads ultimately to a crisis; to the loss of meaning and significance in the very bearer of reason itself. The impressive

commitment and rigour of the *Crisis* is equalled only in Max Weber's sociological writing as a statement, both ironic and despairing, of the inescapable human failure of modernity (Schluchter, 1996: Weber, 1948).

More than this the *Crisis* brings into focus both the historical character of human subjectivity and the subjective character of human history. History is the paradox of subjectivity: 'that of humanity as world-constituting subjectivity and yet as incorporated into the world itself' (Husserl, 1970b: 182). Human history is grasped as self-created Objectivity and Otherness; that is to say, as spirit. The grasping of humanity as spirit penetrates Husserl's work as a whole and comes increasingly into prominence with its development; in *Cartesian Meditations*, for example, he remarks 'we . . . not only have a spiritual heritage, but have become what we are thoroughly and exclusively in a historical-spiritual manner' (Husserl, 1950: 71).

All experience shares to some degree this enigmatic character. The natural scientist, too, deals with spiritual data. Modern science is general and irresistible truth, identical for all and identical over time; uniquely in this field 'repeated production creates not something similar . . . [but] something identically the same, identical in sense and validity' (Husserl, 1970b: 278). But this general validity has a starting point and periods of renewal and rediscovery. Science finds its modern philosophical form in humanism; and humanism traces itself in the Greek world. Now, if we enquire about Greek science we must begin with an understanding of what constituted 'Nature' for the Greeks, what was included in their 'surrounding world' as their 'world representation'. Now, '"Surrounding world" is a concept that has its place exclusively in the spiritual sphere . . . Our surrounding world is a spiritual structure in us and in our historical life' (Husserl, 1970b: 272). The 'eternal validity' of science, in its origins and development as in its confrontation with new infinities and tasks, cannot be removed from the spiritual structure of history. Its truths find their full meaning only in relation to the spiritual 'life-world' and its vast historical transformations.

IMPLICATIONS FOR SOCIAL THEORY

Sociologists and social theorists have found it easier to ignore than to criticize or assimilate phenomenology. It has been (wrongly) identified as both 'psychological' and 'idealist'; positions from which sociology regards itself as having a special responsibility to win conviction. More plausibly, perhaps, it seems that phenomenology 'brackets' just those aspects of experience which are of abiding concern to *social* theorists. The *epoché* considers experience, as it were, artificially removed from its constituting entanglement in society. Yet it has been just the point of the preceding presentation to make clear the connection – and in quite fundamental ways – between phenomenology and the substantive themes of any realistic social theory and any meaningful historical sociology of modernity.

There are three evident ways in which phenomenology in fact became relevant to sociological theory. First, as a distinctive methodological approach to the central problems and tasks of sociology, secondly, as itself a source of sociologically valid insight and, thirdly, as forming the descriptive material for a general sociology of modern experience.

The most notable 'bridge' between the two is to be located in the writings of Alfred Schutz, whose work focuses, as does the majority of (the relatively few) contributions to this dialogue, overwhelmingly on the first and second of these themes.

Schutz's phenomenological approach to social reality, in contrast to Husserl's insistence upon the centrality of the transcendental reduction, might be characterized as immanent and mundane. He is less concerned with revealing the 'given' character of consciousness (whether or not as an historical-social construct) by a rigorous and artificial exclusion of everything immediately available to us within the stream of conscious social life, as of grasping that social world as a thoroughly 'interpreted' reality. His phenomenology does not begin with an act of withdrawal or annihilations so much as with a complicit affirmation of social life as a paramount reality: 'The world of everyday life is . . . man's fundamental and paramount reality' (Schutz and Luckmann, 1973: 3). What Husserl had 'bracketed' in order to reveal the most primitive structure of consciousness becomes the real subject matter for a phenomenological understanding of society. This entirely avoids the difficult analytical problems connected with intersubjectivity. Though making reference at various times to the inadequacy of both Husserl's and other phenomenological treatments of the problem, Schutz himself offers no original solution to the difficulty (Schutz, 1966: 51–83). For Schutz intersubjectivity *is* the givenness of the social world and needs no fundamental explication (Schutz and Luckmann, 1973: 5). We respond to and live in a world that is already formed as a community. The concrete social sciences, thus, deal directly with 'that mundane sphere which transcendental phenomenology has bracketed' (Schutz, 1964: 122).

The first task of a phenomenological sociology, therefore, is to gain insight into the conventional interpreted character of lived social experience. He points out, in this regard, that both scientific concepts and 'everyday' experience are constituted through categories remote from anything immediately given in consciousness; '. . . the so-called concrete facts of common-sense perception are not so concrete as it seems. They already involve abstractions of a highly complicated nature' (Schutz, 1962: 3). Sociology deals with 'second-order' abstractions, with interpretations of those interpretations which constitute the immediate content of social life.

This approach encourages a methodological eclecticism which draws also on the writings of Henri Bergson and, more particularly, of William James. Schutz may thus reasonably be regarded as championing a 'subjective' sociology; that is to say social reality is constituted in and through meaningful actions and relations. There are no wholly 'objective' facts of social life as social life consists exclusively in interpreted behaviour. This brings Schutz's work into a close (but partial and one-sided) relation to that of Max Weber, whom he explicitly acknowledges. This version of phenomenology quickly established itself as a significant critique of positivistic and scientistic trends in American social science research (Cicourel, 1964, 1968).

At a more substantive level of phenomenological insight into the character of social life Schutz may be viewed, otherwise, as drawing heavily on conventional American functionalism rather than on Husserl's critical historical insight into modernity. 'Society' is here viewed as a functional unity; a coherent and ordered whole predicated on a shared body of beliefs and perceptions through which 'reality' is defined as the common property of all its members. The consensual unity of social life, however, rather than being expressed in, and depending upon, a specific body of 'values' is characterized as an 'everyday reality' or common 'lifeworld'. The large-scale coherence of society, that is to say, emerges and is sustained through a multitude of mundane 'taken-for-granted' assumptions. Schutz, returning to the mainstream of modern philosophy, defines this 'taken-for-granted' reality primarily in cognitive terms; as a specific thought world and perceptual community, in which a certain 'stock of knowledge' has been institutionalized, above all in everyday language, as the unreflective foundation of experience.

In terms of social relations a fundamental distinction arises between 'face-to-face' relationships with others directly known and familiar, and relations of a more distant and indirect type. Confirming a tradition deeply rooted in American culture Schutz assumes the former to be the 'real' foundation for social life in general. 'Authentic' social relations express the immediate reciprocity of human contact. All other relations are conducted through a highly differentiated and unequally distributed 'stock of knowledge' through which 'out groups' are defined in terms of a variety of 'typifications': 'The world, the physical as well as the sociocultural one, is experienced from the outset in terms of types' (Schutz, 1970: 119). 'Society' is made possible, in other words, through the sharing of a stock of knowledge within small groups and through reciprocal functional relations among such groups. The consensual unity of society is, thus, assumed as a theoretical necessity rather than taken as an analytical or empirical hypothesis.

In this context social action is not only regarded, in Max Weber's sense, as 'subjectively meaningful', it is interpretable by the sociologist as a consequence of the functional unity of society as a whole; recprocity of action guarantees a certain level of mutual comprehension. Indeed, this unity becomes ever more evident and, therefore, sociology draws ever closer to the everyday common sense of the lifeworld: 'The more these interlocked behaviour patterns are standardized and institutionalized, that is, the more their typicality is socially approved by laws, folkways, mores, and habits, the greater is their usefulness in common sense and scientific thinking as a scheme of interpretation of human behavior' (Schutz, 1962: 62). Modern society, thus, is characterized by a high level of functional integration and unity, and by a growing uniformity of social action as meaningful in terms of 'rational' criteria. Schutz's conception here, though expounded in relation to Weber's sociology is, once again, distinctively American in tone. Rational action is idealized as conscious choice; as an implicit expression of the freedom of the market. Action is defined as 'conduct devised by the actor in advance', and is in principle 'based on a preconceived project' (Schutz, 1962: 19). In contrast, it should be noted, Husserl repeatedly describes action in terms of vague, drifting movements and tentative probings; the partial opening and extending of horizons; continually intermingling tendencies and so on.

Schutz clarifies, simplifies and rationalizes Husserl's endlessly complicating picture of experience. For him 'everyday reality' is of paramount importance and, rather than gaining its depth and solidity through a complex process of modalization and free-variation (themselves, of course, also sociohistorical processes); this reality increasingly takes on the character of the 'given' and unconditional objectivity Husserl was at pains to decompose. Schutz's subjectivism, in practice, consecrates the 'natural attitude', withdrawal from which had been the starting point of the phenomenological movement. By avoiding the difficulties into which Husserl was led by his rigorous analysis of consciousness, Schutz, therefore, also abandons the critical spirit of his master's endlessly nuanced description of experience.

These tendencies become yet more apparent in Peter Berger and Thomas Luckmann's sociological elaboration of Husserl's notion of 'lifeworld'; which is more openly a 'subjective' version of the functionalist paradigm dominant in American sociology in the late 1960s (Berger and Luckmann, 1967). Berger and Luckmann, indeed, reintroduce an object/subject distinction into the heart of their sociological theory of institutionalization. 'Lifeworld' here becomes 'everyday reality', to be understood in terms of a hierarchy of meanings through which its conventional order was realized and maintained – that is, as the *interpretations* of social actors themselves within the natural attitude. Phenomenology, in this version, owed more to Talcott Parsons than it did to Edmund Husserl.

Both the methodological and theoretical implications of this position were further developed in a distinctive fashion by Harold Garfinkel, whose *Ethnomethodology* might be regarded as a further 'secularization' of phenomenology; an approach which restricts itself to conventional criticisms of positivism in the social sciences and to reporting on the everyday worlds of local social actors (Garfinkel, 1967).

Both these examples illustrate the ease with which phenomenological ambitions can be thwarted by a return to either idealism or empiricism. It might reasonably be expected that the results of an 'ethnomethodological' report, or an enquiry into social knowledge, would be the *starting point* rather than the conclusion of a genuine phenomenological sociology. Indeed, phenomenology now appears insignificant as a theoretical perspective in sociology in large measure because it has become exclusively associated with a relatively brief period (late 1960s and early 1970s) whose central sociological ideas have gone out of fashion.

The third approach, it might be argued, has yet to be attempted. Yet it is just such an attempt which Husserl himself makes in his last major work. In this context, it might be asked what is the nature of the social reality which is caught and held in the phenomenological tradition; what turn of modernity gives rise to this philosophy as its valid expression? In this context it is worth noting that a genuine but unacknowledged development of historical phenomenology has in fact been taking place.

More specifically, an historical phenomenology of the senses has been rapidly developing. The rise of visual culture has been a major theme (Brennan and Jay, 1996), and has included important new studies of colour and shadow in the Western history of representations (Gage, 1993; Stoichita, 1997). The emphasis on vision is now in danger of obscuring the importance of changing modes of aural perception and of sound as a metaphor of reality; music and musicology (particularly harmonics) played a foundational role in early modern humanism and in its extension to the new sciences (Crombie, 1995: vol. 2; Hallyn, 1993). Now smell and to a lesser extent taste and touch are being invested as historical and cultural phenomena of the most general type (Classen, 1993). These are studies which progressively turn their attention away from the 'objects' of the senses to investigate the social organization and social meaning of the act of seeing, hearing, touching etc. Less developed but potentially rich fields of historical phenomenology await similar investigations; particularly an historical phenomenology of emotion, feeling, will and action.

In a remarkable way an historical phenomenology of memory is also beginning to emerge. Pioneering studies have begun the process of providing modern memory with a genuine history (Carruthers, 1990; Geary, 1994; Yates, 1966; and for a specific modern content, Mosse, 1990; Samuels, 1994; Winter, 1995). Recently too, and promising far-reaching implications, there has been considerable historical and sociological interest in the central phenomenological theme of embodiment. In these studies both the 'natural attitude' and the 'primal' givenness of the body emerge as distinctive historical phenomena (Elias, 1994; Foucault, 1977; O'Neill, 1985; Vernant, 1991). It is all the more indicative of the penetrating influence of Husserl's philosophical novelties that these recent contributions come from such diverse fields, in complete disregard of phenomenology itself, or, not uncommonly, from quarters hostile to that movement.

Husserl's phenomenology offers a double perspective of the map of contemporary experience. The natural attitude, it might be said, describes the experience of classical modernity in all its aspects; the point-mass vectorial quality of individuated being. The phenomenological reduction, on the other hand, describes the breakthrough into contemporary 'openness'; the streaming fluidity of (post)modern experience. The world of primordial givenness, in fact, is the world of the hypermodern.

The condition of contemporary experience – advanced or (post)modernity – might itself be regarded as an *epoché* or phenomenological reduction. The reduction with which Descartes began, artificially so to speak, surrendering an attitude to the world, refusing momentarily to take a stand in relation to it, and thus transforming its contents into 'mere phenomena' has in fact become the standard practice of everyday life. The withdrawal into doubt crystallizes the ego in its peculiar primordial purity and pregivenness; but does so in a manner detached from the world itself. 'Standing above them all in my posture of *epoché* I may no longer take part in performing them. Thus my whole life of acts – experiencing, thinking, valuing, etc. – remains, and indeed flows on; but what was before my eyes in that life as "the" world having being and validity for me, has become a mere "phenomenon" and this in respect to all determinations proper to it' (Husserl, 1970b: 77/8). In the *Epoché, the world itself* has been transformed into my *ideae*.

But if this becomes a general attitude, then the self as well as the world is negated; the ego can stand apart from the world only in relation to its own validity, only as an interval (like dreaming) between periods of 'real' life. But when 'real life' is *phenomenalized* the *epoché* can no longer take place and self-certainty is assimilated to the insubstantial passage and transitions of that world, to phenomenal moralization rather than to actions properly speaking.

OSCILLATORY MOTION

The most important criticisms of Husserl come from within phenomenology itself. Beginning, it should at once be admitted, with Husserl's own protégé, Martin Heidegger, who quickly abandoned the phenomenological method (or methods) of radical doubt – the 'bracketing' of some aspects of reality. Heidegger's own position, in fact, is more clearly understood in relation to its (almost wholly unacknowledged) inspiration in the work of the Danish religious writer Søren Kierkegaard. For them it is quite inconceivable (and not just practically difficult) to 'suspend all existential position taking'. The essential character of human being is just to be 'interested', continually and irresistibly interested, in its own reality (Kierkegaard), or to 'care' about its own world (Heidegger). In spite of their own denials, existentialists remain much more closely aligned to modern romanticism (which Husserl decisively rejected) than they liked to admit. Though even here, in spite of the self-conscious rejection of Husserl's phenomenology, it is hardly possible to read Heidegger as other than a critical commentary on his original mentor. And, as a guide to contemporary experience, it is Husserl who is surely the more comprehensive and reliable.

Kierkegaard, it should be noted, in offering his own 'Cartesian Meditation', remains a consistent and significant potential critic of Husserl. In his writings 'boredom' and detachment are grasped insightfully as themselves 'positing and existential position taking'; providing an exemplary modern psychology while at the same time subverting the methodological starting point of phenomenology (Ferguson, 1995). Lethargy, depression and melancholy mark the contemporary age as its own (Asendorf, 1993; Rabinbach, 1990). From Pascal onward, a tradition, powerfully renewed in each generation's creative writers, has tirelessly explored the modern fascination with disinterest and self-absorption. Boredom and lethargy have become observable in the most basic phenomenological data of bodily experience – exhaustion, the symptomatology of neuroses, neurasthenias of all kinds – as well as in the deep withdrawness of schizophrenia (Sass, 1992).

An 'existential' variant which is in principle more supportive of Husserl's positions is provided by Karl Jaspers in his neglected masterpiece *General Psychopathology* (1963). An encyclopedic work to which Jaspers added throughout his life, its phenomenological approach to the possible deformations of 'normal' consciousness does more than any other single volume to reveal the extent to which the 'natural atittude' is a conventionalized and fragile structure. All other possibilities, the entire range of modalizations of normal experience, can not only be imagined, they can be experienced as empirical actualities. In that work the enriching penumbra of conventional consciousness is brought fully to light as the inexhaustible variety in the madness of contemporary experience (Sass, 1992).

The most imaginative and compelling of phenomenological writers, Gabriel Marcel, contests Husserl's results rather than his method. In Marcel's view the phenomenological reduction certainly leads to valid insight, but not to certain self-knowledge or self-understanding. What is revealed, rather, is the ineradicable *mystery* of being. Phenomenology, thus, is the foundation of a new theology of contemporary existence rather than the self-clarifying philosophy of modern experience (Marcel, 1949/50, 1952). This is a powerful and beautifully expressed idea, which finds an echo in the equally original writings of Emmanuel Levinas but, once again, must be regarded as a one-sided development rather than a valid rejection, of Husserl's insights. Husserl is determined to trace knowledge back to its intuitive self-founding; he is not concerned to produce 'new' knowledge. There is no need to produce 'knowledge' of the pre-given reality which is, by definition, already heavy with

self-presence. To seek further elucidation at this point is to *create* a mystery and amounts to asking the wrong question; it is rather like trying to 'explain' the fact that we exist, or (as Johann Kepler mistakenly attempted) why there should be just six planets rather than five or seven or any other number. More generally, it should be admitted that Husserl views humanity as spiritual being, and understands science and culture as the work of spirit. The crisis of the sciences is nothing other than the sign of a spiritless age.

The significant insights of phenomenology focus on the 'given' character of experience, yet they also reveal the active role of the experiencing subject in their original constitution as reality. This is just the 'paradox of subjectivity' with which Husserl's work is continually concerned, and a potentially fruitful point of contact, it should be noted, with Marx's analysis of modern society as the commodity mode of production.

Like quantum physics, the essential problem in relation to phenomenology is to interpret its significance, rather than to criticize its internal consistency or reject its assumptions. The 'formalisms' are convincing; they are nothing other than the self-evident; but what does this mean? An historical conceptualization is still possible, albeit this drives it beyond the sphere of original phenomenological insight; this is the route Husserl himself follows. And, like quantum physics, its central dynamical concept is of oscillatory transitions rather than rectilinear motion or developmental growth. Husserl grasps experience through the countless phasic variations in its modalities; and in the ceaseless transitions among perspectives, including the oscillation in his own philosophy from natural attitude to *epoché*. Each transition, incomprehensible in its inner quality and difference, discloses new forms of appearing and new worlds of consciousness.

REFERENCES

Asendorf, Christoph (1993) *Batteries of Life*. Berkeley, CA: University of California Press.

Berger, Peter and Luckmann, Thomas (1967) *The Social Construction of Reality*. New York: Doubleday.

Bergson, Henri (1991) *Matter and Memory* (trans. Nancy Margaret Paul and W. Scott Palmer). New York: Zone Books.

de Boer, Theodore (1978) *The Development of Husserl's Thought* (trans. Theodore Plantinga). The Hague: Martinus Nijhoff.

Brennan, Teresa and Jay, Martin (eds) (1996) *Vision in Context*. New York and London: Routledge.

Brentano, Franz (1973) *Psychology from an Emprical Standpoint*. London: Routledge.

Carr, David (1987) *Interpreting Husserl: Critical and Comparative Studies*. Dordrecht, Boston and Lancaster: Martinus Nijhoff.

Carruthers, Mary (1990) *The Book of Memory: A Study of Memory in Medieval Culture*. Cambridge: Cambridge University Press.

Cicourel, Aaron (1964) *Method and Measurement in Sociology*. Glencoe, IL: The Free Press.

Cicourel, Aaron (1968) *The Social Organization of Juvenile Justice*. London: Heinemann.

Classen, Constance (1993) *Worlds of Sense*. London and New York: Routledge.

Crombie A.C. (1995) *Styles of Scientific Thinking in the European Tradition*, 3 vols. Cambridge: Cambridge University Press.

Daston, Lorraine and Park, Katherine (1998) *Wonders and the Order of Nature*. New York: Zone Books.

Edgerton, Samuel Y. (1991) *The Heritage of Giotto's Geometry; Art and Science on the Eve of the Scientific Revolution*. Ithaca and London: Cornell University Press.

Elias, Norbert (1994) *The Civilizing Process* (trans. Edmund Jephcott). Oxford and Cambridge: Blackwell.

Ellenberger, Henri (1970) *The Discovery of the Unconscious*. London: Allen Lane.

Ferguson, Harvie (1995) *Melancholy and the Critique of Modernity*. London: Routledge.

Foucault, Michel (1977) *Discipline and Punish* (trans. Alan Sheridan). London: Allen Lane.

Gage, John (1993) *Colour and Culture*. London: Thames and Hudson.

Garfinkel, Harold (1967) *Studies in Ethnomethodology*. Englewood Cliffs, NJ: Prentice-Hall.

Geary, Patrick J. (1994) *Phantoms of Remembrance: Memory and Oblivion at the End of the First Millennium*. Princeton, NJ: Princeton University Press.

Gurwitsch, Aron (1964) *The Field of Consciousness*. Pittsburgh: Duquesne University Press.

Gusdorf, Georges (1985) *Le Savoir romantique de la nature*. Paris: Payot.

Hacking, Ian (1995) *Rewriting the Soul*. Princeton, NJ: Princeton University Press.

Hallyn, Fernand (1993) *The Poetic Structure of the World* (trans. Donald M. Leslie). New York: Zone Books.

Hendry, John (1986) *James Clerk Maxwell and the Theory of Electromagnetic Field*. Bristol: Hilger.

Husserl, Edmund (1931) *Ideas: General Introduction to Pure Phenomenology* (trans. W.R. Boyce Gibson). London: Allen & Unwin.

Husserl, Edmund (1950) *Cartesian Meditations* (trans. Dorion Cairns). Dordrecht, Boston and London: Kluwer.

Husserl, Edmund (1969) *Formal and Transcendental Logic* (trans. Dorian Cairns). The Hague: Martinus Nijhoff.

Husserl, Edmund (1970a) *Logical Investigations*, 2 vols (trans. J.N. Findlay). London: Routledge and Kegan Paul.

Husserl, Edmund (1970b) *The Crisis of European Sciences and Transcendental Philosophy* (trans. David Carr). Evanston, IL: Northwestern University Press.

Husserl, Edmund (1973) *Experience and Judgment* (trans. James S. Churchill and Karl Aneriles). London: Routledge and Kegan Paul.

Husserl, Edmund (1977) *Phenomenological Psychology* (trans. John Scanlon). The Hague: Martinus Nijhoff.

Husserl, Edmund (1989) *Ideas Pertaining to a Pure Phenomenology and to a Phenomenological Philosophy: Second Book* (trans. Richard Rojcewicz and André Schuwer). Dordrecht, Boston and London: Kluwer.

Husserl, Edmund (1993) *On The Phenomenology of Internal Time Consciousness* (trans. John Barnet Brough). Dordrechet, Boston and London: Kluwer.

James, William (1950) *Principles of Psychology*, 2 vols. New York: Dover.

Jaspers, Karl (1963) *General Psychopathology* (trans. J. Hoenig and Marian W. Hamilton). Manchester: Manchester University Press.

Judovitz, Dalia (1988) *Subjectivity and Representation in Descartes: the Origins of Modernity*. Cambridge: Cambridge University Press.

Kockelmans, Joseph J. (1994) *Edmund Husserl's Phenomenology*. West Lafayette, IN: Purdue University Press.

Leppert, Richard (1996) *Art and the Committed Eye*. Boulder, CO: Westview Press.

Lotze, Hermann (1885) *Microcosmus: An Essay Concerning Man and His Relation to the World*, 2 vols (trans. Elizabeth Hamilton and E.E. Constance Jones). Edinburgh: T.&T. Clark.

Marcel, Gabriel (1949/50) *The Mystery of Being*. London: Havrill Press.

Marcel, Gabriel (1952) *Metaphysical Journal* (trans. Bernard Wall). London: Rockliff.

Merleau-Ponty, Maurice (1962) *Phenomenology of Perception* (trans. Colin Smith). London: Routledge.

Mosse, George (1990) *Fallen Soldiers: Reshaping the Memory of the World Wars*. New York and Oxford: Oxford University Press.

Nietzsche, Friedrich (1967) *Will to Power* (trans. and ed. Walter Kaufmann). New York: Viking.

O'Neill, John (1985) *Five Bodies: The Human Shape of Modern Society*. Ithaca, NY: Cornell University Press.

Ortega y Gasset, Jose (1957) *Man and People* (trans. Willard R. Trask). London: Allen and Unwin.

Rabinbach, Anson (1990) *The Human Motor: Energy, Fatigue and the Origins of Modernity*. New York: Basic Books.

Ricoeur, Paul (1966) *Freedom and Nature* (trans.

Erazim V. Kohák). Evanston, IL: Northwestern University Press.

Samuels, Raphael (1994) *Theatres of Memory*, Vol. 1: *Past and Present in Contemporary Culture*. London: Verso.

Sass, L. (1992) *Madness and Modernism*. Cambridge, MA: Harvard University Press.

Scheler, Max (1973) *Formalism in Ethics and Non-Formal Ethics of Values* (trans. Manfred S. Frings and Roger L. Funk). Evanston, IL: Northwestern University Press.

Schluchter, Wolfgang (1996) *Paradoxes of Modernity: Culture and Conduct in the Theory of Max Weber* (trans. Neil Solomon). Stanford, CA: Stanford University Press.

Schutz, Alfred (1962) *Collected Papers I*. The Hague: Martinus Nijhoff.

Schutz, Alfred (1964) *Collected Papers II*. The Hague: Martinus Nijhoff.

Schutz, Alfred (1966) *Collected Papers III*. The Hague: Martinus Nijhoff.

Schutz, Alfred (1970) *Alfred Schutz: On Phenomenology and Social Relations* (ed. Helmut R. Wagner). Chicago and London: The University of Chicago Press.

Schutz, Alfred and Luckmann, Thomas (1973) *The Structure of the Life-World* (trans. Richard M. Zaner and H. Tristram Engelhardt Jr). Evanston, IL: Northwestern University Press.

Spariosu, Mihai I. (1989) *Dionysus Reborn*. Ithaca, NY and London: Cornell University Press.

Stoichita, Victor I. (1997) *A Short History of the Shadow*. London: Reaktion Books.

Strasser, Stephen (1977) *Phenomenology of Feeling* (trans. and intr. Robert T. Wood). Pittsburgh: Duquesne University Press.

Strauss, Erwin (1963) *The Primary World of the Senses* (trans. Jacob Needleman). New York and London: The Free Press.

Strauss, Erwin (1966) *Phenomenological Psychology*. London: Tavistock.

Vernant, Jean-Pierre (1991) *Mortals and Immortals*. Princeton, NJ: Princeton University Press.

Weber, Max (1948) *From Max Weber* (eds. H.H. Gerth and C. Wright Mills). London: Routledge and Kegan Paul.

White, John (1957) *The Birth and Rebirth of Pictorial Space*. London: Faber and Faber.

Winter, Jay (1995) *Sites of Memory, Sites of Mourning: The Great War and European Cultural History*. Cambridge: Cambridge University Press.

Yack, Bernard 1992) *The Longing for Total Revolution*. Berkeley, CA: University of Calfornia Press.

Yates, Frances A. (1966) *The Art of Memory*. London: Routledge and Kegan Paul.

19

Fundamentals of Ethnomethodology

WES SHARROCK

AN ALTERNATE, ASYMETRICAL SOCIOLOGY

Ethnomethodology does not sit comfortably in a book like this, for it neither is nor has a theory in the conventional sociological sense, any more than it has a specific or distinct methodology. One way of summarizing ethnomethodology, though not necessarily one that would easily receive the assent of its practitioners, is that it is an attempt at assembling what Ludwig Wittgenstein was apt to call 'reminders'. As such, they serve to clarify our understanding by drawing our attention to things that we already know, but which we are inclined to overlook, or to exile from our attention when we undertake to theorize.

Despite attempts to include it within the 'social action consensus' (as, for example in Colin Campbell's misguided *The Myth of Social Action*, 1996), ethnomethodology remains unreconciled to the prevailing situation in (what remains of) sociology – an unregenerately dissident tendency. It is not dissidence for its own sake, but the result of deep and thorough divergences in the idea of what sociology can be. Invited to see ethnomethodology's influential and beneficial effects, in those recent efforts at theoretical review and synthesis produced by such prominent figures as Jürgen Habermas, Anthon Giddens, Pierre Bourdieu, Jeffrey Alexander and Randall Collins, one can only see, rather, that the essential point has constantly been disregarded, if indeed it has been noticed at all. Forcefully reaffirming ethnomethodology's incongruous character, Harold Garfinkel, the founder of the enterprise, deems it an incommensurable, alternate, asymmetrical sociology (Garfinkel and Wieder, 1992).

One might take Holmwood's (1995) comment about the way theorists have now come to appreciate that members of the society are 'knowledgeable' participants in the same enterprise of theorizing with their professional sociological counterparts as an acknowledgement of, especially, ethnomethodology's critique of the 'cultural dope', of the tendency of sociological theories to portray the members of society as more naïve than they actually are. However, rather than as an appreciation of any such achievement, this could also well seem a direct inversion of the actual point, for, of course, Garfinkel insists that ethnomethodology does not set out to make matters better or worse than they are 'ordinarily cracked up to be' and, in rejecting the 'cultural dope' does not want to make persons out to be more or less smart than they are 'ordinarily cracked up to be'. The correct interpretation of ethnomethodology's lesson is that professional sociological theorists and ordinary members of the society have much more in common than the traditional (professional) sociological contrast between analyst and member makes out. However, that is not because ordinary members have been found to be engaged in theorizing comparable to that conducted in the professional mode, but, instead, because the professional sociologists are (without acknowledgment) much more like the members than they take themselves to be – themselves extensively involved in operating as members immersed in the order of 'practical sociological reasoning'. *Practical* sociological 'theorizing' is not directed toward issuing versions of 'how the society is in general' but involves drawing upon 'common sense understandings of social structures' in order to decide 'what is happening here?', 'what are those people doing?', 'how did things end up this way?' This is not at all comparable to the kind of (upper case) theorizing to be found in those volumes of monumental size, if not significance, that aspire to be the contemporary equivalents of Parsons' *The Structure of Social Action*. It is, however, the kind of (lower case) 'theorizing' that sociological theorists and researchers routinely, ubiquitously and unreflectively do when they speak concretely about the ordinary affairs of the society. There the 'common sense understandings of social structures' come obscurely and ambiguously into play as supplements to the upper case theorizing and the methodological glosses of professionalized enquiry[1] (cf. Bittner, 1974: 70). Further, that reasoning is not 'sociological reasoning' in any specialized and distinctive sense, but is itself integral to and inseparable from the practically saturated concerns in whose service it is done, for example, reasoning during litigation or during jury deliberations, reasoning in the laboratory and observatory over the course of experiments and observations, the following through of the detailed course of mathematical reasoning, reasoning in the management of household arrangements, in the preparation for spiritual and meditative disciplines, in the prevention of accidents in vehicle repair, in the calculation of business costs and profits, in the asking of questions in court, and so on, *ad infinitum*.

To put it another way, the interest resides in the competencies that are required to execute practical affairs, competencies that, of course, range from those that are ubiquitous and commonplace and which 'anyone' might be expected to do, to those of a much more specialized kind and over which only a few might be expected to possess full mastery. Possession and application of these competencies require a grasp upon the fact that they are socially organized, and the effective conduct of these affairs involves the practical management of the course of action in and through a socially organized setting. Consider, Garfinkel's masterful exposition of the competencies of those who work at the determination of suicidal deaths for a Suicide Prevention Centre (SPC):

The work by SPC members of conducting their inquiries was part and parcel of the day's work. Recognized by staff members as constituent features of the day's work, their inquiries were thereby intimately connected to the terms of employment, to various internal and external chains of reportage, supervision, and review, and to similarly organizationally provided 'priorities of relevances' for assessments of what 'realistically,' 'practically,' or 'reasonably' needed to be done and could be done, how quickly, with what resources, seeing whom, talking with whom, talking about what, for how long,

and so on. Such considerations furnished 'We did what we could, and for all reasonable interests here is what we came out with' its features of organizationally appropriate sense, fact, impersonality, anonymity of authorship, purpose, reproducibility – i.e., of a *properly* and *visibly* rational account of inquiry. (1967: 13)

These considerations, including *inter alia* office policy, departmental administration, case load, scheduling, budget and collegial relations, are not conceived as extrinsic to the work of investigating suicidal death. They are rather matters which are integral to forming the course of action that will comprise the investigation and determination of the nature of the death, and that will provide grounds for assessing the adequacy of that enquiry's results. There are numerous other considerations that also enter in: the investigation will consist in some significant part in talking to people, but *which* people, and in what order? Talking to them about what topics? Employing what techniques for getting them to talk at all, or to talk in the way required to make what they have to say useful material for the enquiry? There is also the matter of knowing what to make, with respect to the enquiry's purposes, of what they will or can be brought to say, to know how these conversations individually and cumulatively count as evidence pointing one way or the other to conclusions about the nature of the death under investigation. As well as:

- Knowing one's way around the office, familiarity with the details of the routine arrangement of the office's day and week.
- Knowing how to find a way through the inter-organizational routes for accessing the financial, medical and other circumstances of deceased persons.
- Understanding how particular kinds of, for example, financial and medical situations (typically) affect particular kinds of persons.
- Having a mastery of getting people to talk freely and relevantly when they might be reluctant.
- *Then* knowing how to organize looking into financial and medical circumstances and to understand what is found there.
- Knowing how to make contact with and generate talk from friends and relatives.
- Knowing how to get samples off to and back from the lab.
- *And* knowing how to organize all the things that 'need to be done' into an effectively organized course of action that will
  - fit within the assorted demands of the work load
  - allow the enquiry to be finished in the time available
  - be within budget limits

and in ways that will satisfy those who supervise the work or who otherwise depend upon its outcome that it was done properly, which is the same as effectively.

Knowing how to report – that is, how to present orally or to write up – what has been done in ways that allow one to be left alone to get on with one's own work, to be taken, to be understood by others on the basis of what one says and writes, indeed to have done what one claims to have done, knowing how to write up what has been done so that the conclusion reached will be seen to follow plausibly from what has been reported, being open to other obvious interpretations, are all further matters that are involved in being able to be demonstrably competent in one's work. It is the grasp upon these innumerable, multifarious, detailed, specific and localized considerations, and of the ways in which they figure as grounds for further inference and action, that makes up the sociological competence of the occupants of the coroner's office, the competence which enables them to *see* the phenomenon of a person dead by suicide in the first place. Suicide is, *in this sense*, an *organizational* phenomenon. 'In this sense' here covers the fact that the topic is suicide, the official, legally established fact, the basis on which insurance payments will be made or withheld, decisions as to whether to set criminal investigations in train and so on can be made, and that the ascertaining of this legally established fact is the regular work of the coroner's office and associated investigators. *In this sense*, suicide is nothing other than precisely the investigator's competence applied in accordance with legal standards, office policy, professional good practice and the like in the pursuit of an enquiry to a defensible and acceptable conclusion (the latter itself being relative to circumstance and to exigencies which are not necessarily amenable to anticipation or control by the investigator). The circumstances invoked are the realities, as suicide investigators know them, of the work of identifying suicidal deaths, and the suicidal death is *both* the origin and the outcome of the investigative process conducted under and through those circumstances, with those circumstances being managed by the investigator in assembling the course investigation and in respect of decisions as to what to conclude thus far and what to do next.

NOT A THEORY

Space does not allow me to go into the reasons for and the gross inadequacies in the treatment meted out to the supposed 'agency' position in the one-sided dialectic characterizing recent and contemporary debates about 'structure' and 'agency'. The direct way to highlight the difference as it affects ethnomethodology is to point to the deep ambiguity which cloaks the relationship between the sociological analyst's and the member's point of view. Barely, but simply, one can see the failure to appreciate the character and dimensions of the problem (from ethnomethodology's point of view) in the way that Giddens, Bourdieu and others attempt to resolve their problems by giving 'the member's point of view' an appropriate location within their theoretical scheme, providing acknowledgement of the 'subjective' or 'agency' aspect. As conceived by ethnomethodology, the problem is not one that originates or can be resolved *within* the theoretical framework that attempts an analytical resolution of the issues attending the 'privileging' of the professional sociologist's point of view, for this framework presupposes that there is a clear, sharp or deep distinction between 'the analyst's' and 'the member's' points of view. The question which is raised is not 'Where to place common sense understandings' relative to 'social structural influences' in the determination of persons' conduct?' The question is instead: how much of the freight of *sociological analysis* is carried by the 'common sense understandings' which are tacitly, unreflectively and unsystematically deployed and depended upon in the analyst's purportedly analytical work? It is not easy to find any place in the sociological literature (outside of ethnomethodology's own writings) where this matter is even raised, let alone discussed and dealt with.

Trying to compact the intricate complexities of the reasoning that propels ethnomethodology's dissidence into the space of this short chapter requires real simplification, so for simplicity let it be that ethnomethodology's core problem is: how to track the course of sociological inferences? Rephrased: how to do sociology in a way which allows such tracking? The capacity to undertake such tracking would allow the identification of the points at which 'common-sense understandings' are involved in moving the reasoning forward. *If* this ambiguity is seen to be problematic, then there is a question as to whether it can ever be resolved. At least, whether it can ever be *resolved within the terms of sociological theorizing as those are programmatically conceived within the discipline*. It ought to be obvious that ethnomethodology does not aspire to the formation of *theory*, and that it is not a trivial matter for it that it does not. The undertaking of theorizing in the professionally approved mode would perpetuate, rather than obfuscate the structure of sociolglical inference, of the *inferential* interplay between analyst and member status.

NOT A METHODOLOGY EITHER

However, this does not make ethnomethodology's concerns a set of distinctively methodological ones, engendering a priori deliberation to determine valid procedures for enquiry. It means, rather, that the very idea of what a subject matter for sociology might be is utterly changed. The topic becomes that of *reasoning* – sociological reasoning. This does not, however, mean that reflection on the reasoning of sociological analysts has been substituted for the examination of the life in the society, for one of ethnomethodology's crucial features is its insistence that ordinary members of the society are just as much *sociological* reasoners as are those professionally identified as sociologists. One *can* reflect upon the reasoning of professional sociologists, but *qua* concern with practices of sociological reasoning, such reasoning has no *special* status: it comprises merely one topic amongst others, exhibiting the ways of 'practical sociological reasoning'. The result: motivation for attention to the instantiations of the array of practices comprising *practices of practical sociological* reasoning. Neither more nor less.

ORDINARY SOCIAL ORDER

The relation to the questions that standardly motivate sociological theorizing is now quite attentuated. None the less, there is a continuity, which may be found through the problem of social order. However, even in this connection there is as much discontinuity as continuity, for the problem is transformed. Again, crudely:

- The traditional problem of social order is conceived as the problem of social solidarity, of the unification of the social whole, which is most definitely not ethnomethodology's issue, for that is concentrated upon the order of everyday affairs: the issue of the integration of the social system is displaced by concern with the orderliness of any of the innumerable ordinary affairs of the society: the administrative work of completing forms in social security applications, making a start to a business meeting, directing the flow of air traffic over the South-East of England, dealing with trouble-in-the-making in a classroom, preparing live animals for use in laboratory experiments – an heterogeneous and indefinitely extensible array of topics.

- Secondly, the 'problem of social order' is then conceived as that of identifying the *indigenous* orderliness of such everyday ordinariness, of identifying what comprises, for those who conduct the affairs, the ordinarily orderly, effective, followable orderliness of them: hence the concern with charts, diagrams, written records, counts and other methods-in-use for the tracking and monitoring of courses of action to ensure that all inmates in a cell block are accounted for, or that the working air traffic controller knows at all times just where all the aircraft are in the airspace for which he/she is responsible

- Thirdly, the 'problem of social order' no longer requires theoretical and methodological solution, no longer calls upon the analyst to provide a specification of the principles or mechanisms which ensure, according to the theory, the continuity and stability of everyday affairs.

- Fourthly, the 'problem of social order' is resolved *in practice*, is resolved *in and through* the everyday activities themselves: the orderliness which is recognized amongst participants as the orderliness of these affairs is an order which is, further, endowed upon those activities in whatever ways those conducting the affairs ensure that their activities achieve, *for all practical purposes*, whatever orderliness is appropriate to them.

- Fifthly, social order is indigenous in the sense that social settings are conceived as *self-organizing*, which places the ethnomethodological enquirer in the same informational situation as those participant in and responsible for the affairs under study: the enquirer must identify *from within the scene and amidst its constituent flows of activity* whatever forms of orderliness are indigenously integral to and practically identifiable in those affairs, together with whatever practices are used to effect such orderliness.

- Sixthly, the practices of practical sociological reasoning are those through which the orderlinesses of the setting are identified and the courses of action required to assure, perpetuate, perturb or modify these must be contrived and implemented. The study of practical sociological reasoning is in this sense the study of social order.

- Seventhly, practical sociological reasoning stands, therefore, in a reflexive relationship to the social order. It is reflexive in the sense that it is *embedded within*, is part of and conducted in the course of, the orderly social affairs that it organizes: that is, practical sociological reasoning is done under the auspices of and carried on in pursuit of the affairs of social settings.

This is anything but an attempted reduction of social order to subjective states, as is often critically supposed, being, instead, an attempt to re-identify the phenomena of social order, to identify them in the forms in which they are practically encountered and managed. Talk of 'practical sociological reasoning' should not be mistaken for allusions to inward cognitive computations, but to the depiction of *embodied* and social-organizationally embedded practices. It is risky to lose sight (in the way that Finn Collin, 1997 does) of the fact that sociological reasoning is situated within the world of daily life which itself has anything but a vaporous character (cf. Bittner, 1973). I have tried to suggest the notion of 'reflexive' as it figures significantly in ethnomethodology is less a concern that one's methods of enquiry should apply to oneself just as they do to those who are the subjects of one's studies, than with the fact that activities are embedded in the same social order that they produce.[2] Remember that the enquiry into the 'production of social reality' equates with the assignment of (for brevity) factual status to certain phenomena – such as that this person really is dead and really died by his or her own hand. The point about such a determination is, of course, that the enquiry which undertakes to establish the fact is plainly located within an organizational setting whose ways and features are clearly the real worldly conditions of carrying out the enquiry. The ostensible problem which Collin thinks he finds is a consequence of overlooking the implications of the treatment of *time structures* as matters to be handled in a principled way and, therefore, with the character of *sociological enquiry (lay and professional)* as conducted in real time.

Collin (1997) reads ethnomethodology's writings as a self-defeating portrayal of social reality as being constructed out of nothing, as though the 'negotiation' of factual status were conducted in a vacuum. Unfortunately, the appearance of an impossible conception – reality negotiated out of nowhere and from nothing – is only a result of the neglect of the emphasis noted above upon the irreducibly embedded character of social actions, and of their reflexive relationship to their setting. Were the extent to which the assignment of factual status is conducted under the auspices and by means of the organized ways of a social setting – after all, what else does the above sketch of investigations into suicides show? – fully appreciated, then the apparent difficulty would instantly evaporate. Ethnomethodology's purpose is not to make determinations on its own behalf of the factual status of matters that members address, such as, for example, the nature and cause of an alleged suicidal death, or to second-guess the correctness of some astron-omers finding a pulsar (Garfinkel et al., 1981). The sociologist's examination of those occasions – the determination of cause of death, of the reality of a discovered pulsar – is one step removed from such determinations, itself seeking to highlight the practices through which the parties assure themselves that they *really have* found out how this person died or where a sought-after pulsar is located.[3] The study of the 'night's work' of a team of astronomical observers as they work through the series of observations that results in the discovery of a pulsar shows how it is not possible for anyone to say, at the outset of the observations, how they would turn out, nor, as the realization that the observations were possibly showing the presence of *something*, whether that something was really there, whether the apparent observations were a result of having found something or were merely an effect of the technologies being used for the observations, and whether, further, if the observations were authentic, the phenomenon being observed was actually the thing being sought. It was only over the course of their work, making their observations and reasoning about the significance of these, that they could eventually arrive at the conclusion that they had indeed discovered phenomenon that was theoretically possible, but had not yet actually been found. *In this sense*, the 'pulsar' is a product of their work, something whose existence is established, whose reality is affirmed through the observatory-sited activities of assembling, of building up in an accumulating series, and construing the corpus of materials that comprise a series of astronomical observations (Garfinkel et al., 1981).

Ethnomethodology concerns itself, then, with phenomena as they are encountered from within local social settings, and therefore in terms of the way in which they are 'known' as something to be dealt with in that setting (as the pulsar is something to be found through the use of the technologies and skills of observatory practice). The phenomena which are brought under ethnomethodology's review are often quite commonplace, such as, for example, 'traffic'. The objective is to identify the phenomenon from its very midst, in the way that, for example, traffic is prevailingly (but not exclusively) encountered either from the driving seat, on the road and *en route*, or equally commonly, in the course of pedestrian movement. Again, however, there must be no illusion of reductionism which would insist that traffic is *only* the affair of vehicle and pedestrian movement. Clearly, 'traffic' also features (for example) as an affair of system management. No one of these involvements is to be privileged over any of the others, for they instantiate for ethnomethodology the social order as a *local* production; each instantiates different localities within which the production of orderly traffic movements can be achieved. The two uses of management in this paragraph should not be conflated. The driver-at-the-wheel who is managing the traffic is doing so in the sense of handling or coping with the traffic situation that he or she currently occupies, and it is this kind of management – the practical handling of social affairs – with which ethno-methodological studies are occupied. Those who work as managers – such as someone who, say, directs the Highways Agency or supervises the air traffic control system – represent in ethnomethodology's view just more instances of practical management of everyday affairs rather than a distinct species of it. The study of such managers would be contending with the phenomena of highway or air traffic as, no doubt, those that are found on the desk, in the meeting, in the finding of experts to assure policy etc.[4] The local production of order is undertaken from one or another of a multiplicity of local sites, sites *within* the course of affairs that the activities are managing.

Ethnomethodology, then, deliberately eschews upper-case theorizing of the sort which has lately reasserted itself in the "Return of Ground Theory". It agrees, further, that deep difficulties which sociological projects have conventionally and continuously faced (though the recognition that this is so is periodic and cyclical) are due to the disjunction of theory and research. That theory and research stand in a deeply proble-matic relation is hardly surprising when they are construed as distinct activities which are to be pursued in near-complete autonomy from one another. Why confront this problem in its terms? Why not disregard the traditional distinction of 'theory' and 'method' and engage in 'theorizing' in conjunction with the conduct of research? Why not, further, notice the difference in the 'logic' of enquiry (as formulated by Abraham Kaplan, 1998) between logic-in-use and recon-structed-logic, and abandon a concern for the latter, being concerned with the *actual* methods for 'collecting data', exclusively with the logic-in-use in the actual enquiry. 'Collecting data' is in scare quotes only to emphasize that collecting data *is the very same thing as* finding out about social structures.

Canonical Characteristics of Conversation Analysis

One of the few things which nowadays stirs the blood of ethnomethodologists is the controversy over whether 'conversation analysis' is or is not subsumed under, affiliated with, or even origin-ally indebted to ethnomethodology (cf. for a provactive discussion 'Molecular Sociology' in Lynch, 1993: 203–57). The *historical* merits of insisting upon or denying the existence of such a relationship are one thing, the advantages of using conversation analysis (or at least, the work laid out in Harvey Sacks' (1992) *Lectures on Conversation*) as an exemplification of ethno-methodology's ideas are another. And perhaps by registering some of the reservations about what I'll call 'latter-day CA', I might do even more to clarify what it is that, whilst appreciat-ing that *in other respects* Sacks' meticulous reasoning follows through on ethnomethodolo-gy's project ideas, gives rise to contemporary dissatisfactions.

If you are interested in tracking where, and in what fashion, specific common-sense under-standings enter into the course of sociological reasoning, then there is every advantage to beginning with both materials and problems which are as simplified as possible. Beginning with tape-recordings of (often telephone) con-versations as the *whole* of one's 'materials' will seem perverse from most methodologically informed sociological points of view, but then, it needs to be remembered that Sacks' point of view reciprocated the impression of strangeness about sociology's more usual ways of setting about things. How can we, without knowing something about the identities of these people, their placement in social systems and so on, possibly begin to understand what they are doing in their talk? But suppose we do know things about the identities etc. of the conversationalists, what advantage to us will that be if those identities etc. are introduced into the course of (professional) sociological reasoning in an undisciplined way? The investigative indifference to the possession of such 'ethnographic' riches hardly equates with a denial of the fact that, for example, that the speaker is a police officer ever matters. The question is not one of substance but of procedure: why make presumptions that identities etc. *must* matter, and how they must do so? Why not begin *without* such biographical information and see how far one can get *without* it? and see if one finds it unnecessary to draw upon such information, or whether one finds that one cannot proceed further without such information, specifically what it is that makes such information cogent to the investigation at just this point.

If one works with audio recordings and their transcriptions, what is the data? The point of the enquiry is to find this out, to determine what is on the recording, what is in the transcription. Examining the data is not a preliminary to analysis, it *is* the undertaking of the analysis. The examination of the audio recording must first address the questions: what are these persons saying/doing, and on what basis can one make those identifications?

Note, first, for the conversations that are used as materials, these are commonly transparent to the understanding of the investigator. The talk involved is pretty characteristically plain talk, about commonplace affairs.[5] Much of what is said can be understood without knowing *anything* 'biographically' about the speakers independently of the recording. The talk, as plain talk, makes sense: it does not engender bewilderment – what are they saying, what could they possibly mean, what on earth are these people doing? They are (plainly) arranging to meet for coffee, one is updating the other on what happened at work today, they are telling jokes and stories, they are soliciting assistance from the police, they are getting into an argument about leisure preferences and so on. That is *evidently* what they are doing. No special competence is required to figure out these materials. No specialized kind of expertise, medical, or legal is required for this, and certainly no professionally provided *sociological* expertise is required either. The basis for following the talk and grasping its sense is the fact that these matters are ones that pretty much *anyone* can grasp (anyone who is an ordinary, wide awake member of the society, that is) and it is, of course, upon the basis of one's *common sense understandings* of how *both* talk *and* the everyday affairs of the society are organized that one can make such construals.

However, the point is not to gloss these conversations, listening to/reading through the records to arrive at a neat, concise summary of what the talk amounts to. It is, rather, to examine the conversation in a step-by-step way, to make specific identifications of just what is being said, what is being done by what is being said, and what is being contributed to the conversation by what is being done/said at any specific point. A step-by-step examination of the ways in which the materials are construed for what they are is required. The conversational sequence is treated as a real time construction, one that is put together by the parties to it as it goes along. The alignment between the analyst's and the participants' understandings is a critical consideration, the participants being assumed to act on the basis of knowledge available to them, and the identification of their actions turning, then, upon what they could have known at the moment at which the utterance was spoken. The operation of what Garfinkel termed the 'prospective/retrospective' determination of sense requires attention to the difference between the sense that can be assigned to an utterance at the moment of its production, and the subsequent modification of that sense in the light of what is

said/done subsequently. The treatment of the talk as a real time activity involves a precise tracking of the ways in which individual utterances contribute to the emerging sense of the conversational exchange. The conversational sequence is one which builds-up, with the nature of the identity of any present utterance being tied in multifarious ways to its predecessors. Being tied, furthermore, very much to the specifics of prior utterances.

The recognition that the organization of the talk is done through its specificity acknowledges for the case of conversation the general point that real worldly practical action is invariably a matter of contending with the 'just this' quality of its circumstances. The notion of 'constraint' has been widely adopted as the criterion of demarcation between sociological approaches, between the supposed sides of 'structure' and 'agency' particularly. It is ethnomethodology's misfortune to have been deemed to have fallen on the 'agency' side of this inadequately conceived divide, with (in its terms) the principal failure of the 'agency' approach being its incapacity to acknowledge the extent to which action is constrained. A polarization of positions around the issue of constraint as such is wholly inappropriate, though there may be reasons for differentiation in terms of the kind of interest that is taken in constraint and in the kind of constraint that is of interest. The interest of classical sociological theory is in the question of whether or not the agent is free to act or whether he or she is limited in freedom to act, or is perhaps largely (if not wholly) propelled by causal determination: how free is the agent to do this action rather than that one? Admittedly a crude way of presenting the issue, but sufficient to allow the suggestion that the issue of interest to ethnomethodology (most meticulously reflected in conversational studies) is what goes into the performance of an action: just how is one (here, now, in this place, with these people, having so far done these things, and having all this yet to do) to do the next thing that one does? Just what words, said in what fashion, accompanied by what other doings, in those circumstances, will serve to carry out the action that is on the agenda? Posing the question this way does not entirely reject the question of how actions are selected, but it *demotes* it, in favour of a deeper (that is, otherwise only presupposed) concern with the formation of the course of action: what specifically counts in real world conditions as the doing of action X or Y?

There are, then, multifarious (I might even say, tight) constraints upon what words, gestures, movements etc. can be put together, under these circumstances etc., so as to perform whatever action is to be undertaken. Amongst these constraints, there are, of course, those which pertain to the interactional organization of the occasion and to its collective construction. The formation of the action-to-be-done needs also to be considered from the way in which it contributes to the further organization of the relationships (whatever these might be) with other parties, and to the doing of whatever is required for the continuation of the organization of the occasion that the relationships and actions are carrying through. Saying just what words in just what ways could execute the step of (say) 'answering the police dispatcher's enquiries in the correct manner and in sufficient detail to ensure the initiation of the kind of police action I seek in response to my complaint and thereby close out my telephone call to the emergency number?'

Conversation analysis has a predominant focus on those constraints on the formation (the 'design' as it is often called) of conversational contributions that derive from the turn-taking character of conversations: 'sequencing' considerations most generally, and centrally those involved in the sequencing of turns at talk. The organization of conversation involves the more-or-less alternation of turns at talk (that is, more or less, one person talks at a time, though sometimes several do, and sometimes no one does) and therefore presents the issue of how many turns at talk does it take to do a given action? In other words, the issues arise around accessing the conversational 'floor'. Patently, then, the talking needs to be done in ways that enable taking and keeping 'the floor'. The speaker's utterance may need to be constructed so that it effects either

1 a temporary suspension of the usual turn-taking practices that would license other speakers to talk before the current speaker has finished, allowing that speaker to take a more-than-usually protracted turn at uninterrupted talk; or
2 alternately, the action may be done over several turns at talk, but this requires the speaker to segment the action so that it may be distributed across those turns. How, then, is that segmentation to be shaped so that, having taken a turn at talk to initiate the action, then having ceded a turn at talk to another speaker, can the initiating speaker then be assured of regaining the floor? And how does the speaker then shape his or her utterance to provide the continuity between their previous turn and their current one so as to achieve the continuity of the action begun in that prior turn?

These and a plurality of similar and related questions are not ones that can be answered in the abstract, and in advance, for they require that one look into actual cases to see how, in specific instances, these are done. Moreover (certainly in the beginning), it is not possible simply to pluck out instances of relevant occurrences and examine these for, given that the identity of any utterances hinges upon its contexting circumstances, one must examine much more of the conversational sequence (perhaps the whole of it) to be assured that the correct identification of the utterance's character has been made.

The conversational exchange has provided a perspicuous instance for conveying the idea of self-organizing activities, though, it must be stressed that conversation is not to be conceived as thereby more self-organizing than other activities.

Conversation analysis emphasizes the way in which the conversation which is put together through a succession of alternating turns at talk by different speakers is jointly assembled into a unified structure. The individual utterances are produced so as to comprise unified sub-parts of the conversation, such as, for example, talk unified around a single topic, with these sub-parts being further unified into a whole: the conversation has a beginning-to-end structure. Amongst the constraints which govern the formation of any single turn at talk, then, are those that:

1 relate to the management and manifestation of the utterance's place within the organization of the conversation as a whole;
2 place the utterance relative to that overall structure (for example, is it a beginning, or does it open up a closing?);
3 place the utterance relative to the current phase of the conversation within that overall structure (for example, is it a remark introducing a new topic?);
4 in each case display (through the formatting of the utterance) the nature of the placing within the sectional and overall structures that the speaker of the utterance projects for it within the conversation's organized course for other parties to the conversation (that is, how does it show to other parties that the utterance is proposing a new topic?);
5 effect the development of the further course of talk through the ways in which further turns at talk are projected for other speakers, that is, this turn at talk attempts the assignment of specific next actions to other speakers (as a question directed at another party calls for an answer).

The building of the conversation's organization, whilst it may be projected and anticipated, is none the less something that is constructed over the course of the conversation itself, something that is worked out in and through the talking. Though points (1) to (5) above are cast in terms that apply to a single person, it must be recalled that the production of the unity of the conversation is a collective affair, is done together amongst the participants, and is not, therefore, determined by any single participant. I have preferred the term 'collectively' to 'collaboratively' so as to avoid all implication that the construction of an orderly conversation precludes the possibility of controversy, dispute and conflict, whilst simultaneously stressing conversation's remorselessly interactional character.

Whilst the conversation has an overall organization, this is something that is managed on a turn-by-turn basis, with the form of the conversation's structural sub-divisions and their relation to its overall architecture being worked on as it goes along. The management of the relation between immediate past, the present and the projected next turns provides the place for the local work upon the organization of the conversation's course, for addressing practically, in the formation of the utterance, the issues of the continuation of the current phase of the conversation, the re-orientation of the direction of the course of this phase or its possible closure etc. Nothing about the conversation's course is fixed in advance, for that eventual course is to be worked on in the conversation itself: working out where the conversation is going, where it ought to go, and how to get it to go in the way that it should, *is* holding the conversation, not something done distinctly from talking through the conversation itself.

Plainly it is the case that the purely improvised character of conversations does not parallel the organization of many other kinds of occasions, for these involve doing activities that have been worked out in advance or that follow through routinized and standard courses of action. However, it is not by virtue of its entirely on-the-spot character that conversation provides a perspicuous example. The fact that other occasions are standardized and practised does not obviate the need for examination of their real time organization. The parties to such routinized occasions must none the less reciprocally find where they mutually are in the developing sequence, ready themselves for the anticipated next steps, form and implement the specifics of the action that will place that action in its appropriate, timely and proper place within the interactive progression of the occasion.

Recently, however, the issue of conversation analysis' ethnomethodological provenance has become a disputed issue, and there has been the expression, from the ethnomethodological side, of doubt about conversation analysis' *bona fides.* The controversy around this point is both complex and tangled, and I can only superficially diagnose the source of these doubts. There can

be little doubt but that the publication of a systematizing paper setting out a synthesizing scheme for the depiction of conversational turn-taking provided the turning point (Sacks et al., 1974). The production of this paper signalled great success for conversation analysis, bringing together the detailed analyses of innumerable features of conversation's turn-taking organization within a concise summation. At the same time, it made, or brought to fruition, a transition in the way in which the relation between conversational participant and the conversational analyst was conceived. The work of conversation analysis was becoming more a matter of administering a developed and formal analytical scheme to the further study of conversational materials. The possession and use of the scheme seemed to engender a distinct, specialized and professional competence that distinguished the analyst from the participant. The phenomena in conversation that were being sought and found appeared to be those which could only be noticed and identified by those operating with the guidance of the scheme. Thus, there was a divergence from the initial concerns of conversation analysis with the identification of those phenomena which anyone (at least anyone who could carry on a conversation, preferably in the appropriate natural language) can find, into an interest in phenomena in conversation that can only be found through the use of a specialized investigative apparatus.

I do not here comment on the rights and wrongs of the disagreements on this issue but mention it only to reinforce the point which has provided a central rationale for refusing the stock sociological concerns with the formation of theories and methods, namely, the determined insistence that the phenomena of interest are ones that 'anyone' (with the appropriate practical competences) can find. From this point it follows that ethnomethodology has no phenomena that belong distinctively to it, and that it has no need to develop a theory and method as means toward finding those phenomena, and for discerning their order. It has no version of social reality to offer on its own behalf. It offers only instigation to, and perspicuous examples in, recovering what, in one or another part of the social order, inhabitants already 'know' in the form of practical mastery of their everyday affairs (with 'everyday' being a relative term).

FUNDAMENTALS OF ETHNOMETHODOLOGY

I have sought to draw out as clearly as possible the very distinctive nature of ethnomethodology's central concern, which has generated a pioneering exercise in developing a concern that arguably must underlie any rigorously thorough sociology but which has been – thus far – overwhelmingly distinctive to ethnomethodology, namely, what does it take to carry out a course of activity and, in doing this, to carry out the society's routine, worldly affairs?[6] Ethnomethodology itself and the arguably conjoined field of conversation analysis have been dominated by their two founding figures, Harold Garfinkel and Harvey Sacks, and it is in their work that the basic conception and direction of the approach (as sketched out here) has been formed, with a number of other researchers following through on their initiatives. These researchers have generated a large corpus of studies, under Garfinkel's direct influence, of a wide variety of practical affairs, and under Sacks' influence, of aspects of turn-taking in conversation,[7] though the guiding principles have remained fairly constant. I have sought to draw out some of those central principles here, trying to spell out those that provide the rationale for ethnomethodology's insistence that it does not appropriately fit within the conventional sociological categories of either theory or method. It is not motivated by the aspiration to make *discoveries* about the nature of social phenomena, but to undertake the *recovery* of what is already known – but is 'known' in the form of competent mastery of practical affairs – to the members of society. In its preoccupation with this, it remains unique.

NOTES

1 Bittner says (with organization theory specifically in mind, but making a more general point) that 'in general, there is nothing wrong with borrowing a common-sense concept for the purposes of sociological inquiry. Up to a certain point it is, indeed, unavoidable. The warrant for this procedure is the sociologist's interest in exploring the common-sense perspective. The point at which the use of common-sense concepts becomes a transgression is where such concepts are expected to do the analytical work of theoretical concepts. When the actor is treated as a permanent auxiliary to the enterprise of sociological inquiry at the same time that he is the object of its inquiry, there arise ambiguities that defy clarification.' Ethnomethodology's exercise could be seen as entirely engaged in attempting to achieve clarity with respect to the relationship between analytical and common-sense concepts.

2 This last requirement is assuredly satisfied by ethnomethodology's abjuring of claims to a proprietary methodological apparatus.

3 The requirement for 'unique adequacy' is one which calls for the use of hybrid competence, calling

upon investigators of specialist competences to possess those competences, in order that they may themselves and autonomously make factual determinations of the character of what is done, achieved, found. Eric Livingston acquired mathematical skills in order that he might reflectively rework Godel's proof (Livingston, 1986). It is, however, Livingston's mathematical, not his sociological, competence which assures him of the soundness of the proof. His ethnomethodological reflections are on the ways in which mathematicians, himself now included, assure themselves of the soundness of proofs.

4 Lynch and Bogen (1996) studied the major public 'spectacle' of the Iran–Contra hearings. The fact that theirs was an analysis of a major national affair did not cause them to retract ethnomethodology's study policies. That this was such a national affair made no great analytical difference.

5 In which respect they are scarcely a paradigm of the full range of social phenomena, especially those situations which involve specialized competences and which are extensively opaque to anyone lacking the relevant competence.

6 It would be quite wrong to read into the expression 'to carry out the society's affairs' a preference for the study of compliant conduct, for compliance and defiance surely both number amongst 'the society's affairs'. The differences between them do not entail differences in the mode in which they may be analysed.

7 For a catalogue of writings up to 1990 see B.J. Fehr's bibliography in Coulter, 1990, which features some 3000 items.

REFERENCES

Bittner, Egon (1973) 'Objectivity and Realism in Sociology', in George Psathas (ed.), *Phenomenological Sociology*. Chichester: Wiley. pp. 109–25.

Bittner, Egon (1974) 'The Concept of Organisation', in Roy Turner (ed.), *Ethnomethodology*. Harmondsworth: Penguin. pp. 69–81.

Campbell, Colin (1996) *The Myth of Social Action*. Cambridge: Cambridge University Press.

Collin, Finn (1997) *Social Reality*. London: Routledge.

Coulter, Jeff (ed.) (1990) *Ethnomethodological Sociology*. Aldershot: Elgar.

Garfinkel, Harold (1967) *Studies in Ethnomethodology*. Englewood Cliffs, NJ: Prentice-Hall.

Garfinkel, Harold and Wieder, D. Lawrence (1992) 'Two Incommensurable, Asymmetrically Alternate Technologies of Social Analysis', in Graham Watson and Robert Seiler (eds), *Text in Context*. London: Sage. pp. 175–206.

Garfinkel, Harold, Lynch, Michael and Livingston, Eric (1981) 'The Work of a Discovering Science Construed with Materials from the Optically Discovered Pulsar', *Philosophy of the Social Sciences*, 11 (1): 131–58.

Holmwood, John (1995) 'Feminism, Epistemology and Postmodernism: What Kind of Successor Science?', *Sociology*, 29 (3): 419–20.

Kaplan, Abraham (1998) *The Conduct of Inquiry*. NJ: Transaction Books.

Livingston, Eric (1986) *The Ethnomethodological Foundations of Mathematics*. London: Routledge.

Lynch, Michael (1993) *Scientific Practice and Ordinary Action*. Cambridge: Cambridge University Press.

Lynch, Michael and Bogen, David (1996) *The Spectacle of History*. Durham, NC: Duke University Press.

Sacks, Harvey (1992) *Lectures on Conversation*, 2 vols. Oxford: Blackwell.

Sacks, Harvey, Schegloff, Emmanuel and Jefferson, Gail (1974) 'A Simplest Systematics for the Organization of Turn-taking in Conversation', *Language*, 50: 696–735.

20

Theories of Social Exchange and Exchange Networks

LINDA D. MOLM

As anthropologists first recognized (Lévi-Strauss, 1969), many forms of social interaction outside the economic sphere can be conceptualized as an exchange of benefits. Both social and economic exchange are based on a fundamental feature of social life: much of what we need and value (for example, goods, services, companionship) can only be obtained from others. People depend on one another for these valued resources, and they provide them to each other through the process of exchange.

Social exchange theorists take as their focus this aspect of social life – the benefits that people obtain from, and contribute to, social interaction, and the opportunity structures and relations of dependence that govern those exchanges. Unlike classical microeconomic theories, which traditionally assumed independent transactions between strangers, social exchange theorists are primarily interested in relations of some length and endurance. This emphasis on the history of relations reflects the influence of behavioral psychology, the other discipline that played a key role in the theory's development.

Contemporary social exchange theory diverges from both psychology and microeconomics in its emphasis on the *social structures* within which exchange takes place. Whereas early exchange theorists primarily examined two-party relations, contemporary theorists situate those exchanges in the context of larger networks, and explore how actors' structural opportunities for exchange with alternative partners affect power, coalition formation and related processes.

In this chapter I discuss the scope and accomplishments of contemporary exchange theories in the context of their historical roots and future prospects. I begin with an overview of the basic concepts and assumptions that all approaches share and a brief review of the contributions of early theorists. I then turn to contemporary theories and research programs, considering their similarities and differences, their achievements and the challenges that remain for future work. Because earlier exchange theories are reviewed in depth elsewhere (for example, Molm and Cook, 1995; Ritzer, 1996; Turner, 1986), I focus most of my attention on more recent developments.

BASIC CONCEPTS AND ASSUMPTIONS

All exchange theories share a common set of analytical concepts and certain assumptions. These describe the basic 'building blocks' of social exchange: actors, resources, structures and processes.

Actors and resources

Participants in exchange are called *actors*. Actors can be either individual persons or corporate groups,[1] and either specific entities (a particular friend) or interchangeable occupants of structural positions (the president of IBM). This flexibility allows exchange theorists to move from micro-level analyses of interpersonal exchanges to macro-level analyses of relations among organizations.

When an actor has possessions or behavioral capabilities that are valued by other actors, they are *resources* in that actor's relations with those others. Social exchange resources include not only tangible goods and services, but capacities to provide socially valued outcomes such as approval or status.

Actors who perform an act as part of an exchange incur some *cost* to self and produce some *outcome* for another. The costs incurred always include opportunity costs (rewards forgone from alternatives not chosen) and sometimes investment costs, material loss, or costs intrinsic to the behavior (for example, fatigue). The *outcomes* produced for others can have either positive value (gain or reward) or negative value (loss or punishment).

Exchange theories make no assumptions about *what* actors value; they might value riches and fame, time with family, or environmental causes. But virtually all exchange theories assume that actors are self-interested, seeking to increase outcomes they positively value and decrease those they negatively value.[2] They differ in the extent to which they assume a 'rational actor model', derived from microeconomics, or a 'learning model', adopted from behavioral psychology. In the former, actors cognitively weigh the potential benefits and costs of alternatives and make rational choices that seek to maximize outcomes; in the latter, actors respond only to the consequences of past choices, without conscious weighing of alternatives (and often without maximizing outcomes). Both classical and contemporary theories vary in their relative adherence to these two models.

Exchange structures

Exchange relations develop within structures of mutual dependence, which can take several forms: direct exchange, generalized exchange and productive exchange. In relations of *direct exchange* between two actors, each actor's outcomes depend directly on another actor's behaviors; that is, A provides value to B, and B to A (Figure 20.1a). In relations of *generalized exchange* among three or more actors, the reciprocal dependence is indirect: a benefit received by B from A is not reciprocated directly, by B's giving to A, but indirectly, by B's giving to another actor in the network. Eventually, A may receive a 'return' on her exchange from some actor in the system, but not from B (Figure 20.1b). Finally, in *productive exchange* (Figure 20.1c), *both* actors in the relation must contribute in order for either to obtain benefits (for example, coauthoring a book).

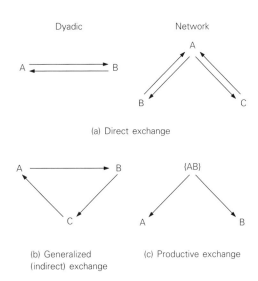

(a) Direct exchange

(b) Generalized (indirect) exchange

(c) Productive exchange

Figure 20.1 *Direct, generalized and productive exchange structures*

Although generalized exchange was a particular interest of early anthropological exchange theorists (and, increasingly, of contemporary sociologists), relations of direct exchange have dominated research and theorizing for the past thirty years. Structures of direct exchange can consist of isolated dyads or networks of connected dyadic relations (Figure 20.1a). Networks can vary substantially in size, shape and type of connection, as I discuss later. These distinctions and their effects on exchange are the focus of many contemporary theories.

Exchange processes

The process of exchange describes how interaction takes place within exchange structures. *Exchange opportunities* provide actors with the occasion to *initiate* an exchange; when an initiation is reciprocated (or an offer accepted), the mutual exchange of benefits that results is called a *transaction*. An ongoing series of transactions between the same actors constitutes an *exchange relation*.

Transactions in direct exchange relations take two main forms: negotiated and reciprocal. In *negotiated transactions* (buying a car, dividing household tasks), actors engage in a joint-decision process, such as explicit bargaining, in which they reach an agreement on the terms of the exchange. Both sides of the exchange are agreed upon at the same time, and the benefits for both partners comprise a discrete transaction. In *reciprocal transactions*, actors' contributions to the exchange are separately performed and non-negotiated. Actors initiate exchanges without knowing whether or when others will reciprocate, and exchange relations – if they develop – take the form of a series of sequentially contingent, individual acts; for example, you comment on a colleague's paper, she lectures in your class, and so forth.

HISTORICAL BACKGROUND

As Turner (1986) has observed, the philosophical roots of social exchange begin with the assumptions of utilitarian economics, broaden to include the cultural and structural forces emphasized by classical anthropologists, and enter sociology after further input and modification from behavioral psychology. The sociological development of the exchange perspective was particularly influenced by Blau (1964), Homans ([1961] 1974) and Thibaut and Kelley (1959), whose theories were published within a few years of one another. These early works demonstrated the ubiquity of exchange processes in social life, introduced key concepts that influenced later theorists and established the importance of the exchange perspective for the study of social interaction.

Despite Blau's efforts to bridge the gap between interpersonal exchanges and more complex social systems, the focus of these early theories remained primarily dyadic. They also tended to stimulate more theoretical controversy than empirical research, as critics raised charges of psychological reductionism, tautological reasoning and the like (Emerson, 1976). Later, more sophisticated theories addressed most of these shortcomings, but some of the breadth and richness of the early theories was also lost and is only now beginning to be reclaimed.

Emerson's contribution: the turning point

The publication of Emerson's exchange formulation (1972a, 1972b) marked the beginning of a new stage in the theory's development. His approach departed from earlier formulations in three important ways. First, Emerson replaced the relatively loose logic of his predecessors with a rigorously derived system of propositions that were more amenable to empirical test. Second, he established power and its use as the major topics of exchange theory – topics that would dominate research for the next twenty-five years. Third, by integrating behavioral psychology with social network analysis, he developed a theory in which the structure of relations, rather than the actors themselves, became the central

focus, and the explanation of structural change the primary aim.

Power-dependence relations

The dynamics of social relations in Emerson's theory revolve around power, power use and power-balancing operations, and rest on the central concept of *dependence*. Emerson recognized that patterns of dependence provide the structural foundation for both integration and differentiation in society. Relations of dependence bring people together (to the extent that people are mutually dependent, they are more likely to form relations and groups and to continue in them), but they also create inequalities in power that can lead to conflict and social change.

Emerson defined an actor's dependence on another by the extent to which outcomes valued by the actor are contingent on exchange with the other. Consequently, he proposed that B's dependence on A increases with the *value* to B of the resources A controls, and decreases with B's *alternative* sources of those resources. Actors' mutual dependence provides the structural basis for their *power* over each other. A's power over B derives from, and is equal to, B's dependence on A, and vice versa.

Power in dyadic relations is described by two dimensions: *balance*, or the relative power of A and B over one another, and *cohesion*, or the absolute power of A and B over each other. If two actors are equally dependent on each other, power in the relation is balanced. But if B is more dependent on A, power is imbalanced, and A has a *power advantage* in the relation equal to the degree of imbalance. The greater the mutual dependence of the two actors on each other – independent of their power imbalance – the greater their cohesion.

According to this formulation, *power* is a structural potential that derives from the relations of dependence among actors, and *power use* is the behavioral exercise of this potential. The more dependent B is on A for rewards, the higher the potential cost that A can impose on B by not providing those rewards. Over time, the structure of power produces predictable effects on the frequency and distribution of exchange as actors use power to maintain exchange or gain advantage: initiations of exchange increase with an actor's dependence; the frequency of exchange in a relation increases with cohesion; and in imbalanced relations, the ratio of exchange changes in favor of the more powerful, less dependent actor.

Emerson also argued that imbalanced relations are unstable and lead to 'power-balancing' processes. These processes reduce imbalance by decreasing the value of exchange to the less powerful actor ('withdrawal'), increasing value to the more powerful actor ('status-giving'), increasing alternatives available to the less powerful actor ('network extension'), or decreasing alternatives available to the more powerful actor (possibly through coalition formation). The latter two strategies represent structural changes in networks and receive more attention in Emerson's analysis of exchange networks and groups.

Exchange networks and groups

Emerson (1972b) was the first to link exchange theory with the growing field of social network analysis, a move that fundamentally changed the nature of exchange research. He began by distinguishing between groups and networks as different structural forms. *Groups* are collective actors (for example, teams, organizations) who function as a single unit in exchange with other actors. *Exchange networks* are sets of direct exchange relations among actors, either individual or collective, that are *connected* to one another. Connected relations are linked by a focal actor (for example, A–B–C), and exchange in one relation (for example, the A–B relation) affects the frequency or value of exchange in the other (the B–C relation). Connections are *positive* to the extent that exchange in one relation increases exchange in the other, and *negative* to the extent that exchange in one decreases exchange in the other.

How relations are connected – positively or negatively – determines the dynamics of exchange. Consider the two networks in Figure 20.2, which are identical in size and shape. In (a), B_1–A and A–B_2 are negatively connected relations, implying that B_1 and B_2 are alternatives for A (the more A exchanges with one B, the less A exchanges with the other), and competitors with each other for exchange with A: for example, A might be an employer and the Bs applicants for the same job, or the Bs might be potential tennis partners for A. In (b), positive connections between B–A and A–C describe a cooperative exchange network, in which exchange between B and A facilitates exchange between A and C (for example, B might give information to A that is useful in A's exchange with C). In some cases, A might act as a 'broker' in the network, with resources flowing from B to C, and back, through A.

Using these basic principles, Emerson proposed that a wide range of social forms could be analysed, including stratified networks, divisions of labor, 'social circles' of intracategory exchanges like cartels, and norm formation. In

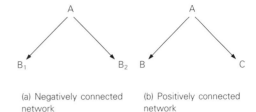

(a) Negatively connected network   (b) Positively connected network

Figure 20.2 *Negatively and positively connected exchange networks. (Note: Actors designated by the same letter (B_1, B_2 etc.) control resources in the same exchange domains; those designated by different letters (A, B, C) control resources in different domains)*

this way, Emerson showed how two main concepts – networks as sets of connected exchange relations, and actors broadly defined to include both individuals and corporate groups – could be used to explain the emergence and change of social structures.

The rise of programmatic research

Emerson's theory initiated a period, still in progress, of sustained, programmatic research on exchange relations and networks. The vast majority of this work uses experimental methods and standardized laboratory settings to test and construct theory. Most of these settings share certain features: subjects in isolated rooms interact via computer to ensure that their behavior is affected solely by structural characteristics of networks (rather than by personal characteristics of actors); they exchange repeatedly with partners over multiple trials; and they engage in exchanges that produce monetary outcomes for each other.[3]

During the 1970s and 1980s several distinct programs of research on power and exchange emerged. Cook, Emerson and their students conducted the first critical tests of power-dependence theory, while other researchers (particularly Lawler and Molm) used it as a framework for developing related theories of power and power processes. As Cook and her associates continued to link the theory with social network analysis, they attracted the attention of other researchers who were interested in developing formal mathematical models of power in exchange networks. These efforts produced a number of alternative approaches. Each of these lines of theoretical development is described below.

THE POWER-DEPENDENCE TRADITION:
CONTEMPORARY DEVELOPMENT

Cook and Emerson: power in exchange networks

In a series of highly influential experiments, Cook, Emerson and their students conducted tests of the major tenets of power-dependence theory in a laboratory setting constructed for that purpose. In contrast to the reciprocal exchanges envisioned by the classical theorists, subjects in Cook and Emerson's setting negotiated the terms of exchange, through offers and counter-offers, to reach binding agreements. Their setting was specifically designed for the study of power in negatively connected networks; to create the negative connections, a subject's exchange with one partner precluded exchange with another partner on that opportunity. The setting was also designed to test Emerson's assertion that power leads to power use, regardless of actors' knowledge or intentions; accordingly, subjects were not informed of the size or shape of the network beyond their immediate connections. To eliminate effects of equity concerns, subjects had no knowledge of the benefits their partners received from exchange agreements. In reality, subjects divided a fixed amount of profit between them, but they were unaware of the division, the total profit or their partners' gain.

Using this setting, Cook and Emerson showed that networks imbalanced on structural dependence produce unequal distributions of benefits, in favor of the less dependent actor, as Emerson predicted (Cook and Emerson, 1978). As he proposed, these effects occur even in the absence of actors' awareness of power. When actors are informed of inequalities, however, normative concerns about the fairness of exchange can inhibit power use. Commitments between exchange partners have a similar effect. Later studies showed that disadvantaged actors can also improve their bargaining position by forming coalitions, which reduce power imbalance and lead to more equal exchanges (Cook and Gillmore, 1984).

In a key 1983 article, Cook, Emerson, Gillmore and Yamagishi demonstrated the critical importance of Emerson's distinction between negatively and positively connected networks. Most social network research has traditionally assumed that network centrality determines structural power. The work reported in Cook et al. (1983) challenged this conception and showed that the relation between centrality and power depends on network connections. In positively connected networks centrality yields power,

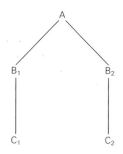

Figure 20.3 *A negatively connected network in which centrality does not determine power*

because central actors can serve as 'brokers' in cooperative relations. But in negatively connected networks, centrality is less important than access to highly dependent actors with few or no alternatives, and the most central actor is not always the one with the most power. In Figure 20.3, for example, the central actor, A, has less power than B_1 or B_2, who have the advantage of being the only partners for C_1 and C_2.

As these ideas suggest, somewhat different principles are required to predict the distribution of power in networks with different connections. Power-dependence theory, which predicts power from access to alternative exchange partners, is really a theory of power in negatively connected networks. The study of these networks has dominated research; far less work has been done on positively connected networks (Yamagishi et al., 1988).

In their 1983 study, Cook and her associates explicitly linked exchange theory and power-dependence concepts with social network research and its structural concepts of density, centrality and the like. But they also acknowledged the theory's inadequacy for analysing complex networks. Although power-dependence theory takes account of the larger network in which actors are embedded, it predicts the distribution of power within dyadic relations, not the network as a whole. Network-level analysis required a new approach.

The publication of their article stimulated a flurry of new theories, particularly new algorithms for measuring power in networks, that became one of the most significant developments to emerge from contemporary exchange theory. Cook and her associates were involved in these efforts, first proposing a preliminary measure based on the graph-theoretic concept of 'vulnerability' (Cook et al., 1983), and later introducing a new algorithm, called the equi-dependence exchange ratio, to predict the distribution of power in negatively connected networks (Cook and Yamagishi, 1992). This algorithm determines the exchange ratios that will produce 'equal dependence' of actors on each other in all relations throughout a network, based on iterative calculations of the value of their exchanges with each other relative to the value of exchanges with their best alternatives.

Lawler: power processes in bargaining

Lawler's work brings together power-dependence theory's analysis of structural power with bargaining theories' analyses of tactical power. Traditional work on bargaining neglected the social structure within which parties negotiate, and paid scant attention to the role of power. Lawler and Bacharach (Bacharach and Lawler, 1981) used ideas from power-dependence theory to fill that gap, and tested their predictions in a series of experiments modeled after intergroup bargaining (for example, between labor and management). The focus of their work was the dyadic relation, embedded in a hypothetical network. Later work by Lawler (1992) further developed the theoretical integration of these two traditions.

Several features distinguish this approach from other work on negotiated exchanges. First, for Lawler and his associates, the questions of whether an agreement will be reached and how, and not simply what the terms of the agreement will be, are central issues. Secondly, Lawler and his colleagues have primarily been interested in the relation between structural power – both total (absolute) power and relative power – and the *power tactics* that actors use to reach agreements. Thirdly, in contrast to the strongly structural position of Emerson, Lawler sees actors' perceptions of power as mediating between structural power and its use. The use of power is more conscious in this formulation, and issues of saving face and impression management affect choices of tactics.

This program is also one of the few to investigate systematically both reward- and punishment-based power. Different branches of the research program have investigated reward power, conceptualized in power-dependence terms, and punitive power, based on Lawler's extension of bilateral deterrence theory. As Lawler (1992) notes, power-dependence and bilateral deterrence theories predict similar effects of some dimensions of the two bases of power. When power in a relation is equal, high absolute power – on either base – should increase positive, conciliatory actions (rewards and concessions) and decrease negative, hostile tactics (threats and punishments). Unequal (imbalanced) power on either base should produce more hostility and less conciliation (that is,

fewer frequent rewards and greater conflict) than equal power. Their research findings have generally supported these predictions.

Molm: coercive power in social exchange

Molm's work also investigates both reward and punishment power, but departs from the bargaining approaches of Cook and Lawler. Rather than negotiating the terms of exchange, actors engage in reciprocal exchanges in which each actor individually makes choices that produce consequences for another. Actors do not know whether or when others will reciprocate their rewarding acts, and their relations develop gradually over time. This conception of social exchange is closer to that of the classical theorists than to most contemporary programs on negotiated exchange.

The classical theorists, however, excluded punishment and coercion from the scope of exchange theory. In a decade-long program of research, Molm sought to bring coercion within the theory's scope, arguing that both reward power and coercive power are derived from dependence on others, either for obtaining rewards or avoiding punishment (Molm, 1997). In exchange networks in which actors have the capacity to both reward and punish, the two bases of power have vastly different effects. The structure of reward power dominates interaction, and punishment and coercion are rarely used.

Molm's work showed that these differences are not the result of differences in the *effects* of rewards and punishments on exchange, as Blau and Homans assumed, but of differences in the relation between the *structure* of power and the *use* of power. Unlike reward power, the use of coercive power is not structurally induced by power advantage, but strategically enacted as a means of increasing an exchange partner's rewards. Decisions to use coercion are made under conditions of uncertainty and risk: both gain and loss are possible, and fear of loss constrains the use of coercion. Actors who are disadvantaged on reward power have the strongest incentive to use coercion, but also stand to lose the most if the partner retaliates. Rather than risk the loss of the partner's rewards, they forgo coercion and accept the status quo. Justice norms reinforce these effects. Actors perceive coercive tactics as unjust, and as their sense of injustice increases, so does their resistance to coercion. These reactions are strongest when advantaged actors, who expect rewards rather than punishments from their partners, are targets of coercion (Molm et al., 1994).

Molm's analysis highlights the role of risk in coercive power relations and, more generally,

in non-negotiated exchanges in which reciprocity is secured only by concerns with future
exchanges rather than by binding agreements.
As discussed below, risk and uncertainty are also
key factors in generalized exchange and some
negotiated exchanges in which agreements are
not binding or deception is possible.

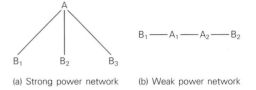

(a) Strong power network   (b) Weak power network

Figure 20.4   *Examples of strong and
weak power networks*

NEW THEORIES OF NETWORK EXCHANGE AND POWER

In the same way that Thibaut and Kelley's (1959)
outcome matrix stimulated research on dyadic
relations, the laboratory setting that Cook and
Emerson designed became the blueprint for a
decade of research on power in exchange networks. Cook et al.'s (1983) linkage of exchange
theory with social network research and graph-
analytic techniques, and their introduction of a
new (but inadequate) measure of power in
networks, prompted a sustained theory competition to see who could develop the best algorithm
for predicting the distribution of power in
exchange networks. This work concentrates
almost exclusively on negotiated exchanges in
negatively connected networks that vary in size,
shape and complexity.

Many of the researchers who participated in
this competition came from traditions outside of
social exchange theory, and the algorithms they
developed were derived from different theories.
The major competitors to emerge were based on
elementary theory (Willer and Markovsky,
1993), expected value theory (Friedkin, 1993),
and game theory (Bienenstock and Bonacich,
1993). All of these approaches used formal
mathematical models to predict the distribution
of power in negatively connected networks. All
adopted the basic parameters of Cook and
Emerson's setting – the negotiated exchanges,
the division of points (which became explicit,
rather than implicit), and even the number of
points – even though that setting had been
designed to operationalize specific concepts of
power-dependence theory, which the new theories did not always share. Consequently, the
setting came to take on something of a life of its
own, and substantially influenced the direction
of the new research programs.

Markovsky and Willer: elementary/resistance theory

The most active and well known of the alternative approaches to power in exchange networks
is the theory developed by Markovsky, Willer
and colleagues from the basic concepts of

elementary theory and resistance theory (Willer
and Markovsky, 1993). Variously called by those
names as well as the more general label of
network exchange theory, the theory uses two
algorithms – a graph-theoretical power index
(GPI) based on a network path-counting algorithm, and a resistance model based on actors'
expectations about outcomes – to predict
relative power and profit in exchange networks.

The theory assumes that structural power is
derived from the availability of alternative
partners, as determined by the structure of the
network and the connections among actors.
Alternatives are more 'available' to an actor if
they lie on odd- rather than even-length paths.
Differences in availability affect the likelihood
that some actors will be excluded from negotiated agreements, creating what Markovsky et al.
(1993) call 'strong power' or 'weak power'
networks. In Figure 20.4, network (a) is a strong
power network (all of A's alternatives lie on
paths of length 1 and are highly available), and
network (b) is a weak power network (A's
immediate alternative to B – the other A – lies
on a path of length 2 and has another potential
partner). In strong power networks, one or more
disadvantaged actors (for example, the Bs in
Figure 20.4a) are excluded on every opportunity
from exchanges with a powerful actor (A).
Exclusion increases power use by driving up the
offers that the Bs make to A. In weak power
networks, no position can consistently exclude
another without incurring cost to itself. For
example, in Figure 20.4b the two As can exclude
the Bs only by exchanging with each other, but
this action is costly because agreements between
the equal-power As should provide each with no
more than half the benefits.

The GPI calculates the relative power of positions in networks by counting paths out from a
position and then summing 'non-intersecting'
paths. Odd-length paths increase power; even-
length paths decrease it. Positions with higher
GPI scores are predicted to receive a larger share
of the profit from agreements. In weak power
networks, the GPI scores of all positions are
equal, but profit differences (while smaller)
still occur. New versions of the theory explain
these differences by incorporating a 'resistance'

model, which considers how actors' beliefs about their best and worst possible outcomes affect bargaining.

Friedkin: expected value model

While Markovsky and associates incorporated bargaining processes in later versions of their theory, the joint role played by structure and process was the central issue of expected value theory from the beginning. Friedkin (1993) developed his expected value approach from a broader model of social power based on French's formal theory. The broader model applies to a variety of different social relations, including interpersonal influence, information flow, social support and social exchange.

The most distinctive feature of the expected value model is its emphasis on the interplay between structure and process. Rather than assuming that exchange outcomes can be predicted solely from network structure, Friedkin argues that the opportunity structure of exchange networks and the actual process of actors' bargaining jointly determine exchange outcomes. The probabilities of alternative exchange patterns (which are structurally determined) affect actors' bargaining positions and payoffs, which in turn affect the probabilities of future exchange transactions, and so on, in an iterative process.

Bienenstock and Bonacich: game theoretic solutions

In contrast to the other approaches, Bienenstock and Bonacich (1993) argue that no new theory is required to predict the distribution of power in negatively connected exchange networks. As they point out, negotiated exchanges in negatively connected networks are equivalent to N-person cooperative games. Consequently, it should be possible to apply existing game-theoretic solutions to make predictions about resource distributions. They do not argue that game-theoretic solutions are necessarily better; rather, their advantage lies in their wide applicability and well-established solutions.

Whereas power-dependence theory and elementary/resistance theory are based on loose assumptions of 'rational actors', including both behavioral learning and cognitive calculation, game-theory models are based explicitly on assumptions of rational choice. The game-theoretic solution on which Bienenstock and Bonacich have focused most of their attention is the *core*: the set of payoffs in a game (that is, profits obtained by actors in an exchange network) that satisfies assumptions of individual, coalition (relation) and group (network) rationality. For networks that have no core outcomes, other game-theoretic solutions (for example, the Shapley value and the Kernel) are possible.

Evaluation and comparison

All four network approaches – equi-dependence, elementary/resistance, expected value, and game theory – offer sophisticated mathematical models for predicting the distribution of power in exchange networks. Intense competition among them has spurred refinements that now enable all of the approaches to make point predictions of the profits that actors in different structural positions will receive from negotiated transactions. Some theories have also focused on other outcomes, particularly the frequencies of agreements between exchange partners.

Comparative tests of their predictions have produced varying results. Skvoretz and Willer (1993) found that which theory performed best depended on whether predictions were based solely on structural potentials for exclusion, or observed instances of exclusion. Elementary/resistance theory performed best in the former instance, and expected value theory in the latter. Lovaglia et al. (1995), comparing three different versions of GPI/resistance models with the other approaches, found the most recent version of GPI/resistance to be most accurate. Because the various algorithms for predicting power are frequently revised, and the experimental tests are conducted under varying conditions, claims to empirical superiority by one approach are often refuted by another.

The theoretical implications of these comparisons are somewhat difficult to interpret. Because of the focus on accuracy of predictions, there has been little discussion of exactly *which* differences in assumptions or algorithms account for the variations in success, or why predictions are far more similar in some networks than in others. In addition, the competition among the approaches tends to obscure the principles they hold in common. Most of the theories are based on the notion that actors' relative power depends, at least in part, on the availability of their alternative partners (Skvoretz and Willer, 1993). This emphasis on alternatives is reflected in the theoretical concepts of dependence and exclusion, one or both of which is used by most of the theories. In networks with strong variations in availability of alternatives across positions ('strong power' networks), the GPI appears to be the best algorithm. In networks with weak variations in availability, prediction becomes more complex and depends on assumptions about actors' bargaining strategies. Again, the theories are all based on fairly similar assumptions about actors' behavior, but differ in how they model that behavior and, consequently, the specific predictions they make.

The theoretical programs on power in exchange networks have expanded the size and range of networks studied, increased the precision of predictions about the terms of negotiated exchange, and reinforced the linkage of exchange theory with social network analysis. Nearly all of these efforts, however, have concentrated on a specific problem in exchange theory: (a) predicting how actors divide profits, (b) in negatively connected networks of direct exchange, (c) when transactions are negotiated and agreements are binding. How well the various models will do in predicting other forms of exchange, in other types of networks, remains to be seen.

Emerging perspectives on neglected topics

While research on power and exchange networks continues to focus on the particular questions of that tradition, social exchange theorists have begun to examine other issues. These include some of the long-neglected concerns of the classical theorists: the risk and uncertainty inherent in exchange (particularly generalized exchange and reciprocal exchange) and its effect on trust and commitment, the emergence of affective ties between exchange partners and their ability to transform the structure and form of exchange, and the relation between structure and agency.

Uncertainty and risk in social exchange

As Kollock (1994) has noted, the study of negotiated exchanges with binding agreements tends to obscure the uncertainty and risk of many social exchanges. Exchanges that are not secured by binding agreements, or that involve exchanges of goods of uncertain value, are risky: one actor can produce value for another but receive nothing in return.

Although all exchanges involve some uncertainty and risk, the risk of incurring a net loss varies systematically with the form of exchange (Molm, Takahashi and Peterson, 2000). In general, reciprocal exchange is riskier than negotiated exchange, and generalized exchange is riskier than reciprocal exchange. These variations in risk result from differences in outcome structure and information among the three forms

of exchange. In negotiated exchange, actors make joint decisions about known terms of exchange. Binding agreements make defections from these agreements impossible. In contrast, in both reciprocal and generalized exchange, actors initiate exchanges individually without knowing what, if any, returns they will receive. Thus, in both, actors risk incurring the costs of initiating exchange while receiving nothing in return.

Generalized exchange is riskier than reciprocal exchange because reciprocity – if it occurs – is indirect. When A and B exchange directly and repeatedly with each other, they can respond contingently to one another in ways that increase the probability of the other's reciprocity. But when A gives to B in a network of generalized exchange, A's influence over B has no direct effect on the actor who eventually returns benefit to A (see Figure 20.1b). Sanctioning systems may encourage individuals to participate in a generalized exchange system, but such systems entail the classical problems of 'second-order' free-riding.

Risk and trust

The classic solution to overcoming risk and uncertainty in exchange is trust. Blau (1964) proposed that exchange relations typically begin with minor transactions that involve little risk and require little trust; trust develops and exchange expands as partners prove themselves trustworthy.

Other theorists have proposed that exchange under risk and uncertainty not only *requires* trust, but *promotes* trust (Lévi-Strauss, 1969). At the same time that risk provides the opportunity to exploit another, it also provides the opportunity to demonstrate one's trustworthiness. Without risk, attributions of trust are impossible. Yamagishi and Yamagishi (1994) make this same point by distinguishing between *trust* (expectations of benign behavior based on a partner's personal traits) and *assurance* (expectations of benign behavior based on the existing incentive structure). As long as an 'assurance' incentive structure is present, there is no opportunity for trust to develop. In general, negotiated exchange provides greater assurance than reciprocal exchange, and reciprocal exchange provides greater assurance than generalized exchange.

Recent tests support this predicted relation between risk and trust. Kollock (1994) found that ratings of partners' trustworthiness were greater when subjects negotiated exchanges under conditions of uncertainty about the quality of goods they were buying than under certainty. And Molm, Takahashi and Peterson (2000) found that reciprocal exchanges produced higher levels of trust than equivalent negotiated exchanges. Of course, risk creates a breeding ground not only for trust but for exploitation; both Kollock and Molm et al. found that trust varies more with behavior under conditions of risk. In generalized exchange systems like the one in Figure 20.1b, Yamagishi and Cook (1993) caution that participants must have a relatively high level of general trust in others initially, or the system will collapse. More recently, Takahashi (2000) has shown that pure generalized exchange systems can develop and persist without high levels of trust or central sanctioning systems, as long as actors selectively give to others whose behavior meets a personal criterion of fairness.

Risk and commitment

In direct exchange relations, actors can reduce risk and promote trust by forming behavioral *commitments*: relations in which two persons exchange repeatedly with one another while forgoing other profitable alternatives. Cook and Emerson (1978) first conceptualized commitments as a means of uncertainty reduction. Because commitments can reduce power use by curtailing the exploration of alternatives, they are generally beneficial to low-power actors and costly to high-power actors. Kollock (1994) directly tested the effects of uncertainty on commitment, and found, as predicted, significantly higher levels of commitment (and trust) under uncertainty.

In a comparison of reciprocal and negotiated exchange, Molm et al. (2000) found that although subjects reported greater *feelings* of commitment and trust when exchanges were reciprocal (and therefore riskier), their actual behavioral commitments were no greater than when exchanges were negotiated, with binding agreements. These results suggest that commitment may be multi-faceted, with distinct behavioral and affective components.

Affect and social exchange

In a theoretical tradition that assumes self-interested actors, the development of affective ties and emotional expressions has generally received short shrift. Lawler and Yoon (1993, 1996), however, have developed a theory that seeks to explain affective ties and emotional expressions as emergent properties of relations, initially based on instrumental considerations. They propose that frequent, successful negotiations between two actors produce positive emotions that are attributed, in part, to the relationship itself. As a result, the relationship becomes an object of affective attachment, distinct and valued in its own right: an outcome they define as relational cohesion.

Experimental tests support the theory's logic (Lawler and Yoon, 1993, 1996). Both higher absolute power and more equal (balanced) power promote more frequent agreements, which in turn produce more positive emotions, and these emotions increase relational cohesion and commitment behaviors. Lawler and Yoon's work also illustrates how the structure of relationships can change and resource domains expand as a result of repeated interactions. When relationships become objects that are valued in their own right, they take on characteristics of 'productive exchange'; that is, the benefits each actor obtains from exchange are based partly on what the two actors give each other (direct exchange), and partly on what they jointly contribute to their collective good (productive exchange). Those benefits include not only the original domains of extrinsic value, but new, emergent domains of intrinsic value.

Structure and agency

Developing a theoretical framework that links structures with actors has been the goal of exchange theory since its inception. While conceptions of structure have become quite sophisticated, conceptions of actors remain underdeveloped. Most contemporary theories are loosely based on assumptions derived from either rational choice or learning theories, often without being very explicit about whether one or both is involved. Rational choice theories of exchange are an exception (for example, Coleman, 1990).

In part, this was intentional: since Emerson, most exchange theorists have sought to develop structural theories of exchange, with only a minimal conception of actors. One of Emerson's best known assertions is that power use is *structurally induced* by power advantage, regardless of actors' motives. Even that assertion rests on certain assumptions about actors, however; for example, that they follow the behavioral principles of increasing more rewarding patterns and decreasing less rewarding ones, or, in negotiated exchanges, that they raise or lower offers according to their success in securing agreements.

In addition to structurally induced power use, however, actors can use power strategically, by selectively giving and withholding rewards, contingent on the partner's behavior (Molm, 1997; Thibaut and Kelley, 1959). Such strategies *create* contingencies that produce consequences for others' behaviors. Actors' strategies can also include attempts to change the structure of power itself, as Emerson's 'power-balancing' processes illustrate. Coalition formation, for example, requires both purposive action and collective action.

To the extent that actors can or must engage in strategic action to use power or effect structural change, processes of learning and decision-making become important. Cognitive biases such as loss aversion, referent dependence and framing effects (Kahneman and Tversky, 1984) may influence perceptions and actions. Research to date suggests these considerations are more important under some conditions than others. When variations in structural power are weak, for example, actors' strategies have more effect on power use (Markovsky et al., 1993). Similarly, when power is based on control over punishments rather than rewards, strategies are more important and predictions require more assumptions about actors' decision-making processes (Molm, 1997).

CONCLUSIONS AND FUTURE DIRECTIONS

As long as people are dependent on each other for meeting their material and social needs, the exchange of valued benefits will constitute an important part of social life. These exchanges take different forms – direct or generalized, negotiated or reciprocal – and they occur within networks of varying sizes, shapes and connections. As a result, actors vary in their opportunities to obtain benefits and in the control they exert over others' benefits.

Since the earliest formulations, these considerations have led theorists to focus on the relations between exchange and power. Today, the study of power continues to dominate the field; consequently, a review of theories of exchange is in many respects a review of power. As we have seen, researchers have approached this topic in different ways. Some have concentrated on developing precise predictions under fairly restrictive conditions, others have settled for ordinal predictions but explored a broader range of conditions, and still others have used the study of power as a springboard for investigating related areas such as commitment, trust and affective ties.

This multiplicity of approaches has produced a much richer understanding of exchange and contributed to the remarkable progress of the past twenty-five years. The sheer quantity of programmatic research during this period stands in sharp contrast to the earlier years of exchange theory in sociology, when little empirical work was conducted. In a relatively short time, the combined efforts of a number of researchers

have produced a strong empirical base that offers substantial support for the perspective.

Because of the dominant focus on power and related issues, however, some important questions have received little attention. These neglected areas offer promising avenues for future theory development. We have already seen renewed interest in some understudied topics, such as the role of affect, emotion, commitment and trust in social exchange. It is likely that work in these areas will continue to grow during the next decade, thus linking social exchange theory with work in the sociology of emotions and theories of trust.

Several other areas also deserve attention. One is Emerson's original aim of studying structural change. For the past two decades, most exchange researchers have studied how static network structures affect the distribution of exchange benefits. But networks are rarely static; instead, they expand and contract, network connections change and the value of resources attached to different positions varies. Studying what produces structural change, how change affects established patterns of interaction, and how the structural history of a network alters its current impact are all questions worth more attention.

As we have seen, the linkage of social exchange theory with social network analysis has been valuable for both traditions. But one important difference remains: the vast majority of social exchange theorizing and research has addressed networks with negatively connected relations, that is, networks in which some actors are pitted against each other in competition for the resources of others. In contrast, social network researchers primarily study positively connected networks, in which actors exchange information, opinions and so forth that flow across relations and build cooperation and solidarity. Positively connected and mixed networks are at least as common in social life as negatively connected networks, and they deserve greater attention from exchange theorists. The type of network connection is likely to have important implications not only for power, but for the development of affective ties, perceptions of fairness and the like.

Finally, to return the theory to its original roots as a theory of *social* exchange, more attention should be paid to some of the dimensions that typically distinguish social from economic exchanges. These include greater consideration of reciprocal exchanges, of exchange relations with multiple domains of value, and of developmental stages in exchange relations. Although social exchange is distinguished by its emphasis on 'more or less enduring relations between specific partners' (Molm and Cook, 1995), contemporary theorists have paid relatively little attention to how relationships change over time.

Many of these suggestions involve greater recognition of the ways in which social exchanges are embedded not only in structure, but in time. For the past twenty years exchange theorists have concentrated on developing sophisticated theories of exchange structures; perhaps the next twenty years will see the rise of equally advanced theories of exchange dynamics. Whatever its future, the current vibrancy of the field suggests that Emerson's 1976 statement that '. . . exchange theory is still growing; it still contains diversity and sparks of controversy' (1976: 1) is likely to be as apt in another twenty years as it is today.

NOTES

1 Corporate actors are more complex than individual actors and are distinct in many ways. The two are assumed to be analytically equivalent only when groups act as a single unit, in exchange with other groups or individuals.

2 Some of the classical 'collectivist' theories (e.g., Lévi-Strauss, 1969) are exceptions.

3 The use of money in exchange experiments often gives the mistaken impression that researchers are studying economic exchange, not social exchange. But researchers use money solely because of its advantages for experimental control: money is widely valued, quantifiable and resistant to satiation effects. The resource in exchange experiments is not money (money is not transferred from one actor to another), but the capacity to produce valued outcomes – operationalized as money – for another. Because exchange theories assume that the domain of value does not affect theoretical predictions, results obtained from experiments using money can be generalized to other outcomes.

REFERENCES

Bacharach, Samuel B. and Lawler, Edward J. (1981) *Bargaining: Power, Tactics, and Outcomes*. San Francisco: Jossey-Bass.

Bienenstock, Elisa Jayne and Bonacich, Phillip (1993) 'Game Theory Models for Social Exchange Networks: Experimental Results', *Sociological Perspectives*, 36: 117–36.

Blau, Peter M. (1964) *Exchange and Power in Social Life*. New York: Wiley.

Coleman, James S. (1990) *Foundations of Social Theory*. Cambridge, MA: Harvard University Press.

Cook, Karen S. and Emerson, Richard M. (1978) 'Power, Equity and Commitment in Exchange Networks', *American Sociological Review*, 43: 721–39.

Cook, Karen S. and Gillmore, Mary R. (1984) 'Power, Dependence, and Coalitions', in Emerson J. Lawler (ed.), *Advances in Group Processes*, vol. 1. Greenwich, CT: JAI Press. pp. 27–58.

Cook, Karen S. and Yamagishi, Toshio (1992) 'Power in Exchange Networks: A Power-Dependence Formulation', *Social Networks*, 14: 245–65.

Cook, Karen S., Emerson, Richard M., Gillmore, Mary R. and Yamagishi, Toshio (1983) 'The Distribution of Power in Exchange Networks: Theory and Experimental Results', *American Journal of Sociology*, 89: 275–305.

Emerson, Richard M. (1972a) 'Exchange Theory, Part I: A Psychological Basis for Social Exchange', in Joseph Berger, Morris Zelditch Jr and Bo Anderson (eds), *Sociological Theories in Progress*, vol. 2. Boston, MA: Houghton-Mifflin. pp. 38–57.

Emerson, Richard M. (1972b) 'Exchange Theory, Part II: Exchange Relations and Networks', Joseph Berger, Morris Zelditch Jr and Bo Anderson (eds), *Sociological Theories in Progress*, vol. 2. Boston, MA: Houghton-Mifflin. pp. 58–87.

Emerson, Richard M. (1976) 'Social Exchange Theory', *Annual Review of Sociology*, 2: 335–62.

Friedkin, Noah E. (1993) 'An Expected Value Model of Social Exchange Outcomes', in Emerson J. Lawler, Barry Markovsky, Karen Heimer and Jodi O'Brien (eds), *Advances in Group Processes*, vol. 10. Greenwich, CT: JAI Press. pp. 163–93.

Homans, George C. ([1961] 1974) *Social Behavior: Its Elementary Forms*. New York: Harcourt Brace and World.

Kahneman, Daniel and Tversky, Amos (1984) 'Choices, Values, and Frames', *American Psychologist*, 39: 341–50.

Kollock, Peter (1994) 'The Emergence of Exchange Structures: An Experimental Study of Uncertainty, Commitment, and Trust', *American Journal of Sociology*, 100: 313–45.

Lawler, Edward J. (1992) 'Power Processes in Bargaining', *The Sociological Quarterly*, 33: 17–34.

Lawler, Edward J. and Yoon, Jeongkoo (1993) 'Power and the Emergence of Commitment Behavior in Negotiated Exchange', *American Sociological Review*, 58: 465–81.

Lawler, Edward J. and Yoon, Jeongkoo (1996) 'Commitment in Exchange Relations: Test of a Theory of Relational Cohesion', *American Sociological Review*, 61: 89–108.

Lévi-Strauss, Claude (1969) *The Elementary Structures of Kinship*, rev. edn. Boston, MA: Beacon.

Lovaglia, Michael J., Skvoretz, John, Willer, David and Markovsky, Barry (1995) 'Negotiated Exchanges in Social Networks', *Social Forces*, 74: 123–55.

Markovsky, Barry, Skvoretz, John, Willer, David, Lovaglia, Michael and Erger, Jeffrey (1993) 'The Seeds of Weak Power: An Extension of Network Exchange Theory', *American Sociological Review*, 53: 220–36.

Molm, Linda D. (1997) *Coercive Power in Social Exchange*. Cambridge: Cambridge University Press.

Molm, Linda D. and Cook, Karen S. (1995) 'Social Exchange and Exchange Networks', in Karen S. Cook, Gary Alan Fine and James S. House (eds), *Sociological Perspectives on Social Psychology*. Boston, MA: Allyn and Bacon. pp. 109–235.

Molm, Linda D., Peterson, Gretchen and Takahashi, Nobuyuki (2000) 'Risk and Trust in Social Exchange: An Experimental Test of a Classical Propsition', *American Journal of Sociology*, 105: 1396–1427.

Molm, Linda D., Quist, Theron M. and Wiseley, Phillip A. (1994) 'Imbalanced Structures, Unfair Strategies: Power and Justice in Social Exchange', *American Sociological Review*, 59: 98–121.

Ritzer, George (1996) *Sociological Theory*, 4th edn. New York: McGraw-Hill.

Skvoretz, John and Willer, David (1993) 'Exclusion and Power: A Test of Four Theories of Power in Exchange Networks', *American Sociological Review*, 58: 801–18.

Takahashi, Nobuyuki (2000) 'The Emergence of Generalized Exchange', *American Journal of Sociology*, 105: 1105–34.

Thibaut, John W. and Kelley, Harold H. (1959) *The Social Psychology of Groups*. New York: Wiley.

Turner, Jonathan H. (1986) *The Structure of Sociological Theory*. Homewood, IL: Dorsey.

Willer, David and Markovksy, Barry (1993) 'Elementary Theory: Its Development and Research Program', in Joseph Berger and Morris Zelditch Jr (eds), *Theoretical Research Programs: Studies in the Growth of Theory*. Stanford, CA: Stanford University Press. pp. 323–63.

Yamagishi, Toshio and Cook, Karen S. (1993) 'Generalized Exchange and Social Dilemmas', *Social Psychology Quarterly*, 56: 235–48.

Yamagishi, Toshio and Yamagishi, Midori (1994) 'Trust and Commitment in the United States and Japan', *Motivation and Emotion*, 18: 129–66.

Yamagishi, Toshio, Gillmore, Mary R. and Cook, Karen S. (1988) 'Network Connections and the Distribution of Power in Exchange Networks', *American Journal of Sociology*, 93: 833–51.

21

Sociological Rational Choice

DOUGLAS D. HECKATHORN

Many discussions of contemporary sociological theory are infused with a sense of disenchantment (Alexander, 1998). The expectation that theoretic development would prove cumulative is now seen by many theorists as a mirage. The field grows increasingly theoretically fragmented. Luminaries in one sub-field are frequently unaware of their contemporaries in other sub-fields. Theoretic fragmentation and micro-specialization divide the field into ever smaller and more isolated islands. These developments in sociology mirror larger intellectual trends. For example, a symposium of historians studying different facets of the French Revolution concluded that they had nothing to learn from one another.

Intellectual fragmentation due to micro-specialization is compounded by an additional fault line. Writing in the 1950s, C.P. Snow described the emergence of two cultures, science and humanities, which had become so divergent in language and world-view that they had lost even the ability to communicate with one another. This division corresponds to a major fault line in sociology. As Alexander (1998: 26) notes, the field is being pulled in opposite directions, between those who view sociology as a literary and humanistic enterprise, versus those who view it as a science. Thus multiple centripetal forces would appear to make the prospect for unified theory ever more remote.

The emergence of rational choice is a stunning exception to this trend toward ever-increasing fragmentation. Rational choice has always dominated economics, but economists are using this perspective to analyse subjects beyond their discipline's traditional domain, including the family (Becker, 1981), revolution (Kuran, 1995),

and emotions (Frank, 1988). During the last two decades, rational choice has emerged as the dominant perspective within political science, and it is now entering areas of the discipline, such as area studies, that had initially resisted it (Johnson and Keehn, 1994). Rational choice remains the foundation for most experimental social psychology, and recent work focuses on developing theories that are relevant at the macro-social level (Lawler et al., 1993). The growth of rational choice sociology is reflected in institutional developments such as the founding of the journal *Rationality and Society* in 1989 and the formation of a rational choice section in the American Sociological Association in 1994. Rational choice is also a force in anthropology (e.g., see Hopcroft, 1999), though it is so closely related to rational choice sociology that the two will be treated together. Because of its role in providing theoretic integration across the social science disciplines, rational choice has been described as *the interlingua of the social sciences.*

In addition to providing theoretic cohesion in the social sciences, rational choice also extends into the humanities, providing the basis for much current work in the philosophies of ethnics and law (Frey and Morris, 1994). Therefore, it bridges C.P. Snow's two cultures, providing integration across the boundary separating the humanities and the sciences.

WHAT IS RATIONAL CHOICE?

Despite rational choice's visibility as an intellectual movement and the emergence of an associated set of institutions and publication outlets, no clear boundary differentiating rational choice from other theoretic perspectives is generally recognized. Indeed, there is no consensus regarding whether it can best be understood as a theory that is testable and hence potentially falsifiable, or whether it can better be understood as a theoretic perspective from which substantive theories can be derived. Here I adopt the latter, more common, interpretation.

Definitions of rational choice vary enormously in breadth. Some scholars define rational choice so broadly as to encompass the majority of sociological research, by equating it with any analysis in which behavior is viewed as purposive (Huber, 1997). In contrast, others employ a definition so restrictive that it would exclude virtually all sociological rational choice, by requiring that actors be viewed as motivated exclusively by self interest. (For a discussion of this latter position, see Mansbridge, 1990.) This chapter will focus on the intellectual movement involving scholarly works that are both self-identified as embodying a rational choice approach, and viewed by others as exemplifying that approach.

CONTINUITIES BETWEEN RATIONAL CHOICE AND TRADITIONAL SOCIOLOGICAL THEORY

Rational choice is frequently seen as differing from other theoretic approaches in sociology in two ways, a commitment to methodological individualism, and a view of choice as an optimizing process. However, on examination, neither suffices to differentiate rational choice from most other current work in the social sciences, including sociology.

Methodological individualism

Methodological individualism has been traditionally attacked within sociology because it undercuts the discipline's distinct area of investigation and threatens to dissolve it in favor of psychology. A commitment to at least some form of methodological individualism, in contrast, is often seen as a defining characteristic of rational choice (see Coleman, 1990: 5). The issue of methodological individualism is complex, so assessing and examining this issue requires clarification of terms. Joseph Schumpeter coined the term methodological individualism in 1908, though it was anticipated in the works of Jeremy Bentham and John Stuart Mill (Hodgson, 1986). The classic statement of methodological individualism is attributed to Ludwig von

Mises (1949). He argues that social, economic, and other societal-level phenomena can only be adequately explained in terms of the actions of individuals. Societal-level phenomena can therefore be explained exclusively in terms of micro-level events. The opposite form of explanation, in which macro-level events affect the individual, is thereby excluded. As a result, in von Mises' view causality lies exclusively at the micro-level, and macro-level events are mere epiphenomena. This is a statement of what may be termed *strict methodological individualism*.

Methodological individualism is frequently confused with a less stringent position that Lukes (1968) terms 'truistic social atomism'. According to Lukes, as its name implies, this position is expressed in truisms from which no reasonable person could dissent, such as 'society consists of individuals', and 'institutions consist of people plus rules and roles'. Even methodological holists do not claim that social institutions take on a physical reality divorced from their constituent individuals. The Leviathan, after all, is only a metaphor. For example, by viewing persons as 'empty vessels' whose contents are provided socially, they thereby recognize that social and institutional action is ultimately individual action. There are also many intermediate conditions between strict methodological individualism and truistic social atomism. However, no consensus exists regarding the point on this continuum at which a departure from strict methodological individualism fails to constitute a form of methodological individualism.

Contemporary sociological rational choice scholars do not embrace the strict form of methodological individualism. For example, James Coleman (1990: 5) described himself as committed to a 'special variant' of methodological individualism. An examination of his analyses show that this variant is closer to truistic social atomism than to the strict position. For example, Coleman argues that macro-level events cannot be adequately explained in terms of other macro-level events, a position consistent with methodological individualism. However, when Coleman describes the ideal form of explanations of macro-level events he argues that such explanations should combine three types of propositions: macro-to-micro propositions which express the effects of societal level factors upon individuals; micro-to-micro propositions which describe micro-level processes; and micro-to-macro propositions which show how individual level events aggregate to produce societal level changes. Hence, for Coleman, micro-level processes serve as the intermediate terms through which macro-level events are causally linked, but contrary to strict methodological individualism, the analysis includes macro to micro propositions.

To find strict methodological individualists, one must look to economics, and yet even here the position is increasingly abandoned (for example, see Arrow, 1994). There are indications that even von Mises would have abandoned strict methodological individualism had he chosen to analyse sociological rather than economic problems. For example, he (1949: 41–2) states that 'in the sphere of human action social entities have real existence. Nobody ventures to deny that nations, states, municipalities, parties, religious communities, are real factors determining the course of human events.' Hence, at least within sociology and perhaps even somewhat beyond, truistic social atomism is the consensus position shared by rational choice and traditional theorists.

Optimization

A second trait of rational choice that is often viewed as distinct from traditional sociological theory is the view of choice as an optimizing process. This is the sense in which choice is viewed as *rational*. It is important to note here that unlike classical microeconomics, contemporary sociological rational choice does not assume that income or profit is maximized. Hence, these rational choice theorists have moved far from the classical microeconomic assumption that individuals seek to maximize income, to recognition of the multiplicity of egoistic and altruistic goals that can direct behavior. This is the form of analysis that Jane Mansbridge (1990: 20–1) terms 'inclusive' modeling, because analysts 'are in principle happy to abandon the claim that self-interest is the sole operative motive and willing to work with any motive, provided only that the decision-maker maximize and be consistent'. This is a category in which she includes herself. The category also includes contemporary sociological rational choice scholars. Furthermore, these scholars all view rationality as 'bounded', in the sense that decision-makers are seen as having limited information of uncertain validity, and limited abilities to acquire and process information – hence they have also moved far from the classic microeconomic assumption of complete information. Because of the boundedness of rationality, actors are frequently unable to anticipate the effects of their actions. Many of the consequences of their actions are therefore unintended. The result may be positive, as in invisible hand systems, or the result may be disaster.

Given the recognition that preferences need not exclude altruistic motivations and information

need not be complete, the question remains as to whether conceptualizing choice as an optimizing process constitutes a point of essential differentiation between rational choice and traditional theory. Addressing this question requires an examination of the concept of purposive action shared by both approaches. Attribution of purpose to explain behavior involves a form of teleology. Two forms of teleological explanation can be distinguished (Elster, 1990). *Objective teleology* refers to processes such as Darwinian evolution, in which the appearance of purpose arises despite the absence of an intentional actor. For example, wings evolved as though their purpose were to fly. This is functionalist explanation. In contrast, *subjective teleology* refers to the actions governed by a system of values, goals, or aims, and hence to purposive action. This link between purposiveness and teleology is significant, because according to philosophers or science, any teleology implies some form of extremal principle (Nagel, 1953). This is a principle of maximization (for example, striving to attain a goal) or, what is the same thing from a formal standpoint, minimization (for example, striving to avoid falling short of a goal). Hence, purposive action entails maximization. The implication is that maximization principles are not merely used by rational choice theorists. They are also used implicitly by others who view behavior as purposive.

From a mathematical standpoint, the demonstration that purposive action entails maximizing assumptions should not be surprising, because in principle, any well-defined system can be described in maximizing terms. Hence the use of maximizing principles does not impose significant constraints upon an analyst. It merely requires that system dynamics be well described. The use of maximizing principles therefore does *not* constitute a point of essential differentiation between traditional and rational choice theory.

This examination of methodological individualism and optimization serves to emphasize the continuities between traditional and rational choice theory. This leaves us with the difference between traditional sociological theory and rational choice that they describe, that the latter makes explicit that which is implicit in the former.

WHAT IS UNIQUE ABOUT RATIONAL CHOICE ANALYSIS?

Given the substantive overlap in core assumptions regarding actors and their relationship to structure of rational choice and traditional sociological theory, it might seem that the differences are inessential. As Hechter and Kanazawa (1997: 192) note, 'many sociologists, like the character in Moiré's *Bourgeois Gentilhomme* who was startled to learn that he was speaking prose, unwittingly rely on rational choice mechanisms in their own research'. Is rational choice then merely a new label, albeit a provocative and controversial label, by which to describe what may sociologists have been doing all along? Though exaggerating the discrepancy between the two would be a mistake, so too would it be a mistake to fail to appreciate the distinctiveness of rational choice.

What makes rational choice distinctive is that the conception of choice as an optimizing process is made *explicit*. It might seem that making an assumption explicit would be a minor matter. However, it has important implications, for it imposes a common structure on rational choice models. Each must specify a core set of theoretic terms, including (1) the set of actors who function as players in the system, (2) the alternatives available to each actor, (3) the set of outcomes that are feasible in the system given each actor's alternatives, (4) the preferences of each actor over the set of feasible outcomes, and (5) the expectations of actors regarding system parameters. Rational choice models can also vary along many dimensions. They may be expressed mathematically or discursively, they can correspond to one-shot games in which actor makes only a single choice, or processual models in which each actor's choices affect the conditions under which they and others will make subsequent choices, they may assume materially based instrumental preferences or include preferences for social approval, altruism, or justice; they may assume information is complete (that is, knowing the structure of the game, including others' preferences), perfect (that is, also knowing others strategies), or information may be incomplete and reflect either risk (that is, knowing the probability of occurrence for each uncertain event) or uncertainty (that is, not knowing these probabilities); they may include individual actors, corporate actors, or a combination of both types of actors. Despite such variations, due to the common structure of rational choice theories, they share a common theoretic vocabulary. It is this common vocabulary that permits rational choice to function as the interlingua of the social sciences, and ensures that theoretic developments in one substantive area will have implications in other substantive areas.

Due to the common structure of rational choice theories, analysis revolves around a limited set of issues. One central issue concerns the relationships among preferences. If individual preferences are convergent, the system is guided to optimality by an invisible hand, so individually rational actions lead to outcomes that are also collectively rational. However, such situations are rare empirically. In the absence of an invisible hand, everyone acting rationally could lead to an outcome that is collectively irrational, in that everyone is worse off relative to other feasible outcomes. Such situations, where a potential conflict exists between individual and collective rationality, are termed *social dilemmas*. A substantial part of rational choice theory concerns how actors resolve, or fail to successfully resolve, these dilemmas.

Social dilemmas

Three social dilemmas have received special attention in the literature (for a typology see Heckathorn, 1996). These focus on issues of trust, competition, and coordination. The best known of these is the Prisoner's Dilemma (PD) (see Figure 21.1A). It is named for a vignette in which two criminal suspects are questioned separately about a crime. Their interests derive from the preference order of the core game's payoffs. The most preferred outcome is unilateral defection ('Temptation', T), where one benefits from confessing when the other remains quiet; then comes Universal Cooperation (the 'reward', R) where both remain quiet and receive

Prisoner's Dilemma	C	D
C	3, 3	0, 5
D	5, 0	1, 1

Chicken Game	C	D
C	3, 3	1, 5
D	5, 1	0, 0

Assurance Game	C	D
C	5, 5	0, 3
D	3, 0	1, 1

Invisible Hand (Privileged) Game	C	D
C	5, 5	1, 3
D	3, 1	0, 0

Figure 21.1 *Social dilemma games. The number on the left in each cell is Row's payoff, the number on the right is Column's payoff. Each player has a choice between cooperation (C) and defection (D). Four outcomes are possible in each. These are generally designated Reward (universal cooperation), Sucker (unilateral cooperation), Temptation (unilateral defection), and Punishment (universal defection)*

light sentences; next comes Universal Defection ('punishment', P) where both confess and are severely punished; and the worst is Unilateral Cooperation ('sucker', S), where only the other confesses so one's own penalty is most harsh. A second requirement is that the reward from universal cooperation is preferable to any mix of unilateral cooperation and defection (i.e., R > (T+S)/2). The essential problem is one of *trust*. If the prisoners can trust one another to act on their common interest in remaining quiet, they can escape with a light sentence. A marker indicating the presence of this dilemma is the potential for hypocrisy. Whenever individuals are tempted to act in ways they would prefer others not adopt, the presence of a PD should be suspected. This game has become the paradigm for cases where individually rational actions lead to a collectively irrational outcome.

The PD can affect dyads or larger groups. A group version arises when a group seeks to produce a *public good.* A public good is defined by two characteristics. First, excluding anyone from its benefits would be impractical. Examples include police protection and national defense. Second, public goods are characterized by jointness of supply, for example, the cost of national defense does not increase along with population. Because of these two attributes, provision of public goods faces a free-rider problem, in that even those who did not contribute to their production none the less enjoy their benefits. For example, even tax evaders benefit from police protection and national defense.

The literature focuses on two distinct means by which PDs can be resolved. First, incentives can serve to either reward those who cooperate or punish those who free-ride. An example of the latter is punishment for theft. Reciprocity includes another example of an incentive system, in which trustworthy or untrustworthy behavior is reciprocated in kind. Second, reputation systems provide information about who can and cannot be trusted, and thereby provide the means by which cooperators can locate and interact with one another.

A second social dilemma, which can be described in game theoretic terms as a Chicken Game, concerns competition for some form of scarce resource. In this game, the order of the two least valued payoffs are reversed from their position in the PD, that is, the new order is T > R > S > P. This reversal of preferences occurs, in essence, because less than universal cooperation suffices to produce most of the gains attainable from cooperation. This game is named for a contest in which drivers test their courage by driving straight at one another. Each player chooses between two strategies, Chicken (swerve to avoid a collision) or Daredevil (do not

swerve). Thus the order of preferences is: Temptation, the other swerves; then Reward, both swerve; then Sucker, ego swerves; and the worst of all is Punishment, a head-on collision. The essential problem in a Chicken Game is *allocation of concessions.* Players combine a common interest in avoiding conflict, with competing interests regarding the terms of agreement, such as the allocation of courage, honor, or profit. This game fits systems where a common interest in collective action coexists with opposed preferences regarding the precise direction that action should take. Examples include the hawk–dove split that arises in many social movements, in which purists claim that pragmatists are selling out by forsaking the movement's essential goals, and pragmatists claim that purists' unwillingness to compromise will lead the movement into ruinous conflict.

The literature on this dilemma focuses on two ways in which it can be resolved. First, theories of bargaining seek to explain how actors assess the strengths of their strategic positions when deciding how many concessions to offer, and thereby seek to explain the allocation of concessions that make agreement possible, and the origins of conflict when efforts to reach agreement fail. Examples of these models include Harsanyi's (1977) model, resistance theory (Heckathorn, 1980) and Rubinstein's (1982) model. The various models agree on some principles, such as that all else equal, an increase in the costliness of conflict will weaken an actor's strategic position and lead to more concessions. A second resolution of the dilemma precludes or narrows the scope for bargaining by defining rights to scarce resources, as in a system of property rights. Thus a property rights system confers legitimacy on particular allocations of resources (Alchian and Demsetz, 1973).

A third type of social dilemma, which is a game theoretically described as an assurance game, arises when coordination is required for some joint endeavor. The effect in games such as those depicted in Figure 21.1 is to make universal cooperation preferred to unilateral defection, thereby reversing the order of the two most highly valued outcomes from their position in the PD, that is, the new order is R > T > P > S. This game derives its name from the fact that each player can be motivated to cooperate by the mere assurance that the other will do the same. A collective action system fits it if participation with others is valued, participation can take multiple forms, and therefore coordination regarding the form of participation is required. For example, if two people want to meet at a restaurant for lunch, they must coordinate their choice of restaurant. Though it might seem that resolution of the coordination problem would be

		Target of impact	
		Single actor	Multiple actors
Source	Single actor	Market	Hierarchy
	Multiple actors	Normative System	Electoral System

Figure 21.2 *Institutional form as a function of source and target of impact of action*

trivial, it has proven especially challenging for rational choice theorists. One approach focuses on the identification of focal points around which coalitions of cooperators can rally.

Institutional forms

Rational choice models can be differentiated based on the institutional form to which they refer. Four basic institutional forms are possible based on whether the choices through which the institution is constituted are the product of a single actor or multiple actors, and whether the target of impact of the action is single or multiple actors. The logical possibilities can be expressed in the form of a two-by-two table (see Figure 21.2). A distinct rational choice literature has arisen focusing on each of these four institutional forms.

Norms have long been an important focus of sociological investigation. Whereas a view of social actors as rule followers has been a traditional part of sociological theory, rational choice sociology tends to focus on the emergence and enforcement of norms. The interactional structure on which norms are based involves multiple actors exerting control over a single actor, as when a norm violation triggers collective expressions of disapproval. In normative systems, power relations have a unique feature, wherein *power is everywhere elsewhere*. Even the most powerful individual is controlled by the actions of the others, so from the standpoint of each individual, power lies elsewhere, that is, within the remainder of the group. This form is quintessentially sociological, in that the group takes on a reality – that is, it exerts a form of control – that is independent of each of the individuals in the group. Hence, it should not be surprising that sociologists have been especially heavy contributors in this area.

A distinct type of norm corresponds to each of the three types of social dilemma (Ulmann-Margalit, 1977). First, PD norms, as the name implies, serve as a means for resolving that dilemma. These involve either normatively

punishing defectors or rewarding cooperators. Violation of these norms entail hypocrisy. For example, usually, murderers do not want to be murdered, burglars do not want their own homes burgled, rapists do not want to be raped, and liars do not want others to lie to them. Every society contains a variant of the golden rule, which codifies such norms. Secondly, Ullmann-Margalit (1977) identified what she termed inequality-preserving norms. These *allocation norms* legitimize the current distribution of scarce resources, including property, power and prestige, and thereby define a system of *property rights*. In a system without property rights, such as the hypothetical Hobbesian war of all against all, resources would be continually reallocated based on relative physical strength, threat capability and other coercive measures. In contrast, in a system with property rights, only transfers deemed legitimate are subject to negotiation. The effect is to narrow radically the scope for bargaining by precluding non-legitimate transfers of resources. Thirdly and finally, Ullmann-Margalit (1977) defined coordination norms as those that solve coordination problems. These include norms specifying the meaning of symbols, for example, the meanings of words. Thus a language can be seen as a vast system of coordination norms. Other coordination norms regulate turn-taking in conversation, body language, clothing styles, table manners, standards for weights and measures, and the innumerable rules that each generation of parents must struggle to teach their children.

The emergence and enforcement of norms entails a form of *collective action* because of the inherently cooperative nature of normative regulation. Building on the pioneering work of Mancur Olson (1965), a large literature on collective action has emerged (Hardin, 1982) to which sociologists have emerged as major contributors (Heckathorn, 1996; Macy, 1990; Marwell and Oliver, 1993). This literature focuses on the emergence and maintenance of social cooperation, including resolution of the free-rider problem that arises because norms themselves constitute a public good, a benefit that can be enjoyed even by those who do not contribute to their production. The result can be free-rider problems at multiple levels (Hecka-thorn, 1989). Free-riding is possible at either the primary level (for example, stealing), or at a second level (for example, failing to help enforce norms against theft). Resolving the first-order collective action problem (prohibiting theft) therefore requires resolving the second-order free-rider problem (motivating individuals to participate in norm enforcement). A regress arises because were the second-order problem to be resolved normatively, for example, a norm mandating participation in norm enforcement, this would produce a third-order free-rider problem, and so forth to ever-higher levels. A number of solutions to this problem have been proposed. For example, Taylor (1982) argues that the second-order free-rider problem is not a true social dilemma because the cost of parti-cipating in norm enforcement is generally trivial. The cost of participating in norm enforcement may even be negative. For example, gossip is both an important mechanism of norm enforce-ment, and a common though often deplored form of recreation. The implication is that the second-order collective action problem is not a social dilemma. Another solution (Heckathorn, 1989) suggests that hypocrisy may play a con-structive social role by facilitating the emergence of norms. For example, lawmen in the old American West were frequently brutally corrupt, violating the very rules they imposed on others, but their cumulative effect was to increase the level of social order, eventually bringing one another into control. Thus 'hypocritical coop-erators', persons who defect at the first level but cooperate at the second, can trigger a norm emergence process that eventually brings them under control. Alternatively, a division of labor between first and second level cooperation can persist, as in the emergence of a hierarchy. For in a hierarchy, superordinates specialize as second-level cooperators by establishing and enforcing the regulations that govern the labor of their subordinates, the first-level cooperators. As this example illustrates, hypocritical cooperation, as theoretically defined, need not have negative connotations, but rather can merely reflect a special form of division of labor. In this division of labor, higher-level cooperators are compen-sated for that cost by being able to defect at the lower level. Both these approaches to revolving the second-order free-rider problem view the actions by which norms are created and enforced as purposive.

Markets are the second basic institutional form. They are based on aggregations of exchanges between single actors, where these exchanges may involve individuals, as in peasant markets, corporate actors, as in capital markets, or a mix of individual and corporate actors, as when individuals make purchases from corpora-tions. Markets as thus conceived include not only the systems of monetary transactions upon which economists have traditionally focused, but also phenomena of traditional sociological concern. For example, marital choices aggregate to form a marriage market (Coleman, 1990) in which an individual's market value depends on a variety of factors, including employment pro-spects, physical attractiveness, and personality attributes. An important focus of socialization is the effort to instill attributes that will increase the person's value in the marriage market. Similarly, friendship choices aggregate to form a status market, in which high status is definable as high value in the friendship market (Coleman, 1990).

The relationship between individual and collective interests in markets is highly variable. In the fortunate and unlikely event of perfect convergence, no social dilemma arises, and the result is the invisible hand, a *non*-dilemma. In contrast, when convergence is imperfect, one or more of the three above-described social dilem-mas can arise. The problematic nature of trust marks the presence of a Prisoner's Dilemma. For example, fortune hunters marry for money rather than love. Bargaining marks the presence of another social dilemma. For example, in dowry systems, the amount of the dowry is generally negotiated. Similarly, when marriages are arranged, arranging a suitable match for a child can become a means by which parents enhance their wealth or social position, thereby providing the basis for competition and conflict between parents and children. Coordination problems are prominent in consensual marriage systems. The result tends to be assortative mating, in which partners tend to have equal values in the marriage markets. However, the complexity of the information upon which marriages are based means that any marriage system includes a coordination problem of enormous complexity. Thus marriage markets entail problems of trust, competition, and coordination, which reflect each of the above three social dilemmas.

Studies of non-economic markets, such as Coleman's (1990) use of neoclassical economic theory to analyze marriage markets, may appear to provide support for the stereotype of rational choice as a form of economic imperialism, wherein rational choice sociology would thereby be reduced to the application to sociological phenomena of economic theory. However, this concern about economic imperialism is invalid for two reasons. First, neoclassical economic theory is most powerful when applied to perfect and near-perfect markets, in which the above-described social dilemmas are resolved by the market's invisible hand. Contributions to the understanding of how social dilemmas are resolved have come from many disciplines, and few of these analyses are grounded in neoclassical economic analysis. Second, most phenomena of traditional sociological concern cannot be usefully conceptualized as markets but instead correspond to other institutional forms.

Consistent with the traditional sociological focus on norms, a special focus for rational choice sociology concerns the embeddedness of norms in markets. This is a major theme in the rapidly growing field of economic sociology (Smelser and Swedberg, 1994). Markets are not the self-sufficient entities presumed in classical and neo-classical economics. Instead, they depend on a host of underlying norms, including the system of property rights upon which transactions are based, and norms structuring the transactions. The dependence of markets on a system of underlying norms was an important theme in Durkheim's ([1893] 1947) analysis of markets. However, this insight has now become the basis for a growing body of work. Similarly, in Coleman's (1990) analysis of social capital, he emphasized the importance of norms for economic growth and development. These include norms which require that obligations be fulfilled, and even norms that make it safe to walk at night.

Hierarchies are a third institutional form for which rational choice theories have been developed. Here the fundamental principle of organization is for a single actor to exert power or influence over a set of subordinate actors. In the simplest structure, subordinates in one relationship function as superordinates in other relationships, to form a pyramidal structure. Agency theory (Eisenhardt, 1985; Jensen and Meckling, 1976; White, 1985) is one of the rational choice theories used for analyzing hierarchical relationships. The theory focuses on *informational asymmetries* between individuals who contract for a service (principals), and those who hire them (agents). For example, in the relationship between patients (principals) and physicians (agents), the latter's vastly greater access to specialized medical knowledge creates opportunities to control the patient through evasion, dissimulation, mystification and many other deceptive practices (Waitzkin, 1991). Similarly, in the relationship between clients (principals) and lawyers (agents), the latter can use their specialized legal knowledge in ways that lead clients to act against their own interests (Bok, 1978). More generally, any bureaucracy can be seen as a chain of principal–agent relationships that link principals ('superordinates') to agents ('subordinates') charged with fulfilling their delegated responsibilities. However, subordinates' differential control over information frequently enhances their power and provides the opportunity to manipulate their superordinates, so all hierarchical relationships include some scope of negotiation.

According to agency theory, two fundamental types of problems inevitably arise when the agent's interests fail to coincide with those of the principal. The first problem occurs *ex ante*, before the agent's services are retained. It is termed *adverse selection*, because the agents with the strongest incentives to offer their services to the principal tend to be those who are least well qualified or motivated. For example, when advertising for a job, the applicants who respond do not come from a random sample of all people who are qualified for the job, because most such people are satisfied with their current employment. Instead, responses come differentially from people who are unemployed or are in the process of losing their current jobs. This group contains a larger proportion of workers with problems in competence or reliability than does the working population at large. Identifying the true suitability of candidates for a job is difficult; because applicants who are least qualified have the greatest incentive to withhold information that reveals their deficiencies, so a coordination problem is complicated by a problem of trust.

A second type of agency problem occurs *ex post*, after an agent's services have been retained. If a principal lacks the means to monitor an agent's performance, the latter may act in ways that serve his or her interest at the principal's expense, thus a second problem of trust arises. This risk stems from postcontractual opportunism and is termed 'moral hazard', though it need not entail behavior that is either immoral or illegal. Problems of moral hazard arise to some extent in all organizations. Businesses lose far less money to robbery than embezzlement, for it is impossible to watch all employees all the time, especially those in positions of trust.

It might seem that suitably structured incentives could resolve agency problems; thereby creating the hierarchical equivalent of a perfect market that resolved all potential social dilemmas. However, just as perfect markets have characteristics that are seldom approximated in the real world, such as full information and the inability of individual buyers or sellers to affect aggregate price or demand, so too is a perfect incentive system impossible in realistic contexts. According to Holstrom (1982), an ideal incentive system would have three characteristics: (1) working effectively must be individually rational, (2) the outcome must be collectively rational, and (3) its costs must not exceed the enterprise's revenues. However, he proved that these three conditions are incompatible. This arises, in essence, because ensuring that a worker will be motivated to work effectively requires incentives equal to that person's marginal product, that is, the difference between the product with and without that person's effort. However, when the level of interdependence is high, and hence the efforts of all are necessary to achieve a desired outcome, each individual's marginal product approximates the entire product, so each individual would have to be paid an amount approximating the total product. Given these constraints, no magic bullet (that is, no perfectly designed incentive system) with which to resolve social dilemmas in hierarchies appears possible. Therefore, institutional measures with which to resolve issues of trust, to limit the potentially destructive effects of competition and allocate scarce resources, and to resolve cooperation problems, will remain important features affecting the operation of hierarchies.

Hierarchies, like markets, can be combined with other institutional forms. For example, many firms contain an 'internal labor market', in which individuals compete for promotions. Therefore, a market can be embedded in a hierarchy (Miller, 1992). Yet, many markets have hierarchical elements, as in a 'price leader' system in which a specific firm decides when to raise prices and others in the industry follow. A hierarchy is then embedded in a market.

The embeddedness of norms in hierarchies is another important focus of rational choice sociology. It has long been recognized that parallel to each organization's formal structure, is an informal normative structure. Analyzing such organizationally embedded norms has now become central to what Nee and Ingram (1998) term the 'new institutionalism' in sociology, in which institutions are defined as networks of formal and informal norms. They reject the 'structural embeddedness paradigm' in which individuals are embedded in structures so inflexible as to preclude meaningful choice. Instead, their essential argument is that norms provide the missing link, with which to integrate a *choice within institutional constraints perspective* with the *network embeddedness approach*.

Elections are a fourth institutional form, in which multiple actors (the voters) take actions that affect the collectivity. All three types of dilemmas can occur in electoral systems. PD problems arise when candidates use deceptive or dirty campaign tactics, logrolling and the exchange of political favors involves bargaining, and when the electorate uses simplistic criteria to make choices among numerous issues and candidates that reflects coordination problems. This institutional form has been a traditional focus of rational choice analysis in political science, though given the importance of political sociology as an area within the discipline, it should not be surprising that sociologists have also contributed in this area. For example, Kanazawa (1998) proposed a solution to the paradox of voter turnout, the problem of explaining why people would bother to vote given that the chance of influencing the outcome is null in systems with large numbers of voters.

The core–periphery structure in rational choice analysis

Traditionally, economists studied markets, political scientists studied elections and governmental hierarchies, and sociologists studied norms and hierarchies, including both systems of inequality and organizations. This rough division of labor how now blurred, reflecting the greater permeability of the division among the disciplines. The advent of rational choice has contributed to this process of integration. Because of its common theoretic vocabulary and focus on a central set of theoretic issues, theory development in rational choice exhibits a core–periphery structure. The core consists of bodies of theories and the associated common theoretic vocabulary, for example, general theories regarding social dilemmas and their modes of resolution. The periphery consists of substantive applications of rational choice theory to particular institutional forms, including tests of previously developed theory and analyses of specific phenomena. In this system, core and periphery are mutually interdependent, because substantive applications of rational choice theory draw on the core, and new theoretic developments frequently originate from research in substantive areas. Furthermore, because most rational choice scholars are involved both in development and elaboration of core theories and in substantive applications, there is no clear division of labor between theoretic and applied work. Yet the conceptual distinction between theoretic core and substantive periphery is none the less instructive, because a theoretic contribution resulting from substantive analysis radiates inward, affecting the body of core theory, and this in turn has implications that radiate outward to the array of other substantive areas in which rational choice analysis is pursued. For example, studies of social cooperation employing evolutionary game theory (Axelrod, 1984) have impacted fields ranging from evolutionary psychology and social movements to the philosophy of ethics. Thus, theoretic contributions arising in one substantive area can have implications in many other substantive areas. This process provides theoretic integration and coherence to rational choice as an intellectual movement that transcends disciplines.

CONCLUSION

By way of conclusion, let us consider critiques of rational choice. Four traditional critiques of rational choice are now widely recognized as misconceptions. First, rational choice is not wedded to a grim view of actors as ruthless opportunists. Indeed, much sociological rational choice analysis focuses on altruistic and other non-egoistic behaviors (Hechter, 1987). Secondly, rational choice is not wedded to any particular political position. Rational choice scholars range from free-market conservatives to Marxists (Elster, 1990). Thirdly, rational choice theory does not require that actions have only intended consequences; indeed, enormous emphasis has been placed on analyzing social dilemmas such as the prisoner's dilemma, in which individually rational actions combine to produce a collective loss. Finally, rational choice is not an alien import, but has deep roots within sociology, in particular the methodological individualism of Max Weber (Swedberg, 1998).

Other critiques remain contested. One that has gained increasing prominence during the past decade holds that rational choice scholars are so excessively concerned with abstract theory that they avoid the deep engagement with empirical data that is essential to any adequate analysis. This argument was put forth independently by Green and Shapiro (1994) in a critique of political science applications of rational choice, and by Johnson and Keehn (1994) in a critique of applications to area studies. Both critiques received wide attention and produced a debate that included a book-length response to Green and Shapiro (Friedman, 1995). In evaluating this debate, it is important to distinguish between critiques that bear directly on the theoretical approach, versus critiques that bear on particular applications. The former are more important, because even the best theoretic approaches can be applied badly.

When applications of rational choice in sociology are examined, what is striking are the numbers that are rich in empirical detail. This is consistent with the sociological tradition of deep engagement with empirical data. Examples include Jankowski's (1991) book *Islands in the Street*, in which he reports the results of more than a decade of ethnographic study of thirty-seven street gangs in Boston, Los Angeles and New York. This included, for example, studies

of the choice to join a gang, which involved assessments by his ethnographic informants of a complex combination of costs and benefits. Costs included having to share income from criminal endeavors with other gang members, and a greater chance of being caught by police because greater numbers of persons would have detailed knowledge of the endeavor. Compensatory benefits included earnings that were more regular, less individual effort, smaller risk of physical harm when part of a gang action, protection for family members, and money for family emergencies. He studied the processes by which individuals climb the gang hierarchy and the alternative forms of gang hierarchies, which ranged from flat but rather autocratic structures, to steep and highly bureaucratized structures that included written bylaws and formal elections. An important focus of his analysis was the emergence and enforcement of norms within the gangs, focusing on issues such as trust, allocation of authority, and coordination. These norms limited violence and predation within the gang, and forbade activities that would harm the relations with the community on which gang stability rests. Other empirically rich applications of rational choice in sociology include Hechter's (1987) analysis of group solidarity, Brinton's (1993) analysis of gender roles in Japan, Kiser and Schneider's (1994) analysis of pre-modern states, Opp's (1988) analysis of political protest, Nee's (1996) studies of development in China, Brustein's (1996) analysis of the social origins of the Nazi party, and Anthony et al.'s (1994) analysis of the ratification debate following the US constitutional convention of 1787. In light of such studies, it is surprising that the view of rational choice as theory obsessed has gained such support. However, the role of rational choice as the *interlingua of the social sciences* may provide the answer. The language of rational choice can serve as the basis for richly textured descriptions, however when it does so, the use of theoretically grounded terms also serves to point to the bodies of rational choice theory that would be relevant to an explanation. Hence, theory in rational choice analyses never can recede into the background, so a feature of rational choice descriptions that should be regarded as positive may be misjudged as a deficiency.

Rational choice theories are currently in a state of flux. This includes areas of theoretic development designed to broaden the perspective beyond its traditional limits. For example, rational choice has been criticized for ignoring emotions, but several distinct rational choice theories of emotion have now been proposed (Brams, 1997; Frank, 1988; Hirshleifer, 1987; Lawler and Yoon, 1998). Countering the view of rational choice as excessively rationalistic, rational choice theories of religion have also been proposed (Iannaccone, 1988; Stark 1999). Similarly, rational choice is sometimes criticized for treating preferences as fixed, and thereby ignoring preference change that is an important part of socialization, yet sociological rational choice theorists have offered several models intended to explain preference change (for example, see Lindenberg and Frey, 1993). Theories of socialization (Morgan, 1998; Yamaguchi, 1998) have also been proposed, and Rambo (1999) proposed a partial integration of rational choice and cultural sociology. Given the rate at which rational choice theory and applications are advancing, it is impossible at this time to offer a definitive assessment of its ultimate potential. However, two developments appear to be clear. First, a distinctively sociological form of rational choice analysis is in the process of development; a body of work that both reflects two important traditions within sociology, a substantive emphasis on norms and inequality and a commitment to deep engagement with empirical data. Second, this development will occur, not in isolation, but in a manner that draws upon and enriches theory-driven empirical research in other disciplines.

Acknowledgements

This research was made possible by grants from the Centers for Disease Control (U62/CCU114816-01) and the National Institute on Drug Abuse (RO1 DA08014).

REFERENCES

Alchian, Armen and Demsetz, Harold (1973) 'The Property Rights Paradigm,' *Journal of Economic History*, 33: 16–27.

Alexander, Jeffrey (1998) *Neofunctionalism and After*. Malden, MA: Blackwell.

Anthony, Denise L., Heckathorn, Douglas D. and Maser, Steven M. (1994) 'Rational Rhetoric in Politics: the Debate Over Ratifying the U.S. Constitution', *Rationality and Society*, 6 (4): 489–518.

Arrow, Kenneth J. (1994) 'Methodological Individualism and Social Knowledge', *American Economic Review*, 84: 1–9.

Axelrod, Robert (1984) *The Evolution of Cooperation*. New York: Basic Books.

Becker, Gary S. (1981) *A Treatise on the Family*. Cambridge, MA: Harvard University Press.

Bok, Sissela (1978) *Lying: Moral Choice in Public and Private Life*. New York: Random House.

Brams, Steven J. (1997) 'Game Theory and Emotions,' *Rationality and Society*, 9: 91–124.

Brinton, Mary C. (1993) *Women and the Economic Miracle: Gender and Work in Postwar Japan*. Berkeley, CA: University of California Press.

Brustein, William (1996) *The Logic of Evil: The Social Origins of the Nazi Party, 1925 to 1933*. New Haven, CT: Yale University Press.

Coleman, James S. (1990) *Foundations of Social Theory*. Cambridge, MA: Belknap Press.

Durkheim, Emile ([1893] 1947) *Division of Labor*. New York: The Free Press.

Eisenhardt, K. (1985) 'Control: Organizational and Economic Approaches', *Management Science*, 31: 134–49.

Elster, Jon (1990) 'Marxism, Functionalism, and Game Theory', in Sharon Zukin and Paul DiMaggio (eds), *Structures of Capital: The Social Organization of the Economy*. Cambridge: Cambridge University Press. pp. 87–117.

Frank, Robert H. (1988) *Passions within Reason: The Strategic Role of the Emotions*. New York: Norton.

Frey, R.G. and Morris, Christopher W. (1994) *Liability and Responsibility: Essays in Law and Morals*. Cambridge: Cambridge University Press.

Friedman, Jeffrey (ed.) (1995) *The Rational Choice Controversy: Economic Models of Politics Reconsidered*. New Haven, CT: Yale University Press.

Green, Donald P. and Shapiro, Ian (1994) *Pathologies of Rational Choice Theory: A Critique of Applications in Political Science*. New Haven, CT: Yale University Press.

Hardin, Russell (1982) *Collective Action*. Baltimore, MD: Johns Hopkins University Press.

Harsanyi, J.C. (1977) *Rational Behavior and Bargaining Equilibrium in Games and Social Situations*. New York: Cambridge University Press.

Hechter, Michael (1987) *Principles of Group Solidarity*. Berkeley, CA: University of California Press.

Hechter, Michael and Kanazawa, Satoshi (1997) 'Sociological Rational Choice Theory', *Annual Review of Sociology*, 23: 191–214.

Heckathorn, Douglas D. (1980) 'A Unified Model for Bargaining and Conflict', *Behavioral Science*, 25: 261–84.

Heckathorn, Douglas D. (1989) 'Collective Action and the Second-order Free-rider Problem', *Rationality and Society*, 1 (1): 78–100.

Heckathorn, Douglas D. (1996) 'Dynamics and Dilemmas of Collective Action', *American Sociological Review*, 61: 250–78.

Hirshleifer, Jack (1987) 'On Emotions as Guarantors of Threats and Promises', in *The Latest on the Best: Essays in Evolution and Optimality*. Cambridge, MA: MIT Press.

Hodgson, Geoff (1986) 'Behind Methodological Individualism', *Cambridge Journal of Economics*, 10: 211–24.

Hopcroft, Rosemary L. (1999) *Regions, Institutions,*

and Agrarian Change in European History. Ann Arbor: University of Michigan Press.

Huber, Joan (1997) 'The Place of Rational Choice in Sociology', *American Sociologist*, 28: 55–60.

Iannaccone, Laurence R. (1988) 'A Formal Model of Church and Sect', *American Journal of Sociology*, 94: 241–68.

Jankowski, Martin Sanchez (1991) *Islands in the Street: Gangs and American Urban Society*. Berkeley, CA: University of California Press.

Jensen, Michael C. and Meckling, William H. (1976) 'Theory of the Firm: Managerial Behavior, Agency Costs, and Ownership Structure', *Journal of Financial Economics*, 3: 305–60.

Johnson, Chalmers and Keehn, E.B. (1994) 'A Disaster in the Making: Rational Choice and Asian Studies', *National Interest*, 36: 14–22.

Kiser, Edgar and Schneider, Joachim (1994) 'Bureaucracy and Efficiency: An Analysis of Taxation in Early Modern Prussia', *American Sociological Review*, 59: 187–204.

Kuran, Timur (1995) *Private Truths, Public Lies: The Social Consequences of Preference Falsification*. Cambridge, MA: Harvard University Press.

Lawler, Edward J. and Yoon, Jeongkoo (1998) 'Network Structure and Emotion in Exchange Relations', *American Sociological Review*, 63: 871–94.

Lawler, Edward J., Ridgeway, Cecelia and Markovsky, Barry (1993) 'Structural Social Psychology and the Micro-Macro Problem', *Sociological Theory*, 11: 268–90.

Lindenberg, Seigwart and Frey, Bruno S. (1993) 'Alternatives, Frames, and Relative Prices: a Broader View of Rational Choice Theory', *Acta Sociologica*, 36: 191–209.

Lukes, Steven (1968) 'Methodological Individualism Reconsidered', *British Journal of Sociology*, 19: 119–29.

Macy, Michael W. (1990) 'Learning Theory and the Logic of Critical Mass', *American Sociological Review*, 55: 809–26.

Mansbridge, Jane J. (1990) 'The Rise and Fall of Self-Interest in the Explanation of Political Life', in Jane J. Mansbridge (ed.), *Beyond Self-Interest*. Chicago, IL: University of Chicago Press. pp. 3–22.

Marwell, Gerald and Oliver, Pamela (1993) *The Critical Mass in Collective Action: A Micro-Social Theory*. Cambridge: Cambridge University Press.

Miller, Gary J. (1992) *Managerial Dilemmas: The Political Economy of Hierarchy*. Cambridge: Cambridge University Press.

Morgan, Stephen L. (1998) 'Adolescent Educational Expectations: Rationalized, Fantasized, or Both?', *Rationality and Society*, 10: 131–62.

Nagel, Ernest (1953) 'Teleological Explanation and Teleological Systems', in Herbert Feigl and May Broadbeck (eds), *Readings in the Philosophy of Science*. New York, NY: Appleton-Century-Crofts. pp. 537–58.

Nee, Victor (1996) 'The Emergence of a Market Society: Changing Mechanisms of Stratification in China', *American Journal of Sociology*, 101: 908–49.

Nee, Victor and Ingram, Paul (1998) 'Embeddedness and Beyond: Institutions, Exchange, and Social Structure', in Mary C. Brinton and Victor Nee (eds), *The New Institutionalism in Sociology*. New York: Russell Sage Foundation. pp. 19–45.

Olson, Mancur (1965) *The Logic of Collective Action*. Cambridge, MA: Harvard University Press.

Opp, Karl-Dieter (1988) *The Rationality of Political Protest*. Boulder, CO: Westview Press.

Rambo, Eric H. (1999) 'Symbolic Interests and Meaningful Purposes: Conceiving Rational Choice as Cultural Theory', *Rationality and Society*, 11: 317–42.

Rubinstein, Ariel (1982) 'Perfect Equilibrium in a Bargaining Model', *Econometrica*, 50: 97–110.

Stark, Rodney (1999) 'A Theory of Revelations', *Journal for the Scientific Study of Religion*, 38: 287–308.

Smelser, Neil J. and Swedberg, Richard (1994) *The Handbook of Economic Sociology*. Princeton, NJ: Princeton University Press.

Swedberg, Richard (1998) *Max Weber and the Idea of Economic Sociology*. Princeton, NJ: Princeton University Press.

Taylor, Michael (1982) *Community, Anarchy, and Liberty*. Cambridge: Cambridge University Press.

Ullmann-Margalit, Edna (1977) *The Emergence of Norms*. Oxford: The Clarendon Press.

von Mises, Ludwig (1949) *Human Action: A Treatise on Economics*. London: William Hodge.

Waitzkin, Howard (1991) *The Politics of Medical Encounters*. New Haven: Yale University Press.

Watters, John K., Downing, Moher, Case, Patricia, Lorvick, Jennifer, Cheng, Yu-Teh and Fergusson, Bonnie (1990) 'AIDS Prevention for Intravenous Drug Users in the Community: Street-Based Education and Risk Behavior', *American Journal of Community Psychology*, 18: 587–96.

White, H. (1985) 'Agency as Control', in J. Pratt and R. Zeckhauser (eds), *Principals and Agents: The Structure of Business*. Boston: Harvard Business School Press.

Yamaguchi, Kazuo (1998) 'Rational-Choice Theories of Anticipatory Socialization and Anticipatory Non-Socialization', *Rationality and Society*, 10: 163–99.

22

Contemporary Feminist Theory

MARY F. ROGERS

Over the past forty or so years feminist theorists have advanced critical social theory along path-breaking lines. Challenges to liberal feminist theory, in particular, have stimulated note-worthy developments during this period. These challenges have taken most visible shape around postmodernism as an anti-Enlightenment per-spective, yet the most consequential resistance comes from multicultural and postcolonial theorists demanding attention (postmodernist or not) to racial/ethnic and other hierarchies.

Two other varieties of feminist theorizing have also challenged liberal feminist theory, namely, lesbian and psychoanalytic perspectives. Adrienne Rich's (1980) *lesbian continuum*, ranging from sexual to emotional bonds between women that exert priority in women's lives, raises issues that liberal feminist theory largely ignores or even resists. Similarly, feminist psychoanalytic perspectives such as Nancy Chodorow's (1978) or Jessica Benjamin's (1988, 1995) introduce conceptual and political baggage that liberal feminists often find problematic, if not repugnant. Thus, four forms of theoretical resistance to liberal feminist theory account, I argue, for the growing diversity and vitality of feminist theory.

THE LIBERAL CONTINUUM

Over the past several centuries Enlightenment values, such as freedom and rights, evolved into a politically foundational liberalism in North America and Western Europe. Gaining ascendance during the nineteenth century as a centrist ideology alongside socialism to its left and conservativism to its right (Wallerstein, 1995: 1), liberalism helped to spawn *first-wave feminism*, which eventually gained Western women the franchise. Although such liberal feminism has 'been a constant feature of modern societies' (Frazer, 1998: 52), even liberal versions of feminism involve a 'critique of the Enlightenment' (Waugh, 1998: 177). Enabled yet constrained by Enlightenment discourses, feminism has had an ambivalent connection with the liberalism rooted there. Kate Nash (1998: 1) sees ambivalence as 'highly productive for feminism', perhaps impelling transformative resistance to liberal feminist theory.

Also stimulating resistance has been the waning influence of liberalism itself. Having peaked between 1946 and 1968 (Wallerstein, 1995: 2), liberalism faced continual challenges in the wake of the 1960s. Second-wave feminism was perhaps its first serious challenger inasmuch as it reworked key liberal notions such as rights (for example, Okin, 1998) and public/private spheres (for example, Duncan, 1996; Pateman, 1979). By the 1980s, if not earlier, communitarianism and postmodernism had also emerged as serious challengers to the liberal hegemony in social theory, as had postcolonial social theory. During the 1990s the deepening crisis in liberalism (Digeser, 1995; McCallister, 1996; Ramsay, 1997) fueled further resistance to it.

All the while, liberal feminist theory continued wielding considerable influence. Carol Robb's (1998) work on woman-friendly economies or Arlie Russell Hochschild's (1989) on most women's second (domestic) shift of work are illustrative. What gets challenged in such theorizing is some fine print on the social contract, not its fundamental terms. Social theory, which has a long history of social critique, can accommodate such feminist theorizing. In effect, liberal feminist theory deflates the gendered character of social theory by rendering it less masculinist or androcentric. It mostly fails, however, to challenge bases of inequality other than the gender hierarchy, such as racial, sexual, or class hierarchies. Put differently, liberal feminist theory has a shape not unlike that of most social theory today, which reflects a 'relatively privileged' perspective as well as 'European cultural traditions' (Sprague, 1997: 95).

Yet liberal feminist theory is no one-size-fits-all knowledge. Heuristically, a *liberal continuum* makes sense insofar as it delineates diverse stances among feminist theorists who fundamentally accept institutionalized hierarchies other than the *gender order* (Connell, 1987). As Zillah Eisenstein (1981: 229) implies, a liberal feminist continuum comprises at least three groupings. At one end are *radical liberal* theorists; at the other end, *status quo liberal* theorists. Between these two groupings stand *progressive liberal* feminist theorists. What puts these feminist thinkers on the same terrain is that they retain liberal notions of 'freedom of choice, individualism, and equality of opportunity', even while disagreeing 'about the patriarchal, economic, and racial biases of these ideas' (Eisenstein, 1981: 229). Robb and Hochschild, for instance, occupy the middle ground on the liberal continuum, with Robb leaning more toward the radical liberal pole insofar as she takes class and sexual orientation as well as gender into sustained account.

In stark contrast to such reformist theorizing stand status quo liberal feminists whose work gets little attention within feminist theory. Camille Paglia (1992, 1994) and Elizabeth Fox-Genovese (1996) exemplify dramatically distinct versions of status quo liberal theorizing. Neither thinker gives women-centered attention to lesbians, straight women of color or low-income women and women with disabilities of whatever racial/ethnic group or sexual orientation. Terms such as exploitation, oppression and injustice serve no positive theoretical functions at this end of the liberal continuum, where 'postfeminism' is the order of the day now that equality of opportunity is supposedly in place.

At the radical liberal end of the continuum one finds feminist theorists who insist that feminism is about more than gender inasmuch as women make up substantial proportions of nearly every subordinate group in society, such as minimum-wage workers or welfare recipients. In large measure feminist theorists who focus on issues of race, class *and* gender occupy this part of the liberal continuum (see, for example, Dill, 1994; Gilkes, 1994; Hurtado, 1996; Mullings,

1994). Such theorists may also attend to sexuality, age or disability, but their main preoccupation is that triad of social formations.

Perhaps exemplifying this part of the continuum is Patricia Hill Collins. Collins (1990), who probes the situated knowledges available to those occupying institutional sites as outsiders, that is, as *outsiders-within*. Women of color laboring in white households illustrate the outsider-within perspective that Collins (1990: 95ff.) deploys in tandem with the notion of *safe spaces* to theorize African American women's struggles for self-definition. Of late, says Collins (1998), a new *politics of containment* uses surveillance-driven modes of controlling African American women, whether they be mothers on welfare or professors in academe. Collins (1998: 34, 35) sees racism, mixed with sexism and classism, in current trends toward privatization in the United States as 'market forces' appear to displace policy-makers and corporate executives as agents in inequality. Under these circumstances the public sphere increasingly functions as a site of subordination as well as surveillance. Calling for 'new forms of visionary pragmatism', Collins (1998: 228, 153) also calls for critical attention to the 'mutually constructing nature of systems of oppression'.

Earlier (1990) conceptualized as a *matrix of domination*, that web of interlocking hierarchies now commands Collins' (1998) attention as *intersectionality* (see Crenshaw 1991). Whichever term is used, that focus is capable of moving her beyond the liberal continuum, but for the most part it does not. At root, Collins' recurrent attention to social class, sexual orientation and other women of color besides African Americans remains secondary. That circumstance, coupled with Collins' failure to challenge hierarchy generically, leaves her on the liberal continuum, albeit at its left end.

ANTI-LIBERAL FEMINIST THEORY

African American feminists such as bell hooks and Audre Lorde go where Collins does not. They represent a strand of multicultural feminist theorizing that is more revolutionary than reformist. Even before African American feminism began establishing itself with such works as Barbara Smith's (1983) *Home Girls: A Black Feminist Anthology* (Kanneh, 1998: 91), this anti-liberal strand had been influential. During the 1960s and 1970s Angela Davis' activism and streetwise theorizing exemplified this strand, as did her later work (1981, 1998) insisting on social class as a central dynamic in African American women's lives.

Multicultural feminists like hooks (1989: 20, 22) theorize feminism as a transformative antidote to the 'politics of domination'; 'as liberation struggle'; 'as a part of the larger struggle to eradicate domination *in all its forms*' (emphasis added). Hooks (1989: 21, 22) gives priority to fighting gender oppression 'because it is that form of domination we are most likely to encounter in an ongoing way in everyday life'. Moreover, it infiltrates people's intimate, especially familial, relationships where care is supposed to predominate. All the while hooks consistently focuses on other hierarchies that also constrain people, including racial, class, sexual and age hierarchies. Her comprehensive analysis of social injustices also includes a great deal of attention to consumer culture and the corporate media as conduits of domination (hooks, 1993, 1994).

Lorde's framework is as multicultural as but narrower than hooks'. Typically writing as an African American lesbian feminist, Lorde (1984) insists on bringing social class to the fore alongside gender, sexuality and race. Like hooks, she is unafraid to criticize those of her white counterparts (liberal or not) whose privilege inscribes their feminist theorizing. Both Lorde and hooks, like Collins, theorize marginality as a site of potential resistance and positive self-definition. Unlike Collins, though, these anti-liberal theorists make patently clear their commitment to remaining outsiders, whether within or beyond mainstream structures like academe. (Yet 'insider' and 'outsider' are far from straightforward terms, as Susan Moller Okin (1998) and Diana Fuss (1991), among others, have theorized.) Thus, these theorists' work problematizes 'equal opportunity' and related liberal ideas more thoroughly than Collins and other radical liberal theorists do.

Multicultural feminist theorists thus perpetuate some anti-liberal values that found expression as second-wave feminism emerged in the 1960s in North America and Western Europe. Those second-wave feminist theorists who emerged out of *dissensus politics* (Piven and Cloward, 1997), such as anti-war and civil rights struggles, tended toward radical thinking (Echols, 1989). Other theorists emerged out of *consensus politics* (Piven and Cloward, 1997), comprising such developments as President Kennedy's appointment of a commission on the status of women in 1960. (Resonant with such political developments were cultural eventualities such as Betty Friedan's (1963) *The Feminine Mystique*.) These liberal-minded theorists came to predominate. Never, though, did they overcome resistance from other feminists whose discontent with the status quo ran wider and deeper.

Dissensus politics and anti-liberal values are also implied or espoused in postcolonial feminist theory, which like postcolonial theorizing in general, blurs distinctions among the center, the right and the left (Giroux, 1994: 149). Such theorizing involves cognitive *decolonization*, or 'unlearning historically determined habits of privilege and privation, of ruling and dependency' (Mohanty, 1995: 110). Postcolonial theorizing also involves critically examining social realities within 'the fields of transnational economic relations and diasporic identity constructions' (Grewal and Kaplan, 1994: 15). Postcolonial feminist theory has 'brought about a "worlding" of mainstream [that is, liberal] feminist theory' (Mills, 1998: 98). At the same time it has impelled feminists toward 'theoriz[ing] heterogeneity in place of binaries so that the complicated relationships between men and women of oppressed races and nationalities might be more accurately described' (Alcoff, 1996: 26).

Particularly influential among postcolonial feminist theorists is Gayatri Chakravorty Spivak (1993: 187), who, resonant with other anti-liberal theorists, sees the postcolonial person as an *outside/insider*. From that perspective Spivak problematizes much that liberal First World or Northern feminists take for granted. Spivak (1987: 130, 133) emphasizes that feminism cannot operate as a 'special-interest glamorization of mainstream discourse' whose 'academic inceptions' make it 'subject to correction by authoritative men'. She (1987: 136, 153) challenges First World feminists to confront the 'inbuilt colonialism of First World feminism toward the Third World'. For Spivak (1990: 42) and other postcolonial feminists, then, feminist theory necessitates 'the unlearning of one's privilege' so that one might be 'taken seriously' by the 'female constituency of the world' beyond academe. Spivak (1990: 102–3) thus theorizes with a view toward and concern for 'the one most consistently exiled from episteme', namely, 'the disenfranchised woman, . . . called the "gendered subaltern"' (cf. Narayan, 1998a, 1998b). In her own fashion she promotes a cognitively nomadic perspective much like that of Gloria Anzaldua's (1987) *mestiza consciousness*.

Such consciousness is a border-crossing, hybrid consciousness forged out of struggles to be both/and in the face of either/or geopolitical realities. Such border-crossing, even border-defying, consciousness sometimes finds parallel expression in lesbian feminist theorizing as well, albeit with primary reference to heteronormative rather than geopolitical boundaries. Often cast as and feeling like feminist outsiders-within, lesbian feminist theorists have created theoretical momentum around such matters as compulsory heterosexuality, heterosexuality as an institution, sadomasochistic sexual practices and separatism. Their theorizing makes an issue of how straight feminists' heterosexual privilege – deflated as it may be by their gender – infiltrates their work so as to erase, marginalize or exoticize lesbians.

Rich's (1980) delineation of *compulsory heterosexuality* concerns the diverse practices and penalties deployed to ensure that virtually everyone either become a practicing heterosexual or feel ambivalent or guilty for failing to become one. Just as the notion of compulsory hetero-sexuality de-naturalizes heterosexuality, so does *heterosexuality as an institution*. Like other insti-tutions, heterosexuality here gets theorized as a historically and culturally variable array of norms and practices associated with different-sex coupling. Wilkinson and Kitzinger (1993) have helped to lead the charge along this front, inspired in large measure by Rich's path-break-ing work.

Also pivotal along these lines has been Sarah Lucia Hoagland's theorizing. Hoagland proble-matizes heterosexual femininity by implying that in the end it amounts to a redundant phrase. She (1988: 7) sees 'heterosexualism' as a normal-ization of one person's dominance over another person and 'femininity' as a means of 'normal-iz[ing] female subordination'. Judith Butler (1990: 6), whose work we later examine, has also contributed to such theoretical advances with formulations like this: 'Taken to its logical limit, the sex/gender distinction suggests a radical discontinuity between sexed bodies and culturally constructed genders.' Butler thus presses forward along theoretical lines that lay bare the connections between gender and sexuality while rejecting the once commonplace distinction between sex as a physical phenom-enon and gender as a cultural one.

Sexual agency is also a matter that lesbian feminist theorists emphasize more sharply than their heterosexual counterparts. This difference is most evident with respect to sadomasochistic practices. While lesbian theorists themselves debate these practices, as a group they are more attuned to them than are straight women theorists. Gayle Rubin (1987, 1989) occupies a prominent position here, as do Pat Califa (1981, 1987) and various contributors to the Samois anthology *Coming to Power: Writings and Graphics on Lesbian S/M*. (Samois is a San Francisco-based lesbian s/m group.) These and other lesbian feminist theorists also see issues about sexual agency in practices such as pornography and safe-sex education.

Lisa Duggan (1995: 5), another theorist addressing sexual agency, sees sexual dissent as the core idea conjoining these and closely related sexual issues. By *sexual dissent* she means 'a concept that invokes a unity of speech, politics, and practices and forges a connection among sexual expressions, oppositional politics, and claims to public space'. With this conceptualiza-tion Duggan threatens to upset the liberal, feminist, (often) heterocentrist applecart. By linking sexual expressions with oppositional politics she both affirms and complicates a stance common among feminists. To wit, feminist theorists characteristically construct typologies of feminism as oppositional and political in varying degrees and forms. Further, they typically imply some connection between feminist values and (hetero)sexual practices, routinely problematizing feminists' heterosexual (and other) relationships. Lesbian feminist theorists like Duggan radically extend these characteristic stances by arguing for expanded rights to public sexual dissent (Duggan, 1995: 5), which unnerves some straight liberal feminists who balk at public displays – any 'displays' – of non-normative sexual practices (see LeMon-check, 1997).

In the end, some lesbian feminist theorists' advocacy of separatism most divides them from their liberal counterparts. Here we encounter *cultural feminism*, which also informs a great deal of *ecofeminist theory* focused broadly on how the domination of 'nature' correlates with that of women and other subordinated groups (Adams, 1993; Warren, 1994). Centered on the assumption that women and men are different enough to construct and inhabit distinctive cultural worlds, cultural feminism inherently opposes liberal feminism which typically empha-sizes the basic 'sameness' of women and men. Like liberal feminism, though, cultural feminism comes in various versions. Broadly, its 'strong' version emphasizes that women's characteristics are superior or preferable to men's. Adrienne Rich (1980) and Mary Daly (1978) were early proponents of strong cultural feminism, which not only valorizes what patriarchy has devalued but also advocates separatism, whether holisti-cally (separate communities) or partially (sepa-rate liturgies or schooling, for example).

'Weak' cultural feminism is less radical. It is not separatist and often leaves room for or even advocates that men adopt some of women's values and practices or at least accommodate women's ways across various institutional sites such as schools, workplaces and houses of worship. Here one finds feminist theorists such as Mary Field Belenky and her colleagues (1986) who argue that women's styles of learning and knowing are distinct from men's (also see Goldberger et al., 1996); Carol Gilligan (1982, 1995) who has traced the distinctive features of women's moral reasoning; Virginia Held (1993), whose 'feminist morality' rests on a critique not only of Enlightenment individualism but also of communitarian selfhood; and Sara Ruddick (1989), who theorizes that mothering gives most of the world's women a distinctive slant on everyday life and on politics, too.

Strong cultural feminists are likelier than weak cultural feminists to identify as lesbian feminists. By and large, the strong cultural feminists of interest here part company with theorists like Rubin and Duggan by advancing a cultural feminism centered on women's institution building in connection with an 'alternative culture'. As Verta Taylor and Leila Rupp (1998: 346, 347) go on to emphasize, in the 'sex wars' of the 1980s these cultural feminists came to be seen as 'antisex' (in contrast with feminists like Rubin who got portrayed as 'sex radicals'). Greta Gaard's (1997: 133) conceptualization of the *erotic* illustrates such cultural feminists' stances. She sees eroticism not only in sexuality but also in 'sensuality, spontaneity, passion, delight, and pleasurable stimulation'. Thus, lesbian feminist theorizing has contributed to, as well as contested, the warm, fuzzy sexuality often associated with middle-class women in modern Western cultures.

Besides reinforcing commonplace notions about women's sexuality, cultural feminism has reinforced the grounds of feminism during periods of feminist retrenchment or stasis. By theorizing 'belief in female difference, the practice of limited or total separatism, belief in the primacy of women's relationships, and the practice of feminist ritual', strong cultural feminists have bolstered the bases whereon 'women can claim feminism as a political identity' (Taylor and Rupp, 1998: 355). At the same time they challenged the 'sameness' thinking characteristic of liberal feminist theory.

Such thinking also gets challenged by psychoanalytic feminist theorists. As I (Rogers, 1998: 291) have pointed out elsewhere, theorists like Chodorow see a *maternal continuum* where those like Rich postulate a lesbian one. Broadly, Chodorow (1978) argues that the institutionalized division of childrearing labor in the heteronormative family ensures that women's and men's *unconscious* psychic structures will differentiate them in socially and psychologically consequential ways. Typically raised by mothers and destined to mother, women develop impressive relational skills, while men – needing to disidentify with their mothers (and other women) in order to become masculine – develop autonomy and deny their dependence on or interdependence with others. Chodorow (1978: 200, 203) argues that women wanting emotional closeness seek it in bonds with their children. Without a 'fundamental reorganization of parenting' (Chodorow, 1978: 215), women and men can never be equal, then. Overall, frame-

works like Chodorow's imply the need for fundamental institutional change more than frameworks like those of Collins and other radical liberal feminist theorists.

Though more subtly, Benjamin's work also implies the need for institutional changes, particularly changes in the knowledge systems whereby we claim to grasp human subjectivity. Interested foremostly in women's, especially mothers', subjectivity, Benjamin reorients the psychoanalytic perspective along lines that intersect with the work of feminist epistemologists and standpoint theorists, who will focus our attention before long. Benjamin (1988) argues, for example, that mothers have in common the fate of having their singular, irreplaceable subjectivity disregarded so that others might more readily ignore mothers' needs. Maternal subjectivity is elusive for having been ignored or denied even by 'good' daughters and sons. To illuminate the unique subjectivities – the full otherness – associated with women's mothering requires revamping psychoanalytic and related perspectives.

Benjamin (1997: 782, 284) recalls that 'psychoanalysis began as a marginal, radical enterprise' centered on subjectivity and concerned with 'what lies behind knowledge and values', especially 'psychic motives'. Believing that it could yet be a 'force of radical social critique', Benjamin (1997: 785, 789) aligns herself with postmodernist stances toward objectivity, subjectivity and knowledge. She believes that 'it may be possible to transcend the split between intellect and emotion, between subjectivity and objectivity'. Such transcendence is a common aspiration among feminist theorists, especially those identifying themselves as postmodernists or standpoint theorists.

POSTMODERNIST FEMINIST THEORY AND FEMINIST STANDPOINT THEORY

As I hinted earlier, postmodernism opposes liberalism as a modernist myopia, a failed experiment, an array of false hopes, a colonialist rationale. As with liberalism itself, postmodernism presents itself in multiple guises (see Lemert, 1997: 36–52). Whatever the version, postmodernism presupposes that some time during the twentieth century modernist values and dreams began losing their grip on people's consciousness. In their wake came an appetite for ambiguity, irony and paradox and a feel for how localized and situated our knowledge is in the end and for all practical purposes. As postmodernism gained ground, many feminist theorists developed love–hate or ambivalent relationships with it. Often fearful that post-modernist skepticism toward modern values such as equality might feed resistance to feminism, for example, some theorists (Hart-sock, 1990; Minnich, 1990) advocate skepticism toward postmodernist stances. Others embrace postmodernism, while still other feminist theorists carve out more nuanced reactions such as making their 'political project . . . one of discursive destabilization' (Gibson-Graham, 1996: 241).

Prominent among postmodernist feminist theorists are Judith Butler, Donna Haraway and Laurel Richardson. Some of Butler's (1990) most important work centers on showing how cultures make only certain identities 'intelligible' so that other enactments of identity get siphoned off the mainstream heap as abnormal, perverse, unsuccessful or weird. In Butler's hands identity is a performative phenomenon that is heavily regulated. Institutionalized regimes render some enactments of identity 'real' – that is, recognizable – versions of X, Y or Z and other enactments something *other than* versions of X, Y or Z. For example, only culturally approved ways of enacting womanhood get seen as expressions of femininity; other ways of enacting it get seen as selfishness, man-hating, feminist stridency, or bitchiness rather than as more ways of enacting womanhood and expressing 'femininity'. As Butler (1992: 15–16) sees it, 'part of the project of postmodernism . . . is to call into question the ways in which such 'examples' and 'paradigms' serve to subordinate and erase that which they seek to explain'. More generally, for Butler (1992: 15–16), 'Identity categories are never merely descriptive, but always normative, and as such, exclusionary.'

For Haraway (1993: 257, 258), feminist post-modernism or postmodernist feminism revolves around 'politics and epistemologies of location, positioning and situating, where partiality and not universality is the condition of being heard to make rational knowledge claims'. Her feminism favors 'the sciences and politics of interpretation, translation, stuttering, and the partially understood'. Haraway ([1985] 1990: 190–1) adopts irony both as a 'rhetorical strategy' and as a 'political method', and she puts the cyborg – a machine/organism hybrid – 'at the center of [her] ironic faith'. Yet that center also has modernist ingredients. Haraway (1997: 269) stresses, for instance, that 'valid witness depends not only on modesty but also on nurturing and acknowledging alliances with a lively array of others'.

Richardson's (1997: 55) theoretical projects revolve around 'refram[ing] sociological discourse as a feminist-postmodernist practice'. While interrogating narratives, Richardson

(1997: 57) looks at 'issues of representation', particularly at which hierarchies they reproduce. More than any other contemporary social theorist, Richardson (1988, 1990, 1992) has probed writing practices for their political baggage and transformative promise *and* experimented with diverse genres in her own theoretical endeavors. In constructing her 'feminist speaking position', Richardson (1997: 59, 123) thus cultivates a 'postmodern sensibility [that] celebrates multiplicity of method and multiple sites of contestation'.

Richardson's bold explorations of non-traditional genres for writing social theory puts her in the camp of feminist theorists committed to bursting representational boundaries as well as discipline-based ones. Some feminist theorists (Alfonso and Trigilio, 1997: 7–16) have, for example, published their work in dialogical form as electronic-mail exchanges. Others (for example, Rinehart, 1998) talk about feminist theorizing as a 'conversation'. At least two feminist social theorists – Katherine Gibson and Julie Graham – have done their collaborative theorizing using a combined-name pseudonym (J.K. Gibson-Graham) to designate the authorship of their texts. They then write substantially in the first-person *singular*! (Gibson-Graham, 1996). What Richardson and others are theorizing, in effect, are profound connections between narrative conventions and what can be said, who can credibly say it and who can hear it in meaningful, practical ways.

Mapping the terrain of feminist epistemology in resonant fashion are standpoint theorists such as Sandra Harding, Dorothy Smith and Nancy Hartsock. Patricia Hill Collins has also contributed to this body of feminist theorizing with her explorations of the situated knowledges and distinctive perspectives of African American women. Collins (1998: 195) refuses, however, to identify herself as a standpoint theorist despite her joining the three aforementioned standpoint theorists in responding to Susan Hekman's (1997: 341–65) critique of standpoint theory. Yet Collins' work illustrates Helen Longino's description of standpoint theory:

> By valorizing the perspectives uniquely *available* to those who are socially disadvantaged, standpoint theorists turn the tables on traditional epistemology; the ideal epistemic agent is not an unconditioned subject but the subject conditioned by the social experiences of oppression. (1993: 105; emphasis added)

As Longino implies, standpoint theorists assume not that subordinate social positioning determines consciousness but that it makes specific sorts of knowledge available as experiences of subordination get interwoven with pervasive exposure to hegemonic beliefs. To that extent, members are not cognitively interchangeable.

Yet as Sandra Harding (1991: 51) emphasizes, 'The methodology and epistemology of modern science assume that people are interchangeable as knowers.' Standpoint theorists like her reject that assumption in favor of some notion that 'the subject of feminist knowledge . . . must be multiple and contradictory' (Harding, 1991: 284). Harding (in Hirsh and Olson, 1995: 25) sees standpoint theory as both drawing from and rejecting various Enlightenment theories but having clearly begun with Marxian epistemology. Her own work has centered on diverse women's standpoints as correctives to (non-feminist) science. Harding (1986: 10) aims to rid the scientific world of androcentrism, not 'systematic inquiry'.

Smith's concerns are similar, namely, those

> practices of thinking and writing . . . that convert what people experience directly in their everyday/everynight world into forms of knowledge in which people as subjects disappear and in which their perspectives on their own experiences are transposed and subdued by the magisterial forms of objectifying discourse. (1990a: 4)

Like other feminist standpoint theorists, Smith (1990b: 1) sees 'objectified knowledges' as 'essential constituents' of what she calls the *relations of ruling* in modern societies. Institutionalized, hegemonic knowledge is thus a tool of domination and a precious one at that. For Smith (1990b: 11) and other feminist standpoint theorists, women's lived experiences provide correctives to hegemonic texts 'as constituents of ongoing social relations into which our own practices of reading enter us'. Ultimately, women's standpoints disturb not only 'ruling' texts but also commonplace ways of reading.

More than other standpoint theorists, Hartsock (1998b: 406) emphasizes that both Marxian and feminist standpoint theories presuppose that what is most readily available to consciousness are the notions of dominant groups in society. Moreover, power relations infiltrate perceptions of and judgements about reality, knowledge and objectivity. Following Marx, Hartsock (1998b: 408) sees the criteria for assessing knowledge as ethical and political as well as epistemological. She (1998b: 410) also stresses that subordinated members cannot flatly reject hegemonic versions of the world as 'false'. Instead, 'the understanding *available* to the oppressed must be struggled for' (emphasis added) until a distinctive sort of 'privileged knowledge' takes shape, namely, knowledge 'that takes nothing of the dominant culture as self-evidently true' (1998b: 410, 411).

Thus, 'a standpoint is not generated unproblematically by simple existence in a particular social location' (Hartsock, 1998a: 237). A standpoint 'represents an achievement' most likely to come from members of dominated groups whose experiences of 'inversions, distortions, and erasures . . . can be epistemologically constitutive' (Hartsock, 1998a: 229, 241). From this perspective, social theory is a kind of 'appropriation, a way of taking up and building on our experience' (1998a: 39). The more inclusive or multicultural it is, the more rigorous and useful our theorizing will be. As Joy James (1993: 34) puts it, 'The point is to stand at the crossroads' or, to invoke earlier terminology, to cultivate intersectional thinking. In Hartsock's (1998a: 58) view, our 'differences' thus provide 'potential grounds for creativity, connection, and complementarity', especially as we struggle against 'truths' handed to us rather than forged from our own experiences.

The matter of struggling to express the truth of one's own experiences *against* the ready-made truths inherent in the relations of ruling raises among many feminists the issue of generations. Over the past decade much has been said, especially in the corporate media, about young women's apparent disidentification with feminism, signified mostly (and simplistically) by their common unwillingness to call themselves 'feminists'. Yet 'postfeminist' stances find clearest expression in polemical works like self-identified feminist Katie Roiphe's (1993) *The Morning After*. Among most young women a more complex stance toward feminism seems to predominate. In large measure that complexity derives from feminism's oppositional character. As Lisa Maria Hoagland (1994: 21) reminds us, 'To stand opposed to your culture, to be critical of institutions, behaviors, discourses – when it is clearly *not* in your immediate interest to do so – asks a lot of a young person.'

In other words, the struggle for an antihegemonic standpoint is particularly hard for young women. In addition, 'once equal access to jobs, pay, credit, and education was legislated, once abortion was at least protected by law and women could begin to take more control of their lives' (Tobias, 1997: 171), a diversification of feminist stances, especially among younger women, was likely. Nevertheless, energized by the contradictions and ironies of their own experiences as well as second-wave feminist ideas, many young women are diversely positioning themselves within the *third-wave feminism* being shaped by post-Baby Boom women born after 1964 and Generation X women born even later. To be sure, their voices are seldom heard in academe or on the evening news, but these feminist voices resound in 'transnational popular cultural productions such as comics, zines, music videos, and films' (Bhavnani et al.,

1998: 578). For third-wave feminists, in fact, 'the embrace of popular culture is tantamount to a kind of populism' (Orr, 1997: 41). Increasingly, too, third-wave feminists' voices are finding some limited academic sponsorship, for example, the University of Minnesota Press' *Third Wave Agenda: Being Feminist, Doing Feminism* (Heywood and Drake, 1997). Not surprisingly, then, feminist scholars such as Nancy Whittier (1995: 2–3, 25) consider 'postfeminism' a sociopolitical myth that obfuscates 'the continual infusion of new participants who simultaneously challenge and carry on the feminist legacy'.

Whittier's perception holds up well now, even in academic circles. In the late 1990s at least two feminist journals devoted entire issues to third-wave developments. *Signs* (Spring, 1998) focused its issue on 'feminisms and youth cultures'. There, for example, Kelly O'Neill (1998: 611, 615), then the director of a 'nonprofit organization run for and by young women (from thirteen to twenty-four years old)', notes the age biases within feminist organizations and sees much mentoring as 'a one-way, patronizing, class-based approach' that often serves as a mechanism of control. Such stances illustrate how young women's struggles can constitute a distinctive standpoint that both carries on and contests their feminist heritage.

The third-wave issue of *Hypatia* also illustrates the continuities and contestations linking second- and third-wave feminisms. In that issue Cathryn Bailey (1997: 25) theorizes that young women's standpoints may illuminate the lived meanings of feminist identity in a society where 'postfeminism' has been widely declared. Moreover, forging a feminist identity today may necessitate 'navigating feminism's contradictions' (Orr, 1997: 35) more than older feminists had to, since the latter grouping inherited a less developed legacy. Older feminists were also likelier to theorize, at least initially, on the basis of substantial activism, whereas younger feminists often begin with theory that they encounter in 'institutional space' (Siegel, 1997: 62). In any event generational differences among feminists appear to be significant but not yet well understood (Findlen, 1995).

MATERIALIST FEMINISMS AND FEMINIST STATE THEORY

Within as well as beyond feminism, multiplicity is the order of the day. Feminist theorists grapple with it, as we have seen, using such concepts as 'matrix of domination', 'intersectionality', and 'relations of ruling'. Yet the multiplicity representing a site of theoretical struggle and progress typically centers on gender, race and ethnicity, with sexual orientation getting only secondary attention outside of lesbian feminist theory. Age, too, mostly gets relegated to supposedly special-interest theorists such as those currently shaping the third wave, and disability gets only sporadic attention within feminist theory.

To my way of thinking, though, the single most consequential gap in feminist theory is the absence of *sustained, detailed* attention to social class. To be sure, a rich feminist literature on low-income women, including mothers on welfare, does exist, but it comprises mostly empirical studies (Edin and Lein, 1997; Polakow, 1993) of low-income mothers and their children. When one looks for feminist theories of social class, one finds little. Less ambitious theoretical works are also in short supply, for example, theoretical works on interclass interactions among women, on the exploitation of lower-income by higher-income women, on the politics of childcare as a class-skewed women's issue, or on the class origins of influential feminist theorists. To my ear the relative silence about women and class among feminist theorists is debilitating. Particularly rankling are some theorists' swift mention of their 'middle-class' status among their litany of standpoint-related self-attributions, as if 'middle class' meant much of anything besides 'not poor' and 'not wealthy'. Since I am speaking in relative terms, the picture I sketch is partly impressionistic. Yet it repeatedly strikes me that feminist theorists need to catch up with feminist empiricists in shedding light on social class.

What this overall state of affairs amounts to is the historically diminishing role of materialist feminisms among First World or Northern feminist theorists (cf. Jackson, 1998: 25). Materialist concerns have not lost ground across the board, however, as the 'new phenomenologies of embodiment' (Alcoff, 1996: 21) advanced by Iris Marion Young (1990), Sandra Lee Bartky (1990), and to a lesser extent Susan Bordo (1993) illustrate. For the most part, though, Marxian, socialist and other materialist feminisms exhibit considerably more vitality in other parts of the world (Chinchilla, 1991; Hennessey and Ingraham, 1997). Beyond the First World, in other words, no 'cultural turn' in feminist theory (Barrett, 1992) is evident. Even in the First World, though, that turn has been sharper in some areas of feminist theorizing than in others. Feminist state theories (for example, Haney, 1996) and feminist jurisprudence (for example, Fineman, 1995) neither turn away from material realities and social structures in favor of culture nor consistently give social class secondary attention.

In particular, (socialist-)feminist political theorizing about whether patriarchy and capitalism represent a single system or dual-systems of domination has tended to keep class issues – that is, issues of production, profit, and capitalist power – at the fore (Brenner and Laslett, 1991). Similarly, theorizing about the welfare state, wherein women occupy distinctive positions both as employees and recipients, typically includes attention to social class. Nancy Fraser's (1988) theorizing about 'rights' and 'needs' is illustrative. In the political sphere 'rights' rhetoric often earmarks 'deserving', higher-class individuals, while 'needs' rhetoric targets undeserving, lower-class individuals. The latter individuals, disproportionately women, exhibit visible dependence evocative of scorn, while the former individuals, disproportionately men, are rarely *seen* as dependent at all. Linda Gordon (1990: 10) points out that in spite of these woefully gender-skewed perceptions non-feminist scholars largely ignore gender in their analyses of the welfare state.

What more generally gets ignored, even among feminist theorists, are the diffuse, complex connections between gender and social class – connections between gender and career trajectories, single motherhood and downward social mobility, gender and career planning, and so forth. Yet the intersections between gender and social class are at least as consequential as those between gender and race or gender and disability. Thus, feminist theorists cannot remain softspoken or relatively silent about social class. In particular, they cannot in good faith refuse to theorize poverty as 'the radical, unrepresentable, suppressed other to bourgeois pleasure' (Ebert, 1996: 121). Disproportionately women's burden, albeit in different ways around the planet, poverty is in my view feminist theorists' most promising, pressing topic in the new millennium. Much feminist theory and debate already implies the economic ramifications of being feminine, that is, enacting womanhood in institutionally mandated ways. Theorizing about the economic vulnerabilities of single mothers, the demise of a 'family wage', the nature of 'work', the financial ramifications of divorce, the feminization of poverty, comparable worth, sexual harassment and other matters implies that people's economic prospects and outcomes – thus, their class positions – are profoundly gendered.

A theoretical focus on poverty, including attention to the working poor, would perhaps bring the insights of all this extant work into a bold, path-breaking framework centered on the economic sanctions that keep women subordinated to men. With poverty seen as the ultimate such sanction, other economic penalties take on significance as key elements in the relations of ruling. In the end well-founded anxieties about downward social mobility – often soft-pedaled as a 'lifestyle change' – may well have kept modern women subordinated more than feminist theory has yet delineated. Exploring that possibility may catapult feminist theorists of the twenty-first century into the limelight as they continue demasculinizing the materialist legacy that social theorists since Marx have both carried forward and resisted.

REFERENCES

Adams, Carol J. (ed.) (1993) *Ecofeminism and the Sacred*. New York: Continuum.

Alcoff, Linda Martin (1996) 'Feminist Theory and Social Science: New Knowledges, New Epistemologies', in Nancy Duncan (ed.), *Bodyspace: Destabilizing Geographies of Gender and Sexuality*. London: Routledge. pp. 13–27.

Alfonso, Aita and Trigilio, Jo (1997) 'Surfing the Third Wave: A Dialogue Between Two Third Wave Feminists', *Hypatia: A Journal of Feminist Philosophy*, 12 (3): 7–16.

Anzaldua, Gloria (1987) *Borderlands/La Frontera: The New Mestiza*. San Francisco: Aunt Lute Books.

Bailey, Cathryn (1997) 'Making Waves and Drawing Lines: The Politics of Defining the Vicissitudes of Feminism', *Hypatia: A Journal of Feminist Philosophy*, 12 (3): 17–28.

Barrett, Michele (1992) 'Words and Things: Materialism and Method in Contemporary Feminist Analysis', in Michele Barrett and Anne Phillips (eds), *Destabilizing Theory*. Stanford, CA: Stanford University Press.

Bartky, Sandra Lee (1990) *Femininity and Domination: Studies in the Phenomenology of Oppression*. New York: Routledge.

Belenky, Mary Field, McVicker Clinchy, Blythe, Goldberger, Nancy Rule and Mattuch Tarule, Jill (1986) *Women's Ways of Knowing: The Development of Self, Voice, and Mind*. New York: Basic Books.

Benjamin, Jessica (1988) *The Bonds of Love: Psychoanalysis, Feminism, and the Problem of Domination*. New York: Pantheon.

Benjamin, Jessica (1995) *Like Subjects, Love Objects: Essays on Recognition and Sexual Difference*. New Haven, CT: Yale University Press.

Benjamin, Jessica (1997) 'Psychoanalysis as a Vocation', *Psychoanalytic Dialogues*, 7 (6): 781–802.

Bhavnani, Kum-Kum, Kent, Kathryn R. and Winddance Twine, Frances (1998) 'Editorial', *Signs*, 23 (3): 575–83.

Bordo, Susan (1993) *Unbearable Weight: Feminism, Western Culture, and the Body*. Berkeley, CA: University of California Press.

Brenner, Johanna and Laslett, Barbara (1991) 'Gender, Social Reproduction, and Women's Self-Organization: Considering the U.S. Welfare State', *Gender & Society*, 5 (3): 311–33.

Butler, Judith (1990) *Gender Trouble: Feminism and the Subversion of Identity*. New York: Routledge.

Butler, Judith (1992) 'Contingent Foundations: Feminism and the Question of "Postmodernism"', in Judith Butler and Joan W. Scott (eds), *Feminists Theorize the Political*. New York: Routledge.

Califa, Pat (1981) 'Feminism and Sadomasochism', *Heresies*, 3 (4): 30–4.

Califa, Pat (1987) 'A Personal View of the History of the Lesbian S/M Community and Movement in San Francisco', in Samois (ed.), *Coming to Power: Writings and Graphics on Lesbian S/M*. Boston, MA: Alyson Publications. pp. 245–82.

Chinchilla, Norma Stoltz (1991) 'Marxism, Feminism, and the Struggle for Democracy in Latin America', *Gender & Society*, 5 (3): 291–310.

Chodorow, Nancy (1978) *The Reproduction of Mothering: Psychoanalysis and the Sociology of Gender*. Berkeley, CA: University of California Press.

Collins, Patricia Hill (1990) *Black Feminist Thought: Knowledge, Consciousness, and the Politics of Empowerment*. New York: Routledge.

Collins, Patricia Hill (1998) *Fighting Words: Black Women and the Search for Justice*. Minneapolis: University of Minnesota Press.

Connell, R.W. (1987) *Gender and Power: Society, the Person and Sexual Politics*. Stanford, CA: Stanford University Press.

Crenshaw, Kimberle Williams (1991) 'Mapping the Margins: Intersectionality, Identity, Politics, and Violence Against Women of Color', *Stanford Law Review*, 43 (6): 1241–99.

Daly, Mary (1978) *Gyn-Ecology: The Metaethics of Radical Feminism*. Boston, MA: Beacon.

Davis, Angela Y. (1981) *Women, Race & Class*. New York: Random House.

Davis, Angela Y. (1998) *Blues Legacies and Black Feminism: Gertrude (Ma) Rainey, Bessie Smith, and Billie Holiday*. New York: Pantheon Books.

Digeser, Peter (1995) *Our Politics, Our Selves? Liberalism, Identity, and Harm*. Princeton, NJ: Princeton University Press.

Dill, Bonnie Thornton (1994) 'Fictive Kin, Paper Sons and *Compadrazgo*: Women of Color and the Struggle for Family Survival', in Maxine Baca Zinn and Bonnie Thornton Dill (eds), *Women of Color in U.S. Society*. Philadelphia: Temple University Press. pp. 149–70.

Duggan, Lisa (1995) 'Introduction', in Lisa Duggan and Nan D. Hunter (eds), *Sex Wars: Sexual Dissent and Political Culture*. New York: Routledge. pp. 1–15.

Duncan, Nancy (1996) 'Renegotiating Gender and Sexuality in Public and Private Spheres', in Nancy Duncan (ed.), *Bodyspace: Destabilizing Geographies of Gender and Sexuality*. London: Routledge. pp. 127–45.

Ebert, Teresa L. (1996) *Ludic Feminism and After: Postmodernism, Desire, and Labor in Late Capitalism*. Ann Arbor, MI: University of Michigan Press.

Echols, Alice (1989) *Daring to Be Bad: Radical Feminism in America, 1967–1975*. Minneapolis: University of Minnesota Press.

Edin, Kathryn and Lein, Laura (1997) *Making Ends Meet: How Single Mothers Survive Welfare and Low-Wage Work*. New York: Russell Sage Foundation.

Eisenstein, Zillah R. (1981) *The Radical Future of Liberal Feminism*. New York and London: Longman.

Findlen, Barbara (ed.) (1995) *Listen Up: Voices from the Next Feminist Generation*. Seattle: Seal Press.

Fineman, Martha Albertson (1995) *The Neutered Mother, the Sexual Family, and Other Twentieth Century Tragedies*. New York: Routledge.

Fox-Genovese, Elizabeth (1996) *'Feminism Is Not the Story of My Life': How Today's Feminist Elite Has Lost Touch with the Real Concerns of Women*. New York: Doubleday.

Fraser, Nancy (1988) 'Talking About Needs', *Public Culture Bulletin*, 1 (1): 44–57.

Frazer, Elizabeth (1998) 'Feminist Political Theory', in Stevi Jackson and Jackie Jones (eds), *Contemporary Feminist Theories*. New York: New York University Press. pp. 50–61.

Friedan, Betty (1963) *The Feminine Mystique*. New York: Norton.

Fuss, Diana (1991) 'Inside/Out', in Diana Fuss (ed.), *Inside/Out: Lesbian Theories, Gay Theories*. New York: Routledge.

Gaard, Greta (1997) 'Toward a Queer Ecofeminism', *Hypatia*, 12 (1): 114–37.

Gibson-Graham, J.K. (1996) 'Reflections on Postmodern Feminist Social Research', in Nancy Duncan (ed.), *Bodyspace: Destabilizing Geographies of Gender and Sexuality*. London: Routledge.

Gilkes, Cheryl Townsend (1994) '"If It Wasn't for the Women . . .": African American Women, Community Work, and Social Change', in Maxine Baca Zinn and Bonnie Thornton Dill (eds), *Women of Color in US Society*. Philadelphia: Temple University Press.

Gilligan, Carol (1982) *In a Different Voice: Psychological Theory and Women's Development*. Cambridge, MA: Harvard University Press.

Gilligan, Carol (1995) 'Hearing the Difference: Theorizing Connection', *Hypatia*, 10 (2): 120–7.

Giroux, Henry A. (1994) *Disturbing Pleasures: Learning Popular Culture*. New York: Routledge.

Goldberger, Nancy, Tarule, Jill, Clinchy, Blythe and Belenky, Mary (eds) (1996) *Knowledge, Difference, and Power: Essays Inspired by Women's Ways of Knowing*. New York: Basic Books.

Gordon, Linda (1990) 'The New Feminist Scholarship on the Welfare State', in Linda Gordon (ed.), *Women, the State, and Welfare*. Madison, WI: University of Wisconsin Press.

Grewal, Inderpal and Kaplan, Caren (1994) 'Introduction: Transnational Feminist Practices and Questions of Postmodernity', in Inderpal Grewal and Caren Kaplan (eds), *Scattered Hegemonies:*

Postmodernity and Transnational Feminist Practices. Minneapolis: University of Minnesota Press.

Haney, Lynne (1996) 'Homeboys, Babies, Men in Suits: The State and the Reproduction of Male Dominance', *American Sociological Review*, 61 (5): 759–78.

Haraway, Donna ([1985] 1990) 'A Manifesto for Cyborgs: Science, Technology, and Socialist Feminism in the 1980s', in Linda J. Nicholson (ed.), *Feminism/Postmodernism.* New York: Routledge.

Haraway, Donna (1993) 'Situated Knowledges: The Science Question in Feminism and the Privilege of Partial Perspective', in Evelyn Fox Keller and Helen E. Longino (eds), *Feminism and Science.* Oxford and New York: Oxford University Press.

Haraway, Donna (1997) *Modest_Witness@Second_ Millennium.FemaleMan_Meets_OncoMouse: Feminism and Technoscience.* New York: Routledge.

Harding, Sandra (1986), *The Science Question in Feminism.* Ithaca, NY: Cornell University Press.

Harding, Sandra (1991) *Whose Science? Whose Knowledge? Thinking from Women's Lives* . Ithaca, NY: Cornell University Press.

Hartsock, Nancy C.M. (1998a) *The Feminist Standpoint Revisited and Other Essays.* Boulder, CO: Westview Press.

Hartsock, Nancy (1998b) 'Marxist Feminist Dialectics for the 21st Century', *Science & Society*, 62 (3): 400–13.

Hartsock, Nancy C.M. (1990) 'Foucault on Power: A Theory for Women?', in Linda J. Nicholson (ed.), *Feminism/Postmodernism.* New York: Routledge.

Hekman, Susan (1997) 'Truth and Method: Feminist Standpoint Theory Revisited', *Signs: A Journal of Women in Culture and Society*, 22 (2): 341–65.

Held, Virginia (1993) *Feminist Morality: Transforming Culture, Society, and Politics.* Chicago: University of Chicago Press.

Hennessey, Rosemary and Ingraham, Chrys (1997) 'Introduction: Reclaiming Anticapitalist Feminism', in Rosemary Hennessey and Chrys Ingraham (eds), *Materialist Feminism: A Reader in Class, Difference, and Women's Lives.* New York: Routledge.

Heywood, Leslie and Drake, Jennifer (1997) *Third Wave Agenda: Being Feminist, Doing Feminism.* Minneapolis: University of Minnesota Press.

Hirsh, Elizabeth and Olson, Gary A. (1995) 'Starting from Marginalized Lives: A Conversation with Sandra Harding', in Gary A. Olson and Elizabeth Hirsh (eds), *Women Writing Culture.* Albany, NY: State University of New York Press. pp. 3–42.

Hoagland, Lisa Maria (1994) 'Fear of Feminism: Why Young Women Get the Willies', *Ms.*, 5 (3): 18–21.

Hoagland, Sarah Lucia (1988) *Lesbian Ethics: Toward New Value.* Palo Alto, CA: Institute of Lesbian Studies.

Hochschild, Arlie Russell (1989) *The Second Shift: Working Parents and the Revolution at Home.* New York: Viking.

hooks, bell (1989) *Talking Back: Thinking Feminist, Thinking Black.* Boston, MA: South End Press.

hooks, bell (1993) *Sisters of the Yam: Black Women and Self-Recovery.* Boston, MA: South End Press.

hooks, bell (1994) *Outlaw Culture: Resisting Representations.* New York: Routledge.

Hurtado, Aida (1996) *The Color of Privilege: Three Blasphemies on Race and Feminism.* Ann Arbor, MI: University of Michigan Press.

Jackson, Stevi (1998) 'Feminist Social Theory', in Stevi Jackson and Jackie Jones (eds), *Contemporary Feminist Theories.* New York: New York University Press. pp. 15–33.

Kanneh, Kadiatu (1998) 'Black Feminisms', in Stevi Jackson and Jackie Jones (eds), *Contemporary Feminist Theories.* New York: New York University Press. pp. 86–97.

Kaplan, E. Ann (1997) 'Introduction 2: Feminism, Aging, and Changing Paradigms', in Devoney Looser and E. Ann Kaplan (eds), *Generations: Academic Feminists in Dialogue.* Minneapolis: University of Minnesota Press. pp. 13–54.

Lemert, Charles (1997) *Postmodernism Is Not What You Think.* New York: Blackwell.

LeMoncheck, Linda (1997) *Loose Women, Lecherous Men: A Feminist Philosophy of Sex.* New York: Oxford University Press.

Longino, Helen E. (1993) 'Subjects, Power, and Knowledge: Description and Prescription in Feminist Philosophies of Science', in Linda Alcoff and Elizabeth Potter (eds), *Feminist Epistemologies.* New York: Routledge. pp. 101–20.

Lorde, Audre (1984) *Sister Outsider: Essays and Speeches.* Freedom, CA: The Crossing Press.

McAllister, Ted V. (1996) *Revolt Against Modernity: Leo Strauss, Eric Voegelin, and the Search for a Postliberal Order.* Lawrence, KS: University Press of Kansas.

Mills, Sara (1998) 'Post-Colonial Feminist Theory', in Stevi Jackson and Jackie Jones (eds), *Contemporary Feminist Theories.* New York: New York University Press. pp. 98–112.

Minnich, Elizabeth Kamarck (1990) *Transforming Knowledge.* Philadelphia: Temple University Press.

Mohanty, Satya P. (1995) 'Colonial Legacies, Multicultural Futures: Relativism, Objectivity, and the Challenge of Otherness', *PMLA*, 110 (1): 108–18.

Mullings, Leith (1994) 'Images, Ideology, and Women of Color', in Maxine Baca Zinn and Bonnie Thornton Dill (eds), *Women of Color in US Society.* Philadelphia: Temple University Press. pp. 265–90.

Narayan, Uma (1998a) 'Essence of Culture and a Sense of History: A Feminist Critique of Cultural Essentialism', *Hypatia*, 13 (2): 86–106.

Narayan, Uma (1998b) 'The Project of Feminist Epistemology: Perspectives from a Non-Western Feminist', in Mary F. Rogers (ed.), *Contemporary Feminist Theory: A Text/Reader.* New York: McGraw-Hill. pp. 82–8.

Nash, Kate (1998) *Universal Difference: Feminism and*

the Liberal Undecidability of 'Women'. London: Macmillan.

Newton, Esther and Shirley Walton (1989) 'The Misunderstanding Toward a More Precise Sexual Vocabulary', in Carole S. Vance (ed.), *Pleasure and Danger: Exploring Female Sexuality.* London: Pandora Press.

Okin, Susan Moller (1998) 'Feminism, Women's Human Rights, and Cultural Differences', *Hypatia*, 13 (2): 32–52.

O'Neill, Kelly (1998) 'No Adults Are Pulling the Strings and We Like It That Way', *Signs*, 23 (3): 611–18.

Orr, Catherine M. (1997) 'Changing the Currents of the Third Wave', *Hypatia*, 12 (3): 29–45.

Paglia, Camille (1992) *Sex, Art, and American Culture: Essays.* New York: Vintage Books.

Paglia, Camille (1994) *Vamps and Tramps: New Essays.* New York: Vintage Books.

Pateman, Carole (1979) *The Problem of Political Obligation: A Critical Analysis of Liberal Theory.* Chichester and New York: John Wiley & Sons.

Piven, Frances Fox and Cloward, Richard A. (1997) *The Breaking of the American Social Compact.* New York: The New Press.

Polakow, Valerie (1993) *Lives on the Edge: Single Mothers and Their Children in the Other America.* Chicago: University of Chicago Press.

Ramsay, Maureen (1997) *What's Wrong with Liberalism? A Radical Critique of Liberal Political Philosophy.* London: Leicester University Press.

Rich, Adrienne (1980) 'Compulsory Heterosexuality and Lesbian Existence', *Signs*, 5: 631–60.

Richardson, Laurel (1988) 'The Collective Story: Postmodernism and the Writing of Sociology', *Sociological Focus*, 21: 199–208.

Richardson, Laurel (1990) *Writing Strategies: Reaching Diverse Audiences.* Thousand Oaks, CA: Sage.

Richardson, Laurel (1992) 'The Consequences of Poetic Representation: Writing the Other, Rewriting the Self', in Carolyn Ellis and Michael G. Flaherty (eds), *Investigating Subjectivity: Research on Lived Experience.* Thousand Oaks, CA: Sage. pp. 125–40.

Richardson, Laurel (1997) *Fields of Play: Constructing an Academic Life.* New Brunswick, NJ: Rutgers University Press.

Rinehart, Jane A. (1998) 'Feminist Theorizing as a Conversation: The Connections between Thinking, Teaching, and Political Action', *Text and Performance Quarterly*, 18 (1): 59–89.

Robb, Carol S. (1998) 'Principles for a Woman-Friendly Economy', in Mary F. Rogers (ed.), *Contemporary Feminist Theory: A Text/Reader.* New York: McGraw-Hill. pp. 272–82.

Rogers, Mary F. (1998) 'Partnering, Parenting, and Family Making', in Mary F. Rogers (ed.), *Contemporary Feminist Theory: A Text/Reader.* New York: McGraw-Hill. pp. 283–97.

Rogers, Mary F. (ed.) (1998) *Contemporary Feminist Theory: A Text/Reader.* New York: McGraw-Hill.

Roiphe, Katie (1993) *The Morning After: Sex, Fear and Feminism on Campus.* Boston, MA: Little, Brown and Company.

Rubin, Gayle (1987) 'The Leather Menace: Comments on Politics and S/M', in Samois (ed.), *Coming to Power: Writings and Graphics on Lesbian S/M.* Boston: Alyson Publications.

Rubin, Gayle (1989) 'Thinking Sex: Notes for a Radical Theory of the Politics of Sexuality', in Carole S. Vance (ed.), *Pleasure and Danger: Exploring Female Sexuality.* London: Pandora Press.

Ruddick, Sara (1989) *Maternal Thinking.* Boston, MA: Beacon Press.

Siegel, Deborah L. (1997) 'The Legacy of the Personal: Generating Theory in Feminism's Third Wave', *Hypatia*, 12 (3): 46–75.

Smith, Barbara (ed.) (1983) *Home Girls: A Black Feminist Anthology.* New York: Kitchen Table Women of Color Press.

Smith, Dorothy E. (1990a) *The Conceptual Practices of Power: A Feminist Sociology of Knowledge.* Boston, MA: Northeastern University Press.

Smith, Dorothy E. (1990b) *Texts, Facts, and Femininity: Exploring the Relations of Ruling.* New York: Routledge.

Spivak, Gayatri Chakravorty (1987) *In Other Worlds: Essays in Cultural Politics.* New York: Methuen.

Spivak, Gayatri Chakravorty (1990) *The Post-Colonial Critic: Interviews, Strategies, Dialogues* (ed. Sarah Harasym). New York: Routledge.

Spivak, Gayatri Chakravorty (1993) *Outside in the Teaching Machine.* New York: Routledge.

Sprague, Joey (1997) 'Holy Men and Big Guns: The Can(n)on in Society Theory', *Gender & Society*, 11 (1): 88–107.

Taylor, Verta and Rupp, Leila J. (1998) 'Women's Culture and Lesbian Feminist Activism: A Reconsideration of Cultural Feminism', in Mary F. Rogers (ed.), *Contemporary Feminist Theory: A Text/Reader.* New York: McGraw-Hill. pp. 346–63.

Tobias, Sheila (1997) *Faces of Feminism: An Activist's Reflections on the Women's Movement.* Boulder, CO: Westview Press.

Wallerstein, Immanuel (1995) *After Liberalism.* New York: The New Press.

Warren, Karen J. (ed.) (1994) *Ecological Feminism.* New York: Routledge.

Waugh, Patricia (1998) 'Postmodernism and Feminism', in Stevi Jackson and Jackie Jones (eds), *Contemporary Feminist Theories.* New York: New York University Press.

Whittier, Nancy (1995) *Feminist Generations: The Persistence of the Radical Women's Movement.* Philadelphia: Temple University Press.

Wilkinson, Sue and Kitzinger, Celia (eds) (1993) *Heterosexuality: A Feminism & Psychology Reader.* London: Sage.

Young, Iris Marion (1990) *Throwing Like a Girl and Other Essays in Feminist Philosophy and Feminist Theory.* Bloomington, IN: Indiana University Press.

23

Multiculturalism

CHARLES LEMERT

'Multiculturalism' – the term is among the most confusing and misused in the language of social theory. 'Multiculturalism' confuses because it makes obstinate reference to two things at once – reality and a theory of reality. The same has been said (Lemert, 1997) of another trouble-maker of this sort, 'postmodernism', with which 'multiculturalism' is often, usually incorrectly, taken as a cognate of some kind.

Though there is a close lexical kinship, the two terms are separated by an important semantic space arising upon their different conjunctions of attributes. 'Postmodernism', when used naively, is thought to be 'nothing more' than a theoretical term. It is true, of course, that the word may be used as the name for a kind of theory. But this is properly done only when the use embraces, with delicate care, plausible statements of fact about the 'real world'. Just the same, any number of wise-guys (and, remarkably, a few wise-gals) go about using the word 'postmodernism' (or, worse yet, the appalling adjective 'postmodernist') in reference to what in their own minds is 'nothing more than a theoretical fad' of vaguely French provenance. (Near the end of the modern half-millennium, the most notable wise-guy of this sort was someone who called himself 'Alan Sokal', the improbability of whose linguistic practices are discussed in Lemert, 1997: 7–11.) That some people who ought to know better speak or write this way does not excuse the irre-sponsibility of their misuse – hence, abuse – of the word. In this connection, it is proper, at this point, to note for future reference that the diffi-culty otherwise literate people have in getting these two terms in their proper semantic spaces is associated by custom with a studied confusion of other terms of notable ability to trouble – 'theory', 'fact' and 'science' among others (of which Abbott, (1998) among examples too depressingly many to list). Fortunately, those who abuse the language in such ways, occasion-ally have friends who take pains to encourage them to do better; for example, in reference at least to the last three terms mentioned, Alan Sica's undeservedly generous ministry to Abbott (Sica, 1999; in reply to Abbott, 1998).

The trouble with 'multiculturalism' among all the troubling terms used in and about social theory is that its corruption requires an altogether inexcusable, even malicious, misun-derstanding of the facts of the world (Fish, 1998). It is relatively easy to forgive those so alarmed by the *possibility* that the modern world might be drawing to a close that they would use the word 'postmodernism' pejoratively in the sense of 'only a theory, and an obscure French one at that!' One can well understand why those in social positions well respected in a given cultural arrangement such as the modern one might fear the loss of position that would follow a decline in the fortunes of the arrangement itself.

'Multiculturalism', on the other hand, if it is to be used at all, can only be used to characterize, at most, a generalized attitude toward actual and unforgiving facts. Whereas 'postmodernism', when properly used, refers to a factual *possibi-lity*, 'multiculturalism' can only be well used in reference to facts so evidentally accepted as to be beyond necessity of reference; not even to works written by those who would never, normally, be thought of as 'multiculturalists' – Samuel Huntington's (1996) *The Clash of Civilizations and the Remaking of World Order* or Nathan Glazer's (1997) *We Are All Multiculturalists* [sic] *Now*. (For a discussion of the 'apparent' victory of 'multiculturalism' in the culture wars begun in 1987 by Allan Bloom's *The Closing of the American Mind*, see Buell, 1998: 553–61.) Still, evident or not, the term 'multiculturalism', when used indefinitely as a substantive, remains controversial against a growing accord over the facts of the matter.

The most general of those facts may, however, be adequately summarized in the following: *The world at large and the social worlds of most societies in it are affected by global (as distinct from nationalizing) forces that can be called 'multicultural' in the sense that 'peoples of different and often incommensurable cultural affinities' live in sufficiently real – or, at least televisual – proximity to each other as to be well aware of each other, and their differences – often to the point of open civil or, even, armed conflict.'* It is possible, of course, to propose a theory of such a state of affairs, but one would hardly be well advised to present himself as, say, a 'multiculturalist' in the sense that persons who are thought to suppose the modern world is coming to an end are referred to as 'postmodernists'. This may be why two of the more ambitious theories of the present, end-of-millennium world are decidedly not 'postmodernist', even though both argue that with the end of the Cold War in 1990 the world itself changed decisively – either by a clearing of the decks so that the true monoculture may thrive (Fukuyama, 1992), or by the end of the West's cultural dominance (Huntington, 1996).

Hence, the dilemma attendant upon any serious consideration of the word 'multiculturalism'. It is a word so embedded in 'facts' (in, that is, warrantable presumptions about the 'real world') that one might have a theory in its name only when one's feet are planted on some factual ground similar to the kind that would be required to support some other person's 'postmodernism'. The two terms, and their factual subject matters, are empirically allied, which accounts for the tendency to treat them as virtual cognates, thus to ignore that their respective relations to fact are distinguishable by the kind of fact entailed – certain and available in the one case ('multiculturalism'); possible and presently unavailable in the other ('postmodernism'). Those who might wish to use either term are well advised to use either or both cautiously (if only because, in a multicultural world, the unglossed use of such terms exposes one to the threat of being thought of as a 'postmodernist').

Therefore, a premise: *Though the world today may or may not be postmodern, it is certainly multicultural.* This distinction, along with the troubles involved, does not mean it is impossible to speak of such a practice as 'multicultural theory' (though, if one must, one should avoid at all costs the usage 'multiculturalist theory', which, apart from the inelegance, is a slur of sorts). It is possible, however, to 'have' or 'hold' a 'multicultural theory' in the sense of sharing an empirically reliable, if not universally held, attitude with respect to the world's current state of being whatever it is becoming. Still, even this expression requires great care. Theories of the world as it is, whether professional or practical ones, are always, at best, representations of the world. They are, thus, no better and no worse than the facts upon which they rely – and everyone knows that all facts are ever vulnerable to question, even doubt.

Therefore: here, for once, the proper and classic sense of the word 'theory' applies strictly. As is seldom noted, the original Greek *theoros* meant 'one who travels in order to see things'. Hence, if one wants to use the term 'theory' properly there is no better field of facts in respect to which it might be used than this, present and (presumably) actually, existing, multicultural world. A theory of the multicultural word would be something that could only be accomplished by traveling about in order to see the varieties of things practiced in the name of the world's multiple cultures. This is why one who speaks of 'multicultural theory' is always at risk of contradiction (if not down right embarrassment). The use of the word 'multicultural' requires a settled opinion, based on reliable (if not incontrovertible) facts as to the state of the real world. Hence, to be a 'multiculturalist' [sic] – as in Glazer (1997) – is to purport to be a proper member of 'reality'. This is plainly absurd. What is neither absurd nor embarrassing is to believe that people, including oneself, are not wrong to have and hold theories of their world that would account for its many-cultured nature. Therefore, a theory may be 'multicultural' only because it is agreed that 'multicultural' is a proper word with which to modify the term 'world' (on which, more soon).

It is true that, as in many things, modern times (even postmodern ones) have lost much of what was sensible and good in olden times such as those of ancient Greece. Today, sadly, theories claim to be able to analyse and organize vast reaches of observable social realities – a practice outlandishly alien to the original practices done in the name of theory. The Greeks were never so much theorists, as they were philosophers – lovers of the wisdom of their own powerful, but local culture. 'Theory', as we have come to use it today, has broken all relations with philosophy – as, indeed, if Richard Rorty (1979) is to be trusted, philosophy itself has long since broken off with its own foundational practices.

So, to speak today of 'multicultural theory' one must not speak any too modernishly, as if 'theory' *only* referred to a certain high discourse associated with claims to general truth about very large categories of things like justices, recognitions, welfares and the like. To attempt to speak, or write, this way, even theoretically, of the varieties of cultures inhabiting the world today, would be imprudent for reason of the certainty that the behavior will redouble one's trouble by virtue of misusing 'theory' as a substantive available for modification by the adjective 'multicultural' – hence, to err twice in one move.

To allude to the Greeks in this way is not to trifle with meanings or common sense. It may very well be that it is impossible to use the word 'theory' as it has descended into modern usages in reference to the subject immediately at hand. Hence, irony, once again: at the very moment when the world, being multicultural, presents itself ready for the original Greek sense of 'theory', modernists (having lost their habit of studying the Greeks) no longer trust them to know what they are talking about as they did even in the earliest days when a person or persons we know as 'Homer' taught them a theory of what came to be their civilization by telling stories of travels he, or they, either undertook or heard reports of. Homer's stories were, in every respect, shocking, upsetting and entertaining. We would not know these stories if the Greeks had not first loved them and incorporated them into their own surprisingly multicultural dramas (Constantinidis, 1996, who, otherwise, and prudently, objects to 'multiculturalism').

By contrast, against every shred of common sense, some moderns (or modernists, if you choose) consider 'multicultural' stories told by authors probably as multiple as those who told the Homeric fables to be of surprising, arbitrary and of recent origin – and, thus, as intrusions upon their values. This is why, as any wide awake reader of the newspapers of the last years of the second post-Hellenic millennium knew, those who used the words 'multiculturalism' and 'postmodernism' as invective meant also to attack those who think of themselves as doers of 'theory' in other than the official Enlightenment sense (as, that is, the general organizing truth of a category of officially sanctioned facts).

Hence, one can hardly speak of 'theory' in relation to the 'multicultural' without examining the thing, the multiplicities of which make for the shockingly aggressive adjective 'culture', which forms the basis for 'multicultural theory'. Even the Greeks, and certainly the Romans, understood very well that their manners of worship were opposed by those of alien social and political groups. I use here the word 'worship',

because that indeed was the earliest, now obsolete, sense of our word 'culture'. It was only very late in the nineteenth century that the idea of 'culture' as a sustained order of common intellectual habit came into use. Only a truly modernist cast of mind could pervert so lively a word as 'culture' to such administrative purposes. Today's idea of 'culture' (which came into its own about the same century as did today's idea of 'theory') was taken, it seems, at close range in the late nineteenth century from the biologist's idea of a 'culture' as a medium in which one can grow microbes and other sometimes dangerous organisms. The current meaning in use among social theorists, including various social scientists, fell out of the sky after a long semantic journey from the cultivation of crops to the cultivation of the minds of human individuals. What can be learned from this passing glance at the word's history in the *Oxford English Dictionary* (2nd edition) is that 'culture' refers to very local stuff – as in, those idols worshipped in a given temple, the crops grown in a specific field, the mind (or at best class of minds) educable in a given pedagogic practice, or the stuff that grows in this or that petri dish. To speak of 'culture' in a global sense is to speak nonsense – particularly so when the culture in question is the purported totality of global cultures.

The problem here, of course, is with the term 'world', which finally I get to after having, at the outset, said that a multicultural theory, if any, must be grounded upon the facts of the 'real world'. Is it by accident that this word derives from the Teutonic *weorld* (for which, just as curiously, there is no Gothic equivalent) that came into something like its current usage only after Charlemagne established the Holy Roman Empire? Then, and for most of its history through Old English, 'world' meant something like 'this life' as opposed to the 'other' – or, in the *OED* meaning: 'the earthly state of human existence'. In other words, the very idea of 'world' – whether multicultural or not – assumes some limiting condition in time, and perhaps space as well, on the human order. To speak of a 'world' is to speak of limits, or finitude. Worlds recognize their borders with other worlds. In the beginning of semantic time, the recognition was of transcending worlds (as in the distinction most social theorists learn from Max Weber's *Protestant Ethic and the Spirit of Capitalism* between 'this worldly' and 'other worldly' ascetic practices). Today, when some still want to argue about the meaning of the word 'multicultural' as affixed to 'world' (hence to suggest something real in itself), the distinctions implied are ironic. Since the high modern era, just before the word 'culture' became necessary in the sociological sense in the nineteenth century, 'world' took a perverse turn into its present confused state of meaning. As the colonial regimes of Europe and America sought to organize the many 'cultures' of the earth over which they were extending the arm of Enlightenment policing, the word 'world' came to designate the idea that all things human were naturally subsumable under a term that (again Weber) referred not to the other world but to the varieties of this worldly ethical conduct. In the nineteenth century 'world' came to carry a secularized sense of the 'profane' or 'mundane' – as in: 'The guests were often this-worldly, often profane' (Mark Twain, *Life on the Mississippi* [1883]).

About the same time, which was also when 'culture' and 'theory' came into their 'modern' meanings, 'world' took on the absurd meaning the modernizers meant it to have, something like: 'the unifying state of all human cultures'. At first, such a meaning was limited enough to allow that those colonized were different in some measurable degree from the colonizers. The main idea was that the missionaries, slave traders and early anthropologists among others who traded for profit beyond the seas were offering a unifying 'culture' in exchange for the goods and services extracted from the regions they overran with their marvelous horses and superior firepower. Hence, the modern, quasi-secularized idea of '*the* world' is at best a ruse covering the unholy motives of the colonial system – which are currently disguised in such forms as the vestigial modernization theory that continues to influence the lending policies of the World Bank.

To speak of 'a world', then, is to speak of some or another distinction or set of distinctions organizing the volume of presumed social spaces that might be said to be 'real' in some sense. Here, more trouble, still. If social theorists are honest with themselves, they will admit that they don't really know what they are talking about when they use the word 'reality'. Today, not even the philosophers can help very much on this score. But even if they could, social theorists who aim to satisfy an empirical impulse would ignore them. This is why, in the hollowed hallways and lecture rooms, sometimes even in books, one encounters the expression 'real world'. This is actually a very hip expression – one that serves simultaneously to let the auditors of professorial wisdom know that the professor means to 'speak to them', even as he nods in the direction of whichever colleague may be within hearing, thus to suggest that the speaker holds himself to the high standard of certifiable truth-giving – that is, 'reality' (Locke, [1690]).

The problem here is that, though there may well be a reality out there beyond the apperceptive competencies in which normal human beings trust, there is no 'world' in the sense the term is used. The world that is still to be distinguished as 'this world' from '*the* other world' can only be considered a Unity in relation to a possibly transcendent one. To use the word 'world' as we so blithely do to imply some coherence in the sphere of social and other things that transpire around the earth is, as I said, to speak nonsense. This nonsense, however, has been a very powerful one. It is the nonsense of the modern which, until recently, operated without too much resistance under the illusion that its truth was Truth itself, from which there were but a few steps to the quasi-scientific idea that what grows in European or American petri dishes will and should grow in all petri dishes.

This is why, when all is said and done, one cannot even speak of a 'multicultural theory' in the sense of a theory apt to a practical world in which all things therein are 'multicultural'. If the 'world' is multicultural, then, strictly speaking, it is no longer a 'world', in the current common sense of the term.

But, in current, turn-of-millennium usage, one could speak of the 'multicultural' in relation to 'the globe', which surprisingly early in the sixteenth century came into currency out of the prior and proper sense of 'a globe', that is: 'a body having (accurately or approximately) the form of a sphere' – for which the *OED* lists the first occurrence as 1551, two years before its first recorded use with the definite article: '*the* globe'. It would be, however, some centuries yet, at the height of Enlightenment faith, before the explorations of the sixteenth century on a physical 'globe' would come to produce '*the* globe' as a surface upon which 'culture' ought be spread. Hence, in 1752, even so skeptical a party to enlightenment as David Hume would say: 'The same set of manners will follow a nation over *the* whole globe' (*OED*, 2nd edition; emphasis added). It was, thus, during the eighteenth century that 'world' and 'globe' came to be united, as they are today, by sly first appearances of what, a century after, came to be known as 'culture'. The foundational principle of Enlightenment doctrine was, simply but honestly enough, that everything in the 'world' is governed by intelligible laws the knowledge of which is, thus, the basis for reason, hence civilization.

In Isaiah Berlin's succinct words (1999: 119), the 'essence' of Enlightenment, indeed of the whole of Western rationality that came clear in the eighteenth century, 'is that there is a body of facts to which we must submit. Science is submission, science is being guided by the nature of things, scrupulous regard for what there is, non-deviation from the facts, understanding, knowledge, adaptation.' Thus it became possible to speak confidently of 'the globe' only when the political economy of the colonial system drew up over its brutish shoulders the mannered cloak of a one, and true, 'culture' which was thought to be the scientific essence of *the* 'real' world. Or, as Ralph Waldo Emerson would put it in *Nature* in 1836: 'All science has but one aim, namely, to find a theory of nature.' This entailed, of course, the beginning of the end of 'worship' as the desideratum of necessity for 'culture', allowing 'culture' to become the more rigorous term for the 'manners' that would follow 'a' nation across the globe, in Hume's word. Emerson, thus, had left the religious ministry eventually to become the acknowledged founder of the uniquely American 'culture' he announced in *The American Scholar*, presented at Harvard the year following his remark on nature, which at the time referred to 'nature' as we know it, but also to 'life' as such.

The word 'multiculturalism', therefore, leads the social theorist in many directions at once. Its connotative risks owe, curiously, to its denotative necessity. It may well be that those few who would prefer that the world were not 'multicultural' win the day even as they are losing it. The word would not appear in conversation as it does were it not controversial in 'fact'. Part of that controversy is, of course, over the 'facts' of the world.

Theoretical troubles caused by multiculturalism

Trouble associated with the history of the term is real trouble as much because of what 'multiculturalism' entails about the facts of the world as for what the word means. To be sure, some – for example, Glazer (1997: esp. ch. 4) – are famously upset by the way the word is sometimes used as a political weapon. Arthur Schlesinger, for another example, writes of the prevailing multiculturalism of ethnic groups that were freshly in evidence in America in the 1980s: 'The ethnic revolt against the melting pot has reached the point, in rhetoric at least, though not I think in *reality*, of a *denial of the idea of a common culture* and a single society' (1991: 76; emphasis added). Schlesinger bemoans the threats to his society's national identity by the rise of group loyalties to ethnic identities among African, Asian, Native, Caribbean and other Latin Americans, among numerous others. (But, for the other side see, among many examples, JanMohamed and Lloyd, 1990; Lowe, 1996.)

By extension, and in actual political practice, the sense of threat to national identity can be associated with others who swear an allegiance to some or several social groups not necessarily ethnic or racial, but also evidently not nationalist – notably, the varieties of what are sometimes called queer identities (especially gay and lesbian), feminisms of various kinds and what may roughly be called 'identities owing to a sense of post-colonial experience'. For an admirably respectful objection to these kinds of identity movements, see Jean Bethke Elshtain's *Democracy on Trial* (1995: ch. 2).

Obviously, what is particularly unnerving to strong monoculturalists like Schlesinger and gentler ones like Elshtain is that multiculturalism as it applies to groups of individuals in a society is never simple. It is entirely possible that individuals may identify themselves with a considerable number of social and ethnic groups long before they come to think of themselves as 'American' or, for that matter, Dutch or British, Russian or Congolese. An individual born and bred within the territories of the United States may – for example, Anzaldúa (1987) – think of herself as Chicana, lesbian, *mestiza* and *tejana*, among other possibilities, without ever supposing that she is significantly 'American'. The unnerving wrought by strong identity politics like Anzaldúa's arises upon the impression that identity choices are simply 'choices' and, thus, are 'merely personal' or even psychological – thus all the more a decline along the slippery slope away from the monocultural ideal thought to hold a nation together. Anyone who reads Anzaldúa, or *any* of those in the border-culture tradition, understand very well that, though she writes personally, she is writing of the politics of social exclusions.

By further extension, the logic of fear associated with multicultural reality is that the world as a whole is as subject to these new allegiances as is even so radically multicultural a society as the United States (Habermas, 1994). When the idea of a world culture of any kind is subjected to scrutiny, it becomes an uncertain possibility – at least relative to the world system to which it would presumably apply (Appadurai, 1996; Wallerstein, 1991, ch. 12; 1998). Still, the prospect of an unqualifiedly multicultural world calls into question the supposed unity of humankind, just as in a given society like the American it threatens, in Schlesinger's words, 'the idea of common culture' – which is to say: 'the idea that what grows in one's national petri dish is good once and for all, and probably good for all humankind'.

'Common culture' is, thus, the social ethical foundation of Western culture since, at least, the eighteenth century. It is, in short, that by which the goodness of a society, or of *the* society of all humans, is determined. But, ideals are always subject to argument, even among those who profess to share them. Those arguments may be said to be the principal topic of the gossip – or, in the word used at the end of the millennium, the 'discourse' – of civil society. Those who enter the argument in their local coffee shops, cocktail parties, or taverns do so from the points of view of their actual concrete lives. As a result, local talk of the good society always turns toward other, more arguable, subjects: general principles, applicable values and specific social policies.

Western culture in modern times has considered it important that there be universal principles on the basis of which the good society may be established. The literature on this subject is too vast, and in some respects too familiar, to permit, or require, elaboration (still, for a succinct summary of the issues in relation to multiculturalism, see Charles Taylor, 1994). Without going into the long history of this discussion, going back at least to Hobbes and Augustine, not to mention Aristotle and Plato, it is sufficient to say that, at the turn of the twentieth century, the wider argument about the multicultural turned on two general kinds of universal principles.

The one concerned the universality of *rights*; the other, universal principles of *justice*. Evidently, as much as some have tried, the two are inseparable. They are two sides of any argument over the principles at stake in the ethics of organized society, as in the familiar argument that good rights policies yield good justice outcomes (Rawls, 1971). Still, the two principles invite legitimate disagreement over emphasis, even when they are not used in mutual exclusion.

Those who emphasize *rights* tend to think of the political and economic individual as the moral force behind (hence as the effective, if not the original, source of) whatever may be good in the good society. Their politics tend toward the protection of the rights of the individual. 'Rights' people are, therefore, typically associated with political opinions Americans think of as 'conservative' and Europeans think of as 'liberal', in the classic, nineteenth century sense. (On the historic convergence of conservative, liberal, and socialist principles, see Wallerstein, 1995, and esp. 1998: 15–33.)

By contrast, those who emphasize *justice* generally believe that when many individuals are left to pursue their well-protected rights they will sort themselves into stronger and weaker groups; hence into a social arrangement wherein the stronger will deprive the latter of their rights. Justice-people, therefore, are inclined to trust some larger social entity (in modern times, usually the well-managed state, whether socialist or social democratic, even liberal) as the guarantor of individual rights or, more robustly, of social outcomes in respect to many, if not all, of the goods thought to be necessary or desirable in the good society. An emphasis on justice,

therefore, is typically associated with politics that Americans think of as 'left-liberal' and Europeans think of as just plain 'left' or 'social democratic', occasionally still 'socialist'.

One of the not very well thought through consequences of the necessary, if variable, relationship of rights to justices is that, when the discussion attends to the specific goods, or social and economic outcomes, assured by the general principles, distinctions are very much more clear, to the point of incommensurability. Hence, those who speak earnestly of *rights* almost always consider the primary good in any society to be *freedoms*. Freedom may seem to be an abstraction, but in practice it demands very specific policies with respect to privacy, speech, property, mobility. When freedoms are entertained in public, the freedom (for example) of a pregnant woman to pursue her right to bodily privacy can come up against rival claims on behalf of the right to life of her fetus (a freedom that becomes public because of the proven wisdom of seeking an abortion at the hands of a qualified physician).

Whereas rights-people usually (though not exclusively) think of freedoms, those who speak of justice as the ultimate principle in a good society tend to think of *equality* as the more applicable value. Justice-people would think of the good society as one that guarantees basic equalities with respect to outcomes, ranging from civil rights and certain social opportunities (such as education in the United States) to more comprehensive social and economic outcomes (as in certain Scandinavian societies). Obviously, though distinguishable, arguments emphasizing equalities can be used against strong freedoms arguments. One of the stronger arguments in support of a woman's right to terminate her pregnancy is framed against the specific history of *unequal* access to information, health care and social supports available to women, especially poor women, most especially poor women of color, that may render them less able to protect the long-term right to life of a child (including the child's rights or alleged rights to health, education, safety and other social goods). Injustices demand a correction in the unequal availability of social goods, including certain goods deemed to be actual or virtual rights.

Still, the argument gets even more harsh, when the principles that issue in applicable values come to entail local social policies. Though people may share a principled appreciation for rights *and* justices, and may sing the virtues of freedoms *and* equalities, they will seldom agree on specific policies governing the local administration of the social goods glorified in principles or hinted at in values. In practice – that is, in real arguments in coffee shops in Des Moines or bars in Palaiseau – it is seldom the case that a strong justice argument will trump a strong rights argument; or vice-versa. Opponents move to the barricades, or the picket lines, even the bricks or bullets, with frightful ease.

As a result, any theoretical argument over multiculturalism, if it is to stop short of violence, must be moved with dispatch to concrete cases. Ultimately, when people are ready to fight over the facts of the multicultural world they live in, they are in actual practice ready to fight over specific (even if imagined) assaults upon their freedoms, or specific (even if imagined) deprivations in their equal access to social goods (including freedoms). Arguments turn to fights when real or allegedly real freedoms and equalities are at stake. As a result, a clear-headed understanding of the specific social policies by which social goods are distributed in a multicultural society is doubly difficult. In an uncontestedly modern culture there is a *presumption* of agreement over the principles, values and policies in question. In a multicultural society the modernist ideal of a stabilizing common culture is held in doubt. One might even say that a multicultural society (whether global or national; whether modern or postmodern) is one in which there is no presumption of prior accord over such questions as these: what are the social goods? who should get which ones? – and in what proportions? As a result, multiculturalism makes less sense as a theory of societies (including purportedly global ones) than as a study of the applicable values governing specific social policies by which the goods of a good society are distributed.

Here is where the argument turns dirty. Struggles over freedoms and equalities, in addition to being struggles over social goods or necessities, are always also struggles over social life itself. Individuals never enter society clean and clear of enquiries into their right to belong. The right to belong may be distinguished from rights to the social goods normally associated with belonging. Membership (sometimes called 'citizenship') is the first condition for rights-eligibility. Or, put cynically, the first recourse of those in a position of power sufficient to protect their freedoms and unequal advantages is to deny membership to evident or potential rivals for the goods they consider theirs – by right or otherwise. Liberals, in the broad and inclusive sense of the word, have done this by using citizenship as much to exclude as to include (Wallerstein, 1995, 1998: 21–5). Hence, the first question put to all, whether implicitly or explicitly, is the question of one's right to identify oneself as a claimant on fair shares of the goods available in the social entities to which one petitions for inclusion.

Here is where the debate turns dirty because here is where it turns from principles of rights or justices, even from the specific value of freedoms against equalities, even from this or that policy, to the down-right ugly question of *identities* – as in 'identity politics' (of which the first known use is Goffman, 1963: 123–5). Far from being, as so many think, a matter of personal self-understanding, identity is always political because declarations of identity, when made, are always and necessarily made on the verge of demanding membership. The demand is freedom itself; the membership is *always* the demand for an equal share of whatever may be the social goods of value in this or that locale.

When all is said and done, the important questions associated with political discussions of 'identity' are, first: 'How does the human individual understand herself in relation to which social things?', and secondly: 'What rights and claims are associated with her identity claims?' In the real world of scarcities, declarations and investigations of identities are *always*, immediately or ultimately, claims on goods that disturb prevailing social policies and practices. Questions of identity are of intense, often vicious, public interest because it is widely recognized (though seldom discussed) that when members of established human groups require certifications from petitioners for inclusion by enquiries on the theme 'who they think they are', this requirement extends well beyond its superficial spiritual values into the realm of real or potential demands for material, as well as social (and spiritual), inclusion. When, for an example, those previously excluded from, say, a fair share of competent education demand an equal share of the goods associated with a so-called 'educational opportunity', they are simultaneously saying: 'I belong; therefore I am a rightful claimant, on my own terms.' This is the point all too often overlooked by those like Schlesinger and Glazer (not to mention Gitlin, 1995) when they complain about the identity demands of those previously dealt unequal access to social and economic goods for which a proper 'education' is expected.

This is where those who object to identity politics as overly personal go wrong. Those who hate (or fear, or doubt) multiculturalism tend most of all to object to identity politics as a trivializing of real politics by a petulant insistence upon personal recognition. Elshtain (1995: 58), referring to queer identity politics, says, disapprovingly: 'If politics is reducible to the "eruption of radical feelings", something as seemingly "ordinary" as protest against an unjust war lacks radical panache. Personal authenticity becomes the test of political credibility.' It is true that identity politics involve radical feelings and questions of personal authenticity, but it is not true that they involve 'nothing more' than a preoccupation with the personal. The problem arises in most cases by a misunderstanding of the essentially social and political nature of the identity question.

The 'Who am I?' question is, of course, subject to abuses of all kinds. Still it must be answered because one cannot get round it. Were it the case that individuals were utterly and unqualifiedly self-sufficient, then there would be no question of their identity. Curiously, in the whole of Western literature only one being was ever considered utterly self-sufficient – and he is one whose precise status in being is open to doubt (in large part because of his claim to self-sufficiency). When Moses enquired (Exodus 3:14) as to the identity of the being by whom he was being addressed through the mediation of a burning bush, God answered, 'I am who I am.' Except in comedies of various kinds, no ordinary human would think to respond in this fashion because all humans recognize the need to 'identify' themselves, especially upon presentation in foreign crowds where rights of membership are open to inspection (Goffman, 1963). It might, therefore, be said that the ability to recognize responsibility for answering this question – if only by providing a name, even an alias – is what makes us human. One might even say that a 'human being' is 'that creature sufficiently conscious of its individual limitations as to be capable of representing himself as a proper member of associations of other creatures of like kind – with all the duties and privileges appertaining thereto.'

'Identity', therefore, is one of the more abstract names humans may use in recognition that they are wittingly 'who they are' by consequence of the choices they make (among those available, *when* they are made available) to associate with other humans (Taylor, 1989, 1994). The types of choices vary over time (in respect to which, a recent succinct summary is Walzer, 1997: ch. 2). In ancient Greece, among other traditional social orders, it was common to identify with one's kin group (or family) and one's polis (or societal community). In modern times, it was expected that one would identify with one's 'nation-state'. In multicultural (whether modern or postmodern) times, it is said that people are inclined to identify with their ethnic, sexual-orientational, racial, religious, immigrant or engendered social groups. The list of possibilities is, in principle, indefinitely long. For an individual to declare him- or herself an Athenian, an American, a follower of Christ, a Lakota, a bisexual, a Jew, a feminist and so on (and not to mention, several at once), is to acknowledge membership or memberships by which those interested are meant to derive an answer to the question 'Who are you?' The 'Who am I?' question, thus, bears with it an ever ready (even if provisional) answer, poised in anticipation of the inevitable enquiry from another, 'Who are you?' To be human is to have an answer at the ready.

Ultimately, identity politics are the politics that more sternly test principles, values and policies. An individual's freedoms and equalities are made known in the first instance by entry into foreign company: Who possesses the right to inspect the candidate? How does she reply? And with what answer or answers? And, is she accredited (or not) to answer as she does? Is the answer acceptable? These are the proper, first questions for a sociological investigation of just how freedoms and equalities are distributed in a society. They are often precisely the questions asked in the study of what academic sociologists call social stratification, for which the first empirical line is always the basic demographics: Name? Address? Class? Race? Ethnicity? – and so forth and so on!

If, then, the identity question is so essential (possibly the only completely essential human question), why then does 'identity' – or more precisely, 'identity politics' – drive some people nuts when they are confronted with the reality of a multicultural world? At first blush, the answer would seem to be simple, and may well be. The inspection of the identity cards of the newly immigrant, or the recently assertive, is *only* a troubling political questions when those groups are either palpably ignorant of (by virtue of immigrant status) or morally resistant to (by virtue of their assertiveness) the prevailing rules of social order. In principle this is a problem for any social group of any size, but at the end of the millennium it became an especially troubling problem for those with vested interests in the nation-state as the principal unit of social membership (hence, of privilege and its attendant duties).

'Multicultural', to repeat (and to amplify), is a proper adjective in reference to any world in which there is widespread dissensus with respect to membership rules, which is to say: principles, values, policies – and, above all, proper identity confessions. That the United States, a good number of European nation-states and perhaps the cultures of the world taken as a global whole might be called 'multicultural' is tribute to the indisputably *social and political* (as opposed to 'personal') value of identity. There are no identity politics (at least not in visible public) in social arrangements (including nation-states) when members of subordinate groups are sufficiently deprived of equal access to the social goods as to be unfree to claim their memberships as they see them.

Hence, the irony of identity politics at the end of the twentieth century. This was a time when, for a number reasons, confidence in universal principles of humankind fell into grave doubt. The nation-state regimes of the modern world system had proven themselves since the long sixteenth century, perfectly capable of atrocities equal to the worst of the premodern systems. Yet, they prided themselves in somehow being morally better than the others, which pride extended to the presumption that their principles were *truly* universal; hence of considered value to all humankind. These were, in effect, values of the sort that claimed to have reduced the identity question to its thinnest possible value. The expectation was that, in the liberal modern regime, all humans would gladly reply that they were, of course, 'simply human'. Since the expectation and, where given with a straight face, the reply are on the face absurd, it is remarkable that until recently so few groups laughed out loud. They did not, of course, because the politically weaker among them were vulnerable to the protections and regulations of the nation-state and its various economic, military and judicial instrumentalities.

Or, to put the matter from the point of view of those in the weaker positions in such an arrangement, members of many social groups – ethnic, racial, gender, sexual, economic and others – were in effect deprived of the right to answer the identity question freely. It is entirely reasonable to assume that they might have, in principle, honestly replied by affirming their identification with the democratic values of this or that nation-state had anything in their experience caused them to believe that the universal principles of either rights or justices of those states merited their loyalty. In fact, little in the actual experience, over many years of most immigrant groups, most minority ethnic groups, most minority racial groups, all gays and lesbians, most women (so on and so forth) would truly have inspired confidence in the democratic principles of *any* of the major democratic societies of the European Diaspora. On the contrary, the actual, practical experience of those whose migrations and assertions have created the multicultural world is one of injury – and most especially the injury of exclusion which, in effect, is the injury of non-recognition.

Hence, the situation as it stood at the turn of the last millennium: 'multicultural', insofar as it then referred to a theoretical claim, referred in effect to an argument among loyalists to the centrist liberal state, which had already entered into its decline. The grounds for argument were complicated by the evidence since the revolutions of 1968 of the precarious promise and unpredictability of liberal democracy (Elshtain, 1995; also Wallerstein, 1995, 1998). Those who complain about the culture of complaint (Hughes, 1993) or the loss of a common vision miss the fundamental fact of the world as it is. Even the most injured by injustice, even the most deprived of their rights, affirm the ideals of the democratic order – and do so with a courage that puts the lie to those who claim that, somehow, the principles of that order are in effect long-proven, well-established and true in practice.

A multicultural social theory?

Insofar as the multicultural world affects social theory, it does so by transposing social ethical questions of rights and justices into questions of the nature of social and political membership and participation. In so doing a multicultural social theory reveals the necessarily left-leaning nature of social theory itself. Though the expression 'social theory' is sometimes used duplicitously by conservatives to claim membership in a conversational circle to which they have no natural affinity, conservative politics and 'social theory' mix poorly. 'Social theory' may be distinguished from any specific instance of theory in a social 'science' (as in 'sociological theory') by virtue of its willingness to abandon the favors of a strict scientific presentation for an analysis of social reality that permits, even welcomes, a frankly political and normative commitment.

This is why what passes for multicultural social theory is always entirely an argument between and among proponents of various left, or as some would say 'progressive' (for example, Unger and West, 1998: 25) or 'radical' (for example, Giddens, 1994: 11–21), social theorists. Social theory, thus, as it had come to be understood at the end of the twentieth century, devolved in some more or less direct fashion from the 'personal politics' ideal of the revolutions of 1968. Why that social moment in particular led to such a dramatic transformation of the social and political debates of the previous two centuries is hard to say. The answer may lie in the exhaustion of the traditional categories of liberal culture (Wallerstein, 1995) – of, that is, attempts to resolve questions of rights and justices by formal references to the preferences for individuals or societies as the rival causal sources for the origins of social life (not to mention the long-standing tensions between Enlightenment and Romanticism, Berlin, 1999). Though the rivalries and tensions remain, the only truly informative social theoretical instances of multicultural theory take the form of arguments over the relative merits of a politics of recognition (or identity politics) and the politics of redistribution (or post-socialist socialism).

On the surface, this would appear to be 'nothing more' than a rehash of the rights or justice debate. But, it is more. Proponents of the politics of recognition assert that identity politics entail a real political struggle to overcome the effects of injuries inflicted by well-structured social (as opposed to interpersonal) insults (Taylor, 1994: 25–44, 63). Though the injury is experienced qua individual and usually entails a deprivation of rights, it is understood to be a consequence of membership in a social group (such as African guest workers in France) subjected to injustices at the hand of the host society. On the other side, those who are fixed on a post-socialist politics of redistribution are justice people who recognize, however awkwardly, that the politics of recognition must be taken into any viable account of redistributive justice (for examples, Fraser, 1997; Young, 1990).

Though, as the millennium ended, there was far from perfect resolution of the debates *among* multicultural social theorists – or *about* multiculturalism and the multicultural world – it did seem that within the proper domain of social theory there was an important, if incomplete, transformation in the way social things, and their ethical and political consequences, were thought. One (but only one) sign of that change was recognition of real human differences that appeared in the wake of a lessening of hard commitments to categorical differences – those *between* rights and justices, *between* freedoms and equalities, and those *between* the individual and his or her societal world.

However high the moral principle, however true the theoretical concept, the plain fact is that there are mothers whose babies cry for milk. And cry they do *because* those charged with feeding the hungry refuse to recognize the essential membership, even of the babies, in the community of humans. The mothers do not give a damn about principles, values, or concepts. They care about life, which in this world is never so much supported by animal instincts as by social memberships. The growing recognition of the multicultural world accompanies a declining commitment to categories of all kinds.

In the new times, it remains to be seen if the multiculturalism debate at the end of the old millennium truly led to more milk for all babies.

REFERENCES

Abbott, Andrew (1998) 'Engaging Exemplars or Touting the Top Ten?', *Perspectives: American Sociological Association Theory Section Newsletter*, 20 (4): 4–8.

Anzaldúa, Gloria (1987) *Borderlands/La Frontera*. San Francisco: Aunt Lutte Books.

Appadurai, Arjun (1996) *Modernity at Large: Cultural Dimensions of Globalization*. Minneapolis, MN: University of Minnesota Press.

Berlin, Isaiah (1999) *The Roots of Romanticism*. Princeton, NJ: Princeton University Press.

Buell, Frederick (1998) 'Nationalist Postnationalism: Globalist Discourse in Contemporary American Culture', *American Quarterly*, 50 (3): 548–91.

Constantinidis, Stratos (1996) 'Greek Drama and Multiculturalism', *Journal of Modern Greek Studies*, 14 (1): 1–30.

Elshtain, Jean Bethke (1995) *Democracy on Trial*. New York: Basic Books.

Fish, Stanley (1998) 'Boutique Multiculturalism, or Why Liberals Are Incapable of Thinking about Hate Speech', in Philip Lopate (ed.), *The Anchor Essay Annual: Best of 1998*. New York: Anchor/Doubleday. pp. 31–54.

Fraser, Nancy (1997) *Justice Interruptus: Critical Reflections on the 'Postsocialist' Condition*. New York: Routledge.

Fukyama, Francis (1992) *The End of History and the Last Man*. New York: The Free Press.

Giddens, Anthony (1994) *Beyond Left and Right: The Future of Radical Politics*. Stanford, CA: Stanford University Press.

Gitlin, Todd (1995) *Twilight of Common Dreams*. New York: Metropolitan Books.

Glazer, Nathan (1997) *We Are All Multiculturalists Now*. Cambridge, MA: Harvard University Press.

Goffman, Erving (1963) *Stigma*. New York: Simon and Schuster.

Habermas, Jürgen (1994) 'Struggles for Recognition in the Democratic Constitutional State', in Charles Taylor et al. (eds), *Multiculturalism: Examining the Politics of Recognition*. Princeton, NJ: Princeton University Press.

Hughes, Robert (1993) *The Culture of Complaint*. New York: Warner Books.

Huntington, Samuel (1996) *The Clash of Civilizations and the Remaking of World Order*. New York: Simon and Schuster.

JanMohamed, Abdul R. and Lloyd, David (1990) *Nature and Context of Minority Discourse*. New York: Oxford University Press.

Lemert, Charles (1997) *Postmodernism Is Not What You Think*. Oxford: Basil Blackwell.

Locke, John ([1690]) *An Essay Concerning Human Understanding*.

Lowe, Lisa (1996) *Immigrant Acts: On Asian American Cultural Politics*. Durham, NC: Duke University Press.

Rawls, John (1971) *Theory of Justice*. Cambridge, MA: Harvard University Press.

Rorty, Richard (1979) *Philosophy and the Mirror of Nature*. Princeton, NJ: Princeton University Press.

Schlesinger, Arthur Jr (1991) *The Disuniting of America*. Knoxville, TN: Whittle Direct Books.

Sica, Alan (1999) 'Mr. Abbott's Miss Bennet: So Much Not to Read; So Little Time in Which Not to Read It', *Perspectives: American Sociological Association Theory Section Newsletter*, 21 (1): 1–8.

Taylor, Charles (1989) *Sources of the Self*. Cambridge, MA: Harvard University Press.

Taylor, Charles (1994) 'The Politics of Recognition', in Charles Taylor et al. (eds), *Multiculturalism: Examining the Politics of Recognition*. Princeton, NJ: Princeton University Press.

Unger, Roberto M. and West, Cornel (1998) *The Future of American Progressivism*. Boston, MA: Beacon Press.

Wallerstein, Immanuel (1991) 'The National and the Universal: Can There Be Such a Thing as World Culture?', in Immanuel Wallerstein (ed.), *Geopolitics and Geoculture*. New York: Cambridge University Press.

Wallerstein, Immanuel (1995) *After Liberalism*. New York: The New Press.

Wallerstein, Immanuel (1998) *Utopistics*. New York: The New Press.

Walzer, Michael (1997) *On Toleration*. New Haven, CT: Yale University Press.

Young, Iris Marion (1990) *Justice and the Politics of Difference*. Princeton, NJ: Princeton University Press.

24

Social Theory and the Postmodern

STEPHEN CROOK

INTRODUCTION

The idea of the postmodern is no longer a novelty in social theory. Themes that had been the recondite concerns of an avant-garde in the 1980s and exploded into an intellectual craze-cum-publishing bonanza in the early 1990s are now part of the standard repertoire of social theory and cognate disciplines. Undergraduate students in cultural studies and sociology learn to distinguish the postmodern from other theoretical 'frameworks' or 'perspectives', ably assisted by the textbooks, readers and websites now available. At the same time, the idea of the postmodern sits at the heart of contemporary 'culture wars', where it is attacked variously as the bearer of cognitive relativism, ethical nihilism, political quietism, aesthetic triviality and historical anachronism, The question arises, now that the postmodern has become both such a familiar and such a contentious part of the intellectual landscape, of how we should assess its significance for social theory. The assessment developed in this chapter can be summarized in four linked propositions.

1   Themes strongly associated with the postmodern are now inescapable problems and resources for any serious attempt to engage theoretically (or empirically) with the contemporary social world. To that degree, social theory cannot ignore or reject the postmodern while retaining its salience.
2   Despite this, the modern–postmodern contrast remains troublesome. Clear formal or historical ruptures between modern and postmodern are difficult to draw and to defend, producing obvious anomalies. Claims for distinctively postmodern analytic

procedures, poltical strategies or social forms often – and paradoxically – turn on the surreptitious borrowing of modern tropes.
3   Social theory requires an orientation to the postmodern that refuses the caricatures of modern and postmodern that have dominated recent culture wars. One route to such a sober and pragmatic orientation is a recognition that many themes now associated with the postmodern – and many of the anxieties provoked by those themes – have broad and deep roots in the histories of social theory and its cognate disciplines.
4   A modestly postmodern social theory that is alert to the complexities and the ironies of its present situation will be uniquely well placed to chart the contemporary mutations of the field that it once confidently labelled 'the social' and in so labelling claimed as its own.

These propositions are explored in five sections below. The first sketches the recent history of the idea of the postmodern in social theory and briefly draws some terminological distinctions. The next three sections address the first three propositions and assess the significance of the postmodern in relation to epistemology and method, values and politics, and change in culture and society. A concluding section pulls together the threads of the argument and spells out what the fourth proposition might entail.

THE ADVENT OF THE POSTMODERN

Introducing a 1986 edition of *Theory, Culture & Society* devoted to 'French social theory', Featherstone outlines a genealogy of postmodernism. A New York based artistic movement of the 1960s known as 'postmodernism' was exported to France where it was taken up by intellectuals such as Kristeva and Lyotard. It was eventually re-exported to the USA 'with added epochal meaning' (Featherstone, 1986: 2). This trajectory helps to explain the conjunction, in most of what was presented as postmodernist analysis to Anglophone audiences in the 1980s, of three elements: a focus on aesthetic or cultural issues, the intimation of an immanent epochal threshold and an emphasis on the work of French 'post-structuralist' theorists. Taking a rather longer and broader view, other developments in Anglophone social theory prepared the ground.

For example, the influential form of 'cultural studies' associated with the (British) Centre for Contemporary Cultural Studies insisted during the 1970s and early 1980s on its Marxist credentials (see, for example, Hall and Jefferson, 1975; Hall et al., 1980; McLennan et al., 1977). However, the dominant legacies of CCCS were its refusal to 'reduce' cultural to socioeconomic processes, its emphasis on the effectivity of language and textuality, and its documentation of the heterogeneous forms of popular 'resistance'. Sociological studies of value change, environmentalism and 'new social movements' familiarized their readers with the possibility of an intense but fluid and fragmentary radical politics disconnected from the clear structuring principles of class (or, indeed, of gender) (see, for example, Cotgrove, 1982; Inglehart, 1977; Milbrath, 1984). Theoretical models of 'post-industrial society' (notably Bell, 1973 but also Touraine, 1974) thematized epochal change and introduced the trope of 'post-ing'. The curious episode of the unfolding deconstruction of Althusserian Marxism in successive books by Hindess and Hirst (for example, 1977) dominated British social theory for a while and popularized an analytic position close to that associated with post-structuralism and postmodernism (see Crook, 1991: ch. 5). These developments were clearly related to the spiralling crises of Marxism and socialism that culminated in the 1989 collapse of the Soviet bloc. It is a striking feature of the respective accounts that Nicholson and Seidman give of their 'conversions' to postmodernism (in Nicholson and Seidman, 1995: 1–7) that for each, disillusionment with an erstwhile Marxism broadened into a critique of enlightened modernity.

In the early 1980s the terminology of the postmodern became more familiar as a set of labels for trends that in various ways upset received ideas about the structures and dynamics of the modern. Foster's (1983) collection *The Anti-Aesthetic* played an important role in linking debates about a postmodern aesthetic to broader cultural and social issues. Dews (1980) was among those who introduced to Anglophones (even if he did not endorse) the ideas of French anti-leftist 'new philosophers'. The new journal *Theory, Culture & Society* included from the outset (in 1982) papers on topics that helped to define the themes of the postmodern turn: advertising, consumer culture, diet, embodiment, sexuality and sport (to take examples from the first two volumes). The appearance in English of Lyotard's *The Postmodern Condition* in 1984 helped to focus the idea of postmodernity as an historically emergent social configuration.

Social theory in the 1970s had been dominated by variants of Marxism and neo-Marxism and the responses of Marxist theorists to postmodern themes ranged from overt hostility to cautious attempts at convergence. Callinicos (1982) polemicized against all post-structuralist, postmodernist trends while Smart (1983) explored convergences between Marx and Foucault. Early versions of Jameson's influential model of the postmodern as the 'cultural logic' of consumer capitalism were published in the Foster collection and in *New Left Review* (Jameson, 1983, 1984). Berman's (1982) book on Marx came close to portraying his 'melting vision' as a postmodern theory of flux and disorder. At the same time, the main elements of Habermas' defence of the 'uncompleted project' of modernity were appearing in English through the translation of papers such as 'Modernity versus postmodernity' and 'Neo-conservative culture criticism' (1981, 1983). (See the account in Ashley, 1990.)

The difficulty of defining the 'postmodern' is notorious, a reference point for almost all commentators. As Hassan famously expressed the problem, 'in the last two decades the word postmodernism has shifted from awkward neologism to derelict cliché without ever attaining the dignity of a concept' (Hassan, 1985: 119). In Lemert's more recent *bon mot*, 'postmodernism . . . like sin and Russia is something that tends to excite the development of theories inversely to the availability of the thing itself to be satisfactorily described by any known theory of it' (Lemert, 1997: xi). Despite these well-known warnings, it will be difficult to take the argument of this chapter any further without offering at least some provisional definitions of key terms and at least a sketch map of the terrain over which they operate.

The term *postmodernism* originates, for practical purposes, in the artistic milieu identified by Featherstone (above). Aesthetic postmodernism constitutes itself after and in crucial respects against what it takes to be an exhausted modernism (see Crowther, 1990; Harvey, 1989: ch. 3; Jencks, 1987). If modernism is marked by a commitment to aesthetic 'progress' and to 'working out the possibilities in the aesthetic material' (Lash, 1990: 14), postmodernism reacts against the intellectualism and formalism that so often results. It is marked by playfulness, anachronistic pastiche, parody and populism. This distinction between an earnestly progressive, unitary modernism and a populist, heterogeneous postmodernism plays out by analogy in other fields of practice. In politics, the totalizing modernist progressivisms of Marxism and social democracy are contested by the multiple postmodernist resistances of diverse social movements and neo-tribes. In social theory, the unifying, rationalist structural schemes and grand narratives of modernists from Hegel to Parsons or Althusser give way to postmodernist celebrations of the local, the subordinated, the non-rational. So, if modernists are committed to modernism understood as a project aiming to realize the potential of the modern in some field, postmodernists are committed to postmodernism understood as the advocacy of plural alternatives to modernism in that field. The symmetry is not precise because postmodernists reject the model of an unfolding and unitary 'logic of development' that they discern in modernism.

If the 'ism/ist' of postmodernism/ist signifies a self-conscious advocacy, the adjective *postmodern* does not. It simply designates its object as belonging to a configuration that comes after the modern. So, Tony Blair or Bill Clinton may be 'postmodern' politicians but not 'postmodernists'. If that distinction is clear in principle, it becomes blurred in practice because the question of whether any social or cultural phenomena are really 'postmodern' divides postmodernists from modernists. It may be more apt to define 'postmodern' as the way in which postmodernists describe the contemporary world than to define 'postmodernism' as an orientation towards an already constituted postmodern.

Postmodernity generally designates 'a social and political epoch that is . . . seen as following the modern era in an historical sense' (Ritzer, 1997: 5). To that degree, postmodernity is a synonym of 'the postmodern'. However, two specific inflections should be noted. First, the term is often used to imply that a specific ethos, or way of experiencing the world, or *Zeitgeist* is in play in the postmodern (see Bauman, 1992; Lemert, 1997; Lyotard, 1992a). Secondly, it is also used by theorists for whom the postmodern constitutes a new and distinctive social order (see Bauman, 1988; Featherstone, 1991; Ritzer, 1997: ch. 11). Finally, the term *postmodernization* has been used to denote the complex of intersecting

processes responsible for the radical reconfiguration of modernity (see Crook et al., 1992).

The ambiguities of the idea of the postmodern are legendary, of course, so that the definitions and distinctions proposed here will be an imperfect guide through the literature. The difficulties are compounded by the equally legendary refusal of many major 'postmodern/ist' theorists to concede that they are anything of the kind (see, for example, Kumar, 1995: 139). Nevertheless, it will be clear that the distinctions outlined above make available a range of postmodern positions. So, the reluctance of a Baudrillard, Derrida or Foucault to accept the label 'postmodern' when their orientations seem so close to what was defined as 'postmodern*ist*' above can be linked to a fear of complicity in an idea of 'postmodern*ity*' that seems to derive from modernist models of historical evolution and social system (see Ritzer, 1997: 8). In a mirror image, many analysts of postmodern*ity* reject as subversive of, or indifferent to, all coherent social analysis the methodological prescriptions and proscriptions of postmodern*ists* (see Featherstone, 1988: 127; Nicholson and Seidman, 1995: 8). These matters lead directly to the concerns of the next section.

EPISTEMOLOGY AND METHOD

The best-known charge against postmodern*ism* is that it subverts objective standards of truth and thus the distinction between knowledge and belief. Recently this charge has been levelled by protagonists in the so-called 'science wars', in which 'postmodernism' has become a term of abuse akin to 'political correctness'. The well-known polemic from Gross and Levitt (1994: 11) accuses postmodernist critics of science of a 'radical epistemological skepticism' that subverts the cognitive authority of science although 'rarely is it seen to impeach their own researches'. In earlier critiques, the charge of relativism came as often from the left. For example, Norris (1990: 121) associates Baudrillard, Rorty and Fish with variants of the claim that 'it is no longer possible to maintain the old economy of truth and representation'. He notes that this stance relativizes all social criticism, including Marxism, and he turns to the language philosophies of Putnam and Davidson to save the concept of truth. Callinicos (1982: 178) had earlier used similar resources to argue that recognition that all knowledge is mediated by discourse 'does not lead to scepticism, but merely to fallibilism'.

The many variants of postmodernist relativism share a critique of claims to authoritative knowledge in the social (and natural) sciences. Those claims are said to be based on a series of illicit assumptions: that language and textuality are transparent media through which knowing subjects can articulate the essential nature of a known object; that authoritative knowledge arises from concepts that are either truly timeless and universal (as in the natural sciences) or whose universality is underwritten by a rational logic of historical development (as in the social sciences); that the 'will to knowledge' in science is disinterested and uncontaminated by desire or power. The critique takes too many forms to review exhaustively here. However, two pairs of themes have been especially influential.

The first pair might be labelled 'physicalism' and 'textualism'. Physicalist themes debunk the claim that knowledge of the social has rational foundations by postulating quasi-physical principles that are the real origin (note the irony and difficulty) of both the social and knowledge. Florid examples include the idea of a material 'intensity' in the work of Deleuze (1994) and Guattari (1984), Baudrillard's flirtations with figures drawn from astro-physics (see Baurillard, 1983) and Maffesoli's (1996) re-cycling of a Bergsonian *elan vital*. Textualist themes suggest that language and textuality are not a transparent window onto the real but opaque media in and by which versions of the real are constructed. As Lemert has noted (1997: 80), the post-structural and then postmodern emphasis on textuality must be considered in the context of the broader 'linguistic turn' in philosophy and social analysis. Derrida's critique of the 'metaphysics of presence' and his alternative account of language as the play of 'difference' (Derrida, 1976) has played a pivotal role, but his direct influence has been more marked in literary than social theory. Textualism and physicalism are often combined. Baudrillard's early work (1981) argued for the 'materiality' of signifying systems and that idea survives the abandonment of its Marxist roots in his later accounts of the simulatory hyperreal (Baudrillard, 1983). Foucault's studies of 'power/knowledge' combine in the compound term a model of 'power' that verges on the physicalist in its ubiquity and productivity with a significantly textualist account of the discursive elaboration of knowledges (see Foucault, 1980).

The second pair of themes can be termed 'anti-historicism' and 'anti-universalism'. Lyotard's influential (1984, 1992b) critique of 'grand' or 'meta-' narratives draws the two together. In his view, the cognitive, as well as the political, projects of the past two centuries have legitimated themselves through meta-narratives of enlightenment, emancipation and progress. The unity of modern forms of knowledge has been guaranteed in the convergence and realization of these long-term historical projects. In the late twentieth century such narratives lost their legitimating force: science and technology as well as progressive politics revealed their dark side, so that 'it is no longer possible to call development progress' (Lyotard, 1992b: 91–2). Now, legitimation of knowledge is de-historicized and localized in small-scale language games. Vattimo (1992: 8–9) also links anti-historicism to anti-universalism in his model of a 'transparent' postmodern. 'With the demise of the idea of a central rationality of history, the world of generalized communication explodes like a multiplicity of "local" rationalities – ethnic, sexual, religious, cultural or aesthetic minorities – that finally speak up for themselves.' This anti-universalism is perhaps the best known and most scandalous epistemic theme in postmodernism. The direct targets of science warriors are what they construe as claims that 'Science' is inherently masculine (see, for example, Harding, 1991), or an effect of the local rationalities of laboratories (see, for example, Latour and Woolgar, 1986), or anthropologically equivalent to a variety of ethno-sciences (see Watson-Verran and Turnbull, 1995).

So, how should social theory respond to these claims? The propositions set out in the introduction can shape the answer. First, social theory cannot simply ignore the epistemological and methodological dimensions of the postmodern. Even from the standpoint of the most objectivist social science, the de-legitimation, fragmentation and re-composition of previously authoritative knowledges must be signficant data for the sociology of knowledge. Even from such an objectivist standpoint, an unsettling feedback loop is built into the problem. If it transpires that major transformations are under way in the production, exchange and consumption of knowledge (as argued by Gibbons et al., 1994 and Stehr, 1992, among others), then why should social scientific knowledge expect to be immune? To put it another way, the postmodernization of knowledge must be a resource as well as a problem for social science and social theory.

But what degree of epistemological and methodological reflexivity is required of social theory in its attempt to grapple with the postmodern? In an influential paper that specifically posed that question of sociology, but has a much wider relevance, Featherstone (1988) distinguished between 'a sociology of the postmodern' and a 'postmodern sociology'. The former enterprise finds an exemplar in Bauman's (1988: 811) claim that 'post-modernity is an aspect of a fully fledged, viable social system which has come to replace the "classical" modern capitalist society and thus needs to be theorized in its own terms'. A 'postmodern sociology' 'would abandon its generalizing social science ambitions and instead parasitically play off the ironies, inconsistencies and intertextuality of sociological writings' (Featherstone, 1988: 127). Kumar's (1995: 139) observation that 'it is very hard indeed to find anyone who declares unequivocally for the postmodernist position' certainly applies to a 'postmodern sociology' as defined by Feather- stone. Perhaps Game's (1991) *Undoing the Social* comes closer than any other text. By contrast, the convergence of Bauman's and Featherstone's substantive contributions with those of anti- postmodernists, such as Beck and Giddens, suggests that a 'sociology of the postmodern' represents only a modest break with mainstream sociological practices and assumptions. The idea that a 'sociology of the postmodern' could remain uncontaminated by 'postmodern*ist*' themes was criticized by Smart (1990: 26) and Crook et al. (1992: 232–3) as implausible on the sociology of knowledge grounds noted above and unhelpful in placing a priori limits on the analysis of postmodernizing change. As Kellner (1998: 79) has recently observed, echoing those earlier critiques, Bauman's conception of the postmo- dern 'makes it appear that the postmodern paradigm is already fixed and established and is clearly at work establishing its dominance'.

These difficulties are linked to the second proposition from the introduction. Just what does the 'post' in postmodern mean in relation to epistemological and methodological debates? One seductive answer that Lemert (1997: 36) labels as 'radical postmodernism' would be to posit a double great divide, or rupture, in socio- cultural development and in knowledge, so that a new kind of theory and analysis is needed to comprehend a new kind of society. The problem here, and the reason why few postmodernist theorists would explicitly endorse this view, is that it almost directly replicates the defining moves of modern social theory a century and more before (see Crook, 1991: 24–9). Lyotard (1992b: 93) is alive to the problem: at the pro- cedural level, the 'post' of postmodern becomes 'ana-' 'a procedure of analysis, anamnesis, ana- logy and anamorphosis'. As he recognizes elsewhere, such a definition of the analytic post- modern ties it directly to the modern. 'What place, if any, does [the postmodern] occupy in the vertiginous work of questioning the rules that govern images and narratives? It is undoubtedly part of the modern' (Lyotard, 1992a: 21). Kumar (1995: 109) has underlined the point, arguing that 'the antinomian, anarchic, anti-systemic character of postmodernism seems at one with both the form and spirit of what we understood as modernism'. Either way – in 'radical post- modernism' or in attempts to evade its implica- tions – the analytic postmodern seems unable to draw the line that divides it from the modern.

This point is not made in an attempt to argue (following anti-postmodernists from Callinicos to Habermas to Gross and Levitt) that the analy- tic postmodern is in some way self-contradictory and therefore impossible. On the contrary, its procedures and outcomes merit close attention. The difficulty runs the other way: it is not plausible to represent the analytic postmodern as a generic and debunking critique of all other procedures in social theory and empirical social science. To do so is to recapitulate the defining modernist myth of a pure and redemptive critique that found its 'thinnest' and most sophisticated formulations in Adorno's critiques of 'identity thinking'. It is notable that many commentators have drawn parallels between Adorno and the analytic postmodern (see, for example, Callini- cos, 1990: 98; Dews, 1987; Jay, 1984: 510–37; Lemert, 1997: 41).

The third proposition from the introduction connects to these difficulties: the epistemological arguments and controversies associated with postmodernism have a pedigree at least as long as that of social theory itself. For example, Jones et al. (1993: 2) argue that postmodernist themes are linked to a 'line of prominent European thinkers stretching from the late Eighteenth Cen- tury to the present'. Drawing on Mannheim's analysis of conservatism, they point out that most of the 'thinkers' in this line have been conservative 'in the ontological-epistemological sense' (Jones et al., 1993: 5). Of course, Nietzsche is almost universally accepted as a parent of the postmodern, by its friends (Antonio, 1995 for example) and enemies (most notably Habermas, 1987). Others make strong claims for Rousseau, Schiller and 'romanticism' (Beilharz, 1994), for Schopenhauer (Mestrovic, 1993) and for Hei- degger (Vattimo, 1992). Social theory and my own discipline of sociology have engaged with this conservative 'line of thinkers' throughout their history. Simmel and Weber were both markedly influenced by Nietzsche while, in their different ways, Durkheim and Marx took up 'romantic' themes. Durkheim, Mannheim, Marx, Simmel, Weber and other 'founders' all advanced variants of the claim that 'being' deter- mines 'consciousness' and all faced accusations that they destructively relativized knowledge.

Since at least the time of Mannheim, some social theorists have argued that 'the objectivity of [scientific] knowledge' and 'the existential determination of all knowledge' are not mutually exclusive claims. The view that the merest hint of a 'social' influence on a knowledge claim must destroy its validity is a variant of what Smith (1988) has termed the 'egalitarian fallacy'. This variant holds that unless the objectivity of science is completely independent of existential determinations, then science is no different from common sense or ideology. On a more balanced view, to consider scientific (or any other) knowledge as a 'construct' is not to debunk it, but to focus attention on the way it is produced. So, in most contemporary relativistic sociologies that have an empirical focus – for which ethnomethodology/conversation analysis set the basic pattern – 'relativism' is a methodological device that makes available a region of practices for sociological analysis. There are clear parallels here with the practice of deconstruction in postmodernisms deriving from Derrida and others, where deconstruction is a critical method that makes the practice of writing available to analysis and exposes its ontological complicities. Shared roots in Heidegger's later analyses of language also link deconstruction to the 'reflexive sociologies' that flourished in the 1970s (see Blum, 1974; McHugh et al., 1974; Sandywell et al., 1975). These approaches were as 'postmodern' before the letter in their text-centricity as any later 'postmodern sociology', such as Game's (1991).

VALUES AND POLITICS

The charge that postmodernism relativizes truth has been broadened to include the relativization of all values, and hence nihilism. It comes in two variants. In one, nihilism results from the inability of deconstructionist and post-structuralist postmodernisms to set limits to the scope of their radical critiques of knowledge and value. As Billig and Simon (1994: 6) put it, 'no voice is secure in this mood of promiscuous critique'. In O'Neill's critique, the post-rationalist critique of foundations has consumed all commonality, so that the 'sparkling signifiers' of postmodernism are 'flashing out momentary values against a great black sky of nonsense' (O'Neill, 1995: 191). A second variant of the charge is made against postmodernist physicalisms: Foucault's concept of power, Deleuze and Guattari's 'intensity', Baudrillard's treatment of 'the masses', the varied 'problematics of desire' and related figures. These are versions of a monistic, physicalistic metaphysics incapable of sustaining distinctions of value. So, in perhaps the most systematic treatment of this theme Rose (1984: 197) notes the 'scandalous consequence' that Foucault's concept of power cannot 'distinguish between fascist *ressentiment* and the Freudian analysis of *ressentiment*'. Callinicos (1990: 102) reads Deleuze and Guattari's work as a 'bizarre if often entertaining neo-romantic *Naturphilosophie*', while Crook (1990: 62) argues more generally that 'postmodernism's reliance on either reductionist or formalist monisms renders it nihilistic'.

In Crook's (1990: 59) account, the nihilism of postmodernism links to an inability to explain how change happens and an inability to explain why change is either desirable or undesirable. In these circumstances, the political options for postmodernism are either a nihilistic endorsement of action – as in Foucault's 'resistance' or Guattari's 'experimentation' or a quietist withdrawal from political engagements. O'Neill (1995: 18) parodies the triviality of postmodernism as a 'will to willessness', while Squires (1993: 1) complains that while deconstruction may be 'liberating, even democratizing' up to a point, 'it is paralysing in its destruction of all "principled positions"'. In stronger versions of this argument, the alleged postmodernist substitution of word-play for political engagement is an explicit and deliberate 'sell-out'. For Callinicos (1990: 115) 'the term "postmodern" would seem to be a floating signifier by means of which [part of the] intelligentsia has sought to articulate its political disillusionment and its aspiration to a consumption-oriented lifestyle'. Callinicos' view converges here with Lash's less judgemental (1990: 20, 18) account of a postmodernist culture favoured by the 'newer, post-industrial middle classes' and serving as a vehicle for the 'restabilization' of bourgeois identity. The arguments of Jameson (1984, 1991) and Harvey (1989) that postmodern culture articulates with the configuration of late or consumer capitalism have clearly shaped many of the stronger critiques of the (non-) politics of postmodernism.

Turning again to the propositions from the 'introduction', a first point is that the postmodern problems of value and politics clearly cannot be ignored by social theory. It is difficult to deny that both the idea of universal and binding norms and values and the idea of a unified progressive political practice have lost their force: any social theory conceived with 'practical intent' must engage with these circumstances. On the second and third propositions, away from the clamour of 'culture wars' debates, there are productive convergences between postmodern positions and other strands in social theory. As a rule of thumb, postmodern approaches are particularly fruitful on the 'value' question while other theoretical and empirical resources perhaps have more to contribute to the question of politics.

Classical social theory was subject to the charge of nihilism just as postmodern theory has been more recently. Strauss famously charged Weber's value doctrine with nihilism: the residual exhortation 'thou shalt have ideals' has lost the capacity to distinguish between the excellent and the base (Strauss, 1953: 44–6). More ambiguously, Rose (1984: 211) portrays Weber, and sociology more generally, as delicately poised on the brink of nihilism in its defining operation of 'turning juridicial things into social interaction'. Weber grappled with the problem of value in two registers. In the register of method, sociology must be both 'value neutral' and 'value relevant' if it is to constitute a science of social action. In the register of historical sociology, the rationalizing disenchantment of the world engenders incommensurable value-spheres and erodes the grounds of rational value-choices. For a Weberian, Strauss' condemnation of Weber's decisionism shoots the messenger: it is history, not Weber, that produces nihilism. Postmodern theorists might plausibly make a similar claim.

Social theory has never finally resolved its post-Weberian value dilemma. If it works too hard to establish foundations for its value commitments, it stands accused of an illicit dependence on anachronistic metaphysical formulae. If it opts simply for 'value neutrality' in the manner of radical empiricisms, or founds itself in directly political commitments, it opens itself to charges of nihilism and decisionism (see Crook, 1991). The attempts by Adorno, Horkheimer and their colleagues to establish a 'critical theory of society' represented the most significant and sustained effort to find a way out of this post-Weberian corner. For Habermas (1987: 119) their failure turns on a 'performative contradiction'. In the figure of a nihilistic 'dialectic of enlightenment' Adorno and Horkheimer claim on the one hand that instrumental reason has abolished the distinction between validity and power, destroying the basis of critique. On the other hand Adorno, particularly, commits to a totalizing and relentlessly negative critique – which ought to be impossible on his own diagnosis. The contradiction arises, argues Habermas (1987: 113), because Adorno and Horkheimer 'do not do justice to the rational content of cultural modernity that was captured in bourgeois ideals (and also instrumentalized along with them)'. However, Habermas' stupendous attempt to overcome nihilism in a critical theory that preserves an 'affirmative' dimension has won more respect than acceptance. It is not clear that it evades the 'metaphysical' arm of the dilemma noted above.

If modern – and modernist – social theory has not been strikingly successful in handling the problem of nihilism there has been a vigorous debate about value-questions among approaches usually classified as postmodern. Lyotard (1992a: 13) engages with the Weberian problem of value-fragmentation as well as the Habermasian plea for 'unity' when he asks what type of unity Habermas has in mind: 'the constitution of a sociocultural unity at the heart of which all elements of daily life and thought would have a place, as though within an organic whole?' or alternatively 'the path to be cut between heterogeneous language games – knowledge, ethics, politics . . .?' Habermas opts for the former when only the latter is available. Lyotard's emphasis on heterogeneity overlaps with Rorty's (1989) pragmatism of foundation-less 'conversations', the bearers of values with no guarantees. Fekete's (1988) introduction to an influential collection of essays on value problems characterizes postmodern approaches in terms of their passage beyond a neurotic obsession with 'the Good–God–Gold standards' (1988: xi). In the same collection, Barbara Smith also identifies modern ethical theories with anxieties summed up in what she terms (1988: 6) the 'egalitarian fallacy': 'unless one judgement can be said or shown to be more "valid" than another, then all judgements must be "equal" or "equally valid"'. For Smith as for Lyotard or Rorty, the work of evaluation-without-guarantees goes on regardless of the anxieties of the philosophers.

This more relaxed approach to matters of value meets objections from within the camp of postmodern/ism/ity itself. For Baudrillard (1994: 11, 26, 35), postmodern ethics are implicated in a suspect 'curving back of history': 'it is as though history were rifling through its own dustbins and looking for redemption in the rubbish'. Postmodernity is marked by 'the recycling of past forms, the exalting of residues, rehabilitation by *bricolage*, eclectic sentimentality'. Bauman's cautious endorsement of a postmodern ethics of being together recognizes that both modern and postmodern configurations have their unavoidable pathologies. 'Just as the modern adventure with order and transparency bred opacity and ambivalence, postmodern tolerance breeds intolerance' (Bauman, 1993: 238). The range of views held within the camp of postmodern/ism/ity only underlines two critical points: that modern and postmodern approaches to problems of nihilism and value are intertwined within social theory, and that little purpose is served by the more zealous attempts to disentangle them.

A similar conclusion holds for the problem of the relations between sociocultural analysis and political action. Indeed, the naivety of the view that there might be a single authoritative answer, or even a single authoritative question, is even more striking in this field. In Lemert's (1997: 149) tart formulation, 'resistance is the foremost social problem of late modern, or early postmodern societies. But resistance to what?' Once, Marxists of various stripes were able to give an authoritative and general answer to this question: resistance to the economic and political power of the bourgeois class. Contemporary animal rights activists, environmentalists, feminists or indigenes can also give reasonably precise, but more circumscribed answers. Notoriously, extremely vague answers are furnished by some postmodernisms of resistance. Foucauldians once urged resistance to 'power', while a cluster of French writers including de Certeau (1984), Lyotard (1993) and Maffesoli (1996) urge resistance by the 'weak' against the 'strong'. Rorty (1982) refuses to align a postmodern politics with resistance, preferring the pragmatist tradition of cautious social engineering. In a variant of Smith's diagnosis of 'the egalitarian fallacy', Rorty questions the obsession of French intellectuals with revolutionary politics. In Kumar's (1995: 181) summary, 'if revolutionary politics cannot be justified, there is no politics. The choice for them is total revolution or total nihilism.' Hence, one might add, the stress on 'resistance', however imprecisely drawn its target. There is a clear parallel with problems in the epistemic postmodern considered in the previous section: postmodern approaches are at their least compelling when they seem to be in the grip of attenuated, residual ghosts of modern dreams of purity – whether in epistemology and method or values and politics. Of course, this model of an attenuated but pure radicalism is not confined to the postmodernist side of the fence. Habermas' reconstruction of critical theory may be more subtle and thorough than the postmodernisms of resistance, but (in Rorty's terms) it is the thinnest possible version of the German project to specify the philosophical foundations of modernity (see also Crook, 1991: ch. 4).

It has become conventional among both critics and supporters to align postmodernism with the progressive politics of multiculturalism, new social movements and 'political correctness' (among the critics see Gross and Levitt, 1994: ch. 2; among the friends see Nicholson and Seidman, 1995). While the link is well established empirically, it is rather radically underdetermined by the methods and themes of major postmodernist texts. The analyses of Baudrillard, Derrida, Deleuze, Foucault or Rorty can as well be aligned with 'conservative' as 'progressive' themes and resources. This is a central plank in Habermas' attempted (1987) debunking of the postmodern, of course. By contrast to the rather 'thin' treatment of politics in most postmodernisms, recent years have seen the rise of the 'new political sociology' (see Nash, 2000) and politically oriented social theory. Beck's (1994) model for the 're-invention' of politics under conditions of risk and reflexivity, Etzioni's (1993) embrace of 'communitarianism', Giddens' (1991) postulate of the emergence of 'life politics' and his subsequent (1998) embrace of the British New

Labour 'third way', Inglehart's (1990) 'post-materialism' hypothesis, the examination of the cultural politics of globalization (see Featherstone et al., 1995) and the re-awakening of interest in the analysis of 'civil society' (see Alexander, 1998) are all elements in a rich and vital 'conversation' about the prospects for a political re-making of contemporary societies. Within that conversation, some (for example, Boggs, 1995, 1997) take a gloomy view of the new politics as a collapse of the public sphere. Others (such as Beilharz, 1994) more optimistically fold new politics and postmodern themes into a new socialist programme. Few of the writers cited above would regard themselves as postmodernists, but the themes they address place their work at the heart of debates about the complex of postmodern/ism/ity.

CHANGE IN CULTURE AND SOCIETY

Within a very few years during the early 1990s, the question of the postmodern came to dominate social theory. As late as 1990, Smart was able to note that 'relatively little consideration' had been given thus far to the implications for sociology of 'movement beyond the social, political and epistemological limits of modernism' (Smart, 1990: 25). Only two years later, Rosenau (1992: 3) could write that 'post-modernism haunts social science today'. Kumar (1995: 194) was soon able to present the question of whether social and cultural changes were 'fundamentally a new departure or . . . simply another twist in the capitalist tale' as 'perhaps the central question of contemporary social theory'. The defining and – for some – scandalous novelty of the postmodern/ism/ity complex lies in the links it has forged between long-standing debates in the social sciences and allegedly immanent epochal change. As Whitebook (1982: 53) put it quite early on, 'while the announcement that Minerva's owl is about to depart may be premature, one is increasingly struck by the sense of living in the closing of an epoch'. The idea of the postmodern drew together all of the 'ends' that were fiercely debated during the last quarter of the twentieth century in the different regions of academic and, in some cases public, cultures: ends of art, of class, of history, of the human, of literature, of the nation-state, of science, of socialism and of society.

However, for reasons considered above, many theorists associated with the idea of the postmodern, such as Baudrillard, Derrida and Foucault, are reluctant to address epochal change directly, or even at all. To do so smacks of the speculative philosophies of history that they reject. Yet postmodernist writing gets its edge from showing (if not saying) that the way things are now is radically different from the way things were then. We attend to Baudrillard's analyses of the hyperreal, Foucault's dissections of power/knowledge or Lyotard's critiques of meta-narrative at least in part for the clues they give us to the specificity and direction of the present. The slightly teasing rhetorics of showing or intimating but never (quite) stating plainly links the question of historical ruptures to the epistemic themes discussed above. Maffesoli's physicalism (1996) is buttressed by the suggestion that the collapse of Apollonian modernity allows Dionysian 'sociality' to re-assert itself. The privilege given to textualist themes and methods gains plausibility from assertions that the contemporary world is the outcome of a transition to generalized communication in Vattimo's account or to a generalized logic of simulation in Baudrillard's. Both anti-historicism and anti-universalism draw strength from intimations that a linear and progressive universal history is at an end.

Critics have repeatedly argued that the millennial strain in postmodernism is anachronistic. Perhaps the most influential critique has been Habermas' (1987) argument that modernity remains an 'uncompleted project'. Both 'neo-conservative' and 'anarchist' versions of postmodernity treat the horizon of 'the self-understanding of European modernity' as the 'horizon of a past epoch', but both remain dependent on modern presuppostions, both dress up 'counter-Enlightenment in the garb of post-Enlightenment' (Habermas, 1987: 4–5). Other commentators and critics have pointed to supposedly discrediting continuities between 'postmodern' and 'modern' themes. For example, Lyotard's critique of a modernity premised on 'meta-narratives' replicates Comte's distinction between metaphysical and postive stages of evolution (Crook, 1991: 155) while Foucault's concept of discipline 'merely adds a third stage to Durkheim's two laws of penal evolution' (Rose, 1984: 176). These claims are themselves close to the spirit of Kumar's critique of postindustrial theorizing as a reiteration of the pattern and politics of theories of industrial society, simply adding another stage (Kumar, 1978: 191). While they are less polemical, influential theorists of change such as Beck (1992) and Giddens (1990) have argued that the present is still to be understood as a variant of modernity. Finally, even sympathetic commentators frequently concede that historical and thematic ruptures between modern/ism/ity and postmodern/ism/ity are blurred (see Boyne and Rattansi, 1990: 9; Lash, 1990: 172–3; Lemert, 1997: 24; Smart, 1990: 20–2).

To amplify Kumar's claim, the questions raised in these debates are surely the most fundamental faced by contemporary social theory. What kind of social and cultural world do we now inhabit? What continuities and what ruptures mark its relations with the worlds of the recent and distant past? What forms of theory and analysis will help us to answer those questions? To what degree are those forms shaped by the processes they seek to comprehend? It is clear that the first proposition from the introduction holds good here: social theory cannot reject or ignore the 'problematic' of the postmodern and retain its salience. However, and in relation to the second proposition, it is not clear that postmodernist answers to the questions above command the same assent. As indicated in the third proposition, a much broader range of social theoretical resources may be brought to bear on the problems. Debates about postmodernist aesthetics and an aestheticized postmodernity are at the centre of the problem of postmodernizing change and can provide a point of entry to the more general question.

The playfulness of postmodernist critique and the accessibility of postmodernist cultural products are among the more obviously attractive aspects of the postmodern/ism/ity complex. As Lyon (1999: 97) puts it, it can seem as if 'postmodernists relax in a playground of irony and pastiche, where pluralism and difference contrast with the older "terrorism" of totalizing discourses'. However, the critical positions that condemn postmodernism as relativist, nihilist and quietist also portray its aesthetic as a trivialization. For example, Harris and Lipman (1986) condemn the triviality of postmodern architecture that has abandoned the link between design and the socialist project. This theme was prominent in many early critical responses to the postmodern from Callinicos (1982) through Jameson (1983) to Norris (1990). In O'Neill's recent version, triviality is a symptom of nihilism. Disconnected from history and community, postmodernism can align itself only with the dross of consumer capitalism: 'the footings of postmodernism are sunk in fast food, information desks, rattling waterfalls, lifeless plants and indifferent elevators that marry time and money to the second' (O'Neill, 1995: 197). However, the aesthetic turn of postmodernism also attracted the attention of theorists who found in it a clue to the apparent decomposition of socio-cultural structures defined by relations of production. Bell's (1976) pessimistic diagnosis of a contradiction between a postmodern culture and a modern economy, recently re-stated by Saunders (1995: ch. 5), set the pattern for subsequent – but less overtly conservative – theories of the postmodern that turned on the transformation of 'society' into 'culture' (as in Bauman, 1992; Crook et al., 1992; Featherstone, 1990).

In cultural studies, social theory and sociology the most obvious symptom of this aestheticization of the social is the development of new areas of research and teaching which turn away from classical and structural conceptions of 'society' as something ontologically or epistemologically distinct from 'culture': consumption, embodiment, food, popular culture, tourism and the like. A more overt rejection of classical models is implied in announcements of the 'death of class' (see Pakulski and Waters, 1996). Class, after all, was the quintessential socio-structural concept: hidden from immediate view, the fundamental cleavages of class produced the structural arrangements in which they were reflected. To an important degree, the decomposition of class would be the decomposition of social structure. More radically still, the recent focus on global structures and processes requires, in the words of Featherstone and Lash (1995: 2), 'that we must now embark on the project of understanding social life without the comforting term "society"'. For Touraine (1998: 127) it is the late twentieth-century retreat from projects for the intellectual and political 'reconstruction' of society that has led to its decomposition, so that we 'have learned to do without the idea of society as it was . . . renovated and reinforced by the theorists of modernity, of industrial society, of the welfare state and also of national development policies'. Crook, Pakulski and Waters (1992: 229) have argued that the twin processes of 'the increasing effectivity of culture' and 'the return of nature' play a critical role in a process of postmodernization that not only moves away from modern and towards postmodern configurations but also transforms what we can mean by society and 'the social'. The argument that we must look not only to the cultural but to the technological and natural dimensions of social relations is well established in actor network approaches (see Bijker and Law, 1992, for example) and has recently been taken up by analysts such as Knorr Cetina (1997).

As Lyon (1999: 105) has observed, there is 'much agreement on what are the crucial analytic issues . . . on the eve of the third millennium', surely the issues noted in the previous paragraph would no doubt figure in most lists. But not only is there disagreement, as Lyon notes, about 'whether our social condition is "postmodernity", or "high", "late", "radicalized" or "reflexive" modernity', there is also disagreement about the legitimacy of any such periodizations. Students of Foucault are among the most radical sceptics on this question. Their 'histories of the present' refuse typification and

generalization. For example, Dean (1996: 212–13) suggests that the Foucauldian 'ethos' shares some concerns with social theory, but 'without its will to represent world-historical epochs, conflicts, powers and processes, and without its godlike perspective over the destiny and attributes of humanity'. In similar vein, Barry et al. (1996: 7) dismiss 'grand genealogies of the present moment'.

Rhetorics of this type must be assessed with care. Sweeping historical narratives of social evolution were substantially discredited well before Foucauldian or other postmodern positions were formulated. Adorno and Benjamin were among the pre-war critics of both Hegelian and 'scientific' Marxism, while Weber's historical sociology can be read as a refutation of sociological models of 'stages of development'. More recently, Althusserian Marxism has been a significant influence on anti-historicism. For all its fame, Lyotard's (1984) announcement of the death of meta-narratives can have surprised few of its readers: it re-packaged what had already become received wisdom in a variety of traditions. In that context, terms such as 'godlike' and 'grand' are elements in the rhetorical production of an exaggerated disjunction between careful attention to micro-level contingencies (good and Foucauldian) and the formulation of general theoretical propositions (bad and social-theoretic). The use of theoretical concepts in narrative accounts of social change need be neither a symptom of a closet Hegelianism nor a reversion to grand narratives. The production of provisional and qualified diagnoses of the times that draw on equally provisional and qualified middle-range historical schema is a quite legitimate theoretical pursuit.

The question of historical thresholds made its way back to the centre of attention in social theory, in association with the problem of the postmodern, during the late 1980s. Lash and Urry's (1987) *The End of Organized Capitalism* and Harvey's (1989) *The Condition of Postmodernity* followed Jameson's lead in offering middle-range compromises in debates about postmodernity. Significant transformations of social relations were, indeed, under way but their roots lay in processes that could be grasped by established theoretical concepts and arguments. Capitalist disorganization follows the period of organization as a result of developments in the global economy, changes in the class structures of advanced societies and new spatial divisions of labour. In Harvey's account, Fordism gives way to 'flexible accumulation' in an example of a secular pattern of oscillation between structure and flexibility in capitalist development and crisis management. Each book takes the idea of the postmodern seriously, but nests it inside a middle range historical sequence. For Lash and Urry (1987: 7) it is a 'cultural ideological configuration' correlated with other features of disorganization. For Harvey (1989: 328), it is a 'historical – geographic condition' fused with flexibility, just as mature modernity is fused with Fordism.

When these modestly discontinuist accounts are compared with the explicitly continuist theories of late modernity offered by Beck (1992) and Giddens (1990 and subsequent texts) the interesting thing is that, if anything, the supposedly continuist texts offer the more radical departures from previously mainstream views. Beck's model of late modernity as 'risk society' and Giddens' explorations of 'reflexive' post-traditionalism are less respectful of conventional models of structure and established hierarchies of determination than are Lash and Urry or Harvey. The radicalism of their departure from standard accounts of industrial capitalism is masked by their insistence that they are analysts of an only now maturing modernity. Among the discontinuists, there is a tendency for breaks from the grid of modernity to become more radical over time. So, Lash and Urry's (1994) *Economies of Signs and Space* is a more radical enterprise than their first book, embracing a strong version of 'post-societal sociology' and implying a sharper distinction between 'now' and 'then'. Bauman (1988) embraced a version of the postmodern early in the piece, but as Kellner (1998: 76) points out, his critique of 'modern' ideals and frameworks becomes much sharper over the years.

The elusive thematic boundaries between modernity and postmodernity place formidable difficulties in the way of attempts to locate postmodernity as an historical phase placed after the modern. For any given attempt to specify definitively 'postmodern' themes, examples can be found which locate those themes firmly within historical periods that are clearly 'pre-postmodern'. In response to that difficulty, many commentators have argued that postmodern*ism* is clearly an aspect of modernity itself – perhaps one that is now more prominently, now less prominently displayed. So, for Boyne and Rattansi (1990: 9) postmodernism, like modernism, is a critique of modernity. For Beilharz (1994: 15), 'perhaps postmodernism is the self-styled *doppelgänger* of modernity'. But these moves do not finally determine the location of postmodern*ity* in its troublesome double relation – historical and thematic – to modernity. If the model of postmodernity as an already formed 'social system' (see Bauman, 1992) cannot be defended, some analysts have offered more cautious accounts of posteriority to the modern. For example, Turner (1990) suggests that we renounce the idea of a postmodern that is thematically opposed to the modern while retaining the sense of posteriority – the postmodern is after, not against, the modern. Lyon (1999: 95) is among those who link the posteriority of the postmodern to an internal unravelling of the modern – 'the very items that modernity used to banish ambivalence and uncertainty' have the effect of undermining 'the modern sense of reality'. The account of 'postmodernization' developed by Crook, Pakulski and Waters (1992) generalizes a similar point: the modernity-constituting processes of commodification, differentiation, organization and rationalization accelerate and intensify within modernity, producing effects that radically disrupt and eventually decompose modernity itself.

These positions loop back to a familiar paradox: the real contribution that the idea of the postmodern has made to social theory has been its interrogation of modernity as a category of history and society. To paraphrase Hegel, you don't quite know what you've got 'til its gone. The view that the postmodern is – at present – primarily a passage out of modernity gives rise to two rather distinct perspectives on the receding modern. In one, the defining contours of modernity emerge more sharply, like the skyline of a city seen from some kilometres away. So, modernity was rational, organized, Fordist-industrial, class-divided etc. while our present conditions seem less clear-cut. This view, often linked to 'middle-range' periodizations such as organization–disorganization and Fordism–postFordism, is probably dominant. But from an alternative perspective, the opposite effect is observed: far from becoming sharper, the boundaries of modernity become blurred as we move away, like Los Angeles seen from the air on a smoggy day. To paraphase Lemert, maybe modernity wasn't what you thought. It is an interesting feature of 'continuist' accounts of the present, such as Giddens' and Beck's, that they re-interpret the 'industrial society' of the late nineteenth and early twentieth centuries as not fully modern. For example, Beck (1992) emphasizes the quasi-feudal character of class cultures and family networks in the industrial period.

More generally, the benefit of hindsight might show that cultures and societies of the modern period were always more multi-dimensional, and always had more in common with earlier configurations, than was allowed in theoretical constructs of 'the modern' (see also Seidman, 1991). For example, in Maffesoli's (1996) account it is a waning of the grip of an Apollonian model of the modern that allows us to re-assess the force of an archaic Dionysian sociality. The pattern of trying to link the themes of a postmodern order to pre- or at least early modernity is by now well established. Turner (1990) is among those who saw an analogy between our present condition and the crises of the Baroque period. There too, rapid change and marked dislocation was matched by highly decorative cultural forms and an unstable mixture of the rational and the non-rational in religion and politics. Lyon (1999) is among those who has drawn attention to the recent popularity of premodern – especially Greek – models in ethics, politics and religion among social theorists.

The claim that 'we have never been modern', associated with Baudrillard (1983), Latour (1993) and Maffesoli (1996), dramatized a growing sense that models of 'modern society' were always highly selective, marginalizing processes, experiences and practices that were constitutive of everyday life. Here, the idea of the postmodern is linked to the recognition that the modern was always in crucial respects premodern. A similar challenge to the idea of 'modern society' arises in some studies of change in non-Western societies. Brazilian, Chinese or Indonesian 'modernities' cannot be trimmed on the Procrustean bed of the Anglo-American West. The case of Japan is particularly interesting because the global power of the Japanese economy makes it difficult to marginalize Japan as a case of defective or incomplete modernity. On one plausible diagnosis (see Clammer, 1995), Japan should be regarded as postmodern in its mix of traditionalism, economic hypermodernity and simulatory popular culture. If, as Clammer suggests, Japan has passed directly from its own 'premodernity' to 'postmodernity' without experiencing an Anglo-American 'modernity' it poses a double challenge to social theory. It undermines models of modernity as a necessary and universal stage of development while it equally undermines accounts of the postmodern as a stage located after the modern.

Conclusion: social theory and the postmodern

How, then, are we to answer the question, posed in the introduction, of the significance of 'the postmodern' for 'social theory'? The three main sections of the chapter have set out to demonstrate that three propositions hold good for each of three major areas of concern to social theory: epistemology and method, values and politics, and change in culture and society. The propositions, set out in full in the introduction, are that postmodern themes are inescapable problems and resources for contemporary social theory, that the modern–postmodern distinction is nevertheless troublesome, and that postmodern

themes have deep roots in social theory. To the degree that those propositions hold, the phrase 'postmodern social theory' is really a pleonasm: any social theory that engages with the contemporary world is 'postmodern'. Two qualifications to that statement might reduce the risk of misunderstanding. First, it does not imply that all social theory must be postmodern*ist* as that term is usually understood. It is possible to engage theoretically with the postmodern without buying one of the packaged positions usually termed 'postmodernist' in epistemology, methodology, ethics, politics, aesthetics and history. At the same time, our understanding of the world has not been markedly advanced by attempts to demonize those positions, to use the guilt of postmodernism as an alibi for the innocence of non-postmodern social theory.

Second, the argument that social theory cannot help but be postmodern is not intended to beg periodizing questions about whether the contemporary world 'is' postmodern, high modern, neotraditional or whatever. There can be little serious doubt that the social world, and the ways in which social theory has tried to engage with that world, have changed in significant ways over a relatively brief period of thirty or forty years. For example, how many contemporary social theorists still align themselves with a triumphal, enlightened Western modernity? How many still maintain that 'class' is the template for all inequalities of gender and race? How many maintain that the key to the analysis of consumption lies in the analysis of production? How many take their object of study to be integrated and autonomous national societies? The claim that social theory cannot but be postmodern says no more initially than that social theory must engage with the complex transformations that are shaping both the contemporary world and the ways in which we apprehend it. Perhaps the claim implies a little more than that: naturally enough, social theorists who have directly addressed the idea of the postmodern have made major contributions to clarifying the complex of issues that have been labelled 'postmodern themes' here. But the match is not exact: some notable postmodern*ists* do not address the idea of the postmodern other than in passing, while anti-postmodernists such as Beck and Giddens do address important 'postmodern themes'. So, a range of positions that apply differing labels to the present can contribute to social theoretical debate on the postmodern.

The fourth proposition in the introduction calls for a 'modestly postmodern' social theory, focused on the shifting shapes and textures of 'the social'. That proposition can be addressed by posing two questions. First, in what ways has the postmodern made a decisive difference to social theory? Secondly, in what ways might social theory productively turn away from what are usually understood as postmodern positions? The materials for an answer to each question have been provided in the preceding sections.

On questions of epistemology and method, the postmodern has focused efforts to re-assert in contemporary conditions the fundamental insight of social theory that knowledge is relative to the context and the means of its production. There can be legitimate debate as to which version of this insight is to be preferred, but social theory cannot now credibly ignore its reflexive dimension. So here the postmodern has made a difference. But at the same time, post-modern approaches that mobilize the reflexive moment to debunk all knowledge claims – other than those produced by their own deconstructive or genealogical procedures – are implausible. They recapitulate modernist mythologies of pure critique, fail to distinguish between methodo-logical and other variants of relativism and commit epistemological variants of Smith's 'egalitarian fallacy'. So social theory need not consider itself bound by the more strident postmodernist positions on these questions. To be 'modestly postmodern' here is to trace the ways in which the reflexivity of knowledges of the social constitutes and limits, but does not destroy, modes of validity. One effect of such a positioning would be to draw postmodern social theory back towards a closer relationship with the social sciences. Here, the point is not to mock the methodological naivety of 'positivism', but to understand what can legitimately be inferred from particular empirical studies and how the inferences might inform theory. Social theory has a legitimate synthetic, as well as analytic, moment.

A symmetrical case holds for questions of value and politics. On value questions, particu-larly, the postmodern has reminded social theory of the potential nihilism of value relativism and re-awakened interest in the attempt to resolve the problem. If some variants of the postmodern stand charged with nihilism – like some variants of non-postmodern social theory – others have made significant contributions to a post-founda-tional ethics. On questions of politics, the postmodern stress on the multiple forms and sites of subordination and on the repressed voices of the subordinate has become a significant resource for the post-Marxist left. However, in contemporary debates about value and politics little purpose is served by the search for a clear, sharp line that divides postmodern from other approaches. In the hands of critics, it produces only the slogans and caricatures of culture warriors. In the hands of advocates, it produces

positions that parallel the epistemological mythologies noted above and give credibility to the culture warriors. Strident postmodernisms of 'resistance' perpetuate the idea of a 'pure' politics uncontaminated by tendencies to oppression or compromise. Such positions misconstrue the nuances of value relativism, commit ethical and political variants of the 'egalitarian fallacy' and endorse resistance in a way that drifts towards nihilism. A modestly postmodern social theory must begin from the diagnosis that there are no historical or universal principles that can stand as guarantor for its ethical or political positions. But rather than embrace the problematic certainties of postmodernisms of resistance it should range more widely across contemporary 'conversa-tions' about post-foundational ethics and poli-tics. Its engagement should include both a careful assessment of programmes of social scientific research and attention to the whole gamut of political activities, including electoral politics.

Questions of social and cultural change are the elusive core of the postmodern. They are the core because it is the assertion, or frequently the intimation, of immanent epochal thresholds that defines the 'post' in postmodern and holds together postmodern positions on aesthetic, epistemological, ethical and political matters. The questions are elusive because, in any register we choose, it turns out to be extremely difficult to align thematic and historical disjunctions to produce unambiguous boundaries between the modern and postmodern. This difficulty leads many critics to reject the idea of the postmodern out of hand as vague and incoherent. As we have seen in the previous section, there are ample grounds for such impatience. But at the same time, even if the answers given are unsatisfac-tory, the questions posed by the postmodern will not go away. Social theory cannot abandon the attempts to determine what kind of world we now inhabit and to trace its relations of con-tinuity and discontinuity with the worlds of the past.

So, what would be the tasks of a 'modestly postmodern' social theory that took up these questions? An obvious first task must be to find a way of addressing change theoretically that neither falls back into historicist grand narra-tives nor remains fixed on genealogical particu-larities. Unfashionable as it may be to say so, the historical and methodological texts of Marx and Weber provide important pointers here, since each in his own way tried to find a path between unpalatable alternatives similar to those we now face. A second task must be to determine what remains of 'the social' after we have given away the defining idea of 'society'. Here, classical authorities are of less help. One important possibilty is that 'the social' becomes the way in which natural, technical, discursive and psychic processes hang together, to the extent that they do hang together. In the vocabulary of Latour, Law and their colleagues, the social then inheres in the production of 'networks' or 'chains of association'. In Lyotard's vocabulary, the social becomes the 'path' between language games. One implication of this approach is that the social is neither a predetermined terrain, always available as a scene for action, nor a fixed quantum. Understood in this way, the sphere of the social expands or contracts depending on the length of the chains or paths. If such a possibility were pursued, it would generate a third and related task. If we can no longer take 'society' as a given reality in the Durkheimian sense, and if the space of the social can both expand and contract, how do we account for the orderliness of social and cultural life? We can no longer answer that question plausibly by constructing a model of a unitary, homogeneous and hegemonic order or structure. The task, rather, must be to explore the ways in which multiple programmes for the ordering of social life interesect with, contest and accommodate each other. Of course, these tasks do not begin to capture the great diversity of projects that are carried on, and should continue to be carried on, under the rubric of social theory. However, a case can be made that they must be addressed if social theory is to engage with the contemporary world in a way that is both adequate to the challenge of the postmodern and also merits the dignity of the title 'theory'.

REFERENCES

Alexander, J. (ed.) (1998) *Real Civil Societies*. London: Sage.

Antonio, R. (1995) 'Nietzsche's Antisociology: Subjectified Culture and the End of History', *American Journal of Sociology*, 101: 1–43.

Ashley, D. (1990) 'Habermas and the Completion of "the Project of Modernity"', in B. Turner (ed.), *Theories of Modernity and Postmodernity*. London: Sage. pp. 88–107.

Barry, A., Osborne, T. and Rose, N. (1996) 'Introduction', in A. Barry, T. Osborne and N. Rose (eds), *Foucault and Political Reason*. London: UCL Press. pp. 1–17.

Baudrillard, J. (1981) *For a Critique of the Political Economy of the Sign*. St Louis: Telos Press.

Baudrillard, J. (1983) *In the Shadow of the Silent Majorities*. New York: Semiotext(e).

Baudrillard, J. (1994) *The Illusion of the End*. Cambridge: Polity Press.

Bauman, Z. (1988) 'Sociology and Postmodernity', *Sociological Review*, 36: 790–813.

Bauman, Z. (1992) *Intimations of Postmodernity*. London: Routledge.

Bauman, Z. (1993) *Postmodern Ethics*. Oxford: Blackwell.

Beck, U. (1992) *Risk Society: Towards a New Modernity*. London: Sage.

Beck, U. (1994) 'The Reinvention of Politics: Towards a Theory of Reflexive Modernization', in U. Beck et al., *Reflexive Modernization*. Cambridge: Polity Press. ch. 1.

Beilharz, P. (1994) *Postmodern Socialism: Romanticism, City and State*. Melbourne: Melbourne University Press.

Bell, D. (1973) *The Coming of Post Industrial Society*. New York: Basic Books.

Bell, D. (1976) *The Cultural Contradictions of Capitalism*. New York: Basic Books.

Berman, M. (1982) *All That is Solid Melts into Air: The Experience of Modernity*. New York: Simon and Schuster.

Bijker, W. and Law, J. (eds) (1992) *Shaping Technology/Building Society*. Cambridge, MA: MIT Press.

Billig, M. and Simon, H. (1994) 'Introduction', in H. Simon and M. Billig (eds), *After Postmodernism: Reconstructing Ideology Critique*. London: Sage. pp. 1–13.

Blum, A. (1974) *Theorizing*. London: Heinemann.

Boggs, C. (1995) 'Socialist Decline and the Radical Challenge', in *The Socialist Tradition: From Crisis to Decline*. New York: Routledge. ch. 6.

Boggs, C. (1997) 'The Great Retreat: Decline of the Public Sphere in Late Twentieth-century America', *Theory and Society*, 26: 741–80.

Boyne, R. and Rattansi, A. (1990) 'The Theory and Politics of Postmodernism: By Way of an Introduction', in R. Boyne and A. Rattansi (eds), *Postmodernism and Society*. London: Macmillan. pp. 1–45.

Callinicos, A. (1982) *Is There a Future for Marxism?* London: Macmillan.

Callinicos, A. (1990) 'Reactionary Postmodernism?', in R. Boyne and A. Rattansi (eds), *Postmodernism and Society*. London: Macmillan. pp. 97–118.

Clammer, J. (1995) 'From Modernity to Postmodernity?', in *Difference and Modernity: Social Theory and Contemporary Japanese Society*. London: Kegan Paul International. ch. 2.

Cotgrove, S. (1982) *Catastrophe or Cornucopia?*. Chichester: John Wiley.

Crook, S. (1990) 'The End of Radical Social Theory?', in R. Boyne and A. Rattansi (eds), *Postmodernism and Society*. London: Macmillan. pp. 46–75.

Crook, S. (1991) *Modernist Radicalism and its Aftermath: Foundationalism and Anti-Foundationalism in Radical Social Theory*. London: Routledge.

Crook, S., Pakulski, J. and Waters, M. (1992) *Postmodernization: Change in Advanced Society*. London: Sage.

Crowther, P. (1990) 'Postmodernism and the Visual Arts: a Question of Ends', in R. Boyne and A.

Rattansi (eds), *Postmodernism and Society*. London: Macmillan. pp. 237–59.

Dean, M. (1996) 'Foucault, Government and the Enfolding of Authority', in A. Barry, T. Osborne and N. Rose (eds), *Foucault and Political Reason*. London: UCL Press. pp. 209–29.

De Certeau, M. (1984) *The Practice of Everyday Life*. Berkeley: University of California Press.

Deleuze, G. (1994) *Difference and Repetition*. London: Athlone Press.

Derrida, J. (1976) *Of Grammatology*. Baltimore: Johns Hopkins University Press.

Dews, P. (1980) 'The "New Philosophers" and the End of Leftism', *Radical Philosophy*, 24: 2–11.

Dews, P. (1987) *Logics of Disintegration*. London: Verso.

Etzioni, A. (1993) *The Spirit of Community*. New York: Touchstone.

Featherstone, M. (1986) 'French Social Theory: an Introduction', *Theory, Culture & Society*, 3 (3): 1–5.

Featherstone, M. (1988) 'In Pursuit of the Postmodern', *Theory, Culture & Society*, 5: 195–215.

Featherstone, M. (1990) 'Perspectives on Consumer culture', *Sociology*, 24 (1): 5–22.

Featherstone, M. (1991) *Consumer Culture and Postmodernism*. London: Sage.

Featherstone, M. and Lash, S. (1995) 'Globalization, Modernity and the Spatialization of Social Theory: an Introduction', in M. Featherstone, S. Lash and Robertson, R. (eds), *Global Modernities*. London: Sage. pp. 1–24.

Featherstone, M., Lash, S. and Robertson, R. (eds) (1995) *Global Modernities*. London: Sage.

Fekete, J. (1988) 'Introductory Notes for a Postmodern Value Agenda', in J. Fekete (ed.), *Life After Postmodernism: Essays on Value and Culture*. London: Macmillan. pp. i–xix.

Foster, H. (ed.) (1983) *The Anti-Aesthetic*. Port Townsend: Bay Press.

Foucault, M. (1980) *Power/Knowledge*. Brighton: Harvester Press.

Game, A. (1991) *Undoing the Social: Towards a Deconstructive Sociology*. Milton Keynes: Open University Press.

Gibbons, M., Limoges, C., Nowotny, H., Schwartzman, S., Scott, P. and Trow, M. (1994) *The New Production of Knowledge*. London: Sage.

Giddens, A. (1990) *Consequences of Modernity*. Cambridge: Polity Press.

Giddens, A. (1991) *Modernity and Self-Identity*. Cambridge: Polity Press.

Giddens, A. (1998) *The Third Way*. Cambridge: Polity Press.

Gross, P. and Levitt, N. (1994) *Higher Superstition: The Academic Left and Its Quarrels with Science*. Baltimore: Johns Hopkins University Press.

Guattari, F. (1984) *Molecular Revolution*. Harmondsworth: Penguin.

Habermas, J. (1981) 'Modernity versus Postmodernity', *New German Critique*, 22: 3–14.

Habermas, J. (1983) 'Neoconservative Culture Criticism in the United States and West Germany', *Telos*, 56. (Reprinted in R. Bernstein (ed.) (1985) *Habermas and Modernity*. Cambridge: Polity Press. pp. 78–95.)

Habermas, J. (1987) *The Philosophical Discourse of Modernity*. Cambridge: Polity Press.

Hall, S. and Jefferson, T. (eds) (1975) *Resistance Through Rituals*. London: Hutchinson.

Hall, S. et al. (eds) (1980) *Culture, Media, Language*. London: Hutchinson.

Harding, S. (1991) *Whose Science? Whose Knowledge?*. New York: Cornell University Press.

Harris, H. and Lipman, A. (1986) 'A Culture of Despair: Reflections on Postmodern Architecture', *Sociological Review*, 34: 837–54.

Harvey, D. (1989) *The Condition of Postmodernity*. Oxford: Blackwell.

Hassan, I. (1985) 'The Culture of Postmodernism', *Theory, Culture & Society*, 2 (3): 119–31.

Hindess, B. and Hirst, P. (1977) *Mode of Production and Social Formation*. London: Routledge and Kegan Paul.

Inglehart, R. (1977) *The Silent Revolution*. Princeton, NJ: Princeton University Press.

Inglehart, R. (1990) *Culture Shift in Advanced Industrial Society*. Princeton, NJ: Princeton University Press.

Jameson, F. (1983) 'Postmodernism and Consumer Society', in H. Foster (ed.), *The Anti-Aesthetic*. Port Townsend: Bay Press.

Jameson, F. (1984) 'Postmodernism, or, the Cultural Logic of Late Capitalism', *New Left Review*, 146: 53–92.

Jameson, F. (1991) *Postmodernism, or, The Cultural Logic of Late Capitalism*. Durham, NC: Duke University Press.

Jay, D. (1984) *Marxism and Totality*. Berkeley, CA: University of California Press.

Jencks, C. (1987) *What is Post-Modernism?* (2nd edn). London: Academy Editions.

Jones, J., Natter, W. and Schatzki, T. (1993) '"Post"-ing Modernity', in J. Jones, W. Natter and T. Schatzki (eds), *Postmodern Contentions*. New York: Guilford Press. pp. 1–16.

Kellner, D. (1998) 'Zygmunt Bauman's Postmodern Turn', *Theory, Culture & Society*, 15 (1): 73–86.

Knorr-Cetina, K. (1997) 'Sociality with Objects: Social Relations in Postsocial Knowledge Societies', *Theory, Culture & Society*, 14 (4): 1–30.

Kumar, K. (1978) *Prophecy and Progress: the Sociology of Industrial and Post-Industrial Society*. Harmondsworth: Penguin.

Kumar, K. (1995) *From Post-Industrial to Post-Modern Society: New Theories of the Contemporary World*. Oxford: Blackwell.

Lash, S. (1990) *Sociology of Postmodernism*. London: Routledge.

Lash, S. and Urry, J. (1987) *The End of Organized Capitalism*. Cambridge: Polity Press.

Lash, S. and Urry, J. (1994) *Economies of Signs and Space*. London: Sage.

Latour, B. (1993) *We Have Never Been Modern*. Cambridge, MA: Harvard University Press.

Latour, B. and Woolgar, S. (1986) *Laboratory Life*, 2nd edn. Princeton, NJ: Princeton University Press.

Lemert, C. (1997) *Postmodernism is Not What You Think*. Malden, MA: Blackwell.

Lyon, D. (1999) *Postmodernity*, 2nd edn. Buckingham: Open University Press.

Lyotard, J.-F. (1984) *The Postmodern Condition: A Report on Knowledge*. Manchester: Manchester University Press.

Lyotard, J.-F. (1992a) 'Answer to the Question: What is Postmodernism?', in *The Postmodern Explained to Children*. London: Turnaround. ch. 1.

Lyotard, J.-.F (1992b) 'Note on the Meaning of "Post"', in *The Postmodern Explained to Children*. London: Turnaround. ch. 7.

Lyotard, J.-.F (1993) 'On the Strength of the Weak', in *Toward the Postmodern*. Atlantic Highlands, NJ: Humanities Press. ch. 5.

McHugh, P., Raffel, S., Foss, B. and Blum, A. (1974) *On the Beginning of Social Enquiry*. London: Routledge and Kegan Paul.

McLennan, G. et al. (eds) (1977) *On Ideology (Working Papers in Cultural Studies 10)*. Birmingham: CCCS, University of Birmingham.

Maffesoli, M. (1996) *The Time of the Tribes*. London: Sage.

Mestrovic, S. (1993) *The Barbarian Temperament: Towards a Post Modern Critical Theory*. London: Routledge.

Milbrath, L. (1984) *Environmentalists: Vanguard for a New Society*. Albany, NY: State University of New York Press.

Nash, K. (2000) *Contemporary Political Sociology*. Oxford: Blackwell.

Nicholson, L. and Seidman, S. (1995) 'Introduction', in L. Nicholson and S. Seidman (eds), *Social Postmodernism: Beyond Identity Politics*. Cambridge: Cambridge University Press. pp. 1–35.

Norris, C. (1990) 'Lost in the Funhouse: Baudrillard and the Politics of Postmodernism', in R. Boyne and A. Rattansi (eds), *Postmodernism and Society*. London: Macmillan.

O'Neill, J. (1995) *The Poverty of Postmodernism*. London: Routledge.

Pakulski, J. and Waters, M. (1996) *The Death of Class*. London: Sage.

Ritzer, G. (1997) *Postmodern Social Theory*. New York: McGraw-Hill.

Rorty, R. (1982) 'Method, Social Science and Social Hope', in *The Consequences of Pragmatism*. Brighton: Harvester Press. ch. 11.

Rorty, R. (1989) 'The Contingency of a Liberal Community', in *Contingency, Irony, Solidarity*. Cambridge: Cambridge University Press. ch. 3.

Rose, G. (1984) *Dialectic of Nihilism*. Oxford: Blackwell.

Rosenau, P. (1992) *Post-Modernism and the Social Sciences: Insights, Inroads and Intrusions*. Princeton, NJ: Princeton University Press.

Sandywell, B., Silverman, D., Roche, M., Filmer, P. and Phillipson, M. (1975) *Problems of Reflexivity and Dialectics in Sociological Enquiry*. London: Routledge and Kegan Paul.

Saunders, P. (1995) *Capitalism: A Social Audit*. Buckingham: Open University Press.

Seidman, S. (1991) 'The End of Sociological Theory: the Postmodern Hope', *Sociological Theory*, 9: 131–46.

Smart, B. (1983) *Foucault, Marxism and Critique*. London: Routledge and Kegan Paul.

Smart, B. (1990) 'Modernity, Postmodernity and the Present', in B. Turner (ed.), *Theories of Modernity and Postmodernity*. London: Sage. pp. 14–30.

Smith, B. (1988) 'Value Without Truth Value', in J. Fekete (ed.), *Life After Postmodernism: Essays on Value and Culture*. London: Macmillan. pp. 1–21.

Squires, J. (1993) 'Introduction', in J. Squires (ed.), *Principled Positions: Postmodernism and the Rediscovery of Value*. London: Lawrence and Wishart.

Stehr, N. (1992) 'Experts, Counsellors and Advisers', in N. Stehr and R. Ericson (eds), *The Culture and Power of Knowledge*. Berlin: de Gruyter. pp. 107–92.

Strauss, L. (1953) *Natural Right and History*. Chicago: University of Chicago Press.

Touraine, A. (1974) *The Post Industrial Society*. London: Wildwood House.

Touraine, A. (1998) 'Sociology Without Society', *Current Sociology*, 46 (2): 119–43.

Turner, B. (1990) 'Periodization and Politics in the Postmodern', in B. Turner (ed.), *Theories of Modernity and Postmodernity*. London: Sage. pp. 1–13.

Vattimo, G. (1992) *The Transparent Society*. Cambridge: Polity Press.

Watson-Verran, H. and Turnbull, D. (1995) 'Science and Other Indigenous Knowledge Systems', in S. Jasanoff et al. (eds), *Handbook of Science and Technology Studies*. Thousand Oaks, CA: Sage. pp. 115–39.

Whitebook, J. (1982) 'Saving the Subject: Modernity and the Problem of the Autonomous Individual', *Telos*, 50: 79–102.

25

Michel Foucault: 'A Man in Danger'

MITCHELL DEAN

> Our societies have proved to be really demonic since they happen to combine those two games – the city–citizen game and the shepherd–flock game – in what we call modern states.

(Foucault, 1988c: 71)

What could Michel Foucault have meant by this statement delivered in his Tanner lectures to his audience at Stanford University in October 1979? Was it a case of hyperbole, an attempt to catch the ear of an indifferent American audience, designed to convince them of his critical intent and credentials? Was it something we were meant to pass over quickly and move on to the more detailed analysis of different forms of what he called 'political rationality'? Or was this statement meant to summarize and to a certain extent encapsulate Foucault's understanding of the nature of 'modern societies'? Does it thereby stand as testimony to Foucault's abiding preoccupations that persisted despite all apparent ruptures and revisions?

The variety and sheer volume of commentary on Foucault's work suggests that there is no single way of understanding or encapsulating his theoretical contribution.[1] In this chapter, I present an interpretation of Foucault's legacy that challenges one contention that runs through much of this literature, that Foucault's work can be characterized foremost in terms of its discontinuities. While accepting that there are discontinuities of subject matter and perspective within his work, I want to suggest that it can be characterized in terms of at least one fundamental continuity. That continuity resides, not in Foucault's general theoretical pronouncements

concerning power but in an 'analytics' of the regulation – or as he would have it, 'government' – of human beings according to forms of truth in what might be loosely described as 'modern' societies. From *Madness and Civilization* (1965) to the *The Care of the Self* (1986), Foucault is centrally concerned, in much more concrete terms, with the question of what he occasionally calls the 'society of normalization' (for example, Foucault, 1980: 107), with the regulation of human individuals and populations according to practices that divide and group them according to certain norms, and the identities they assume or are furnished with in relation to such norms. Without denying the specific concerns of the final published volumes of his *History of Sexuality*, these last works can be understood as an attempt to contribute to the genealogy of this 'society of normalization' in at least one way – to show how it is possible to conceive and govern oneself outside the framework of the norm and identity.

To make this argument I focus on one point of supposed rupture: that between the first volume of the *History of Sexuality* (hereafter referred to as *The Will to Knowledge*, to use its less clumsy French title), published in France at the end of 1976, and the lecture series of 1977–8 and 1978–9 which elaborate the concept of 'governmentality'. I suggest here that the reflection on the arts of government in the latter lectures does not erase the earlier discussions of bio-politics, sovereignty and discipline but places them within the development of the modern government of the state. It is thus not possible to contrast an earlier, more 'radical' Foucault with a more cautious, pragmatic analyst of the arts of government, to reprise something of Richard

Rorty's distinction between a Nietzschean Foucault and a liberal Foucault (1992). Foucault remained concerned throughout his intellectual life with the manner in which human beings are divided and governed according to certain forms of knowledge, how the 'dividing practices' of modern societies often accomplish this through furnishing individuals and groups with various identities, and with the attendant dangers inherent in this process. The ethical and political impulse of his work remained one of a mood of recognition that we live in perpetual danger even, and particularly, when we try to enact a normative political vision. The symbol and catastrophic eventuation of that danger remained, more than anything else, I shall suggest, the Final Solution.

The chapter is divided into three parts: first, an investigation into continuity and discontinuity in Foucault's analysis of forms of power during the 1970s; secondly, an elaboration of his general framework for the analysis of power and rule in modern societies, including a discussion of the relationship between such concepts as biopolitics, sovereignty and liberalism; and finally, an exploration on the possibility of the use of this framework to analyse authoritarian forms of rule, and to begin to offer an account of modern political evil.

CONTINUITY AND DISCONTINUITY IN FOUCAULT'S DISCUSSION OF POWER

Discontinuity

Several commentators, including those who closely collaborated with him, suggest that there are important discontinuities within Foucault's work. Dreyfus and Rabinow (1982), in their justly famous commentary, find a fundamental discontinuity between Foucault's archaeology of discourse formations and his genealogy of power relations. On their reading, the discovery and thematization of power answers the problem of the 'outside' of discourse, of the articulation of the procedures for the production of truth and value with social and institutional relations of domination and power. Pasquale Pasquino (1993), while acknowledging this first shift, suggests a disjunction of a rather different kind: between Foucault's discussions of power and his analytics of government. He recollects:

> It became clear during our discussions of the second half of the 1970s that the discourse on disciplines had reached an impasse and could go no further. That it threatened above all to lead to an extremist denunciation of power – envisioned according to a *repressive* model – that left us both dissatisfied from a theoretical point of view. If a close analysis of discipline opposed the Marxist thesis of economic exploitation as a principle for understanding the investigation of the mechanism of power, this analysis by itself was not enough and required the investigation of global problems of the regulation and ordering of society as well as the modalities of conceptualizing this problem. Hence the question of *government* – a term Foucault gradually substituted for what he began to see as the more ambiguous word, 'power'. (1993: 79; emphasis in original)

Foucault maintained several theses about power during the final decade of his life, namely, that power should be regarded as multiple, positive, productive and relational.[2] That is to say, there is no single form of power for Foucault. It is pervasive, present in all social relations and is exercised at innumerable points and in heterogeneous forms. Moreover, power does not primarily operate through the repressive form of interdiction and law, but is creative of forms of subjectivity, of capacities, and of modes of action. Nor does it exist as a substance that can be possessed by a particular party. Rather, it is conceived as a balance of forces, an overall complex strategical situation between parties in complex relations of contestation and resistance. Nevertheless, there are three important shifts in Foucault's conceptualization of power that stand in support of Pasquino's thesis of discontinuity.

First of all, Foucault removes an assumption which is present in much of the conventional literature on power – that power and liberty exist in an inverse and, in a sense, quantitative relationship. The exercise of power, in this view, entails the subtraction of liberty. While Foucault had already rejected the idea that power works through a 'deductive' subtraction of forces and capacities, he only later draws out the implications of that idea. Instead of an inverse, quantitative relationship between power and liberty, Foucault now suggests that the exercise of power presupposes liberty in the sense that it is possible for the subject of power to act in more than one way. Such a notion is entailed in his various characterizations of relationships of power as 'strategic games between liberties' (1988a: 19) and 'a total structure of action brought to bear upon the actions of others' (1982: 220). Such conceptions of power are interesting because they presuppose the existence of free subjects, that is, subjects who are, to use the sociological term, 'agents' in that they are able to act in a number of ways even while they are acted upon. Power in this regard is an aspect of all social relations and may take the form of open and reversible relationships.

This leads Foucault to a second move: it is possible, he continues, to distinguish among these relations of power those that take a relatively fixed, irreversible and hierarchical form. When such a form is combined with a high degree of circumscription of the possibilities of action because the 'margin of liberty is extremely limited', we have what Foucault calls 'domination' (1988a: 12). Thus Foucault uses the term domination to designate 'what we ordinarily call power' (1988a: 12), and argues that power should be viewed as an aspect of all social relationships. Indeed, one of the consequences of this approach is that we cannot say very much at all about power in general, and that our investigations should concentrate on 'what happens' in social and political relationships and focus on the means by which power is exercised. For Foucault, 'power as such does not exist' (1982: 217). This is the third shift in Foucault's approach to power. Instead of a 'microphysics' (or, indeed, macrophysics) of power, he offers us an analytics of all the ways in which various political and social actors seek to affect the action of others – an analytics of government, 'government' defined as the 'conduct of conduct'.

There is more to support a picture of discontinuity. If one wanted to find the tendency to an 'extremist denunciation of power', as Pasquino put it, one could do no better than to look to Foucault's lectures at the Collège de France of the year 1975–6. There he contrasts conventional approaches to power based on the 'juridical-political theory of sovereignty' with the 'discourse of war'. He makes an effort to displace the traditional questions of the legitimacy of power, of the right of the sovereign, and of the consent and obligation of subjects, by questions of tactics and strategies, of domination and subordination. This entails not only cutting off the King's head in our political thought – an image from interviews about this time (for example, Foucault, 1980: 121) – but attending to the mobile relations of domination, of tactics and strategy within the social body. It entails viewing the condition of peace within a given territory as the disposition of forces engaged in a permanent state of struggle and war. Casting for an alternative conception of power to that grounded in the figure of the legitimate sovereign and its law-making right, Foucault asks 'who imagined that the civil order was an order of battle, who perceived war in the watermark of peace, who has sought the principle of intelligibility of order, of the state, of its institutions and its history, in the outcry, in the confusion and in the mud of battles?' (Foucault, 21 January 1976, cited in Stoler, 1995: 64). His search for alternative perspectives is captured in the suggestion

that it is necessary to reverse Clausewitz's aphorism that war is politics continued by other means (1980: 90–1). Such a reversal means, first, that politics is viewed as 'sanctioning and upholding the disequilibrium of forces that was displayed in war', second, that the phenomena of 'civil peace' should be interpreted but as episodes in the continuation of the same war, and third, that the end result can only be decided by a 'recourse to arms'.

These lectures cover such concerns as the seventeenth-century historical-political narratives of the 'war of the races', first at the time of the English revolution (in the work of Coke and Lilburne) and later at the time of aristocratic struggle against the French monarchy (with Boulainvilliers and Buat-Nançay), its various political uses, and the biological and social class re-inscriptions of racial discourse in the nineteenth century, beginning with Augustin and Thierry (Stoler, 1995: 55–88; Foucault, 1997a, 1997b: 60–5). He concludes with the development of the biological state racisms and the genocidal politics of the twentieth century. The final lecture, which is recapitulated in the last and important chapter in *The Will to Knowledge*, ends on a radical analysis of the Nazi state and of varieties of socialism. When Foucault sought to give examples of the form of power, 'biopower' (or the power over life), he was examining at this time, he found them in the most terrible regimes and events of the twentieth century. As if to underline the importance of these themes, Foucault said of the last chapter of *The Will to Knowledge* that 'no-one wants to talk about that last part . . . All the same it's the fundamental part of the book' (1980: 222).

More evidence is added to the thesis of discontinuity by Foucault's return to the lecture podium in 1978. Now the topic is not the development of the great genocidal state racisms of the twentieth century, but the development of early modern conceptions of the government of the state, of what he would call 'governmentality', under the title of 'Security, Territory, and Population' (1991; 1997a: 67–71). In the following year, despite the title of the course being 'The Birth of Bio-politics', Foucault's course summary suggests he turns to a discussion of liberalism and forms of neo-liberalism (1997a: 73–9). We also notice at this time Foucault has given up on his earlier project of a seven volume *History of Sexuality* and has begun to investigate ancient Greek and Roman notions of the government of the self. The drama of the discourse of war, the theme of race and the emblem of National Socialism and the Holocaust, has been replaced by the analysis of government, the concern with population and a focus on liberalism. 'Power–knowledge' had given way to 'governmentality'. The six volume series of the *History of Sexuality* had apparently been abandoned. Not only the content, but also the temper and tone, had apparently changed.[3]

There is some justice in noticing the movement of such a lively form of thought as Foucault's. The years 1975 to 1978 seem to reflect a change in the political temper among Parisian intellectuals. We witness the move from the ultra-leftism of the early 1970s and engagement with the ideas of the Maoist *Gauche Prolétarienne* to the participation in the discovery of dissidence within the Soviet Union and its satellites, the publicity stunt of the 'new philosophers', the final discrediting of institutional forms of Marxism, and the French publication of Alexander Solzheitsyn's *The Gulag Archipelago*.[4] All these had no doubt an impact on Foucault and were the context in which he spoke at the Collège de France. Without doubt, all of this occasions a more recursive approach to political pronouncements in Foucault's thought, a shifting within his problematics of power, and a realization that the question of the 'society of normalization' must be posed in terms that are more nuanced and subtle than some of his (and others') formulations at that time.[5]

'Demonic societies'

Despite this argument and this evidence, I think that what we witness in these crucial years is less of a break in Foucault's thought and more an unfolding, an elaboration, a refinement and a repositioning of certain of its elements. The extraordinary statement with which we began this chapter stands in evidence of this view, perhaps more than any other. From a philological perspective, the timing of this statement is interesting and suggests that Foucault had not given up his concern for the 'extreme' forms taken by more mundane political thought. This statement is found in lectures delivered in October 1979, well after any supposed break between an extremist Foucault and a more liberal one. With their focus on pastoral power, reason of state and German police science (*Polizeiwissenschaft*), the Tanner lectures appear to be based on material from Foucault's Collège de France course of 1977–8 (1997a: 67–73). There is thus more than a trace of the same problem of political evil that we saw was in evidence in the final lecture of his previous course in 1975–6 (1997b: 213–35) and in the final chapter of *The Will to Knowledge*. Writing of the paradoxes of the 'life-administering power' or 'bio-power', he notes the apparent paradox that 'wars were never as bloody as they have been since the nineteenth century, and all things being

equal, never before did regimes visit such holocausts on their own populations' (1979: 136–7). That the problem posed by National Socialism and the Final Solution remained as a dark shadow across his analysis of political rationality is borne out by a part of the Stanford lectures which was not included in the final published form, in which he concludes a discussion of the importance of life as a political problem with the following: 'Both the development of the human and social sciences, and the simultaneous possibility of protecting life and of the holocaust make their historical appearance' (quoted in Dreyfus and Rabinow, 1982: 138). If anything, the use of the singular noun, 'the holocaust', bears out a central contention of a number of commentators and biographers that 'Foucault was tormented by Auschwitz' (Bernauer, 1992; Milchman and Rosenberg, 1996: 102) and that he was 'haunted by the memory of Hitler's total war and the Nazi death camps' (Miller, 1993: 171).

The term 'demonic' itself perhaps draws together a complex of meaning that includes this sense in which the exploration of politics for Foucault must be haunted by the Nazi extermination of millions of Jews and other people. It would perhaps be permissible to read this term as analogous to Socrates' *daimon*, which, as Pierre Hadot puts it, was both a kind of inspiration that came over him in an irrational manner and his real 'character' (Hadot, 1995: 164–5). The demonic would thus be the inspirational character of modern states, accounting for something of their dynamism and capacity for political invention. However, the occasion of Foucault's statement is of a discussion of a 'strange game whose elements are life, death, truth, obedience, individuals and self-identity' (1988c: 71). Life and death figure prominently in the discussions of bio-politics and sovereignty of 1975–6. This not only suggests a continuity of certain fundamental themes but thereby provides a warrant for an interpretation of the term in the much stronger sense as referring to the possibility of great political evil. Foucault sought to pose the problem of political evil as that which lurks in our rationalities and techniques of government and in the various attempts to combine elements of the 'shepherd–flock' and 'city–citizen games'. The terms have certainly changed, but the perspective seems relatively unmodified. In 1976, the 'shepherd–flock game' took the form of the modern life-politics, bio-politics, and the 'city–citizen game' was cast in the language and practice of sovereignty. The idea that the attempted combination of these trajectories of rule was both a fundamental component of modern regimes of the government of the state, and the reason for their proneness to extreme and totalitarian forms – even within societies that regard themselves as liberal – remains.

The statement advances our understanding of Foucault's analytics of power and rule in modern societies in two ways. First, it establishes the importance of the *longue durée* of two very broad trajectories of rule and ways of thinking about rule. Second, it argues that many of our current problems and dangers are located not in one or other of these trajectories but in the attempt to put together elements of the rationalities found along these trajectories in the government of the state. This is to say that, whether political actors take the form of an incumbent regime, a party, or social movement, those who attempt to affect the government of the state are bound, in very different contexts, to try to force together aspects found along these two trajectories.

Foucault's statement, then, poses the dual and interrelated problems of political invention and political evil in the 'tricky adjustment' between two modes of exercising rule. The 'shepherd–flock game' – or what he elsewhere calls 'pastoral power' (for example, Foucault, 1982) – has its birth in Hebraic and early Christian religious communities. Its genealogy concerns its transformation into a centralized and largely secular exercise of power over populations concerned with the life and welfare of 'each and all' with the development of the administrative state in Europe in the seventeenth and eighteenth centuries. The 'city–citizen' game has its sources in Greco-Roman antiquity and notions of the *polis* and *res publica* and concerns the treatment of individuals as autonomous and responsible political actors within a self-determining political community. This mode of exercising and thinking about power has been transformed by modern liberal and republican doctrines, notions of direct and representative democracy, and by the key status of the citizen being granted to certain members of the population within the territorial state.

One way in which the attempted articulation of these elements may be viewed as 'demonic' concerns the vacillation over the status of the welfare state. Here we are closer to the inventive side of the *daimon* of modern politics. On the one hand, national governments are loath – for a variety of reasons – to do anything that might undermine the responsible freedom of those who can exercise active citizenship, and even seek to reform social provision so that it might transform certain groups into active citizens. On the other, they must find a way of providing for those with needs whether due to human frailty and mortality or the nature of the capitalist labour market itself. The genealogy of the welfare state seems to be indeed bedeviled by this problem of trying to find a norm of provision that can adjust the competing demands of a subject of needs with the free political citizen. We can note that that genealogy would also show that this problem of welfare states is also a problem of the relations and competition between sovereign states, most recently reconfigured as an issue of economic globalization.

Important as this 'welfare-state problem' and its ramifications are, I want to focus here on the other aspect of this demonic character of modern states. This is the character of what I shall call, for want of a better term, authoritarian forms of rule. This term encompasses those practices and rationalities immanent to liberal government itself, which are applied to certain populations held to be without the attributes of responsible freedom. More directly, it refers to non-liberal and explicitly authoritarian types of rule that seek to operate through obedient rather than free subjects, or, at a minimum, endeavor to neutralize opposition to authority. Foucault is often recognized as having made a distinctive contribution to the study of liberal rule in modern societies;[6] as we shall see here, his same concepts can be used to indicate a singular approach to non-liberal forms.

Very broadly, then, Foucault's sentence on the demonic nature of modern states can be taken to mean something like the following. All versions of what might loosely be called modern arts of government must articulate a bio-politics of the population with questions of sovereignty. And, it is the combination of these elements of bio-politics and sovereignty that is fraught with dangers and risks, with potential for invention and for extraordinary evil of the kind that is unimaginable before it has occurred and, even more frighteningly, remains so afterwards.

LIBERALISM, BIO-POLITICS, SOVEREIGNTY

The question of whether there is a significant break in Foucault's analytics of power around the mid-1970s is a matter that will no doubt be revisited by historians and commentators. If, however, we are concerned with using rather than commenting on his ideas, an interesting and intelligible framework of contemporary forms and rationalities of power and rule emerges when we refuse to accede to the supposition of a break. According to Foucault, from the end of the eighteenth century until perhaps quite recently, there has existed a common conception of the government of the state. This was true for those who criticized and sought to limit existing forms of government and those who argued for its extension, its co-ordination and centralization.

Government would be regarded as a unitary, centralized and localized set of institutions that acted in a field that was exterior to itself. It would no longer be purely concerned with 'the right disposition of things arranged to a convenient end' as Guillame La Perrihre had argued in the sixteenth century (cited by Foucault, 1991: 93), that is, it would no longer be concerned with the detailed regulation of heterogeneous and localized minutiae of manners and morals, with the activities and resources within a territory, in the manner of 'police'. The government of things would meet and be re-inscribed within the government of processes. To govern would mean to cultivate, facilitate and work through, the diverse processes that were to be found in this domain exterior to the institutions of government. These processes would variously be conceived as vital, natural, organic, historical, economic, psychological, biological, industrial, cultural or social. They would be processes that established the paradoxical position of life as at once an autonomous domain and as a target and objective of forms of politics and systems of administration.

Biopolitics

One key domain in which these processes exterior to but necessary to government are constituted is 'bio-politics'. Bio-politics is a politics concerning the administration of life, particularly as it appears at the level of populations. It is 'the endeavor, begun in the eighteenth century, to rationalize problems presented to governmental practice by the phenomena characteristic of a group of living human beings constituted as a population: health, sanitation, birthrate, longevity, race' (Foucault, 1997a: 73). It is concerned with matters of life and death, with birth and propagation, with health and illness, both physical and mental, and with the processes that sustain or retard the optimization of the life of a population. Bio-politics must then also concern the social, cultural, environmental, economic and geographic conditions under which humans live, procreate, become ill, maintain health or become healthy, and die. From this perspective bio-politics is concerned with the family, with housing, living and working conditions, with what we call 'lifestyle', with public health issues, patterns of migration, levels of economic growth and the standards of living. It is concerned with the biosphere in which humans dwell.

Bio-politics is a fundamental dimension or even trajectory of power from the eighteenth century concerned with a government of and through the processes of life and the evolution of life. It constitutes as its objects and targets such entities as the population, the species and the race. In Foucault's narrative, however, the detailed administration of life by bio-political and, it should be added, disciplinary, practices is not coextensive with the entire field of politics and government. There are at least two other dimensions of rule that are important here: *economic government*, which is internal to the field of government conceived as the art of conducting individuals and populations; and the theory and practices of *sovereignty*. Both provide liberalism with means of criticizing and halting the effects of the generalization of the norm of the optimization of life.

Bio-politics then first meets quite distinct forms of political rationality and knowledge concerned with the role of commerce in civil society. This leads Foucault to undertake a charting of the different events in the emergence of the theoretical and programmatic reality of the economy as a self-regulating system largely coincident with the boundaries of the nation (Dean, 1999: 114–15; Gordon, 1991: 15–18). By the formation of classical English political economy in the first quarter of the nineteenth century we find clearly delineated limits to the bio-political aim of the optimization of the life of the population. These limits are most marked in Thomas Malthus' pivotal discovery, in the relation between the processes that impel the growth of population and those natural ones that provide the subsistence for the increasing quantity of human life, of a realm of scarcity and necessity. The bio-economic reality discovered and enshrined in the work of the English political economists of the early nineteenth century will be used to generate new norms of government that must be factored against the optimization of the life of the population. The administration of the life of the population would hence meet a concern to govern economically. That would entail a government through the economic realities, commercial society and the market; it would also entail a concern to govern efficiently, to limit waste and restrict cost, a concern with what Benjamin Franklin called 'frugal government' (Foucault, 1997a: 77).

Sovereignty

The notion of sovereignty is above all characterized as a power of life and death that, according to Foucault, was 'in reality the right to *take* life and *let* live' (1979: 136; emphasis in original), or, '*le droit de faire mourir ou de laisser vivre*' to cite the lecture of 17 March, 1976 (1997b: 214). Sovereignty undergoes its own transformation: in the juridical theories of the seventeenth and eighteenth centuries, such as those of Thomas Hobbes and Samuel von Pufendorf, Foucault finds a more limited account of the sovereign right of death as 'conditioned by the defense of the sovereign' (1979: 135). The end of sovereignty is, however, the continuation of sovereignty itself – it is caught in a kind of 'self-referring circularity' (Foucault, 1991: 94–5). Thus Foucault argues that, if we take Pufendorf's definition of the end of sovereign authority as 'public utility' and seek to define the content of 'public utility', we find little more than that subjects obey laws, fulfil their expected tasks, and respect the political order.

Throughout the period of his work we are concentrating on, Foucault maintains an extraordinarily constant understanding of sovereignty (for example, in 1979: 135–5, 144–5; 1980: 103–6; 1991: 94–102). He suggests that in Western European societies from the Middle Ages sovereignty is principally conceived as a transcendent form of authority exercised over subjects within a definite territory. Its main instruments are laws, decrees and regulations backed up by coercive sanctions ultimately grounded in the right of death exercised by the sovereign. Sovereignty is a 'deductive' exercise and relies on a technology of subtraction levied on its subjects (Foucault, 1979: 136). It subtracts products, money, wealth, goods, services, labour and blood. Its symbolic language is one of the sword, of blood, of family and alliance (1979: 148–9).

Foucault also maintains that sovereignty is far from a universal and, like other concepts, should be understood in its historical singularities according to specific regimes of practices and forms of political rationality. Thus, in one lecture, Foucault summarizes some of the shifts and uses of the language and theory of sovereignty (1980: 103). He distinguishes four roles in European history: as an effective 'mechanism of power' in the feudal monarchy; as an 'instrument' and 'justification' in the construction of the administrative institutions of absolutism; as a 'weapon' in the hands of different parties to the wars of religion of the sixteenth and seventeenth centuries; and as an 'an alternative model', that of parliamentary democracy, in opposition to those 'administrative, authoritarian and absolutist monarchies' at the time of the French Revolution. In certain states, from the end of the eighteenth century, we know that sovereignty has been 'democratized' in that they have witnessed the development of mechanisms of representation by which those deemed to possess the required attributes can participate in the choice of who should stand in place of the sovereign.

The other aspect of sovereignty mentioned by Foucault is that the notion of a nominally separate state with territorial integrity, subject to non-interference by outside powers, is itself a governmental product, and a consequence of the 'external' dimension of doctrines such as 'reason of state' (Foucault, 1991: 104). The city–citizen game not only entails relations between putatively self-governing citizens, but also the formation of and relations between what aspire to be self-governing political communities. One of the features of the modern political world – which we date quite precisely to the agreements of Westphalia concluded in 1648 following the Thirty Years War – is that these fictive self-governing political communities have come to be represented as independent states, that is, political unities with definite territorial boundaries, secured by the principle of non-interference of one sovereign state in the internal affairs of another. Claims to sovereignty by such communities have thus become identical with claims to be a state. The 'city–citizen' game, therefore concerns the panoply of techniques by which the members of a population are formed or form themselves into a political community, and by which they seek to exercise sovereignty. It also includes the arts of international government by which certain populations are assigned to these nominally independent sovereign states and which regulate the coexistence of states with one another. We might conclude that securing the sovereignty of states is an end of these arts of international government. The existence of a system of sovereign states has as its condition a form of governmental regulation of the international order.

Liberalism

We are now in a position to locate the third term of our triad, liberalism. As Foucault puts it in regard to bio-political problems,

> 'Liberalism' enters the picture here, because it was in connection with liberalism that they began to have the look of a challenge. In a system anxious to have the respect of legal subjects and to ensure the free enterprise of individuals, how can the 'population' phenomenon, with its specific effects and problems, be taken into account? On behalf of what, and according to what rules, can it be managed? (1997a: 73)

According to Foucault, liberalism can be understood as a form of critique of excessive government (1997a: 74–5). It should be approached, however, not only as a critique of earlier forms of government such as police and reason of state, but of existing and potential forms of bio-political government. This is to say that liberalism criticizes other possible forms that the government of the processes of life might take. It might criticize those forms, for example, in which bio-political norms will be compromised by a lack of understanding of economic norms. It might also criticize the detailed regulation of the biological processes of the species, and the tendencies toward state racism found in bio-politics, by an appeal to the framework of right – either legal or natural – that it will codify as the theory and practice of democratic sovereignty. If liberalism emerged less as a doctrine or form of the minimal state than as an ethos of review, this ethos needs to be situated in the rationalization of the field of bio-political problems. If, for liberalism, it is always necessary to suspect that one is governing too much, this is because the imperatives of bio-political norms that lead to the creation of a coordinated and centralized administration of life need to be weighed against the norms of economic processes and the freedoms on which they depend and the norms derived from the sovereign subject of rights. This is why, for liberalism, the problem will not be a rejection of bio-political regulation but a way of managing it.

There are other aspects of Foucault's complex account of the formation of liberalism that deserve some mention in this context. While it can be posed as a critique of reason of state and police doctrines, liberalism retains a concern with security and advances a novel conception of the objective of government as 'setting in place mechanisms of security . . . whose function is to assure the security of those natural phenomena, economic processes, and the intrinsic processes of population' (Foucault, 5 April 1978, cited in Gordon, 1991: 19). Further, Foucault suggests that liberty becomes a condition of security in so far as a central component of securing economic and demographic processes is effectively working through the exercise of freedom by responsible, rational individuals. Finally, while liberalism would adopt a legal and parliamentary framework, this is less due to an affinity with juridical thought than because of law's generality and exclusion of the particular and exceptional, and because through the parliamentary system, liberalism permits (and, one might add, regulates) the participation of the governed in liberal government (Foucault, 1997a: 77). Indeed, Foucault seems to suggest that liberalism has more of an affinity with the norm than with the law (1979: 149; Ewald, 1990). This is because, first, it constantly seeks a norm of good government in the changing balance between governing too much and governing too little and, second, it employs mechanisms that strive to stabilize and normalize subjects in such a way that they exercise freedom in a responsible and disciplined manner (Dean, 1999: 121–2; Ewald, 1990).

Liberalism thus participates in and fosters the 'society of normalization'. In its emphasis on the formation of the responsible exercise of freedom as necessary to the security of autonomous processes of economy, society and population, liberalism multiplies and ramifies what Foucault (1982: 208) calls 'dividing practices', that is, practices in which 'the subject is either divided inside himself or divided from others'. Mariana Valverde (1996), for instance, has recently shown how the liberal conception of the juridical and political subject has a form of ethical despotism at its core, contained in notions of the possibility of improvement and habit. Moreover, the history of liberalism shows how a range of illiberal techniques can be applied to those individuals and populations who are deemed to be capable of improvement and of attaining self-government (from women and children to certain classes of criminals and paupers). As a form of colonial governmentality, liberalism can justify authoritarian types of government for those regions deemed unimproved, like Africa, or degenerate and static, like China, to use John Stuart Mill's judgements. For such nations, Mill suggests, 'their only hope of making any steps in advance depends on the chances of a good despot' (cited by Valverde, 1996: 361).

Foucault's account of liberal governmental formations suggests a complex articulation of issues of bio-politics and sovereignty. It is an articulation of elements of the shepherd–flock game concerned in its modern form to optimize the life of the population and normalize the identities of individuals within it, and of the city–citizen game in which the individual appears as an active and responsible citizen within a self-governing political community and within commercial society. Nevertheless, while liberalism may try to make safe the bio-political imperative of the optimization of life by deploying the notion of rights and framework of law it has inherited from forms of sovereign rule, it has shown itself permanently incapable of arresting – from eugenics to contemporary genetics – the emergence of forms of knowledge that make the optimization of the life of some dependent upon the disallowing of the life of others. This is because of a number of reasons. First, because liberalism is concerned to govern through what it conceives as processes that are external to the formal sphere of government, it thus must foster forms of knowledge and expertise of vital processes, and seek to govern through their application. Moreover, to the extent that liberalism depends on the formation of responsible and autonomous subjects, it relies upon and multiplies the disciplinary and bio-political practices that are the ground of those rationalities that seek to divide, transform, prevent and even eliminate the categories of individuals within populations. Finally, we might consider the possibility that sovereignty and bio-politics are so heterogeneous to one another that the derivation of political norms from the democratization of the former cannot act as a prophylactic for the possible outcomes of the other. The framework of right and law can act as a resource for forces engaged in contestation of the effects of bio-power; it cannot provide a guarantee as to the efficacy of such struggle.

SOVEREIGNTY AND BIO-POLITICS IN NON-LIBERAL RULE

There are, of course, plenty of examples of the exercise of sovereignty in the twentieth century that have practiced a decidedly non-liberal form and program of national government both in relation to their own populations and those of other states. Does this mean that the form of government of such states is assembled from elements that are radically different from the ones that we have discussed here? Does this mean that state socialism and National Socialism, for example, could not be subject to an analysis of the arts of government in societies of normalization? The answer to both these questions, I submit, is no. The general argument of this chapter is that Foucault's analysis rests on a thesis that the exercise of rule in all modern states entails the articulation of a form of pastoral or bio-power with one of sovereign power. Liberalism, as we have just seen, makes that articulation in a specific way. Other types of rule have a no less distinctive response to the combination of elements of a bio-politics concerned with the detailed administration of life and sovereign power that reserves the right of death to itself.

Consider again the contrastive terms in which it is possible to view bio-politics and sovereignty. The final chapter in the *The Will to Knowledge* which contrasts sovereignty and bio-politics is called 'Right of Death and Power over Life'. The initial terms of the contrast between the two registers of government is thus between one that could employ power to put subjects to death, even if this right to kill was conditioned by the defense of the sovereign, and one that was concerned with the fostering of life. Nevertheless, each part of the contrast can be further broken down. The right of death can also be understood as 'the right to take life or let live'; the power over life as the power 'to foster life or disallow it'. Thus the contrast concerns the way in which the different forms of power treat matters of life

and death. Thus bio-politics re-inscribes the earlier right of death and places it within a new and different form. It is no longer so much the right of the sovereign to put to death its enemies but to disqualify the life of those who are a threat to the life of the population, to disallow those deemed 'unworthy of life'.

This allows us first to consider what might be thought of as the dark side of bio-politics (Foucault, 1979: 136–7). In Foucault's account, bio-politics does not put an end to the practice of war. It provides it with new and more sophisticated killing machines. These machines allow killing itself to be re-posed at the level of entire populations. Wars become genocidal in the twentieth century. The same state that takes on itself the duty to enhance the life of the population also exercises the power to put to death whole populations. Atomic weapons are the ultimate weapons of this process of the power to put whole populations to death. We might also consider here the aptly named biological and chemical weapons that seek an extermination of populations by visiting plagues upon them or polluting the biosphere in which they live to the point at which life is no longer sustainable. Nor does the birth of bio-politics put an end to the killing of one's own populations. Rather it intensifies that killing – whether by an 'ethnic cleansing' that visits holocausts upon whole groups or by the mass slaughters of classes and groups conducted in the name of the utopia to be achieved. As Foucault put it to his audience at the University of Vermont in 1982, 'since population is nothing more than what the state takes care of for its own sake, of course, the state is entitled to slaughter it, if necessary. So the reverse of biopolitics is thanatopolitics' (1988b: 160; cf. Milchman and Rosenberg, 1996: 104–5). The 'counterpart of a power that exerts a positive influence on life', as he wrote six years earlier, was 'this formidable power of death' (1976: 137).

There is a certain restraint in sovereign power. The right of death is only occasionally exercised as the right to kill. More often sovereign power is manifest in the *refraining* from the right to kill. The bio-political imperative knows no such restraint. Power is exercised at the level of populations and hence wars will be waged at that level, on behalf of everyone and their lives. This point brings us to the heart of Foucault's provocative thesis about bio-politics: that there is an intimate connection between the exercise of a life-administering power and the commission of genocide:

If genocide is indeed the dream of modern powers, this is not because of a recent return of the ancient right to kill: it is because power is situated and exercised at the level of life, the species, the race, and the large-scale phenomena of population. (1979: 137)

Foucault completes this same passage with an expression that deserves more notice: 'massacres become vital'.

There is thus a kind of perverse homogeneity between the power over life and the power to take life characteristic of bio-power. The emergence of a bio-political racism in the nineteenth and twentieth centuries can be approached as a trajectory of the 'statization of the biological [*l'étatisation du biologique*], in which this homogeneity always threatens to tip over into a dreadful necessity' (Foucault, 1997b: 213). This racism can be approached as a fundamental mechanism of power that is inscribed in the bio-political domain (Stoler, 1995: 84–5). For Foucault, the first function of this form of racism is to establish a division between those who must live and those who must die (1997b: 227). It is to introduce a series of caesura into the biological continuum between those who are superior and those who are inferior, and to make possible the treatment of human species as a series of sub-groups, a *mélange* of races. The series, 'population, evolution and race', is not simply a way of thinking about the superiority of the 'white races', or of justifying colonialism, but also of thinking about how to treat the degenerates and the abnormals within one's own population and prevent the further degeneration of the race.

The second and most important function of this bio-political racism in the nineteenth century for Foucault is that 'it establishes a positive relation between the right to kill and the assurance of life' (Stoler, 1995: 84). The life of the population, its vigor, its strength, its health and its capacities to survive and proliferate, becomes necessarily linked to the elimination of internal and external biological threats: the abnormal individual, inferior species, degenerates. The racism that is compatible with bio-power is one that asserts a biological relation between the fostering of 'my life and the death of the other' (1995: 85). This power to disallow the life of the other in order to foster one's own life is perhaps best encapsulated in the injunctions of the eugenic project: identify those who are degenerate, abnormal, feeble-minded, or of an inferior race, and subject them to forced sterilization; encourage those who are superior, fit and intelligent to propagate. But this last example does not necessarily yet mobilize the bio-political recuperation of the right to kill, only the right to disallow life. The most fundamental example of the former are the genocidal regimes of the twentieth century. When such regimes seek to justify their actions it will be through race. As Foucault suggests: 'Racism is the condition of acceptability of putting to death in a society of normalization' (1997b: 228).

If we are to begin to understand the type of racism engaged in by Nazism, we need to take into account a somewhat different kind of denouement between the bio-political management of population and the exercise of sovereignty than the one we found in Foucault's account of liberalism. This version of sovereignty is no longer the transformed and democratized form of sovereignty founded on the liberty of the juridical subject, as it is for liberalism, but a sovereignty that takes up and transforms a further element of sovereignty, its 'symbolics of blood' (Foucault, 1979: 148).

For Foucault, sovereignty is grounded in blood just as one might say that sexuality becomes the key field upon which bio-political management of populations is articulated with the disciplinary normalization of individuals. In a society in which power was exercised primarily through sovereign instruments, through the juridical model of law, with its symbol of the sword, and in which relations between households and families were forged through the deployment alliance, 'blood was *a reality with a symbolic function*'. By contrast, for bio-politics with its themes of health, vigor, fitness, vitality, progeny, survival and race, 'power spoke *of* sexuality and to sexuality' (Foucault, 1979: 147).

The novelty of National Socialism, for Foucault (1979: 149–50), was the way it articulated 'the oneiric exaltation of blood', of fatherland and of the triumph of the race, in an immensely cynical and naive fashion, with the paroxysms of a disciplinary power concerned with the detailed administration of the life of the population and the regulation of sexuality, family, marriage and education.[7] Nazism may have generalized bio-power without the limit-critique posed by the juridical subject of right. Nevertheless, rather than doing away with sovereign forms, it re-inscribed some of its most characteristic elements. It established a set of permanent interventions into the conduct of the individual within the population and articulated this with the 'mythical concern for blood and the triumph of the race'. Thus the shepherd–flock game and the city–citizen game are transmuted into the eugenic ordering of biological existence and articulated upon the themes of the purity of blood and the myth of the fatherland.

In such an articulation of these elements of sovereign and bio-political forms of power, the relation between the administration of life and the right to kill entire populations is no longer simply one of a dreadful homogeneity. It has become a necessary one. The symbolics of blood comes to require a blood-bath. It is not simply that power – and therefore war – will be exercised at the level of entire populations. It is that the act of disqualifying the right to life of other races becomes necessary for the fostering of the life of the ('superior') race. Moreover, the elimination of other races is only one face of the purification of one's own race (1997b: 231). The other part is to expose the latter to a universal and absolute danger, to expose it to the risk of death and total destruction. For Foucault (1997b: 232), with the Nazi state we have an 'absolutely racist state, an absolutely murderous state and an absolutely suicidal state', all of which are superimposed and converge on the Final Solution. With the Final Solution, it tries to eliminate, through the Jews, all the other races, for whom Jews were the symbol and the manifestation. This includes, in one of Hitler's last acts, the order to destroy the bases of life for the German people itself. 'Final Solution for other races, the absolute suicide of the German race' is inscribed, according to Foucault, in the functioning of the modern state (1997: 232).

Foucault's analysis of the political rationality of National Socialism finds confirmation in the work of recent German historians on at least one point, that of the fundamental role of the human sciences in the atrocities of that regime (Peters, 1995). The late Detlev Peukert drew upon studies of psychiatry under National Socialism, the history of compulsory sterilization programs, genetics, eugenics, medicine, social policy and education, and his own work on social-welfare education, to argue that 'what was new about "Final Solution" in world-historical terms was the fact that it resulted from the fatal racist dynamism present within the human and social sciences' (1993: 236). Again we witness a fundamental division of the population, on this occasion made on a particular qualitative distinction between 'value' and 'non-value' and a treatment of the *Volkskörper* or body of the nation that consisted in 'selection' and 'eradication'. Peukert argues that twentieth-century medical and human sciences are confronted by what he calls a 'logodicy' that tries to resolve the dilemma between the rationalist dream of the perfectibility of human kind and the empirical existence of human finitude, of illness, suffering and death. One resolution of this dilemma is the projection of the rationalist project away from the finite individual onto a potential immortal body. In the German case, what Foucault called the 'species body' of the population is mapped onto the body of the *Volk* or race. The bio-political imperative is re-articulated with a kind of 'mythisized' version of sovereignty. Like Foucault, Peukert argues (1993: 242) that the logic of

National Socialism, with its concern for the nurture and improvement of the immortal *Volkskörper* had a double significance: heroic death on one side and eradication on the other.

National Socialism is one contingent, historical trajectory along the development of the bio-political dimension of the social, medical, psychological and human sciences that occurs under a particular set of historical circumstances. One should not underestimate either the factors operative in German society – the historical legacy of the Great War and the Treaty of Versailles, the revolutionary movements, the fragile nature of German state-formation and the economic crises of the early twentieth century. Nevertheless, Peukert and Foucault would both agree that the kind of state racism practiced by the Nazis, that would lead to the Final Solution, was quite different from traditional anti-semitism insofar as it took the forms of a 'biological politics', as the German historians call it, that drew upon the full resources of the human, social and behavioral sciences. According to Peukert, Nazi social policy was a policy of eradication of those who, in the language of the order that represents the crucial step in the Final Solution, are deemed 'unworthy of life' (*lebensunwertes Leben*). The bio-political government of life had arrived at the point at which it decided who was worthy of living. The phrase 'those unworthy of life' is striking because it so clearly resonates with the bio-political attempt to govern life. We should be clear that there was nothing necessary in the path of National Socialism, and that there were crucial steps in the conversion of knowledge and services concerned with the care of the needy into a technology of mass annihilation. However, given that many, if not all, the forms of knowledge and technologies of government (eugenics, the concentration camp) were the product of polities characterized at least broadly by liberal forms of rule, its does suggest there is no room for complacency and that the liberal critique of bio-politics cannot offer the kind of guarantees it claims to. Foucault is right to provoke us with the idea that the 'assurance of life' is connected with the 'death command' and to claim that 'the coexistence in political structures of large destructive mechanisms and institutions oriented toward the care of individual life is something puzzling and needs some investigation' (1988a: 147). Mass slaughters may not necessarily or logically follow from the forms of political rationality and types of knowledge we employ, but they do not arise from a sphere that is opposed to that rationality and knowledge.

What Peukert cannot address is the rationality of what he conceives as the irrational component of Nazism. While he understands the role of the human sciences in the formation of Nazi bio-logical politics, he tends to consign the themes of blood, race and *Volk* to an irrational sublimation contained within them rather than viewing them, as Foucault does, as re-articulated elements of sovereign power. This brings us to the singularity of Foucault's comments. National Socialism is not regarded as the pinnacle of the total administration of life undertaken with the help of the human sciences and bio-political technologies, as it might be by the Frankfurt School and their descendants. The key point for Foucault is that National Socialism is regarded as a particular articulation of specific elements of bio-politics, and its knowledge of populations and individuals, and sovereignty. It is not simply the logic of the bureaucratic application of the human sciences that is at issue but the re-inscription of racial discourse within a bio-politics of the population and its linkage with themes of sovereign identity, autonomy and political community. This form of sovereignty has been drained of all its potential to claim and protect rights by the removal, following Bauman (1989: 111), of all counterbalancing resourceful and influential social forces.[8] A political discourse that divides populations on the basis of race has certain fairly obvious political dangers. However, one that makes the welfare and life of a racialized population the basis for national sovereignty and political community could be viewed as more clearly 'demonic'.

A man in danger

Unfortunately, this story of bio-political racism does not end with Nazism. Foucault also insists that the possibilities of state racism are found in many versions of the articulation of bio-politics and sovereignty, including many varieties of popular nineteenth-century socialist movements, for example, Blanquism, the Communards and anarchism (1997b: 233–4; Stoler, 1995: 86–7). The problem with socialism for Foucault is that it has a kind of state racism inscribed in its premises and that, even if it has sometimes criticized bio-power, it has not re-examined the foundations and modes of functioning of racism. When socialism analyses its own emergence as a result of economic transformation, it does not have need for an immediate recourse to these racist motifs. When it insists on the necessity of struggle to socialist transformation, a struggle that is against the enemies within the capitalist state, Foucault argues, it necessarily revives the theme of racism. Moreover, when socialism takes upon itself the task of managing, multiplying and fostering life, of limiting chances and risks, and

governing biological processes, it ends up practicing a form of racism that is not strictly ethnic but evolutionary and biological.[9] The enemies within on which this racism will be practiced are the mentally ill, the criminal and political adversaries and – with, say, China's one-child policy – imprudent parents and their potential offspring (Sigley, 1996). In the latter case, we find a form of government that combines market-based norms and bio-political interventions into the intimate life of the population in a non-liberal manner in order to realize the objective of the quantity and quality of the population necessary for the socialist plan.

Foucault's analysis of National Socialism and his comments on the history of socialism are a striking event within the series of utterances that make up his thought. They should be approached neither as an expression of an entire oeuvre nor as an irruption of temporary folly unrelated to more sober judgements. While they do not simply repeat what is said before, nor contain all that will be said after, they are a singular point within a trajectory, a link within a chain. This trajectory is one of the government of individuals and populations in a 'society of normalization' that he pursued from *Madness and Civilization* (1965) to the lectures on governmentality. This trajectory is present in the last volumes of his *History of Sexuality* by virtue of the search for an intelligibility of forms of self-government outside the regime of norm, identity and truth.

Foucault (1980: 78) opened his lectures in 1976 by pointing to the 'repetitive and disconnected' nature of his research into penality, psychiatry and abnormality in the previous five years: 'Since indeed it never ceases to say the same thing, it perhaps says nothing. It is tangled up into an indecipherable, disorganised muddle.' Yet at the end of these lectures, he recuperates these earlier themes by suggesting that madness, criminality and abnormality all become re-inscribed within the genealogy of bio-politics, the birth of state racism and the right to kill (Foucault, 1997b: 230). In his 1978–9 course, the last to directly deal with issues of power and government, he situates liberalism as the rationality in which these bio-political problems of population will first appear. As those lectures show, the problem of population leads in multiple and heterogeneous directions, not just toward the birth of state racism but also toward modern notions of economic and social government. There may be a re-balancing of the theme of the modern government of the population in the later 1970s, but there is no attempt to erase or disown the perspectives of 1976. The attempt to articulate elements in the trajectory of sovereignty and bio-politics leads not simply to state racism, ethnic cleansing, the Soviet gulags and the Final Solution, but also to the welfare state, to liberalism and neo-liberalism. The important point to note, for Foucault, is that there is a common pool of resources by which all these programs are made thinkable and practicable, and that these are summarized by the trajectories he calls the 'shepherd–flock' and 'city–citizen' games.

These explorations of the *daimon* of modern societies is continuous with Foucault's work in another, perhaps more fundamental way. While they may not try to work as 'effective history', as Stoler points out (1995: 88) they certainly do work as a 'history of the present': 'Foucault's analysis has an almost eerie quality. It speaks to, and even seems to anticipate, the conditions for "ethnic cleansing" in Eastern Europe's fractured state.' They are a component of a 'history of the present' rather than a critical theory of the present. These substantive analyses exemplify Foucault's rejection of universal normative foundations and adoption of an ethos of 'hyper- and pessimistic activism' (1997a: 256). Politics is far too dangerous an enterprise to seek to rationalize it according to any set of norms, however derived, with any guarantee that those norms will not become components of dividing practices. It is, however, far too important an enterprise to ignore or defer, and it is for that reason that its practice must be accompanied by at least one signal technique of self-government, the constant reminder that this 'strategic game between liberties' is also a sphere that contains the potential for the generation of enormous and unthinkable horror.

Foucault's broad schemata for the analysis of modern societies insists that they are possessed by a *daimon*, which accounts for both their political inventiveness and their propensity for political evil. This *daimon* lies in the fact that the modern government of the state is formed from resources that articulate a productive bio-political government of processes based on population, life, procreation and sexuality with the deductive logic of sovereignty based on right, territory, death and blood. There is no necessity that this *daimon* will ineluctably lead to the really demonic eventualities we have continued to witness right to the end of the twentieth century. Nor, however, is there any guarantee that the appeal to rights within liberal democracies and the international community of states will guard against such eventualities. Elements within sovereignty and bio-politics will continue to provide resources for political rationality and invention. But there can be no system of safeguards that offers us a zone of comfort when we engage in political action. When we do so, Foucault's position here seems to suggest, we enter a zone of

uncertainty and danger because of the governmental resources we have at our disposal. We might add that the price of not engaging in political action is equally great, if not greater. A condition of informed political action remains an analysis of the rationalities and technologies that made politics thinkable and practicable and that act as its resources, and the manner in which these are deployed in particular programmes seeking various ends, by particular actors in a field of contestation, alliances, tactics and strategy. Foucault's genealogy of modern political rationality does not offer us a totalizing vision that excuses us from the detailed and meticulous work of analysis. It is precisely because the attempt to combine the 'shepherd–flock' and 'city–citizen' games contains the possibility of unimaginable and unspeakable evil, while simultaneously accounting for the political inventiveness of modern societies, that the kind of ethico-politico-historical study that made Foucault himself famous remains necessary.

Foucault was 'a man in danger', to quote Maurice Blanchot (1987: 68), 'who, without making a display of it, had an acute sense of the perils to which we are exposed, and sought to know which ones are the most threatening and with which it is possible to compromise'. As such, he is often accused of documenting only the dark side of modernity. One wonders, however, what could be more optimistic than the meticulous historical and theoretical study of all the different ways in which we govern and are governed in a 'society of normalization' without acceding to a specification of truth, norm and identity. A study, moreover, conducted as a vigil to the subject populations of the Holocaust.

NOTES

1 This is made absolutely plain by the extraordinary compendium edited by Barry Smart (1994–6), *Michel Foucault: Critical Assessments*.

2 For an excellent summary of these themes see Foucault, 1979: 94–7.

3 The original series was to be: *La Volonté de savoir* ('The Will to Knowledge'), *La Chair et le corps* ('The Flesh and the Body'), *La Croissade des enfants* ('The Children's Crusade'), *La Femme, la mère, l'hystérique* ('Woman, Mother, Hysteric'), *Les Pervers* ('Perverts') and *Population et races* ('Population and Races'). See David Macey, 1993: 353–5. While the abandonment of the series might be thought to be a key signal of discontinuity, the title of the final volume might also stand in evidence of a certain continuity, i.e. around a central concern with the manner in which the emergence of population as a domain of knowledge

is linked to modern forms of power and government. The theme of population is crucial to Foucault's notion of governmentality (1991).

4 The context of Foucault's thought during these years is dealt with in admirable detail by David Macey (1993).

5 Even in January 1976, however, we find Foucault entertaining doubts about his approach to power through the discourse of war: 'It is obvious that all my work in recent years has been couched in the schema of struggle–repression, and it is this which I have now been forced to reconsider . . . because I believe that these two notions of repression and war must themselves be considerably modified, if not ultimately abandoned' (1980: 92).

6 See, for example, many of the contributors to three recent collections: Burchell et al., 1991; Barry et al., 1996; Dean and Hindess, 1998.

7 For a recent admirably documented account, see Pine, 1997.

8 I have not the space here to discuss the similarities and differences between Zygmunt Bauman's (1989) important account of the Holocaust and the present understanding of the specific character of Nazi racism as a rationality of extermination. Bauman's account concurs with the one presented here insofar as it presents the Holocaust as something that must be understood as endogenous to Western civilization and its processes of rationalization rather than as an aberrant psychological, social or political pathology. Moreover, to the extent that his account stresses the collapse or non-emergence of democracy, it indicates the failure of the democratization of sovereignty as a fundamental precondition of Nazi rule, a theme which echoes those of Hannah Arendt's famous book, *The Origins of Totalitarianism* (1958). Foucault's brief remarks seem to add to or qualify Bauman's account in two ways. They first offer the possibility of a closer specification of the kind of rationality and technology that makes possible a racialized politics and policy by demonstrating its bio-political character. Such a view enables us to get a clearer understanding of the role of the human sciences in such a politics. They also suggest that Nazi politics articulates this biological politics with alternative traditions and frameworks of sovereignty such as those of fatherland, *Volk* and blood. It is not simply the imperative of the totalistic administration of life which accounts for the mentality of Nazi rule, but the way the bio-political discourses and sovereign themes are re-inscribed and modified within one another.

9 Note that Foucault's point here extends one made by Hannah Arendt (1958: 313). 'Practically speaking', she states 'it will make little difference whether totalitarian movements adopt the pattern of Nazism or Bolshevism, organize the masses in the name of race or class, pretend to follow the laws of life and nature or of dialectics and economics.' Bio-political state racism can be justified in terms of the goal of the evolution to an ideal society or optimizing the quality of the population as much as the evolution of the race. The practice of state racism upon populations retarding social and political evolution does not necessarily always speak the language of race.

REFERENCES

Arendt, H. (1958) *The Origins of Totalitarianism*, 2nd edn. London: Allen and Unwin.

Barry, A., Osborne, T. and Rose, N. (eds) (1996) *Foucault and Political Reason: Liberalism, Neo-liberalism and Rationalities of Government.* London: UCL Press.

Bauman, Z. (1989) *Modernity and the Holocaust.* Ithaca, NY: Cornell University Press.

Bernauer, J. (1992) 'Beyond Life and Death: on Foucault's Post-Auschwitz Ethic', in T.J. Armstrong (ed.), *Michel Foucault Philosopher.* London: Harvester Wheatsheaf. pp. 260–79.

Blanchot, M. (1987) 'Michel Foucault as I Imagine Him', in *Foucault/Blanchot.* New York, Zone Books. pp. 61–109.

Burchell, G., Gordon, C. and Miller, P. (eds) (1991) *The Foucault Effect: Studies in Governmentality.* London: Harvester Wheatsheaf.

Dean, M. (1999) *Governmentality: Power and Rule in Modern Society.* London: Sage.

Dean, M. and Hindess, B. (eds) (1998) *Governing Australia: Studies in Contemporary Rationalities of Government.* Melbourne: Cambridge University Press.

Dreyfus, H. and Rabinow, P. (1982) *Michel Foucault: Beyond Structuralism and Hermeneutics.* Brighton: Harvester.

Ewald, F. (1990) 'Norms, Discipline and the Law', *Representations*, 30: 138–61.

Foucault, M. (1965) *Madness and Civilization: A History of Insanity in the Age of Reason.* London: Tavistock.

Foucault, M. (1979) *The History of Sexuality*, vol. 1: *An Introduction.* (Translation of *La Volonté de savoir* ['The Will to Knowledge']. London: Allen Lane.

Foucault, M. (1980) *Power/Knowledge: Selected Interviews and Other Writings, 1972–1977* (ed. C. Gordon). Brighton: Harvester.

Foucault, M. (1982) 'The Subject and Power', in H. Dreyfus and P. Rabinow, *Michel Foucault: Beyond Structuralism and Hermeneutics.* Brighton: Harvester. pp. 208–26.

Foucault, M. (1986) *The Care of the Self.* New York: Pantheon.

Foucault, M. (1988a) 'The Ethic of the Care of the Self as a Practice of Freedom', in J. Bernauer and D. Rasmussen (eds), *The Final Foucault.* Cambridge, MA: MIT Press. pp. 1–20.

Foucault, M. (1988b) 'The Political Technology of Individuals', in L.H. Martin, H. Gutman and P.H.

Hutton (eds), *Technologies of the Self: a Seminar with Michel Foucault*. London: Tavistock. pp. 145–62.

Foucault, Michel (1988c) 'Politics and Reason', in L.D. Kritzman (ed.), *Politics, Philosophy, Culture: Interviews and Other Writings, 1977–1984*. Routledge: New York. pp. 57–85.

Foucault, M. (1991) 'Governmentality', in G. Burchell, C. Gordon and P. Miller (eds), *The Foucault Effect: Studies in Governmentality*. London: Harvester Wheatsheaf. pp. 87–104.

Foucault, M. (1997a) *The Essential Works, 1954–1984*, vol. 1: *Ethics, Subjectivity and Truth* (ed. Paul Rabinow). New York: The New Press.

Foucault, M, (1997b) '*Il faut défendre la société*'. Paris: Gallimard/Seuil.

Gordon, C. (1991) 'Introduction', in G. Burchell, C. Gordon and P. Miller (eds), *The Foucault Effect: Studies in Governmentality*. London: Harvester Wheatsheaf. pp. 1–51.

Hadot, P. (1995) *Philosophy as a Way of Life*. Oxford: Blackwell.

Macey, D. (1993) *The Lives of Michel Foucault*. London: Hutchinson.

Milchman, A. and Rosenberg, A. (1996) 'Michel Foucault, Auschwitz and Modernity', *Philosophy and Social Criticism*, 22 (1): 101–13.

Miller, J. (1993) *The Passion of Michel Foucault*. New York: Simon and Schuster.

Pasquino, P. (1993) 'The Political Theory of War and Peace: Foucault and the History of Modern Political Theory', *Economy and Society*, 22 (1): 77–88.

Peters, M. (1995) '"After Auschwitz": Ethics and Educational Policy', *Discourse*, 16 (2): 237–51.

Peukert, D. (1993) 'The Genesis of the "Final Solution" from the Spirit of Science', in T. Childers and J. Caplan (eds), *Reevaluating the Third Reich*. New York: Holmes and Meier. pp. 234–52.

Pine, L. (1997) *Nazi Family Policy, 1933–45*. Oxford: Berg.

Rorty, R. (1992) 'Moral Identity and Private Autonomy', in T.J. Armstrong (ed.), *Michel Foucault Philosopher*. London: Harvester Wheatsheaf. pp. 328–34.

Sigley, G. (1996) 'Governing Chinese Bodies: the Significance of Studies in the Concept of Governmentality for the Analysis of Government in China', *Economy and Society*, 25 (4): 457–82.

Smart, B. (ed.) (1994–6) *Michel Foucault: Critical Assessments*, 7 vols. London: Routledge.

Stoler, A.L. (1995) *Race and the Education of Desire*. Durham, NC: Duke University Press.

Valverde, M. (1996) '"Despotism" and Ethical Governance', *Economy and Society*, 25 (3): 357–72.

26

The Macro/Micro Problem and the Problem of Structure and Agency

BARRY BARNES

THE GENERAL FORM OF THE MACRO/MICRO PROBLEM

All fields of empirical enquiry face a macro/micro problem in some form. Typically, such a field will concern itself with the study of things or processes of some particular kind, and their complexity and variability will lead to the thought that they are composite, and to conjectures about the nature and properties of their components. Or else it may be obvious from the start that this is the case, that the organisms being dissected, or the chemical substances being experimented on, or the nebulae being photographed, or the communities being studied, are made of smaller things.[1] Similarly, although in practice less significantly, the things that a field studies may be themselves recognized as parts of a larger whole. Either way, the question arises as to how the properties and propensities of 'macro' things are related to those of 'micro' things, and how the enquiries of fields studying the one should be related to enquiries in fields that study the other. Of course, we cannot simply presume that there are general answers to these questions, but it is worthwhile, none the less, to look at the very general theoretical responses that have been made to them. In practice, they have tended to fall into one of three kinds. Nearly all accounts of the macro/micro relation involve reductionism, or dualism or else some form of pragmatism or constructivism.

Suppose we have two accounts, both of which refer to the same observable state(s)-of-affairs. One speaks of a single object perhaps, with such-and-such properties and propensities; the other speaks of many things, in proximity to and interacting with each other. Reductionism typically asserts that one of the accounts should be replaceable 'in principle' by a sufficiently elaborated version of the other. It may assert, for example, that an account of a biological organism as an integrated system reduces 'in principle' to an account of a cluster of molecules. This kind of example, wherein the thing described in the macro-account is held to be reducible to those encountered in the micro-one, is the most relevant to the present discussion. But there are also 'reductions' that move in the other direction, and seek to assimilate the micro to the macro. It may be suggested, for example, that particles are but the local properties of a field; or that colonies of coral, or of ants, are really extended single organisms; or that there are no such things as individuals, but only societies.

A macro-object, on a standard reductionist account, can be no better than some composite entity, attention to which is drawn purely for convenience. The world could be described, 'in principle', without reference to the 'macro-object' at all. Indeed such a description, sidestepping it in favour of its 'fundamental' constituents, would not merely substitute for the original description without loss or remainder, it would improve on that description in accuracy and detail and hence be preferable to it and more trustworthy than it. On this account, it is only because the 'in principle' reduction is in practice too difficult or time-consuming that the macro-level description is persisted in, if indeed it is persisted in at all; for this, of course is only the best case scenario. In the worst case, a reductionist analysis may claim to have exposed the fantastical character of the macro-account, and the non-existence of the macro-object. And between the best and the worst case are positions that may render the macro-object as a reification or hypostatization, or as a distorted and misleading representation of what is really the case.

Renditions of this last kind are particularly common in the social sciences, but in the natural sciences a more accommodating reductionism exists as a widely diffused ideology, employed to justify the disciplinary hierarchy. The familiar, longstanding ranking, wherein, for example, physics stands above chemistry, which in turn stands above biology, is often made out as a hierarchy of dependence wherein those who study small things are needed by, but themselves have no need of, those who study the larger things that the small things make up. Whether or not this familiar picture could be elaborated into an empirically adequate account, encompassing, for example, celestial mechanics and molecular genetics, is moot. And how far the picture will continue widely to be credited, as greater and greater prestige accrues to work in the biological sciences is, similarly, an open question. But for all that, the hierarchy continues to command significant credibility.

At the other extreme from reductionism are radical dualist positions that insist on the independence and autonomy of both micro- and macro-accounts, and on the irreducibility of the distinct and separate phenomena they describe.[2] In practice, the task that dualism faces is that of acknowledging the composite character of macro-objects, and the fact that micro-objects and/or micro-processes are encountered within them, whilst at the same time insisting on their 'irreducibility'. Reference to the existence of 'emergent properties' is probably the most widespread method of accomplishing this task. These properties are said to come into existence only as and when macro-objects do, and to be unpredictable from, and irreducible to, the properties, proclivities and interrelations of the smaller objects or entities 'within' them. Distinctive emergent properties of this kind may be attributed to macro-objects as diverse as chemical compounds, biological organisms, human brains, crowds of people and social systems. But at the same time it is interesting to note a certain deference to reductionism in the very language here, which invites us to imagine the macro, as it were, arising out of the micro. Why, for example, do we not speak instead of the 'emergent' properties of isolated, individual micro-entities, created by our acting upon 'fundamental' macro-objects?

How should we compare and evaluate reductionism and dualism? If our criterion is that of conformity to the contingent features of empirical enquiries themselves, it is arguable that both reductionism and dualism are inadequate. Even in the more recondite areas of the physical sciences there are 'composite' objects (benzene rings, electron beams, etc.) that must not be 'reduced', where the very equations acknowledged to apply to them scream holism, as it were. Yet it would be ludicrous to hold that those who have studied, say, benzene rings, have needed to take no interest in work on carbon atoms. Thus, reductionism faces fundamental difficulties even with (accounts of) atoms and molecules in the favourable context of physics and chemistry; but it does none the less point up the interconnectedness of fields of empirical enquiry, and the salience of claims made at one 'level' of description for those 'above' and 'below' it. Dualism, in contrast, whilst it rightly emphasizes the problems of reductionism, has difficulty in explaining why claims or findings made in one domain may be consequential in another supposedly autonomous one.

Let us assume that there are things like carbon and benzene in the world, and, more, that there really are atoms of carbon and molecules of benzene. We may still ask what in the world insists that atoms are 'fundamental' and that molecules are not; and what in the world tells us that anything we might conceivably ever learn about the one can, or cannot, be reduced 'in principle' to knowledge of the other. Questions of this kind, asked in a spirit of empirical curiosity, quickly prompt the thought that nothing in the world so insists, and that reductionism and dualism are alternative metaphysical accounts, or ontologies. And this is indeed what they are often understood to be. But this opens the possibility of walking away from both ontologies, and adopting instead a pragmatic view, wherein the relation of macro- and micro-things, being a matter of indifference to the world, is decided by people for their own convenience. On this view, the ontologies of reductionism and dualism take on the character of dogmas, or postulates accepted by convention. Of course, a pragmatic approach of this kind entails a changed understanding of the *nature* of macro- and micro-things as well as of their relationship. Just as the world itself no longer tells us about the reality of their relation, so it no longer tells us about their reality *per se*. Macro- and micro-things both become the products of the classifying activities we decide to employ in our dealings with the world. This entails monism, but not reduction. Both kinds of thing have the same standing. As to their relationship, that is a wholly contingent matter.

If we wish, we may address this contingent matter, and ask what as a matter of history has most often inclined people working at different levels of enquiry to take account of each others' findings? Common sense would suggest that a need for consistency in practical inference is perhaps the dominant consideration. The thought here is that a certain kind of consistency has to exist between micro- and macro-descriptions, because these descriptions do not relate to distinct and separate states-of-affairs (Barnes, 1995: 85–8). The cat on the mat may be described as an organism, a system of cells, a molecular system, or even as a cat, but these descriptions must not place conflicting demands on the 'cat itself' that is all these things. Thus, whereas no practical difficulty need arise if, for example, the cat as specific organs were observed to be far more stable than the cat as specific molecules; if the cat were apparently far more massive as organs than as molecules then serious questions would arise, however much dualists insisted on the independence of organic and molecular phenomena.

As an illustration of more obvious relevance to sociology and social theory, it is worth noting that suicides as suicides, and the same suicides as a suicide rate, are not independent states-of-affairs, and that to treat them as independent micro- and macro-phenomena risks creating just this kind of practical difficulty. And, finally, to illustrate the real historical importance of the point in the natural sciences, it is worth mentioning that the planet earth described as a physical system is no other than the earth described as a life-supporting system. The particular fascination of this lies in the fact that, according to the accepted science of the late-nineteenth century, the age of the earth as a life-supporting system was orders of magnitude greater than its age as a physical system of sufficient temperature to be such. What we have here is the only major historical episode wherein knowledge of physical and chemical materials and processes has come into conflict with biological and geological accounts of living things and their history. As it happens, the outcome of that clash was clearcut: biology won (Burchfield, 1975).

THE MACRO/MICRO PROBLEM IN SOCIOLOGY AND SOCIAL THEORY

For those working in a specific field of empirical enquiry, weakly linked to other specialized fields by modest interdependence and a modicum of mutual respect as is typical, the macro/micro problem might be thought of little moment. The patient observer of the three-toed sloth need not consider whether said sloth is a real essence, or a reified process, or a complex aggregate of molecules; or whether the resulting observation-reports are simple truths, or convenient simplifications, or illegitimate constructs. It suffices for her to speak of the sloth as sloth, even if her reports describe its responses to adrenaline, say, and are consciously intended to be of interest to chemists as well as biologists. The relative merits of different descriptions here, and the relationships between them, are likely to appear as 'merely philosophical' issues. Yet controversy about these 'philosophical' issues has frequently erupted in the natural sciences. And it has engendered debate in sociology and social theory as long as these fields have existed. Indeed, controversy over the macro/micro problem remains remarkably intense in these last fields, wherein merely pragmatic considerations are often overshadowed by 'fundamental' arguments about ontology. Although it is far from being a universal obsession, many macro-sociologists and social theorists, in contrast to observers of the three-toed sloth, are anxious to establish the reality of the macro-objects they describe, and eager to broadcast the defects of reductionism.

It is not hard to see why macro-sociologists are sensitive on this matter. On their right, they face the individualistic reductionism of what in terms of external recognition is the most successful of all the social science fields, economics. On their left, they face deconstruction by micro-sociologists and their allies and affines. And neither of these sources of difficulty seems sufficiently well disposed towards them to allow their references to institutions, or classes, or cultures, or social systems, any standing as 'convenient simplifications'. In macro-economics, firms, markets and currency flows represent an alternative 'convenient simplification', whilst for many micro-sociologists no simplification is ever convenient, and interest in macro-objects tends to be confined to identifying the precise way in which they are harmful.

It is not only problems with the neighbours, however, that give macro-sociologists a sense of vulnerability. In most fields, however much macro-descriptions may over-simplify by ignoring the composite character of macro-objects, they do at least remain less problematic epistemologically than reductionist micro-accounts; for macro-objects are easier to see, as it were, than micro-objects. But in sociology and macro-social theory this compensating virtue of macro-descriptions does not exist. Here, macro-objects are the harder to see, and indeed they often have the standing of invisible theoretical entities and not of objects that may be seen at all. Whilst individuals, and situations, and encounters, are by no means unproblematically 'there', they give rise to fewer practical-epistemological problems, as it were, than institutions and social systems do.

None the less, sociologists and social theorists remain reluctant to renounce macro-entities. Social theorists, in particular, often regard their references to invisible entities and mechanisms as essential to their central task of critical evaluation, and associate micro-description with the uncritical acceptance of appearances. Whether they are right to do so is, however, another matter. If critical potency and profundity are indeed to be taken as the primary criteria of good work here, then nowhere is honour more deserved than in the various traditions of micro-sociology, where careful descriptive studies remain able to inspire deep-seated insecurity in apologists for existing institutions and hierarchies. In contrast, the most eminent practitioners of what currently passes for critical social theory belong amongst those apologists. In the macro-theory of Jürgen Habermas, for example, we find an account of how modern capitalist societies embody a balance between the spheres of 'system' and 'lifeworld' that is pretty well just right. And this anodyne vision of how we currently stand is, if anything, even more clearly apparent in the recent writing of Anthony Giddens. Both these 'critical' social thinkers now deploy theory to identify and applaud in capitalist societies a politics that represents the apotheosis of the one great resilient and enduring moral ideal of our century, that of 'bourgeois equality'.[3]

Be that as it may, it remains the case that many macro-sociologists and social theorists currently regard the macro/micro problem as that of maintaining the defence against reductionism. And they are surely right in one respect: there is a lot of reductionism around to defend against, particularly in the guise of rational choice theory and related forms of individualism. Enthusiasts for this theory have long entertained the ambition of rendering the whole of our social life as so many calculated individual actions, and whatever macro-order there might be as the unlooked-for by-product of the relevant calculations. Conversely, critics have often regarded it as an imperialistic and undiscriminating intellectual movement lacking any genuine empirical curiosity – one that has sought to make sense of all it has encountered within a pre-ordained framework, rather as Marxism used to do. There is certainly some justice in this description. But imperialistic tendencies and the urge to a thoroughgoing reduction have also had the beneficial effect of bringing the theory into prolonged and fruitful confrontation with its most serious difficulties and most recalcitrant counter-examples.[4] In my judgement, it is greatly to the credit of rational choice theorists that they

have themselves focused attention on these difficulties and opened the way to the conclusion that they are insuperable, and fatal to their position. The powers of human beings to engender shared understandings across cultures, and coordinated action for the indivisible good of collectives, is simply unintelligible on the assumption that they are independent individuals.

Of course the irreducibility of macro-social phenomena to the actions and calculations of independent individuals does not preclude the possibility of alternative reductions. All the micro-objects of sociology are possible resources here: we may explore whether macro-entities are perhaps 'really' sets of encounters, or chains of interactions, or discursive exchanges or sequences of practices. And it is hard to see how we might identify any macro-entity or property, by inspection as it were, as 'emergent' and 'irreducible in principle', and thereby confound reductionist aspirations altogether in relation to it. None the less, whilst it is perfectly possible in a formal sense, it would be seriously misleading to render the relationship of micro- and macro-sociology as if it turned on the philosophical issue of reductionism.[5] Unlike the argument with rational choice, the 'internal' arguments between macro- and micro-sociologists and social theorists have not been dominated by metaphysical and ontological issues. Indeed pragmatist and constructivist perspectives have been and remain well represented in this context, and their characteristic methods of understanding objects as secondary to processes – not as entities self-evidently there in the world, but as the products of human activity ongoing in the world – are much in evidence.

Pragmatist and constructivist orientations to macro- and micro-objects, and hence to the macro/micro problem, have interesting implications for all fields of enquiry, but they have a special significance in social theory and sociology. For these fields have a special responsibility to provide an understanding of activities, and if objects are constituted through activities then both those objects and the relations between them become foci of sociological curiosity. The macro/micro problem is then not a problem *within* theory, of the relations of those levels of theory associated with different real-world objects; it is a problem *for* theory, an observable product of human theorizing activity which has to be made intelligible in and through that very activity. It must now be asked how and why human beings choose to set different orderings on the world, and why they relate those orderings to each other as they do, for example, as micro- and macro-orderings.

Interesting illustrations of how a perspective of this kind may address the macro/micro distinction can be found in the work of Michel Callon and Bruno Latour, who have repeatedly confronted this issue from the perspective of their 'actor–network' theory (Callon, 1986; Callon and Latour, 1981). In their studies, 'the observer follows the actors in order to identify the manner in which these define and associate the different elements by which they build and explain their world, whether it be social or natural' (Callon, 1986: 197). In the course of this defining and associating by actors both micro- and macro-objects are constituted; their properties are attributed; and the relations between them are established. No intrinsic differences are presumed between macro- and micro-objects. Objects of different 'sizes' are alike in being the products of the 'associations and definitions' that actor network theorists seek to describe. And they are alike in their standing: neither kind of object is reducible to the other; neither has ontological priority over the other. Although given macro-objects may be the products of the growth of smaller objects as a matter of history, all objects are the products of the same kinds of processes. The macro/micro distinction dissolves into an uncompromising monism.

The monism of Callon and Latour is indeed all-pervading. Not only do they treat micro- and macro-objects as equivalent, they try to treat humans and non-humans as equivalent as well and to mark no distinction between natural and social objects. For them all objects are alike in being the products of associations, and in their work associations created by scientists and engineers figure especially prominently. They have sought to emphasize how social and natural orders are simultaneously constituted in and as these associations, along with all the range of objects, large and small, they are acknowledged to contain. A major part of the message of this work is indeed that the (scientific) study of the natural world constitutively involves sociological enquiry, that social life similarly involves the (scientific) study of natural phenomena and that the macro-objects engendered in the course of all this are hybrid 'quasi-objects, neither 'natural' nor 'social'.

Actor–network theory is now very widely used in studies that seek to document how macro-objects get constituted. It has, of course, been subjected to extensive technical criticism, like any theory, but it also faces formal difficulties because of its status as a theory of theories. The objects and entities 'created' by use of the theory, and in that sense internal to it, can be addressed in just the way that the theory itself addresses objects and entities external to it. Callon (1986: 200) gives a clear response to the problem of justification implicit here: 'our narrative is no more, but no less valid, than any other'. What he does not clarify, however, is what pragmatic or practical considerations make this particular narrative preferable to 'no less valid' alternatives.[6]

Actor–network theory is sometimes defended as the most rigorous extant expression of the principle that all accounts and all actions, including those of the sociologists themselves, must be treated equally in sociological study. But there are difficulties here. Objects are said to be the creations of the actors being followed, and the properties of the objects to be those that actors assign to them. But at the same time, actors are amongst the created objects and their agency is just such an assigned property; indeed agency may be assigned to non-humans, whereupon they become actors, presumably with powers of assignation themselves, whatever that may imply. The evident circularity here – wherein actors are the creations of actors, that are the creations of actors, that . . . – gives no concern to users of the theory. They simply decide for themselves which actors they will follow, and proceed. But in making prior decisions of this kind actor–network theorists come very close to deciding in advance just how the historical episodes they are about to address will be made visible.

It is important to notice how much of what Callon and Latour describe as they 'follow the actors' is preordained, as it were, rather than 'found'. In practice, prior external decisions fix not only which actors will be followed, but also what theoretical schemes will be used to make sense of what those actors do. These schemes seem predominantly to be drawn from economic and political theory; and on the face of it they offer unedifying visions of human beings as Hobbesian warriors, or ruthless entrepreneurs, or Machiavellian calculators. The stories constructed from these theories, however, never aspire to a systematic explanation of what the actors are doing. Instead, they render events *ex post facto*, as displays of human activity and potency, and this is perhaps what makes them so attractive.

It is intriguing to notice here how their inclination to render humans as active is related to the conception of social order favoured by Callon and Latour. For them, the social order is the entirety of manifest social activity, which means that more or less by definition anything that an agent does reconstitutes and in a sense transforms the social order. Notice the intensified sense of agency conveyed by this vision of things, in comparison with that encouraged by the alternative vision wherein a stable social structure underlying manifest activity is the central macro-social object.[7] It is a nice illustration of how prior decisions on frame can have profound remote consequences as theories unfold.

In the narratives of actor–network theory human beings construct and manipulate their world, overcome resistance, create and then realize interests, all with amazing facility. It is indeed a valid cause of dissatisfaction with these narratives that justice is not done to the manifest difficulty of carrying out such projects. These are projects involving learning about and acting upon real-world objects, or so those engaged in them might want to say, and they are as likely to end in frustration and failure as in success. But actor–network studies seem attracted to success and pleased to fashion it into mock-heroic history (Latour, 1988). For all that at one level actor–network theory modestly 'follows the actors' and marks no distinction of its own between humans and things, at another level it is a profoundly intrusive monism engaged in the celebration of human agency. For many readers it provides a narrative of contingency revelatory of how things could have happened otherwise (Michael, 1996).

'STRUCTURE' AND 'AGENCY' IN SOCIOLOGY AND SOCIAL THEORY

Sociology and social theory have always been interested in the nature of voluntary action and in how, if at all, to take account of the free agency of human beings whilst constructing theoretical accounts of their actions. Currently, however, these issues are being debated as never before. Perhaps a spreading sense of empowerment has something to do with this; especially through the way that empowerment engenders negative attitudes to the burgeoning ranks of bureaucrats and technical professionals whose knowledge is structured in terms of the institution of causal connection. But whatever the reason (or the cause) may be, it is clear that there is now an unprecedented level of interest in the nature of human agency, and that macro/micro debates have largely become debates about the relationship of agency and structure.

To grasp what is at issue in the structure/agency debates it is necessary to glance back to the sociology that established itself in the English-speaking world half a century or so ago, and sought acknowledgement as an authentic science. Human societies, so it seemed to its practitioners, were ordered and patterned. The order and pattern was evident in the voluntary actions from which they were made. The task of a science faced with such a pattern was to explain it or account for it. Accordingly, the task of sociology was to establish why voluntary actions were patterned as they were. There was a need for voluntary actions to be explained, and, by analogy with other sciences, explanation meant linking the actions to causes, or influences, independent of them. Among the cited influences were class interests, external coercive powers, social pressures and, in the structural functional sociology that came to dominate the field, rules and social norms. Curiosity was satisfied by appeal to these kinds of things as externalities. What is making people act thus and so? They are conforming to norms. Why is there an overall pattern in their actions? Because there is an overall pattern in the norms. What is the pattern? It is that of the social system or structure of the society in question; and by reference to that system or structure, wherein rules and norms are ordered around statuses to form social institutions, actions may be understood and explained. Thus emerged the vision of social structure famously associated with the work of Talcott Parsons and long the theoretical mainstay of sociological work in the English-speaking world.

It is worth noting the oddity of this version of structure. Cut down a tree and the eye remarks the ringed structure of the trunk, the array of concentric circles visible in the cellulose fibres that make it up. There is a standard macro/micro problem here. Are the rings really there, or can accounts of them be 'reduced' to accounts of cellulose fibres? Will the growth of the fibres explain or fail to explain the existence of the rings? What we don't tend to ask is whether the ringed structure explains the growth of the fibres, as if the structure is there in advance, as it were, and the fibres grow as it requires or specifies. Yet this is how social structure has sometimes been understood; as real, separate, prior, macro and explanatory. Actions manifest pattern; the pattern is described; the pattern is taken as a separate real macro-entity; the macro-entity explains the actions. This, at least, is how critics of this form of macro-sociology have seen it, and why they have dismissed it as illegitimate reification.

As it happens, this peculiarity of social structure and of 'social-structural explanation', did not prevent their constituting a perfectly acceptable macro-sociology for a considerable period, and thereby constituting the backdrop to the debates here discussed. And indeed it is tempting to suggest that a secular pattern of social change involving an ever-increasing concern with the dignity and standing of 'the individual' is what brought about its demise, and not its inherent inadequacies. In any event, distaste for the passive role allegedly being accorded to the individual 'human subject', did eventually become irresistibly strong, and the offending 'structural functional' theories were set aside. Indeed the reaction against the institution of causal connection and the urge to stress internal autonomy and activity came to encompass far more than human beings. Entire monistic cosmologies of agency were constructed, and accepted as appropriate descriptions of objects of all kinds, animate and inanimate. The move to celebrate human agency now to be discussed was actually part of a larger, possibly still more fascinating, shift of perspective.[8]

One famous formulation of what was wrong with the older causal theories was that of the ethnomethodologist Harold Garfinkel. He denounced them for making out individual human beings as 'dopes', that is as 'passive producers of actions to the specification of whatever structural or cultural models of their conduct were available in the cultural setting, rather than as knowledgeable human beings aware of and able to take account of the existence of those models' (1967: 68). Consider now a macro-sociologist, disinclined to doubt the large-scale orderliness of human societies or that it has something to do with norms or rules, but impressed notwithstanding by the ethno-methodological argument and by the lovely studies of the artful and reflexive character of human actions that Garfinkel's work inspired. For such a sociologist at least three problems are likely to arise. First, how might human beings be understood, other than as dopes of some kind? Secondly, what new account of the relationship of human beings and social norms or rules might such an alternative understanding lead to? Thirdly, will the evident macro-orderliness of societies be intelligible on the basis of any such new account? The case studies of ethnomethodologists offered direct assistance on the first two problems. They documented human beings taking account of rather than merely 'following' rules , and actively construing and interpreting them in ways that suited their practical purposes. In effect, rules were more the outcomes than the determinants of actions, and in that guise they were known of and utilized by human beings actively pursuing their practical purposes.

Much the most widely known attempt to reconceptualize macro-sociology on this kind of basis is Anthony Giddens' structuration theory.[9] Giddens refers to language to convey his thoughts about rules. Human beings draw upon the resources of language in all kinds of ways, for all kinds of purposes. The language does not tell them what they may or may not say. They may use it how they will. And in using it as they will, however that may be, they reconstitute the language as a set of resources available for use. Similarly, a set of rules may persist as something that is drawn-upon in and by a collective. In an idiosyncratic departure from normal usage that has sometimes caused confusion, Giddens calls such a set of rules a social *structure*.[10] A social structure both facilitates and constrains action that draws upon it; it facilitates action by virtue of what it makes available and constrains action by virtue of what it lacks and cannot make available. It does not, however, stand as a determinant or even as a cause of that action, since it does not 'make' the active agents who engender it do one thing rather than another. Indeed it is those agents, deciding to do whatever they decide to do by drawing upon structure, and thereby manifesting their *agency*, who reconstitute structure through their actions and secure its continued existence. Thus, Giddens is able to give both the macro (structure) and the micro (agency) an essential role, whilst rejecting any causal connection between the two, and in particular any suggestion that the operation of human reason may be externally determined.

There is no point in this brief space in attempting either to review or to add to the innumerable commentaries on structuration theory, but some remarks on its macro and micro dimensions may be worthwhile. It is important to note, first of all, that 'structure' is not the only macro-entity in structuration theory. Just as the members of a language-sharing community routinely continue to say some things and not others, to use language in some patterns and not others, so it is with those who draw upon the repertoire of rules that is social structure. The *particular* patterns thereby engendered and reproduced are *social systems*, and the persistence of social systems needs to be accounted for as well as that of structures. What is necessary here is an account or explanation of the *particular* ways in which agents choose to draw upon the resources of structure. Giddens' response is to suggest that individual agents have a need for *ontological security*, essential to tension management and anxiety reduction within themselves, and itself dependent on their implicit faith in 'the conventions (codes of signification and forms of normative regulation) via which, in the duality of structure, the reproduction of social life is effected' (1979: 218–19). In order to sustain this sense of ontological security agents tend to act to reproduce the specific social system they inhabit as it already exists, and this is how the system persistence observable almost everywhere is to be explained.

It needs to be asked whether this does not return the analysis very close to the point whence it started. Accounts of anxiety-reduction and the maintenance of ontological security are drawn from a broadly Freudian tradition of psychology, and what they refer to are causes of, or causal influences upon, how individual persons act. So it could be said that implicit here is an individualistic micro-causal account of how social systems are reproduced. Indeed, it could be said that the need for ontological security makes persons act in accordance with the system-status-quo, that it disposes them to conform to system requirements and existing 'forms of normative regulation'. This makes the account look very like the outmoded functionalism of Talcott Parsons, wherein the reproduction of the status quo was similarly linked to 'forms of normative regulation'.[11] And the resemblance becomes still more striking when it is recalled that what Giddens calls 'system' is very like what earlier theorists called 'social structure'. Indeed, the enduring value of earlier theories, which rendered social structures in terms of statuses, institutions and other macro-objects, is readily appreciated once this line of thought is pursued. That human beings everywhere orient to each other in terms of social statuses, for example, must be accounted for in any sociology; but it cannot be accounted for simply by reference to the individual agents and rules that dominate a 'structurationist' perspective. There is currently a manifest need to renew and reinvigorate the traditional macro-sociology of statuses and institutions.[12]

Now to the micro level, where Giddens' account of the notion of agency may be taken as typifying that now favoured by large numbers of theorists. Clearly, it is necessary for his theory that individuals are not the dopes of rules, that they 'have agency' in the specific, narrow sense of being active in relation to rules and norms and not predictably compliant with them. But his actual vision of agency far transcends this necessity: it is a larger vision of agency altogether, of the kind we often entertain in everyday life when we speak of someone as a free agent. Agency in this large sense is the independent power of the individual human being to intervene in the ongoing flow of events and make a difference to them, her power to 'act otherwise' as Giddens sometimes says. This assertion, in effect, of the freedom of the individual and her ability to change things, is a metaphysical postulate, not an empirically plausible claim. It expresses a *prior* belief in 'the freedom of the acting subject' and in the standing of that subject as an undetermined source of power. 'It is *analytical* to the concept of agency', Giddens says, 'that a person (i.e. an agent) "could have acted otherwise"' (1976: 75; emphasis added). And it is similarly held to be true of action, even

routine action, that in being action and not mere behaviour it 'could have been otherwise' by virtue of the agency of its performer.

This characterization of human beings as active agents who can 'make things happen' is unquestionably the source of much of the very widespread appeal of structuration theory. But it is important to ask what considerations might dispose us to accept it. There is indeed reason to believe that persons are active in relation to norms and rules. But whilst we might consequently wish to speak of agency in relation to rules and norms, why would we want to go further and speak of agency *per se*? Giddens himself offers us nothing here. Indeed, his efforts are largely confined to explaining why agency is so rarely manifest as a transformative power; why, even in relation to rules, it is the routine and familiar modes of use that are overwhelmingly in evidence and relatively little that is new is 'made to happen'. On 'agency' in its unrestricted sense, the agency of his metaphysics, he is unenlightening.

It is interesting to notice that the 'agency' of this metaphysics is very close to the 'agency' of everyday discourse – to the metaphysics of everyday life as it were. We routinely say of other people, 'she was a free agent', or 'she didn't have to do it; she could have acted otherwise', or 'it was her choice to do it'; and we do not speak in this way of objects. It is, of course, the everyday use of such notions in the context of references to voluntary actions that makes theoretical discussions of 'agency' and 'choice' so readily intelligible. Thus, having asked what the metaphysics of agency does for social theorists, and found it hard to arrive at a satisfactory answer, it is worth asking what that metaphysics does for us as ordinary members.

'AGENCY' AND THE INSTITUTION OF RESPONSIBLE ACTION

Custom has it that writers of pieces such as this may conclude with some of their own ideas and reflections, and I shall grasp the opportunity custom presents to offer some thoughts of my own on 'agency'. The discussion will, however, differ radically both in form and focus from what has gone before. The initial form will not be provided by macro/micro, or structure/agency, or individual/society, or any other pair of distinctions, but by a monistic vision of interacting human beings presumed to be intrinsically sociable and interdependent. And the initial focus will be on 'agency' as used in the context of ordinary life, wherein it is deployed along with a number of other notions, sometimes called 'voluntaristic' notions, as a constituent of the institution of responsible action. Naturally, these changes in the initial frame of reference produce changed conclusions. The conception of agency that then emerges (which I discuss in detail in Barnes, 2000) contrasts sharply with those that dominate the current literature (Emirbayer and Mische, 1998).

First, form. Imagine that the social world is formed of sociable, interacting, interdependent human beings. This is more than mere assumption. There are good empirically grounded arguments for it, although these will be passed over here save only for one that is particularly relevant in this context. Think of the relationship of people with rules and norms again. Older macro-social theories rendered people as the 'dopes' of rules, or so it is now claimed. More recent theories have them 'drawing-upon' rules. But what and where are these rules? Just what is it that we are said to be dopes of, or to draw upon? This is an unresolved issue of enormous sociological importance, that continues to engender controversy between rule realists, rule individualists, rule collectivists and so forth.[13]

The crucial thing in any attempt to grasp what rules are is to keep the imagination, and ideally the senses, close to the actual business of their invocation and use. Look at people driving cars perhaps, or exchanging courtesies, or eating a meal together, or participating in a march, or even individually, adjusting dress, or measuring a carpet or drawing a circle. All that will be found in this way is instances cited as examples of rule use, and clustered into sets by being so cited. It is through examples that rules are learned and as examples that they are encountered from that point on. This does not imply, necessarily, that 'there are no such things as rules', although it does point up their character as reifications. What is implied, however, if rules are only apprehended through instances, is that their application must consist in the making of *analogies* with existing instances. The importance of this point is that persons are liable to differ on how to extend analogies, and if they were to proceed as so many independent, isolated individuals, even if they were to start with identical examples or instances, they would lose coordination and be liable to disagree. Because examples differ in detail from each other, and what constitutes proper analogy between them is always contestable, uniformity in the following of a rule shared by many individuals cannot be put down to their common awareness of some essential feature or property of 'the rule itself'. If a continuing sense that there is 'a rule there' is to be generated, and a right way of extending the rule to future cases and

situations is to be identified, all the various attempts at correct rule use across the collective will have to be considered by its members; a sense of which of these attempts are right and which wrong will have to be engendered; and a shared sense of how to move from agreed 'right' instances to new applications will continually have to be sustained.

In all manifestations of social life, what would otherwise be diverse individual inclinations in the specification and application of rules must be ordered into a tolerably coherent collective practice. Without this there can be no sense that one way of continuing to follow a rule is better than another, and hence there can be no rule. But independent individuals have no incentive to do the work of evaluation and standardization constantly necessary to sustain a sense of 'what the rules are'. Only non-independent human beings will do this work, human beings who are indeed active and independent in relation to rules but not in relation to each other. Sociable human beings, capable of affecting each other implicitly, causally and continuously in their communicative interaction, may coordinate their understandings and their actual implementations of rules in this way, whilst independent individuals may not. And this coordination is, of course, just what is invariably found in practice.

There are many forms and varieties of the argument given above, but all point in the same direction. They evoke a vision of people disposed all the time to retain coordination in their practical sense of what rules amount to, what their implications are, what their normativity consists in, and of their managing to do so through interacting together and influencing and being influenced by each other. It is important to be clear as well that coordination of *understandings* is involved here, and not just coordination of physical actions. Shared understandings are the products of the effort to coordinate, not its basis, which means that 'rational' verbal exchanges, reliant upon 'shared meanings', are only possible, if at all, when coordination already exists; they can in no way be understood as the means of securing it. This is a point of major importance. If it is correct then rationalist versions of communicative action, and notably that of Habermas (1984, 1987, 1990, 1992), are fundamentally flawed, and indeed the rationalist theory of individual human agency so persuasively advanced by Habermas is revealed as fundamentally defective as well.[14] Proponents of this kind of theory should steel themselves to recognize that there must be something *causal* at work, all the time in the course of communicative interaction, that keeps people sufficiently well aligned with each other for mutual intelligibility to continue. People must be *mutually susceptible*, in a causal sense, in their interactions and communications. Susceptibility of this kind has, of course, long been recognized and documented in the classical interactionist studies of micro-sociology. In Erving Goffman, for example, it is visible as the concern of members to avoid loss of face. The ubiquitous need to keep face is what constitutes mutual susceptibility.[15]

Let us put that on hold, now, and switch attention from the form to the focus of the discussion. In everyday life we speak of and to each other as responsible agents, deploying all the familiar concepts of everyday voluntaristic discourse. We describe each other as acting voluntarily, or else under constraint, as making choices, as seeing reason, or else of not seeing it or having lost it. It is common to codify this discourse of responsible agency using an individualistic idiom, wherein the state of individual responsibility involves the possession of two key powers or attributes: the capacity for rational conduct and freedom of will. Indeed, rational choice theory is very close to being an individualistic codification of this kind, wherein action is related to the internal individual states of rationality and power to choose. But there is a notorious problem associated with these internal states. Not merely are they invisible: there seems to be no fact of the matter to tell us when they are operative and when not, or indeed whether or not they 'really' exist. It is difficult, for example, to understand just how we distinguish in practice between chosen and caused behaviour, or voluntary actions that 'could have been otherwise' and behaviours that could not. These are crucial distinctions; and we make them all the time, as we must, usually with consummate ease. On what basis we make them, however, is highly problematic, and not even systematic studies by psychologists have thrown much light on the matter. None the less, we evidently do believe that a distinction is there to be made, and indeed we evidently do make it and imagine ourselves guided by empirical considerations when we do so.

Let me now bring the form and the focus of the discussion together. We are given to speaking of ourselves as responsible agents, and to deploying the notions of our everyday voluntaristic discourse in characterizing ourselves as such. A widespread individualistic codification of that discourse renders us as independent agents, possessed of rationality and free will. But rationality and free will, understood as the internal states of independent individuals, are elusive, and just what prompts our use of these notions in this sense is notoriously hard to discern. Nor ought this to surprise anyone who

recognizes that social life is actually constituted as interacting, non-independent, mutually susceptible human beings. However, if this is indeed the case, then it must be asked how voluntaristic discourse actually maps onto such human beings, and what it is about them that prompts us to describe them in voluntaristic terms.

Human beings are properly described, let us agree, as sociable creatures whose interactions are characterized by mutual intelligibility and mutual susceptibility. Human beings none the less describe each other as responsible agents, possessed of rationality and free will. Both descriptions refer to the same human beings. The conjecture must accordingly be that responsible agency, as specified in everyday discourse, comprises mutual intelligibility and mutual susceptibility, the basic necessities for the maintenance of coordinated interaction. And we can conjecture further that, in a rough and ready way, the rationality of the responsible agent is her intelligibility (or accountability), and the free will of the responsible agent is her susceptibility. But of course it is not merely that we describe each other (in our normal 'responsible' state) with this voluntaristic discourse; it is that we communicate in terms of it and *affect* each other through these communications. To identify someone as a normal responsible agent is to recognize her as open to influence, as capable of being affected, by our communications; and to remind her in those communications that she is a responsible agent is part of the business of affecting her through them.

Voluntaristic discourse needs to be understood primarily as the medium through which our sociability is expressed, not the medium in which our independence is celebrated. And the sociability so expressed needs to be recognized as a distinctive strength of our species. Most of the order in our social and mental life is sustained by mutually susceptible responsible agents who press each other to do what is necessary to create it, continue it and change it. Communicating and evaluating, learning and suffering, in the course of our social interaction, our collective accomplishment far transcends anything that could be hoped for from independent individuals. Parts of this accomplishment are groups and collectives, offices and hierarchies, institutions and organizations, all recognizable in turn as features of the landscape in which we live our social lives, and hence as loci of responsibility and accountability in their own right. In this way the everyday voluntarism of the institution of responsible action now expresses itself in the complex and elaborate systems of practice we recognize as those societies in which we presently live. The simple institution allows the elaboration of the larger society: the larger society is the simple institution elaborated. And voluntaristic discourse is the medium through which all this is achieved and sustained, the characteristic form of communication in which the inherent sociability of human beings is so potently expressed.

In modern theorists such as Anthony Giddens (just as in Immanuel Kant), agency is the individual capacity to act otherwise. This alleged capacity is amongst the most opaque and obscure of all the inner states, or powers, or capacities, spoken of in voluntaristic discourse. What there is, we might say, is all there is; what is otherwise, if it were, would not be otherwise. But we have a strong sense that human action 'could have been otherwise' none the less. What prompts it? Consider whether it is not an awareness that the action 'could have been otherwise' if only communication, or persuasion, or some kind of symbolically mediated 'pressure', had been directed toward the agent involved. Consider, in other words, whether normal free action is not that which we regard as capable of modification through communication. This is what is being suggested here. And if correct, it transforms a vision of agency as a mysterious independent uncaused power into one where all actions can be understood, if that is what we wish, by routine recourse to the institution of causal connection. Free action need no longer be an uncaused intervention; it may be action with whatever causal antecedents, given only that we reckon it readily variable by use of the causal powers of communicative interaction. In that interaction we *do* things with voluntaristic notions; we do things to and with those we address as responsible agents.

To suggest this, of course, is no small matter, since it is to deny an individualistic conception of agency long accepted amongst us and with significant implications for how we live our lives. But the account being proposed, whilst it does indeed deny individual agency as generally understood, will provide more than sufficient compensation if it has correctly identified the interactive basis of the collective agency that engenders the cultural and institutional order intrinsic to human life. And of course if it has correctly done this, then it will also have identified the appropriate starting point for reflection on macro/micro problems in the context of sociology and social theory. There is no space here to explore the many macro-sociological implications of the inherent sociability and susceptibility of human beings, but what follows above all is that macro-entities should be identified by attending, not to similarities in the characteristics of individuals, or even to similarities in their situations, but to the connections and relations between those 'individuals'. Consistent with this, I have suggested elsewhere that status groups and extended status orderings will be extremely important elements of any macro-theory designed to be consistent with a micro-sociology of interacting sociable agents. Indeed, a micro-sociology of face and a macro-sociology of status could well prove amenable to synthesis into a coherent overall perspective that could underpin and inform social theory as a whole.[16]

There remains one final point to be dealt with if these brief suggestions are to carry plausibility. If we are agents in the sense outlined here, why do we not explicitly recognize ourselves as such? Why instead do we reify our collective agency into an individual power? Part of the answer may be that reifications of this kind are extremely common in our culture, and that the conversion of accountability and susceptibility into rationality and free agency exemplifies a common process. We are very prone to render the relational properties of things in context as the internal powers or properties of the things. We render statuses as states. The responsible agent possesses the rudimentary relational properties to count as being of that status, whereupon the status is misread as a part of her nature, as her internal state. Similar reifications include the value of money and the power of political leaders. It is important, however, to recognize the special importance of what is reified here. The status of the responsible agent is the most rudimentary of all social statuses, and the crucial default status of the institution of responsible action. As such, it is a vital focus for the attribution of responsibilities, for praise and blame according to how they are met and for demands for response when failure to fulfil them gives rise to damage to others. But responsibility must be localized, whereas causal connection delocalizes. The ideal carrier of responsibility is an uncaused cause, a clearly distinguished and demarcated target for demands and expectations (and, as optional extras, rights and powers). And even if in reality human beings are buffeted by causes like flotsam in foam, it may still be that these causes are largely discounted, or airbrushed from reality by various devices, for this reason. It may be indeed that such devices have always and everywhere been employed to identify 'individuals' and their powers, since all societies attach responsibilities to individual persons. But their deployment surely reached a zenith of skill and sophistication in our own recent history: the myth of individual agency as an independent power is, after all, the very essence of the myth of the Enlightenment.

NOTES

I would like to thank John DuPre, Adrian Haddock and Nigel Pleasants for helpful comment and criticism that enabled me to improve an earlier draft of this chapter.

1 There is no theory-independent terminology available here, and my talk of 'things' should be given no particular significance.

2 Bhaskar (1979) gives the basic dualist/emergentist position. But for a sense of the complication and elaboration possible on the basis of it, and hence of the difficulty of a brief appraisal of it, see for example Bhaskar (1986). Note also that pluralist ontologies are possible, which seems implicit in Bhaskar and is explicit in DuPre (1993). For present purposes pluralism may be understood as iterated dualism. Historically, dualism and reductionism have often been found locked in opposition, as the expanding discourses and practices of colonizing fields have been opposed and resisted by those they have threatened. Matter/spirit dualism, for example, has long been deployed to resist the encroachment of 'science' into the 'proper spheres' of religion and philosophy, as well as to oppose politically threatening versions of materialism. And similarly, in the micro-political context of the social sciences, dualists have asserted the independence of macro-social objects in opposing the imperialistic individualism of economics.

3 See Habermas (1984, 1987) and Giddens (1994, 1998). For relevant criticism of these alternative up-market and down-market versions of uncritical critical theory see Pleasants (1999).

4 For rational choice a vast literature includes Coleman (1990), and Abell (1991). For its reflexive criticism, see Elster (1989), Friedman (1995), Green and Shapiro (1994) and Hardin (1995).

5 Certainly, the history of the older micro-sociologies in the USA shows them content to take a secondary role in relation to a macro-sociology they none the less believed to be profoundly misconceived (Rock, 1978). And whilst today micro-theory can be far more confident, aggressive and even evangelical, the discourse of reductionism remains alien to it, and whatever encroachments it makes into other 'levels' of enquiry are rationalized by other means.

6 Those with an interest in constructivist accounts should note that one of these alternatives is the finitist sociology of knowledge that I myself have helped to develop (Barnes et al., 1996). Latour (1993) misrepresents this as a dualist account when in truth it is entirely monistic. It is a monism that differs from Latour's in being based not on actants and agency (see main text), but on the institution of causal connection. The grounds for my recommending it over 'no less valid alternatives' are that it consistently extends the established approach of the natural sciences, precisely by rendering scientists' own classifications in terms of a conceptual relativism and characterizing them as human inventions sustained by authority. Scientists themselves unfortunately are liable to lapse into megalomania when making this kind of extension, as is apparent in the literature of the 'science wars' (see Gieryn, 1999).

7 An anecdote in a talk on sexuality attended during the writing of this chapter comes to mind as embodying a vividly contrasting approach. Roughly it went as follows: 'A woman straps on a dildo and fucks her male partner. Its common enough today. But so what? Half an hour later she descends from the bedroom to do the washing up. Nothing at all has changed.' The sense of social structure implicit here remains quite widespread.

8 The work of Callon and Latour already referred to is an illustration of this, as also are the many strands of work inspired by Harre and Madden (1977). Indeed, as the institution of causal connection increasingly prevails as the discourse of those technical specialists whose knowledge is overwhelmingly dominant as power, so talk of agency and empowerment dominates the discourse of other, often relatively powerless and marginalized, intellectuals.

9 At least in so far as sociology and social theory in Britain is concerned, the structuration theory set out by Giddens in the early 1980s has long been at once the most lauded and influential of all theoretical perspectives (Clark et al., 1990; Giddens, 1984; Held and Thompson, 1989). A great deal of what once was discussed under the rubric of the macro/micro problem is now debated as the problem of structure and agency, and indeed, all the familiar elements of the quarrels between dualists and reductionists are to be found in the context of the structure/agency debates, despite the apparent intention of its initiator to take theory beyond those modes of thought; see, for example, Archer, 1988, 1995; Loyal, 1997; Willmott, 1986.

10 See Giddens, 1984. I have simplified somewhat in that Giddens thinks of social structure as 'rules and resources' and not rules alone.

11 The argument here is Loyal's (1997).

12 For analyses of statuses as macro entities, see Barnes, 1983, 1988, 2000, where they are treated as elements of an institutional order constituted as a self-referring distribution of knowledge. For a closely analogous account, superior in clarity but at the cost of a more limited scope and a little too much reification see Searle, 1994.

13 See Bloor, 1997, both for a general discussion, and a defence of rule collectivism linked to Wittgenstein, 1968. See also Kripke, 1982.

14 There is no space here to discuss Habermas on individual agency, but even though they have their idiosyncrasies, his views are close enough to those of Giddens in the aspects taken to be central in the main text.

15 See, for example, Goffman, 1967, and also Scheff, 1988 and Barnes, 1995: ch. 3 and 2000: ch. 5.

16 For macro-sociology that exemplifies the suggestion see Banton, 1983 and Collins, 1986; and for an extended argument on its behalf Barnes, 1995, 2000.

REFERENCES

Abell, P. (1991) *Rational Choice Theory*. Aldershot: Elgar.

Archer, M. (1988) *Culture and Agency*. Cambridge: Cambridge University Press.

Archer, M. (1995) *Realist Social Theory: the Morphogenetic Approach*. Cambridge: Cambridge University Press.

Banton, M. (1983) *Racial and Ethnic Competition*. Cambridge: Cambridge University Press.

Barnes, B. (1983) 'Social Life as Bootstrapped Induction', *Sociology*, 17: 524–45.

Barnes, B. (1988) *The Nature of Power*. Champaign-Urbana, IL: University of Illinois Press.

Barnes, B. (1995) *The Elements of Social Theory*. Princeton, NJ: Princeton University Press.

Barnes, B. (2000) *Understanding Agency: Social Theory and Responsible Action*. Beverly Hills, CA: Sage.

Barnes, B., Bloor, D.C. and Henry, J. (1996) *Scientific Knowledge: a Sociological Analysis*. Chicago: University of Chicago Press.

Bhaskar, R. (1979) *The Possibility of Naturalism*. Brighton: Harvester.

Bhaskar, R. (1986) *Scientific Realism and Human Emancipation*. London: Verso.

Bloor, D. (1997) *Wittgenstein, Rules and Institutions*. London: Routledge.

Burchfield, J. (1975) *Lord Kelvin and the Age of the Earth*. New York: Science History Publications.

Callon, M. (1986) 'Some Elements of a Sociology of Translation', in J. Law (ed.), *Power, Action and Belief. Sociological Review Monograph 34*. London: Routledge and Kegan Paul.

Callon, M. and Latour, B. (1981) 'Unscrewing the Big Leviathan', in K. Knorr Cetina and A. Cicourel (eds), *Advances in Social Theory and Methodology: Toward an Integration of Micro and Macro Sociologies*. London: Routledge.

Clark, J., Modgil, C. and Modgil, S. (eds) (1990) *Anthony Giddens: Consensus and Controversy*. London: Falmer Press.

Coleman, J. (1990) *Foundations of Social Theory*. Cambridge, MA: Harvard University Press.

Collins, R. (1986) *Weberian Sociological Theory*. Cambridge: Cambridge University Press.

DuPre, J. (1993) *The Disorder of Things*. Cambridge, MA: Harvard University Press.

Elster, J. (1989) *The Cement of Society: a Study of Social Order*. Cambridge: Cambridge University Press.

Emirbayer, M. and Mische, A. (1998) 'What is Agency?', *American Journal of Sociology*, 103: 962–1023.

Friedman, J. (ed.) (1995) *The Rational Choice Controversy*. New Haven, CT: Yale University Press.

Garfinkel, H. (1967) *Studies in Ethnomethodology*. Englewood Cliffs, NJ: Prentice-Hall.

Giddens, A. (1976) *New Rules of Sociological Method*. London: Hutchinson.

Giddens, A. (1979) *Central Problems in Social Theory*. London: Macmillan.

Giddens, A. (1984) *The Constitution of Society*. Cambridge: Polity Press.

Giddens, A. (1994) *Beyond Left and Right*. Cambridge: Polity Press.

Giddens, A. (1998) *The Third Way*. Cambridge: Polity Press.

Gieryn, T. (1999) *Cultural Boundaries of Science*. Chicago: University of Chicago Press.

Goffman, E. (1967) *Interaction Ritual: Essays on Face-to-Face Behavior*. New York: Doubleday.

Green, D. and Shapiro, I. (1994) *Pathologies of Rational Choice Theory*. New Haven, CT: Yale University Press.

Habermas, J. (1984) *The Theory of Communicative Action*, vol. I: *Reason and the Rationalization of Society*. London: Heinemann.

Habermas, J. (1987) *The Theory of Communicative Action*, vol. 2: *Lifeworld and System: a Critique of Functionalist Reason*. Cambridge: Polity Press.

Habermas, J. (1990) *Moral Consciousness and Communicative Action*. Cambridge: Polity Press.

Habermas, J. (1992) *Postmetaphysical Thinking*. Cambridge: Polity Press.

Hardin, R. (1995) *One for All*. Princeton, NJ: Princeton University Press.

Harre, R. and Madden, E.H. (1977) *Causal Powers*. Oxford: Blackwell.

Held, D. and Thompson, J.B. (eds) (1989) *Social Theory of Modern Society: Anthony Giddens and his Critics*. Cambridge: Cambridge University Press.

Knorr Cetina, K. and Cicourel A. (1981) *Advances in Social Theory and Methodology: Toward an Integration of Micro and Macro Sociologies*. London: Routledge.

Kripke, S. (1982) *Wittgenstein on Rules and Private Language: an Elementary Exposition*. Oxford: Blackwell.

Latour, B. (1988) *The Pasteurisation of France*. Cambridge, MA: Harvard University Press.

Latour, B. (1993) *We Have Never Been Modern*. London: Harvester.

Law, J. (ed.) (1986) *Power, Action and Belief. Sociological Review Monograph 32*. London: Routledge and Kegan Paul.

Loyal, S. (1997) 'Action, Structure and Contradiction: a Contextual Critique of Giddens' Theory of Structuration', PhD thesis: Exeter University.

Michael, M. (1996) *Constructing Identities*. London: Sage.

Parsons, T. ([1937] 1968) *The Structure of Social Action*. New York: The Free Press.

Pleasants, N. (1999) *Wittgenstein and the Idea of a Critical Social Theory*. London: Routledge.

Rock, P. (1978) *The Making of Symbolic Interactionism*. London: Macmillan.

Scheff, T.J. (1988) 'Shame and Conformity: the Deference–Emotion System', *American Sociological Review*, 53: 395–406.

Searle, J. (1994) *The Construction of Social Reality*. London: Allen Lane.

Willmot, H.C. (1986) 'Uncovering Sources of Motives in the Theory of the Subject: an Exposition and Criticism of Giddens' Dualistic Models of Action and Personality', *Journal of the Theory of Social Behaviour*, 16: 105–21.

Wittgenstein, L. (1968) *Philosophical Investigations*, 3rd edn. Oxford: Blackwell.

27

Norbert Elias and Process Sociology

ROBERT VAN KRIEKEN

An interviewer once drew Norbert Elias' (1897–1990) attention to a comment made on his work by Zygmunt Bauman, that he was 'perhaps the last representative of classical sociology, someone striving after the great synthesis'. Elias' response was to say that he did not appreciate the observation, because he 'would rather be the first one to open up a new path' (1994b: 75). This exchange actually captures one of the more arresting features of his work. Elias combines a synthesis of the most powerful elements of classical sociological thought with a strongly independent and intellectually rigorous mobilization of that synthesis in relation to a wide range of empirical evidence.

Although he began writing in the 1930s – he was in Heidelberg at the same time as the young Talcott Parsons – Elias has only recently begun to be recognized as a major sociologist. He had only an underground reputation in the 1950s among some of his English colleagues and a scattering of scholars in Europe who had managed to obtain a copy of his major work, *Über den Prozeß der Zivilisation*. In the 1960s, word gradually spread in Western Europe about the importance of his approach to sociology and history, and interest grew in the English-speaking world from the time translation of his work into English began to accelerate in the 1980s. In Germany, students read the 1969 re-issue of *Über den Prozeß der Zivilisation* alongside Foucault's (1977) book *Discipline and Punish* as an account of the increasingly disciplined character of modern social life; by 1993 Elias was leading German publisher Suhrkamp's best seller, out-selling Jürgen Habermas (Taschwer, 1994).

The substantive issues Elias dealt with – including the history of subjectivity, power,

knowledge, violence, state formation, attitudes towards the body and sexuality – anticipated later historical and sociological scholarship, often providing a more systematic and effective approach to the same problems. His analysis of the historical development of emotions and psychological life is particularly important in relation to the connections he established with larger-scale processes such as state formation, urbanization and economic development. The aim of this chapter, then, is to provide a basic sketch of Elias' sociological perspective and his approach to sociological theory and research, as well as to locate and position his ideas within broader debates in social science and social theory.[1]

TOWARDS A THEORY OF HUMAN SOCIETY

Elias always resisted making the claim that he was a 'social theorist', because he wanted to avoid the tendency towards fetishising theory, theorists and theoretical perspectives, at the expense of getting on with the practice of sociological investigation. Elias preferred simply to develop his conceptual framework in the process of conducting his research. But it was, none the less, an ambitious theoretical position. As he put it, he saw his task as one of drawing on the work of Marx, Weber and Freud, *inter alia*, and 'elaborating a comprehensive theory of human society, or, more exactly, a theory of the development of humanity, which could provide an integrating framework of reference for the various specialist social sciences' (1994b: 131). Although he was willing to present his socio-

logical theory for some time as organized around
the concept of 'figuration', he grew to dislike the
term 'figurational sociology' and ended up pre-
ferring 'process sociology' as a label.

Elias was also concerned to develop a different
form of *perception* of the social world (1969:
127). He believed that many of the problems and
obstacles in contemporary social science were
built into the very categories and concepts which
thought about society and human behaviour
was organized around. To a large extent, his
work constitutes an argument for a particular
sociological vocabulary and conceptual framework, which in turn has embedded within it a
form of social perception he believed would
get closer to the reality of human social life. A
number of concepts are important here: figuration, process, habitus, civilization, relation,
network/web, power-ratio, interdependence,
established/outsiders, involvement/detachment,
not only in themselves, but also as radical alternatives to the standard concepts used by most
sociologists in the second half of the twentieth
century: society, system, structure, role, action,
interaction, individual, reproduction.

Unplanned 'order' and the question of agency

Elias shares with most sociologists a concern
with explaining the orderliness of social life, and
he sees sociology as fundamentally concerned
with a 'problem of order', but from a very particular perspective. He did not see the very
existence of 'social order' itself as problematic,
saying that he understood the concept 'in the
same sense that one talks of a natural order, in
which decay and destruction as structured processes have their place alongside growth and
synthesis, death and disintegration alongside
birth and integration' (1978a: 76). He directed his
attention to a very different question, namely,
the apparent *independence* of social order from
intentional human action. For Elias, the question
was: 'How does it happen at all that formations
arise in the human world that no single human
being has intended, and which yet are anything
but cloud formations without stability or
structure?' (1994a: 443–4).

The thinkers who first contributed to a developing understanding of this problem included
Adam Smith, Hegel, the Physiocrats, Malthus,
Marx and Comte. Hegel's concept of the
'cunning of reason' was one of the first attempts
to capture this 'ordered autonomy' of social life
from the individuals who make it up:

> Again and again . . . people stand before the
> outcome of their own actions like the apprentice
> magician before the spirits he has conjured up and
> which, once at large, are no longer in his power.

They look with astonishment at the convolutions
and formations of the historical flow which they
themselves constitute but do not control. (Elias,
1991: 62)

The most acute question for Elias was the
apparent *lack* of relationship between social
order and human intentions, the seemingly *alien*
character of the social world to the individuals
making it up. He saw 'society' as consisting
of the structured interweaving of the activity of
interdependent human agents, all pursuing their
own interests and goals, producing distinct social
forms such as what we call 'Christianity',
'feudalism', 'patriarchy', 'capitalism', or whatever culture and nation we happen to be part of,
which cannot be said to have been planned or
intended by any individual or group.

In analysing the relationship between intentional human action and unplanned surrounding
social preconditions and outcomes, Elias emphasized, on the one hand, the dependence of any
given individual, no matter how central a
position they held, on the surrounding network
of social, economic and political relations (1991:
50). He indicated a very clear preference for
understanding social transformations in terms of
changes in social conditions, or in the structuring
of social relationships, rather than attributing
very much causal significance to the decisions
and actions of particular, supposedly powerful
individuals or groups (1994a: 266).

On the other hand, although within the broad
sweep of history it is apparent how much
individuals are buffeted by forces beyond their
control, 'the person acting within the flow may
have a better chance to see how much can
depend on individual people in individual
situations, despite the general direction' (1991:
48). It is equally unrealistic to believe 'that
people are interchangeable, the individual being
no more than the passive vehicle of a social
machine' (p. 54). Elias saw social life as both
'firm' and 'elastic': 'Crossroads appear at which
people must choose, and on their choices,
depending on their social position, may depend
either their immediate personal fate or that of a
whole family, or, in certain circumstances, of
entire nations or groups within them' (p. 49).
Agency thus consisted of the strategic seizure of
opportunities that arise for individuals and
groups, but not in the actual creation of those
opportunities, which 'are prescribed and limited
by the specific structure of a person's society and
the nature of the functions the people exercise
within it' (p. 49). Moreover, once an opportunity
is taken, human action 'becomes interwoven
with those of others; it unleashes further chains
of actions', the effects of which are based not on
individual or group actors, but 'on the distribu-

tion of power and the structure of tensions within this whole mobile human network' (pp. 49–50).

One of the primary focuses of sociological analysis is, then, the *relationships* between intentional, goal-directed human activities and the unplanned or unconscious process of interweaving with other such activities, past and present, and their consequences. Often Elias emphasized the unplanned character of social life, largely because he was concerned to counter the notion that there can ever be a direct and straightforward relationship between human action and its outcomes. However, all his observations taken together indicate a more complex understanding, for he always believed that improved human control of social life was the ultimate objective of sociological analysis. In his words, 'people can only hope to master and make sense out of these purposeless, meaningless functional interconnections if they can recognize them as relatively autonomous, distinctive functional interconnections, and investigate them systematically' (1978a: 58). Elias saw an understanding of long-term unplanned changes as serving both 'an improved orientation' towards social processes which lie beyond human planning, and an improved understanding of those areas of social life which can be said to correspond to the goals and intentions of human action (1997a: 370). In relation to technological change, he commented: 'From the viewpoint of a process theory what is interesting is the *interweaving of an unplanned process and human planning*' (1995: 26; 1997a: 370).

Interdependence – figurations – habitus

For Elias, the structure and dynamics of social life could only be understood if human beings were conceptualized as *interdependent* rather than autonomous, comprising what he called *figurations* rather than social systems or structures, and as characterized by socially and historically specific forms of *habitus*, or personality-structure. He emphasized seeing human beings in the plural rather than the singular, as part of collectivities, of groups and networks, and stressed that their very identity as unique individuals only existed within and through those networks or figurations.

The civilizing process itself, argued Elias, had produced a capsule or wall around individual experience dividing an inner world from the external world, individuals from society. Rather than seeing individuals as ever having any autonomous, pre-social existence, Elias emphasized human beings' interdependence with each other, the fact that one can only become an

individual human being within a web of social relationships and within a network of interdependencies with one's family, school, church, community, ethnic group, class, gender, work organization and so on. The essential 'relatedness' of human beings, said Elias, began with being born as a helpless infant, over which we have no control: 'Underlying all intended interactions of human beings is their unintended interdependence' (1969: 143).

He developed this point in part through his critique of what he called the *homo clausus*, or 'closed personality' image of humans. Elias argued for a replacement of this *homo clausus* conception with its emphasis on autonomy, freedom and independent agency with:

> the image of man as an 'open personality' who possesses a greater or lesser degree of relative (but never absolute and total) autonomy *vis-à-vis* other people and who is, in fact, fundamentally oriented toward and dependent on other people throughout his life. The network of interdependencies among human beings is what binds them together. Such interdependencies are the nexus of what is here called the figuration, a structure of mutually oriented and dependent people. (1994a: 213–14)

Elias introduced the concept of 'figuration' in the 1960s because it 'puts the problem of human interdependencies into the very heart of sociological theory' (1978a: 134) and he hoped it would 'eliminate the antithesis . . . immanent today in the use of the words "individual" and "society"' (1994a: 214).

Elias regarded societies as basically 'the processes and structures of interweaving, the figurations formed by the actions of interdependent people' (1978a: 103). He also believed that it made it easier to overcome the tendency to apparently deny human agency and individuality with the use of concepts like 'society' or 'social system'. Indeed, 'it sharpens and deepens our understanding of individuality if people are seen as forming figurations with other people' (1983: 213).

He used the analogy of dance to illustrate the concept figuration, saying that 'the image of the mobile figurations of interdependent people on a dance floor perhaps makes it easier to imagine state, cities, families, and also capitalist, communist, and feudal systems as figurations' (1994a: 214). Although we might speak of 'dance in general', 'no one will imagine a dance as a structure outside the individual'. Dances can be danced by different people, 'but without a plurality of reciprocally oriented and dependent individuals, there is no dance'. Figurations, like dances, are thus 'relatively independent of the specific individuals forming it here and now, but not of individuals as such' (p. 214). In other words, although it is true that figurations 'have the peculiarity that, with few exceptions, they can continue to exist even when all the individuals who formed them at a certain time have died and been replaced by others' (1983: 142), they only exist in and through the activity of their participants. When that activity stops, the figuration stops, and the continued existence of the figuration is dependent on the continued participation of its constituent members, as the East European regimes discovered in 1989.

The dynamics of figurations also depend on the formation of a shared social *habitus* or personality make-up which constitutes the collective basis of individual human conduct. In Elias' words:

> This make-up, the social habitus of individuals, forms, as it were, the soil from which grow the personal characteristics through which an individual differs from other members of his society. In this way something grows out of the common language which the individual shares with others and which is certainly a component of his social habitus – a more or less individual style, what might be called an unmistakable individual handwriting that grows out of the social script. (1991: 182)

Elias gave the example of the concept of 'national character', which he called 'a habitus problem *par excellence*' (1991: 182). He also referred to it as 'second nature', or 'an automatic, blindly functioning apparatus of self-control' (1994a: 113, 446). The organization of psychological make-up into a *habitus* was also a continuous *process* which began at birth and continued throughout a person's life, 'for although the self-steering of a person, malleable during childhood, solidifies and hardens as he grows up, it never ceases entirely to be affected by his changing relations with others throughout his life' (1994a: 455).

The relational view of social life

Elias maintained that it was necessary for sociologists to avoid seeing social life in terms of states, objects or things, what Georgy Lukács called the *reification* ('turning into a thing or object') of what are in fact dynamic social relationships.[2] His attempt to transcend reification in sociological theory consisted of a double movement: the first was towards a consistent emphasis on social life as *relational*, and the second was an insistence on its *processual* character. We will look at the first in this section and the second in the following section. It is important to emphasize both sides of this double movement away from reification, because many sociologists undertake one or the other (for

example, Berger and Luckmann, 1971), but very few pursue both.

The principle is simple enough, that it is necessary in sociology 'to give up thinking in terms of single, isolated substances and to start thinking in terms of relationships and functions' (Elias, 1991: 19). A 'person' or 'individual' is thus not a self-contained entity or unit, she or he does not exist 'in themselves', they only exist as elements of sets of relations with other individuals. The same applies to families, communities, organizations, nations, economic systems, in fact to any aspect of the world, human or natural, for the concept arose from Einstein's physics. Relations between people, the ties binding them to each other are, for Elias, the primary object of sociological study, the very stuff of historical change: 'The "circumstances" which change are not something which comes upon men from "outside": they are the relationships between people themselves' (1994a: 480).

Recently the significance of this has been underlined by Pierre Bourdieu, who defines this form of perception as thinking in terms of *fields*, a mode of thought which 'requires a conversion of one's entire usual vision of the social world, a vision which is interested only in those things which are visible' (Bourdieu, 1990: 192). Referring to Elias, he points out that thinking non-relationally also has the effect of treating social units as if they were themselves human actors, and mentions the possible 'endless list of mistakes, mystifications or mystiques created by the fact that the words designating institutions or groups, State, bourgeoisie, Employers, Church, Family and School, can be constituted . . . as historical subjects capable of posing and realizing their own aims' (Bourdieu, 1990: 192; for a discussion of Elias within 'relational sociology' generally, see Emirbayer, 1997).

What Elias found most important about relationships between people was the way in which they were constituted as *power* relations, so that he develops this argument in most detail with reference to 'the relational character of power' (1978a: 75). 'The whole sociological and political discussion on power', he wrote, 'is marred by the fact that the dialogue is not consistently focused on power balances and power ratios, that is, on aspects of relationships, but rather on power as if it were a thing' (1987: 251). If we see it more as a relation, it also becomes possible to recognize that questions of power are quite distinct from questions of 'freedom' and 'domination', and that all human relationships are relations of power (1978a: 74).

Elias understood power in terms of *power-ratios* or 'shifting balances of tensions' (1983: 145), and regarded these concepts as the best successors to debates about freedom and determinism. He said that the recognition that all human beings possess some degree of freedom or autonomy 'is sometimes romantically idealized as proving the metaphysical freedom of man', its popularity arising primarily from its emotional appeal (1983: 144). However, he argued that it was important to go beyond thinking in terms of a fictional antithesis between 'freedom' and 'determinism' – fictional because of human beings' essential interdependence – and move to thinking in terms of power-balances.

Elias also stressed the *reciprocal* workings of power, so that within the network of relations binding the more and less powerful to each other, apparently less powerful groups also exercise a 'boomerang effect' back on those with greater power-chances (1983: 265). This was, he felt, a problem with concepts like 'rule' or 'authority', since they 'usually make visible only the pressures exerted from above to below, but not those from below to above' (p. 265). He gave the example of the relation between parents and children: parents clearly have greater power-chances than their children, but because children fulfil particular functions and needs for their parents, they also have power over their parents, such as calling them to their aid by crying, requiring them to reorganize their lives (1997b: 195).

Against process-reduction

The second step Elias took away from the reification of social life was to see it as having an inherently *processual* character. Figurations of interdependent individuals and groups can only be properly understood as existing over time, in a constant process of dynamic flux and greater or lesser transformation. The analysis of the interrelationships between intentional action and unplanned social processes had to be undertaken over periods of time, for as Johan Goudsblom has put it, 'yesterday's unintended social consequences are today's unintended social conditions of "intentional human actions"' (1977: 149). Elias spoke of the 'transformational impetus (*Wandlungsimpetus*) of every human society', and regarded 'the immanent impetus towards change as an integral moment of every social structure and their temporary stability as the expression of an impediment to social change' (1997a: 371).

The expression Elias used to identify the tendency in sociological thought which he was arguing against was *Zustandsreduktion* – literally, 'reduction to states', although in English he preferred 'process-reduction', that is, the 'reduction of processes to static conditions'

(1978a: 112). A manifestation of process-reduction was sociologists' turning-away from historical analysis, the emphasis by both functionalists and structuralists on synchronic rather than diachronic analysis, and the assumption that stability was the normal condition of social life, and change a 'disruption' of a normal state of equilibrium. By 'long-term' Elias meant periods of not less than three generations (1986: 234).

Just as individuals, families, communities and so on should be conceived as embedded within a network of relations, rather than being seen as isolated objects, Elias argued that they should also be seen as *dynamic*, in a state of flux and change, as processes. Individuals, for example, rather than having a fixed identity, move from being dependent infants, to adolescents, mature adults and then to old age and death. An individual, then, 'may justifiably be seen as a self-transforming person who, as it is sometimes put, goes through a process' (1978a: 118). Indeed, suggested Elias, although it is not how we are used to thinking about ourselves, 'it would be more appropriate to say that a person is constantly in movement; he not only goes through a process, he *is* a process' (p. 118). We can only understand and explain any given sociological problem if it is seen as the outcome of some long-term process of development, if we trace its *sociogenesis*.

Instead of speaking of static 'states' or phenomena such as capitalism, rationality, bureaucracy, modernity, postmodernity, Elias would always wish to identify their processual character, so that he would think in terms of rationalization, modernization, bureaucratization and so on. Often it is difficult to come up with the appropriate concept. For example, 'capitalism' is difficult to render in this way – but the point is to attempt a conceptualization along these lines, to identify the process underlying what one was studying. If, for example, one observes what appear to be a large number of single parents in Western societies, a productive approach for Elias would be to look for the long-term trends in marriage and fertility, to see how this current phenomenon fits in with other processes of social development, in order to possibly explain its occurrence. This example also illustrates Elias' emphasis on the existence of a *plurality* of processes, all of which interweave with each other, with no causal primacy being given to any one of them. Transformations in social relationships are thus intertwined with a variety of other processes of change: economic, political, psychological, geographical, and so on.

Although Elias distanced himself from theories of social progress which simply assumed that all social change was progressive, he did feel that, overall, humanity was in fact progressing.

It is important to bear his fundamentally *ambiguous* attitude to progress in mind, because it helps explain why so many of his critics accuse him of reverting to nineteenth century evolutionary perspectives. He was also confident that human beings have gradually developed more control over the natural world, and that this increased control could be put in the category of 'progress'. Despite the barbarism which Western 'civilized' people were capable of, for Elias (1984) this meant merely that 'we have not learnt to control ourselves and nature enough', for he was insistent that the contemporary world was considerably less brutal and violent than it had been in the ancient or medieval world. He felt that relations between classes, men and women, superordinates and subordinates, adults and children, were gradually becoming increasingly equal and democratic, and that the point of identifying those instances where this was not the case was to *further* the process of 'functional democratization', not to suggest its impossibility.

On the other hand, he also argued that processes of integration could at any time be accompanied by those of disintegration, civilizing processes by decivilizing processes (1986: 235), and he placed more emphasis on these in his later work, such as *The Germans*. Elias should be read both ways, as optimistic about the progress of humanity, and as acutely aware of how easily we can descend to barbaric cruelty.

Sociology and 'object-adequacy': between involvement and detachment

Questions of objectivity and values, the position of the social scientist in society, the relation between the natural and social sciences, were all central to Elias' understanding of the role that knowledge plays in the historical development of humanity. He emphasized the *historical development* of human knowledge, and argued for seeing science as a social and collective endeavour, consisting of sets of social institutions located within a particular process of social development, rather than springing from the mind of an idealized 'subject' of scientific activity. As a result, he rejected both the concept of 'truth' as absolutely distinct from 'falsity' and a relativistic conception of knowledge, in favour of the concept of a greater or lesser 'object adequacy' in human knowledge, lying somewhere between 'involvement' and 'detachment'.

Elias was concerned to identify how the knowledge available to members of any given society is both *built upon* and *advances on* previous generations' attempts to comprehend the world around them. Rather than engaging in arguments about the 'truth' or 'falsity' of knowledge, Elias thought it was more appropriate to assess the relationship of any given idea or theory with its predecessors, with specific reference to its 'object-adequacy' or 'reality-congruence', and its 'survival value' (1971: 358).

For Elias, scientific 'advance' has two features: first, it consists of the attainment of *relative autonomy* in relation to the specific human groups engaged in the production of scientific knowledge. An exemplary case for Elias was the progressive de-centring of the physical world, the development from geocentric to heliocentric, and finally to relationist conceptions of the universe. In the work of Aristotle and Ptolemy, human beings were conceived as constituting the centre of the physical universe. The work of Copernicus, Galileo and Newton, in contrast, 'shows in a paradigmatic manner the crucial changeover from the dominance of a subject-centred to that of a more object-oriented orientation' (1971: 359). However, even this model is still subject-centred to the extent that it presumes a single frame of reference for the entire universe, whereas Einstein's theory of relativity allows for an infinite number of frames of reference, putting forward 'a model of a universe without an absolute centre' (p. 360).

Second, Elias explained the basis of greater or lesser 'object-adequacy' in terms of an opposition between what he called 'involvement' and 'detachment', and he used the example of Edgar Allan Poe's story of two fishermen caught in a maelstrom to illustrate his argument. In the story the elder brother was so overcome by the immediacy of the situation and his direct emotional response, his 'involvement', that he was unable to formulate any course of action to avoid his fate. The younger brother, on the other hand, was able to exercise greater self-control and develop some detachment from his terror, observing how the maelstrom actually worked, in particular that cylindrical objects descended more slowly, as did smaller objects. Tying himself to a cask, he jumped out of the boat, failing to persuade his brother to do the same. The elder brother in the larger object, the boat, was dragged under, while the younger managed to stay on the water's surface until the maelstrom subsided. This does not mean that a cool head is always what a situation demands, and Elias commented that there will be times when 'force, skill, courage and a hot temper may be . . . of greater value than a high capacity for sustained self-control', although he could not help adding 'even though a bit of reflection may still help' (1987: 47). The point is a more complex one that particular situations will demand particular *balances* of involvement and detachment, and we can judge the adequacy of our conceptions by the effects they have – in the case of the fisher-men, whether one goes under or not.

Despite Elias' argument that scientific knowl-edge is distinguished from ideology by its degree of relative autonomy and detachment, he also believed that scientists can never achieve abso-lute autonomy from their social location. In the first of his articles on the sociology of knowl-edge, Elias began the piece referring to a passage from Ernest Hemingway's *Death in the After-noon*, where a character responds to the question, 'Are you not prejudiced?' as follows: 'Madame, rarely will you meet a more pre-judiced man nor one who tells himself he keep his mind more open. But cannot that be because one part of our mind, that which we act with, becomes prejudiced through experience, and still we keep another part completely open to observe and judge with?' (Elias, 1956: 226). For Elias, all scientific endeavour is characterized by this permanent tension between the reality of 'pre-judice', what many sociologists refer to as the socially constructed nature of all knowledge, and the possibility of a responsiveness to the observation and analysis of an ever-changing surrounding world, a balance between 'involve-ment' and 'detachment'.

CIVILIZING AND DECIVILIZING PROCESSES

Elias' focus on the concept 'civilization' in analysing the origins of contemporary Western societies was rooted in dual synthesis of Freud with Marx on the one hand, and with Weber on the other. He drew on Marx's materialism to explain the development of a particular person-ality structure, emphasizing its 'production' by particular sets of social relations, and elaborated on Freud's understanding of the effects of developing civilization on psychic life in terms of Weber's conception of the state as organized around a monopoly of the means of violence. Elias' historicization of human psychology provides empirical support for an understanding of the processes by which changes in social relations are interwoven with changes in psychic structure.

Processes of civilization

What Elias felt sure was the product of a long historical process had, by the end of the eighteenth century, come to be defined by Euro-peans 'simply as an expression of their own high gifts' (1994a: 41). Civilization became a crucial part of Europeans' sense of superiority over all other peoples in the world: 'the consciousness of their own superiority, the consciousness of this "civilization," from now on serves at least those nations which have become colonial conquerors, and therefore a kind of upper class to large sections of the non-European world, as a justification of their rule' (p. 41). It was Euro-peans' perception of themselves as particularly 'civilized', at the very hour of their indulgence in a horrific barbarism, around which Elias organized his observations about the develop-ment of modern social life, because he felt it went to the heart of the constitution of the psychic structure characteristic of contemporary Wes-tern societies.

Elias believed that what we experience as 'civilization' is founded on a particular habitus, a particular psychic structure which has changed over time, and which can only be understood in connection with changes in the forms taken by broader social relationships. Elias insisted that 'the moulding of instinctual life, including its compulsive features, is a function of social interdependencies that persist throughout life', and these interdependencies change as the structure of society changes. 'To the variation in this structure correspond,' wrote Elias, 'the differences in personality structure that can be observed in history' (p. 249). The first point was explored by Elias in relation to the successive editions of a variety of etiquette manuals, and the second in relation to the history of state formation in Britain, France and Germany.

The first volume of *The Civilizing Process* traces gradual changes in expectations of people's interpersonal conduct in European societies, as well as the way they approached their own bodily functions and emotions. In outlining 'correct' behaviour, Erasmus pointed to 'attitudes that we have lost, that some among us would perhaps call "barbaric" or "unciv-ilized"', and it spoke 'of many things that have in the meantime become unspeakable, and of many others that are now taken for granted' (p. 44). Elias suggested that typical medieval conduct was characterized by 'its simplicity, its naïvete', emotions were 'expressed more vio-lently and directly' and there were 'fewer psychological nuances and complexities in the general stock of ideas' (p. 50).

As time went by, he found that the standards applied to violence, sexual behaviour, bodily functions, eating habits, table manners and forms of speech became gradually more sophis-ticated, with an increasing threshold of shame, embarrassment and repugnance. Gradually more and more aspects of human behaviour become regarded as 'distasteful', and 'the distasteful is *removed behind the scenes of social life*'.

Again and again, wrote Elias, we see 'how characteristic is this movement of segregation, this hiding "behind the scenes" of what has become distasteful' (p. 99). For example, a French etiquette manual from 1729 advises its readers as follows:

> It is very impolite to keep poking your finger into your nostrils, and still more insupportable to put what you have pulled from your nose into your mouth . . .
>
> You should avoid making a noise when blowing your nose . . . Before blowing it, it is impolite to spend a long time taking out your handkerchief. *It shows a lack of respect toward the people you are with* to unfold it in different places to see where you are to use it. You should take your handkerchief from your pocket and use it quickly in such a way that you are scarcely noticed by others.
>
> After blowing your nose you should take care not to look into your handkerchief. It is correct to fold it immediately and replace it in your pocket. (1994a: 120–1; emphasis in original)

'Formerly,' suggested another etiquette manual in 1672, 'one was allowed to take from one's mouth what one could not eat and drop it on the floor, providing it was done skilfully. Now that would be disgusting' (1994a: 76).

Elias described medieval society as being characterized generally by 'a lesser degree of social control and constraint of instinctual life' (p. 159), in particular by a *violence* which dominated everyday life and was rarely subject to much social or self-control. His interpretation of his evidence was that it suggested 'unimaginable emotional outbursts in which – with rare exceptions – everyone who is able abandons himself to the extreme pleasures of ferocity, murder, torture, destruction, and sadism' (1978b: 248). Elias felt that there was great pleasure in killing and torturing, describing it as 'a socially permitted pleasure'; indeed, to some degree 'the social structure even pushed its members in this direction, making it seem necessary and practically advantageous to behave in this way' (1994a: 159).

The social process of 'courtization' subjected first knights and warriors, and then ever-expanding circles of the population (p. 88), to an increasing demand that such expressions of violence be regulated, that emotions and impulses be placed more firmly in the service of the long-term requirements of complex networks of social interaction. Slowly and gradually, argued Elias, 'the code of behaviour becomes stricter and the degree of consideration expected of others becomes greater', and 'the social imperative not to offend others becomes more binding' (p. 64). In court society we see the beginnings of a form of mutual and self-observation which Elias referred to as a 'psychological' form of perception (p. 63). Elias did not see courts as the 'cause' or driving force of this process, but as its *nucleus*, and he drew a parallel with the form taken by a chemical process like crystallization, 'in which a liquid . . . [being] subjected to conditions of chemical change . . . first takes on crystalline form at a small nucleus, while the rest then gradually crystallized around this core' (p. 95).

The result was a particular kind of habitus or 'second nature', an 'automatic self-restraint, a habit that, within certain limits, also functions when a person is alone' (p. 113). Elias argued that the restraint imposed by increasingly differentiated and complex networks of social relations became increasingly internalized, and less dependent on its maintenance by external social institutions, developing what Freud was to recognize as a super-ego (p. 154).

He did say that these developments in habitus were not unilinear, that 'the civilizing process does not follow a straight line' and that 'on a smaller scale there are the most diverse criss-cross movements, shifts and spurts in this or that direction' (p. 153). None the less, at this point he felt that there was a more significant overall tendency with a particular direction, towards increasing 'regulation of affects in the form of self-control' (p. 153). 'Regardless', then, 'of how much the tendencies may criss-cross, advance and recede, relax or tighten on a small scale, the direction of the main movement – as far as is visible up to now – is the same for all kinds of behaviour' (p. 154).

The second volume of *The Civilizing Process* dealt with the *explanation* of the transformation of psychic structure revealed by the etiquette books and other historical evidence. 'When enquiring into social processes', he wrote 'one must look at the web of human relationships, at society itself, to find the compulsions that keep them in motion, and give them their particular form and their particular direction' (p. 288).

Among those changes in the 'web of human relationships' there was, first, 'the process of state-formation, and within it the advancing centralization of society' (p. 269), especially as it was expressed in the absolutist states of seventeenth and eighteenth century Europe. Second, he stressed the gradual differentiation of society, the increasing range, diversity and interdependence of competing social positions and functions composing European societies. There were other, related changes which he also mentioned, such as the development of a money economy and urbanization, but it was these two processes of social development which he emphasized most (p. 457).

There was, Elias believed, a powerful 'logic' built into any configuration of competing social units, such as states, towns or communities, towards an increasing monopolization of power and, correspondingly, of the means of violence. He saw this 'logic' as emerging from the dynamics of social, political and economic competition, and saw it as being organized around two 'mechanisms': the 'monopoly mechanism', which 'once set in motion, proceeds like clockwork' (p. 343), and the 'royal mechanism'. The operation of the 'monopoly mechanism was that as social units competed with each other, 'the probability is high that some will be victorious and others vanquished, and that gradually, as a result, fewer and fewer will control more and more opportunities, and more and more units will be eliminated from the competition, becoming directly or indirectly dependent on an ever-decreasing number' (p. 347). Unless some countervailing process is set in motion, argued Elias, competition would generally drive any human figuration towards 'a state in which all opportunities are controlled by a single authority: a system with open opportunities has become a system with closed opportunities' (p. 347).

Accompanying the monopoly mechanism was another tendency, that of what Elias called the 'royal mechanism', which was a feature of the *evenness* or *indecisiveness* of any pattern of competition. If social conditions are not bad enough for any one group to risk the loss of their current position, and power is distributed so evenly that every group is fearful of any other group gaining the slightest advantage, 'they tie each other's hands' and 'this gives the central authority better chances than any other constellation within society' (p. 397). The position of a central authority is not based simply on some greater power that they might have over any other social unit, but on their function as a mediator or nodal point for the conflicts between the other groups in society, which can neither individually overcome any of the others, nor stop competing to the degree required to form an effective alliance with each other.

The consequence of these mechanisms in terms of power relations was not, however, simply to increase the power-chances of those individuals and groups in more central positions of authority and influence, which is how we usually think of any process of monopolization. Elias emphasized that 'the more people are made dependent by the monopoly mechanism, the greater becomes the power of the dependent, not only individually but also collectively, in relation to the one or more monopolists'. This was because those in the more central, monopoly positions were also made increasingly dependent on 'ever more dependents in preserving and exploiting the power potential they have monopolized' (p. 348). The greater monopolization of

power-chances is thus accompanied by a greater *collective* democratization, at least, because a monopoly position is itself dependent on a larger and more complex network of social groups and units. Examples here would include the position of the head of government in any of the advanced industrial countries, or the managing director of a large corporation.

The state-formation process in Europe was accompanied, necessarily, by an increasing monopolization of the means of violence, and a pressure towards other means of exercising power in social relations. Rather than the use of violence, social 'success' became more and more dependent on 'continuous reflection, foresight, and calculation, self-control, precise and articulate regulation of one's own affects, knowledge of the whole terrain, human and non-human, in which one acts' (p. 476). Elias argued that this 'rationalization' of human conduct, its placement at the service of long-term goals and the increasing internalization of social constraint was closely tied to the process of state formation and development of monopolies of physical force (p. 447). The 'requirement' placed on each individual is not a direct one, but one mediated by the individual's own reflection on the consequences of differing patterns of behaviour (p. 450).

Underlying the processes of state-formation and nation-building were also others of increasing social *differentiation*, increasing density, complexity and what Elias called 'lengthening chains of social interdependence' (p. 448). A central developmental process in European societies was their increasing density, produced by a combination of population growth and urbanization, and the ever-larger circles of people that any single individual would be interdependent with, no matter how fleetingly.

He spoke of the 'conveyor belts' running through individuals' lives growing 'longer and more complex' (p. 452), requiring us to 'attune' our conduct to the actions of others (p. 445), and becoming the dominant influence on our existence, so that we are less 'prisoners of our passions' and more captive to the requirements of an increasingly complex 'web of actions' (p. 445), particularly a demand for 'constant hindsight and foresight in interpreting the actions and intentions of others' (p. 456). Just as important as the 'length' of chains of interdependence was the increasing *ambivalence* of overlapping and multiple networks: as social relations become more complex and contradictory, the same people or groups could be 'friends, allies or partners' in one context and 'opponents, competitors or enemies' in another. 'This fundamental ambivalence of interests,' wrote Elias, is 'one of the most important structural characteristics of more highly developed societies, and a chief factor moulding civilized conduct' (p. 395).

All of these processes of civilization 'tend to produce a transformation of the whole drive and affect economy in the direction of a more continuous, stable and even regulation of drives and affects in all areas of conduct, in all sectors of his life' (p. 452). We are all compelled more and more to regulate our conduct 'in an increasingly differentiated, more even and more stable manner'. Elias referred to this increasing self-regulation as a process of 'psychologization' and 'rationalization', because it revolved around the growing reflexive understanding of our own actions, those of others, their interrelationships and their consequences. 'The web of actions grows so complex and extensive,' wrote Elias, and 'the effort required to behave "correctly" within it becomes so great, that beside the individual's conscious self-control an automatic, blindly functioning apparatus of self-control is firmly established' (pp. 445–6).

It is useful, too, to recall the qualifications which Elias added in response to his critics. First, his concept of a civilizing process in European social history did not imply the existence of any sort of original 'state of nature' in some early historical period. There is no 'zero point in the historicity of human development' (p. 131), no example of human existence without social constraints. Second, there was no particular *beginning* to civilizing processes, so that in any given period people will regard themselves as more civilized than the peoples in the preceding periods. 'Wherever we start,' he wrote, 'there is movement, something that went before' (p. 48). Third, civilizing processes were *never-ending*, and we can never regard ourselves as having attained a state of 'true' civilization. Although he was confident that considerable social development had taken place since antiquity, he was equally sure that we had by no means stopped 'civilizing' ourselves and each other, which was why the final line in *The Civilizing Process* included these words from Holbach: 'la civilisation . . . n'est pas encore terminée' (p. 524; see also Elias, 1996: 173).

Decivilizing processes

The Civilizing Process was completed in 1939, and both Elias himself and his interpreters, supportive as well as critical, have often tended towards the view that his understanding of the development and dynamics of Western societies did not change substantially afterwards. The development of Elias' ideas between the 1960s and 1980s reveals, however, a more nuanced picture, and his writings can be regarded as ranging from a reiteration of his arguments in *The Court Society* and *The Civilizing Process*, through a development or refinement of his ideas, to a distinct change of direction and emphasis.

One of the themes running through the way that Elias changed and developed his approach after *The Civilizing Process* was an examination of the contradictory and ambivalent character of processes of civilization, their 'dark' sides and the question of 'civilized barbarism'.

In *The Civilizing Process*, the relationship between barbarism and civilization had been presented largely as mutually exclusive, one turning into the other, with possible 'reversals' of direction. To a large extent *The Germans* is consistent with this line of argument, raising the possibility that specific processes of state-formation produce either a 'deficient' process of civilization, or result in a clear process of decivilization encouraging the more widespread manifestation of brutal and violent conduct. However, Elias also raised the possibility that civilization and decivilization can occur *simultaneously*. For example, he made the point that the monopolization of physical force by the state, through the military and the police, cuts in two directions and has a Janus-faced character (1996: 175), because such monopolies of force can then be all the more effectively wielded by powerful groups within any given nation-state, as indeed they did under the Nazi regime. Pursuing a line of thought he had been developing since the 1970s (Wouters, 1977: 448), in one of his entries to a German dictionary of sociology published in 1986 he argued for the reversibility of social processes, and suggested that 'shifts in one direction can make room for shifts in the opposite direction', so that 'a dominant process directed at greater integration could go hand in hand with a partial disintegration' (Elias, 1986: 235). Similarly, in *The Germans* he remarked that the example of the Hitler regime showed 'not only that processes of growth and decay can go hand in hand but that the latter can also predominate relative to the former' (1996: 308). In a critique of Kingsley Davis' understanding of social norms, he argued that Davis emphasized the integrative effect of norms at the expense of their 'dividing and excluding character'. Elias pointed out that social norms had an 'inherently double-edged character', since in the very process of binding some people together, they turn those people against others (Elias, 1996: 159–60). Critics like Stefan Breuer, however, have remarked that a central problem with Elias' work overall is his disinclination to perceive processes of social integration as being accompanied by other, equally significant processes of social disintegration and decomposition (Breuer, 1991: 405–6).

Elias had pointed out that a large part of his motivation in writing *The Civilizing Process* was precisely to come to a better understanding of the brutality of the Nazi regime, since 'one cannot understand the breakdown of civilized behaviour and feeling as long as one cannot understand and explain how civilized behaviour and feeling came to be constructed and developed in European societies in the first place' (1994a: 444–5). In other words, Elias was advancing the very important argument that barbarism and civilization are part of the same analytical problem, namely how and under what conditions human beings satisfy their individual or group needs 'without reciprocally destroying, frustrating, demeaning or in other ways harming each other time and time again in their search for this satisfaction' (p. 31). The problem for Elias was both to make events such as the Holocaust – and one could add any number of other examples of 'modern barbarism' – understandable as the outcome of particular social figurations and processes of sociohistorical development, and also to explain what it was about the development of modern state-societies which generated organized *critical* responses to such large-scale genocide (p. 445).

CRITIQUE

There are, of course, a range of critiques of Elias' work (Mennell, 1992: 227–50), including the question of continuity versus change, or whether there has been the degree and kind of transformation in human conduct that Elias argues for, the issue of contradictions and conflicts within civilizing processes, and the question of 'civilized barbarism', but it is not possible to do justice to all of them here (see van Krieken, 1989, 1998). The topic I will use as an example is Elias' stress on the unplanned character of civilizing processes, and the possibility that intentional, deliberate action has been neglected. Should we speak of civilizing *processes* or civilizing *offensives*?

Although Elias did explicitly argue that we should analyse the interweaving of intentional action with unplanned social processes, in the substance of his analyses he laid far greater stress on the unplanned character of social change. A number of commentators, such as Haferkamp, Arnason and Chartier, argue that the result is a relative neglect of the organizing interventions of powerful social groups into the form and direction of civilizing processes. Elias' understanding of European history, suggests Arnason, 'seems to leave no place for a relatively autonomous, let alone a "pace-setting" development

of world views' (1989: 56). Haferkamp also argues that Elias did not 'give much weight to the success of intentions and plans', nor did he 'check to see when the planning of associations of action has been successful' (1987: 556). When Chartier speaks of self-discipline and emotional management as having been 'instituted' by the state (1989: 16), he is actually using a logic which is very different from Elias' in *The Civilizing Process*, where the emphasis is placed on the requirements of particular types of social figuration. Most social historians also paint a picture of European history where particular groups of lawyers, inquisitors, clergy, judges, entrepreneurs and so on played an active, constitutive role in shaping history, rather than merely reflecting their social context. The argument can be summarized as revolving around whether we should speak of civilizing *processes* or civilizing *offensives* (van Krieken, 1990).

The major conclusions we can draw from this and other criticisms are, first, that there seems to be a need to push Elias' own work towards a more *dialectical* understanding of social relations and historical development, one which grasps the often contradictory character of social and psychic life. This applies both in relation to social relations and the conflicting consequences of state societies organized around the logic of the market, as well as in relation to psychic processes and the contradictory dynamics between our affects, desires and impulses and the requirements of social relationships. Elias himself moved in this direction in his later writings, and the issue can be seen as one of 'reading back' this conceptual shift into his earlier writings. This issue is particularly significant in coming to an adequate understanding of 'civilized barbarism', of how it is possible for dehumanizing violence to continue at both an individual and collective level at the very same time that we appear to be becoming increasingly civilized. An important question, then, is the extent to which civilization in Elias' sense actually *generates* barbaric conduct, rather than simply being its opposite.

Second, Elias' concentration on state-formation and social differentiation in his earlier writings appears to require modification, to take account both of alternative aspects of social organization which can have almost identical civilizing effects, and of the diverse, often barbaric effects of state-formation, indeed the brutality lying at the heart of almost every nation-state (van Krieken, 1999). This is particularly significant in relation to developing a less linear view of European history, to the ways in which we approach non-Western societies and the relations between civilizations and cultures across the globe. An important area of research will thus be working through many of these arguments in relation to parts of the world other than Europe. For example, it is debatable how well Elias' analysis works even for the United States, with its weaker centralization of authority and a state with a much shakier hold on the monopoly of the means of violence. The way in which one might analyse civilizing processes outside Western Europe remains an under-examined area of study. Central here is the question of colonialism and imperialism, the ways in which nation-states have established a brutal and violent relationship between their own 'civilization' and the supposedly 'barbaric' cultures of subjected peoples. This applies both to the ways in which Europeans dealt with their colonies, and the ways in which nation-states such as the USA, Canada and Australia based their civilization on an essentially violent and barbaric relationship with their respective indigenous peoples.

Third, the theoretical injunction to see planned, intentional action as interwoven with unplanned social processes can be explored in much greater detail in analyses of processes of civilization. Dealing with this problem will also establish much clearer linkages between Elias' work and that of social and cultural historians generally, as well as the arguments of thinkers such as Weber and Foucault (van Krieken, 1990).

ELIAS AND SOCIOLOGY TODAY

Because of the comparative lateness of both his own university career and his appearance within English-language sociology, Elias' presence in sociological thought is not as strong as it might have been. Although leading sociologists like Lewis Coser have been generally supportive, there has been no real 'champion' of Elias' work in the United States, as Parsons was for Weber, Mills and Gouldner for Marx, or Levine and Coser for Simmel. Despite this late start, Elias' work has had a powerful impact on sociology worldwide since the 1970s, and it also has enormous potential to contribute even more, both to a reorientation of contemporary sociological theory, and to a wide range of topics in empirical social research, with great promise of generating powerful lines of enquiry, explanation and debate.

Lewis Coser referred to him as 'one of the most significant sociological thinkers of our day' (1980: 194) and Zygmunt Bauman described him as 'indeed a great sociologist' (1979: 123). 'Long before American scholars had discovered the idea of historical sociology,' wrote Christopher

Lasch, 'Elias understood the possibilities of this new genre and worked them out with an imaginative boldness that still surpasses later studies in this vein' (1985: 705). Anthony Giddens describes his work as 'an extraordinary achievement, anticipating issues which came to be generally explored in social theory only at a much later date' (1992: 389). Elias' teaching, writing and ideas are gradually exercising an increasingly pervasive influence on an ever-widening circle of sociologists as well as a broader lay public, in an expanding number of countries and languages, and he is now starting to take his place in the sociology textbooks and dictionaries (Ritzer, 1996: 511–24; Waters, 1994: 196–8). Intellectual 'impact' is notoriously difficult to measure, but one can look, just as an indication, at citations in *Sociological Abstracts*, where Elias is referred to at a rate similar to Bourdieu, Giddens, Goffman, Luhmann, Mannheim, Derrida, Merton, Mills, Althusser, Baudrillard and Wallerstein.[3]

In relation to the research utility of Elias' ideas, a growing number of books and articles on topics including sexuality (Hawkes, 1996), crime (Pratt, 1998, 1999), national and ethnic identity (Stauth, 1997), globalization (Mignolo, 1998), in a variety of disciplines, make positive reference to Elias as an important reference point if not an authority on the history of emotions, identity, violence (Fletcher, 1997), the body (Turner, 1984) and state formation (de Swaan, 1988).

His analysis of court society, for example, has significant implications for the sociology of organizations, especially organizational culture and power relations within organizations (Dopson and Waddington, 1996; Newton, 1999; van Krieken, 1996). His ideas are important for the analysis of consumption and the role of representation in the construction of subjective identity (Finkelstein, 1991, 1996; Ogborn, 1995). The work of Steven Shapin (1994) and Mario Biagioli (1993) in the history of science has indicated the importance of the development of particular types of 'civility' for the emergence of the practices of modern science. His sociology of sport and leisure serves as a springboard for detailed studies of the intersection between increasingly globalized and commercialized forms of sport and the formation of national and individual identities – the Olympic Games are only the most obvious example here (Dunning, 1999; Dunning and Rojek, 1992).

The position of concepts such as 'progress' and 'evolution' has never been satisfactorily resolved in theories of social change, and as sociologists continue to wrestle with their possible utility, Elias' approach to long-term processes of development and change remains a useful reference point. Civilizing processes have often operated through the prism of 'health', which serves as an organizing principle for what constitutes 'civilization', so that the sociology of health and illness is an arena in which Elias' concepts are being used to analyse the long-term development of health, medical knowledge and public health (Pinell, 1996). In general his work has played a central role in the resurgence of historical sociology over the past few decades. As Goudsblom (1997) has argued recently, one useful way to think of Elias' work is in terms of a linkage of historical sociology with symbolic interactionism, a combination which develops the strengths of both fields of scholarship in a way which neither does on its own.

The theory of established-outsider relations also has potential for a deeper sociological understanding of the dynamics of multiculturalism and racism, especially in the current context of increasing international migration and mixtures of cultural identities within nation-states (Wacquant, 1997). As social interaction becomes increasingly organized around computers and the Internet, the sociological understanding of this development will benefit enormously from seeing it as a particular social figuration based on changing patterns and lengthening chains of interdependency. Computer-mediated communication and social interaction can thus be seen as exercising a particular kind of civilizing, and decivilizing, effect, constructing a corresponding 'net habitus' among increasing numbers of people around the globe. As a set of sensitizing concepts, then, Elias' ideas have been exercising a gradually widening influence on contemporary sociological theory and research. Like Foucault, with whom he is often compared (Burkitt, 1993; Dean, 1994; Ogburn, 1995; Smith, 1999; van Krieken, 1990), more and more sociologists and social theorists are finding that Elias is 'good to think with'.

well before social scientists started using the term 'globalization'. His conceptualization of history in terms of long-term processes subjects, arguably more effectively than any of the existing critiques, the self-assessment of 'modernity' itself to critical analysis. This also means that he did not accept the notion that we have entered a 'postmodern' period; indeed, he preferred to describe us today as 'late barbarians' (1988: 190) living at the closing of the Middle Ages. Like Bruno Latour (1993), Elias felt that 'we have never been modern', let alone become postmodern.

The overarching theme of Elias' sociology was the question of human barbarism and its relation to whatever we might wish to call civilization. Alvin Gouldner once complained about Elias' work that violence had not been eliminated in contemporary civilizations, it had simply been transformed from explicit ferocity to 'passionless, impersonal callousness, in which more persons than ever before in history are now killed or mutilated with the flick of a switch . . . where killing occurs without personal rancour and the massacre of nations may be ordered without a frown' (1981: 418). This was, however, exactly the point Elias was trying to address: how to understand such a development and, more importantly, to develop a sense of what it was about the way our social relations are ordered, and have developed in the long term, which may make it possible to move beyond the mere 'civilization' of barbarism to its genuine elimination. His theory of civilizing processes was above all concerned with the *problem* of when and how civilization takes place, an analysis of the extent to which we have come to treat each other more humanely, precisely in order to identify how we might continue such a change into the future and live with each other with neither ferocity nor callousness.[4]

CONCLUSION

Elias himself would not have used the term 'radical', but it may be the best way to describe his approach to sociology. At a time when most sociologists turned away from history and poured scorn on the dangers of evolutionism, he insisted on placing historical analysis and a concern with directional social development at the centre of sociological thought. He maintained a linkage between sociology and other human sciences such as psychology and history while the discipline became increasingly isolated and fragmented. He argued for the importance of transcending the boundaries of nation-states and thinking in terms of 'humanity as a whole'

NOTES

1 Parts of which are drawn from my 1998 book, *Norbert Elias*, with the kind permission of Routledge. See also Mennell, 1992, and Mennell and Goudsblom, 1998.

2 The concept of reification was in turn stimulated by Georg Simmel's (1990) analysis of objective and subjective culture in, *inter alia*, *The Philosophy of Money*.

3 At the time of writing (August 1999), I searched in Sociofile for the number of citations of a range of theorists, in any language, between 1963 and 1999, in the 'Abstract' and 'Text Word' fields. The results were: Weber 2298; Marx 1774; Durkheim 1251; Habermas 102; Foucault 933; Parsons 783; Simmel 655; Bourdieu

408; Giddens 354; Goffman 339; Luhmann 337; Elias 301; Mannheim 296; Derrida 267; Merton 264; Mills 225; Althusser 178; Baudrillard 152; Wallerstein 137.

4 The Norbert Elias and Process Sociology web site is: http://www.usyd.edu.au/su/social/elias/eliasframe.html

REFERENCES

Arnason, J. (1989) 'Civilization, Culture and Power: Reflections on Norbert Elias' Genealogy of the West', *Thesis Eleven*, 24: 44–68.

Bauman, Z. (1979) 'The Phenomenon of Norbert Elias', *Sociology*, 13 (1): 117–25.

Berger, P. and Luckmann, T. (1971) *The Social Construction of Reality*. Harmondsworth: Penguin.

Biagioli, M. (1993) *Galileo, Courtier*. Chicago: University of Chicago Press.

Bourdieu, P. (1990) *In Other Words*. Cambridge: Polity Press.

Breuer, S. (1991) 'The Denouements of Civilization: Elias and Modernity', *International Social Science Journal*, 128: 405–6.

Burkitt, I. (1993) 'Overcoming Metaphysics: Elias and Foucault on Power and Freedom', *Philosophy of the Social Sciences*, 23 (1): 50–72.

Chartier, R. (1989) 'Introduction', in R. Chartier (ed.), *A History of Private Life*, vol. III: *Passions of the Renaissance*. Cambridge, MA: Harvard University Press.

Coser, L. (1980) 'Review of *What is Sociology?* and *Human Figurations*', *American Journal of Sociology*, 86 (1): 192–4.

Dean, M. (1994) *Critical and Effective Histories: Foucault's Methods and Historical Sociology*. London: Routledge.

de Swaan, A. (1988) *In Care of the State: Health Care, Education and Welfare in Europe and the USA in the Modern Era*. Cambridge: Polity Press.

Dopson, S. and Waddington, I. (1996) 'Managing Social Change: A Process-Sociological Approach to Understanding Organisational Change within the National Health Service', *Sociology of Health and Illness*, 18 (4): 525–50.

Dunning, E. (1999) *Sport Matters: Sociological Studies of Sport, Violence, and Civilisation*. New York: Routledge.

Dunning, E. and Rojek, C. (eds) (1992) *Sport and Leisure in the Civilizing Process: Critique and Counter-Critique*. Toronto: University of Toronto Press.

Elias, N. (1969) 'Sociology and Psychiatry', in S.H. Foulkes and G.S. Prince (eds), *Psychiatry in a Changing Society*. London: Tavistock. pp. 117–44.

Elias, N. (1971) 'Sociology of Knowledge: New Perspectives. Part One', *Sociology*, 5: 149–68.

Elias, N. ([1970] 1978a) *What is Sociology?*. London: Hutchinson.

Elias, N. (1978b) 'The Civilizing Process Revisited: Interview with Stanislas Fontaine', *Theory and Society*, 5: 243–53.

Elias, N. (1983) *The Court Society*. Oxford: Blackwell.

Elias, N. (1984) 'We Have Not Learnt to Control Ourselves Enough: an Interview with Norbert Elias', *De Groene Amsterdammer*, 16.5.84: 10–11.

Elias, N. (1986) 'Soziale Prozesse', in B. Schäfers (ed.), *Grundbegriffe der Soziologie*. Opladen: Leske en Budrich. pp. 234–41.

Elias, N. (1987) *Involvement and Detachment*. Oxford: Blackwell.

Elias, N. (1988) 'Wir sind die späten Barbaren: Der Sociologe Norbert Elias über die Zivilisationsprozeß und die Triebbewältigung', *Der Spiegel*, 42 (21): 183–90.

Elias, N. (1991) *The Society of Individuals*. Oxford: Blackwell.

Elias, N. ([1993] 1994a) *The Civilizing Process*. Oxford: Blackwell.

Elias, N. ([1987] 1994b) *Reflections on a Life*. Cambridge: Polity Press.

Elias, N. (1995) 'Technization and Civilization', *Theory, Culture and Society*, 12 (3): 7–42.

Elias, N. (1996) *The Germans*. Cambridge: Polity Press.

Elias, N. (1997a) 'Towards a Theory of Social Processes', *British Journal of Sociology*, 48 (3): 355–83.

Elias, N. (1997b) 'The Civilizing of Parents', in J. Goudsblom and S. Mennell (eds) *The Norbert Elias Reader*. Oxford: Blackwell. pp. 189–211.

Emirbayer, M. (1997) 'Manifesto for a Relational Sociology', *American Journal of Sociology*, 103 (2): 281–317.

Finkelstein, J. (1991) *The Fashioned Self*. Philadelphia: Temple University Press.

Finkelstein, J. (1996) *After a Fashion*. Melbourne: Melbourne University Press.

Fletcher, J. (1997) *Violence and Civilization*. Cambridge: Polity Press.

Foucault, M. (1977) *Discipline and Punish*. London: Allen Lane.

Giddens, A. (1992) 'Review of *The Society of Individuals*', *American Journal of Sociology*, 98: 388–9.

Goudsblom, J. (1977) *Sociology in the Balance*. Oxford: Blackwell.

Goudsblom, J. (1997) 'Norbert Elias and American Sociology', paper delivered at the 92nd American Sociological Association Conference, Toronto, Canada, 9–13 August 1997.

Gouldner, A. (1981) 'Doubts about the Uselessness of Men and the Meaning of the Civilizing Process', *Theory and Society*, 10 (3): 413–18.

Haferkamp, H. (1987) 'From the Intra-state to the Inter-state Civilizing Process?', *Theory, Culture and Society*, 4: 545–57.

Hawkes, G. (1996) *A Sociology of Sex and Sexuality*. Philadephia: Open University Press.

Lasch, C. (1985) 'Historical Sociology and the Myth of

Maturity: Norbert Elias's "Very Simple Formula"', *Theory and Society*, 14 (5): 705–20.

Latour, B. (1993) *We Have Never Been Modern*. Cambridge, MA: Harvard University Press.

Mennell, S. (1992) *Norbert Elias; An Introduction*. Oxford: Blackwell.

Mennell, S. and Goudsblom, J. (1998) 'Introduction', in N. Elias, *On Civilization, Power, and Knowledge* (ed. by S. Mennell and J. Goudsblom). Chicago: University of Chicago Press. pp. 1–45.

Mignolo, W.D. (1998) 'Globalization, Civilization Processes, and the Relocation of Languages and Cultures', in F. Jameson and M. Miyoshi (eds), *The Cultures of Globalization*. Durham, NC: Duke University Press. pp. 32–53.

Newton, T. (1999) 'Power, Subjectivity and British Industrial and Organisational Sociology: the Relevance of the Work of Norbert Elias', *Sociology*, 33 (2): 411–40.

Ogborn, M. (1995) 'Knowing the Individual: Michel Foucault and Norbert Elias on *Las Meninas* and the Modern Subject', in S. Pile and N. Thrift (eds), *Mapping the Subject: Geographies of Cultural Transformation*. London: Routledge. pp. 57–76.

Pinell, P. (1996) 'Modern Medicine and the Civilising Process', *Sociology of Health and Illness*, 18 (1): 1–16.

Pratt, J. (1998) 'Towards the "Decivilizing" of Punishment?', *Social and Legal Studies*, 7 (4); 487–515.

Pratt, J. (1999) 'Norbert Elias and the Civilized Prison', *British Journal of Sociology*, 50 (2): 271–96.

Ritzer, G. (1996) *Sociological Theory*, 4th edn. New York: McGraw-Hill.

Shapin, S. (1994) *A Social History of Truth*. Chicago: University of Chicago Press.

Simmel, G. (1990) *The Philosophy of Money*, 2nd edn. London: Routledge.

Smith, D. (1999) '*The Civilizing Process* and *The History of Sexuality*: Comparing Norbert Elias and Michel Foucault', *Theory and Society*, 28 (1): 79–100.

Stauth, G. (1997) '"Elias in Singapore": Civilizing Processes in a Tropical City', *Thesis Eleven*, 50: 51–70.

Taschwer, K. (1994) 'Wie Norbert Elias trotzdem zu einem soziologischen klassiker wurde', *Amsterdams Sociologisch Tijdschrift*, 20: 43–69.

Turner, B. (1984) *The Body and Society*. Oxford: Blackwell.

van Krieken, R. (1989) 'Violence, Self-discipline and Modernity: Beyond the "Civilizing Process"', *Sociological Review*, 37: 193–218.

van Krieken, R. (1990) 'The Organisation of the Soul: Elias and Foucault on Discipline and the Self', *Archives Europeénnes de Sociologie*, 31 (2): 353–71.

van Krieken, R. (1996) 'Proto-governmentalization and the Historical Formation of Organizational Subjectivity', *Economy and Society*, 15 (2): 195–221.

van Krieken, R. (1998) *Norbert Elias*. New York: Routledge.

van Krieken, R. (1999) 'The Barbarism of Civilization: Cultural Genocide and the "Stolen Generations"', *British Journal of Sociology*, 50 (2): 295–313.

Wacquant, L.J.D. (1997) 'Elias in the Dark Ghetto', *Amsterdams Sociologisch Tijdschrift*, 24 (3–4): 340–8.

Waters, M. (1994) *Modern Sociological Theory*. London: Sage.

Wouters, C. (1977) 'Informalization and the Civilising Process', in P. Gleichman, J. Goudsblom and H. Korte (eds), *Human Figurations*. Amsterdam: Amsterdams Sociologisch Tijdschrift. pp. 437–53.

Part Three
ISSUES IN SOCIAL THEORY

28

Positivism in the Twentieth Century

PETER HALFPENNY

Comte coined both the terms 'positivism' and 'sociology' in the early nineteenth century and their development has been intertwined ever since. The twentieth-century history of sociology is a prolonged engagement with positivism, attempting either to consolidate sociology's positivist inheritance or repudiate it. Given the multifarious forms which positivism takes, this history is convoluted, with critical rejection of one strand of positivism often leaving other strands untouched. Moreover, especially over the past twenty-five years, the number of practitioners of sociology has increased enormously, and they speak with proliferating voices. There has been no consolidation of the discipline into a dominant paradigm, instead diversity has increased. Some of this diversity has been expressed in terms of multiplying challenges to positivism. This chapter describes various twists and turns in the twentieth-century debates over positivism which are, essentially, driven by one central methodological question: is sociology a science? But first it is necessary to go back to Comte and review his legacy to the twentieth century.

COMTE'S LEGACY

Comte's positivism drew on earlier ideas, combining in particular notions of science influenced by seventeenth-century empiricism and a commitment to progress emerging from the eighteenth-century Enlightenment (Comte, [1830] 1970). The result was enthusiastic avowal of the modernist project: the goal is orderly progress towards a better future for humankind and the means to accomplish this is the practical application of science (Becker and Barnes, 1938). Scientific knowledge is achieved by the rational evaluation of empirical evidence. Application of this knowledge enables us to control both the natural and the social worlds, to bend them to our needs. All vestiges of unscientific thought, and especially traditional religion as a guide to human action, are to be abandoned. Instead, a scientific sociology is to be our guide. Indeed, in Comte's later writings, his positivist science of society took on the form of a secular religion of humanity devoted to moral regeneration through the worship of society organized by the positivist church (Wright, 1986).

To these strands – of progress, scientism and humanist religion – Comte added another. His 'law of three states' provided an interpretation of the history of ideas which he believed gave empirical support to a unity of science thesis (or naturalism). All domains of knowledge progress from an initial theological stage, in which events are explained by appeal to other-worldly beings, through the metaphysical stage, where religious superstitions are repudiated, to the final positive stage, where science is ascendant but limits itself to the systematic ordering of empirical knowledge in general laws. In their mature form, all disciplines become, in essence, the same. In particular, there are no differences in principle between the natural and social sciences, a claim which is an enduring aspect of positivist sociology.

Each of the various strands of Comte's positivism was carried forward into the twentieth century, often by thinkers who developed one strand but rejected others, and who disagreed with each other about which strands were the crucial elements of the positivist legacy. As a result, his influence on the subsequent development of sociology is more indirect than direct. For example, Spencer's evolutionary sociology became a popular characterization of the idea of progress in the late nineteenth century. But Spencer turned away from Comte's view that progress relied on increasing individuals' conformity to the harmonizing laws uncovered by the science of society (Spencer, 1864). Instead, Spencer proposed a theory of historical development in which competition between individuals was the motor of progress. This dovetailed with both the social Darwinism and the *laissez-faire* ethos of the day and, for many, provided a more acceptable account of progress than an alternative which was attracting increasing attention at the time: the revolutionary theory proposed by Marx and Engels.

J.S. Mill was a leading exponent of Comte's early work, playing a major role in bringing it to the attention of British thinkers, though he distanced himself from the later religion of humanity (Simon, 1963). Mill was attracted to the idea that the study of society would benefit from the application of scientific methods, meaning the systematic collection and analysis of empirical data, oriented towards the production of laws summarizing the regular association of observables. Mill developed an account of the methods of the moral sciences (his term for the disciplines that study humans) in the sixth book of his *System of Logic*, setting out there the principles of induction through which the truth of laws is empirically justified (Mill, [1843] 1961). This laid the ground for later developments in both the positivist philosophy of science and the statistical analysis of data.

Although for many the positivist church was an aberration at odds with the tenets of Comte's own positive science, it was popular with others. It had a troubled history but its adherents played an active role in keeping positivist ideas in the public eye. Its influence extended to early twentieth-century British sociologists such as Geddes and Hobhouse, and the first issues of *Sociological Review* (which began publication in 1908) contained sympathetic articles, including one that argued that positivism had permeated prevailing currents of thought so thoroughly that its continuation as a distinctive faith and separatist organization was redundant (Oliphant, 1909).

Even though he rejected other aspects of Comte's work, Durkheim subscribed to the unity of science thesis, and together with Spencer he is often identified as one of the more important sources of twentieth-century positivist sociology. To naturalism, Durkheim added the idea that society is *sui generis*, a causal force independent of its component individuals, resulting in a sociology with no place for human agency (Benoit-Smullyan, 1948). This *sociologism*, according to which social forces precede and constitute the human psyche, is often identified as another strand of the positivist legacy to the twentieth century, alongside its *empiricism*, whereby human sensory experience is the arbiter of factual knowledge, *scientism*, which maintains that the growth of knowledge is for the benefit of humankind, *naturalism*, which argues that there is no essential difference between the social and natural sciences, and *progressivism*, according to which the goal of steadily improving society while maintaining social order is to be achieved by adjusting human desires to the scientifically established laws of society.

This rather loosely woven perspective was not the only intellectual bequest of the nineteenth century. Positivist ideas were in competition with many others as the social sciences crystallized and became institutionalized in university curricula at the beginning of the new century. However, the positivist view of science was revitalized in the 1920s and 1930s by a group of philosophers, scientists and mathematicians which became known as the Vienna Circle.

THE POSITIVIST MODEL OF SCIENCE

The members of the Vienna Circle, the logical positivists, gave new impetus to the nineteenth-century social theorists' modernist programme (Feigl, 1969a; Kolakowski, 1972). Committed to scientism, they were optimistic that if all disciplines could be made truly scientific, they would provide the basis for rational social reforms and avoid disastrous social dislocations – such as recently experienced in the First World War (Wartofsky, 1982). In their manifesto, entitled 'The Scientific Conception of the World', they expressed high hopes that, through advances in the natural sciences and by extending science into the social arena and into the heart of philosophy would accelerate towards its goal of universal enlightenment (Neurath et al., [1929] 1973).

Crucial to the logical positivists was the demarcation of knowledge that was properly scientific from opinion and superstition, and from metaphysics more generally. This they believed could be achieved by refining earlier empiricist accounts of science and merging them with new ideas from logic and mathematics. Empiricism can be specified in several different ways and the logical positivists adopted a radical, phenomenalist version, according to which the foundational experiences of science are elements of scientists' own perceptions, such as sounds and colours. This phenomenalism is anti-realist, because experiences of sensations do not justify claims that lying beyond them are real objects that they reflect or represent or which cause them. Particular groupings of sensory elements may be referred to as physical or mental objects but this is a mere convenience. Concepts of purported real objects inaccessibly beyond experience are complex ideas, and they must be exhaustively analysable in terms of simple sensations if they are to be admitted to science. Although phenomenalism avoided some of the characteristic problems of less radical forms of empiricism, such as the relation between an independent reality and human experiences of it, it posed problems of its own which later became insurmountable barriers to the further development of the logical positivist programme.

The second central component of the Vienna Circle's programme was logic which, in general terms, is the study of argument and sound reasoning. Following Frege's and Russell's and Whitehead's work on the foundations of mathematics, the Vienna Circle took the narrow view that logic is concerned with the formal analysis of implication relations, rather than the older, broad view that it involves the study of the human activity of inferring – which leads in the direction of empirical psychology. Logic in the narrow sense is an ideal language in which the meanings of logical connectives are precisely defined, just as in mathematics the algebraic operators $+$, $-$, $\times$ and $\div$ have a precise meaning. By adopting the narrow view, the logical positivists could relinquish the empiricist interpretation of logic and mathematics, according to which they comprise empirical generalizations liable to refutation by countervailing evidence, which seems too weak a basis on which to build the certainties of logic and mathematics. At the same time they could avoid what previously had appeared to be the only alternative, the rationalist interpretation which captures the inviolability of logic and mathematics, but at the expense of rendering them beyond experience and therefore unacceptably metaphysical. Instead, for the logical positivists mathematics and logic comprise analytic a priori statements, necessarily true or false solely by virtue of the definitions of the operators they contain, independent of their factual content. For example, $4 + 3 = 7$ is true and $4 - 3 = 7$ is false irrespective of whether they refer to humans or horses or hairbrushes.

Logical analysis became a central resource for the Vienna Circle (Carnap, [1932] 1959). They used it to overcome previous philosophical paradoxes. Issues were investigated by reconstructing them in a formal language, which cleared away conceptual confusions by setting out the issues in simple propositions linked by precisely defined relations. Philosophy, the logical positivists maintained, should concern itself solely with clarifying the logic of scientific enquiry. By deploying phenomenalism and logical analysis, they argued that the whole of the language of scientific theories could be analysed into or constructed out of sets of atomic propositions that describe immediate experience, linked by the rules of logic.

This combination of phenomenalism and logical analysis is captured in the principle of verifiability, which is often identified as the defining characteristic of logical positivism. It is this principle which provides the criterion for demarcating between scientific language and metaphysical chatter. To have descriptive meaning, a proposition must be verifiable – at least in principle – by experience. If it is unverifiable, either because it is ill-formed, violating the syntactical rules of logic, or because it is ungrounded, employing concepts beyond the hold of experience, then it is neither true nor false, but meaningless. Propositions that are properly scientific are factual or logical, and all other expressions are without sense, that is, nonsensical. Non-scientific, nonsensical expressions might have some non-descriptive function, such as the display of emotion, but they are not cognitively significant. Since they are meaningless, arguments for and against them are undecidable and therefore pointless. They must be purged from positive science. In this way, moral discourse was expunged, since statements about what ought to be cannot be logically derived from empirically grounded statements about what is. Moral theory is metaphysical nonsense because it is impossible to deduce what is morally desirable from scientific knowledge of the facts. This argument forms another strand of positivism: science is value-free. Scientific study can reveal possibilities and identify limits, but it does not provide an evaluation of alternatives.

Logical positivism was far more rigorous and narrowly focused than any earlier form of positivism, and it had enormous influence because it set the agenda for the philosophy of science for a large part of the twentieth century, not least because most of the Vienna Circle's members fled Nazism and settled in other European countries and the United States, where they continued to develop and promulgate their ideas (Ayer, 1959; Feigl, 1969b). Although further articulation of their programme to purge science of metaphysics, by both sympathizers and critics, increasingly revealed problems, the general tenor of their approach became established as the 'received view' of the methodology of the natural sciences by the middle of the twentieth century (Putnam, 1962). So entrenched did their model of science become that it was often forgotten that it was a *theory* of science and taken instead to be a description of scientific practice. Accordingly, it was commonly argued that if sociology were to be a science, it would have to conform to the positivist image of scientific enquiry.

One of the Vienna Circle, Neurath, addressed the question of how such conformity might be achieved. He suggested that sociology, like other sciences, aims to establish regularities between observables, the ultimate aim being a unified science connecting together all logically compatible laws. Marx's materialism comes close, he thought, to the required form for sociology. However, if the sciences were to be unified, all would need to deploy the same lexicon to describe experience, that is, all the non-logical primitive concepts of the sciences must be interpreted in the same observational vocabulary. Members of the Vienna Circle had different views as to what this vocabulary should be; Neurath (1931a) favoured the language of physics. His view of positivist sociology was then a reductionist one (in stark contrast to the sociologism of Durkheim), limited to the study of social behaviour. Not only were ephemeral social forces excluded from sociology but so too were all references to apparently mental events; both banished as metaphysical unless they could be replaced by behaviours describable spatio-temporally in the language of physics. Although Neurath's writings had little direct influence on twentieth-century sociology, they did reinforce the general view that in order for 'backward' disciplines to enjoy the success and prestige of the natural sciences they had only to articulate their problems in precise terms, preferably physicalist (or behaviourist) and mathematical, and pursue their enquiries along strictly empiricist lines (Taylor, 1920).

The logical positivist image of science was codified in the 1940s by Hempel (1942), whose deductive-nomological schema sought to capture the essence of explanation and prediction common to all the sciences: past events were explained and future events predicted by deduction from universal laws and antecedent conditions. The idea of unifying all the sciences around this schema was accepted by some sociologists, most notably Homans ([1961] 1974), who offered an extended analysis of several empirical sociological studies in an attempt to show that their findings could be explained by subsumption under five general laws of human behaviour, which he took from behavioural psychology and utilitarian economics. The schema also featured

widely as a characterization of science in philosophy of social science and social research methods textbooks, and several authors gathered together lists of putative sociological laws (Berelson and Steiner, 1964; Joynt and Rescher, 1959: 386-7; Popper, [1944–5] 1961: 62–3).

Hempel's schema focused attention on universal laws as the vital ingredient of scientific explanation. By what procedures were they to be produced? Older empiricist accounts had relied on induction: the accumulation of single instances of co-occurrence was thought to justify the truth of the universal generalization. Mill's methods ([1843] 1961) summarized the rules of inference used in scientific enquiries to inductively discover laws and prove their truth. However, the problem of induction obtrudes: although observations of A1 co-occurring (or co-varying) with B1, A2 with B2, and so on, license the inference that all observed As are Bs, it is not self-evident that the accumulation of singular observations of co-occurrence (or covariation) directly justifies accepting the truth of the unrestricted universal law that all As are Bs. Yet it is just such unrestricted universals that are required if the deductive-nomological schema is to carry explanatory force: given A, B *must* follow in all cases. Despite intense philosophical efforts, including an ingenious attempt by Carnap (1950), one of the original members of the Vienna Circle, to construct a logic of induction comprising precise rules for calculating the degree of confirmation that a particular set of evidence propositions give a particular conclusion, no empiricist solution to the problem of induction has gained widespread support. Instead, the inductivist conception of scientific method has largely been abandoned in favour of the hypothetico-deductivist account, popularized by Popper.[1] Test implications are deduced from conjectured laws and compared with experience. If the evidence conflicts, the hypothesized law is rejected or modified; if experience accords with the test implications, the hypothesized universal is corroborated and accepted for the present, though it remains open to falsification by subsequent evidence (Popper, [1963] 1969). Induction, argues Popper, plays no part in the logic of science. The source of conjectured laws is a psychological or sociological matter and of no interest to the philosophy of science, which restricts itself to analysing the justification for rejecting or retaining hypotheses, however scientists come by these.

Popper's account of scientific method is widely known among sociologists, often being identified as the characteristic *modus operandi* of natural scientists, rather than the theory of scientific method that it is. Sociologists are perhaps less attentive than philosophers of science to the problems with his account, which arise because it is not individual law-like propositions that are subject to empirical test, but whole logically connected systems of hypotheses and additional conditions. It is then not clear which part of the system is in error when falsifying evidence is presented, and which corroborated. Popper himself warned against protecting theoretical systems from falsifying evidence by introducing ad hoc hypotheses or by redefining terms or by any other stratagems. He thought that the mark of science, as opposed to pseudo-science, was its openness to refutation and revision, its willingness to abandon hypotheses in the face of disconfirming evidence. Others have taken the failure of both inductivism and hypothetico-deductivism to provide a satisfactory account of the empirical status of scientific laws as indicating more generally the failure of the logical positivist ambition to demarcate science from metaphysics through the application of logical analysis and radical empiricism (Quine, 1951). Ironically, many sociologists remained committed to extending the Popper–Hempel vision of science to their own discipline long after logical positivism as a philosophical school had become mired in internal difficulties by the mid-century (Black and Champion, 1976; Rudner, 1966).

THE CHALLENGE OF CRITICAL THEORY

As a social movement, the Vienna Circle, though committed to the value neutrality of science, was modernist in the sense of believing that the growth of science could contribute to human progress through social reform. Moreover, some of its original members were sympathetic to the left wing theories prevalent in Vienna at the time. Neurath (1931b), for example, thought that Marx's materialism was the most credible existing attempt to create a scientific sociology. Yet logical positivist conceptions of social science came under sustained attack by the critical theorists of the Frankfurt School in the 1950s (Marcuse, [1941] 1955). Turning Marxist tools of analysis to cultural products, they insisted that because scientific knowledge is a product of human activity, like all such products it should be subject to critique, to an analysis of how and why it arose and whose interests it serves. Their critique of the positivist theory of scientific knowledge found it one-dimensional, for it reduced everything it investigated, including human beings, to objects to be manipulated and controlled. Positivism is a form of instrumental rationality. Positivist science has an intrinsic interest in technical control and is

therefore oppressive, an outgrowth of the class oppression at the heart of capitalism. Supposed value freedom is a value itself, sinisterly hiding behind a façade of neutrality.

Ironically, when these attacks were at their most virulent, logical positivism as a philosophy of science was already losing its force because of the internal contradictions identified as much by its adherents as their critics. Moreover, it was Popper, not a logical positivist, who defended the philosophy of science, most notably in the methodological dispute or *positivismusstreit* played out in the 1960s, prompted by a debate between Adorno and Popper at a conference organized by the German Sociological Association (Adorno et al., 1977). Popper set out his own view of science, critical rationalism, in twenty-seven theses. Adorno did not respond directly to these, but instead put the case that sociology, as well as analysing its own and other sciences' theories and methods, must also offer a critique of the sciences' objects of enquiry which, in the case of sociology, are the social structures within which it is practised. Critical analysis must not be purely formal, limited to the logic of science, but also material, a critique of society.

What the debate highlighted was that more was at stake than identifying an adequate philosophy and methodology for the social sciences. The disputants subscribed to fundamentally opposed orientations towards political activity, progress and scientism. For Popper and most twentieth-century positivists, problems in the social sciences are technical ones, soluble by more careful attention to sciences' inner workings, and problems in society are to be overcome by piecemeal social reforms, guided by scientific enquiry. For the Frankfurt School and the Hegelian–Marxist tradition, problems in the social sciences are manifestations of the fractured and contradictory nature of the social structures within which they are practised and they are to be overcome by radical transformations in society. This fundamental difference goes back to the rival views of Comte and Marx, the former concerned with orderly progress, the latter with revolutionary social transformation.

QUANTITATIVE RESEARCH AND STATISTICAL ANALYSIS

A unity of science thesis or naturalism has been an enduring strand of positivism and the discussion above has revealed that it has taken a variety of bases, including a common grounding of all sciences in sensory experience, a unified logical structure for the language of science, a common lexicon as in physicalism, a shared model of explanation, and the same method of enquiry, either inductive or hypothetico-deductive. A more prosaic form of naturalism is the claim that scientific enquiry involves the collection and manipulation of quantified facts, a view that has become closely associated with positivism, especially in the social sciences. Nevertheless, the practice of counting features of societies, their citizens and their resources – what we now call descriptive social statistics – goes back to antiquity and followed a trajectory quite separate from the other strands of positivism until the twentieth century (Lazarsfeld, 1961). In particular, the administrators and social reformers who gathered numerical information on a wider and wider range of issues in the nineteenth century, either to administer the state or to document their concerns about the fate of the urbanized industrial workers, largely limited themselves to immediate practical issues and did not construct general social theories about the processes they documented so thoroughly. Conversely, the early sociologists like Comte and Spencer, if they used evidence at all, relied on qualitative comparative material from historical and anthropological sources, which they used to arrange societies in an order of progression. It was Durkheim who merged descriptive statistics and the abstract, philosophical strands of nineteenth-century positivism. His book *Suicide* ([1897] 1970) is often taken as the exemplar of the positivist study of society, making central the collection of and commentary on quantitative data about society to demonstrate how various social forces encouraged or checked suicides.

Durkheim appears to have been innocent of the rapid developments occurring at this time in a second branch of statistics: relational statistics. At the turn of the century, Pearson, building on the work of the British eugenicists, especially Galton, formalized procedures for establishing the strength of relationship between variables, that is, assessing how much of the variation in one factor could be accounted for by variations in the others (Pearson, 1938). Pearson argued that causality was only the limit of the broader notion of correlation. He introduced numerous formal techniques for testing empirically hypotheses about the relationships between variables, adding a degree of precision to the informal analyses of earlier descriptive statisticians, exemplified by Durkheim's *Suicide*.

The third branch of statistics – probability or inductive statistics – also has a history separate from that of other strands of positivism (Hacking, 1975). Probability theory has its roots in the analysis of games of chance – cards and dice – in the eighteenth century. It became relevant to eugenicists and biologists at the turn of the century because their empirical

work involved samples of plants and animals, whereas they wanted empirical justification for their claims about whole populations or species. They used relational statistics to formulate and test substantive hypotheses about the relations between different characteristics of their samples, but they also needed to test hypotheses about the likelihood that their findings for samples were true for the populations from which the samples were drawn and were not merely specific to the particular sample they had selected. These statistical hypotheses about the generalizability of sample findings could be formulated and tested once the sampling distributions for the sample measures had been mathematically derived from assumptions about the population and the sampling procedure used. Rapid advances were made in the first third of the century, including the extension of statistical inference from large samples collected from naturally occurring populations to small samples used in controlled experiments. These experiments were initially on plant breeding, but subsequently came to dominate psychology.

Although the developments in relational and inductive statistics provided the tools to make radical changes in the organization and analysis of social surveys, which were well-established as a tool of social enquiry by the beginning of the twentieth century, they were slow to make an impact on survey practice (Selvin, 1976). In Britain, the newly developed statistical methods were tainted by their association with the eugenics movement, which was opposed by early academic sociologists like Hobhouse because eugenics seemed to reduce social science to biology (Collini, 1979). The large-scale surveys addressing social problems organized by the German Association for Social Policy (of which Weber was a member) were unsystematic and indifferently analysed by today's standards (Lazarsfeld and Oberschall, 1965). The combination of statistics and social theory pioneered by Durkheim gradually dissipated in France after his death. But a similar synthesis, in a Spencerian individualistic guise as opposed to Durkheim's sociologistic one, became firmly established in America. There the men who headed the new sociology departments founded during the rapid expansion of universities at the end of the nineteenth century believed that academic acceptability relied on demonstrating that their discipline was scientific (Walker, 1929). This was particularly the case with Franklin Giddings at Columbia, who believed that statistical analysis of precisely measured social facts was central to science. Giddings and his students were instrumental in professionalizing American sociology around survey research and statistical analysis (Oberschall, 1972). A major demonstration of the power of this approach was the extensive study of the American army undertaken during the Second World War under the direction of Stouffer. Lazarsfeld also played a prominent part in establishing what he called the empirical social research tradition. He was trained as a mathematician in Vienna in the 1920s and 1930s, and although he had virtually no direct contact with the Vienna Circle, he described himself as a European positivist and recorded that he was influenced by the Circle's convenor, Mach (Lazarsfeld, 1969). Lazarsfeld established the Bureau of Applied Social Research at Columbia University in 1937. He was committed to using statistical techniques to separate causal relationships from spurious co-variation, where two variables co-vary not because one causes the other but because both are caused by a third variable.

The explanatory survey became a standard part of sociology from the middle of the twentieth century, forming a core element of the curriculum in many sociology departments around the world, serviced by an endless stream of research methods textbooks which gave advice on how to select random samples, how to collect quantitative data systematically through questionnaires and structured interviews, and how to deploy statistics to analyse the data, with the emphasis on the statistical significance of results. Over the past half century, there have been further technical developments in statistics, particularly relevant to the nominal and ordinal measures that are more common in sociology than interval and ratio measures. Important too has been the very rapid growth in computing power and the development of wide-ranging statistical analysis packages, which allow complex analyses of very large datasets to be undertaken with relative ease.

This 'professional practice' positivism has not been without criticism. For example, the descriptive adequacy of social statistics, especially official statistics gathered by government agencies, has been found wanting because of definitional inadequacies and measurement errors (Levitas and Guy, 1996) or – echoing the critical theorists – because they inherently serve political interests (Dorling and Simpson, 1999). Adherents counter that the statistics can be improved by proper attention to estimating the reliability and validity of the measures used and that the statistics themselves are neutral tools even though they can be deployed to serve political ends. Inductive statistics and especially statistical significance testing have been subject to a battery of criticisms: confusing a statistically significant result (where there is a high probability that the correct decision has been made in generalizing the sample finding to the population) with a

substantively significant one (that is theoretically tenable or has important practical implications), confusing the level of significance with the strength of relationship, distorting results by focusing only on statistically significant ones, failing to take account of the power of statistical tests, failing to note that there are important and often substantial sources of error other than sampling error, and employing statistical tests when the data are about non-random samples or whole populations (Morrison and Henkel, 1970). Supporters counter that such problems can be overcome by more careful and informed use of inductive statistics. They argue that problems involved in extending all three branches of statistics to social research are merely technical ones and that advances have been made, and will continue to be made, in resolving them. For critical theorists, as already noted, such technical advances miss the point, for what is needed is not improvements in the technology of instrumental control, but a critique of that form of knowledge. For other critics, the problems raised about statistics are indicators of more fundamental problems with empiricism, induction and causality in sociology.

THE CHALLENGE OF QUALITATIVE APPROACHES[2]

At no time in its history has positivism been free from challengers adopting alternative perspectives on the nature of sociology. Each strand loosely woven into the positivist tradition has had its opponents – the challenge to value-freedom by critical theorists has already been noted. At the time the discipline of sociology was forming in the nineteenth century there was a strong current of idealism abroad among social theorists, especially in Germany. In the 1890s this prompted a 'revolt against positivism' (Hughes, 1958) which swept even Britain, the bastion of empiricism. Vehemently against naturalism and empiricism, it proposed a radical distinction between the natural and cultural (or human or moral) sciences in direct opposition to the unity of science thesis adopted by positivism. The realm of human culture, and in particular the generation and transmission of social meanings, was to be protected from positivists' reductionist explanations of behaviour, especially if these led ultimately to physical or biological causes. Central to the human sciences is interpretive understanding or the method of *verstehen*, for it is this that provides access to the shared meanings and interpretive frameworks which pervade the human but not the natural worlds and through which people make sense of their social activities. This idealist tradition had a major impact on nascent sociology through the works of Dilthey and especially Weber, whose stress on human agency was in direct contrast to Durkheim's sociologism (Outhwaite, 1975).

Skirmishes between positivism and the equally loose bundle of strands that make up the qualitative tradition have been played out in sociology across the twentieth century in a variety of different ways. For example, the idealist philosophy of the beginning of the century is the butt of much of the logical positivists' antipathy to metaphysics, since they found it obscure, urgently in need of logical analysis and the application of verifiability principle in order to separate out any scientific knowledge it might contain. Similarly, the alliance formed by the critical theorists between idealism and Marxism and their critique of positivist science for its rational instrumentalism have already been noted.

After the Second World War, a new wave of qualitative criticisms of positivism emerged whose source lay in linguistic philosophy. This was inspired by the later work of Wittgenstein and it came to dominate English-language philosophy over the middle decades of the century. It abandoned the empiricist understanding of language, according to which language's primary function is to capture our experiences, to give names to objects that pre-exist the language. Instead, linguistic philosophy's starting point was the observation that ordinary language serves a multiplicity of functions; language is a rule-guided social activity and the philosophers' task is to examine linguistic customs within particular language communities (Austin, 1962). By this means are traditional philosophical puzzles dissolved when the customary uses of the words and sentences in which they are couched are properly understood.

This mode of analysis was extended to the social sciences by Winch (1958). He argued that the notion of a *science* of social action was based on a misunderstanding of the nature of action because it failed to take into account action's key feature, which is its meaningfulness among the community of actors where it takes place. He maintained that not just language but all human activities are embedded social practices and their meanings must be understood by careful attention to the local rules that guide the practices. Actors' conceptions of their own actions are central and the sociologists' task is to understand and describe those culturally specific conceptions in terms intelligible to the actors under study. In such an interpretivist sociology, contextualized shared meanings are the central focus of enquiry. This has relativist implications: because the meanings of actions sought out by the interpretivist

sociologist are tied to the group within which they are constructed and sustained, then there is no fixed point from which to assess the meanings of one group against those of another. Nothing could be further from the positivist image of a value-free social science founded on the bedrock of experience and committed to identifying the universal, law-governed patterns of social interaction.

Positivists responded to the revitalized interpretivist sociology by suggesting that it might be a source of hypotheses about the determinants of action, but these must subsequently be subject to empirical test in the same way as hypotheses generated any other way (Abel, 1948). They attempted to reconstruct *verstehen* as a method of generating hypotheses about the regularities connecting social events to mental events and, in turn, mental events to behaviours. In other words, in its positivist reformulation, *verstehen* was a procedure for inserting intervening mental events between social causes and behavioural effects. Nevertheless, more radical empiricists among positivists remained sceptical about 'hidden' mental events playing any role in an explanatory science of social action. Philosophical attention focused on whether reasons are antecedent, independent causes of actions, which (leaving aside empiricist arguments about there being no evidence for reasons) might allow them a place in positivist sociology, or whether they are inseparable, logical parts of the actions in the sense of being one way of describing the meaning of the action, as interpretivist sociologists would maintain (Taylor, 1964). While these abstract arguments continued, enthusiasm for interpretivist sociology had a marked impact on substantive areas of enquiry, which turned to documenting actors' own understandings of their milieux, be that the work place, classroom, religious sect, deviant subgroup or whatever.

This interpretivist empirical work drew strength from other sources as well as the ordinary language philosophy of the 1950s. The works of continental thinkers were influential, especially those who drew on the hermeneutic tradition to challenge the extension of the Popper–Hempel vision of science to sociology. Schutz (1954), for example, returned to Husserl's phenomenology to defend Weber's *verstehende* sociology from the positivist misconstrual of it. Also influential in the 1960s was symbolic interactionism, an older anti-positivist tradition of studying groups and communities that had emerged in the 1920s and 1930s out of Chicago School sociology in the United States (Blumer, 1969). This stressed the necessity for first-hand engagement with the people under study, through participant observation, life histories and depth interviews, in order to obtain an intimate understanding of the meanings that they give to their activities, and how these meanings are constructed, negotiated and modified through processes of everyday social interaction.[3]

Towards the end of the twentieth century, several strands of qualitative sociology coalesced around 'social constructionism' (Hacking, 1999). In its more radical, universal form, this maintains that all human activities are contingent practices whose sense is constructed in the ebb and flow of social interaction. All our representations of the natural and social world – all our claims to truth – are arbitrary and could have been different had the historical and social circumstances in which they formed been other than they were. Pushed this far, social constructionism is a variant of idealism – all that exists are ideas – and it quickly falls prey to the many arguments that have been marshalled throughout the history of philosophy against idealism and for the existence of a world independent of our ideas about it. In a less radical form, social constructionism focuses on particular aspects of the world and suggests that our characterizations of these are contingent, the outcomes of social arrangements, rather than inevitable, determined by the nature of things. This has been liberating in debates about gender and ethnicity, where it has been demonstrated that gender and ethnic attributes and relations are not biologically determined but socially constructed. They need not take the form that they currently do; they can be socially constructed in other ways (and political activists insist that they must be). Even this more modest, localized social constructionism discomforts positivists because it rejects several of positivism's core strands, empiricism and naturalism in particular. When social constructionism is extended to aspects of the natural sciences, and it is argued that particular concepts and theories in, say, physics are the outcome of historically contingent social processes of negotiation between scientific investigators rather than determined by the nature of the real world, then this discomfort becomes heightened and manifests itself in what have become known as the 'science wars'.[4] These involve natural scientists heatedly rejecting social constructionist claims because they violate the scientists' understanding of their science as a broadly positivist enterprise, conducted along Popper–Hempel lines. In particular, the natural scientists usually take the view that their science discovers and reflects an independent reality rather than constructs the things they study, and they deplore social constructionism because it seems to devalue science or, worse, lend support to anti-science movements.

THE CHALLENGE OF SCIENTIFIC REALISM

Prompted by alarm over the anti-naturalism of the various interpretivist sociologies which were challenging the dominance of positivist approaches in the 1960s, a new argument for a science of society emerged in the 1970s, based on a scientific realist critique of positivism (Bhaskar, [1975] 1978; Harré, 1961). Realists applaud positivism's naturalism but reject its dependence on empiricism, especially the more radical forms, and the deductive-nomological model of explanation. Adopting a notion of ontological depth, that is, of layers of reality beyond that accessible to sensory experience, for realists the essence of scientific explanation is the discovery of underlying real generative mechanisms and causal powers, which are responsible for producing directly experienced events. This reformulation of the philosophy of science gained support because it seemed to capture, better than the positivist account, some notable episodes in the natural sciences, such as the discovery of atomic structure and its place in the explanation of, for example, the observable behaviour of gases. However, the extension of realism to the social sciences raises problems, in particular about the nature of the postulated generative mechanisms. Some scientific realists appeal to the sorts of structures identified by Marx as having a determinate effect on social relations. Others appeal to structures of the mind, or even the brain. But the issue then arises of how to justify the existence claims for the proposed mechanisms. Any such claims are prone to objections from positivists that the purported explanatory mechanisms are metaphysical and can play no part in science.

There are analogies between scientific realism and French structuralism, another family of anti-positivist attempts to construct a science of society in which explanations of human activities appeal to 'deep structures' and not the surface meanings which people give to their actions. These structures, it is argued, play themselves out in human activities, though the actors are unaware of this. Well-known examples are the structures of myths, analysed by Lévi Strauss ([1958] 1968), and Althusser's re-statement of Marxism ([1966] 1969). However, structuralist studies came under criticism by the late 1970s for their lack of reflexivity, that is, for failing to account for their own scientific status. While emphasizing the unconscious structuring of the activities and beliefs of those they studied, they seemed to exempt their own activities and beliefs from structural analysis. This contributed to the rise of postmodernism, which is considered shortly.

THE CHALLENGE OF FEMINIST APPROACHES

There has been a ferment of feminist writing since the 1960s and this has had a substantial, enlivening impact on academic disciplines, especially sociology. An early strand of feminism, 'feminist empiricism', found fault with traditional sociology on the grounds that it ignored women as a topic of enquiry. An example is the study of work up to the 1960s which focused mainly on men's jobs; women's paid employment outside the home barely featured, let alone their domestic labour and care work inside the home. The criticism was that the science of society omitted to investigate half the population and, worse, the experience of men was presented as if it were the whole of human experience. The remedy was to extend the discipline's scope to include women. This strand of feminism made no challenge to the positivist ambitions of sociology. Instead, it insisted that the positivist programme be more completely embraced: the discipline was to be extended to include scientific knowledge about women's activities, which was needed in order to guide social reforms. The existing science of society still contained gaps due to androcentric biases which feminists were more likely than sexist men to notice and strive to overcome. Such biases must be eliminated from science by more careful attention to all the evidence, about women as well as men. Only then are the inequalities between men and women revealed, in employment and earnings for example. Once soundly established by the unbiased application of broadly positivist principles, scientific knowledge of such disparities provides the grounds on which to introduce political programmes to overcome them, such as equal opportunities legislation.

However, other feminists mounted challenges to the positivist science of sociology. The liberation strand of feminism, for example, promoted an approach similar to critical theory: sociology is not a value-free, self-certifying science but a cultural product, a socially constructed institution. Given male dominance of most areas of society, sociology like other cultural products is mostly by men for men, it serves their interests. Men wield power in the social institution of sociology (and other sciences) to their own advantage. This disciplinary 'malestream' should be subject to critique in order to reveal how its sexist biases contribute to or collude in women's oppression. Such a critique serves the practical purpose of increasing the self-understanding of its female practitioners and therefore enhancing their potential to empower and emancipate themselves and their sisters. 'Feminist standpoint epistemology' maintains that, by virtue of their collective experience of subjugation,

women are in a privileged position to engage in this critique of the sciences' intrinsic androcentrism (Harding, 1987). Through feminists' struggles against male domination, they gain a more empirically adequate understanding of patriarchal society (or more generally of the social and even the natural world) than is available through the social experience of men, just as Marxists argue that it is through class struggle that the proletariat gains a privileged understanding of the workings of capitalist society. Feminist standpoint theorists nevertheless retain commitment to the modernist project – the application of science to achieve a better future – even if they are critical of the androcentric biases that have, historically, distorted the practice of sociology and limited its utility to support progress.

Other feminists have been drawn to the qualitative challenges to positivist sociology. It is not that the technical, instrumental, patriarchal science of society must be subject to critique and then corrected. Instead it must be abandoned and replaced by the sort of sociology that recognizes the fundamental divide that separates the natural and social worlds because of the meaningfulness that pervades the latter. It is argued that women's distinctive qualities, cognitive capacities, personality traits, upbringing, education or social roles make them particularly sensitive to the necessity of constructing an interpretivist sociology which is engaged, subjective, committed and passionate. In contrast, it is masculinst values of detachment, objectivity, impartiality and rationality that encourage men to mistakenly believe that a positivist science of society incorporating these qualities is possible (Smith, 1989). Similarly, it is argued at the level of research practice that women, by virtue of their familiarity with sharing experiences through women's everyday talk, are particularly adept at qualitative data collection techniques like informal interviewing, and that women's everyday lived experiences, which are the foundation of a feminist sociology, are more adequately represented in qualitative than quantitative terms. All these various arguments emphasize the meaningfulness of social action and maintain that qualitative sociology is more fitted to feminism than quantitative, positivist sociology. Sociology's goal should be a participatory, anti-sexist understanding of the interpretive frameworks through which the women whose activities are of interest make sense of their lives. In other words, the positivist science of society should be relinquished in favour of qualitative (or interpretivist) sociology.

As with the more general upsurge in qualitative sociology over the second half of the twentieth century, its feminist version has taken a social constructionist turn. This has been particularly successful in challenging previously taken for granted gender roles, showing how these were the contingent outcome of historical and social processes rather than determined by biological differences between women and men. However, arguments that gender can be completely divorced from biology have contributed to the 'culture wars', analogous to the 'science wars',[5] with proponents of a broadly positivist view of biology insisting that obdurate facts place limitations on gender behaviour, and that cultural variation is thereby constrained.

Also radically opposed to the implicit cultural relativism of social constructionism, and of interpretivist sociology more widely, is the realist strand in feminism, which seeks to establish a scientific feminist sociology, though on realist as opposed to positivist principles. Its central proposal is that underlying patriarchal structures generate gender inequalities and exploitation (Walby, 1990). This strand offers an explanation which parallels the realist Marxist explanation of class inequalities. It is the role of the analyst to discern the mechanisms that alienate people within the exploited group (class, gender) from their own everyday experiences and create false consciousness that hides from them the source of their own oppression. Knowledge about these mechanisms is potentially transformative, enabling the exploited group to combat their oppression.

Even this fleeting review of some of the strands that comprise the broad church of feminism reveals that it embraces most of the responses and challenges to positivism that have emerged since its first formulation in Comte's writings. These range from feminist empiricists who are effectively professional practice positivists urging that the quantitative science of society be applied more systematically to embrace all human activities, female as well as male; through feminist critical theory-like critique of positivism's one-sided androcentric instrumental rationality; and through feminist realists' argument that positivism misconstrues the basis of naturalism, which is not empiricism but the search for underlying generative mechanisms within the structure of patriarchy; to feminist interpretivists' rejection of naturalism because sociology should be concerned with the distinctive feature of the social world, its meaningfulness, which women are more able to apprehend than men; and to social constructionists' arguments that apparently determinate facts about women are the upshot of contingent historical and social processes.

These and other variants of feminism have heightened awareness of how people at different intersections of class, gender, ethnicity and sexuality in particular, but also nationality, religion,

language and so on, have widely varied lived experiences (feminist standpoints, in the plural) that deny validity to generalizations about social phenomena. Confidence in the modernist programme, of which positivism is a prime component, has ebbed away in the face of the diversity of human lives and the failure of the social sciences to develop uncontested general theories to guide successful social reforms.

THE CHALLENGE OF POSTMODERNISM

As emphasized throughout this chapter, positivism arose as part of the modernist project, the ambition to replace superstition, religion and metaphysics by science, to ground science indubitably in experience, to extend science to human affairs, and to apply science to achieve progressive control of natural and social forces and to further the emancipation of humankind. At the end of the twentieth century, in dramatically changed social, political, economic and cultural circumstances from when the modernist project initially emerged out of the Enlightenment, and in the face of continuing disasters such as major wars and environmental degradation, which erode our faith in human progress, many commentators have expressed 'incredulity' towards such 'grand narratives' (Lyotard, 1984), especially foundational theories of knowledge and stories of social progress. No longer in these fractured and fluid postmodern times does it seem that history has an over-arching coherence or direction, or that any theory of knowledge can legitimate itself by appeal to universal standards, or that any particular knowledge claim can be securely substantiated. Similarly, it does not seem that advances in science guarantee progressive emancipation, because science is often deployed as a tool of social control, domination and destruction. Facts and values cannot be separated, knowledge and power are entangled (Foucault, [1972] 1980).

All the various challenges to positivism documented in the preceding pages have contributed to the loss of faith in the ability of science to provide us with truths about reality: the failure of the philosophy of science to provide an uncontested foundation for the authority of science and demarcate it clearly from – and demonstrate its superiority to – metaphysics and other belief systems; the critique of the one-sidedness of instrumental reason; the cultural relativism that seems to follow from embracing the intrinsic meaningfulness of social phenomena; the social constructionists' unmasking of the contingent nature of many characterizations of the social and natural world previously taken for granted to be inevitable because determined by the nature of things; the many diverse lived experiences of women, and men, depending how gender intersects with ethnicity and class and other individual characteristics; the claims of realism and structuralism that explanations of the surface features of the world are to be found in generative underlying structures. These challenges to positivism are taken up and amplified by postmodernist analysts, who devote themselves to confronting and deconstructing what they claim are misleading appearances of coherence in all of the grand narratives' attempts to develop and legitimate systematic, scientific representations of the world. The postmodernists' critical enterprise seeks to show how theory and philosophy are inevitably engaged in exercising power, in attempting to elevate necessarily contingent, context-bound, historically situated beliefs to universal status (Seidman, 1994). Postmodernists reconfigure knowledge so that its uncertainty and incompleteness is acknowledged. Disciplinary boundaries, the separation of science from ideology and the division between power and knowledge are all challenged. In human studies, absolute knowledge, universal categories and grand theories are abandoned in favour of local, historical and pragmatic enquiries that alert us to and encourage tolerance of social differences. The abstracted rational knowing subject is replaced by multiple subjects in multiple local situations with multiple identities and multiple knowledges. This, the postmodernists argue, enables us to recognize and aspire to altered relations between knowledge and power, and provides a critical edge, an opportunity to live our lives differently.

This is, of course, too ephemeral and playful for the positivist, who strikes back with the argument that without sound knowledge, firmly grounded, we lack the basis to make progressive social reforms. Scientific ideas have a social history, but this does not undermine their truth, which is determined by the way the world is. (This does not deny that in some cases investigating its social history might reveal *some* science to be false.) Once its truth is dispassionately established, science is the neutral tool of progress. These claims draw attention to the issue that has exercised positivism since its inception – how do we demarcate science from ideology? – and to which it has sought a universally applicable answer. Postmodernism insists that it is a question that cannot be answered except partially and provisionally, in a local historical and social context. For postmodernism, the Enlightenment's science, like God before it, cannot provide us with a definitive route to a better future. The modernist project is a failure.

POSITIVISM'S PROSPECTS

If the postmodernists are correct in their diagnosis that the modernist project faced failure in the closing decades of the twentieth century, what role, if any, does its central doctrine – positivism – have left to play? In sociology, arguments about the rival merits of positivism, interpretivism, realism and feminism in various guises and under various descriptions continue at both the abstract and substantive levels. The debates are complicated because each perspective is a loose bundle of strands, and the perspectives shade into one another. Moreover, within each perspective commitment to one strand does not entail commitment to another; and mixed and muddled positions are proposed and defended. Because of the cacophony, it is impossible to discern any clear trends. Many have pronounced positivism dead, almost from the moment it was born in name in the nineteenth century and in spirit much earlier. Yet for many it lives on, at least in an everyday commitment to science, a belief that reality can by and large be truthfully and systematically represented in reason, and the acceptance that, for all its faults, as a practical enterprise science remains generally successful. This commitment may be less zealous, less self-confident than in an earlier age; after all, the sociology of science has shown science to be as liable to the influence of politics, fashion and whim as any other human enterprise, scientific knowledge has been revealed as oppressive and limiting as well as emancipatory, and there is no uncontested philosophical demonstration that science is epistemically special. Empiricism, scientism, naturalism and progressivism – core strands of positivism – are nowadays hedged with doubts and qualifications. Nevertheless, our daily round largely confirms that, more rather than less, the sciences fulfil the requirements of what we expect of well-founded empirical beliefs: they deliver the goods.

It is this that inspires some sociologists to continue the defence of positivism and search for its distinctive qualities. At the abstract level, this manifests itself in attempts to unpick postmodernist and other critical challenges scientifically, that is, by application of reason and logic and appeal to empirical evidence. Examples are provided by Haack's (1992) careful appraisal of the claim that science is masculine and Devaney's (1997) logical analysis of postmodernists' rhetorical tools. At the substantive end of the discipline, large numbers of investigators continue to produce research that conforms to the positivist image of science, explaining social activities in loosely deductive–nomological terms, and these explanations are used to guide and evaluate a wide variety of social programmes. The current clamour to ensure that professional practice in a wide range of applied fields is evidence-based is an indicator of the attraction of this type of enquiry. And so there is every likelihood that positivism will live on into the twenty-first century, for some the best hope for the future, for others the Beelzebub to be beaten.

NOTES

Some of the discussion in this chapter is a rehearsal of ideas presented in Halfpenny, 1982 and many of the source materials are reprinted in Halfpenny and McMylor, 1994.

1 Popper, though he communicated with several of the Vienna Circle, strenuously distanced himself from logical positivism, rejecting the verifiability principle and doubtful about the capacity of logical analysis to contribute to what, for him, was the central question of the philosophy of science, namely the growth of scientific knowledge. Nevertheless, his work falls within the positivist spirit of the century.

2 The challenges to positivist approaches briefly reviewed in this section have been given a wide variety of different names in different contexts, including idealist, conventionalist, humanist, hermeneutic, neo-Kantian, interpretivist, interactionist, symbolic interactionist and phenomenological. Like positivism itself, they contain a variety of different strands which are given different emphases by different authors.

3 Interestingly, there was a positivist variant of symbolic interactionism, the Iowa School, which sought to establish testable generalizations, though this had less long-term impact than the Chicago School variant.

4 The 'science wars' became particularly intense after Sokal (1996) succeeded in having an article that was a mischievous pastiche of cultural theory published in Social Text, an academic journal for cultural studies.

5 The 'culture wars' are, more generally, over literary and aesthetic canons, as well as theories of knowledge.

REFERENCES

Abel, T. (1948) 'The Operation Called Verstehen', American Journal of Sociology, 54: 211–18.

Adorno, T.W., Albert, H., Dahrendorf, R., Habermas, J., Pilot, H. and Popper, K. (eds) (1977) The Positivist Dispute in German Sociology (trans. G. Adey and D. Frisby). London: Heinemann. pp. 68–86.

Althusser, L. ([1966] 1969) For Marx (trans. B. Brewster). Harmondsworth: Penguin.

Austin, J.L. (1962) How to Do Things with Words. Oxford: Clarendon Press.

Ayer, A.J. (1959) 'Editor's Introduction', in Logical Positivism. Glencoe, IL: The Free Press.

Becker, H. and Barnes, H.E. (1938) Social Thought: From Lore to Science. New York: Dover.

Benoit-Smullyan, E. (1948) 'The Sociologism of Émile Durkheim and his School', in H.E. Barnes (ed.), An Introduction to the History of Sociology. Chicago: University of Chicago Press. pp. 499–537.

Berelson, B. and Steiner, G.A. (1964) Human Behaviour: An Inventory of Findings. New York: Harcourt, Brace and World.

Bhaskar, R. ([1975] 1978) A Realist Theory of Science. Hassocks: Harvester.

Black, J.A. and Champion, D.J. (1976) Methods and Issues in Social Research. New York: Wiley.

Blumer, H. (1969) Symbolic Interactionism. Englewood Cliffs, NJ: Prentice-Hall.

Carnap, R. ([1932] 1959) 'The Elimination of Metaphysics through the Logical Analysis of Language', in A.J. Ayer (ed.), Logical Positivism. Glencoe, IL: The Free Press. pp. 165–98.

Carnap, R. (1950) Logical Foundations of Probability. Chicago: University of Chicago Press.

Collini, S. (1979) Liberalism and Sociology. Cambridge: Cambridge University Press.

Comte, A. ([1830] 1970) Introduction to Positive Philosophy (trans. F. Ferré). Indianapolis: Bobbs-Merrill. [First two chapters of Cours de philosophie positive, Vol. 1.]

Devaney, M.J. (1997) 'Since at Least Plato . . .' and other Postmodernist Myths. Houndmills: Macmillan.

Dorling, D. and Simpson, S. (eds) (1999) Statistics in Society: The Arithmetic of Politics. London: Arnold.

Durkheim, É. ([1897] 1970) Suicide: A Study in Sociology. London: Routledge and Kegan Paul.

Feigl, H. (1969a) 'The Origin and Spirit of Logical Positivism', in P. Achinstein and S.F. Barker (eds), The Legacy of Logical Positivism: Studies in the Philosophy of Science. Baltimore, MD: Johns Hopkins University Press. pp. 3–24.

Feigl, H. (1969b) 'The Wiener Kreis in America', in D. Fleming and B. Bailyn (eds), The Intellectual Migration: Europe and America, 1930–1960. Cambridge, MA: Harvard University Press. pp. 630–73.

Foucault, M. ([1972] 1980) Power/Knowledge: Selected Interviews and Other Writings. New York: Pantheon.

Haack, S. (1992) 'Science "From a Feminist Perspective"', Philosophy, 67: 5–18.

Hacking, I. (1975) The Emergence of Probability: A Philosophical Study of Early Ideas about Probability, Induction and Statistical Inference. Cambridge: Cambridge University Press.

Hacking, I. (1999) The Social Construction of What? London: Harvard University Press.

Halfpenny, P. (1982) Positivism and Sociology: Explaining Social Life. London: George Allen and Unwin.

Halfpenny, P. and McMylor, P. (eds) (1994) Positivist

Sociology and Its Critics, vols. I, II and III. Aldershot: Edward Elgar.

Harding, S. (ed.) (1987) *Feminism and Methodology*. Milton Keynes: Open University Press.

Harré, R. (1961) *Theories and Things: A Brief Study of Prescriptive Metaphysics*. London: Sheed and Ward.

Hempel, C.G. (1942) 'The Function of General Laws in History', *Journal of Philosophy*, 39: 35–48.

Homans, G.C. ([1961] 1974) *Social Behaviour: Its Elementary Forms*. New York: Harcourt, Brace and World.

Hughes, H.S. (1958) *Consciousness and Society: The Reorientation of European Social Thought, 1890–1930*. London: McGibbon and Kee.

Joynt, C.B. and Rescher, N. (1959) 'On Explanation in History', *Mind*, 68: 383–8.

Kolakowski, L. (1972) *Positivist Philosophy: From Hume to the Vienna Circle*. Harmondsworth: Penguin.

Lazarsfeld, P. (1961) 'Notes on the History of Quantification in Sociology – Trends, Sources and Problems', *Isis*, 52: 277–333.

Lazarsfeld, P. (1969) 'An Episode in the History of Social Research: A Memoir', in D. Fleming and B. Bailyn (eds), *The Intellectual Migration: Europe and America, 1930–1960*. Cambridge, MA: Harvard University Press. pp. 270–337.

Lazarsfeld, P. and Oberschall, A. (1965) 'Max Weber and Empirical Social Research', *American Sociological Review*, 30: 185–99.

Lévi Strauss, C. ([1958] 1968) *Structural Anthropology* (trans. C. Jacobson and B.G. Schoepf). London: Allen Lane.

Levitas, R. and Guy, W. (1996) *Interpreting Official Statistics*. London: Routledge.

Lyotard, J-F. (1984) *The Postmodern Condition: A Report on Knowledge* (trans. G. Bennington and B. Massumi). Manchester: Manchester University Press.

Marcuse, H. ([1941] 1955) 'The Foundations of Positivism and the Rise of Sociology', in *Reason and Revolution: Hegel and the Rise of Social Theory*, 2nd edn. London: Routledge and Kegan Paul. pp. 323–88.

Morrison, D.E. and Henkel, R.E. (eds) (1970) *The Significance Test Controversy: A Reader*. London: Butterworth.

Mill, J.S. ([1843] 1961) *A System of Logic*. London: Longman.

Neurath, O. (1931a) 'Sociology and Physicalism', in A.J. Ayer (ed.), *Logical Positivism*. Glencoe, IL: The Free Press. pp. 282–317.

Neurath, O. (1931b) 'Empirical Sociology: The Scientific Content of History and Political Economy', in M. Neurath and R.S. Cohen (eds), *Empiricism and Sociology*. Dordrecht: Reidel. pp. 319–421.

Neurath, O., Hahn, H. and Carnap, R. ([1929] 1973) 'The Scientific Conception of the World: The Vienna Circle', in M. Neurath and R.S. Cohen (eds),

Empiricism and Sociology. Dordrecht: Reidel. pp. 299–317.

Oberschall, A. (1972) 'The Institutionalisation of American Sociology', in *The Establishment of Empirical Sociology: Studies in Continuity, Discontinuity and Institutionalisation*. New York: Harper and Row. pp. 187–251.

Oliphant, J. (1909) 'The Present Position of Positivism', *Sociological Review*, 2: 179–80.

Outhwaite, W. (1975) *Understanding Social Life: The Method Called Verstehen*. London: Allen and Unwin.

Pearson, E.S. (1938) *Karl Pearson: An Appreciation of Some Aspects of His Life and Work*. Cambridge: Cambridge University Press.

Popper, K. ([1944–5] 1961) *The Poverty of Historicism*, 2nd edn. London: Routledge and Kegan Paul.

Popper, K. ([1963] 1969) *Conjectures and Refutations: The Growth of Scientific Knowledge*, 3rd edn. London: Routledge and Kegan Paul.

Putnam, H. (1962) 'What Theories are Not', in E. Nagel, P. Suppes and A. Tarski (eds), *Logic, Methodology and Philosophy of Science: Proceedings of the 1990 International Congress*. Stanford, CA: Stanford University Press. pp. 240–51.

Quine, W.V. (1951) 'Two Dogmas of Empiricism', *Philosophical Review*, 60: 20–43.

Rudner, R.S. (1966) *Philosophy of Social Science*. Englewood Cliffs, NJ: Prentice-Hall.

Schutz, A. (1954) 'Concept and Theory Formation in the Social Sciences', *Journal of Philosophy*, 51: 257–73.

Seidman, S. (1994) *Contested Knowledge: Social Theory in the Postmodern Era*. Oxford: Blackwell.

Selvin, H.C. (1976) 'Durkheim, Booth and Yule: The Non-Diffusion of an Intellectual Innovation', *European Journal of Sociology*, 17: 39–51.

Simon, W.M. (1963) *European Positivism in the Nineteenth Century*. New York: Cornell University Press.

Sokal, A. (1996) 'Transgressing the Boundaries: Toward a Transformative Hermeneutics of Quantum Theory', *Social Text*, Spring/Summer: 217–52.

Spencer, H. (1864) 'Reasons for Dissenting from the Philosophy of M. Comte', appended to *The Classification of the Sciences*. London: Williams and Norgate.

Smith, D.E. (1989) 'Sociological Theory: Methods of Writing Patriarchy', in R.A. Wallace (ed.), *Feminism and Sociological Theory*. London: Sage. pp. 34–64.

Taylor, C. (1964) *The Explanation of Behaviour*. London: Routledge and Kegan Paul.

Taylor, C.C. (1920) 'The Social Survey and the Science of Sociology', *American Journal of Sociology*, 25: 731–56.

Walby, S. (1990) *Theorising Patriarchy*. Oxford: Blackwell.

Walker, H.M. (1929) *Studies in the History of Statistical Method*. Baltimore, MD: Williams and Wilkins.

Wartofsky, M.W. (1982) 'Positivism and Politics: The Vienna Circle as a Social Movement', R. Haler (ed.), *Grazer Philosophische Studien: Schlick und Neurath – Ein Symposion*, 16: 79–101.

Winch, P. (1958) *The Idea of a Social Science and Its Relation to Philosophy*. London: Routledge and Kegan Paul.

Wright, T.R. (1986) *The Religion of Humanity: The Impact of Comtean Positivism on Victorian Britain*. Cambridge: Cambridge University Press.

29

Metatheorizing in Sociology

SHANYANG ZHAO

Metatheorizing is a common practice in the field of sociology. While sociological theorizing attempts to make sense of the social world, metatheorizing in sociology attempts to make sense of sociological theorizing. Theorizing the practice of theorizing also takes place in other academic fields, but it has been particularly prevalent in sociology. The objective of this chapter is to examine the phenomenon of metatheorizing in sociology. More specifically, the chapter looks at (1) the definition of metatheorizing, (2) the prevalence of metatheorizing and (3) the central issues of metatheorizing. It concludes with a brief discussion on the future prospects of metatheorizing in sociology.

DEFINITION OF METATHEORIZING

The prefix 'meta' connotes 'after', 'about', and 'beyond', which is often used in describing 'second order' studies (McMullin, 1970). Let S denote a given subject of study. The study of S constitutes a first order study, S_1; and the study of S_1 constitutes a second order study, S_2. The second order study, or metastudy, is thus the study of the study, which transcends as well as succeeds the first order study. The transcendental nature of metastudy entails a high level of *reflexivity* embodied in the critical self-examination by those engaged in the first order studies.

Not all studies of studies fall into the category of metastudy. A given S_1 can be a legitimate subject of such fields as history, literature, logic and philosophy. The historical study of sociology, for example, is not necessarily metasociological, for it may lack the kind of reflexivity or

self-monitoring that is required of metastudy. Any first order study consists of at least the following three elements – purpose, process and product. The *purpose* of S_1 defines the aim of study or the type of knowledge to be gained through the study; the *process* of S_1 refers to the way in which the goal of study is to be reached; and the *product* of S_1 includes everything resulting from the study. The reflexivity of metastudy involves the continuous monitoring of the first order study by the practitioners through self-examination and self-direction. Self-examination entails (1) empirical assessment of the accomplishment (products) of the first order study and (2) critical evaluation of the appropriateness of the aim of study (purpose) as well as the effectiveness of the means of study (processes). The outcome of such examinations serves as the basis for self-direction, for example, either to continue the ongoing research activities or to make necessary changes. In sum, metastudy is the reflexive monitoring of the purpose, process and product of the first order study in the form of self-examination and self-direction by the practitioners.

Metastudy thus defined is distinguishable from 'research reviews', that also takes as its subject matter the first order studies. Harris Cooper (1984: 11) divides research reviews into three basic types: (1) the theoretical review that involves the study of extant theories 'with regard to their breadth, internal consistency, and the nature of their predictions'; (2) the methodological review that involves the study of 'the research methods and operational definitions that have been applied to a problem area'; and (3) the integrative research review that involves the synthesis of research findings 'by drawing overall conclusions from many separate studies that are believed to address related or identical hypotheses'. The crucial difference between research reviews and metastudy lies in the fact that the former lacks an essential element of reflexivity, which is the defining characteristic of the latter. While the objective of research reviews is mainly to summarize by comparison and contrast the research findings on a given subject, metastudy involves critical reflections on the ongoing research in terms of 'where we have been, where we are, [and] where we seem to be going' (Fuhrman and Snizek, 1990: 27).

Metatstudy is therefore a normative endeavor aiming to make sense of and give directions to the first order studies. Metasociology is a sub-type of metastudy, focusing on research activities in the field of sociology. Paul Furfey (1965: 8) defined metasociology as 'an auxiliary science whose function is to determine for sociology criteria of scientific quality and criteria of relevance together with their practical application'. Furfey began his metasociological treatise with an assumption that 'sociology is a science' and admitted that this untested postulate would 'affect all decisions as to the nature of sociology and the methods appropriate for developing it' (1965: 1). Furfey saw metasociology as composed of two major realms: logic and axiology, with the former furnishing the criteria of scientific quality and the latter providing the criteria of relevance and value judgement. Furfey was well aware that sociologists were not guided exclusively by the logic of science, for 'extra-logical' factors such as usefulness, practicality and convenience would inevitably affect sociological practice. The purpose of metasociology was to examine those logical and extralogical presuppositions held by the sociologists.

Sociological metatheory is a subdomain of metasociology that examines research activities in theorizing within sociology. George Ritzer (1988: 188) defines metatheory as 'the study of the underlying structure of sociological theory'. Quoting Gouldner (1970: 46), Ritzer points out that metatheory is interested in getting at the 'subtheoretical level of the "infrastructure" of theory'. However, unlike Furfey, Ritzer opposes the metatheoretical attempt to lay down the prerequisites for doing theory. Ritzer argues that metatheorizing should concentrate on reflexive analysis of extant sociological theory rather than formulating a priori rules for theoretical practice. Ritzer (1990b) divides sociological metatheory into three types according to differences in the aim of metatheorizing. The first type of metatheory is a means of attaining a deeper understanding of theory (M_u) which involves the effort to uncover the underlying structure of extant sociological theory. The second type of metatheory is a prelude to theory development (M_p) which involves the study of sociological theory in order to produce new sociological theory. The third type of metatheory is a source of overarching perspective (M_a) in which the study of theory is oriented to the goal of producing a perspective that overarches some part or all of sociological theory. All these three types of metatheory take extant sociological theories as their subject matter and examine them reflexively.

Reflexivity is also an important component of Bourdieu's conception of metatheory. Bourdieu believes that reflexive self-monitoring is required of all scientific enquiry, because 'the scientific project and the very progress of science presuppose a reflective return to the foundation of science and the making explicit of the hypotheses and operations which make it possible' (Bourdieu, 1971: 181). For Bourdieu, metatheory is a form of *socioanalysis* where the sociologist is to the social unconscious of society as the psychoanalyst is to the patient's unconscious (Swartz, 1997). A reflexive return upon the practice of theorizing is a necessary means for freeing sociologists from the constraints of symbolic struggle in the domain of social science.

The term 'metatheory' has sometimes been equated with overarching theoretical perspectives or 'frames of reference' (Parsons, 1979/80). Metatheory in this sense becomes philosophical presuppositions about the social world rather than reflexive monitoring of the practice of theorizing about the social world. To avoid this terminological confusion, metatheory is used here to mean reflexive understanding of theorizing only, with metatheorizing referring to the activity of such reflections. The following section looks at the prevalence of metatheorizing in the field of sociology.

PREVALENCE OF METATHEORIZING

The practice of metatheorizing has encountered several sharp criticisms in sociology. A major objection to metatheorizing is that metatheory makes no substantive contributions to the understanding of the real world because it mostly 'consists of commentaries on works of the past rather than constructions that are creative in their own right' (Collins, 1986: 1343). Another critique is that metatheoretical reflections are often too philosophical or normative, which 'embroils theorists in inherently unresolvable and always debatable controversies' (Turner, 1991: 9). A third criticism is that metatheoretical analysis, conducted at the empirical level, usually involves nothing but stuffing the work of other sociologists into grossly oversimplified 'pigeon-holes' (Skocpol, 1986). Metatheorizing has therefore been seen by some as a non-productive or even counter-productive intellectual exercise. Although the aforementioned charges are not entirely unfounded, they are not fair criticisms of metatheorizing as a whole. As is true of any other field of academic research, there are good as well as bad practices in metatheorizing. It is to be argued here that good practices of metatheorizing are not only possible but also indispensable in sociology.

According to the structuration theory, reflexivity is a defining character of human actors. Reflexivity involves the constant monitoring of the ongoing flow of social action that is essential to the continuity of social life. 'To be a human being is to be a purposive agent, who both has reasons for his or her activities and is able, if asked, to elaborate discursively upon those reasons (including lying about them)' (Giddens, 1984: 3). The knowledgeability of human agents takes the forms of both discursive and practical consciousness. Under the normal condition of theory construction, the continuous monitoring of theorizing is largely maintained at the practical consciousness level. Although not engaged in direct metatheoretical discourse, most theorists are able, if asked, to articulate what they are doing, how they are doing it, and why they do what they are doing. Any theorist in this sense is potentially a metatheorist. The reflexive monitoring, however, takes a discursive turn when the taken-for-granted routine of theory construction becomes problematic, in which case intense episodes of explicit metatheoretical discourse inevitably 'erupt' (Weinstein and Weinstein, 1992).

While it is true that metatheoretical discourses also take place in other fields (Connolly, 1973; Fiske and Schweder, 1986; Noblit and Hare, 1988; Radnitzky, 1973), it has been particularly common and frequent in sociology. The prevalence of sociological metatheorizing has been attributed, among other things, to the lack of a unified disciplinary matrix (Wallace, 1988), weak institutional control (Turner and Turner, 1990), and the proliferation of specialties and sub-fields (Collins, 1986). A main argument to be advanced in this chapter is that the fundamental cause of the prevalence of metatheorizing in the field of sociology lies in the ontology of the social world rather than in the epistemology of sociological research.

First of all, sociologists are dealing with a subject matter that is culturally diverse and historically specific (Calhoun, 1992). The human world consists of a multitude of meaningful contexts in which social reality is being defined and redefined by individuals located within different segments of a given social structure. The existence of multiple and contradictory meanings, values and interests both within and across cultural boundaries invalidates many universal truth claims. Furthermore, the meaning context of a given social structure is not invariant. Each generation, or each cohort within a generation, reconstructs the manifold sociocultural world as its members interact with one another and with the changing historical contingencies in which they all find themselves. The mutability of meaning contexts and social practices makes the laws of society inconstant. The persistent failure to discover universal truth and invariant laws in the social world has awakened the metatheoretical consciousness of many sociological theorists.

Secondly, in the realm of sociology, the knower and the known are intricately interconnected. Sociologists are an integral part of the social reality they attempt to theorize. Being encapsulated in a unique cultural tradition, located within a given sociopolitical structure, and affected by various personal interests in the lifeworld, no sociologists are able to escape the grip of certain types of prejudice and bias that come with their situatedness. As a result, theoretical stances taken in sociological discourse are invariably bound up with practical options in life. The clashes of multiple paradigms and grand narratives competing for authenticity and symbolic power in the realm of sociological theorizing create a perfect condition for the emergence of metatheoretical discourse. 'The ground for the possibility of metatheory is the multiplicity of theorization in sociology, which permits a second-level theorization about the process of constituting and the form of the theoretical object' (Weinstein and Weinstein, 1992: 140).

Finally, in sociology not only is the knower related to the known but also is theory integrated with practice. As the knowledge of a situation affects the decision of an actor, social theory constitutes an essential part of the condition of social action. Social theories do more than explain social reality; they define situations for the members of a society and orient them in action. Thus, 'discourse *about* society reflects and engenders discourse *within* society' (Brown, 1992: 237), and 'accepting a theory can itself transform what that theory bears on' (Taylor, 1985: 101). This constitutive power of theory obliges many sociologists to engage in metatheorizing, where 'it continually turns back onto itself the scientific weapons it produces. It is fundamentally reflexive in that it uses the knowledge it gains of the social determinations that may bear upon it . . . in an attempt to master and neutralize their effects' (Bourdieu, in Wacquant, 1996: 226–7).

To a large extent, the ontological conditions for active self-examination outlined above exist in most other social sciences, and it is perhaps the primary reason why metatheoretical debates have taken place in virtually all branches of social enquiry. Sociology, however, stands out as a field where metatheorizing has been particularly prevalent. It can be argued even that the founding of sociology itself was a product of metatheorizing. Auguste Comte ([1830–1842] 1974) pronounced the birth of sociology through reflecting on the trajectory of the progress of human knowledge. According to Comte, the development of science is incomplete until it covers the domain of human society. Sociology, or 'social physics' as he first called it, is to be the culmination of the advancement of positive science. Comte's metatheoretical prophecy inspired generations of sociologists in search of a scientific theory of human society which is comparable to the theory of the physical world. However, the failure to construct such a theory after persistent efforts made by many generations of devoted theorists has resulted in a growing sense of disciplinary crisis leading to waves of intense metatheoretical confrontations.

Incessant metatheoretical discourse is, therefore, a reflection of prolonged disciplinary crises. The crisis of sociological theorizing has resulted from the unresolved controversies over the purpose, process and product of theorizing. The practice of theorization is regarded as normal or routine if the majority of the practitioners are satisfied with the outcome of theorizing. Problems occur, however, when significant numbers of the practitioners become dissatisfied with what they end up with and start to question either the appropriateness of the purpose, or the effectiveness of the process, of their theorization. An even graver situation emerges when the practitioners begin to question *both* the purpose and the process of theorizing. And this is precisely what has happened in the realm of sociological theorizing.

The coming of age of metatheorizing in American sociology, for example, can be traced to the collapse of the dominant sociological paradigm during the 1960s. The social facts paradigm, especially its theoretical component, Parsonian functionalism, had dominated American sociology for more than two decades before it was seriously challenged by two rival paradigms: the social definition paradigm and the social behavior paradigm (Ritzer, 1975). The emergence of a multiparadigmatic structure in sociology in the late 1960s destroyed the unity of the discipline and fragmented sociological research. There was a widespread feeling that a general crisis of sociology was on the horizon (Gouldner, 1970). It was this sense of imminent disciplinary crisis that aroused interest in metastudy. 'Thus, only as the discipline discovered its consolidated paradigm – system – in grave difficulty was it tempted to open the Pandora's box that was the sociology of sociology' (Friedrichs, 1970: 31).

A major eruption of discipline-wide metatheorizing in sociology began with an outburst of interest in the methodology of theory construction (Blalock, 1969; Dubin, 1969; Gibbs, 1972; Hage, 1972; Mullins, 1971; Reynolds, 1971; Stinchcombe, 1968; Willer, 1967; Zetterberg, 1954/1963/1965). The inability to discover scientific laws of society had been initially attributed to the deficiencies in the methodology of theory construction. Only when the allegedly improved techniques again failed to produce the desired theory, did sociologists begin to look beyond methodology for an explanation. This new effort resulted in what has since been known as the sociology of sociology, which links the disciplinary problems of sociology to changes in the larger society (Friedrichs, 1970; Gouldner, 1970). The findings of metatheorizing damaged the cherished image of sociology as a science, which, along with the influence of Kuhn's ([1962] 1970) popular work on paradigms in the natural sciences, led to vigorous debates over the paradigmatic status of sociology (Eckberg and Hill, 1979; Effrat, 1972; Friedrichs, 1970; Ritzer, 1975). These debates eventually developed into a full-scale meta-analytic examination of the discipline that covered not only theory but also methods and data analysis (Brewer and Hunter, 1989; Fiske and Schweder, 1986; Hunter and Schmidt, 1989; Osterberg, 1988; Ritzer, 1988; Wolf, 1986).

Metatheorizing was formalized as a sub-field within sociology in the early 1990s. Toward the end of the 1980s, Ritzer (1988) published an influential article in *Sociological Theory*, delineating for the first time the parameters of metatheory as a sub-field in sociology. In the subsequent years, Ritzer edited two high-profile journal symposia (1990, 1991a) and published a series of articles and books (1991b, 1992), all devoted to the topic of metatheorizing in sociology. These publications, along with the ensuing commentaries, ushered in the coming of age of sociological metatheorizing, which finally came out of the closet of sociology and became a legitimate field of intellectual enquiry in social research.

CENTRAL ISSUES OF METATHEORIZING

Metatheoretical discourse in sociology has touched on a wide range of issues that are central to sociological theorizing. This section is devoted to the examination of three such issues. The first is related to the purpose of sociological theorizing, namely, the question of what sociological theory is and what it is for. The second issue deals with the process of sociological theorizing, focusing on the methodology of theory construction and verification. The third issue involves the evaluation of the product or the outcome of sociological theorizing. None of these issues has been satisfactorily resolved, but reflections on them have increased our understanding of the nature of sociological theorizing.

Purpose of sociological theorizing

The field of sociology since the collapse of the Parsonian paradigm has been marked with an impressive boom in empirical research but an increasing fragmentation in theorizing. Up to this point, sociologists have been unable to reach a consensus on such fundamental issues as what constitutes sociological theory and what sociological theorizing is supposed to accomplish. Based on answers to these questions, three major metatheoretical positions can be identified, which are labeled here nomological, interpretive and normative, respectively.

Those who hold the *nomological* position argue that the goal of sociological theorizing is to discover universal laws of the social, and theory is nothing but a concise summary of such laws. The following quotations from Zetterberg ([1954] 1963/1965) best represent this perspective:

> I want to pursue sociological theory in the sense of systematically organized law-like propositions about society and social life. As a reminder that this is a different breed of animal, I shall speak of it as 'theoretical sociology' rather than 'social theory'. (p. 5)

> The assumption here is that sociology will eventually discover a small number of propositions that are valid in several diverse contexts . . . This approach represents what we see as the main task of the sociological theorist – that is, the discovery of general propositions. (pp. 8–9)

For nomological theorists, therefore, the goal of theorizing is to discover general laws of human society and to put them together systematically in the form of sociological theory which is distinguishable from discursive social theory.

In recent years a mechanism-based approach to theorizing has emerged as an alternative to the search for general laws of society. This approach 'seeks to explicate the social mechanisms that generate and explain observed associations between events' (Hedstrom and Swedberg, 1998: 1). Theories of social mechanisms are

distinguished from variable-based statistical analysis on the one hand and narrative accounts for unique events on the other. The objective of this approach is to discover causal mechanisms capable of explaining a wide range of social situations. Mechanisms are a special type of causal laws that operate in systems like biology, machines and human society (Luhmann, 1995). A mechanism generates a predictable outcome in a given environment. In the sense that like mechanisms produce like outcomes in like environments, theories of social mechanisms are nomological in nature.

The nomological approach to theorizing has been criticized by the *interpretive* sociologists who argue that the aim of sociological theorizing is not to uncover laws of society but to interpret the meaning of human action and to understand the lifeworld in which human actors live. As Taylor (1985: 91) put it:

> There is a constant temptation to take natural science theory as a model for social theory: that is, to see theory as offering an account of underlying processes and mechanisms of society, and as providing the basis of a more effective planning of social life. But for all the superficial analogies, social theory can never really occupy this role.
>
> Social theory is . . . concerned with finding a more satisfactory fundamental description of what is happening. The basic question of all social theory is in a sense: what is really going on?

Sociological theories are therefore narrative tales about human society and tradition. Levine (1995), for example, subsumes extant sociological theories under six 'narrative types': positivist, pluralist, synthetic, humanistic, contextualist and dialogical. The dialogical narrative is regarded as most appropriate for sociology because it is able to 'make respectful contact with each of the other narratives and to bring them into fruitful conversation with one another' (Levine, 1995: 327).

Normative theorists, however, differentiate themselves from both nomological and interpretative sociologists in seeing sociological theorizing as a form of social practice. Most Marxian sociologists and critical theorists belong to this camp. For them, sociological theory does not answer the question of 'What is?' but rather 'What ought to be?' The purpose of sociological theorizing is to articulate and advocate positions for social action. Steven Seidman (1991: 132) describes this metatheoretical position in the following way:

> I'd like to posit a distinction between social theory and sociological theory. Social theories typically take the form of broad social narratives. They relate stories of origin and development, tales of crisis,

decline, or progress. Social theories are typically closely connected to contemporary social conflicts and public debates. These narratives aim not only to clarify an event or a social configuration but also to shape its outcome – perhaps by legitimating one outcome or imbuing certain actors, actions, and institutions with historical importance while attributing to other social forces malicious, demonic qualities. Social theory relates moral tales that have practical significance; they embody the will to shape history.

Contrary to Zetterberg, who sought to replace discursive social theory with formalistic sociological theory about half a century ago, Seidman is now seeking to replace sociological theory with social theory. Instead of looking for objective laws of society that are universally valid, Seidman argues for morally charged narratives that are locally based. Sociological theory has thus come full circle, ending where it started.

Disagreements among sociologists on the purpose of theorizing reflect fundamental differences in the understanding of the ontology of human society and the nature of sociological knowledge. Resolution of such disagreements requires a new conceptualization of a manifold social world that calls for the application of a variety of theoretical approaches, including nomological, interpretive and normative perspectives. It is essential as a first step to delineate at the analytical level the conditions under which the application of a given perspective is valid. The responsibility of a theorist is to recognize the given conditions of practice and to determine the appropriateness of the use of a given theoretical approach. The issue is then not which approach is ultimately right for sociological theorizing, but rather which approach is appropriate under the given conditions of social practice.

Process of sociological theorizing

Sociological theorists disagree among themselves not only on the end (purpose) but also the means (process) of theorizing. Those holding the nomological position believe that universal laws of society can be discovered if the correct methodology of theorizing is employed. The reason that so few, if any, universal laws of society have been found is mainly because of sociologists' 'ignorance about what scientific knowledge should look like and how it is created' (Reynolds, 1971: 163). This belief in scientific methodology led to the launching of a theory construction movement in sociology in the 1950s (Zhao, 1996). The objective of this movement was to codify the procedures of sociological theorizing by imposing on the discipline a

verificational approach to theory construction (Merton, 1949/1957/1968). Theories were to be verified by testing the hypotheses derived from them against empirical facts. Although the movement was later declared a failure (Hage, 1994), efforts to look for the right methodology of discovering the laws of the social have continued (Freese, 1980; Turner, 1989).

The interpretive position on sociological theorizing, however, has given rise to an entirely different methodological approach to theoretical development. The inability to understand the lifeworld of others is primarily attributed to the lack of intuitions and to the differences in the way of living. As Taylor (1985) pointed out, hermeneutical understanding requires a certain measure of insight that is inherently 'unformalizable', for the gap in intuitions is a result of 'divergent options in politics and life'. In order to understand others, one needs to sharpen one's intuitions; but to sharpen one's intuitions, one has to change one's way of life, or to live in a way that allows for greater comprehension of others. 'Thus, in the science of man insofar as they are hermeneutical there can be a valid response to "I don't understand" which takes the form, not only "develop your intuitions", but more radically "change yourself"' (Taylor, 1985: 54). Sociological theorizing is, in this sense, an effort to foster the 'fusion of horizons' in social life (Gadamer, 1975).

The normative approach to theorizing differs from both nomological and interpretive positions in that it sees the processes of theorizing as 'enter[ing] constitutively into the world they describe' (Giddens, 1987: 20). By advocating 'what *ought* to be there', instead of uncovering 'what *is* out there', sociological theorizing becomes 'a mode of altering reality, not by the direct application of energy to objects, but by the creation of discourse which changes reality through the mediation of thought and action' (Bitzer, 1968). As the aim of theorizing is no longer to make social theory correspond to the social world but to make the social world 'conform to' social theory, the success of theorizing is marked by the actualization of what is advocated rather than by the verification of what is uncovered. Sociological theorizing thus becomes a form of social practice, where the emphasis is on the advocacy of reality rather than the discovery of reality, on the actualization of ideas rather than the verification of ideas, on manipulation rather than confirmation.

Product of sociological theorizing

Metatheoretical discourse in this realm involves the evaluation of the outcome of sociological theorizing. People from the nomological camp tend to evaluate theoretical progress in terms of the accumulation of empirically tested theories. Theoretical accumulation is taken 'to mean that certain fundamental and crucial problems in theory have been resolved or superseded in such a way as to permit more general, sophisticated and systematic theory to develop as the framework for research activity within the sociology community' (Turner, 1989: 131). David Wagner (1984) broadens the criteria of theory assessment to include the following five dimensions of theoretical development: elaboration, variation, proliferation, integration and competition. Using these criteria, Wagner was able to show that cumulative theoretical growth is not only possible but also occurs frequently in contemporary sociology.

The criteria used by interpretive sociologists for theory evaluation is not the establishment and accumulation of factual interpretation of human action, but the enlightenment the interpretation brings to the audience and the new light the theory sheds upon the understanding of self and society. As understanding is an effort to place oneself 'within a process of tradition, in which past and present are constantly fused' (Gadamer, 1975: 258), knowing is inherently a historical process. Truth is not the imposition of theorists' interpretation on society, nor is it the removal of theorists' subjective bias in order to let social facts 'speak for themselves'. Truth is rather defined by the value the interpretation has for the comprehension of the knower's own being in the world (Hoy, 1978). Good sociological theories should then provide people with a type of knowledge that enables them to see a new horizon of life and to advance beyond their current understanding of themselves and their relationships with others.

To the normative theorists, however, the criterion for theory evaluation is neither factual representation nor enlightening interpretation, but the power a theory possesses to change reality. The integration of knowing and action in the practice of sociological theorizing renders the nomological mode of theory verification inapplicable. The emphasis on changing the object of theorizing rather than on enlightening the knowing subjects also makes the interpretive criterion inadequate, for theory as practice can only be validated by the impact the theory produces on practice. 'To test the theory in practice means here not to see how well the theory describes the practices as a range of independent entities; but rather to judge how practices fare when informed by the theory' (Taylor, 1985: 113). Although social theory alone cannot bring about the success of social practice, social practice cannot

succeed without social theory. To test the validity of a social theory is thus to examine the contribution that the theory made to the outcome of a given social practice.

Although Wagner has been able to show some evidence for a cumulative progress in nomological theorizing, others are less impressed with the limited accomplishment. They point to the paucity of general sociological laws and argue that nomological theoretical formulations in sociology are at best local knowledge limited in its scope of application. James Rule's, for example, describes contemporary sociological theory as 'a succession of short-lived visions, each satisfying a specific and ephemeral theoretical taste' (1994: 244). In cases where the validity of a theory appears to be universal and invariant, the content of such theory is invariably banal and commonsensical. The evaluation of interpretive theory yields a different kind of problem. The shift of focus from factual representation to subjective interpretation removes the foundation upon which the truth claims of a theory can be objectively validated (Antonio, 1991). The same critique can be made of normative theory which in essence defines truth in terms of the outcome of action. These unresolved yet important metatheoretical issues reveal the grave complexity of sociological theorizing which necessitates a heightened level of critical reflection by sociological theorists.

CONCLUSION

Metatheorizing is a constant condition of theorizing in sociology. Metatheorizing involves the reflexive monitoring of the practice of theorizing, the awareness of the intricate connectedness of sociologists with the social world they study, and the concern about the moral responsibilities that sociologists hold for the theories they advocate. Metatheorizing never dies: it comes and goes, erupts and subsides, responding to the changing situations in 'first-order' theorizing. If sociological theorizing is an arduous journey to an unfamiliar territory, then metatheorizing represents frequent pauses for rest, consulting maps, revising travel plans, or even having second thoughts about the final destination. The more difficult the journey is, the more pauses there will be. It is therefore the problematic condition of theorizing that leads to the prevalence of metatheorizing, not the prevalence of metatheorizing that causes the problematic condition of theorizing. As many of the problems associated with sociological theorizing are ontological in nature, metatheorizing will always be a part of sociology.

REFERENCES

Antonio, Robert J. (1991) 'Postmodern Storytelling versus Pragmatic Truth-seeking: The Discursive Bases of Social Theory', *Sociological Theory*, 9: 154–63.

Bitzer, Lloyd (1968) 'The Rhetorical Situation', *Philosophy and Rhetoric*, 1: 1–14.

Blalock, Hubert M. Jr (1969) *Theory Construction: From Verbal to Mathematical Formulation*. Englewood Cliffs, NJ: Prentice-Hall.

Bourdieu, Pierre. (1971). 'Intellectual Field and Creative Project', in M.F.D. Young (ed.), *Knowledge and Control*. London: Collier–Macmillan. pp. 161–88.

Brewer, John and Hunter, Albert (1989) *Multimethod Research: A Synthesis of Style*. Newbury Park, CA: Sage.

Brown, Richard H. (1992) 'Social Science and Society as Discourse: Toward a Sociology for Civic Competence', in Steven Seidman and David G. Wagner (eds), *Postmodernism and Social Theory*. Cambridge, MA: Blackwell. pp. 223–43.

Calhoun, Craig (1992) 'Culture, History, and the Problem of Specificity in Social Theory', in Steven Seidman and David G. Wagner (eds), *Postmodernism and Social Theory*. Cambridge, MA: Blackwell. pp. 244–88.

Collins, Randall (1986) 'Is 1980s Sociology in the Doldrums?', *American Journal of Sociology*, 91: 1336–55.

Comte, Auguste ([1830–1842] 1974) *The Positive Philosophy*. New York: AMS Press.

Connolly, William E. (1973) 'Theoretical Self-consciousness', *Polity*, 6: 5–36.

Cooper, Harris M. (1984) *The Integrative Research Review: A Systematic Approach*. Beverly Hills, CA: Sage.

Dubin, Robert (1969) *Theory Building*. New York: The Free Press.

Eckberg, Douglas L. and Hill, Lester Jr (1979) 'The Paradigm Concept and Sociology: A Critical Review', *American Sociological Review*, 44: 925–37.

Effrat, Andrew (1972) 'Power to the Paradigms: An Editorial Introduction', *Sociological Inquiry*, 42: 3–33.

Fiske, Donald W. and Schweder, Richard A. (eds) (1986) *Metatheory in Social Science: Pluralism and Subjectivities*. Chicago: University of Chicago Press.

Freese, Lee (ed.) (1980) *Theoretical Methods in Sociology*. Pittsburgh: University of Pittsburgh Press.

Friedrichs, Robert W. (1970) *A Sociology of Sociology*. New York: Free Press.

Fuhrman, Ellsworth R. and Snizek, William (1990) 'Neither Proscience nor Antiscience: Metasociology as Dialogue', *Sociological Forum*, 5: 17–36.

Furfey, Paul H. (1965) *The Scope and Method of Sociology: A Metasociological Treatise*. New York: Cooper Square.

Gadamer, Hans-Georg (1975) *Truth and Method*. New York: Seabury Press.

Gibbs, Jack P. (1972) *Sociological Theory Construction*. Hinsdale, IL: The Dryden Press.

Giddens, Anthony (1984) *The Constitution of Society: Outline of the Theory of Structuration*. Berkeley and Los Angeles, CA: University of California Press.

Giddens, Anthony (1987) *Social Theory and Modern Sociology*. Stanford, CA: Stanford University Press.

Gouldner, Alvin (1970) *The Coming Crisis of Western Sociology*. New York: Basic Books.

Hage, Jerald (1972) *Techniques and Problems of Theory Construction in Sociology*. New York: Wiley.

Hage, Jerald (ed.) (1994) *Formal Theory in Sociology*. Albany, NY: State University of New York Press.

Hedstrom, Peter and Swedberg, Richard (eds) (1998) *Social Mechanisms: An Analytical Approach to Social Theory*. New York: Cambridge University Press.

Hoy, David Couzens (1978) *The Critical Circle*. Berkeley, CA: University of California Press.

Hunter, John E. and Schmidt, Frank L. (1989) *Methods of Meta-Analysis: Correcting Error and Bias in Research Findings*. Newbury Park, CA: Sage.

Kuhn, Thomas ([1962] 1970) *The Structure of Scientific Revolutions*, 2nd edn. Chicago: University of Chicago Press.

Levine, Donald N. (1995) *Visions of the Sociological Tradition*. Chicago, IL: The University of Chicago Press.

Luhmann, Niklas (1995) *Social Systems*. Stanford, CA: Stanford University Press.

McMullin, Ernan (1970) 'The History and Philosophy of Science: A Taxonomy', in Roger H. Stuewer (ed.), *Historical and Philosophical Perspectives of Science*. Minneapolis, MN: University of Minnesota Press. pp. 12–67.

Merton, Robert K. (1949/1957/1968) *Social Theory and Social Structure*. New York: The Free Press.

Mullins, Nicholas C. (1971) *The Art of Theory Construction and Use*. New York: Harper and Row.

Noblit, George W. and Hare, R. Dwight (1988) *Meta-Ethnography: Synthesizing Qualitative Studies*. Newbury Park, CA: Sage.

Osterberg, Dag (1988) *Metasociology: An Inquiry into the Origins and Validity of Social Thought*. Oslo: Norwegian University Press.

Parsons, Talcott (1979/1980) 'On Theory and Metatheory', *Humboldt Journal of Social Relations*, 7: 5–16.

Radnitzky, Gerard (1973) *Contemporary Schools of Metascience*. Chicago: Henry Regnery.

Reynolds, Paul D. (1971) *A Primer in Theory Construction*. Indianapolis: Bobbs-Merrill.

Ritzer, George (1975) *Sociology: A Multiple Paradigm Science*. Boston, MA: Allyn and Bacon.

Ritzer, George (1988) 'Sociological Metatheory: A Defense of a Subfield by a Delineation of its Parameters', *Sociological Theory*, 6: 187–200.

Ritzer, George (1990a) 'Symposium: Metatheory: Its

Uses and Abuses in Contemporary Sociology', *Sociological Forum*, 5: 1–74.

Ritzer, George (1990b) 'Metatheorizing in Sociology', *Sociological Forum*, 5: 3–15.

Ritzer, George (1991a) 'Recent Explorations in Sociological Metatheorizing'. A Special Issue of *Sociological Perspectives*, 34: 237–390.

Ritzer, George (1991b) *Metatheorizing in Sociology*. Lexington, MA: Lexington Books.

Ritzer, George (1992) *Metatheorizing*. Newbury Park, CA: Sage.

Rule, James B. (1994) 'Dilemmas of Theoretical Progress', *Sociological Forum*, 9: 241–57.

Seidman, Steven (1991) 'The End of Sociological Theory: The Postmodern Hope', *Sociological Theory*, 9: 131–46.

Skocpol, Theda (1986) 'The Dead End of Metatheory', *Contemporary Sociology*, 16: 10–12.

Stinchcombe, Arthur L. (1968) *Constructing Social Theory*. New York: Harcourt Brace Jovanovich.

Swartz, David (1997) *Culture and Power: The Sociology of Pierre Bourdieu*. Chicago, IL: University of Chicago Press.

Taylor, Charles (1985) *Philosophy and the Human Sciences: Philosophical Papers 2*. New York: Cambridge University Press.

Turner, Jonathan (ed.) (1989) *Theory Building in Sociology: Assessing Theoretical Cumulation*. Newbury Park, CA: Sage.

Turner, Jonathan (1991) *The Structure of Sociological Theory*, 5th edn. Belmont, CA: Wadsworth.

Turner, Stephen P. and Turner, Jonathan H. (1990) *The Impossible Science: An Institutional Analysis of American Sociology*. Newbury Park, CA: Sage.

Wacquant, Loic J.D. (1996) 'Toward a Reflexive Sociology: A Workshop with Pierre Bourdieu', in Stephen P. Turner (ed.), *Social Theory and Sociology: The Classics and Beyond*. Cambridge, MA: Blackwell. pp. 213–28.

Wagner, David G. (1984) *The Growth of Sociological Theories*. Beverly Hills, CA: Sage.

Wallace, Walter (1988) 'Toward a Disciplinary Matrix in Sociology', in Neil Smelser (ed.), *Handbook of Sociology*. Chicago: Aldive. pp. 1–59.

Weinstein, Deena and Weinstein, Michael A. (1992) 'The Postmodern Discourse of Metatheory', in George Ritzer (ed.), *Metatheorizing*. Newbury Park, CA: Sage. pp. 135–50.

Willer, David (1967) *Scientific Sociology: Theory and Method*. Englewood Cliffs, NJ: Prentice-Hall.

Wolf, Frederic M. (1986) *Meta-Analysis: Quantitative Methods for Research Synthesis*. Beverly Hills, CA: Sage.

Zetterberg, Hans L. (1954/1963/1965) *On Theory and Verification in Sociology*. Totowa, NJ: The Bedminster Press.

Zhao, Shanyang (1996) 'The Beginning of the End or the End of the Beginning? The Theory Construction Movement Revisited', *Sociological Forum*, 11: 305–18.

30

Cultural Studies and Social Theory: A Critical Intervention

DOUGLAS KELLNER

Within the traditions of critical social theory and cultural criticism, there are many models of cultural studies. Both classical and contemporary social theory have engaged the relationships between culture and society, have carried out analyses of culture, and have thus enacted some form of 'cultural studies'. From this perspective, there are neo-Marxian models of cultural studies ranging from the Frankfurt School to Althusserian paradigms; there are neo-Weberian, neo-Durkheimian, post-structuralist, feminist and a wide range of approaches that apply specific social theories to the study of culture.

The term 'cultural studies', however, has been most clearly associated in recent years with the work of the Birmingham Centre for Contemporary Cultural Studies and its offshoots, so my discussion will focus on its work and its immediate predecessors – although I will argue that the Frankfurt School anticipated many of the positions of British cultural studies. In the following study, I accordingly examine the specific origins of British cultural studies, its genesis and trajectory, and imbrication with social theory. My argument will be that critical cultural studies requires social theory and that cultural studies in turn is a crucial part of a critical theory of society.

ORIGINS OF BRITISH CULTURAL STUDIES

Operating in a thoroughly British context, immediate precursors of British cultural studies created a critique of mass culture in some ways parallel to the work of the Frankfurt School, while more positively valorizing traditions of working-class culture and resistance. Richard Hoggart, Raymond Williams and E.P. Thompson sought to affirm working-class culture against onslaughts of mass culture produced by the culture industries. Richard Hoggart's *The Uses of Literacy* (1957) contrasted the vitality of British working-class institutions and life with the artificiality of the products of the culture industry that were seen as a banal homogenization of British life and a colonization of its culture by heavily American-influenced institutions and capitalist ideology.

During the same era, Raymond Williams developed an expanded conception of culture that went beyond the literary conceptions dominant in the British academy, conceptualizing culture as 'a whole way of life', that encompasses modes of sensibility, values and practices, as well as artifacts (1958, 1961). Arguing for the need to think together 'culture and society', seeing the importance of media culture, and overcoming the division between high and low culture, Williams produced an impressive series of publications that deeply influenced the trajectory of British cultural studies. He polemicized against the concept of the masses which he claimed was both condescending and elitist – as well as overly homogenizing, covering over real and important differences – a theme that came to run through the cultural populism that helped shape and distinguish British cultural studies.

British cultural studies was also shaped by E.P. Thompson's studies of the English working-class culture and valorization of forms of resistance (1963). The socialist humanism of Thompson, like Williams and Hoggart would influence the later Birmingham project that would seek forms of resistance to capitalist modernization. Williams and Hoggart were deeply involved in projects of working-class education and oriented toward socialist working-class politics, seeing their form of cultural studies as an instrument of progressive social change. Their critiques of Americanism and mass culture paralleled to some extent the earlier critique of the Frankfurt School, yet valorized a working class that the Frankfurt School saw as defeated in Germany and much of Europe during the era of fascism and which they never saw as a strong resource for emancipatory social change. The early work of the Birmingham School was continuous with the radicalism of the first wave of British cultural studies (the Hoggart–Thompson–Williams 'culture and society' tradition) as well, in important ways, as with the Frankfurt School (Kellner, 1997b). Yet the Birmingham project also paved the way, as I suggest below, for a postmodern populist turn in cultural studies, which responds to a later stage of capitalism.

The school of cultural studies that has become a global phenomenon of great importance over the past decade was inaugurated by the University of Birmingham Centre for Contemporary Cultural Studies in 1963/64, led at the time by Rochard Hoggart and Stuart Hall. During its 'heroic period' in the 1960s and 1970s, the Centre developed a variety of critical approaches for the analysis, interpretation and criticism of cultural artifacts, combining sociological theory and contextualization with literary analysis of cultural texts.[1] Curiously, Hoggart and Hall's recollections of the reception of their enterprise by the sociology department vary. Hoggart recalls that: 'the sociologists in fact were very charitable. They said, right through, "this is interesting stuff and we can learn from it"' (cited in Corner, 1991: 146). Hall recollects, however, that Hoggart's inaugural address 'triggered off a blistering attack specifically from sociology [which] reserved a proprietary claim over the territory' and that the opening of the Centre was greeted by a letter from two social scientists who warned: 'if Cultural Studies overstepped its proper limits and took in the study of contemporary society (not just its texts) without "proper" scientific controls, it would provoke reprisals for illegitimately crossing the territorial boundary' (1980a: 21).

Of course, the Birmingham School refused to be policed and resolutely undertook sustained investigation of both culture and society. The now classical period of British cultural studies from the mid-1960s to the early 1980s adopted a Marxian approach to the study of culture, one especially influenced by Althusser and Gramsci (see Hall, 1980a). Through a set of internal debates, and responding to social struggles and movements of the 1960s and the 1970s, the Birmingham group came to concentrate on the interplay of representations and ideologies of class, gender, race, ethnicity and nationality in cultural texts, especially concentrating on media culture. They were among the first to study the effects of newspapers, radio, television, film and other popular cultural forms on audiences. They also engaged how assorted audiences interpreted and used media culture in varied and different ways and contexts, analysing the factors that made audiences respond in contrasting ways to media texts.

From the beginning, British cultural studies systematically rejected high/low culture distinctions and took seriously the artifacts of media culture, thus surpassing the elitism of dominant literary approaches to culture. Likewise, British cultural studies overcame the limitations of the Frankfurt School notion of a passive audience in their conceptions of an active audience that creates meanings and the popular. Building on semiotic conceptions developed by Umberto Eco, Stuart Hall argued that a distinction must be made between the encoding of media texts by producers and the decoding by consumers (1980b).[2] This distinction highlighted the ability of audiences to produce their own readings and meanings, to decode texts in aberrant or oppositional ways, as well as the 'preferred' ways in tune with the dominant ideology.

Despite their differences, like the Frankfurt School, the work of the Birmingham School of cultural studies is transdisciplinary in terms of their metatheory and practice. Subvert existing academic boundaries by combining social theory, cultural critique, and politics, while aiming at a comprehensive criticism of the present configuration of culture and society. Moreover, the Birmingham School attempted to link theory and practice in a project that is oriented toward fundamental social transformation. Situating culture within a theory of social production and reproduction, British cultural studies specifies the ways that cultural forms served either to further social domination, or to enable people to resist and struggle against domination. It analyses society as a hierarchical and antagonistic set of social relations characterized by the oppression of subordinate class, gender, race, ethnic and national strata. Employing Gramsci's model of hegemony and counter-hegemony (1971, 1992), British cultural studies sought to analyse 'hegemonic', or ruling, social and cultural forces of domination and to seek 'counter-hegemonic' forces of resistance and struggle.

For Gramsci, societies maintained their stability through a combination of force and hegemony, with some institutions and groups violently exerting power to maintain social boundaries (that is, the police, military, vigilante groups, etc.), while other institutions (like religion, schooling, or the media) serve to induce consent to the dominant order through establishing the hegemony, or ideological dominance, of a distinctive type of social order (that is, liberal capitalism, fascism, white supremacy, democratic socialism, communism, and so on). Hegemony theory thus involved both analysis of current forces of domination and the ways that distinctive political forces achieved hegemonic power (that is, Thatcherism or Reaganism) *and* the delineation of counter-hegemonic forces, groups and ideas that could contest and overthrow the existing hegemony. Hegemony theory thus requires historically specific sociohistorical analysis of particular conjunctures and forces, with cultural studies highlighting how culture serves broader social and political ends.

British cultural studies aimed at a political project of social transformation in which location of forces of domination and resistance would aid the process of political struggle. Richard Johnson, in discussions at a 1990 University of Texas conference on cultural studies, stressed that a distinction should be made between the postmodern concept of difference and the Birmingham notion of antagonism, in which the first concept often refers to a liberal conception of recognizing and tolerating differences, while the notion of antagonism refers to structural forces of domination, in which asymmetrical relations of power exist in sites of conflict. Within relations of antagonism, oppressed individuals struggle to surmount structures of domination in a variety of arenas. Johnson stressed that the Birmingham approach always defined itself as materialist, analysing sociohistorical conditions and structures of domination and resistance. In this way, it could be distinguished from idealist, textualist and extreme discourse theories which only recognized linguistic forms as constitutive of culture and subjectivity.

Moreover, British cultural studies developed an approach that avoided cutting up the field of culture into high and low, popular versus elite, and to see all forms of culture as worthy of scrutiny and criticism. It advocated approaches that appraised the politics of culture and made political discriminations between different types of culture and their varying political effects. Bringing the study of race, gender and class into the center of the study of culture and communications and adopts a critical approach that, like the Frankfurt School, but without some of

its flaws, interprets culture within society and situates the study of culture within the field of contemporary social theory and oppositional politics.

The Birmingham project was oriented toward the crucial political problems of their age and milieu. Their early spotlight on class and ideology derived from an acute sense of the oppressive and systemic effects of class in British society and the struggles of the 1960s against class inequality and oppression. The work of the late 1950s and early 1960s Williams/Hoggart/Hall stage of cultural studies valorized the potential of working-class cultures and then began, in the 1960s and 1970s, appraising the potential of youth subcultures to resist the hegemonic forms of capitalist domination. Unlike the classical Frankfurt School (but similar to Herbert Marcuse), British cultural studies looked to youth cultures as providing potentially new forms of opposition and social change. Through studies of youth sub-cultures, British cultural studies demonstrated how culture came to constitute distinct forms of identity and group membership and appraised the oppositional potential of various youth sub-cultures (see Hebdige, 1979; Jefferson, 1976).

Cultural studies came to center attention on how sub-cultural groups resist dominant forms of culture and identity, creating their own style and identities. Individuals who conform to hegemonic dress and fashion codes, behavior and political ideologies thus produce their identities within mainstream groups, as members of particular social groupings (such as white, middle-class conservative Americans). Individuals who identify with sub-cultures, like punk culture, or hip hop sub-cultures, look and act differently from those in the mainstream, and thus create oppositional identities, defining themselves against standard models.

British cultural studies was thus engaged in a sustained quest for political agency and new political subjects and movements when they discerned that the working class was integrated into existing capitalist societies. Their studies were highly political in nature and stressed the potentials for resistance in oppositional sub-cultures. The development of cultural studies and search for new political agents were influenced by 1960s struggles and political movements. The turn toward feminism, often conflictual, was shaped by the feminist movement, while the turn toward race as a significant factor of study was fueled by the anti-racist struggles of the day. The move in British cultural studies toward emphasis on education was related to political concern with the continuing bourgeois hegemony despite the struggles of the 1960s. The right turn in British politics with Thatcher's victory led in the late 1970s to concern with understanding the authoritarian populism of the new conservative hegemony.

As it developed into the 1970s and 1980s, British cultural studies successively appropriated feminism, race theory, gay and lesbian theory, postmodern theory and other fashionable theoretical modes. They deployed these theoretical perspectives to examine the ways that the established society and culture promoted sexism, racism, homophobia and other forms of oppression, – or helped to generate resistance and struggle against these phenomena. This approach implicitly contained political critique of all cultural forms that promoted oppression and domination, while positively valorizing texts and representations that produced a potentially more just and egalitarian social order.

Developments within classical British cultural studies have thus been in part responses to struggles by a multiplicity of different groups which have produced new methods and voices within cultural studies (such as a variety of new feminisms, gay and lesbian studies, insurgent multiculturalism, critical pedagogy and critical media literacy). Thus, the center and fulcrum of British cultural studies at any given moment was determined by the struggles in the present political conjuncture and their major work was thus conceived as political interventions. Their studies of ideology, domination and resistance, and the politics of culture directed the Birmingham group toward analysing cultural artifacts, practices and institutions within existing networks of power and showing how culture both provided tools and forces of domination and resources for resistance and struggle. This political optic valorized studying the effects of culture and audience use of cultural artifacts, which provided an extremely productive focus on audiences and reception, topics that had been neglected in most previous text-based approaches to culture.[3] Yet recent developments in the field of cultural studies have arguably vitiated and depoliticized the project.

CULTURAL POPULISM AND THE POLITICS OF THE POPULAR

In the 1980s, there was a turn within British cultural studies and beyond to celebrations of the popular, the pleasures of consumption, and affirmations of a postmodern global culture of multiplicity and difference which led many in the tradition to uncritical celebration of 'popular culture' and the joys of consumption. However, just as the term 'mass culture' is ideologically loaded and overly derogatory, so too is the term

'popular culture' overly positive (see the analysis in Kellner, 1995). In its usage by John Fiske (1989a, 1989b) and other contemporary practitioners of cultural studies, the terms 'popular culture' and 'the popular' suggest that the people themselves choose and construct the popular, covering over that media culture is a top-down form of culture produced by culture industries in a market governed by commercial and ideological imperatives. The discourse of the 'popular' has long been utilized in Latin America and elsewhere to describe culture fabricated by and for the people themselves as an adversarial sphere to mainstream or hegemonic culture. Thus, in many oppositional discourses, 'popular forces' describe groups struggling against domination and oppression, while 'popular culture' describes culture of, by and for the people, in which they create and participate in cultural practices that articulate their experience and aspirations.

The concept of 'popular culture' also encodes a celebratory aura associated with the Popular Culture Association, which often engages in uncritical affirmations of all that is 'popular'. Since this term is associated in the United States with individuals and groups who often eschew critical, theoretically informed and political approaches to culture, it is risky to use this term, though Fiske has tried to provide 'popular culture' with an inflection consistent with the socially critical approach of cultural studies. Fiske defines the 'popular' as that which audiences make of and do with the commodities of the culture industries (1989a and 1989b). He argues that progressives should appropriate the term 'popular', wresting it from conservatives and liberals, using it as part of an arsenal of concepts in a cultural politics of opposition and resistance (discussion in Austin, September 1990). Fiske claims 'there can be no instance of the popular which involves domination', thus excluding the 'popular' from domination and manipulation in principle.

More debate is needed as to whether using the term 'popular culture' in any form risks blunting the critical edge of cultural studies, and whether it is thus simply better to avoid terms like 'mass culture' and 'popular culture'. A possible move within cultural studies would therefore be to take culture itself as the field of one's studies without divisions into the high and the low, the popular and the elite – though, of course, these distinctions can be strategically deployed in certain contexts. Thus, I believe that instead of using ideological labels like 'mass' and 'popular culture', it is preferable to talk of 'media culture' when considering the forms of radio, television, film, journalism, music, advertising and the other modes of culture generated by communications media; further, I would propose developing a cultural studies cutting across the full expanse of culture from radio to opera, rather than bifurcating the field and only focusing on 'popular' forms (Kellner, 1995 and Best and Kellner, forthcoming).

Moreover, especially as it has developed in the United States, many current configurations of cultural studies are too narrow in their optic, either by concentrating solely on cultural texts and/or audience reception, thus occluding the broader terrain of culture and society. In his study of Madonna, for instance, Fiske writes:

> A cultural analysis, then, will reveal both the way the dominant ideology is structured into the text and into the reading subject, and those textual features that enable negotiated, resisting, or oppositional readings to be made. Cultural analysis reaches a satisfactory conclusion when the ethnographic studies of the historically and socially located meanings that *are* made are related to the semiotic analysis of the text. (1989a: 98)

This dialectic of text/audience, however, leaves out many mediations that should be part of cultural studies and a sociology of culture, including analyses of how texts are manufactured within the context of the political economy and system of production of culture, as well as how audiences are formed by a variety of social institutions, practices, ideologies and the uses of different media.

Thus, centering on texts and audiences to the exclusion of analysis of the social relations and institutions in which texts are created and consumed truncates cultural studies, as does analysis of reception that fails to indicate how audiences are produced through their social relations and how to some extent a distinctive culture and society help shape audiences and their reception of texts. Fiske's claim, for instance, that a cultural studies analysis of Madonna merely needs to analyse her texts and the ways that her audiences use the material overlooks the social construction of 'Madonna', her audiences and the ways that her marketing strategies, use of new media technologies and skillful exploitation of themes resonant within her sociohistorical moment all account for important dimensions of the 'Madonna phenomenon'.

Madonna first emerged in the moment of Reaganism and embodied the materialistic and consumer-oriented ethos of the 1980s ('Material Girl'). She also appeared at a time of dramatic image proliferation, associated with MTV, fashion fever and intense marketing and promotion. Madonna was one of the first MTV music video superstars who consciously crafted images to attract a mass audience. She used top production personnel to create her videos and music

and brilliant marketing strategies to incorporate ever-larger and diverse audiences. Her early music videos were aimed at teenage girls (the Madonna 'wannabes'), but she soon incorporated black, Hispanic and minority audiences with her images of inter-racial sex and a multicultural 'family' in her concerts. She also appealed to gay and lesbian audiences, as well as feminist and academic audiences, as her videos became more complex and political ('Like a Prayer', 'Express Yourself', 'Vogue', and so on).

Madonna also had at her disposal one of the top PR firms in the business and probably no one has achieved more publicity and been more in the public eye. Thus, Madonna's popularity was in large part a function of her marketing and promotion strategies, combined with creative fabrication of music videos and images that appealed to diverse audiences. The latter was a function of new technologies of music video and the ascendancy of MTV and a culture of the spectacle which she skillfully exploited. The meanings and effects of her artifacts therefore can best be discerned within the context of their production and reception, which involves discussion of MTV, the music industry, concerts, marketing and the construction of images and spectacle. Understanding Madonna's popularity also requires study of audiences, not just as individuals, but as members of distinctive groups, such as teenage girls, who were encouraged in their struggles for individual identity by Madonna, or gays, who were empowered by her incorporation of alternative images of sexuality within popular mainstream cultural artifacts. Yet appraising the politics and effects of Madonna also requires analysis of how her work might merely reproduce a consumer culture that defines identity in terms of images and consumption (see Kellner, 1995: ch. 7).

FETISHISM OF THE AUDIENCE AND RESISTANCE

Indeed, in many versions of contemporary cultural studies, concentration on the audience and reception is too restrictive. Hence, there is the danger of the fetishism of the audience in the recent emphasis on the importance of reception and generation of meanings. On the whole, there has been a large-scale shift during the past decade within cultural studies from concentrating on texts and the context of their production to centering attention on the audience and reception, in some cases producing a new dogmatism whereby the audience, or reader, alone creates meaning. The texts, society and system of production and reception disappear in the solipsistic ecstasy of the textual producer, in which there is no text outside of reading – resulting in a parody of Derrida's *bon mot* that there is nothing outside of the text.

Furthermore, there has been a fetishism of resistance in some versions of cultural studies. There is a tendency within the cultural studies tradition of reception research to dichotomize between dominant and oppositional readings. Hall's distinctions between 'dominant', 'negotiated' and 'oppositional' readings (1980b) is flattened in Fiske's work to a dichotomy between the dominant and the oppositional. 'Dominant' readings are those in which audiences appropriate texts in line with the interests of the hegemonic culture and the ideological intentions of a text, as when audiences feel pleasure in the restoration of male power, law and order, and social stability at the end of a film like *Die Hard*, after the hero and representatives of authority eliminate the terrorists who had taken over a high-rise corporate headquarters. An 'oppositional' reading, by contrast, celebrates the resistance to this reading in audience appropriation of a text; for example, Fiske (1993) observes resistance to dominant readings when homeless individuals in a shelter cheered the destruction of police and authority figures, during repeated viewings of a video-tape of the film, before the superhero re-establishes law and order – at which time, Fiske claims, the homeless men lost interest in the video.

There is, however, a tendency in cultural studies to celebrate resistance *per se* without distinguishing between types and forms of resistance (a similar problem resides with indiscriminate celebration of audience pleasure in certain reception studies). Thus resistance to social authority by the homeless evidenced in their viewing of *Die Hard* could serve to strengthen brutal masculinist behavior and encourage manifestations of physical violence to solve social problems. Violence, as Sartre, Fanon and Marcuse, among others, have argued, can be either emancipatory, directed at forces of oppression, or reactionary, directed at popular forces struggling against oppression. Many feminists, by contrast, see all violence as forms of brute masculinist behavior and many people involved in peace studies see it as a problematic form of conflict resolution. Moreover, unqualified valorization of audience resistance to preferred meanings as good *per se* can lead to populist celebrations of the text and audience pleasure in its use of cultural artifacts. This approach, taken to an extreme, would lose its critical perspective and would lead to a populist positive gloss on audience experience of whatever is being studied. Such studies also might lose sight of the manipulative and conservative effects of certain types of mass-mediated culture and thus serve the interests of the culture industries as they are presently constituted.

While concentrating on the audience and reception was an important correction to the limitations of purely textual analysis, I believe that in recent years cultural studies has over-emphasized reception and textual analysis, while decentering the production of culture and its political economy. While earlier, the Birmingham group regularly focused on media institutions and practices, and the relations between media culture and broader social structures and ideologies, this theme has waned in recent years, to the detriment of much current work in cultural studies. For instance, in his classical programmatic article 'Encoding/Decoding', Stuart Hall began his analysis by using Marx's *Grundrisse* as a model to trace the articulations of 'a continuous circuit', encompassing 'production – distribution – production' (1980b: 128ff.). He concretizes this model through analysis of how media institutions produce messages, how they circulate and how audiences use or decode the messages to create meaning.

Similarly, Richard Johnson provides a model of cultural studies, analogous to Hall's earlier model, based on a diagram of the circuits of production, textuality and reception, similar to the circuits of capital stressed by Marx (see 1986/ 1987: 47). Although Johnson stresses the importance of analysis of production in cultural studies and criticizes the British film journal *Screen* for abandoning the perspective of production in favor of more idealist and textualist approaches (pp. 63ff.), much work in cultural studies has replicated this omission. One could indeed argue that most recent cultural studies have tended to disregard analyses of the circuits of political economy and production in favor of text and audience-based analyses.

Indeed, the fetishism of the popular in contemporary cultural studies overlooks the role of marketing and public relations strategies in helping to produce the popular. The 'popular' is not just created by audiences alone as Fiske would have it, but is negotiated between audiences and cultural producers with the mediation of cultural industry hype, public relations and media discourses. In other words, part of the popular is produced by advertising, public relations, critics' accolades or generating of controversies, and general media exchange which tells audiences that they *must* see this film, watch this television show, listen to this music, be familiar with this celebrity, to be 'with it', to be in the know. I addressed the role of marketing strategies, public relations, critical hype and media discourses in producing the Madonna phenomenon above, and would argue that other megastars like Michael Jackson, Mariah Carey and popular film stars also benefit from mega-publicity machines.

In addition, films like the *Star Wars* series are hyped in massive advertising campaigns, cross-over promotions with products like Pepsi and Coca-Cola, or food chains like McDonald's and Burger King, as well as articulations with toys and other consumer products. The second *Austin Powers* film was the beneficiary of unprecedented advertising hype in summer 1999 (including appearance in a Madonna music video) which helped produce an opening weekend gross superior to the entire take of the previous *Austin Powers* film, as well as surpassing *Star Wars: The Phantom Menace* as the highest grossing film of the week – before disappearing after its 15 minutes of fame (or 15 days of high gross in this case). Advertising budgets for high-concept films are often a significant part of the film's expenses and elaborate promotional campaigns are an essential aspect of the effort to increase an artifact's popularity (this is also true in the music, television, video game and computer industries).

While many affiliated with British cultural studies in recent years have ignored production, some in the tradition and others outside of it have made important advances by analysing the products and institutions of corporate culture with studies of the Sony Walkman (du Gay, Hall et al., 1997), McDonald's (see Ritzer, 1993/6; Alfino et al., 1998; Smart, 1999) and Nike (Goldman and Papson, 1998), as well as malls, theme parks and new sites of consumption (see Gottdiener, 1997; Ritzer, 1998). Practitioners of media culture studies should likewise concentrate more analysis on media corporations, practices and promotion campaigns to better grasp the ways that media culture is produced, circulated and distributed.

Analysing the marketing and production of stardom and popularity thus demonstrates how the popular is a negotiated interaction between the culture industries and audiences. Obviously, for celebrities or products to be popular they must resonate with audience experiences and fantasies, but the culture industries pay people incredible amounts of money to research precisely what will sell and then aggressively market this product. Breaking with a fetish of the popular can help reveal how the popular is a construct and could also help to demystify the arguably false idols of media culture and to produce more critical audience perception. Analysing the business dimension of media culture can thus help produce critical consciousness as well as better understanding of its production and distribution. Such a dimension enhances cultural studies and contributes to developing a critical media pedagogy that supplements analysis of how to read media texts and how to study audience use of them.

The fetishism of the popular also leads dominant trends in British and North American cultural studies to slighting high culture and the engagement of modernist and avant-garde movements, such as distinguished the work of the Frankfurt School, whose analyses extended from the most esoteric modernist art to the most banal artifacts of media culture. It appears that in its anxiety to legitimate study of the popular and to engage the artifacts of media culture, cultural studies has turned away from so-called high or elite culture in favor of the popular. But such a turn sacrifices the possible insights into all forms of culture and replicates the bifurcation of the field of culture into a 'popular' and 'elite' (which merely inverts the positive/negative valorizations of the older high/low distinction). More important, it disconnects cultural studies from attempts to develop oppositional forms of culture of the sort associated with the 'historical avant-garde' (Bürger, [1974] 1984). Avant-garde movements like Expressionism, Surrealism and Dada wanted to develop art that would revolutionize society, that would provide alternatives to hegemonic forms of culture (see Bronner and Kellner, 1983).

The oppositional and emancipatory potential of avant-garde art movements was a primary emphasis of the Frankfurt School, especially Adorno, and it is unfortunate that British and North American cultural studies have largely neglected engaging avant-garde art forms and movements. This is connected with a failure of many versions of cultural studies and the sociology of culture to develop a radical cultural and media politics, such as is found in the works of Brecht and Walter Benjamin, concerned with cultural politics and the development of alternative oppositional cultures. The ignoring of modernist and avant-garde art and intense focus on the popular was aided and abetted by the postmodern turn in cultural studies which disseminated key positions and strategies of British cultural studies throughout the world but also helped produce an important mutation in the cultural studies project.

THE POSTMODERN TURN IN CULTURAL STUDIES

Although cultural populism, the turn to the audience and fetishism of the popular can be read as part of a postmodern turn in cultural studies, a more explicit version is found in the work of critical critics who wish to revise the project of cultural studies from the perspectives of postmodern theory advanced by Jean Baudrillard (1983a, 1983b, 1993), Fredric Jameson (1991, 1998) and others.[4] One version involves an appropriation of the collapse of high into low culture, of depth onto surface and the audience into the text, such that distinctions within media culture and between texts, audiences and contexts are increasingly difficult to make; in its more extreme versions, the postmodern turn in cultural studies excludes the very possibility of progressive or critical encoding or decoding of cultural texts, or production of alternative cultures.

While Fredric Jameson has developed his own Marxian version of cultural studies that has been immensely influential (see Jameson, 1981, 1991 and the discussions of his work in Kellner, 1989c), his ground-breaking essays on postmodernism claim that postmodern culture manifests 'the emergence of a new kind of flatness or depthlessness, a new kind of superficiality in the most literal sense – perhaps the supreme formal feature of all the postmodernisms' (1991: 9). Existentially, Jameson identifies the 'waning of affect' within fragmented postmodern selves devoid of the expressive energies characteristic of modernism. Such one-dimensional postmodern texts and selves put in question the continued relevance of hermeneutic depth models such as the Marxian model of essence and appearance, true and false consciousness; the Freudian model of latent and manifest meanings; the existentialist model of authentic and inauthentic existence; and the semiotic model of signifier and signified.

For Arthur Kroker and David Cook (1986: 267ff.), following Baudrillard, television is just a sign-machine that spews out image after image whose meanings cancel each other out in a postmodern implosion of noise – a black hole of meaninglessness, imploding into the masses who themselves cancel out and resist meaning, losing themselves in the mediascapes of simulation. In an article on television and postmodernity ([1987] 1997b), Lawrence Grossberg in turn characterizes 'the in-difference of television', which reduces the flow of TV images to mere affect and feeling, disconnected and fragmented signs akin to billboards that drivers glance at as they speed down superhighways. Several articles in a collection of television criticism, *Watching Television* (Gitlin, 1986), aggressively take this position, which builds on McLuhan's theory of 'medium as message', Baudrillard's theory of the media, and Jameson's arguments concerning the depthlessness and waning of affect in postmodern culture.[5] Pat Aufderheide, for example, thinks that music videos abolish 'the kinds of energizing, critical response once called up by rock music' (1986: 112). With Todd Gitlin and

other contributors to the volume, she pursues a formalist analysis which sees television less as a transmission of ideological messages, than a total look or environment. Music videos, with their fantasy structures, rapid, mesmerizing cuts and camera angles, throbbing music soundtracks, and extreme aestheticized environments, offer a total mood or pure environment to be consumed.

A certain version of postmodern cultural criticism thus signifies the death of hermeneutics: in place of what Ricoeur (1970) has termed a 'hermeneutics of suspicion' and the polysemic reading of cultural symbols and texts raises a postmodern view that there is nothing behind the surface of texts, no depth or multiplicity of meanings for critical enquiry to discover and explicate. Postmodern cultural criticism thus renounces hermeneutics and tends to privilege the medium over the message, style over substance, and form over content. For postmodern theorists like Baudrillard, as for McLuhan, 'the medium is the message' and the rise to cultural dominance of media culture is symptomatic of far-reaching social and cultural changes.

Yet many other types of postmodern cultural theory and politics have emerged. Hal Foster (1983) distinguishes between a conservative postmodernism of quotation of past forms and a postmodernism of resistance, championing art works that engage in social criticism and subversion. Indeed, many feminists, people of color, gays and lesbians, multiculturalists, postcolonialists and others have deployed a postmodern cultural studies to stress difference and marginality, valorizing the culture and practices of individuals and groups excluded from mainstream culture, generating a cultural studies of the margins and oppositional voices. Nestor Garcia Canclini (1995), for instance, describes the 'hybrid cultures' and 'oblique powers' of forms of popular art in Latin America, including monuments, graffiti, comic books and songs.

Another version of the postmodern turn in cultural studies involves reconstructing the project of cultural studies in response to the challenges of postmodern theory. Lawrence Grossberg, for instance, has been carrying out a systematic attempt to rethink the project of British cultural studies in response to what he perceived as the new postmodern condition. Having been one of the organizers of the University of Illinois at Urbana conference on Marxism and Postmodernism in 1983, Grossberg heard Jameson's presentation of postmodernism and the response of Hall and others associated with British cultural studies. In a 1986 article, 'History, Politics, Postmodernism', Grossberg is justifiably skeptical about postmodern claims for a radical break in culture or history, arguing: 'I think it unlikely (and certainly too easy a conclusion), but its powerful presence and popularity do suggest a series of questions that must be addressed about the possibilities of communication, opposition, elitism, and self-definition' (1997a: 188).

Noting that British cultural studies 'has been shaped by an almost continuous series of debates and challenges' (p. 187), Grossberg notes that it is now time for cultural studies to enter the fray in the disputes about the postmodern and to respond accordingly. Grossberg asserts that both cultural studies and postmodern theory are anti-essentialist and radically contextualist, and that both reject an extreme deconstructionist rejection of all fixed positions and meanings. Both are concerned 'less with questions of origin and causality than with questions of effectivity, conditions of possibility, and overdetermination' (p. 189). Both are concerned with power, domination and resistance, and can be articulated with radical politics and new social movements, so the possibility of an articulation between postmodern theory and cultural studies is readily apparent.

Grossberg is aware that certain Baudrillardian and extreme versions of cultural studies resist such articulation and in a series of articles argues against what he sees as elitism, excessive pessimism and nihilism, and political deficits within some versions of postmodern theory, calling for development of a more positive postmodernism (1997a, 1997b) – a position shared by Dick Hebdige, Stuart Hall and others associated with British cultural studies.[6] In Hall's words:

> the global postmodern signifies an ambiguous opening to difference and to the margins and makes a certain kind of decentering of the Western narrative a likely possibility; it is matched, from the very heartland of cultural politics, by the backlash: the aggressive resistance to difference; the attempt to restore the canon of Western civilization; the assault, direct and indirect, on the multicultural; the return to grand narratives of history, language, and literature (the three great supporting pillars of national identity and national culture); the defense of ethnic absolutism, of a cultural racism that has marked the Thatcher and the Reagan eras; and the new xenophobias that are about to overwhelm fortress Europe. (1991)

For Hall, therefore, the global postmodern involves a pluralizing of culture, openings to the margins, to difference, to voices excluded from the narratives of Western culture. Moreover, one could argue that a postmodernist cultural studies articulates experiences and phenomena within a new mode of social organization. The emphasis on active audiences, resistant readings, opposi-

tional texts, utopian moments and the like describes an era in which individuals are trained to be more active media consumers, and in which they are given a much wider choice of cultural materials, corresponding to a new global and transnational capitalism with a much broader array of consumer choices, products and services. In this regime, difference sells, and the dissimilarities, multiplicities and heterogeneity valorized in postmodern theory describes the proliferation of otherness and marginality in a new social order predicated on proliferation of consumer desires and needs.

Thus, there are competing versions of the postmodern turn in cultural studies. At its most extreme, the postmodern turn erases economic, political and social dimensions to cultural production and reception, carries out a new form of cultural and technological determinism, engages in theoreticist blather, and renounces the possibility of textual interpretation, social criticism and political struggle. In a more dialectical and political version, postmodern theory is used to rethink cultural criticism and politics in the contemporary era. Indeed, postmodern theory can be useful in calling attention to new configurations and functions of culture, as it charts the trajectories and impacts of new technologies, the emergent global economy and culture and the novel political terrain and movements. In addition, some versions of postmodern theory provide extremely useful interdisciplinary perspectives, as did the Frankfurt School and British cultural studies at their best.

CULTURAL STUDIES UNDER SIEGE

During the 1990s, cultural studies became a target of intense contestation and debate, taken up by individuals in a myriad of disciplines, attacked by more traditionalist defenders of the academy, and often assaulted from the left and right alike. A 1993 ICA (International Communications Association) panel elicited a passionate response with debates between defenders and critics of the current configuration of British cultural studies, and the organizers of the panel, Marjorie Ferguson and Peter Golding, collected papers from the contributors to the panel and others into a book *Cultural Studies in Question* (1997). Citing a 'deep unease' with its current configuration, the editors claim that cultural studies is today a crucial subject of controversy due to its high visibility, which makes it impossible to ignore, and its 'infinite plasticity', which enables the field to absorb any conceivable topic, from its own internal history to 'history and global culture in a postmodern age'

(Grossberg et al., 1992: 18–22, cited in Ferguson and Golding 1997: xiii). And most crucially – in the light of cultural studies' sometimes extravagant claims – the editors warn that we must be aware of its 'failure to deal empirically with the deep structural changes in national and global political, economic and media systems through its eschewing of economic, social or policy analysis' (p. xiii). In this situation: 'As ontology replaces epistemology and interpretation replaces investigation, the embrace of textualism, discursive strategies, representation and polysemic meanings accelerates the elevation of the theoretical over the empirical and the abstract over the concrete' (p. xiv).

Within the volume itself, Todd Gitlin (1997: 25ff.) polemicizes against what he sees as a retreat from politics in cultural studies. Against the more ludic, celebratory and theoretical modes of cultural studies, Angela McRobbie (1997: 170ff.) urges a return to the 'three Es' – the empirical, the experiential, and the ethnographic – calling in effect for a more grounded sociological analysis. Likewise, David Morley criticizes some of the dominant varieties of contemporary cultural studies and argues for 'putting sociology back in' (1997: 121ff.). The editors and other contributors deplore the distancing of cultural studies from political economy and argue for articulating cultural studies with political economy and a social science approach to the study of culture (Ferguson and Golding, 1997; Garnham, 1997; Kellner, 1997a; Murdock, 1997; Thomas, 1997).

In addition, I would argue that critical social theory is necessary to adequately develop cultural studies. Earlier models in the Frankfurt School and British cultural studies made the relationship between culture and society the center of their analysis, utilizing the methods of social theory and more literary and cultural analysis to contextualize the production, distribution and consumption of culture and to critically analyse cultural texts. As British cultural studies developed, it brought more and more theories into its purview, but as its project became globalized and absorbed into a multiplicity of disciplines the connection with social theory has often been attenuated. In some of the ludic, postmodern forms of cultural studies, context, text and the constraints of everyday life disappear in descriptions of the diverse pleasures of consumers or the surfaces of texts. Thus, the relationship between cultural studies and social theory is itself complex, shifting and variable.

In this context, I would propose that cultural studies utilize critical social theory to develop a multiperspectivist approach which includes investigation of a broad expanse of artifacts, interrogating relationships within the three dimensions of: (1) the production and political economy of culture; (2) textual analysis and critique of its artifacts; and (3) study of audience reception and the uses of media/cultural products.[7] This proposal involves suggesting, first, that cultural studies itself be multiperspectivist, getting at culture from the optics of political economy and production, text analysis and audience reception.[8] I would also propose that textual analysis and audience reception studies utilize a multiplicity of perspectives, or critical methods, when engaging in textual analysis, and in delineating the multiplicity or subject positions, or perspectives, through which audiences appropriate culture. Moreover, the results of such studies need to be interpreted and contextualized within critical social theory to adequately delineate their meanings and effects.

One can obviously not deploy the full range of methods and perspectives noted above in each distinctive project that one undertakes and the substance of particular projects will determine which perspectives are most productive. But one should none the less see the dimensions of political economy, textual analysis and audience research as complementing each other rather than as constituting separate domains. I am not, therefore, making the impossible suggestion that one adopt this comprehensive multiperspectivist approach every time that one sets out to do cultural studies or a piece of sociological cultural research. Obviously, intensely focusing on political economy, on audience reception, or on close textual reading and criticism alone can be very valuable and yield important insights. But exclusively and constantly highlighting one of these dimensions to the omitting of others can be destructive for a sociology of culture or cultural studies that aims at developing comprehensive and inclusive approaches to culture and society, which interrogates culture in all of its dimensions.

A critical cultural studies would also pursue certain pedagogical, ethical and political ends. While the early development of British cultural studies was closely connected to adult education and pedagogy, later cultural studies became more academic and disciplinary. In recent years, however, there has been a call to return cultural studies to articulation with a critical pedagogy, a project that I endorse (see Giroux, 1992; Grossberg, 1997b; Kellner, 1995). Since media culture itself is a potent form of pedagogy, cultural studies should develop a counter-pedagogy that teaches audiences how to read cultural texts, how to critically decode and produce oppositional readings, and to understand the effectivity of cultural texts in socialization, the construction of identity and the reproduction of social relations.

I would also argue that critical pedagogy involves what Paolo Freire (1972, 1998) calls reading the world through reading the text, so that gaining critical literacy, the ability to read the word, involves at the same time learning to read the world through the word and text. This injunction is parallel to a basic tenet of critical cultural studies that operates with a dialectic of text and context, situating and reading texts through their social contexts and better understanding context through critical reading of texts. From this perspective, gaining critical media literacy involves learning to read texts through the world and the world through texts. Hence, just as politics is a form of pedagogy, a critical pedagogy is a form of politics, teaching individuals how to situate their forms of culture and their everyday lives in the context of the social and political system in which they live.

Developing critical media literacy also requires creation of a postmodern pedagogy that takes seriously image, spectacle and narrative, and thus promotes visual and media literacy, the ability to read and analyse critically images, stories and spectacles of media culture. Yet a postmodern pedagogy is concerned to develop multiple literacies, to rethink literacy itself in relation to new technologies and new cultural forms, and to develop a cultural studies that encompasses a wide array of fields, texts and practices, extending from popular music to poetry and painting to cyberspace and multimedia like CD-ROMs (see Hammer and Kellner, 1999; Kellner, 1999).

The particular pedagogy employed, however, should be contextual, depending on the concrete situation, interests and problems within the specific site in which cultural studies is taught or carried out. For it will be the distinctive interests of the teachers, students or critics that will help determine what precise artifacts are engaged, what methods will be used and what pedagogy will be deployed. Just as a cultural studies research problem and text is necessarily contextual, so too must be its pedagogy and its politics.

A critical pedagogy also dissects the norms, values, role models and negative and positive representations in cultural artifacts. Rather than focusing on ethics *per se*, British cultural studies and its later variants tend to engage the politics of representation. Employing Gramsci's model of hegemony and counter-hegemony, cultural studies attempts to specify forces of domination and resistance in order to aid the process of political struggle and emancipation from oppression and domination. Their politics of representation thus entailed a critique of cultural representations that promoted racism, sexism, classism, or any forms of oppression.

Representations that promoted domination and oppression were thus negatively valorized, while those that promoted egalitarianism, social justice and emancipation were positively valorized.

In this optic, ethics tends to be subordinated to politics and the moral dimension of culture tends to be underemphasized or downplayed. Thus, one could argue for a cultural studies that more explicitly stresses the importance of ethical analysis, scrutinizing cultural texts for the distinctive ethical norms, ideals and values portrayed and evaluating the work accordingly. Or one could explore in more detail and depth than is usually done in cultural studies the moral and philosophical dimensions of cultural texts, the ways that they carry out moral critiques of society and culture, or embody ethical concerns regarding good and evil, and construct models of moral and immoral behavior or phenomena.

Yet ethical concerns permeated cultural studies from the beginning (see Hoggart, 1957; Williams, 1958). Culture is, among other things, a major transmitter and generator of values and a cultural studies sensitive to the very nature and function of culture should be aware of its ethical dimension. Thus, concern with ethics, with the moral aspects of cultural texts, should be a central and fundamental consideration of cultural studies, as it was with non-formalist literary studies. While it is unlikely that the texts of media culture have the ethical depth and complexity of great literary texts, it is clear that ethical issues are of fundamental importance to the sort of popular cultural artifacts that have been the domain of cultural studies (for proposals for developing the themes of ethics, aesthetics and conceptions of distinction and taste in cultural studies, see McGuigan, 1997a; Mepham, 1991; Stevenson, 1997; Tester, 1994).

But cultural studies has also sought to articulate the thematics and effects of its artifacts with existing political struggles. There have been indeed a significant number of attempts to connect cultural studies with oppositional political movements and, more recently, with more pragmatic involvement in policy issues and debates (see Bennett, 1992, 1997; McGuigan, 1997a). There are thus a heterogeneity of political articulations of cultural studies and, as with its pedagogy, its politics will necessarily be conjunctural and contextual, depending on the particular site and moment of a certain form of cultural studies.

Such a transdisciplinary and political project involves a synthesis of the Frankfurt School, British cultural studies, postmodern theory and other critical approaches, combining empirical research, theory, critique and practice. A revitalized cultural studies would reject the distinction between high and low culture and would study a broad expanse of cultural artifacts. It would use the concept of an active audience and valorize resistance, but also explore manipulation and more passive reception. A political cultural studies would follow earlier trends of British cultural studies with detailed consideration of oppositional sub-cultures and alternatives to mainstream culture, but would also devise strategies of alternative media and an activist cultural politics. It would combine the Frankfurt School focus on political economy, on media manipulation and on the ways that culture reproduces domination, with scrutiny of the emancipatory potential of a wide range of cultural artifacts extending from modernism and the avant-garde to critical and subversive moments in media culture.

A critical sociology of culture and oppositional cultural studies would also draw upon feminist approaches and multicultural theories to fully analyse the functions of gender, class, race, ethnicity, nationality, sexual preference and so on which are so important in constituting cultural texts and their effects, as well as fundamentally constitutive of audiences who appropriate and use texts. British cultural studies progressively adopted a feminist dimension (see Gray, 1997; McRobbie, 1997) paid greater attention to race, ethnicity and nationality, and concentrated on sexuality, as various discourse of race, gender, sex, nationality and so on circulated in responses to social struggles and movements. Indeed, it is of crucial importance for a theoretically responsible cultural studies to continually appropriate the latest theoretical discourses and to modify its assumptions, program and discourses in response to critiques of its previous work, the emergence of new theories that can be used to strengthen one's future work, and new social movements which produce innovative critical political discourses. Both the Frankfurt School and British cultural studies continually modified their work in response to novel theoretical and historical developments and in a period of rapid social-historical change and the proliferation of ever-new theories, engagement with theory and history is of fundamental importance for all disciplines.

But a revitalized cultural studies would also productively engage postmodern theory. We are currently living in a proliferating image culture in which multimedia technologies are changing every dimension of life from the economy to personal identity. In a postmodern media and computer culture, fresh critical strategies are needed to read narratives, to interpret the conjunctions of sight and sound, words and images, that are producing novel cultural spaces, forms and experiences. This project also involves exploration of the emergent cyberspaces and

modes of identities, interaction and production that is taking place in the rapidly exploding computer culture, as well as exploring the new public spaces where myriad forms of political debate and struggle are evolving (Kellner, 1997c). Finally, a future-oriented sociology of culture should look closely at the development of the media and computer industries, the mergers and synergies taking place, and the syntheses of information and entertainment, computer and media culture, that are being planned and already implemented. A global media and cyberculture is our life-world and fate, and we need to be able to chart and map it accordingly to survive the dramatic changes currently taking place and the even more transformative novelties of the rapidly approaching future.

NOTES

1 For accounts of origins and genesis of British cultural studies, see Agger, 1992; Dworkin, 1997; Fiske, 1986; Grossberg, 1997a, 1997b; Hall, 1980b; Johnson, 1986/7; Kellner, 1995; McGuigan 1992; O'Connor, 1989; Turner, 1990. More polemical, alternative genealogies of cultural studies stress the broader historical antecedents, and include Davies (1995), who points to the origins of the problematic of British cultural studies in debates around the journals *University Review* and *New Left Review*. Steele (1997) wishes to go back and retrieve the roots of British cultural studies in an earlier adult education movement that he thinks provides important resources for cultural studies today that have been covered over in the narratives of the progressive appropriations of theory that characterize most genealogies of cultural studies. He argues that the long and heroic march of the 'theory express' of European Marxism and post-Marxism may have dumped 'an extremely ripe mound of manure on the seedling of British cultural studies, only to bury some of their more fragile shoots' (1997: 205). And Ang and Stratton (1996) argue that identification of cultural studies with the British model perpetuates an imperialist ideology that identifies all important cultural creation with the imperial power, relegating broader international developments in cultural studies to the margins. On earlier traditions of US cultural studies, see Ross, 1989 and Aronowitz, 1993. For readers that document the positions of British cultural studies, see the articles collected in Grossberg, Nelson and Triechler, 1992 and During, 1992/1998.

2 It might be pointed out that Walter Benjamin – loosely affiliated with the Frankfurt School, but not part of their inner circle – also took seriously media culture, saw its emancipatory potential, and posited the possibility of an active audience. For Benjamin (1969),

the decline of the aura – the sense of originality, uniqueness and authenticity – under the pressures of mechanical reproduction helped produce a public able to more actively and critically engage a wide range of cultural phenomena. He argued that, for instance, the spectators of sports events were discriminating judges of athletic activity, able to criticize and analyse plays, players, strategies and so on. Likewise, Benjamin postulated that the film audience as well can become experts of criticism and critically dissect the construction, meanings and ideologies of film.

3 'Textualism' was especially one-sided in English and North American versions of 'new criticism' and other literary practices which for some decades in the post-Second World War conjuncture defined the dominant approach to cultural artifacts. The British cultural studies focus on audience and reception, however, was anticipated by the Frankfurt School: Walter Benjamin focused on the importance of reception studies as early as the 1930s, while Adorno, Lowenthal and others in the Frankfurt School carried out analyses of audience reception in the same era. See the discussion in Kellner, 1989a: 121ff. On the turn to the audience within British cultural studies, see Ang, 1991 and 1996; Jensen and Pauly, 1997; Morley, 1997.

4 On the postmodern turn, see Best and Kellner, 1991, 1997, and forthcoming; on Jameson, see Kellner, 1989c; and on Baudrillard, see Kellner, 1989b, 1994.

5 See the critical review of the Gitlin book upon which I draw here in Best and Kellner, 1987.

6 Grossberg comments: 'I choose to use the term [postmodern] because it has already been used, and my argument is that we must win this sensibility back to a more progressive and optimistic articulation' (1997b: 289). Dick Hebdige explains in a similar fashion: 'I take, then, as my (possibly ingenuous) starting point, that the degree of semantic complexity and overload surrounding the term "postmodernism" at the moment signals that a significant number of people with conflicting interests and opinions feel that there is something sufficiently important at stake here to be worth struggling and arguing over' (1988: 182). Grossberg, Hebdige, Stuart Hall and others associated with the Birmingham projects thus propose linking the program of cultural studies to the project of promoting radical social and cultural change, to advance new solidarities and new struggles in the interests of progressive social transformation and are prepared accordingly to transform the project of cultural studies in the new terrain.

7 I set out this multi-perspectivist model in an earlier article and book on the Gulf War as a cultural and media event (Kellner, 1992a), and illustrate the approach in studies of the Vietnam War and its cultural texts, Hollywood film in the age of Reagan, MTV, TV entertainment like *Miami Vice*, advertising, Madonna, cyberpunk fiction and other topics in Kellner, 1995. Thus, I am here merely signaling the metatheory that I have worked out and illustrated elsewhere.

8 Curiously, Raymond Williams (1981) equates precisely this multiperspectivist approach in his textbook on the sociology of culture to a mainstream 'observational sociology' perspective, although I am suggesting more critical and theoretically informed strategies to engage production, textual analysis and audience reception, facilitated by the best work in cultural studies. Interestingly, Williams privileges an institution and production approach in his sociology of culture, whereas British and North American cultural studies have neglected these dimensions for increasing focus on audiences and reception.

REFERENCES

Agger, Ben (1992) *Cultural Studies.* London: Falmer Press.

Alfino, Mark, Caputo, John S. and Wynyard, Robin (eds) (1998) *McDonaldization Revisited: Critical Essay in Consumer Culture.* Wesport, CT: Praeger.

Ang, Ien (1991) *Desperately Seeking the Audience.* London and New York: Routledge.

Ang, Ien (1996) *Living Room Wars. Rethinking Audiences for a Postmodern World.* London and New York: Routledge.

Ang, Ien and Stratton, J. (1996) 'Asianing Australia; Notes Towards a Critical Transnational in Cultural Studies', *Cultural Studies*, 10 (1).

Aronowitz, Stanley (1993) *Roll Over Beethoven.* Hanover, NH: University Press of New England.

Aufderheide, Pat (1986) 'Music Videos. The Look of the Sound', in Gitlin 1986, op. cit.: 111–35.

Baudrillard, Jean (1983a) *Simulations.* New York: Semiotext(e).

Baudrillard, Jean (1983b) *In the Shadow of the Silent Majorities.* New York: Semiotext(e).

Baudrillard, Jean (1993) *Symbolic Exchange and Death.* London: Sage.

Benjamin, Walter (1969) *Illuminations.* New York: Shocken Books.

Bennett, Tony (1992) 'Putting the Policy into Cultural Studies', in L. Grossberg, C. Nelson and P. Treichler (eds), *Cultural Studies.* New York: Routledge.

Bennett, Tony (1997) 'Towards a Pragmatics for Cultural Studies', in Jim McGuigan (ed.), *Cultural Methodologies.* London: Sage. pp. 42–61.

Best, Steven and Kellner, Douglas (1987) '(Re)Watching Television: Notes Toward a Political Criticism', *Diacritics*, (Summer): 97–113.

Best, Steven and Kellner, Douglas (1991) *Postmodern Theory: Critical Interrogations.* London and New York: Macmillan and Guilford Press.

Best, Steven and Kellner, Douglas (1997) *The Postmodern Turn.* New York: Guilford Press.

Best, Steven and Kellner, Douglas (forthcoming) *The Postmodern Adventure.* New York: Guilford Press.

Blundell, Valda, Shepherd, John and Taylor, Ian (eds)

(1993) *Relocating Cultural Studies*. New York: Routledge.

Bronner, Stephen and Kellner, Douglas (eds) (1983) *Passion and Rebellion: The Expressionist Heritage*. New York: Universe Books and Bergin Publishers; London: Croom Helm (2nd edn, New York: Columbia University Press, 1988).

Bronner, Stephen and Kellner, Douglas (eds) (1989) *Critical Theory and Society. A Reader*. New York: Routledge.

Bürger, Peter ([1974] 1984) *Theory of the Avant-Garde*. Minneapolis: University of Minnesota Press.

Corner, John (1991) 'Studying Culture: Reflections and Assessment. An Interview with Richard Hoggart', *Media, Culture, and Society*, 13: 171–92.

Davies, Ioan (1995) *Cultural Studies, and After*. London and New York: Routledge.

du Gay, Paul, Hall, Stuart and Janes, Linda et al. (1997) *Doing Cultural Studies. The Making of the Sony Walkman*. London: Sage.

During, Simon (ed.) (1992) *The Cultural Studies Reader*. London and New York: Routledge (2nd edn, 1998).

Dworkin, Dennis (ed.) (1997) *Cultural Marxism in Postwar Britain: History, the New Left, and the Origins of Cultural Studies*. Durham, NC: Duke University Press.

Ferguson, Marjorie and Golding, Peter (1997) *Cultural Studies in Question*. London: Sage.

Fiske, John (1986) 'British Cultural Studies and Television', in R.C. Allen (ed.), *Channels of Discourse*. Chapel Hill, NC: University of North Carolina Press. pp. 254–89.

Fiske, John (1989a) *Reading the Popular*. Boston, MA: Unwin Hyman.

Fiske, John (1989b) *Understanding Popular Culture*. Boston, MA: Unwin Hyman.

Fiske, John (1993) *Power Plays. Power Works*. New York and London: Verso.

Foster, Hal (1983) *The Anti-Aesthetic*. Washington: Bay Press.

Freire, Paulo (1972) *Pedagogy of the Oppressed*. New York: Herder and Herder.

Freire, Paulo (1998) *The Paulo Freire Reader*. New York: Continuum.

Garcia Canclini, Nestor (1995) *Hybrid Cultures: Strategies for Entering and Leaving Modernity*. Minneapolis: University of Minnesota Press.

Garnham, Nicholas (1997) 'Political Economy and the Practice of Cultural Studies', in M. Ferguson and P. Golding (eds), *Cultural Studies in Question*. London: Sage. pp. 56–73.

Giroux, Henry (1992) *Border Crossings. Cultural Workers and the Politics of Education*. New York: Routledge.

Giroux, Henry (1994) *Disturbing Pleasures. Learning Popular Culture*. London and New York: Routledge.

Gitlin, Todd (ed.) (1996) *Watching Television*. New York: Pantheon.

Gitlin, Todd (1997) 'The Anti-political Populism of Cultural Studies', in M. Ferguson and P. Golding (eds), *Cultural Studies in Question*. London: Sage. pp. 25–38.

Goldman, Robert and Papson, Stephen (1998) *Nike Culture*. London and Thousand Oaks, CA: Sage.

Gottdiener, Mark (1997) *The Theming of America*. Boulder, CO: Westview Press.

Gramsci, Antonio (1971) *Selections from the Prison Notebooks*. New York: International Publishers.

Gramsci, Antonio (1992) *Prison Notebooks*, Volume 1. New York: Columbia University Press.

Grossberg, Lawrence (1997a) *Bringing It All Back Home. Essays on Cultural Studies*. Durham, NC and London: Duke University Press.

Grossberg, Lawrence (1997b) *Dancing in Spite of Myself. Essays on Popular Culture*. Durham, NC and London: Duke University Press.

Grossberg, Lawrence, Nelson, Cary and Treichler, Paula (1992) *Cultural Studies*. New York: Routledge.

Hall, Stuart (1980a) 'Cultural Studies and the Centre: Some Problematics and Problems', in Centre for Contemporary Cultural Studies, *Culture, Media, Language*. London: Hutchinson. pp. 15–47.

Hall, Stuart (1980b) 'Encoding/Decoding', Centre for Contemporary Cultural Studies, *Culture, Media, Language*. London: Hutchinson. pp. 128–38.

Hall, Stuart (1991) Lecture on Globalization and Ethnicity. University of Minnesota, videotape.

Hammer, Rhonda and Douglas Kellner (1999) 'Multimedia Pedagogical Curriculum for the New Millennium', *Journal of Adolescent and Adult Literacy*, 42 (7) (April): 522–6;

Harvey, David (1989) *The Condition of Postmodernity*. Oxford, UK and Cambridge, MA: Basic Blackwell.

Hebdige, Dick (1979) *Subculture. The Meaning of Style*. London: Methuen.

Hebdige, Dick (1988) *Hiding in the Light*. London and New York: Routledge.

Hoggart, Richard (1957) *The Uses of Literacy*. New York: Oxford University Press.

Jameson, Fredric (1981) *The Political Unconscious*. Ithaca, NY: Cornell University Press.

Jameson, Fredric (1991) *Postmodernism, or the Cultural Logic of Late Capitalism*. Durham, NC: Duke University Press.

Jameson, Fredric (1998) *The Cultural Turn*. London: Verso.

Jefferson, Tony (ed.) (1976) *Resistance through Rituals*. London: Hutchinson.

Jensen, Joli and Pauly, John J. (1997) 'Imagining the Audience: Losses and Gains in Cultural Studies', in M. Ferguson and P. Golding (eds), *Cultural Studies in Question*. London: Sage. pp. 155–69.

Jessop, Bob, Bonnett, Kevin, Bromley, Simon and Ling, Tom (1984) 'Authoritarian Populism, Two Nations, and Thatcherism', *New Left Review*, 147: 22–45.

Johnson, Richard (1986/87) 'What is Cultural Studies Anyway?', *Social Text*, 16: 38–80.

Kellner, Douglas (1989a) *Critical Theory, Marxism,*

and Modernity. Cambridge and Baltimore, MD: Polity and Johns Hopkins University Press.

Kellner, Douglas (1989b) *Jean Baudrillard: From Marxism to Postmodernism and Beyond.* Cambridge and Palo Alto, CA: Polity and Stanford University Press.

Kellner, Douglas (ed.) (1989c) *Postmodernism/Jameson/Critique.* Washington, DC: Maisonneuve Press.

Kellner, Douglas (1991) 'Reading Images Critically: Toward a Postmodern Pedagogy', in *Postmodernism, Feminism and Cultural Politics* (ed. Henry Giroux and Peter McLaren). Albany, NY: SUNY Press. pp. 60–82.

Kellner, Douglas (ed.) (1994) *Jean Baudrillard. A Critical Reader.* Oxford: Blackwell.

Kellner, Douglas (1995) *Media Culture. Cultural Studies, Identity, and Politics Between the Modern and the Postmodern.* London and New York: Routledge.

Kellner, Douglas (1997a) 'Overcoming the Divide: Cultural Studies and Political Economy', in M. Ferguson and P. Golding (eds), *Cultural Studies in Question.* pp. 102–19.

Kellner, Douglas (1997b) 'Critical Theory and British Cultural Studies: The Missed Articulation', in Jim McGuigan (ed.), *Cultural Methodologies.* London: Sage. 12–41.

Kellner, Douglas (1997c) 'Intellectuals, the New Public Spheres, and Technopolitics', *New Political Science*, 41–42: 169–88.

Kroker, Arthur and Cook, David (1986) *The Postmodern Scene.* New York: St Martin's Press.

McGuigan, Jim (1992) *Cultural Populism.* London and New York: Routledge.

McGuigan, Jim (1997a) 'Cultural Populism Revisited', in M. Ferguson and P. Golding (eds), *Cultural Studies in Question.* London: Sage. pp. 138–54.

McGuigan, Jim (ed.) (1997b) *Cultural Methodologies.* London: Sage.

McRobbie, Angela (1997) 'The Es and the Anti-Es: New Questions for Feminism and Cultural Studies', in M. Ferguson and P. Golding (eds), *Cultural Studies in Question.* London: Sage. pp. 170–86.

Mepham, John (1991) 'Television Fiction – Quality and Truth-Telling', *Radical Philosophy*, 57 (Spring): 20–7.

Morley, David (1992) *Television, Audiences, and Cultural Studies.* New York and London: Routledge.

Morley, David (1997) 'Theoretical Orthodoxies: Textualism, Constructivism and the "New Ethnography" in Cultural Studies', in M. Ferguson and P. Golding (eds), *Cultural Studies in Question.* London: Sage. pp. 121–37.

Murdock, Graham (1989) 'Cultural Studies at the Crossroads', *Australian Journal of Communication*, 16: 54–77.

Murdock, Graham (1997) 'Base Notes: The Conditions of Cultural Practice', in M. Ferguson and P. Golding (eds), *Cultural Studies in Question.* London: Sage. pp. 86–101.

O'Connor, Alan (1989) 'The Problem of American Cultural Studies', *Critical Studies in Mass Communication*, December: 405–13.

Ricoeur, Paul (1970) *Freud and Philosophy. An Essay on Interpretation.* New Haven: Yale University Press.

Ritzer, George (1993) *The McDonaldization of Society.* Thousand Oaks, CA: Pine Forge Press (rev. edn. 1996).

Ritzer, George (1999) *Encharging a Disenchanted World: Revolutionizing the Means of Consumption.* Thousand Oaks, CA: Pine Forge Press.

Ross, Andrew (1989) *No Respect. Intellectuals and Popular Culture.* London and New York: Routledge.

Smart, Barry (ed.) (1999) *Resisting McDonaldization.* London: Sage.

Steele, Tom (1997) *The Emergence of Cultural Studies 1945–65: Adult Education, Cultural Politics and the English Question.* London: Lawrence and Wishart.

Stevenson, Nick (1997) 'Towards a Pragmatics for Cultural Studies', in Jim McGuigan (ed.), *Cultural Methodologies.* London: Sage. pp. 62–86.

Tester, Keith (1994) *Media, Culture and Morality.* New York and London: Routledge.

Thomas, Sari (1997) 'Dominance and Ideology in Cultural Studies' in M. Ferguson and P. Golding (eds), *Cultural Studies in Question.* London: Sage. pp. 74–85.

Thompson, E.P. (1963) *The Making of the English Working Class.* New York: Pantheon.

Turner, Graeme (1990) *British Cultural Studies: An Introduction.* New York: Unwin Hyman.

Williams, Raymond (1958) *Culture and Society.* New York: Columbia University Press.

Williams, Raymond (1961) *The Long Revolution.* London: Chatto and Windus.

Williams, Raymond (1981) *Communications.* London: Penguin.

31

Theories of Consumption

GEORGE RITZER, DOUGLAS GOODMAN AND WENDY WIEDENHOFT

No serious theory of contemporary society can ignore the importance of consumption. For proof of its significance, we need look no further than the Internet, which has become emblematic of modern society. Although the Internet was originally developed for the scientific/military/industrial complex, its role in production has been eclipsed by its role in consumption. It has been estimated that consumers spent $38–$40 billion on the Internet in 1999 and companies devoted to consumption are the darlings of high-tech investors (Ivey, 1999). The boom in computer- and Internet-related industries played a key role in the unprecedented boom in the American economy and stock market (and those of many other developed nations), which enjoyed breathtaking gains in 1999. This, in turn, fueled a consumer revolution in the United States and other nations; an orgy of consumption unsurpassed in world history. The form and future of the Internet, or of modern society as a whole, cannot be grasped without understanding the forces of consumption that drive it.

However, the significance of consumption seems to have eluded the view of most social theorists (especially those in the United States), who remain wedded to the idea that production in its traditional sense remains the single most fundamental human activity.[1] Nevertheless, there are finally signs of growing theoretical and empirical interest in the study of consumption.[2] This work on consumption has now progressed far enough so that we can offer an overview of its development. We can even suggest an approach that integrates these theoretical developments into the beginnings of a theory of consumption that will be so necessary to understanding what is likely to transpire in the twenty-first century.

This chapter is divided into two parts. In the first section, we look at the historical development of theories about consumption. Because of social theorists' productivist bias, consumption has been greatly undertheorized, especially by the classical theorists. Further undermining the utility of classical theories is the fact that when consumption was addressed, theorists generally operated with a negative predilection. In spite of this, there are still useful ideas about consumption to be derived from the classical theories, and their reinterpretation has provided the beginning of some of the most important approaches to consumption. In some cases, the negative view of consumption has been replaced by a similarly one-sided celebration.

In the second section, we suggest that there is a need for more balanced theorizing of consumption that addresses both its positive and negative aspects. In addition, more balanced theories of consumption need to deal with a wider range of issues including consumers, the objects consumed, sites of consumption and the processes of consumption.

FROM CLASSICAL CRITICISM TO POSTMODERN CELEBRATION

Given the fact that they wrote mainly during the peak of the Industrial Revolution, it is little wonder that the classical theorists devoted most of their attention to the systems of production that were its most obvious feature. Accompanying the change in the mode of production was a large-scale social disruption leading ultimately to the subversion of the traditional way of life that had been based on agricultural production. Capitalism came to dominate the economy. Stable bureaucracies with predictable rules were established. Customary rights and obligations were replaced by rights revolving around private property. There were mass migrations to newly forming urban centers. New social classes emerged as serfs were transformed into wage laborers. And, as Marx ([1848] 1948) said, all that was solid melted into air.

As the old order based on traditions was replaced by economic individualism, there was a growing concern with how social order could be maintained. In response, a new view of social order emerged, most persuasively advocated by Adam Smith (1910), which tied it to production. The 'invisible hand' of the market economy created social order through the individual's production practices. What appeared to be a threat to social order – the individual engaged in production for his own self-interests – promoted, according to Smith (1910: 423), social order 'more effectively than when he really intends to promote it'.[3]

If production contributed to the new social order, consumption appeared to many social thinkers of the day to threaten this order.[4] For example, Weber ([1904] 1958) saw consumption as a threat to the capitalist Protestant ethics. Durkheim (1964) identified consumption with the society-threatening *anomie* that could be remedied by the functional interrelations of the divisions of labor found in production. Rosalind Williams (1982: 271) reports that almost all the social philosophers writing about the rise of mass consumption in late nineteenth-century France saw consumption as primarily an individual phenomenon that threatened social order. Even those who saw the potential for consumer solidarity, such as Charles Gide and Gabriel Tarde, noted the corrosive effect of the inherent individualism of consumption (Rosalind Williams, 1982: chs 7, 8).

Even today, it is common to view consumption as a threat to social order. The consumer's pursuit of choice, pleasure and individual expression encourages individualistic and pluralistic values that are often seen as inimical to the collective norms of society. Consequently, the vast majority of classical, and much contemporary, social theory has either ignored or condemned consumption. However, even in classical works dominated by a concern for production, there were important insights into the nature of consumption and, as we will see, some of the best current theory began by expanding upon the suggestions of the classical theorists.

Marx and the neo-Marxists

Certainly, the heart of Marx's approach lies in production. There is no need to discuss in any detail Marx's productivist concerns, but they include his view that labor and the production of objects (objectification) is central to species being, the labor theory of value, the ideological belief that capital has productive power, his criticisms of the division of labor in capitalism, and so on. Most generally, the focus of Marx's analysis was the capitalist system of production and the fact that it was inherently an exploitative and alienating system.

It was in the *Grundrisse* that Marx ([1857–58] 1973: 83–94) discussed consumption directly and in any detail. Most of that discussion is concerned with establishing a threefold, dialectical relationship between consumption and production. First, consumption is always production and production is always consumption. That is, in producing objects, material and human energies are always consumed; while in consuming objects, some aspect of the consumer is produced. In a statement that could be the hallmark of contemporary studies in consumption, Marx ([1857–58] 1973: 91) writes that every kind of consumption 'in one way or another produces human beings in some particular aspect'.

Second, production and consumption are mutually interdependent. Production creates the necessary object for consumption and consumption creates the motivation for production. Although they are dependent upon one another, Marx ([1857–58] 1973: 93) points out – in agreement with current notions of the autonomy of consumption – that consumption and production remain 'external to one another'.

Finally, in completing themselves, production and consumption create each other. Production is completed through consumption which creates the need for further production. Conversely, consumption is only created as a material reality through production because the need that impels consumption only becomes concrete in relation to particular objects that have been produced. However, after having shown the complex relationship between consumption and production, Marx ([1857–58] 1973: 94) closes the section by declaring, without real argument, that 'production is the real point of departure and hence also the predominant moment'.

However, while Marx was certainly preoccupied with production, he has had more influence on later theorizing about consumption than any other classical theorist. His influence is clearest in the widespread use of his concepts of commodity and commodity fetishism. Marx argued that commodities are much more than economists would have us believe. Commodities are not neutral objects that take on values from their market relations with other objects (or with money which abstractly represents other objects). The market relation between objects obscures the true value of the commodity which is derived from human labor. The capitalist market system makes the relation between objects appear to be more powerful and real than the actual relations between people. Just as Marx believed that certain tribal religions carved fetishes that represented Gods and then worshipped them as though they were more important and real than the people who made them, so we create commodities and markets and believe that they control our lives.

However, even when he discusses a concept like commodities, Marx is far more interested in how it relates to production than consumption. It is the capitalist mode of production that divorces human labor from the objects that human labor produces and results in exploitation, alienation and reification. Marx did not elaborate on how this process affects the sphere of consumption.

Marx operated with a framework that distinguished between true use values and the false characteristics of fetishized and alienated objects. This framework and distinction has defined the Marxist approach where the consumption of something that is functionally defined as useful is legitimated as a necessity, while all other consumption is associated with luxuries and seen as decadent. For example, in his criticism of commodity aesthetics, W.F. Haug (1986: 54) decries the strategy of promoting aesthetics over use value as 'a highly effective strategy because it is attuned to the yearnings, and desires, of the people'. The actual yearnings and desires of individuals are denounced in the name of a theoretically derived use value. The old morally laden dichotomy between luxury and necessity reappears here as aesthetics and use value. As Douglas Kellner (1989: 37) points out, 'commodities have various uses, some defined by the system of political economy and some created by consumers or users'. To label some uses as the true use values and to see others as decadent requires, at the very least, a theoretical defence that Haug never provides. Reducing fashion to an attempt to package humans as if they were commodities (Haug, 1986: 72), robs clothing of a legitimate social dimension. If Haug looks good in his Maoist uniform, that is no reason to condemn the rest of us as decadent.

There are other theoretical problems with the Marxist approach to consumption. The strictly Marxian concept of exploitation is closely tied to the production of surplus value and it is difficult to locate the source of surplus value and therefore exploitation in the realm of consumption.

Neo-Marxist ideas of control (Braverman, 1974) seem to be extended more easily from workers to consumers. The revolution in advertising in the 1920s was based on the fact that capitalists had begun to realize that they could no longer leave consumers alone to make their own decisions (Ewen, 1976). Consumers, like workers, can be seen as controlled by capitalists with the objective of increasing the profits capitalists reap from their enterprises. Even here, there are theoretical difficulties. The line between persuasion and control is much more difficult to define in consumption than in production. Strategies to influence consumers must recognize a freedom of choice that has few analogies on the shop floor. Also, as in the other condemnations of consumption, the concept of control requires an explanation for the apparent pleasure of consumers, not only from consumption itself, but the pleasure that is found even in the very advertisements that seek to control consumers.

The critical theorists, in many ways, continued the Marxist critique that saw consumption primarily as an opportunity for greater control and manipulation. Their most famous contribution to this perspective is found in their discussion of the 'culture industry' (Horkheimer and Adorno, [1944] 1972). If art and music were once thought to be 'pure' and 'authentic' objects of culture, we have come to recognize that not only these objects, but culture itself, has been commodified and reduced to the value of exchange. Thus, the cultural sphere has come to be dominated by the same instrumental rationality that dominates industrial production.

Horkheimer and Adorno describe the culture industry as organized around the Fordist model of mass production. Fordism led not only to homogeneous consumer goods but also to the standardization and commodification of prefabricated cultural products. Consumer goods and the mass culture that accompanies it can be seen from this viewpoint as a means of reproducing social order as well as class relations. As Marcuse (1964: 9) states, 'the people recognize themselves in their commodities – social control is anchored in the new needs which it has produced'. We all watch the latest sit-com, drink bottled water and wear running shoes. In mass culture, this is the basis of our equality. And, of course, we can all change the channels or change our brands. This is the basis of our freedom. Cable TV and superstores mean more choices among consumer goods, that is, more freedom. When this is what 'equality' and 'freedom' mean, there is no reason to rebel against the culture industry much less to overthrow capitalism.

Traditional forms of culture, from high art to family organizations, retreat before the onslaught of a mass-produced, ersatz commodity culture. Without these traditions, the individual is left impoverished and defenceless against the unmediated power of the capitalist economy. Personal identity is no longer formed through the internalization of the family structure nor is it expanded and disrupted through encounters with the utopian art projects. In the commodity culture, identity is derived from the commodity itself – you are what you purchase – and art no longer expands and disrupts, instead it soothes and distracts. The realm of consumption supplies an illusion of freedom and pleasure in exchange for the alienation necessary for capitalist production.

However, and in anticipation of more recent theoretical developments discussed below, the critical theorists recognized the novel character of consumption and they, more than any other neo-Marxists, attempted to explicitly account for the consumer's experience of pleasure. Critical theorists, especially Marcuse (1955, 1964), were able to free themselves of the underlying assumption of many studies of consumption, that pleasure itself is morally suspect. In an interesting reversal, Marcuse diagnosed the problem of consumer society as not enough pleasure. Consumer culture in contemporary capitalism is not a place of an unbridled hedonism, but of rationalized, bureaucratically controlled pleasures. The repetitive, superficial pleasures of contemporary society distract us from the possibility for unalienated pleasure which would require a restructuring of society. It was certainly this theme that attracted the student revolutionaries of the 1960s. The promise of greater pleasure brought the United States closer to a revolution than any promise of fulfilling 'authentic' needs ever had. It is likely that this revolution failed because Marcuse's promise of greater pleasure appeared less realistic than the pleasures promised by advertising and already found in consumption. While the latter forestalled a revolution in the United States, it could be argued that those same forces led to the demise of the Soviet Union.

Weber and a neo-Weberian approach

Weber (whose ideas were a second powerful input into critical theory) similarly focused on issues relating to production – especially rationalization in general, and bureaucratization in particular. While Weber did not do it, it is possible to relate his concepts to consumption. First, the much-emphasized asceticism of Calvinism and its role in the rise of capitalism involves a focus on the importance of an ethic that is *opposed* to consumption. Second, his inclusion of status groups based on lifestyles as a form of stratification is easily applied to consumption. Third, Weber's thinking on bureaucracy is certainly relevant since so much of consumption is shaped by, and takes place in, bureaucratized structures. Finally, and ultimately most important, his theory of rationalization (which encompasses his thinking on bureaucratization) has come to be seen as applicable to many aspects of consumption, especially the settings in which consumption takes place.

Ritzer (1993, 1996, 1998, 2000) has developed the concept of 'McDonaldization' as a contemporary variant of Weber's notion of (formal) rationalization (relatedly, see Bryman, 1999 on 'Disneyization'). This term obviously indicates a shift from a focus on bureaucracies to the fast-food restaurant as the paradigm for the process of rationalization. This, of course, moves us out of the realm of production (and the state and its bureaucracy) and into the realm of consumption. Contemporary sites of consumption have been McDonaldized. That is, they have come to be characterized by an emphasis on efficiency, calculability, predictability and control. More generally, we can say that vast areas of contemporary consumption are likely to be defined by these characteristics. While Ritzer acknowledges the positive aspects of McDonaldization, his greatest interest is in the irrationalities of these rational systems. Thus, he can be seen as continuing, at least in part, the classical propensity to be critical of consumption.

Simmel

While there are many critical thrusts in Georg Simmel's thinking on consumption, it is best to think of him as ambivalent about consumption, as he was about most aspects of modernity (Levine, 1985; and see Birgitta Nedelmann's contribution to this volume). Take, for example, his analysis of the role of money in modernity. A money economy forces us to be more dependent upon people who are increasingly distant from us. On the other hand, 'we are compensated for the great quantity of our dependencies by the indifference towards the respective persons and by our liberty to change them at will' (Simmel, [1907] 1978: 298). Furthermore, consumers develop a cynical and blasé attitude because of the reduction of all human values to money terms. But these very characteristics allow for the development of individuality and the freedom to 'unfold the core of our being with all its individual desires and feeling' (Simmel, [1907] 1978: 298).

This same ambivalence is found in the 'tragedy of culture'. Simmel argues that there is a growing gap between, on the one hand, the objective culture of material and immaterial human productions that are available to people and, on the other hand, those cultural objects that people actually are able to use for self-development. On the favorable side, we have more products than ever before, but the tragedy is that objective culture grows exponentially while our capacity to understand, use and control those objects – what Simmel calls subjective culture – increases only minimally. As a result, people grow increasingly distant from their products and unable to control or even understand them. Individuals are overwhelmed by the 'vast supplies of products . . . which call forth an artificial demand that is senseless from the perspective of the subject's culture' (Simmel, [1907] 1978: 43). There is certainly a similarity between the tragedy of culture and Marx's concept of commodity fetishism. However, Simmel's point, in contradiction to Marx, is that the growth and even reification of objective culture is also a good thing providing individuals with more opportunities for the expression of freedom and individuality.

Simmel's conception of the tragedy of culture is productivist in the sense that through their subjective culture people produce the bewildering array of objects that becomes objective culture and that comes to be beyond their control and even to exercise control over them. Nevertheless, the concept of the tragedy of culture is of great relevance to a sociology of consumption where the growth of commodities overwhelms our ability to use them and calls forth a diffuse and senseless desire for more. Instead of using this enormous array of commodities, we often seem to be used by them.

Veblen

While the study of consumption was secondary in the work of many of the classical theorists, it played a significant part in the work of Thorstein Veblen and it is in his book *The Theory of the Leisure Class* ([1899] 1994), that a sociology of consumption has its real beginnings. Although production was a primary concern in most of Veblen's writing, the *Theory of the Leisure Class* is known for its historical model of a change from conspicuous leisure (waste of time) to conspicuous consumption (waste of money). Veblen focused on people's need to make invidious social distinctions through the display of consumer objects. The upper class uses ostentatious consumption to distinguish itself from those situated below it in the social hierarchy, while the lower classes attempt (and usually fail) to emulate those who rank above them. The drive to emulate initiates a 'trickle

down' effect in which the upper class sets the tone for all consumption that takes place below it. However, once the lower classes successfully imitate the status objects of the upper class, the latter abandons the objects and selects new objects that, once more, distinguish it from those below.

While Veblen may be celebrated as one of the founders of a sociology of consumption, his productivist bias should not be ignored. We certainly see in his work the moral condemnation that has long characterized the sociological view of consumption. Veblen was critical of the consumption practices of the leisure class because of the value he placed on workmanship and production. Veblen viewed conspicuous consumption as wasteful and unproductive – thus, contributing little to society as a whole. However, his work also represents an important shift away from analysing commodities and towards understanding their meanings. Rather than focusing exclusively on commodities, Veblen theorized that class (and status) were important 'objects' of consumption. Thus, in consuming objects we are, in fact, consuming various class-linked meanings.

Although there is some ambivalence among classical theorists (and their followers), in the main they adopted a negative view of consumption. That view tends to ignore or explain away the pleasurable experiences of the consumer. There are several reasons why this is ultimately an unsatisfactory theoretical position. First, while the sociology of consumption should not pretend to an amoral positivism, it would be better to make consumption the object of moral investigations rather than of moral assumptions. Second, since consumption constitutes such a central, necessary and, for many, pleasurable process in everyday life, the moral tone of sociologists may come across as the ranting of elitist intellectuals about the 'vulgar' practices of the common people. Finally, standing up to the ineffectual moral condemnations of experts and intellectuals may be one of the factors that makes unbridled consumption so much fun. In response to the moral denouncements of consumption by many early social theorists, a new image of the consumer has emerged. Rather than being condemnatory, some theorists have attempted to redeem and even celebrate consumption.

Rewriting the classical tradition

Although there are still a number of approaches that view consumption negatively (among more recent examples are Frank, 1999; Schor, 1991, 1999), some contemporary theorists have attempted to redeem consumption through a re-interpretation of the sociological classics. For example, Colin Campbell (1987) seeks to correct Weber's productivist bias through a historical analysis of hedonism's role in the birth of modern capitalism. Campbell argues that Weber did not take his historical analysis of the spirit of capitalism far enough. Later developments revealed that, in addition to a rationalistic Calvinism, the Protestant movement also contained a Pietism that focused on an emotional hedonism. The latter led to a 'romantic ethic' that extolled the virtues of passion, subjective experience and imagination, which in turn supported a consumer culture that was as necessary to modern capitalism as any work ethic. Therefore the Weberian thesis that a Protestant ethic of frugality and self-denial is at the heart of capitalist development is one-sided. The development of modern capitalism required changes in both production and consumption. Early rational Calvinism contributed to the development of the productive side of modern Western capitalism while later Pietistic Calvinism contributed to the development of the consumption side.

Another example of a positive re-working of a classical critique can be found in Daniel Miller's (1987) *Material Culture and Mass Consumption.* Here Miller picks up on Simmel's theme of the tragedy of culture attempting to examine the impact of the increase in the production of material goods in modern society. Miller (1987: 1) is concerned foremost with the way in which 'our culture has become to an increasing degree a material culture based on an object form'. Tracing the concept of objectification from Hegel to Marx to Simmel, Miller develops a theory of objectification that cuts through the subject–object dualism of these classical theorists. Miller's non-dualistic model of objectification stresses the way subjects–objects, society–culture are mutually constitutive. Thus, he sees material objects of mass consumption as necessary in the construction of society. Miller is extremely critical of reducing consumption to the commodity form, as do both economists and Marxists. Instead of creating alienation or fetishism, consumption creates conditions where objects are 'so firmly integrated in the development of social relations and group identity as to be as clearly generative of society' (1987: 204). Miller views consumption in a positive light, 'as the continual struggle to appropriate goods and services made in alienating circumstances and transform them into inalienable culture' (1987: 193). Mass consumption has laid a new kind of foundation for a process of democratization that can be extended to the realm of politics and knowledge.

However, the most influential reworking of a classical perspective has been the reinterpretations and critiques of Veblen's approach. Even though he focused too narrowly on the message of class, the fact that Veblen recognized the ability of consumer objects to function as signs that convey social meanings has been enormously influential. The *Theory of the Leisure Class* seems to us now to describe a very circumscribed period which has long since been surpassed by a fashion system better understood by its subtlety of taste (Bourdieu, 1984) than by its overt waste. Both the 'trickle down theory' of consumer objects and the premise that emulation is the force steering modern consumption have come under criticism. A number of theorists (Blumberg, 1974; Field, 1970; Sproles, 1981) have pointed to the elite consumer objects, fashions, or styles that have originated from classes below it. Blues jeans, Doc Martens shoes, Harley Davidison motorcycles and jazz music are all objects of consumption that have 'trickled up' from marginal social groups.

Herbert Blumer (1969) argued that Veblen's focus on class was too narrow to encompass the truly dynamic diffusion of consumer objects. Several contemporary social theorists (Baudrillard, [1970] 1998; [1973] 1993; Davis, 1992; Lipovetsky, [1987] 1994) have found that consumer objects, especially fashion, symbolize more than simply social class. Indeed, Featherstone (1991: 83) claims that 'we are moving towards a society without fixed status groups in which the adoption of styles of life (manifest in choice of clothes, leisure activities, consumer goods, bodily dispositions) which are fixed to specific groups have been surpassed'.

Celebrating consumption

The extensions and criticisms of Veblen along with new semiotic, post-structural and postmodern approaches opened the way for a more approving view of consumption and consumers. For example, Michel de Certeau (1984: 34) views consumers as 'unrecognized producers, poets of their own affairs, trailblazers in the jungles of functionalist rationality'. He argues that consumption represents the possibility of the subversion of capitalism, at least temporarily and locally. De Certeau focuses on the practices of everyday life, especially as they relate to consumption. His key point is that consumers are not simply controlled by marketing manipulations as Marxists, neo-Marxists and others would have us believe. Consumers are themselves active manipulators. Instead of meekly using consumer goods and services as intended, consumers use them in unique ways that suit their own needs and interests. Consumers engage in a kind of guerrilla warfare with capitalists by appropriating objects and transforming, twisting or undermining their dominant meanings. Consumption allows even the weakest members of society a space for resistance, although they are rarely allowed to threaten the system as a whole.

> In reality, a rationalized, expansionist, centralized, spectacular and clamorous production is confronted by an entirely different kind of production called 'consumption' and characterized by its ruses, its fragmentation (the result of circumstances), its poaching, its clandestine nature, its tireless but quiet activity, in short by its quasi-invisibility, since it shows itself not in its own products, but in an art of using those imposed on it. (de Certeau, 1984: 31)

Following a similar course is the work of Raymond Williams (1982), Paul Willis (1978), Dick Hebdige (1979), Richard Hoggart (1961), Stuart Hall (1996) and their associates at Birmingham University. They brought together structuralist and Gramscian Marxisms, cultural materialism and semiotics to focus on a concept of culture as irreducibly polysemic and tied to the conflicting and shifting meanings of everyday life. The Birmingham School studied the representations of class, gender and race in cultural texts, including radio, television, film, popular fiction and other forms of popular culture. They were among the first to focus on the way that oppositional subcultures consume these cultural products. Of most interest here was their analysis of the ways that different subcultures create their own style and identity out of consumer objects. For example, even something as mundane as mass-produced safety pins (Clark, 1976) or as class identified as Edwardian suits (Jefferson, 1976) could be taken up by skinheads and Teddy Boys respectively to signify non-conformity and rebellion.

Gilles Lipovetsky goes even further than de Certeau and the Birmingham School. For Lipovetsky, consumption and fashion (Simmel had also made an important contribution to our understanding of this issue) do not simply afford the opportunity for often futile resistance, instead they are the realms of individuality itself. Unlike many postmodernists, Lipovetsky sees individuality as a long-term and mostly positive trend in Western culture. Consumption, especially of fashion, is a reflection of this trend toward individuality, rather than any social hierarchy. Fashion is defined by its relatively unbridled pursuit of novelty, fantasy and subjective expression. And this freedom 'inevitably accompanies the promotion of secular individualism and the end of the immutable preregulated universe of traditional forms of appearance' (Lipovetsky, [1987] 1994: 27–8).

According to Lipovetsky, this frivolous play of fashion has prepared people for our present democratic form of government. The more that fashion dominates the personal realm, 'the more stable, profoundly unified, and reconciled with their pluralist principles the democracies become' (Lipovetsky, [1987] 1994: 7). And fashion can continue to have beneficial political effects in the post-industrial society. 'An age that functions in terms of information, the seductive power of novelty, tolerance, and mobility of opinions is preparing us, if only we can take advantage of its strong points, for the challenges of the future' (Lipovetsky, [1987] 1994: 8).

Perhaps the most extreme perspective in this context is that consumers are replacing workers as the group best able to threaten capitalism and its system of consumption. Consumers are celebrated as the group best able to deal with problems associated with consumerism; they are seen as being capable of much more than the kind of 'guerilla warfare' discussed by de Certeau. In other words, it is possible to think in terms of 'dangerous consumers' (Ritzer, 1999b). Part of the reason that this group can be dangerous is that, following Bauman (1997), they simply do not consume enough. Any drag on the ever-escalating level of consumption poses a threat to those who profit from a robust economy driven by consumerism.

However, the threats posed by the 'dangerous consumer' go beyond merely not consuming enough; dangerous consumers consume the wrong things. For example, because they lack adequate resources, such people consume a variety of public and welfare services that are a drain on the economy. Because they lack the resources but share the goals of a consumer society, they are more likely to engage in criminal activities and thereby to 'consume' the services of the police, the courts and the prisons. Further, when they consume in a more conventional sense, they are more likely to consume the 'wrong' commodities. They tend to consume the 'wrong' drugs, for example, crack instead of powder cocaine. Thus, dangerous consumers are so designated because *both* what they do, and what they do not, consume pose a threat to consumer society.

The broader implication is that those who consume too little (including Schor's (1999) 'downshifters' and 'simple livers') can come together with those who consume the wrong things to overthrow consumer capitalism. However, it is important to recognize that even those who threaten consumer society are themselves consumers. No one is able to escape the imperatives of the consumer society, even those who are seen as threatening it. The fact that they are consumers, and mainly aspire to be bigger and better consumers of conventional goods and services, indicates that ultimately 'dangerous' consumers pose no real threat to consumer society. This complements Bauman's (1997) argument that because consumption is inherently individualizing, it is far less likely to produce a revolutionary class than production which is a collective enterprise and thereby apt to produce collective opposition in the form of a revolutionary social class. At most, dangerous consumers will corrode consumer society, they are unlikely to overthrow it.

FOUR TOPICS IN THEORIZING CONSUMPTION

The celebrations of the consumer as a champion of democracy and as a subversive revolutionary against capitalism were necessary correctives to the pessimism of earlier social theorists. However, most contemporary studies of consumption (Bourdieu, 1984; Campbell, 1987; Featherstone, 1991; Miller, 1987, 1998; Slater, 1997) have tried to steer a middle course that reconciles the more pessimistic classical heritage with a recognition of the fact that consumption is not only indispensable in modernity, but also a domain in which people can express themselves positively.

These newer theories of consumption have not only balanced negatives and positives, but they have also dealt with a wider range of topics. Implicit in much of the current literature is a fourfold distinction among topics – subject, object, setting and process – which should prove useful in theorizing consumption. While they are usually discussed in isolation from one another, it is clear that none makes sense without the others. They are really inseparable components of a single, tightly integrated process. While it is unlikely that we will have one integrated theory of consumption, that should not dissuade us from theorizing connections among these elements. Individual thinkers may want to focus on one element, even on sub-dimensions of that element. Or the focus could be on the relationship between two or three of the elements. But whatever the particular choice, the theorist must always bear in mind that any specific focus is part of a broader whole.

Objects of consumption

Before social theorists reflected on the individual behavior of consumers or the sites where, and processes through which, consumption occurs, most were primarily concerned with the objects of consumption. Early economists, such as Adam Smith, approached the study of objects of consumption with the concept of the commodity. It was Marx, however, who opened up the commodity to sociological analysis by revealing its social dimension. The commodity has both a material character that is able to satisfy human need and a social character through which the exploitative relations between people are expressed as relations between objects.

For both Smith and Marx, the commodity was seen primarily as part of the productive process. The important step that Veblen took was to place the commodity within the circuits of consumption. This opened up the object of consumption to a semiotic approach that looked at the object of consumption primarily as a locus of social meaning.

Semiotics has been an especially useful tool for analysing consumer objects as signs (Fiske, 1989; Gottdiener, 1995). When consumer objects are studied as signs, it appears that the object itself does not have intrinsic properties that make it meaningful, since the same objects can carry diverse and even contradictory social messages. According to semiotics, the meaning of the object is its difference from the meanings of other objects and is therefore derived from the system of objects as a whole.

Jean Baudrillard writes in *The System of Objects* ([1968] 1996: 200) that 'to become an object of consumption, an object must first become a sign'. Thus, to understand consumption, we need to be able to read consumer goods as a series of signs – similar to a language – that requires interpretation. Consumer goods constitute a system of codes that work together so that no particular object can be understood in isolation from the system. But Baudrillard makes it clear that the sign here refers primarily to the flow of difference in the system itself. This would mean, for example, that Veblen's conspicuous consumption only signifies high or low class as a secondary effect. The primary effect of consumption is simply difference and precisely what that difference is can be added later and changed when necessary. Baudrillard tells us that an object becomes an object of consumption when it is no longer determined by any of the following: (1) its place in the production cycle; (2) its functional use; or (3) its symbolic meaning. It is then that it is 'liberated as a sign to be captured by the formal logic of fashion' (Baudrillard, 1981: 67).

In the present-day context, objects of consumption do, in fact, seem to be increasingly autonomous from the conditions of their production, their functional use and their symbolic meaning. More kinds of objects are entering the whirl of fashion. Sex is exemplary of this. Sex can hardly be said to be defined in our society by the ability to produce or, indeed, reproduce (socially or biologically). Even this most central and necessary 'production' is now merely secondary to sex. Similarly, its social functions – for example, binding together the nuclear family – have waned. Furthermore, the symbolic meaning of sex, upon which the entire Freudian edifice is based, seems to be in flux. Sex has entered fashion as part of the system of consumer objects. Everything is sexualized even as sex no longer really means anything in particular. Sex in the system of consumption promises meaning, just as advertised meanings promise sex, but both function merely as lures whose effect is to entice more objects into the fashion system.

Taken to an extreme, consumer goods are seen entirely as signifiers that are completely divorced from any stable signified. If consumer goods are viewed as nothing more than signifiers, then these objects become freed from their signified component, thus emancipated from their obligation to designate (Baudrillard, 1983). One consequence of this emancipation is the reign of the spectacle, or what Debord ([1967] 1994: 15) describes as the 'monopolization of the realm of appearances'. From this perspective, the surface appearance of consumer objects matters much more than any deeper use value or exchange value that may be hidden.

However, Douglas and Isherwood ([1979] 1996: 49) argue that the semiotic approach must go beyond the idea that consumer objects are messages: 'consumption goods are most definitely not mere messages; they constitute the very system itself . . . In being offered, accepted, or refused, they either reinforce or undermine existing boundaries. The goods are both the hardware and the software, so to speak, of an information system whose principal concern is to monitor its own performance.'

Grant McCracken (1990) contends that the metaphor of consumption as the manipulation of signs is more useful for the difference that is revealed between it and language than for their similarity. The materiality of consumer objects makes them both less flexible for communicating idiosyncratic meanings and more stable for passing on culturally central categories such as gender and class distinctions. One difference is that the communication system of language is comprised of rules that allow for novel combinations that, nevertheless, are able to communicate relatively precise meanings. McCracken argues that with consumer objects, there are no rules that allow novel combinations to communicate a meaning. For example, 'the interpreter of clothing examines an outfit not for a new message but for an old one fixed by convention' (McCracken, 1990: 66).

A second difference is that in language, a novel combination is not really reducible to the meaning of the individual elements, the words. Understanding in language must include a holistic approach. With consumer objects, however, novel combinations are usually reducible to a mixture of the meaning of individual objects (a yuppie car, a preppie jacket, intellectual's glasses, etc.) whose overall meaning is, at best, an inventive disdain for communicating through objects and more usually interpreted simply as bad taste. Finally, a novel combination in language is able to communicate an unambiguous meaning that fits its novel context. In consumption, unambiguous meanings that fit the context can only come from the pre-fabricated meanings established by convention. Novel combinations don't really fit any particular context and their meaning is indeterminate and mutable.

Therefore, the system of consumer objects that semiotics sees as relational differences and that Baudrillard sees as the whirl of fashion is better seen, according to McCracken (1990: 119), as a patterned relationship between consumer goods that he calls 'Diderot unity' which takes into account meaning, fashion and the materiality of consumer objects. Consumer goods work in harmony to create a consistent, meaningful whole. Buying a new pair of shoes creates a disharmony with an outfit that is old; thus, one must buy a new skirt, a new blouse and a new purse so all consumer objects can be unified.

The semiotic approach has provided important insights, but it is limited because it tends to neglect the material characteristics of the object of consumption. On the one hand, objects of consumption are the locus for powerful and diverse meanings that are open to both repressive manipulation and individual appropriation (Appadurai, 1986; Baudrillard, [1968] 1996; Douglas and Isherwood, [1979] 1996). On the other hand, objects of consumption deplete limited material resources; their use has environmental effects; they satisfy material human needs; and their materiality limits and modifies their use as signs (Cross, 1997). Although it is often useful to focus on one aspect or the other, the dual nature of objects of consumption as both social sign and material object cannot be forgotten.

Subjects of consumption

Gabriel and Lang (1995) have shown that there is a wide range of types of consumers: victim, chooser, communicator, explorer, identity-seeker, hedonist, artist, rebel, activist, or citizen. This list is far from complete, but it does succeed in communicating the fact that there is great diversity among consumers.

From the standpoint of a system of objects, the individual, the subject of consumption, would be, at most, the necessary environment of the system and may often be reduced to merely an effect of the system of objects. Such an approach leads easily, if not inevitably, to the view of the consumer as a 'judgemental dope' (Garfinkel, 1967) who is manipulated by those who control the system of objects. It is likely, however, that the derivative status of the subject in analyses of consumption is attributable to little more than the theoretical preferences of certain analysts. The purely subjective experiences of the consumer – emotions, fantasies, hedonistic delights and private sensory experiences – seem, if anything, to be intensifying as a lived reality in consumer culture.

A purely object-centered approach, however, has never dominated the sociological approach to consumption and the reasons for this are not entirely scientific. What is most striking about the sociology of consumption is its unabashedly moral tone. Both the left and the right wings of sociology have collaborated to marginalize consumption (Miller, 1995: 2) and this often takes the tone of a moral condemnation of the hedonism that consumption is taken to incarnate.

Any discussion of morality, however, requires a conception of a subject who can be morally responsible. Therefore, those sociological theories that describe the progressive dominance of commodities are usually accompanied by a description of the subject's progressive enslavement. Even if one sees the subject as a dupe, manipulated and enslaved by the commodity system, this only becomes a moral issue if the subject is, at heart, something other than a dupe, so that a system of consumption that treats him or her as a dupe is evil. Colin Campbell describes the pervasive moral dimension of sociology's approach to the consumer:

> This view sometimes places the blame on individuals for engaging in such practices, while at other times it exonerates them by arguing that consumers are typically coerced or manipulated into this form of behavior by others (usually manufacturers or advertisers). In either case, however, consumerism itself is judged to be bad, whether the source of the evil lies in individuals or in the organization of the society. (Campbell, 1998: 152)

Campbell (1998: 139) concludes that 'the tendency to denigrate consumerism derives from the widespread acceptance of sociological theories that represent consumers as prompted by such reprehensible motives as greed, pride, or envy. These theories are largely unsubstantiated and fail to address the distinctive features of modern consumption . . .'

Due to this moralizing tone, the sociology of consumption has, as we have seen, tended to vacillate between the condemnation of consumption and its celebration. In terms of the subject of consumption, she/he is seen either as a judgemental dope or a revolutionary hero.

Although he provides an enormously useful perspective for studying the consumer, we see the same moral tone in the work of Pierre Bourdieu. Bourdieu's own reaction to modern consumers tends toward a mixture of the 'intellectual doxa' of moral condemnation and his own attacks on that aspect of the current intellectual doxa that glorifies populism (Bourdieu, 1993: 268). Nevertheless, a critique of his propensity to economic reductionism and a development of his analysis of the artistic and scientific sphere can provide a powerful approach to the consumer.

It is around the twin concepts of habitus and field that Bourdieu's ideas can make the greatest contribution. Habitus is a system of enduring, primarily embodied, structuring structures created in response to objective conditions and acquired through socialization. Habitus are those mostly unconscious schemata that structure the way in which we acquire other cognitive structures. They reflect and tend to reproduce current social relations but have enough flexibility to be transposable to new relations. The most important feature of habitus is not that it controls the actor, but that it can be transcended through reflexivity. Without this, we would have just a clever reformulation of economic determinism. Since habitus exerts its strongest influence through deep, unconscious structures, reflexivity is able to escape its determinations. We can never be completely free of our habitus, but we can be free enough to interrupt the reproduction of class structures.

A field is a grouping in which each element in the group is subjectively defined in terms of its relations and oppositions to other elements. Any given field is, to varying degrees, autonomous from other social structures. For Bourdieu, autonomy develops on two levels: the subjective level of sociological reflexivity, discussed above; and the objective level of institutions that establish their own separate hierarchies of success. A field is analysed as an arena of conflict, struggle and competition for scarce resources and symbolic recognition related to the specific type of capital that governs success in the field. Although the definition of success in the field and, consequently, what counts as valued capital is related to overarching structures, it is not reducible to them. The field must be analysed in terms of its own internal dynamic processes and structuring principles.

Bourdieu's twin concepts of habitus and field are meant to provide an analysis of culture that avoids, on the one hand, turning it into a 'transcendent sphere, capable of developing in accordance to its own laws' (Bourdieu, 1993: 33) and, on the other hand, reducing it to a mere reflection of the social (especially economic) order. This is a difficult balancing act and Bourdieu often leans toward the latter, especially in his analysis of the consumer. For example, creativity in consumption is analysed purely in terms of an economistic functionality. His focus is on how creativity is used to sell cultural products (Bourdieu, 1993, esp. ch. 1) and is never seen as a value in and of itself. For example, he never considers that the point of consumption may be the creative appropriation by the consumer of the cultural product.

In *Distinction* (1984) Bourdieu relates habitus to taste. If there is no disputing taste, it is, according to Bourdieu, because taste has its foundation in these deep, underlying structures. Through the concept of habitus, Bourdieu is able to relate the apparently voluntaristic micro-practices usually associated with taste to the macrostructures of capitalist classes. Most importantly, he does this without turning agents into dupes or seeing their subjective experience of freedom as illusory. Consumption can be seen, in this view, as conscious, strategic lifestyle choices made by the consumer against a backdrop of mostly unconscious tastes characteristic of a class habitus.

Bourdieu, however, never develops this approach to consumption, because he does not recognize an autonomous field in the sphere of consumption and there is no place in his scheme for consumer creativity. He has a tendency to view consumption as a reflection of the economic hierarchy and any subjective experience that contradicts that is seen as a type of false consciousness.

Featherstone (1991) has applied Bourdieu's ideas in a less moralistic way in order to develop a richer and more complex conception of the consumer. First, Featherstone recognizes the autonomy of the field of consumption. Secondly, Featherstone carves out a place for individual creativity by relying on Bourdieu's analysis of the *petit bourgeois* of cultural intermediaries who provide symbolic goods and services. Motivated by an embodied discomfort and lacking economic and cultural capital, this new *petit bourgeois* 'adopts a learning mode of life . . . consciously educating himself in the field of taste, style, lifestyle' (Featherstone, 1991: 91). Thus the consumer is able to appropriate creatively consumer objects rather than being controlled through them.

Rejecting a moralistic and reductionist approach allows us to look at the relation between the subjects and objects of consumption as a multidimensional process of self relatedness (Falk, 1994). This new approach assumes that consumption has the possibility of constructing a self as well as reflecting one.

Miller and Rose (1997) trace the changing approaches to the consumer in one influential marketing research center. Their study rules out an interpretation of marketing practices as either dominating or simply reflecting consumer's choices. Instead they see marketing techniques as 'mobilizing' the consumer by investigating and creating complex connections between the subject's psyche and the specific characteristics of consumer goods enmeshed in everyday consumption practices. In these studies, the consumer emerges as a highly problematic entity whose consumption activities are bound to an entire way of life. On the one hand, marketing cannot be understood as simply uncovering pre-existing desires, but, on the other hand, neither is it the implantation of manufactured needs. Instead, marketing helps to construct the consumer by assembling the rituals of everyday life and connecting them to a commodity in order to give it meaning.

The recognition of the complex, multidimensional relations between subjects and the objects they consume has led to a focus on what has been called lifestyle shopping (Shields, 1992). In mainstream marketing, lifestyle refers to a method of market segmentation. In this newer analysis, it refers to a set of individual experiences and social practices – especially consumption practices – with meaningful interrelations. Lifestyle *shopping*, then, refers to a series of experimentations with modes of subjectivity, interpersonal relations and social community. What is being consumed are not objects so much as lifestyles with accompanying objects. Consumption is envisioned as a field in which the intentions and objectives of individual actors are both sustained and transformed by experimental manipulations of the system of objects. This field cannot be reduced to either the predefined intentions of the participating subjects or to the structural organization of the objects because both are at stake in lifestyle shopping.

That consumption is now a key process in the construction of self-identity has been recognized by a number of theorists (for example, Featherstone, 1991; Giddens, 1991). Bauman (1988) analyses the effect that this has on our experience of freedom. Bauman notes that historically freedom has faced two problems: that actual freedom requires access to scarce resources; and that the desire for freedom (from others) is compromised by an equally strong desire for social interaction. Bauman argues that the experience of freedom associated with consumption bypasses these two problems. First, since the realm of modern consumption is concerned more with lifestyles than goods, scarcity is less of a problem because 'identities are not scarce goods' (1988: 63). Secondly, those involved in lifestyle shopping can experiment with forms of community which can be slipped in and out of without compromising their individual freedom.

Bauman does not claim that this freedom is complete or entirely good. Freedom through consumption extends to more people than any other form of freedom ever has, but it has the disadvantage of making those to whom it does not extend virtually invisible as a political problem. Because freedom through consumption is depoliticized, it makes it appear that non-freedom is an inescapable side effect of the market. Sociology's relative lack of attention to consumption is complicit with this. Since consumption is seen as frivolous and morally bankrupt, exclusion from the practices of freedom associated with it can hardly be taken as a serious problem.

Alan Warde (1994) points out a deficiency in Bauman's analysis and other celebrations of the consumer. There is little evidence that intrepid consumers boldly experimenting with radically different brands of cereal, identities, hairstyles and lifestyles actually exist in significant numbers. While this is true, Warde misses the larger theoretical point. The stability of the consumer along with the complexity and dimensionality of the relationship between the consumer and the objects of consumption are now an empirical question in need of investigation rather than a theoretical assumption. Sociologists can no longer build a theory of consumption by assuming either rational or identity-shopping or status-driven consumers. Undoubtedly, there are rational consumers comparing quantity and quality in order to satisfy their essential needs. There are, also, many whose identity is defined primarily by their work or community traditions rather than their consumption. Similarly, there are those who steadfastly consume in order to fulfill a never-changing passion, whether it be status or greed or psychosocial pathologies. But the point is that none of these can serve as the assumption from which a study of consumers can begin. The prevalence of any given type of consumer in a particular social setting requires investigation. The lack of lifestyle shoppers is just as much in need of explanation as is their presence. At least for a *theory* of consumption, the subject of consumption is highly complex, problematic and unstable. If in practice the consumer is simple, self-evident and stable, this now requires explanation.

Sites of consumption

While the analysis of objects and subjects of consumption has a rich history from which to draw new theories, the sites of consumption have been relatively neglected. That is not to say, however, that they have been totally ignored. Worth singling out in this domain is the work of a fellow traveler of the Critical School, Walter Benjamin (Buck-Morss, 1989). His concern for sites of consumption is illustrated by his interest in the Parisian arcades and the world exhibitions; he described the latter as 'sites of pilgrimages to the commodity fetish' (Benjamin, 1986: 151). While Marx and many of his early followers discussed the fetishism of commodities from the viewpoint of production and workers, Benjamin approached it from the other side – from consumption and consumers.

Central to Benjamin's approach to consumption was the role played by technological change. For example, gas lighting was first used in a site of consumption. Similar technological developments were affecting other aspects of Western culture, such as the arrival of the photograph and the threat it posed to painting. The fact that photographs, unlike paintings, could be reproduced again and again threatened the mystical 'aura' of genius and uniqueness that surrounded the artistic object, at the same time that it made possible a great expansion in commodity trade. The mass production of large numbers of often identical cultural products lured more consumers into the new sites of consumption.

Technological changes not only made the new sites of consumption (and the goods they proffered) possible, they also helped to make them more fantastic. Benjamin often uses the term 'phantasmagoria' to describe the developments in France in the 1800s, including the new consumption settings. Art was brought together with technology to produce increasingly fantastic settings, or dream worlds, that were oriented to entertaining and amusing the consumer in order to increase consumption. Merchandise was enthroned in these settings and wrapped in an aura of entertainment. Produced, in the process, was a 'phantasmagoria of capitalist culture' (Benjamin, 1986: 153). This is an early stage in the long-term trend toward merging amusement and consumption; indeed making them virtually indistinguishable from one another.

The emergence of the new sites of consumption was linked by Benjamin to another locale, the private living space, which for the first time had come to stand as distinct from the place of work. Here, dwellers sought to create fantasy spaces of their own – 'phantasmagorias of the interior' (Benjamin, 1986: 154). In order to do so, they were driven as consumers to the new sites of consumption in order to obtain what they needed to turn their living spaces into dream worlds, even if most lacked the resources to fully succeed in this.

The structures of concern to Benjamin (1986: 162), including the new sites of consumption, were viewed as 'monuments of the bourgeoisie' and from his perspective they are 'ruins even before they have crumbled'. Given the later history of consumer capitalism, and the explosive growth of such sites of consumption, they might better have been seen as the modest ancestors of the palaces of consumption that have supplanted, and far outdone, them.

Rosalind Williams' (1982) historical study of social theory and consumption can be seen as linking Benjamin's work with Emile Durkheim's concept of anomie. Like Benjamin, she stresses the role that these specific sites (world's fairs, department stores) played in creating and fueling consumer desire, as well as in the generation of the consumer society. Williams looks at Paris during the same period examined by Benjamin. She argues that it was during this period that the French pioneered the twin pillars of modern consumer life – advertising and retail consumption settings. While the north of England had been the site and symbol of the Industrial Revolution, it was Paris that emerged as the modern capital of consumption. It was here that we had the first 'planned environment of mass consumption' (Rosalind Williams, 1982: 12).

The world expositions and department stores (for example, Bon Marché) of the period were dream worlds designed to inflame consumers' interest in consumption, to entertain them and to provide settings and goods and services that could fulfill the needs of their imagination. They lured and seduced consumers with fantasies and, in that sense, functioned like the simultaneously developing movie industry. Both sought to market dreams, to offer a uniform experience based on powerful images and to induce passivity among consumers. The dream worlds offered hope and they made it accessible to the masses by offering large numbers of inexpensive imitations, as well as credit so that a lack of available resources would not stand in the way of consumption.

While Williams emphasized the romantic aspect of her dream worlds, the fact is that these settings were also bureaucratized and rationalized. This point is made by Michael Miller (1981). The early Bon Marché was a fusion of the emerging rationalized world with more traditional elements of French bourgeois culture; over the years it moved increasingly in the direction of becoming a rationalized, bureaucratized structure. That is, it encountered 'an incessant push towards greater efficiency' (Miller, 1981: 168). Among the rationalized elements of the store were its division into departments; its partitioning of Paris for the purposes of making deliveries; its files and statistics,

records and data; its telephone lines, sliding chutes, conveyor belts, and escalators; and its 'blanc', or great white sale, 'the most organized week of the store' (Miller, 1981: 71).

Taken together, the work of Williams and Miller indicate that the early French department store, like contemporary sites of consumption, was both enchanted and disenchanted (for more on this, see below). Perhaps the most general conclusion to be drawn from this discussion is that enchantment and disenchantment are not easily distinguished from one another; one does not necessarily preclude the other. There is a reciprocal relationship between them. Fantasies draw people into sites of consumption, and those fantasies can be rationalized in order to continue to draw people in and to reinforce their Weberian cage-like qualities. The cage quality of consumption sites can itself be a fantasy; the fantasy of being locked into one of those cages with ready access to all of its goods and services. As Colin Campbell (1987: 227) suggests, 'Modern individuals inhabit not just an "iron cage" of economic necessity, but a castle of romantic dreams, striving through their conduct to turn the one into the other.'

Ritzer (1999a) offers a more contemporary effort to balance traditional concerns with the consumer, consumer objects and the process of consumption, with more attention to the sites of consumption (see, also Gottdiener, 1997 on the 'theming' of these sites). John Urry (1995: 1) has referred to these sites as 'consuming places', or, 'centres for consumption . . . the context within which goods and services are compared, evaluated purchased and used'.[5] On the one hand, these sites are forced to rationalize and bureaucratize, especially if they seek to serve a large clientele and to operate in a number of different geographic settings. While this makes for effective operations, it has the tendency to be off-putting to consumers who may find the coldness and impersonality of these settings at variance with their desire to have them function as dream worlds. As a result, these rationalized settings are led into efforts to enchant, or re-enchant, themselves in order to attract and retain consumers. This is most often done by the creation of spectacles of various types (Debord, [1967] 1994). The spectacle of a mega-mall, a Las Vegas casino (Gottdiener et al., 1999), or Disney World (Bryman, 1995) serves to enchant these settings and to bring in large numbers of consumers.

However, the large numbers lead to an increased need to rationalize and bureaucratize the spectacle and the settings themselves. This, in turn, serves to alienate consumers and to lead to a new round of efforts to re-enchant these settings. This dialectic between rationalization and enchantment is seen by Ritzer within the context of the rise of what he calls 'cathedrals of consumption'. The idea of 'cathedrals of consumption' allows us to see these sites as enchanted settings that must always be careful to maintain enchantment as a way of continuing to lure large numbers of consumers. Much like religious cathedrals in the past, these sites of consumption have come to be the center of our lives, even if they cannot possibly fill the same spiritual role.

These are new versions of sites of consumption with a long history – county fairs, general stores, world's fairs, department stores and super-markets (Humphrey, 1998). Ritzer focuses on a wide range of new sites ('means') of consumption that came into existence in the United States in the decade, or two, after the end of the Second World War – enclosed shopping malls, mega-malls, discount malls, fast-food restaurants and other franchises and chains, superstores, cyber-malls, the home shopping TV network, cruise ships, Disney World, Las Vegas-style casino-hotels, and so on. As huge organizations attracting hordes of consumers, these settings are particularly prone to bureaucratization and rationalization. Yet, these must lure large numbers of consumers and they do so by offer-ing enchantment through a wide range of spectacles that dwarf those offered by earlier means of consumption.

While they have been described, at least in part, as dream worlds, the sites of consumption discussed thus far have been quite material – fast-food restaurants, department stores, cruise ships and the like. However, one of the most important trends is in the direction of the emergence of 'dematerialized' means of con-sumption (Ritzer, 1999c). Slater (1997: 193–5) has discussed dematerialization primarily in terms of consumer goods and the fact that more of them are non-material (that is, in the form of services), the idea that even material goods have more non-material elements (for example, advertising imagery, design and packa-ging elements), the fact that we are more likely to encounter goods in terms of representations of them, and the increasing relationship of such goods to non-material labor involving knowl-edge, science and so on. But just as consumer goods are increasingly dematerialized, so are the settings in which they can be obtained. Import-ant new non-material means of consumption are to be found on television in the form of home shopping networks, infomercials and the like. However, the big growth area in the future is likely to be in the non-material sites to be found on the Internet, including cybermalls, cyber-shops ('e-tailers') of all types (Amazon.com is a good example), on-line gambling, as well as on-line pornography. It is not likely that people will give up the joys of traveling to the more material means of consumption, but it is likely that more goods and services, especially of a non-material form, will be obtained through de-materialized means of consumption.

Of relevance here is Fredric Jameson's work on 'the cultural logic of late capitalism'. For example, the idea of 'late capitalism' (drawn from Mandel) involves the view that we have witnessed 'a prodigious expansion of capital into hitherto uncommodified areas' (Jameson, 1984: 78). Clearly, the expansion of the consumer society has commodified many things not here-tofore commodified and it has brought com-modification into more and more areas of the world as well as into more realms of everyday life.

This is in line with Ritzer's argument that many other settings are coming to emulate the new means of consumption. Included here would be baseball stadiums, universities, hospitals, museums and churches. Consumers, accustomed to the spectacles offered in mega-malls and casinos, are demanding the same kinds of things in other settings. In addition, the advent of home shopping television and cybermalls has brought commodification into the home to an unprece-dented degree.

Processes of consumption

Changes in the sites of consumption have produced complementary changes in the process of consumption. One of the most significant was related to the mid-nineteenth-century emergence of the department store. Before the dominance of the department store, shopping often meant entering a specialized small shop already having decided what to purchase and haggling over the price. As we all know, shopping now generally means something entirely different. Shopping can mean wandering through displays of objects, trying on goods (or trying on fantasies); it need not include an actual purchase. The practice of shopping encompasses experiences that exist at the periphery of consumption in the strictest sense. Shopping sites are full of those who would describe themselves as 'window shopping', but who leave empty-handed (Fried-berg, 1993).

One of the more interesting studies of the process of consumption is Daniel Miller's *A Theory of Shopping* (1998). His ethnography of the shopping experiences of consumers in North London reveals three stages to consumption. The first stage is a vision of the pure shopping experience which exists primarily at the level of discourse and not of practice. This is a vision of pure waste and excess usually referred to as 'real shopping' or 'power shopping'. In this vision, hedonistic consumers irresponsibly plunder the world and exhaust resources, collaborating with capitalism in their own and the earth's degradation. It is interesting to note the similarity between the mostly imaginary description of the pure shopping experience by Miller's subjects and what most sociologists think is the actual practice of consumption.

In stage two, Miller found that the actual practice of consumption was, in fact, a negation of the image of pure shopping. In their actual practices, consumers exercised the strategies and skills of thrift. Shopping, in practice, was usually described as an opportunity for saving money rather than spending it. Thrift was a central element of shopping even for those who had absolutely no need to practice it. Of course, there are elements of the hedonistic first stage in actual shopping. Many shopping trips include an expensive treat; some vacation shopping features excessive expenditures, as does special event shopping such as in courtship. But for the bulk of shopping, the strategies, skills and expertise are devoted to saving rather than spending.

In the third stage, the processes of consumption are connected to the real and ideal social relationships that make up the shopper's world. The typical and, especially at this stage, very gendered consumer, 'buys this particular brand or flavour, in relation to her sense of not only what the individual wants, but her reasoning as to what would improve that individual. In practice the two may be compromised in the form of what she can get that wretched object of love to actually eat!' (Miller, 1998: 108).

Miller (1998: 148) concludes that the primary 'purpose behind shopping is not so much to buy the things that people want, but to strive to be in a relationship with subjects that want these things'. Love and devotion play important roles in consumption for Miller (1998: 147), as he suggests that consumer objects can mediate our personal, even romantic, relationships with other people. Thus, the process of shopping helps to reproduce and maintain human relationships as well as the inequalities that they reflect.

The process of consumption has been transformed as a result of a variety of changes, including those in the other realms discussed in this section. For example, the development of cathedrals of consumption has greatly altered the process of consumption. Ritzer (1999a) has identified four such changes. First, instead of needing to go to many different settings, sites like shopping malls and mega-malls (as well as supermarkets and hypermarkets) have made for the possibility of 'one-stop shopping'. Second, many of the cathedrals of consumption (such as mega-malls, Disney World, cruise ships, Las Vegas and its hotel-casinos) have become 'destinations' in their own right and people go there as much to consume the sites as they do the goods and services offered by them. Third, instead of having employees do things for consumers, much of consumption now involves consumers doing many things for themselves, and for no pay. Examples include picking up our own groceries in the supermarket, serving as our own wait-persons in fast-food restaurants, pumping our own gasoline in contemporary filling stations, getting cash from ATMs and the like. Finally, the cathedrals of consumption have altered social relations so that consumers are more likely to interact with the sites and what they have to offer than they are with people who work in those sites or with fellow consumers.

Of course, the very newest means of consumption – home shopping television and e-commerce – are having an even more profound effect on the process of consumption. Obviously, an increasing amount of consumption is taking place in the home as the home is fast becoming a cathedral of consumption. Among other things, this is 'no-stop' shopping, consumers do even more tasks for no pay (for example, much of the work involved in ordering books from Amazon.com and even the writing of free on-line book reviews), and social relations are so altered that they become 'virtually' non-existent.

Changes in the 'facilitating means of consumption', for example, the introduction of the credit card, have also altered the process of consumption (Ritzer, 1995). The credit card frees practices of consumption from the need for planning and responsibility before the act of consumption. For example, consuming when on vacation no longer requires bringing large amounts of money or making sure that a site will accept an out-of-town check. One does not even need to have access to the amount of money necessary for the purchase. Planning and responsibility are shifted to the post-purchase period when the consumer must plan how to handle the 'easy monthly payments'. The process empties the moment of consumption of the need for responsibility and allows debt to multiply as full responsibility is perpetually postponed. This is especially likely to happen because credit card companies encourage minimum payments and target immature consumers such as students.

More analysis of the process of shopping is needed. There is obviously more involved than simply purchasing necessities. A focus on the processes of consumption reminds us that the everyday practice of consumption is strongly shaped by historical trends and socioeconomic forces. Consumption is clearly not the transparent ahistorical process that we tend to assume.

Conclusion

Even with the current upturn in interest, consumption remains a minor subject in social theory. Yet, as we have said before, that must and will change. Theorists cannot afford to continue to remain so far out of touch with the new realities of the socioeconomic world.

Consumption has arguably come to define contemporary American society. This makes it somewhat puzzling that European theorists have been much more active in developing theories of consumption than Americans. American sociology continues to be dominated by a productivist bias – as evidenced by such specialties as industrial sociology, sociology of work, organizational sociology, as well as the absence of a specialization in the sociology of consumption. Ironically, part of the reason for the concern of European theorists is American consumerism and its exportation to Europe and the rest of the world. American theorists may not be much interested in American consumerism, but others are acutely concerned about its implications for an emerging global culture. Thus, we have the paradox of a virtual absence of a sociology of consumption in a nation which is without doubt the world leader in consumption and is aggressively exporting its consumer goods and its means of consumption to much of the rest of the world.

That leads to the question: Why have social theorists (especially Americans) paid so little attention to consumption? Three factors suggest themselves. The first is the productivism that has historically dominated social theory. This was easily understandable during the nineteenth century and until the end of the Second World War. Throughout these years, one could defend the idea that production was predominant. But what about since 1945? How could social theory ignore or simplistically condemn the world-transforming changes in consumption over the past half century? While there has been an upturn in theorizing consumption, it has a long way to go to approximate the amount of theorizing on production. Productivism still lingers in social theory because the training of social theorists involves, in large part, reading the giants of the nineteenth century. And what they find when they read them is productivism. To break that habit, social theorists will need to learn to spend at least as much time gazing at the world around them as they do on the works of the predecessors. Perhaps more difficult, they will have to develop new tools and vocabularies that break with the production paradigm and are more appropriate to an analysis of consumption.

A second and related factor is that social theorists have the belief that serious theory deals with production while trivial theory deals with consumption. This is undoubtedly related to the gendered division of labor where men work and women shop. A sociologist is a serious thinker when studying the factory, but a dilettante when studying the shopping mall. This continues to this day, even though it is clear, at least in the United States and Western Europe, that the shopping mall has become an infinitely more important place than the factory and, more generally, consumption is of greater importance to more people than production.

Finally, theorists tend to think of their professional careers in terms of production rather than consumption. Status and salaries are related to what they write, not what they read. Furthermore, to recognize consumption is to acknowledge that their own contributions will be consumed in ways that they do not intend and cannot control. The meaning of any consumer product, including social theory, derives as much from the consumer as the producer. So long as theorists see themselves as producing social theory, can they ever accord consumption a central place?

The past three decades have brought forth some new theoretical (and empirical) work on consumption, but it nonetheless remains greatly subordinated to thinking on production. There is no question that given current social and economic trends, theorizing consumption will eventually exceed thinking on production, but not now and not soon. Social theory continues to be characterized by 'cultural lag' – our thinking continues to lag behind the changing social world.

Notes

1 Sociology is far from the only field to neglect consumption. This is also true of economics, and Calder (1999) documents a similar lack of interest in consumption in history.

2 This is reflected in the growing number of overviews of the field, including those by Corrigan (1997), Miles (1998) and Slater (1997).

3 In fact, Albert Hirschman (1977) has shown that Smith's vision of the contribution of production to social order was decidedly less optimistic than his immediate predecessors and contemporaries. The common view of social philosophers even before the 'triumph of capitalism' was that the new era of trade and industry would deliver humankind from the evils associated with the individualistic pursuit of passion.

4 Others simply ignored consumption, more or less. For example, Spencer (1908) welcomed the evolution to an industrial society which he believed tamed militancy and created a more harmonious and economically interdependent world through an increasing division of labor and the improvement in production technology. There is no analogous interest in his work in the evolution of consumption.

5 Urry also uses this term in three other senses. First, the settings themselves may be consumed, especially visually. Secondly, the sites can be literally consumed, that is used up and destroyed by consumers, over time. Thirdly, the settings can become so important to people that they become all-consuming, such as the shopping malls that some people simply cannot resist.

REFERENCES

Appadurai, Arjun (ed.) (1986) *The Social Life of Things*. Cambridge: Cambridge University Press.

Baudrillard, Jean ([1968] 1996) *The System of Objects*. London: Verso.

Baudrillard, Jean ([1970] 1998) *The Consumer Society: Myths and Structures*. London: Sage.

Baudrillard, Jean ([1973] 1993) *Symbolic Exchange and Death*. London: Sage.

Baudrillard, Jean (1981) *For a Critique of the Political Economy of the Sign*. St Louis, MO: Telos.

Baudrillard, Jean (1983) *Simulations*. New York: Semiotext(e).

Bauman, Zygmunt (1988) *Freedom*. Milton Keynes: Open University Press.

Bauman, Zygmunt (1997) *Postmodernity and Its Discontents*. New York: New York University Press.

Benjamin, Walter (1986) 'Paris, Capital of the Nineteenth Century', in *Reflections: Essays, Aphorisms, Autobiographical Writings*. New York: Schocken. pp. 146–62.

Blumberg, Paul (1974) 'The Decline and Fall of the Status Symbol', *Social Problems*, 21: 480–98.

Blumer, Herbert (1969) 'Fashion: From Class Differentiation to Collective Selection', *Sociological Quarterly*, 10: 275–91.

Bourdieu, Pierre (1984) *Distinction: A Social Critique of the Judgement of Taste*. Cambridge, MA: Harvard University Press.

Bourdieu, Pierre (1993) *The Field of Cultural Production: Essays on Art and Leisure*. New York: Columbia University Press.

Braverman, Harry (1974) *Labor and Monopoly Capital: The Degradation of Work in the Twentieth Century*. New York: Monthly Review Press.

Bryman, Alan (1995) *Disney and His Worlds*. London: Routledge.

Bryman, Alan (1999) 'The Disneyization of Society', *Sociological Review*, 47: 25–47.

Buck-Morss, Susan (1989) *The Dialects of Seeing: Walter Benjamin and the Arcades Project*. Cambridge, MA: The MIT Press.

Calder, Lendol (1999) *Financing the American Dream: A Cultural History of Consumer Credit*. Princeton, NJ: Princeton University Press.

Campbell, Colin (1987) *The Romantic Ethic and the Spirit of Modern Consumerism*. Oxford: Blackwell.

Campbell, Colin (1998) 'Consuming Goods and the Good of Consuming', in D. Crocker and T. Linden (eds), *Ethics of Consumption: The Good Life, Justice and Global Stewardship*. New York: Rowman and Littlefield. pp. 151–73.

Clark, John (1976) 'The Skinheads and the Magical Recovery of Community', in S. Hall and T. Jefferson (eds), *Resistance Through Rituals: Youth Subculture in Post-war Britain*. London: HarperCollins. pp. 99–102.

Corrigan, Peter (1997) *The Sociology of Consumption*. London: Sage.

Cross, Gary (1997) *Kid's Stuff: Toys and the Changing World of American Childhood*. Cambridge, MA: Harvard University Press.

Davis, Fred (1992) *Fashion, Culture, and Identity*. Chicago: University of Chicago Press.

Debord, Guy ([1967] 1994) *The Society of the Spectacle*. New York: Zone Books.

De Certeau, Michel (1984) *The Practice of Everyday Life*. Berkeley, CA: University of California Press.

Douglas, Mary and Isherwood, Baron ([1979] 1996) *The World of Goods*. London: Routledge.

Durkheim, Emile (1964) *The Division of Labor in Society*. New York: The Free Press.

Ewen, Stuart (1976) *Captains of Consciousness*. New York: McGraw-Hill.

Falk, Pasi (1994) *The Consuming Body*. London: Sage.

Featherstone, Mike (1991) *Consumer Culture and Postmodernism*. London: Sage.

Field, George (1970) 'The Status Float Phenomenon: The Upward Diffusion of Innovation', *Business Horizon*, 12: 45–52.

Fiske, John (1989) *Reading the Popular*. Boston, MA: Unwin Hyman.

Frank, Robert H. (1999) *Luxury Fever: Why Money Fails to Satisfy in an Era of Excess*. New York: The Free Press.

Friedberg, Anne (1993) *Window Shopping: Cinema and the Postmodern*. Berkeley, CA: University of California Press.

Gabriel, Yiannis and Lang, Tim (1995) *The Unmanageable Consumer: Contemporary Consumption and Its Fragmentation*. London: Sage.

Garfinkel, Harold (1967) *Studies in Ethnomethodology*. Englewood Cliffs, NJ: Prentice-Hall.

Giddens, Anthony (1991) *Modernity and Self-identity: Self and Society in the Late Modern Age*. Cambridge: Polity Press.

Gottdiener, Mark (1995) *Postmodern Semiotics: Material Culture and the Forms of Postmodern Life*. Oxford: Blackwell.

Gottdiener, Mark (1997) *The Theming of America: Dreams, Visions, and Commercial Spaces*. Boulder, CO: Westview Press.

Gottdiener, Mark, Collins, Claudia C. and Dickens, David R. (1999) *Las Vegas: The Social Production of an All-American City*. Oxford: Blackwell.

Hall, Stuart (1996) *Stuart Hall: Critical Dialogues in Cultural Studies* (eds David Morley and Kuan-Hsing Chen). New York: Routledge.

Haug, W.F. (1986) *Critique of Commodity Aesthetics: Appearance, Sexuality and Advertising*. Cambridge: Polity Press.

Hebdige, Dick (1979) *Subculture: The Meaning of Style*. London: Methuen.

Hirschman, Albert (1977) *The Passions and the Interests: Political Arguments for Capitalism Before Its Triumph*. Princeton, NJ: Princeton University Press.

Hoggart, Richard (1961) *The Uses of Literacy*. Boston, MA: Beacon Press.

Horkheimer, Max and Adorno, Theodor ([1944] 1972) *Dialectic of Enlightenment*. New York: Seabury.

Humphery, Kim (1998) *Shelf Life: Supermarkets and the Changing Cultures of Consumption*. Cambridge: Cambridge University Press.

Ivey, Catherine (1999) 'Survey Shows Online Sales Up Plenty', *Minneapolis St Paul Star Tribune*, December 30: A1.

Jameson, Fredric (1984) 'Postmodernism, or the Cultural Logic of Late Capitalism', *New Left Review*, 146: 53–92.

Jefferson, Tony (1976) 'Cultural Responses of the Teds: The Defence of Space and Status', in S. Hall and T. Jefferson (eds), *Resistance Through Rituals: Youth Subcultures in Post-war Britain*. London: Harper Collins. pp. 81–6.

Kellner, Douglas (1989) *Jean Baudrillard: From Marxism to Postmodernism and Beyond*. Stanford, CA: Stanford University Press.

Levine, Donald (1985) *The Flight from Ambiguity: Essays in Social and Cultural Theory*. Chicago: University of Chicago Press.

Lipovetsky, Gilles ([1987] 1994) *The Empire of Fashion*. Princeton, NJ: Princeton University Press.

Marcuse, Herbert (1955) *Eros and Civilization*. Boston, MA: Beacon Press.

Marcuse, Herbert (1964) *One Dimensional Man*. Boston, MA: Beacon Press.

Marx, Karl ([1857–58] 1973) *The Grundrisse: Foundations of the Critique of Political Economy*. New York: Random House.

McCracken, Grant (1990) *Culture and Consumption*. Bloomington, IN: University of Indiana Press.

Miles, Steven (1998) *Consumerism as a Way of Life*. London: Sage.

Miller, Daniel (1987) *Material Culture and Mass Consumption*. Oxford: Blackwell.

Miller, Daniel (ed.) (1995) *Acknowledging Consumption: A Review of New Studies*. London: Routledge.

Miller, Daniel (ed.) (1998) *A Theory of Shopping*. Ithaca, NY: Cornell University Press.

Miller, Michael B. (1981) *The Bon Marché: Bourgeois Culture and the Department Store, 1869–1920*. Princeton, NJ: Princeton University Press.

Miller, Peter and Rose, Nikolas (1997) 'Mobilizing the Consumer: Assembling the Subject of Consumption', *Theory, Culture & Society*, 14 (1): 1–36.

Ritzer, George (1993) *The McDonaldization of Society*. Thousand Oaks, CA: Pine Forge Press.

Ritzer, George (1995) *Expressing America: A Critique of the Global Credit Card Society*. Thousand Oaks, CA: Pine Forge Press.

Ritzer, George (1996) *The McDonaldization of Society*, rev. edn. Thousand Oaks, CA: Pine Forge Press.

Ritzer, George (1998) *The McDonaldization Thesis*. London: Sage.

Ritzer, George (1999a) *Enchanting a Disenchanted World: Revolutionizing the Means of Consumption*. Thousand Oaks, CA: Pine Forge Press.

Ritzer, George (1999b) 'Obscene from Any Angle: Fast Food, Credit Cards, Casinos and Consumers', Plenary address presented at the conference on 'Obscene Powers: Corruption, Coercion and Violence', John Hansard Gallery, University of Southampton, Southampton, England, December, 1999.

Ritzer, George (1999c) 'Ensnared in the E-Net: The Future Belongs to the Immaterial Means of Consumption', Plenary address presented at the conference: Sociality/Materiality: the Status of the Object in Social Science, Brunel University: Uxbridge, England, 9–11 September 1999.

Ritzer, George (2000) *The McDonaldization of Society: New Century Edition*. Thousand Oaks, CA: Pine Forge Press.

Schor, Juliet (1991) *The Overworked American: The Unexpected Decline of Leisure*. New York: Basic Books.

Schor, Juliet (1999) *The Overspent American*. New York: Harper Collins.

Shields, Rob (ed.) (1992) *Lifestyle Shopping: The Subject of Consumption*. London: Routledge.

Simmel, Georg ([1907] 1978) *The Philosophy of Money*. London: Routledge.

Slater, Don (1997) *Consumer Culture and Modernity*. Cambridge: Polity Press.

Smith, Adam (1910) *The Wealth of Nations*. Harmondsworth: Penguin Books.

Spencer, Herbert (1908) *The Principles of Sociology*, vol. 1. New York: Appleton.

Sproles, George B. (1981) 'Analyzing Fashion Life Cycles – Principles and Perspectives', *Journal of Marketing*, 45: 116–24.

Urry, John (1995) *Consuming Places*. London: Routledge.

Veblen, Thorstein ([1899] 1994) *The Theory of the Leisure Class*. New York: Penguin Books.

Warde, Alan (1994) 'Consumers, Identity and Belonging: Reflections on Some Theses of Zygmunt Bauman', in R. Keat, N. Whiteley and N. Abercrombie (eds), *The Authority of the Consumer*. London: Routledge. pp. 58–74.

Weber, Max ([1904] 1958) *The Protestant Ethic and the Spirit of Capitalism*. New York: Scribner's.

Williams, Raymond (1982) *The Sociology of Culture*. New York: Schocken Books.

Williams, Rosalind (1982) *Dream World: Mass Consumption in Late 19th Century France*. Berkeley, CA: University of California Press.

Willis, Paul (1978) *Profane Culture*. London: Routledge and Kegan Paul.

32

Sexualities: Social Theory and the Crisis of Identity

ANTHONY ELLIOTT

In the past few decades, sexuality has become a topic that is increasingly discussed and debated among social theorists. Indeed, sex and desire have become the focus of intense social-theoretical, philosophical and feminist fascination, and it is against this backcloth that social theorists have sought to rethink the constitution and reproduction of sexualities, bodies, pleasures, desires, impulses, sensations and affects. How to think sexuality beyond the constraints of culture is a question that is increasingly crucial to the possibilities of political radicalism today. The cultural prompting for this turn towards sexuality in social theory is not too difficult to discern. In the aftermath of the sexual revolution of the 1960s, and particularly because of the rise of feminism, sexuality has come to be treated as infusing broad-ranging changes taking place in personal and social life. The politics of identity, sexual diversity, postmodern feminism or post-feminism, gay and lesbian identities, the crisis of personal relationships and family life, AIDS, sexual ethics and the responsibilities of care, respect and love: these are core aspects of our contemporary sexual dilemmas.

This turn to sexuality in social theory, as I have said, is relatively recent. Social theorists, for many years, largely ignored sex. This neglect is perhaps less odd than it first appears, since the pleasures of the flesh were not considered a substantive or proper scientific matter for the social sciences – especially at a time when positivistic or naturalistic philosophies of natural science dominated the methods of the social sciences and humanities. There were, it is true, scattered texts – Wilhelm Reich's *The Function*

of the Orgasm (1961) or Norman O. Brown's *Love's Body* (1966). Yet it was only in the wake of social protests and movements in the 1960s and 1970s that sociologists and social theorists turned their attention to the analysis of sexuality in any detailed fashion.

In this chapter, I shall explore the central discourses of sexuality that dominate contemporary social theory and the social sciences. These approaches can be grouped under five broad headings – psychoanalytic, Foucauldian, feminist, sociological and queer theory. I make no claim in this analysis to discuss all the significant themes raised by these discourses or theories. Rather, I seek to portray the contributions of particular theorists in general terms, in order to suggest some central questions that the analysis of sexuality raises for social theory today.

FREUD AND PSYCHOANALYSIS

The founder of psychoanalysis, Sigmund Freud, initiated a trend in twentieth-century thought which attributed primary place to human sexuality in the organization of culture and society. The theory Freud developed views the mind as racked with conflicting desires and painful repressions; it is a model in which the self, or ego, wrestles with the sexual drives of the unconscious on the one hand, and the demands for restraint and denial arising from the superego on the other. Freud's account of the complex ways in which the individual is tormented by hidden sources of mental conflict provided a source of inspiration for the undoing of sexual repression in both personal and social life. In our therapeutic culture, constraints on, and denials of, sexuality have been (and, for many, still are) regarded as emotionally and socially harmful. The Freudian insight that personal identity is forged out of the psyche's encounter with particular experiences, especially those forgotten experiences of childhood, has in turn led to an increasing interest in the secret history of the self (see Elliott, 1998).

Many psychoanalytic critics working in the humanities and social sciences have sought to preserve the radical and critical edge of Freud's doctrines for analysing the discourse of subjectivity and desire (see Elliott, 1994, 1999). For these theorists, psychoanalysis enjoys a highly privileged position in respect to social critique because of its focus on fantasy and desire, on the 'inner nature' or representational aspects of human subjectivity – aspects not reducible to social, political and economic forces. Indeed, social theorists have been drawn to psychoanalytic theory to address a very broad range of issues, ranging from destructiveness (Erich Fromm) to desire (Jean-François Lyotard), communication distortions (Jürgen Habermas) to the rise of narcissistic culture (Christopher Lasch). It is perhaps in terms of sexuality, however, that Freud and psychoanalysis have most obviously contributed to (and some would also say hampered) social and cultural theory. Psychoanalysis has certainly been important as a theoretical resource for comprehending the centrality of specific configurations of desire and power at the level of 'identity politics', ranging from feminist and post-feminist identities to gay and lesbian politics. It is possible to identify three key approaches through which psychoanalytic thought has been connected to the study of sexuality in social theory:

1 as a form of social critique, providing the conceptual terms (repression, unconscious desire, the Oedipus complex and the like) by which society and politics are evaluated;
2 as a form of thought to be challenged, deconstructed and analysed, primarily in terms of its suspect gender, social and cultural assumptions;
3 as a form of thought that contains both insight and blindness, so that the tensions and paradoxes of psychoanalysis are brought to the fore.

While I cannot do justice here to the full range of psychoanalytic-inspired social theories of sexuality, I shall in what follows concentrate on the seminal contributions of Herbert Marcuse and Jacques Lacan.

Herbert Marcuse

A member of the Frankfurt School, Herbert Marcuse developed a radical political interpretation of Freud that had a significant impact upon those working in the social sciences and humanities, as well as student activists and sexual liberationists. Marcuse added a novel twist to Freud's theory of sexual repression, primarily because he insisted that the so-called sexual revolution of the 1960s did not seriously threaten the established social order, but was rather another form of power and domination. Instead of offering true liberation, the sexual revolution was defused by the advanced capitalist order, through its rechanneling of released desires and passions into alternative, more commercial outlets. The demand for individual and collective freedom was seduced and transfigured by the lure of advertising and glossy commodities, the upshot of which was a defensive and narcissistic adaptation to the wider world. This narcissistic veneer characterizing contemporary social relations, Marcuse argued, was in fact evident in the conservative rendering of Freudian psychoanalysis as ego psychology in the United States – a brand of therapy in which self-mastery and self-control were elevated over and above the unconscious and repressed sexuality.

A range of psychoanalytic concepts – including repression, the division between the pleasure principle and the reality principle, the Oedipus complex, and the like – have proven to be a thorn in the side of political radicals seeking to develop a critical interpretation of Freud. Freud's theories, many have argued, are politically conservative. Marcuse disagrees. He argues that political and social terms do not have to be grafted onto psychoanalysis, since they are already present in Freud's work. Rather, social and political categories need to be teased out from the core assumptions of Freudian theory. The core of Marcuse's radical recasting of Freud's account of sexuality lies in his division of repression into basic and surplus repression, as well as the connecting of the performance principle to the reality principle. Basic repression refers to that minimum level of psychological renunciation demanded by collective social life, in order for the reproduction of order, security and structure. Repression that is surplus, by contrast, refers to the intensification of self-restraint demanded by asymmetrical relations of power. Marcuse describes the 'monogamic-patriarchal' family, for example, as one cultural form in which surplus repression operates. Such a repressive surplus, he says, functions according to the 'performance principle', defined essentially as the culture of capitalism. According to Marcuse, the capitalist performance principle transforms individuals into 'things' or 'objects'; it replaces eroticism with masculinist genital sexuality; and it demands a disciplining of the human body (what Marcuse terms 'repressive desublimation') so as to prevent desire from disrupting the established social order.

What chance for personal and social emancipation? Marcuse is surprisingly optimistic about socio-sexual change. He argues that the performance principle, ironically, opens a path for the undoing of sexual repression. The material affluence of the advanced capitalist societies, says Marcuse, is the basis upon which a reconciliation between culture and nature can be undertaken – the ushering in of a stage of social development he calls 'libidinal rationality'. Although maddeningly vague about this undoing of sexual repression, Marcuse sees the emergence of emotional communication and mature intimacy issuing from a reconciliation of happiness with reason. 'Imagination', writes Marcuse (1956: 258), 'envisions the reconciliation of the individual with the whole, of desire with realization, of happiness with reason.'

Jacques Lacan

Perhaps the most influential author who has influenced recent debates about sexuality in social theory is the controversial French psychoanalyst Jacques Lacan. Like Marcuse, Lacan criticizes the conformist tendencies of much psychoanalytic therapy; he was particularly scathing of ego psychology, a school of psychoanalysis that he thought denied the powerful and disturbing dimensions of human sexuality. Also like Marcuse, Lacan privileges the place of the unconscious in human subjectivity and social relations. Unlike Marcuse, however, Lacan was pessimistic about the possibilities for transforming the sexual structure of modern culture and the dynamics of gender relationships.

In an infamous 'return to Freud', Lacan attempts to read psychoanalytic concepts in the light of structuralist and post-structuralist linguistics – especially such core Saussurian concepts as system, difference and the arbitrary relation between signifier and signified. One of the most important features of Lacan's psychoanalysis is the idea that the unconscious, just like language, is an endless process of difference, lack and absence. For Lacan, as for Saussure, the 'I' is a *linguistic shifter* that marks difference and division in interpersonal communication; there is always in speech a split between the self which utters 'I' and the word 'I' which is spoken. The individual subject, Lacan says, is structured by and denies this splitting, shifting from one signifier to another in a potentially endless play

of desires. Language and the unconscious thus thrive on difference: signs fill-in for the absence of actual objects at the level of the mind and in social exchange. 'The unconscious', Lacan argues, 'is structured like a language.' And the language that dominates the psyche is that of sexuality – of fantasies, dreams, desires, pleasures and anxieties.

This interweaving of language and the unconscious is given formal expression in Lacan's notion of the Symbolic Order. The Symbolic Order, says Lacan, institutes meaning, logic and differentiation; it is a realm in which signs fill-in for lost loves, such as one's mother or father. Whereas the small child fantasizes that it is at one with the maternal body in its earliest years, the Symbolic Order permits the developing individual to symbolize and express desires and passions in relation to the self, to others and within the wider culture. The key term in Lacan's theory, which accounts for this division between imaginary unity and symbolic differentiation, is the phallus, a term used by Freud in theorizing the Oedipus complex. For Lacan, as for Freud, the phallus is the prime marker of sexual difference. The phallus functions in the Symbolic Order, according to Lacan, through the enforcement of the Name-of-the-Father (*nom-du-père*). This does not mean, absurdly, that each individual father actually forbids the infant/mother union, which Freud said the small child fantasizes. Rather, it means that a 'paternal metaphor' intrudes into the child's narcissistically structured ego to refer her or him to what is outside, to what has the force of law – namely, language. The phallus, says Lacan, is fictitious, illusory and imaginary. Yet it has powerful effects, especially at the level of gender. The phallus functions less in the sense of biology than as fantasy, a fantasy which merges desire with power, omnipotence and mastery.

It is against this complex psychoanalytic backdrop that Lacan develops a global portrait of the relation between the sexes. Males are able to gain phallic prestige, he says, since the image of the penis comes to be symbolically equated with the phallus at the level of sexual difference. 'It can be said that the phallic signifier', comments Lacan (1977: 287), 'is chosen because it is the most tangible element in the role of sexual copulation . . . it is the image of the vital flow as it is transmitted in generation.' Masculinity is thus forged through appropriation of the sign of the phallus, a sign that confers power, mastery and domination. Femininity, by contrast, is constructed around exclusion from phallic power. Femininity holds a precarious, even fragile, relation to language, rationality and power. 'There is no woman,' says Lacan (1975: 221), 'but excluded from the value of words.'

This viewpoint, as the reader might have already gathered, is hardly likely to win much support from feminists; and, in fact, Lacan has been taken to task by many feminist authors for his perpetuation of patriarchal assumptions within the discourse of psychoanalysis. However, it is perhaps also worth holding in mind that more fluid possibilities for gender transformation are contained within Lacan's formulation of sexual difference and its cultural consequences. Beyond the bleak Oedipal power of the phallus, Lacan deconstructs sexuality identity as fiction or fraud. Desire, he maintains, lurks beneath the signifiers upon which identity and sex are fabricated. Gender fixity is always open to displacement.

Lacan's 'return to Freud' has exercised an enormous influence upon debates over sexuality in social theory, especially in the area of feminist studies – of which more shortly. However, his work has also been criticized for its structuralist leanings, its failure to attend to the inner complexities of emotion and affect, and its pessimistic account of the possibilities for personal and social change (see Elliott, 1994, 1999; Frosh, 1987).

FOUCAULT ON THE DISCURSIVE PRODUCTION OF SEXUALITY

For the French philosopher and historian Michel Foucault, sexuality is intricately bound up with advanced systems of power and domination within our broader culture. Foucault's major studies in the 1960s and 1970s, such as *Madness and Civilization*, *The Archaeology of Knowledge* and *Discipline and Punish*, examine the deeper social implications of configurations of knowledge and power in the human sciences – for example, psychiatry, sexology, criminology, penology and demography. Giving a novel twist to Bacon's dictum that 'knowledge is power', Foucault argues that scientific discourses, while aiming to uncover the truth about 'the criminal' or 'madness' or 'sex', are in fact used to control individuals. In his genealogies of power/knowledge networks, he argues that scientific disciplines and discourses shape the social structures in which culture defines what is acceptable and unacceptable; of what can be said from a position of authority, and by whom and in what social conditions. In a society such as ours, writes Foucault (1980a: 93):

> There are manifold relations of power which permeate, characterize and constitute the social body, and these relations of power cannot themselves be established, consolidated nor implemented without

the production, accumulation, circulation and functioning of a discourse. There can be no possible exercise of power without a certain economy of discourses of truth which operates through and on the basis of this association. We are subjected to the production of truth through power and we cannot exercise power except through the production of truth.

The production of discourses, texts and knowledges is deeply interwoven with the operation of power in society. The individual subject is viewed by Foucault, in this early phase of his career, as an upshot or product of discursive positioning and fixation; the individual is increasingly subjected to new forms of power and control in what Foucault terms our 'disciplinary society'; in Weberian terms, the Foucauldian subject is caught up in the iron cage of modernity (see O'Neill, 1986; Turner, 1993).

In the later part of this career, Foucault problematized global conceptions of sexuality (such as those portrayed in psychoanalytic, social-constructivist and feminist theories), and developed powerful genealogies of the self and subjectivity. He explained his shift of analytical focus from power and domination to sexuality and the self in the following terms:

> If one wants to analyse the genealogy of the subject in Western civilization, one has to take into account not only techniques of domination, but also techniques of the self. One has to show the interaction between these two types of the self. When I was studying asylums, prisons and so on, I perhaps insisted too much on the techniques of domination. What we call discipline is something really important in this kind of institution. But it is only one aspect of the art of governing people in our societies. Having studied the field of power relations taking domination techniques as a point of departure, I should like, in the years to come, to study power relations, especially in the field of sexuality, starting from the techniques of the self. (Foucault 1985: 367)

Foucault's concerns about the culture of sexuality were prompted, in part, by his own homosexuality; in particular, he was troubled by what he saw as the intolerant and repressive heterosexual regime governing sex in French society. He became increasingly fascinated with the sexual liberation movements of the 1970s and 1980s, especially the politicization of gay and lesbian identities; he regarded political demands for sexual liberation, as defined by theorists like Marcuse, to be of crucial importance in redefining configurations of normal and pathological desires, acts and identities. However he was suspect of the claims of various sexual liberationists that desire was repressed in Western societies; he was even more troubled by the notion that, if sexuality were released from existing personal and social constraints, society might achieve greater levels of autonomy. Rejecting what he described as 'the Californian cult of the self' – the notion that the scrutinizing of sexuality would reveal the essence of the 'true self' – Foucault sought to develop a radically different approach to analysing the culture of sexuality, desire, and sexual identity.

At the core of Foucault's approach was a rejection of the modernist assumption that sex should be understood as a natural or biological foundation, upon which an imprinting of 'sexuality' and 'gender' is added. Turning such conventional wisdom on its head, Foucault argues that the idea of sex as origin, as base, or as given to identity and social relations is itself the outcome of a discursive regime of sexuality. As Foucault (1980b: 155) explains:

> We must not make the mistake of thinking that sex is an autonomous agency which secondarily produces manifold effects over the entire length of its surface of contact with power. On the contrary, sex is the most speculative, most ideal, and most internal element in a deployment of sexuality organized by power in its grip on bodies and their materiality, their forces, energies, sensations and pleasures.

Pre-existing types of sensual pleasure, says Foucault, become 'sex' as the creation of discourses about it – such as medical texts, therapeutic books, self-help manuals and the like – bring about an ordering of 'normal' and 'pathological' sexual practices. The human subject, according to Foucault, is not 'sexed' in any meaningful sense prior to its constitution within a discourse through which it becomes a carrier of a natural or essential sex.

In *The History of Sexuality*, Foucault sets out to overturn what he calls 'the repressive hypothesis'. According to this hypothesis, the healthy expression of sexuality has been censured, negated, forbidden; at any rate, this is held to be the case in the West. Sexuality as repressed: this theorem has been crucial not only to Freudian and post-Freudian theory, but also to various sexual liberationists. Foucault, however, rejects the thesis of sexual repression. Sex, he says, has not been driven underground in contemporary culture. On the contrary, there has been a widening discussion of sex and sexuality. Sexuality, says Foucault, has flourished. Sexuality for Foucault is an end-effect, a product, of our endless monitoring, discussion, classification, ordering, recording and regulation of sex. As an example, Foucault considers attitudes toward sexuality in the Victorian age of the late

nineteenth century. Victorianism, writes Foucault, is usually associated with the emergence of prudishness, the silencing of sexuality, and the rationalization of sex within the domestic sphere, the home, the family. Against such conventional wisdom, though, he argues that the production of sexuality during the Victorian era as a secret, as something forbidden or taboo, created a culture in which sex then had to be administered, regulated and policed. For example, doctors, psychiatrists and others catalogued and classified numerous perversions, from which issues about sex became endlessly tracked and monitored with the growth of social medicine, education, criminology and sexology.

According to Foucault, this fostering of a science of sexuality arose from the connection of confession to the growth of knowledge about sex. The Roman Catholic confessional, Foucault contends, was the principal means of regulating the individual sexuality of believers; the Church was the site in which subjects came to tell the truth about themselves, especially in relation to sexuality, to their priests. The confessional can be regarded as the source of the West's preoccupation with sex, particularly in terms of the sanctioned inducement to talk of it. Confession became disconnected from its broad religious framework, however, somewhere in the late eighteenth century, and was transformed into a type of investigation or interrogation through the scientific study of sex and the creation of medical discourses about it. Sexes became increasingly bound up with networks of knowledge and power, and in time a matter for increasing self-policing, self-regulation and self-interrogation. In other words, instead of sex being regulated by external forces, it is much more a matter of attitudinal discipline, which is in turn connected to issues of, say, knowledge and education. Psychotherapy and psychoanalysis, says Foucault, are key instances of such self-policing in the contemporary era. In therapy, the individual does not so much feel coerced into confessing about sexual practices and erotic fantasies; rather the information divulged by the patient is treated as the means to freedom, the realization of a liberation from repression.

Foucault's writings have been sharply criticized on the grounds of sociological determinism – that is, that his definition of power primarily in terms of its disciplinary consequences on passive bodies denies the active place of human agency (Giddens, 1981; Habermas, 1987). His writings on sexuality and the self have also been criticized for their neglect of gender dynamics (see McNay, 1992). Notwithstanding these criticisms, however, many social theorists, ranging from sociologists to literary critics, have drawn from

Foucault's critique of sexuality to debunk traditional notions of rationality, the unified subject, and sexuality as the foundation of identity.

FEMINISM AND SEXUALITY

There are many different approaches that feminists have adopted in exploring the theme of sexuality and gender. Some feminists have offered perspectives on the social role of women from the viewpoint of our patriarchal society, in which women are the targets of sexual oppression, abuse, harassment and denigration. Other feminists have concentrated on, say, the regimes of beautification or modes of self-presentation to which women submit in adopting 'masks of femininity', in order to function as objects of men's sexual desire. Still other feminists have examined the broader influences of economics and public policy in the reduction of women's sexuality to the tasks of child rearing and household duties. In these contrasting approaches, the issues of sexual difference, gender hierarchy, social marginalization and the politics of identity achieve different levels of prominence. For the purposes of this brief discussion here, I will explore the crucial links between sexual subjectivity and gender practices as elaborated in contemporary feminist thought, cultural analysis and psychoanalysis.

The interlocking relations of subjectivity, gender and society were powerfully theorized in the late 1970s by the American feminist sociologist Nancy Chodorow. In *The Reproduction of Mothering* (1978), which is now considered a classic feminist statement on sexuality and gender, Chodorow combines sociological and psychoanalytic approaches to study the reproduction of gender asymmetries in modern societies. Her idea was to focus on the emotional, social and political ramifications of exclusive female mothering, giving special attention to the construction of masculinity and femininity. Against the tide of various socialization theories, Chodorow contends that gender is not so much a matter of 'role' as a consequence of the ways in which mothers emotionally relate to their children.

In explaining the sex roles to which women and men are expected to conform, Chodorow argues that the developing infant acquires a core gender identity that functions as a psychological force in the perpetuation of patriarchy. The core of her argument concerns gender difference. Mothers, she says, experience their daughters as doubles of themselves, through a narcissistic projection of sameness. The mother emotionally relates to her daughter as an extension of herself, not as an independent person; the daughter, as a consequence, finds it extremely difficult to emotionally disengage from her mother, and to create a sense of independence and individuality. Chodorow sees gains and losses here. Empathy, sensitivity and intimacy are the gains that flow from this narcissistic merging of mother and daughter. Daughters, she argues, are likely to grow up with a core sense of emotional continuity with their mother, a continuity that provides for strong relational connections in adult life. In this account, girls become mothers since their mothers' feminine selves are deeply inscribed within their psyche. However the losses are that, because daughters are not perceived as separate others, women consequently lack a strong sense of self and agency. Feelings of inadequacy, lack of self-control and a fear of merging with others arise as core emotional problems for women.

By contrast, Chodorow sees masculine sexual identity as based upon a firm repression of maternal love. Boys, she says, must deny their primary bond to maternal love – thus repressing femininity permanently into the unconscious. This is not a psychic task that boys complete by themselves, however. Mothers, according to Chodorow, assist boys in this painful process of psychic repression through their own tacit understanding of gender difference. That is to say, because mothers experience sons as other, mothers in turn propel their sons towards individuation, differentiation and autonomy. Mothers thus lead their sons to emotionally disengage from intimacy. The mother, in effect, prepares her son for an instrumental, abstract relation to the self, to other people and to the wider society; and this, of course, is a relation that males will be expected to maintain in the public world of work, social relations and politics.

Chodorow's work is an important contribution to feminist scholarship; her psychoanalytically orientated sociology has influenced many feminists researching gender identity in the wider frame of families and communities. Her general claim that women mother in order to recapture an intensity of feeling originally experienced in the mother/daughter relation has been especially fruitful. For such a claim connects in Chodorow's work to a wider social explanation of gender alienation and oppression. Women's emotional lives are drained and empty since men are cut off from interpersonal communication and sexual intimacy. From this angle, the desire to have a child is, in part, rooted in the repression and distortion of the current gender system. Against this backdrop, Chodorow argues for shared parenting as a means of transforming the current gender regime.

A similar focus on the mother/daughter relationship is to be found in the writings of the French philosopher Luce Irigaray. Like Chodorow, Irigaray is out to analyse the deeper symbolic forces that limit or constrain women's autonomy and power. Unlike Chodorow, however, Irigaray proposes a more formalistic or structuralist thesis. Taking her cue from Lacan, Irigaray contends that woman is, by definition, excluded from the Symbolic Order. On this view, the feminine cannot be adequately symbolized under patriarchal conditions. As Irigaray (1985: 143) argues: 'there is no possibility whatsoever, within the current logic of sociocultural operations, for a daughter to situate herself with respect to her mother: because, strictly speaking, they make neither one nor two, neither has a name, meaning, sex of her own, neither can be "identified" with respect to the other'. Similarly, the French psychoanalytic feminist Julia Kristeva (1984) argues against the patriarchal bent of the Lacanian Symbolic Order, to which she contrasts the 'semiotic' – a realm of pre-oedipal prolinguistic experience, consisting of drives, affects, rhythms, tonalities. According to Kristeva, semiotic drives circle around the loss of the pre-oedipal mother, and make themselves felt in the breakup of language – in slips, silences, tonal rhythms. These semiotic drives, she suggests, are subversive of the symbolic Law of the Father since they are rooted in a pre-oedipal connection with the maternal body. The subversive potential of the semiotic is thus closely tied to femininity, and Kristeva devotes much of her psychoanalytic work to the analysis of motherhood and its psychical consequences.

Most recently, the development of a social theory of sexuality has been transformed by the writings of the American feminist post-structuralist Judith Butler. Butler seeks to debunk the work of theorists, such as Chodorow, who appeal to women as a foundation or basis for feminist theory and politics. She argues that notions of 'identity' or 'core gender identity' serve to reinforce a binary gender order that maintains women's oppression. Like Kristeva and Irigaray, Butler sees sexual identity as shot through with desire, fantasy, emotion, symbol, conflict and ambivalence. Unlike Kristeva and Irigaray, however, Butler argues that desire is not so much some inner psychic force as a result of the internalization of gender images upon the surface of our bodies. Drawing upon the work of Foucault, Butler contends that the link between sex and gender power is produced, not through nature, biology or reason, but through the deployment of knowledge, discourses and forms of power, actualized through acting bodies and sexual practices.

In *Gender Trouble: Feminism and the Subversion of Identity* (1990) and *Bodies That Matter*

(1993), Butler argues that sex and sexuality are constituted and reproduced through the body that performs – the production of masculine and feminine bodies, lesbian and gay bodies, the sexy body, the fit and healthy body, the anorexic body, the body beautiful. Gender, says Butler, is not the outcome of the 'true self' or 'core sex identity', but rather a matter of performance, the performance of a corporeal style. Individuals for Butler model their gender performances after fantasies, imitations and idealizations of what we think it means to be a 'man' or 'woman' within the range of cultural representations of sex in the current gender regime. Butler's notion of performance, of the body that performs, encompasses the copying, imitation and repetition of cultural stereotypes, linguistic conventions and symbolic forms governing the production of masculinity and femininity.

THE SOCIOLOGY OF SEX

Among changes now pervading our culture, sociologists argue that few are more profound than those transforming the texture of family life. In many advanced societies, we are moving to a situation in which nearly half of first marriages end in divorce, and the statistics are even worse for second and subsequent marriages. Among conservatives, this decline is often cast as a sign of society's moral decay; the lament is attributed to several sources. From sexual permissiveness to feminism, from new parenting arrangements to the spread of overt homosexuality: our new era, so many conservatives argue, is one that spells the end of family ties that bind.

A key reference point here is a recent study of American families, *A Generation at Risk: Growing Up in an Era of Family Upheaval*. Paul Amato and Alan Booth, the authors of the study, argue that the costs of our separating and divorcing society are simply too high. Divorce might suit adults, but not children. For it is children that suffer the painful and destructive long-term impact of divorce in their own sense of self, sexuality and intimate relationships. Based on an analysis of couples married for over 15 years, the authors of *A Generation at Risk* suggest that unhappy parents should try to stay together for the sake of their children. It is acknowledged that children can suffer if they remain with parents in what is termed a 'high-conflict marriage', but the authors argue that in most 'low-conflict marriages' couples ought to make certain sacrifices in order to fulfil their parental and societal responsibilities.

There are some rather obvious criticisms that might be made of this argument. For one thing, it pays little or no attention to the emotional damage sustained by children living in family contexts of disrespect, to say nothing about lack of love. For another, it seems excessively prescriptive and moralistic. Who, exactly, is to say whether conflicts experienced in marriage are to count as 'low-level' or 'high-level'? Emotions, after all, are not exactly skilled workers. On a deeper sociological level, there is something awry with arguments about 'the breakdown of the family'. Certainly the rise of one-parent families, as well as the dramatic increase of births outside of marriage, indicates that broad-ranging changes are sweeping through society. And divorce undeniably looms as a feature of family and domestic arrangements. Yet liberal and conservative critics do not readily acknowledge the fact that people very often remarry. The implications of this are far-reaching, and some sociologists are now suggesting that, rather than family breakdown, the family is undergoing a constructive renewal.

Sexual relationships today, conducted inside and outside of marriage, embrace what has been called the movement toward 'individualization'. Individualization refers principally to self-construction and self-design, in which the forging of identity and sexuality becomes less dependent on social traditions and customs and organized instead around personal decision-making and choice. The self-staging of individualization is inevitably undertaken through a host of traditional social, economic, political and cultural constraints. However, individualization, as the German sociologist Ulrich Beck argues, is a paradoxical compulsion that takes the individual into a post-traditional social setting, a setting where the person must live as an individual agent and designer of her or his biography. There is a new contingency at the level of the self, identity and sexuality, says Beck. What this means as far as families and domestic arrangements are concerned is that the stress today on choice and individual autonomy provides a radicalizing dynamic that, in turn, alters the interpersonal realm in which relationships are rooted.

Beck claims there are many patterns of family development which suggest that traditional expectations ('till-death-us-do-part') are being put aside, and instead that domestic relationships are increasingly based upon the growth of the individual as well as the care of others. The individualized individual, says Beck, engages in relationships in which trust is the key anchor. If trust evaporates so too does the relationship; traditional ties no longer bind in the way they once did. Beck connects this redesign of family living to the changing ways in which individuals experience sex, sexuality, relationships and intimacy. 'The traditions of marriage and the family', writes Beck (1997: 96), 'are becoming dependent on decision-making, and with all their contradictions must be experienced as personal risks.'

Beck's social theory permits the illumination of very broad transformations at the level of personal and social relationships. Many parents are now step-parents as well as biological parents, and the clear trend is toward new commitments to others across family boundaries. This can be viewed positively for children, in so far as it involves an 'opening out' of childhood to relationships in the deepest sense of the term. As Beck notes, there are many social forces at work here, including more flexible employment options, recent gains in autonomy for women, newly emerging definitions of masculinity, as well as rising experimentation across diverse heterosexual and homosexual lifestyles. Add to this the variety of options in the area of reproductive technologies – such as in vitro fertilization and embryo freezing – and changes in human attitudes to sexual reproduction become increasingly transparent. These developments usher in a world of new possibilities and risks for people.

The British sociologist Anthony Giddens also sees the modern social world as unleashing positive and negative developments at the level of the self, sexuality and intimacy. Like Beck, Giddens argues that the self is increasingly individualized today – the self becomes something that is reflected upon, reworked, altered, even reshaped. 'The self', writes Giddens (1991: 32), 'becomes a reflexive project.' By reflexivity, Giddens means to underscore a disposition of continuous self-monitoring, in which social practices are constantly examined and reformed in the light of new information and fresh developments about those very practices. Again, marriage is a key example. According to Giddens, statistics about marriage and divorce do not exist in a separate realm from the flesh-and-blood human agents that comprise those statistics. On the contrary, Giddens' sociology emphasizes the knowledgeability of social agents, and in particular the manner in which social transformations affect the reflexive organization of the self. The coming of a divorcing society, says Giddens, penetrates to the core of our personal lives, such that it is virtually impossible to equate romantic love with the 'forever' or permanence of the marriage contract. When people marry today, they do so against a backdrop of high divorce statistics – knowledge that, in turn, alters their conception and understanding of the permanence of relationships. 'In struggling with intimate problems', writes Giddens (1991: 12), 'individuals help actively to reconstruct the universe of social activity around them.'

In *The Transformation of Intimacy: Sexuality, Love and Eroticism in Modern Societies* (1992), Giddens speaks of 'the pure relationship', a relationship created and maintained through the mutual trust of partners. As Giddens (1992: 58) explains:

> A pure relationship has nothing to do with sexual purity, and is a limiting concept rather than only a descriptive one. It refers to a situation where a social relation is entered into for its own sake, for what can be derived by each person from a sustained association with another; and which is continued only in so far as it is thought by both parties to deliver enough satisfactions for each individual to stay within it.

At the heart of this account of contemporary, postmodern intimacy and life-style there lies a radicalization of gender and sex. For if relationships are indeed designed and maintained through personal commitment, trust and emotional satisfaction, then it follows that contemporary men and women are demanding equality in order to provide ongoing consent to the post-traditional world of intimacy in which they find themselves. Feminism and the women's movement, says Giddens, are crucial to this process of democratization in the sphere of gender, sexuality and intimacy.

A related emphasis upon reflexivity in the construction and deconstruction of sexuality is to be found in the work of the British social theorist and cultural historian Jeffrey Weeks. In a series of publications (1977, 1985, 1995), Weeks developed a social constructivist approach to the study of sexuality, in which sex is less a matter of inner desires and personal behavior than a site where ideologies, cultural norms and institutions interweave. Weeks contends that the notion that homosexual practices reveal a distinct identity – 'the homosexual' – did not arise in the West until the late nineteenth century. Prior to this, the policing of homosexuality were undertaken not through the monitoring of deviant persons, but through the punishing of particular acts, organized under the general category of sodomy. By drawing attention to the ways in which homosexuality was socially fashioned in relation to specific identity traits, psychological dispositions and cultural markers, Weeks attempts to underscore the patterns of social fabrication underpinning modernity's regimes of sexuality.

QUEER THEORY

The history of the label 'queer theory' is set against a backdrop of the radical sexual politics of the 1970s, in particular the assumption that homosexuality is a foundation or identity of minority sexual experience in the sociocultural order. The development of this theoretical approach to sexuality arose not only from emerging social divisions around the meaning of homosexuality throughout the 1980s, but also from new attempts to avoid exclusionist and separatist strategies of political opposition to the masculinist, heterosexual dynamic of Western culture. If the first generation of gay, lesbian and feminist activists and theorists sought to analyse homosexuality as a minority experience, then the focus of queer theorists has been to contest the binary divide between majority and minority experience, as well as the social dynamics of heterosexuality and homosexuality.

The theoretical grounding of queer theory lies in post-structuralism and literary deconstructionism, and the influence of social theorists such as Foucault, Lacan and Derrida looms large. Less a unitary coherent body of thought than an assemblage of conceptual tools and political strategies, queer theory attempts to subvert the cultural stereotypes used to understand gays, lesbians, or bisexuals – in order to bring into focus the 'queer knowledges' which modernity has unleashed in its framing of sexual identities and differences. As Teresa de Lauretis (1991: v) explains this transgressive edge of queer theory:

> Today we have, on the one hand, the term 'lesbian' and 'gay' to designate distinct kinds of lifestyles, sexualities, sexual practices, communities, issues, publications, and discourses; on the other hand, the phrase 'gay and lesbian', or more and more frequently, 'lesbian and gay' (ladies first), has become standard currency . . . In a sense, the term 'Queer Theory' was arrived at in an effort to avoid all of these fine distinctions in our discursive protocols, not to adhere to any one of the given terms, not to assume their ideological liabilities, but instead to both transgress and transcend them – or at the very least problematize them.

So queer theory embraces not only lesbians, gays and bisexuals, but also sadists, fetishists, voyeurs, drag queens, transsexuals, transvestites, butches, gender benders, and all other practices that attract the label 'deviant sexualities' within the asymmetrical power relations of patriarchy.

In *Essentially Speaking* (1989), Diana Fuss develops a post-structuralist critique of the homosexual/heterosexual binarism. Heterosexuality, says Fuss, derives meaning in relation to its opposite, homosexuality; the sexual foundation of the former is framed upon an exclusion and repression of the latter; the production of hetero/homosexual divisions and differences is crucial to the workings of sexual oppression. This carries radical implications for understanding sexual identity, and especially the construction of gay and lesbian identities. Fuss argues that the hetero/homosexual opposition constitutes a fixed normativity for sexual identities, a rigid cultural order in which sexual differences are forever displaced and denied. Thus, the assertion of identity-based gay and lesbian communities has the paradoxical effect of reinforcing heterosexuality and homophobia as the key dynamics of socio-sexual organization. In contrast to the politics of identity, Fuss (1991) urges sexual radicals to contest, and hence destabilize, the hetero/homosexual hierarchy. She urges, in short, a politics of relational identities.

Eve Kosofsky Sedgwick, sometimes dubbed 'the mother of queer theory', goes one step further. In *The Epistemology of the Closet* she argues that the hetero/homosexual binarism not only shapes and structures sexual identities and differences, but informs key categories of Western thought and culture. For Sedgwick, the hetero/homosexual binarism organizes people's experience and knowledge of the world, particularly forms of self-knowledge, self-disclosure and self-revelation. 'Coming out' and the 'closet' are key terms for understanding the experiences of gay and lesbian people; but these broad categories of self-definition also deeply affect heterosexuals, who situate their own identities and practices in relation to homosexuality, especially the power of homosexuality to disturb and displace. The contemporary crisis of homo/heterosexual definition is at root a desire for certainty at the level of sexual knowledge. Following Foucault, Sedgwick argues that the secrecy surrounding knowledge of the closet is both maintained and frustrated because of the risk of the secret's disclosure. Somewhat akin to Lacan's description of the phallus as a 'master signifier', Sedgwick describes the hetero/homosexual division as pivotal to the cultural logic of the advanced societies. Knowledge of the closet and its secrets, Sedgwick says, is invested with much energy and anxiety, a set of fears and fantasies, which underwrites spacings between appearance and reality, norm and pathology, power and powerlessness.

Sedgwick's work has been very influential in queer theory, primarily since she has moved debate beyond narrow definitions of the politics of identity, as well as the basic oppositions of oppression and resistance. Refusing to accept that the world can be easily divided between homosexuals and heterosexuals, Sedgwick seeks to underline (a) that knowledge is the consequence of bodies, (b) that sex is not the center or foundation of the human subject, (c) that sexual identities are fundamentally provisional, mobile and fractured, and (d) that the instability of the hetero/homosexual binary opposition holds out possibilities for the reinvention of identities, desires, practices, communities, knowledges and social structures.

Concluding remarks

In this chapter I have conducted a survey of recent work on sexuality in social theory. Situating sexuality in the discursive spaces of psychoanalysis, Foucauldian analysis, feminism, sociological thought and queer theory, we find issues of the foremost importance for the social sciences. Though the foregoing approaches share little in common in analytical terms, they are all concerned with questioning the constitution of sexuality, as well as the interpersonal social, cultural, political and epistemic contexts on which sexuality is produced.

REFERENCES

Beck, U. (1997) *The Reinvention of Politics.* Cambridge: Polity Press.

Butler, J. (1990) *Gender Trouble: Feminism and the Subversion of Identity.* New York: Routledge.

Butler, J. (1993) *Bodies That Matter: On the Discursive Limits of 'Sex'.* New York: Routledge.

Chodorow, N. (1978) *The Reproduction of Mothering.* Berkeley, CA: University of California Press.

de Lauretis, Teresa (ed.) (1991) 'Queer Theory', *Differences*, 3 (2).

Elliott, A. (1994) *Psychoanalytic Theory: An Introduction.* Oxford: Blackwell.

Elliott, A. (ed.) (1998) *Freud 2000.* Oxford and New York: Routledge.

Elliott, A. (1999) *Social Theory and Psychoanalysis in Transition: Self and Society from Freud to Kristeva,* 2nd edn. London: Free Association Books; New York: New York University Press.

Foucault, M. (1980a) 'Two Lectures' (trans. C. Gordon et al.), in C. Gordon (ed.), *Power/Knowledge: Selected Interviews and Other Writings, 1972–1977.* New York: Pantheon.

Foucault, M. (1980b) *The History of Sexuality: An Introduction.* Harmondsworth: Penguin.

Foucault, Michel (1985) 'Sexuality and Solitude', in M. Blonsky (ed.), *On Signs: A Semiotic Reader.* Oxford: Blackwell.

Frosh, S. (1987) *The Politics of Psychoanalysis.* London: Macmillan.

Fuss, D. (1989) *Essentially Speaking.* New York: Routledge.

Fuss, D. (1991) *Inside/Outside: Lesbian Theories, Gay Theories.* New York: Routledge.

Giddens, A. (1981) *Profiles and Critiques in Social Theory.* London: Macmillan.

Giddens, A. (1991) *Modernity and Self-Identity.* Cambridge: Polity Press.

Giddens, A. (1992) *The Transformation of Intimacy: Sexuality, Love and Eroticism in Modern Societies*. Cambridge: Polity Press.

Habermas, J. (1987) *The Philosophical Discourse of Modernity*. Cambridge: Polity Press.

Irigaray, L. (1985) *This Sex Which Is Not One*. Ithaca, NY: Cornell University Press.

Kristeva, J. (1984) *Revolution in Poetic Language*. New York: Columbia University Press.

Lacan, J. (1975) *Encore: Le Seminaire XX*. Paris: Seuil.

Lacan, J. (1977) *Ecrits: A Selection*. London: Tavistock.

McNay, L. (1992) *Foucault and Feminism*. Cambridge: Polity Press.

Marcuse, H. (1956) *Eros and Civilization*. London: Ark.

O'Neill, J. (1986) 'The Disciplinary Society: From Weber to Foucault', *British Journal of Sociology*, 37: 42–60.

Sedgwick, E.K. (1990) *The Epistemology of the Closet*. Berkeley, CA: University of California Press.

Turner, B.S. (1993) *Max Weber: From History to Modernity*. London: Routledge.

Weeks, J. (1977) *Coming Out*. London: Quartet Books Limited.

Weeks, J. (1985) *Sexuality and Its Discontents*. London: Routledge.

Weeks, J. (1995) *Invented Moralities: Sexual Values in an Age of Uncertainty*. Cambridge: Polity Press.

33

The Embodied Foundations of Social Theory

CHRIS SHILLING

It is something of an irony that 'the body' has become an established, highly popular object of study in the social sciences since the 1980s. Issues central to the embodied constituents of agency and interaction, and the bodily referents of social structures, were evident in the origins of Western thought and maintained their place in the modern development of social theory (Snell, [1948] 1960). Earlier in the twentieth century, for example, the corporeal foundations of human agency had been examined by Marcel Mauss ([1934] 1973) in his analysis of 'techniques of the body', while Maurice Merleau-Ponty's (1962) phenomenology suggested our bodies provide us with our 'opening onto', our 'vehicle of being in' and our 'means of communication with' the world. Erving Goffman's (1963) concern with 'shared vocabularies of body idiom' highlighted the constraints of the 'interaction order' for those seeking to maintain a social self as a morally worthy member of society, while Max Weber (1968: 975) had earlier analysed how bureaucratic structures depended on 'eliminating from official business love, hatred, and all purely personal, irrational, and emotional elements' characteristic of embodied relationships. Emile Durkheim ([1912] 1995), in contrast, highlighted what he considered to be the *enduring* somatic foundations of social orders through his evaluation of the collective effervescence which turned a group of individuals into a community of people united by a morally binding collective consciousness (Shilling and Mellor, 2001).

Such developments occurred before the recent 'discovery' of the body, but have only been received gradually as important contributions towards a research programme on the embodied bases of social life. This can be attributed in part to the mind/body dualism characteristic of that tradition in Western thought which has marginalized body matters on the assumption that the mind makes us distinctively human. Snell ([1948] 1960) traces this dualism to ancient Greece. Soma, which subsequently came to mean 'body', referred to the corpse, while Socrates argued that lasting happiness came not from the (perishable) body, but through the (immortal) soul; a division later mapped onto that between the 'irrational passions' and 'rational thought'. More generally, Greek ethics held that the soul's aspirations should be guided by a self-control termed 'healthy thinking' which opposed itself to the inevitable 'sufferings' of the bodily instincts and emotions, while the eye was frequently viewed as the mind's neutral gateway to knowledge.

This philosophical legacy helped devalue the body and promoted a related tendency to distrust the senses and interpret 'seeing' as a rational process: a 'highway' for the transport of knowledge between the 'outside' world and the 'inside' mind (Jenks, 1995). In devaluing the body, Kant ([1785] 1964) rejected the possibility that criteria for the good are grounded in the natural properties of humans, and sought a rational foundation for universal laws which elevated duty above desire. In distrusting the senses, Descartes' *Cogito ergo sum* ('I think, therefore I am') involved at one level a dismissal of all the body's senses. Descartes doubted the existence of his senses and argued in *The Meditations* that 'I am . . . only a thing that thinks', and that 'my mind . . . is entirely and truly distinct from my body and may exist without it' (Descartes, [1634] 1974: 105, 156). This philosophical approach was modified by an ultimate acceptance of the eye as a neutral conveyor of rational knowledge which promoted an 'I'll believe it when I see it' mentality (Classen, 1993; Slater, 1995; Synnott, 1991). Locke's *Essay on Human Understanding* emphasized the visual basis of mental activity, while Descartes ultimately accepted sight as the most important sense for science and technology.

There have, of course, been exceptions to this prioritization of minds over bodies. Hume ([1739–40] 1985) suggested that the 'light of reason' was only to be tolerated on a full stomach, and is part of a minority tradition in Western thought which posited 'passions' or 'sentiments' as bases of thought. Distinctive versions of the mind/sight/thought equation continue to be popular, however, while cognitive views of the human agent have exerted an enduring influence on modern thought. While this chapter is concerned with the embodied foundations of social theory, this emphasis can be highlighted via the specific development of sociological theory.

THE COGNITIVE AGENT IN SOCIOLOGICAL THEORY

Sociological theory emerged from a dissatisfaction with the utilitarian emphasis on the rational pursuit of egoistic interest as the basis of society. The theoretical syntheses proposed by Talcott Parsons held that classical sociology converged on the understanding that shared *values* underpinned social action. Parsons' work has influenced theories of embodiment, as we examine later in this chapter, but despite discussing the expressive, ritual and affective aspects of socialization, he attributed most importance to *information* as a motive in individual choice. Drawing on cybernetics theory (the science of systems), Parsons suggested that cultural information in general, and 'ultimate values' in particular, became increasingly dominant in steering individual behaviour and social development. That element of the individual constituting an energy-rich behavioural organism, in contrast, is both low in information and important to the social system only as a constraining factor. The physiological body becomes a 'unit point of reference' whose study belongs to the natural sciences or psychology (Parsons, [1951] 1991: 541–2, 547–8).

With this formulation, Parsons was accused of proposing an 'oversocialized', disembodied conception of the individual whose internalization of norms was a predominantly cognitive process.

His inability to deal fully with the creativity of embodied human interaction was evident in his eventual rejection of Simmel (a sociologist whose concern with the dynamism of human vitalism incorporated an interest in the senses) from his grand synthesis, and was reflected in Wrong's (1961) suggestion that sociology might avoid the limitations of Parsonian theory by starting from the suggestion that 'in the beginning there is the body'.

Parsons encouraged sociology to develop as 'the study of the rules and normative behaviour that proceed from people's beliefs' and not from their bodies (O'Neill, 1985: 18), while alternatives to his normatively driven actor did little to 'reclaim' the body for the discipline. Wrong's suggestion to start with the body, for example, was actually a call to incorporate psychology into sociology. Homans' (1958, 1961) insistence that 'social structures' and 'norms' should be accounted for by the cumulative results of individual decision-makers paved the way for recent versions of rational choice sociology, but constitutes a partial return to utilitarianism in suggesting action is motivated by a rationality underpinned by only a limited, under-explored set of 'bodily passions'. As Joas (1983, 1996) points out, theories of rational action tend to make several questionable assumptions about the body of the actor. They assume actors cognitively establish goals before acting (and thereby propose that the normal state of the body is lethargy). They view the body as a permanently available instrument of action (that is, autonomous *vis-à-vis* other people and the environment). Finally, and they reduce the body to a mere medium of self-expression (underestimating the importance of human frailty and the unintended and unexpected events of life). These assumptions inadequately represent the varieties of human action and complexities of human life by implying that an actor who displays any loss of concentration on purposive action, any loss of bodily control, or any sign of dependency on others, departs from the norm of rational action. Human development is reduced to acquiring the capacities for rational action, while individuals who persist in acting non-rationally, whose actions cannot even be judged as exhibiting a 'masked' rationality, are evaluated as 'malfunctioning' actors (Coleman, 1990: 504).

This marginalization of the embodied nature of action was not overcome fully by interactionist sociology. Emphasizing *inter*subjectivity rather than normative or rational subjectivity, it nevertheless continued to emphasize action as driven by the cognitive mind rather than the sensuous body. A creative engagement with Mead's work has been central to recent writings on the corporeality of social action, as we examine later in this chapter, yet the essence of the modern self for Mead (1934: 173) was primarily 'cognitive', involving 'thought or reflection', rather than bodily affects. Aaron Cicourel (1974) has redefined ethnomethodology as 'cognitive sociology' (Wrong, 1994: 60–1), while Berger and Luckmann's (1966) sociology of knowledge reinforced this prioritization of the mind over the body by suggesting society could be understood in terms of cognitive processes. Goffman's work was more satisfactory, formulating a battery of concepts designed to examine the constraints placed on the 'presentation of self' within the parameters of bodily co-presence. Nevertheless, Goffman's analysis of the bodily foundations of human being, social selves and interaction has been criticized for proposing a theoretically 'shallow' view of the body. Hochschild (1983), for example, argues that for all Goffman's focus on embarrassment, we get little sense that his presentationally capable actors are deeply motivated by a range of emotions which may sometimes overwhelm cognitive responses to situations (C.F. Shilling, 1998).

Contemporary theoretical projects frequently incorporate similarly cognitive conceptions of agency. Structuration theories and analytical dualism constitute two of the most influential attempts to overcome the reductionism of collectivist and individualist approaches to society by analysing the interplay between structures and agents. Analytical dualism is best known through the sociology of Archer (1995), while structuration theory has been formulated most coherently in the writings of Giddens (1984). Neither structuration theory nor analytical dualism, however, attribute to the body a productive role in mediating the formation of social structures (Shilling, 1997a). The body remains an 'organic constraint' (Giddens, 1984), providing us with 'non-social experiences of non-social reality' (Archer, 1995), constituting only a constraining condition for the constitution of society.

THE RISE OF THE BODY

Despite these cognitive conceptions of social action, the 1980s witnessed rising criticism of the mind/agency equation from within sociology, and a transdisciplinary explosion of work questioning the assumption that 'society operates upon us intellectually and consensually rather than directly upon our bodies' (O'Neill, 1985: 48). This avalanche of literature carved out a distinctive theoretical terrain. Writings on the social and medical consequences of interactions between culture and biology (e.g. Freund, 1982;

Hirst and Woolley, 1982; Oudshoorn, 1994; Turner, 1991a), were accompanied by studies on the structural, communicative, political and interpretive dimensions of embodiment (e.g. Johnson, 1983; O'Neill, 1985), collections of essays (e.g. Davis, 1997; Featherstone et al., 1991; Nettleton and Watson, 1998; Scott and Morgan, 1993), books on the medical management of bodies (Martin, 1989, 1994); works that drew on and constructed histories of the body (Brown, 1988; Feher et al., 1989; Hillman and Mazzio, 1997; Laqueur, 1990; Sawday, 1995; Sennett, 1994; Synnott, 1993), reviews of the literature (e.g. Frank, 1990; Freund, 1988), distinctive theoretical approaches to the construction of embodied social theories (e.g. Burkitt, 1999; Butler, 1993; Falk, 1994; Grosz, 1994; Mellor and Shilling, 1997; Shilling, 1993; Turner, 1984), feminist theories of the body (e.g. Butler, 1990, 1993; Diprose, 1994; Grosz, 1994; Leder, 1990; Kirby, 1997; Shildrick, 1997), studies of health, illness, disability and the body (e.g. Frank, 1991, 1995; Freund and McGuire, 1991; Peterson and Bunton, 1997; Seymour, 1998; Turner, 1987), analyses of the senses and the irreducibly embodied nature of emotions (e.g. Bendelow and Williams, 1998; Classen, 1993; Craib, 1998; Howes, 1991; Scarry, 1985); cultural geographies of embodiment (e.g. Ainley, 1998; Bale and Philo, 1998; Nast and Pile, 1998; Rodaway, 1994); assessments of ageing and of masculinity, femininity and the body (Connell, 1995; Davis, 1995; Featherstone and Wernick, 1995; Peterson, 1998); studies of biotechnologies and cyberbodies (e.g. Featherstone and Burrows, 1995; Kimbrell, 1993), and the establishment in 1995 of the journal *Body & Society*.

Four major factors assisted this development and stimulated distinctive lines of enquiry traversing important social issues and academic concerns. First, the prominence of the body in consumer culture provided an obvious focus of interest. Within advanced capitalist societies during the second half of the twentieth century there was a move away from the focus on hard work in the sphere of production coupled with frugality in the sphere of consumption. Instead, the proliferation of production oriented toward leisure helped promote the 'performing self' which treats the body as a machine and symbol to be finely tuned and cared for; an approach reinforced by the body's status as a ubiquitous sign in advertising culture. Featherstone (1982) argues that the cumulative effect of these changes is that the body ceases to be a vessel of sin, as posited in Christianity, and presents itself as an object for display inside and outside the bedroom.

It is in this context that Tönnies' ([1887] 1957) *Gemeinschaft/Gesellschaft* distinction was drawn on by analysts concerned with the changing social importance and increased individualization of the body. Giddens (1991: 7, 98, 102) suggested the body was a 'given' in traditional societies, marked by communal signs of status, yet had been colonized by modernity and 'drawn into the reflexive organization of social life' to the extent that we are 'responsible for the design of our bodies'. This responsibility is facilitated by advances in modern science and technology, yet is qualified morally by the absence of answers to fundamental questions. Turner (1984: 108–9) makes a related point in contrasting the premodern 'housing' of the person in a persona, a public mask incorporated into the honour of a heraldic sign, with the modern concept of dignity based on the 'presentational body'. Similarly, Falk (1994) analyses modern and premodern bodies by drawing on Durkheim's understanding of mechanical and organic solidarity. Falk conceptualizes traditional society as an 'eating community'; a two-way order structured by the communal feast. Within modernity, however, the boundaries of self became detached from the bonds of community and centred around the 'bodily surface and its sensory openings', while human association is facilitated by individualizing 'communicative (speech) acts' (Falk, 1994: 12–13, 36).

Second, since the 1960s 'second wave' feminism emphasized through a critical interrogation of the sex/gender divide that there was nothing natural about women's corporeality which justified their public subordination (Oakley, 1972). Various strands of feminist thought examined technology's potential to liberate women from the constraining effects of biology (Firestone, 1971; Haraway, 1985); traced the legal history of the female body as male property (Eisenstein, 1988; Williams, 1997); and highlighted the bodily bases of female oppression through the construction of 'compulsory heterosexuality' (Mackinnon, 1989), and the marginalization or 'erasure' of female sexuality in male culture (Irigaray, [1977] 1985; Kristeva, [1977] 1987).

The body was not, however, welcomed uncritically into feminist thought. This was partly because 'malestream' philosophers traditionally associated men with freedom and the mind, and women with 'unreason associated with the body' (Grosz, 1994: 4). Women were seen as '*more* biological, *more* corporeal and more natural than men', and therefore more suited to the world of private existence than men (1994: 4). This ambivalence to the body also derived from the influence of de Beauvoir's 1949 *The Second Sex*. Drawing on Sartre's existentialism, de Beauvoir suggested women's bodies made them amenable to being constructed as Other (sentenced to a life of immanence) for use by the male Self (de Beauvoir, [1949] 1993: 31, 214, 281). Despite such negative associations, however, feminists helped place on the agenda the project of 'reexploring, reexamining, notions of female corporeality' (Grosz, 1994: 14), and have interrogated the body in analysing sexuality, ethics and standpoint epistemologies.

Changes in governmentality provided a third impetus for the body's prominence. Instrumental here is Foucault's (1970, 1979a, 1979b) analysis of how modernity's creation of 'man' was accompanied by a shift in the *target* of governmental discourses (the fleshy body gave way to the mindful body as a focus of concern); in the *object* of discourse (preoccupation with matters of death was replaced by interest in structuring life); and in the *scope* of discourse (the control of anonymous individuals gave way to the management of differentiated populations). The eighteenth century witnessed a large increase in discourses on sexuality, for example, which linked the sex of individual bodies to the management of national populations (Foucault, 1981).

While these modes of power were facilitated by developments in welfare provision (teaching hospitals, for example, were instrumental in developing medical norms), fiscal crises have highlighted the financial burdens associated with monitoring and managing, educating and caring for dependent groups. These are associated with declining infant mortality rates in the West, increasing life expectancies, medical advances and the rise of diseases such as AIDS requiring long-term care. Issues concerning the prioritization and distribution of particular treatments and medicines inevitably raise questions concerning whose bodies should/should not be treated. Viewed in a global context in which most of the world's population has inadequate supplies of food and clean water, this emphasizes the importance of the body to the structuring of social inequalities and 'risk societies' (Beck, 1992).

A fourth factor to raise the analytic profile of the body is a growing uncertainty about the 'reality' of the body. Advances in technology, transplant surgery, *in vitro* fertilization and genetic engineering have weakened the boundaries between bodies and machines. But while we may have the means to exert an unprecedented amount of control over bodies, including the ability to redesign them in particular ways, we are living in an age which has thrown into radical doubt our knowledge of what bodies are and how we should control them. Turner (1984: 7), for example, states that 'In writing this study of the body, I have become increasingly less sure of what the body is.' Such considerations have contributed towards an additional 'decentering' of the subject. The principle of individuality accepted by Enlightenment thought depended on identifying what was unique to a person across the contingencies of date and location, yet the malleability of the body threatens such constancies. This is reflected in postmodernist writings which have abandoned the modernist project of 'knowing' what the body is, and which threaten the body with the same fate as befell humanistic versions of the 'subject' or 'author'. The body becomes a 'blank screen' or 'sign-receiving system' ever open to being (re)constructed by social forces beyond its control (Kroker and Kroker, 1988), or alternatively, in the work of Deleuze and Guattari, an elusive 'body without organs'.

This 'uncertain body' has also been interpreted in aesthetic, sensual terms by those unhappy with postmodern attempts to dissolve the facticity of the embodied subject. Berger ([1967] 1990) and Giddens (1991: 45–7), for example, suggest that it is the contingencies and frailties associated with our embodied selves that can stimulate a loss of 'basic trust' or 'ontological security' leading to the experience of 'paranoid horrors' (Tudor, 1995). In this context, a 'will to purity' in the treatment, punishment and categorization of bodies has been associated with particular events that threaten the borders of the social body (Douglas, 1966; Theweleit, [1977] 1987). Placing this 'uncertain body' within such social and corporeal parameters relativizes the relativistic claims of postmodern writings on embodiment, suggesting, for example, that recent concern with the 'disappearing body' signifies not a permanent dissolution of the body's integrity but a resurgence of effervescent experiences of the sacred in a modern world in which the profane has become banal (Mellor and Shilling, 1997).

RESOURCES FOR SOCIAL THEORIES OF THE BODY

While contemporary writings suggest that social theory has traditionally treated the body as the province of another discipline, as an uninteresting prerequisite of human action, or simply has a target of social control, I have already noted the presence of body matters in the early development of Western thought. Indeed, a long tradition of writings has provided valuable resources for contemporary discussions of embodiment, and lends support to the argument that recent enthusiasm for this subject area is as much a recovery of important issues as it is the discovery of a new theoretical terrain. This becomes evident in a selective overview of writings drawn on by theorists of embodiment.

Feuerbach ([1841] 1957) turned to sensualism in criticizing the rationalist legacy of German philosophy developed by such writers as Hegel, and in contesting idealist conceptions of the agent with a more materialist emphasis (Turner, 1996). Marx engaged with this debate in constructing a *historical* materialism which proceeded on the basis that 'The chief defect of all hitherto existing materialism (that of Feurbach included) is that the thing, reality, sensuousness, is conceived only in the form of the *object or of contemplation*, but not as *sensuous human activity, practice*, not subjectively' (Marx, 1970: 121). Humans had first to produce the means of satisfying their basic needs, but *transformed* their corporeal capacities and desires, as well as their natural environment, through the social relations they entered into in satisfying these needs. The extent to which Marx's later writings were dependent on a prior view of human nature has been contested by Althusser and debated by other writers (Geras, 1983; McLellan, 1985). Nevertheless, Marx's ([1844] 1975) theory of alienation had as its referent a clear view of the bodily capacities of humans that were stunted by the instrumental nature of labour under capitalism and its associated division of labour.

Durkheim insisted that the subject matter of the discipline be kept separate from that of biology and psychology. Nevertheless, he associated social facts with moral rules which arise from and are consolidated through the 'special energy' of collective sentiments which transform the *homo duplex* nature of humans (Durkheim, [1914] 1973; 1982: 50–6). While accepting a nature/culture distinction which is anathema to most current theorists on the body, Durkheim was concerned with the ritual socialization of individuals and the interrelationship between the experience of collective effervescence, and the production and maintenance of social solidarity and the *conscience collective*.

Nietzsche's ([1871] 1993) contrast between Apollo and Dionysus has often been utilized in analysing Western culture, but has also been employed to analyse the 'internally divided' nature of human beings. The Apollo/Dionysus contrast may encapsulate struggles within humans, and between individuals and society, by illuminating the division between instrumental rationalism and sensual satisfaction. Weber continued to see the influence of Dionysus in the restricted spheres of eroticism and charisma within rationalized society, and his account of the sublimation of salvation anxiety within a work ethic can be read as a description of the non-rational, corporeal foundations of modern society which provides for a productive comparison with Durkheim. Additionally, the placing of Weber within the tradition of philosophical anthropology, rather than as a value-free socio-logist of social action, has been used to empha-size his understanding of asceticism as both 'the basis of our modern civilization and as the necessary denial of our ontology' (Turner, 1991b: xxvi).

Adopting a distinctive approach toward the rational/sensual aspects of life, Marcuse (1955, [1964] 1972) warned that emotional responses had been harnessed to the ordering properties of markets in which the body is dominated by a 'performance principle' resulting in 'surplus repression'. The 'triumph of form over vitalism' that had occurred in postliberal capitalism was associated with a one-dimensional society in which the possibility of class conflict, as Marx envisaged it, was no longer possible (Marcuse, [1964] 1972). Freud (psychologically) and Elias (sociologically) analysed humans' turbulent inner life as a necessary cost of civilizing processes which could sometimes break through the con-trolled 'presentation of self' prized within modernity. While Freud tended to construct a universalistic view of human psychology, how-ever, Elias linked the minutiae of individual consciousness and behaviour to large-scale changes in monopolies of violence and the division of labour.

Having already mentioned the emphasis placed on culture in Parsons' view of action, it appears odd to list his writings as a resource for theories of the body. Parsons recognized the importance of the biological organism as a constraining sub-system of action, however, and provided fasci-nating analyses of the major existential predica-ments of the human condition such as sickness and death. Proposing a different approach to the body, recent critiques of Parsons have drawn on American pragmatism in order to focus on 'situated creativity'; on how 'new variations of action are generated by the tension of problems contained in situations' (Joas, 1996: 139). Here, bodily doing and problem-solving is an integral part of human action in a way that was missing from Parsons' sociology. Dewey's writings on ethics, education and play, for example, ascribe a more important role to experiential creativity than that contained within notions of normative action.

From a feminist perspective, the writings of de Beauvoir ([1949] 1993) did much to promote the 'Other' as a unit idea for feminist sociology. The embodied construction of the 'Other' is also relevant to historical writings on colonialism utilized by theorists of race. Central to imperi-alist thought was a process of associating 'racial Otherness' with bodily characteristics. European colonial powers did not initiate representations of physical Otherness, but embodiment and skin colour became central to these images, and proved suitable ways of indicating and legitimiz-ing colonial rule. Bastide (1968), for example, shows how the symbolic import of 'black' was invested with a monstrousness in the Christian West even in medieval times. Jordan (1974) suggests this Otherness existed before contact with Africans (black was associated with biblical narratives of evil and beneficence, the devil and God), but was subsequently used to justify slavery. Associations between blackness and a dreaded Otherness continued in a non-biblical vein in the work of later political thinkers. As Gilroy (1993: 9–10) notes, the eighteenth-century philosopher Edmund Burke's discus-sions of the sublime link blackness with the experience of horror and darkness. Blackness, then, existed as a visual, symbolic resource facilitating the 'racialization' of peoples as slaves and primitive 'Others', and contrasting with positive constructions of whiteness.

Finally, the work of Foucault has proved to be an almost infinitely flexible resource: being used by theorists interested in any amount of body-related matters, such as discourses of sexuality, technologies of power and techniques of the self. The influence of Foucault becomes evident when we examine the major thinkers to have shaped social constructionist approaches to the body.

SOCIALLY CONSTRUCTED BODIES

The roots of recent theories of the body are diverse, but the most influential have drawn on those literatures that facilitate social construc-tionist analyses of the body. Minimally, all social theories of the body are constructionist in recognizing that society exerts *some* influence in shaping bodies. In this section, however, I reserve the term for theories that assert most strongly that human physicality can be derived from, or explained by, social phenomena; for theories which are powerfully deconstructive of conventional assumptions about the body's biological facticity.

The influence of social constructionism derived significantly from its apparent ability to combat naturalistic views of the body. These remain significant in sociobiology (if not in natural sciences with a more dynamic view of their subject matter), inform much popular thought, and view the body as a pre-social, bio-logical entity which determines self-identity and social institutions. Culture does not create differ-ences, it merely 'replicates' them within the social sphere or, at most, 'amplifies' them. Social con-structionism, in contrast, has enabled critics to deconstruct such accounts by examining the historical, categorical and discursive creation of bodily differences (Laqueur, 1990).

Two authors have been particularly influential in shaping recent constructionist writings on the body. I focus initially on Foucault, and on an influential development of Foucault's concerns in the writings of Butler, and then examine the strong Parsonian influence in Turner's structuralist theory of 'bodily order'.

Post-structuralism and the deconstructed body

Foucault's post-structuralism highlights the ubiquity of power within the 'discursive formations' that construct human embodiment. The importance of the body to Foucault is such that he described his work as constituting a '"history of bodies" and the manner in which what is most material and vital in them has been invested' (Foucault, 1981: 152). Central to this history is a mapping of 'the body and the effects of power on it' (Foucault, 1980: 58). This includes examining how the 'micro-physics' of power operates in institutional formations 'through progressively finer channels, gaining access to individuals themselves, to their bodies, their gestures and all their daily actions' (Foucault, 1980: 151–2).

There is, however, a tension in Foucault's approach. On the one hand, there is a real substantive concern with the body as an actual product of constructing discourses. Somewhat ironically, given the emphasis Foucault places on historical discontinuity, this leads him to treat the body as a transhistorical and cross-cultural unified phenomenon *insofar* as the body is always already to be constructed by discourse. Such a view provides no room for recognizing that different aspects of embodiment, such as illness and death, may be more or less open to discursive reconstruction depending on the specific characteristics of an era. On the other hand, Foucault's epistemological view of the body means that it disappears as a material and phenomenological entity; its existence and experience is permanently deferred behind the grids of meaning imposed by discourse (Butler, 1990: 129–30; Shilling, 1993: 79–80). Foucault (1977: 153) makes promising mention of how 'The body is moulded by a great many distinct regimes', but this moulding turns out to be a deconstruction whose effects can only be accessed via discourse. Turner (1984: 245) suggests such features mean Foucault's approach is insufficiently concerned with 'lived experience', while Dews (1987: 163) notes: 'Without some theory which makes the corporeal more than a tabula rasa, it is impossible to reckon the costs imposed by "an infinitesimal power over the active body".' Foucault's position changes significantly in his later volumes on the history of sexuality, in which the material body comes more into view, but problems of discursive reductionism characterize what have been the most popular developments of Foucault's analyses.

Feminist scholars have made much of Foucault's work in arguing that power is invested in and exercised through bodies in ways that produce gender differences (e.g. McNay, 1992; Nicholson, 1990; Sawicki, 1991), and that 'the biological' is simply a manifestation of 'the social' and does not need theorizing as an 'objective' extra-discursive field of knowledge (Delphy, 1984; Wittig, 1982). Butler (1990, 1993) has been one of the most influential feminist interrogators of Foucault, and is centrally concerned with Foucault's aim 'To substitute for the enigmatic treasure of "things" anterior to discourse, the regular formation of objects that emerge only in discourse' (Foucault, 1989: 47). Critical of the Cartesianism governing de Beauvoir's analysis of the mind as freedom and the (female) body as constraint, Butler (1990) deconstructs the opposition between the sexual body (as foundational and natural) and normative gender (as product and cultural) by arguing that 'sex', 'body', 'gender' and 'identity' are *equally constructed* by the dominant matrix of heterosexuality.

Butler's (1990) *Gender Trouble* focuses on gender as stylized acting; 'a set of repeated acts within a highly rigid regulatory frame that congeal over time to produce the appearance of substance' (Butler, 1990: 33). There is no subject or sexed body prior to this stylized, regulated action and it is gender, therefore, which constructs sexual identity (e.g. Butler, 1990: 71, 88, 93; 1997). Butler's (1993) *Bodies That Matter*, in contrast, focuses on the category of sex. Sex refers to the *discursively constituted* materiality of the sexed body, 'a process whereby regulatory norms materialize "sex" and achieve this materialization through a forcible reiteration of those norms' (Butler, 1993: 1). Foucault (as well as Derrida and Lacan) remains influential in Butler's theorization of sexed bodies, but Althusser is also deployed to reveal how bodies are produced as sexed in order for them to engage in gendered doings. Althusser suggests subjects are 'hailed' or 'interpellated' to assume certain positions: ideological and repressive institutions participate in the 'girling' of the infant, a 'founding interpellation' reiterated to produce a 'naturalized effect' which sets boundaries and norms (Butler, 1993: 7–8). Once again, it is the power of discursive authorities to *construct* materiality that interests Butler (1993: 68). Indeed, Butler (1993: 29, ix) doubts whether feminists need to talk about the materiality of sex, and admits that in seeking to consider the materiality of bodies, she found herself moving to other domains and 'kept losing track of the subject'.

Butler's work has proved productive in rethinking the sex/gender/body distinctions prominent in contemporary feminist theory. Her writing is by no means restricted to or uncritical of Foucault's analyses, but shares with them the problem of being unable to conceptualize the body distinct from *extant* power relations. This ignores the thousands of years of 'socio-natural' (Burkitt, 1999) evolutionary history that equipped humans with particular capacities, and makes it impossible to evaluate cultural practices in relation to people's bodily well-being.[1] If we do not have some idea of our body's *own* needs and abilities at a particular time, how can we judge whether an institution or a society is good or bad for our well-being? Soper (1995: 138), for example, argues that if we reject the idea of embedded, bodily pleasures and pains, 'we remove the objective grounds for challenging the authority of custom and convention, and must accept that it is only on the basis of personal preference (or prejudice) that we can contest the "necessity" of a practice such as clitorectomy or foot binding, challenge the oppression of sexual minorities, or justify the condemnation of any form of sexual abuse or torture.' Post-structuralism may have been promoted with the aim of 'freeing up the subject from the policing of cultural norms' but ends up ceding to culture the right to arbitrate on matters bodily (1995: 138).

Structuralism and the ordered body

If Foucault's writings constitute an influential source for social constructionist analyses, Parsonian theorizing is also important. It is rare for Parsons to be associated explicitly with theories of the body, for reasons already outlined, but his work informs many sociological assumptions about the ability of bodies to be socialized and the social system's importance in this socialization.

Despite his consistent espousal of a voluntarist theory of action, Parsons is perhaps best known for his 'structural functionalism'; a functionalism that suggests social systems possess a structure that confronts them with a set of 'core problems' that have to be overcome if they are to survive. This feature of his work is central to Turner's (1984) structuralist theory of 'bodily order', but Turner combines it with a resiting of Parsons' analysis of the behavioural organism. Instead of being a sub-system of action, the behavioural organism becomes for Turner the model for his analysis of the *overarching environment in which action occurs*. While maintaining

its Parsonian form, this contrasts with Parsons' eventual positioning of culture as the environment for action (Alexander, 1998).

Turner examines the structural problems posed by the body for the government of social systems by combining Parsons' 'core problems' perspective with Hobbes' concern with the 'geometry of bodies'. For Turner, all social systems must solve 'the problem of the body' which has four dimensions: the reproduction of populations through time; the restraint of desire; the regulation of populations in space; and the representation of bodies. Having established this typology, Turner emphasizes the critical intent to his work and examines the control of sexuality by men exercising patriarchal power.

The scope of Turner's analysis ranges far and wide, examining a *mode of control* by which society has sought to manage each dimension of the government of the body, a *dominant theorist* of each dimension, and a *paradigmatic disease* liable to 'break down' bodies as a result of society's imposition of these tasks. Having learnt what gets 'done to' the body though, we get little sense of the agentic body or the 'lived experience' of what it is like to be an embodied subject at a particular time. Turner's 'core problems' approach might enable us to 'work down' from the problems confronting social systems to the choices confronting individuals but, like Parsons' 'voluntaristic theory of action', this is vulnerable to the criticism that these 'choices' only exist in relation to the norms of the social system rather than being concerned, at least in part, with the passions, emotions and conflicts within the embodied individual.

Structuralist approaches have instituted a valuable 'epistemological break' from common-sense thinking about the relationship between the body, self-identity and society, but ultimately produce unsatisfactory engagements with the social consequences of the body's materiality by substituting social reductionism for biological reductionism. Indeed, theorists such as Turner (1991a) have supplemented their work with foundationalist perspectives that distinguish between how the body is *classified*, what the body *is*, and how it is *experienced*. This accepts that the experience of ageing, for example, can be shaped by gender and ethnicity, but insists that 'The human body has definite and distinctive biological and physiological characteristics' (Turner, 1996: 30). In highlighting people's *experiences* of their bodies, Turner also points us in the direction of phenomenological approaches developed by such theorists as Merleau-Ponty. The question of how these epistemological, ontological and phenomenological dimensions are articulated remains to be answered. Nevertheless, as Turner (1996: 28) points out, for theorists who refuse any significant notion of the experienced, sensuous materiality of the body, and remain entirely within the parameters of (post-) structuralism, 'the lived body drops from view as the text', or discourse, or the structural 'interpellation' of subjects 'becomes the all-pervasive topic of discourse'. This leaves us with a major gap as 'what differentiates the body as it is lived from any artificially constructed object is precisely the fact that it is a vital organism which is experienced subjectively' (Soper, 1995: 135), even if this organism is itself subject to re-formations over time (Mellor and Shilling, 1997: 18–31).

EMBODYING SOCIAL THEORY

Studies of the body have been concerned with, and influenced by, a range of issues central to social theory; provide distinctive interpretations of what classical theorists have to offer our understanding of modernity; and often contain within them a creative tension between traditional social theory and contemporary cultural theory. In what follows, I want to illustrate these features by focusing on recent debates on the consequences of corporeality for theories of social action, for theories of self-identity and (post-) modernity, for the sociology of knowledge, and for social theory's enduring concern with the relationship between the human organism and the social organism.

Embodiment and social action

Hans Joas' (1983, 1993, 1996) analyses of the intersubjective constitution of body-image, pragmatism and the creativity of action have done much to consolidate the argument that satisfactory theories of social action require an account of the embodied actor. Social theories that conceive action as taking place in relation to either a normative system or a criteria of rationality formulated outside of the actor tend to presuppose the body as a factual basis of action, and as inert matter motivated by the mind. In contrast, Joas (1996: 158) draws on the work of Merleau-Ponty and the American pragmatists in suggesting that our corporeal-practical being makes it essential to recognize the 'situated creativity' involved in our bodily coming to terms with the world, and that the practical mediacy of the human organism and its situations precede all conscious goal-setting.

Taking account of this bodily being in the world has important implications for theories of social action. First, our practical ability to come to terms with reality is more immediately important to our social existence than any clearly defined value system. Instead of basing our action on fully elaborated cognitive maps, we are able to face the world with relatively few fixed cognitive expectations (Joas, 1996: 159). In Giddens' (1984) terms, practical consciousness is more important to our daily lives than discursive consciousness. Secondly, our corporeal-practical being in the world also allows us to switch between various forms of sensory perception and action. Sight can be supplemented by touch if we wish to find out more about an object while the knowledge we gain about the social world is not abstract-rational, but is related to the bodily modes by which we engage with objects and other people. Thirdly, opposing the idea that all action can be defined along a rational/irrational continuum, our perception of a situation 'is pre-defined in our capacities for action and our current dispositions for action' (Joas, 1996: 161; see also Bourdieu, 1984). Action is not subsequent to thought but is integral to thought.

Having established that our corporeal-practical being in the world is actively implicated in the creative and situated nature of social action, Joas argues for the necessity of ascertaining how the body becomes present to ourselves. This involves investigating how we acquire a body-image (an individual's awareness of the morphological structure of their body, its parts and postures, its capacities and limitations) that allows us to coordinate our actions and make our way in the world (Joas, 1996: 175). Referring us to the psychiatrist Schilder's work on the subject, for example, Grosz (1994: 83) notes that body-image is a necessary precondition for undertaking voluntary action as it 'unifies and coordinates postural, tactile, kinesthetic, and visual sensations so that these are experienced as the sensations of a subject coordinated into a single space'. Research on such issues as phantom arms and legs of amputees, on the inability to tell left from right, and on disturbances in locating sensations in the body show that body-image is not unproblematically given to people.

The phenomenology of Merleau-Ponty (1962) provides us with one approach to the acquisition of body-image. Body-image is pre-reflective for Merleau-Ponty: intentionality can only exist as incarnate intentionality and there is a 'pregiven interrelatedness between our own kinesthetic processes and the laws of nature that surrounds us' (Joas, 1983: 200). Every conscious intention refers back to this structure which is constituted by the pre-reflective interaction of the body with itself (for example, when one part touches another) and with its environment. Merleau-Ponty (1962) also recognizes the importance of accounting for changes in body-image and distinguishes between a habitual body and an actual body when dealing with transformations brought about by ageing or infirmity. Joas (1983: 200–1) remains unhappy with this general approach, however, and argues that the pre-reflective field must itself have a genesis: 'it is biologically impossible for the human species to come to a self-control of the body and social abilities by mere maturation, without socialization.' Merleau-Ponty draws on Lacan in tying the constitution of body-image to the infant's experience of the mirror image, but Joas (1996) argues that this exaggerates the importance of visual experience and downplays the importance of emotional relationships. Instead, it is Mead who provides a way of developing Merleau-Ponty's concern with 'intercorporeite' (the interrelatedness of our experience of our bodies to our experience of others' bodies) (Joas, 1983: 200–1; 1996: 181).

The crucial idea Joas takes from Mead's published (1934, 1938) and unpublished work is that the process of constituting objects as permanent already presupposes elementary structures of role-taking engaged in by the pre-linguistic infant (Joas, 1983: 203). Opposing the priority of self-experiences in phenomenology, Mead suggests that the constitution of one's own body, and the constitution of permanent objects, are shaped through communicative interaction. Even to be able to identify a perception or sensation as coming from within oneself requires an attitude towards one's body mediated by significant gestures. Similarly, in the case of interaction between an embodied actor and the outside world, it is only the gestures involved in role-taking that 'renders possible the coordination of hand and eye and the transference into the objects of a substance that has an active effect' (Joas, 1983: 202–3; 1996: 182).

Joas concludes by arguing that if the relation of an individual to their body, and, therefore, to action, is not given but is shaped by pre-linguistic intersubjective structures, there must be a foundational sociality based on corporeal interaction. As Joas (1996: 184) puts it,

> If an actor does not perceive his [sic] own body directly as present, but rather via a body schema . . . constituted in an intersubjective process, then any ability to act rests on a further tacit assumption, namely that there is a *primary sociality* which has not yet been generated by conscious intentionality but has preceded such, in other words a structure of common action which initially consists solely of our interaction with other bodies.

This creative deployment of Mead's work seeks to overturn the assumptions of theories of social action which marginalize the body. Nevertheless, Joas' emphasis on primary sociality as a precursor to creative bodily action could be opposed if we accept there are natural propensities to act associated with a naturally generated body-image. This prompts Joas (1983: 203) to recognize the emphasis on social-cognitive development in Mead's work and to look elsewhere to integrate his analysis with a study of motivational and affective processes. It is writers like Durkheim, Joas suggests, who enable us to see that body-image and the ability to act are not given once and for all but are dependent on foundations that are periodically refreshed through the revitalization of collectivities.

Embodiment and self-identity

Mead's (1913) analysis of the emergence of the social self through the 'me'/'I' relationship, a relationship central to the role-taking discussed above, helped open a space for post-structuralists and postmodernists to more radically destabilize the notion of any durable identity, body-image or human agent. The advance of biotechnologies and the supposed disappearance of 'the social' as a durable system have informed arguments suggesting that identity and capacities for action are no longer given, or even dependent on a 'primary sociality', but have become a potentially infinitely flexible resource for either the individual or for technologies of control (Featherstone and Burrows, 1995). The question posed by theories of embodiment, however, is whether the constitution of our corporeal being places any limits on this fragmentation of identity or on our capacities as actors.

In a strong version of the argument that embodiment provides a foundational basis for identity, Archer (1995: 287–8) proposes a 'body + consciousness' view of human beings: the body provides us with non-social experiences of non-social reality whose stability is complemented by a fundamental 'continuity of consciousness'. Drawing on the anthropology of Mauss, Archer (1995: 383) argues that this corporeal and cognitive continuity equips humans with a 'Universal Sense of Self' over and above historically specific conceptions of personhood. Bourdieu's (1984) theory of the relationship between *habitus*, taste and social space also posits a strong relationship between people's embodied upbringing and their identity even if it opposes the universalism of Archer's work. Bourdieu argues that a 'socially constituted set of cognitive and motivating structures' result in a bodily *hexus* that provides people with class-dependent, pre-disposed ways of relating to and categorizing both familiar and novel situations (Brubaker, 1985: 758). The habitus is formed in the context of people's social location and inculcates in them an orientation to life based on and reconciled to these positions. As such, it tends toward reproducing the status quo (Bourdieu, 1984: 190, 466).

The idea that identities may involve a potentially intransigent structuring of bodily dispositions is repeated in recent writings on habit (Camic, 1986) and sexuality. Connell (1995) suggests that physical apprenticeships into masculinity result in deeply engrained and highly restrictive orientations to the flesh and emotions (see also Wacquant, 1995). Grosz's (1994: 117) analysis of theories of the sexed body as a text also suggests society can appear to shape the 'body permanent': 'the tools of body engraving – social, surgical, epistemic, disciplinary – all mark, indeed constitute, bodies in culturally specific ways . . .' Coupled with her opposition to the view that sexual difference is forged out of undifferentiated bodies, and her statement that the possession of certain genitals 'must play a major role in the type of body imagery one has' (Grosz, 1994: 58), one argument of her book suggests an important degree of sexual stability in the link between embodiment and gendered identity.

While social theory has employed the body to critically engage with the postmodern decentring of the subject, other work suggests current forms of embodiment contribute to the *fluidity* of identity. Grosz, for example, shuttles between suggestions of fixity to analyses of fluidity in her model of the body as a 'Möbius strip' (the inverted three-dimension figure eight) used to mirror how flesh and mind flow into each other to produce a flexible body image which serves as a basis for sensory interaction and the production of a contingently coherent view on the world (Grosz, 1994: 36–43, 66, 99–100). The flexibility of self-identity is also central to Giddens' writings on modernity. While Giddens structuration theory proposes a view of the body as an 'organic constraint', as a container of self-identity, he later argues that the chronic reflexivity and corporeal malleability characteristic of high modernity destabilizes identity. The ability to mould the body in line with our sense of self means identity is not located in an intransigent habitus, but 'in the capacity to keep a particular narrative going' – a capacity always at risk as a result of the 'until further notice' character of (self) knowledge (Giddens, 1991: 53–4).

Such contrasting views of embodied identity appear irreconcilable, yet we can establish a dialogue between them by looking historically at themes and metaphors of bodily fixity and fluidity. Such a perspective may suggest that any single formulation of embodied identity is incapable of dealing with the diverse forms of bodily-being-in-the world, but that simple modern body/premodern body distinctions fail

to grasp some of the shared potentialities characteristic of embodied identities over time.

Elias' ([1939] 1978; [1939] 1982) study of the relationship between state and personality formation argues that medieval persons possessed instinctual and emotional responses to events which tended to be more fluid (more impulsive, volatile and unpredictable) than their modern counterparts. The medieval habitus was formed in an environment characterized by intermittent violence and disease, where struggle for survival loomed large in people's actions, and where magic and superstition were aides to knowledge. Outside of the relatively controlled environments provided by Court Societies, these conditions did not promote the considered adoption of habits designed to cultivate the 'presentation of self' (Elias, 1983). Nevertheless, the volatility of the medieval era could co-exist with the flesh becoming a site for the pursuance of religious 'body regimes' (Mellor and Shilling, 1997). Body regimes are aggressive, if structured, flights into physicality which sought to harness the emotional and physical extremes characteristic of the medieval era to religious goals. Body regimes were associated with the Catholic Church and pursued by a minority of the population (Bynum, 1987), but their adoption represented the development and restructuring of *already existing*, popular ways of implicating the body in magical and superstitious activities as routes to meaning and material benefit.

The development of the *early modern body* has been associated with various factors, centuries apart, but Protestant attempts to re-form medieval bodies accelerated extant processes. First, by seeking to dislocate people from their natural, supernatural and social environments, and in prioritizing cognitive belief and thought as routes to knowledge, Protestantism made linguistic symbols and narratives a central source of people's self-identity. Secondly, the Protestant flesh had to be made subordinate to these (religiously justifiable) narratives; the body had, in other words, to be controlled by the mind. Thirdly, the inability of these narratives to control fully human emotions helps us understand the enormous anxiety stimulated in Protestants over those sinful aspects of their bodily selves (and the bodies of others) which threatened to become grotesque and out of control (Roper, 1994).

While Reformers tended to be suspicious of feelings, the arts, and entertainment, certain scripturally justifiable 'industrious pastimes' and 'rational recreations' were encouraged (Hill, 1966). The personal pursuit of healthy bodies also became important to many Puritans (dirt was symbolically linked with sin, while cleanliness and sobriety were markers of righteous living), and has been associated with post-reformation medical regimes and the development of capitalism (Turner, 1983). Indeed, the idea that Protestant sectarianism unwittingly provided capitalism with a sober, honest and industrious labour force is a general theme in historical sociology (Hobsbawm, 1964; Thompson, 1963).

In contemporary Western societies, it has been argued that the continuing development of certain rationalizing aspects of embodiment are matched by altogether different expressions of human corporeality marked by a sensualization of experience. What has been referred to as a 'baroque modern' form of embodiment (Mellor and Shilling, 1997) combines aspects of both these orientations. On the one hand, the pervasiveness of chronic reflexivity, the growing number of experts ready to proffer guidance for all aspects of life, and the technologies which increase our ability to alter our bodies in line with our *ideas*, point to the extension of the cognitive characteristics of the early modern body. On the other hand, a new fluid sensuality is also increasingly evident, as explored in Ferguson's (1992) discussion of a 'recovered sensuousness', Lash and Urry's (1994) analysis of the emergence of 'aesthetic reflexivity', the notion of the reappearance of the baroque (Buci-Glucksmann, 1994; Turner, 1994), and Maffesoli's (1996) account of the spread of a Dionysian, irrational and emotional resacralization of contemporary bodies.

Bodies and knowledge

In examining the embodied bases of knowing, theories of the body have challenged the dominant tradition in Western philosophy which associates the mind with what makes us human, and rational thought with our ability to acquire knowledge and control. I have already mentioned the philosophical influence of Descartes' principle *cogito ergo sum* as the foundation for knowledge, and Kant's ranking of duty over bodily desire. Of most interest to social theorists, however, are the practical uses to which such perspectives have been put. Turner (1996: 9) argues that an adapted Cartesian 'world-view' became part of early modern individualism, 'scientific rationalism and [a] Protestant spirit which sought to dominate external nature' through instrumental rationality. He also suggests this facilitated the growth of colonialism in which 'other cultures were subordinated to the instrumental control of Western technology and civilization' (Turner, 1996: 10).

In deconstructing the objectivist view of the world behind Western modes of control and oppression, postmodern thought sought to destabilize metanarratives which have the potential to be associated with 'final solutions' (Bauman, 1989); relativize the foundations of 'knowledge' and 'truth'; and promote deconstructionist epistemologies. Deconstructionism relativized knowledge, while standpoint epistemology prioritizes experience and has its roots in Marx and Engels' (1970: 51) argument that 'Consciousness is . . . from the very beginning a social product.' As Gilroy (1993: 52) points out, standpoint epistemologies are often based on essentialist premises which divide people on the basis of their gendered or racial identities. Other theories concerned with explicating the shared bodily bases of knowledge, however, have sought to develop a *corporeally situated* theory of knowledge in which communication is possible because of what unites us as humans, as much as what divides us into social groups.

Elias' (1991) theory of 'symbol emancipation' starts by emphasizing the links between knowledge and embodiment; links characteristic of the entire human species. Symbol emancipation results from evolutionary processes which provided humans with the physical means of communicating, thinking and orienting themselves to reality via symbols. This gave humans the ability to act in the light of learned knowledge and provided them with an evolutionary advantage over other species. Humans have a unique ability to learn and synthesize symbols, to develop these into language marked by reflexivity, variability, precision, flexibility and a high degree of 'reality congruence', and to transmit accumulated knowledge between generations in the form of symbols (Elias, 1991: 31–2, 43, 131). Symbol emancipation enabled humans to reflexively monitor their own behaviour, to adapt to new circumstances independently of biological changes, and represented a breakthrough of the evolutionary process to a 'post animalistic' level (Elias, 1991: 43, 31–2).

This is no sociobiological conception of human communication, but suggests that if we are to understand the social world we have to take notice of the intertwining of social and natural processes, transformed as they are by the historical relationships of interdependent individuals. Symbol use may be impossible for Elias without minimal biological equipment, but it remains dependent on individuals learning language and an array of social contingencies that have their own impact on the bodily basis of knowledge. In their study of a divided community, for example, Elias and Scotson ([1965] 1994) show how spatial separation and contact based on limited sensory information can lead to the stigmatization of social groups and the proliferation of 'fantasy knowledge' about others.

Related observations have been made in Hirsch's (1976) study of the defensiveness represented by the construction of 'armoured villages' and Sennett's (1994: 366) suggestion that 'The fears of touching which gave rise to the Venetian Ghetto have been strengthened in modern society as individuals create something like ghettos in their own bodily experience when confronted with diversity.'

The 'experiential realism' of Johnson (1987) and Lakoff (1987) reinforces this view of the embodied bases of knowledge; emphasizing that explanations of meaning and rationality should account for the sensory structures through which we grasp our world. Johnson focuses on 'imagination' (how we abstract from certain sensory experiences and contexts to others in making sense of new situations) and 'categorization' (how the classificatory schemes we use typically depend on our perceptual capacities and motor skills). In contrast to objectivist theories of knowledge, Johnson and Lakoff demonstrate how 'Thought begins at a pre-verbal level, in a primary experience of embodiment' and suggest that our basic bodily experiences form 'image schemata' which enable us to 'connect up a vast range of different experiences that manifest this same recurring structure' (Frank, 1988: 158; Johnson, 1987: 2).

These perspectives suggest that instead of discourse determining the body, the body is integrally involved in the *construction* of discourse; we can talk literally of 'bodies of thought' (Burkitt, 1999). Distinctive forms of knowing are integrally related to those shifting forms of embodiment that have formed bases for, and are subsequently transformed by, successive historical epochs. Historical re-formations of embodiment involve changing sensory hierarchies, techniques of the body, and types of *habitus*, which provide people with distinctive means of acquiring knowledge about the world (Mellor and Shilling, 1997).

The problems associated with ignoring the embodied bases of human knowledge can be illustrated with reference to writings on communicative rationality and moral development. Habermas ([1981] 1984, 1987) prizes the capacity of linguistic communication and argumentation to enable people to transcend the particularities of their own situation and reach agreement. As Young (1990) points out, though, his account of communicative rationality tends to ignore the social actor as an emotional being. Reason is opposed to affectivity and desire and, in contrast to earlier critical theorists such as Marcuse, there is little recognition of how the repressive socialization of the body can depress people's capacity for rational thought. Habermas' theory presupposes concrete speakers but, as Crossley

(1997: 27) notes, having rejected Freud's theory of the instinctual basis of personality, Habermas provides us with no account of the 'pre-linguistic mutuality' of speakers, or of how perceptual awareness and body language enters into communication and understanding. There is a need here to explain how people with radically different forms of *habitus*, for example, can be represented adequately as 'a community of scholars rationally debating a problem which can be objectively described in a theoretical manner' (Delanty, 1997: 34).

Gilligan's (1982) critique of moral philosophy makes a related point. In highlighting the limitations of traditional, cognitivist and masculinist accounts of moral development, Gilligan distinguishes between an 'ethics of justice and rights', and a contrasting 'ethics of care and responsibility'. For Benhabib (1987), this distinction reflects divergent forms of embodied development: traditional moral philosophy relies on a conception of the moral agent disembedded from emotional, personal relationships and able to take the stance of the 'universal other'. The sphere of moral justice, from Hobbes, through Locke and Kant, is here pictured as involving independent, cognitive beings released from obligations of 'the domestic-intimate sphere' which might interfere with their universalizing impartiality. Yet this vision serves to exclude 'An entire domain of human activity, namely, nurture, reproduction, love and care . . . from moral and political considerations' (Benhabib, 1987: 83). It proposes an analysis of the universal moral agent which might be theoretically coherent, but which threatens to have little relation to the embodied, interdependent character of humans. As Benhabib (1987: 89) puts it, 'The conception of selves who can be individuated prior to their moral ends is incoherent. We could not know if such a being was a human self, an angel, or the Holy Spirit.' Gilligan's concern to explicate a theory of moral development from the multiple contextual commitments which humans are immersed in from birth, in contrast, proposes a view of the moral agent as a *concrete other*. This possesses a flesh and blood, sensual and emotional existence which Benhabib (1987: 95) suggests must be incorporated into moral philosophy if it is to develop 'a more integrated vision of ourselves and of our fellow humans as generalized as well as "concrete" others' (Benhabib, 1987: 95).

Individual bodies and social bodies: the embodied bases of community

Recent writings on images of the body in consumer culture have explored the flow of symbolic interchanges between the individual and social body, but have taken less note of classical theory's implicit concern with *emotional exchanges* between individuals and social systems. In seeking to emancipate the new discipline of sociology from moral philosophy, Comte linked the 'science of society' to biology and invoked the 'organismic analogy' in which 'a true correspondence between Statistical Analysis of the Social Organism in Sociology, and that of the Individual Organism in Biology' could be developed (Turner and Maryanski, 1988: 110). Spencer continued Comte's tendency to analogize from animal organisms to social systems, and a long tradition in sociological theory has taken 'literally the metaphor of society as a body' (Levine, 1995: 168). Especially prominent in, but not confined to, French sociology, this was associated with the conception of society as a 'system' with its own 'needs', which possessed characteristics that could be evaluated as 'normal' or 'pathological'.

Symbolic analogizing between human and social bodies was not new. The doctrine of the 'King's Two Bodies' provided a convenient justification for monarchical power by suggesting the King possessed a political, sovereign and permanent body which received its authority from God, as well as an earthly body subject to death (Kantorowitz, 1957). This conjoined the ideas of Christ's mortal and eternal body with a 'sociological distinction between an individual body and a collective body', and developed 'when the doctrines of corporational and organic structure of society began to . . . mould most significantly . . . political thinking in the high and late middle ages' (Kantorowitz, 1957: 198–9).

Prominent in political and sociological thought, this symbolic exchange was also influential in anthropology. Douglas' ([1970] 1996) theory of the 'body as classification system', for example, is predicated on the assumption that the human body is the most ubiquitous image of a system available to people. Douglas suggests that the structuring of social systems, and the delineation of established and outsider groups, are reflected in dominant attitudes toward the body.

This focus on the body as symbolically 'good to think with' captures only one side of the human body/social body relationship, however, and illustrates the cognitive bias characteristic of much theoretical work on the subject. Douglas' concern with the body as symbol draws on Durkheim, but her suggestion that his appeals 'to the emotions' have 'to be eliminated' as 'psychologistic waverings' overlooks the embodied foundations of what Durkheim referred to as the 'precontractual foundations of social contract' (Durkheim, [1893] 1984; Douglas, 1996: xv). Durkheim is often interpreted as a positivist theorist of social facts, yet this marginalizes his

complementary analysis of society as a 'fiery furnace' whose formal features are dependent on the 'recharging capacities' of collective effervescence (Durkheim, [1912] 1995; Shilling, 1997b).

Durkheim intended 'collective effervescence' to capture the idea of social force at birth, and his analysis suggests individual-social body relations be analysed in terms of their emotional as well as their symbolic dimensions. Collective effervesence works on people mentally and emotionally in their confrontations with sacred phenomena, mediates tensions between non-rational passions and rational thought, and between individuals and society, and can, during times of social change, stimulate acts of 'super-human heroism and bloody barbarism' (Durkheim's, [1912] 1995: 213; [1914] 1973: 152, 162).

Durkeim's analysis has been developed through theories of how effervescent manifestations of the sacred can result in virulent conflict as well as communal cohesion, and is being increasingly utilized by theoretical work on the body. Callois (1950), Hertz (1960), Bataille (1962) and Girard ([1972] 1995) all provide distinctive developments of the emotional flows between human and social bodies, while Maffesoli and Mestrovic' provide contrasting recent examples of the potential of this approach.

Maffesoli (1991, 1996) discusses the 'reinvigoration' of *puissance* in modernity; a revitalization of the sacred, the appearance of new forms of sociality, and the return of an emotionally grounded category of the moral. Maffesoli suggests this morality is shaped by an 'ethic of aesthetics' based on the body, experienced through fleeting participation in various 'neo-tribal' groups (Maffesoli, 1991, 1996), and rooted in a deep vitalism apparent in the structural changes of Western societies and in 'the smallest details of everyday life lived for their own sake' (Maffesoli, 1996: 32). This accords with Durkheim's ([1912] 1995: 209) assertion that the spread of effervescent vitalism, and its effects on social solidarity, occurs irrespective of utilitarian considerations. Nevertheless, Maffesoli marginalizes Durkheim's emphasis on the contrasting social consequences of effervescent manifestions of the sacred, and thereby neglects its potentially violent characteristics. Maffesoli's (1996) 'keeping warm together', for example, is a process which one-sidedly shields people against the impersonality and 'cold winds' of modernity. This is provocative, but overlooks the fact that neo-tribes may 'get burnt together' and may also enjoy *'burning others* together'. The effervescence produced by the Freikorps, by gangs, by para-military survivalists and by the Ku Klux Klan, for example, is based on a hatred and fear that can undermine broader collectivities (Shields, 1996).

In opposition to Maffesoli's optimism, Městrovic' (1991, 1993, 1994) concentrates on the promotion within modernity of effervescent manifestations of fear and hatred. Městrovic''s (1991, 1993) analysis is also rooted in a Durkheimian framework, but Městrovic' argues that the sensual and cognitive experience of modern societies is bound up with ethnic and racial conflict (Městrovic', 1993, 1994). In this respect, Městrovic' (1994: 2) observes a scenario which is not confined to North America when he notes 'the race riots that spread from Los Angeles to many other cities in the USA in April 1992 led many commentators to remark . . . that America suddenly seemed like the Balkans . . . they could not believe that the US of A could be racked by ethnic conflict this late in its historical development.'

This focus on the relationship between diverse social groups and distinctive forms of collective effervescence has been supplemented by the methodologically individualistic analyses of Collins (1993) and Scheff (1990) which suggest humans are emotional beings wedded to particular interactional contexts and social bodies by the accumulation and discharge of emotional energies. This concern with emotions and social order has strong roots in the sociological tradition and can be traced not only to Comte's and Durkheim's concern with the effervescent forces that connect individuals to collectivities, but to Weber's analysis of the processes involved in charismatic leadership, and Simmel's ([1908] 1971; [1918] 1971) concerns with social forms and the vitalism of life that sustains and supersedes the parameters of these forms.

CONCLUDING REMARKS

This chapter has sought to situate the recent growth of writings on the body in a broader context, and to suggest that a theoretical understanding of embodiment is central to mapping the constitution of society. There are, however, important issues that remain to be addressed in advancing this area of thought. Turner (1996: 33–4) suggests that we need a more comprehensive philosophical understanding of embodiment; a view of how the body functions in social space; an understanding of the communal nature of embodiment; and a greater historical sense of the body's cultural formation. Turner (1996: 34) further argues that 'We do not have to develop a sociological appreciation of the physicality of the body since the "natural body" is always and already injected with cultural understandings and social history.' Now, 'Natural', physical bodies

are indeed pervaded by cultural understandings, and contain a social history. As Benton (1991) implies, the evolution and generational development of human bodies involves processes that cannot be located unambiguously in either the social or the natural world. Nevertheless, the body's social history is irreducibly bound up with human physicality and it is the history of this physicality that is central to understanding how bodies both shape and are shaped by the structures of society into which we are born. Bodies may be extremely flexible and subject to all kinds of cultural representation, but the fact that 'all human bodies are subject to process of growth, reproduction, illness and mortality' remains consequential for social theory as it is just such processes which provide the preconditions for the construction and decline of particular social systems (Soper, 1995: 133).

The body has been evolving for thousands of years and forms a basis for human societies: those species capacities we have at birth (for example, the potential for walking, speech and tool use) allow us to forge particular types of social and cultural structures. Clearly we are, to some degree, 'fated' to live in particular bodies, but it is also important to recognize that the parameters of this fate change historically and culturally. Firestone's (1971) study of the social consequences of biological reproduction and reproductive technologies may exaggerate the social inequalities deriving from sexual difference, for example, but recognizes the potential of technology for reducing these differences; a potential which has further been explored by Haraway (1985). At the same time, however, bodies continue to shape the limits of these developments. Recent discussions of biotechnologies and cyberspace, for example, suggest that 'virtual reality' and other developments that reduce the boundaries between humans and machines may significantly transform modes of work and sociality. Nevertheless, the time people spend in virtual environments is limited by their biological need for food and drink and by the difficulties people have in adapting to these environments (Heim, 1995). As long as the body remains irreducible to both society and nature, then, it will remain necessary for theorists to examine how human embodiment is partly shaped by society, yet also influences its social development.

NOTE

1 The use of 'evolution' or 'socio-natural' history by theorists of the body does not invoke a crude sociobiology, but points to the interrelation of long-

term processes relevant to the development of humans which cannot be located unproblematically within the conventional categories of 'social' or 'natural' (Benton, 1991), but which may nevertheless highlight the intransigence of the body in relation to a specific social system or discursive order. This has the analytical benefit of suggesting that while the body may be resistant to certain forms of social construction, it also constitutes an important agentic basis for the reproduction of institutions and knowledges.

REFERENCES

Ainley, R. (ed.) (1998) *New Frontiers of Space, Bodies and Gender*. London: Routledge.

Alexander, J. (1998) *Neofunctionalism and After*. Oxford: Blackwell.

Archer, M. (1995) *Realist Social Theory. The Morphogenetic Approach*. Cambridge: Cambridge University Press.

Bale, J. and Philo, C. (1998) *Body Cultures*. London: Routledge.

Bastide, R. (1968) 'Colour, Racism and Christianity', in J. Franklin (ed.), *Colour and Race*. Boston, MA: Houghton-Mifflin.

Bataille, G. (1962) *Eroticism*. London: John Calder.

Bauman, Z. (1989) *Modernity and the Holocaust*. Cambridge: Polity Press.

de Beauvoir, S. ([1949] 1993) *The Second Sex*. London: Everyman.

Beck, U. (1992) *Risk Society*. London: Sage.

Bendelow, G. and Williams, S. (1998) *Emotions in Social Life*. London: Routledge.

Benhabib, S. (1987) 'The Generalized and the Concrete Other: The Kohlberg–Gilligan Controversy and Feminist Theory', in S. Benhabib and D. Cornell (eds), *Feminism as Critique*. Cambridge: Polity Press.

Benton, T. (1991) 'Biology and Social Science: Why the Return of the Repressed Should Be Given a (Cautious) Welcome', *Sociology*, 25 (1): 1–29.

Berger, P. ([1967] 1990) *The Sacred Canopy*. New York: Anchor Books.

Berger, P. and Luckmann, T. (1966) *The Social Construction of Reality*. New York: Doubleday Anchor Books.

Bourdieu, P. (1984) *Distinction. A Social Critique of the Judgement of Taste*. London: Routledge.

Brown, P. (1988) *The Body and Society*. London: Faber and Faber.

Brubaker, R. (1985) 'Rethinking Classical Theory', *Theory and Society*, 14 (6): 745–75.

Buci-Glucksmann, C. (1994) *Baroque Reason. The Aesthetics of Modernity*. London: Sage.

Burkitt, I. (1999) *Bodies of Thought*. London: Sage.

Butler, J. (1990) *Gender Trouble*. London: Routledge.

Butler, J. (1993) *Bodies That Matter*. London: Routledge.

Bynum, C.W. (1987) *Holy Feast and Holy Fast. The Religious Significance of Food to Medieval Women*. Berkeley, CA: University of California Press.

Callois, R. (1950) *L'Homme et le sacré*. Paris: Gallimard.

Camic, C. (1986) 'The Matter of Habit', *American Journal of Sociology*, 91 (5): 1039–87.

Cicourel, A. (1974) *Cognitive Sociology*. New York: The Free Press.

Classen, C. (1993) *Worlds of Sense. Exploring the Senses in History and Across Cultures*. London: Routledge.

Coleman, J.S. (1990) *Foundations of Social Theory*. Cambridge, MA: Belknap/Harvard University Press.

Collins, R. (1993) 'Emotional Energy as the Common Denominator of Rational Action', *Rationality and Society*, 5 (2): 203–30.

Connell, R. (1995) *Masculinities*. Cambridge: Polity Press.

Craib, I. (1998) *Experiencing Identity*. London: Sage.

Crossley, N. (1997) 'Corporeality and Communicative Action: Embodying the Renewal of Critical Theory', *Body & Society*, 3 (1): 17–46.

Davis, K. (1995) *Reshaping the Female Body. The Dilemmas of Cosmetic Surgery*. London: Routledge.

Davis, K. (ed.) (1997) *Embodied Practices*. London: Sage.

Delanty, G. (1997) 'Habermas and Occidental Rationalism: The Politics of Identity, Social Learning and the Cultural Limits of Moral Universalism', *Sociological Theory*, 15 (1): 30–59.

Delphy, C. (1984) *Close to Home. A Materialist Analysis of Women's Oppression*. London: Hutchinson.

Descartes, R. (1973) *The Philosophical Works of Descartes*, Vol. 1 (trans. E. Haldane and G.R.T. Ross). Cambridge: Cambridge University Press.

Descartes, R. ([1634] 1974) *Discourse on Method and the Meditations* (trans. F.E. Sutcliffe). Harmondsworth: Penguin.

Dews, P. (1987) *Logics of Disintegration. Post-Structuralist Thought and the Claims of Critical Theory*. London: Verso.

Diprose, R. (1994) *The Bodies of Women: Ethics, Embodiment and Sexual Difference*. London: Routledge.

Douglas, M. (1966) *Purity and Danger. An Analysis of the Concepts of Pollution and Taboo*. London: Routledge and Kegan Paul.

Douglas, M. ([1970] 1996) *Natural Symbols. Explorations in Cosmology*. London: Routledge.

Douglas, M. (1996) 'Introduction to the 1996 edition', *Natural Symbols. Explorations in Cosmology*. London: Routledge.

Durkheim, E. ([1893] 1984) *The Division of Labour in Society*. London: Macmillan.

Durkheim, E. ([1912] 1995) *The Elementary Forms of Religious Life*. New York: The Free Press.

Durkheim, E. ([1914] 1973) 'The Dualism of Human Nature and its Social Conditions', in R.N. Bellah (ed.), *Emile Durkheim on Morality and Society*. Chicago: University of Chicago Press.

Durkheim, E. (1982) *The Rules of Sociological Method*. London: Macmillan.

Eisenstein, Z. (1988) *The Female Body and the Law*. Berkeley, CA: University of California Press.

Elias, N. ([1939] 1978) *The Civilizing Process*, Vol. 1: *The History of Manners*. New York: Pantheon Books.

Elias, N. ([1939] 1982) *The Civilizing Process*, Vol. 2: *State Formation and Civilization*. Oxford: Blackwell.

Elias, N. (1983) *The Court Society*. Oxford: Blackwell.

Elias, N. (1991) *The Symbol Theory*. London: Sage.

Elias, N. and Scotson, J. ([1965] 1994) *The Established and the Outsiders*. London: Sage.

Falk, P. (1994) *The Consuming Body*. London: Sage.

Featherstone, M. (1982) 'The Body in Consumer Culture', *Theory, Culture and Society*, 1: 18–33.

Featherstone, M. and Burrows, R. (eds) (1995) *Cyberspace/Cyberbodies/Cyberpunk*. London: Sage.

Featherstone, M. and Wernick, A. (1995) *Images of Aging*. London: Routledge.

Featherstone, M., Hepworth, M. and Turner, B.S. (eds) (1991) *The Body. Social Process and Cultural Theory*. London: Sage.

Feher, M. Naddaff, R. and Tazi, N. (1989) *Fragments for a History of the Human Body*, 3 vols. New York: Zone.

Ferguson, H. (1992) *The Religious Transformation of Western Society*. London: Routledge.

Feuerbach, L. ([1841] 1957) *The Essence of Christianity* New York: Harper and Row.

Firestone, S. (1971) *The Dialectic of Sex*. London: Johnathon Cape.

Foucault, M. (1970) *The Order of Things. An Archaeology of the Human Sciences*. London: Tavistock.

Foucault, M. (1977) 'Nietzsche, Genealogy, History', in D.F. Bouchard (ed.), *Michel Foucault. Language, Counter-Memory, Practice*. Oxford: Blackwell.

Foucault, M. (1979a) *Discipline and Punish. The Birth of the Prison*. Harmondsworth: Penguin.

Foucault, M. (1979b) 'Governmentality', *Ideology and Consciousness*, 6: 5–22.

Foucault, M. (1980) 'Body/Power', in C. Gordon (ed.), *Michel Foucault: Power/Knowledge*. Brighton: Harvester.

Foucault, M. (1981) *The History of Sexuality*. Vol. 1: *An Introduction*. Harmondsworth: Penguin.

Foucault, M. (1989) *The Archaeology of Knowledge*. London: Routledge.

Frank, A. (1990) 'Bringing Bodies Back In: A Decade Review', *Theory, Culture and Society*, 7: 131–62.

Frank, A. (1991) *At the Will of the Body*. Boston, MA: Houghton-Mifflin.

Frank, A. (1995) *The Wounded Storyteller. Body, Illness and Ethic*. Chicago: University of Chicago Press.

Freund, P. (1982) *The Civilized Body: Social Domination, Control and Health*. Philadelphia, PA: Temple University Press.

Freund, P. (1988) 'Understanding Socialized Human Nature', *Theory and Society*, 17: 839–64.

Freund, P. and McGuire, M. (1991) *Health, Illness and the Social Body*. Englewood Cliffs, NJ: Prentice-Hall.

Geras, N. (1983) *Marx and Human Nature*. London: Verso.

Giddens, A. (1984) *The Constitution of Society*. Cambridge: Polity Press.

Giddens, A. (1991) *Modernity and Self Identity*. Cambridge: Polity Press.

Gilligan, C. (1982) *In A Different Voice*. Cambridge, MA: Harvard University Press.

Gilroy, P. (1993) *The Black Atlantic. Modernity and Double Consciousness*. London: Verso.

Girard, R. ([1972] 1995) *Violence and the Sacred*. London: Athlone.

Goffman, E. (1963) *Behaviour in Public Places*. New York: The Free Press.

Goodchild, P. (1996) *Deleuze and Guattari*. London: Sage.

Grosz, E. (1994) *Volatile Bodies. Toward a Corporeal Feminism*. Bloomington, IN: Indiana University Press.

Habermas, J. ([1981] 1984, 1987) *The Theory of Communicative Action*, 2 vols. Cambridge: Polity Press.

Haraway, D. (1985) 'A Manifesto for Cyborgs', *Socialist Review*, 80: 65–170.

Heim, M. (1995) 'The Design of Virtual Reality', *Body and Society*, 1 (3–4): 65–77.

Hertz, R. (1960) *Death and the Right Hand*. London: Cohen and West.

Hill, C. (1966) *Society and Puritanism in Pre-Revolutionary England*. London: Secker and Warburg.

Hillman, D. and Mazzio, C. (1997) *The Body in Parts*. London: Routledge.

Hirsch, F. (1976) *Social Limits to Growth*. Cambridge, MA: Harvard University Press.

Hirst, P. and Woolley, P. (1982) *Social Relations and Human Attributes*. London: Tavistock.

Hobsbawm, E.J. (1964) *Labouring Men. Studies in the History of Labour*. London: Weidenfeld and Nicolson.

Hochschild, A. (1983) *Managed Heart. Commercialization of Human Feeling*. Berkeley, CA: University of California Press.

Homans, G.C. (1958) 'Social Behaviour as Exchange', *American Journal of Sociology*, 63: 597–606.

Homans, G.C. (1961) *Social Behaviour: Its Elementary Forms*. New York: Harcourt Brace.

Howes, D. (ed.) (1991) *The Varieties of Sensory Experience*. Toronto: University of Toronto Press.

Hume, D. ([1739–40] 1985) *A Treatise of Human Nature*. Harmondsworth: Penguin.

Irigaray, L. ([1977] 1985) *This Sex Which is Not One* (trans. C. Porter with C. Burke). Ithaca, NY: Cornell University Press.

Joas, H. (1983) 'The Intersubjective Constitution of the Body-image', *Human Studies*, 6: 197–204.

Jenks, C. (1995) 'The Centrality of the Eye in Western

Culture: An Introduction', in C. Jenks (ed.), *Visual Culture*. London: Routledge.

Joas, H. (1993) *Pragmatism and Social Theory*. Chicago: University of Chicago Press.

Joas, H. (1996) *The Creativity of Action*. Cambridge: Polity Press.

Johnson, D. (1983) *Body*. Boston, MA.

Johnson, M. (1987) *The Body in the Mind: The Bodily Basis of Meaning, Imagination and Reason*. Chicago: University of Chicago Press.

Jordan, W.D. (1974) *The White Man's Burden*. Oxford: Oxford University Press.

Kant, I. ([1785] 1964) *Groundwork of the Metaphysics of Morals*. New York: Harper and Row.

Kantorowitz, E.H. (1957) *The King's Two Bodies. A Study in Medieval Political Theology*. Princeton, NJ: Princeton University Press.

Kimbrell, A. (1993) *The Human Body Shop*. London: Harper and Collins.

Kirby, V. (1997) *Telling Flesh. The Substance of the Corporeal*. London: Routledge.

Kristeva, J. ([1977] 1987) 'Talking about Polylogue', in T. Moi (1987) *French Feminist Thought. A Reader*. Oxford: Basil Blackwell.

Kroker, A. and Kroker, M. (1988) *Body Invaders: Sexuality and the Postmodern Condition*. Basingstoke: Macmillan.

Lakoff, G. (1987) *Women, Fire and Dangerous Things*. Chicago: University of Chicago Press.

Laqueur, T. (1990) *Making Sex: Body and Gender from the Greeks to Freud*. Cambridge, MA: Harvard University Press.

Lash, S. and Urry, J. (1994) *Economies of Signs and Space*. London: Sage.

Leder, D. (1990) *The Absent Body*. Chicago: The University of Chicago Press.

Levine, D. (1995) *Visions of the Sociological Tradition*. Chicago: University of Chicago Press.

Mackinnon, C. (1989) *Towards a Feminist Theory of the State*. Cambridge, MA: Harvard University Press.

McLellan, D. (1985) 'Marx's Concept of Human Nature', *New Left Review*, 149: 121–4.

McNay, L. (1992) *Foucault and Feminism*. Cambridge: Polity Press.

Maffesoli, M. (1991) 'The Ethic of Aesthetics', *Theory, Culture and Society*, 8: 7–20.

Maffesoli, M. (1996) *The Time of the Tribes*. London: Sage.

Martin, E. (1989) *The Woman in the Body: A Cultural Analysis of Reproduction*. Milton Keynes: Open University Press.

Martin, E. (1994) *Flexible Bodies*. Boston, MA: Beacon Press.

Marcuse, H. (1955) *Eros and Civilization. A Philosophical Inquiry into Freud*. London: Allen Lane.

Marcuse, H. ([1964] 1972) *One Dimensional Man*. London: Abacus.

Marx, K. ([1844] 1975) 'Economic and Philosophic Manuscripts of 1844', in *Karl Marx. Early Writings*. Harmondsworth: Pelican.

Marx, K. (1970) 'Theses on Feuerbach', in *Early Writings* (introduced by Lucio Colletti). Harmondsworth: Penguin.

Marx, K. and Engels, F. (1970) *The German Ideology* (edited and introduced by C. Arthur). London: Lawrence and Wishart.

Mauss, M. ([1934] 1973) 'Techniques of the Body', *Economy and Society*, 2: 70–88.

Mead, G.H. (1913) 'The Social Self', in A. Reck (ed.), *Selected Writings: George Herbert Mead*. Chicago: University of Chicago Press.

Mead, G.H. (1934) *Mind, Self and Society*. Chicago: University of Chicago Press.

Mead, G.H (1938) *The Philosophy of the Act*. Chicago: University of Chicago Press.

Mellor, P.A. and Shilling, C. (1997) *Re-forming the Body: Religion, Community and Modernity*. London: Sage.

Merleau-Ponty, M. (1962) *Phenomenology of Perception*. London: Routledge and Kegan Paul.

Městrovic', S. (1991) *The Coming Fin de Siècle: An Application of Durkheim's Sociology to Modernity and Postmodernity*. London: Routledge.

Městrovic', S. (1993) *The Barbarian Temperament*. London: Routledge.

Městrovic', S. (1994) *The Balkanization of the West*. London: Routledge.

Nast, H. and Pile, S. (1998) *Places Through the Body*. London: Routledge.

Nettleton, S. and Watson, J. (1998) *The Body in Everyday Life*. London: Routledge.

Nicholson, L. (ed.) (1990) *Feminism/Postmodernism*. London: Routledge.

Nietzsche, F. ([1871] 1993) *The Birth of Tragedy and the Genealogy of Morals*. Harmondsworth: Penguin.

Oakley, A. (1972) *Sex, Gender and Society*. London: Temple Smith.

O'Neill, J. (1985) *Five Bodies: The Human Shape of Modern Society*. Ithaca, NY: Cornell University Press.

Oudshoorn, N. (1994) *Beyond the Natural Body*. London: Routledge.

Parsons, T. ([1951] 1991) *The Social System*. London: Routledge.

Parsons, T. (1969) *Politics and Social Structure*. New York: The Free Press.

Parsons, T. (1970) 'On Building Social System Theory: A Personal History', *Daedalus*, 99 (4): 826–81.

Peterson, A. (1998) *Unmasking the Masculine*. London: Sage.

Peterson, A. and Bunton, R. (eds) (1997) *Foucault, Health and Medicine*. London: Routledge.

Rodaway, P. (1994) *Sensuous Geographies*. London: Routledge.

Roper, L. (1994) *Oedipus and the Devil. Witchcraft, Sexuality and Religion in Early Modern Europe*. London: Routledge.

Sawday, J. (1995) *The Body Emblazoned*. London: Routledge.

Sawicki, J. (1991) *Disciplining Foucault: Feminism, Power and the Body.* New York: Routledge.

Scarry, E. (1985) *The Body in Pain.* Oxford: Oxford University Press.

Scheff, T.J. (1990) *Microsociology: Discourse, Emotion and Social Structure.* Chicago: University of Chicago Press.

Scott, S. and Morgan, D. (eds) (1993) *Body Matters.* London: Falmer Press.

Sennett, R. (1994) *Flesh and Stone. The Body and the City in Western Civilization.* London: Faber and Faber.

Seymour, W. (1998) *Remaking the Body.* London: Routledge.

Shields, R. (1996) 'Foreword: Masses or Tribes?', to M. Maffesoli (1996), *The Time of The Tribes.* London: Sage.

Shildrick, M. (1997) *Leaky Bodies and Boundaries.* London: Routledge.

Shilling, C. (1993) The *Body and Social Theory.* London: Sage.

Shilling, C. (1997a) 'The Undersocialized Conception of the Agent in Modern Sociology', *Sociology,* 31 (4): 737–54.

Shilling, C. (1997b) 'Emotions, Embodiment and the Sensation of Society', *Sociological Review,* 45 (2): 195–219.

Shilling, C. (1999) 'Towards an Embodied Understanding of the Structure/Agency Relationship', in *The British Journal of Sociology,* 50(4): 543–562.

Shilling, C. and Mellor, P.A. (2001) *Sociological Theory. The Elementary Forms of Social and Moral Life.* London: Sage.

Simmel, G. ([1908] 1971) 'Social Forms and Inner Needs', in D. Levine (ed.), *Georg Simmel On Individuality and Social Forms.* Chicago: University of Chicago Press.

Simmel, G. ([1918] 1971) 'The Transcendent Character of Life', in D. Levine (ed.), *Georg Simmel On Individuality and Social Forms.* Chicago: University of Chicago Press.

Slater, D. (1995) 'Photography and Modern Vision: The Spectacle of "Natural Magic"', in C. Jencks (ed.), *Visual Culture.* London: Routledge.

Snell, B. ([1948] 1960) *Discovery of the Mind. The Greek Origins of European Thought.* Oxford: Blackwell.

Soper, K. (1995) *What is Nature?* Oxford: Blackwell.

Synnott, A. (1991) 'Puzzling over the Senses: From Plato to Marx', in D. Howes (ed.), *The Varieties of Sensory Experience.* Toronto: University of Toronto Press.

Synnott, A. (1993) *The Body Social. Symbolism, Self and Society.* London: Routledge.

Theweleit, K. ([1977] 1987) *Male Fantasies,* vol. 1: *Women, Floods, Bodies, History.* Cambridge: Polity Press.

Thompson, E.P. (1963) *The Making of the English Working Class.* Harmondsworth: Penguin.

Tönnies, F. ([1887] 1957) *Community and Association.* Michigan: Michigan State University Press.

Tudor, A. (1995) 'Unruly Bodies, Quiet Minds', *Body and Society,* 1 (1): 25–41.

Turner, B. (1983) *Religion and Social Theory.* London: Sage.

Turner, B.S. (1984) *The Body and Society.* Oxford: Blackwell.

Turner, B.S. (1987) *Medical Power and Social Knowledge.* London: Sage.

Turner, B.S. (1991a) *Regulating the Body.* London: Routledge.

Turner, B.S. (1991b) 'Preface to the New Edition', in H.H. Gerth and C. Wright Mills (eds), *From Max Weber: Essays in Sociology.* London: Routledge.

Turner, B.S. (1994) 'Introduction', to C. Buci-Glucksmann, *Baroque Reason. The Aesthetics of Modernity.* London: Sage.

Turner, B.S. (1996) 'Introduction to the Second Edition', *The Body and Society.* London: Sage.

Turner, J.H. and Maryanski, A.R. (1988) 'Is "Neofunctionalism" Really Functional?', *Sociological Theory,* 6: 110–21.

Wacquant, L. (1995) 'Pugs at Work: Bodily Capital and Bodily Labour among Professional Boxers', *Body and Society,* 1: 65–93.

Weber, M. (1968) *Economy and Society.* Berkeley, CA: University of California Press.

Williams, W.W. (1997) 'The Equality Crisis', in L. Nicholson (ed.), *The Second Wave. A Reader in Feminist Theory.* New York: Routledge.

Wittig, M. (1982) 'The Category of Sex', *Feminist Issues,* Fall: 63–8.

Wrong, D. (1961) 'The Oversocialized Conception of Man in Modern Sociology', *American Sociological Review,* 26 (2): 183–92.

Wrong, D. (1994) *The Problem of Order.* Cambridge, MA: Harvard University Press.

Young, I.M. (1990) *Throwing Like a Girl and Other Essays in Feminist Philosophy and Social Theory.* Bloomington, IN: Indiana University Press.

34

Globalization Theory 2000+: Major Problematics

ROLAND ROBERTSON

SENSITIZATIONS

There has been a veritable explosion of interest in the theme of globalization and adjunct matters in recent years. Much of this has been confined to academia, but rapidly at the end of the twentieth century it became very much more than an academic issue. From the late 1980s it became a topic of great political and economic policy concern and, in fact became one of the most frequently used terms in political and business discourse. In turn it penetrated the discourse of ideological and everyday life. Thus to survey the present debate about globalization in a relatively short space is a daunting task. While the same might well be said of a number of other areas of sociology, there are features of the explosion of interest in and discourse about globalization that tend to make comprehensive discussion of this theme rather different.

First, the debate about globalization cuts across a considerable number of disciplines – including sociology, anthropology, political science and international relations, comparative literature, religious studies, business studies, cultural and communication studies, geography, feminist studies, ethnic studies and history. This gives rise to the issue of transdisciplinarity – not simply interdisciplinarity or even multidisciplinarity. Transdisciplinarity means a *transcendence* of disciplinarity, although it certainly does *not* mean the obliteration of perspectives deriving from the conventional academic disciplines. Secondly, even within the social sciences, as normally conceived, the discussion of globalization

has become remarkably extensive and is embracing an increasingly broad range of general themes, such as globality, modernity and postmodernity, globalism, capitalism and culture. To encompass just this literature succinctly would be very difficult in my allotted space. Thirdly, there is a particularly formidable hurdle to surmount in coming to terms with the intellectual complexity of globalization as an analytical viewpoint. This has much to do with the disjunction between the political, journalistic and financial rhetoric of globalization and serious 'academic debate as to whether globalization . . . delivers any added value in the search for a coherent understanding of the historical forces which, at the dawn of the new millennium, are shaping the socio-political realities of everyday life' (Held et al., 1999: 1).

The third of these problems centres upon the extensive representation of globalization as an economic – at best, a politicoeconomic – phenomenon. The current tendency to regard globalization in more or less exclusively economic terms is a particularly disturbing form of reductionism, indeed of fundamentalism. Nowadays invocation of the word 'globalization' almost automatically seems to raise issues concerning so-called economic neoliberalism, deregulation, privatization, marketization and the crystallization of what many call a global economy (or global capitalism). Indeed, this is an important topic in its own right – namely, how and why the notion of globalization has come to be used so economistically, most notably in the field of business studies, even though during the early 1980s a much more comprehensive perspective had been developed in such disciplines as sociology (particularly the sociology of religion) and anthropology.[1]

But it is an undeniable fact that around the world the idea of globalization very often now connotes the shifting of control and influence over economic affairs from the local (including the national) to the global, with an attendant sense that 'no one person, country or institution can exert exclusive political control . . .' (T.L. Friedman, 1999: 161); even though the rapidly increasing thematization of governance in an era of globalization (however defined) constitutes a growing academic and political response to the latter (Held, 1995; Sassen, 1998). This is also true of the spread of anti-global movements (Castells, 1997: 68–109; Robertson, 1992). These have been evident for some time, but they came dramatically into view at the controversial meetings of the World Trade Organization in Seattle in December 1999. These involved large but not complementary, demonstrations against the WTO and a rift within the WTO between relatively rich and poorer, 'developing' countries. That these demonstrations should have taken place on American soil is not surprising. The most obvious reason is the blame heaped upon the government of the USA for its dominance within the WTO. But a second reason is less obvious and more interesting. This concerns the strength and extent of political and religious anti-globality in the USA itself. It might well be said that the USA is the *home of opposition and resistance to globalization*, in spite of the widely held view that globalization is an American project. In fact, it has by now become appropriate to talk of the globalization of anti-globalism. Mention of anti-globalism – a major problematic in its own right at this time – raises the question as to what in fact we mean by globalism. Beck (2000: 117–28) rightly, in my view, highlights what he calls 'the errors of globalism' in terms of its strong support for world marketization, 'so-called' free world trade, and the like. But while this is, indeed, a core aspect of globalism and (anti-globalism) at this time, we would be remiss sociologically were we not to think also of globalism and anti-globalism in more directly cultural (including religious) terms. For there is a widespread view that globalization, however defined, is crushing 'local' traditions and identities. People adhering to this position frequently speak of their opposition to globalism or, particularly in the USA, to 'one-worldism' (Robertson, 2000). On the other hand, the slogan 'global resistance to global attack' was evident in some May Day demonstrations in 2000.

In spite of objections to economistic reductionism, it should be made clear that I most certainly take the socioeconomic consequences of globalization, as it is widely (if misleadingly) understood in primarily economic terms, with great seriousness. To state this in a very different way, much of the current debate about globalization now takes the form of analyses of global capitalism and the inequalities and social tensions that it is seemingly producing both *intra*-societally and *inter*-societally. These are very significant issues and to neglect them would be myopic and, indeed, irresponsible (Mazur, 2000). Having said this, it should also be noted that the opposition to what is often called the neoliberal economic conception of the global economy is in some respects a calculated vehicle for the revival of Marxist or neo-Marxist perspectives in the world arena. (This is not to condemn such opposition but merely to underline the broad significance of it.) From yet another perspective, the promotion of and the opposition to neoliberal conceptions of globality increasingly constitute an ideological battleground. In the present context my strategy is to consider these sorts of issue from an analytic perspective – in the belief that social scientists should never suspend or bracket this in the service of ideological polemic; regardless of their moral and ideological commitments or, for that matter, their opportunistic ambitions. As I have remarked before, the discourse of globalization inherently carries with it the danger that it may become (is becoming?) a 'playground' – as well as an ideological battleground – for the display of all kinds of self-indulgent, solipsistic statements about the time in which we live (Robertson, 1992). Thus the debate about the globalization paradigm (Robertson, 1991) urgently requires analytical, or analytical-critical, rigour in the face of chicness, as well as ideological flippancy, and talk of 'the third way'. The latter, associated particularly in the UK with the names of Blair and Giddens, is an impediment to serious confrontation with the theme of globalization.

An example of the confusion we now face is provided, within the domain of social theory, by the influential figure of Bourdieu, who seemingly adheres to the crudest of anti-globalization postures. While we may well have no weighty objection to his suggestion that global neoliberalism is 'the utopia (becoming a reality) of unlimited exploitation' (Bourdieu, 1998: 94–105) it is, on the other hand, almost impossible to believe that such a widely acclaimed and influential sociologist should be so out of touch with the discussion of globalization and global change that has increasingly come to the forefront of much of social-scientific debate, as well as the discourse of the humanities, during the past thirty years or more. The French intellectual and political tendency to conceive of globalization as an

American project partly accounts for this (cf. Mathy, 1993). None the less, Bourdieu's ignorance of the work of major sociologists and anthropologists not only in the USA, but also in Europe, Oceania and elsewhere, on such issues as globalization, globality and globalism is, unfortunately, not unsymptomatic of the perspectives of some other major figures in contemporary social theory. The fact is that the study of globalization – more generally, global change – has been promoted or, at least, adopted by leading social scientists (whose numbers are undoubtedly growing fast) but is still neglected by others.

This reluctance on the part of some conspicuous and/or highly regarded social theorists to engage directly with the globalization debate is regrettable for a number of reasons. Among the latter should be emphasized the following. Social theory still suffers – at least, implicitly – from a confinement to *national* or *societal* contexts, in spite of the continuing interest in the work of the classical theorists of the late nineteenth and early twentieth centuries. In fact, much of the work of the classical theorists did neglect crucial features of globalization, but none the less much of classical sociology of the period 1880–1920 and of the sociology that immediately preceded it was extensive in spatial, not to say temporal, scope.[2] Some of those sociologists, particularly Weber, did not even acknowledge *en passant* some of the most crucial developments that were – even in his own time – making the entire world into a single place (Robertson, 1993). It would appear that the problem of Orientalism (as well as Occidentalism) played an important role in this. Weber's attitude towards the 'Orient' constituted a modified extension of the relegation by Hegel and Marx of the latter to a less than significant role in world history. Marx's Asiatic mode of production finds a strong echo in Weber's claim that the mystical otherworldliness of Hinduism and Buddhism constituted a barrier to general global-human progress (Robertson, 1985). In this connection it is crucial to recognize the 'cultural dynamics' involved in the making of contemporary 'world society'. The 'invention' of Europe, Africa and Latin America and North America and so on are examples of global cultural dynamics (cf. Lewis and Wigen, 1997).

The fashionable concern with Eurocentrism and Orientalism (in the negative sense) has blinded us to the (mis)representation of 'the West' (Europe minus USA or USA minus Europe) in Asia (including the Middle East), Africa and in Latin America. To put it as simply as possible, we now have to deal with the 'deconstruction' and the various, competitive forms of 'construction' of the whole world in which we live and have our being (Lewis and Wigen, 1997).

Having said this, it seems clear that as the concern with globalization, in its comprehensive and multidimensional sense, grows those aspects of the pre-classical and classical sociologists' work that did involve globalization-relevant themes are now being given increasing attention. This is particularly true of Marx, on the one hand, and Durkheim and Mauss, on the other. While little attention was paid to such developments as faster sea and land travel, the telegraph, the time-zoning of the world, and numerous other phenomena so crucial to the pace and extent of globalization during much of the nineteenth and the early years of the twentieth centuries (Kern, 1983), the increasing compression of the world was an evident feature of their work (Kilminster, 1997). Nevertheless much needs to be done in promoting discussion of the work of early sociologists from a global standpoint.

KEY PROBLEMS OF THE INCLUSIVE GLOBALIZATION PARADIGM

The discourse of globalization in sociology, anthropology, cultural studies and political science, including international or postinternational relations (Rosenau, 1990: 3–20), and other disciplines, by now extends well beyond the discussion of globalization *per se*. The actual word 'globalization' is not always in favour among writers who none the less have made significant inputs to the field of what might loosely be designated as global studies. Within sociology this is true of the major contributions from the world-systems analysis of Wallerstein (for example, 1974/1980/1989) and his followers, which have focused almost entirely upon the economic aspect of the long making of the modern world capitalistic system (Chase-Dunn, 1989). Nor has globalization been prominent in the lexicon of world society theory, whose leader has been Meyer, with his emphasis on cultural and institutional aspects of the consolidation of 'world society' (Boli and Thomas, 1999; Meyer et al., 1997). It should be noted that world society theory was in its origins a cultural-institutional reaction to the economic emphasis of the world-systems school(s), the latter evolving basically from the fundamental Marxian problems of accounting for the transition from feudalism to capitalism and the possibility of socialism-in-one-country (Stalin) versus the view that socialism can only succeed on a global scale (Trotsky).

One could continue at length in indicating the ways in which contributions to the debate about globalization do not involve the use of this actual word. Indeed, it is possible to detect an increasing reluctance to use the term even among those who previously used it eagerly – precisely because of the distortions and reductions involved in its 'popular' usage, which has by now most certainly been globalized! Some scholars now prefer 'transnational' to global or 'transnationalization' to globalization, precisely in order to avoid the simplistic global-capitalistic connotations of the latter term or to get away from its buzzword status. This is so even though economic globalization does not necessarily have to mean capitalistic globalization (sustained ironically by heavily bureaucratic apparati such as the World Trade Organization, the International Monetary Fund and the World Bank), as world-systems analysis has shown. For the latter is for the most part dedicated to world *socialism*. None the less the extensive use of the notion of globalization to refer to the growth of bureaucratically sustained world capitalism *or* to the heavily economic concerns of the world-systems approach has resulted in large part in the preference in some quarters for the focus on transnationality rather than globality (for example, Hannerz, 1996). However, the position adopted here is that the idea of globalization as strongly thematized in the early 1980s by sociologists, anthropologists and a few others should be upheld – if necessary, in direct defiance of those who would reduce it mainly to economic processes.[3]

In any case, regardless of the degrees to which globalization as a motif is embraced or eschewed, a number of pivotal issues have emerged in the mounting debate about *the interconnectedness of the world as a whole* and *the concomitant increase in reflexive, global consciousness*, these being the two essentially defining features of globalization (Beck, 2000; Robertson, 1992). These include the following.

When did globalization trends begin?

The contention here is that globalization has been a very long historical process, extending over many hundreds, indeed thousands, of years. In very sharp contrast there are those who see it as a distinctively recent process, confining it, in its narrowest sense, to the so-called post-Cold War years since 1989 and the rapid spread subsequently of organized global capitalism.[4] There are also some discussants who see globalization as something which has been occurring particularly during the past two hundred years or so – making it, in effect, almost synonymous in origin with what is frequently referred to as the Industrial Revolution in the West (notably Britain) of the late eighteenth century. The preference for the view that globalization has been a very long-term process should become more apparent in the pages which follow.

Having said that, however, it is necessary to emphasize that globalization has only taken a particular, discernible *form* during the past five centuries or so (Robertson, 1992). In this context, form involves the idea that the world has increasingly taken a particular overall shape consisting of nation-states; individual selves; the system of international relations; and humankind. Alternatively, when people define what they mean by the (human) world they may well use one or more of these basic components of the form of the world as their basic image of what the world consists of in the most elemental sense. There are, then, four fundamental ways of viewing the world as a whole. But to insist that one of them, or less than four of them, *is* the world, constitutes a type of reductionist fundamentalism (Robertson, 1992: 61–84).

What drives the globalization process? What is its 'motor force'?

For many contributors to the globalization debate, to those who might prefer to talk more generally about global change or the formation of Wallerstein's modern world-system (Wallerstein, 1974/1980/1989) the answer is, in diffuse terms, economic change – more specifically, the inexorable development and spatial expansion of world capitalism. The present author has not infrequently been accused of neglecting the economic, capitalistic factor; and, in a certain way, I plead guilty to this lacuna in my work over the past thirty years or more. However, there are specific reasons for this downplaying of the economic, in favour of the cultural. One of these arises from weariness with the economic determinism of much of social science – not in the sense that the significance in sociocultural change of the 'march' of capitalism is denied, but rather because of my objections to the reification of the very notion of capitalism in general, as well as the closely related reification of modernity.

Even more important, it is becoming clear to an increasing number of analysts that the economic is becoming cultural and the cultural is becoming economic (Jameson, 1998a, 1998b; Ray and Sayer, 1999). Hence my own emphasis upon the different forms of capitalism is closely intertwined with what has often been cast as 'the cultural turn'. The latter is itself bound-up with the matter of commodification. The recognition, in recent years, of commodification as a central feature of the connection between culture and the economy is closely related to globalization, particularly because transnational corporations have a vested interest in promoting sales in a variety of different cultural contexts in an age of consumerism. Jameson (1998b: 69) makes an important point when he argues that 'the libidinalization of the market . . . – the reason why so many people feel that this boring and archaic thing is sexy – results from the sweetening of this pill by all kinds of images of consumption as such: the commodity, as it were, becoming its own ideology . . .'.

There is no straightforward answer to the question as to *the* driving force of globalization. One dimension, such as the cultural (or religious) has been more important than others at certain historical moments, while the economic or the political have been powerful at other times. But generally it is best to say that over the long haul there has been no single motor force (cf. Held et al., 1999) and that the question of causation in this respect is a matter for comparative and historical study with regard to particular places and periods.

Does global change involve increasing homogeneity or increasing heterogeneity, or a mixture of both?

Here the proposition is that it is a mixture of both, but given the very widespread support for the homogenization position it is crucial to consider carefully the heterogeneity aspect, in terms of the idea of difference-within-sameness (Robertson, 1995a). I have developed the concept of *glocalization* in order to deal systematically with specific aspects of this characteristic of the world arena. This is closely connected to the relation between culture and economy which has just been mentioned. It has also been proposed that the ongoing interpenetration of the universal and the particular is the most general character-istic of global change (Robertson, 1992, 1994, 1995a). The concept of glocalization is vital in coming to terms with the homogeneity vs. heterogeneity dispute (cf. Barber, 1995; Robert-son, 1995a). And it must be acknowledged that in this respect we have much to learn, ironically, from the discipline of business studies, in spite of the latter's central role in the promotion of the idea that globalization is basically a matter of economic policy and strategy. Specifically, *global marketing* requires, in principle, that each product or service requires calculated sensitivity to local circumstances, identities, practices and so on. This approach to the practical implications of globalization teaches us that globalization is not an all-encompassing process of homogenization but a complex mixture of homogenization and heterogenization.

What is the relation between the local and the global?

To some extent I have indicated my position on this question in the preceding paragraph.

However, it may be best here to express my stance by invoking its opposite. In their import-ant book *Global Transformations*, Held, McGrew, Goldblatt, and Perraton ask the question 'what is "global" about globalization?' (1999: 15). They state that 'globalization can be taken to refer to those spatio-temporal processes of change which underpin a transformation in the organization of human affairs by linking together and expanding human activity across regions and continents'. This somewhat parallels Urry's (2000) emphasis upon 'scopes and flows' as the pivotal characteristics of globalization. However, the perspective of Held and his co-writers more definitely suggests, unlike Urry, that the local stands at one end of a continuum, at the opposite end of which is the global. Suffice it to say at this juncture that there are good grounds for arguing that in a certain sense the local is an extra-local product. To put it very simply the local is globally – certainly translo-cally – produced and reproduced. The crucial question which Held et al. pose concerning the meaning of the term global must be deferred, although at this stage the preliminary point should be made that the degree of systemicity suggested by the employment of this word is a crucial issue. In other words, when we speak of worldwide change moving in a certain direction, how do we characterize the 'entity' which is changing or being formed? Or is the word global to be viewed more as a condition, the condition of globality (Robertson, 1984)?

Is the modern nation-state being undermined by processes of globalization?

Here the thesis is that the nation-state has been a critical *aspect* of globalization during the past two and a half centuries and that is has been sustained and encouraged by a global political culture (Meyer, 1980; Robertson, 1992). This stands in sharp contrast to the frequently advanced claim that there is an inevitable opposition between nationalism and globaliza-tion. However, the strength of the *globewide norm* of national self-determination which has underpinned the ubiquity of the nation-state since around the mid-nineteenth century, accel-erating sharply as part of the peace settlement following the World War of 1914–1918, sig-nificantly weakens this claim. This is not to deny that there are some respects in which the nation-state *is* being undermined by specific features of the globalization process.

Overall, my view is that the nation-state is being simultaneously weakened and strengthened (Sassen, 1996). The respects in which it is being weakened include the following: (a) the increas-ing significance of transnational corporations

(Sklair, 1991); (b) migration flows and the rise of post-national membership (cf. Soysal, 1994) and forms of citizenship, including the increasingly discussed notion of global citizenship which take citizenship out of its traditional national 'iron cage'; (c) the mounting concern with issues that transcend the nation-state's effective reach, notably environmental matters and the rise of megacities which straddle two or more nation-states, thus leading to crucial problems of governance (Held, 1995); (d) the growing strength of supranational institutions – the UN and its various affiliated organizations (such as UNESCO), the IMF, GATT, the World Bank, the World Trade Organization, and so on; (e) the striking increase in and the influence of international non-governmental organizations (INGOs); (f) the crystallization of an extensive concern with human rights issues, this being a vital example of the increasing penetration of the internal affairs of nation-states by external agencies; and (g) the rapid increase of political interest over the past twenty years or so in the rights of 'first nations' (or indigenous peoples), the globally co-ordinated presence of these on the international scene presenting a threat to the conventional form of the nation-state.

However, in spite of these, and still other, trends the nation-state remains the central and most formidable actor in world affairs generally. A good example of this is the degree to which national interests and conflicts between states continue to dominate the functioning of the European Union (EU). Or, to take another case, it is *nation-states* which are held responsible for the implementation of human rights, even though there are cases – for example, within the European Union – where the legal decisions of the relevant agency within the EU are directly binding. Generally, it can be said that in spite of a salient erosion of some of the nation-states functions by and large those who speak of the demise of the nation-state do not have a convincing case. The viability of the nation-state depends to some extent on its ability to increase its tolerance for what McNeill (1986) has called the polyethnic norm, as opposed to the ethnic cleansing which we have witnessed in the Balkans, Central Africa and elsewhere in recent years.

How does modernity relate to globalization and globality?

This is a question of considerable importance in contemporary social and cultural analysis, one which has been high on the agenda of debate since the publication of Giddens' *The Consequences of Modernity* (1990). In this book the author argues that globalization has been a consequence of modernity, a position which has great weaknesses (for example, Robertson, 1992: 138–45). Contra Giddens, it is the condition of globality and the process of globalization which have constituted the vital setting for the emergence of modernity and for modernization. Indeed, it was largely the failure to attend carefully to the global circumstance which led to the demise of the modernization theory of the 1950s and 1960s (Nettl and Robertson, 1968; Wallerstein, 1974/1980/1989); and it is more than ironic that the revival of interest in modernization – be it all in the form of 'reflexive' modernization – should have as one of its major advocates a sociologist who has become well-known, in large part, through his opposition to the kind of sociology underlying the idea of societal and individual modernization. (For a much more positive view of Giddens on globalization, see Tomlinson, 1999.) Clearly, such crucial aspects of the overall globalization process as the growth of the 'world religions', voyages of discovery, early map-making, the spread of the Gregorian calendar, and so on were both pivotal attributes of globalization and preconditions of *different types* of modernity. One should also take into account in discussing the relationship between modernity and globality recent claims that we are entering a 'global age' (Albrow, 1996), an age which supersedes the epoch of modernity. We also cannot entirely ignore the subsiding claim that we now live in a postmodern age, for whereas 'the global turn' has largely subsumed and 'defeated' the interest in postmodernity and postmodernism of the mid-1980s to mid-1990s, much of analytic and interpretive value has been acquired from the postmodern moment. Much of what has been discussed in the debate about postmodernity and postmodernism has been incorporated into and recast in the contemporary debate about globality, globalization and globalism (Beck, 1992; 2000: 86ff.).

The list of issues which I have identified above as 'key problems of the globalization paradigm' is by no means exhaustive. During the past few years numerous theoretical and/or empirical topics have been added to the agenda of global studies. On the theoretical side mention should be made of the ideas concerning risk society and of reflexive modernization (e.g. Beck, 1992, 1999, 2000) and a cluster of closely intertwined and contested perspectives such as subaltern and postcolonial studies. On the more empirical side mention should be made of the increasing interest in migration and the creation of diasporas, these having a strong bearing on the question of the future of the nation-state (Sassen, 1999); postnational and global citizenship (e.g.

Soysal, 1994; van Steenburgen, 1994); the new electronic media and global mass media (e.g. Porter, 1997); new social movements; human rights (e.g. Lauren, 1998); ecology and the environment (e.g. Elliott, 1998); and so on. In fact there are few areas of contemporary social science that have not been greatly affected by the globalization paradigm. There are by now numerous individuals applying one or another form of globalization theory *inter alia* to sport, science, museums, the novel, the cinema, cuisine, health and medicine, the heritage industry and tourism; while few disciplines in the social sciences and humanities remain insulated from the global perspective. And this list could easily be extended. In sum, most of the central topics in the social sciences, contemporary history and cultural studies are increasingly connected to the issues involved in or surrounding the theme of globalization and globality. As was argued at the outset in the broadest sense globalization is a dominant site of transdisciplinarity – a site upon which very significant disciplinary mutations are occurring and where borders between disciplines which have been rigidified during the twentieth century are being loosened and transcended.

The three themes I wish now to consider in closer detail are the following: the homogeneity vs. heterogeneity dispute; the relationship between the global and the local; and the connection between globality and modernity.

More on the homogeneity vs. heterogeneity dispute

This is perhaps the most contentious of the debates in the current discussion and analysis of globalization and it is in part related to the economic – or as I have described it, economistic – conception of globalization. This is because those who regard globalization as an economic process – as opposed to a more encompassing one – tend also to think that with (capitalistic) economic globalization there also comes a homogenizing tendency, which in its strongest form amounts to the Americanization of the world – a view which can be found on both the ideological left and the right (Robertson and Khondker, 1998). To repeat, the economistic conception of globalization goes more or less hand in hand with the homogenization thesis. However, this is not to say that there is a perfect one-to-one relationship here anymore than there is pure symmetry between those who lean toward the heterogenization thesis and a more-than-economic conception of globalization. In addition, we have to be mindful of the point that was made earlier concerning global marketing and advertising. In his important book on this theme, de Mooij argues against business schools holding

to the 'common assumption that there are a few global, homogenous target groups' (1998: 287). Giving the example of jeans (often held up as a paradigmatic case of Americanization and global standardization), de Mooij (1998: 288) maintains that 'students worldwide wear jeans, but the type of jeans they wear and personal grooming are slightly different'. He goes on to point out that Spanish students do not wear torn jeans, unlike Dutch students. Designer jeans are preferred by Spanish students and they are typically worn, says de Mooij, with fashionable jackets. But in spite of the 'stylishness' of jean-wearing among young Spanish people, students from El Salvador are found to be critical of Spanish students for being badly dressed.

Thus there are an increasing number of people directly involved in global marketing and advertising who emphasize strongly that the production and promotion of goods and services on a global scale requires close, ongoing attention to cultural differences. As is insufficiently recognized, relatively few global or near-globally marketed goods or services are in fact sold in a standardized form. Thus, the frequent talk about the McDonaldization of the world (Ritzer, 1997, 2000) has to be strongly tempered by what is increasingly known about the ways in which such products or services are actually *the basis for localization*, as is well demonstrated in the recent book edited by Watson titled *Golden Arches East: McDonald's in East Asia* (1997) and by surveys of the various ways in which American films and TV programmes are received and interpreted in different parts of the world (e.g. Tomlinson, 1991).

The book by Tomlinson which I have just mentioned is in fact titled *Cultural Imperialism*. It is a sophisticated discussion of the main discourses of cultural imperialism, each of which the author finds to have deficiencies. In the last chapter of his book Tomlinson persuasively concludes that globalization, in its most comprehensive sense, transcends the debate about cultural imperialism and is a preferable term. This, broadly speaking, is the position advocated here. The stance of the present chapter with respect to the homogenization argument, which is often stated as Westernization, or even simply Americanization, is, then, that the argument is remarkably unsubtle and lacking in a seriously analytical mode of enquiry. One of the most basic – perhaps the most fundamental – of the relevant deficiencies is the equation of globalization with Westernization, or Americanization. One should conceptually separate these two notions and thereby acknowledge that globalization has to do with the making of the world as a whole into a single place. The process of globalization when considered multidimensionally – as having political, cultural and further aspects other than the economic – then includes numerous phenomena that are not related, certainly not directly, to what is problematically called Westernization. Use of the concept of globalization thus provides an exploratory space in which one can include all kinds of cultural flows from Asia to the West or from the South to the West and so on (Tomlinson, 1999).

This kind of consideration also raises the issue as to whether the USA is culturally *isolated*, as opposed to hegemonic in the world as a whole. For while much of what has originated in the contemporary world – films, music, fast-food restaurants and the like – has done so in the USA, the USA is, on the other hand, relatively isolated from the world in a variety of respects, including the display of the erotic; the practice of killing young legal offenders and capital punishment generally; its gun culture, and so on. That Hollywood films, American popular music, etc. have had a great impact in the shaping of world culture cannot be denied, but flows *into* the USA have been substantial: Chinese, Italian and various other cuisines; African, Latin American and European music; and various other cultural forms. And it should not be forgotten that Hollywood was largely shaped by Jewish immigrants from Central and Eastern Europe.

What is often interpreted as 'Americanization' in the UK and continental Europe is really a pastiche of American popular culture, unrecognizable in its crassness as 'American' to anybody who has lived in the USA for any length of time. Thus what we see in various parts of the world is a series of hyper-American theme parks. This is not the same as the oft-mentioned Americanization.

There are, in any case, a number of ways in which the world is displaying increasing heterogeneity, as opposed to sameness. Tourism, with its standardized way of emphasizing alleged uniqueness, is a particularly good manifestation of the *difference-within-sameness* that increasingly characterizes the modern world, along with 'strange' conjunctions of cultural phenomena conventionally thought of as incompatible. This is often referred to as hybridization.

More on the relationship between the global and the local

As I argued earlier, the spatial conceptualization of the local standing at the opposite end of a continuum from the global is deficient – although the significance of the spatial dimension of the globalization process certainly cannot be eschewed (Robertson, 1995a). The attractions of making a clear distinction between the local and the global are based upon the widespread perception that the global, or even the regional or the national, constitutes an undermining of control on the part of much smaller social collectivities. Thus there is much current literature of a broadly economic or ecological nature which is directed against the global economy or the processes of globalization (e.g. Mander and Goldsmith, 1996). I can readily sympathize with this in the relatively simple terms in which polemics of this type are stated. Disempowering local collectivities or localized individuals is not something to be desired. The idea that globalizing forces are overwhelming not merely local control but also what are often called indigenous culture and tradition is certainly very widespread. But, again, as superficially attractive as this standpoint may be, it fails to get at the analytic problems with enough sophistication.

For a start, it must be recognized that ideas about home, locality and community have been extensively spread around the world in recent years. In a word, the local has been globalized and *the stress upon the significance of the local or the communal can be viewed as one ingredient of the overall globalization process* (Robertson, 1997). This surely attenuates the tendency to think of the local as the opposite of the global. Secondly, it is virtually a commonplace to say that when we talk about the process of globalization or the condition of globality we are speaking in macro-sociological terms, while in speaking of quotidian, 'small-scale' interaction we are operating in a micro-sociological frame. Yet these characterizations are very misleading. Much of what is thought of as being personal or as pertaining to the individual life cycle is in fact sustained by a global culture and transmitted mainly through the educational institutions of contemporary societies (Meyer et al., 1997), institutions which are remarkably isomorphic on a global scale. In other words, notwithstanding significant and particular differences from society to society there is much *general* similarity between the various institutionalized individualisms of the contemporary world.

Globalization is as much about *people* as anything else. And it is this very issue that Lin (1998: 191) invokes in addressing the theme of 'bringing the local back in' in her study of the nexus between the transnational and the local in New York's Chinatown. The biographies and interactions of migrants, to look at people from different vantage points, are equally a crucial feature of globalization (cf. Sassen, 1999). This is to be seen in such different contexts as the experiences and writings of foreign correspondents (Hannerz, 1996: 112–26), the everyday interactions between participants in the affairs of a large stock exchange, or encounters between tourists from very different cultural backgrounds. Once one has begun to appreciate this so-called micro dimension then one can very easily produce a multitude of examples of 'the local in the global and the global in the local' (Robertson, 1995a: 32). As Susan Stanford Friedman (1998: 110) has said, we must 'break down the geopolitical boundaries between home and elsewhere by locating the ways the local and the global are always interlocked and complicitous'.

This brief review of the major problems involved in the relationship between the global and the local would most definitely be incomplete without pointing up the significance of the human 'creation' of locality, for many people speak as if locality is something that is, so to speak, given to us. This is what may be called *geographic essentialism* (Robertson, 1995a). Locality is actually the product of boundary-making, including map-making, that has proceeded over the centuries. Moreover, in relatively recent times, during the past one hundred years or so, the world as a whole has been subjected to the institutionalization of World Time, involving the establishment of the Greenwich Meridian, the International Dateline, and the time-zoning of the world and the countries (with changing borders) within it. The everyday conception of the local is contingent upon the idea that there is indeed something beyond the local. Or, to put it another way, the universal must precede the particular – a proposition which may well run contrary to everyday common sense, but which is, none the less, not easily refuted.

Appadurai's discussion of the production of locality (see also Robertson, 1995a) is centred upon 'locality as a phenomenological property of social life, a structure of feeling that is produced by particular forms of intentional activity and that yields particular sorts of material effects' (Appadurai, 1996: 182), to which he adds, in connection with the link between neighbourhood and locality, the importance of *contexts*. Appadurai also explores the idea of neighbourhoods as translocalities. The latter are neighbourhoods which in one sense are in particular nation-states but which in another sense extend well beyond that context. Tourist locations constitute but one example of translocalities (Appadurai, 1996: 192). In addition, as part of the general globalization process, the new forms of electronic communication are giving rise to *virtual* neighbourhoods or communities, these being examples of the way in which identification and participation are increasingly deterritorialized (Porter, 1997).

Early in this discussion it was declared that the question of what is meant by the word 'global' must be addressed. Broadly speaking, there are two general meanings of the term global, used adjectivally. On the one hand, it can refer, as it all too often does, simply to geographical range. Thus, there is a growing tendency for sociology textbooks to claim to be global merely because a considerable number of societies are invoked. At its best, this approach represents an increasing concern with *comparison*. But comparative analysis is by no means the same as global analysis; although, unfortunately, there is very little opportunity here to consider the complex and critical question of the difference between the two (cf. Crow, 1997). At this point it can only be said here that globalization greatly affects canonical forms of comparative analysis, because the latter have in effect depended on the idea that all societies are 'islands' – with little, if any, direct interaction among them.

On the other hand, 'global' should have a direct reference to an entity, usually to the world as a whole. Moreover this entity should have some degree of systemicity. This does not mean that one has to go to the lengths of conceiving of the world as a world-system, as Wallerstein has advocated. It is preferable to speak of the world as becoming a 'single place' or to speak of globalization as a process of formation of a global field (Robertson, 1992).

Anti-global sentiments, actions and movements will certainly persist, probably grow. None the less the analyst of such phenomena and of global life generally must be careful to explore – indeed convey to the wider public – the drastic simplifications involved in seeing the local–global distinction in dichotomous terms. Emphasizing the inevitable global dimension of very many contemporary sociocultural phenomena should not be interpreted as an ideological decision in favour of the global over the local. Our definitions and our concepts have not yet been sufficiently refined so as to deal with, for example, the ways in which the spread of anti-global movements inexorably involves them in becoming global. This is the case with indigenous movements which have banded together on a worldwide basis to oppose the destruction of local life by global and globewide agencies.

More on the relationship between modernity and globalization

The book which sparked much of the recent discussion of this issue was, as has been indicated, Giddens' *The Consequences of Modernity* (1990). It should be remarked initially that there is something unsatisfactory about thinking of a process – namely, globalization – being a consequence of a condition, modernity. With this in mind, perhaps the more fruitful way of tackling the issue would be in terms of exploring the relationship between modernity and globality.

Having said this one can see, however, how all three terms *can* be used together, as in Albrow's conception of globalization as a transitional process between modernity and globality (Albrow, 1996: 75–96).

Much of what is meant by the term globality is implied in my present discussion, but I have said virtually nothing concerning modernity – about which many hundreds, if not thousands, of books or articles have been published just in the past fifteen years or so. I will restrict myself here to a tiny portion of the debate about modernity and globality.

In great contrast to the multitude of attempts to define a single modernity (and/or postmodernity), there is a strong counter-position. Graubard (1998: viii) argues that 'only in superficial ways is the contemporary world uniform, where earlier traditions and habits have for all practical purposes been extinguished'. Graubard goes on to maintain that 'the concept of *difference* may be as essential to an understanding of contemporary modernities, of late-twentieth century societies, as it was of earlier ones, less obviously joined by advanced communication technologies'. While Graubard appears to be lacking an understanding of the 'thickness' of the uniformity of the late-twentieth-century world as a whole, as well as an appreciation of the complexity of comparison in a rapidly globalizing world, his position is none the less a welcome antidote to those who depict it as a single homogenous globalized modernity. In fact Giddens' talk of the consequences of modernity is deficient on its face precisely because he apparently sees only one modernity – that which has issued from the West during the past two hundred years or so. The most cogent position is one that emphasizes that even though Europe was the site of 'original' modernity, it has expanded to different parts of the world in different ways, in conjunction with relatively autonomous change in different areas of the world. To be even more specific, prior to the modern period of the past two hundred years or so, the various civilizational complexes of the world had been moving along their own trajectories of change but within the overall context of a more and more compressed global arena.

Eisenstadt and Schluchter (1998: 5) have convincingly argued that what they call the 'cultural codes' of modernity have been formed by the ongoing interaction between those codes, as well as their encounters with new and external challenges. The centrepiece of their contribution to this theme is that 'several modern civilizations have emerged, all multicentred and heterogeneous, all generating their own dynamics' (Eisenstadt and Schluchter, 1998: 3). More succinctly, 'modernity has spread to most of the world but has not given rise to a single civilization' (1998: 5). There are undoubtedly a number of purely semantic issues at stake in this general debate. But perhaps the following will make matters more clear.

In their helpful statement on paths to early modernities Eisenstadt and Schluchter (1998: 3) state that the relationships between civilizations, particularly modern ones, have 'never been stable' and that what has been considered 'the reference society for others has shifted continuously'. The introduction of the theme of 'reference societies' is crucial. In fact it has been a pivotal theme in some of the work on globalization over the past thirty years or so (cf. Nettl and Robertson, 1968). What I call either selective emulation (cf. Cohen, 1987) or cross-societal emulation (Westney, 1987) is probably the central empirical phenomenon in the multidimensional, long historical theory of globalization. For it encapsulates the dynamics of the ways in which social formations imitate (to varying degrees selectively) or reject cultural, social, political and other attributes from different areas of the world – from near or from far. This historically continuous process has over hundreds, or thousands, of years cumulatively created the condition of globality, which, to repeat, may be defined, on the one hand, as increasingly reflexive consciousness across the world of both variety as well as global singularity, and, on the other hand, as concrete institutional interdependence and isomorphism.

Selective emulation (or rejection) precedes and has helped make modernity – more accurately, modernities. Cross-societal emulation has become an *institutionalized* feature of all forms of modernity (Robertson, 1995b). It is the primary dynamic of globalization, in the sense that the processes of imitation and rejection have been so crucial in the history of civilizations and societies. Not that all of this has been undertaken voluntarily. A great deal of contemporary modernity has been imposed – as in the case of the virtual extinction of indigenous people in much of the Western hemisphere; or it has arisen in response to the Western challenge (Therborn, 1995). None the less, a critical attribute of the contemporary world as a whole is the global institutionalization of quotidian comparison. This ranges from the tourist or traveller comparing the attractions of different locations to the league tables that are compiled by governments or supranational agencies. This, incidentally, brings us again into contact with the way in which considering the world as a whole affects comparative sociology. For the focus on 'world society' means that we must now pay much more attention to the ways in which various categories of collective and individual actors make comparisons. We must compare comparisons. We must also address much more the interactions between social formations, both small and large.

Returning directly to the issue of modernity and its forms, one can do no better than quote Appadurai and Breckenridge (1995: 1), who argue strongly against the widespread idea that 'Americanization or commodification or McDonald's . . . is seducing the world into sameness and creating a world of little Americas . . .' Their assumption, then, is that modernity is indeed a global experience, but that 'this experience is as varied as magic, marriage, or madness, and thus worthy of scholarly attention and, more generally, of comparative study'.

CONCLUSION

At this time, when there are almost 10 million entries for 'global' on the World Wide Web (and undoubtedly this number is growing on a daily, if not hourly, basis), I have attempted to distill the paramount concerns in the debate among academics in this 'Tower of Babel'. As has been pointed up at various places in my discussion, the overriding difficulty in the analysis of globalization at present is the disjunction between those who take an inclusive, multidimensional approach to globalization and those who focus almost entirely upon economic globalization. The fact that the latter word has become so prominent in political and everyday talk about economic change has made the situation much more complicated. Even those – such as the present author – who are convinced that globalization is far more encompassing than the growth of modern globe-wide capitalism have now to face the fact that reactions to globalization as seen in these narrow terms are unavoidably objects of sociological study, as is the way in which this 'thin' economistic approach has gained so much ground during the past fifteen years or so.

The study of and the normative advocacy of resistance to what some have called 'globalization from above' (for example, Falk, 1999: 127–36) is clearly providing a relatively new perspective on the themes I have been addressing in this chapter. Against the idea of globalization from above has been counter-posed the conception of 'globalization from below'. The advocacy of globalization from below takes, to put it all too simply, two major forms. On the one hand there is the right-wing, often violent and racist, form which has become particularly evident in the USA in recent years. On the other hand, there is the left wing perspective, of which Falk is a good example. Falk (1999: 134) argues that 'the democratic spaces available to resist globalization-from-

above tend to be mainly situated at either local levels of engagement or transnationally'. In this connection, Falk rightly draws attention to the 'flow of gatherings' which have accompanied a considerable number of recent international conferences some of them under the auspices of the United Nations. Among these have been the recent, somewhat dramatic, meeting of the World Trade Organization in Seattle (1999), the Rio Conference on the Environment and Development (1992), the Vienna Conference on Human Rights and Development (1993), the Istanbul Conference on Habitat and Development (1996), and a number of conferences on women and development (the most recent being the meetings in New York). Falk sees the activities of groups attending these conferences, but denied formal access because of their not having 'statist credentials', as none the less having considerable impact. He goes so far as to say, perhaps a little optimistically, that these extra-conference activities represent 'a new sort of participatory politics that had little connection with the traditional practices of politics within states and could be regarded as fledgling attempts to constitute "global democracy"' (Falk, 1999: 134).

Thus what Falk (1999: 137) calls 'the historical unfolding of *economic* globalization in recent decades' (emphasis added) has become the focus of attempts to address such themes as global civil society and global citizenship. These important issues should not, however, blind us to the wider and long-historical matters which fall under the rubric of globalization. By now there have appeared a considerable range of books dealing synoptically with globalization in its broadest sense (for example, Appadurai, 1996; Axford, 1995; Axtman, 1998; Beyer, 1994; Buell, 1994; Held et al., 1999; Lechner and Boli, 2000; Robertson, 1992; Sklair, 1991; Waters, 1995 – to name but a small number). These arrive at such problematics as global civil society, global citizenship and human rights and global ethics via intellectual routes other than the nature and consequences of global or inter-national capitalism (Hirst and Thompson, 1996). These routes include such issues as direct interests in dealing analytically with a particular topic such as sport (for example, Maguire, 1999), a concern with civilizational differences (e.g. Huntington, 1996; Roudometof and Robertson, 1995), normative commitment to an aspect of the future of the human species (for example, Sachs, 1993), and religiomoral commitment to peace and justice (for example, Dower, 1998; Kung, 1991, 1998). Here, again, this is a highly and almost randomly selective list.

There is obviously a plethora of themes and problems associated with the global turn.[5] And it must be stressed strongly that the global turn is not simply an *aspect* of contemporary sociology. Whether one uses the specific term, globalization, or not, an expanding number of individuals from a wide spectrum of disciplines are currently speaking, in different ways, of our now being in a global age, or epoch. This is also leading to a questioning of many canonical assumptions and viewpoints and is creating a new sociologically informed concern with global history (Robertson, 1998) as well as a sociological history which rejects the conventional society-centred sociology of much of the twentieth century (Mann, 1986/1993). The idea of the end of societality in sociology, however, is not the same as subscription to the end-of-the-nation-state thesis.

The approach adopted here has been primarily sociological. However, as has been intermittently remarked, the study of globalization and related themes, is of increasing necessity, transdisciplinary.

NOTES

1 It is important to note that the concept of globalization and even discussion of the global economy is not a prominent feature of the academic discipline of economics *per se*. There is further discussion later in this chapter of the ways in which business studies has, in spite of its consideration of globalization as an economic phenomenon, also promoted an interest in globalization which must take culture into account.

2 In the phase preceding the classical period, apart from Marx, such key figures as Saint-Simon and Comte took what one would now call a global perspective.

3 But this is easier said than done, as will become apparent towards the end of this chapter.

4 This claim that what we have now is *organized* capitalism at the global level deliberately runs counter to the well-known thesis of Lash and Urry (1987).

5 Many of these are explored with great sensitivity in Urry, 2000.

REFERENCES

Albrow, M. (1996) *The Global Age: State and Society Beyond Modernity*. Stanford, CA: Stanford University Press.

Appadurai, A. (1996) *Modernity at Large*. Minneapolis, MN: University of Minnesota Press.

Appadurai, A. and Breckenridge, C.A. (1995) 'Public Modernities in India', in C.A. Breckenridge (ed.), *Consuming Modernity: Public Culture in a South Asian World*. Minneapolis, MN: University of Minnesota Press. pp. 1–20.

Axford, B. (1995) *The Global System*. Cambridge: Polity Press.

Axtman, R. (1998) *Globalization and Europe: Theoretical and Empirical Investigations*. London: Pinter.

Barber, B. (1995) *Jihad vs. McWorld*. New York: Ballantine Books.

Beck, U. (1992) *Risk Society: Towards a New Modernity*. London: Sage.

Beck, U. (1999) *World Risk Society*. Cambridge: Polity Press.

Beck, U. (2000) *What Is Globalization?* Cambridge: Polity Press.

Beyer, P. (1994) *Religion and Globalization*. London: Sage.

Boli, J. and Thomas, G.M. (eds) (1999) *Constructing World Culture*. Stanford, CA: Stanford University Press.

Bourdieu, P. (1998) *Acts of Resistance: Against the Tyranny of the Market*. Cambridge: Polity Press.

Buell, F. (1994) *National Culture and the New Global System*. Baltimore, MD: Johns Hopkins University Press.

Castells, M. (1997) *The Power of Identity*. Oxford: Blackwell.

Chase-Dunn, C. (1989) *Global Formation*. Oxford: Blackwell.

Cohen, E. (1987) 'Thailand, Burma and Laos – an Outline of the Comparative Social Dynamics of Three Theravada Buddhist Societies in the Modern Era', in S.N. Eisenstadt (ed.), *Patterns of Modernity*. Vol. II: *Beyond the West*. New York: New York University Press. pp. 192–216.

Crow, G. (1997) *Comparative Sociology and Social Theory: Beyond the Three Worlds*. London: Macmillan.

de Mooij, M. (1998) *Global Marketing and Advertising: Understanding Cultural Paradoxes*. Thousand Oaks, CA: Sage.

Dower, N. (1998) *World Ethics: The New Agenda*. Edinburgh: Edinburgh University Press.

Eisenstadt, S.N. and Schluchter, W. (1998) 'Introduction: Paths to Modernity: A Comparative View', *Daedalus*, 127 (3): 1–18.

Elliott, L. (1998) *The Global Politics of the Environment*. London: Macmillan.

Falk, R. (1999) *Predatory Globalization: A Critique*. Cambridge: Polity Press.

Friedman, S.S. (1998) *Mappings: Feminism and the Cultural Geographies of Encounters*. Princeton, NJ: Princeton University Press.

Friedman, T.L. (1999) *The Lexus and the Olive Tree*. New York: Farrar, Straus, Giroux.

Giddens, A. (1990) *The Consequences of Modernity*. Cambridge: Polity Press.

Graubard, S.R. (1998) 'Preface to the Issue "Early Modernities"', *Daedalus*, 127 (3).

Hannerz, U. (1996) *Transnational Connections: Culture, People, Places*. London: Routledge.

Held, D. (1995) *Democracy and the Global Order: From the Modern State to Cosmopolitan Governance*. Stanford, CA: Stanford University Press.

Held, D., McGrew, A., Goldblatt, D. and Perraton, J.

(1999) *Global Transformations: Politics, Economics and Culture*. Stanford, CA: Stanford University Press.

Hirst, P. and Thompson, G. (1996) *Globalization in Question*. Cambridge: Polity Press.

Huntington, S. (1996) *The Clash of Civilizations and the Remaking of World Order*. New York: Simon and Schuster.

Jameson, F. (1998a) *The Cultural Turn: Selected Writings on the Postmodern, 1983–98*. London: Verso.

Jameson, F. (1998b) 'Notes on Globalization as a Philosophical Issue', in F. Jameson and M. Miyoshi (eds), *The Cultures of Globalization*. Durham, NC: Duke University Press. p. 70.

Kern, S. (1983) *The Culture of Time and Space 1880–1918*. Cambridge, MA: Harvard University Press.

Kilminster, R. (1997) 'Globalization as an Emergent Concept', in A. Scott (ed.), *The Limits of Globalization*. London: Routledge. pp. 257–83.

Kung, H. (1991) *Global Responsibility: In Search of a New World Ethic*. New York: Crossroad.

Kung, H. (1998) *A Global Ethic for Global Politics and Economics*. New York: Oxford University Press.

Lash, S. and Urry, J. (1987) *The End of Organized Capitalism*. Cambridge: Polity Press.

Lauren, P.G. (1998) *The Evolution of Human Rights: Visions Seen*. Philadelphia: University of Pennsylvania Press.

Lechner, F.J. and Boli, J. (eds) (2000) *The Globalization Reader*. Oxford: Blackwell.

Lewis, M.W. and Wigen, K.E. (1997) *The Myth of Continents: A Critique of Metageography*. Berkeley, CA: University of California Press.

Lin, J. (1998) *Reconstructing Chinatown: Ethnic Enclave, Global Change*. Minneapolis, MN: University of Minnesota Press.

Maguire, J. (1999) *Global Sport: Identities, Societies, Civilizations*. Cambridge: Polity Press.

Mander, J. and Goldsmith, E. (eds) (1996) *The Case Against the Global Economy: And For a Turn Toward the Local*. San Francisco: Sierra Club Books.

Mann, M. (1986/1993) *The Sources of Social Power*, 2 vols. Cambridge: Cambridge University Press.

Mathy, J-P. (1993) *Extreme Occident*. Chicago: University of Chicago Press.

Mazur, J. (2000) 'Labor's New Internationalism', *Foreign Affairs*, 79 (1): 79–93.

McNeill, W. (1986) *Polyethnicity and National Unity in World History*. Toronto: University of Toronto Press.

Meyer, J. (1980) 'The World Polity and the Authority of the Nation State', in A. Bergesen (ed.), *Studies of the Modern World System*. New York: Academic Press. pp. 109–37.

Meyer, J., Boli, J., Thomas, G. and Ramierz, F. (1997) 'World Society and the Nation State', *American Journal of Sociology*, 103 (1): 144–81.

Nettl, J.P. and Robertson, R. (1968) *International Systems and the Modernization of Societies*. New York: Basic Books.

Porter, D. (ed.) (1997) *Internet Culture*. London: Routledge.

Ray, L. and Sayer, A. (eds) (1999) *Culture and Economy After the Cultural Turn*. London: Sage.

Ritzer, G. (1997) *The McDonaldization Thesis: Explanations and Extensions*. London: Sage.

Ritzer, G. (2000) *The McDonaldization of Society: New Century Edition*. London: Sage.

Robertson, R. (1984) 'Interpreting Globality', in *World Realities and International Studies Today*. Glenside, PA: Pennsylvania Council on International Education.

Robertson, R. (1985) 'Max Weber and German Sociology of Religion', in N. Smart et al. (eds), *Nineteenth Century Religious Thought in the West*, Vol. III. Cambridge: Cambridge University Press. pp. 263–304.

Robertson, R. (1991) 'The Globalization Paradigm: Thinking Globally', in D. Bromley (ed.), *Religion and the Social Order*, Vol. I: *New Developments in Theory and Research*. Greenwich, CT: JAI Press. pp. 1–10.

Robertson, R. (1992) *Globalization: Social Theory and Global Culture*. London: Sage.

Robertson, R. (1993) 'Globalization and Sociological Theory', in H. Martins (ed.), *Knowledge and Passion: Essays in Honour of John Rex*. London: I.B. Tauris. pp. 174–96.

Robertson, R. (1994) 'Globalisation or Glocalisation?', *Journal of International Communication*, 1 (1): 33–52.

Robertson, R. (1995a) 'Glocalization: Time–Space and Homogeneity–Heterogeneity', in M. Featherstone, S. Lash and R. Robertson (eds), *Global Modernities*. London: Sage. pp. 25–44.

Robertson, R. (1995b) 'Theory, Specificity, Change: Emulation, Selective Incorporation and Modernization', in B. Grancelli (ed.), *Social Change and Modernization: Lessons from Eastern Europe*. Berlin: W. de Gruyter. pp. 213–31.

Robertson, R. (1997) 'Values and Globalization: Communitarianism and Globality', in L.E. Soares (ed.), *Identity, Culture and Globalization*. Rio de Janeiro: UNESCO. pp. 73–97.

Robertson, R. (1998) 'The New Global History: History in a Global Age', *Cultural Values*, 2 (2 and 3): 368–84.

Robertson, R. (2000) 'Globalization and the Future of Religion', in M. Stackhouse with P.J. Paris (eds), *God and Globalization: Religion and the Powers of the Common Life*. Vol. I. Harrisburg, PA: Trinity Press International. pp. 53–68.

Robertson, R. (forthcoming) 'Opposition and Resistance to Globalization', in J.R. Short and R. Grant (eds), *Globalization at the Margins*. Syracuse, NY: Syracuse University Press.

Robertson, R. and Khondker, H.H. (1998) 'Discourses of Globalization: Preliminary Considerations', *International Sociology*, 13 (1): 25–40.

Rosenau, J.N. (1990) *Turbulence in World Politics: A Theory of Change and Continuity*. Princeton, NJ: Princeton University Press.

Roudometof, V. and Robertson, R. (1995) 'Globalization, World-System Theory, and the Comparative Study of Civilizations: Issues of Theoretical Logic in World-Historical Sociology', in S.K. Sanderson (ed.), *Civilizations and World Systems: Studying World-Historical Change*. Walnut Creek, CA: Altamira Press. pp. 273–300.

Sachs, W. (1993) *Global Ecology: A New Arena of Political Conflict*. London: Zed Books.

Sassen, S. (1996) *Losing Control? Sovereignty in an Age of Globalization*. New York: Columbia University Press.

Sassen, S. (1998) *Globalization and its Discontents*. New York: The Free Press.

Sassen, S. (1999) *Guests and Aliens*. New York: The Free Press.

Sklair, L. (1991) *Sociology of the Global System*. Baltimore, MD: Johns Hopkins University Press.

Soysal, Y.K. (1994) *Limits of Citizenship: Migrants and Postnational Membership in Europe*. Chicago: University of Chicago Press.

Therborn, G. (1995) 'Routes to/through Modernity', in M. Featherstone, S. Lash and R. Robertson (eds), *Global Modernities*. London: Sage. pp. 124–39.

Tomlinson, J. (1991) *Cultural Imperialism*. Baltimore, MD: Johns Hopkins University Press.

Tomlinson, J. (1999) *Globalization and Culture*. Cambridge: Polity Press.

Urry, J. (2000) *Sociology Beyond Societies: Mobilities for the Twenty-First Century*. London: Routledge.

van Steenburgen, B. (1994) *The Condition of Citizenship*. London: Sage.

Wallerstein, I. (1974/1980/1989) *The Modern World-System*, 3 vols. New York: Cambridge University Press.

Waters, M. (1995) *Globalization*. London: Routledge.

Watson, J. (ed.). (1997) *Golden Arches East: McDonald's in East Asia*. Stanford, CA: Stanford University Press.

Westney, D.E. (1987) *Imitation and Invention: The Transfer of Western Organizational Patterns to Meiji Japan*. Cambridge, MA: Harvard University Press.

35

Nationalism: Between Nation and State

GERARD DELANTY

In recent years nationalism and the discourse of the nation has become a central concern of sociology and no study of the contemporary world is complete without it. Yet there is little consensus on how it should be studied and the very concept is undoubtedly one of the contested terms which seem to make up the theoretical vocabulary of the social sciences. However, one thing is clear: in the past nationalism was related to the rise of the modern state under the conditions of modernization while today its resurgence is somehow connected to the decline of the modern nation-state under the conditions of globalization. The central argument in this chapter is that today we are witnessing the decoupling of nation from state, and with the decline of the nation-state both nation and state are undergoing different developmental logics. The current situation is seemingly characterized by a paradox: the idea of the nation seems to be very much alive, yet the state is allegedly in decline or at least no longer enjoys the powerful position it once held. One way of looking at this is to see a gradual shifting of the discourse of the nation away from the state which, under the conditions of globalization, is becoming detached from cultural legitimation but is having constantly to face the recalcitrance of the nation.

In this chapter I will outline the central themes in the study of nationalism concentrating on the main theorists and theoretical approaches. In order to execute this I will organize the discussion around the following ten problematics: constructivism versus realism; modernity and nationalism; power and the imaginary; state versus nation; agency and structure; inclusion and exclusion; identity formation and mobilization;

mobilization and institutionalization; progress and regression; and nationality and citizenship. By way of conclusion, I discuss the question of postnationalism. These debates by no means summarize everything that has been written on nationalism but they capture the core of the central theoretical debates on the subject.[1]

HOW REAL IS THE NATION?

One of the central debates in the study of nationalism is a reflection of one of the main philosophical-methodological problems in the social sciences, namely are social entities such as nations and other social identities real or constructed?[2] This may be expressed like this: identities can be seen either as deriving from an underlying essence, which constitutes their basic reality, or they are constructed by social actors and are therefore socially specific. The former view takes for granted the authenticity of identities which can claim a certain reality while the latter sees identities as constructed and therefore lacking any real authenticity. An essentialist view of identity entails a strict separation of culture from agency for cultural entities such as identities are prior to agency and are not therefore the fabrications of social actors. According to this view, then, social actors are the recipients or addressees of cultural traditions and not the active codifiers of them. In contrast, a constructivist view sees social actors as having an active relation to culture which does not derive from its own internal developmental logic but from the ability of social actors to construct creatively their world with the aid of the cognitive, normative, aesthetic and symbolic resources that culture makes available. It would appear, then, that a realist view of culture and identity differs from a constructivist position in the degree of autonomy culture is given with respect to agency. In sum, what is at stake is the relationship between culture and agency: a realist/essentialist view sees a strong causal link between culture and agency, whereas a constructive position sees this as largely contingent.[3]

This debate is particularly relevant to nationalism. According to some theorists, the nation is based on a primordial essence which is the basis of its popularity. Nations are held to be authentic cultural traditions which can be explained by history and the power of enduring traditions. From a different perspective, one which is more or less constructivist, nations are inventions; they are conceived, constructed even fabricated by social actors and consequently cannot be explained by reference to an underlying historical essence which simply unfolds in history. The first position, frequently called 'essentialism' or 'primordialism', sees nations as long-term historical 'grand' narratives deriving from an origin, while the latter approach argues for a stronger sense of rupture and renewal in historical narratives. According to the constructivist view the author of the narrative has virtually disappeared, leaving just the narrative as an open discourse. If nations are stories about the real world, a constructivist would argue, we must not forget about the story-teller who frequently subverts the plot and even re-writes it to make it resonate with the world of the listener. A constructivist view of nationalism suggests less a notion of *narrative* than of *discourse*: nations are discourses which are always open to new formulations and inventions.[4] Whether nations are basically primordial narratives or constructed discourses is an issue that has cut across a wide range of debates on nationalism in recent times and has strong political implications, since on the whole constructivists tend to be critical of nationalism while those who argue for a realist or essentialist position tend to be defensive of nationalism.

These positions can be attributed to the accounts of Anthony Smith and Eric Hobsbawm, who respectively argue from essentialist and constructivist perspectives. Smith (1986, 1991a, 1991b, 1995a, 1995b) insists on the prior existence of an ethnic and historical core to nationalism, which in his view is never a pure construction. Hobsbawm (1990, 1992, 1993), in contrast, sees nationalism as primarily a modern construction, a creation of strategic elites who use nationalism for the mobilization of the masses. Nationalism is akin to an 'invented tradition' (Hobsbawm and Ranger, 1983).

It is not my intention to resolve this question here since it involves complex philosophical questions – which neither Smith nor Hobsbawm address – as well as necessitating detailed empirical attention to specific cases, but two observations can be made. First, with respect to the theoretical problematic of realism and essentialism and constructivism, it may be suggested that the latter is always the perspective of the theorist while the former is the perspective of the social actor. The theoretical perspective is not the one adopted in everyday life, for social actors do not normally reflect on the constructed nature of their identities which, in the pre-theoretical mode of action, assumes a certain continuity of narrative and authenticity in its claims. In my view this is the only way to resolve the theoretical dimension to the debate: national identities are constructions from the perspective of the social scientist, while from the perspective of the social actor they are essentialist.[5] The second observation I wish to make relates to the notion of nations and nationalism as discourses. If we see the idea of the nation less as a narrative struggling with the forces of history – whether one characterized by continuity with history as essentialists would argue or characterized by discontinuity and invention as constructionists would claim – than as a *discourse* the problem can be further relativized. The discourse of the nation has both a real and a constructed dimension to it. For example, the idea of the nation, like the perception of injustice or historical grievance, may reflect something real but can take a constructed form when it is interpreted through cultural models which have the feature of selecting certain aspects of the phenomenon in question and giving it a symbolic existence. Constructed in the cognitive structures of a discourse, a new level of symbolic reality emerges.

HOW MODERN IS THE NATION?

A theme closely related to the problematic of constructivism is the question whether nationalism is a product of modernity or a product of premodern tradition: is nationalism modern or a product of long-run identities? A conventional view is that nationalism derives its strength from tradition, a position more or less held by Anthony Smith. States are modern, the argument goes, but are anchored in tradition, and one of the most powerful traditions is that of the nation. This view would see nations as secular religions, and in the case of Islamic nationalism as coeval with religion. Jewish nationalism, for instance, would see the idea of the nation going back to the biblical Israelites, Japanese cultural nationalism claims that Japan is culturally unique because of its ancient civilization, Irish nationalists have often claimed continuity with the ancient Gaelic civilization and English nationalism has claimed continuity with the early Anglo-Saxons. In short, virtually every national culture claims continuity of the modern nation with a primordial community and believes its traditions to be in some way authentic, even if historians have demonstrated their frequently fabricated nature and the fact that much of what we take to be traditional is very often the product of the recent past. Thus Eugene Weber (1976) in a classic work argued that French national identity was not consolidated until as late as the end of the nineteenth century when an infrastructure of compulsory schooling, military conscription and modern means of communication emerged. Local and regional identities were much stronger than national identities, he argued, which depended on a uniform society and common language.[6]

The historical literature on nationalism would suggest that the idea of the nation, while having its antecedents in premodern traditions, is on the whole a modern creation.[7] Hans Kohn (1944), in one of the early studies of nationalism, denied that it could be traced back to the middle ages, claiming that religion was a far more important mark of identity.[8] Moreover, the idea of the nation in the Holy Roman Empire of the German Nation was very different from the modern notion of the nation, referring largely to the aristocratic order (Alter, 1989: 56). The medieval term *natio* referred to a birthright and not to a particular cultural or political community as is suggested by the modern term, the nation.[9] In the eighteenth century the German elite was predominantly French-speaking and many, including Frederick the Great, had contempt for the German language. This was also the case in England from the Norman Conquest until the fourteenth century, when the Anglo-Saxon elite was replaced by a French-speaking elite. The nation was precisely designed to exclude the masses. Some historians, for instance William McNeill (1986), have argued that polyethnicity and not the nation has been the norm in history, for territory and culture have rarely been coeval.

In a famous essay on nationalism, originally published in 1882, Ernst Renan (1990) argued that 'forgetting', not remembering, history was central to nationalism. Nationalism is a kind of historical amnesia, for far from being a remembered history from times immemorial, a crucial dimension to nationalism is the forgetting of history in the invention of new myths. Since many nations came into existence as a result of violence, war and the brutal repression of

minorities, the forgetting, even repression or sublimation, of the origin has been important for nationalism to survive. Thus Karl Deutsch once claimed: 'A Nation is a group of persons united by a common error about their ancestry and a common dislike of their neighbors'. In this sense the discourse of the nation is a constructed reality.

NATIONS AS IMAGINED COMMUNITIES

If nations are not fabrications in Hobsbawm's sense, and if they are not entirely real in the way Smith would claim they are, they may be seen as imaginary discourses. This is the position taken by Benedict Anderson (1983) in his famous book, *Imagined Communities*. His thesis is not as explicitly constructivist as Hobsbawm in that he sees nations as being more than mere fabrications by elites. He criticizes Gellner for conflating 'invention' with 'falsity' and 'fabrication' and for assuming that there is such a thing as a 'true' community. 'Communities are to be distinguished, not by their falsity/genuineness, but by the style in which they are imagined' (Anderson, 1983: 15). For Anderson, the nation is above all an imagined community which is able to provide a narrative of meaning for individuals. It is imagined because its members will never meet most of their fellow-members. He thus downplays the role of intentional agency and does not address the question of exclusion, which is central to Hobsbawm's approach. According to Anderson, nationalism is above all a response to the disappearance of community as a shared face-to-face world and its replacement by large-scale territorial societies organized around a state. Nationalism provides a kind of imagined community as opposed to a real community; it allows individuals to imagine the territory of the nation without having personally to encounter it and its inhabitants. The emergence of print-mediated experience, in particular novels and newspapers, and clock time was crucial for the articulation of imagined communities, giving them a foundation in narrative: 'the convergence of capitalism and print technology on the fatal technology of human language created the possibility of a new form of imagined community, which in its basic morphology set the stage for the modern nation' (Anderson, 1983: 49).

Anderson's approach thus does not see nationalism as a discourse of power or one of ideology but one of cultural meaning and cognition. He leaves open the question of power and the role of agency in codifying the discourse of nationalism. While being very influential in studies on nationalism, Anderson's work has not succeeded in explaining how actually nationalist mobilizations occur. The explanatory power of his thesis is largely confined to a very long historical view of the genesis of nationalism as a cognitive structure. However, when it comes to explaining the actual dynamics by which a nationalist movement or changes in the codification of nationalism arise we need a perspective on agency and how different and opposed discourses of the nation emerge and compete with each other for supremacy.[10]

Despite these limits, his approach has the advantage that it can alert one to the role of nationalism in everyday life. Thus Billig (1995) proposes the term 'banal nationalism' to describe the nationalism inherent in everyday life. Arguing that too often nationalism is seen as the identity of the periphery, whereas in fact it is deeply engrained in the dominant discourses of society. Thus the separatists in Quebec or in the Basque country in Spain are nationalists while the state and the main parties are somehow supposed to be free of nationalism. Nationalism, he argues, has been rendered natural or normalized in most parts of the world with its banal moments filling everyday life by means of media messages. Undoubtedly tourism and sport (which are frequently related) are among the most powerful means of articulating images of the nation today. In the past the imagined community of the nation was a product of industrialization and nation-state-building, in other words, it was a creation of a society of producers; today, it is a product of a society of consumers. Thus one of the most powerful expressions of French national identity in recent times was the celebrations in Paris when France won the soccer World Cup in 1998. What is remarkable about this is the shifting of the discourse of the nation from history – the equation of the Revolution of 1789 with the nation – to post-industrial popular culture, creating what might be called a kind of post-historical nationalism.

DEFINING THE NATION: STATE VERSUS NATION

Before we proceed further we need to give some thought to basic questions of definition. The words nation, nationality, national identity, nationalism, nation-state are often used imprecisely and have a wide range of applicability, with the term 'nation' being used to refer to 'societies' and 'nationality' to mean citizenship. The term 'nationalism' can mean nationalism as a movement or nationalism as an ideology or idea and is often equated with the more diffuse term 'national identity' while the term nation is often used when what is meant is clearly the state, as for example in the 'United Nations' (which is in fact an organization of states). Mindful of these problems in the actual use of terms, I wish to look at the problem in defining the nation, in the most general sense of the term, with respect to its cultural or ideological content. What defines a nation?

Two ways of looking at this have prevailed: the state creates the nation or the nation creates the state. According to the first position, the nation is defined by the state. Typical examples of this would be the older European territorial states, such as France, Spain, England where the state form preceded the discourse of the nation, or at least the modern idea of the nation.[11] According to the second position, the state is the creation of the nation, typical examples here being Ireland, Italy, Israel and Germany where the idea of the nation is allegedly older than the particular form of the state. There are clearly a whole range of historically specific issues at stake here, largely concerned with definitions of exactly what is a nation and the process by which nation and state become fused in the formation of the modern nation-state. One way of looking at this is to see the first case in terms of a project of state-building – as in England, Japan and France where national identity was a project largely forged by the state and the elites[12] – whereas in the case of Ireland and many central and east European countries national identity was forged against the existing state and came from 'below'.

Nations have mostly been defined by reference to either an *ethnos* or a *demos*, the nation is either a cultural community or a political community, or as Friedrich Meinecke ([1907] 1970) expressed it in a classic work, a 'cultural nation' and a 'state nation' (or 'political nation'). Of course it can also be both. The ethnos of the nation is its cultural foundation in language, religion, a shared sense of history or a myth of descent or origin. Of these, undoubtedly language has been the strongest in maintaining the spirit of the nation, either as a functional prerequisite or as a reference point for identification. Most nationalist movements have been in some way linguistic. In the case of some, such as the Irish revival movement at the beginning of the twentieth century, this was the language of a minority and the preoccupation of elites, but in the majority of cases language has been central to the definition of the nation, with Quebec being the best contemporary example.[13] Religion has played a role too, but this has mostly been marginal, exceptions being Ireland, Poland and Israel. Important as language is, the cultural component of nationalism more or less always contains an identification with history in the sense of a myth of origins. Mention must also be made of the role of territory in defining the nation, relevant in the case of Serbia (Hooson, 1994). However, it is important to stress that the nation as a cultural community is more than an ethnos: nationalism and ethnicity are not coeval. The nation is also a political community, a dimension which is closely related to the state, though is not reducible to the state. In this context the nation is closely identified with a particular territory, a legal order, a state, and even a governing elite.

Nations can thus be defined in terms of the kind of community to which they give substance. Closely related to the political dimension of community there is the additional question of the role of ideology. Nationalism can be put alongside liberalism, conservatism and socialism as one of the great ideological doctrines of modern times. As a political ideology, nationalism is a doctrine codified by elites who sought to mobilize the masses or, in other cases, sought to provide a system of legitimation for a political order. Of particular importance in this regard is the pivotal role of intellectuals in the codification of nationalism (Giesen, 1993).

Arguably, the two most influential ideologies of modern nationalism were those of Giuseppe Mazzini and Woodrow Wilson. Mazzini was the apostle of modern republican nationalism and argued that nations of a certain size have a right to states of their own. In his conception the nation is essentially a territorially large cultural community which has a historical right to be realized in a sovereign state. This doctrine of nationalism, which derives from the Enlightenment's emphasis on self-determination, was immensely influential in the second half of the nineteenth century, giving rise to many nationalist movements such as Young Italy, Young Poland and Young Ireland (though curiously Mazzini denied the claim of the Irish nationalists to an independent state on the dubious grounds that Ireland was too small). However, despite some sessionist movements and the creation of modern Greece, nationalism in the nineteenth century was for the most part the nationalism of the established territorial states. The twentieth century marked the birth of sessionist nationalism, and as a result of the circumstances in the aftermath of the First World War, principally the problem of the dissolution of the Habsburg and Ottoman Empires, new states were created. The criteria for the formation of these new states were laid down by the American president Woodrow Wilson whose famous Thirteen Point Plan, which included a commitment to the principle of self-determination, gave a powerful ideological legitimation – and supported by V.I. Lenin – to the idea that nations must be realized in states. In this case the problem was that it was

never clear exactly what a nation was and as a result many ethnically defined identities suddenly found themselves declared 'nations' and then transformed into states, since it was easier to create a state than a nation. The doctrine of self-determination assumes that a nation can be definable territorially and that it consists of only one ethnicity, or a single cultural community. This doctrine thus rests on the equation of nation, state and culture. But the problem of course has been, with some few exceptions, that cultural community never translates so neatly into political community and as a result the struggle for self-determination has frequently been associated with violence, both political and cultural. The solutions states have found to this problem of incongruity of state, nation and culture have been various, including genocide, expulsion, partition, population exchange, marginalization and forcible assimilation.

THE SOCIAL DIMENSION: STRUCTURAL FACTORS

While much of the debate on nationalism has been focused on the political and cultural dimensions concerning the role of elites in the invention of the nation or on the relationship of the nation to the state, a major area of debate has been on the social structural basis of nationalism. Can nationalism be explained by reference to social structures or is it to be explained by the power of its ideological message? Sociologists such as Karl Deutsch and Ernst Gellner have stressed the social origins of nationalism as a response to the need of modern societies for cultural cohesion. According to Karl Deutsch (1953), who wrote one of the most influential sociological books on nationalism, it is the need of modern societies for intense communication that gives rise to nationalism. Modernization, in his account, brings about more and more communication and nationalism can be seen as a response to the need of modern society for a common medium of political communication. While being an explicitly sociological account, Deutsch tended to stress nationalism only in terms of its structural effects: nationalist ideas meet with widespread acceptance when there is dense communication. Missing was any sense of the role of agency or a sense of ideological competition. Moreover, Deutsch confined his analysis to the impact of the *idea* of nationalism and did not show how that idea is itself actually constructed and why nationalism takes different forms.

Ernst Gellner's (1983; see also 1987, 1994) sociology of nationalism was a considerable improvement on the older, highly functionalist accounts such as those of Deutsch. He viewed nationalism as related to industrialization which had the effect of uprooting large segments of the population leading to the decline of traditional forms of cohesion. Nationalism can be seen as a post-traditional form of cohesion. Basically accepting Deutsch's account, Gellner brought the discussion one step further in stressing the importance of industrialization which produces the need for a new system of homogeneous integration based on communication. Nationalism, he argued, offers a principle of cultural homogeneity, generally one related to a common language; 'nationalism is not the awakening of an old latent, dormant force, though that is how it does indeed present itself. It is in reality the consequence of a new form of social organization, based on deeply internalized, education-dependent high cultures, each protected by its own state' (Gellner, 1983: 48). However, while taking the debate on nationalism much further than earlier studies, his approach remained largely structural and functionalist, though he did recognize the constructivist element to nationalism as well. Like Hobsbawm, he was a trenchant critic of nationalism, which he regarded as a construction of elites, the enemy of liberal enlightenment, and one of the most destructive forces in the modern world. His view of nationalism was that it was a fabricated ideology and a false resolution to the problems of modernity: 'Nationalism is not the awakening of nations to self-consciousness. It invents nations where they do not exist' (Gellner, 1964: 168). However, it must be said that Gellner was more distinctively a structuralist than a constructivist in that his aim was primarily to explain the socio-structural factors in the genesis of nationalism rather than the actual codifications of elites.

Structural explanations of nationalism typically downplay the role of agency. As with all structural explanations, nationalism is explained by reference to the functional needs of society – or its dysfunctions[14] – and not by reference to the actions of social actors who tend to be reduced to structure. Obviously a complete view of nationalism must entail a synthesis of structure, culture and agency. Missing from Gellner's work on nationalism was an appreciation of the popularity of nationalism, its ability to strike powerful chords of emotional attachment and resonate with cultural identities.[15] On the whole, he tended to overemphasize structural factors, neglecting both the autonomy of culture (which is better illustrated by Anderson) and the role of agency in interpreting and transforming cultural codes. Thus while industrialization may have provided the structures for much of modern nationalism, we also have to recognize the relative autonomy of culture. Clearly modern

nationalism did emerge in preindustrial situations, for example late nineteenth-century Ireland, Tokugawa Japan and eastern Europe, and in the developed West today nationalism has enjoyed a resurgence under the condition of what might be called 'deindustrialized'. Obviously, then, we need a more finely worked theory of the interrelations of agency, structure and culture in the explanation of the genesis of nationalism. The studies of George Mosse (1975, 1985, 1993) can be cited as an example of an approach that is more sensitive to the *cultural* logic of nationalism. Mosse emphasized such factors as the lower middle-class ethic of respectability, the aesthetization of politics and the fusion of nature and nation in the discourses of nationalism, which was originally a progressive-leftist movement but gradually became a right wing and fascist movement by the early twentieth century. Mention can also be made of the work of John Breuilly (1982), for whom nationalism is to be explained as a means of conducting politics by mass mobilization.

INCLUSION AND EXCLUSION

The difficulty with many conventional accounts of nationalism is that they neglect the role of agency as a mediator of structure and culture. Structural accounts, such as Gellner, neglect the autonomy of agency, more culturalist approaches such as Anderson's confine the analysis to the cultural content of nationalist discourse, and more historically inclined authors such as Hobsbawm stress the role of agency to the neglect of both culture and structure. A fruitful approach is the anthropological theory of Frederick Barth (1969). In his influential book, he looked at how social actors deploy cultural constructs in order to set up and maintain group symbolic boundaries which in time become real ones. His point, which places him theoretically in the constructivist camp, is that cultural boundaries do not derive from cultural tradition as such but are set up by groups seeking to establish their difference from others. For Barth, there is not a direct causal relationship between culture and agency, as in the work of Smith, but a creative one. The main dimension to this is the Self/Other dichotomy, which for Barth derives from boundary maintenance and not from cultural traditions. Thus what counts is the ability to make a 'difference', even if this is a very small difference.[16] The importance of his approach is that he can show how social actors – who have different social locations – manipulate cultural codes in order to maintain group boundaries.[17] In this approach, nationalism is less driven by the Enlightenment's ideal of 'self-determination' than by the dynamics of group formation, which require the 'self' to determine the 'other'.

IDENTITY FORMATION AND MOBILIZATION

A theme in the recent literature on nationalism is the sociological question of how a movement arises, gains public support and leads to the establishment of a new institutional framework. The emphasis in the older literature on nationalism was on the ideology and cultural content of nationalism – in particular on national identity – and on the political role of nationalist movements. Only recently have studies on nationalism progressed to look at exactly how nationalist movement arises.[18] Does nationalism derive its strength from interests or from identities, for instance? This is an area of huge debate, with some approaches emphasizing the role of interests and others the role of identity. Rational choice theorists, such as Hechter (1975), have looked at nationalism in terms of the strategic goals of nationalist leaders. For Hechter, the success of a nationalist movement is to be explained by reference to its ability to maximize benefits for its supporters who respond to grievances. One of the problems with a social interest approach – that is, the assumption that grievances led to the articulation of identities which give expression to social interests – is that it cannot provide a satisfactory account of how nationalist mobilization actually occurs since interests have to be interpreted through cultural models in which grievances are amplified (or even invented). Nor can it explain the genesis of values and the desirability – that is, the cultural and institutional selectivity – of certain normative goals over others. It is particularly weak in explaining how nationalist agencies are themselves formed.

Other traditional approaches which stressed the content of nationalist discourse as opposed to external interests have tended to remain at the level of an analysis of ideology. Thus, for Elie Kedourie (1993), in his influential book, nationalism is primarily an ideology whose force is simply compelling. Put more sociologically, his argument was nationalism as a movement is caused by the ideology of nationalism. Again, missing from this account is a theory of agency and structure. We need to understand the relationship between social agents such as nationalist elites and movements on the one side, and on the other how these relate to both the socio-structural context and pre-existing discourses of the nation. As we have seen, Gellner's work was an important step in this direction but suffered from the limits of his structural and somewhat functionalist modernization bias.

Recent literature on social movements shifts the focus from identity to *mobilization*. Identity is theorized as emanating from the actual dynamics of mobilization; it is seen less as an underlying essence which somehow causes action than as a product of action and the existence of certain opportunity structures. According to this approach, which has moved beyond constructivism and essentialism, identities are 'projects' and are constructed in a relational field which is created when groups mobilize to win support for their view of the world. In this struggle, to impose new definitions of reality, interests and identities are articulated together. Thus identities are less resources than projects. According to O'Mahony and Delanty (1998), adopting this analysis, the most important identity formations of Irish nationalism did not precede the mass mobilization of the late nineteenth century but were created in the period of mobilization itself, including the key grievances that fuelled nationalism. This approach, which challenges the conventional view that a nationalist movement is the product of deeply entrained historical identities which derive from grievances – allows us to see identity as something that is always open to strategic change and symbolic reinterpretation as circumstances change. As Rogers Brubaker (1996: 17) argues, nationalism is not engendered by nations but is produced by political fields of particular kinds. His approach, which is influenced by the sociology of Bourdieu, sees the dynamics of nationalism being governed by the properties of political fields, not by the properties of collectivities.

A central question in this approach is under which conditions nationalist interpretation models, attempting to make sense of a given situation, acquire societal validity. How does nationalist ideology resonate with segments of the population and gain widespread support? To answer this question it is necessary to have recourse to the idea of opportunity structures. Following Kitschelt (1986), the concept of an opportunity structure – political, cultural and social – has become influential in recent literature on nationalism (Brand, 1992; Hooge, 1992; O'Mahony and Delanty, 1998). In contrast to the structuralist approach, which places too much emphasis on the functionalist nature of nationalism, the idea of opportunity structures describes how institutional conditions offer opportunities or barriers to the realization of a movement's goals, for instance, the degree of institutional access to state (political opportunity structures), the openness of the public sphere to the identity projects of the nationalist movement (for their message must resonate in the society linking up with other identities and interests, cultural and social opportunity structures); and the receptivity of the movement's project with other movements. The latter opportunity structure is particularly important in the case of nationalism, which often needs the emergence of a 'discourse coalition' where a variety of social movements unite behind a common programme leading to the building of a consensus movement and a master frame of identity. It may be argued that the key to the success of nationalism is precisely the construction of such a consensus movement.

One of the implications of the emphasis on mobilization strategies in the context of opportunity structures is a multidimensional view of nationalist movements, which are rarely unitary. In a study of European smaller-country nationalisms, Hroch (1985; see also 1993) identifies three vertical periods and four typical factions in nationalist mobilizations. The temporary distinctions are Enlightenment cultural nationalism, the elite nationalist movements of the mid-nineteenth century, which had a more pronounced political dimension, and finally the emergence of a mass movement from the end of the nineteenth century. In the latter phase there are four principal wings, the clerical-conservative, liberal democratic, socialist and revolutionary. Each of these emerges from different contexts and acts in the name of different and frequently incompatible interests and identities. Hroch, however, does not use mobilization theory as such and his work does not actually explain how mobilization occurs. Mobilization theory stresses the role of social actors in taking advantage of certain structural conditions and also has the advantage of relating cultural models to relational fields in which social actors struggle in the context of open structural situations. Combined with a discourse theory of nationalism, this is undoubtedly a promising approach to the study of nationalism since it combines structure, agency and culture.

MOBILIZATION AND INSTITUTIONALIZATION

The relationship between identity formation and the emergence of a movement has been a concern of a great deal of recent work on nationalism. Another key concern, though one which has received less attention, is the question of the institutionalization of a project of nation-building in a state, for a successful nationalist mobilization leads to the establishment of a state. Obviously this is going to be heavily influenced by the mobilization phase. However, one of the main differences between the mobilization phase and the phase of institutionalization is that in the latter there is likely to be a more pronounced tendency towards the emergence of a master frame, or a discourse coalition. New elites will emerge; frequently after an initial civil war when marginal elites significant during the mobilization phase are isolated in the struggle for the acquisition of economic and political power as well as social influence. The establishment of a nation-state involves the creation of a new system of regulating interests within an institutional order and a new cultural imaginary which will bind the new elites together. The elites who codify this imaginary will also have an opportunity to define the institutional rules of the new order.

Recent literature on nationalism emphasizes very strongly the importance of an institutional analysis to nationalism. For instance, Rogers Brubaker (1996) has shown how the seeds of post-communist nationalism were sown by the policies of institutionalizing nationhood and nationality in the Soviet Union. The Soviet Union was based on institutionalized multi-nationality, which not only tolerated national identification but institutionalized it, establishing nationhood and nationality as central institutional categories, and in doing so, Brubaker argues, it prepared the way for its own demise.

PROGRESS AND REGRESSION

An unavoidable theme in the debate is the question of whether nationalism is a progressive force, or more generally, whether there are progressive forms of nationalism. There is a tendency in the literature to assume that certain forms of nationalism are more progressive than others.[19] Thus Hobsbawm dismisses the nationalism of the periphery – but not that of the existing nation-state as an unrealistic aspiration for an impossible statehood. However, it is evident that for him nationalism is a deeply destructive force and is best combated with a more cosmopolitan consciousness. We are not told what this could be, but there is a certain nostalgia in his writings for a lost socialist consciousness. This brings us back to one of the older debates on nationalism, whether class or nation is the primary social actor in advancing progress. For Marx it was clearly class.[20] It was his view that nationalism was a useful resource for the attainment of an international proletarian class consciousness. Engels famously dismissed the 'unhistorical' peoples of eastern Europe and, with Marx, assumed that the initiative would come from the industrially advanced nations. In general, Marxists have regarded nationalism as secondary to the class struggle but have positively appraised it as a progressive movement since the national and the class struggle were putatively connected.

The idea of history entailing progress was central not only to the Marxist theory of society but to liberal social science. Nation-state building and the shaping of nationally specific political cultures was regarded as an essential dimension to the process of modernization. One of the main debates on German history has been on the so-called 'Sonderweg' thesis, namely the argument that there is an ideal or normal path to modernity which offers a normative reference point to assess other paths.[21] Thus, it has been argued Germany's path to modernity was an aberration from the norm which was allegedly characterized by the established nation-states (England, the Netherlands, France). The difficulties with this position are obvious. For instance, the history of Britain can be seen as a series of failed attempts to institutionalize federalism, for it is by no means apparent that the nation-state has been a success, as has been illustrated by Anglo-Irish relations. More generally, there is the question as to from where do normative alternatives come? Do they come from the society's own learning structures or from outside?

NATIONALISM, NATIONALITY AND CITIZENSHIP

According to a particular tradition associated with the Enlightenment, the nation is an idea of universalistic significance. The idea of the nation was synonymous with society and far from being the ideology of a particular state it was associated with the universalism of civil society. The ideas and ideals of the American and French Revolutions promoted a view of the nation as the voice of civil society. This conception of the nation was concretely realized in notions of citizenship and human rights. The ideals of modern constitutional law and democracy, which stressed the formal equality of all individuals and their right to autonomy, provided the foundation for the idea of the civic nation. Modern republicanism was the first nationalist movement in this universalistic sense of the term. This univeralistic sense of nationalism associated with the Enlightenment is often termed patriotism and can be contrasted to the particularism of late forms of nationalism which fostered strong identification with the state and equated the nation with a culturally or ethnically defined people or *Volk*.

With the growing identification of the nation with the state, the republican spirit of patriotism and civic identity waned. Henceforth there was an increasing emphasis on the territorial nation-state, on the one side, and on the other the culturalist-historicist interpretation of the nation began to overtake the civic interpretation. In the twentieth century nationalism – in its explicitly political and cultural forms – has been mostly associated with strategies of exclusion rather than ones of inclusion. With the exception of pan-nationalist movements, it has mostly been a particularist ideology seeking a close identification of the cultural community with a particular geographical territory or, more commonly, with a state. The rise of the *national* has been at the cost of *civil* society.

The universalistic core of nationalism has mostly disappeared today, though in certain forms of civic nationalism (as opposed to political or cultural nationalism) and in 'cosmopolitan' forms of identification a degree of universalism is retained. In sum, what is happening is that nationality and citizenship have become interchangeable. In modern society citizenship, as membership of a political community, came to be defined in terms of membership of a territorial nation-state. National identification and citizenship identification became one and the same, even though the distinction for many is contingent rather than necessary.[22] What is at stake in this distinction is exactly what membership of a community entails. Is the community a political entity defined by the polity, a cultural community defined by a shared framework of norms and values or a civic community defined by something that goes beyond nationality and entailing a deeper kind of citizenship? This is much evidence today that nationality and citizenship are losing their close connection and that consequently the discourse of the nation is losing its power to define social reality.

CONCLUSION: NATIONALISM AND POSTNATIONALISM

From about the end of the 1980s, nationalism has been on the rise throughout the world, in particular in the former communist countries but also in Western Europe there is also a pronounced increase in nationalism (Ignatieff, 1994; Judt, 1994; Kaldor, 1993). There is one major difference between nationalism today and in the past: today it is mostly an expression of conflicts *within* nation-states rather than *between* them. In the classical period of nation-state-building in the late nineteenth century nationalism was an expression of the growing identification of the masses with the state. An important part of this was 'social imperialism', the cultivation of a patriotism around the nascent empires the Western states were amassing. If the old nationalism was primarily jingoistic, the new nationalism is xenophobic. Nationalism today is more about exclusion than inclusion; it is heavily focused on immigrants and minorities within the state rather than on other states. Equality and modernity had been central to the old nationalism whereas 'ethnic cleansing' has become a metaphor of the new nationalism.

In many parts of the world nationalism is related to the growing incidence of civil wars rather than wars between the nation-states (Enzensberger, 1994). There are also major changes in its social composition. In the past nationalism was primarily an ideology of elites who competed for mass support; in other cases it was an ideology imposed from above by the state upon society. Today nationalism on the whole derives from 'below' and is generally anti-statist. The anti-statist component in the new nationalism is illustrated in the Northern League, for whom the Italian state is disloyal, and, in the extreme case, in the American militias, for whom the Federal government has betrayed the American nation.

It may be suggested that the new nationalism gains its impetus from the decoupling of nation and state. The nation is mobilizing against the state which is losing its connection with society. The resurgence of nationalism can be seen as the product of the growing alienation of society. In their analysis of right-wing voting in Western Europe Jürgen Falter and Markus Klein (1996) argue right-wing voting is to be explained less as an ideological phenomenon than as a reaction to economic insecurity. Economic crises combined with ideological predispositions channel support into the extreme right. Thus the decline in the vote for the German Republikaner in the 1994 election may be seen as a decline in political dissatisfaction rather than a decline in right-wing political attitudes, for this potential always exists. This would suggest extreme right-wing parties are likely to succeed if they can find a way of linking xenophobia to material interests. This has indeed been the case with the 1998 elections, when the support of the extreme right dropped due, it may be suggested, to the ability of the SPD and left alliance to offer a successful challenge to the neoliberal position represented by the government. Therefore, it may be argued that nationalism today is less the expression of notions of cultural superiority or political ambition than an expression of the decline of the social and the exhaustion of the civic component of political community.

One dimension to this is the crisis of the welfare state. In the period that followed the Second World War Western societies succeeded in creating welfare states that were also the social basis of Western multiculturalism. The economic boon of the postwar years allowed Western societies to achieve full employment, with many countries importing immigrant labour. The decline of the welfare state is inseparably linked to the crisis of multiculturalism and the emergence of growing nationalism. Extreme nationalist parties have gained huge support due less to the inherent belief in nationalism than in growing social discontent with the mainstream parties. This is evident in the tendency of nationalists, including extreme nationalists, to deny the racist component in their discourses. The issues, it is alleged, are merely about immigration and the restriction of citizenship to nationals. The new nationalism thus might be called a 'materialistic' nationalism as opposed to one that is explicitly cultural or political (Habermas, 1991).

Another factor is undoubtedly the reaction to the global context. In Europe the momentum towards European integration occurred at a time when welfare states were under attack from neoliberal-influenced strategies. Combined with the spectre of large-scale immigration following the collapse of communism, the secure foundations of Western societies suddenly became questioned. Transnational processes, such as European integration, notwithstanding the case of German unification, appeared to undermine the cultural models of national societies which were also reaching the limits of their capacity to provide an enduring form of social citizenship. The motivational forces of nationalism are fear, trauma, resentment and disappointment. Nationalism provides an ethos of security in a world that is fraught with anxiety, risk and insecurity. In the former communist countries the loss of economic security that communism and exposure to neoliberal economics and a culture of consumption led to a major feeling of economic and cultural insecurity.

Earlier in this chapter I suggested that a major dimension to nationalism today is the disjuncture of citizenship and nationality. We are no longer living in a world in which nation and state are secure entities. It is in this sense that we can speak of postnationality. Societies are no longer defined by exclusive reference to states or nations. In the global era citizenship is becoming increasingly de-territorialized, with transnational communities becoming more and more able to appeal to human rights and citizenship rights which are not specific to nation-states (Soysal, 1994). Many theorists have observed that the consequence of globalization is more and more particularism (Robertson, 1992). Globalizing trends in politics and law give nationalism a major impetus. For instance, the decline of the state releases the nation, as is illustrated in the fact that much of world politics is about the regulation of ethnic nationalism (Barkin and Cronin, 1994). It has been frequently argued that globalization entails the mobilization of the local and the regional against the centre. But this dynamic is also one that provides a tremendous boost to nationalism (Castells, 1997).

In what sense, then, is it meaningful to speak of postnationalism? It is clear that nationalism is not going to decline but it is unlikely to become a dominant identity. Unlike in the past, when nationalism had few competitors – its main adversary being class – today it is forced to live in a world in which many identities exist. According to Habermas and others, modernity contains a self-reflective component that cannot be simply avoided: the critique of cultural traditions and the reflexivity of ideology is built into the self-understanding of modern conceptions of the world. The postnational position would argue that no cultural tradition is able to withstand self-examination (Delanty, 1995). Habermas defends the plausibility of a 'constitutional patriotism' – an identification with the principles of the constitution rather than an identification with the state, territory or history – as the basis of a postnational political culture. This might also be conceived as a new cosmopolitan 'imaginary', but it is evident that such an identity can only be a minimal one.

Notes

1 For some general surveys which provide good introductions to the study of nationalism see Calhoun, 1997, Guibernau, 1996, Hutchinson, 1994, Llobera, 1994 and McCrone, 1998.

2 For more on constructivism and realism, see Delanty, 1997.

3 See Archer, 1988 for an account which stresses the contingency of the relationship between culture and agency. See also Swidler, 1986 and Hedetoft, 1999.

4 For a more constructivist view of narrative see Bhabha, 1990.

5 A similar argument has been proposed by Benhabib (1998: 90–5).

6 See also Watkins, 1990.

7 Some historians, however, have disputed this, for instance Marc Bloch, Seton-Watson and Johan Huizinga, who believed national consciousness was highly developed well before the modern period. This thesis is generally disputed. See Connor, 1991.

8 This was also the view of Hayes (1931).

9 On premodern nationalism, see Amstrong, 1982, Marcu, 1976, Ranum, 1975 and Tipton, 1972. For a more traditional approach, see Coulton, 1933.

10 For an interesting view of power and the imaginary in nationalist discourse, see Salecl, 1993.

11 For approaches that stress the priority of the state, see Breuilly, 1982 and Carr, 1945.

12 See Colley, 1992 and Corrigan and Sayer, 1985.

13 However, it must be mentioned that cultural nationalism and political nationalism have frequently clashed, as in Ireland in the early twentieth century.

14 Some studies prefer to stress uneven development as a cause of nationalism. See Miller, 1978 and Nairn, 1977.

15 For an account which takes the emotional appeal of nationalism seriously, see Calhoun, 1997 and Greenfield, 1992.

16 For a similar apporach see Eriksen, 1993. See also Blok, 1998, who argues the 'narcisism of the small difference' plays a greater role in conflict than big differences.

17 In this context mention can be made of the work of Eisenstadt and Giesen (1995) on the construction of collective identity codes.

18 This largely derives from the historical sociological school of Tilly, see for example Tilly, (1994) and the more political science-dominated school of mobilization analysis associated with authors such as Tarrow (1994).

19 See Roudometof, 1999. Some accounts emphasize the pathological dimension of nationalism, see Rothchild and Groth, 1995.

20 For an interesting reappraisal of the debate on nationalism and class, see Szporluk, 1988.

21 See Evans, 1987 and Wehler, 1988.

22 For some of the literature on citizen and nationality, see Brubaker, 1992.

References

Alter, P. (1989) *Nationalism*. London: Edward Arnold.

Anderson, B. (1983) *Imagined Communities: Reflections on the Origin and Spread of Nationalism*. London: Verso.

Armstrong, J. (1982) *Nations before Nationalism*. Chapel Hill, NC: University of North Carolina Press.

Archer, M. (1988) *Culture and Agency*. Cambridge: Cambridge University Press.

Barkin, S. and Cronin, B. (1994) 'The State and the Nation: Changing Norms and the Rules of Sovereignty in International Relations', *International Organization*, 48: 107–30.

Barth, F. (ed.) (1969) *Ethnic Groups and Boundaries*. Boston, MA: Little, Brown and Co.

Benhabib, S. (1998) 'Democracy and Identity', *Philosophy and Social Criticism*, 24 (2/3): 85–100.

Bhabha, H. (1990) *Nation and Narration*. London: Routledge.

Billig, M. (1995) *Banal Nationalism*. London: Sage.

Brand, K.-W. (1992) 'Zur Neustrukturierung kolletiver Identitäten', in B. Schäfers (ed.), *Lebensverhältnisse und soziale Konflike im neuen Europa*. Frankfurt a.M.: Campus Verlag.

Breuilly, J. (1982) *Nationalism and the State*, 2nd edn. Manchester: Manchester University Press.

Brubaker, R. (1992) *Citizenship and Nationhood in France and Germany*. Cambridge, MA: Harvard University Press.

Brubaker, R. (1996) *Nationalism Reframed*. Cambridge: Cambridge University Press.

Calhoun, C. (1997) *Nationalism*. Buckingham: Open University Press.

Carr, E. (1945) *Nationalism and After*. London: Macmillan.

Castells, M. (1996) *The Rise of the Network Society*. Oxford: Blackwell.

Castells, M. (1997) *The Power of Identity*. Oxford: Blackwell.

Colley, L. (1992) *Britons: Forging the Nation, 1707–1837*. New Haven, CT: Yale University Press.

Connor, W. (1991) 'From Nation to Tribe', *History of European Ideas*, 13: 5–18.

Corrigan, P. and Sayer, D. (1985) *The Great Arch: English State Formation as a Cultural Formation*. Oxford: Blackwell.

Coulton, G. (1933) 'Nationalism in the Middle Ages', *Cambridge History Journal*, 5: 14–40.

Delanty, G. (1995) *Inventing Europe: Idea, Identity, Reality*. London: Macmillan.

Delanty, G. (1997) *Social Science: Beyond Constructivism and Realism*. Buckingham: Open University Press.

Deutsch, K. (1953) *Nationalism and Social Communication*. Cambridge, MA: MIT Press.

Eisenstadt, S.N. and Giesen, B. (1995) 'The Construction of Collective Identity Codes', *European Journal of Sociology*, 26 (1): 72–102.

Enzensberger, H.M. (1994) *Civil War*. London: Granta.

Eriksen, T.H. (1993) *Ethnicity and Nationalism*. London: Pluto.

Evans, R. (1987) *Rethinking German History*. London: Harper Collins.

Falter, J. and Klein, M. (1996) 'The Mass Basis of the Extreme Right in Contemporary Europe in a Comparative Perspective', in D. Weil (ed.), *Research on Democracy*, vol. 3. *Extremism, Protest, Social Movements and Democracy*. London: JAI Press.

Gellner, E. (1964) *Thought and Change*. London: Weidenfeld and Nicolson.

Gellner, E. (1983) *Nations and Nationalism*. Oxford: Blackwell.

Gellner, E. (1987) *Culture, Identity and Politics*. Cambridge: Cambridge University Press.

Gellner, E. (1994) *Encounters with Nationalism*. Oxford: Blackwell.

Giesen, B. (1993) *Die Intellektuelen und die Nation*. Frankfurt, a.M.: Suhrkamp.

Greenfeld, L. (1992 *Nationalism: Five Roads to Modernity*. Cambridge, MA: Havard University Press.

Guibernau, M. (1996) *Nationalism: The Nation-State and Nationalism in the Twentieth Century*. Cambridge: Polity Press.

Habermas, J. (1991) 'Yet Again: German Identity – A Unified Nation of Angry DM-Burghers', *New German Critique*, 52: 84–101.

Habermas, J. (1994) 'Struggles for Recognition in the Democratic Constitutional State', in A. Gutmann (ed.), *Multiculturalism: Examining the Politics of Recognition*. Princeton, NJ: Princeton University Press.

Hayes, C. (1931) *The Historical Evolution of Modern Nationalism*. New York: Macmillan.

Hedetoft, U. (1999) 'The Nation-State Meets the World: National Identities in the Context of Transnationality and Cultural Globalization', *European Journal of Social Theory*, 2 (1): 71–94.

Hobsbawm, E. (1990) *Nations and Nationalism Since 1780*. Cambridge: Cambridge University Press.

Hobsbawm, E. (1992) 'Ethnicity and Nationalism in Europe', *Anthropology Today*, 8: 3–8.

Hobsbawm, E. (1993) 'The New Threat to History', *New York Review of Books*, 16 (December): 62–4.

Hobsbawm, E. and Ranger, T. (eds) (1983) *The Invention of Tradition*. Cambridge: Cambridge University Press.

Hooge, L. (1992) 'Nationalist Movements and Social Factors: a Theoretical Perspective', in J. Coakeley (ed.), *The Social Origins of Nationalist Movements*. London: Sage.

Hooson, D. (ed.) (1994) *Geography and National Identity*. Oxford: Blackwell.

Hroch, M. (1985) *Social Preconditions of National Revival in Europe*. Cambridge: Cambridge University Press.

Hroch, M. (1993) 'From National Movement to the Fully-formed Nation', *New Left Review*, 198: 1–20.

Hutchinson, J. (1994) *Modern Nationalism*. London: Fontana.

Ignatieff, M. (1994) *Blood and Belonging: Journeys into the New Nationalism*. London: Chatto and Windus.

Judt, T. (1994) 'The New Old Nationalism', *New York Review of Books*, 26 (May): 44–51.

Kaldor, M. (1993) 'Yugoslavia and the New Nationalism', *New Left Review*, 197: 96–112.

Kedourie, E. (1993) *Nationalism*, 4th edn. London: Hutchinson.

Kitschelt, H. (1986) 'Political Opportunity Structures and Political Protest', *British Journal of Sociology*, 16: 57–85.

Kohn, H. (1944) *The Idea of Nationalism*. New York: Macmillan.

Llobera, J. (1994) *The God of Modernity: The Development of Nationalism in Western Europe*. Oxford: Berg.

McCrone, D. (1998) *The Sociology of Nationalism*. London: Routledge.

Marcu, E. (1976) *Sixteenth-Century Nationalism*. New York: Abaris.

McNeill, W. (1986) *Polyethnicity and National Unity in World History*. Toronto: University of Toronto Press.

Meinecke, F. ([1907] 1970) *Cosmopolitanism and the National State*. Princeton, NJ: Princeton University Press.

Miller, D. (1978) *The Queen's Rebels: Ulster Loyalism in Historical Perspective*. Dublin: Gill and Macmillan.

Mosse, G. (1975) *The Nationalization of the Masses*. New York: Fertig.

Mosse, G. (1985) *Nationalism and Sexuality*. Madison, WI: University of Wisconsin Press.

Mosse, G. (1993) *Confronting the Nation: Jewish and Western Nationalism*. London: Briadeis University Press.

Nairn, T. (1977) *The Break-Up of Britain*. London: New Left Books.

O'Mahony, P. and Delanty, G. (1998) *Rethinking Irish History: Nationalism, Identity and Ideology*. London: Macmillan.

Ranum, O. (ed.) (1975) *National Consciousness, History and Political Culture in Early Modern Europe*. Baltimore, MD: Johns Hopkins University Press.

Renan, E. (1990) 'What is a Nation?', in H. Bhabha (ed.), *Nation and Narration*. London: Routledge.

Robertson, R. (1992) *Globalization*. London: Sage.

Rothchild, D. and A. Groth (1995) 'Pathological Dimensions of Domestic and International Ethnicity', *Political Science Quarterly*, 110 (1); 69–82.

Roudometof, V. (1999) 'Nationalism, Globalization and Eastern Orthodoxy', *European Journal of Social Theory*, 2: 2.

Salecl, R. (1993) 'The Fantasy Structure of Nationalist Discourse', *Praxis International*, 13: 213–23.

Smith, A. (1986) *The Ethnic Origins of Nations*. Oxford: Blackwell.

Smith, A. (1991a) *National Identity*. London: Penguin.

Smith, A. (1991b) 'The Nation: Invented, Imagined, Reconstructed', *Millennium*, 13 (2): 200–17.

Smith, A. (1995a) 'Gastronomy or Geology? The Role of Nationalism in the Reconstruction of Nations', *Nations and Nationalism*, 1 (1): 3–23.

Smith, A. (1995b) *Nations and Nationalism in the Global Era*. Cambridge: Polity Press.

Soysal, Y. (1994) *Limits of Citizenship: Migrants and Postnational Membership in Europe*. Chicago: University of Chicago Press.

Swidler, A. (1986 'Culture in Action, Symbols and Strategies', *American Sociological Review*, 51: 273–86.

Szporluk, R. (1988) *Communism and Nationalism: Karl Marx and Friederich List*. Oxford: Oxford University Press.

Tarrow, S. (1994) *Power in Movement: Collective Action, Social Movements and Politics*. Cambridge: Cambridge University Press.

Tilly, C. (1994) 'States and Nationalism in Europe, 1492–1992', *Theory and Society*, 23 (1): 131–46.

Tipton, C. (ed.) (1972) *Nationalism in the Middle Ages*. New York.

Watkins, S. (1990) *From Provinces into Nations*. Princeton, NJ: Princeton University Press.

Weber, E. (1976) *Peasants into Frenchmem: The Modernization of Rural France, 1877–1914*. Stanford, CA: Stanford University Press.

Wehler, H.-U. (1988) *Aus der Geschichte Lernen?* Munich: Beck.

36

Socialism: Modern Hopes, Postmodern Shadows

PETER BEILHARZ

Socialism, today, may seem to be part of the past; perhaps this is necessarily so. To begin to consider the arguments involved across various socialisms as social theory already means to begin to break up these firm, if imaginary distinctions between past, present and future. For if the socialist traditions often think back, they also necessarily reach forward. Socialism is one central trend in the critique of modernity, for socialism rests on the image of modernity as it is and as it might be. Its main strength has been its capacity to call out the critique of the present by comparing it with senses of pasts and distinct possible futures, or else by comparing innovative experiences in some times and places with more routine achievements elsewhere. Socialism thus functions as critique, via utopia; and at the end of the twentieth century we might conclude that it works better in this critical register than as a politics aimed at the possession of state power. Socialism is, as Zygmunt Bauman puts it, the counter-culture of modernity (Bauman, 1976, 1982). Into the millennium, the presence of socialism may be more discernible as a culture than as a politics. In this broader sense socialist argument replays various claims and counter-claims associated with modernity and critique via Romanticism and Enlightenment. Both rural and urban, modern and anti-modern, socialist theory remains the alter ego of capitalism (Beilharz, 1994b). Thus socialism runs parallel arguments to many of capitalism's claims, including its obsession with economy and, into the middle of the twentieth century, with the state. Similarly socialism runs a dialogue of its own with America and Americanism as the putative model and future of modernity.

To begin, it is important to register two historical facts. First, socialism has a history, a plurality of traditions across place and time. Second, the fact that Marxism comes to dominate socialism does not mean that the two are identical. Socialism has a history; of which Marxism is a part. Socialism precedes, and postdates Marxism (see generally Sassoon, 1996). These facts raise other issues, such as the extraordinary power of local cultures, to the extent that, for example, some communist traditions remain far more deeply marked by local stories than by the grand narratives of Soviet Marxism (Beilharz, 1994a; Davidson, 1982; Tiersky, 1983; Touraine et al., 1987).

Socialism as a social theory coincides not only with the radical aspirations of the French Revolution but also with the earliest reactions against the Industrial Revolution. Arguably there are two streams of development. Socialist argument has a local, practical current which emerges into the 1830s and emphasizes cooperation, contrasting socialism to individualism and hoping for a maintenance of the older orders and habits against modernization (Bauman, 1982; Wright, 1986). It also has an intellectual, or middle-class stream which incorporates these local insights often into more ambitious schemes or hopes for the future. Robert Owen and Charles Fourier were earlier representatives of this intellectual stream, which really comes into its own with Marx, where for the first time the socialist project becomes a property dispute between warring intellectuals. Marxism in a sense abducts socialism, but especially after 1917, when the Bolsheviks pin the Marxist flag to their own attempt to seize power and construct the socialist order in the Soviet Union. Socialism consequently is identified with Marxism and with the Soviet and subsequent claimed socialist roads from China to Cuba and elsewhere into the Third World. Marxism thus becomes an ideology itself, and sacrifices its capacity to criticize the present.

Does this mean, however, that socialism can only ever be a negative or oppositional trend? The point for any consideration of socialism as social theory is that politics and critique do not get on well together, at least when it comes to state power. But this obsession with the state came late, discernibly into the interwar period of the twentieth century. Socialism is often identified with statism, but this is misleading. The earliest socialists like Owen and Fourier favoured the local level of analysis and viewed cooperation or self-management as crucial, and Marx follows them in this; even Marx's greatest work, *Capital* itself, presents its theoretical object at the level of the capitalist factory, and the socialist regime of associated producers as its alternative. Early socialists worked more at the level of the exemplary politics of the commune than at the level of large-scale organization, and again Marx follows them in this, for he fails to bridge intellectually the gap between the individual factory and the globalized world-system. Local socialism thus historically coincides with the idea that small is beautiful, and thus reveals the power of its own romanticism or anti-modernism. For it is only with the work of Weber, Simmel and Durkheim in different ways that sociologists centre upon scale and complexity as irreversible features of modern social organization. Marx's social theory is still guided by the spirit of Rousseau, in that problems of scale and complexity are largely withered away. This is exactly what motivates later turns to market socialism in Eastern Europe, and marketism, say, with the later work of Alec Nove: the recognition that markets deal better with scale than bureaucracies do (see, for example, Nove, 1983).

Socialists from the beginning, then, are active in dispute as to whether socialism involves more progress or modernity or less. Some, like Saint-Simon, anticipate Durkheim in presuming that socialism will be modern or it will not be at all, presuming therefore in this that socialism is a state of affairs to be achieved rather than an ethic or an attitude. Marx's own work indicates the shift from romanticism to modernism. Others dug in on different positions. Thus Ferdinand Tönnies' incredibly influential defence of community, *Gemeinschaft*, versus association, or *Gesellschaft*, was a leading example of the romantic socialist case, where socialism was the opposite of everything that capitalism indicated – size, mobility, speed, rootlessness, restlessness, dirt, promiscuous sex, legalism, money and contract, and urban frenzy (Tönnies, [1887] 1974). Tönnies' views in turn called out Durkheim's modernist socialism in *The Division of Labour in Society* (1893) and in his Bordeaux lectures on socialism (1894–5), where Durkheim sends Rousseau and Tönnies back to the eighteenth century and insists instead that the idea of the whole Romantic personality be replaced by the expanded solidarity afforded by industrialism.

Today we forget that Durkheim and Tönnies were both socialists, and this is one reason why we fail sufficiently to think of socialism as a social theory. Perhaps the more explicitly recognized period dispute here was that between William Morris and Edward Bellamy, whose competing images of the socialist future clearly indicate corresponding critiques of the present and social theories appropriate to their understanding. Bellamy published his sleeper wakes novel, *Looking Backward*, in 1888. Constructed against the image of capitalist waste and disorganization, Bellamy posited the image of socialism as highly organized, without friction, and in effect militarized, nationalized, well-fed, fit and, to our eyes, grey (Bellamy, [1888] 1989). William Morris hit the roof at this philistine good news, and wrote in return 'News from Nowhere', an explicitly rural, Thames Valley utopia where modernity was not celebrated but pushed away, small was beautiful and beauty was central to the quality of living, as Ruskin before him had insisted (Morris, [1890] 1962).

The history of socialisms since has worked this contradiction, among others, between the sense that the idea of socialism involved more modernity, or less. The significance of Marx's work here emerges most fully, for it covers both aspects, a fact which his followers generally avoided. Marx offers at least five images of utopia. To track them is to witness Marx's own embrace of modernity as industrialism, or his transition from green to grey. The Marx known to us in the English language from the 1960s was different to the Marx of the Soviets. The extraordinary efflorescence of Marxism into the 1970s involved a humanist phase, manoeuvred by the *1844 Manuscripts*, followed by a structuralist moment led by Louis Althusser. But in the 1960s the Marx for today was deeply romantic in spirit, more in tune with Schiller's lament for human fragmentation than Levi-Strauss' science of the human mind. The great Marx of the period was the Marx set against alienation, implying a wholeness and authenticity which capitalism had destroyed, making it necessary to destroy the

Destroyer in turn. The utopia implicit in Marx's *1844 Manuscripts* was one of guild labour, where the medieval connotations denied the very idea of the division of labour. Marx put a Fourier spin on this in the famous passage in *The German Ideology* (1845), where the good society, playfully pictured, would involve hunting, herding, fishing and criticism – a horticultural life, not a smokestack in sight (Beilharz, 1992: 7–8). All this changes across the period that Marx leaves the green of the Rhine for the dirt of Dean Street and the British Museum. His subsequent images of utopia evoke automation, and the trade off between boredom and free time in the *Grundrisse* (1857–8), and the self-managed factory in the third volume of *Capital*. A fifth possible utopia is glimpsed in Marx's correspondence with his Russian admirers into the 1870s, where Marx allows the dispensation that communal socialism might still be feasible in Russia (Beilharz, 1992: 11).

Marx, of course, denied utopia, but dealt in it every day of his life, again, necessarily so. For his purpose was to show, at first, that capitalism was a blot on the natural landscape, and then, later, that it was not the only possible way to organize modernity or industrialism. Marx's social theory remains central not only because of its critical power and influence, but because of its capacity to contain this contradiction as it coincides with the progressive entrenchment of industrialism. The young Marx, like Owen and Fourier, can still imagine that industrialism is reversible. By *Capital* (1867), the realization has changed; already in *The Communist Manifesto* (1848) this other modernist stream is apparent, that the real challenge is to harness the forces of production to popular need. But there are other transformations across Marx's work as well. One is powerfully apparent in the 1859 Preface to *A Contribution to the Critique of Political Economy*, where Marx makes plain his substitution of political economy for the earlier, Hegelian curiosity about civil society. This is a landmark in the history of Marxism, for it indicates plainly that henceforth Marxism's concern is within political economy itself. Marx and subsequent Marxists became the wizards of economic analysis, predicting capitalist breakdown, falling profit rates and inevitable proletarian revolution. This logical turn away from politics or culture within Marxism was not to be remedied until the later appearance of Antonio Gramsci. Culture and politics became epiphenomenal, within Marxism, the result of economics rather than realms in their own right. Socialism became a result of capitalism, as classes had their interests inscribed into them by the structural relationship of exploitation between bourgeoisie and proletariat. Marxists spent their lives trying to work out why the proletariat failed to live up to these projections, rather than wondering about the logic or interests of the projectors themselves. As later critics such as Castoriadis and Baudrillard would put it, Marxists were neither historical nor materialist and were not revolutionary but messianic; they had succumbed to their own mirrors of production (Baudrillard, 1975; Castoriadis, 1987).

Marxisms proliferated after Marx, not least with the political success of the Bolsheviks. The diversity of Marxisms did not generally acknowledge the diversity in Marx's own work, partly because it was unknown, and remained so until the Marx renaissance of the 1960s. Marx's influence touched his contemporaries, but Marxism did not take off as a political force until its institutionalization by the German Social Democrats closer to the turn of the century. Certainly Marx influenced those with whom he came into creative contact, such as William Morris, though the content of Morris' socialism, sometimes referred to as his Marxism, was also thoroughly local. Romantic and technologically sensitive by turns, Morris was made to look like Marx because both insisted on the necessity of revolution. But revolution was not the property of Marxism, even if gradualism or enthusiasm for reform was the more common attitude among English socialists.

Marxism emerged as the ideology and theory of the first mass political party, the German Social Democrats (SPD). The SPD became widely known as a kind of counter-society or state within the Prussian state. Its greatest strength also proved to be its greatest weakness; its ghetto-nature made it vulnerable to the Nazis on their road to power after 1933, and its own messianism fed into the fatalistic slogan of the German Communists, 'first Hitler, then us'. Marx's legacy had left unresolved the exact question of how socialism would emerge. Would it automatically follow the collapse of socialism? Would it, instead, be the conscious result of self-organized activity? Or would it, as the 1859 Preface implied, involve some combination of these, where the correct economic conjuncture would call out the appropriate political intervention? Marx's inattention to the theory of politics left the question of the party unresolved, or absent. Marx's party, like Rosa Luxemburg's, looked like the whole working class. Only classes did not act, as such, so that political representation became necessary. Modernity caught Marx napping, together with Rousseau. The Bolsheviks closed this political hiatus by inserting themselves into it as the combat, vanguard party. The German Social Democrats set out practically to make another culture, working in general on the sense of maturational reformism

– sooner or later, socialism would come, whether out of crisis or a gradual growing over, whether by electoral means or collapse.

The larger political legacy of Marxism left a dual possibility, reform or revolution. In *The Communist Manifesto* Marx and Engels had sketched out a ten-point, minimum programme of reforms; yet their tougher stance, outlined by Marx in the penultimate chapter of *Capital*, clearly indicated that socialism would arrive through revolutionary apocalypse. The German Social Democrats grew apart on the basis of this split. Some, like Eduard Bernstein, came to view socialism as a project of citizenship to be achieved by civilizing capitalism. Others, like Karl Kautsky, were happy to combine revolutionary rhetoric with reformist activity, while others again, such as Rosa Luxemburg, wanted to adjust reformist reality to fit revolutionary theory (Beilharz, 1992: ch. 4).

The SPD turned Marxism into catechism so that its rank and file members would have the revolutionary science at its fingertips. Marxist dogma insisted that the two basic classes, bourgeoisie and proletariat, would dichotomize until the vast majority of the working masses would bump off the capitalists. The 'Bernstein Controversy' over reform versus revolution involved two distinct issues; one, whether reformism was to be preferred, and two, whether Marxism must be revised in order to register this political recognition theoretically (Beilharz, 1992; Steger, 1996, 1997). Was Marxism a set of axioms, beyond challenge, or was it a method of analysis open to necessary revision? The process in which Marxism became an ideology also involved its consolidation into scholastics. This is one of the clearest of historical cases in which a social theory intended to help explain and even change the world becomes an impediment to these processes. Marxism became, especially in the hands of Kantsky, a general theory of social evolution where each mode of production emerged triumphantly out of its precedent. Kautsky set these formulae out in *The Class Struggle* (1895), an unrepentantly modernist text, where all that is missing from capitalism's industrial achievement is the crown of socialization. Kautsky therefore set out to prove that all would become proletarians, peasants included, before the bourgeoisie could simply be shown the door. At the same time, it was Kautsky who insisted that left to their own resources, the workers would never achieve more than trade union or economistic consciousness, so they would always need good theoretical leaders like himself. Lenin agreed, and built an ideology on this view in *What is to Be Done* (1902). Kautsky eventually came to the opposite conclusion after 1917, like Bernstein, arguing that history could not be forced.

In effect Bernstein and Kautsky formed a long-term intellectual alliance, as Bernstein continued the Marxian impulse of reforms in the ten-point programme while Kautsky carried on the revolutionary rhetoric of *Capital*. Bernstein's position was closer to the ethics of Kantianism or new liberalism, while Kautsky's sociology shifted in the direction of a Weberian Marxism in his 1930 magnum opus, *The Materialist Conception of History*.

Max Weber had taken sides with Bernstein, however, in preferring revision as the normal attitude for social science and theory. Kautsky, for his part, agreed with Weber that specialization was our fate, and therefore that modernity would overdetermine socialism rather than the other way around. Lenin's utopia, best formally revealed in *State and Revolution* (1916) still sought a new world characterized by simplicity rather than adjusting to complexity, something of a contradiction given the driving modernism which otherwise characterizes his work. When it comes to Bolshevism and the massive shadow which it casts over the twentieth century, it is Lenin who is dominant as actor but Trotsky who is the imposing theorist. What was Bolshevism, as a social theory? Like other streams of socialism, Bolshevism is plural and its paths were many, though Lenin and Trotsky still stand out, together with Bukharin, to Lenin's right and Preobrazhensky, to Trotsky's left. Lenin's theoretical writing is more occasional, and less systematic than Trotsky's. Lenin in a sense combines Luxemburg's desire to radicalize practice with a kind of pragmatism which values political expediency above all else. Unlike Luxemburg, Lenin was always a Jacobin, for whom one wise man was worth a hundred fools. His ultra utopia in *State and Revolution* combines the putative libertarianism of 'all cooks can govern' with the grim insistence that the practical model for socialism would be the post office. This futuristic or modernizing scenario stands in contrast to Lenin's other views of the prospect of socialism, which tend to be populist and rural or at least based upon the idea that Soviet socialism will remain agrarian and not only industrial. Lenin dreamed of extending direct democracy into Soviet experience, but the challenges of modernization without democracy became overwhelming (Arnason, 1993; Beilharz, 1992: ch. 2). While his final utopia looked more distinctly Maoist, accommodating Russian agrarian realities rather than forcing them, Lenin's high Bolshevik utopia was something more like the image of German capitalism, symbolized by Americanism ascendant. Like Trotsky, Lenin's belief that the success of the Russian Revolution depended on the German Revolution was not merely strategic, or even economic; Lenin viewed the 'organized capitalism' analysed by Hilferding to be the basic model for Soviet modernization (Beilharz, 1992: 24). Lenin's model of socialism as modernity was something like capitalism without democracy, or with the lure of an impossible, direct democracy held over it by the Bolsheviks. Its political logic remains populist, in that it pits the people against their exploiters and renders the alternative exploiters – the Bolsheviks – invisible in the process.

Lenin's response to various failures and setbacks was to introduce the New Economic Policy, which in 1921 recognized the status quo as the framework for future Soviet efforts. Trotsky, in contrast, accepted NEP with hesitance, for his model of socialism had always been industrialist and modernizing. Trotsky's was a Faustian Bolshevism, one prepared even to risk life and limb for the thrill, the prospect of even glimpsing what men and technology could do. Trotsky hoped not merely to follow the Germans and Americans, but to outdo them, not least through developing enthusiasms for the principles of Taylorism and scientific management. Americanized Bolshevism – that was the way forward (Beilharz, 1992: 30). Anything is possible – this is the motivation; the rational mastery of nature, and thereby of humanity itself, this is the canvas. Trotsky's impulse is a kind of developmental romanticism, where the frenzy of creation reaches out into the sublime.

The image of socialism in the Bolshevik tradition thus disperses across a spectrum, even if we consider Lenin and Trotsky alone, from a modest hope of feeding people on the one extreme to the project of endlessly reconstructing the world, on the other. The futurism of Trotsky embodies something of the productivism, or obsession with technology, which becomes characteristic of Marxism into the twentieth century. Socialism becomes a matter of harnessing the best of capitalist technology to what are claimed to be more benign ends. The line back to Marx is plain: if abundance is the practical precondition of socialism, then socialism becomes another way of doing capitalism, or at least another form of organising capitalist technology. The producer, or more specifically the proletarian, becomes not only the subject of history but also the citizen; and his incapacity to rule as well as to produce at the same time quietly keeps the Bolsheviks in the business of 'politics'.

Russian radicals had long been divided into localists and westernizers; the distinction was by no means peculiar to Russia. British socialism, too, divided between those who sought more wilfully to return to or to extend the past, and those who sought to modernize it. The conflict between traditionalists and modernizers was acted out in various British sites, not least of them Fabianism. The Fabians became known into the 1930s as progressivists, reformers and statists, sometime apologists for authoritarian regimes or at least for the principles of social engineering which underpinned them. Fabianism began as an alternative life movement, caught up as various European socialisms were in the 1880s with vegetarianism, alternative dress and bicycling (Britain, 1982). Its substantive theoretical impulse came not only from John Stuart Mill and Owen but from Cobbett, Carlyle, Ruskin and indirectly Morris, for whom the old image of England's green and pleasant land looked more interesting than the prospect of Coketown or the Satanic Mills. The opposition to modernity or civilization became major themes of social criticism across socialisms and kindred positions such as Distributism and Catholic ruralism. More recently, these kinds of issues have been pursued with regard to broader questions of British industrial culture and the residual presence of Romanticism even among the captains of industry (Wiener, 1985). British socialisms have long been more heavily influenced by medieval than modernizing claims and motifs, at least until Wilson and then Blair.

The strongest English variant of medievalism was Guild, or Gild socialism, associated with various theorists such as Sam Hobson and Orage and Penty and *The New Age*, but defended most ably by G.D.H. Cole, who took its legacy into Fabianism, where it was lost as statism triumphed with the Beveridge Report into the 1940s. The guild socialists viewed utopia as a coalescence of local unions modelled on the medieval guilds, autonomous and capable of holding together the moments of conception and execution or head and hand. The image of society involved would be based on direct democracy, only the producer would remain privileged; after all, Adam Smith's jibe against trade unions was more accurately addressed to guilds, that they were conspiracies against the public, closed and traditionalistic in the absolute sense. Cole's early hope was for the federation of these self-governing units, a veritable example of small is beautiful (Wright, 1979). Different local English lineages also claimed that the way back opened the way forward; the ethical or Christian socialism based on the idea of fellowship among men and stewardship of nature led by R.H. Tawney was a major contributor to the labourism associated with the British Labour Party into the 1930s (Wright, 1987).

While Tawney worried about compassion and mutual responsibility, and Cole echoed the early Marx's enthusiasm for the autonomy of labour, others like the Webbs puzzled over waste and inefficiency. Beatrice and Sidney Webb began

from positions closer to liberalism or cooperation, with the added sense of evolutionism
associated with the work of Beatrice's childhood
tutor, Herbert Spencer. The idea of evolution
alone – progress from lower forms to higher –
plainly locates the Webbs on different terrain to
that inhabited by the guildists. This point of their
mentality was closer to Marx's, that the development of society made progress possible. Only the
Webbs' image of utopia lacked the monomania-
cal developmentalism of Trotsky; their hope was
rather to service such a minimum of provision as
might enable all to flourish in their interdependence (Beilharz, 1992: ch. 3). Revolutionaries
have enjoyed the prospect of casting Fabianism
as mere 'gas and water socialism'; the problems
of provision, of health, education and housing
nevertheless remain fundamental. Socialism for
the Webbs, then, consisted largely in practical
terms of reorganizing the wealth that society
already possessed. Social problems could be
measured, their existence publicized and appropriate reforms enacted to see to their resolution.
Social solidarity could be developed upon the
emerging patterns of social evolution, so that, as
in Durkheim's view, each would depend on all
the rest. All citizens, in this view, would have a
place in the division of labour; the middle
classes, tempted by their location and tradition
to social parasitism, would also need to find their
social vocation.

The opposition to social parasitism motivated
various different kinds of socialism. Some, like
Marx, viewed the bourgeoisie as implicitly
parasitic, or without social function. Others,
like Lenin, viewed aristocrats, fat capitalists or
coupon-clippers as parasites; for the Webbs, it
was middle-class folks lacking in social conscience who were parasites, at least until they
took up the cause of reform. For others, like
Lenin and Trotsky, again the *kulaks* or rich
peasants became the enemy. And for socialists
and radicals of anti-semitic bent, from Hilaire
Belloc to Werner Sombart, it was finance-capital
which was parasitic (Belloc, 1913; Sombart,
[1911] 1951). Socialists had their distinct
enemies, then, as well as their heroes, proletarian
or mock-proletarian for the Bolsheviks, factory-
inspectors for the Webbs, savants for Kautsky,
scientists for Wells or Trotsky. But for Fabians
the citizen would not be conceived as the
proletarian, as in Bolshevism. Indeed, as the
Webbs went on to suggest in their *Constitution
for the Socialist Commonwealth of Great Britain*
(1920), vocational electorates should be developed alongside geographical forms of representation in order fully to register the significance of
work in political life (Beilharz, 1992: 62). The
evident weakness in this, as in much else of
socialist theory, is the failure to take seriously

the private sphere and the gender consequences
thereof. 'Work', in this discourse as in most
others, refers to paid public work, rather than to
the labours of the home. Not that socialists
failed to address domestic labour, which they did
from Bebel through to Wells; only they continued to presume its gendered nature, themselves reflecting the traditionalism of patriarchy
which itself violates the ethics of modernity and
yet holds it up.

Fabianism in effect dissolved into the state,
victim, like British liberalism, of its own success
with the 1945–51 Labour Government. Fabianism had better articulated the common sense of
the labour movement referred to historically as
labourism, where the politics of socialism was
constructed in terms of the defence and protection of workers and their families. Fabianism
built upon labourism an infrastructure of
research, organization and agitation, pushing
an ethic which sought to tie together the gradual
modernization of society and the solidarity
imputed to its traditional forms. All this
became fundamental to the postwar regimes of
reconstruction, until they were washed away by
the processes of crisis and globalization which
ran through the 1970s to the 1990s.

The idea of the Russian Revolution was
exhausted by the 1940s, being replaced in
romantic Western imaginations by images of
Chairman Mao or Che Guevara. Yet the image
of October excited many earlier, including Shaw
and in Italy the young Antonio Gramsci. The
younger Gramsci was a council communist,
taking up a position for the new proletarian, self-
organized order, espousing a kind of social
democratic syndicalism not unlike the view of
G.D.H. Cole. Gramsci embraced the October
Revolution as 'The Revolution Against Capital',
by which he referred both to the power of capital
and to the fatalistic influence of Marx's *Capital*.
His view was that the Marxism of Kautsky and
his Russian equivalent, Plekhanov, had become
a deadweight on Marxists, who passively
accepted Kautsky's maxim that their job was
to wait for the revolution. Gramsci insisted on
extending the voluntaristic and democratic
element in Marx, that which indicated that
socialism was only possible as a result of the
action of self-organized masses of men and
women. Gramsci insisted that Marxism was a
politics, and not just a political economy: a
statement of will, and not only a recognition of
constraint, and he was stubborn in this insistence
until he was personally constrained within
Mussolini's prison walls, where he wrote the
famous (if thematically scattered) *Prison Notebooks*. Gramsci's *Prison Notebooks* reinstate the
Marxian formula of the 1859 *Preface*, that
people make history but not just as they choose.

The *Notebooks* also reconfigure Marxist politics by placing Machiavelli at the fore, and conceptualizing the Italian Communist Party as the New Prince. More significantly, the *Notebooks* foreground culture, ideology and common sense as the practical field within which bourgeois societies ensure their self-reproduction. Hegemony, and not only force, ensures social coherence; socialism, conceived as the practical project of a new class alliance, or new historic bloc, therefore depends on the possibility of counter-hegemony (Davidson, 1978; Gramsci, 1971).

Gramsci was a revolutionary communist, who was subsequently reinvented as a culturalist predecessor of the Birmingham School of Cultural Studies. He was not only Italian, but more specifically Sardinian, a peripheral Marxist who understood uneven development without falling for the hypermodern cosmopolitanism of a Trotsky. Vital to his legacy is not only *The Prison Notebooks* (1971), but also *The Southern Question* (1926), where Gramsci opened the case that modernity would always ever be traditionalistic as well as progressive. Gramsci's contemporary, often grouped with him and the German philosopher Karl Korsch in the retrospective category of 'Western Marxism', was Georg Lukács. The Hungarian Marxist Lukács not only founded the later Budapest School after 1956, but also was a central voice in the formation of the Frankfurt School in the 1920s, for Lukács was the pioneer of a kind of Weberian Marxism, refracting together (as differently did Simmel) the themes of commodification (Marx) and instrumental reason (Weber) to develop the theme of reification (Lukács, [1923] 1971). The so-called Western Marxists therefore developed the political and cultural spheres of analysis which had been neglected since Marx's call, that vision lay in the analysis of political economy rather than civil society. In the case of Lukács' analysis, culture emerged only to show, by other means, the impossibility of socialism except at the hands of a magically endowed intellectual proletariat. The legacies of Gramsci and Lukács were either institutionalized or ignored by their respective communist parties. Korsch wrote one of the best books on Marx, *Karl Marx*. in 1936 before taking up American exile, where his influence was negligible except for the impact upon marginal local council communists such as Paul Mattick.

The critical theorists of the Frankfurt School, most notably Theodor Adorno, Max Horkheimer and Herbert Marcuse, migrated to America to escape Nazism. There they cultivated the anti-modern or at least anti-American thread of the German tradition, viewing American culture as either candy floss or televisual totalitarianism (Jay, 1973; Wiggershaus, 1994). The Frankfurt School, in common with Lukács, pursued a kind of aristocratic radicalism quite at odds with Gramsci's curiosity about popular culture and folk wisdom. The trajectory of Critical Theory, in contrast, was influenced not only by the failure of socialist revolution in the West, but also by the outcome of Nazism in the Holocaust. 'Western Marxism', so-called because of its guiding sense that Western cultures offered different challenges to those facing others like the Bolsheviks seeking socialism in the 'East', was also deflated by those developments in the West, where the prospects of socialism gave way to the power of barbarism.

In the meantime, German Social Democracy became historically institutionalized as a form of social management into the 1960s, as did labourism in Britain. The extraordinary extent of the postwar boom and the arrival of mass consumerism through the 1950s combined with the effects of the Cold War saw socialism lose impetus again until the 1960s, when critical theory and Western Marxism were revived or reconstructed especially by student radicals from Berkeley to the London School of Economics (the latter, founded by the Webbs). Radicalism rode the wave, perhaps especially in the United States. American socialisms are long of lineage and rich in variety, though they have often been marginalized within scholarship by academics with short memories. The famous question put by Sombart in 1906 was, *Why is There no Socialism in the United States?* ([1906] 1976), presuming that socialism was something necessarily to be measured by its presence or absence at the level of central state power, rather than within civil society or as a counter-current to modernity. Yet far from being a mere absence, socialism has a rich American history, from nineteenth-century utopian experiment, through Bellamy and the Bellamy Clubs, to the Industrial Workers of the World and various intellectual permutations from Lewis Mumford to the pragmatism of Max Eastman and Richard Rorty. If the answer to Sombart's question, rephrased as why was there not *more* socialism in the United States, was material abundance, then the real tease was yet to come, as more of that material abundance into the 1960s brought out the New Left with a vengeance. With Marcuse, Habermas, Gorz and Mallet, traffic increased both into English-speaking cultures and back to the centres as radicals struggled for equal rights and dreamed, still, of the end of alienation.

The Marx of the 1960s conjured up themes going back to alienation as well as commodification. Indeed, whether via Marcuse in *One Dimensional Man* (1964) or the newly translated Marx of the *1844 Manuscripts*, the essential message provided by radical social theory often seemed singular: the world needed to be changed all at once, which in effect, given the power of capital and its culture, meant not at all. Other socialisms were eclipsed by Marxism, and Marxist humanism was scorned by the rising star of structuralism, which also established an image of structure or history as unshiftable (Dosse, 1997). Reformisms could easily be made to look feeble by armchair revolutionaries who claimed a radical distance from the Soviet experience but whose vocabularies were basically Bolshevik (Beilharz, 1987).

Marxism revived as a critical theory, perhaps for the last time before expiring, as State Theory (Frankel, 1983; Jessop, 1982). State Theory was often caught up with the idea that a theory of politics could be derived from the analysis of capital. Thus, again, was Gramsci rediscovered as a political theorist (Sassoon, 1987). Thus, for example, Laclau and Mouffe sought to use Gramsci as a way out of the impasse in *Hegemony and Socialist Strategy* (1985). The sticking point in Gramsci remained that of Bolshevism, or Jacobinism; was the party still the key agent of social transformation, or was it merely a collective noun for the various related social movements which held it up?

The collapse of Marxism as the key presence within socialist social theory at this point came in at least two different forms. The first involved the rediscovery of methodological pluralism, in principle available in Weber but politically accessible through the work of Foucault. Foucault widely replaced Althusser, who had replaced Marx. Power was discovered to exist throughout modernity, and not only in economy. The second point of erosion involved the rediscovery or renegotiation of democracy, via liberalism as political theory in the re-emergence of social movements and the reappraisal of civil society (Arato and Cohen, 1992). On both these accounts, Marxism now appeared to be a regional theory rather than a general theory. The fact that liberalism could be seen as radical again gave a second chance to various non-Marxian socialist alternatives.

The general problem, inasmuch as it could be named, was now reidentified as the problem not of capitalism but of modernity. Working out of the Budapest School tradition of Weberian Marxism, Agnes Heller and Ferenc Feher identified the field of modernity as at least threefold, characterized by the differing logics or dynamics of capitalism, industrialism and democracy (Heller and Feher, 1983). This was, in effect, to return to one of the earliest socialist sensibilities, that socialism was less a state of affairs to be achieved upon the negation of private property than it was a restatement of the priority of the social against individualism. The striking loca-

tional difference was that, by the end of this century, socialism lived in the academy perhaps more than anywhere else, as its claims to being taken seriously as a culture of social theory had outgrown its street credentials as a practical politics. After all that has occurred in its name, socialism remains the kind of critique and utopia which it began as, diminished in its certainty just as its existence is warranted by what surrounds it, part of the past and thereby of our present. Formally speaking, socialism might be said to have returned to the civil societies and social movements which originally called it forth. For as socialists have declared that the core of their utopia is democracy, and not only equality, so have their ambitions returned to the horizons of social democracy and the radical liberal heritage which often informs it. If socialism began as the claim to pursue the ideals of the French Revolution, supporting the expansion of democracy against power or capitalism, then its Marxian claims to absolute difference may have been illusory. Socialism remains part of the critique of modernity; neither term seems possible without the other.

REFERENCES

Arato, A. and Cohen, J. (1992) *Civil Society and Political Theory*. Boston, MA: MIT Press.

Arnason, J.P. (1993) *The Future that Failed*. London: Routledge.

Baudrillard, J. (1975) *The Mirror of Production*. St Louis, MO: Telos.

Bauman, Z. (1976) *Socialism – The Active Utopia*. London: Allen and Unwin.

Bauman, Z. (1982) *Memories of Class*. London: Routledge.

Beilharz, P. (1987) *Trotsky, Trotskyism and the Transition to Socialism*. London: Croom Helm.

Beilharz, P. (1992) *Labour's Utopias: Bolshevism, Fabianism, Social Democracy*. London: Routledge.

Beilharz, P. (1994a) *Transforming Labour*. Cambridge: Cambridge University Press.

Beilharz, P. (1994b) *Postmodern Socialism: Romanticism, City and State*. Melbourne: Melbourne University Press.

Bellamy, E. ([1888] 1989) *Looking Backward*. Harmondsworth: Penguin.

Belloc, H. (1913) *The Servile State*. London: Constable.

Britain, I. (1982) *Fabianism and Culture*. Cambridge: Cambridge University Press.

Castoriadis, C. (1987) *The Imaginary Institution of Society*. Cambridge: Polity Press.

Davidson, A. (1978) *Antonio Gramsci*. London: Merlin.

Davidson, A. (1982) *The Theory and Practice of Italian Communism*. London: Merlin.

Dosse, F. (1997) *History of Structuralism*. Minneapolis, MN: University of Minnesota Press.

Frankel, B. (1983) *Beyond the State?* London: Macmillan.

Gramsci, A. (1971) *Selections from the Prison Notebooks*. London: Lawrence and Wishart.

Heller, A. and Feher, F. (1983) 'Class, Democracy, Modernity', *Theory and Society*, vol. 12. pp. 211-44.

Jay, M. (1973) *The Dialectical Imagination*. Boston, MA: Little Brown.

Jessop, B. (1982) *The Capitalist State*. London: Martin Robinson.

Korsch, K. (1936) *Karl Marx*. New York: Chapman and Hall.

Laclau, E. and Mouffe, C. (1985) *Hegemony and Socialist Strategy*. London: Verso.

Lukács, G. ([1923] 1971) *History and Class Consciousness*. London: Merlin.

Morris, W. ([1890] 1962) 'News from Nowhere', in A. Briggs (ed.), *William Morris – Selected Writings*. Harmondsworth: Penguin. pp. 183–301.

Nove, A. (1980) *Economics of Feasible Socialism*. London: Allen and Unwin.

Sassoon, A. Showstack (1987) *Gramsci's Politics*. London: Hutchinson.

Sassoon, D. (1996) *One Hundred Years of Socialism*. London: Tauris.

Sombart, W. (1906/1976) *Why is There no Socialism in the United States*. New York: ME, Sharpe.

Sombart, W. ([1911] 1951) *The Jews and Modern Capitalism*. New York: The Free Press.

Steger, M. (ed.) (1996) *Selected Writings of Eduard Bernstein*. Atlantic Highlands, NJ: Humanities Press.

Steger, M. (1997) *The Quest for Evolutionary Socialism: Eduard Bernstein and Social Democracy*. New York: Cambridge University Press.

Tiersky, R. (1983) *Ordinary Stalinism*. London: Allen and Unwin.

Tönnies, F. ([1887] 1974) *Community and Association*. London: Routledge.

Touraine, A., Wieviorka, M. and Dubet, F. (1987) *The Workers Movement*. Cambridge: Cambridge University Press.

Wiener, M. (1985) *English Culture and the Decline of the Industrial Spirit*. Cambridge: Cambridge University Press.

Wiggershaus, R. (1994) *The Frankfurt School*. Boston, MA: MIT Press.

Wright, A. (1979) *G.D.H. Cole and Socialist Democracy*. Oxford: Oxford University Press.

Wright, A. (1986) *Socialisms*. Oxford: Oxford University Press.

Wright, A. (1987) *R.H. Tawney*. Manchester: Manchester University Press.

37

Modern Societies as Knowledge Societies

NICO STEHR

New social realities require a new perspective. In advanced societies, the capacity of the individual to say no has increased considerably. At the same time, the ability of the large social institutions that have significantly shaped the nature of the twentieth century to get things done has diminished in the past couple of decades. Or, appropriating Adolp Lowe's (1971: 563) astute insights, we are witnessing a change from social realities in which 'things', at least from the point of view of most individuals simple 'happened' to a social world in which more and more things are 'made' to happen. In this contribution, these new realities are described as representing the emergence of advanced societies as knowledge societies.

I will describe some of these transformations that constitute a real and unprecedented gain from the perspective of the individual and small groups but also what may be described as a rise in the fragility of society. The stress on rights and the growing ability to assert and claim such rights is one of the salient manifestations of the transformations I examine. The same developments are responsible for a crisis in mastering, planning and managing common problems and for a decline in the sense of individual responsibilities. However, there is a trade-off; the decline in the steering capacity of large social institutions and their growing difficulty in imposing their will on society leads to a rise of the importance and efficacy of civil society.

First, I will refer to the concept of knowledge societies and examine the notion of knowledge. I propose to define knowledge as a capacity to act. I will describe the reasons for the importance of scientific knowledge as one among various forms of knowledge in advanced societies. I also

examine the limits to the power of scientific knowledge as well as the emergence of the fastest growing segment of the labor force, namely knowledge-based occupations. The transformation of modern societies into knowledge societies manifests itself most importantly in the sphere of economic activities. I therefore describe some of the features of the changing economy before turning to those consequences of the advancing 'knowledgeability' of actors in modern society that give rise to the growing fragility of modern society.

INTRODUCTION

John Stuart Mill, in *The Spirit of the Age* (1831), published after his return to England from France, where he had encountered the political thinking of the Saint-Simonians and of the early Comte, affirms his conviction that the intellectual accomplishments of his own age make social progress somehow inevitable (cf. Cowen and Shenton, 1996: 35–41). But progress in the improvement of social conditions is not, Mill argues, the outcome of an 'increase in wisdom' or of the collective accomplishments of science. It is rather linked to a general diffusion of knowledge:

> Men may not reason better, concerning the great questions in which human nature is interested, but they reason more. Large subjects are discussed more, and longer, and by more minds. Discussion has penetrated deeper into society; and if greater numbers than before have attained the higher degree of intelligence, fewer grovel in the state of stupidity, which can only co-exist with utter apathy and sluggishness. (Mill, [1831] 1942: 13)

Mill's observations in the mid-nineteenth century, a period he regarded as an age of moral and political transition, and in particular his expectation that increased individual choice (and hence emancipation from 'custom') will result from a broad diffusion of knowledge and education, strongly resonate with the notion of present-day society – the social structure that is emerging as industrial society gives way – as a 'knowledge society'.

The foundation for the transformation of modern societies into knowledge societies is to a significant extent also based, as was the case for industrial society, on changes in the structure of the economies of advanced societies. Economic capital – or, more precisely, the source of economic growth and value-adding activities – increasingly relies on knowledge. The transformation of the structures of the modern economy by knowledge as a productive force constitutes the 'material' basis and justification for designating advanced modern society as a 'knowledge society'. The significance of knowledge grows in all spheres of life and in all social institutions of modern society.

KNOWLEDGE SOCIETIES

Both the greatly enhanced social, political and economic significance of science and technology and the often narrow, even scientistic conception of knowledge generated by modern science call for a careful sociological analysis of knowledge itself. Knowledge has, of course, always had a major function in social life.[1] That human action is knowledge-based might even be regarded as an anthropological constant. Social *groups*, social *situations*, social *interaction* and social *roles* all depend on, and are mediated by, knowledge. Relations among *individuals* are based on knowledge of each other.[2] Indeed, if (as in the interactionist tradition in sociology) such a general notion of knowledge is regarded as the foundation of social interaction and social order, we find that the very possibility of social interaction requires situation-transcendent knowledge that is deployed by the individuals engaging in social action.[3] Power too has frequently been based on knowledge advantages, not merely on physical strength. Societal reproduction, furthermore, is not just physical reproduction but has always also been cultural, that is, it involves reproduction of knowledge.

The historical emergence of 'knowledge societies' does not occur suddenly; it represents not a revolutionary development, but rather a gradual process during which the defining characteristics of society change and new traits emerge. Even today, the demise of societies is typically as gradual as was their beginning, even if some social transformations do occur in spectacular leaps. But most major social changes continue to evolve gradually, at an uneven pace, and they become clearly visible only after the transition is already over. The proximity of our time to significant social, economic and cultural changes, however, makes it highly likely that what is now beginning to come into view is of extraordinary present and future significance.

Moreover, knowledge societies do not come about as the result of some straightforward common pattern of development. They are not a one-dimensional social figuration. Knowledge societies become similar by remaining or even becoming dissimilar. New technological modes of communication break down the distance between groups and individuals, while the isolation of particular regions, cities and villages remains. The world opens up and creeds, styles and commodities mingle, yet the walls between incompatible convictions about what is sacred do not come tumbling down. The meaning of time and place erodes even while boundaries are celebrated.

Until recently, modern society was conceived primarily in terms of property and labor. Labor and property (capital) have had a long association in social, economic and political theory. Work is seen as property and as a source of emerging property. In the Marxist tradition, capital is objectified, encapsulated labor. On the basis of these attributes, individuals and groups were able or constrained to define their membership in society. In the wake of their declining importance in the productive process, especially in the sense of their conventional economic attributes and manifestations, for example as 'corporeal' property such as land and manual work, the social constructs of labor and property themselves are changing. While the traditional attributes of labor and property certainly have not disappeared entirely, a new principle, 'knowledge', has been added which, to an extent, challenges as well as transforms property and labor as the constitutive mechanisms of society.

Theories of societies, depending on their constitutive principles, mirror these quintessential social mechanisms in the chosen shorthand for the historical era they claim to describe and represent. Thus, bourgeois or capitalist society was originally viewed as a society of owners. Later it became a 'laboring society' (*Arbeitsgesellschaft*), and it is now evolving into a knowledge society.

In retrospect, even some ancient societies (Rome, China, the Aztec Empire), that gained and maintained power in part as a result of their superior knowledge and information technology, may be described as knowledge societies of sorts. Ancient Israel was founded upon its lawlike Torah-knowledge, and in ancient Egypt religious, astronomical and agrarian knowledge served as the organizing principle and basis of authority. In this sense knowledge has had an important function throughout history, and humans have always lived in 'knowledge societies'. But in present-day society knowledge has clearly become much more fundamental and even strategic for all spheres of life, greatly modifying and in some cases replacing factors that until recently had been constitutive of social action.

Thus, and despite the fact that there also have been societies in the past that were based on knowledge-intensive action, the idea that modern society increasingly is a knowledge society is meaningful and has practical relevance. It is as meaningful to refer to modern society as a knowledge society as it made sense to refer to industrial societies even though there had been past social systems that were based on the work of 'machines'.

KNOWLEDGE ABOUT KNOWLEDGE

The focus of sociological analysis must therefore increasingly be the peculiar nature and function of knowledge in social relations as well as the carriers of such knowledge together with the resulting changes in power relations and sources of social conflict.[4] In sociology, however, virtually all classical theorists are proponents and even architects of scientism. This also applies to the ways in which knowledge is conceptualized in theories of society designed to capture the unique features of present-day society.

Marxist theories of society have assigned decisive importance to the (cultural) forces or means of production for societal development since 'man's understanding of nature and his mastery over it by virtue of his presence as a social body . . . appears as the great foundation-stone (*Grundpfeiler*) of production and of wealth', so that general knowledge becomes a direct force of production (Marx, [1939–1941] 1973: 705). Max Weber's seminal enquiry into the unique features of Western civilization stresses the pervasive use of reason to secure the methodical efficiency of social action. The source of rational action and, therefore, of rationalization is located in particular intellectual devices. The theory of industrial society, as developed by Raymond Aron, which encompasses both socialist and capitalist forms of economic organization as a single social reality

of industrial civilization, accentuates first and foremost the extent to which science and technology shape the social organization of productive activities.

More recent theories of postindustrial society, in particular those of Daniel Bell, have elevated theoretical knowledge to an axial principle of society.[5] Scholars like Bell, for whom knowledge is an axial principle, nevertheless treat knowledge as a kind of black box. In often polemically charged circumstances, they have tended to defend positive knowledge as non-problematic, inherently practical, efficient, powerful and even ethical. That 'rational knowledge', fabricated in one system, apparently travels with great ease and without loss across the boundaries of social systems, for instance, from science into the economy or state institutions, is hardly ever questioned.

The knowledge referred to in virtually all theories of society that elevate knowledge to prominence, and the groups of individuals that are seen as acquiring influence and control by means of this knowledge, tend to be conceptualized narrowly. This does not mean, however, that such a concept lacks cultural centrality and public or political influence. On the contrary, the narrower notion of knowledge that attributes enormous efficacy to scientific and technical knowledge resonates strongly with the dominant public conception of knowledge and its tasks. This concept of knowledge is a testimonial of the success of the scientific community in installing a particular conception of knowledge as the dominant public concept of knowledge. Whatever the limitations of this 'scientistic' conception of knowledge, its centrality clearly reflects the diminishing role of the non-scientific conception of knowing. The scientization of everyday life, for example in the fields of health or the assessments of risks, manifests the cultural centrality of a particular conception of knowledge that has been assimilated by the theories of modern society described above.

There exists, then, a perhaps paradoxical tendency to overestimate the efficacy of 'objective' technical-scientific or formal knowledge. Theories of modern society generally lack sufficient detail and scope in their conceptualizations of 'knowledge' in order to provide explanations for the causes of the increasingly greater demand for ever more knowledge, the ways in which knowledge travels, for the rapidly expanding groups of individuals in society who in some way or another live off knowledge, for the many forms of knowledge considered pragmatically useful and the various effects knowledge may have on social relations. Since the constitutive mechanism of 'knowledge' is defined in a restrictive objectivist manner, the social, political and economic consequences to which these theories allude tend to be confined to rather straightforward effects that include the hope for (or the fear of) highly rationalized forms of social action.

KNOWING AND THE KNOWN

The changes that should be examined are developments that occur with respect to the forms and dominance of knowledge itself. The focus should be on the relationships between scientific knowledge and everyday knowledge, declarative and procedural knowledge, knowledge and non-knowledge, and on knowledge as a capacity for social action. In order to demonstrate the significance of knowledge for social action, particularly in advanced societies, it is necessary to formulate a sociological concept of knowledge. What is it that we do know? Knowing represents a relation to things and facts, but also to laws and rules. Knowing involves participation: knowing things, facts, rules means to 'appropriate' them, to include them in our field of orientation and competence.

Knowledge can of course be objectified, that is, the intellectual appropriation of things, facts and rules can be established symbolically. In order to know it is not necessary to get into intimate contact with the things themselves, but only with their symbolic representations. This is precisely the social significance of language, of writing, printing and data storage. Most of what is called knowledge and learning today is not direct knowledge of facts, rules and things, but objectified knowledge. Objectified knowledge is the highly differentiated stock of intellectually appropriated nature and society that constitutes society's cultural resource.

However, such participation is subject to stratification; the life chances, the life style and the social influence of individuals depend on access to the stock of knowledge at hand. Modern societies have made dramatic advances in the intellectual appropriation of nature and society. There exists an immense stock of objectified knowledge that mediates our relation with nature and with ourselves. In a general sense, this advancement used to be seen, in earlier contexts, as a form of modernization and rationalization that would lead to a 'unity of civilization'.[6] This second nature now overshadows the primary nature of humans. The real and the fictional merge and become indistinguishable. Theories become facts, yet facts cannot police theories.

It is only after the societal significance of such opposites and oppositions has been understood that the full sociological significance of

knowledge can become clear. Such a perspective leads to the realization that knowledge is increasingly the foundation of authority, that access to knowledge becomes a major societal resource as well as the occasion for political and social struggles.

Although knowledge has always had a social function, it is only recently that scholars have begun to examine the structure of society and its development from the point of view of the production, distribution and reproduction of knowledge.[7] Applied to present-day society, the question arises if knowledge can provide a foundation for social hierarchies and stratification, for the formation of class structure, for the distribution of chances of social and political influence and also for personal life and, finally, whether knowledge may prove to be a normative principle of social cohesion and integration, even though the variations and alterations in the reproduction of knowledge appear to be enormous. Paradoxically, efforts to entrench necessity in history or eliminate the role of chance from it has produced, at least at the collective level, the very opposite tendency. The role of chance, ambiguity and 'fragility' at the collective level, continues to be an increasingly important part of the way society is organized.

KNOWLEDGE AS A CAPACITY FOR ACTION

Knowledge may be defined as a *capacity for action*. The use of the term 'knowledge' as a capacity for action is derived from Francis Bacon's famous observation that knowledge is power (a somewhat misleading translation of Bacon's Latin phrase: '*scientia est potentia*'). Bacon suggests that knowledge derives its utility from its capacity to set something in motion. The term potentia, that is *capacity,* is employed to describe the power of knowing. More specifically, Bacon asserts at the outset of his *Novum Organum* that 'human knowledge and human power meet in one; for where the cause is not known the effect cannot be produced. Nature to be commanded must be obeyed; and that which in contemplation is the cause is in operation the rule.'

The definition of knowledge as capacity for action has multifaceted implications and consequences. *Capacity* for action signals that knowledge may in fact be left unused, or that it may be employed for 'irrational' ends. The thesis that knowledge invariably is pushed to its limit, that it is often translated into action without regard for its possible consequences (as argued, for instance, by C.P. Snow; cf. Sibley, 1973), represents a typical view among observers of

technological development. However, the claim
that science and technology invariably push for
the practical implementation of scientific and
technical knowledge does not give proper
recognition to the context of implementation
of such knowledge. Such a conception of the
immediate practical efficacy of scientific and
technological knowledge, furthermore, vastly
overestimates the inherent practicality of the
knowledge claims fabricated in science.

The definition of knowledge as capacity for
action strongly indicates that the material
realization and implementation of knowledge is
open, that it is dependent on or embedded within
the context of specific social, economic and
intellectual conditions. Knowledge, as a capacity
for action, does not signal that *specific* knowledge claims always possess a fixed 'value' or even
a distinct practical dimension. We cannot, as a
result, stipulate a priori that some knowledge
claims, for example, those that issue from
disciplines in the humanities, are less practical
than knowledge that originates in the natural
sciences.[8] Inasmuch as the realization of knowledge is dependent on the active elaboration of
knowledge[9] within specific networks and social
conditions, a definite link between knowledge
and social power becomes evident because the
control of conditions and circumstances requires
social power. The larger the scale of a project,
the greater the need for social power to control
the actual realization of knowledge as capacity
for action.

Knowledge is a peculiar entity with properties
unlike those of commodities or of secrets, for
example. Knowledge exists in objectified and
embodied forms. If sold, it enters other domains
– and yet it remains within the domain of its
producer. Knowledge does not have zero-sum
qualities. Knowledge is a public as well as
private good. When revealed, knowledge does
not lose its influence. While it has been understood for some time that the 'creation' of
knowledge is fraught with uncertainties, the
conviction that its application is without risks
and that its acquisition reduces uncertainty has
only recently been debunked. Unlike money,
property rights and symbolic attributes such as
titles, knowledge cannot be transmitted instantaneously. Its acquisition takes time and often is
based on intermediary cognitive capacities and
skills. But acquisition can be unintended and
occur almost unconsciously. Neither the acquisition nor the transmission of knowledge is always
easily visualized. The development, mobility and
reproduction of knowledge are difficult to
regulate. It is 'troublesome' to censor and control knowledge. It is reasonable to speak of limits
to growth in many spheres and resources of life,
but the same does not appear to hold for

knowledge. Knowledge has virtually no limits to
its growth, but it takes time to accumulate.

Knowledge is often seen as a collective commodity par excellence; for example, the ethos of
science demands that it be made universally
available, at least in principle. But is the 'same'
knowledge available to all? Is scientific knowledge, once transformed into technology, still
subject to the same normative conventions? The
answer provided by one economist is that
technology must be considered a 'private capital
good'. In the case of technology, disclosure is
uncommon, and rents for its use can be privately
appropriated (cf. Dasgupta, 1987: 10). But the
potentially unrestricted universal availability of
knowledge makes it, in peculiar and unusual
ways, resistant to private ownership (Simmel,
[1907] 1978: 438). Modern communication technologies ensure that access becomes easier, and
may even subvert remaining proprietary restrictions; however, concentration rather than dissemination is also possible and certainly feared
by many, including the late Marshall McLuhan.
But it is equally possible to surmise that the
increased social importance of knowledge in
the end undermines its exclusiveness. Yet the
opposite appears to be the case and therefore
raises anew the question of the persisting basis
for the power of knowledge. Despite its reputation, knowledge is virtually never uncontested.
In science, its contestability is seen as one of its
foremost virtues. In practical circumstances, the
contested character of knowledge is often
repressed and/or conflicts with the exigencies of
social action.

Scientific and technical knowledge, while
clearly representing such 'capacities for action',
does not thereby become uncontestable, no
longer subject to challenge and interpretation.[10]
Scientific and technical knowledge is uniquely
important because it produces *incremental*
capacities for social and economic action or an
increase in the ability of 'how-to-do-it' that may
be 'privately appropriated', at least temporarily.[11] And contrary to neoclassical assumptions,
the unit price for knowledge-intensive commodities and services decreases with increased
production, reflecting 'progress down the learning curve' (cf. Schwartz, 1992).

Knowledge constitutes a basis for power. As
Galbraith (1967: 67) stresses, power 'goes to the
factor which is hardest to obtain or hardest to
replace . . . it adheres to the one that has greatest
inelasticity of supply at the margin'. But knowledge as such is not a scarce commodity, though
two features of certain knowledge claims may
well transform knowledge from a plentiful into a
scarce resource. First, what is scarce and difficult
to obtain is not access to knowledge *per se* but to
incremental knowledge, to a 'marginal unit' of

knowledge. The greater the *tempo* with which incremental knowledge ages or decays, the greater the potential influence of those who manufacture or augment knowledge, and correspondingly, of those who transmit such increments. Secondly, if sold, knowledge enters the domain of others, yet remains within the domain of the producer, and can be spun off once again. This signals that the transfer of knowledge does not necessarily include the transfer of the cognitive ability to generate such knowledge, for example the theoretical apparatus or the technological regime that yields such knowledge-claims in the first place and on the basis of which it is calibrated and validated. Cognitive *skills* of this kind, therefore, are scarce.

KNOWLEDGE AS CAPITAL

Among knowledge-based approaches and concepts in social theory, *cultural capital* and *human capital* theories stand out. Pierre Bourdieu distinguishes between different forms of cultural capital – its embodied or symbolic form as internalized culture, its objectified form in material objects and media, and its institutionalized form (for example, as academic certificates).[12] These distinctions signal the ways in which cultural capital is stored and passed on by way of becoming an integral habitus of the individual. Bourdieu identifies two additional forms of capital – economic and social capital. These two forms of capital refer to the gains individuals may derive from their network of social relations. I will focus on Bourdieu's concept of cultural capital since it resonates more closely with the concept of knowledge.

In Bourdieu's sense, cultural capital[13] as a form of *symbolic capital* is much broader than the concept of human capital as developed in economic discourse. Modern human capital theory relates deliberate and measurable educational investments (and achievements) in the acquisition of useful skills and knowledge to their *monetary* gains or losses. Skills and knowledge have grown in Western societies at a much faster rate than non-human capital, as one of the originators of this idea in economics, Theodore W. Schultz (1961) contends. Investment in human capital (that is, capital embodied in human beings), Schultz argues, has driven much of the growth in real earnings per worker in recent decades.

In strong contrast, cultural capital theory does not proceed from the assumption of a kind of *tabula rasa* that allows every individual to participate in the competitive market where human capital is allocated and where success or failure is at most affected by unequal natural aptitudes.

Cultural capital theory acknowledges not only pre-existing unequal access to the distributional channels for its accumulation, but also the different ways in which the 'market' from the beginning favors the chances of particular players. In a largely undifferentiated society or community, of course, culture does not function as a vehicle for the emergence of cultural capital. There the social conditions of its transmission tend to be much more disguised than those that govern economic capital. The portion of individual lives that can be afforded for the acquisition of cultural capital is regarded as highly significant. Cultural capital yields benefits of distinction for its owner.

The most evident drawback of Bourdieu's explication of cultural capital theory is, first, its strong individualistic bias, that is, the extent to which Bourdieu stresses the fusion of cultural capital and the personality of the individual owner. The emphasis remains for the most part on cultural capital as an inherent attribute of the *individual* carrier. Cultural capital declines and dies with its bearer since both have identical biological limits. Bourdieu's individualistic conception of cultural capital appears to be linked to his determination not to dispossess cultural capital theory of the ability to calculate and attribute investment gains that derive from cultural capital. And such returns of investment are seen to accrue primarily to the investor. In this sense, cultural capital theory resonates with human capital theory. It contains crucial residues of economic discourse.[14]

It is important to recognize that cultural capital is embodied in collective processes and structures; hence the benefits often do not accrue only to those who have invested resources. The production as well as consumption of such capital is not charged to the individual. It is borne by the collectivity. At one extreme, such capital can even be seen to be entirely free, in that its use by certain individuals does not diminish its utility or availability to others. Cultural capital is human-made capital and as such subject to limits applicable to all human products and creations. Secondly, Bourdieu discovers and utilizes the concept of cultural capital in the context of social inequality research. The concept derives its coherence from this context in which distinction, processes of inclusion and exclusion, cultural frames and meaning production are the hallmark of the work that cultural capital accomplishes for individuals. Bourdieu thereby implies the continued social, economic and political relevance of social class in modern society.[15] But it must be asked if class divisions are not undermined by virtue of the transformation of economic realities. Distinctions linked to cultural processes are not merely derivative but foundational. Thirdly, although the notion of human cultural capital is not employed in a fully ahistoric manner, it is for the most part devoid of historical specificity. Bourdieu ([1983] 1986: 255) refers to relatively undifferentiated societies in which embodied culture, since not stratified, does not function as cultural capital; however, this does not permit differentiation between various forms of society beyond a straightforward dichotomy of 'simple' and 'complex' societies. New 'structures of consciousness' (to use Benjamin Nelson's phrase) cannot be captured by this term. In many ways, the structure of consciousness of knowledge societies is not novel. It resonates with the consciousness of modernity that dates – although this too is a highly contested question – at least from the sociohistorical context of the French Revolution. In other respects, the *conscience collective* in knowledge societies is at variance with the belief systems and mental sets that are usually identified as uniquely modern and therefore warrants the designation of a new structure of consciousness. In any event, the notion of cultural capital is not well designed to capture such transformations.

THE LIMITS OF THE POWER OF (SCIENTIFIC) KNOWLEDGE

A critical analysis of the limits of the social power of scientific knowledge requires an understanding of the special nature as well as the similarities of scientific and non-scientific knowledge and action. Classifying scientific knowledge as a unique form of human knowledge is of little value. Such a classification is too closely linked to now obsolete epistemological conceptions of science – to such notions and ideals as universality, experience, rationality, necessity and practicality. Conceptions of scientific knowledge that adhere to such notions tend to deny that scientific knowledge is socially based and a collective as well as historical enterprise.

Robert K. Merton ([1942] 1973) has suggested that for most people everyday knowledge provides greater plausibility and more useful means of comprehension than scientific knowledge, as well as considerable substantive affinity to existing cultural 'prejudices', thereby constituting a potential source of competition for scientific knowledge claims. Merton's is an early theoretical conception of the limits of scientific knowledge and goes far beyond considerations primarily driven by epistemological concerns.

Stephen Toulmin's (1972: 378) useful characterization of organized human activities generally may be taken as a description of the social conditions within which the social production of scientific knowledge occurs: '[H]uman activities and enterprises . . . in which decisions are made, procedures followed, considerations taken into account, conclusions arrived at, new possibilities entertained, and "reasons" given for the resulting conclusions or actions.' The *special* social and intellectual circumstances that prevail in the manufacture of scientific knowledge affect the structure and the possibility of reproducing such knowledge.

Among the special conditions that should be noted here are that knowledge claims or knowledge effects produced under special conditions in scientific laboratories can, first, only be reproduced outside the laboratory if the special conditions that allowed such outcomes are also reproduced outside the laboratory. That is, the special circumstances that led to the original observation of the effect must be extended to the context in which a successful transfer is to be made (see Rouse, 1987: 227). The notion that scientific knowledge, unlike other forms of knowledge, is not bound or limited institutionally has to be questioned in light of the conditions necessary for the reproduction of scientific knowledge claims outside the circumstances of their initial discovery.

Secondly, knowledge claims not only take on features derived from the material conditions of their production, but also reflect institutionally bound cognitive attributes. These attributes include, importantly, a suspension of the pressure to act as constitutive of scientific discourse. Knowledge produced within the scientific community is released from the tasks it must perform outside of science.

One of the most salient attributes of everyday life situations is, in contrast, the persistent pressure to reach a decision, to observe a specific rule, to follow a particular course of action by discarding alternative possibilities, or to provide an account of completed action *ex post facto*. This suspension of the constraint to act within scientific discourse may be described, on the one hand, as a virtue of intellectual activity taking place under privileged conditions that moderate the effect of the pressing interests, rapidly passing opportunities and ambiguous dependencies of everyday contexts on the production of scientific knowledge claims. On the other hand, the result of this suspension of the pressure to act is that scientific knowledge takes on qualities of incompleteness, provisionality, fragmentariness or expansiveness that reduce its effectiveness as knowledge in circumstances in which action is the foremost requirement. As Durkheim ([1912] 1965: 479) observed so well: 'Life cannot wait' (cf. also Gehlen, [1940] 1988: 296–7).[16] Finally, knowledge must be made available and interpreted, and also linked to local, contingent circumstances. The complexity of the linkages and the volume of resources required delineate further limits of the power of scientific and technical knowledge.

The set of limits to the social power of scientific knowledge constitutes an inevitable part of the fabrication and the utilization of scientific knowledge. But they also explain why the knowledge work performed by the stratum of experts of knowledge-based occupations, generally speaking, attains greater and greater centrality in advanced society. The knowledge work performed by knowledge-based occupations or by experts, counselors and advisors, is crucial in that their work 'heals' some of the practical deficiencies of scientific knowledge. For example, a chain of interpretations must come to an 'end' in order for knowledge to become relevant in practice and effective as a capacity for action. This function of ending reflection or remedying the lack of immediate practicability of scientific and technical knowledge – as it emerges from the scientific community – for the purpose of action is largely performed by various groups of experts in modern society.

The centrality of knowledge-based occupations or, using a narrower term, experts in knowledge societies, does not mean that we are on the way, as social theorists have feared in the past, to a technocratic society. A technocratic model of society and its major social institutions which 'sees technicians dominating officials and management, and which sees the modern technologically developed bureaucracies as governed by an exclusive reliance on a standard of efficiency' (Golden, 1976: 257) is but a nightmare, an ideal type or a utopia. Quite a number of arguments can be deployed to demystify the threat of technocracy and a new ruling class made up of faceless experts. The most persuasive argument is social reality itself, which has failed to support the transformation of society in this direction. The emergence of technocratic regimes long predicted has not materialized.

THE KNOWLEDGE-BASED ECONOMY

The emergence of knowledge societies signals first and foremost a radical transformation in the *structure of the economy*. Productive processes in *industrial society* are governed by factors that – relative to the increasing importance of the exchange of symbolic goods – have greatly changed and for the most part declined in significance as preconditions for economic growth: the dynamics of the supply and demand for primary products or raw materials; the dependence of employment on production; the import-

ance of the manufacturing sector that processes primary products; the role of manual labor and the social organization of work; the role of international trade in manufactured goods and services; the function of time and place in production and of the nature of the limits to economic growth.

The most common denominator of the changing economic structure is a shift away from an economy driven and governed by 'material' inputs into the productive process and its organization, towards an economy in which the transformations of productive and distributive processes are increasingly determined by 'symbolic' or knowledge-based inputs. The development and impact of modern information technology exemplifies these transformations (and not just in the sphere of economic activities). They include the dematerialization of production that represents diminished constraints on supply, lower and still declining cost, and a redefinition of the social functions of time, place and the increasing acceleration of change (cf. Miles et al., 1988; Perez, 1985).

The economy of industrial society, in short, is primarily a *material economy* on the way of becoming a monetary economy. Keynes' economic theory, particularly his *General Theory* (1936), reflects this transformation of the economy of industrial society into an economy substantially affected by monetary matters. But, as more recent evidence indicates, the economy described by Keynes is best understood as a *symbolic economy*. The structural changes of the economy and its dynamics increasingly reflect the fact that *knowledge* is emerging as the leading dimension in the productive process, the primary condition for its expansion and for a change in the limits to economic growth in the developed world. In the knowledge society, most of the wealth of a company is embodied in its creativity and information. In short, for the production of goods and services, with the exception of the most standardized commodities and services, factors other than 'the amount of labor time or the amount of physical capital become increasingly central' (Block, 1985: 95) to the economy of advanced societies.[17]

INDIVIDUAL AND COLLECTIVE SOCIAL CONDUCT IN KNOWLEDGE SOCIETIES

The transformation of modern societies into knowledge has profound consequences aside from those that pertain to its economic structure. One of the more remarkable consequences is the extent to which modern societies become fragile societies. This observation has to be qualified.

Modern societies tend to be fragile from the viewpoint of those large and once dominant social institutions that find it increasingly difficult to impose their will on all of society, to give direction and determine the fate of its individual components. From the perspective of small groups and social movements more and uncoupled from the influence of the traditional large-scale social institutions, however, modern societies are not particularly fragile at all. For such groups and social movements, the social transformations under way mean a distinct gain in their relative influence and participation, even if typically mainly in their ability to resist, delay and alter the objectives of the larger institutions. I regard precisely the growing importance of such knowledge in modern society as the prime and immediate reason for the enlargement of the capacity of individuals and social movements to assert themselves in traditional as well as new contentious circumstances. The increase in the 'knowledgeability' of actors and the decrease or static capacity to act of large collectivities have to be seen as complementary developments since the decline in the ability of large institutions to impose their will is linked to the enlargement of the capacity to act by individuals and small groups in society, for instance, in their capacity to say no or mobilize effective strategies of contention.

Knowledge societies are (to adopt a phrase from Adam Ferguson) the results of human action, but not of deliberate human design. They emerge as adaptations to persistent but evolving needs and changing circumstances of human conduct. Among the most significant transformations in circumstances that face human conduct is the continuous 'enlargement' of human action, including an extension of its 'limits to growth'. Modern societies as knowledge societies are becoming more fragile. But this does not mean that they are disintegrating. Increased individualism, for example, does imply an uncoupling from certain collective obligations and constraints and the distinct possibility that the role of the stranger becomes less and less strange for more and more individuals. But it does not suggest a complete uncoupling from collective consciousness and action restraints. In much the same way, while knowledge societies become more fragile, they do not lead to an arrest of social action. On the contrary, they lead to an enlargement and extension of forms of conduct, forms of life, chains of social interaction and channels of communication.

The enlargement in capacities to act occurs at an uneven pace and to an uneven degree. The outcome is a hitherto unknown contradiction: An increasingly larger proportion of the public acquires and exercises political skills, for example – including the choice of non-participation (cf. Stehr and Meja, 1996), or the denial that political activities are indeed political (cf. Magnussson, 1996: 29–32) – while the ability of the state and its agencies to 'impose its will' or to exercise sovereignty is arrested, and typically even decreases.[18] This leads to more fragile and volatile forms of legitimate authority and more fragile powers of the state and of other major social institutions. In that sense the growth and broader dissemination of knowledge paradoxically produces greater uncertainty and contingency rather than providing a resolution of disagreements or the basis for a more effective domination by central societal institutions.

Modern societies are also increasingly *vulnerable* entities. More specifically, the economy, the communication or traffic systems are vulnerable to malfunctions of self-imposed practices typically designed to avoid breakdowns. Modern infrastructures and technological regimes are subject to accidents as the result of fortuitous, unanticipated human action,[19] to non-marginal or extreme natural events that may dramatically undermine the taken-for-granted routines of everyday life in modern societies or to deliberate sabotage.[20] That societies appear to be assailable and sometimes even defenseless in the face of damaging or murderous attacks launched by dedicated individuals represents a fear as well as a now taken-for-granted risk. However, my analysis of modern societies as fragile societies does not extend to its vulnerability in the face of attacks launched by 'rebel' groups, revolutionary dissidents, extremists, assassins, terrorists bent on destroying the institutions they choose to assault, accidents or extreme natural events. It may indeed be difficult to clearly separate the profound susceptibility and vulnerability of modern society to such assaults and forms of aggression from what I am describing and analysing here as the essential fragility of modern society. However, the two refer to entirely different sets of processes, motives and consequences. A society is vulnerable because – prompted by profound disagreements about its very fabric and legitimacy – large or small groups of individuals are determined to negate it. 'Extraordinary' events[21] that occur as the result of such a constellation of motives may be anticipated in principle; at least many large social institutions act and plan as if such events can be anticipated. The state for one prepares itself for events of this kind. 'Revolutionary' activities are not new. In short, we cannot say with any confidence that modernity equals stability as Samuel Huntington (1968: 47), for example, proposed.

Present-day social systems may be seen to be fragile and vulnerable entities in yet another sense. Such fragility results from conduct as well as the deployment of artifacts designed to stabilize, routinize and delimit social action. I am referring specifically to what Rochlin (1997) has called the 'computer trap' or the unintended outcomes and secondary effects of computerization. In the process of even more deeply embedding computers into the social fabric of society, that is, re-designing and re-engineering large-scale social and socio-technical systems in order to manage the complexities of modern society, novel risks and vulnerabilities are created. Computerization becomes more and more invisible but the potential consequences as the result of a breakdown are enlarged. The long-term secondary and destabilizing consequences range from 'the loss of the basis from which such skills can be constructed to the creation of a socio-technical dependency on operating at such high levels of efficiency and complexity that human beings will not be able to manage or control the effects, intended or unintended, whether the computers break down or not'; the increased tightness of linkages, lack of back-up systems, and the speed of response of such systems will make 'human intervention or control difficult at best when (and not if) something goes wrong' (Rochlin, 1997: 217). Hence, one might argue, a basic fragility is inscribed into social systems via the deployment of technical regimes designed to achieve the opposite, namely to stabilize, constrain, routinize and even control conduct. Such an outcome of computerization might be particularly unexpected, cataclysmic and far-reaching but does not differ in principle from the unintended and unanticipated consequences of the widespread deployment of other technical devices in the past.

The fragility of modern societies as described here, however, is a unique condition. Societies are fragile because – propelled by a marked enlargement of their capacities to act – individuals are capable, within certain established rules, to assert their own interests by opposing or resisting the – not too long ago – almost unassailable monopoly of truth of major societal institutions. That is to say, legitimate cultural practices based on the enlargement and diffusion of knowledge enable a much larger segment of society to effectively oppose power configurations that turned out or are apprehended to be tenuous and brittle.[22]

Among the major but widely invisible social innovations in modern society is the immense growth of the 'civil society' sector. The civil society sector recognizes the 'plethora of private, nonprofit, and nongovernmental organizations' (Salomon and Anheier, 1997: 60) that have emerged and grown considerably both in volume and in public influence in recent years in many countries of the developed world. This sector provides an organized basis through 'which citizens can exercise individual initiative in the private pursuit of public purposes' (Salomon and Anheier, 1997: 60).[23]

I also interpret the considerable enlargement of the informal economy, crime, corruption and the growth of wealth in modern society as well as increasing but typically unsuccessful efforts to police these spheres as evidence of the diverse as well as expanded capacity of individuals, households and small groups to take advantage of and benefit from contexts in which the degree of social control exercised by larger (legitimate) social institutions has diminished considerably.[24]

The enlargement of the various social activities known as the informal economy or the growth of wealth, despite the ambiguity of its connotations, constitutes a major structural feature of advanced societies. Among the consequences is a distinctive shift in value-orientations in advanced societies. In political terms, this represents a displacement of the prominence of leftist by more centrist and conservative agendas in all political parties and no longer a trend to the left, as may have been the case in the decades of the 1960s and 1970s.[25]

However, much of social science discourse has been preoccupied with the opposite phenomenon,[26] namely the probable and dangerous enlargement of the ability of modern social institutions, especially various state institutions but also the economy, to more ruthlessly impose its will on its citizens. Thus, the classical social theorists as well as many of their more recent successors were concerned with discovering the conditions that produce and reproduce domination and repression rather than greater autonomy, freedom and independence. Modern science and technology typically were viewed, in the context of such analyses, as the handmaidens of regressive civilizational developments.

But whether the kinds of societal developments we are sketching constitute, as John Stuart Mill anticipated one hundred and fifty years ago, a reconciliation of order and progress remains in doubt. Today, in fact, order and progress are essentially contested concepts and objectives. What is reconciliation to some invariably represents an unsustainable agenda for others. We are living in an age in which the expansion of individual choices is in conflict with traditional sentiments as well as with objectives that favor their restriction.

PROSPECTS

History has by no means ended, but it certainly has changed. The old rules, certainties and trajectories no longer apply. Of course, there are few opportunities of fresh starts in history. None the less, the future of modern society no longer mimics the past to the extent to which this has been the case. That is to say, the future is made from fewer fragments of the past. As a result, sentiments with respect to history that are becoming more pervasive are those of fragility and dislocation. History will increasingly be full of unanticipated incertitudes, peculiar reversals, proliferating surprises, and we will have to cope with the ever-greater speed of significantly compressed events. The changing agendas of social, political and economic life as the result of our growing capacity to make history will also place inordinate demands on our mental capacities. The fit or lack of fit between our knowledgeability and what society, the economy and culture mentally demands is one of the major challenges of knowledge societies.

NOTES

1 A more extended discussion of the sociological meaning of the term 'knowledge' as used in this context may be found in Stehr, 1994: 5–17. Robert Lane (1966: 650) first employed the term 'knowlegeable society', but it was Peter Drucker (1969) who first specifically referred to 'knowledge society', a term used later also by Daniel Bell (1973) and, more recently, by Gernot Böhme (1997). There have been various other attempts to find a term suited to describe the new type of social structure, including 'science society' (Kreibich, 1986), 'information society' (e.g. Nora and Minc, 1980), 'postindustrial society' (Bell, 1973), 'postmodernization' (e.g. Inglehart, 1995), 'technological civilization' (Schelsky, 1961), and 'network society' (Castells, 1996).

2 Cf. Georg Simmel's ([1908] 1992: 383–455) analysis of the secret and the secret society in his *Soziologie*.

3 Cf. Barry Barnes' (1995: 85–93) sympathetic account of the interactionist perspective in sociology and the prominent role of shared knowledge in its thick description of elementary social interaction. However, Barnes (1995: 111) dismisses any designation of modern society as knowledge-based, precisely because he is convinced that shared knowledge is an anthropological constant. In this sense, Barnes echoes Florian Znaniecki's (1940: 23) observation 'that every individual who performs any social role is supposed by his social circle to possess and believes himself to possess the knowledge indispensable for its normal performance'. 'It is sometimes said', Barnes writes, that 'we are living in an increasingly knowledge-based society, which is a profoundly misleading way of describing the proliferation of technical knowledge, the extraordinary division of mental labor and the ever-

growing dependence on specialized expertise, all of which are undoubtedly in evidence.' Barnes limits his enumeration of the possible reasons for designating modern society a knowledge-based society to cognitive transformations and he therefore misses most changes that result from the increased penetration of social structure and culture by knowledge as well as the impact this may have on individuals and major social institutions.

4 Alain Touraine ([1984] 1988: 111) captures well some of the long-term changes in social relations and goals. In mercantile societies, the 'central locus of protest was called *liberty* since it was a matter of defending oneself against the legal and political power of the merchants and, at the same time, of counterposing to their power an order defined in legal terms. In the industrial epoch, this central locus was called *justice* since it was a question of returning to the workers the fruit of their labor and of industrialization. In programmed [or, post-industrial] society, the central place of protest and claims is *happiness*, that is, the global image of the organization of social life on the basis of the needs expressed by the most diverse individuals and groups.' Touraine ([1969] 1971: 3) employs the term 'programmed' society for the new, emerging type of society in order to refer to the 'nature of their production methods and economic organization'.

5 An appreciation as well as a more extensive critique of the theory of postindustrial society is contained in Stehr, 1994: 42–90. Daniel Bell (1971) discusses the more distant as well as immediate intellectual antecedents of his theory of modern society a postindustrial society in an essay published in 1971. Daniel Bell's (1999) book has now been re-issued with a new foreword by the author.

6 Cf. the critique of the unity of civilization thesis by Arnold Toynbee (1946: 36–41).

7 E.g. Malinowski, 1955 and Machlup, 1962, 1981, 1984.

8 It is a widely shared assumption that social science knowledge and knowledge from the humanities is somehow less useful than natural science knowledge, and perhaps increasingly so as 'modernization' advances: 'The more post-industrial society becomes intellectualized, the more it tends to displace traditional value-oriented intellectual disciplines to the benefit of action-oriented ones, that is, those disciplines that can play a direct role in policy-making' (Crozier, 1975: 32). For Crozier, the societal debasement of knowledge from the humanities produces a widespread sense of alienation among its carriers, namely intellectuals, and a general drift toward protest and even revolutionary posture.

9 Compare Lazega's (1992) essay on the 'information elaboration' in work groups and the relations between information and decision-making in and dependent on 'local' contexts.

10 If knowledge indeed 'traveled' almost without impediments and could be reproduced largely at will,

the idea would make considerable sense that scientists and engineers, as the creators of the 'new' knowledge in modern society, should be located at the apex of power.

11 Peter Drucker (1993: 184) observes, however, that initial economic advantages gained by the application of (new) knowledge become permanent and irreversible. What this implies, according to Drucker, is that imperfect competition becomes a constitutive element of the economy. Knowledge can be disseminated or sold without leaving the context from which it is disseminated or sold. The edge that remains is perhaps best described as an advantage based on cumulative learning.

12 Bourdieu's discussion of cultural capital resonates with Simmel's observations ([1907] 1978: 439–40) in *The Philosophy of Money* about the role of the 'intellect'. Simmel notes that 'the apparent equality with which educational materials are available to everyone interested in them is, in reality, a sheer mockery. The same is true of the other freedoms accorded by liberal doctrines which, though they certainly do not hamper the individual from gaining goods of any kind, do however disregard the fact that only those already privileged in some way or another have the possibility of acquiring them. For just as the substance of education – in spite of, or because of its general availability – can ultimately be acquired only through individual activity, so it gives rise to the most intangible and thus the most unassailable aristocracy, to a distinction between high and low which can be abolished neither (as can socioeconomic differences) by a decree or a revolution, nor by the good will of those concerned . . . There is no advantage that appears to those in inferior positions to be so despised, and before which they feel so deprived and helpless, as the advantage of education.'

13 Bourdieu ([1983] 1986: 243) first encountered the usefulness of the notion of 'cultural capital' in social inequality research designed to explain the unequal scholastic achievement of children from different social classes; unequal academic success or the 'specific profits' (failures) students are able acquire in the academic market, are related to the stratified distribution of cultural capital among social classes and the unequal chances of acquiring such capital domestically. One might say that the benefits that derive from the unequal distribution of cultural capital represent a form of unearned income.

14 It needs to be recognized, however, that the actual acquisition of capital, even if the quantity of capital acquired depends on capital previously accumulated by the family of an individual, is – as Simmel ([1907] 1978: 439) observed – ultimately an individual activity.

15 Sympathetic critics of Bourdieu's capital theory have pointed to other attributes of his approach as problematic, for example, the holistic presupposition as a general theoretical assumption. Bourdieu tends to postulate cultural capital as a generalized medium of

accumulation and distinction ill-suited for the analysis of a society with multiple cleavages and divisions (see Hall, 1992; Lamont and Lareau, 1988).

16 Incompleteness or the lack of any impetus to action is constitutive for scientific knowledge: 'Faith is before all else an impetus to action, while science, no matter how far it may be pushed, always remains at a distance from this. Science is fragmentary and incomplete; it advances but slowly and is never finished' (cf. also Luhmann, [1986] 1989: 154–9). The probability that myths and half-truths are employed by large segments of the population in 'advanced' societies may well be even more characteristic of crisis situations in which various dangers appear to be imminent, as Norbert Elias ([1989] 1996: 500–1) argues, for example. In this respect, present-day societies do not differ from 'primitive' societies in which similar responses were elicited by the dangers brought about by illness, draught, thunderstorms or floods. However, Elias is convinced that this state of affairs can be corrected in principle as adequate knowledge is diffused more widely throughout society.

17 See especially Drucker, 1986 and Lipsey, 1992.

18 As Michel Crozier ([1979] 1982: 5) observes, 'the average citizen has never been so free in the range of choices as he is now and has never been able to exert so much influence when grouped together with others as he currently can'. Ronald Inglehart (1990: 335–70) examines the enlargement of political skills of the public in Western societies in terms of a shift from 'elite-directed' to 'elite-challenging' politics.

19 The *Globe and Mail* (17 July 1999, National News) describes the breakdown of much of the communications system in the City of Toronto on 16 July 1999 as the result of an accidentally dropped tool that was the beginning of a chain-reaction disaster affecting not only Canada's largest city as 'a series of failures that revealed the fragility of the complex communications society takes for granted'.

20 My conception of fragility therefore excludes what are clearly *illegal* activities that could hamper and interfere with establish patterns of social conduct, for example, the consequences that follow on the fabrication and at times fast spread of computer viruses (such as the one dubbed Melissa in early 1999; cf. 'Melissa virus suspect caught', *New York Times*, 3 April 1999).

21 Charles Euchner (1996) in his study *Extraordinary Politics* analyses protest movements of recent decades and stipulates that their common denominator is that their members reject or violate the rules of conventional politics. Aside from the distinct possibility that modern protest movements change the rule of politics (cf. Clark and Hoffmann-Martinot, 1998) and are themselves transformed in the course of their struggles, the list of movements Euchner develops shows that it is very difficult to clearly distinguish between 'ordinary' and extraordinary' political events.

22 My emphasis on the individual ability to oppose and contest established power resonates with recent

research that shows power relations to be multidimensional configurations. Such a perspective stresses, for
example, that the notion of resistance must be
redefined so 'that it can be applied to a much wider
range of sociocultural practices and take into account
the ways in which the subjectivity of the dominated is
constrained, modified and conditioned by power
relations' (Haynes and Prakash, 1992: 2).

23 Salomon and Anheier (1997: 62) have attempted
to quantify the growth and presence of the civil society
sector in different countries: 'In France, over 60,000
associations were created in 1990 alone, compared to
less than 18,000 in 1961. Similarly, in Germany the
number of associations per 100,000 population nearly
tripled from 160 in 1960 to 475 in 1990. Even Hungary,
within two years of the fall of communist rule, boasted
over 13,000 associations. And Sweden, often regarded
as the prototypical welfare state, displays some of the
highest participation rates in civil society worldwide.'
The growth of international non-governmental organizations is sketched in Boli and Thomas, 1997.

24 The point is made very well in a study of street
vendors and the state administration in Mexico City or
the political economy of informality as the author calls
it. Cross (1998: 228) observes that street vending in
Mexico City has 'experienced vigorous growth despite
state policies designed to control it and even, at times,
to reduce or eliminate it'. The growth of street vending
activity the author describes certainly has economic
reasons but what is important as well, and perhaps
more significant in this context, is the 'ability of street
vendors collectively to thwart or reverse administrative
attempts to control them that would, if successful, have
prevented such an explosive growth' (Cross, 1998: 228).

25 Bialer (1977: 36–9) tries to account for the
'resurgence and changing nature of the left' in the 1960s
and 1970s. He argues that he is not convinced that either
'the stress on the structural societal changes and on the
growth of the "knowledge industry"' which various
observers (for example, Peter Berger) invoked at the
time should count as adequate explanations nor should
the reference to the cyclical nature of the interest in and
attraction to socialism. For Bialer, the key development
that accounts for the shift toward the political left is
ideological, namely the dissatisfaction with the political
status quo which in turn reflected a fundamental discontinuity in the economic, social and political
developmental base of industrialized democracies.

26 A growing number of studies are investigating
these structural changes in industrialized and less
developed countries. The informal economy, for
example, is examined in the form of a number of case
studies in Portes et al., 1989.

References

Barnes, Barry (1995) *The Elements of Social Theory*.
Princeton, NJ: Princeton University Press.

Bell, Daniel (1971) 'The Post-industrial Society: the
Evolution of an Idea,' *Survey*, 17: 102–68.
Bell, Daniel (1973) *The Coming of Post-Industrial
Society. A Venture in Social Forecasting*. New York:
Basic Books.
Bell, Daniel (1999) *The Coming of Post-Industrial
Society. A Venture in Social Forecasting*. New York:
Basic Books.
Bialer, Seweryn (1977) 'The Resurgence and Changing
Nature of the Left in Industrialized Democracies', in
Seweryn Bialer and Sophia Sluzar (eds), *Radicalism
in the Contemporary Age*, Volume 3: *Strategies and
Impact of Contemporary Radicalism*. Boulder, CO:
Westview Press. pp. 3–82.
Block, Fred (1985) 'Postindustrial Development and
the Obsolescence of Economic Categories', *Politics
and Society*, 14: 416–41.
Böhme, Gernot (1997) 'The Structure and Prospects of
Knowledge Society', *Social Science Information*, 36:
447–68.
Bourdieu, Pierre ([1983] 1986) 'The Forms of Capital',
in J.G. Richardson (ed.), *Handbook of Theory and
Research for the Sociology of Education*. New York:
Greenwood Press. pp. 241–58.
Castells, Manuel (1996) *The Rise of the Network
Society*. Oxford: Blackwell.
Clark, Terry N. and Hoffmann-Martinot, Vincent (eds)
(1998) *The New Political Culture*. Boulder, CO:
Westview Press.
Cowen, Michael P. and Shenton, Robert W. (1996)
Doctrines of Development. London: Routledge.
Cross, John C. (1998) *Informal Politics. Street Vendors
and the State in Mexico City*. Stanford, CA: Stanford
University Press.
Crozier, Michel (1975) 'Western Europe', in M.
Crozier, S.P. Huntingdom and J. Watanuki
(eds), *The Crisis of Democracy. Report on the
Governability of Democracies to the Trilateral
Commission*. New York: New York University
Press. pp. 11–57.
Crozier, Michel ([1979] 1982) *Strategies for Change:
The Future of French Society*. Cambridge, MA: MIT
Press.
Dasgupta, Partha (1987) 'The Economic Theory of
Technology Policy', in P. Dasgupta and P. Stoneman
(eds), *Economic Policy and Technological Perfor-
mance*. Cambridge: Cambridge University Press.
pp. 7–23.
Drucker, Peter (1969) *The Age of Discontinuity.
Guidelines to our Changing Society*. New York:
Harper and Row.
Drucker, Peter (1986) 'The Changed World Economy',
Foreign Affairs, 64: 768–91.
Drucker, Peter (1993) *Post-Capitalist Society*. New
York: HarperBusiness.
Durkheim, Emile ([1912] 1965) *The Elementary Forms
of Religious Life*. New York: The Free Press.
Elias, Norbert ([1989] 1996) *The Germans. Power
Struggles and the Development of Habitus in the*

Nineteenth and Twentieth Centuries. New York: Columbia University Press.

Euchner, Charles C. (1996) *Extraordinary Politics. How Protest and Dissent are Changing American Democracy.* Boulder, CO: Westview Press.

Galbraith, John K. (1967) *The New Industrial State.* New York: Houghton-Mifflin.

Gehlen, Arnold ([1940] 1988) *Man. His Nature and Place in the World.* New York: Columbia University Press.

Hall, John R. (1992) 'The Capital(s) of Cultures: A Nonholistic Approach to Status Situations, Class, Gender, and Ethnicity', in M. Lamont and M. Fournier (eds), *Cultivating Differences. Symbolic Boundaries and the Making of Inequality.* Chicago: University of Chicago Press. pp. 257–85.

Haynes, Douglas and Prakash, Gyan (1992) 'Introduction: The Enlargement of Power and Resistance,' pp. 1–22 in Douglas Haynes and Gyan Prakash (eds.), *Contesting Power. Resistance and Everyday Social Relations in South Asia.* Berkeley: University of California Press.

Huntington, Samuel P. (1968) *Political Order in Changing Societies.* New Haven, CT: Yale University Press.

Inglehart, Ronald (1990) *Culture Shift in Advanced Industrial Society.* Princeton, NJ: Princeton University Press.

Inglehart, Ronald (1995) 'Changing Values, Economic Development and Political Change', *International Social Science Journal*, 145: 379–403.

Keynes, John M. (1936) *The General Theory of Employment, Interest and Money.* London: Macmillan.

Kreibich, Rolf. 1986. *Die Wissenschaftsgesellschaft. Von Galilei zur High-Tech Revolution.* Frankfurt a.M.: Suhrkamp.

Lamont, Michèle and Lareau, Annette (1988) 'Cultural Capital: Allusions, Gaps and Glissandos in Recent Theoretical Developments', *Sociological Theory*, 6: 153–68.

Lane, Robert E. (1966) 'The Decline of Politics and Ideology in a Knowledgeable Society', *American Sociological Review* 31: 649–62.

Lazega, Emmanual (1992) *Micropolitics of Knowledge. Communication and Indirect Control in Workgroups.* New York: Aldine de Gruyter.

Lipsey, Richard G. (1992) 'Global Change and Economic Policy', in N. Stehr and R. Ericson (eds), *The Culture and Power of Knowledge: Inquiries into Contemporary Societies.* Berlin and New York: de Gruyter. pp. 279–99.

Lowe, Adolph (1971) 'Is Present-day Higher Learning "Relevant"?', *Social Research*, 38: 563–80.

Luhmann, Niklas ([1986] 1989) *Ecological Communication.* Chicago: University of Chicago Press.

Machlup, Fritz (1962) *The Production and Distribution of Knowledge in the United States.* Princeton, NJ: Princeton University Press.

Machlup, Fritz (1981) *Knowledge and Knowledge Production.* Princeton, NJ: Princeton University Press.

Machlup, Fritz (1984) *The Economics of Information and Human Capital.* Princeton, NJ: Princeton University Press.

Magnusson, Warren (1996) *The Search for Political Space. Globalization, Social Movements, and the Urban Political Experience.* Toronto: University of Toronto Press.

Malinowski, Bronislaw (1955) *Magic, Science and Religion.* Garden City, NY: Doubleday Anchor.

Marx, Karl ([1939–1941] 1973) *Grundrisse. Introduction to the Critique of Political Economy.* New York: Vintage Books.

Merton, Robert K. ([1942] 1973) 'The Normative Structure of Science', in *The Sociology of Science. Theoretical and Empirical Investigations.* Chicago: University of Chicago Press. pp. 267–78.

Miles, Ian, Rush, Howard, Turner, Kevin and Bessant, John (1988) *Information Horizons. The Long-Term Social Implications of New Information Technology.* London: Edward Elgar.

Mill, John Stuart ([1831] 1942) *The Spirit of the Age.* Chicago: University of Chicago Press.

Nora, Simon and Minc, Alain (1980) *The Computerisation of Society.* Cambridge, MA: MIT Press.

Perez, C. (1985) 'Microelectronics, Long Waves and World Development', *World Development*, 13: 441–63.

Portes, Alejandro, Castells, Manuel and Benton, Lauren A. (eds) (1989) *The Informal Economy. Studies in Advanced and Less Developed Countries.* Baltimore, MD: Johns Hopkins University Press.

Rochlin, Gene I. (1997) *Trapped in the Net. The Unanticipated Consequences of Computerization.* Princeton, NJ: Princeton University Press.

Rouse, Joseph (1987) *Knowledge and Power: Toward a Political Philosophy of Science.* Ithaca, NY: Cornell University Press.

Salomon, Lester M. and Anheier, Helmut K. (1997) 'The Civil Society Sector', *Society*, 34: 60–5.

Schelsky, Helmut (1961) *Der Mensch in der wissenschaftlichen Zivilisation.* Köln/Opladen: Westdeutscher Verlag.

Schultz, Theodore W. (1961) 'Investment in Human Capital', *American Economic Review*, 51: 1–17.

Schwartz, Jacob T. (1992) 'America's Economic-Technological Agenda for the 1990s', *Daedalus*, 121: 139–65.

Sibley, Mulford Q. (1973) 'Utopian Thought and Technology', *American Journal of Political Science*, 17: 255–81.

Simmel, Georg ([1908] 1992) *Soziologie. Untersuchungen über die Formen der Vergesellschaftung.* In *Gesamtausgabe*, Band 11. Frankfurt a.M.: Suhrkamp.

Simmel, Georg ([1907] 1978) *The Philosophy of Money.* London: Routledge and Kegan Paul.

Stehr, Nico (1994) *Knowledge Societies.* London: Sage.

Stehr, Nico and Meja, Volker (1996) 'Die Zerbre-chlichkeit der modernen Gesellschaft', *Vorgänge*, 35: 114–20.

Toulmin, Stephen (1972) *Human Understanding.* Princeton, NJ: Princeton University Press.

Touraine, Alain ([1969] 1971) *Post-Industrial Society. Tomorrow's Social History.* New York: Random House.

Touraine, Alain ([1984] 1988) *Return of the Actor. Social Theory in Postindustrial Society.* Minneapolis, MN: University of Minnesota Press.

Toynbee, Arnold (1946) *A Study of History.* Abridge-ment of vols I–IV. New York: Oxford University Press.

Znaniecki, Florian (1940) *The Social Role of the Man of Knowledge.* New York: Columbia University Press.

38

Sociology, Morality and Ethics: On Being With Others

BARRY SMART

In a critical historical study of the life and work of Emile Durkheim, Steven Lukes comments that it is 'astonishing how little attention has been given to . . . questions [of morality] in twentieth-century sociology . . . Indeed, it is not an exaggeration to say that the sociology of morality is the great void in contemporary social science' (1973: 432 n.19). In a similar manner, Pickering remarks on the 'dearth of classics in the sociology of morals' and wonders why morality 'has not attracted a large number of scholars devoted to sociology' (1979: 26) and Ossowska (1970) laments the marginal status of morality within sociology and calls for the development of a sociology of morality. Unease about the general relation of the social sciences to the realm of ethics and morality informs the work of several contributors to *Social Science as Moral Inquiry* (Haan et al., 1983) and disquiet about moral life has been a dominant theme in the work of a number of other prominent social and philosophical analysts (Bernstein, 1995; MacIntyre 1982, 1990; Rorty, 1989). A comparable concern emerges from Zygmunt Bauman's critical reflections on the way in which the issue of morality has been virtually silenced within a sociological discourse bent on promoting its modern scientific credentials. Indeed, in his powerful study of the respects in which the Holocaust can be considered to be bound up with modernity and its consequences, Bauman (1989) sets out to explain why ethical problematics and moral questions have generally been treated as inadmissible within sociology and then proceeds to outline an argument for a sociology that might be more appropriately attentive to ethical and

moral concerns. While Bauman's (1991, 1993, 1995a) critical engagement with the consequences and discontents of modern civilization and associated ethical reorientation of social enquiry demonstrates that questions of ethics and morality are no longer quite as marginal within contemporary sociological discourse as they might once have been, it nevertheless remains indisputable that 'insufficient attention' has been devoted to such matters within contemporary social theory (Lash, 1996).

Questions of ethics and morality have featured in some form in some of the works of prominent classical sociological figures: Georg Simmel's two-volume *Einleitung in die Moralphilosophie Eine Kritik der ethischen Grundbegriffe* (1892–3) and Max Weber's *Protestant Ethic and Spirit of Capitalism* (1904–5) represent two significant examples. In turn, the respective works of Karl Marx and Sigmund Freud, while not specifically analytically orientated towards sociology or necessarily directly preoccupied with questions of ethics and morality, might be argued to have contributed significantly to a sociological understanding of the 'moral landscape' (Rieff, 1965; Sayer, 1991). However, a sustained and explicit sociological engagement with questions of morality is perhaps most evident in the work of Emile Durkheim and it is his work, in the first instance, to which attention is directed below.

What consideration has been given to morality in contemporary social analysis and how, if at all, things have fared since Lukes drew attention to the moral void at the heart of modern sociology are matters to which the second half of my discussion is directed. It will suffice here to add that a number of commentators have remarked on the ways in which questions of ethics and morality have been marginalized within modern sociological discourse (Gouldner, 1971; Levine, 1995). The marginalization of ethics and morality has assumed two particular forms: a relative neglect of ethics and morality as social phenomena *for* sociological analysis and a parallel avoidance of potentially controversial ethical and moral matters *within* the practice of social enquiry. Belated recognition of this state of affairs has caused unease about both 'the moral meaning of modern society' and 'the moral meaning of social science' (Haan et al., 1983: 1), an unease that has perhaps proven to be analytically productive insofar as it has led to increasing attention being directed to the moral dilemmas of modernity and the prospects for a postmodern ethical turn (Bauman, 1993).

SOCIOLOGY, PHILOSOPHY AND MORALITY

Morality and ethics, formerly regarded as primarily, if not entirely, the province of philosophy, are represented in Durkheim's work as empirical matters amenable to social scientific analysis. In his work, Durkheim makes reference to the need to distinguish between the constitution of a science of morality and the deduction of morality from science, but it is evident that his analysis of the reality of moral life also had as one of its objectives the achievement of moral improvement. While Durkheim remarked that 'science must resolutely and definitively be dissociated from practice' and that the types of morality associated with different societies 'should be studied for the sole purpose of understanding them, of learning how they are made up and what factors condition them', he also argued strongly that a sociological science of morals – a particular branch of sociology – promised to provide a 'rational basis for practical applications', to put us 'in a position to undertake a rational modification of . . . [moral reality], *to say what it should be*' (1979: 31, 32; emphasis added). In a subsequent, more detailed treatment of the subject Durkheim remarks, in a characteristically legislative manner, that 'the science of reality puts us in a position to modify the real and to direct it. The science of moral opinion furnishes us with the means of judging it and the need of rectifying it' (1974: 60). In a similar vein, Durkheim comments that 'the science of moral facts puts us in a position to order and direct the course of moral life' (1974: 65). In sum, it can be argued that throughout Durkheim's reflections on morality there is an implied articulation between the 'theoretical' and the 'practical', the

ambition driving his work being 'to arrive at practical conclusions which should bear fruit in social action' (Bougle, 1974: xxxvi). However, as I will endeavour to demonstrate below, Durkheim's sociological reflections on the foundation of morality are not easily reconciled with his less frequently expressed views on the possibility of judging, rebelling against, and/or combating moral ideas deemed inappropriate.

In his reflections on the nature of moral facts Durkheim identifies two characteristics: obligation and desirability. For an action to count as moral it needs must involve duty or obligation, but in contrast to Kant, it is argued that such an action must also be characterized by a 'degree of desirability'. Duty or obligation alone is not enough, a moral act must appeal, it must, as Durkheim states, 'interest our sensibility to a certain extent' (1974: 36). As Bernstein argues, by 'phenomenologically building into the obligatory force of moral norms their desirability, Durkheim constrains their theoretical reconstruction such that Kantian-style analyses that turn on the logical and rational vindication of universalistic claims are dropped from serious consideration' (1995: 93). Furthermore, it is suggested by Durkheim that the idea of the moral presents a comparable duality to the idea of the sacred, insofar as it commands authority or respect while simultaneously appealing to us, while being an 'object of love and aspiration' (1974: 48), and this in turn leads reference to be made to close links between moral and religious life. Indeed, making explicit reference to the 'sacred character of morality' Durkheim adds that it is impossible for morality and religion to be 'dissociated and become distinct' and that '[m]orality would no longer be morality if it had no element of religion' (1974: 68, 48, 69). The basis for the association between morality and religion drawn by Durkheim is that both are set apart from other orders of phenomena, that is, there is a relationship of incommensurability between the 'sacred' (religion; morality) and the 'profane'. Insofar as it is argued that 'sacredness and morality are closely related' (1974: 71), Durkheim's work has been considered to be vulnerable to the charge that it neglects to satisfactorily distinguish between morality and religion (Lukes, 1973: 432). How justified is this line of criticism?

In addressing the question of the relationship between religious symbols and moral reality Durkheim comments that the 'two systems of beliefs and practices' have been historically closely articulated, that 'moral ideas became united with certain religious ideas to such an extent as to become indistinct from them' (1972: 109, 110). However, responding to a period of crisis in which traditional forms of morality were being undermined and displaced, Durkheim proceeds to argue that 'we must discover the rational substitutes for those religious notions that have, for so long, served as the vehicle for the most essential moral ideas' (1972: 110). In short, it is the achievement of '*reasoned* evaluations' towards which Durkheim argues a science of morals is to be directed, but such a science while permitting 'empirical study of moral facts' does not apparently destroy the '*sui generis* religious character which is inherent in them and which distinguishes them from all other human phenomena' (1974: 62).

A closely related criticism to which Durkheim's work is vulnerable is that the relationship he sought to establish between 'society' and 'morality' remains ambiguous and that promotion of the potential benefits of scientific analysis for the practice of morality betrays an inadequate understanding of both the moral condition itself and the relationship between philosophy and sociology. Certainly the relationship between science and morality has proven to be far more complex and uneven than is acknowledged in references to 'the science of morality . . . [teaching] us to respect moral reality [as] it affords us the means of improving it' (Durkheim, 1984: xxviii–xxix).

Both the characteristics of moral action identified above – intrinsic desirability or a shared sense of the virtue or goodness attached to a course of conduct, and duty or obligation – are considered to derive from 'society'. As Durkheim states, 'society . . . for me is the source and the end of morality' (1974: 59), and again, 'society . . . is . . . a moral power superior to the individual, enjoying a sort of transcendence analogous to that which religions ascribe to divinity' (1979: 138). But what does this tell us about 'morality' and its relationship with 'society'? And how are we to make sense of the other, less attractive face of morality, exemplified by moral indifference and/or immoral behaviour? How are we to account for the absence, suppression or silencing of moral responsibility? Frequent reference is made by Durkheim to different social types having their own particular 'moral discipline', and that there is no one 'single morality which is valid for all men at all times and in all places' (1979: 31, 130). The observation that moral systems have varied and continue to vary is not contentious, neither is the idea that as a society changes, so may its morality. However, what is open to question is the quasi-legislative status accorded to the sociological science of morals outlined by Durkheim, a status that has become more contentious as everyday life is lived amidst a diversity of different, if not divergent and conflicting, moralities, in respect of which judgements have to be made concerning 'right' and

'wrong'. Durkheim remarked that 'we cannot aspire to a morality other than that which is related to the state of our society' (1974: 61). But such an observation begs more questions than it resolves. In an increasingly fragmented and diverse late modern capitalist society in which it might be argued that 'anything goes', to what morality can, do and *should* we aspire?

SOCIETY, MORALITY AND SOCIALITY

For Durkheim morality is necessarily bound up with society: it is by virtue of society that morality is possible. In short, 'Man is only a moral being because he lives in society, since morality consists in solidarity with the group, and varies according to that solidarity' (Durkheim, 1984: 331), or as he notes in a subsequent paper on the determination of moral facts, 'society is the end of all moral activity . . . [m]orality begins with life in the group, since it is only there that disinterestedness and devotion become meaningful' (1974: 54, 52). In a series of clarificatory remarks on the relationship between society and morality Durkheim states that his concern is to understand 'objective moral reality, that common and impersonal standard by which we evaluate action' (1974: 40). Durkheim asserts that the individual, whether acting as agent or object, cannot be a measure of the 'moral value of conduct', for moral value derives from a 'higher source', namely society, 'the *sui generis* collective . . . formed by the plurality of individuals associated to form a group' (1974: 51). Society for Durkheim is a 'moral power', it transcends the individual and constitutes 'the source and the guardian of civilization . . . It is a reality from which everything that matters to us flows' (1974: 54). It is argued that 'each society has in the main a morality suited to it' (1974: 56) and that any other would be 'impossible' or 'fatal'. However, after emphasizing yet again that moral systems are a function of social organization, that they are bound to specific 'social structures and vary with them' (1974: 56), Durkheim is forced to confront reality and to briefly acknowledge the possibility that there might be exceptions, 'abnormal cases', but the references made to such 'exceptions' are for the most part brief and enigmatic. The prospect that moral indifference or immoral behaviour may not be a temporary symptom of an in principle remedial societal pathology, but a direct consequence or corollary of modern culture and a particular modern form of societal organization, is not considered.

Insofar as the impact of modernity is recognized to have loosened ties between people by undermining traditional sources of solidarity, then modern societies are acknowledged to be morally uncertain – '[t]he old duties have lost their power without our being able to see clearly and with assurance where our new duties lie' (Durkheim, 1974: 68). The reality of modern life according to Durkheim is that 'we do not feel the pressure of moral rules as they were felt in the past' (1974: 68–9), however this is not experienced as greater freedom or liberation, but as 'crisis', as 'anomie', a condition that may be alleviated if not resolved by a 'special science of moral facts'.

Although Durkheim is frequently credited with analysing the reality of emerging modern forms of social life a significant part of his narrative is preoccupied with outlining prescription, with articulating what needs to be done to compensate for the anomic consequences following the 'disappearance of the segmentary type of society' (1984: 333). In his first major work the key proposition is that 'the division of labour becomes the predominant source of social solidarity, at the same time [as] it becomes the foundation of the moral order' (1984: 333). But this is merely speculation, for as the concluding paragraphs of the text acknowledge, 'morality . . . is in the throes of an appalling crisis' (1984: 339). Concern over the weakening of the foundations of morality also informs Max Weber's (1976) reflections on the consequences arising from the development of the modern economic order, in particular the 'inexorable power' exercised by 'material goods' over people's lives. Max Weber notes how 'the refusal of modern men to assume responsibility for moral judgements tends to transform judgements of moral intent into judgements of taste' (1970: 342). For Emile Durkheim, the loosening of traditional ties has 'irretrievably undermined' morality and as a result it is suggested that 'our first duty at the present time is to fashion a morality for ourselves' (1984: 340). In a related text Durkheim notes that 'we are passing through a period of crisis' and that in such circumstances morality appears to us 'less as a code of duties' and more as a 'sort of aspiration towards an elevated but vague objective' (1974: 69).

It is in the Preface to the Second Edition of his narrative on the division of labour that Durkheim turns directly to address the legal and moral anomie to which modern economic life is considered to be subject and remarks on the lack of any clearly articulated 'boundary between the permissible and the prohibited, between what is just and what is unjust' (1984: xxxii). In a context where economic functions are recognized to have become of 'prime importance' morality is described as at best 'vague' and 'inconsistent': the development of an industrial

and commercial economic environment is considered to have become the source of 'moral deterioration', to have left social life without an adequate moral framework. The picture painted is one in which there is a lack of regulation and an absence of self-control. The predominance of self-interest is portrayed as having the effect of undermining 'public morality'. Seemingly anticipating 'communitarian' sentiments articulated by contemporary analysts addressing the moral malaise of late modern consumer capitalist forms of life in which the habits of individualism predominate (Bellah et al., 1996: Etzioni, 1994), as well as analyses that have drawn attention to a crisis in the public domain following the promotion of self-interest and the stimulation of private appetites (Bell, 1976), Durkheim calls upon the collectivity to reconstitute cohesion and regulation. However if, as Durkheim argues, political society or the state is unable to fulfil such a role – '[e]conomic life, because it is very special and is daily becoming increasingly specialised, lies outside their authority and sphere of action' (1984: xxxv; see also 297) – from where is the impetus for a remoralization of social life to come? The answer forthcoming from Durkheim is that professional groups and professional ethics may provide a 'moral force capable of curbing individual egoism' (1984: xxxix).

What is outlined is the possibility of professional groups being constituted – 'between the state and individuals' – as a system of corporations with a variety of functions, including the exercise of moral regulation over members. With the benefit of hindsight Durkheim's account of the ways in which the disorganizing, disorderly and disembedding consequences of modernity might be remedied appears excessively optimistic. The idea that a network of corporations, in addition to exercising 'moral influence' over members, might also in good faith adopt and apply general principles formulated by the state in respect of 'mutual assistance', education and other activities, is strikingly at odds with the reality of late twentieth-century life. Durkheim may have been sufficiently perceptive to recognize that 'the corporation is destined to assume an ever more central and preponderant place in society' (1984: liii), but the conduct and consequences of corporate affairs have been quite different from those anticipated. Far from contributing to a remoralization of social life, economic corporations have contributed to the development of a seductive consumer society and an associated pervasive cult of individual self-interest which serve to weaken 'the impulse of responsibility for the integrity and well-being of other people' (Bauman, 1998: 77). In short, increased demoralization rather than re-moralization would appear to have been the outcome of the modern reconstitution of the corporation.

Reflecting on events at the beginning of the twentieth century Durkheim speculated that the corporation might become 'the elementary division of the state' and that society 'would become a vast system of national corporations'. At the beginning of the twenty-first century it is increasingly evident that the sovereignty of the modern nation-state has been diminished by the development of transnational or global economic corporations whose relationships to any specific territorial location have become weak at best. In turn, given the increasing globalization of economic production, finance and cultural communications, and the extension of social relations beyond the territorial borders of the nation, society can no longer be assumed to be synonymous with the geopolitical formation of the modern nation-state. In such circumstances, where 'the nation-state's economic sovereignty is thinned' and 'state-endorsed nationhood is increasingly contested as the principal frame of cultural identity', it is not surprising to find that the moral community is considered to be 'fragmented and pluralized' (Bauman, 1995b: 152). Durkheim had hoped to help put an end to such moral uncertainty; we seem to be reconciled to living with it.

As I have indicated, recognition of the dynamism of modern society leads Durkheim to an acknowledgement of the difficulties that arise with the erosion of 'morality maintained by the forces of tradition' and the emergence of 'new tendencies'. The implication is of an interregnum between two moral orders in respect of which the moral science of sociology might serve to render new moral ideas more precise and help to direct 'the process of becoming' or 'moral remaking'. Although there is an associated reference to resistance to moral ideas being justified insofar as they are 'out of date', such an observation avoids the important, albeit complex, question of the grounds on which 'datedness' is to be determined and a related and increasingly pressing, if not more difficult issue, that is the presence of competing, if not conflicting systems of contemporary moral ideas claiming to meet the criteria advanced by Durkheim, namely of being appropriately 'related to the state of our society' (1974: 61). The question of conflicting modern moral values and ideas and the associated problem of contrasting accounts of the condition of modern society is not a matter to which Durkheim devotes much, if any, attention. The process of understanding and accounting for the state of our society is not, as Durkheim seems to assume, independent of ethical and moral aspects, and as such it cannot constitute 'an objective standard with which to compare our evaluations', and in consequence the attempt to demonstrate that a sociological science of moral facts can provide reasoned evaluations of morality and thereby guide conduct proves to be highly problematic. Modern scientific reason does not provide a secure basis from which to judge moral matters; to the contrary, as Bauman (1989: 18) argues, its 'spirit of instrumental rationality' has been directly implicated in the 'moral mediocrity', if not the silencing of moral voices and the de-moralization, characteristic of modern social life.

There is a lack of clarity in Durkheim's work in respect of the 'various different relations between "society" and "morality"', and Steven Lukes suggests a particular 'confusion between "end"', "objective" or "object"; "interest"; "motive"; "ideal"; "precondition"; and "cause"' (1973: 416). There is also another possible confusion between 'societal' and 'social' context that leads Zygmunt Bauman (1989) to propose a reorientation of the sociological theorizing of morality away from a Durkheimian focus on society and towards a consideration of a Levinasian conception of 'pre-societal sources of morality'.

DUALISM OF HUMAN NATURE – DURKHEIM, FREUD AND LEVINAS

For Durkheim the human condition is riven by a tension between the demands arising from 'society', from the regulation that is a corollary of communal existence, from sociality, and the 'organic' characteristics of human beings, their 'nature'. Implied here is a close parallel with the work of Freud on the association between civilization and instinctual repression (Coser, 1960). In a text originally published in 1914 Durkheim makes reference to the 'constitutional duality of human nature', to the substantially different, contrasting, if not conflicting, qualities of body and soul – 'sensations and sensory appetites, on the one hand, and the intellectual and moral life, on the other' (1960: 326, 338). Just as Freud comments on the 'antagonism between civilization and instinctual life' (1985: 30), so Durkheim argues that we are unable to 'pursue moral ends without causing a split within ourselves, without offending the instincts and the penchants that are the most deeply rooted in our bodies' (1960: 328). For Durkheim we are 'double'; 'we are the realization of an antimony' – profane body and sacred soul; inferior sensations and sensory appetites on the one hand and the higher faculties of reason and moral activity on the other. When Durkheim turns to account for this duality he argues that 'human dualism has always expressed itself in religious form' and that even where explicit religious belief does not seem to be present morality remains 'infused with religiosity'. In short, the dualism of human nature is considered to be simply 'a particular case of that division of things into the sacred and profane that is the foundation of all religions' (1960: 335). As Durkheim makes clear in *The Elementary Forms of the Religious Life* (1995), sacred forms are collective representations, they are products of group life. The force of morality, its authority and ability to move, lead and direct conduct, does not originate from within individuals but 'from the outside'. The duality identified is depicted as an inescapable feature of human being – on the one hand existence appears to be 'purely individual and rooted in our organisms', on the other 'social and nothing but an extension of society' (Durkheim, 1960: 337). As with Freud's analysis, for Durkheim our passions and egoistic inclinations emanate from the former, from our individual constitutions, while rational activity ('concepts, the material of all logical thought') and morality are deemed to be manifestations of society, of social causes. The relationship between the two is identified as one of tension, antagonism and struggle, the maintenance of social life being considered to require 'perpetual and costly sacrifices' on the part of individuals. From such a standpoint moral life is inevitably a *socialized* life.

A Durkheimian approach to the sociological study of moral life places emphasis upon the requirements of society, 'social needs' and the accommodations and adaptations demanded of individuals to meet and maintain these. Above all it is to the achievement and maintenance of one central need, the need of social integration or societal unity, that moral ordering is considered to be directed. In a brief critical address of Durkheim's sociological view of moral life, Zygmunt Bauman makes a series of telling observations and raises a number of significant questions about 'the conception of society as, essentially, an actively moralizing force' (1989: 172). Pre-social, a-social, if not anti-social, our 'natural' inclinations are represented by Durkheim as in need of socialization, as requiring moral regulation and constraint, if society is to be sustained. In this context social integration appears to be the end and measure of morality. The problem with this, as Bauman rightly argues, is that if 'the only existential foundation of morality is the will of society, and its only function is to allow the society to survive, then the very issue of substantive evaluation of specific moral systems is effectively removed from the sociological agenda' (1989: 172).

Insofar as the analytic agenda is conditioned by an uncritical acceptance of the idea that there are as many moralities as there are social types and a parallel assumption that any existing morality practised by a people needs must have a purpose, namely 'to enable it to live', analysis necessarily appears to be confined to simply studying the various types of morality in order to learn 'how they are made up and what factors condition them' (Durkheim, 1979: 130, 31). Such a line of argument, developed in a discussion on moral doctrines first published in 1909, leads Durkheim to express the view that notwithstanding knowledge of variations in moral life, and an appreciation that 'the morality of the future will probably not be that of today', existing morality is 'worthy of respect' and 'children must be bound . . . to the morality of their own time and country' (1979: 131). This point of view provides little scope for a critical analytical address of a prevailing system of morality. As Bauman suggests, given the above 'there is no way in which various moral systems can be compared and differentially evaluated. The need each system serves arises inside the society in which it is nested, and what matters is that there must be a moral system in every society, and not the substance of moral norms this or that society happens to enforce in order to maintain its unity' (1989: 172).

Durkheim was clearly aware that his view of moral reality was vulnerable to the criticism that it precluded the possibility of judgement and in a 1906 seminar discussion of his ideas he sought to counter objections by arguing that they rested upon a misunderstanding. However, the counter-argument raises more questions than it resolves, for it amounts to little more than an expression of faith in the potential ability of what Durkheim describes as 'the science of reality', 'the science of moral opinion', and 'the science of morals' to provide the means of judgement and rectification when we encounter a 'troubled moral condition'. The science of morals is credited by Durkheim with the capacity to resolve the dilemmas of moral life. Whether it is the retrieval of an inappropriately abandoned moral principle, one that can be shown to be still 'related to . . . essential and ever-present conditions of our social organization and collective mentality' (1974: 60), or facilitating adjustment to an interregnum between 'two divergent moralities, the one now existing and the one in the process of becoming' (1974: 61), it seems that the science of morals is able to provide a resolution of moral dilemmas. Durkheim adds that '[w]e are not then obliged to bend our heads under the force of moral opinion' (1974: 61). It seems that we may take issue with a specific prevailing regime of morality. But the bottom line remains, namely that 'we cannot aspire to a morality other than that which is related to the state of our society'

(1974: 61). Such a statement begs the question of how the vague criterion advanced allows the appropriateness of different, possibly overlapping, perhaps competing, if not conflicting, simultaneously present moralities to be compared and evaluated. On what basis, following Durkheim, can we take issue with a prevailing moral order, make clear that it is not worthy of respect, and refuse to be bound by it, even if it is the morality of our own time and country? Following Durkheim, is it possible to develop a critical analysis of morality?

Towards the conclusion of his discussion Durkheim remarks that the science he proposes is insufficiently advanced to guide us and that in such circumstances we are forced to do what we can, to operate with a 'more summary and premature science', and to look 'in moments of doubt to the inspirations of sensibility' (1974: 61–2). Durkheim does not elaborate on the 'inspirations of sensibility', but such a remark opens up the issue of our ability to perceive or feel and a cluster of related possibilities, including the capacity of responding to emotion, and the habits of the heart documented and explored to such critical effect by Bellah et al. (1996), as well as moral feelings. It is evident from Durkheim's discussion of human nature and moral activity that any inspiration needs must derive from society, for morality can only come from society. From such a standpoint symptoms of 'immorality' necessarily signify deficiencies in the social processing of moral behaviour and there is little, if any prospect, as Bauman warns, of recognizing the respects in which society 'may, at least on occasion, act as a "morality-silencing" force' (1989: 174). If morality is considered to be a consequence of society, a social product, then 'moral behaviour becomes synonymous with social conformity and obedience to the norms observed by the majority' (Bauman, 1989: 175). The significant limitations of this conception of moral life, in particular for generating appropriate criticisms of problematic social norms and for promoting resistance to questionable standards promoted by society, leads Bauman to explore a radically different perspective on the subject of moral sensibility.

In his critical confrontation with the Durkheimian perspective on moral life Bauman raises the question of the 'possibility that . . . certain moral patterns may be rooted in existential factors unaffected by contingent social rules of cohabitation', but that these may 'be neutralized or suppressed by countervailing social forces' (1989: 174). Drawing on events associated with the Holocaust, Bauman argues that the civilizing process of modernity needs must be recognized now to include 'death camps and *Muselmanner* among its material and spiritual products'(1989: 176); conformity with the moral norms of a particular modern society leading in the case of Nazi Germany to genocide and other forms of immoral conduct. The events of the Holocaust undermine the idea of society as the foundation of morality, in particular the punishment of individuals for war crimes, and other political and legal responses following the defeat of Germany testify to the existence of legitimate grounds for distinguishing good from evil that are not 'fully and solely at the disposal of the social grouping able to "principally co-ordinate" the social space under its supervision' (Bauman, 1989: 176). Citing Hannah Arendt's powerful reflections on the moral implications of the prosecution of defendants for following orders, for engaging in forms of conduct unopposed, if not accepted and endorsed by the 'unanimous opinion of . . . all around them', Bauman suggests that what is at issue is 'the question of *moral responsibility for resisting socialization*' and by implication the presence of non-societal or pre-societal sources of morality. Insofar as the conduct of an individual may be moral, notwithstanding condemnation by the group, and in turn, conduct advocated by the whole of society may be immoral, it is necessary, as Bauman argues, to rethink the sociology of morality. Rather than the process of socialization being the source of the solution to immorality it may be responsible for 'the manipulation of moral capacity' (Bauman, 1989: 178), for the neutralization, if not the perversion, of morality. Such an awareness leads Bauman to argue that 'the factors responsible for the presence of moral capacity must be sought in the *social*, but not *societal* sphere. Moral behaviour is conceivable only in the context of coexistence, of "being with others", that is, a social context; but it does not owe its appearance to the presence of supra-individual agencies of training and enforcement, that is of a societal context' (1989: 178–9). It is the primary existential condition of our 'being with others' which is fundamental to the ethical philosophy of Emmanuel Levinas, a philosophy that Bauman argues is able to provide the basis of a significantly 'different and original sociological approach to morality' (1989: 182).

ETHICAL RESPONSIBILITY, MORAL LIFE AND THE POLITICAL WORLD OF SOCIETY

In his discussion of the model of the civilizing process which has informed our understanding of the development of modernity, Bauman argues that critical consideration needs to be given to the way in which the 'promotion of rationality' has marginalized, if not excluded altogether, alternative criteria of action, particularly ethical motivations for action. A marginalization or neglect of ethical and moral problematics has been a feature of modern sociological enquiry as it has worked to establish its place within an increasingly morally silent scientific culture. As Bauman remarks, '[t]he nature and style of sociology has been attuned to the selfsame modern society it theorized and investigated' (1989: 29), a society which has revered the rational to the detriment of 'ethical norms or moral inhibitions'. The work of Levinas, on which Bauman draws, stands in stark contrast to the discourse of modern sociology insofar as it presents a relationship of ethical responsibility for the other as constitutive of subjectivity. Sociality, the condition of being *with* another, is from this standpoint primarily a matter of being *for* the other.

In the work of Levinas the inter-human relationship of proximity with the other constitutes the analytic focus. Subjectivity is conceived in ethical terms, 'the very node of the subjective is knotted in ethics understood as responsibility'. In turn, the latter is described as 'the essential, primary and fundamental structure of subjectivity' (Levinas, 1992: 95). In contrast to the mainstream philosophical tradition of the West, which makes a correlation between '*knowledge*, understood as disinterested contemplation, and *being* . . . the very site of intelligibility, the occurrence of meaning' (Levinas, 1989: 76), it is *ethics* which constitutes first philosophy for Levinas. However, the relationship of ethical responsibility that constitutes our human being is recognized by Levinas to become occluded the moment sociality extends beyond face-to-face interaction. As soon as there are more than two people the ethical relationship changes and becomes political. It is here in 'the socio-political order of organizing and improving our human survival' that morality, 'a series of rules relating to social behaviour and civic duty' (Levinas and Kearney, 1986: 29) comes into play. Levinas argues that ethics, the sensitivity of the subject to the call of the other, 'becomes morality and hardens its skin as soon as we move into the political world of the impersonal "third" – the world of government, institutions, tribunals, prisons, schools, committees, and so on' (Levinas and Kearney, 1986: 30). The critical task of ethics as 'first philosophy' is to seek to unsettle this ontologically naturalized form of being-in-the-world by continually reminding us of our fundamental ethical responsibility for the other. A sense of our ethical responsibility for the other provides a foundation and a resource from which the prevailing moral-political order of the state may be challenged and resisted. Indeed, Levinas describes ethical responsibility as 'a perpetual duty of vigilance and effort' (Levinas and Kearney, 1986: 30) that needs to be continually ready to hold the political world of government to account. As such ethics represents for Levinas not so much a metaphysical 'what ought to be' as a critical disturbance of our being, of the complacency of our being, and as such Levinasian ethics constitutes a potentially powerful form of critique.

In an explication of the work of Jacques Derrida, Simon Critchley argues that Levinas attempts to 'build a bridge from ethics understood as a responsible, non-totalizing relation with the other, to politics, conceived of as a relation to the third party . . . to all the others, to the plurality of beings that make up the community' (1992: 220). The sociological significance of a transformation of this order in the magnitude or scale of a social group for the relations between its elements has been addressed by Georg Simmel. Reflecting on the significance of numbers for social life Simmel argues that the 'simplest sociological formation . . . remains that which operates between two elements' (1950: 122). Simmel argues that this formation, the dyad, is distinctive, that it has 'a different relation to each of its two elements than have larger groups to *their* members . . . each of the two feels himself confronted only by the other, not by a collectivity above him . . . The dyad, therefore, does not attain that super-personal life which the individual feels to be independent of himself' (1950: 123). As soon as an additional member or third party enters the scene the intimacy, closeness and sense of responsibility associated with the dyad is dissolved; the relationship is transformed with the formation of an 'objective unit up and above its members . . . an objective, super-individual structure which they feel exists and operates on its own' (Simmel, 1950: 127–8). Simmel proceeds to argue that such an objective structure may lead individuals to pass responsibility for 'performances which really are the business of individual members . . . over to society' (1950: 133). In turn, Simmel identifies other features, such as the erosion or elimination of moral restraint and the possible anonymity associated with group membership, leading 'the individual to commit acts for which, *as an individual*, he does not care to be responsible' (1950: 134). What is clearly at issue here is the qualitative transformation of the basis of individual conduct arising from an expansion in the scale of social interaction, precipitating in particular what Simmel describes as 'disturbance and distraction of pure and immediate reciprocity' (1950: 136).

While Simmel's references to 'dyads, triads and larger groups' may suggest a degree of convergence with the views of Levinas on the significance of the move into 'the political world of the impersonal "third"', beyond superficial similarities in respect of the significance of numbers for social life, there are really relatively few parallels to be found in their respective works. Although Simmel seems to acknowledge the way in which the size of a social group may affect 'the individual's group behavior' and that this may have 'normative and moral significance', ultimately such concerns receive merely the briefest of consideration and then only in relation to the 'ties of the individual to a super-individual order of life' (1950: 99), rather than through a more sustained consideration of the question of ethical relationships of responsibility towards others which Levinas has identified as primary.

When Simmel does directly address questions of ethics and morality it is in the relatively familiar sociological context of a consideration of the way in which relations between 'individual and society' and the distinction between 'the social' and 'the human' have been articulated in eighteenth and nineteenth-century thought. However, Simmel's reflections on 'the ethics of the individual and . . . the ethics of society' (1950: 60) do extend beyond a predictable discussion of the 'egoism–altruism dichotomy' and acknowledge the existence of other significantly different philosophical positions. In contrast to the assumption of the necessity of individual egoism being contained and altruistically re-ordered or re-directed within society, Simmel at least opens up the issue of the violence to which the individual may be subject 'for the benefit and utility of the many' and, in turn, raises the question of the possibility that the individual's strivings may not be an expression of egoism but rather a manifestation of the pursuit of a 'super-personal value' (1950: 59). What is placed on the agenda here is the potential discrepancy and conflict between the claims made by society upon the individual and the attempts that may be made by the individual to 'realize a value . . . or . . . an accomplishment that is unappreciated . . . [and] not rewarded by society' (1950: 61). Elaborating on this theme, Simmel makes reference to Nietzsche's identification of possible differences between the interests of humanity and society respectively, in particular the fact that society is merely one of the forms in which human development is realized and that other objective orders in which we are involved may not have anything 'intrinsically and essentially . . . whatever to do with "society"' (1950: 62). Simmel notes that such 'personal qualities' as 'depth of thought, greatness of conviction, kindness, nobility of character, courage, purity of heart – have their autonomous significance which likewise is entirely independent of their social

entanglements' (1950: 62). The contrast presented is between values of human existence and social values, it being argued that the former allow us to entertain claims that 'go far beyond any given society . . . and may even be in pointed conflict with the more specific claims of the group that for any given man represents "his society"' (Simmel, 1950: 63).

The pressures on the individual are, as Simmel recognizes, to accommodate to the demands and standards of society, 'to differentiate himself from the humanly general' but to submit to the 'socially general'. There is an underlying current here that has been articulated in terms of notions of the 'freedom of the individual', 'natural-law man' and an abstract individualism, notions that suggest we are 'ethically the more valuable, charitable, and good, the more each of us is purely himself . . . Inasmuch as he is more than sheer empirical individuality, the true individual has in this "more" the possibility to give of himself and thus to overcome his empirical egoism' (1950: 70). In these eighteenth-century views discussed by Simmel there is a sense of an essential nature imperfectly (re)present(ed) in reality, the objective being to achieve 'the ego which we already are . . . because we are it not yet purely and absolutely but only in the disguise and distortion of our historical destinies' (1950: 71). In short, to achieve with others 'the true equality of all that is man'.

Simmel notes that this conception finds its 'abstract perfection' in the work of Kant, for whom moral value is predicated upon personal freedom, including equality. In the course of the nineteenth century a significant transformation is evident in the relationship that is assumed to exist between the qualities of freedom and equality, literally a shift from potential 'harmony' to perceived 'antagonism', and two other tendencies emerge placing emphasis on 'equality without freedom' and 'freedom without equality' respectively. The first of these Simmel notes is characteristic of socialism, the second of a new individualism – a qualitative individualism stressing incomparability, uniqueness and specificity. A socialized system necessarily encounters the impossibility of reconciling freedom and equality and is 'forced to resort to an *adjustment* to equality, which, as an overall satisfaction, is supposed to reduce the desires for freedom that go beyond it' (Simmel, 1950: 75). With the new individualism, 'the individualism of difference', there is an implied 'constitution of a more comprehensive whole that is composed of the differentiated elements' (Simmel, 1950: 82), a societal collective that unifies heterogeneous elements.

In contrast to the qualities identified above, qualities, that is, of reciprocity, freedom and equality that inform our understanding of the

relationship between individual and society, there
is another relevant position, to which I have
already drawn attention, one that operates on
radically different terms. Rather than 'reciprocity', Emmanuel Levinas places emphasis on an
ethical relationship of responsibility for the other
as constitutive of subjectivity, a relationship that
is not one of 'symmetrical co-presence' but of
'essential asymmetry' (Levinas and Kearney,
1986: 31), or as he states in *Ethics and Infinity*,
'the intersubjective relation is a non-symmetrical
relation' (1985: 98). Instead of 'freedom' Levinas
speaks of duty, responsibility and obligation.
And rather than 'equality', Levinas makes clear
that 'I must always demand more of myself than
of the other' (Levinas and Kearney, 1986: 31). In
short there is an inequality of responsibility, such
that 'I and the Other are in this sense not equals. I
am infinitely more responsible than the Other'
(Llewelyn, 1995: 139). Implied here is a very
different conception of the relationship between
individual and society to the one that has tended
to underpin sociological reflection. Levinas
demands,

> It is extremely important to know if society in the
> current sense of the term is the result of a limitation
> of the principle that men are predators of one
> another, or if to the contrary it results from the
> limitation of the principle that men are *for* one
> another. Does the social, with its institutions,
> universal forms and laws, result from limiting the
> consequences of the war between men, or from
> limiting the infinity which opens in the ethical
> relationship of man to man. (1985: 80)

For Freud, Durkheim and Simmel it is the
former view that predominates, it being argued
that in the 'development of the individual as of
the species, ethical obedience to the claims of the
"thou" and of society characterizes the first
emergence from the pre-ethical stage of naïve
egoism' (Simmel, 1950: 261). In the respective
works of Levinas and Bauman it is evident that
the latter view prevails, in short that 'moral
responsibility . . . is the first reality of the self, a
starting point rather than a product of society'
(Bauman, 1993: 13). Indeed, reflecting on the
question of the relationship with the other
Levinas remarks that Durkheim has 'misunderstood the specificity of the other when he asks in
what Other rather than myself is the object of a
virtuous action' and that he is mistaken to
regard '"morality . . . [as] the product of the
collective" and not the result of the face to face
encounter' (1987: 84:). For Bauman it is clear
that the sources of morality are to be regarded as
'pre-societal' and that rather than being a
product of society', morality may in fact be
something society manipulates – exploits, re-
directs, jams' (Bauman, 1989: 183).

CONCLUDING REMARKS – QUESTIONING ETHICS, CRITICAL THEORIZING AND MORAL LIFE

Traumatized by 'the administered nightmare of
the twentieth century' (Jay, 1973: 280), Theodor
Adorno and Max Horkheimer raised questions
about the status and purpose of social enquiry
and the fate of morality. The question of what
remains of morality after Auschwitz is one to
which both Levinas and Bauman have
responded. For Levinas it is a question of
whether we can 'speak of morality after the
failure of morality?' The cautious answer
provided is that it 'cannot be concluded that
after Auschwitz there is no longer a moral law, as
if the moral or ethical law were impossible without promise' (Levinas, 1988: 176). The notion of
'ethics as first philosophy' outlined by Levinas
represents a more positive response to the same
question, a response that promotes the idea of the
continuing 'primacy of the ethical, . . . of the
relationship of man to man – signification,
teaching, and justice – a primacy of an irreducible
structure upon which all other structures rest'
(1969: 79). The ethical demand to recall and live
with our responsibility for the other articulated
by Levinas achieves a wide-ranging, if not
universal, critical analytical and political value
in a context where the articulation of an increasingly global neocapitalism with a culture of
individualism has promoted self-fulfilment as the
primary preoccupation and produced moral
indifference as a consequence. As Robert Bellah
and his colleagues suggest, it is important to
recognize the extent to which our 'basic sense of
solidarity with others' has been and continues to
be undermined; how our sense of 'solidarity with
those near to us . . . [and] those who live far from
us, those who are economically in situations very
different from our own' (1996: xxx) continues to
be eroded. For Bauman too it is important to
understand how the modern civilizing process
has produced moral indifference, eroded moral
inhibitions, and rendered victims of exploitation
and dehumanization morally invisible. Now that
it is no longer possible to treat the incidence of
immoral conduct as symptomatic of a breakdown of '"normal" social arrangements'
(Bauman, 1989: 198) a new sociological theory
of morality is required to account for the social
production of immorality and to assist in the
recovery of ethical life.

REFERENCES

Bauman, Z. (1989) *Modernity and the Holocaust.*
     Cambridge: Polity Press.

Bauman, Z. (1991) *Modernity and Ambivalence*. Cambridge: Polity Press.

Bauman, Z. (1993) *Postmodern Ethics*. Oxford: Blackwell.

Bauman, Z. (1995a) *Life in Fragments – Essays in Postmodern Morality*. Oxford: Blackwell.

Bauman, Z. (1995b) 'Searching for a Centre that Holds', in M. Feathertone, S. Lash and R. Robertson (eds), *Global Modernities*. London: Sage.

Bauman, Z. (1998) *Work, Consumerism and the New Poor*. Buckingham: Open University Press.

Bell, D. (1976) *The Cultural Contradictions of Capitalism*. New York: Basic Books Inc.

Bellah, R.N., Madsen, R., Sullivan, W.M., Swidler, A. and Tipton, S.M. (1996) *Habits of the Heart – Individualism and Commitment in American Life*. London: University of Californiia Press.

Bernstein, J.M. (1995) *Recovering Ethical Life – Jurgen Habermas and the Future of Critical Theory*. London: Routledge.

Bougle, C. (1974) 'Preface to the Original Edition', in E. Durkheim, *Sociology and Philosophy*. New York: The Free Press.

Coser, L. (1960) 'Durkheim's Conservativism and its Implications for His Sociological Theory', in K.H. Wolff (ed.), *Essays on Sociology and Philosophy by Emile Durkheim et al.* New York: Harper and Row. pp. 211–32.

Critchley, S. (1992) *The Ethics of Deconstruction: Derrida and Levinas*. Oxford: Blackwell.

Durkheim, E. (1960) 'The Dualism of Human Nature and its Social Conditions', in *Essays on Sociology and Philosophy by Emile Durkheim et al.* (ed.) K.H. Wolff. New York: Harper and Row. pp. 325–40.

Durkheim, E. (1972) *Emile Durkheim: Selected Writings* (edited with an introduction by A. Giddens). London: Cambridge University Press.

Durkheim, E. (1974) *Sociology and Philosophy*. New York: The Free Press.

Durkheim, E. (1979) *Durkheim: Essays on Morals and Education* (edited and with introductions by W.S.F. Pickering). London: Routledge.

Durkheim, E. (1984) *The Division of Labour in Society*. London: Macmillan.

Durkheim, E. (1995) *The Elementary Forms of the Religious Life*. New York: The Free Press.

Etzioni, A. (1994) *The Spirit of Community – The Reinvention of American Society*. London: Simon and Schuster.

Freud, S. (1985) *Civilization, Society and Religion*, Volume 12. The Pelican Freud Library. Harmondsworth: Penguin.

Gouldner, A. (1971) *The Coming Crisis of Western Sociology*. London: Heinemann.

Haan, N., Bellah, R.N., Rabinow, P. and Sullivan, W.M. (1983) (eds), *Social Science as Moral Inquiry*. New York: Columbia University Press.

Jay, M. (1973) *The Dialectical Imagination – A History of the Frankfurt School and the Institute of Social Research 1923–50*. London: Heinemann Educational Books.

Lash, S. (1996) 'Introduction to the Ethics and Difference Debate', *Theory, Culture and Society*, 13 (2): 75–7.

Levinas, E. (1969) *Totality and Infinity – An Essay on Exteriority*. Pittsburgh: Duquesne University Press.

Levinas, E. (1987) *Time and the Other (and Additional Essays)* (trans. R.A. Cohen). Pittsburgh: Duquesne University Press.

Levinas, E. (1988) 'The Paradox of Morality: An Interview', in R. Bernasconi and D. Wood (eds), *The Provocation of Levinas – Rethinking the Other*. London: Routledge. pp. 168–80.

Levinas, E. (1985) *Ethics and Infinity – Conversations with Philippe Nemo* (trans. R.A. Cohen). Pittsburgh: Duquesne University Press.

Levinas, E. (1989) 'Ethics as First Philosophy', in Hand, S. *The Levinas Reader*. Oxford: Blackwell.

Levinas, E. and Kearney, R. (1986) 'Dialogue with Emmanuel Levinas', in R.A. Cohen (ed.), *Face to Face with Levinas*. Albany, NY: State University of New York Press.

Levine, D.N. (1995) *Visions of the Sociological Tradition*. Chicago: University of Chicago Press.

Llewelyn, J. (1995) *Emmanuel Levinas – The Genealogy of Ethics*. London: Routledge.

Lukes, S. (1973) *Emile Durkheim: His Life and Work*. London: Penguin.

MacIntyre, A. (1982) *After Virtue: A Study in Moral Theory*. London: Duckworth.

MacIntyre, A. (1990) *Three Rival Versions of Moral Enquiry – Encyclopaedia, Genealogy, and Tradition*. Notre Dame, IN: University of Notre Dame Press.

Ossowska, M. (1970) *Social Determinants of Moral Ideas*. Philadelphia: University of Pennsylvania Press.

Pickering, W.S.F. (1979) 'Introduction', in *Durkheim: Essays on Morals and Education*. London: Routledge and Kegan Paul.

Rieff, P. (1965) *Freud: The Mind of the Moralist*. London: Methuen.

Rorty, R. (1989) *Contingency, Irony and Solidarity*. Cambridge: Cambridge University Press.

Sayer, D. (1991) *Capitalism and Modernity – An Excursus on Marx and Weber*. London: Routledge.

Simmel, G. (1950) *The Sociology of Georg Simmel* (trans., ed. and with an introduction by Kurt H. Wolff). London: The Free Press.

Weber, M. (1970) *From Max Weber – Essays in Sociology* (ed. and trans. H.H. Gerth and C. Wright Mills). London: Routledge and Kegan Paul.

Weber, M. (1976) *The Protestant Ethic and the Spirit of Capitalism*. London: Allen and Unwin.

39

Postsocial Relations: Theorizing Sociality in a Postsocial Environment

KARIN KNORR CETINA

What is more evident than the boundaries of the social world? The social world is the domain of human interaction, human institutions, human rationality, human life. As Luckmann pointed out in 1970, we take it for granted that social reality is the world of human affairs, exclusively. But why should we take this for granted? Why has no one 'in the main traditions of Western philosophy' (1970: 73) ever seriously questioned these boundaries? Luckmann raised the issue from a phenomenological perspective, arguing that the boundary we see between the human social and the non-human, non-social was not an essential structure of the lifeworld. One reason for this was that our sense of humanness itself is not an original or universal projection but arises from revisions and modifications of other distinctions, for example that between living and non-living things. Since living things tend to be seen as social beings, as the evidence of animism, totemism and early childhood classifications suggests, our own narrowing-down of the social to the human must be the result of historical and ontogenetic processes of 'de-socialization'. Scheler ([1913] 1948: 257f.) saw it as given that (cultural) learning was a process of mounting disappointment with the fact that so little remained of the animated social worlds of more original states of humanity.

This chapter is based on the assessment of two structural conditions of Western societies which render Luckmann's question about the boundaries of the social world more acute today than when he posed it. The first is the current process of de-socialization; a process not bearing on the world of living things which Luckmann had in mind but on the human world itself, in which the social principles and structures we have known 'empty out', lose some of the meaning and relevance they had. The second structural condition is that of an enormous expansion of object words within the social world – of consumer goods, technological devices and scientific objects; an expansion in sheer volume, but also in the value we attribute to these things. Natural objects have also become, if not more numerous, then at least more 'present' in public discourse and concern. The two conditions provide the backdrop to the idea of a postsocial environment. In a postsocial environment, social principles are not simply thinned out; 'other' cultural elements and relationships take their place, mediate between them, and in some measure collapse in on social relations and structures. Among these 'other' elements I want to include objects; in this chapter, I shall develop an analysis of object-relations as a social form that constitutes something like the reverse side of the coin of the contemporary experience of de-socialization. Postsocial theory analyses the phenomenon of a disintegrating 'traditional' social universe, the reasons for this disintegration and the direction of changes. It attempts to conceptualize postsocial relations as forms of sociality which challenge core concepts of human interaction and solidarity, but which none the less constitute forms of binding self and other. The changes also affect human sociality in ways which warrant a detailed analysis in their own right. Though I cannot offer this analysis within the confines of this chapter, I will briefly come back to this issue at the end.

In the following, I will first discuss several dimensions along which the current retraction of social principles and structures can be made apparent. I will then go on to place these retractions in the context of the enlargement of the space of the individual subject and the rise of a 'subjective imagination' in social theory and practice. In the third section I will begin to develop a framework for the analysis of postsocial environments by proposing a conception of the subject that contrasts with the 'I–you–me' system that dominates the literature. The fourth extends the analysis to non-human objects, which we can no longer understand, I maintain, as material entities of a fixed nature. The following two sections put the pieces together by addressing postsocial relations. To provide a sense of how we might conceive of them, I will pick my way through different interpretations of binding self and other. The final section summarizes the argument and points to a more general understanding of postsocial environments.

SOCIALITY AS A HISTORICAL PHENOMENON: EXPANSIONS AND RETRACTIONS

Sociality is very likely a permanent feature of human life. But the forms of sociality are none the less changing, and the regions of social structuring may expand or contract in conjunction with concrete historical developments. Modernity has often been associated with the collapse of community and tradition and the onset of individualization. Central to our experience today are similar retractions of social principles in different regions of social life. These are not usually discussed together, and they do not have the same roots. But they may none the less work together in emptying out previous categories of social ordering, and in creating the space in which postsocial developments take hold. In evaluating these developments, we need to be careful to place them in a larger historical context not only of retractions of social principles but also of expansions, and of the changing institutional focus of these movements. While a systematic history of these movements has yet to be written, we can at least say that the current retraction of social principles comes in the wake of an apparent expansion of the regions of social structuring during the course of the nineteenth century and throughout the early decades of the twentieth. These expansions refocused social definitions and social thinking on the newly emerging nation-state and on modern organizations. Thus, while communities and traditions may have been emptied of social meanings

during industrialization, the larger scale social organizations attracted and expanded such meanings. Before considering the current situation, let us briefly review this expansion.

The first region of expansion of social principles in the nineteenth century was that of social policies, and it is intricately linked to the rise of the nation-state. According to many authors, social policies and social problem solutions took shape as nation-states (which may themselves have been formed by such interventions)[1] attempted to deal with the social consequences of capitalist industrialization. Social policies as we know them today derive from what Wittrock and Wagner (1996: 98ff.) call the 'nationalization of social responsibility'. What these authors mean is the formulation of social rights alongside individual rights and the positing of the state as the 'natural container' and provider of labour regulations, pension and welfare provisions, unemployment insurance, public education and so on. Social policies existed at the local level before, but increases in social mobility and migration and the related changes in production patterns made these practices appear inadequate and often unjust. Wittrock and Wagner accordingly see the construction of national social policies as an extension of the idea of community. A second region of expansion, connected to the first, is that of social thinking and social imagination. A corollary of the institutionalization of social policies were new concepts of the forces that determine human destiny: they were now more likely to be thought of as impersonal, social forces. Rabinbach has argued that the idea of individual risks, poverty and inequality as a socially induced phenomenon entailed a decisive break with preceding individualist liberal ideas (e.g. Rabinbach, 1996). Rather than assuming the automatic adaptation of individuals to changing environmental conditions these ideas focused on the prevailing imbalances and their social causes, for example on the social causes of occupational accidents. Sociology played an important role in bringing about the shift in mentality through which individuals came to be seen as the bearers of the individual costs of collective structures. For example, the German Verein für Sozialpolitik and the English Fabian Society played critical roles in bringing to public attention the problems created by capitalist industrialization as the central challenge of the new industrial order, and in the initiation of modern social policies in their countries (Rueschemeyer and Van Rossem, 1996). Durkheimian sociology and its grounding of a theory of society in 'social facts' exemplifies the new attention to the social as a distinctive layer of relationships with causal efficacy, which Durkheim and Mauss (1963) held responsible for the structuring of cosmological beliefs. When Mills argued for a 'sociological imagination' (1959), he tried to capture in one concept the phenomenon of societal processes which individuals do not recognize but which affect and change their lives.

A third area of expansion of social principles and structures is that of social organization. The modern nation-state has its roots in the history of European societies, with the reference case being France with its tradition of early centralization and political consolidation. This consolidation dates back to the period after the French Revolution when Napoleon 'set in motion ... a modern institutional and administrative structure [that] was superimposed on the society' (Ashford, 1982: 13). The social form brought into existence at the time was that of public bureaucracies, forms of collective organization based on the formalization of procedures and authority and underpinned by institutions for socialization and rule enforcement that reached deep into society (Wittrock and Wagner, 1996: 105). As Rueschemeyer and Van Rossem (1996) argue, state structures preceded industrial society in continental Europe, while the reverse appears to have been the case in Anglo-American societies. If the rise of the nation-state implied the rise of bureaucractic institutions, the growth of industrial production brought with it the emergence of the factory and the modern corporation. Similar organizational forms also characterize modern science, which became embodied in the research university and the scientific laboratory. The rise of health care corresponds to the establishment of the clinic, and the disciplining of a modern workforce was accompanied by the expansion of the prison (Foucault, 1977). Industrial, nation-state societies are unthinkable without complex modern organizations. Complex organizations are localized social arrangements serving to manage work and services in collective frameworks with the help of social structural means.

Now the contemporary situation. Central to our experience today is that these expansions of social principles and of socially constituted environments have come to some sort of a grinding halt. In many European countries and in the the United States the welfare state, with its many chapters of social policy and collective insurance against individual disaster, is in the process of being 'overhauled', some would say 'dismantled'. In Bauman's words, the new constellation is one of nations divided between premium payers and benefit recipients in which the services for those who do not pay are resented by those who do (1996: 56). Social explanations and social thinking run up against, among other things, biological accounts of human behaviour against which they have to prove their worth. If

Freud thought that the fixations and nervous ailments he studied resulted from individuals not coming to terms with a rigorous inner 'censor' that represented society (Lasch, 1978: 37), today's psychologists are more likely to seek the cause of compulsive disorders in the expression of genes. The mobilization of a social imagination was an attempt to identify the collective basis for individuals' predicaments and dispositions to react. This collective basis is now more likely to be found in the similarity of the genetic make-up of socially unrelated members of the population. Most interesting, perhaps, is the phenomenon that social structures also seem to be losing some of their hold. When complex organizations are dissolved into networks of smaller independent profit centres, some of the layered structural depth of the hierarchically organized social systems that organizations used to represent gets lost on the way. When person-provided services are replaced by automated electronic services, no social structures at all need to be in place – only electronic information structures (see Lash and Urry, 1994). The main arena and site of some global transactions such as stock or forex market trading appears to be the electronically mediated computer- or telephone-conversation. In these cases, the massive social resources of multinationally operating corporations are replaced by conversational and interactional microstructures which carry the transactions. The expansion of societies to global societies does not imply, it appears, further expansions of social complexity. The installation of a 'world-society' would seem to be feasible with the help of individuals and social microstructures, and perhaps becomes plausible only in relation to such structures (see Bruegger and Knorr Cetina, 2000).

The retraction of social principles and structures also manifests itself in new problems of individualization, having to do with primordial social relations. Individualization is not, of course in itself a new phenomenon. In fact, individualization is frequently considered to be the immediate result of industrialization and modernization. One of the great legacies of classical social thought is the idea that the development of modern societies involves the transformation of traditional, group-based, kinship-dominated communities into systems characterized by the growing dominance of private ownership, profit motives, industrial production, mobility, large urban centres and bureaucratic professionalism – all undermining the embeddedness of individuals in traditional communities (MacFarlane, 1978).[2] Berger et al. (1974) portrayed the individual of an industrialized, technological society as a 'homeless mind' – an uprooted, confused and inchoate self, whose predicaments contributed to the expansion of social principles discussed before. But well into this century, this self found refuge in the private spheres of life and was sustained by traditional family relations. What analysts see disintegrating today are these 'primordial social relations' (Coleman, 1993). Recent individualism can be distinguished from earlier breakdowns of community by what Lasch considers the 'collapse' of the private sphere, the 'devastations' of married and family life (see also Giddens, 1994a). Bauman puts this in a broader context:

> Everything seems to conspire these days against . . . lifelong projects, lasting commitments, eternal alliances, immutable identities. One cannot build long-term hopes around one's job, profession, skills even; one can bet that, before long, the skills will cease to be in demand . . . One cannot build the future around partnership or the family either: in the age of 'confluent love,' togetherness lasts no longer than the satisfaction of one of the partners, commitment is from the start 'until further notice', and today's intense attachment may only intensify tomorrow's frustrations. (1996: 51f.)

Beck and Beck-Gernsheim (1994, 1996) see the historically new in contemporary individualization in the challenges this poses for individuals: 'something that was earlier expected of a few – to lead a life of their own – is now being demanded of more and more people'. Individuals are thrown back on their own resources to construct forms of togetherness, and a coherent life course and identity. Like others (Hage and Powers 1992: 133f., 179f.), Beck and Beck-Gernsheim emphasize the difficulties this presents. The demise of tradition leaves the individual in the lurch – without the psychological means to deal with the great freedom of choice and the contingencies of modern life, in which this freedom rebounds (Bauman, 1996: 50f.). The 'do-it-yourself' biography, they say, is always a risk biography, a state of permanent endangerment (Beck and Beck-Gernsheim, 1996: 25).

It may be interesting to note that at least some authors 'blame' some of this development on the nation-state itself and its bureaucratic institutions. Thus Berger et al. (1974) borrowing a notion from Gehlen, maintain that the private sphere has been 'deinstitutionalized' in part as a result of the dominance of large-scale bureaucratic organizations. Foucault's notion of a pastoral state can be seen as a variant of this position. Bureaucratic state organizations are continuous with industrial organizations not only in institutional form, but also in that they drain areas of social life of the meaning content they once had (see also Beck, 1992). Already a generation ago, Giddens (1990: 116) reminds us, Horkheimer argued that 'personal initiative plays an ever smaller role in comparison to the plans of those in authority'. The result is a turning inward toward human subjectivity and the search for meanings in the inner self.

THE RISE OF A SUBJECT-CENTRED IMAGINATION

One of the most important elements in the development described so far may well be the loss of a social imagination, the slow erosion of the belief in salvation by society. The expansion of a social imagination involved, from the beginning, not only the idea of impersonal social forces affecting the individual but also the notion of universal human perfection through society. This idea was put forward by Rousseau and Enlightenment thinkers such as Condorcet ([1795] 1955: 173, 193), who announced the possibility of an ever-more rapid progress towards a perfect form of human society marked by 'the abolition of inequality between nations, the progress of equality within each nation, and the true perfection of mankind'. The notion is best epitomized by Marx's vision of a socialist age which he thought would begin once capitalism reached its peak and collapsed under its own self-created contradictions. The collapse of Marxism as a creed signifies the end of the belief in salvation by society, the end of a social imagination that transposed itself into a 'secular religion' (Drucker 1993: ch. 1).

Marxism also failed in practice, but its failure as a creed that supports the belief in society may be vastly more consequential. The modern welfare state is a massive machinery for the redistribution of resources based on solidarity principles. This solidarity, however, is not rooted in the experience of community as perhaps it was in premodern times. It is an abstract principle instituted in tax systems and legally based welfare provisions that rest at best on the ideals of the 'commonality of fate' of the imagined community of nation-state societies.[3] Without visions of the possibility of 'social salvation' within these communities, the redistribution of resources which lies at the core of the modern welfare state loses legitimacy. What gains legitimacy, one assumes, are theories of utilitarian and expressive individualism – theories of the desires associated with self-interest of individuals and the feelings or intuitions associated with self-expression and authenticity. The phantasized unit, in such a scenario, is the person and his or her relational options.

If we are adequately to grasp postsocial environments, I want to argue, we have to start from the emptying out of the social imagination of the past and to consider its replacement by an imagination centred more strongly on individuals. One can think of several developments that support such a view. First, even from within the state-oriented political camp, voices and slogans have emerged which advocate individual self-reliance in regard to personal welfare and non-governmental avenues to the achievement of collective goals. The former is illustrated by Etzioni's new golden rule (1996), offered to a democratic government, which urges individuals to commit themselves voluntarily to a moral order that society cannot enforce; the latter by the attempt, in the United States, to implement market mechanisms for the purpose of environmental protection. Another example is Tony Blair's model of a deinstitutionalized welfare state and a socialism that reinstitutes individual responsibility while curtailing the possibilities for benefit seeking and social rights.

Secondly, just as a social mentality was elaborated and extended by social science, so individualizing ideas are unfolded by particular disciplinary traditions. Such ideas are constitutive of disciplines such as psychology; but there has also been a seemingly unprecedented growth of such programmes in sociology and social theory. One example is the rise of rational choice theory (e.g. Coleman, 1990), which draws on concepts long prominent in economics that have been imported into sociology and political science. Self-interest concepts of rationality define rational action as that which serves the actor's interest. The approach rules out self-damaging and irrational preferences, and has often been criticized for its inability to comprehend moral or cooperative choices which actors also seem to make. The model also suffers from assuming too much about the information a rational actor must have or find in order to infer from it which is the best course of action. Rational choice theory can be discussed by reference to a long tradition of such criticisms, as it usually is (e.g. Coleman and Fararo, 1992), but within the present framework we can also see it as a programme that contributes to an individual-centred imagination. It empowers the individual as the unit that seeks information, calculates behavioural outcomes, engages in rational deliberation, and through all these mechanisms, engineers his or her fate. It contributes a strong model of 'agentic actorhood' which has been unfolded further over time to include individual 'non-rational' functions such as emotions (e.g. Barbalet, 1998: ch. 2). The exaggerated emphasis in these models on 'high reason' and complete information, and the attempt to translate collective and cooperative choices into individual utilities may be 'phantasmatic' (not warranted by data or plausible argument) from a traditional sociological perspective, but these phantasms are

also the ones that empower subjectivity thinking and cast doubt on social thinking. Theories of identity and identity politics (e.g. Calhoun 1994a), of the self and subjectivity (e.g. Calhoun, 1994b; Giddens, 1991; Lash, 1999: parts III and IV; Wiley, 1994) provide other examples of such trends.

Thirdly, subjectivity thinking and subjectivity imagination is manifest in the vast numbers of self-help books and manuals that counsel individuals on self-improvement and engage them in the discovery of their own selves:

> As the world takes on a more and more menacing appearance, life becomes a never-ending search for health and well-being through exercise, dieting, drugs, spiritual regimens of various kinds, psychic self-help and psychiatry. For those who have withdrawn interest from the outside world except in so far as it remains a source of gratification and frustration, the state of their own health becomes an all-absorbing concern. (Lasch, 1977: 140)

This literature is massive and diverse and requires an analysis in its own right. But some principles are recurrent; for example, the literature consistently affirms individuals' right and obligation to make a strong commitment to themselves. A person who loves him/herself, who makes a commitment to him/herself before making a commitment to others, who is in touch with him/herself, so the argument goes, will not only experience more self-fulfilment and satisfaction in life but will also be able to love, help and manage others better than someone whose first commitment is to others. The literature affirms subjectivity thinking rather than social thinking by theorizing sociality as something that flows from self-commitment and is secondary to it. The popular literature on the self is often esoteric in its claims but it may play a considerable role in shaping people's self-understanding. Giddens offers an interpretation of this role through his version of a theory of reflexive modernization. Post-traditional societies, in his view, are marked by expert systems, 'systems of technical accomplishment of professional expertise that organise large areas of the material and social environments in which we live today' (1990: 27). Such systems are, for example, technological complexes such as airports and planes and everything associated with air travel, but Giddens also means the softer forms of professional advice to which people turn in confronting the 'ontological insecurities' of modern life. For him, 'a world of intensified reflexivity is a world of clever people', of individuals who engage with the wider environment and with themselves through information produced by specialists which they routinely interpret and act on in everyday life (1994b: 7).

The conclusion I want to draw from the contemporary re-imagining of the individual contradicts postmodern social theories which tend to postulate the eclipse and death of the subject. As a first approximation, we can associate a postsocial environment with an expanding sphere of the subject, where 'subject' stands not only for mental or existential conceptions of individuals but for an open-ended series of individual-centred significations and processes. The remarkable rise of subjectivity thinking and the concomitant emptying out of a social imagination and of social principles and structures act in concert, so to speak, to create and unfold the space for this expansion. Postmodern thinkers understand the death of the subject in a variety of ways. For example, the literature on 'cyborgs' (e.g. Haraway, 1991; Heim, 1993: ch. 7; Virilio, 1995) is concerned with 'endocolonization', the colonization of the human body from within through such things as the implantation of various microtechnologies, the replacement of body parts by transplants and machines, etc. Other variants of the death of the subject theme include Jameson's, which speaks of the extinction of such figures as prophets, seers, great cultural producers or charismatic leaders in our 'post-individualistic age' (1991). A third group of authors takes the 'decentring' of the Enlightenment version of the subject as an autonomous, self-conscious agent as an indication of its end. Thus, the discovery of the unconscious by Freud, or Foucault's conception of the subject as produced in networks of power, or the subject's 'fragmentation' into multiple functions and selves, may be taken as requiring us to abandon ideas of agency (Ashe, 1999). Enlightenment thinkers drew the 'circle of humanity' tightly, as Seidler puts it (1994: 16), defining the subject in terms of reason that underpinned the subject's capacity to exercise agency. It seems plain that current thinking, in making claims about the unconscious and emotional sides of the individual, about his or her technoscientific and biological parts and his or her normalized features and fragmented self, is drawing the circle much more widely, opening up the notion of subjectivity and in fact enlarging the space of individuals in society by working out their 'non-rational' aspects and processes. The traditional sociological notion of an actor, with its emphasis on subjective intentions, may indeed be too limited to allow us to conceptualize this enlarged space. But the rise of the individual subject, however technologically (and biologically) enhanced, cognitively distributed and emotionally torn, needs to be recognized as structural 'presence' and 'node' in postsocial environments, a density region in which things cross and to some degree converge.

FROM THE INNER CENSOR TO THE MIRROR IMAGE SELF: THE SELF AS A STRUCTURE OF WANTING

One of the elements of the subjectivity thinking presented so far is that the modern and postmodern individual is conceptualized in terms of relational deficiencies (the terms used were 'uprooted', 'disembedded', 'thrown back upon its own resources', 'inward turning', 'individualized', 'atomized', 'ontologically insecure'). The individual is swept out of all traditional types of relationships and ends up recoiling in his or her own inner space. But this view of the subject as the bearer of relational deficiencies is selective and plausible only if we focus exclusively on human relationships. It ignores the degree to which the modern untying of identities has been accompanied by an expansion of object-centred environments which situate and stabilize selves, define individual identity just as much as communities and families used to do, and promote forms of binding self and other that supplement the human forms of sociality studied by social scientists. In this section, I want to propose a conception of the self that allows us to explore these postsocial relations.

I shall begin by distinguishing two models that have been used to understand the self. One is the idea of the self as composed of an ego and an inner censor, which we can associate with Peirce, Mead and Freud, among others. In Mead, the inner censor is called the 'generalized other', by which he means the internalized norms of the community or society. The 'generalized other' in Mead's terminology is closely coupled to what he calls the 'me'; the self as object and as the intrasubjective conformist past of the self. At the opposite end of the 'generalized other' and the 'me' lies what Mead calls the 'I', the spontaneous, unpredictable, disobeying side of the self. The 'I' has the power to construct reality cognitively, and by redefining situations, can break away from the 'me' and the norms of society. The 'me' and the 'generalized other' can be likened to Peirce's 'you'; Peirce held the 'you' to be a critical self that represented society and to which all thought was addressed. These notions are also roughly similar to Freud's 'super-ego', the rule-carrier which functions as a regulative principle in an internal dynamic of morality and deviance. In Mead's theory, the self first originates from such a dynamic. The internal conversations we engage in when we think are transformed versions of interpersonal communication. The self arises from role-taking, from taking the perspective of the other first interpersonally, when engaged with a close caretaker, and then also intrapersonally. Wiley

(1994: 34ff., 44ff.), merging Mead and Peirce, elaborates this structure into what he calls the 'I–you–me' system of the self.

The second model understands the self not as a relation between the individual and society but as a structure of wantings in relation to continually renewed lacks. The notion of the self as a structure of wantings can be derived from Lacan (e.g. 1975), but it can also be linked to Baldwin ([1899] 1973: 373ff.) and Hegel.[4] Like Freud, the psychoanalyst Lacan is concerned with what 'drives' the subject, but he derives this wanting not as Freud did from an instinctual impulse whose ultimate goal is a reduction in bodily tension, but rather from the mirror stage of a young child's development. In this stage the child becomes impressed with the wholeness of his or her image in the mirror and with the appearance of definite boundaries and control – while realizing that she/he is none of these things in actual experience. Wanting or desire is born in envy of the perfection of the image in the mirror (or of the mirroring response of the parents); the lack is permanent, since there will always be a distance between the subjective experience of a lack in our existence and the image in the mirror, or the apparent wholeness of others (e.g. Alford, 1991: 36ff.; Lacan and Wilden, 1968).

The two conceptions may seem similar in that both emphasize the discrepancy between the I and a model, but they are in fact quite different. From the idea of the self as composed of an inner censor results an ego subjected to feelings of guilt, experiencing rebellion and attempting to 'live up' to social expectations. In contrast, the self as a permanently reiterated lack gives rise to the desire, also permanent, to eliminate the lack. The former model would seem to result in actions that are perpetually curtailed as an ego attempts to adapt them to internalized norms; it will also result in deviant actions that transgress boundaries of which the actor is well aware. The second model yields actions spurred on by the unfulfillability of lacks, or by new wants opening up simultaneously with the (partial) fulfilment of old ones. In the first model, the actor's free fall from society is continually broken as she/he catches himself (or is caught by others) in compliance with social rules and traditions, and returns to their ontological security. In the second case, no society of this sort is in place any longer to provide ontological security. The 'you' is the idealized self in the mirror or the perfect other. The actor would seem to be freed from any guilt complexes; but she/he is like a vagrant in a state of perpetual search, stringing together objects of satisfaction and dismantling the structure again as she moves on to other goals. With the first model, we can associate primordial social relations of a kind that foster normative models,

compliance and security. With the second model, we can perhaps associate postsocial relations.

Having said this I should add immediately that if these two conceptions make sense as models of the self they make sense in conjunction; in Western societies, both the I–you–me system of the socialized self and the lack–wanting system of the reflexive (mirror image) self would seem to identify important features of identity. On the other hand, one can make the argument that the lack–wanting system is better suited to characterizing self-feelings and self-problems in a general way in contemporary societies than the I–you–me system. To historicize the argument, one might venture the hypothesis that the lack–wanting system of self-formation is in the process of displacing and reshaping the I–you–me system. Why would this be the case? Possible reasons for such a scenario are not difficult to come by. If the lack–wanting system describes contemporary selves better than the I–you–me system then this might result at least in part from the problems of primordial social relations, which no longer offer the kind of normative models and tight structures of social control that are needed to give rise to an inner censor and a dynamic of guilt and rebellion, compliance and transgression. The liberalization of partnership and family life which Beck and Beck-Gernsheim (1994, 1996), Coleman (1993), Lasch (1978) among others describe, the detraditionalization of education and the individualization of choice (Gross, 1994), all conspire to prevent a strong I–you–me dynamic founded on the internalization of a censor. Mead, Freud and others contributing to the I–you–me model were not only proposing abstract theories of the self. Their conceptions were also rooted in existence, in particular patterns of attachment and socialization practices which are no longer dominant in contemporary society.

There is also a second development that may account for the declining grip of the I–you–me system on the self. This is what we may call the 'exteriorization' of the 'mirror' that psychoanalysts and social psychologists deem important, its institutionalization and professionalization in the external society. For the analysts concerned with self-formation, the mirror is either a physical mirror or the caretakers' activity of 'back-projecting'; their activity of 'reflecting', like a mirror, the child's being through responding to it as a person and through articulating and defining the child's behaviour in relation to parental idealizations and expectations. These reflexive 'judgements' should not be seen as reflected upon opinions of the sort reached through thinking. A caretaker's mirroring response that matters to a child may be entirely emotional as opposed to cognitive, or as in Cooley's looking-glass self analysed by Wiley (1994: 111), it may contain ideas associated with feeling, but not be based on distantiated thinking. The source of the power of the mirror lies not in the cognitive superiority or objectivity of the judgements made but in its projection of an (idealized) image that differs from the subject's self-feeling and self-experience. The mirror reveals the subject to him/herself as a piece of unfinished business composed of ever new lacks.

Now in today's societies, this sort of projection is no longer only supplied by primary reference persons who do their work in the initial stages of life. The mirror is instituted in the media and other displays which project images and stage 'wholeness', and it is permanent: the media provide a continual flow of images of the sort Lacan attributes to the early childhood. The mirror also is present in the 'cathedrals of consumption' Ritzer analyses (1999: 8ff.), in the shopping malls and other places that offer enchanted displays of possible selves. And it is there in simulations, the life-like reality processes in a purely symbolic space in which many of the insufficiencies of real life can easily be forgotten and erased (Baudrillard, 1983; Turkle, 1995). To a considerable extent, the mirror response has changed hands altogether and is now articulated by complicated and dispersed machineries of professional image production – of industries that produce movie stars and fashion models, TV programmes and films, shopping catalogues and advertisements. These industries are, of course, not motivated by parental considerations but by a variety of other goals which include extending the subject's lacks and desires.

To conclude this section, I want to make one point about the model I have foregrounded. While the mirror idea appears plausible as a characterization of fictive external elements around which we build an ego as a life project, it may be less plausible when it is applied in the way Lacan intended it, as a description of what happens to the infant when it first recognizes itself in a real mirror. As Anderson (1983), Wiley (1994: 172) and others have stressed, no one knows what the child experiences at this stage, and what the consequences of this experience are. We need not find Lacan's account of the lack of subjectivity as rooted in the child's narcissistic relationship to him/herself persuasive in order to find the idea of a structure of wanting plausible. The latter is simply a convenient way to capture the way wants have of continually searching out new objects and of moving on to them – a convenient way, if you wish, to capture the volatility and unstoppability of desire. The idea of a structure or chain of wantings has the advantage of bringing into view a whole series of

moves and their underlying dynamic rather than isolated reasons, as the traditional vocabulary of motives and intentions does. Plainly, one can make the argument that these moves, or the unstoppability of wants, is continually re-incited by the lures and images that society generates. Accordingly, the self need not be seen as frozen into a lacking subjectivity for life at the mirror stage. It is at least as plausible to conceive of lacks in a more sociological idiom as permanently recreated by relevant institutional processes in a post-industrial society.

OBJECTS ARE UNFOLDING STRUCTURES OF ABSENCES

We have now discussed the reflexive mirror image self which we have moved away from the mirroring response of particular or generalized others, emphasizing instead the pervasiveness of the images themselves in a media and information society. In a world that is continually formulated and exhibited through object displays and technological processes, humans take second place as mirror response providers. What we are hitting here is another source of the retraction of social principles and structures, but also, at the same time, the rise of object worlds (in the form of displays) that take the place of these principles and structures. These object worlds are also manifest in the displays themselves: the mirror images tend to point to objects we are missing and which others have. They rarely base their messages on moral virtues or social behaviour. The exteriorized mirror foregrounds objects at the expense of social principles and structures. What we need to do in this section is to conceptualize these objects.

Let us remind ourselves of why these objects are important in the present context. Postsocial transitions imply that social forms as we knew them are becoming flattened, narrowed and thinned out. But as indicated before, they do not imply a straightforward loss of sociality in the areas marked above. What one needs to put forward against the scenario of simple 'desocialization' is that the flattened structures, the narrowed principles, the thinned out social relations also coincide with, and are propelled by, the expansion of 'other' cultural elements and practices in contemporary life. The retraction of social principles leaves no holes, one imagines, in the fabric of cultural patterns. There has been no loss of texture for society, though what the texture consists of may need rethinking. If this view is correct, the idea of postsocial transitions no longer simply describes a situation where the social is shut out of history. Rather, it describes a situation where social principles and structures (in the old sense) become intermeshed with and perhaps displaced by 'other' cultural principles and structures to which the term social has not been extended in the past. In this scenario, postsocial forms are not a-social or non-social forms. Rather, they are forms specific to late modern societies, which are marked by a massive expansion and recasting of object worlds in the social world. While postsocial relations are not limited to object relations and postsocial theory pertains to a much wider nexus of developments, I am confining my attention in this chapter to object relations.

But what do we mean by objects? To start things off we can simply consider objects as non-human things. As indicated before, there has been an enormous increase in the volume of such non-human things in the social world – technological objects, consumer goods, instruments of exchange, scientific things, all exemplify this expansion. Consider just briefly scientific objects such as biologists' molecular structures, physicists' quarks or their Higgs mechanisms, astronomers' black holes and dark matter of the universe. Most of these objects (and they are internally differentiated further) have become available to us for discussion and enquiry only relatively recently, and they enrich and enlarge the natural world as a conglomerate of ever-more detailed, more distant and invisible things. The social world has equally been enlarged by consumer objects and exchange commodities (for example, the objects of financial markets), whose role in Western societies can easily be glossed by simply comparing their presence everywhere in our daily life with the massive gap their absence has created in the former socialist states.

The expanded presence of objects in the social world offers a sort of background substantiation for the claims made in this chapter, but it does not provide a conceptual basis for the discussion of postsocial relations. The second point I want to make is more pertinent to this issue, and it has to do with the features of objects which we encounter today in professional and daily life. The definition I want to offer of large classes of objects in contemporary life breaks away from received concepts of objects as fixed things of a material nature. In fact, I want to go in the opposite direction, and characterize the objects relevant here by their indefiniteness of being. To make this clearer let us turn for a moment to scientific objects as defined by Rheinberger (1992: 310). Scientific objects lie at the centre of a process of investigation; they are characteristically open, question-generating and in the process of being materially defined. They are processes and projections rather than definite

things. The central characteristic of these kinds of objects, from a theoretical point of view, is their changing, unfolding character – in the present terminology, their lack of 'object-ivity' and completeness of being, and their non-identity with themselves. The lack of completeness of being is crucial: objects of knowledge in many fields have material instantiations, but they must simultaneously be conceived as unfolding structures of absences – as things that continually 'explode' and 'mutate' into something else, and that are as much defined by what they are not as by what they are.

I want to propose that technological objects, consumer goods and exchange commodities also show these qualities. Consider first technological objects, which are often perceived as fixed; Rheinberger considers them to be the stable moments in an experimental arrangement. But this conception is highly problematic, in light of contemporary technologies which are simultaneously things-to-be-used and things-in-a-process-of-transformation: they undergo continual processes of development and investigation. Computers and computer programs are typical examples; they appear on the market in continually changing 'updates' (progressively debugged issues of the same product) and 'versions' (items marked for their differences from earlier varieties). These objects are both present (ready-to-be-used) and absent (subject to further research), the 'same' and yet not the same. They have a dual structure that was not available to thinkers like Heidegger, who drew a sharp contrast between instruments and knowledge objects. In sum, technologies must be included in the category of unfolding objects.

If we turn now to consumer objects, we can also put them in this category. There is, of course, a great variety of consumer objects that matter in day-to-day life. But a significant portion of these objects are subject to transformations and to 'technological development'; many of them are in fact technologies, or are technologically prepared and upgraded goods. They are changing as we buy them and their changed versions stimulate further demand. Fruit and vegetables are as much examples of this as are television sets or software programs. We can perhaps say that in a knowledge economy, most objects will be mass-produced 'copies' of techno-scientific originals that undergo continuous transformation and exemplify the lack of completeness of being described above. This dual structure contradicts notions of consumer society such as Baudrillard's, which conceptualize the objects of mass-consumption as copies without original (see Ritzer, 1999: 97). But then Baudrillard ignores the knowledge base of contemporary products. There are also consumer objects that are not technological or knowledge-driven in the sense indicated. One example is perhaps fashion products, but their continual transmutation and indefiniteness is even more apparent than that of other objects. Fashion pieces are always in the process of being materially defined through activities of 'design' which lean toward art (or are art) and about which we know little (but see Henderson, 1998). The important point here is that objects of design are continually redesigned; their fixedness is a matter of moments of stability in a chain of changes and it is always in danger of disappearing.

A similar situation obtains with many objects of exchange that are not subject to consumption. Consider, for example, the financial 'instruments' that are traded in stock, option and foreign exchange markets. These are 'instruments' in the sense that they insure the owner against the risks of adverse currency movements, allow bets in speculative activities, faciliate shifts between financial positions and so on. But these instruments are also knowledge-based. They are developed by specialists in the research and development centres of large investment banks and similar institutions. Their 'indefiniteness of being', the changing risk calculations they involve, lies at the heart of these instruments' adaptability to changing financial scenarios and needs.

Are there objects in contemporary society that still have the stability of fixed material structures? There are, and we can give an example of them by considering 'tools' like the Heideggerian hammer, which we need to distinguish from the technical and financial instruments discussed before. In his analysis of thinghood and equipment ([1927] 1962), Heidegger proposes that equipment (*Zeug*, the term he uses for tools), has the property of being not only ready-to-hand but transparent: it has the tendency to disappear and become a means when we are using it. Equipment becomes problematic only when it is unavailable, when it malfunctions, or when it temporarily breaks down. Only then do we go from 'absorbed coping' to 'envisaging', 'deliberate coping' and to the scientific stance of 'theoretical reflection' of the properties of entities. Heidegger's goal here is to contrast tool-use with the 'theoretical attitude' that we bring to bear on objects of knowledge, and that entails a 'withholding' of practical reason. This view is limited when it comes to understanding science, which can no longer be equated with theorizing as a by now substantial number of empirical studies demonstrates (e.g. Galison, 1997; Geison, 1997; Knorr Cetina, 1981, 1999; Latour, 1988; Latour and Woolgar, 1979; Lynch, 1985; Todes, 1997; Traweek, 1988). It is suggestive with regard to tool-use and objects like a hammer.

Heidegger also had something to say on the existence of 'things' within systems of objects (see also Baudrillard, 1996) which should be mentioned. The indefiniteness of objects comes about through their manufacture in series and models, as suggested. But it also comes about through the referential nexus of objects, the phenomenon that one object refers to another, and this one to a third, in an unending series of referrals. Heidegger tried to capture this with his notion of a referential whole ([1927] 1962). He used the idea to suggest that our instrumental being in the world implies not a single tool but the 'whole' of a workshop, where one tool refers to another and the whole constitutes an instrumental environment in which we are embedded. In a similar vein, we can argue that the objects we want to complete our being always refer to further objects in an unending series. When an advertisement suggests 'all we need' is a car of a particular brand which has completeness of being in that it satisfies all wants and will very nearly run forever, then other images suggest that with the car go other objects enmeshed in particular lifestyles and career trajectories, and so on. If a fashion model projects the perfect look, his or her visually suggested completeness of being always rests on further products and qualities which she/he has, and which may become foregrounded as our lacks. This referential nexus of objects can be seen as an unfolding series, much like single objects.

To return now to single consumer objects: these should not be seen as expandable only through new models and versions. The notion we started out with is that many consumer goods have a dual structure of the sort where these objects can simultaneously be ready-to-hand usable things and absent objects of enquiry developed further by research. The point is that this duality repeats itself, so to speak, in the ready-to-hand state in an interesting way. Consider again a computer or a software program. These instruments are by now at least moderately 'ready' to be used even by the uninitiated when they are bought, but their potential is often much larger than what we can do with them in one or even many tries. The object has an interior indefiniteness of being in the sense of a potential for further 'discovery' and extension. As we 'discover' the object, it may change, for example when we go from using the computer to entering the Internet made accessible by it – the situation is much like in science, where knowledge objects are similarly changeable. But even within the 'same' umbrella object like a computer the possibilities of extension seem inexhaustible. The lack of completeness of being can literally mean a lack or insufficiency of some consumer object which begs to be replaced by a newer version. But the notion also allows us to see objects as expanding environments of realization. This is perhaps most obvious in the case of scientific objects which almost always 'lack' completeness in the sense that they have vast undisclosed areas of further parts and mechanisms. What I want to claim is that many contemporary consumer objects also are expanding objects – and they make relational demands associated with their expandability.

POSTSOCIAL RELATIONS

We now have all the ingredients in place to discuss postsocial relationships more directly, while at the same time summarizing the discussion thus far. Consider again the referential connectedness of objects, their existence in temporal series and their extendability into the depths of a dark closet. Objects melt into indefinite beings and become transmutable for different reasons. In a knowledge economy goods tend to be knowledge-based and bear the characteristics of knowledge objects. This is significant, since it not only accounts for the changeability and sophistication of a vast number of consumer objects, it also legitimizes the constant turnover of products through which consumption is stimulated under market conditions. The market itself is, in some domains, an object of interest to which buyers and sellers (traders, investors) are oriented, and which continually changes its shape and moves in new directions (Knorr Cetina and Bruegger, 2000). Finally, the objects of science are transmutable entities on yet other grounds, having to do with the complexity and connectedness of natural objects. The point is that all these conditions converge in contributing to the phenomenon that the objects sought can never be fully attained, that they are, if you wish, never quite themselves. What we encounter are representations or stand-ins which compensate for a more basic lack of completeness of the objects we encounter. On the subject side, this lack corresponds to a structure of wanting, a continually reiterated interest and desire that appears never to be fulfilled by a final object. Some theories see the self as frozen into a lacking subjectivity for life at the infant stage, but we can also link the self as a structure of wanting to the mimetic reflexivity (see Lash, 1994, 1999: ch. 9) of contemporary society and its 'mirroring' projections and images.

The argument about the ties that bind subjects to objects builds on the correspondence between the two series. In a nutshell, the argument is that the incompleteness of being which I have attributed to contemporary objects uniquely matches the structure of wanting by which I have characterized the self. The touchstone of the argument is what we mean by this 'match'. As we shall see, what is involved is a form of reciprocity: of objects providing for the continuation of a chain of wantings, through the signs they give off of what they still lack and 'hide' within themselves; and of subjects providing for the continuation of objects which only exist as a sequence of absences, as unfolding possibilities. To start from the beginning, I will first examine the structural affinity between subject and object, which provides a sort of backbone for the idea of a reciprocity, and then go on to discuss the deeper sense of the mutualities involved. I will then bring into play a sense in which solidarity can be a defining characteristic of object relations, and argue that object worlds can be embedding environments for individuals. Postsocial relations and postsocial forms, I maintain, are 'social' in all of these senses. But they are also *post*social in that not all of the links in the patterns of human sociality readily apply. If recent assessments are right, some links may also be lost or replaced in human sociality, which is changing as people encounter each other in new ways in, for example, the purely symbolic space of electronically mediated communication. In the next section, I will draw attention to such postsocial human relations.

The notion of a structural affinity between subject and object captures the equivalence in form between subjects conceived as structures of wanting and objects that are unfolding things, continually in the process of being defined. Both are moving entities that provide 'ports' and targets for one another. A subject that develops an intrinsic connection to a consumer object like a car, a computer or a fashionable outfit will be lured into further pursuits by the referential nexus of objects and their continuous transmutation into more attractive successor versions. In that sense objects not only attract a person's desire, they also allow wanting to continue, giving it its 'serial', chain-like structure. On the subject side, a string of vagrant, insatiable wants, in demanding new things, provides for the creation of new object varieties. Note that this structural equivalence fulfils one condition of a relationship, which is that it should continue over time and not be reducible to a short experience.

The significance of the formal correspondence of two structures which I have outlined lies in what this correspondence facilitates – a potential binding of a subject to an object in which the two sides 'feed' and sustain one another. But when this binding relationship comes about, it always involves more than the formal equivalence. It has, for example, a semiotic dimension: for the relationship to continue, the object must be signalling what it still lacks and the subject must be interpreting these signals (and his or her own wants or dissatisfactions). Moreover, for the interlocking of signs and interpretations to come about we may need to introduce something like role-taking or perspective-taking. For how is the subject to interpret the signals if not by putting him/herself in the position of the object? Mead devised his famous role-taking formula for an interpersonal sociality, which he thought comes about when a person sees the world from the perspective of the other, includes in his or her perspective-taking the other's attitude toward him/herself, and when the process is mutual, involves both parties in an interaction. Mead meant his formula to extend to physical objects (1938: 426ff.; Heintz, 2000; Joas, 1980); he thought that the child that treats objects as if they were human beings, putting gestures if not words 'into their mouths' and anticipating what they were about to say, illustrated role-taking (Wiley, 1994: 34). But childplay or anthropo- morphization is not crucial to the applicability of role-taking to non-human others. On the basis of what we know about how experts 'figure out' their objects of knowledge, it seems plain that we can do even less without positioning ourselves on the object's side when the object is non-human than when it is human. We do not have the same natural familiarity with a Higgs mechanism or a chromosome that we have with a fellow human being from our culture, a familiarity that may allow us to understand the other 'instantly' and shortcut role-taking. Initially anyway, we will have to make an effort to apprehend the object's behaviour by placing ourselves in its position, by somehow cognizing and visualizing its needs and dispositions.

The process of position-taking involves the subject's 'becoming the object', a sort of cross- over through which the subject attempts to see the object world from the inside, to 'think' as it does, and to feel its reactions. In the words of a biologist, 'if you want to really understand about a tumor, you've got to *be* a tumor' (Fox Keller, 1983: 207). But is the object also taking the subject's position and 'becoming the subject', as Mead's notion of reflexive role-taking in inter- subjective communication suggests? We can only make sense of this by applying Mead's formula in a less than completely symmetric way. A knowledge object may indeed be seen to come to the subject to 'live in it'. As the biologist Barbara McClintock put it, 'as you look at these things (tumours, chromosomes, etc.) they become part of you. And you forget yourself' (Fox Keller, 1983: 117ff.). McClintock describes how the object occupies her mind and attention until she

disappears into an 'I am not there' state. My way of putting this is to say that the object of knowl- edge has become an internal object situated within a person's processing environment. It may preoccupy the subject even when the subject is unaware of it, working away in a person's unconscious. Many scientists have commented on sudden surprise insights seemingly arising from such subconscious preoccupations. Now Mead's formula would seem to apply to this if we could say that an object occupying the subject takes over the person's attitude toward it. But can we say this? What objects will find in a person's mind is their thinking oriented toward them. Yet non-human objects do not generally take over these thoughts, rather they are taken over by them, they become defined in terms of them and in that sense a person's attitude is transferred onto them. But on the other hand, something other than a subject ruminating on his or her own thoughts must occur when an object comes to the subject. McClintock, for example, appears to have felt that the object transferred some of its patterns of existence onto her mind in the process of 'occupation'. What we can perhaps say is the subject partakes in the object world and the object world partakes in the subject in different ways. The reciprocity is there but it is somewhat skewed, since the subject and the object are not structurally doing the same thing. Perhaps we can summarize this in the notion of a *crossover* that takes place through two different mechanisms – position-taking and transference.

We have now added a form of symbolic exchange 'between species' to the interlocking of wants and lacks we started out with, and from here it is only a small step to considering the idea of solidarity as also relevant to conceptualizing postsocial relations. But first we must bring out a dimension implicit in the discussion thus far, which I think is a major source of postsocial relations as solidarity relations. Mead's ideas about perspective-taking imply a standpoint theory according to which one's thoughts and viewpoints are dependent upon one's social or existential position in life – and they imply that the ensuing differences of viewpoints between different persons must somehow be recognized and perhaps smoothed out for something like sociality to come about (I am ignoring here Mead's concern with self-formation to which his insights were also linked). But with many non-human objects, the problem would not seem to be merely different standpoints but different worlds which need to be bridged. Such a bridging process involves knowledge in a much more extensive and direct sense than the standpoint scenario. In order to take an object's position, we must already know something about it, and we extend this knowledge through position-taking and by opening ourselves up for transference. The interlocking of wants and lacks is intermeshed with knowledge processes which make the interlocking possible. Mead could ignore this to some degree since a massive amount of shared knowledge can be presupposed in intracultural human relations.

Now the point I want to make is that the knowledge we acquire of non-human things can also give rise to sociality with objects as a form of solidarity with them. Solidarity has been conceptualized in various ways in social theory (e.g. Durkheim, [1893] 1964); but the notion may be most widely applicable to object relations when the moral dimension is foregrounded; when solidarity means cooperation and altruism between self and other. When applied to objects, this sense of solidarity easily extends itself to human relationships to nature, to the environmental attitudes of social movements, etc. The knowledge base of this sort of postsocial relatedness through feelings of solidarity with objects can best be made apparent by a further illustration – by working our way through another set of quotes from McClintock, the scientist mentioned before (Fox Keller, 1983: 198f.).

> Every time I walk on grass I feel sorry because I know the grass is screaming at me.

Why does McClintock feel sorry for the grass? The answer appears to lie not simply in the civility of her character or her general love of nature (though she might have had both), but rather in her knowledge of plants and their 'ingenious mechanisms' of responding to an environment. McClintock made the above utterance in the context of a series of others in which she describes these reaction mechanisms as extraordinary:

> Plants are extraordinary. For instance . . . if you pinch a leaf of a plant you set off electrical pulses. You can't touch a plant without setting off an electrical pulse . . . There is no question that plants have all kinds of sensitivities. They do a lot of responding to an environment. They can do almost anything you can think of.

If my interpretation is right, then we have hit here the epistemic source of an object-centred solidarity – its rootedness in knowing something about an object. I do not wish to argue that feelings of moral solidarity toward nature cannot also spring from, or be accompanied by, a lack of knowledge, for example in the case of romanticism or rapturousness about the world. But I would argue that the latter kind of relationship lays itself open to critique and dismissal precisely on the grounds of its lack of knowledge. In a knowledge society, deep emotional investments

in nature draw their legitimation from knowledge rather than from 'blind' admiration; the two processes of solidarity become interwoven, reinforcing one another.

An individual looping his or her desire through an object and back is not only likely to learn something about the object in the process. He or she is also likely to develop a shared lifeworld with these objects, a larger context of practices and things within which the relationship is enacted. A shared lifeworld that is continually reaffirmed through the sort of processes described would also seem to provide embeddedness to individuals, even if the embedding environment is non-human. I will turn to embeddedness now because the notion has been strongly associated with human sociality in the past, yet it also provides another way of filling in what we might mean by postsocial relatedness. In the current literature, embeddedness tends to be associated with networks of social ties. An individual that has at his or her disposal a network of human relationships into which he or she is tied is embedded; the network provides a resource on which the individual can draw (e.g. Granovetter, 1985). Embeddedness is also linked to human 'traditions', seen as traces of practices, signs of beliefs and images of continuity revealed in human thought or action (Luke, 1996). Accordingly, we have been embedded in the past when traditions were intact, but experience disembeddedness as previous traditions disintegrate and our age moves beyond tradition (Heelas et al., 1996). But it seems plain that traces and continuities of the sort found in traditions can also arise from interactions with non-human environments. In fact, this possibility is implicit in the detraditionalization literature; what prevents it from being recognized is the tendency to focus on individualization as a direct consequence of detraditionalization. Here theories of integration may be better positioned to recognize this possibility, for example when they address common prosperity as a new form of integration (e.g. Peters, 1993). Turning now to network concepts of embeddedness, object worlds can also be conceived as networks into which individuals are tied, as indeed they are by the actor-network theory (e.g. Callon, 1986; Latour and Johnson, 1988). If the criterion for embeddedness is the existence of networks, then object-dominated networks should deliver the embeddedness experience.

POSTSOCIAL HUMAN FORMS

The understanding of 'postsociality' is not only pertinent to human–object relations but also to domains that are both human and non-human or even exclusively human. I want to emphasize this in concluding, and, starting from the idea of embeddedness just discussed, give some illustrations by turning to studies of Internet users. What these studies emphasize are the spatial features of this 'environment' and the virtual (disembodied) interactions in it as giving rise to community (Hornsby, 1998; Jones, 1998; Stone, 1996: 36f.). These ideas of collective disembodied systems generated in a symbolic space illustrate an important instance of what we might mean by postsocial forms – forms of human interaction mediated by and constituted through communication technologies. We may call these postsocial forms since they arise in circumstances where interaction, space and even communication appear to mean something different from our accustomed understanding of the terms. But what exactly are the new characteristics of these forms? How do the characteristics of social interaction change when the technological is the natural, and 'social space is a computer code, consensual and hallucinatory' (Stone, 1996: 38)? Empirical studies of this question are only beginning to emerge, and we will have to await their results. But as this author suggests, one chief difference is the decreased density of the communication, coming about through the narrower bandwidth of electronic communication, where fewer signalling channels are availabe than in face-to-face interaction. In narrow bandwidth communication the interpretative faculties of the person become more powerfully, even obsessively engaged in the effort to provide closure on a set of signals. Perhaps a more powerful engagement, and the interpretative fantasies opened up, translate *not* into the poorer experiential quality of virtual systems but into 'higher' experience and greater attraction.

It is not difficult to find evidence of this attraction. Heim provides indications of it in his work on virtual reality (e.g. 1993: ch. 7), as does Turkle (1995: ch. 3). An early, more literary rendering can be found in Gibson (1984: 4–5):

A year [in Japan] and he still dreamed of cyberspace, hope fading nightly . . . [S]till he'd seen the matrix in his sleep, bright lattices of logic unfolding across that colorless void . . . [H]e was no [longer] console man, no cyberspace cowboy . . . But the dreams came on in the Japanese night like livewire voodoo, and he'd cry for it, cry in his sleep, and wake alone in the dark, curled in his capsule in some coffin hotel, his hands clawed into the bedslab, . . . trying to reach the console that wasn't there.

As Turkle (1995: 83ff.) aptly suggests, during the early stages of the personal computer's entrance into everyday life, the young person's

response to computers centred around the question of whether or to what extent the computer was alive, and adults and philosophers were concerned with the degree to which computers could or could not emulate human beings (Dreyfus, 1967, 1972; Searle, 1980). These issues have moved into the background in the countries where computers have gained wide acceptance, and where their 'future presence' in every household and every aspect of our life seems inevitable. In these countries the notion of the machine has been expanded to include enough features of social actors to make them acceptable as business partners in all kinds of interaction, even intimate ones. Turkle describes a new pragmatism and nonchalance with a view to expert systems in the 1990s, as people come to terms with the idea that machines can be intelligent, helpful, trustworthy etc. They have, one might add, in any case become a 'presence' against which our defensive redefinitions of what is special about people may be the wrong track to take. And while they may have become the 'selfless and loyal butler' (Turkle, 1995: 123) for some, for others they offer the possibility of the sort of intimate relationships described by Heim (1993), of self-experience and parallel lives.

Could postsociality also be understood as a negative social form, a form of human relatedness not based on 'crossovers', reflexivity and solidarity but on hatred and self-negation? Could it be 'post' in the sense of new and beyond received concepts of sociality? Consider a fictional case.[5] In the movie *Fight Club* which was screened at the turn of the millennium, aggression and violence between persons were portrayed as something that binds self and other. The forms of violence were physical and extreme; binding seemed to be based on others providing for the self the negative part that perhaps a parent once played, the part of an interiorized, alien 'other' who refused to recognize the self, behaved in ways the self admired *and* dreaded, and to whom the self was related in a dynamic of challenges and fights. These fights when exteriorized became a force that bound the self to others with similar tendencies, and that was instituted in fight clubs. The deliberate interpersonal violence was also made plausible as an alternative to one kind of object relations, that of consumer objects. One can intepret the resorting to violence as an attempt to 'break out of' some kind of lack–wanting dynamic with objects, human or non-human, to free oneself of its holding power by resorting to the level of what Gibson (1984) called 'the meat', the level of the physical suffering (and inflicting) of pain and blows. Goffman saw physical assault as the stopping point for all symbolic exchanges; as a way, we might say, to absorb all lacks and erase all meaning (Goffman, 1974; see also Baudrillard's notion of a fatal strategy, 1990).

At the same time, this sort of symbolic disintegration simply gives rise to another variant of a postsocial form. Fighting might not be based on role-taking, but in the case of fight clubs, it easily fits the Meadean idiom of a 'conversation of gestures' that involves turn-taking, rules, limits, reciprocity and an audience (it is structured like a spectacle or an 'event'). Here we can see a variety of mechanisms which have traditionally been associated with social forms at work. These are also evident when we consider the fact that fights are staged in cycles that establish the continuity and expectedness of the behaviour. Where things begin to differ somewhat from the conventional picture is the point at which we consider the mechanism that gives rise to the other. In the case portrayed, this mechanism is transference; the other is constituted as a fighter by the projection onto the other of experiences of the self. A second distinction concerns the content of the exchanges, which are physical. As indicated, participants make the attempt to deliberately 'reduce' exchanges to non-symbolic levels of interaction. Though gangs and violent activities have long been analysed by sociologists, they are often seen to enact status concerns, engage in 'deep play' (Geertz, 1973) or profit-seeking and the like – this points to motives which are entirely conventional but are enacted in the alternative world of deviant behaviour. Yet such interpretations would not seem adequately to capture the sort of 'opting out' and 'letting go' of senseless fighting.

CONCLUSION

We have come full circle now, returning from postsocial reciprocity, solidarity and embeddedness to the self as a structure of wanting that plays itself out as it 'moves into' object worlds, and to forms of self-relatedness realized in violent physical engagement with others. Postsocial relations are relations to computers and expert systems and their holding power. They are forms of attraction articulated in relation to shopping malls of the sort described by Ritzer (1999; see also Falk and Campbell, 1997; Miller, 1994, 1997) in which we feel embedded, 'mirror' our identity and spend our time. They include attachments to nature and the environment whose characteristic feature may be the moral slant that sociality takes in this case, and which perhaps indicates the continued relevance of the inner censor model of the self (discussed above). Postsocial forms address the fascination the market has for traders and investors, who perceive the market as a 'greater being' which

they enter as they strap themselves to their seats in front of dealing screens (Knorr Cetina and Bruegger, 2000). But they also encompass understandings of human relatedness and engagement that stand as alternatives to, or perhaps supplant, traditional understandings of human sociality. Note that in all these cases, I have not derived relatedness from the satisfaction postsocial individuals may experience from the attachment. We should be careful not to construe object relationships simply as positive emotional ties, or as being symmetric, non-appropriative, etc. The characterization one must look for should be more dynamic, allow for ambivalence and account for the durability of people's engagement with objects and the sort of symbolic environments described. I have suggested that we can theorize postsocial relations more through the notion of a lack, and a corresponding structure of wanting, than through positive ties and fulfilment.

I have also argued in this chapter that postsocial forms 'step into the place' of social relations where these empty out, where they lose some of the thickness and meaningfulness they have had in earlier periods. These forms and the objects they involve may also simply be the risk winners of the relationship risks and failures that many analysts of contemporary life associate with human relations. A condition for understanding this role of objects is that we develop, in social theory, concepts that break with the tradition of seeing objects in certain ways. In the past, we have seen them as abstract technologies that promote the alienation of the worker (e.g. Berger et al., 1974), as fetishized commodities (Marx [1887] 1968) and spectacles that freeze and numb any human or political potential (Baudrillard, [1976] 1993), or as transparent tools which theory can disregard if only it focuses on instrumental action (Habermas, 1981). In this chapter, I have tried to provide an initial framework for a different conception of objects; one that sees their 'hooking power' as lying with their indefiniteness of being and their expanding potential in contemporary life. This power matters in relation to a self that is structured by a dynamic of reiterated wantings and lacks of fulfilment – in addition to other dynamics it may also be caught in. From a sociological perspective, this dynamic is sustained by the mimetic reflexivity of contemporary society and by changes of socialization practices that only recreate a waning version of the 'inner censor' self.

The shift from social to postsocial relations is not the only way of envisaging the epic character of the changes now in the making, but it is one that 'specializes', as it were, in shining the analytic torch on the concept of the social. This view of things does not stand in any necessary contrast or contradiction to assessments that associate current transitions with a shift from industrial to postindustrial life, from nation-states to global societies, or from modernity to postmodernity. What it stands in contrast to are attempts to hold on to the concepts of the social which have been important to us in the past. Interestingly, such tendencies are quite prominent in what Ritzer aptly calls the 'gloomy view of postmodernists' – of thinkers who denigrate trends like the consumerist bent of Western democracies (1996: 256; see also Lipovetsky, 1994) or the evanescence of contemporary human relations (Bauman, 1993, 1996). To develop an understanding of current changes in sociality, I maintain, we need to mobilize new concepts and to refuse to adopt an attitude of denigration.

I want to emphasize in concluding that the changes in the way we live and understand sociality also pertain to human relations. Jameson, who has no nostalgia for modernism, has characterized postmodern life as a waning of emotion or affect, a tiring of the search for meaning associated with the modern world, a wanting 'to live on the surface for a while' (1991: 151; Ritzer, 1996: 182). Such characterizations may be joined by those of other theorists who take as their starting point a shift in authority from without to within, from a pre-given social order to authority resting with the self (Heelas, 1996: 2), and who analyse the type of marriage and family relations that ensue from such shifts (e.g. Beck and Beck-Gernsheim, 1996). Other bits and pieces for an understanding of post-social forms of human collectivity are beginning to emerge from the studies of Internet communities and shopping malls I have cited. The characteristics of all these forms of human collectivity may not be discerned easily through the mists of history and of existing concepts. Yet we ought to develop a sense of postsocial forms in social theory if we are not to ignore significant assessment of postmodern life by authors who are not sociologists, and who challenge our conceptions.

NOTES

1 See, for example, the recent volume by Rueschemeyer and Skocpol (1996), which brings together many recent interpretations of the history of welfare institutions. See also Giddens, 1994b: 134ff.

2 MacFarlane also argues controversially that individualism is much older than the Renaissance in England (1978: 196).

3 See Bauman 1996: 55 for the notion of a commonality of fate and Anderson, 1983 for the idea of 'imagined communities'.

4 Baldwin's and Hegel's notion of desire are summarized by Wiley, 1994: 33. See also Hegel, (1807) 1979 and Baldwin (1899) 1973.

5 I am grateful to Urs Bruegger who alerted me to the following example.

REFERENCES

Alford, C.F. (1991) *The Self in Social Theory*. New Haven, CT: Yale University Press.

Anderson, B. (1983) *Imagined Communities*. London: Verso.

Ashe, F. (1999) 'The Subject', in F. Ashe, A. Finlayson, M. Lloyd, I. Mackenzie, J. Martin and S. O'Neill, *Contemporary Social and Political Theory*. Buckingham and Philadelphia: Open University Press. pp. 88–110.

Ashford, D. (1982) *Policy and Politics in France*. Philadelphia: Temple University Press.

Baldwin, J.M. ([1899] 1973) *Social and Ethical Interpretations of Mental Development*. New York: Arno Press.

Barbalet, J.M. (1998) *Emotion, Social Theory, and Social Structure: A Macrosociological Approach*. Cambridge: Cambridge University Press.

Baudrillard, J. ([1976] 1993) *Symbolic Exchange and Death*. London: Sage.

Baudrillard, J. (1983) *Simulations*. New York: Semiotext(e).

Baudrillard, J. (1990) *Fatal Strategies*. New York: Semiotext(e).

Baudrillard, J. (1996) *The System of Objects*. London: Verso.

Bauman, Z. (1993) 'Wir sind wie Landstreicher – Die Moral im Zeitalter der Beliebigkeit', *Süddeutsche Zeitung*, 16/17 (November).

Bauman, Z. (1996) 'Morality in the Age of Contingency', in P. Heelas, S. Lash and P. Morris (eds), *Detraditionalization: Critical Reflections on Authority and Identity*. Oxford: Blackwell. pp. 49–58.

Beck, U. (1992) *Risk Society: Towards a New Modernity*. London: Sage.

Beck, U. and Beck-Gernsheim, E. (1994) *The Normal Chaos of Love*. Cambridge: Polity Press.

Beck, U. and Beck-Gernsheim, E. (1996) 'Individualization and "Precarious Freedoms": Perspectives and Controversies of a Subject-Oriented Sociology', in P. Heelas, S. Lash and P. Morris (eds), *Detraditonalization: Critical Reflections on Authority and Identity*. Oxford: Blackwell. pp. 23–48.

Berger, P., Berger, B. and Kellner, H. (1974) *The Homeless Mind: Modernization and Consciousness*. New York: Vintage Books.

Bruegger, U. and Knorr Cetina, K. (2000) 'Global Microstructures: The Interaction Practices of Financial Markets' (forthcoming).

Calhoun, C. (1994a) 'Social Theory and the Politics of Identity', in C. Calhoun (ed.), *Social Theory and the*

Politics of Identity. Cambridge, MA: Blackwell. pp. 9–36.

Calhoun, C. (ed.) (1994b) *Social Theory and the Politics of Identity.* Cambridge, MA: Blackwell.

Callon, M. (1986) 'Some Elements of a Sociology of Translation: Domestication of the Scallops and the Fishermen of St. Brieuc Bay', in J. Law (ed.), *Power, Action and Belief: A New Sociology of Knowledge?* London: Routledge and Kegan Paul. pp. 196–233.

Coleman, J. (1990) *The Foundations of Social Theory.* Cambridge, MA: Belknap Press.

Coleman, J. (1993) 'The Rational Reconstruction of Society: 1992 Presidential Address', *American Sociological Review,* 58: 1–15.

Coleman, J. and Fararo, T.J. (eds) (1992) *Rational Choice Theory: Advocacy and Critique.* London: Sage.

Condorcet, M. de ([1795] 1955) *Sketch for a Historical Picture of the Progress of the Human Mind.* London: Weidenfeld and Nicolson.

Dreyfus, H. (1967) 'Why Computers Need Bodies in Order to Be Intelligent', *Review of Metaphysics,* 21: 13–32.

Dreyfus, H. (1972) *What Computers Can't Do: A Critique of Artificial Reason.* New York: Harper and Row.

Drucker, P.F. (1993) *Post-Capitalist Society.* New York: Harper Collins.

Durkheim, E. ([1893] 1964) *The Division of Labor in Society.* New York: The Free Press.

Durkheim, E. and Mauss, M. (1963) *Primitive Classifications* (trans. R. Needham). Chicago: University of Chicago Press.

Etzioni, A. (1996) *The New Golden Rule: Community and Morality in a Democratic Society.* New York: Basic Books.

Falk, P. and Campbell, C. (eds) (1997) *The Shopping Experience.* London: Sage.

Foucault, M. (1977) *Discipline and Punish.* New York: Random House.

Fox Keller, E. (1983) *A Feeling of the Organism: The Life and Work of Barbara McClintock.* San Francisco: Freeman.

Galison, P. (1997) *Image and Logic.* Chicago: University of Chicago Press.

Geertz, C. (1973) 'Deep Play: Notes on the Balinese Cockfight', in C. Geertz, *The Interpretation of Cultures.* New York: Basic Books. pp. 412–53.

Geison, G. (1997) *The Private Science of Louis Pasteur.* Princeton, NJ: Princeton University Press.

Gibson, W. (1984) *Neuromancer.* New York: Ace Books.

Giddens, A. (1990) *The Consequences of Modernity.* Stanford, CA: Stanford University Press.

Giddens, A. (1991) *Modernity and Self-Identity.* Cambridge: Polity Press.

Giddens, A. (1994a) 'Living in a Post-Traditional Society', in U. Beck, A. Giddens and S. Lash (eds), *Reflexive Modernization.* Stanford, CA: Stanford University Press. pp. 56–109.

Giddens, A. (1994b) *Beyond Left and Right: The Future of Radical Politics.* Stanford, CA: Stanford University Press.

Goffman, E. (1974) *Frame Analysis: An Essay on the Organization of Experience.* Cambridge: Harvard University Press.

Granovetter, M. (1985) 'Economic Action and Social Structure: The Problem of Embeddedness', *American Journal of Sociology,* 91 (3): 481–510.

Gross, P. (1994) *Die Multioptionsgesellschaft.* Frankfurt a.M.: Suhrkamp.

Habermas, J. (1981) *Theorie des kommunikativen Handelns.* Frankfurt a.M.: Suhrkamp.

Hage, J. and Powers, C.H. (1992) *Post-Industrial Lives: Roles and Relationships in the 21st Century.* London and Newbury Park, CA: Sage.

Haraway, D. (1991) 'A Cyborg Manifesto: Science, Technology and Socialist-Feminism in the Late Twentieth Century', in D. Haraway, *Simians, Cyborgs, and Women.* New York: Routledge. pp. 149–81

Heelas, P. (1996) 'Introduction: Detraditionalization and its Rivals', in P. Heelas, S. Lash and P. Morris (eds), *Detraditionalization: Critical Reflections on Authority and Identity.* Oxford: Blackwell. pp. 1–20.

Heelas, P., Lash, S. and Morris, P. (eds) (1996) *Detraditionalization: Critical Reflections on Authority and Identity.* Oxford: Blackwell.

Hegel, G.W.F. ([1807] 1979) *Phenomenology of Spirit.* Oxford: Oxford University Press.

Heidegger, M. ([1927] 1962) *Being and Time.* New York: Harper and Row.

Heim, M. (1993) *The Metaphysics of Virtual Reality.* Oxford: Oxford University Press.

Heintz, B. (2000) *Die Innenwelt der Mathematik: Zur Kultur und Praxis einer beweisenden Disziplin.* Berlin: Springer.

Henderson, K. (1998) *On Line and on Paper: Visual Representations, Visual Culture, and Computer Graphics in Design Engineering.* Boston, MA: MIT Press.

Hornsby, A. (1998) 'Surfing the Net for Community', in P. Kivisto (ed.), *Illuminating Social Life.* Thousand Oaks, CA: Pine Forge Press. pp. 63–106.

Jameson, F. (1991) *Postmodernism or the Cultural Logic of Late Capitalism.* London: Verso.

Joas, H. (1980) *Praktische Intersubjektivität.* Frankfurt a.M.: Suhrkamp.

Jones, S. (1998) 'Information, Internet and Community: Notes Toward an Understanding of Community in the Information Age', in *Cybersociety 2.0.* London: Sage. pp. 1–34.

Knorr Cetina, K. (1981) *The Manufacture of Knowledge: An Essay on the Constructivist and Contextual Nature of Science.* Oxford: Pergamon Press.

Knorr Cetina, K. (1999) *Epistemic Culture. How the Sciences Make Knowledge.* Cambridge, MA: Harvard University Press.

Knorr Cetina, K. and Bruegger, U. (2000) 'The Market as an Object of Attachment: Exploring Postsocial

Relations in Financial Markets', *Canadian Journal of Sociology*, 25 (2): 141–68.

Lacan, J. (1975) *The Language of the Self.* New York: Dell.

Lacan, J. and Wilden, A. (1968) *Speech and Language in Psychoanalysis.* Baltimore, MD: Johns Hopkins University Press.

Lasch, C. (1977) *Haven in a Heartless World.* New York: Basic Books.

Lasch, C. (1978) *The Culture of Narcissism.* New York: Norton.

Lash, S. (1994) 'Reflexivity and its Doubles: Structure, Aesthetics, Community', in U. Beck, A. Giddens and S. Lash (eds), *Reflexive Modernization.* Stanford, CA: Stanford University Press. pp. 110–73.

Lash, S. (1999) *Another Modernity, a Different Rationality.* Oxford: Blackwell.

Lash, S. and Urry, J. (1994) *Economies of Signs and Space.* London: Sage.

Latour, B. (1988) *The Pasteurization of France.* Cambridge, MA: Harvard University Press.

Latour, B. and Johnson, J. (1988) 'Mixing Humans with Non-Humans: Sociology of a Door-Opener', Special issue on Sociology of Science, L. Star (ed.), *Social Problems*, 25: 298–310.

Latour, B. and Woolgar, S. (1979) *Laboratory Life: The Social Construction of Scientific Facts.* Cambridge: Cambridge University Press.

Lipovetsky, G. (1994) *The Empire of Fashion: Dressing Modern Democracy.* Princeton, NJ: Princeton University Press.

Luckmann, T. (1970) 'On the Boundaries of the Social World', in M. Natanson (ed.), *Phenomenology and Social Reality. Essays in Memory of Alfred Schutz.* The Hague: Nijhoff. pp. 73–100.

Luke, T.W. (1996) 'Identity, Meaning and Globalization: De-traditionalization in Postmodern Space–Time Compression', in P. Heelas, S. Lash and P. Morris (eds), *Detraditionalization. Critical Reflections on Authority and Identity.* Oxford: Blackwell. pp. 109–33.

Lynch, M. (1985) *Art and Artifact in Laboratory Science: A Study of Shop Work and Shop Talk in a Research Laboratory.* London: Routledge and Kegan Paul.

MacFarlane, A. (1978) *The Origins of English Individualism: The Family, Property and Social Transition.* New York: Cambridge University Press.

Marx, K. ([1887] 1968) *Das Kapital. Kritik der politischen Ökonomie.* Hamburg: Europäische Verlagsanstalt.

Mead, G.H. (1938) *The Philosophy of the Act.* Chicago: University of Chicago Press.

Miller, D. (1994) *Modernity – An Ethnographic Approach.* Oxford: Berg.

Miller, D. (1997) *Capitalism – An Ethnographic Approach.* Oxford: Berg.

Mills, C.W. (1959) *The Sociological Imagination.* Oxford: Oxford University Press.

Peters, B. (1993) *Die Integration moderner Gesellschaften.* Frankfurt a.M.: Suhrkamp.

Rabinbach, A. (1996) 'Social Knowledge, Social Risk, and the Politics of Industrial Accidents in Germany and France', in D. Rueschemeyer and T. Skocpol (eds), *States, Social Knowledge, and the Origins of Modern Social Policies.* Princeton, NJ: Princeton University Press. pp. 48–89.

Rheinberger, H.-J. (1992) 'Experiment, Difference, and Writing: I. Tracing Protein Synthesis', *Studies in the History and Philosophy of Science*, 23 (2): 305–31.

Ritzer, G. (1996) *Postmodern Social Theory.* New York: McGraw-Hill.

Ritzer, G. (1999) *Enchanting a Disenchanted World.* Thousand Oaks, CA: Pine Forge Press.

Rueschemeyer, D. and Skocpol, T. (eds) (1996) *States, Social Knowledge, and the Origins of Modern Social Policies.* Princeton, NJ: Princeton University Press.

Rueschemeyer, D. and Van Rossem, R. (1996) 'The Verein für Sozialpolitik and the Fabian Society', in D. Rueschemeyer and T. Skocpol (eds), *States, Social Knowledge, and the Origins of Modern Social Policies.* Princeton, NJ: Princeton University Press. pp. 117–62.

Scheler, M. ([1913] 1948) *Wesen und Formen der Sympathie*, 5th edn. Frankfurt: Schulte–Bulmke.

Searle, J. (1980) 'Minds, Brains and Programs', *The Behavioral and Brain Sciences*, 3: 417–24.

Seidler, V. (1994) *Unreasonable Men: Masculinity and Social Theory.* London: Routledge.

Stehr, N. (1994) *Arbeit, Eigentum und Wissen. Zur Theorie von Wissensgesellschaften.* Frankfurt a.M.: Suhrkamp.

Stone, A.R. (1996) *The War of Desire and Technology at the Close of the Mechanical Age.* Boston, MA: MIT Press.

Todes, D. (1997) 'Pavlov's Physiology Factory', *ISIS*, 88 (2): 205–46.

Traweek, S. (1988) *Beamtimes and Lifetimes: The World of High Energy Physics.* Cambridge, MA: Harvard University Press.

Turkle, S. (1995) *Life on the Screen.* New York: Simon and Schuster.

Virilio, P. (1995) *The Art of the Motor.* Minneapolis: University of Minnesota Press.

Wiley, N. (1994) *The Semiotic Self.* Chicago: University of Chicago Press.

Wittrock, B. and Wagner, P. (1996) 'Social Science and the Building of the Early Welfare State', in D. Rueschemeyer and T. Skocpol (eds), *States, Social Knowledge, and the Origins of Modern Social Policies.* Princeton, NJ: Princeton University Press. pp. 90–113.

Index